CONTENTS

SCHEME OF EXAMINATION

1. The AFCAT Question Paper will have 100 questions. All questions will be of three marks each. For every correct answer the candidate will get three marks and for every wrong answer one mark will be deducted under negative marking. The total time allotted for the paper is two hours.
2. Each Question Paper will have questions from the following topics:
   A. **General Awareness**
   B. **Verbal Ability in English**
   C. **Numerical Ability**
   D. **Reasoning and Military Aptitude Test**

R. Gupta's®

POPULAR MASTER GUIDE

AFCAT

Air Force Common Admission Test

For

FLYING & TECHNICAL BRANCH

- Specialised Study Material Prepared by Experts
- Solved Multiple Choice Questions

by

RPH Editorial Board

RAMESH PUBLISHING HOUSE, NEW DELHI

Published by

O.P. Gupta *for* Ramesh Publishing House

Admin. Office

12-H, New Daryaganj Road, Opp. Officers' Mess

New Delhi-110002 ✆ 23275224, 23245124

E-mail: info@rameshpublishinghouse.com

For Online Shopping: www.rameshpublishinghouse.com

Showroom

- Balaji Market, Nai Sarak, Delhi-110006 ✆ 23282525 📱 9354373464
- 4457, Nai Sarak, Delhi-110006

Book Code: R-1436

ISBN: 978-93-5012-141-2

Price: ₹ 520

Printed at: S.K. Graphics, Delhi

Previous Years' Paper

AIR FORCE COMMON ADMISSION TEST (AFCAT)—01/2026

(Exam held on 31-01-2026)

1. Read the sentence to find out whether there is any grammatical error in it. The error, if any, will be part of the sentence. Spot the error from the given options.

The chairperson of the ethics committee, (*a*)/ as well as several senior advisors, were present (*b*)/ during the confidential deliberations that followed the inquiry. (*c*)/ No error (*d*)

1. (*a*) 2. (*b*)
3. (*d*) 4. (*c*)

2. Select the option that best completes the analogy.

CONSTITUTION : GOVERNANCE :: ______ : INTERPRETATION

1. Lexicon 2. Archive
3. Canon 4. Grammar

3. Select the correct one-word substitute for the given group of words.

A remedy or solution believed to cure all diseases or resolve all problems.

1. Palliative 2. Panacea
3. Succor 4. Elixir

4. An idiom is given below, followed by four possible meanings. Select the option that best conveys the meaning of the idiom.

To throw the helve after the hatchet

1. To act impulsively without regard for long-term consequences
2. To abandon a task midway due to excessive difficulty
3. To worsen a situation by incurring further loss after an initial failure
4. To escalate a dispute by responding with disproportionate force

5. The following question consists of an incomplete sentence with a fixed beginning and a fixed ending. The middle portion of the sentence is divided into four parts labelled P, Q, R and S. These four parts are given in a jumbled order. Arrange P, Q, R and S in the correct sequence to form a meaningful and grammatically correct sentence. Choose the correct combination from the options given.

To address the reviewer's concerns, ... coherence of the dissertation significantly.

P. too many theoretical directions
Q. the scholar revised two core arguments,
R. simultaneously could weaken the overall
S. yet acknowledged that pursuing

1. R P Q S 2. S P R Q
3. P S R Q 4. Q S P R

1. 2 **2.** 4 **3.** 2 **4.** 3 **5.** 4

6. In the following sentence, choose the option that expresses the antonym of the underlined word.

The narrative presents an archetypal hero whose journey conforms precisely to established mythic patterns rather than deviating into idiosyncratic or experimental forms of characterisation.

1. fortuitous 2. anomalous
3. immutable 4. recondite

7. In the following question, a complex sentence is given. Choose the option that best transforms it into a simple sentence without altering its meaning, logical emphasis, or syntactic correctness.

Though the theoretical framework appeared robust, anomalies in empirical observations necessitated a reassessment of the underlying assumptions and methodological approach.

1. The theoretical framework appeared robust, but anomalies in empirical observations necessitated reassessment of the underlying assumptions and methodological approach.
2. The theoretical framework appeared robust, and anomalies in empirical observations necessitated reassessment of the underlying assumptions and methodological approach.
3. Robust theoretical framework notwithstanding, anomalies in empirical observations necessitated reassessment of the underlying assumptions and methodological approach.
4. Appearing robust, anomalies in empirical observations necessitated reassessment of the underlying assumptions and methodological approach.

8. Choose the option which best replaces the given group of words.

The practice of gaining advantage through flattery or excessive compliance

1. Normativity
2. Sycophancy
3. Equivocation
4. Consequentialism

9. Select the best one word substitute for the given group of words.

Someone who demands strict compliance with rules even when it is unnecessary

1. Martinet 2. Disciplinarian
3. Dogmatic 4. Iconoclast

10. The following question consists of an incomplete sentence. The missing part of the sentence has been split into four parts. All four parts are jumbled up and labelled P, Q, R, S. Arrange the jumbled parts of the sentence and find out which of the four combinations from the given options will correctly complete the sentence.

Postcolonial literary criticism has repeatedly challenged the neutrality of narrative voice .... within texts long regarded as formally objective.

P. revealing how stylistic transparency can function as ideological concealment
Q. when imperial epistemologies are naturalised as universal experience
R. through close attention to perspective, silence, and narrative authority
S. rather than as an absence of mediation

1. P – R – Q – S
2. Q – R – P – S
3. R – Q – P – S
4. R – P – S – Q

6. 2 **7.** 3 **8.** 2 **9.** 1 **10.** 4

11. Read the sentence to find out whether there is any error in it. The error, if any, will be in one part of the sentence. Spot the error from the given options.

The analyst cautioned against excessive (A) reliance on anecdotal indicators masquerading (B) as statistically representative evidence. (C) No Error (D)

1. (B) 2. (C)
3. (A) 4. (D)

12. Select the most appropriate homonyms to complete the sentence.

_____ the researcher went _____ a _____ review, she deliberately _____ the outdated assumptions aside.

1. Though /through / thorough / threw
2. Through / thorough /threw / though
3. Thorough / threw / though / through
4. Threw / though / through / thorough

13. An idiom is given below, followed by four possible meanings. Select the option that best conveys the meaning of the idiom.

To ride on Shank's mare

1. To move independently without external support
2. To undertake a journey without adequate preparation
3. To rely on personal effort rather than material resources
4. To travel on foot

14. Read the sentence carefully and choose the option that best completes both blanks. Only one option fits the intended evaluative meaning in both blanks.

In the final review the panel deliberately avoided ________ language while offering ________ criticism so that the assessment conveyed intellectual rigour without appearing dismissive or ideologically entrenched to external evaluators.

1. caustic / superficial
2. equivocal / judicious
3. acerbic / restrained
4. trenchant / measured

15. Read the sentence carefully to find out whether there is any grammatical error in it. The error, if any, will be in one part of the sentence. Spot the error from the given options.

The supervisor disapproved of the researcher submitting sensitive data (*a*)/ without proper authorisation (*b*)/ during the preliminary phase of the study. (*c*)/ no error (*d*)/

1. (*c*) 2. (*d*)
3. (*b*) 4. (*a*)

16. In the following question, out of the given alternatives, choose the best one which expresses the synonym of the underlined word.

The tribunal dismissed the preliminary indictment after the emergence of <u>exculpatory</u> evidence, whose probative force effectively dismantled the prosecution's circumstantial narrative and undermined its inferential coherence.

1. Tendentious 2. Premonitory
3. Duplicitous 4. Exonerative

17. Read the sentence carefully and fill in the blanks with the most appropriate words. Only one option correctly completes both blanks.

The committee objected to the ______ of critical data during peer review, arguing that such ______ compromised transparency and academic integrity across institutions.

1. researcher's withholding / behaviour
2. researchers withholding / behaviours
3. researcher's withhold / behaviour
4. researcher withholding / behaviour

11. 4	**12.** 1	**13.** 4	**14.** 4	**15.** 4	**16.** 4	**17.** 1

18. The following question consists of an incomplete sentence. The missing part of the sentence has been split into four parts. All four parts are jumbled up and labelled P, Q, R, S. Arrange the jumbled parts of the sentence and find out which of the four combinations from the given options will correctly complete the sentence.

In policy debates on artificial intelligence, ethical oversight is frequently invoked ________ that lack both enforcement authority and democratic accountability.

P. as a compensatory gesture for rapid technological deployment

Q. that remains largely procedural rather than substantively transformative

R. allowing innovation to proceed without structural restraint

S. while responsibility is dispersed across advisory frameworks

1. S – P – Q – R
2. Q – P – S – R
3. P – Q – S – R
4. P – S – R – Q

19. In the following sentence, a phrase has been underlined. You are required to replace it with the most appropriate idiom.

Excessive justification in the report threatened entirely <u>to spoil what was already attractive</u> during the final evaluation process.

1. to drop like flies
2. to sour the grapes
3. to throw the baby out with the bathwater
4. to take the gilt off the gingerbread

20. Read the sentence carefully and choose the option that best completes both blanks. Only one option results in grammatically correct subject verb concord throughout.

An understanding of how competing theoretical paradigms intersect, rather than their individual merits alone, ______ shaped the committee's evaluation and ______ decisive in determining the final recommendation.

1. has / was
2. have / were
3. have / was
4. has / were

21. Choose the option that correctly transforms the given complex sentence into a simple sentence without changing its meaning.

When the researcher realised that the data were inconsistent, she revised the analytical framework.

1. The researcher revised the analytical framework as the data had been inconsistent.
2. The researcher revised the analytical framework because the data were inconsistent.
3. On realising the inconsistency of the data, the researcher revised the analytical framework.
4. The researcher revised the analytical framework while realising the data inconsistency.

22. In the following sentence, choose the option that expresses the antonym of the underlined word.

The researcher responded with notable <u>alacrity</u> to methodological criticism, demonstrating an eagerness that contrasted sharply with the usual deliberative pace of academic revision.

1. disinclination
2. buoyancy
3. exuberance
4. amelioration

18. 3 **19.** 4 **20.** 1 **21.** 3 **22.** 1

23. Read the sentence carefully and choose the option that best completes both blanks. Only one option correctly completes the sentence.

Managers ___________ criticism but decide to ________ training programs so teams improve performance, resilience, morale, and accountability across departments during rapid organisational change.

1. bristle among / beef between
2. bristle at / beef up
3. bristle in / beef upto
4. bristle on / beef on

24. Choose the most appropriate one-word substitute for the given phrase from the options provided.

Study of election trends

1. phraseology 2. pyrology
3. posology 4. psephology

Directions: (Qs. No. 25-27): *In the following passage, some words have been deleted. Fill in the blanks with the most appropriate word from the options given for each number.*

Colonial administrations often _________ (1) indigenous customs, imposing foreign ideologies that __________ (2) existing social structures. These policies frequently _________ (3) nationalist movements, leaving enduring legacies of both resistance and adaptation throughout the subcontinent's complex historical landscape, affecting generations in cultural, political, and social spheres.

25. Select the most appropriate option to fill in blank (1).

1. valorized 2. subverted
3. extolled 4. perpetuated

26. Select the most appropriate option to fill in blank (2).

1. dislocated 2. enshrined
3. fortified 4. accentuated

27. Select the most appropriate option to fill in blank (3).

1. obliterated 2. mollified
3. engendered 4. obviated

Directions (Qs. No. 28-30): *Read the given passage carefully and answer the questions that follow:*

Confidence and determination, though frequently invoked as personal virtues, operate less as innate endowments than as rigorously cultivated dispositions forged under conditions of uncertainty and resistance. Confidence, in its substantive sense, does not arise from the absence of doubt but from the disciplined capacity to act despite cognitive hesitation and anticipated failure. It is sustained by an internal economy of judgment wherein selfappraisal remains neither indulgently affirmative nor corrosively self-negating. Determination, closely allied yet conceptually distinct, functions as the temporal extension of confidence, manifesting not in episodic resolve but in the sustained endurance of purpose across protracted intervals of adversity. Where confidence enables initiation, determination secures continuation, converting provisional intent into durable praxis. Together, they constitute a dialectical apparatus through which individuals negotiate structural impediments, recalibrate objectives, and persist without succumbing to either reckless optimism or paralyzing self-doubt. Importantly, neither quality guarantees success; rather, they recalibrate the individual's orientation toward failure, transforming it from a terminal verdict into a provisional datum within an iterative process of refinement. In social and professional contexts, confidence devoid of determination collapses into performative bravado, while determination without confidence risks degenerating into unreflective obstinacy. Their productive convergence lies in an adaptive equilibrium that balances assertive agency

23. 2 **24.** 4 **25.** 2 **26.** 1 **27.** 3

with reflective restraint. Thus, confidence and determination should be understood not as emotive states or motivational slogans but as ethically charged practices, continuously enacted, revised, and disciplined through action, setback, and reassessment.

28. Two statements labelled Assertion (A) and Reason (R) are given below. Read the statements carefully and select the correct option.

Assertion (A): Confidence, as described in the passage, is compatible with the presence of doubt rather than dependent on its elimination.

Reason (R): Confidence is presented as a regulated form of self-judgment that enables action even when certainty is incomplete.

1. A is true, but R is false.
2. Both A and R are true, and R is the correct explanation of A.
3. Both A and R are true, but R is not the correct explanation of A.
4. A is false, but R is true.

29. How do confidence and determination function together within the framework outlined in the passage?

1. By eliminating uncertainty through repeated affirmation
2. By balancing initiation of action with sustained endurance
3. By ensuring success through disciplined persistence
4. By prioritizing emotional assurance over reflective judgment

30. Why does the passage reject the idea that confidence and determination inherently guarantee success?

1. Because failure is described as irrelevant to personal development
2. Because success is portrayed as structurally inaccessible in most contexts
3. Because perseverance is shown to undermine adaptive judgment
4. Because both qualities are framed as situational and ethically constrained practices

31. With reference to Flying Officer Nirmal Jit Singh Sekhon and the Param Vir Chakra, consider the following statements.

1. He was the first individual from the Indian Air Force to be awarded India's highest gallantry award, the Param Vir Chakra.
2. The Param Vir Chakra is octagonal in shape, made of silver, and bears a single Vajra with the Ashoka Chakra embossed at the centre.

Which of the statements given above is/are correct?

1. Neither 1 nor 2
2. 1 only
3. 2 only
4. Both 1 and 2

32. The Sumi tribe's energetic war dance performed to celebrate victory in battle and the Lotha women's Mungyanta harvest dance, performed during the Tokhu Emong festival, are mainly associated with which Indian state?

1. Arunachal Pradesh
2. Mizoram
3. Odisha
4. Nagaland

33. Which of the following is the primary function of AILA, the AI agent introduced by IIT (Indian Institute of Technology) Delhi in 202[illegible]

1. Carrying out scientific experiments from start to finish, much like a human scientist
2. Automating daily class schedule, routine laboratory maintenance, and equipment handling
3. Assisting researchers with literature review and data collection
4. Simulating virtual experiments without physical laboratory involvement

28. 2	**29.** 2	**30.** 4	**31.** 2	**32.** 4	**33.** 1

34. With reference to Aero India, Asia's Largest Air Show, consider the following statements.

1. Aero India is an annual air show and aviation exhibition held in Bengaluru and is organised by the Defence Exhibition Organisation under the Department of Defence Production, Ministry of Defence.
2. Aero India 2025, the 15th edition of the event, had a broad theme, "The Runway to a Billion Opportunities".

Which of the statements given above is/are correct?

1. 2 only
2. Both 1 and 2
3. 1 only
4. Neither 1 nor 2

35. "Layup" and "Three-point shot" are terms commonly associated with which of the following sports?

1. Basketball
2. Ice Hockey
3. Volleyball
4. Futsal

36. Siliserh Lake, which has been designated as a Ramsar site and recognised as India's 96th wetland of international importance, is located in which State?

1. Rajasthan
2. Madhya Pradesh
3. Gujarat
4. Haryana

37. The battle of Stalingrad was famously associated with which of the following events?

1. Cold War
2. World War II
3. French Revolution
4. Russian Revolution

38. Which of the following is a cartilaginous organ in the human body that helps in sound production and hence called the sound box?

1. Bronchioles
2. Pharynx
3. Larynx
4. Epiglottis

39. The 22nd ASEAN–India Summit held in 2025 declared the year 2026 as which of the following?

1. The ASEAN-India Year of Economic Collaboration
2. The ASEAN-India Year of Digital Connectivity
3. The ASEAN-India Year of Cultural Engagement
4. The ASEAN-India Year of Maritime Cooperation

40. Which institution set up in 1990 under an Act of the Indian Parliament, acts as the principal financial institution for promotion, financing and development of the Micro, Small and Medium Enterprise (MSME) sector?

1. Small Industries Development Bank of India
2. National Bank For Agriculture And Rural Development
3. Industrial Development Bank of India
4. Small Industries Credit and Investment Corporation of India Ltd

41. What are the regions called that lie between the Tropic of Cancer and the Arctic Circle in the Northern Hemisphere, and between the Tropic of Capricorn and the Antarctic Circle in the Southern Hemisphere?

1. Temperate Zones
2. Equatorial Zones
3. Frigid Zones
4. Torrid Zones

42. Which of the following ocean relief features has pointed summits that rise from the seafloor but do not reach the ocean's surface, often attaining heights of 3,000–4,500 metres?

1. Continental shelf
2. Seamount
3. Mid-oceanic ridge
4. Guyot

34. 1 **35.** 1 **36.** 1 **37.** 2 **38.** 3 **39.** 4 **40.** 1 **41.** 1 **42.** 2

43. With reference to India's legacy in United Nations peacekeeping operations, consider the following statements.

1. The term Blue Helmets for UN peacekeepers is derived from the light blue colour of the United Nations flag.
2. In 2023, the Dag Hammarskjöld Medal was posthumously awarded to Indian peacekeepers Shishupal Singh and Sanwala Ram Vishnoi, and civilian UN worker Shaber Taher Ali for their sacrifice in the Democratic Republic of the Congo.
3. Major Radhika Sen was named the UN's "Military Gender Advocate of the Year 2023".

Which of the statements given above are correct?

1. 1 and 2 only 2. 2 and 3 only
3. 1, 2 and 3 4. 1 and 3 only

44. Which famous sports personality was awarded the Laureus World Comeback of the Year award in 2025?

1. Rebeca Andrade 2. Sky Brown
3. Max Parrot 4. Christian Eriksen

45. Match List-I (Air Exercise) with List-II (Participating Countries) and select the correct option.

List-I (Air Exercise)	**List-II** (Participating Countries)
(A) Exercise Indradhanush	(I) India and Japan
(B) Exercise Desert Knight	(II) India and Oman
(C) Exercise Eastern Bridge	(III) India and United Kingdom
(D) Exercise Veer Guardian	(IV) India, France and United Arab Emirates

1. A- I B- IV C- III D- II
2. A- III B- II C- IV D- I
3. A- III B- IV C- II D- I
4. A- IV B- III C- I D- II

46. Consider the following statements about the Rowlatt Satyagraha.

(1) The Rowlatt Act authorized the British Government to arrest and imprison any Indian without trial.

(2) In April 1917, Gandhiji gave a call for a satyagraha against the Rowlatt Act.

Which of the above given statements is/are correct?

1. 2 only 2. 1 only
3. Neither 1 nor 2 4. Both 1 and 2

47. How does the Sustainable Harnessing and Advancement of Nuclear Energy for Transforming India (SHANTI) Bill, 2025 affect the involvement of private sector in India's nuclear industry?

1. Enables limited private participation under regulatory oversight
2. Authorises private firms to control all strategic nuclear assets for modernisation
3. Strictly maintains Government monopoly without exceptions
4. Permits private companies to independently undertake the full nuclear fuel-cycle including enrichment, reprocessing, and waste management

48. Which Indian Navy vessel, an indigenously built traditional stitched sailing ship undertook its maiden overseas voyage from Porbandar to Muscat in December 2025 to revive and celebrate India's ancient maritime heritage?

1. Indian Naval Sailing Vessel Tarangini
2. Indian Naval Sailing Vessel Mhadei
3. Indian Naval Sailing Vessel Sudarshini
4. Indian Naval Sailing Vessel Kaundinya

43. 3 **44.** 1 **45.** 3 **46.** 2 **47.** 1 **48.** 4

49. World Polio Day is observed every year on October 24 to raise awareness about polio eradication. Which theme was selected for World Polio Day in 2025?

1. End Polio: Every Child, Every Vaccine, Everywhere
2. Eradicate Polio: Polio Free Future for All Families
3. A Global Mission to Reach Every Child
4. Vaccinate to Protect Every Generation

50. In the context of India's maritime capability development, consider the following statements regarding Indian Coast Guard Ship (ICGS) Samudra Pratap.

1. ICGS Samudra Pratap is India's first indigenously designed pollution control vessel, with more than 60% indigenous content.
2. It is the largest ship in the Indian Coast Guard fleet and was built by Goa Shipyard Limited.

Which of the statements given above is/are correct?

1. 2 only
2. Both 1 and 2
3. 1 only
4. Neither 1 nor 2

51. In August 2025, a former Governor of the Reserve Bank of India was appointed as an Executive Director at the International Monetary Fund for a three-year term. Identify the person among the following.

1. Raghuram Rajan
2. Urjit Patel
3. Shaktikanta Das
4. Viral Acharya

52. In January 2026, Bulgaria became the 21st member of the eurozone. Which of the following European Union countries have NOT adopted the euro by January 2026?

1. Poland, Czech Republic, Hungary
2. Slovenia, Slovakia, Croatia
3. Slovenia, Latvia, Estonia
4. Lithuania, Austria, Belgium

53. In December 2025, during a ceremony at Rashtrapati Bhavan, the President of India released a new edition of the Constitution written in the Ol Chiki script. In which language was this edition of the Constitution published?

1. Santhali
2. Bodo
3. Dogri
4. Konkani

54. Select the correct option based on the given Assertion (A) and Reason (R).

Assertion (A): The 43rd Constitutional Amendment Act introduced the concept of Fundamental Duties into the Indian Constitution.

Reason (R): Fundamental Duties were added to promote responsible citizenship and encourage individuals to contribute to national development.

1. A is false but R is true.
2. Both A and R are true, and R is the correct explanation of A.
3. Both A and R are true, but R is not the correct explanation of A.
4. A is true but R is false.

55. Which two states secured the top two ranks at the Sixth National Water Awards in 2025?

1. Maharashtra and Gujarat
2. Uttar Pradesh and Kerala
3. Gujarat and Rajasthan
4. Maharashtra and Rajasthan

56. The simplified form of $\frac{\left(6^{-1} \times \sqrt{216}\right)^4}{1296}$ is:

1. $\frac{1}{6}$
2. $\frac{1}{36}$
3. $\frac{1}{1296}$
4. $\frac{1}{216}$

49. 1	**50.** 2	**51.** 2	**52.** 1	**53.** 1	**54.** 1	**55.** 1	**56.** 2

57. A car covers a distance of 750 km at a constant speed. Had the car increased the speed by 10 kmph, it would have taken 2.5 hours less to cover the same distance. Find the original speed of the car.

1. 40 kmph
2. 75 kmph
3. 50 kmph
4. 60 kmph

58. Mehul buys an antique vase for ₹ 4,800. He sells it to Raghav at a loss of 20%. Raghav repairs it for ₹ 600 and then sells it to Farhan at a profit of 25% on his total cost. What is the final selling price?

1. ₹ 5,250
2. ₹ 5,600
3. ₹ 5,550
4. ₹ 5,680

59. If 12 workers can build a wall in 15 days, working 6 hours per day, then in how many days can 10 workers build two such walls, if they work for 4 hours per day?

1. 54 days
2. 52 days
3. 27 days
4. 26 days

60. A bakery sources flour from two mills; one supplies flour with 2% impurity, and the other with 8%. After mixing flour from both mills, the combined impurity rate is found to be 6.5%. What percentage of the total mixture of the flour came from the second mill?

1. 25%
2. 78%
3. 75%
4. 22%

61. A mixture of two sugar solutions contains 26% sugar in the first solution and 60% sugar in the second solution. The overall sugar concentration in the mixture is 43%. If 150 liters of the mixture is prepared, what is the quantity (in liters) of the second solution used? If the sugar concentration of the mixture was 55%, what would have been the quantity (in liters) of the second sugar solution in the mixture? (Round off your answer to the nearest integer.)

1. 75, 118
2. 75, 128
3. 72, 118
4. 72, 128

62. A researcher has a median "p" for the data set 15, 12, 14, 28, 16, 28, 32, 36, 13, 12, 34, 39. If the 16 is replaced by 19, and 13 by 31 in the above data set, then the median of the resulting data set is "q". The arithmetic mean of "p" and "q" is:

1. 28
2. 25
3. 56
4. 50

63. The cost price of 6 articles is equal to the selling price of 10 articles. Find the gain or loss per cent.

1. 60% gain
2. 40% gain
3. 60% loss
4. 40% loss

64. The simplified value of $\dfrac{7.2 \times 0.28 \times 5}{0.8 \times 0.12 \times 0.25}$ is:

1. 4.2
2. 420
3. 0.42
4. 42

65. A solid cuboid of dimensions 20 cm × 15 cm × 10 cm is melted and recast into small cubes of side 2.5 cm each. If 10% of the material is lost during recasting, the number of whole (complete) cubes cast is:

1. 175
2. 172
3. 170
4. 173

66. A bag contains 3 red, 5 blue, and 2 green balls. Two balls are drawn one after another without replacement.

Find the probability that both balls are blue.

1. $\dfrac{2}{5}$
2. $\dfrac{5}{18}$
3. $\dfrac{2}{9}$
4. $\dfrac{1}{6}$

57. 3 **58.** 3 **59.** 1 **60.** 3 **61.** 2 **62.** 2 **63.** 4 **64.** 2 **65.** 2 **66.** 3

67. Three numbers are in the ratio 2 : 3 : 4. If their LCM is 480, then their HCF is ________.

1. 2
2. 40
3. 20
4. 80

68. An amount of ₹ 5,000 is invested at 8% per annum for 2 years. If the investment is made under both compound interest and simple interest at the same rate and for the same period, what is the difference between the compound interest and the simple interest?

1. ₹ 36
2. ₹ 35
3. ₹ 38
4. ₹ 32

69. The sum of two natural numbers, x and y, is 324, and the HCF of x and y is 18. If $x < y$, how many such possible pairs of x and y are there?

1. 2
2. 4
3. 5
4. 3

70. A can complete a piece of work in 10 days, and B can do the same work in 15 days. They work together for 5 days, and then C finishes the remaining work in 2 days. How long would C alone take to complete the entire work?

1. 12 days
2. 14 days
3. 18 days
4. 16 days

71. A tower stands vertically on the ground. From a point on the ground, the angle of elevation. If the distance from the point to the foot of tower is 27 m, find the height of the tower.

1. 22.95 meters
2. 25.65 meters
3. 45.9 meters
4. 43.2 meters

72. If $a^2 + b^2 = 50$ and $a \times b = 7$, find $\frac{a-b}{a+b}$, where $a > b > 0$

1. $\frac{5}{3}$
2. $\frac{3}{4}$
3. $\frac{4}{3}$
4. $\frac{3}{5}$

73. A person spends 70% of his income in a month. In the next month, if his income increases by 40% and his expenditure increases by 30%, then his savings increase by ₹ 1,216. What is the person's original income?

1. ₹ 3,475
2. ₹ 8,960
3. ₹ 2,482
4. ₹ 6,400

74. Among three partners A, B and C in a business, the capital of B is equal to half the difference between thrice the capital of C and twice the capital of A. If at the end of the year, they received a profit of ₹ 27,460, what is the share of C (in ₹)?

1. ₹ 10,984
2. ₹ 9,976
3. ₹ 16,476
4. ₹ 12,484

75. A regular hexagon has the same perimeter as a square whose side is 36 m.

Find the area (in m^2) of the hexagon.

1. $54\sqrt{3}$ m^2
2. $864\sqrt{3}$ m^2
3. $324\sqrt{3}$ m^2
4. $468\sqrt{3}$ m^2

76. A dice has its faces named by two letters (P, Z), two numbers (2, 7) and two symbols (μ, Ω). Two positions of the same dice are given below. Which face is opposite to face μ?

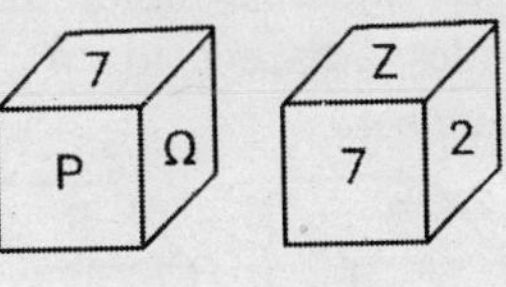

1. P
2. 2
3. 7
4. Ω

67. 2 **68.** 4 **69.** 4 **70.** 1 **71.** 3 **72.** 2 **73.** 4 **74.** 1 **75.** 2 **76.** 3

77. In a certain code language, 'camera angle reverse settings' is coded as '*p6 a5 q7 y4*' and 'methods shown before work' is coded as '*u3 z5 k6 q4*'.

What is the probable code for 'venn diagram'?

1. *t3 b6*
2. *u5 c6*
3. *b6 u5*
4. *c6 u3*

78. Identify the figure given in the options which when put in place of the question mark (?) will logically complete the series.

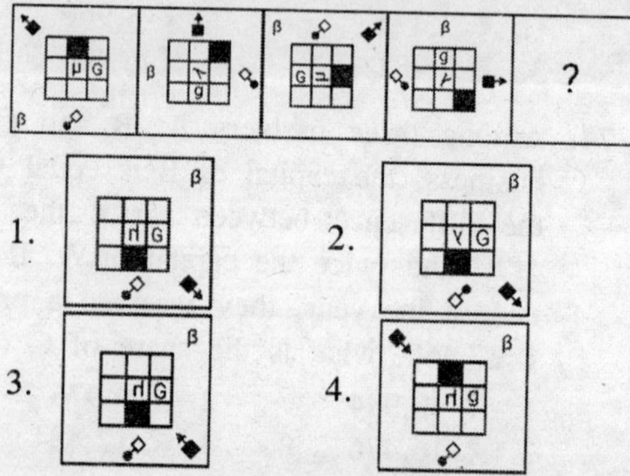

79. A dice has its faces marked by digits 1, 2, 5, 6, 8 and 9. Three positions of the dice are given below. One of the faces in the second image of the dice is masked by '#'.

Which of the following statements is/are true?

(I) The product of the values of '#' and the side opposite to it is 54.

(II) The sum of the values of '#' and the side opposite to '6' is a prime number.

(III) The square root of the sum of all the sides adjacent to '#' gives a rational number.

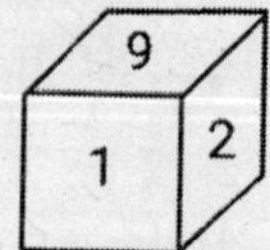

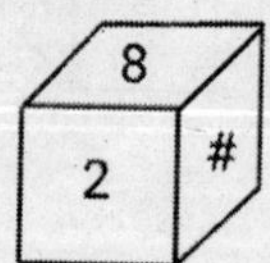

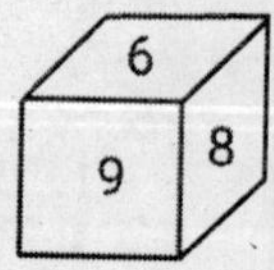

1. Both II and III
2. Only II
3. Only III
4. Both I and II

80. Study the given pattern carefully and select the number that is the product of P and Q (Different operations when performed on the two numbers given in each of the sectors in figure X yield the same result P. Similarly, different operations when performed on the two numbers given in each of the sectors in figure Y yield the same result Q.)

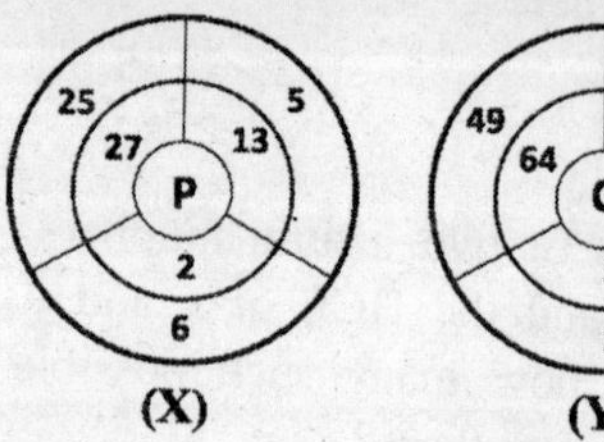

1. 54
2. 40
3. 88
4. 10

81. Which of the given options correctly defines the relationship between x and y, if '× means ÷', '÷ means +', '+ means −', and '− means ×'?

$x = 40 \times 5 \div 12 - 2 + 22$

$y = 60 \times 10 \div 2 - 3 + 4$

1. $\sqrt{(x^2 - y^2 - 11)} = \pm 5$
2. $4x^2 > y^3$
3. $(3/2)x > 2y$
4. $\sqrt{(x^2 - y^2)} = 36$

82. Four groups of letters are given in jumbled form in the options. In each of them, a meaningful English word can be made by rearranging the letters. Find the odd one out after making the meaningful words.

1. RMOOT
2. EGNIEN
3. XARBOGE
4. IENBRTU

77. 1 **78.** 1 **79.** 2 **80.** 3 **81.** 1 **82.** 3

83. In a certain code language,

F @ G means 'F is greater than G',
F % G means 'F is less than G' and
F & G means 'F is equal to G'.

If:

P = 14 × 5 − (10 × 4) ÷ 8
Q = 120 ÷ 3 − 40 + 15 × 2
R = 6 × 4 − 20 + 27 ÷ 3

Which of the following statements is/are true?

Statement I: P & 2Q % 5R
Statement II: P % 3Q % 7R

1. Only II
2. Neither I nor II
3. Both I and II
4. Only I

84. Study the given pattern carefully and select the letters that can replace the symbols in the last figure.

1. $ = U, % = Q, @ = O
2. $ = V, % = P, @ = O
3. $ = V, % = Q, @ = P
4. $ = V, % = Q, @ = N

85. A malfunctioning analogue clock gains 5 minutes per hour of operation. Given that it was initially accurately set to 8:00 AM and subsequently shows 6:00 AM the following day, determine the additional angle traversed by the hour hand of the clock.

1. 86°
2. 62°
3. 55°
4. 75°

86. J is the father of L. N is the daughter of K. Z is the son of P. J is married to K. L is the brother of O. P is married to N. Which of the following statements is/are true?

(I) J is the father-in-law of P.
(II) Z is the niece of O.
(III) K is the grandmother of Z.

1. Both I and III
2. Both I and II
3. All of them (I, II, and III)
4. Only II

87. This question contains three categories. These categories may or may not be linked to one another. Each category may fit into one of the diagrams given below in the options. Select the diagram which most aptly represents the relationship among the given categories.

Prime numbers, Even numbers, Perfect squares

1. 

2. 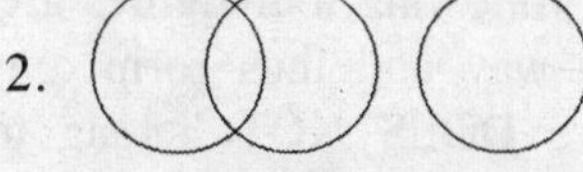

3. 

4.

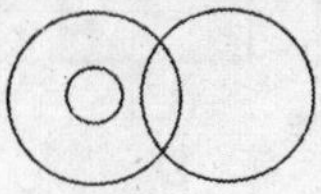

88. In a code language, 'TIMBER' is coded as "2064141121" and "JUNGLE" is coded as "7139152311". Which of the following are correct matches as per the given code language?

WORD	CODE
(*i*) STAR	(X) 2220715
(*ii*) NEST	(Y) 616413
(*iii*) LAND	(Z) 2022220

1. (*i*)-Z, (*ii*)-X only
2. (*i*)-Z, (*ii*)-X, (*iii*)-Y
3. (*iii*)-Y, (*i*)-Z only
4. (*iii*)-Y only

83. 1 **84.** 2 **85.** 3 **86.** 1 **87.** 3 **88.** 1

89. In a row of students facing north, Rahul is 22nd from the left end and Diya is 16th from the right end. If there are exactly 8 people sitting between them, what are the maximum (x) and minimum (y) possible numbers of students in the row?

1. $x = 46, y = 28$
2. $x = 46, y = 24$
3. $x = 44, y = 24$
4. $x = 45, y = 28$

90. SILENT is related to ROCMGT in a certain way based on the English alphabetical order. In the same way, FRIDGE is related to CHBJPG. To which of the following is SHADOW related, following the same logic?

1. BFTUPB
2. UPBBFT
3. VBFTVQ
4. FTBBUP

91. Three of the following four figures are alike in a certain way and thus form a group. Which figure DOES NOT belong to that group?

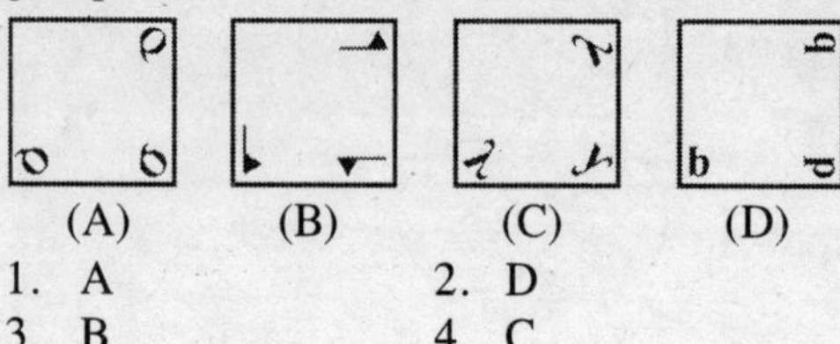

(A) (B) (C) (D)

1. A
2. D
3. B
4. C

92. From the given options, select the option in which the dots can be placed in the same way as shown in the question figure below.

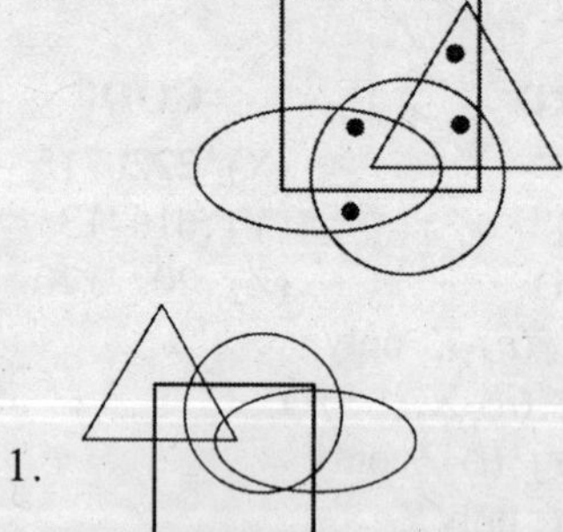

1.

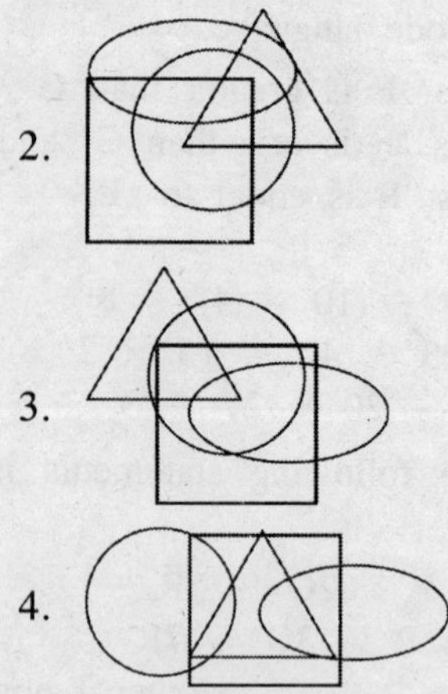

2.

3.

4.

93. In the given diagram, the square represents Technicians, the triangle represents Botanists, the circle represents Managers, and the pentagon represents Physicists. A research institute plans to recruit personnel for various positions based on the following criteria.

(*i*) Managers who are also Botanists but not Technicians

(*ii*) Technicians who are either Botanists or Physicists but not Managers.

Find the number of people in the Venn diagram who are eligible according to the criteria.

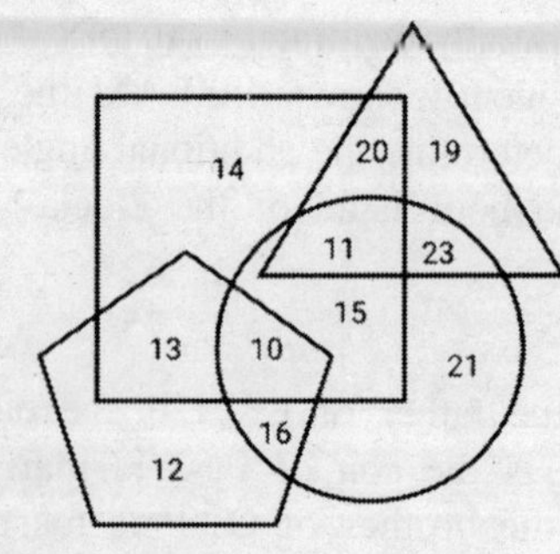

1. 35
2. 54
3. 36
4. 56

89. 1 **90.** 2 **91.** 3 **92.** 1 **93.** 4

94. P + Q means P is the brother of Q,
P % Q means P is the son of Q,
P & Q means P is the wife of Q,
P = Q means P is the husband of Q and
P @ Q means P is the daughter of Q

If 'S & T + U @ V = W @ X', then which of the following statements is not correct?

1. T is the son of W
2. U is the granddaughter of X
3. V is the mother of U
4. S is the daughter-in-law of V

95. Choose the option which is related to the third word in the same way as the second word is related to the first word and the sixth word is related to the fifth word.

Love : Tennis : : Chukker : ? : : Offside : Football

1. Hockey 2. Swimming
3. Rugby 4. Polo

96. Select the option figure that will replace the question mark (?) in the figure given below to complete the pattern.

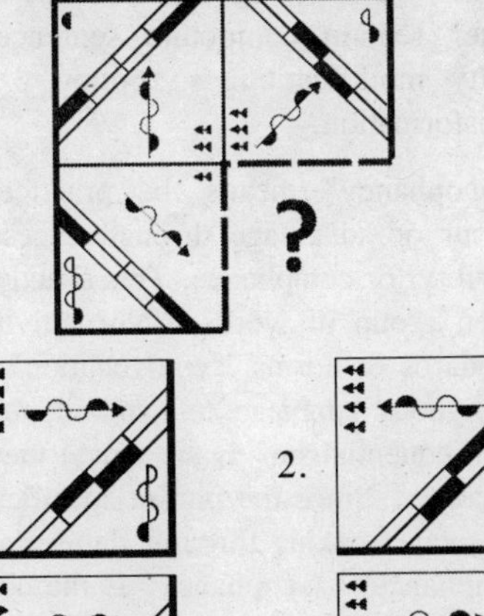

97. A scout starts walking in the forest starting from Point A towards the east for 5 m, then turns 60° left at Point P and walks for 15 m to reach Point C. She then turns 60° left and walks for 15 m to reach Point D.

What is the shortest distance the scout can take to reach Point P again from Point D?

1. $5\sqrt{2}$ m 2. $2\sqrt{5}$ m
3. 20 m 4. 15 m

98. Saravana drives 15 km West from his office to the gym. He then turns left and drives 10 km to a supermarket. Next, he turns left and drives 39 km to a petrol pump. Finally, he takes a right turn and drives 22 km to reach his friend's house. In which direction and at what shortest distance is Saravana's office from his friend's house? (All turns are 90° unless specified.)

1. $\sqrt{40}$ km, North-west
2. 40 km, North-west
3. 40 km, North-east
4. $4\sqrt{20}$ km, South-east

99. If 14 November 1989 was a Tuesday, then what was the day of the week on 26 April 2013?

1. Friday 2. Sunday
3. Saturday 4. Thursday

100. In the following triads, each group of letters is related to the subsequent one following a certain logic.

REST - THOO - PKMP
FARM - HDNH - DGLI

Which of the following are correct matches as per the given code language?

(*i*) TRIM	(W) VVFI	(A) FOGQ
(*ii*) HINT	(X) JMJP	(B) RXCI
	(Y) JLJO	(C) QYCJ
	(Z) VUEH	(D) FOHP

1. (i)-(W)-(A), (ii)-(Y)-(C)
2. (i)-(X)-(A), (ii)-(Y)-(B)
3. (i)-(X)-(D), (ii)-(Z)-(C)
4. (i)-(Z)-(B), (ii)-(Y)-(D)

94. 3 **95.** 4 **96.** 4 **97.** 4 **98.** 2 **99.** 1 **100.** 4

EXPLANATORY ANSWERS

1. The error lies in the part "as well as several senior advisors, were present." The main subject of the sentence is "The chairperson of the ethics committee," which is singular. The phrase "as well as several senior advisors" is only an additional phrase and does not make the subject plural. Therefore, the verb should be "was present" instead of "were present." Hence, option 2 is the correct answer.

2. A constitution provides the foundational rules, principles, and structural framework according to which governance is carried out. In the same way, grammar provides the foundational rules and structural framework according to which language is correctly interpreted. The relationship is therefore not merely between two related words, but between a rule-based framework and the process it regulates or enables. Hence, "Grammar" best completes the analogy with "Interpretation."

3. A panacea means a remedy or solution that is believed to cure all diseases or solve all problems. The word exactly matches the given group of words. "Palliative" only gives temporary relief, "succor" means help or assistance, and "elixir" may mean a magical or medicinal liquid but is not as exact as "panacea." Therefore, option 2 is the correct answer.

4. The idiom "to throw the helve after the hatchet" means to add to one's loss after already suffering an initial loss. The "hatchet" represents the first loss, and the "helve" or handle being thrown after it suggests further waste or damage. It is close in meaning to acting in a way that makes a bad situation worse after an earlier failure. Therefore, option 3 is the correct answer.

5. The correct sentence is: "To address the reviewer's concerns, the scholar revised two core arguments, yet acknowledged that pursuing too many theoretical directions simultaneously could weaken the overall coherence of the dissertation significantly." The sentence must begin with the main action, so Q comes first. S naturally follows Q because it introduces what the scholar acknowledged. P completes the idea after "pursuing," and R connects "simultaneously" with "could weaken the overall coherence." Therefore, option 4 is the correct answer.

6. The word "archetypal" means typical, representative, or conforming to a standard model or pattern. In the sentence, the hero is described as following established mythic patterns, which reinforces the idea of being typical or model-like. The antonym should therefore mean unusual, irregular, or deviating from the norm. "Anomalous" best expresses this opposite meaning, while "fortuitous" means accidental, "immutable" means unchanging, and "recondite" means obscure or difficult to understand.

7. The original sentence is a complex sentence because it contains the concessive clause "Though the theoretical framework appeared robust." To transform it into a simple sentence, the subordinate clause must be reduced to a phrase without changing the meaning. "Robust theoretical framework notwithstanding" correctly preserves the concessive sense of "though the framework appeared robust." The other options either remain compound sentences or create faulty modification, so option 3 is the best transformation.

8. "Sycophancy" means the practice of gaining favour or advantage through excessive flattery, servility, or compliance. This exactly matches the given group of words. "Normativity" refers to standards or norms, "equivocation" means using ambiguous language to avoid commitment, and "consequentialism" is an ethical theory based on outcomes. Since the phrase specifically refers to advantage-seeking through flattery and excessive compliance, "sycophancy" is the correct choice.

9. A "martinet" is a person who demands strict discipline and rigid obedience to rules, often in an unnecessarily harsh or excessive manner. This precisely fits the description of someone who insists on strict compliance even when it is not needed. A "disciplinarian" may enforce discipline, but the word is broader and not necessarily excessive. "Dogmatic" refers to being rigid in beliefs, and "iconoclast" means someone who attacks established traditions, so "martinet" is the best answer.

10. The correct completion is: "Postcolonial literary criticism has repeatedly challenged the neutrality of narrative voice through close attention to perspective, silence, and narrative authority, revealing how stylistic transparency can function as ideological concealment rather than as an absence of mediation when imperial epistemologies are naturalised as universal experience within texts long regarded as formally objective." Part R correctly explains the method by which neutrality is challenged. Part P then states what this method reveals, S completes the contrast after "rather than," and Q gives the condition under which this concealment operates. Therefore, the sequence R – P – S – Q forms the most meaningful and grammatically correct sentence.

11. The sentence has no grammatical error. The expression "cautioned against excessive reliance" is correct because "against" is properly followed by the noun phrase "excessive reliance." The phrase "anecdotal indicators masquerading as statistically representative evidence" is also grammatically and semantically correct. "Masquerading as" correctly means pretending to be something that it is not, so option 4 is the correct answer.

12. The correct sentence is: "Though the researcher went through a thorough review, she deliberately threw the outdated assumptions aside." "Though" introduces contrast, "went through" means underwent or experienced, "thorough review" means a complete and careful review, and "threw aside" means rejected or discarded. All four words are correctly placed according to both meaning and grammar. Hence, option 1 is the correct answer.

13. The idiom "to ride on Shank's mare" means to walk or travel on foot. "Shank" refers to the leg, so the idiom humorously suggests using one's own legs as the means of transport. The other options are either too broad or only indirectly related to self-effort. Since the exact idiomatic meaning is travelling by walking, option 4 is the correct answer.

14. The sentence requires a pair that shows a careful balance between intellectual sharpness and professional restraint. "Trenchant" means sharply incisive, forceful, or strongly critical, so the panel deliberately avoided trenchant language to prevent the assessment from seeming dismissive or ideologically rigid. "Measured" means carefully considered, moderate, and controlled, which fits the idea of offering criticism that still conveys intellectual rigour without becoming harsh. Therefore, "trenchant / measured" best completes both blanks according to the intended evaluative meaning.

15. The error is in the phrase "the researcher submitting sensitive data." After "disapproved of," the more grammatically precise possessive construction is required before a gerund: "the researcher's submitting sensitive data." The corrected sentence would be: "The supervisor disapproved of the researcher's submitting sensitive data without proper authorisation during the preliminary phase of the study." Parts (b) and (c) are grammatically correct. Hence, option 4 is the correct answer.

16. The underlined word "exculpatory" means serving to clear someone from blame, guilt, or accusation. In the sentence, the evidence helps dismiss the indictment and weakens the prosecution's case, so the word clearly has a guilt-removing sense. "Exonerative" has the same meaning, as it refers to something that absolves or clears a person of blame. "Tendentious," "premonitory," and "duplicitous" do not convey this meaning, so option 4 is the correct answer.

17. The phrase "the researcher's withholding of critical data" is grammatically correct because "withholding" is a gerund, and a possessive noun before a gerund is the more precise formal construction. The second blank requires a singular abstract noun referring to the act just mentioned, so "behaviour" is correct. "Researcher's withhold" is grammatically wrong because "withhold" is a verb, not a noun or gerund in that position. "Researchers withholding" and "researcher withholding" are less formally correct in this structure, so option 1 is the best answer.

18. The most coherent arrangement is: "In policy debates on artificial intelligence, ethical oversight is frequently invoked as a compensatory gesture for rapid technological deployment that remains largely procedural rather than substantively transformative while responsibility is dispersed across advisory frameworks allowing innovation to proceed without structural restraint that lack both enforcement authority and democratic accountability." The sequence begins properly with P because "invoked as" forms the required grammatical structure after "ethical oversight is frequently invoked." Q then qualifies the gesture as procedural rather than transformative, S introduces the dispersal of responsibility, and R explains the result of that dispersal. The sentence as printed appears to contain a concord problem at the end because "that lack" most naturally refers to "advisory frameworks," but the given options make P – Q – S – R the best available logical sequence.

19. The idiom "to take the gilt off the gingerbread" means to spoil the attractiveness, charm, or appeal of something that is otherwise pleasing. The sentence says that excessive justification threatened entirely to spoil what was already attractive, which directly matches this idiom. "To throw the baby out with the bathwater" means to discard something valuable along with what is unwanted, which is not the intended meaning here. The other options also do not express the idea of reducing the charm of something attractive, so option 4 is correct.

20. The subject of the sentence is "An understanding," which is singular. The intervening phrase "of how competing theoretical paradigms intersect, rather than their individual merits alone" does not change the number of the subject. Therefore, the first verb must be singular, "has," and the second verb must also agree with the same singular subject, so "was" is required. Hence, the grammatically correct sentence is: "An understanding of how competing theoretical paradigms intersect, rather than their individual merits alone, has shaped the committee's evaluation and was decisive in determining the final recommendation."

21. The original sentence is complex because it contains the subordinate clause "When the researcher realised that the data were inconsistent." To convert it into a simple sentence, the subordinate clause must be changed into a phrase without changing the meaning. "On realising the inconsistency of the data" correctly preserves the time relationship and the cause implied in the original sentence. The other options either remain complex sentences or distort the meaning, so option 3 is correct.

22. "Alacrity" means cheerful readiness, promptness, or eagerness in responding to something. The sentence itself supports this meaning by saying that the researcher showed "an eagerness" in contrast with the usual slow academic pace. The antonym must therefore express unwillingness, lack of readiness, or reluctance. "Disinclination" means unwillingness or lack of inclination, so it is the correct opposite of "alacrity."

23. The correct expression is "bristle at criticism," which means to react angrily or defensively to criticism. The phrasal verb "beef up" means to strengthen, improve, or increase something. Therefore, the sentence correctly means that managers may react defensively to criticism but decide to strengthen training programs for better team outcomes. The other options use incorrect prepositions or incorrect phrasal verb forms, so option 2 is correct.

24. "Psephology" means the statistical or analytical study of elections, voting patterns, and election trends. This exactly matches the given phrase "study of election trends." "Phraseology" refers to the manner of wording or expression, "pyrology" relates to fire, and "posology" refers to the study of drug dosage. Therefore, "psephology" is the most appropriate one-word substitute.

25. The most appropriate word for blank (1) is "subverted," which means undermined, disrupted, or weakened. The passage says that colonial administrations imposed foreign ideologies, so the context is negative and suggests interference with indigenous customs. "Valorized" and "extolled" mean praised, which would not fit the colonial imposition described here. "Perpetuated" means continued or preserved, but the sentence implies that native customs were disturbed rather than maintained.

26. The most appropriate word for blank (2) is "dislocated," which means disrupted, displaced, or thrown out of normal arrangement. The phrase "foreign ideologies that dislocated existing social structures" correctly conveys the disturbance caused by colonial policies. "Enshrined" and "fortified" would suggest preserving or strengthening social structures, which is opposite to the intended meaning. "Accentuated" means highlighted or intensified, but it does not express the structural disruption as accurately as "dislocated."

27. The most appropriate word for blank (3) is "engendered," which means produced, caused, or gave rise to. The sentence says that colonial policies frequently led to nationalist movements, so "engendered" fits both the meaning and historical logic of the passage. "Obliterated" means destroyed, "mollified" means pacified, and "obviated" means made unnecessary. Since the passage refers to the emergence of resistance and adaptation, "engendered" is the correct answer.

28. The assertion is true because the passage clearly states that confidence does not arise from the absence of doubt. Instead, it is described as the disciplined capacity to act despite hesitation and anticipated failure. The reason is also true because confidence is presented as a balanced internal form of self-judgment that avoids both excessive self-approval and destructive self-negation. This reason directly explains why confidence can exist along with doubt, so option 2 is correct.

29. The passage explains that confidence enables initiation, while determination secures continuation. This means confidence helps a person begin action despite uncertainty, and determination helps that person persist through adversity over time. Their combined function is not to remove uncertainty or guarantee success, but to sustain purposeful action with reflective restraint. Therefore, option 2 best captures how confidence and determination work together in the passage.

30. The passage rejects the idea that confidence and determination guarantee success because it presents them as disciplined practices rather than magical assurances of outcome. It says that neither quality guarantees success; instead, they change the individual's orientation toward failure by treating it as part of refinement. The passage also stresses that confidence without determination can become bravado, and determination without confidence can become obstinacy. Therefore, both qualities must operate within adaptive, reflective, and ethical limits, making option 4 the best answer.

31. Statement 1 is correct because Flying Officer Nirmal Jit Singh Sekhon was the first and only Indian Air Force personnel to receive the Param Vir Chakra. He was awarded it posthumously for his extraordinary bravery during the 1971 Indo-Pak war. Statement 2 is incorrect because the Param Vir Chakra is not octagonal and made of silver; it is a circular bronze medal. Therefore, only statement 1 is correct, making option 2 the correct answer.

32. The Sumi and Lotha are major Naga tribes associated with Nagaland. The Sumi tribe's energetic war dance is connected with celebrations of victory and martial tradition. The Lotha women's Mungyanta harvest dance is performed during Tokhu Emong, which is an important festival of the Lotha Nagas. Since both the Sumi war dance and the Lotha Mungyanta dance belong to the cultural traditions of Nagaland, option 4 is correct.

33. AILA, introduced by IIT Delhi, is an Artificially Intelligent Lab Assistant designed to conduct real scientific experiments autonomously. Its importance lies in going beyond ordinary assistance such as literature review or data collection. It can operate laboratory instruments, make decisions, run experiments, and analyse results in a manner comparable to a human scientist. Therefore, option 1 is the most appropriate answer.

34. Statement 1 is incorrect because Aero India is not an annual event; it is generally organised as a biennial air show and aviation exhibition in Bengaluru. The part about its organisation by the Defence Exhibition Organisation under the Department of Defence Production is correct, but the statement becomes incorrect due to the word "annual." Statement 2 is correct because Aero India 2025 was the 15th edition and its broad theme was "The Runway to a Billion Opportunities." Therefore, only statement 2 is correct, making option 1 the correct answer.

35. "Layup" and "three-point shot" are standard terms used in basketball. A layup is a close-range shot taken near the basket, usually while moving toward it. A three-point shot is a shot made from beyond the three-point line and is worth three points if successful. These terms are not associated with ice hockey, volleyball, or futsal in their standard sporting usage, so option 1 is correct.

36. Siliserh Lake is located in Alwar district of Rajasthan. It is associated with the Aravalli landscape and lies near the Sariska region, making it ecologically significant. The question specifically asks the state in which this newly recognised Ramsar wetland is located. Since Siliserh Lake belongs to Rajasthan, option 1 is the correct answer.

37. The Battle of Stalingrad was one of the most decisive and famous battles of World War II. It was fought between Nazi Germany and the Soviet Union and marked a major turning point on the Eastern Front. The battle is not associated with the Cold War, French Revolution, or Russian Revolution. Therefore, option 2 is the correct answer.

38. The larynx is a cartilaginous organ in the human body and is commonly called the sound box. It contains the vocal cords, which vibrate to produce sound when air passes through them. The bronchioles are air passages in the lungs, the pharynx is a passage for food and air, and the epiglottis helps prevent food from entering the windpipe. Hence, option 3 is the correct answer.

39. The 22nd ASEAN–India Summit held in 2025 declared 2026 as the ASEAN-India Year of Maritime Cooperation. This reflects the importance of maritime connectivity, security, and cooperation between India and ASEAN countries. The other options referring to economic collaboration, digital connectivity, or cultural engagement do not match the declared theme. Therefore, option 4 is the correct answer.

40. The Small Industries Development Bank of India, commonly known as SIDBI, was established in 1990 under an Act of the Indian Parliament. It acts as the principal financial institution for promotion, financing, and development of the MSME sector. NABARD is mainly associated with agriculture and rural development, while IDBI and the other option do not fit the specific MSME role described in the question. Hence, option 1 is the correct answer.

41. The regions lying between the Tropic of Cancer and the Arctic Circle in the Northern Hemisphere, and between the Tropic of Capricorn and the Antarctic Circle in the Southern Hemisphere, are called the Temperate Zones. These regions are neither as hot as the Torrid Zone nor as cold as the Frigid Zones. They generally experience moderate climatic conditions with seasonal variation. Therefore, option 1 is the correct answer.

42. A seamount is an underwater mountain rising from the ocean floor with a pointed or conical summit that does not reach the ocean surface. Such features can attain great heights, often around 3,000 to 4,500 metres above the seafloor. A guyot is different because it has a flat top, while a continental shelf is a shallow submerged margin of a continent. Therefore, the feature described in the question is a seamount, making option 2 correct.

43. Statement 1 is correct because UN peacekeepers are popularly called Blue Helmets due to the distinctive light blue colour associated with the United Nations. Statement 2 is also correct in the intended exam sense because, in 2023, the Dag Hammarskjöld Medal was posthumously awarded to Indian personnel Shishupal Singh, Sanwala Ram Vishnoi, and civilian UN worker Shaber Taher Ali; Shishupal Singh and Sanwala Ram Vishnoi served in the Democratic Republic of the Congo, while Shaber Taher Ali served in a civilian capacity with the UN Assistance Mission for Iraq. Statement 3 is correct because Major Radhika Sen was named the UN's Military Gender Advocate of the Year 2023. Therefore, all three statements are correct, making option 3 the correct answer.

44. Rebeca Andrade was awarded the Laureus World Comeback of the Year award in 2025. She is a Brazilian artistic gymnast and received the honour for her remarkable return and achievements after serious injury setbacks. The other listed names are associated with different years of the same award or other sporting achievements. Hence, option 1 is the correct answer.

45. Exercise Indradhanush is conducted between India and the United Kingdom, so A matches III. Exercise Desert Knight involves India, France, and the United Arab Emirates, so B matches IV. Exercise Eastern Bridge is conducted between India and Oman, so C matches II. Exercise Veer Guardian is conducted between India and Japan, so D matches I, making option 3 the correct answer.

46. Statement 1 is correct because the Rowlatt Act empowered the British Government to arrest and detain Indians without trial. It was strongly opposed because it continued wartime repressive measures even after the First World War. Statement 2 is incorrect because Gandhiji gave the call for Rowlatt Satyagraha in 1919, not in April 1917. Therefore, only statement 1 is correct, making option 2 the correct answer.

47. The SHANTI Bill, 2025, opens India's nuclear energy sector to private participation, but not in an unrestricted manner. It allows private entities to participate under licensing, safety, and regulatory controls while strategic nuclear activities remain under state oversight. It does not authorise private firms to control all strategic nuclear assets or independently handle the entire nuclear fuel cycle. Therefore, option 1 is the correct answer.

48. INSV Kaundinya is the indigenously built traditional stitched sailing ship associated with the revival of India's ancient maritime heritage. Its maiden overseas voyage from Porbandar to Muscat was intended to symbolically retrace historical maritime links between India and West Asia. The vessel is different from Tarangini, Mhadei, and Sudarshini, which are modern Indian naval sailing vessels. Therefore, option 4 is the correct answer.

49. Every Child, Every Vaccine, Everywhere: The theme selected for World Polio Day 2025 was "End Polio: Every Child, Every Vaccine, Everywhere." The theme emphasised the need to vaccinate every child and ensure that no community is left unprotected. It also reflected the continuing global commitment to complete polio eradication. Hence, option 1 is the correct answer.

50. Statement 1 is correct because ICGS Samudra Pratap is India's first indigenously designed pollution control vessel and has more than 60% indigenous content. Statement 2 is also correct because it is the largest ship in the Indian Coast Guard fleet and was built by Goa Shipyard Limited. The vessel marks an important step in India's maritime pollution-control and shipbuilding capability. Therefore, both statements are correct, making option 2 the correct answer.

51. Former Reserve Bank of India Governor Urjit Patel was appointed as Executive Director at the International Monetary Fund for a three-year term in August 2025. He had earlier served as the 24th Governor of the RBI, which makes him the correct former RBI Governor among the given options. Raghuram Rajan, Shaktikanta Das, and Viral Acharya do not fit this specific appointment mentioned in the question. Therefore, option 2 is the correct answer.

52. Bulgaria adopted the euro on 1 January 2026 and became the 21st member of the eurozone. By January 2026, Poland, Czech Republic, and Hungary had not adopted the euro, so they correctly fit the question. Slovenia, Slovakia, Croatia, Latvia, Estonia, Lithuania, Austria, and Belgium are already eurozone members. Therefore, option 1 is the correct answer.

53. The Constitution written in the Ol Chiki script was released in the Santhali language. Ol Chiki is the script specifically associated with the Santhali language, and the President released this edition at Rashtrapati Bhavan in December 2025. Bodo, Dogri, and Konkani are not written in Ol Chiki as their primary script in this context. Therefore, option 1 is the correct answer.

54. The Assertion is false because Fundamental Duties were introduced into the Indian Constitution by the 42nd Constitutional Amendment Act, 1976, not by the 43rd Constitutional Amendment Act. The Reason is true because Fundamental Duties were added to promote responsible citizenship and remind citizens of their duties toward the nation. However, since the Assertion contains the wrong amendment number, it cannot be accepted as correct. Therefore, option 1 is the correct answer.

55. At the Sixth National Water Awards, Maharashtra secured the first rank in the Best State category, while Gujarat secured the second rank. Haryana was placed third, so Rajasthan, Kerala, and Uttar Pradesh do not form the correct top-two combination in the given options. The pair asked in the question is therefore Maharashtra and Gujarat. Hence, option 1 is the correct answer.

56. $\dfrac{\left(6^{-1} \times \sqrt{216}\right)^4}{1296}$

$$\sqrt{216} = \sqrt{36 \times 6} = 6\sqrt{6}$$

$$6^{-1} \times \sqrt{216} = \frac{1}{6} \times 6\sqrt{6} = \sqrt{6}$$

$$\frac{\left(\sqrt{6}\right)^4}{1296} = \frac{36}{1296} = \frac{1}{36}$$

Therefore, the simplified form is $\frac{1}{36}$, so option 2 is correct.

57. $\dfrac{750}{x} - \dfrac{750}{x+10} = 2.5$

$$\frac{7500}{x(x+10)} = 2.5$$

$$x(x + 10) = 3000$$

$$x^2 + 10x - 3000 = 0$$

$$x = 50$$

Therefore, the original speed of the car is 50 kmph, so option 3 is correct.

58. Mehul's CP = 4800

Mehul's SP to Raghav = 4800 × 80% = 3840

Raghav's total cost = 3840 + 600 = 4440

Raghav's SP = 4440 × 125% = 5550

Therefore, the final selling price is ₹ 5,550, so option 3 is correct.

59. Work for 1 wall = 12 × 15 × 6

= 1080 worker-hours

Work for 2 walls = 2 × 1080

= 2160 worker-hours

Daily work by 10 workers = 10 × 4 = 4(worker-hours

$$\text{Required days} = \frac{2160}{40} = 54$$

Therefore, 10 workers will build two such wall in 54 days, so option 1 is correct.

60. Let flour from second mill = x%

$$\frac{8x + 2(100 - x)}{100} = 6.5$$

$$8x + 200 - 2x = 650$$

$$6x = 450$$

$$x = 75$$

Therefore, 75% of the total mixture came fror the second mill, so option 3 is correct.

61. Quantity of second solution for 43%

$$= \frac{43 - 26}{60 - 26} \times 150$$

$$= \frac{17}{34} \times 150 = 75$$

Quantity of second solution for 55%

$$= \frac{55 - 26}{60 - 26} \times 150$$

$$= \frac{29}{34} \times 150 = 127.94 \approx 12$$

Therefore, the required quantities are 75 litr and 128 litres, so option 2 is correct.

62. Original data in ascending order: 12,12,13,1 15,16,28,28,32,34,36,39

$$p = \frac{16 + 28}{2} = 22$$

New data in ascending order: 12,12,14,15,1 28,28,31,32,34,36,39

$$q = \frac{28 + 28}{2} = 28$$

Arithmetic mean of p and q = $\frac{22 + 28}{2}$ = 2

Therefore, the arithmetic mean is 25, so opti 2 is correct.

63. CP of 6 articles = SP of 10 articles

$$6 \text{ CP} = 10 \text{ SP}$$

$$\text{SP} = \frac{6}{10} \text{ CP} = \frac{3}{5} \text{ CP}$$

Loss = CP − SP = $CP - \frac{3}{5}CP = \frac{2}{5}CP$

Loss percentage = $\frac{2}{5} \times 100 = 40\%$

Therefore, there is a 40% loss, so option 4 is correct.

64. $\frac{7.2 \times 0.28 \times 5}{0.8 \times 0.12 \times 0.25}$

$= \frac{7.2}{0.8} \times \frac{0.28}{0.12} \times \frac{5}{0.25}$

$= 9 \times \frac{28}{12} \times 20 = 9 \times \frac{7}{3} \times 20$

$= 3 \times 7 \times 20 = 420$

Therefore, the simplified value is 420, so option 2 is correct.

65. Volume of cuboid = $20 \times 15 \times 10 = 3000 \text{ cm}^3$

Usable volume after 10% loss

$= 3000 \times \frac{90}{100} = 2700 \text{ cm}^3$

Volume of each small cube

$= 2.5^3 = 15.625 \text{ cm}^3$

Number of complete cubes

$= \frac{2700}{15.625} = 172.8$

Only whole complete cubes can be counted, so the number of cubes cast is 172, making option 2 correct.

66. Total balls = 3 + 5 + 2 = 10

P(first blue) = $\frac{5}{10}$

P(second blue after first blue) = $\frac{4}{9}$

P(both blue) = $\frac{5}{10} \times \frac{4}{9} = \frac{1}{2} \times \frac{4}{9} = \frac{2}{9}$

Therefore, the probability that both balls are blue is $\frac{2}{9}$, so option 3 is correct.

67. Let the numbers be $2x$, $3x$, $4x$

LCM of $2x$, $3x$, $4x$ = $12x$

$12x = 480$

$x = 40$

Since x is the common factor of the three numbers, their HCF is 40, so option 2 is correct.

68. Difference between CI and SI for 2 years

$= P\left(\frac{r}{100}\right)^2 = 5000\left(\frac{8}{100}\right)^2$

$= 5000 \times \frac{64}{10000} = 32$

Therefore, the difference between compound interest and simple interest is ₹ 32, so option 4 is correct.

69. $x + y = 324$, HCF = 18

$x = 18a$, $y = 18b$, $\gcd(a, b) = 1$

$18a + 18b = 324$

$a + b = 18$, $a < b$

Possible coprime pairs are (1,17),(5,13),(7,11). Therefore, there are 3 possible pairs, so option 4 is correct.

70. A's 1 day work = $\frac{1}{10}$, B's 1 day work = $\frac{1}{15}$

A+B 1 day work = $\frac{1}{10} + \frac{1}{15} = \frac{1}{6}$

Work done in 5 days = $5 \times \frac{1}{6} = \frac{5}{6}$

Remaining work = $1 - \frac{5}{6} = \frac{1}{6}$

C completes $\frac{1}{6}$ work in 2 days, so C's 1 day work = $\frac{1}{12}$

Therefore, C alone would complete the entire work in 12 days, so option 1 is correct.

71. AB = 27 m, ∠A = 59.5°

$\tan\theta = \frac{\text{Perpendicular}}{\text{Base}}$

$\tan 59.5° = \frac{BC}{AB}$

$BC = AB \times \tan 59.5°$

$BC = 27 \times \tan 59.5°$

$\tan 59.5° \approx 1.7$

$BC = 27 \times 1.7 = 45.9$ m

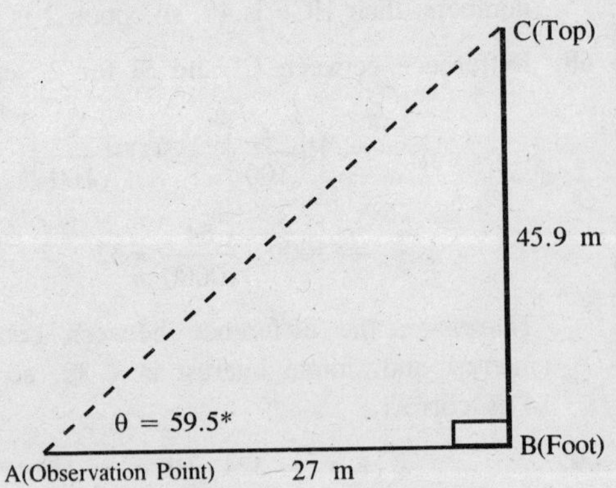

In the given diagram, AB is the horizontal distance from the observation point to the foot of the tower, and BC is the height of the tower. Since the angle of elevation from A to the top C is 59.5°, the tangent ratio is used. Therefore, the height of the tower is 45.9 meters, so option 3 is correct.

72. $a^2 + b^2 = 50, ab = 7$

$(a - b)^2 = a^2 + b^2 - 2ab$

$(a - b)^2 = 50 - 2(7) = 50 - 14 = 36$

$a - b = 6$

$(a + b)^2 = a^2 + b^2 + 2ab$

$(a + b)^2 = 50 + 2(7) = 50 + 14 = 64$

$a + b = 8$

$$\frac{a-b}{a+b} = \frac{6}{8} = \frac{3}{4}$$

Therefore, the value of $\frac{a-b}{a+b}$ is $\frac{3}{4}$, so option 2 is correct.

73. Let original income $= x$

Original expenditure $= 70\%$ of $x = 0.7x$

Original savings $= x - 0.7x = 0.3x$

New income $= 1.4x$

New expenditure $= 1.3 \times 0.7x = 0.91x$

New savings $= 1.4x - 0.91x = 0.49x$

$0.49x - 0.3x = 1216$

$0.19x = 1216$

$x = 6400$

Therefore, the person's original income is ₹ 6,400, so option 4 is correct.

74. $B = \frac{3C - 2A}{2}$

$2B = 3C - 2A$

$2A + 2B = 3C$

$A + B = \frac{3C}{2}$

$A + B + C = \frac{3C}{2} + C = \frac{5C}{2}$

$$\text{C's share} = \frac{C}{\frac{5C}{2}} \times 27460$$

$$= \frac{2}{5} \times 27460 = 10984$$

Therefore, C's share is ₹ 10,984, so option [illegible] is correct.

75. Perimeter of square $= 4 \times 36 = 144$ m

Perimeter of regular hexagon $= 144$ m

Side of regular hexagon $= \frac{144}{6} = 24$ m

Area of regular hexagon $= \frac{3\sqrt{3}}{2}a^2$

$= \frac{3\sqrt{3}}{2} \times 24^2 = \frac{3\sqrt{3}}{2} \times 576 = 864\sqrt{3}$ m

Therefore, the area of the regular hexagon [illegible] $864\sqrt{3}$ m^2, so option 2 is correct.

76. In the first position of the dice, the faces [illegible] P, and Ω are visible together, so all three a[illegible] adjacent to one another. In the second positio[illegible] the faces Z, 7, and 2 are visible together, [illegible] 7 is also adjacent to Z and 2. Therefore, fa[illegible] 7 is adjacent to P, Ω, Z, and 2. The on[illegible] remaining face is μ, so μ must be opposite 7. Hence, the face opposite to μ is 7, maki[illegible] option 3 correct.

77. In "venn", unique letters are $v,e,n = 3$

So, the number code for "venn" is 3

In "diagram", unique letters are $d,i,a,g,r,m =$ [illegible]

So, the number code for "diagram" is 6

The letter-code pattern is not completely fix[illegible] from the two given examples, so the answ[illegible] is based on the most probable coding structu[illegible] available in the options. The only option t[illegible]

gives the natural unique-letter counts in the same word order is *t*3 *b*6, so option 1 is the best answer.

78. In the figure series, the symbol β moves step by step along the outer boundary and therefore reaches the top-right position in the missing figure. The black square inside the 3 × 3 grid also follows a positional movement pattern and is expected at the bottom-middle cell in the next figure. The letter G/*g* alternates in case, so after small *g* in the fourth figure, the next figure should contain capital G. The outer arrow and diamond symbols also match the required placement and orientation most appropriately in option 1, so option 1 correctly completes the series.

79. From the first and third dice positions, the common face is 9, and the arrangement gives the opposite pairs as 2 opposite 6, 1 opposite 8, and 5 opposite 9. In the second dice position, the hidden face marked # is 9. Therefore, the face opposite to # is 5, and their product is 9 × 5 = 45, not 54, so statement I is false. The face opposite to 6 is 2, and # + 2 = 9 + 2 = 11, which is prime; however, the faces adjacent to 9 are 1,2,6,8, whose sum is 17, and $\sqrt{17}$ is irrational, so only statement II is true.

80. In figure X:

$\sqrt{25} + \sqrt[3]{27} = 5 + 3 = 8$

$13 - 5 = 8$

$6 + 2 = 8$

$\therefore \quad P = 8$

In figure Y:

$\sqrt{49} + \sqrt[3]{64} = 7 + 4 = 11$

$17 - 6 = 11$

$8 + 3 = 11$

$\therefore \quad Q = 11$

$P \times Q = 8 \times 11 = 88$

Therefore, the product of P and Q is 88, so option 3 is correct.

1. ×→÷,÷→+,+→–,–→×

$x = 40 \div 5 + 12 \times 2 - 22$

$x = 8 + 24 - 22 = 10$

$y = 60 \div 10 + 2 \times 3 – 4$

$y = 6 + 6 - 4 = 8$

$\sqrt{(x^2 - y^2) - 11} = \sqrt{(10^2 - 8^2) - 11}$

$= \sqrt{100 - 64 - 11} = \sqrt{25} = 5$

Thus, the first relation fits the values of x and y, so option 1 is correct.

82. The meaningful words formed are "MOTOR" from RMOOT, "ENGINE" from EGNIEN, "GEARBOX" from XARBOGE, and "TURBINE" from IENBRTU. Motor, engine, and turbine are power-producing or power-converting machines. A gearbox, however, is mainly a transmission mechanism used to change speed and torque. Therefore, "GEARBOX" is the odd one out, so option 3 is correct.

83. P = 14 × 5 – (10 × 4) ÷ 8

P = 70 – 40 ÷ 8 = 70 – 5 – 65

Q = 120 ÷ 3 – 40 + 15 × 2

Q = 40 – 40 + 30 = 30

R = 6 × 4 – 20 + 27 ÷ 3

R = 24 – 20 + 9 = 13

Statement I: P & 2Q % 5R

65 = 60 < 65

This is false because 65 ≠ 60.

Statement II: P % 3Q % 7R

65 < 90 < 91

This is true.

Therefore, only statement II is true, so option 1 is correct.

84. In the left sector, the letters follow the pattern P,R,T, increasing by +2 each time in alphabetical order, so the next letter is V. In the right sector, the letters follow the pattern Y,V,S, decreasing by –3 each time, so the next letter is P. In the bottom sector, the letters follow the pattern F,I,L, increasing by +3 each time, so the next letter is O. Therefore, $ = V, % = P, @ = O, making option 2 correct.

85. Clock gains 5 minutes per hour

Time from 8:00 AM to 6:00 AM next day = 22 hours

Extra time gained = 22 × 5 = 110 minutes

Hour hand moves 0.5° per minute

Additional angle = 110 × 0.5° = 55°

Therefore, the additional angle traversed by the hour hand is 55°, so option 3 is correct.

86. J is married to K, and N is the daughter of K, so N is treated as the daughter in that family relation. Since P is married to N, J becomes the father-in-law of P, making statement I true. Z is the son of P and, through the marital relation, belongs to the next generation after N and P; hence K is the grandmother of Z, making statement III true. Statement II is false because Z is stated to be the son of P, so Z cannot be called the niece of O. Therefore, both I and III are true, so option 1 is correct.

87. Prime numbers, even numbers, and perfect squares have a partial relationship that is best shown by a chain-type Venn diagram. Prime numbers and even numbers overlap because 2 is both prime and even. Even numbers and perfect squares also overlap because numbers such as 4,16,36 are both even and perfect squares. However, prime numbers and perfect squares do not overlap directly, and there is no common element among all three categories. Therefore, option 3 correctly represents the relationship among the given categories.

88. The coding rule is that the word is first reversed, and then the letters are coded by adding +2, +1, +2, +1,...alternately to their alphabetical positions. For "STAR," the reverse is RATS, so the code is R + 2 = 20, A + 1 = 2, T + 2 = 22, S + 1 = 20, giving 2022220, which matches Z. For "NEST," the reverse is TSEN, so the code is T + 2 = 22, S + 1 = 20, E + 2 = 7, N + 1 = 15, giving 2220715, which matches X. For "LAND," the reverse is DNAL, giving 6,15,3,13, not 616413, so only (*i*)-Z and (*ii*)-X are correct.

89. Rahul's position from left = 22

Diya's position from right = 16

Diya's position from left = N − 16 + 1

= N − 15

Exactly 8 students between them

$$|(N - 15) - 22| - 1 = 8$$

$$|N - 37| = 9$$

$$N = 46 \text{ or } 28$$

Therefore, the maximum possible number of students is 46, and the minimum possible number is 28, so option 1 is correct.

90. The rule is that the given word is first written in reverse order, and then the letters are alternately shifted by −2, +1, −2, +1, −2, +1. For example, "SILENT" becomes "TNELIS," and applying the shifts gives T − 2 = R, N + 1 = O, E − 2 = C, L + 1 = M, I − 2 = G, S + 1 = T, forming "ROCMGT." Similarly, "SHADOW" becomes "WODAHS," and applying the same shifts gives W − 2 = U, O + 1 = P, D − 2 = B, A + 1 = B, H − 2 = F, S + 1 = T. Therefore, SHADOW is related to UPBBFT, making option 2 correct.

91. In figures A, C, and D, the three symbols are placed at the three corner positions: top-right, bottom-left, and bottom-right. Their symbols are also formed as rotated or changed orientations of similar curved/letter-like forms. In figure B, however, one of the symbols is placed at the middle-left side rather than at the bottom-lef corner. This makes figure B different from th other three figures in its positional arrangement Therefore, figure B does not belong to the group so option 3 is correct.

92. In the question figure, the dots occupy fou specific types of regions formed by the overla of the square, triangle, circle, and ellipse. On dot lies in the region common to the squar and triangle only, another in the common regic of square, triangle, and circle, another in th common region of square, circle, and ellips and another in the common region of circle ar ellipse only. Among the given options, optic 1 provides all these required overlapping a non-overlapping regions in the same manne Therefore, the dots can be placed in option 1 the same way as shown in the question figu

93. The square represents Technicians, the trian represents Botanists, the circle represents Manage and the pentagon represents Physicists.

For criterion (*i*), Managers who are also Botani but not Technicians are represented by the reg common to the circle and triangle but outs the square, which is 23.

For criterion (*ii*), Technicians who are eit Botanists or Physicists but not Managers represented by the square-triangle region outs the circle and the square-pentagon region outs the circle, which are 20 and 13.

Total eligible people = 23 + 20 + 13 = 56

Therefore, the number of eligible people is 56, so option 4 is correct.

94. In the relation S & T + U @ V = W @ X, S & T means S is the wife of T, so T is male. T + U means T is the brother of U, and U @ V means U is the daughter of V. Also, V = W means V is the husband of W, so V is male and is the father, not the mother. Hence, the statement "V is the mother of U" is not correct, making option 3 the correct answer.

95. "Love" is a term used in tennis, and "offside" is a term used in football. In the same way, "chukker" is a term used in polo. A chukker refers to a period or division of play in a polo match. Therefore, the word related to "Chukker" in the same way is "Polo," making option 4 correct.

96. In the given pattern, the missing lower-right square must continue the symmetry of the already given three squares. The diagonal band in the missing part should run from bottom-left to top-right, matching the continuation required from the lower-left and upper-right portions. The small arrow cluster must be placed on the left side, and the horizontal wavy arrow should point towards the right to balance the corresponding figure arrangement. The musical-like symbol should appear on the lower-right side, which is correctly shown only in option 4.

97. AP = 5 m

PC = 15 m

CD = 15 m

After reaching P, the scout turns 60° left and walks 15 m to C. Then she again turns 60° left and walks another 15 m to D. These two equal sides with successive 60° turns form an equilateral-triangle relation between P,C,D.

PD = 15 m

Therefore, the shortest distance from D to P is 15 m, so option 4 is correct.

98. Let office be (0,0)

15 km West (–15,0)

Left from West = South, 10 km ⇒ (–15, –10)

Left from South = East, 39 km ⇒ (24, – 10)

Right from East = South, 22 km ⇒ (24, – 32)

Friend's house is 24 km east and 32 km south of the office, so the office is 24 km west and 32 km north of the friend's house.

Shortest distance = $\sqrt{24^2 + 32^2} = \sqrt{576 + 1024}$

$= \sqrt{1600} = 40$ km

Therefore, Saravana's office is 40 km to the north-west of his friend's house, so option 2 is correct.

99. 14 November 1989 = Tuesday

Required date = 26 April 2013

Counting the net day shift from 14 November 1989 to 26 April 2013

The remainder day shift gives Friday.

Therefore, 26 April 2013 was a Friday, so option 1 is correct.

100. REST → THOO

+2, +3, –4, –5

THOO → PKMP

–4, +3, –2, +1

TRIM → VUEH (Z),VUEH → RXCI (B)

HINT → JLJO (Y), JLJO → FOHP (D)

Therefore, the correct matches are (*i*)-(Z)-(B) and (*ii*)-(Y)-(D), so option 4 is correct.

YOUR SPACE

Previous Years' Paper

IR FORCE COMMON ADMISSION TEST (AFCAT)—2/2025*

(Exam held on 23-08-2025)

VERBAL ABILITY IN ENGLISH

Select the option that can be used as a one-word substitute for the given group of words:

A person who has both introvert and extrovert qualities.

A. Philanthropist B. Ambivert
C. Altruist D. Misanthrope

Choose the word which is most opposite in meaning to "Malevolent".

A. Vindictive B. Benevolent
C. Spiteful D. Malicious

Choose the option that best explains the meaning of the idiom:

"To take/carry coal to Newcastle"

A. To engage in a profitable business
B. To do something superfluous or unnecessary
C. To take risk in a dangerous place
D. To supply a scarce commodity

Choose the option that best explains the meaning of the idiom:

"To throw up the sponge"

A. To surrender or give up a contest
B. To insult an opponent
C. To hide one's true feelings
D. To celebrate a victory

5. Select the option that can be used as a one-word substitute for the given group of words:

A person who is fearless and adventurous is called:

A. Pusillanimous B. Intrepid
C. Timorous D. Diffident

6. Choose the word which is the most appropriate synonym of "Quash".

A. Perpetuate B. Nullify
C. Substantiate D. Endorse

7. Spot the error in the following sentence:

The two (A)/ brother in laws (B)/ attended the wedding ceremony together. (C)/ No error (D)

A. A B. B
C. C D. D

8. Select the option that can be used as a one-word substitute for the given group of words:

An act of violating or showing disrespect towards something sacred or holy is called:

A. Heresy
B. Sacrilege
C. Discrimination
D. Defamation

. B	**2.** B	**3.** B	**4.** A	**5.** B	**6.** B	**7.** B	**8.** B

d on Memory.

9. Choose the synonym of "Cognoscenti":

A. Connoisseurs B. Novices
C. Laymen D. Amateurs

10. Choose the word which is the most appropriate synonym of "Reckless".

A. Rash
B. Prudent
C. Circumspect
D. Wary

Directions (Qs. No. 11-15): *Read the following passage and answer the given questions.*

The concept of zero, often taken for granted in modern mathematics, is a relatively recent intellectual achievement in the long history of human civilization. While ancient cultures like the Babylonians used a placeholder symbol to indicate an empty position in their sexagesimal system, this was not equivalent to our modern notion of zero as a number. The true mathematical zero, representing both "nothingness" and functioning as an independent number with arithmetic properties, was first developed in India around the 5th century CE.

The Indian scholar Brahmagupta formalized rules for arithmetic involving zero, including addition, subtraction, and multiplication, though he struggled with division by zero.

From India, the idea spread to the Islamic world, where scholars translated and expanded upon Indian texts, integrating zero into the Arabic numeral system. The Arabic term "sifr", meaning empty, eventually evolved into the word "zero" in European languages. By the 12th century, with the translation of Arabic mathematical works into Latin, zero entered European thought, profoundly transforming mathematics, commerce, and science.

Zero's adoption met resistance in Europe; it was considered mysterious and even dangerous, partly because it was linked to Arabic cult and partly because its abstraction defied comr sense. Yet, once fully accepted, zero beca indispensable, enabling advancements in algel calculus, and eventually, modern computing. Tl what began as a humble placeholder evolved a cornerstone of human intellectual progress

11. The Babylonians' use of zero was prima as:

A. A true number with independent v
B. A placeholder in positional notatio
C. A symbol of infinity
D. A representation of division by ze

12. Who is credited with formalizing arithmetic rules of zero?

A. Aryabhata
B. Euclid
C. Brahmagupta
D. Al-Khwarizmi

13. The word "zero" in European langu evolved from:

A. Latin "nihil"
B. Greek "kenon"
C. Arabic "sifr"
D. Sanskrit "shunya"

14. Resistance to zero in medieval Europe due to:

A. Lack of translation of Indian text
B. Its association with Arabic culture abstract nature
C. Its inability to be used in multiplic
D. The prohibition of symbols in mather

15. According to the passage, zero's accep was crucial in the advancement of:

A. Geometry and Trigonometry
B. Algebra, Calculus and Computing
C. Astronomy and Architecture
D. Literature and Philosophy

9. A	10. A	11. B	12. C	13. C	14. B	15.

ections (Qs. No. 16-18): *Read the following sage and answer the given questions.*

The following question consists of an mplete sentence or a sentence which is split four parts. All four parts are jumbled up and named as P, Q, R and S. These four parts not given in their proper order. Arrange the bled parts of the sentence and find out which he four combinations from the given options correctly complete the sentence.

. India has been a land __________ than the warrior or the administrator.
P. but in the sense that learning has always been very highly valued
Q. not indeed, in the sense that education has been universal
R. and the learned man has been held in higher esteem
S. of learning throughout the ages,

A. SPRQ B. RQPS
C. RSQP D. SQPR

While the recent __________.
P. century show that the June rainfall is
Q. of a drought, India's rainfall data for over a
R. rain may have soothed concerns
S. no predictor of the monsoon's outcome

A. PSRQ B. RQPS
C. PQRS D. RSPQ

For some people patriotism __________ as much as to any one country.
P. today man belongs to the whole world
Q. should be condemned because
R. type of patriotism is an evil and it
S. means hatred for other countries, but this

A. SRQP B. PQSR
C. RSPQ D. QPSR

Directions (Qs. No. 19-21): *Read the following passage and answer the given questions.*

In the following question, there is a related pair of words given. Each pair is followed by four other pairs of words. Choose the pair from the given option that best expresses the relationship like the original pair.

19. Bee : Honey :: Cow : ____
A. Grass B. Milk
C. Horns D. Farm

20. Oven : Bake :: Knife : ____
A. Slice B. Cook
C. Kitchen D. Heat

21. Finger : Hand :: Leaf : ____
A. Plant B. Branch
C. Tree D. Flower

Directions (Qs. No. 22-24): *Read the following passage and answer the given questions.*

Each item in this section has a sentence with three parts (A), (B), and (C). Read each sentence to find out whether there is any error in any part and indicate your response on the answer sheet against the corresponding letter, i.e., (A) or (B) or (C). If you find no error, your response should be indicated as (D).

22. Ten kilometers (A)/ are a long distance (B)/ to walk on foot. (C)/ No error (D)
A. A B. B
C. C D. D

23. Neither of the students (A)/ have completed (B)/ the assignment yet. (C)/ No error (D)
A. A B. B
C. C D. D

24. She did not know (A)/ to whom should she (B)/ address the letter. (C)/ No error (D)
A. A B. B
C. C D. D

. D **17.** B **18.** A **19.** B **20.** A **21.** C **22.** B **23.** B **24.** B

Directions (Qs. No. 25-27): *Each of the following sentences in this section has a blank space and four words are given after the sentence. Select whichever word you consider most appropriate for the blank space and indicate your response on the Answer Sheet accordingly.*

25. The judge remained completely _____ while giving his verdict.

A. impartial B. biased
C. emotional D. hesitant

26. Hardly _____ the train left the platform when it began to rain heavily.

A. has B. will
C. had D. does

27. During his visit to the museum, he __________ some rare paintings of the Mughal period.

A. came across B. came by
C. came out D. came into

Directions (Qs. No. 28-30): *Read the following passage and answer the given questions in the blanks given in the passage with a proper words:*

Most of our food comes from agriculture, so we tend to believe that it is independent of natural biota. This is not true. In nature, both plants and animals _______(1)_______ to the rigo of natural selection. Only the fittest survive.

Consequently, wild populations have numer traits for competitiveness, resistance to parasit _______(2)_______ to adverse conditions, a other aspects of vigour. In contrast, populati grown for many generations under the pampe conditions of agriculture tend to lose th traits, because they are selected for producti not resilience. For example, a high-produc plant that lacks resistance to drought is ___ (3)______ and the resistance to drought ignored. Also, in the process of breeding pl for maximum production, all genetic varia is eliminated.

28. What will come in blank (1)?

A. had been continuously subjected
B. will be continuously subject
C. continuously subjected
D. are continuously subjected

29. What will come in blank (2)?

A. withdrawal B. tolerance
C. adaptable D. compliance

30. What will come in blank (3)?

A. heated B. irrigated
C. showered D. deserted

GENERAL AWARENESS

31. The languages used in the inscriptions of Ashoka is:

A. Sanskrit B. Prakrit
C. Pali D. Hindi

32. Consider the following statements regarding the Nidhi Scheme:

1. The scheme was launched in 2014 by the Ministry of Human Resource Development.
2. It aims to support higher educa institutions to set up start-ups thr incubation and innovation.
3. The full form of NIDHI is Nat Initiative for Developing and Harne Innovations.
4. The scheme is implemented by Department of Science & Technol

Which of the above statements is/are co

A. 1, 2 and 3 B. 1, 3 and 4
C. 2, 3 and 4 D. 1, 2, 3 and

25. A	26. C	27. A	28. D	29. B	30. B	31. B	32.

3. The RailOne App, launched by Indian Railways in 2025, primarily aims to:
   A. Provide passengers with a single-window platform for integrated services.
   B. Replace the IRCTC e-ticketing website completely.
   C. Facilitate only freight and cargo tracking.
   D. Operate as an exclusive platform for railway staff communication.

. General Bipin Rawat, the first Chief of Defence Staff (CDS) of India, was commissioned into which regiment of the Indian Army?
   A. Rajput Regiment B. Gorkha Rifles
   C. Sikh Regiment D. Jat Regiment

. Which of the following is the primary cause of acid rain formation?
   A. Carbon monoxide emissions
   B. Deforestation
   C. Sulphur dioxide and nitrogen oxides emissions
   D. Ozone depletion

Which Indian writer was awarded the International Booker Prize for the year 2025?
   A. Girish Karnad
   B. Geetanjali Sri
   C. Banu Mushtaq
   D. K. Shivaram Karanth

Exercise PRALAY was carried out by which armed force?
   A. Indian Army
   B. Indian Navy
   C. Indian Air Force
   D. Indian Coast Guard

Project 75, under which India is constructing Scorpene–class submarines, is being executed by which company?
   A. Hindustan Aeronautics Limited (HAL)
   B. Mazagon Dock Shipbuilders Limited (MDL)
   C. Bharat Electronics Limited (BEL)
   D. Garden Reach Shipbuilders & Engineers (GRSE)

39. Which rocket is used to launch the Axiom Mission 4 (Ax-4) to the International Space Station?
   A. PSLV B. GSLV Mk III
   C. Ariane 5 D. Falcon 9 Block 5

40. Recently launched, which among the following was the purpose of 'Operation Sindhu'?
   A. To send relief material to flood affected areas.
   B. To protect the sea coasts.
   C. To hold peace talks in Afghanistan.
   D. To safely evacuate Indians stranded in Iran.

41. Who established the Archaeological Survey of India (ASI)?
   A. Lord Dalhousie
   B. Sir Alexander Cunningham
   C. Lord Curzon
   D. James Prinsep

42. With reference to the "DAKSH" portal, consider the following statements:
   1. The portal was launched by the Reserve Bank of India.
   2. 'DAKSH' stands for the Reserve Bank's Advanced Supervisory Monitoring System.
   3. It is a web-based workflow application for monitoring compliance requirements of supervised entities.

   Which of the statements given above is/are correct?
   A. 1 and 2 only B. 2 and 3 only
   C. 1 and 3 only D. 1, 2 and 3

A **34.** B **35.** C **36.** C **37.** C **38.** B **39.** D **40.** D **41.** B **42.** D

43. What is the primary aim of the "100 Million for 100 Million" campaign launched in 2016?

A. To provide free meals to 100 million children worldwide
B. To mobilize 100 million youth to support 100 million children denied basic rights and freedom
C. To vaccinate 100 million children against deadly diseases
D. To build schools for 100 million poor children

44. Who is known as the "Father of the Lok Sabha"?

A. Ganesh Vasudev Mavalankar
B. Hukam Singh
C. Ananthasayanam Ayyangar
D. N. Sanjiva Reddy

45. The working principle of washing machine is:

A. Centrifugation B. Reverse osmosis
C. Dialysis D. Diffusion

46. Cumulonimbus clouds are typically associated with which type of weather?

A. Fair weather
B. Thunderstorms
C. Drizzle
D. Fog

47. What was the position of the Indian football team in the 1956 Melbourne Olympics?

A. 1st B. 2nd
C. 3rd D. 4th

48. With reference to isotopes, isobars, and isotones, consider the following statements:

1. Isotopes have the same atomic number but different mass numbers.
2. Isobars have the same number of neutrons but different atomic numbers.
3. Isotones have the same number neutrons but different atomic and n numbers.

Which of the statements given above is correct?

A. 1 and 2 only B. 1 and 3 only
C. 2 and 3 only D. 1, 2 and 3

49. The Pechora surface-to-air missile syst currently in service with the Indian Force, was originally developed by w country?

A. United States of America
B. Israel
C. Russia (former Soviet Union)
D. France

50. The Subroto Cup was started in which y

A. 1949 B. 1958
C. 1960 D. 1965

51. Who persuaded Mahatma Gandhi to to Champaran to take up the caus exploited indigo planters?

A. Bal Gangadhar Tilak
B. Raj Kumar Shukla
C. Gopal Krishna Gokhale
D. Acharya J.B. Kripalani

52. Consider the following statements rega the DIKSHA (Digital Infrastructur Knowledge Sharing) Scheme:

1. It is a national platform develop the Ministry of Education to pr digital resources for school educa
2. It provides e-content and QR- Energised Textbooks (ETBs) for te and students across states and U

Which of the above statements is/are co

A. 1 only
B. 2 only
C. Both 1 and 2
D. Neither 1 nor 2

43. B **44.** A **45.** A **46.** B **47.** D **48.** B **49.** C **50.** C **51.** B **52**

. Which of the following reactions involves a chain reaction mechanism that starts with a ketone group?

A. Aldol condensation
B. Wolff–Kishner reduction
C. Base-catalyzed haloform reaction
D. Tollen's test

. With reference to Biomagnification, consider the following statements:

1. Biomagnification refers to the increase in the concentration of a toxic substance at successive trophic levels in a food chain.
2. Water-soluble pollutants are more likely to undergo biomagnification than fat-soluble pollutants.
3. Top carnivores are generally the most affected organisms in a food chain due to biomagnification.

Which of the statements given above is/are correct?

A. 1 and 2 only
B. 1 and 3 only
C. 2 and 3 only
D. 1, 2 and 3

55. Which of the following features best describes the Nirbhay missile?

A. Ballistic missile
B. Cruise missile
C. Anti-tank missile
D. Surface-to-air missile

NUMERICAL ABILITY

. If the simple interest (SI) on a sum of money for 2 years at a rate of 5% per annum is ₹ 6000, what will be the compound interest (CI) on the same sum, at the same rate and time?

A. ₹ 6150
B. ₹ 6000
C. ₹ 5250
D. ₹ 3150

1234567891011121314151617181920 divided by 16 then remainder is?

A. 4 B. 2
C. 6 D. 0

In a box 3 yellow balls, 5 red balls, 4 green balls are there. If 3 balls are taken out randomly then what is the probability of getting 2 green balls?

A. $\frac{4}{15}$ B. $\frac{12}{55}$
C. $\frac{8}{15}$ D. $\frac{2}{7}$

59. The area of the floor of a rectangular hall of length 40 m is 960 m². Carpets of size 6 m × 4 m are available. Then, how many carpets are required to cover the hall?

A. 20 B. 30
C. 40 D. 45

60. A person travels a certain distance at 3 km/hr and reaches 15 minutes late. If he travels at 4 km/hr, he reaches 15 minutes earlier. The distance he has to travel is:

A. 4.5 km B. 6 km
C. 7.2 km D. 12 km

61. A rectangular sheet has a length of 30 cm and a breadth of 15 cm. A margin of 2.5 cm from the length side and 1.5 cm from the breadth side is cut out on all sides. What percentage of the original area is left for writing?

A. 66.66%
B. 50%
C. 80%
D. 75%

. C **54.** B **55.** B **56.** A **57.** D **58.** B **59.** C **60.** B **61.** A

62. Ram and Shyam weight ratio is 6 : 5. After 2 months Ram's weight increases by 20% and overall average weight increase by 15%. By what percentage is Shyam's weight increased?

A. 12% B. 9%
C. 10% D. 15%

63. 2 mixtures of milk and water are given. One is 8 litre has 2 litre water while another mixture is 14 litre with ratio of milk and water 6 : 1. After mixing both find ratio of water to milk in a new mixture.

A. 2 : 9 B. 2 : 7
C. 5 : 7 D. 7 : 5

64. P calculates his profit % on cost price while Q calculates his profit % on the selling price. They find that the difference in their profits is ₹ 600. If the selling price of both the men are the same, Q gets 50% profit and P gets 40% profit. Find their selling price.

A. ₹ 3600 B. ₹ 2500
C. ₹ 2000 D. ₹ 2800

65. 8 years ago a family of 5 members had an average age of 25 years. Since then, two children have been born with an age difference of 4 years. Currently, the average age of the family remains the same. What is the age of the youngest child?

A. 6 years B. 3 years
C. 2 years D. 5 years

66. A truck travelling at 70 kilometres per hour uses 30% more diesel to travel a certain distance than it does when it travels at the speed of 50 kilometres per hour. If the truck can travel 19.5 kilometres on a litre of diesel at 50 kilometres per hour, then how far can the truck travel on 10 litres of diesel at a speed of 70 kilometres per hour?

A. 150 km B. 200 km
C. 250 km D. 300 km

67. At what time between 2 and 3 o'clock the minute hand be exactly 1 minute sp ahead of the hour hand?

A. 2 : 12 B. 2 : 15
C. 2 : 13 D. 2 : 14

68. Suppose, C1, C2, C3, C4, and C5 are companies. The profits made by C1, and C3 are in the ratio 9 : 10 : 8 w the profits made by C2, C4 and C5 in the ratio 18 : 19 : 20. If C5 has m a profit of ₹ 19 crore more than C1, the total profit (in ₹) made by all companies is:

A. 441 cr B. 444 cr
C. 438 cr D. 435 cr

69. 15 years ago the average age of a fa of 4 members was 40 years, and durin years 2 children born but the average remain same. If the older child is 8 y older than younger one then find the of ages of both child.

A. 7 : 3 B. 8 : 5
C. 5 : 3 D. 3 : 2

70. Rakesh and Ramesh both sell an artic the same selling price. Ramesh calcu profit on cost price i.e., 25% while R. calculates profit on selling price i.e., If the difference in their profit is ₹ Find the selling price.

A. ₹ 3000 B. ₹ 2000
C. ₹ 4000 D. ₹ 1000

71. A person read 18 books in $\frac{2}{3}$ days. many books he can read in $\frac{1}{4}$ days

A. 5 B. 4
C. $\frac{27}{4}$ D. $\frac{15}{7}$

62. B **63.** A **64.** D **65.** B **66.** A **67.** A **68.** C **69.** A **70.** B **71.**

72. A boat goes 140 km upstream in 7 hours and a distance of 210 km downstream in 7 hours. Find the speed of the boat in still water.

A. 30 km/h B. 25 km/h
C. 20 km/h D. 24 km/h

73. A circle of radius 21 cm is converted into a rectangle. If the length and breadth are in the ratio 6 : 5, find the area of the rectangle.

A. 1124 cm^2 B. 1056 cm^2
C. 1024 cm^2 D. 1080 cm^2

74. What will be the value of x in the following?

$\sqrt{1225} \div \sqrt[3]{343} \times 45\%$ of 760

$= x \times 66.67\%$ of 45

A. 48 B. 50
C. 57 D. 64

75. A and B undertook a work for ₹ 4000. A alone can do that work in 20 days and B alone can do the same work in 30 days. If they work together, then what will be the difference in the amount they receive?

A. ₹ 800 B. ₹ 1050
C. ₹ 900 D. ₹ 880

REASONING AND MILITARY APTITUDE TEST

76. At what time between 3 and 4 o'clock is the minute hand 7 minute ahead the hour hand?

A. 3 : 12
B. 3 : 24
C. 3 : 30
D. 3 : 42

77. Find the Next Set

ST, ND, RD, TH, ?

A. TH B. HT
C. TN D. NT

78. From the following questions, choose the figure that best depicts the relationship between the three objects?

River water, Liquid, Milk

A. 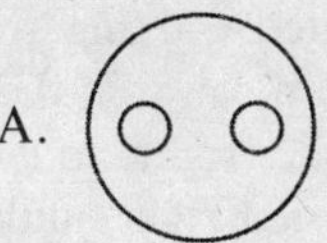

B. 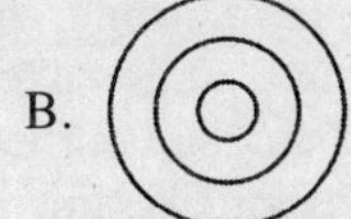

C. 

D. 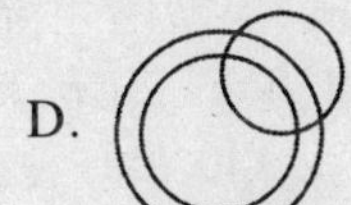

79. If the first half of the English alphabet is reversed and then the second half is reversed, which letter will be the 10th from the right?

A. Z B. D
C. Q D. W

80. From the given options, select the option in which the dot can be placed in exactly the same way as shown in the figure (X) below.

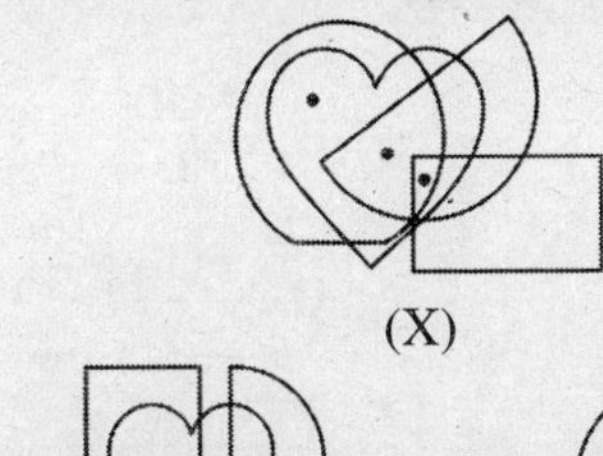

(X)

A. 

B. 

C. 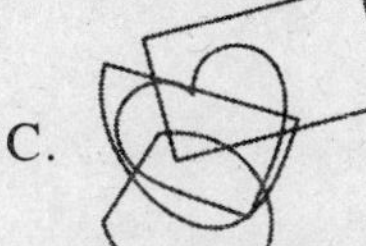

D. 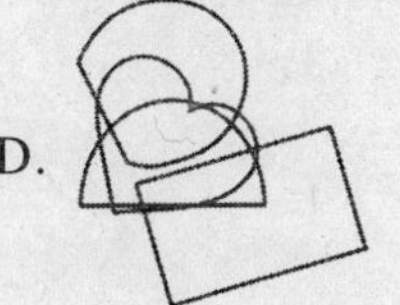

72. B 73. D 74. C 75. A 76. B 77. A 78. A 79. D 80. C

81. Select the figure which satisfies the same condition of placement of the dots as figure–X.

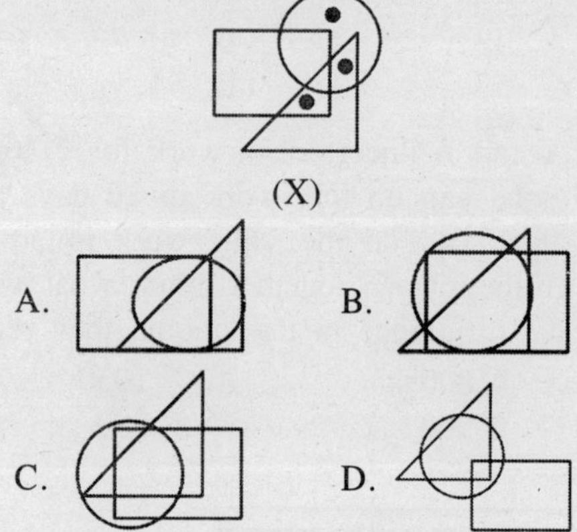

82. P and Q are brothers. P is the father of S. R is the only son of Q and is married to U. How is U related to S?

A. Sister-in-law B. Mother-in-law
C. Sister D. Mother

83. In the same manner that the second term is connected to the first term, pick the option that is associated with the third phrase.

$\frac{FNB}{V} : \frac{EMA}{S} :: \frac{GPC}{Z} : ?$

A. $\frac{EOB}{V}$ B. $\frac{FOB}{W}$
C. $\frac{GOB}{W}$ D. $\frac{FOB}{B}$

84. In the question figure given below, two pairs of figures are given. Find the shape of the second pair based on the same relation as the shapes of the first pair are related to each other.

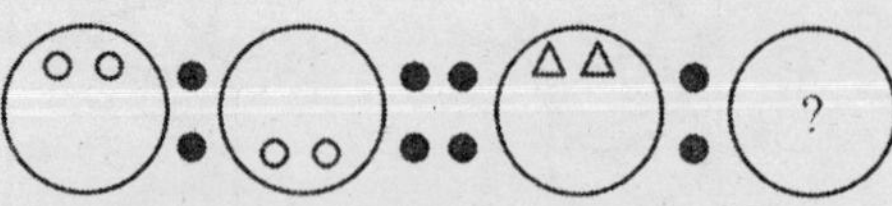

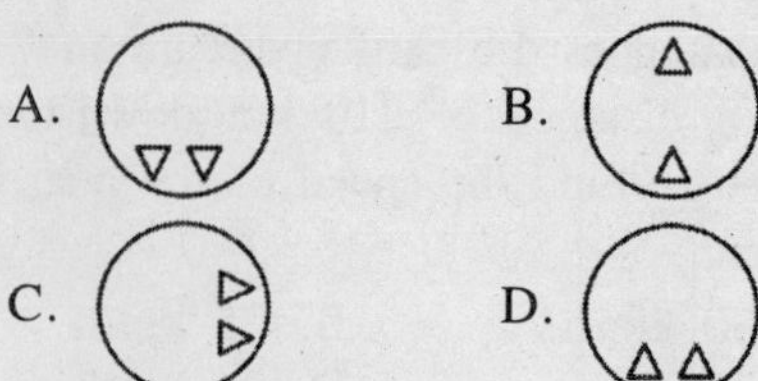

85. Three of the following four words are ali in a certain way and one is different. P the odd word out.

A. Political Science B. Biology
C. History D. Sociology

86. Select the odd number from the giv alternatives.

A. 10 B. 20
C. 15 D. 30

87. In a certain code language, 'MOBILE' coded as BJFZLK and 'TABLET' is co as QCIZXR. How will 'KINDLE' be co in the same language?

A. BJALFI B. BJBKFI
C. CIBKGC D. CJBLGI

88. 'A + B' means 'A is the brother of
'A – B' means 'A is the wife of B'
'A × B' means 'A is the son of B'
'A ÷ B' means 'A is the husband of
If P + Q – S + R × L ÷ M, then wh of the following statements is correct?

A. Q is the sister of M.
B. P is S's wife's brother.
C. L is the father of P.
D. P is the brother of S.

89. Shilpa goes to a park every day for walk One morning, she started walking from home and walked 40 km towards the nc Then she turned to the right and wa 60 km. Again, she turned right and wa 40 km. Lastly, she took a left turn and wa 30 km. How far is she from her ho

A. 140 km B. 90 km
C. 100 km D. 60 km

81. C **82.** A **83.** B **84.** A **85.** B **86.** C **87.** A **88.** B **89.**

90. The water image of the given below figure is:

A.  B. 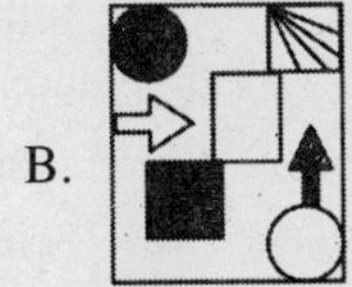

C. 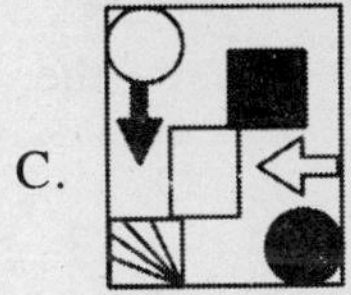 D. 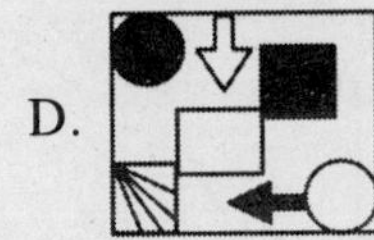

91. In the following figure, the triangle represents 'football players', the circle represents 'kho-kho players', and the rectangle represents 'kabaddi players'. How many players play both kabaddi and football only?

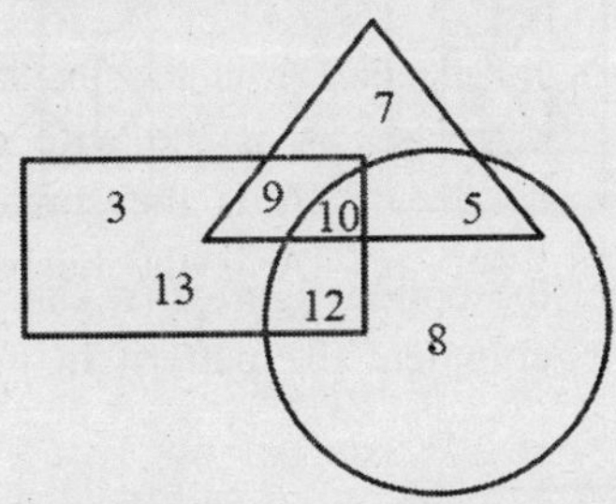

A. 9 B. 26
C. 13 D. 19

92. Select the number from among the given options that can replace the question mark (?) in the following series.

39, 53, ?, 108, 149, 199

A. 81
B. 72
C. 79
D. 76

93. Select the figure from the given options that will replace the question mark (?) in the figure given below and complete the pattern.

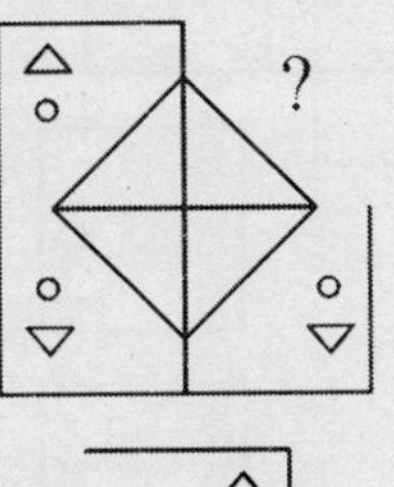

A. B.

C. D.

94. What will come in the place of the question mark (?) in the following equation, if '+' and '×' are interchanged and '–' and '÷' are interchanged?

$105 - 15 \div 13 + 3 \times 27 = ?$

A. 58 B. –5
C. 16 D. 23

95. Select the option that will come next in the following figure series.

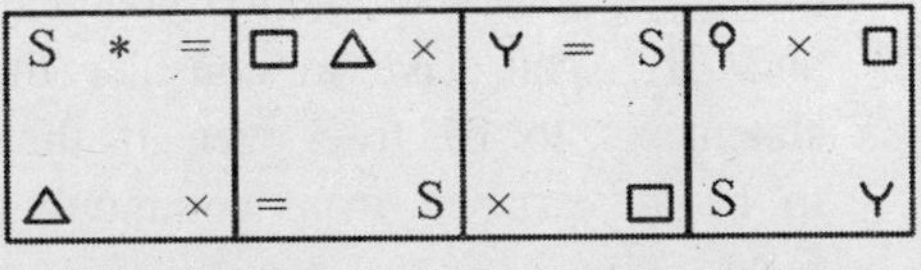

A. 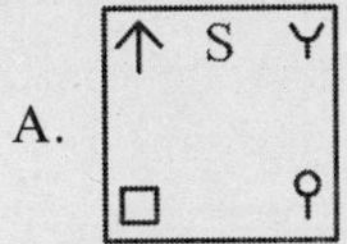

B. 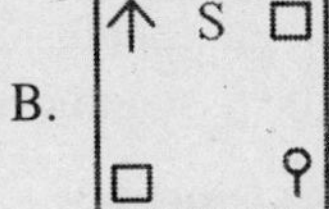

C. 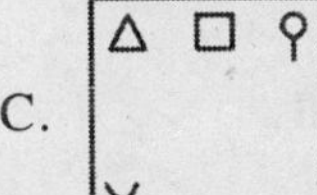

D. 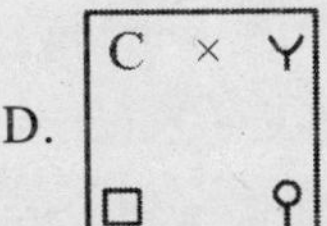

90. D	**91.** A	**92.** D	**93.** A	**94.** B	**95.** A

96. Which figure should replace the question mark (?) if the series were to be continued?

T	N	△	N	
A O Z	△ T A	O A T	E △ O	?
N	O	N	A	

A.
A
N O △
E

B.
E
A O △
N

C.
A
△ O E
N

D.
A
O N E
△

97. Five girls, Amita, Fauzia, Gargi, Ranjita and Sucheta, are sitting in a straight line. All are facing the north direction. Sucheta sits second to the left of Gargi. Fauzia sits third to the right of Sucheta. Only one girl is sitting between Amita and Ranjita. Amita is not sitting at any of the extreme ends. Which two girls are sitting at the extreme ends?

A. Ranjita and Fauzia
B. Gargi and Sucheta
C. Sucheta and Fauzia
D. Ranjita and Gargi

98. In the following question, three statements are given followed by two conclusions (I) and (II). You have to consider the three statements to be true even if they seem to be at variance from commonly known facts. You have to decide which of the given conclusions, if any, follow from the given statements.

Statements:

50% windows are benches.

Some benches are walls.

50% walls are bus.

Conclusions:

I. All bus are benches.

II. At least some buses are bench possibility.

A. Only I follows.
B. Only II follows.
C. Both I and II follow.
D. None of these follows.

99. Select the option figure in which given figure is embedded (rotation is N allowed).

A. 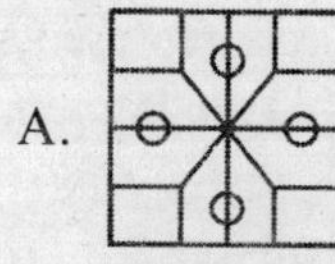

B. 

C. 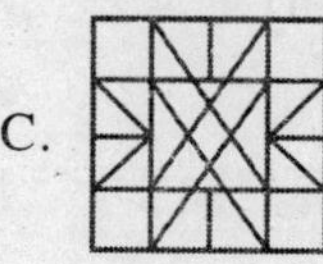

D. 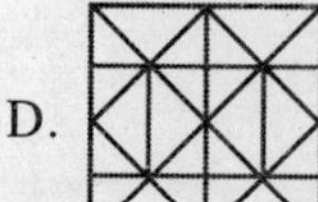

100. Select the option figure that can replace '?' to complete the pattern in the ques figure.

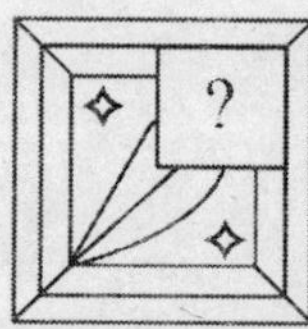

A. 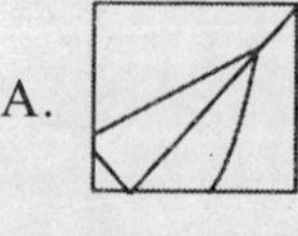

B. 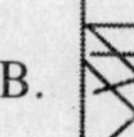

C. 

D. 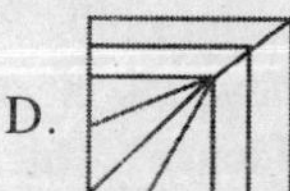

96. B **97.** A **98.** B **99.** B **100.**

EXPLANATORY ANSWERS

. A person who shows both introvert (shy, reserved) and extrovert (outgoing, sociable) tendencies is called an *ambivert*. A philanthropist is one who loves mankind and gives in charity, an altruist is selflessly concerned for others, and a misanthrope dislikes people, so they do not match the given description.

Malevolent means having or showing a desire to do evil or harm others. *Benevolent* means kind, well-meaning and wishing good for others, which is the direct opposite in sense. *Vindictive*, *spiteful* and *malicious* all carry the meaning of wishing to harm, so they are similar to "malevolent", not opposite.

Newcastle was historically a major coal-producing centre in England, so taking coal there is pointless because it is already abundant. Thus, the idiom "to take/carry coal to Newcastle" means to do something needless or redundant. The other options talk about profit, danger or scarcity, which are not implied.

"To throw up the sponge" comes from boxing, where throwing the sponge or towel into the ring signals defeat. So, the idiom means to admit defeat, stop resisting and give up the struggle or contest. It has nothing to do with insulting, hiding feelings or celebrating.

A person who is fearless and willing to take risks in adventurous situations is called intrepid. *Pusillanimous*, *timorous* and *diffident* all mean timid, fearful or lacking confidence, which are opposite in meaning to fearless and adventurous.

"Quash" means to reject, annul, or put an end to something, especially a decision, order, or legal proceeding. "Nullify" also means to make legally void or invalidate. The other words—perpetuate (continue), substantiate (prove), and endorse (approve)—do not match this meaning.

7. The error lies in part (B). The correct plural of "brother-in-law" is *brothers-in-law*, not *brother in laws*. Only the main noun (brother) is pluralised, not "law". Hence, part (B) contains the grammatical mistake.

8. The act of violating, dishonouring, or showing disrespect towards something holy or sacred is called sacrilege. *Heresy* refers to beliefs contrary to established religious doctrine, discrimination relates to unfair treatment, and defamation means harming someone's reputation. Only "sacrilege" expresses disrespect to something sacred.

9. "Cognoscenti" refers to people who are experts or have specialized knowledge in a particular field. "Connoisseurs" means knowledgeable experts, especially in arts or fine matters. "Novices", "laymen", and "amateurs" are inexperienced or non-expert groups, so they do not match.

10. "Reckless" refers to acting without thinking about danger or consequences. "Rash" also means acting hastily or without caution. The other options—prudent, circumspect, and wary—convey careful or cautious behaviour, which are antonyms of reckless, not synonyms.

11. The passage clearly states that the Babylonians used a symbol only to mark an empty position in their sexagesimal system. It did *not* represent a true numerical zero with value; it was merely positional. Therefore, the correct meaning is "placeholder in positional notation".

12. The passage explicitly mentions that Brahmagupta formalized arithmetic rules involving zero, including addition, subtraction, and multiplication. Hence, he is credited with establishing these rules. Aryabhata and Euclid are not associated with this development, and Al-Khwarizmi worked later with Indian concepts.

13. The passage explains that the Arabic term sifr, meaning empty, evolved into the word "zero" in European languages after translations of Arabic mathematical works into Latin. Thus, "zero" originated from the Arabic term.

14. The passage states that zero's adoption met resistance in Europe, because it was considered mysterious and dangerous, partly due to its link with Arabic culture and partly because its abstract nature defied common sense. The other options are not mentioned as reasons.

15. The passage states that once accepted, zero became indispensable in enabling advancements in algebra, calculus, and modern computing. Therefore, these are the disciplines most crucially advanced by the acceptance of zero.

16. India has been a land of learning throughout the ages, not indeed in the sense that education has been universal, but in the sense that learning has always been very highly valued, and the learned man has been held in higher esteem than the warrior or the administrator.

The order S → Q → P → R produces a smooth and logically connected sentence showing contrast between universal education and the high regard for learning.

17. While the recent rain may have soothed concerns of a drought, India's rainfall data for over a century show that the June rainfall is no predictor of the monsoon's outcome.

Here, part R ("rain may have sooth concerns") fits naturally after "While recent ...". It is then logically followed Q ("of a drought, India's rainfall data over a"), which links those concerns the longer record. Part P ("century sh that the June rainfall is") completes clause about the data, and finally S (" predictor of the monsoon's outcome") gi the conclusion. Thus, the only seque that forms a grammatically correct meaningful sentence is R → Q → P →

18. For some people patriotism means hatred other countries, but this type of patrioti is an evil and it should be condem because today man belongs to the wh world as much as to anyone country. H S ("for some people patriotism means ha for other countries") introduces the wr notion of patriotism, R ("but this type patriotism is an evil and it") brings in contrast, Q ("should be condemned bec today man belongs to the whole wor gives the reason, and P ("as much a anyone country") logically completes reason.

Thus, the only sequence that gives a smo logically connected and grammatic correct sentence is S → R → Q → i.e. option A (SRQP).

19. A bee produces honey, and similar cow produces milk. The relationshi both pairs is producer → product. G horns, and farm do not represent somet produced by a cow, so they do not m the analogy.

20. An oven is used to bake, and a kni used to slice. The relationship in the ori pair is instrument → specific primary a performed with that instrument. Jus baking is the typical function of an slicing is the typical function associated a knife. "Cook", "kitchen", and " do not express this direct, specific action relationship.

A finger is a part of the hand, and similarly a leaf is a part of a tree. The relationship is part → *whole*. Branch and plant do not represent the immediate whole to which a leaf belongs, and "flower" is unrelated.

The verb "are" is incorrect because "Ten kilometers" refers to a single distance and must take a singular verb. The correct construction is "Ten kilometers is a long distance to walk on foot". Therefore, the error lies in part B.

"Neither" is always singular, so the verb must also be singular: "Neither of the students has completed..." Thus, the error is in part (B), where "have" is incorrectly used.

The sentence should read: "She did not know to whom she should address the letter". The inversion "to whom should she" is incorrect in a statement. Therefore, the error is in part (B).

A judge is expected to remain completely impartial while giving a verdict. "Biased", "emotional", or "hesitant" would contradict the required neutrality of a judge.

The correct structure for "Hardly...when..." is Hardly had + subject + past participle + when + simple past.

Thus, "Hardly had the train left the platform when it began to rain heavily".

The phrasal verb "came across" means to find something by chance. This fits the sentence: he discovered rare Mughal paintings during his museum visit.

The sentence refers to a general truth about plants and animals in nature. Therefore, simple present passive ("are continuously subjected") is correct. Other options violate tense or meaning.

29. The sentence describes traits such as competitiveness, resistance to parasites, and tolerance to adverse conditions. The word "tolerance" matches the context of survival traits.

30. A high-producing plant lacking drought resistance is irrigated — meaning it must be supplied water artificially because natural drought resistance is absent. The other words do not fit the agricultural context.

31. The inscriptions of Ashoka were primarily written in Prakrit, using the Brahmi and Kharosthi scripts. Sanskrit and Pali were not used for the majority of Ashokan edicts, and Hindi did not exist at that time.

32. Statement 1 is incorrect: NIDHI was launched by the Department of Science & Technology (DST), not by the Ministry of HRD, and not in 2014.

Statement 2 is correct: NIDHI supports start-ups through incubation and innovation.

Statement 3 is correct: NIDHI stands for National Initiative for Developing and Harnessing Innovations.

Statement 4 is correct: It is implemented by DST.

Thus, only 2, 3 and 4 are correct.

33. RailOne App (2025) is designed to integrate multiple railway services—ticketing, catering, parcel, enquiry, tracking—into one unified platform. It does not replace IRCTC, nor is it restricted to freight, nor is it for railway staff alone.

34. General Bipin Rawat, India's first Chief of Defence Staff (CDS), was commissioned into the 5th Battalion of the 11 Gorkha Rifles of the Indian Army.

35. Acid rain is primarily caused by SO_2 and NO_2 gases, which react with atmospheric moisture to form sulphuric and nitric acids. Carbon monoxide, deforestation, and ozone depletion do not directly cause acid rain.

36. The International Booker Prize 2025 was awarded to Banu Mushtaq, making her the correct answer.

37. Exercise PRALAY was carried out by the Indian Air Force, focusing on readiness and rapid response operations. It was not conducted by the Army, Navy, or Coast Guard.

38. Project 75, which involves the construction of Scorpene-class submarines for the Indian Navy, is being executed by MDL in collaboration with Naval Group (France). Therefore, MDL is the correct answer.

39. Axiom Mission 4 (Ax-4) to the International Space Station was launched using SpaceX's Falcon 9 Block 5 rocket. PSLV, GSLV Mk III, and Ariane 5 were not used for this mission.

40. Operation Sindhu was launched to rescue and safely evacuate Indians stuck in Iran. It was not related to flood relief, coastal protection, or Afghan peace talks.

41. The Archaeological Survey of India (ASI) was established by Sir Alexander Cunningham in 1861. He is known as the "Father of Indian Archaeology".

42. All statements about the DAKSH portal are correct:

1. It was launched by the Reserve Bank of India.
2. DAKSH stands for RBI's Advanced Supervisory Monitoring System.
3. It is a web-based workflow application used to monitor compliance requirements of supervised entities.

Thus, all three statements are correct.

43. The "100 Million for 100 Million" campaign (launched in 2016 by Kailash Satyarthi) aims to bring 100 million youth together to fight for 100 million children who are deprived of rights, freedom, and safety. is not about meals, vaccination, or scho construction.

44. G.V. Mavalankar was the first Speaker the Lok Sabha, and due to his foundatio role in shaping parliamentary procedur he is known as the "Father of the L Sabha".

45. A washing machine works on the princi of centrifugation, where rapid spinni forces water out of clothes through outw centrifugal force. Reverse osmosis, dialys and diffusion are unrelated processes.

46. Cumulonimbus clouds are large, toweri clouds that typically produce thunderstorr heavy rain, lightning, and sometimes hail tornadoes. They do not form fair-weath drizzle, or fog.

47. In the 1956 Melbourne Olympics, Indian football team achieved its best-e performance, finishing in 4th place, a reaching the semifinals.

48. Statement 1 is correct because isotopes h the same atomic number but different m numbers due to differing neutrons. Staten 2 is incorrect because isobars share same mass number, not the same nun of neutrons, and they always have diffe atomic numbers. Statement 3 is cor because isotones have the same nun of neutrons but different atomic and n numbers. Therefore, only statements 1 3 are correct.

49. The Pechora surface-to-air missile sy (also known as SA-3 Goa) was origir developed by the former Soviet Unio remains in service with several count including India. The USA, Israel, France have no link to its origin.

50. The Subroto Cup began in 1960 afte formation of the Subroto Mukerjee S

Education Society following Air Marshal Subroto Mukerjee's death. Although the idea was conceived in 1958, the first national inter-school football tournament was actually held in 1960, making 1960 the correct answer.

It was Raj Kumar Shukla, an indigo farmer from Champaran, who persistently persuaded Mahatma Gandhi to come and take up the cause of exploited indigo cultivators, leading to Gandhi's first major satyagraha in India. Tilak, Gokhale, and Kripalani were not involved in this event.

Statement 1 is correct: DIKSHA is a national digital platform developed by the Ministry of Education to provide school-level digital learning resources.

Statement 2 is correct: It provides e-content and QR-coded Energised Textbooks (ETBs) across states and UTs.

Hence, both statements are correct.

The haloform reaction involves a chain reaction mechanism beginning with a ketone (or methyl ketone) group and proceeding through halogenation in the presence of a base. Aldol condensation and Wolff-Kishner reduction follow different mechanisms, and Tollen's test is specific for aldehydes, not ketones.

Biomagnification is the increase in concentration of toxic substances at higher trophic levels, so statement 1 is correct. Fat-soluble pollutants biomagnify far more than water-soluble ones, so statement 2 is incorrect. Top carnivores are the most affected, making statement 3 correct. Therefore, only statements 1 and 3 are correct.

Nirbhay is India's long-range, subsonic cruise missile, capable of low-altitude terrain-hugging flight. It is not ballistic, anti-tank, or surface-to-air.

56. Given, SI = ₹ 6000 at 5% for 2 years

$$SI = \frac{P \cdot R \cdot T}{100}$$

$$6000 = \frac{P \cdot 5 \cdot 2}{100}$$

$$P = 60000$$

CI for 2 years:

$$CI = P\left(1+\frac{R}{100}\right)^2 - P$$

$$= 60000(1.05)^2 - 60000$$

$$= 60000(1.1025) - 60000$$

$$= 66150 - 60000 = 6150.$$

57. A number modulo 16 depends only on its last four digits.

The last four digits of 1234567891011...181920 are 1920.

$$1920 \div 16 = 120 \text{ exactly}$$

So, remainder = 0.

58. Total balls = 3 yellow + 5 red + 4 green = 12

Probability of choosing 2 green and 1 non-green:

Ways to choose 2 green:

$$\binom{4}{2} = 6$$

Ways to choose 1 non-green from 8:

$$\binom{8}{1} = 8$$

Total favourable outcomes:

$$6 \times 8 = 48$$

Total ways to choose any 3 balls:

$$\binom{12}{3} = 220$$

Probability: $\frac{48}{220} = \frac{12}{55}$

Thus, answer $= \frac{12}{55}$.

59. The area of the hall is 960 m^2.

Each carpet has area $6 \times 4 = 24$ m^2.

The total carpets required are $\frac{960}{24} = 40$.

60. Let the distance be D.

He is 15 minutes late at 3 km/hr and 15 minutes early at 4 km/hr; difference

$$= 30 \text{ minutes}$$
$$= 0.5 \text{ hr.}$$

$$\frac{D}{3} - \frac{D}{4} = \frac{1}{2}$$

$$\frac{D}{12} = \frac{1}{2}$$

$$\Rightarrow \quad D = 6.$$

61. Original area $= 30 \times 15$

$= 450$ cm^2

Margins removed:

new length $= 30 - 5 = 25$

new breadth $= 15 - 3 = 12$

New area $= 25 \times 12 = 300$

Percentage left:

$$\frac{300}{450} \times 100 = 66.66\%.$$

62. Let Ram $= 6x$, Shyam $= 5x$

After increase:

Ram $= 6x \times 1.20$

$= 7.2x$

Let Shyam increase $= a\%$

$$\text{New Shyam} = 5x\left(1 + \frac{a}{100}\right)$$

Overall average increase $= 15\%$

Total after increase:

$$11x \times 1.15 = 12.65x$$

Equation:

$$7.2x + 5x\left(1 + \frac{a}{100}\right) = 12.65x$$

$$7.2 + 5 + 0.05a = 12.65$$
$$0.05a = 0.45$$
$$\Rightarrow \quad a = 9.$$

63. First mixture:

8 L $\rightarrow$ milk = 6, water = 2.

Second mixture: 14 L with ratio 6:1

$\rightarrow$ milk = 12, water = 2.

Total milk = 18,

total water = 4.

Water : milk

4 : 18 = 2 : 9.

64. Let selling price = S

P gets 40% profit on cost:

$$S = 1.40C_P$$

$$\Rightarrow \quad C_P = \frac{S}{1.40}$$

Q gets 50% profit on selling price:

$$\text{Profit}_Q = 0.50S$$

Difference of profits = 600:

$$0.50S - 0.40\left(\frac{S}{1.40}\right) = 600$$

$$0.50S - 0.2857S = 600$$
$$0.2143S = 600$$
$$\Rightarrow \quad S = 2800.$$

65. 8 years ago the total age of 5 memb

$= 5 \times 25 = 125$

After 8 years total age

$= 125 + 40 = 16$

Now there are 7 members and av remains 25 $\rightarrow$ total present age

$= 7 \times 25 = 175$

So, ages of two children

$= 175 - 165 = 1$

Let younger child $= x$,

older child $= x + 4$

$$x + x + 4 = 10$$
$$\Rightarrow \quad x = 3.$$

Therefore, youngest child = 3 years

ileage at 50 km/hr = 19.5 km/litre.

t 70 km/hr diesel use increases by 30%

mileage = 19.5 ÷ 1.3

= 15 km/litre.

n 10 litres distance = 15 × 10

= 150 km.

: 2 o'clock the hour hand is 10 minute-aces ahead of the minute hand.

e minute hand must gain 11 minute-spaces be 1 minute-space ahead.

otal angle to gain = 11 × 6° = 66°

Relative speed = 5.5° per minute.

Time taken = 66 ÷ 5.5

= 12 minutes.

erefore, the time is 2 : 12.

C1 : C2 : C3 = 9 : 10 : 8

C2 : C4 : C5 = 18 : 19 : 20

ake C2 common → combined ratio:

: C2 : C3 : C4 : C5

16.2 : 18 : 14.4 : 19 : 20.

fference

5 – C1 = 19

3.8k = 19

k = 5.

Profits = 81 + 90 + 72 + 95 + 100

= 438 cr.

years ago total age = 4 × 40 = 160.

er 15 years

160 + 60 = 220.

sent total (6 people) = 6 × 40 = 240

ages of children = 240 – 220 = 20.

Let younger = x,

older = x + 8

$x + x + 8 = 20$

$x = 6$

Older = 14

Ratio = 14 : 6

= 7 : 3.

70. Let the selling price be S.

Ramesh's profit is 25% on cost price, so

$$CP = \frac{S}{1.25}$$

$$Profit_{Ramesh} = S - \frac{S}{1.25}$$

$$= S - 0.8S = 0.2S$$

Rakesh's profit is 25% on selling price, so

$$Profit_{Rakesh} = 0.25S$$

Difference in profits =

$$0.25S - 0.2S = 0.05S$$

Given, $0.05S = 100$,

$$\Rightarrow \quad S = \frac{100}{0.05} = 2000.$$

71. Books read per day

$$\frac{\frac{18}{2}}{3} = 18 \times \frac{3}{2} = 27$$

Books read in 1/4 day

$$27 \times \frac{1}{4} = \frac{27}{4}.$$

72. Upstream speed

$$\frac{140}{7} = 20 \text{ km/h}$$

Downstream speed

$$\frac{210}{7} = 30 \text{ km/h}.$$

Speed in still water

$$\frac{20+30}{2} = 25 \text{ km/h}.$$

73. Circumference of circle

$$2\pi r = 2 \times \pi \times 21$$

$$= 132 \text{ cm}$$

(since $\pi = 22/7$).

This equals perimeter of the rectangle:

$$2(L + B) = 132$$

$\Rightarrow \quad L + B = 66$

Given ratio,

$L : B = 6 : 5$

Let, $L = 6k$

$B = 5k$

Then, $6k + 5k = 66$

$\Rightarrow \quad 11k = 66$

$\Rightarrow \quad k = 6$

Thus, $L = 36, \ B = 30.$

$\text{Area} = 36 \times 30 = 1080.$

74. $\sqrt{1225} = 35$

$\sqrt[3]{343} = 7$

$\text{Left side} = 35 \div 7 \times 0.45 \times 760$

$35 \div 7 = 5$

$0.45 \times 760 = 342$

So, $\text{LHS} = 5 \times 342 = 1710$

$\text{Right side} = x \times 0.6667 \times 45$

$0.6667 \times 45 = 30$

So, $\text{RHS} = 30x$

Equating: $30x = 1710$

$\Rightarrow \quad x = \frac{1710}{30} = 57.$

75. A's 1-day work $= \frac{1}{20}$

B's 1-day work $= \frac{1}{30}$

Combined 1-day work

$$\frac{1}{20}+\frac{1}{30} = \frac{3+2}{60} = \frac{5}{60} = \frac{1}{12}$$

So, total work (₹ 4000) completed in 12 days.

$$\text{A's share} = \frac{1}{20}\times 12 = \frac{12}{20}$$

$= 0.6$ of work

$$\text{B's share} = \frac{1}{30}\times 12 = \frac{12}{30}$$

$$\frac{1}{30}\times 12 = \frac{12}{30} = 0.4 \text{ of w}$$

A's amount $= 0.6 \times 4000 =$

B's amount $= 0.4 \times 4000 =$

Difference $= 2400 - 1600 =$

76. At 3 o'clock the hour hand is 15 m spaces ahead of the minute hand, ar minute hand must become 7 minute-s ahead, so it must gain a total of 15 = 22 minute-spaces.

One minute-space $= 6°$,

so, the total angular gain required i

$22 \times 6° = 132°$

The relative angular speed of the and hour hands is $6° - 0.5° = 5.5$

The time taken is

$$t = \frac{132°}{5.5°/\text{min}}$$

$$= \frac{132}{11/2} = \frac{264}{11}$$

$= 24$ minutes,

so, the required time is 3 : 24.

77. The pattern uses ordinal suffixes in ST for "1st", ND for "2nd", RD for TH for "4th". The suffix for "5th" TH, so the next term in the sequen be TH.

78. River water and milk are both speci of liquids, so both must lie entirel the larger set "Liquid", but they subsets of each other because river not milk and milk is not river wa correct diagram must show one lar representing "Liquid" and two smal overlapping circles inside it repr "River water" and "Milk", which i the structure shown in option A.

79. The alphabet has 26 letters, so half A–M is reversed to form M

H G F E D C B A, and the second half N–Z is reversed to form Z Y X W V U T S R Q P O N.

The combined sequence becomes M L K J I H G F E D C B A Z Y X W V U T S R Q P O N.

Counting from the right, N is 1st, O is 2nd, P is 3rd, Q is 4th, R is 5th, S is 6th, T is 7th, U is 8th, V is 9th, and W is 10th from the right, making W the correct letter.

80. The required figure must match the exact relative placement of the dot within the overlapping heart shape, the semicircle-like curve, and the rectangle in figure (X).

Option C preserves the same tilt of the rectangle, the same overlap order of shapes, and the same internal positioning of the dot within the intersection region.

The other options change the orientation or relative overlap of the shapes, causing the dot to fall in a different region, so only option C replicates the configuration correctly.

81. In figure X, all three dots lie inside the circle but each dot touches a different boundary formed by the intersection of the circle, rectangle, and the slanted triangle. One dot is near the upper curved boundary of the circle, the second lies inside the circle but close to the rectangle's side, and the third lies in the overlapping region of the circle and the slanted triangular shape. The correct option must reproduce the same three-region placement inside the circle with identical boundary relationships.

Option C is the only figure where the circle overlaps both the rectangle and the triangular shape in the same pattern as figure X, creating three distinct intersection zones inside the circle where the dots can be placed exactly as in X.

82. P and Q are brothers, so both belong to the same generation. P is the father of S. R is the only son of Q, meaning R and S are cousins.

R is married to U, so U becomes the wife of R. Since R is the son of Q, U is Q's daughter-in-law.

From S's point of view, R is his cousin, and the wife of a cousin is referred to as a sister-in-law.

Hence, U is the sister-in-law of S.

83. The transformation follows two independent rules—one for the three-letter group and one for the single letter below it.

In the first term, FNB becomes EMA by shifting each letter one step backward in the alphabet:

F → E, N → M, B → A.

Applying the same rule to GPC gives G → F, P → O, C → B, forming FOB.

For the denominator, V shifts three steps backward: V → S.

Applying this to Z gives Z → W.

Thus, the required pair is $\frac{\text{FOB}}{\text{W}}$.

84. The transformation in the first pair shows that the two circles differ only in the orientation and arrangement of the shapes inside them—specifically, the small shapes shift their positions while maintaining the same quantity and same type.

In the second pair, the third figure contains two identical triangles pointing upward; following the same transformation pattern, the required fourth figure must contain the same two triangles but shifted to the same relative positions as in the first pair's transformation.

Option A shows this exact positional change of the two triangles, matching the relation demonstrated in the example pair.

85. Biology is the odd word out because it belongs to the category of natural sciences, dealing with living organisms and biological processes.

The other three—Political Science, History, and Sociology—are social sciences or humanities, dealing with human society, political structures, cultural evolution, and social behaviour.

Thus, Biology stands apart from the other disciplines in nature and methodology.

86. Among the given numbers 10, 20, 15, 30, all except 15 are divisible by 10.

$10 \div 10 =$ integer,

$20 \div 10 =$ integer,

$30 \div 10 =$ integer,

but $15 \div 10 \neq$ integer.

Thus, 15 does not follow the same pattern.

87. To decode the pattern, compare

MOBILE → BJFZLK

and TABLET → QCIZXR.

Each letter is shifted backward by fixed positions according to its alphabetical order pattern.

Applying the same backward shifts to KINDLE:

K → B

I → J

N → A

D → L

L → F

E → I

Thus, KINDLE becomes BJALFI.

88. Given relations:

$P + Q \Rightarrow P$ is brother of Q.

$Q - S \Rightarrow Q$ is wife of S.

$S + R \Rightarrow S$ is brother of R.

$R \times L \Rightarrow R$ is son of L.

$L \div M \Rightarrow L$ is husband of M.

From $Q - S$, Q is female (wife of S).

From $P + Q$, P is brother of Q.

Thus, P is the brother of Q, who is the wife of S.

Hence, P is S's wife's brother.

89. Shilpa walks 40 km north from home, then 60 km east, then 40 km south which brings her back to the original east–west line but still 60 km east of home.

Finally, she turns left and moves 30 km further east.

Her total displacement from home is purely horizontal:

$60 + 30 = 90$ km east.

So, she is 90 km away from her home.

90. A water image is obtained by reflecting the given figure across a horizontal axis (as if the figure is placed above water and its reflection appears below). In the original figure, the upward-pointing arrow becomes a downward-pointing arrow, the black and white circles interchange their vertical positions, and every element is flipped top-to-bottom while maintaining left-right orientation. Among the given choices only option D accurately preserves all these vertically inverted positions and shapes exactly as a true water reflection, making it the correct image.

91. The question asks for players who play kabaddi and football only, meaning those who lie in the overlap of the rectangle (kabaddi) and the triangle (football) but not inside the circle (kho-kho).

In the Venn diagram, the region common to triangle + rectangle only is represented by the number 9.

The number 10 lies in triangle + rectangle + circle, so it must be excluded.

Therefore, the only value that satisfies the condition of "kabaddi and football only" is 9.

92. The series is:

39, 53, ?, 108, 149, 199

To find the missing term, examine the first differences between terms:

53 – 39 = 14

Let the next differences be d_2, d_3, 41, 50.

Try to establish a consistent rule. Test each option by computing the differences and their second differences.

Testing Option D (76):

53 → 76: 76 – 53 = 23

76 → 108: 108 – 76 = 32

108 → 149: 149 – 108 = 41

149 → 199: 199 – 149 = 50

So, the differences become:

14, 23, 32, 41, 50

Now compute second differences:

23 – 14 = 9

32 – 23 = 9

41 – 32 = 9

50 – 41 = 9

A perfect constant second difference of 9 appears, which confirms a valid quadratic pattern.

This makes the sequence mathematically consistent and uniquely correct.

Thus, the missing number must be: 76.

The given figure is divided into four quadrants around a central diamond. Three quadrants already contain small shapes (triangles and circles) arranged in a balanced rotational pattern, meaning the missing quadrant must mirror the orientation and position of the shapes found in the opposite quadrants.

In the top-left quadrant, a triangle points towards the center, and in the bottom-right quadrant, a similar triangle also points towards the center.

Thus, the top-right quadrant must contain a triangle that also points towards the center, maintaining the rotational consistency of the figure.

Among the options:

Option A shows the required inward-pointing triangle along with the correct circle placement and matching corner lines.

Options B, C, and D either have incorrect triangle orientation or incorrect circle alignment relative to the central figure.

Therefore, only Option A completes the pattern accurately.

94. The symbols '+' and '×' must be interchanged, and the symbols '–' and '÷' must be interchanged, so the given expression

105 – 15 ÷ 13 + 3 × 27

changes to

105 ÷ 15 – 13 × 3 + 27

Now solving step-by-step in mathematical style:

105 ÷ 15 = 7

13 × 3 = 39

Substituting: 7 – 39 + 27

7 – 39 = –32

–32 + 27 = –5

95. The series is governed by cyclic positional shifts of all symbols, especially the rotational movement of the arrow, square, and triangle around the four side-center and four corner positions.

The upward arrow moves counter-clockwise around the four mid-edge positions in the order Top → Right → Bottom → Left → Top, so the next figure must place the arrow again at the top-center.

The square moves clockwise among the four corner positions in the order Top-Right → Bottom-Right → Bottom-Left → Top-Left → Top-Right, so in the next figure it returns to the top-right corner.

The triangle similarly cycles clockwise among the remaining corner positions, returning to the bottom-left.

The fixed letters S and Y retain their respective stable opposite-corner placements. When all symbol-trajectories are followed simultaneously, the configuration of the next diagram matches exactly with Option A, including the correct placement of the central symbol at the bottom as it recurs from earlier in the sequence.

96. The sequence rearranges the five symbols (T, A, O, N, △) by rotating them downward one position in each step, while the top row letters slide left in a repeating pattern. In each frame the bottom element moves to the top position, creating a continuous clockwise rotation. Applying the same transformation to the last shown box results in the order E at the top, followed by A, O, △, and N downward. Option B matches this continuation exactly.

97. Sucheta sits second to the left of Gargi, so the relative order must be S_G.

Fauzia sits third to the right of Sucheta, so counting three seats to the right of S fixes Fauzia at the rightmost position in a 5-seat row.

This forces the arrangement into the pattern _S_G F.

Only Amita and Ranjita remain to be placed, with exactly one girl between them and with Amita not at an extreme end.

The only way to satisfy both conditions is to place Ranjita in the first seat and Amita in the second seat, giving the final line-up (left to right): Ranjita, Amita, Sucheta, Gargi, Fauzia.

Thus, the two girls sitting at the extr ends are Ranjita (left end) and Fauzia (r end).

98. "50% walls are bus" means half of wall set is inside the bus set, but it c not mean all buses are walls or all w are benches.

So, Conclusion I ("All bus are bench does not follow.

But since "Some benches are walls" "50% walls are bus", there is a v possibility that some buses may alsc benches.

Hence, Conclusion II is possible, so II follows.

99. The given figure consists of two interse slanted line segments forming a s angular shape.

Without rotation allowed, only optic contains the exact same oriented s clearly embedded within its grid patte

Options A, C, and D contain sir directions but not the same angled s without rotation.

100. In the question figure, each quadrant cor curved strokes increasing in count a move clockwise, along with thick bour lines that must continue seamlessly.

The missing quadrant must match curved–line progression and bour alignment.

Option C exactly continues both the direction and the boundary alignr matching the rotational and structural of the other three quadrants.

Options A, B, and D either break curv symmetry or border continuity.

Previous Years' Paper

Air Force Common Admission Test (AFCAT)—1/2024*

Select the most appropriate meaning of the given idiom:

Under the weather

A. To feel sad
B. To feel ill
C. To feel cheated by friends
D. Under suspicion

Select the option that is nearest in the meaning to the underlined word:

<u>Pallid</u>

A. Old B. Sanguine
C. Pale D. Grumpy

n questions given below, out of the four lternatives, choose the one which can be ubstituted for the given words:

That which cannot be corrected

. Incorrigible B. Infallible
. Tangible D. Unintangible

he following sentence has been divided nto parts. One of them contains an error. elect the part that contains the error from e given options.

either the doctors (*a*)/ nor the nurse (*b*)/ e availaible. (*c*)/ No error (*d*)

. (*a*) B. (*b*)
. (*c*) D. (*d*)

elect the most appropriate meaning of the ven idiom:

Achilles' heel

A. A funny part of a movie
B. Weakness
C. Sarcasm
D. Long heels worn by ladies

6. Select the option that is nearest in the meaning to the underlined word:

<u>Omnipresent</u>

A. Powerful
B. Unique
C. Universal
D. Modern

7. The following sentence has been divided into parts. One of them contains an error. Select the part that contains the error from the given options.

She was asked (*a*) /that why she had (*b*)/ not attended the class. (*c*)/ No error (*d*)

A. (*a*) B. (*b*)
C. (*c*) D. (*d*)

8. Select the most appropriate meaning of the given idiom:

Turn a blind eye

A. To ignore something that you know is wrong
B. Stay away from bad habits.
C. Hide the ugly truth from someone
D. To feel happy

B	**2.** C	**3.** A	**4.** C	**5.** B	**6.** C	**7.** B	**8.** A

on memory

9. Select the option that is nearest in the meaning to the underlined word:

Pillage

A. Buffet B. Pilgrimage
C. Voyage D. Plunder

10. In the following question there is a related pair of words given. Each pair is followed by four other pairs of words. Choose the pair from the given option the pair of words that best expresses the relationship like the original pair.

Abjure : Renounce : : Alleviate : ?

A. Lessen B. Amplify
C. Simplify D. Nationalise

11. Select the option that is nearest in the meaning to the underlined word:

Fret

A. Laugh B. Hinder
C. Aid D. Worry

12. Select the option that is opposite in the meaning to the underlined word:

Anathema

A. Blessing B. Asthma
C. Purity D. Curse

13. In the following question there is a related pair of words given. Each pair is followed by four other pairs of words. Choose the pair from the given option the pair of words that best expresses the relationship like the original pair.

Sculptor : Clay : : Author : ?

A. write B. story
C. play D. words

14. Fill in the blank with the most appropriate word from the given options.

His neighbour created chaos regularly so he decided to ....

A. blow a whistle
B. blow a baloon
C. take a rain decision
D. read the riot act

15. Select the option that is nearest in meaning to the underlined word:

Asunder

A. Thunder B. Into pieces
C. Bravery D. Baptism

16. Select the option that is nearest in opposite meaning to the given word:

Craving

A. Like B. Dislike
C. Discomfort D. Complacency

Directions (Qs. No. 17-19): *The follo question, consists of an incomplete senten a sentence which is split into four parts four parts are jumbled up and are named Q, R and S. These four parts are not gi their proper order. Arrange the jumbled of the sentence and find out which of th combinations from the given options will co complete the sentence.*

17. Two people argue about .... green gas rich atmosphere.

P: The first argues that it's because is closer
Q: The second argues that it's b Venus has a thick,
R: why Venus is so much warm the Earth.
S: to the Sun, so it absorbs more solar

A. PQRS B. RPSQ
C. RQSP D. SRQP

18. Climate change is .... global temp and weather patterns.

P: causing significant changes in
Q: a major environmental issue
R: that is
S: the increase in greenhouse gas

A. PSRQ B. SRQP
C. QRPS D. PQRS

9. D	10. A	11. D	12. A	13. D	14. D	15. B	16. B	17. B

Electric vehicles are .... emissions.

P: and reduce air pollution
Q: a sustainable transportation option
R: that can help mitigate climate change
S: by lowering greenhouse gas

A. RPSQ B. PQRS
C. QRSP D. QRPS

That which cannot be corrected.

A. Unintelligible B. Indelible
C. Illegible D. Incorrigible

Which word has a similar meaning as:

OMNIPRESENT

A. Ubiquitous B. Good
C. Vanish D. Knowing

Identify the segment in the sentence which contains a grammatical error. If there is no error, then select the option "No error".

We talked about writing a will, but it/ was one of those thing you never/ get around to doing.

A. was one of those thing you never
B. No error
C. get around to doing.
D. We talked about writing a will, but it

Choose the word that can substitute the given sentence.

Study of living organisms

A. Biology B. Zoology
C. Epistemology D. Ecology

Choose the word that is opposite in meaning to the given word.

Suspicion

A. Niggle B. Tremor
C. Conviction D. Incertitude

Choose the incorrectly spelt word.

A. Positon B. Source
C. Serious D. Continue

26. The motto of G-20 Summit 2023 is:

A. Recover Together, Recover Stronger
B. One Earth, One Family, One Future
C. People, Planet, Prosperity
D. Realizing Opportunities of the 21st Century for All

27. The Operation Zindagi was launched for:

A. Bring back Indian Nationalists from Afghanistan.
B. Rescue operation in Lhonak Lake
C. Rescue operation in Silkyara Bend - Barkot tunnel collapse
D. Distribution of covid-19 vaccine

28. Operation Vajra Prahar, which is a bilateral Indo-US Joint Special Forces exercise, was held in:

A. Umroi B. Bakloh
C. Ranikhet D. Goa

29. Who among the following is appointed as the head of the railway board?

A. Jaya Varma Sinha
B. Ayesha Khan
C. Priya Sharma
D. Deepika Gupta

30. Fifth scorpene class submarine commissioned by the Indian Navy is:

A. INS Vagir B. INS Vagshir
C. INS Virat D. INS Arihant

31. Alaknanda and Bhagirathi meeting point is known as:

A. Devprayag B. Nandprayag
C. Karnaprayag D. Vishnuprayag

32. Tawa river is a tributary of which of the following river?

A. Chambal river B. Tapi River
C. Narmada river D. Johilla river

D	20. D	21. A	22. A	23. A	24. C	25. A
B	27. C	28. A	29. A	30. A	31. A	32. C

33. Largest Salt Lake in India is:

A. Sambhar Lake B. Wular Lake
C. Kolleru Lake D. Vembanad Lake

34. What is the designated landing site of Chandrayaan-3, India's lunar mission?

A. Shiv Shakti Point
B. Chandranagar Point
C. Indira Point
D. Vikram Point

35. In cricket match, while catching a fast-moving ball, a fielder in the ground gradually pulls his hands backwards with the moving ball to reduce the velocity to zero. The act represents:

A. Newton's first law of motion
B. Newton's second law of motion
C. Newton's third law of motion
D. Law of conservation of energy

36. The number of pair of chromosomes in humans is:

A. 46 B. 22
C. 23 D. 44

37. Strait of Malacca separates which of the following two countries?

A. Sumatra and Malaysia
B. Java and Brunei
C. Sumatra and Java
D. Malaysia and Brunei

38. Which of the following day "World Environment Day" celebrated?

A. 5 June B. 5 May
C. 5 March D. 5 April

39. 'Discovery of India' book written by Jawaharlal Nehru in which of the following jail?

A. Madras Central Jail
B. Ahmadnagar Fort Jail
C. Tihar Jail
D. Bombay Jail

40. Which one of the following coalfiel
not located in Jharkhand?

A. Jharia B. Ramgarh
C. Deogarh D. Umaria

41. First Battle of Panipat was fought be
Babur and ....

A. Ibrahim Lodhi B. Sikandar L
C. Bahlol Lodhi D. Sher Shah S

42. Who has the power to advise the pre
of India under Article 143?

A. Supreme Court of India
B. High Court of India
C. District Courts
D. All of the above

43. 1st women won gold medal i
Commonwealth boxer by:

A. MC Mary Kom
B. Nikhat Zareen
C. Lovlina Borgohain
D. Jaismine Lamboria

44. Tasveer Khana started by which
following ruler?

A. Akbar B. Humanyun
C. Jahangir D. Aurangzeb

45. 1st greenfield airport in India was
by:

A. Donyi Polo Airport, Itanagar
B. Lokpriya Gopinath Bordoloi Inte
Airport
C. Lengpui Airport, Mizoram
D. Dibrugarh Airport

46. Anti-defection is present in which
of the constitution?

A. 10th schedule B. 11th sche
C. 12th schedule D. 9th sche

33. A	**34.** A	**35.** B	**36.** C	**37.** A	**38.** A
40. D	**41.** A	**42.** A	**43.** A	**44.** A	**45.** A

Terrestrial ecosystem mostly affected by:

A. Water B. Temperature
C. Sunlight D. Wind

C-295 Aircraft is a joint venture between India and:

A. Israel B. USA
C. Spain D. Russia

Which of the following country is **not** a member of SAARC?

A. Sri-Lanka B. India
C. Bangladesh D. China

Mickey Mouse cartoon designed by which of the following cartoonist?

A. Walt Disney and Ub Iwerks
B. Chuck Jones and Ub Iwerks
C. Chuck Jones
D. Tex Avery

There are some people standing in front of the two counters. In the first counter girl 1 rank is seventh from the counter and eighteenth from the back, in the second counter girl 2 rank is third from the front and thirteen from the back. Find the total number of people standing in both the counters?

A. 49 B. 36
C. 46 D. 39

In a certain code language "MANGO" is written as "PHOBN" and "ORANGE" is written as "FHOBSP". How will "GRAPES" be written in that code language?

A. TFQASH B. TFQBHS
C. TFQBSH D. TFRBSH

A car is parked in front of the office facing north. Driver drives the car for some distance and takes a right turn, then after driving a few distance he takes a right turn, then after a few distance he takes a left turn and reaches his home. Now in which direction the car is facing?

A. North B. West
C. South D. East

54. Three of the following four are alike in a certain way and so form a group. Which one does not belong to that group?

A. AUAGRJ B. ATJES
C. AEGIRM D. NDIAI

55. How many tablet are only car?

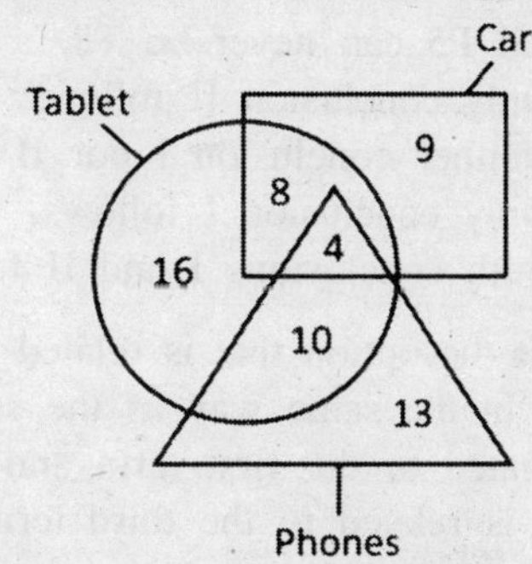

A. 4 B. 12
C. 8 D. 17

56. Three statements are given followed by two conclusions numbered I and II. Assuming the statements to be true, even if they seem to be at variance with commonly known facts, decide which of the conclusions logically follow(s) from the statements.

Statements:

Some towns are cities.
Some cities are villages.
All villages are states.

Conclusions:

I. Some towns are not villages.
II. Some states are cities.

A. Only conclusion II follows
B. Only conclusion I follows
C. Both conclusions I and II follow
D. Neither conclusion I nor II follows

B 48. C 49. D 50. A 51. D 52. C 53. D 54. D 55. C 56. A

57. Read the given statements and conclusions carefully. Assuming that the information given in the statements is true, even if it appears to be at variance with commonly known facts, decide which of the given conclusions logically follow(s) from the statements.

Statements:

Only a few A1 are P5.

Only a few P5 are T8.

Conclusions:

I. Some A1 are T8.

II. All P5 can never be T8.

A. Only conclusion II follows.

B. Neither conclusion I nor II follow.

C. Only conclusion I follows.

D. Both conclusions I and II follow.

58. Select the option that is related to the fifth term in the same way as the second term is related to the first term and the fourth term is related to the third term.

ERA : ETA : : HONEST : JOPEUV : : GRAIN : ?

A. GTCIN B. ITCIP

C. IRAKP D. ITAIP

59. Four letter-clusters have been given, out of which three are alike in some manner and one is different. Select the letter-cluster that is different.

A. HKMR B. BJPV

C. DLRT D. FMNQ

60. Select the figure that will come in place of the question mark (?) in the following figure series.

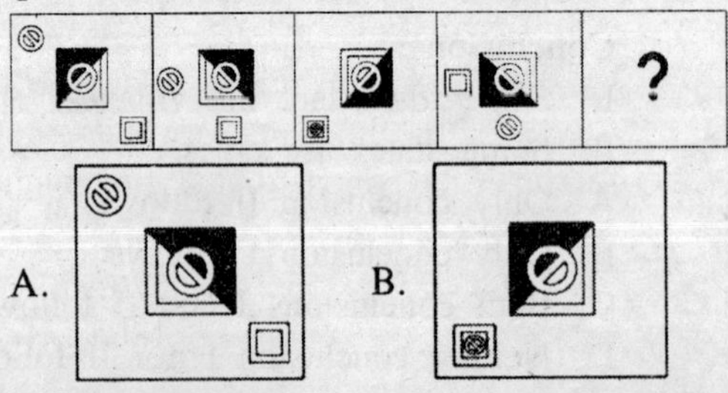

61. Select the letter-cluster from among given options that can replace the que mark (?) in the following series.

YCLE, DWQJ, IQVO, ?, SEFY

A. HLAW B. NHKR

C. HDLA D. NKAT

62. In a certain code language. 'HUM written as 'GTLO' and 'LIKE' is w as 'KHJD'. How will 'PLAY' be w in that language?

A. OJZX B. QKZX

C. OKZX D. OKYX

63. In a family of 5 members, X is the of Y. M has two children and he son of E, who is the father-in-law H has only one son. Y is not the daughter of E. How is X related to

A. Sister B. Daughter

C. Grand-daughter D. Grandson

64. Select the Venn diagram that best rep the relationship between the foll classes.

Mango, Fruit, Banana

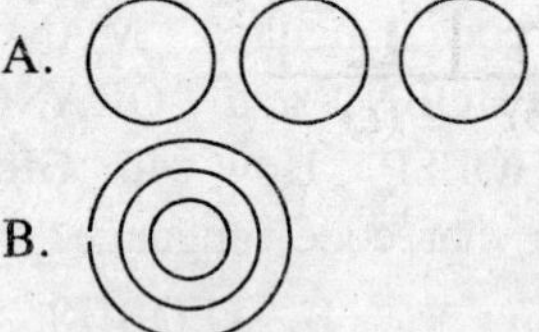

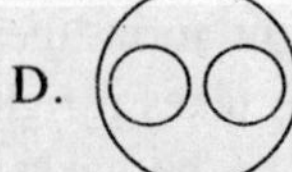

57. A	58. D	59. C	60. C	61. D	62. C	63. C	6

. Select the figure that will come next in the following figure series.

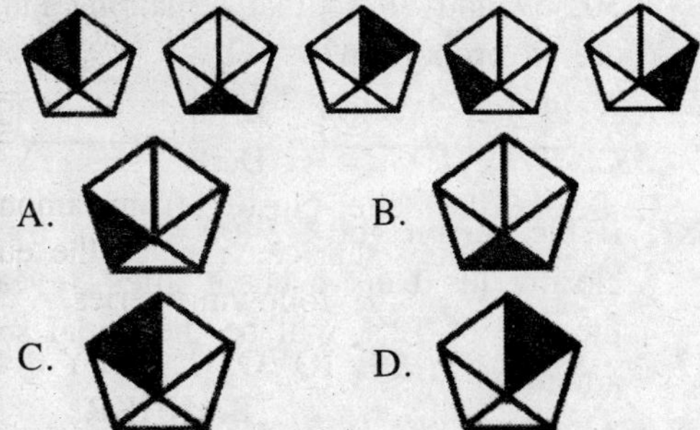

A.

B.

C.

D.

. Find the perfect figure from the option figure that will replace the question mark(?) from the problem figure.

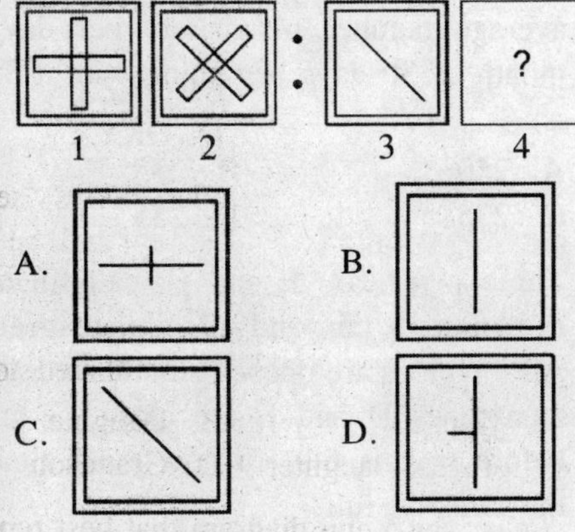

Select the figure that does not belong in the following series.

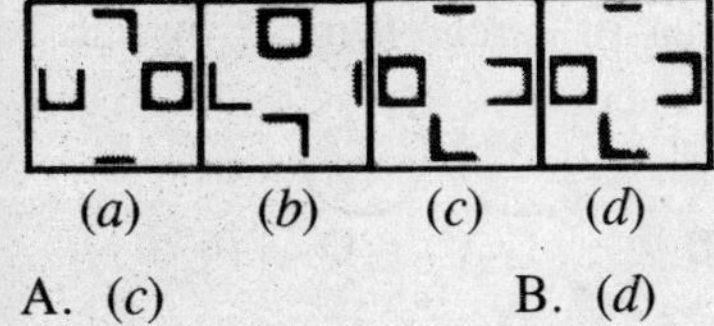

A. (*c*) B. (*d*)

C. (*b*) D. (*a*)

In each of the following questions, a matrix of certain characters is given. These characters follow a certain trend, row wise or column wise.

Find out this trend and choose the missing character accordingly.

862	2	761	875	2	972	963	2	844
546	2	652	766	2	566	464	?	903

A. 2 B. 4

C. 6 D. 1

69. Select the figure that will replace the question following figure series.

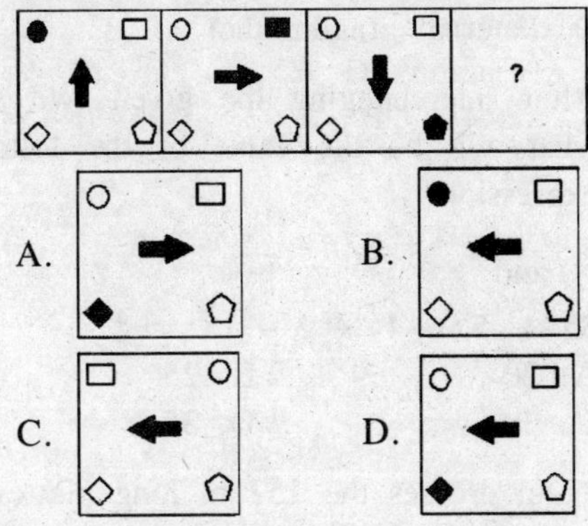

70. If '–' stands for '÷', '+' stands for '×', '÷' stands for '–' and '×' stands for '+', then 80 – 20 + 10 ÷ 8 × 10 is equal to:

A. 42 B. 45

C. 78 D. 68

71. If 'oranges' are 'apples', 'bananas' are 'apricots', 'apples' are 'chillies', 'apricots' are orange and 'chillies' are 'bananas', then which of the following are green in colour?

A. Bananas B. Chillies

C. Apples D. Apricots

72. A series is given with one term wrong select that wrong term from the given alternatives.

MCWH, PFZK, RICN, VLFQ

A. MCWH B. PFZK

C. RICN D. VLFQ

73. Select the option that is related to the third number in the same way as the second number is related to the first number.

5 : 150 : : 8 : ?

A. 864 B. 576

C. 262 D. 186

5. C **66.** B **67.** C **68.** A **69.** D **70.** A **71.** A **72.** C **73.** B

74. Ronita's only brother Vikram is the husband of Kritika's mother Sejal. How is Ronita's mother Chandni related to Kritika?

A. Mother-in-law
B. Maternal grandmother
C. Paternal aunt
D. Paternal grandmother

75. After interchanging the given two signs, what will be the value of the following expression?

× and ÷

35 + 5 ÷ 4 × 2 – 15 = ?

A. 20 B. 25
C. 30 D. 35

76. Train crosses the 153 m long platform in 45 sec if the train length is 747 m then what is the speed of the train?

A. 72 km/hr B. 55 km/hr
C. 75 km/hr D. 90 km/hr

77. What is the largest 4 digit number divisible be 88?

A. 9944 B. 9000
C. 8488 D. 9999

78. A person sold an article for ₹ 3,600 and got a profit of 20%. Had he sold the article for ₹ 3,150, how much profit would he have got?

A. 10% B. 5%
C. 7% D. 7.5%

79. A and B can do a piece of work in 20 hours. B and C can do it in 25 hours, while A and C take 15 hours to complete the work. B independently can complete the work in:

A. 85.71 hrs B. 70 hrs
C. 60 hrs D. 45 hrs

80. Which number should be subtracted from 30, 57 and 78 so that remaining num are in proportion?

A. 9 B. 6
C. 7 D. 8

81. If the person got ₹ 5400 amount by closing his bank account after 3 year the rate of 12% will be the initial sur amount?

A. 15000 B. 14550
C. 16000 D. 13000

82. A Library has an average of 510 vis on Sundays and 240 on other days. average number of visitors per day month of 30 days beginning with a Su is:

A. 250 B. 285
C. 275 D. 255

83. Three pipes, D, E and F, can fill a in 6 min, 8 min and 12 min, respecti All the pipes are opened simultaneously then pipes D and E are closed 3 mi before tank is full. In how much time the tank be full?

A. 4 min B. 11 min
C. 7 min D. 5 min

84. The area of circle formed by the ro length 7 cm will be?

A. 154 B. 156
C. 160 D. 146

85. A sum at simple interest becomes two is 8 years at a certain rate of interes The time in which the same sum will times at the same rate of interest at s interest is:

A. 30 years B. 25 years
C. 24 years D. 20 years

74. D	75. C	76. A	77. A	78. B	79. A
80. B	81. A	82. B	83. D	84. A	85. C

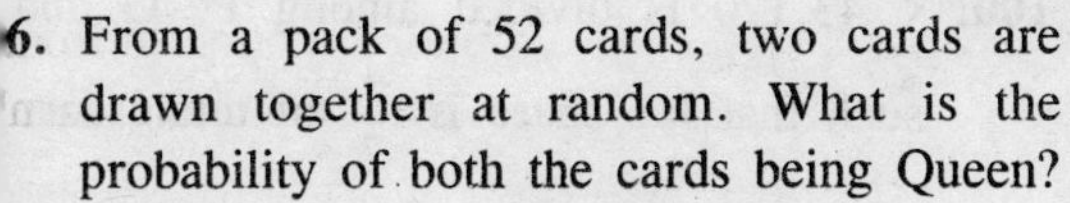

6. From a pack of 52 cards, two cards are drawn together at random. What is the probability of both the cards being Queen?

A. $\frac{1}{221}$ B. $\frac{1}{225}$

C. $\frac{2}{13}$ D. $\frac{1}{13}$

7. What will come in the place of the question mark ? in the following question?

$150 \div 3 \times 12 - (300 \div 6 \times 12) + 1 = ?$

A. 2 B. 1

C. 0 D. –1

8. One dozen notebooks quoted at ₹ 125 are available at 20% discount. How many notebooks can be bought for ₹ 75?

A. 10 B. 6

C. 9 D. 8

. The ratio of milk and sugar in the container is 2 : 3 when 20 L of the mixture is taken out and is replaced by the sugar the ratio becomes 3 : 7. Then the total quantity of the mixture in the container is?

A. 60 B. 80

C. 70 D. 90

. Eight years ago, Ajay's age was 4/3 times that of Vijay. Eight years hence, Ajay's age will be 6/5 times that of Vijay. What is the present age of Ajay?

A. 40 years B. 41 years

C. 42 years D. 43 years

. Tap P can fill a cistern in 6 hours and tap Q can empty the full cistern in 10 hours. If both taps P and Q are kept open simultaneously, then in how many hours will the empty cistern be completely full?

A. 15 B. 18

C. 16 D. 12

92. What will be the value of the expression?

$11122 \div 134 + 26\%$ of 471

A. 207.86 B. 205.46

C. 204.34 D. 203.52

93. A man who is running at the speed of 10 km/hr in the opposite direction of the train. The train at the speed of 60 km/hr crosses the man in 36 seconds. What is the length of the train?

A. 500 m B. 900 m

C. 450 m D. 700 m

94. A candidate scores 25% and fails by 32 marks, while another candidate who scores 40% marks, gets 28 marks more than the minimum required marks to pass the examination. How many marks did a candidate score if he scored 72% marks?

A. 288 B. 275

C. 250 D. 300

95. In a mixture of 160 liters, the ratio of milk and water 3:1. If this ratio is to be 1:3, then find the quantity of water to be further added.

A. 40 liters B. 320 liters

C. 50 liters D. 100 liters

96. A 1800 metres long train crosses a man walking in opposite direction in 10 seconds. If the speed of train is 8 times to the speed of man, then what is the speed of train?

A. 576 km/hr B. 640 km/hr

C. 596 km/hr D. 570 km/hr

97. Distance of a chord RS from the centre is 20 cm. If the length of the this chord is 30 cm, then what will be the diameter of this circle?

A. 45 cm B. 55 cm

C. 60 cm D. 50 cm

86. A	**87.** B	**88.** C	**89.** B	**90.** A	**91.** A
92. B	**93.** D	**94.** A	**95.** B	**96.** A	**97.** D

98. If $\frac{(17)^3-(7)^3}{(17^2+7^2+k)}=10,$ then what is the value of k?

A. 102 B. 119

C. 136 D. 85

99. What is the value of $4^2 - 3^2 + 6^2 - 5^2 + 8^2 - 7^2 + \ldots\ldots 92^2 - 91^2$?

A. 4272 B. 4280

C. 4278 D. 4275

100. ₹ 43,120 is divided among P, Q and such that P's share is $\frac{4}{7}$ of total share Q and R together and Q's share is $\frac{2}{5}$ total share of P and R together. What the share of R?

A. ₹ 15120 B. ₹ 14220

C. ₹ 16400 D. ₹ 18050

EXPLANATORY ANSWERS

1. (B): The idiom "under the weather" means to feel ill. So, the correct answer is: (B) To feel ill. This phrase is commonly used to describe someone who is feeling unwell or sick. It's believed to have originated from maritime language, where sailors who were sick would rest below deck and away from the harsh weather conditions.

2. (C): The option that is nearest in meaning to the underlined word pallid is: (C) Pale. Pallid means having an abnormally pale or wan complexion, often suggesting poor health or lack of colour.

3. (A): The word that can be substituted for "that which cannot be corrected" is: (A) Incorrigible. Incorrigible refers to someone or something that is unable to be corrected, improved, or reformed.

4. (C): The error in the sentence is in part (*c*). The correct form of the verb should be "is" instead of "are" because "neither...nor" construction requires the verb to agree with the subject closest to it, which is "the nurse" (singular). Also, there is a typo in the word "available".

So, the corrected sentence should be: "Neither the doctors nor the nurse is available."

5. (B): The idiom "Achilles' heel" means a weakness. So, the correct answer is: (B) Weakness. The term "Achilles' heel" originates from Greek mythology. Achilles was a hero of the Trojan War whose mother dipped him into the River Styx to make him invulnerable. Howe she held him by his heel, which remained and thus became his only vulnerable spot. ultimately led to his downfall when he struck by an arrow in his heel.

6. (C): The option that is nearest in meaning tc underlined word omnipresent is: (C) Unive Omnipresent means being present everyw at all times, and universal shares a sin meaning, indicating something that is widesp and applicable everywhere.

7. (B): The error in the sentence is in part The correct form should be "why she instead of "that why she had".

So, the corrected sentence should be: "She asked why she had not attended the class

8. (A): The idiom "turn a blind eye" mea ignore something that you know is wrong the correct answer is: (A). To ignore some that you know is wrong.

The phrase "turn a blind eye" is used to de a situation where someone chooses to ign fact or reality, even though they are awa it. It implies a deliberate decision to ove wrongdoing or undesirable situations.

9. (D): The option that is nearest in meani the underlined word pillage is: (D) Pl Pillage means to rob a place using vio

98. B	**99.** D	**100.** A

especially in wartime, and plunder carries a similar meaning, referring to the act of looting or stealing goods, often by force.

10. (A): The pair of words that best expresses the relationship like the original pair Abjure: Renounce is: (A) Lessen. Abjure and Renounce both mean to formally reject or give up something. Alleviate and Lessen both mean to reduce the severity or intensity of something.

The relationship between the words in the original pair is one of synonymy, where both words share similar meanings. The pair Alleviate: Lessen also shares a similar relationship, making it the correct choice.

11. (D): The option that is nearest in meaning to the underlined word fret is: (D) Worry. Fret means to be constantly or visibly anxious or worried.

12. (A): The option that is opposite in meaning to the underlined word anathema is: (A) Blessing. Anathema means something or someone that is intensely disliked or loathed, often to the point of being cursed or condemned. The opposite of this would be a blessing, which is something highly valued or cherished.

13. (D): The pair of words that best expresses the relationship like the original pair Sculptor : Clay is: (D) words.

- **Sculptor:** A sculptor uses clay to create sculptures.
- **Author:** An author uses words to create written works.

The relationship is that the first word is a person who uses the second word as a medium to create something. So, just as a sculptor uses clay, an author uses words.

14. (D): The most appropriate word to fill in the blank is: (D) read the riot act. To "read the riot act" means to reprimand someone severely or issue a strong warning about their behaviour. In this context, it fits perfectly as he decided to confront his neighbour about the chaos they regularly create.

15. (B): The option that is nearest in meaning to the underlined word asunder is: (B) Into pieces. Asunder means to be torn apart or divided into pieces. It is often used to describe something that has been split or separated violently or suddenly.

16. (B): The option that is nearest in the opposite meaning to the given word craving is: (B) Dislike. Therefore, dislike is the opposite of craving, as it indicates an absence of desire or a negative feeling towards something.

17. (B): The sentence "Two people argue about .... greenhouse-gas rich atmosphere." should be completed as follows:

R: why Venus is so much warmer than the Earth. **P:** The first argues that it's because Venus is closer **S:** to the Sun, so it absorbs more solar energy. **Q:** The second argues that it's because Venus has a thick,

So, the correct combination of the jumbled parts to complete the sentence is: (B) RPSQ.

18. (C): The correct sequence to complete the sentence is QRPS:

Q: a major environmental issue

R: that is

P: causing significant changes in

S: the increase in greenhouse gases,

So, the complete sentence is: "Climate change is a major environmental issue that is causing significant changes in the increase in greenhouse gases, global temperatures and weather patterns."

19. (D): The correct sequence to complete the sentence is QRPS:

Q: a sustainable transportation option

R: that can help mitigate climate change

P: and reduce air pollution

S: by lowering greenhouse gas emissions

So, the complete sentence is: "Electric vehicles are a sustainable transportation option that can help mitigate climate change and reduce air pollution by lowering greenhouse gas emissions."

20. (D): The correct answer is: (D) Incorrigible.

Incorrigible means something or someone that cannot be corrected, improved, or reformed.

Unintelligible means not able to be understood.

Indelible means making marks that cannot be removed or forgotten.

Illegible means not clear enough to be read.

21. (A): The word that has a similar meaning to omnipresent is: (A) ubiquitous. Omnipresent means being present everywhere at all times, and ubiquitous shares a similar meaning, indicating something that is found everywhere or is constantly encountered.

22. (A): The segment in the sentence which contains a grammatical error is: (A) was one of those thing you never. The correct phrase should be "was one of those things you never." The noun "thing" should be in its plural form "things" to agree with "those."

So, the corrected sentence should be: "We talked about writing a will, but it was one of those things you never get around to doing."

23. (A): The word that can substitute the given sentence "Study of living organisms" is: (A) Biology.

Biology is the scientific study of living organisms and their interactions with the environment.

Zoology is the study of animals.

Epistemology is the study of knowledge and belief.

Ecology is the study of the relationships between organisms and their environment.

24. (C): The word that is opposite in meaning to suspicion is: (C) Conviction.

Suspicion means a feeling or thought that something is possible, likely, or true, often without certain proof.

Conviction means a firm belief or certainty about something, which is the opposite of doubt or suspicion.

25. (A): The incorrectly spelt word is: (A) Positon. The correct spelling is position.

26. (B): G20 logo is "Bharat", written in the Devanagari script. The theme of India's G20 Presidency - "Vasudhaiva Kutumbakam" or "One Earth, One Family, One Future" – was drawn from the ancient Sanskrit text of t Maha Upanishad.

27. (C): Rescue operation in Silkyara Bend - Bark tunnel collapse. Operation Zindagi was launch as a massive rescue operation to save 41 work trapped in the Silkyara Bend - Barkot tun collapse in Uttarakhand, India.

28. (A): The Indian Army contingent departed to for the 15th edition of India-US joint Spec Forces Exercise VAJRA PRAHAR. The exerc is scheduled to be conducted from 2nd to 2 November 2024 at Orchard Combat Train Centre in Idaho, USA. Last edition of the sa exercise was conducted at Umroi, Meghalaya December 2023. This will be second exercise the year between Indian and the US Army, previous being Exercise YUDH ABHYAS 20 conducted at Rajasthan in September 2024.

29. (A): Jaya Varma Sinha was the first woma hold the topmost post in the Indian Railw as the Chairperson and CEO of the Rail Board. She was succeeded by Satish Kuma September 2024.

30. (A): Indian Navy's fifth stealth Scorpene c Submarine INS Vagir was commissioned the Indian Navy today, 23 January 2023 at Naval Dockyard Mumbai in the presence Adm R. Hari Kumar, Chief of the Naval S the Chief Guest for the ceremony. Six Scor Class submarines are being built in India the Mazagon Dock Shipbuilders Limited (M Mumbai, under collaboration with M/s N Group, France. INS Vagir would form of the Western Naval Command's Subm fleet and would be another potent part of Command's arsenal.

31. (A): Devprayag is one among the list of 'P Prayag, where the holy streams of 'Alakn and 'Bhagirathi' meet, and hereafter the riv called Ganga. One of the major destinatio Devprayag is the sacred temple of Raghun

32. (C): The Tawa River is a tributary of Narmada River of Central India. The Ta the Narmada's largest tributary, at 172 k rises in the Satpura Range of Betul and fl north and west, joins the Narmada at the v of Bandra Bhan in Hoshangabad District.

33. **(A):** Sambhar Lake is the largest inland salt lake in India, located in the state of Rajasthan. It is known for its unique ecology, saline properties, and is an important site for salt production.

34. **(A):** The designated landing site of Chandrayaan-3, India's lunar mission, is: (A) Shiv Shakti Point. Shiv Shakti Point is located between the lunar craters Manzinus C and Simpelius N, approximately 600 km from the south pole of the Moon. The site was named to honour the Hindu deities Shiva and Shakti, symbolizing determination and capability.

35. **(B):** Newton's second law of motion states that the acceleration of an object is directly proportional to the net force acting on it and inversely proportional to its mass. In this case, when a fielder catches a fast-moving ball and pulls his hands backwards, he is applying a force in the opposite direction to the ball's motion, reducing its velocity gradually to zero. This act represents the application of Newton's second law, as the force applied by the fielder results in a change in the ball's momentum.

36. **(C):** Humans have a total of 46 chromosomes, which are organized into 23 pairs. Each pair consists of one chromosome inherited from the mother and one from the father.

37. **(A):** Strait of Malacca, waterway connecting the Andaman Sea (Indian Ocean) and the South China Sea (Pacific Ocean). It runs between the Indonesian island of Sumatra to the west and peninsular (West) Malaysia and extreme southern Thailand to the east and has an area of about 25,000 square miles (65,000 square km).

38. **(A):** World Environment Day is celebrated on 5 June every year. It was established by the United Nations in 1972 and serves as a global platform for raising awareness and taking action on pressing environmental issues.

39. **(B):** Jawaharlal Nehru wrote "The Discovery of India" during his imprisonment at Ahmadnagar Fort Jail from 1942 to 1945. The book provides a comprehensive view of Indian history and culture from ancient times to the British era.

40. **(D):** Umaria coalfield is not located in Jharkhand; it is situated in Madhya Pradesh. The other coalfields mentioned (Jharia, Ramgarh, and Deogarh) are located in Jharkhand.

41. **(A):** The First Battle of Panipat was fought on April 21, 1526, between the forces of Babur and Ibrahim Lodhi, the Sultan of Delhi. Babur's victory in this battle marked the beginning of the Mughal Empire in India.

42. **(A):** Article 143 of the constitution of India points to the Advisory Jurisdiction of the Supreme Court of India. Article 143 confers that the President of the country can ask for the opinion and the advice of the Supreme Court on matters of public importance or certain laws which acts as expedient to the constitution.

43. **(A):** MC Mary Kom became the first Indian woman to win a gold medal in boxing at the Commonwealth Games. She achieved this milestone at the 2018 Gold Coast Commonwealth Games in the 48-kg category.

44. **(A):** Tasveer Khana was started by Emperor Akbar during his reign. He established this artistic studio to promote and develop the arts, including painting and manuscript illustration, within his empire.

45. **(A):** Donyi Polo Airport in Itanagar, Arunachal Pradesh, is the first greenfield airport in India. It is built by the Airports Authority of India, over an area of 320 hectares. The airport is the 16th airport of Northeast India. Prime Minister Narendra Modi laid the foundation stone for the airport on 9 February 2019. Construction was started on 15 December 2020, and was inaugurated on 19 November 2022, with flight services started by IndiGo to Kolkata and Mumbai from 28 November 2022.

46. **(A):** The 10th Schedule of the Indian Constitution, also known as the Anti-Defection Law, was added by the 52nd Amendment Act of 1985. It lays down the process by which legislators may be disqualified on grounds of defection by the Presiding Officer of a legislature based on a petition by any other member of the House.

47. **(B):** Temperature is a major factor that affects terrestrial ecosystems. It influences the distribution and behaviour of organisms, the

timing of biological events (phenology), and the overall functioning of ecosystems. Changes in temperature can have significant impacts on the growth, reproduction, and survival of species within an ecosystem.

48. (C): The C-295 aircraft is a joint venture between India and Spain, with Airbus Defence and Space (Spain) collaborating with Tata Advanced Systems Limited (India) to manufacture and assemble the aircraft for the Indian Air Force.

49. (D): SAARC (South Asian Association for Regional Cooperation) is an organization of South Asian nations established in 1985. The member countries of SAARC are: Afghanistan; Bangladesh; Bhutan; India; Maldives; Nepal; Pakistan; and Sri Lanka, China is not a member of SAARC.

50. (A): Mickey Mouse was co-created by Walt Disney and Ub Iwerks in 1928. Ub Iwerks was responsible for much of the animation and design work, while Walt Disney provided the voice and overall creative direction.

51. (D): In first counter total number of people is:

Total = Top + Bottom − 1
= 7 + 18 − 1
= 24

In second counter total number of people is:

Total = Top + Bottom − 1
= 3 + 13 − 1
= 15

Total people = 24 + 15 = 39

52. (C): Given,

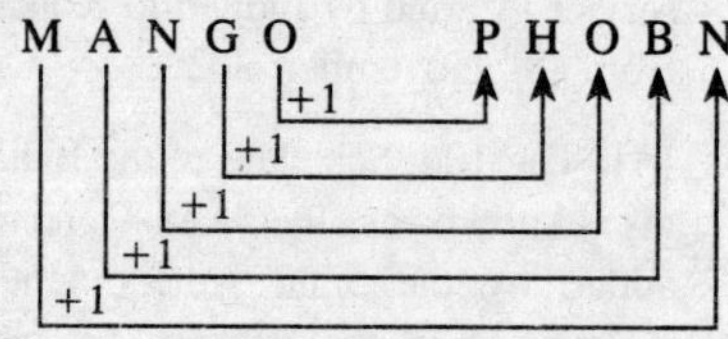

and

O R A N G E F H O B S P

+1 +1 +1 +1 +1 +1

Similarly,

G R A P E S T F Q B S H

+1 +1 +1 +1 +1 +1

∴ GRAPES will be written as TFQBSH.

54. (D): AUAGRJ – JAGUAR
ATJES – TEJAS
AEGIRM – MIRAGE
NDIAI – INDIA (odd one out)

55. (C): In this question we have to find how ma tablet are only car.

According to the Venn diagram:

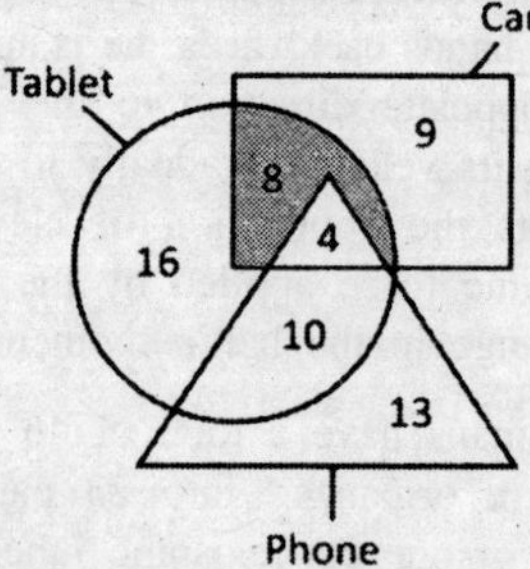

The shaded area shows the total number tablets are only car.

So, the total number of tablets are only car =

Hence, "8" is the correct answer.

56. (A): Possible Venn diagram will be:

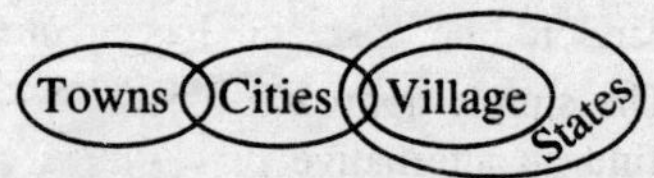

Conclusions:

I. Some towns are not villages. (False, their is no relation given between to and villages)

II. Some states are cities. (True, as some ci are villages and all villages are states t some states are cities).

Hence, only conclusion II follows is the cor answer.

57. (A): Here, in this question we have to find which of the conclusion is followed.

Given:

Statements:

Only a few A1 are P5.

Only a few P5 are T8.

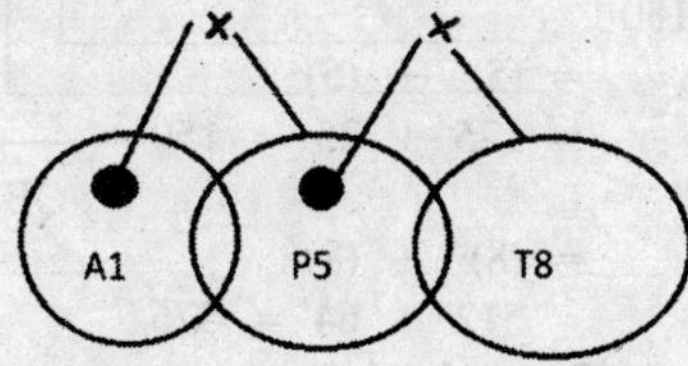

Conclusions:

I. Some A1 are T8 - Does not follow - There is not any direct relationship between A1 and T8. So we cannot say about this conclusion. So conclusion is not follow.

II. All P5 can never be T8 - Follow - As per the given statements, some part of P5 is not T8. So we can conclude the given conclusion. The given conclusion is follow.

Hence, the correct answer is Only conclusion II follows.

. **(C):** In this type of questions, three will be same and one will be different, we have to find the odd one.

The logic is that the sum of the place values of letters in all the given words except DLRT is equal to 50.

H + K + M + R = 8 + 11 + 13 + 18 = 50

B + J + P + V = 2 + 10 + 16 + 22 = 50

D + L + R + T = 4 + 12 + 18 + 20 = 55

F + M + N + Q = 6 + 13 + 14 + 17 = 50

Hence, DLRT is the correct answer.

. **(C):** The simple approach to solve this question is to find an alternative that follows the similar logic of word to letter coding.

The logic used is: Here the place value of each letter is decreasing by (–1).

'HUMP' is written as 'GTLO',

H U M P

–1 –1 –1 –1

G T L O

'LIKE' is written as 'KHJD',

L I K E

–1 –1 –1 –1

K H J D

Similarly, 'PLAY' will be written as:

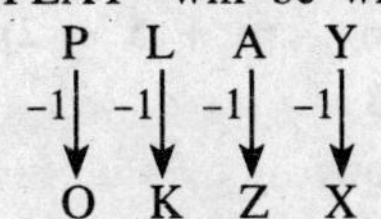

Hence, the correct answer is OKZX.

63. (C):

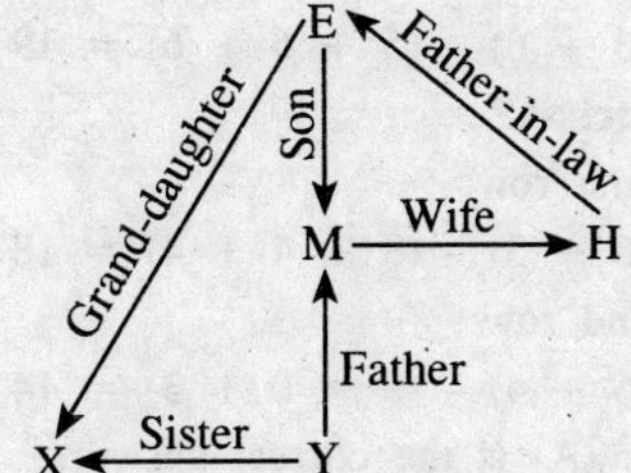

Here, X is related to E as Grand-daughter.

64. (D): The Venn Diagram shows the best relationship between Mango, Fruit, Banana is shown below.

Mangoes comes under Fruits category, Banana comes under Fruits category

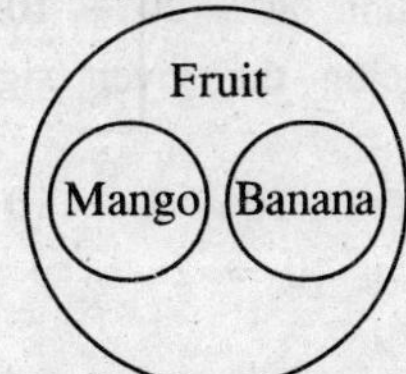

Hence, option 'D' is the correct answer.

65. (C): In the given figure: In each of the diagrams the shaded part is moving with two blocks anticlockwise in each step.

So, the next figure will be:

Hence, option (C) is the correct answer.

67. (C): Here the pattern followed is:

After observing all the figures, we can say that figure (*a*), (*c*) and (*d*) contain four different elements, but figure (*b*) does not contain four different elements.

Therefore figure (*b*) is different in all.

Hence, option (C) is the correct answer.

68. (A): Here the logic is as follows

In matrix-A

In a first row:

(8 + 6 + 2) – (7 + 6 + 1) = 16 – 14 = 2

In a 2nd row:
(5 + 4 + 6) – (6 + 5 + 2) = 15 – 13 = 2

In matrix-B

In a first row:
(8 + 7 + 5) – (9 + 7 + 2) = 20 – 18 = 2

In a 2nd row:
(7 + 6 + 6) – (5 + 6 + 6) = 19 – 17 = 2

In matrix-C

In a first row:
(9 + 6 + 3) – (8 + 4 + 4) = 18 – 16 = 2

In a 2nd row:
(4 + 6 + 4) – (9 + 0 + 3) = 14 – 12 = 2

Hence, (A) is the correct answer.

70. (A): As per the given information:

Given signs:	–	+	÷	×
Replaced by signs:	÷	×	–	+

Given equation: 80 – 20 + 10 ÷ 8 × 10 = ?

After replacing the given signs the equation becomes:

⇒ 80 ÷ 20 × 10 – 8 + 10 = ?

⇒ 40 – 8 + 10 = ?

⇒ 42

Hence, the correct answer is 42.

71. (A): According to the question, 'oranges' are 'apples', 'bananas' are 'apricots', 'apples' are 'chillies', 'apricots' are orange and 'chillies' are 'bananas', then we have to find green in colour.

'Chillies' are green in colour and as given. 'chillies' are 'bananas. So, 'bananas' are green in colour.

Hence, Bananas is the correct answer.

72. (C): Here the logic is as follows

M →(+3) P →(+3) [R] (S) →(+3) V
C →(+3) F →(+3) I →(+3) L
W →(+3) Z →(+3) C →(+3) F
H →(+3) K →(+3) N →(+3) Q

Here we can see place of R should be S.

Therefore RICN is the wrong term.

Hence, RICN is the correct answer.

73. (B): Here, in this question we have to find t correct logic/pattern followed in this questi and find the second pair accordingly.

Logic: (First number)^3 + (First number)^2 Second number.

5 : 150

$= (5)^3 + (5)^2$
$= 125 + 25 = 150$

8 : ?

$= (8)^3 + (8)^2$
$= 512 + 64 = 576$

Hence, 576 is the correct answer.

74. (D): As per the given information:

Chandni(–)
↑ Mother
Ronita ← Brother — Vikram(+) ← Husband — Sejal(–)
↑ Mot
Kritika

{Note: (-) sign indicates female and (+) s indicates male} Thus, Chandni is pare grandmother of Kritika.

Hence, Paternal grandmother is correct ansv

75. (C): Here, in the given question we have interchange two signs and find the value of given equation.

Given equation:

35 + 5 ÷ 4 × 2 – 15 = ?

According to the given question, a interchanging × and ÷ signs, we get:

= 35 + 5 × 4 ÷ 2 – 15
= 35 + 5 × 2 – 15
= 35 + 10 – 15
= 45 – 15 = 30

So, after interchanging × and ÷ the valu the equation is 30.

Hence, 30 is the correct answer

76. (A): Total length = 153 m + 747 m
= 900 m

Time taken = 45 sec.

$\therefore$ Speed of the train $= \frac{900}{45} = 20$ m/s

$= 20 \times \frac{18}{5}$ km/hr

= 72 km/hr

(A): (A + B)'s 1 hr work $= \frac{1}{20}$

(B + C)'s 1 hr work $= \frac{1}{25}$

(A + C)'s 1 hr work $= \frac{1}{15}$

2(A + B + C)'s 1 hr work $= \frac{1}{20}+\frac{1}{25}+\frac{1}{15}$

$= \frac{15+12+20}{300} = \frac{47}{300}$

$\therefore$ (A + B + C)'s 1 hr work $= \frac{47}{600}$

B alone can do this work $= \frac{47}{600} - \frac{1}{15}$

$= \frac{47-40}{600} = \frac{7}{600}$

Hence, B alone can do this work in $\frac{600}{7}$ hrs.

= 85.71 hrs.

(B): The numbers are 23, 30, 57 and 78

Calculation:

Assume that x be subtracted from each term

$23 - x$, $30 - x$, $57 - x$ and $78 - x$ are proportional

It can be written as

$23 - x : 30 - x :: 57 - x : 78 - x$

$\Rightarrow \frac{(23-x)}{(30-x)} = \frac{(57-x)}{(78-x)}$

$\Rightarrow (23 - x)(78 - x) = (30 - x)(57 - x)$

$\Rightarrow 1794 - 23x - 78x + x^2 = 1710 - 30x - 57x + x^2$

$\Rightarrow x^2 - 101x + 1794 - x^2 + 87x - 1710$

So, we get

$\Rightarrow -14x + 84 = 0$

$\Rightarrow 14x = 84$

$\Rightarrow x = \frac{84}{14} = 6$

Therefore, 6 is the number to be subtracted from each of the numbers

Hence, the correct answer is Option (B) i.e., 6.

81. (A): $SI = \frac{P \times r \times t}{100}$

$\Rightarrow P = \frac{SI \times 100}{r \times t}$

$= \frac{5400 \times 100}{12 \times 3} = 15000$

83. (D): Three pipes, D, E and F, can fill a tank in 6 min, 8 min and 12 min respectively.

Total capacity of the tank = LCM of 6, 8 and 12 = 24 unit.

Efficiency of pipe D $= \frac{\text{Total Capacity}}{\text{Time taken by D}}$

$= \frac{24}{6} = 4$

Efficiency of pipe E $= \frac{24}{8} = 3$

Efficiency of pipe F $= \frac{24}{12} = 2$

Let the tank be filled in x min.

According to the question,

$(4 + 3) \times (x - 3) + 2 \times x = 24$

or, $7x - 21 + 2x = 24$

or, $9x = 45$ or, $x = 5$ min

The tank will be filled in 5 min.

84. (A): Area of circle $= \pi r^2$

$= \frac{22}{7} \times 7 \times 7 = 154 \text{ cm}^2$

85. (C): Let $p = x$, $t = 8$ years, $A = 2x$

Then, simple interest $= A - p = 2x - x = x$

$\therefore \quad r = \frac{\text{S.I.} \times 100}{p \times t} = \frac{x \times 100}{x \times 8} = \frac{25}{2}\%$

Again, $p = x$, $A = 4x$, $r = \frac{25}{2}\%$

$t = \frac{\text{S.I.} \times 100}{p \times r}$

$= \frac{(A-p) \times 100}{x \times \frac{25}{2}} = \frac{(4x - x) \times 100}{x \times \frac{25}{2}}$

$= \frac{3x \times 100 \times 2}{x \times 25} = 24$ years

Hence, required time = 24 years

87. (B): $150 \div 3 \times 12 - (300 \div 6 \times 12) + 1 = ?$

$50 \times 12 - (50 \times 12) + 1 = ?$

$? = 1$

88. (C): The cost price of 1 dozen notebook

$$= ₹\ 125 \times \frac{80}{100}$$

$$= ₹\ 125 \times \frac{4}{5}$$

$$= 25 \times 4 = ₹\ 100$$

Hence, the number of notebooks can be bought for ₹ 75

$$= \frac{12}{100} \times 75 = \frac{3}{25} \times 75$$

$$= 3 \times 3 = 9.$$

89. (B): Given:

Milk : Sugar = 2 : 3

When 20 L of the mixture is taken out and replaced with sugar, the ratio becomes 3 : 7.

Calculation:

Let milk be $2x$ and sugar $3x$

When 20 L of the mixture is taken out the ratio remains the same

According to the question

$$\frac{2x}{3x+20} = \frac{3}{7}$$

$\Rightarrow 2x \times 7 = (3x + 20) \times 3$

$\Rightarrow 14x = 9x + 60$

$\Rightarrow x = 12$

Total mixture

$= 2x + (3x + 20) = 5x + 20 = 80$ L

Hence, the correct answer is Option (B) i.e., 80.

90. (A): Concept:

We are using problems on age concept to find the problem.

Formula Used:

If the current age is x, then n times the age is nx.

If the current age is x, then Age n years later hence $= x + n$.

If the current age is x, then Age n years ago $= x - n$.

The ages in a ratio $a : b$ will be ax and bx.

Explanation:

Let the present ages of Ajay and Vijay b and 'V' years.

According to question, we have

$$A - 8 = \frac{4}{3}(V - 8)$$

and $$A + 8 = \frac{6}{5}(V + 8)$$

$$\frac{4}{3}(A - 8) = V - 8$$

and $$\frac{5}{6}(A + 8) = V + 8$$

Then, we get:

$$= \frac{3}{4}(A - 8) + 8$$

$$= \frac{5}{6}(A + 8) - 8$$

From (1) and (2), we get:

$$\frac{3}{4}A - 6 + 8 = \frac{5}{6}A + \frac{20}{3} - 8$$

$$10 - \frac{20}{3} = \frac{10}{12}A - \frac{9}{12}A$$

$$\frac{10}{3} = \frac{A}{12}$$

$$A = 40 \text{ years}$$

91. (A): Part filled in 1 hour by tap P =

and part empted in 1 hour by p Q =

$\therefore$ The net part filled in 1 hour $= \frac{1}{6}$ –

$$= \frac{5-3}{30} = \frac{2}{30} = \frac{1}{15}$$

Hence, the empty cistern will be complet in 15 hours.

93. (D): Given:

Speed of man = 10 km/hr

Speed of Train = 60 km/hr

The train crosses the man in 36 second

Formula Used:

If speed of the two trains be x km/hr and y km/hr respectively, if $x > y$

Relative speed, if opposite directions

$= (x + y)$ km/hr

Relative Speed, if same direction

$= (x - y)$ km/hr

$$\text{Speed} = \frac{\text{Distance}}{\text{Time}}$$

$$1 \text{ km/hr} = \frac{5}{18} \text{ m/s}$$

Calculation:

Relative Speed of train and man, if both running opposite directions

$= (60 + 10)$

$= 70$ km/hr

Let length of train be x m

According to the question

$$70 \times \frac{5}{18} = \frac{x}{36}$$

$$x = 70 \times \frac{5}{18} \times 36 = 700 \text{ m}$$

ength of train is 700 m.

A): A candidate scores 25% and fails by 32 marks

et the maximum marks be $100x$.

Iinimum required number to pass for 1st andidate

$= 25\%$ of $100x + 32$

$= 25x + 32$

nother candidate who scores 40% marks, gets 3 marks more than the minimum required marks pass the examination.

inimum required number to pass for 2nd ndidate

$= 40\%$ of $100x - 28$

$= 40x - 28$

cording to the question,

$25x + 32 = 40x - 28$

$15x = 60,$

$x = 4$

ximum mark $= 100x = 400$

rks of candidate who score 72% marks

$= 72\%$ of $400 = 288.$

95. (B): Given:

Mixture = 160 liters

Ratio of Milk and Water = 3 : 1

Calculation:

Quantity of Milk $= 160 \times \frac{3}{4} = 120$ litres

Quantity of Water $= 160 - 120 = 40$ litres

New Ratio of Milk and Water = 1 : 3

Let quantity of water added in x litres

So, $\frac{120}{40 + x} = \frac{1}{3} \Rightarrow x = 320$

96. (A): Let the speed of man is x m/s

Then, the speed of train is $8x$ m/s

$\because$ Man walking in opposite direction

$\therefore$ Relative speed $= x + 8x = 9x$ m/s

Now, $\frac{\text{distance}}{\text{speed}} = \text{time}$

$\Rightarrow \frac{1800}{9x} = 10$

$\Rightarrow \frac{200}{x} = 10$

$\Rightarrow x = 20$ m/s

$\therefore$ The speed of train $= 8x = 8 \times 20$

$= 160$ m/s $= 160 \times \frac{18}{5}$ km/h

$= 32 \times 18$ km/h $= 576$ km/h.

97. (D): Given, chord RS = 30 cm

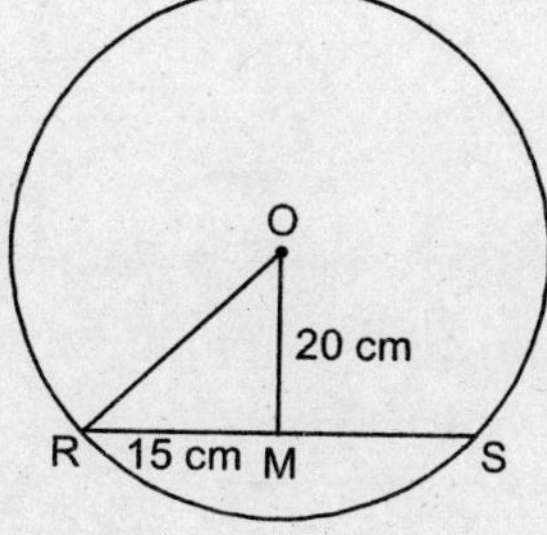

Let OM $\perp$ RS

Then, OM = 20 cm

$\therefore$ RM = MS = 15 cm

Let OR = Radius

In ΔOMR,

$OR^2 = OM^2 + MR^2$

$\Rightarrow OR^2 = (20)^2 + (15)^2$

$\Rightarrow \quad OR^2 = 400 + 225$

$\Rightarrow \quad OR^2 = 625$

$\Rightarrow \quad OR^2 = (25)^2$

$\Rightarrow \quad OR = 25$ cm

$\therefore$ The diameter of the circle $= 2r$

$= 2$ (OR)

$= 2 \times 25$

$= 50$ cm.

98. (B): $[a^3 - b^3 = (a - b)(a^2 + b^2 + ab)]$

Given, $\dfrac{(17)^3 - (7)^3}{(17^2 + 7^2 + k)} = 10$

$\Rightarrow \dfrac{(17-7)(17^2 + 7^2 + 17 \times 7)}{(17^2 + 7^2 + k)} = 10$

$\Rightarrow \dfrac{10(17^2 + 7^2 + 119)}{(17^2 + 7^2 + k)} = 10$

$\Rightarrow \dfrac{(17^2 - 7^2 + 119)}{(17^2 + 7^2 + k)} = 1$

$\Rightarrow 17^2 + 7^2 + 119 = 17^2 + 7^2 + k$

$\Rightarrow k = 119.$

99. (D): $4^2 - 3^2 + 6^2 - 5^2 + 8^2 - 7$ ...... $92^2 - 91^2$

$= 7 + 11 + 15 + ... + 183$

Here, $a = 7$, $d = 4$, th $= 183$

$\because \quad$ th $= a + (n - 1)d$

$\therefore \quad 183 = 7 + (n - 1) \times 4$

$\Rightarrow \quad 4(n - 1) = 183 - 7$

$= 176$

$\Rightarrow \quad n - 1 = 44$

$\Rightarrow \quad n = 45$

Let $\quad S_n = 7 + 11 + 15 + ... +$

then, $\quad S_n = \dfrac{n}{2}[2a + (n-1)d]$

$= \dfrac{45}{2}[2 \times 7 + (45-1) \times 4]$

$= \dfrac{45}{2} \times 2\ [7 + 44 \times 2]$

$= 45[7 + 88]$

$= 45 \times 95$

$= 4275.$

Previous Paper (Solved)

Air Force Common Admission Test (AFCAT)—1/2023*

Select the most appropriate synonym of the given word.

Frugal

A. Economical B. Delicate
C. Splendid D. Hungry

Select the most appropriate synonym for the word given in bold.

Pompous

A. Infected B. Arrogant
C. Fake D. Celebratory

ctions (Qs. No. 3-5): *Select the most appropriate nym of the given word.*

VERACITY

A. mendacity B. truth
C. imperfection D. judgment

PROPENSITY

A. rant B. vilification
C. inclination D. bolster

SAGACIOUS

A. Stagnation B. Defend
C. Transfer D. Wise

ctions (Qs. No. 6-10): *Select the most priate antonym for the given word.*

Embellish

A. Perish B. Disarm
C. Anorn D. Disfigure

Ostentatious

A. Unobtrusive B. Probable
C. Compete D. Obstruct

8. Delusional

A. Pretentious
B. Confused
C. Imaginary
D. Deranged

9. Gentle

A. Tender B. Pleasant
C. Lenient D. Brutal

10. Immure

A. Imprison B. Liberate
C. Detain D. Trap

Directions (Qs. No. 11-13): *Given below are some idioms/phrases followed by four alternative meanings to each. Choose the response A, B, C, or D, which is the most appropriate expression and mark you response in the Answer Sheet accordingly.*

11. French leave

A. Absent from work without asking for permission in French
B. Asking for permission before leaving work
C. Work for permission to get leave
D. Absent from work without asking for permission

12. Select the alternative with the correct meaning of the given idiom/phrase.

Dark horse

A. A person with a bad reputation
B. Sad and depressed
C. An enemy
D. An unexpected winner

. A	2. B	3. B	4. C	5. D	6. D	7. A	8. C	9. D	10. B
. D	12. D								

on memory.

13. In the questions, four alternatives are given for the Idiom/Phrase in 'bold'. Choose the alternative which best expresses the meaning of the idioms/phrase given in bold.

to show a clean pair of heels

A. to hide
B. to escape
C. to pursue
D. to follow

Directions (Qs. No. 14 and 15): *Select the most appropriate meaning of the given idioms & phrases.*

14. A Sine Qua Non

A. To keep at a distance
B. Without any result
C. Frequently
D. An essential condition

15. A Bear with a sore heed

A. A stupid person
B. Bad-tempered
C. A wild bear
D. To be in bad health

16. Select the most appropriate one word substitution for the given words.

Act of giving up the throne

A. Adulation
B. Addiction
C. Admiration
D. Abdication

17. Select the most appropriate one-word substitution for the given group of words.

A person or follower who assists a priest in performing certain religious activities.

A. Acolyte
B. Catholic
C. Amateur
D. Atheist

Directions (Qs. No. 18 and 19): *Find out the error/ no error and indicate your response from the options (A), (B), (C) and (D) on the Answer Sheet.*

18. On a holiday / I prefer watching movies/than meeting friends.

A. On a holiday
B. I prefer watching movies
C. Than meeting friends
D. No error

19. He is the most tallest student in his class.

A. He is the
B. Most tallest student
C. In his class
D. No error

20. Each item in this section has a sentence wh has multiple parts. Find out the error/no e and indicate your response from the opti (A), (B), (C) and (D) on the Answer Shee

Old habits (A)/die (B)/hardly (C)/No Error

A. A
B. B
C. C
D. D

Directions (Qs. No. 21-23): *Read the passage g below and answer the questions that follow.*

The habit of reading is one of the grea resources of mankind; and we enjoy reading bc that belong to us much more than if they borrowed. A borrowed book is like a guest in house; it must be treated with **punctiliousness**, certain, considerate formality. You must see th sustains no damage; it must not suffer while u your roof. You cannot leave it carelessly, you ca mark it, you cannot turn down the pages, you ca use it familiarly. But your own books belon you; you treat them with that affectionate intim that annihilates formality. Books are for use, for show. A good reason for marking favo pages in books is that this practice enables yo remember more easily the significant sayings refer to them quickly.

Everyone should begin collecting a pri library in youth; one should have one's own b shelves, which should not have doors, g windows, or keys; they should be free and acces to the hand as well as to the eye. Books are of people, by the people and for the people. Litera is an immortal part of history; it is the best most enduring part of personality.

21. According to the passage, a borrowed bo like a

A. guest in the house
B. relative in the house
C. host in the house
D. neighbour in the house

13. B	14. D	15. B	16. D	17. A	18. C	19. B	20. C	21. A

According to the passage, books are more enjoyable when they are.
A. in the library
B. borrowed
C. in books shops
D. personal possessions

Select the correct synonym for the word given in bold in the passage.

Punctilious
A. humanity B. dishonesty
C. meticuleus D. Maltreatment

ions (Qs. No. 24-28): *Read the following ge and fill in each blank with words chosen options given.*

is important to remember that overweight besity _______ (1) some of our most able children in struggling communities. Far _ (2) being the result of laziness, ignorance sponsible decisions on the part of children or ___ (3) caregivers, it largely results from a combination ________ (4) financial, social hysical barriers _______ (5) prevent inities from eating well.

elect the most appropriate option to fill in lank No. 1.
. affect B. effect
. result D. cause

elect the most appropriate option to fill in lank No. 2.
. for B. from
. of D. below

elect the most appropriate option to fill in lank No. 3.
him B. its
their D. his

elect the most appropriate option to fill in lank No. 4.
of B. to
with D. into

28. Select the most appropriate option to fill in blank No. 5.
A. who B. whom
C. it D. that

Directions (Qs. No. 29 and 30): *Fill in the blank with the most appropriate answer.*

29. The judge directed the police to ..... the case.
A. Look up B. Look over
C. Look away D. Look on

30. In morning I go _____ through at/by/of ..... the headlines of newspaper.
A. Through B. At
C. By D. Of

31. Who is the recently appointed 50th Chief Justice of India?
A. Justice Nuthalapati Venkata Ramana
B. Justice Uday Umesh Lalit
C. Justice D.Y. Chandrachud
D. Justice Dipak Mishra

32. To oppose which of the following Acts, people gathered at Jallianwala Bagh?
A. Government of India Act, 1915
B. Rowlatt Act
C. Government of India Act, 1919
D. Hindu Inheritance Act, 1928

33. On which date did the famous Dandi March happen?
A. 12th March 1930
B. 29th March 1930
C. 10th March 1930
D. 15th March 1930

34. Which of the following instrument is used to measure blood pressure?
A. Stethoscope B. Manometer
C. Sphygmomanometer D. Hygrometer

35. Which among the following player was awarded the Golden Boot in FIFA World Cup 2022?
A. Mohamed Salah B. Son Heung-min
C. Lionel Messi D. Kylian Mbappe

D **23.** C **24.** A **25.** B **26.** C **27.** A **28.** D **29.** A **30.** A **31.** C
B **33.** A **34.** C **35.** D

36. Which Article of Indian Constitution deals with the President Rule?
A. Article 356 B. Article 352
C. Article 368 D. Article 360

37. What is the value of escape velocity?
A. 11.2 km/sec B. 9.8 m/sec
C. 11.2 m/sec D. 9.8 km/sec

38. Which of the following is not an OPEC founding country?
A. Indonesia B. Russia
C. Nigeria D. Venezuela

39. What is the theme of Yoga Day 2022?
A. Yoga for harmony and peace
B. Yoga for wellness
C. Yoga for health
D. Yoga for humanity

40. Which country manufactured the C Dome Air Defense System?
A. Israel B. Russia
C. USA D. France

41. Recently, Jose Ramos Horta was awarded the Nobel Peace Prize. He was prime minister of which of the following country?
A. East Timor B. Cuba
C. Jamaica D. Honduras

42. Brahmos Extended Version is test fired from which of the following jets?
A. MIG-21 B. Rafaele
C. Mirage-2000 D. SU-30 MKI

43. Who won the 75 kg women National boxing championship?
A. Mary Kom
B. Jigyasa Rajput
C. Puja Nayak
D. Lovlina Borgohain

44. Which of the following Joint Military exercises is conducted between India and Seychelles?
A. CORPAT
B. SIMBEX
C. La Mitye
D. Hand in Hand Exercise

45. Where is Mount Kilimanjaro located?
A. South Africa B. Tanzania
C. Uganda D. Somalia

46. In which of the following state, India's lavender festival was organized?
A. Nagaland
B. Jammu and Kashmir
C. Sikkim
D. Kerala

47. Which of the following is a special for the Air Force?
A. Parachute Regiment
B. Garuda Commando
C. NSG Commando
D. Cobra Commando

48. As per the Indian Constitution, who am the following is the Guardian of Fundan Rights?
A. Supreme Court
B. Election Commission
C. President
D. Parliament

49. What colours do plants absorb most?
A. Blue and red B. Red and yel
C. Yellow and green D. Red and gre

50. Which of the following statements is inc regarding Cathode Ray?
A. Cathode rays can travel in a straigh
B. Cathode rays can ionize gases
C. Cathode rays can heat the material fall on
D. Cathode rays cannot penetrate throug metal foils

51. Where is the National Defense College si in India?
A. Dehradun B. New Delhi
C. Hyderabad D. Noida

36. A	**37.** A	**38.** D	**39.** D	**40.** A	**41.** A	**42.** D	**43.** D	**44.** C	**45.**
46. B	**47.** B	**48.** A	**49.** A	**50.** D	**51.** B				

. Nirmal Jit Singh Sekhon was awarded Param Vir Chakra for which war?
A. Indo-Pakistan War of 1965
B. Indo-Pakistan War of 1971
C. Indo-Chinese War of 1962
D. Kargil War

What is the name of Saina Nehwal's autobiography?
A. But Serious: An Autobiography
B. A Life in Words: Memoirs
C. Playing to Win: My Life On and Off Court
D. Playing It My Way

Which of the following National Parks is a UNESCO World Heritage Site?
A. Jim B. Simplipal
C. Periyar D. Valley of Flower

Who among the following officers holds his office during the pleasure of the President?
A. Chairman of Rajya Sabha
B. Vice Chairman of NITI Aayog
C. Governor
D. Speaker of Lok Sabha

What is the angle between the minute and hour hand of a clock when the clock is showing time 4.20?
A. 22 Degree B. 15 Degree
C. 10 Degree D. 12 Degree

10, 7, 4, ______ –62 then find the 11 number from right.
A. –32 B. 32
C. 38 D. –38

The sum of ₹ 3200 invested at 10% per annum compounded quarterly amounts to ₹ 3362, hen find the time period.
A. 1.5 year B. 0.5 year
C. 1 year D. 2 year

We fold and make a circle from it so the area of that circle is 616 cm^2. Now we made an equilateral triangle then find the circumference of that circle.
A. 74 cm B. 80 cm
C. 82 cm D. 88 cm

60. A can complete a piece of work in 4 days. B takes double the time taken by A, C takes double that of B and D takes double that of C to complete the same task. They are paired in groups of two each. One pair takes two-thirds the time needed by the second pair to complete the work. Which is the first pair?
A. A and C B. B and C
C. A and D D. D and C

61. A tyre has two punctures, first puncture alone would have made the tyre flat in 9 minutes and the second alone would have done it in 6 minutes. If air leaks out at a constant rate, how long does it take both the punctures together to make it flat?
A. 18/5 minutes B. 17/5 minutes
C. 12/5 minutes D. 14/5 minutes

62. The difference between C.I. and S.I. on ₹ 1200 for one year at 10% per annum calculated half-yearly is:
A. ₹ 11 B. ₹ 6
C. ₹ 3 D. ₹ 7

63. The cost of fencing a square field with the rate of ₹ 20 per meter is ₹ 10080. How much will it cost to lay a three-meter-wide pavement along the fencing inside the field at a rate of ₹ 50 per sq meter?
A. ₹ 73700 B. ₹ 73800
C. ₹ 73500 D. ₹ 73400

64. In a box carrying one dozen oranges, one-third have become bad. If 3 oranges are taken out from the box at random, what is the probability that at least one orange out of the three oranges picked up is good?
A. $\frac{53}{55}$ B. $\frac{52}{55}$
C. $\frac{51}{55}$ D. $\frac{54}{55}$

B	53. C	54. D	55. C	56. C	57. A	58. B	59. D	60. C	61. A
C	63. B	64. D							

65. The probability of taking a red king from a pack of 52 cards is?

A. $\frac{1}{13}$ B. $\frac{3}{26}$
C. $\frac{1}{26}$ D. $\frac{5}{26}$

66. A sum of ₹ 1300 is divided between A, B, C and D, such that A's share/B's share = B's share/C's share = C's share/D's share = $\frac{2}{3}$. Then A's share is?

A. 130 B. 160
C. 190 D. 220

67. A sum of ₹ 2500 becomes ₹ 8100 in 2 years at a certain rate of compound interest. What will be the sum (in ₹) after 4 years?

A. 29824 B. 36284
C. 41624 D. 26244

68. A number of friends decided to go on a picnic and planned to spend ₹ 96 on eatables. Four of them, however, did not turn up. As a consequence, the remaining ones had to contribute ₹ 4 each extra. The number of those who were ready for the picnic.

A. 8 B. 12
C. 4 D. 16

69. There are two trains of the same length moving in same direction, the first train cross a post in 7 sec and the second train cross it in 8 seconds, then how much time first train takes to cross second train?

A. 100 B. 110
C. 108 D. 112

70. If the length of rectangle is 60 cm and breadth is 40 cm and a man want to go through the diagonal of that rectangle with the speed of 3 km/h then find the time taken?

A. $\frac{6}{5}$ sec B. $\frac{5}{6}$ sec
C. $\frac{4}{3}$ sec D. $\frac{3}{4}$ sec

71. The average monthly income R and Q ₹ 3000. The average monthly income o and R is ₹ 3250 and the average mon income of P and R is ₹ 4200. The mon income of P is:

A. 2000 B. 3950
C. 5350 D. 2850

72. The speed of a boat downstream is 12 k and the speed of the boat upstrean 6 km/h. Find the speed of the stream?

A. 9 km/h B. 3 km/h
C. 5 km/h D. 7 km/h

73. The sum of four numbers is 64. If you ad to the first number, 3 is subtracted from second number, the third is multiplied b and the fourth is divided by 3, then all result are equal. What is the difference betv the largest and the smallest of the orig numbers?

A. 24 B. 48
C. 12 D. 32

74. The value of $\frac{5}{1\frac{7}{8} \text{ of } 1\frac{1}{3}} \times \frac{2\frac{1}{10}}{3\frac{1}{2}}$ of $1\frac{1}{4}$ is:

A. $\frac{3}{2}$ B. 0.05
C. 1 D. 2

75. If a man buys 12 books in ₹ 100 and a buys 8 books in ₹ 100 now he is se 8 books in ₹ 100. What will his p percentage?

A. 10% B. 16%
C. 20% D. 25%

65. C	**66.** B	**67.** D	**68.** A	**69.** D	**70.** A	**71.** B	**72.** B	**73.**
74. A	**75.** D							

B is the son of A and A is the daughter of C, then what is the relation between B and C ?

A. Mother B. Grandmother
C. Aunt D. Sister

Next term of 61, 68, 82, 92?

A. 101 B. 97
C. 107 D. 103

What is the next term of the number series 66, 36, 18?

A. 12 B. 8
C. 14 D. 16

Odd one out from the following

Penguin, Alligator, Turtle, and Tortoise

A. Penguin B. Alligator
C. Turtle D. Tortoise

What is the suitable Venn diagram for the following.

Criminals, lawyers, bandits

A. 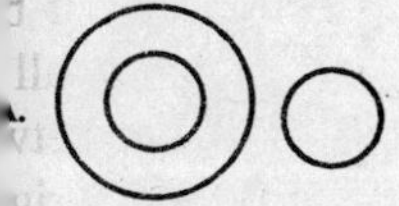

B. 

D. 

dd one out from the following:

ctor, Engineer, and Architecture

Doctor B. Engineer
Architecture D. None of these

hat is the suitable Venn diagram for the lowing:

ver, Pool and Well

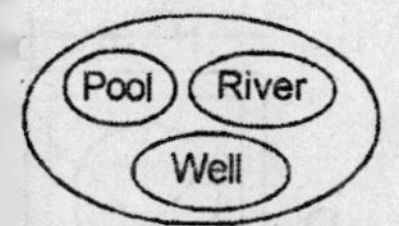

B. 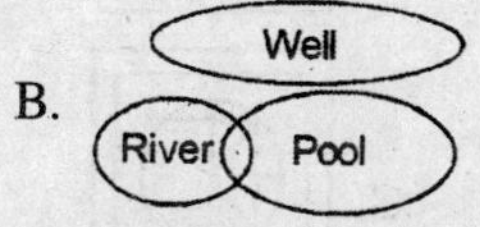

C. 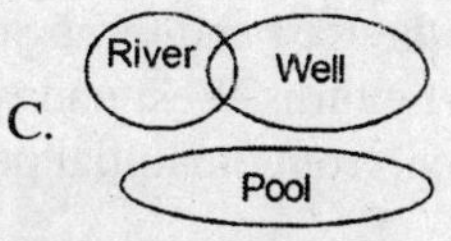

D. 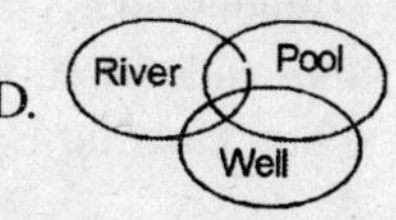

83. If Temple is coded as 71 then Tempest will be:

A. 63 B. 65
C. 98 D. 78

84. A man pointed towards a picture and said she is the only daughter of the only child of my mother. So, what will be the relationship between his wife and that girl?

A. Aunt B. Mother
C. Grandmother D. Niece

85. Dog : Bark :: Bird : ?

A. Bleats B. Howl
C. Grunt D. Chirp

86. Pointing to a man, Rina said, "He is the son of my grandmother's only child". How is the man related to Rina?

A. Son B. Brother
C. Cousin Brother D. Data inadequate

87. Anatomy : Zoology :: Horticulture : ?

A. Chemistry B. Medicine
C. Mechanics D. Botany

88. In a certain code, MOUNTAIN is written as UNMOINTA and OFFICERS is written as FIOFRSCE. Follow the same rule of coding, what will be the code for SERVICES?

A. RVSEESIC B. RVSEESCI
C. VRSEESIC D. RVESESIC

89. A dice is rolled twice and the two positions are shown in the figure below. What is the number of dots at the bottom face when the dice is in position A.

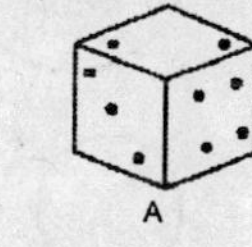

A. 3 B. 4
C. 6 D. 2

77. D	**78.** B	**79.** A	**80.** A	**81.** C	**82.** A	**83.** C	**84.** B	**85.** D
87. D	**88.** A	**89.** C						

90. Mohan walks 3 km to the East and turns South and walk 4 km, again he turns West and walk 6 km. How far is Mohan from the initial point.

A. 4 B. 5
C. 10 D. 8

91. Find the missing number:

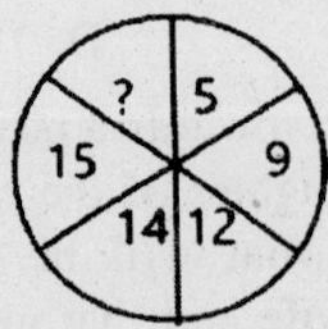

A. 4 B. 2
C. 20 D. 15

92. What is the suitable Venn diagram for Toad (T), Butterfly (B), and Kangaroo (K)

A.
B.

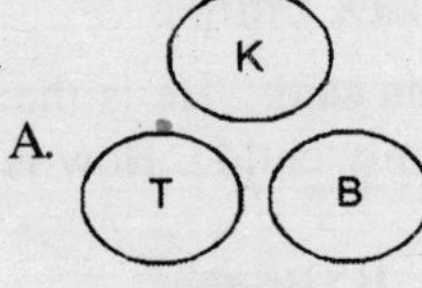

C.
D.

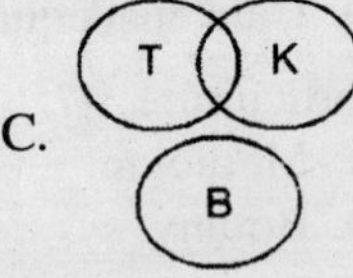

93. Odd one out from the following:

Blue bird, Bare foot, Bristled, and Book worm

A. Blue bird B. Bare foot
D. Bristled D. Book worm

94. Venn diagram for the following:

Daughter, Brother, Males

A.
B.

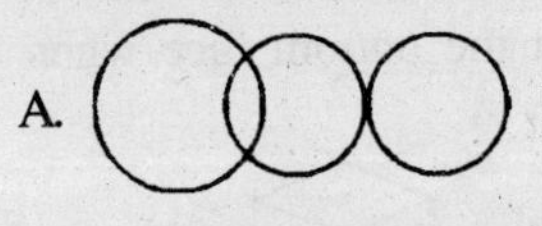

C.
D.

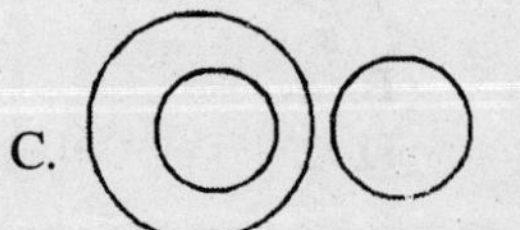

95. From the figure A, B, C, D, select the fig which satisfies the same condition of placen of dots as in the given figure.

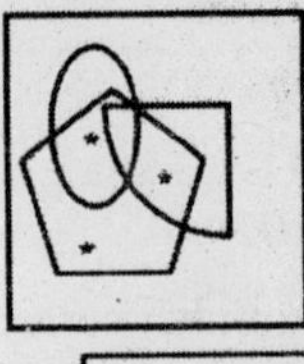

A.

B.

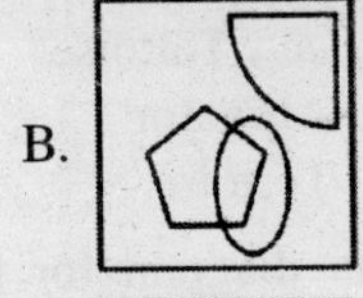

C.

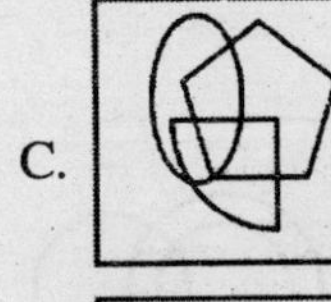

D.

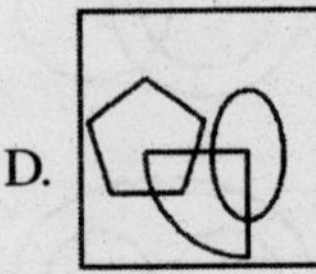

96. From the given answer figures, select th in which the question figure is hi embedded.

A.

B.

C.

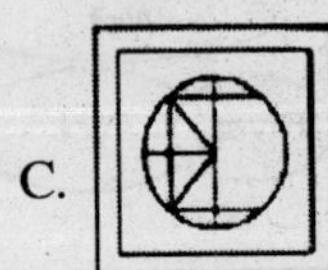

D.

90. B	91. D	92. A	93. B	94. C	95. C	96. D

97. Observe the first two figures. Try to understand how they are related.

Find the figure in the given options that is related to third figure in the same way as the first two figures are related.

Mark the option that completes the analogy.

A. 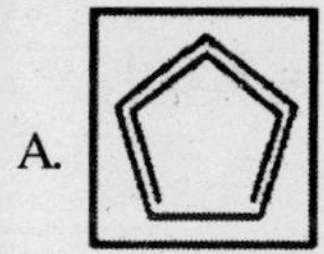 B. 

C. 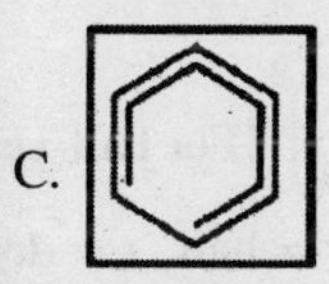 D. 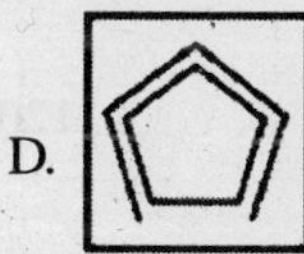

98. Find the odd one out:

A.  B. 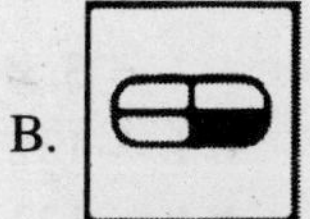

C. 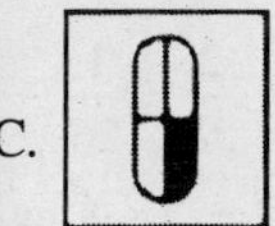 D. 

99. Select a figure from amongst the four alternatives, which when placed in the blank space of fig. (X) would complete the pattern.

A.  B. 

C.  D. 

100. Identify the figure that completes the pattern:

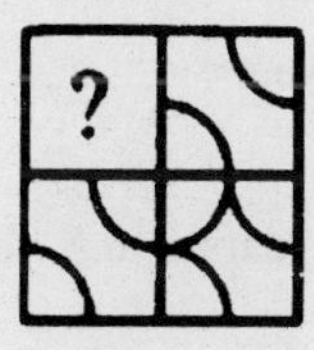

A. 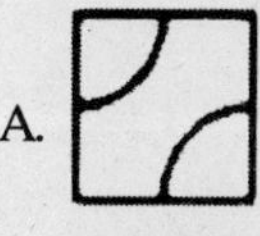 B. 

C. 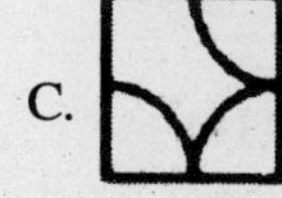 D. 

EXPLANATORY ANSWERS

(C): The minute hand points towards 4 and hour hand shifts from 4th mark onward, the angle which the hour hand shifts through in 20 minutes

$$= 20 \times \frac{1^\circ}{2} = 10^\circ = 10 \text{ degree}$$

(A): 10, 7, 4 ...., – 62 are in A.P.

$a = 10$, $d = -3$

l = last term = –62

11th term from last term = $l - (11 - 1)d$

$= -62 - (10)(-3)$

$= -62 - (-30)$

$= -62 + 30 = -32$

Hence, 11 number from right = –32.

58. (B): P = ₹ 3200, A = ₹ 3362,

$r = \frac{10\%}{4}$ for quarterly and time = 4 years

97. D **98.** A **99.** B **100.** C

$$A = P\left(1+\frac{r}{100}\right)^t$$

$$3362 = 3200\left(1+\frac{5}{200}\right)^t$$

$$\frac{3362}{3200} = \left(\frac{41}{40}\right)^t$$

$$\Rightarrow \quad \frac{1681}{1600} = \left(\frac{41}{40}\right)^t$$

$$\Rightarrow \quad \left(\frac{41}{40}\right)^2 = \left(\frac{41}{40}\right)^t$$

$$\Rightarrow \quad t = 2 \text{ years}$$

For quarterly time $= \frac{2}{4}$ years

$= \frac{1}{2}$ years = 0.5 year

59. (D): Area of the circle $= \pi r^2$

$$\Rightarrow \quad 616 = \frac{22}{7}r^2$$

$$\Rightarrow \quad r^2 = \frac{616 \times 7}{22}$$

$$\Rightarrow \quad = 28 \times 7 = (14)^2$$

$$r = 14 \text{ cm}$$

Circumference of the circle $= 2\pi r$

$$= 2\times\frac{22}{7}\times 14 = 88 \text{ cm.}$$

60. (C): $\because$ A takes to complete work = 4 days

B takes to complete work = 8 days

C takes to complete work = 16 days

D takes to complete work = 32 days

$$A : B = \frac{4}{8} = \frac{1}{2}$$

$$B : C = \frac{8}{16} = \frac{1}{2}$$

$$C : D = \frac{16}{32} = \frac{1}{2}$$

$\therefore$ A, B, C, D are in proportional

$A \times D = B \times C$

$\therefore$ First Pair = A and D.

61. (A): Time taken by both the punctures toge[ther]
to make it flat

$$= \frac{1}{9}+\frac{1}{6} = \frac{2+3}{18} = \frac{5}{18}$$

$$= \frac{18}{5} \text{ minutes.}$$

62. (C): S.I. $= \frac{1200\times 10\times 1}{100} = ₹\ 120$

$$A = P\left(1+\frac{r}{100}\right)^t$$

$= 1200\left(1+\frac{5}{100}\right)^2$ [For half yea[r]
r = half, t = dou[ble]

$$= 1200\times\frac{21}{20}\times\frac{21}{20}$$

$$= 3 \times 441 = 1323$$

C.I. = 1323 − 1200 = ₹ 123

C.I. − S.I. = 123 − 120 = ₹ 3.

65. (C): Required probability $= \frac{2}{52} = \frac{1}{26}$.

66. (B): $\because$ A : B = 2 : 3, B : C = 2 : 3 and
C : D = 2

$\Rightarrow$ A : B = 8 : 12, B : C = 12 : 18 and
C : D = 18

$\therefore$ A : B : C : D = 8 : 12 : 18 : 27

So A's share = ₹ 1300 × $\left(\frac{8}{65}\right)$ = ₹ 160

67. (D): P = ₹ 2500, A = 8100, t = 2 years

$$A = P\left(1+\frac{r}{100}\right)^t$$

$$8100 = 2500\left(1+\frac{r}{100}\right)^2$$

$$\frac{8100}{2500} = \left(1+\frac{r}{100}\right)^2$$

$$\left(\frac{9}{5}\right)^2 = \left(1+\frac{r}{100}\right)^2$$

$$\Rightarrow \quad \frac{9}{5} = 1+\frac{r}{100}$$

$$\Rightarrow \quad \frac{r}{100} = \frac{4}{5} \quad \Rightarrow \quad r = 80\%$$

Now, $\quad A = P\left(1+\frac{r}{100}\right)^t$

$$= 2500\left(1+\frac{80}{100}\right)^4$$

$$= 2500\times\frac{9}{5}\times\frac{9}{5}\times\frac{9}{5}\times\frac{9}{5}$$

$$= 4 \times 81 \times 81$$

$$= ₹\ 26244$$

Hence, the sum will be ₹ 26244 after 4 years.

(D): Let length of the train = x m

$$t = \frac{2\times7\times8}{8-7} = 112 \text{ seconds}$$

Hence, required time = 112 seconds.

(B): Total salary of P and Q = 3000 × 2

= 6000 ...(*i*)

Total salary of Q and R = 3250 × 2

= 6500 ...(*ii*)

Total salary of P and R = 4200 × 2

= 8400 ...(*iii*)

Adding (*i*), (*ii*) and (*iii*)

Total salary of (P + Q + R)

$$= \frac{(6000+6500+8400)}{2}$$

$$= \frac{20900}{2} = 10450$$

Monthly income of P = 10450 – 6500

= 3950.

): Speed of the stream = $\frac{1}{2}(12-6)$ km/hr

$$= \frac{1}{2}\times6 = 3 \text{ km/hr.}$$

74. (A): $\dfrac{5}{1\frac{7}{8} \text{ of } 1\frac{1}{3}} \times \dfrac{2\frac{1}{10}}{3\frac{1}{2}} \text{ of } 1\frac{1}{4}$

$$= \frac{5}{\frac{15}{8}\times\frac{4}{3}}\times\frac{\frac{21}{10}}{\frac{7}{2}}\times\frac{5}{4} = \frac{5}{\frac{5}{2}}\times\frac{\frac{21}{10}\times\frac{5}{4}}{\frac{7}{2}}$$

$$= \frac{10}{5}\times\frac{\frac{21}{10}\times\frac{5}{4}}{\frac{7}{2}} = \frac{10}{5}\times\frac{21}{8}\times\frac{2}{7} = \frac{3}{2}.$$

75. (D): C.P. of 20 books = ₹ 200

S.P. of 20 books = ₹ 250

Profit = 250 – 200 = 50

$$\text{Profit\%} = \frac{50}{200}\times100 = 25\%.$$

76. (B):

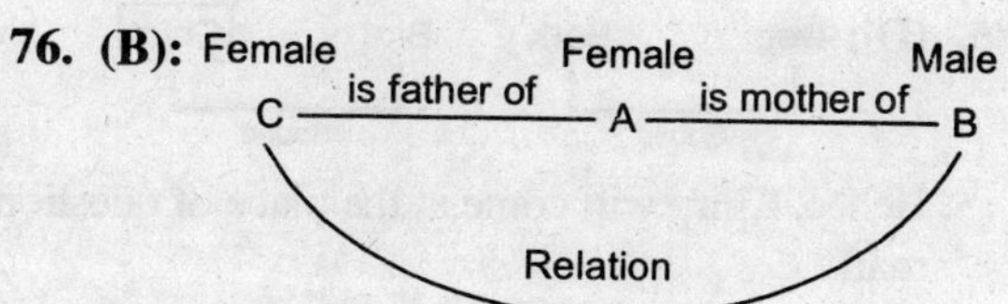

Clearly, C is grandmother of B.

77. (D):

61 68 82 92 **103**

+ (8 × 3)

+ (7 × 3)

+ (7 × 3)

Here, the next term = ? = 103.

78. (B): 66 36 18 **8**

6 × 6 3 × 6 1 × 8

Here, ? = the next term = 8.

80. (A):

Criminals

Bandits

Law-yers

All bandits are criminal, but neither criminals nor bandits can be lawyers.

82. (A): Suitable Venn diagram for River, Pool, Well is:

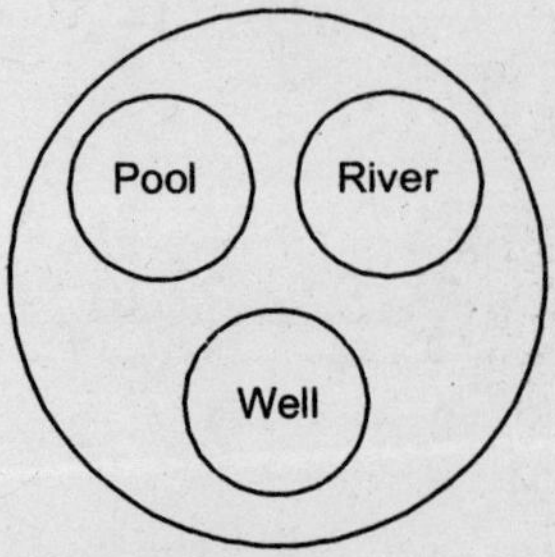
Pool
River
Well

83. (C): Temple is coded as

18 + 5 + 13 + 16 + 12 + 5 = 69 + 2 = 71

[e is 2 times]

Similarly, **Tempest**

18 + 5 + 13 + 16 + 5 + 19 + 18

= 94 + 2e + 2t = 94 + 4 = 98

[e is 2 times, t is 2 times]

Hence, Tempest will be written as 98.

85. (D):

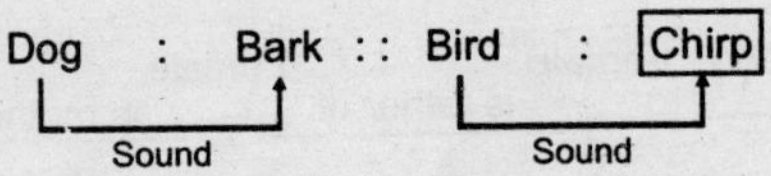
Dog : Bark :: Bird : Chirp
Sound
Sound

Hence, Chirp will come at the place of question mark.

87. (D):

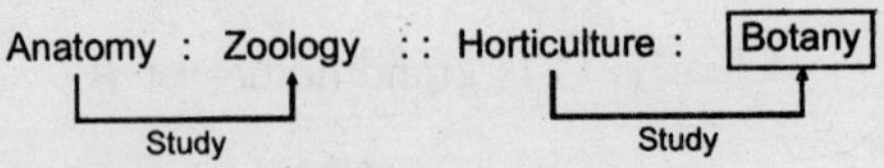
Anatomy : Zoology :: Horticulture : Botany
Study
Study

Hence, Botany will come at the place of question mark.

88. (A): $\frac{MO}{1}\frac{UN}{2}\frac{TA}{3}\frac{IN}{4} = \frac{UN}{2}\frac{MO}{1}\frac{IN}{4}\frac{TA}{3}$

and

$\frac{OF}{1}\frac{FI}{2}\frac{CE}{3}\frac{RS}{4} = \frac{FI}{2}\frac{OF}{1}\frac{RS}{4}\frac{CE}{3}$.

Similarly,

$\frac{SE}{1}\frac{RV}{2}\frac{IC}{3}\frac{ES}{4} = \frac{RV}{2}\frac{SE}{1}\frac{ES}{4}\frac{IC}{3}$

Hence, RVSEESIC will be the code SERVICES.

90. (B):

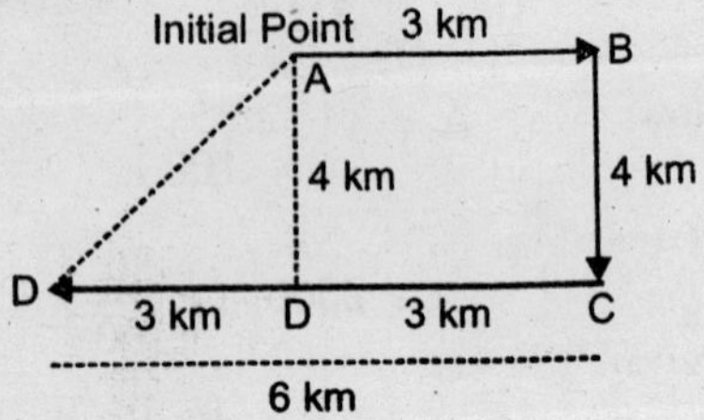
Initial Point
3 km
A
B
4 km
4 km
D
3 km
D
3 km
C
6 km

In ΔAPD,

$(AD)^2 = (3)^2 + (4)^2$

$= 9 + 16 = 25$

$\therefore \quad AD = \sqrt{25}$

$= 5$ km

Hence, Mohan is 5 km far away from i point.

91. (D):

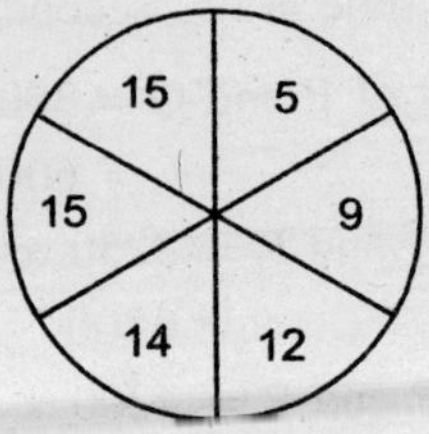
15
5
15
9
14
12

5 + ? + 15 = 9 + 12 + 14

$\Rightarrow$? = 35 − 20

= 15

Hence, 15 will come at the place of qu mark.

Previous Paper (Solved)

Air Force Common Admission Test (AFCAT)—1/2022*

Directions (Qs. No. 1 and 2): *In the following question, select the related word/number from the given alternatives.*

1. Cock : Hen :: ? : ?
A. Horse : Mare B. Rabbit : Goose
C. Bull : Doe D. Boar : Foal

2. Mason : Plumb line :: ? : ?
A. Surgeon : Scalpel
B. Sculptor : Spade
C. Blacksmith : Forcep
D. Gardener : Saw

Directions (Qs. No. 3 and 4): *In the following question, select the odd word/letter/number pair from the given alternatives.*

3. A. Farmer B. Blacksmith
C. Cobbler D. Helper

4. A. Mumbai : President's House
B. Delhi : Parliament
C. Nagpur : Centre Point
D. Hyderabad : Charminar

Directions (Qs. No. 5): *Arrange the given words in the sequence in which they occur in the dictionary.*

5. 1. Clone 2. Climate
3. Clutter 4. Create
5. Clapped
A. 52143 B. 51234
C. 52134 D. 53124

Directions (Qs. No. 6 and 7): *A series is given with one term missing. Select the correct alternative from the given ones that will complete the series.*

6. AAA, BCD, CEG, ?
A. DGI B. DFI
C. DGJ D. DJG

7. 2, 22, 198, 1386, ?
A. 2770 B. 3990
C. 6930 D. 9702

8. A is taller than B, C is taller than D, but shorter than E. B is shorter than D and D is taller than A. Who is the tallest?
A. E B. C
C. B D. D

9. If 'A + B' means 'A is father of B', 'A – B' means 'A is mother of B', 'A * B' means 'A is brother of B' and 'A % B' means 'A is sister of B', then how is Q related to S in 'P + Q * R – S'?
A. Husband B. Uncle
C. Brother D. Father

10. P is shorter than Q but taller than T. R is the tallest and S is shorter than P but not the shortest. Who is second last in the descending order of height?
A. P B. Q
C. S D. T

11. In the following question, select the word which cannot be formed using the letters of the given word.
POSSESSION
A. SESSION B. POSE
C. POISE D. OBSESS

12. If "P" denotes "divided by", "R" denotes "added to", "S" denotes "subtracted from" and "Q" denotes "multiplied by", then
48 P 4 R 3 Q 4 S 6 Q 4 = ?
A. 20 B. 1
C. 6 D. 0

* Based on memory.

13. In the following question, correct the equation by interchanging two numbers.

$9 \times 3 - 8 \div 2 + 7 = 26$

A. 3 and 7 B. 9 and 2
C. 7 and 9 D. 3 and 8

14. If 8 a 48, 12 a 120 and 15 a 195, then what is the value of 'A' in 19 a A?

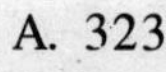

A. 323 B. 347
C. 360 D. 312

15. How many quadrilaterals are there in the given figure?

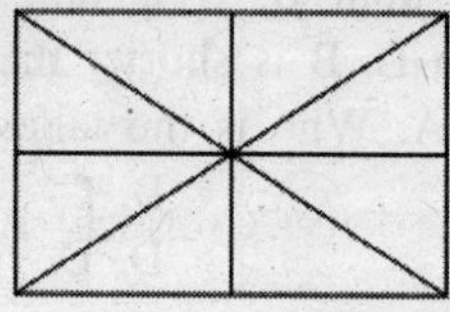

A. 13 B. 15
C. 17 D. 19

16. How many rectangles are there in the given figure?

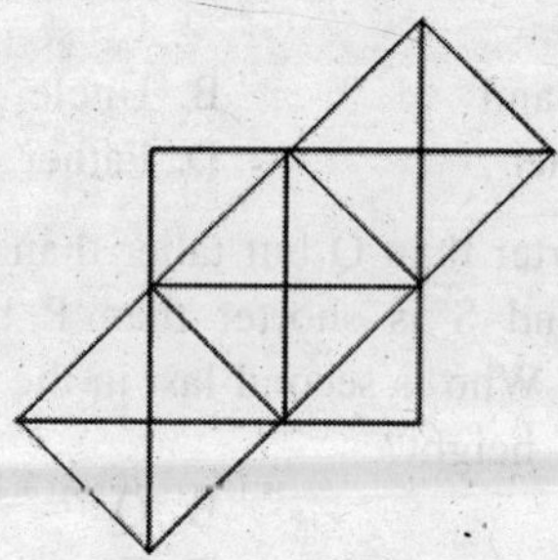

A. 15 B. 17
C. 19 D. 23

17. From the given options, which answer figure can be formed by folding the figure given in the question?

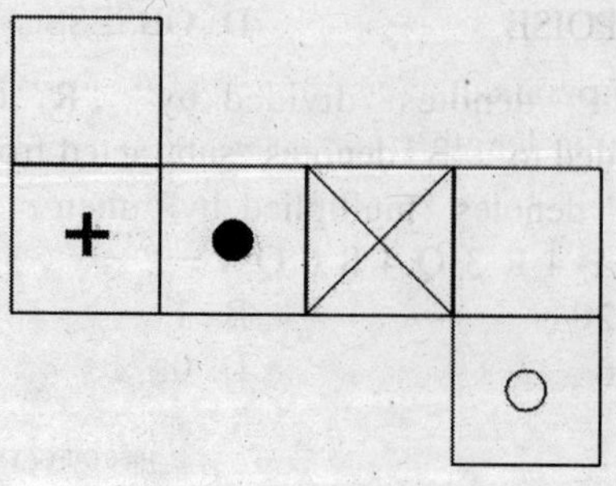

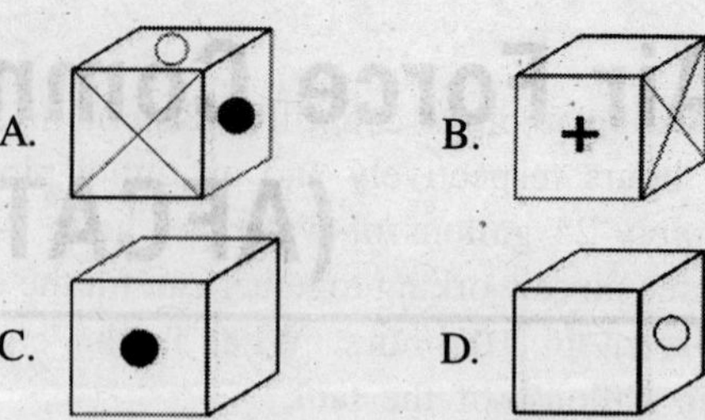

18. A piece of paper is folded and punched as shown below in the question figures. From the given answer figures, indicate how it will appear when opened?

A.

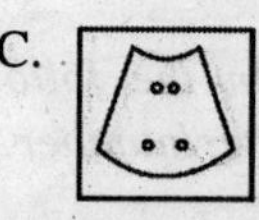

19. What is the value of $2^2 + 6^2 + 10^2 + 14^2 - 1^2 - 5^2 - 9^2 - 13^2$?

A. 0 B. 15
C. 30 D. 60

20. A boy added all natural numbers from 1 to 20, however he missed one number due to which the sum becomes 190. What is the number which the boy missed?

A. 5 B. 10
C. 15 D. 20

21. 3/4 part of a tank is filled with oil. After taking out 60 litres of oil the tank is 2/3 part full. What is the capacity (in litres) of the tank?

A. 240 B. 360
C. 600 D. 720

22. Raman is three times as efficient as Manan. Raman can complete a work in 60 days less than Manan. In how many days the work would be complete if both of them work together?

A. 15 B. 17.5
C. 22.5 D. 27.5

23. Two inlet pipes can fill a cistern in 5 and 6 hours respectively and an outlet pipe can empty 24 gallons of water per hour. All the three pipes working together can fill the empty cistern in 10 hours. What is the capacity (in gallons) of the tank?

A. 90 B. 180
C. 60 D. 120

24. After giving a discount of 44% a cycle is sold for ₹ 17920. What is the marked price (in ₹) of the cycle?

A. 28000 B. 31500
C. 32000 D. 35000

25. The average of 19 results is 111. If the average of first 10 results is 82 and that of the last 10 results is 129, then what will be the 10 result?

A. 0 B. 1
C. 82 D. 111

26. Eleven friends spent ₹ 19 each on a tour and the twelfth friend spent ₹ 11 less than the average expenditure of all twelve of them. What is the total money (in ₹) spent by them?

A. 216 B. 227
C. 236 D. 247

27. Atul sells 12 pencils at ₹ 400. If there is a loss equal to the cost price of 4 pencil, then what is the cost price (in ₹) of a pencil?

A. 30 B. 45
C. 50 D. 60

28. A is 16.66% less than B. If value of A is 500, then what is the value of B?

A. 583.33 B. 566.66
C. 600 D. 620

29. Two trains are moving in the same direction at speed of 60 km/hr and 70 km/hr. The time taken by faster train to cross a man sitting in the slower train is 2 minutes 42 seconds. What will be the length (in metres) of the faster train?

A. 220 B. 330
C. 450 D. 540

30. Two people A and B are at a distance of 110 km from each other at 10:30 AM. After 30 mins, A starts moving towards B at a speed of 20 km/hr while at 12 PM. B starts moving away from A at a speed of 15 km/hr. At what time (in AM) will they meet on the next day?

A. 6:00 B. 8:00
C. 4:00 D. 3:00

31. What will be the amount on ₹ 24000 at the rate of 35% per annum compounded yearly for 2 years?

A. 43740 B. 49870
C. 51785 D. 40890

32. What is the curved surface area (in cm^2 of a cylinder having radius of base as 21 cm and height as 30 cm?

A. 3740 B. 3850
C. 1980 D. 3960

33. A cylindrical well of height 80 metres and radius 7 metres is dug in a field 28 metres long and 22 metres wide. The earth taken out is spread evenly on the field. What is the increase (in metres) in the level of the field?

A. 13.33 B. 26.66
C. 18.17 D. 28.17

34. If $x^2 - x\sqrt{68} + 1 = 0$, then what is the value of $x - \frac{1}{x}$?

A. $\sqrt{66}$ B. 8
C. $\sqrt{62}$ D. 6

35. PQR is an isosceles triangle with such that PQ = PR = 15 cm and QR = 24 cm. PS is a perpendicular bisector of the base QR. What is the length (in cm) of PS?

A. 18 B. 6
C. 12 D. 9

36. ABCD is a cyclic quadrilateral and AB is the diameter of the circle. If ∠CAB = 48°, then what is the value (in degrees) of ∠ADC?

A. 52 B. 77
C. 138 D. 142

37. What is the simplified value of $\left(\frac{\cot\theta + \tan\theta}{\sec\theta}\right)$?

A. $1 - \cos^2\theta$ B. $2 \sin\theta$
C. $\operatorname{cosec}\theta$ D. $\sec^2 \theta$

38. 80 m away from the foot of the tower, the angle of elevation of the top of the tower is 60°. What is the height (in metres) of the tower?

A. 40 B. $60\sqrt{3}$
C. $80\sqrt{3}$ D. $40/\sqrt{3}$

39. The sum of two number is $15\frac{1}{3}$ and their difference is $4\frac{2}{3}$. The product of the numbers is:

A. $53\frac{1}{3}$ B. 60
C. $48\frac{2}{3}$ D. 50

40. The value of:
$(\sqrt{6}-\sqrt{10}+\sqrt{21}-\sqrt{35})$
$(\sqrt{6}+\sqrt{10}-\sqrt{21}-\sqrt{35})$ is:

A. 10 B. 27
C. 18 D. 40

41. If $x+\frac{1}{x}=3$, where $x \neq 0$, then the value of $\frac{x^4+3x^3+5x^2+3x+1}{x^4+1}$ is:

A. 2 B. 7
C. 3 D. 5

42. If 4 men and 6 women can complete a work in 8 days, while 3 men and 7 women can complete it in 10 days, then 10 women complete it in:

A. 40 days B. 45 days
C. 50 days D. 35 days

Directions (Qs. No. 43 and 44): *Select a figure from amongst the answer figures which will continue the same series as established by the five Problem Figures.*

43. Problem Figures

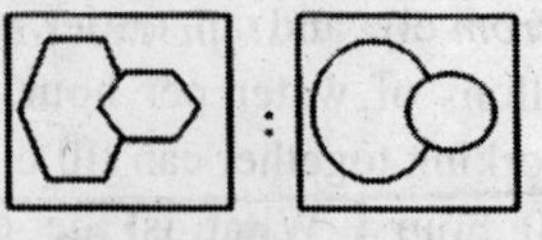

Answer Figures

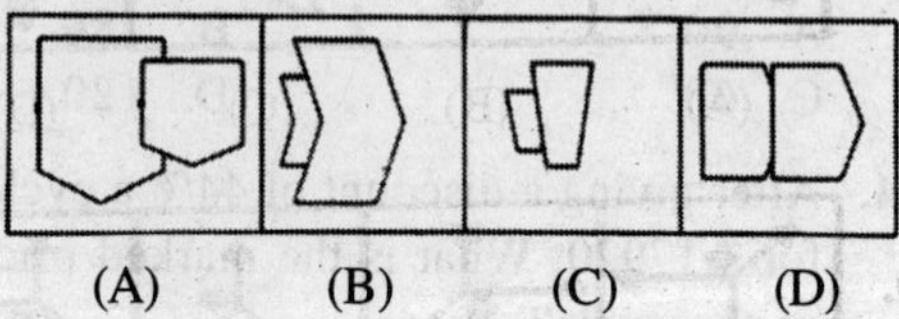

(A) (B) (C) (D)

44. Problem Figures

Answer Figures

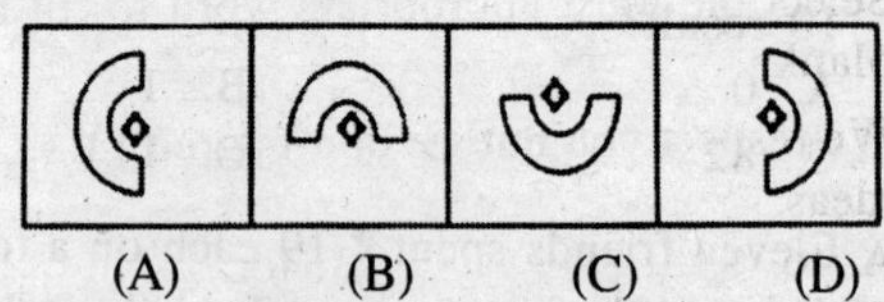

(A) (B) (C) (D)

Directions (Qs. No. 45 and 46): *Select the mirror image of (X) out of the alternatives (A), (B), (C) and (D).*

45.

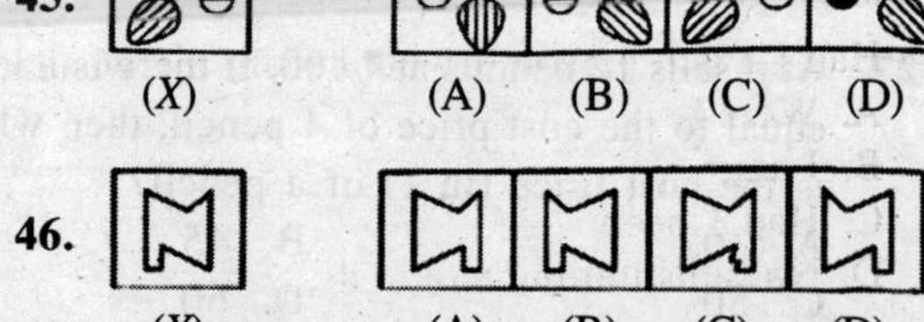

(X) (A) (B) (C) (D)

46.

(X) (A) (B) (C) (D)

Directions (Qs. No. 47 and 48): *Fill in the question mark box with an appropriate option from the given figures.*

47.

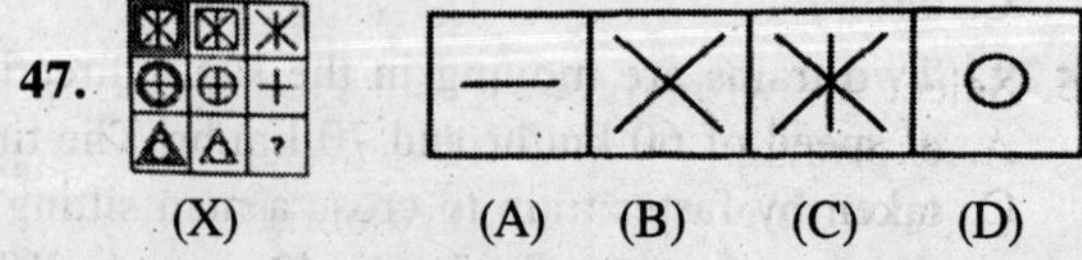

(X) (A) (B) (C) (D)

48.

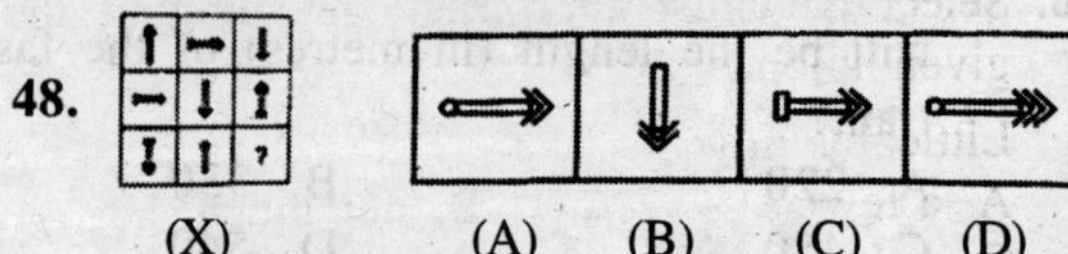

(X) (A) (B) (C) (D)

Directions (Qs. No. 49 and 50): *Choose the figure which is different from the rest in the following figures.*

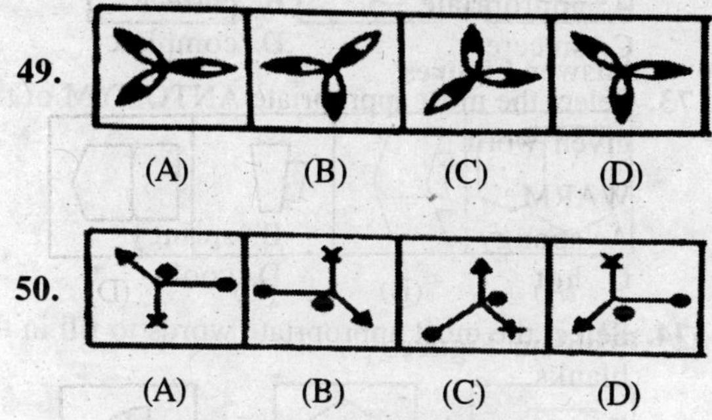

49. (A) (B) (C) (D)

50. (A) (B) (C) (D)

51. Select the wrongly spelt word.
A. capacity B. ablity
C. pupil D. teacher

52. Select the most appropriate word to fill in the blank.

We respect you but we don't agree .... your ideas.

A. to B. for
C. with D. by

53. Select the most appropriate option to substitute the underlined segment in the given sentence. If there is no need to substitute it, select 'No substitution required'.

Had I a rich person, I would share my wealth.

A. Were I
B. I am
C. Had I been
D. No substitution required

54. Select the most appropriate word which means the same as the group of words given.

Extreme mental or physical suffering

A. rapture B. acute
C. agony D. ecstasy

55. Select the wrongly spelt word.
A. exprimant B. sediment
C. occurring D. umbrella

56. Select the most appropriate meaning of the given idiom.

Little by little

A. a few B. not much
C. only once D. gradually

57. Select the most appropriate meaning of the given idiom.

A dry run

A. a rehearsal
B. a run on dry ground
C. a slow run
D. a poor harvest

58. Select the most appropriate word to fill in the blank.

Let us know .... you change your mind.

A. although B. however
C. in case D. suppose

59. Select the most appropriate option to substitute the underlined segment in the given sentence. If there is no need to substitute it, select 'No substitution required'.

Because she didn't love him, she had to marry him.

A. No substitution required
B. Although
C. Since
D. Despite

60. Select the most appropriate option to substitute the underlined segment in the given sentence. If there is no need to substitute it, select 'No substitution required'.

When I left my house this morning, it was raining.

A. rained
B. rains
C. is raining
D. No substitution required

61. Select the most appropriate synonym of the given word.

FOUNDATION

A. top B. base
C. building D. structure

62. Select the most appropriate word to fill in the blank.

I'm sure I .... them at the party last night.

A. am seeing
B. was seeing
C. have seen
D. saw

63. Select the most appropriate synonym of the given word.
IMITATION
A. fake B. real
C. genuine D. original

64. Select the wrongly spelt word.
A. presure B. electric
C. central D. irrigation

65. Select the most appropriate ANTONYM of the given word.
ALIVE
A. active B. dead
C. life D. living

66. Identify the segment in the sentence which contains a grammatical error. If there is no error, then select the option 'No error'.
All of us were a little nervous when we came into this room today.
A. a little nervous when
B. No error
C. when we came into this room today
D. All of us were

67. Select the wrongly spelt word.
A. brakes B. refrence
C. beaker D. solution

68. Select the most appropriate synonym of the given word.
FICTION
A. fact B. truth
C. literature D. fantasy

69. Identify the segment in the sentence which contains a grammatical error. If there is no error, then select the option 'No error'.
Sh! Someone listens to our conversation.
A. Sh! Someone B. our conversation
C. No error D. listens to

70. Select the most appropriate word which means the same as the group of words given.
An exact or a very close copy (of something)
A. forgery B. replica
C. artificial D. substitute

71. Select the most appropriate ANTONYM of the given word.
FERTILE
A. productive B. strong
C. fruitful D. barren

72. Select the most appropriate synonym of the given word.
ACCURATE
A. appropriate B. correct
C. sincere D. complete

73. Select the most appropriate ANTONYM of the given word.
WARM
A. spongy B. springy
C. hot D. cool

74. Select the most appropriate words to fill in the blanks.
Today computer viruses spread .... a dizzying speed .... way of file downloads.
A. in; from B. at; from
C. by; by D. at; by

75. Select the most appropriate meaning of the given idiom.
Give a hand
A. assist B. encourage
C. clap hands D. donate an organ

76. Who was the woman leading Awadh in the 1857 revolt?
A. Kasturba Gandhi
B. Bhikaji Cama
C. Sarojini Naidu
D. Begum Hazrat Mahal

77. Where are the paintings of Bodhisattva Padmapani found?
A. Ajanta B. Badami
C. Bagh D. Ellora

78. Which of the following ministry implements the Mid-day Meal scheme?
A. Ministry of Education
B. Ministry of Social Justice and Empowerment
C. Ministry of Rural Development
D. Ministry of Women and Child Development

79. What is the rate called by which RBI lends money to banks?
A. Prime lending Rate
B. Banker's Rate
C. Reverse Repo Rate
D. Repo Rate

80. Where is the Headquarters of the Organization for Prohibition of Chemical Weapons?
A. Geneva B. Paris
C. The Hague D. New York

81. What was the name of the 1st Nuclear test in India?
A. Chagai 1 – 1 B. Smiling Buddha
C. Project 596 D. Shakti 1 – 1

82. Sakshi Malik is related to which sports?
A. Polo B. Wrestling
C. Judo D. Shooting

83. Which country was not in the support of the Axis powers in World War I?
A. Germany B. France
C. Japan D. Italy

84. Which one is a secondary pollution source:
A. Fog B. Smog
C. Water vapour D. None of these

85. All-weather phenomena occurred in which layer?
A. Troposphere B. Mesosphere
C. Stratosphere D. Thermosphere

86. What is the Indian navy's operation in the strait of Hormuz known as?
A. Operation Calm Down
B. Operation Goodwill
C. Operation Sankalp
D. None of these

87. The tip of the lead pencil is made of:
A. Lead B. Graphite
C. Zinc D. Charcoal

88. Which one of the following is the motto of NCC?
A. Unity and Discipline
B. Unity and integrity
C. Unity and Command
D. Unity and Service

89. Which one is the book written by Ravi Shastri?
A. 281 and Beyond
B. Believe: What Life and Cricket Taught Me
C. The Sardar of Spin
D. Stargazing: The Players in My Life

90. In January 2022, who has been named as the winner of Rachael Heyhoe Flint Trophy for ICC Women's Cricketer of the Year?
A. Smriti Mandhana B. Kavisha Dilhari
C. Ellyse Perry D. Ayesha Naseem

91. Which crop is helpful in Nitrogen fixation?
A. Rice B. Wheat
C. Legume D. Corn

92. Which company has developed the new income tax e-filing portal?
A. TCS B. Infosys
C. Wipro D. Tech Mahindra

93. Which city will host 2022 Asian Games?
A. Guangzhou B. Hangzhou
C. Beijing D. Shenzhen

94. Smallest bone in the human body is:
A. Stapes B. Malleus
C. Patella D. Navicular bone

95. Konkan naval exercise is conducted between which two countries?
A. India-Bangladesh
B. India-Sri Lanka
C. India-United Kingdom
D. India-China

96. Subroto Cup is related to which sports?
A. Tennis B. Football
C. Hockey D. Cricket

97. 1st indigenous rifle used by IAF?
A. AK 203 Assault Rifles
B. AK 47 Assault Rifles
C. AK 56 Assault Rifles
D. None of these

98. In how many states in India have Bicameral legislature?
A. 5 states B. 6 states
C. 7 states D. 9 states

99. Name the British Governor General who introduced railways in India:
A. Lord Auckland B. Sir Charles Metcalfe
C. Lord Hastings D. Lord Dalhousie

100. 'Man Booker Prize' is given in which of the following fields?
A. Journalism B. Science
C. Literature D. Economics

ANSWERS

1	2	3	4	5	6	7	8	9	10
A	A	D	A	C	C	C	A	B	C
11	**12**	**13**	**14**	**15**	**16**	**17**	**18**	**19**	**20**
D	D	C	A	C	A	A	B	D	D
21	**22**	**23**	**24**	**25**	**26**	**27**	**28**	**29**	**30**
D	C	A	C	B	A	C	C	C	A
31	**32**	**33**	**34**	**35**	**36**	**37**	**38**	**39**	**40**
A	D	B	B	D	C	C	C	A	A
41	**42**	**43**	**44**	**45**	**46**	**47**	**48**	**49**	**50**
C	A	A	B	B	D	D	A	D	C
51	**52**	**53**	**54**	**55**	**56**	**57**	**58**	**59**	**60**
B	C	A	C	A	D	A	C	B	D
61	**62**	**63**	**64**	**65**	**66**	**67**	**68**	**69**	**70**
B	D	A	A	B	B	B	D	D	B
71	**72**	**73**	**74**	**75**	**76**	**77**	**78**	**79**	**80**
D	B	D	D	A	D	A	A	D	C
81	**82**	**83**	**84**	**85**	**86**	**87**	**88**	**89**	**90**
B	B	B	B	A	C	B	A	D	A
91	**92**	**93**	**94**	**95**	**96**	**97**	**98**	**99**	**100**
C	B	B	A	C	B	A	B	D	C

EXPLANATORY ANSWERS

3. Farmer, Blacksmith, Cobbler, Helper

Hence, Helper is odd word from the given alternatives.

4. Mumbai : President's House is the odd word pair from the given alternatives.

6.

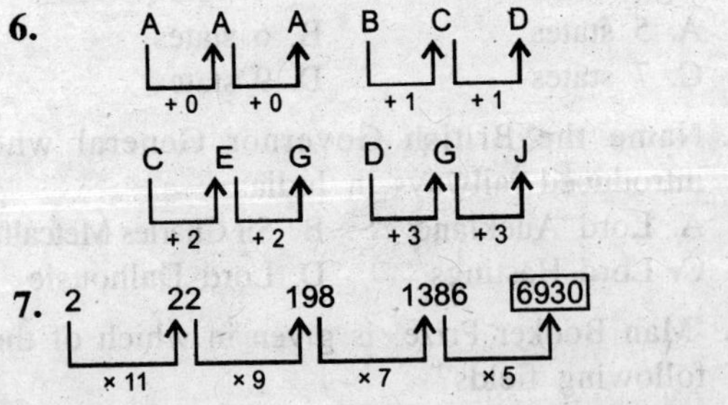

7. Hence, 6930 will come at the place of question mark.

8.

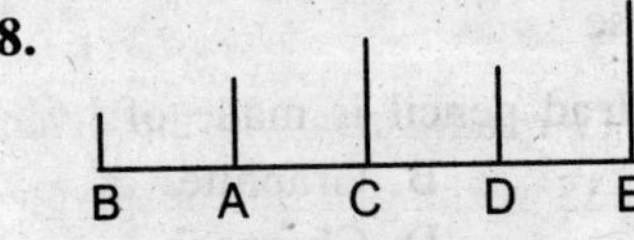

Hence, E is the tallest.

9. A + B means A is father of B

A – B means A is mother of B

A * B means A is brother of B

A % B means A is sister of B

P + Q * R – S

P is father of Q

Q is brother of R

R is mother of S

Hence, Q is Uncle of S.

10. 

In descending order

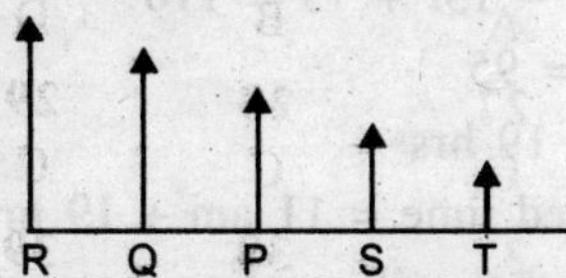

Hence, S is second last in the descending order of height.

11. P O S S E S S I O N

OBSESS can not be formed using the letters of the given word because the letter B is not in the given word.

12. P denotes ÷

R denotes +

S denotes –

Q denotes ×

4 8 P 4 R 3 Q 4 S 6 Q 4

$= 48 \div 4 + 3 \times 4 - 6 \times 4$

$= 12 + 12 - 24 = 24 - 24 = 0$

13. $9 \times 3 - 8 \div 2 + 7 = 26$

Interchange the place of 7 and 9 then we get,

$7 \times 3 - 8 \div 2 + 9$

$= 21 - 4 + 9$

$= 30 - 4 = 26$

15. There are 17 quadrilaterals in the given figure.

16. There are 15 rectangles in the given figure.

19. $2^2 + 6^2 + 10^2 + 14^2 - 1^2 - 5^2 - 9^2 - 13^2$

$= (14)^2 - (13)^2 + 10^2 - 9^2 + 6^2 - 5^2 + 2^2 - 1^2$

$= (27)(1) + (19)(1) + (11)(1) + (3)(1)$

$= 27 + 19 + 11 + 3$

$= 30 + 30 = 60$

Hence, required value = 60

20. Sum of natural numbers from 1 to 20

$= \frac{20 \times 21}{2} = 210$

But by mistake the sum = 190

Hence, the required number which the boy missed = 210 – 190 = 20

21. $\frac{3}{4}x - \frac{2}{3}x = 60$

$\Rightarrow \frac{9x - 8x}{12} = 60$

$\Rightarrow x = 12 \times 60 = 720$

Hence, capacity of the tank = 720 litres

22. Ratio of efficiency of Raman and Manan = 3 : 1

Hence, ratio of their time taking = 1 : 3

Let Raman and Manan can finish the work in x and $3x$ days.

Now, $3x - x = 60$

$\Rightarrow 2x = 60$

$\Rightarrow x = 30$ days and $3x = 3 \times 30 = 90$ days

(Raman + Manan)'s 1 day work $= \frac{1}{30} + \frac{1}{90}$

$= \frac{3+1}{90} = \frac{4}{90} = \frac{2}{45}$

Hence, working together, they will finish the work in $\frac{45}{2} = 22\frac{1}{2}$ days = 22.5 days

23. In 1 hour the part filled by all the three pipes

$= \frac{1}{5} + \frac{1}{6} - \frac{1}{10} = \frac{6+5-3}{30} = \frac{8}{30} = \frac{4}{15}$

Hence, outlet pipe can empty the whole tank in $\frac{15}{4}$ hrs.

Capacity of the tank $= 24 \times \frac{15}{4} = 90$ gallons

24. Let M.P. of the cycle = ₹ x.

Discount $= \frac{44}{100} \times x = \frac{11x}{25}$

S.P. $= x - \frac{11x}{25} = \frac{14x}{25}$ $= \frac{14x}{25} = 17920$

$\Rightarrow x = \frac{17920 \times 25}{14} = 32000$

Hence, the marked price of the cycle = ₹ 32000

25. Sum of 19 results = 111 × 19 = 2109

Sum of first-ten results = 82 × 10 = 820

Sum of last ten results = 129 × 10 = 1290

Hence, the tenth result = (820 + 1290) – 2109
= 2110 – 2109 = 1

26. Let the average expenditure of all the twelve = ₹ x

Amount spent by 11 = 19 × 11 = ₹ 209

Total spent by 12th = x – 11

According to the question,

$12x = x + 198$

$\Rightarrow \; 11x = 198$

$\Rightarrow \; x = 18$

$\therefore$ Total money spent by them = 12 × 18 = ₹ 216

27. Let cost price of each pencil = ₹ x

Cost price of 12 pencils = ₹ $12x$

According to the question,

$12x - 4x = 400$

$\Rightarrow 8x = 400$

$\Rightarrow x =$ ₹ 50

Hence, cost price of each pencil = ₹ 50

28. According to the question,

Let, value of B = x

$$x - \frac{50}{3}\% \text{ of } x = 500$$

$$\Rightarrow \quad x - \frac{50 \times x}{3 \times 100} = 500$$

$$\Rightarrow \quad x - \frac{x}{6} = 500$$

$$\Rightarrow 5x = 6 \times 500$$

$$\Rightarrow x = \frac{6 \times 500}{5} = 600$$

Hence, value of B = 600

29. Relative speed = 70 – 60 = 10 km/hr

$$= 10 \times \frac{5}{18} \text{ m/s} = \frac{25}{9} \text{ m/s}$$

Length of the train = speed × time

$$= \frac{25}{9} \times 162$$

$$= 25 \times 18 = 450 \text{ m}$$

30. Let they will meet after t hours from starting the first man :

According to the question,

$20t - 15(t - 1) = 110$

$\Rightarrow 20t - 15t + 15 = 110$

$\Rightarrow 5t = 95$

$\therefore \; t = 19$ hrs

Required time = 11 am + 19 hrs = 6 am

Hence, they will meet on the next day at 6 am.

31. $$A = P\left(1 + \frac{r}{100}\right)^t$$

$$= 24000\left(1 + \frac{35}{100}\right)^2$$

$$= 24000 \times \frac{27}{20} \times \frac{27}{20}$$

$$= 60 \times 729 = 43740$$

Hence, amount = ₹ 43740

32. Curved surface area of cylinder

$$= 2\pi rh = 2 \times \frac{22}{7} \times 21 \times 30$$

$$= 44 \times 90 = 3960 \text{ cm}^2$$

33. Area of the field = 28 × 22 = 616 m^2

Area of circle = $\pi r^2 = \frac{22}{7} \times 7 \times 7 = 154 \text{ m}^2$

Remaining area of field = 616 – 154 = 462 m^2

$462 \times H = \pi r^2 h = \frac{22}{7} \times 7 \times 7 \times 80$

$$\therefore H = \frac{22 \times 7 \times 80}{462} = \frac{80}{3} = 26.66 \text{ m}$$

34. $x^2 - x\sqrt{68} + 1 = 0 \quad \Rightarrow x^2 + 1 = x\sqrt{68}$

Dividing both sides by x

$$x + \frac{1}{x} = \sqrt{68}$$

Now $$\left(x - \frac{1}{x}\right)^2 = \left(x + \frac{1}{x}\right)^2 - 4 \times x \times \frac{1}{x}$$

$$= \left(\sqrt{68}\right)^2 - 4 = 68 - 4 = 64$$

$$\therefore \quad x - \frac{1}{x} = 8$$

35.

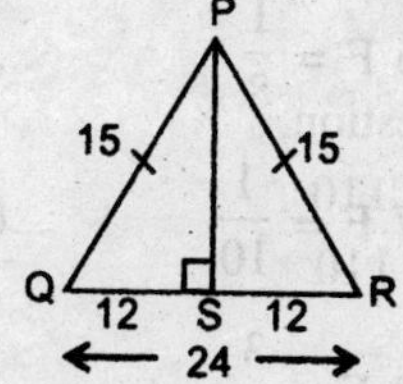

In Δ PQS,

$PS^2 = (15)^2 - (12)^2 = 225 - 144 = 81$

$\Rightarrow PS = 9$

Hence, the length of PS = 9 cm

36.

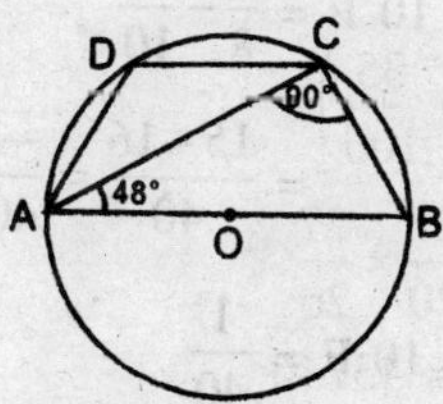

$\because$ ABCD is cyclic quadrilateral and AB is diameter of the circle.

$\therefore \angle ACB = 90°$(Angle in the semi circle = 90°)

$\angle CAB = 48°$ (given)

$\therefore \quad \angle ABC = 180° - (90 + 48°)$

$= 180° - 138° = 42°$

$\because$ ABCD is cyclic

$\therefore \angle B + \angle D = 180°$

$\Rightarrow 42° + \angle D = 180°$

$\Rightarrow \angle D = 180° - 42° = 138°$

Hence, $\angle ADC = 138°$

37. $\dfrac{\cot\theta + \tan\theta}{\sec\theta} = \dfrac{\dfrac{\cos\theta}{\sin\theta} + \dfrac{\sin\theta}{\cos\theta}}{\dfrac{1}{\cos\theta}}$

$= \dfrac{\dfrac{\cos^2\theta + \sin^2\theta}{\sin\theta \cdot \cos\theta}}{\dfrac{1}{\cos\theta}}$

$= \dfrac{1}{\sin\theta . \cos\theta} \times \dfrac{\cos\theta}{1}$

$= \dfrac{1}{\sin\theta} = \text{cosec}\theta$

38.

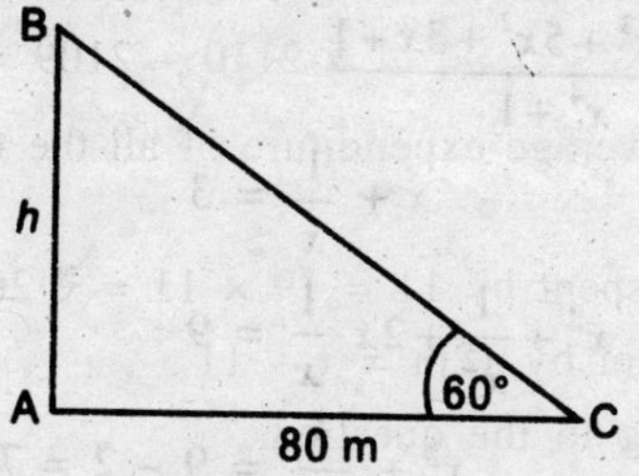

In Δ ABC,

$\tan 60° = \dfrac{h}{80}$

$\Rightarrow \sqrt{3} = \dfrac{h}{80}$

$\Rightarrow h = 80\sqrt{3}$

Hence, height of the tower = $80\sqrt{3}$ m

39. Let numbers are a and b

According to the question,

$a + b = \dfrac{46}{3}$ ...(*i*)

and $a - b = \dfrac{14}{3}$ ... (*ii*)

Adding (*i*) and (*ii*), then we get,

$2a = \dfrac{46}{3} + \dfrac{14}{3} = \dfrac{60}{3} = 20$

$\Rightarrow \quad a = 10$

$b = \dfrac{46}{3} - 10$

$= \dfrac{46 - 30}{3} = \dfrac{16}{3}$

Product of the numbers = $a \times b$

$= 10 \times \dfrac{16}{3} = \dfrac{160}{3} = 53\dfrac{1}{3}$

40. $(\sqrt{6} - \sqrt{10} + \sqrt{21} - \sqrt{35})(\sqrt{6} + \sqrt{10} - \sqrt{21} - \sqrt{35})$

$= (\sqrt{6} - \sqrt{35} - \sqrt{10} + \sqrt{21})(\sqrt{6} - \sqrt{35} + \sqrt{10} - \sqrt{21})$

$= (\sqrt{6} - \sqrt{35})^2 - (\sqrt{10} - \sqrt{21})^2$

$= (6 + 35 - 2\sqrt{210}) - (10 + 21 - 2\sqrt{210})$

$= 41 - 2\sqrt{210} - 31 + 2\sqrt{210}$

$= 41 - 31 = 10.$

41. $\dfrac{x^4+3x^3+5x^2+3x+1}{x^4+1}$

$\because \quad x + \dfrac{1}{x} = 3$

$\Rightarrow \quad x^2 + \dfrac{1}{x^2} + 2x \cdot \dfrac{1}{x} = 9$

$\Rightarrow \quad x^2 + \dfrac{1}{x^2} = 9 - 2 = 7$

$$\frac{\dfrac{x^4}{x^2}+\dfrac{3x^3}{x^2}+\dfrac{3x}{x^2}+\dfrac{5x^2}{x^2}+\dfrac{1}{x^2}}{\dfrac{x^4}{x^2}+\dfrac{1}{x^2}}$$

$$= \frac{x^2+\dfrac{1}{x^2}+3\left(x+\dfrac{1}{x}\right)+5}{x^2+\dfrac{1}{x^2}}$$

$$= \frac{7+3(3)+5}{7} = \frac{7+9+5}{7} = \frac{21}{7} = 3$$

42. $4\,m + 6\text{ F} = \dfrac{1}{8}$ ...(*i*)] × 3

$3\,m + 7\text{ F} = \dfrac{1}{10}$ ...(*ii*)] × 4

$\Rightarrow \quad 12\,m + 18\text{ F} = \dfrac{3}{8}$

$12\,m + 28\text{ F} = \dfrac{4}{10}$

$\quad - \quad\quad - \quad\quad -$

$-10\text{ F} = \dfrac{3}{8} - \dfrac{4}{10}$

$= \dfrac{15-16}{40} = \dfrac{-1}{40}$

$\Rightarrow \quad 10\text{ F} = \dfrac{1}{40}$

∴ 10 female can do this work in 40 days.

Previous Paper (Solved)

Air Force Common Admission Test (AFCAT)—1/2021*

1. Select the alternative to fill in the given blank.

We are ______ by her beauty.

A. Blowed over B. Blown at
C. Blowed D. Blown away

2. Select the opposite of "Kindle":

A. Spark B. Extinguish
C. Ignite D. Torch

3. Select the opposite of "Thrifty":

A. Frugal B. Sparing
C. Extravagant D. Economical

4. Select the nearest of "Antipathy":

A. Liking B. Affinity
C. Kindliness D. Animosity

5. Select the nearest of "Truncate":

A. Elongate B. Decrease
C. Extend D. Lengthen

6. Select the most appropriate meaning for the given Idiom/Phrase.

To Bury the hatchet

A. To bury a dead body
B. To leave someone/something.
C. To end a business deal.
D. To end a quarrel or conflict

7. Select the most appropriate meaning for the given Idiom/Phrase.

To turn over a new leaf.

A. To forget someone
B. To write on a leaf
C. To make a fresh start
D. To plant a new tree

8. Select the most appropriate meaning for the given Idiom/Phrase.

To give currency:

A. To make someone or something popular
B. To give a loan
C. To earn big profits
D. To pay for your sins

9. Select the most appropriate meaning for the given Idiom/Phrase.

To get cold feet:

A. To get too tired
B. To go to the toilet
C. To feel too frightened
D. To feel too cold

10. Select the opposite of "Austerity":

A. Unimportance B. Exactness
C. Formalness D. Rigidity

11. Select the opposite of "Vividly":

A. Sharply B. Vague
C. Distinctly D. Clearly

12. Select the nearest of "Facade":

A. Truth B. Actuality
C. Reality D. Pretence

13. Select the most appropriate meaning for the given Idiom/Phrase.

To miss the boat

A. To be patient
B. To wait for something
C. To work late in the night
D. To fail to take advantage of an opportunity

14. Select the most appropriate meaning for the given Idiom/Phrase.

To get cold feet

A. To get rid of something
B. Lack of confidence or courage
C. To get too cold
D. To get rejected

* Based on memory.

15. Select the nearest of "Eloquent":
A. Inarticulate B. Apathetic
C. Introvert D. Expressive

16. Select the nearest of "Pacify":
A. Inflame B. Calm
C. Provoke D. Enrage

17. Select the opposite of "Inevitable":
A. Avoidable B. Inescapable
C. Assured D. Fated

18. Select the nearest of "Elude":
A. Meet B. Confront
C. Avoid D. Encounter

19. Select the most appropriate meaning for the given Idiom/Phrase.

To spill the beans
A. To reveal secret information
B. To learn how to cook
C. To have no money at all
D. To attract someone's attention

20. Select the most appropriate meaning for the given Idiom/Phrase.

To keep one's head above the water
A. To be unable to sleep
B. To complete a task successfully
C. To stay out of trouble
D. To learn to swim well

21. Select the opposite of "Belligerent":
A. Hostile B. Friendly
C. Aggressive D. Threatening

22. Select the opposite of "Vigilance":
A. Inattention B. Watchful
C. Aware D. Alert

23. Select the opposite of "Blissful":
A. Euphoric B. Miserable
C. Joyful D. Elated

24. Select the nearest of "Industrious":
A. Careless B. Lethargic
C. Diligent D. Indolent

25. Select the nearest of "Mitigate":
A. Diminish B. Intensify
C. Aggravate D. Incite

26. A candidate got 35% vote and lost the election by 450 votes. Then the number of the total voter?
A. 1200 B. 1500
C. 900 D. 1800

27. A shopkeeper marked 30% more than the cost price and gave a discount of 20%. Find the profit percentage:
A. 10% B. 12%
C. 15% D. 20%

28. What will be $\sqrt{29^2 - 2 \times 100 \times 24}$ equal to:
A. 504 B. 416
C. 480 D. 420

29. What will be 23 ÷ 46 × 7.5 + 512 – 251 equal to:
A. 250 B. 264.75
C. 261 D. 3.75

30. A student deposits ₹ 8000 in a bank. He pays 10% of the interest as fee in the college and remains ₹ 900. Find the rate of the interest?
A. 25% B. 12.5%
C. 6.5% D. 8%

31. A policeman started to chase a thief who was running away from 7:00 PM to 9:00 PM. If the speed of the police and the thief are 4.5 kmph and 6 kmph. Then find the time when policeman catches the thief?
A. 4 hr B. 5 hr
C. 6 hr D. 8 hr

32. A man deposits ₹ 3903 in a bank at 4% of interest rate in two schemes. And he gets an equal amount after 7 years and 9 years. Then find the amounts?
A. 1875 : 2028 B. 2028 : 1875
C. 1301 : 2602 D. 2602 : 1301

33. A man goes 12 km upstream and 28 km downstream in 5 hours. Find the speed of the stream?
A. 2 kmph B. 1.6 kmph
C. 1.4 kmph D. 1.8 kmph

34. A man goes 32 km upstream and 40 km downstream in 10 hr. Again he goes 38 km upstream and 50 km downstream in 12 hr, then find the speed of the stream?

A. 8 B. 10

C. 12 D. 15

35. If the average weight of 22 toys is increased by 2 if two of them whose average weight is one-third of the previous are removed. Then the average weight of 20 toys are?

A. 30 B. 32

C. 28 D. 24

36. If profit is 40% for selling an item. If the cost price and selling price are increased by ₹ 50 and ₹ 20 then profit decreases to 20%. Find the cost price?

A. ₹ 100 B. ₹ 150

C. ₹ 200 D. ₹ 120

37. A person buys petrol at the rate of 45, 60 and 90 rupees per litre for three successive years. What is the average petrol he bought if he spent 6000 rupees per year?

A. 133.34 litre B. 120 litre

C. 100 litre D. 66.67 litre

38. If $10.99 \times 10.99 + 10.99 \times x + 0.03 \times 0.03$ then what should be the value of x for this to be perfect square?

A. 0.08 B. 0.06

C. 0.8 D. 0.6

39. If 28016 is divided by 412 then the quotient is 68. Then what will the quotient when 28.016 is divided by 0.68?

A. 0.412 B. 41.2

C. 4.12 D. 412

40. A man's will has 35 L to be given to his daughters of ages 13 and 16 at the rate of 10% when they both turn 21. They get the same amount, then what will be the amount that the elder daughter receives?

A. 17 L B. 20 L

C. 25 L D. 30 L

41. A man runs on a square track of 35 m in length with a speed of 9 kmph. What is the total time taken by him to complete a round of the track?

A. 52 sec B. 54 sec

C. 56 sec D. 58 sec

42. A man bought two T.V. sets and sold at ₹ 3,75,000 for each with 20% profit and 20% loss. Then how much profit or loss gain by that man?

A. 4% gain

B. 4% loss

C. 8% gain

D. Neither profit nor loss

43. A girl goes 6 km against the stream and 10 km with the stream at the same time. If the speed of the stream is $\frac{5}{18}$ m/s, then speed of girl in the still water?

A. 2 kmph B. 3 kmph

C. 4 kmph D. 6 kmph

44. Yakshagana is a traditional dance and theatre form of which state?

A. Karnataka B. Andhra Pradesh

C. Tamil Nadu D. Maharashtra

45. Where is the capital of Zimbabwe?

A. Abuja B. Makati

C. Nairobi D. Harare

46. Indian Independence Act was passed on which date?

A. 16 July, 1947 B. 3 June, 1946

C. 15 August, 1947 D. 14 August, 1947

47. The word SHIRT written as FUVEG then PARTY will be written as:

A. CNEGL B. DMFFM

C. BOEGL D. DMEKM

48. Sculptor : Atelier

A. Painter : Portrait B. Miner : Quarry

C. Poet : Sonnet D. Man : House

49. Vandalism : Property

A. Permission : Testimony

B. Implication : Crime

C. Perjury : Testimony

D. Testify : Reputation

50. Hockey : Game :: Latin : ?

A. Country B. Currency

C. Language D. Capital

51. Newton : Force :: Pascal : ?
A. Work B. Energy
C. Pressure D. Weight

52. Engine : Car
A. Lense : Microscope
B. Day : Night
C. Picture : Frame
D. Club : Member

53. India : Lotus :: Iris : ?
A. Australia B. Germany
C. Japan D. France

54. Cell : Cytology :: Insect : ?
A. Cymology B. Entomology
C. Phycology D. Physiognomy

55. Bihu : Assam :: Kathakali : ?
A. Kerala B. Tamil Nadu
C. Andhra Pradesh D. Karnataka

56. Anthropology : Human Body :: Histology : ?
A. Tissues of the body
B. Fungus
C. Algae
D. History

57. Water : Oxygen :: Salt : ?
A. Hydrogen B. Hydrochloric Acid
C. Sodium D. Chlorine

58. Haemoglobin : Red :: Chlorophyll : ?
A. Black B. Blue
C. Green D. Yellow

Directions (Qs. No. 59-64): *Odd one out.*

59. A. Superior B. Victory
C. Michigan D. Nile

60. A. Kiwi B. Kangaroo
C. Giant panda D. Royal bengal tiger

61. A. Pancreas B. Pituitary
C. Thalamus D. Exocrine

62. A. Temperature : Fahrenheit
B. Distance : Meter
C. Newton : Force
D. Luminous : Candela

63. A. Nebula B. Red Giant
C. Dwarf D. Planet

64. A. Hirakud B. Sutlej
C. Bhakra Nangal D. Tehri

65. Venn diagram between girl, athlete and singer?
A.  B. 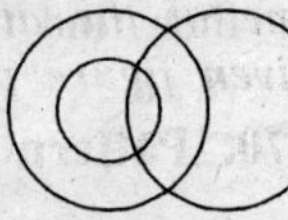
C. 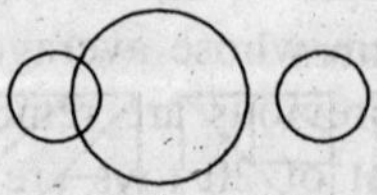 D.

66. Venn diagram instrumentalist, vionalist and musician?
A.  B. 
C. 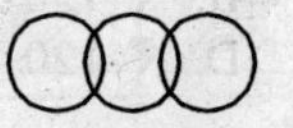 D.

67. Venn diagram between men, rodents, living beings?
A.  B. 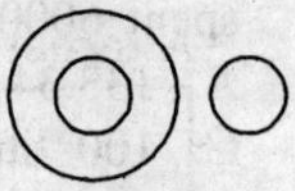
C.  D.

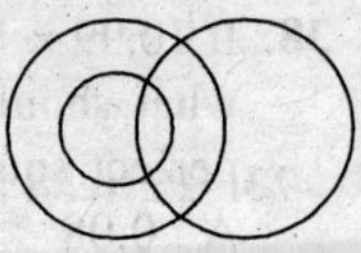

68. Venn diagram between vertebrate, non-vertebrate and turtle?
A.  B. 
C. 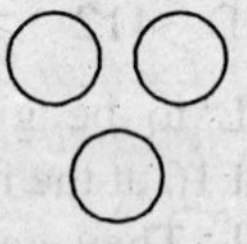 D.

69. Venn diagram between navy, commodore and captain?
A.  B. 
C. 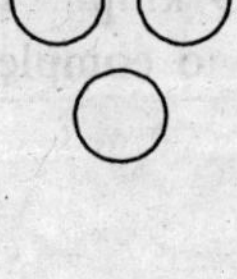 D.

Directions (Qs. 70 to 73): *In each question, which one of the alternative figures will complete the given figure pattern?*

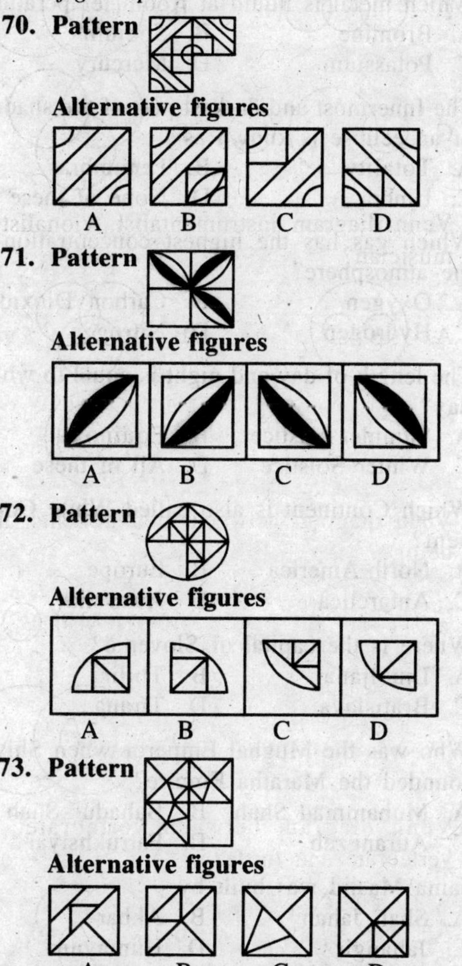

Directions (Qs. No. 74-78) : *Each of the following questions consists of five figures marked 1, 2, 3, 4 and 5 called the Problem Figures followed by four other figures marked A, B, C and D called the Answer Figures. Select a figure from amongst the Answr Figures which will continue the same series as established by the five Problem Figures.*

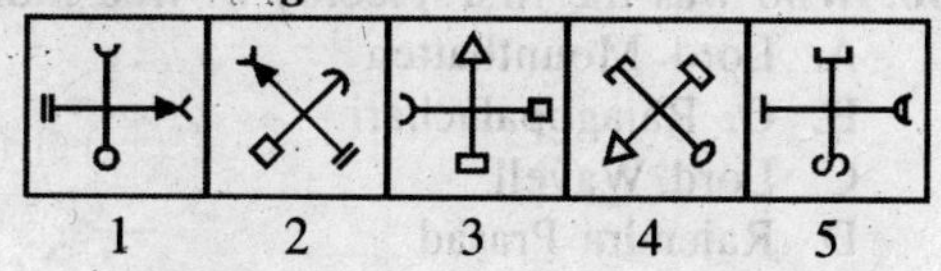

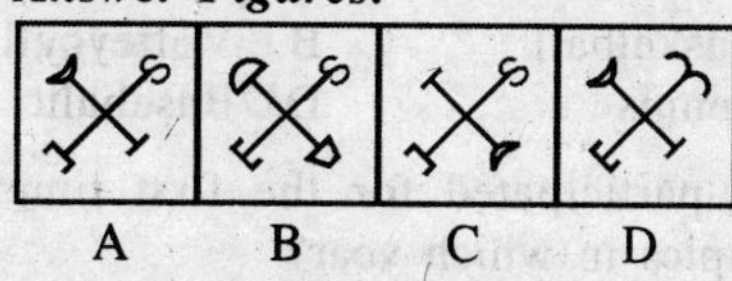

75. *Problem Figures:*

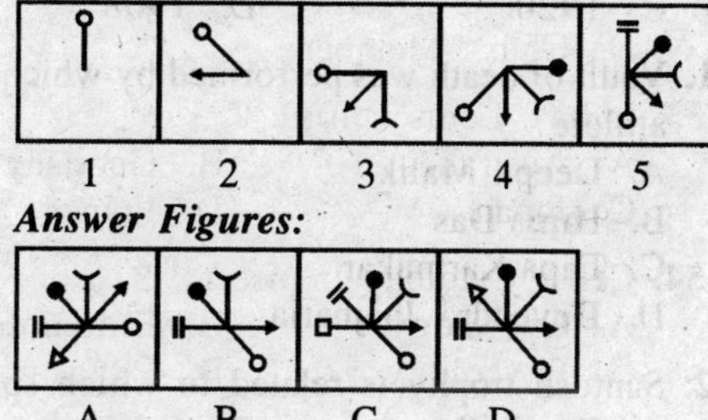

76. *Problem Figures:*

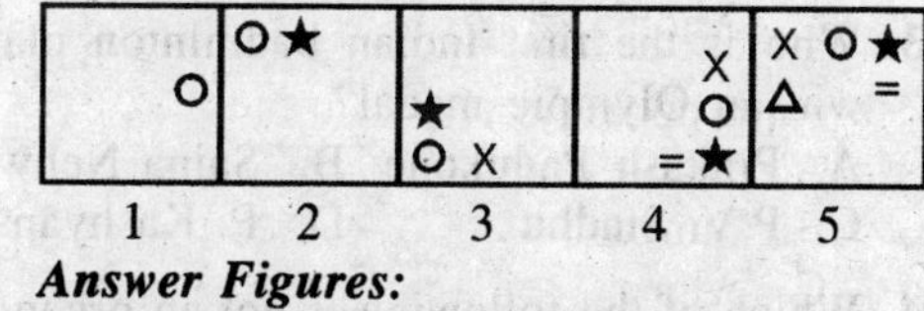

Answer Figures:

A B C D

77. *Problem Figures:*

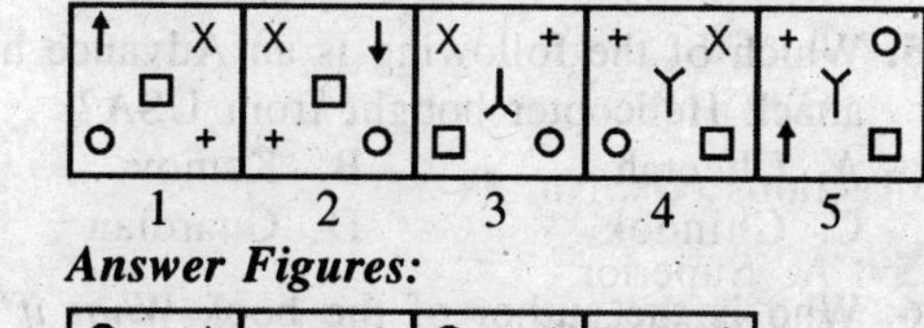

Answer Figures:

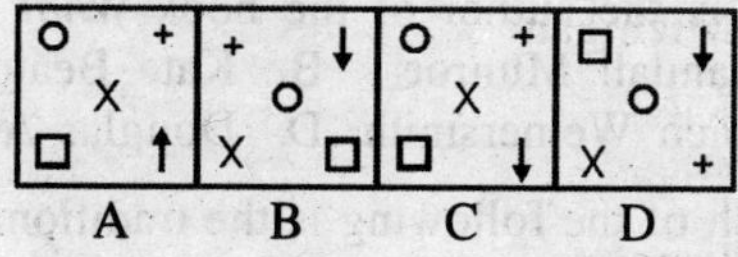

78. *Problem Figures:*

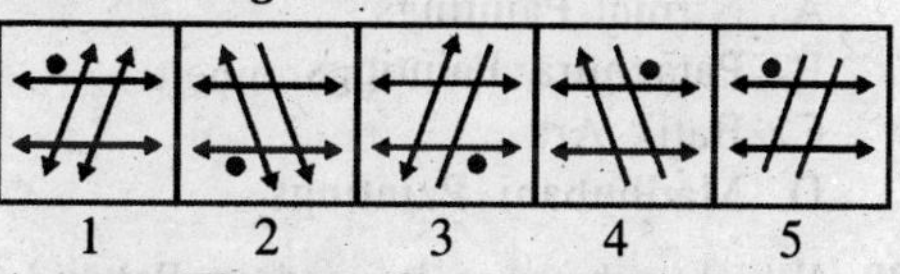

Answer Figures:

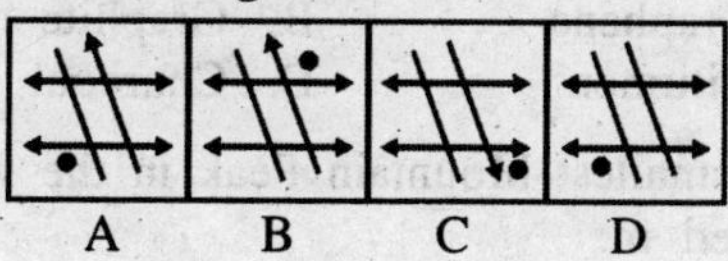

79. Joust is related to which sports?
A. Basketball B. Volleyball
C. Tennis D. Baseball

80. India participated for the first time in the Olympics in which year?
A. 1900 B. 1930
C. 1920 D. 1908

81. Vault of death was performed by which Indian athlete?
A. Deepa Malik
B. Hima Das
C. Dipa Karmakar
D. Devendra Jhajharia

82. Santosh trophy is related to which sports?
A. Football B. Cricket
C. Tennis D. Badminton

83. Who is the first Indian badminton player to win an Olympic medal?
A. Prakash Padukone B. Saina Nehwal
C. P.V. Sindhu D. P. Kashyap

84. Which of the following is not an organ of the UN?
A. ECOSOC
B. UNSC
C. General Assembly
D. Permanent Court of Justice

85. Which of the following is an Advance heavy attack Helicopter bought from USA?
A. Cheetah B. Kamov
C. Chinook D. Guardian

86. Who is the author of the book *What if*?
A. Randall Munroe B. Kate Beaton
C. Zach Weinersmith D. Douglas Adams

87. Which of the following is the traditional cloth painting in Bihar?
A. Nirmal Paintings
B. Patachitra Paintings
C. Batik Art
D. Madhubani Paintings

88. Which substance is used in Pencil?
A. Graphene B. Graphite
C. Bitumen D. Charcoal

89. The smallest Mountain Peak in the world is located in:
A. Australia B. Antarctica
C. South America D. Africa

90. Which metal is liquid at Room temperature?
A. Bromine B. Sodium
C. Potassium D. Mercury

91. The Innermost and darkest part of the shadow of an eclipse is known as:
A. Totality B. Penumbra
C. Umbra D. None of these

92. Which gas has the highest concentration in the atmosphere?
A. Oxygen B. Carbon Dioxide
C. Hydrogen D. Nitrogen

93. The length of day and night is equal to which day?
A. Summer solstice B. Equinox
C. Winter Solstice D. All of these

94. Which Continent is also called White Continent?
A. North America B. Europe
C. Antarctica D. Australia

95. Where is the capital of Slovenia?
A. Ljubljana B. Tbilisi
C. Bratislava D. Tirana

96. Who was the Mughal Emperor when Shivaji founded the Maratha Empire?
A. Muhammad Shah B. Bahadur Shah
C. Aurangzeb D. Farrukhsiyar

97. Jama Masjid was built by:
A. Shah Jahan B. Akbar
C. Jahangir D. Humayun

98. Indus Valley Civilization belongs to which age?
A. Paleolithic Age B. Bronze Age
C. Mesolithic Age D. None of the above

99. Who was the first woman CM of India?
A. Sarojini Naidu
B. Vijayalaxmi Pandit
C. Sucheta Kriplani
D. J. Jayalalitha

100. Who was the first Viceroy of free India?
A. Lord Mountbatten
B. C. Rajagopalachari
C. Lord Wavell
D. Rajendra Prasad

ANSWERS

1	2	3	4	5	6	7	8	9	10
D	B	C	D	B	D	C	A	C	A
11	**12**	**13**	**14**	**15**	**16**	**17**	**18**	**19**	**20**
B	D	D	B	D	B	A	C	A	C
21	**22**	**23**	**24**	**25**	**26**	**27**	**28**	**29**	**30**
B	A	B	C	A	B	B	A	B	B
31	**32**	**33**	**34**	**35**	**36**	**37**	**38**	**39**	**40**
C	B	B	A	B	C	C	B	B	B
41	**42**	**43**	**44**	**45**	**46**	**47**	**48**	**49**	**50**
C	B	C	A	D	A	A	B	C	C
51	**52**	**53**	**54**	**55**	**56**	**57**	**58**	**59**	**60**
C	A	D	B	A	A	C	C	D	C
61	**62**	**63**	**64**	**65**	**66**	**67**	**68**	**69**	**70**
C	C	A	B	D	D	A	D	A	C
71	**72**	**73**	**74**	**75**	**76**	**77**	**78**	**79**	**80**
B	C	B	D	C	C	C	D	B	A
81	**82**	**83**	**84**	**85**	**86**	**87**	**88**	**89**	**90**
C	A	B	D	C	A	D	B	A	D
91	**92**	**93**	**94**	**95**	**96**	**97**	**98**	**99**	**100**
C	D	B	C	A	C	A	B	C	A

EXPLANATORY ANSWERS

26. Candidate got 35% and other candidate got 65% vote.

Then, 65% of x – 35% of x = 450

Let number of voter be x

30% of x = 450

$$x = \frac{450}{30} \times 100,\ x = 1500.$$

27. Let the cost price = x

Then, marked price = $1.4x$

And selling price = $0.8 \times 1.4x = 1.12x$

Hence,

Profit = $0.12x$ and profit percentage = 12%.

28. $\sqrt{29^2 - 2 \times 200 \times 24}$

$\Rightarrow \sqrt{841 - 400 \times 24} \Rightarrow \sqrt{441} \times 24$

$\Rightarrow 21 \times 24 \Rightarrow 504.$

29. $23 \div 46 \times 7.5 + 512 - 251$

$\Rightarrow \frac{23}{46} \times 7.5 + 261 \Rightarrow 3.75 + 261 \Rightarrow 264.75.$

30. Let he deposits at $r\%$ of interest rate

Then, Interest = $\frac{8000 \times r \times 1}{100} = 80r$

He pays 10% as fee and 90% remains as ₹ 900.

$0.9 \times 80r = 900 \Rightarrow r = 12.5\%.$

31. Let after t hr policeman catches the thief. They both must have run an equal distance. So,

$(t + 2) \times 4.5 = t \times 6 \Rightarrow t = 6$ hr.

32. Let he deposits ₹ x and ₹ y in two schemes at 4% rate for 7 years and 9 years.

Then, $x + y = 3903$ ...(*i*)

And, $x\left(1 + \frac{4}{100}\right)^7 = y\left(1 + \frac{4}{100}\right)^9$

$$\frac{x}{y} = \frac{676}{625} \quad ...(ii)$$

After solving the above equations, we get $y = 1875$ and $x = 2028$.

33. Let the speed of the man is x kmph and the speed of the stream is y kmph. Then

Time, $$5 = \frac{12}{x-y} = \frac{28}{x+y}$$

Or, $x - y = 2.4$ and $x + y = 5.6$

After solving the above equations, we get the speed of the stream is 1.6 kmph.

34. Let the speed of the man is x kmph and the speed of the stream is y kmph. Then

$$10 = \frac{32}{x-y} + \frac{40}{x+y} \Rightarrow 16X + 20Y = 5 \quad ...(i)$$

$$\left[\frac{1}{x-y} = X, \frac{1}{x+y} = Y\right]$$

And,

$$12 = \frac{38}{x-y} + \frac{50}{x+y} \Rightarrow 19X + 25Y = 6 \quad ...(ii)$$

By both equations, we get

$$X = \frac{1}{x-y} = \frac{1}{4} \Rightarrow x - y = 4$$

And, $$Y = \frac{1}{x+y} = \frac{1}{20} \Rightarrow x + y = 20$$

After solving, we get the speed of the stream is 8 kmph.

36. Let the cost price $= x$

Then, the selling price $= 1.4x$

New cost price $= x + 50$

New selling price $= 1.4x + 20$

Now profit,

$$\frac{(1.4x+20)-(x+50)}{x+50} = 20\%$$

$$\frac{0.4x-30}{x+50} = \frac{1}{5}$$

$$2x - 150 = x + 50$$

$$x = 200.$$

37. Quantity of petrol he bought in first year

$$= \frac{6000}{45} l = 133.33 l$$

Quantity of petrol he bought in second year

$$= \frac{6000}{60} l = 100 l$$

Quantity of petrol he bought in third year

$$= \frac{6000}{90} l = 66.67 l$$

So average $= \frac{133.33+100+66.67}{3} = 100\ l.$

38. $\Rightarrow 10.99 \times 10.99 + 10.99 \times x + 0.03 \times 0.03$

$$\Rightarrow (10.99)^2 + (0.03)^2 + 2(10.99)\left(\frac{x}{2}\right)$$

For this to be a perfect square

$$\frac{x}{2} = 0.03 \Rightarrow x = 0.06.$$

39. Given that $\frac{28016}{412} = 68$

Dividing both side by 1000,

$$\frac{28016}{412\times1000} = \frac{68}{1000}$$

$$\frac{28.016}{412} = \frac{0.68}{10}$$

$$\frac{28.016}{0.68} = \frac{412}{10} = 41.2.$$

40. Total amount = 35 L

Let he gives to younger and elder daughter of amount are x and y. They take 8 years and 5 years to be 21. The rate of interest is 10%, then

$$x\left(1+\frac{10}{100}\right)^8 = y\left(1+\frac{10}{100}\right)^5$$

$$\frac{x}{y} = \left(\frac{10}{11}\right)^3$$

$$\frac{y}{x} = \frac{1331}{1000}$$

As $x + y = 35$ L, then $x = 15$ L and 20 L.

41. The perimeter of the track $= 4 \times 35 = 140$ m

Speed of the man $= 9$ kmph $= 2.5$ mps

Total time is taken by him to complete around

$$= \frac{140}{2.5} = 56 \text{ sec.}$$

Previous Paper (Solved)

Air Force Common Admission Test (AFCAT)—1/2020*

1. Select the synonym of "Cajole":

A. bash B. bully
C. wheedle D. decline

2. Select the synonym of "Baulk":

A. accept B. pursue
C. eschew D. increase

3. Select the synonym of "Parochial":

A. conservative B. tremendous
C. liberal D. cosmopolitan

4. Select the synonym of "Jibe":

A. sneer B. flatter
C. blarney D. request

5. Select the antonym of "Naive":

A. sophisticated B. artless
C. credulous D. callow

6. Select the antonym of "Sporadic":

A. random B. erratic
C. steady D. uneven

7. Select the antonym of "Dodge":

A. avoidance B. clear
C. evade D. confront

8. Select the antonym of "Enjoin":

A. direct B. counsel
C. forbid D. none of these

9. In the question, four words are given, out of which only one word is correctly spelt. Find the correctly spelt word.

A. Locuacious B. Lokuacious
C. Locvacious D. Loquacious

10. In the question, four words are given, out of which only one word is correctly spelt. Find the correctly spelt word.

A. Impugn B. Impagn
C. Impegn D. Impeign

Directions (Qs. No. 11-14): *In these questions, four alternatives are given for the idiom/phrase given in bold. Choose the alternative which best expresses the meaning of the idiom/ phrase given in bold.*

11. At close quarters:

A. From a very short distance
B. To miss a big opportunity
C. To argue with someone
D. To fight over a trivial issue

12. Bring to book:

A. To gift a book to someone
B. To keep an account of all the expenses
C. To demand an explanation from
D. To read a book enthusiastically

13. Blaze the trail:

A. To erase the evidences
B. To start a movement
C. To put something on fire
D. To win a case in the court

14. Hit below the belt:

A. To do something thoroughly
B. To strike unfairly
C. To end up in an awkward situation
D. To let someone commit mistakes

Directions (Qs. No. 15-17): *In the following questions, out of the four alternatives choose the one which can be substituted for the given words/ sentence.*

15. To delay or prevent someone or something by obstructing them:

A. to perturb B. to impede
C. to irk D. to faze

* Based on memory.

16. A period of time during which a person that might have a disease is kept away from other people so that the disease cannot spread:

A. solitude B. seclusion
C. quarantine D. desolate

17. A heavy blow or the sound of such a blow.

A. lop B. slop
C. flop D. whop

Directions (Qs. No. 18 & 19): *In the following question, a sentence has been given in Active/ Passive voice. Out of four alternatives suggested, select the one, which best expresses the same sentence in Passive/Active voice.*

18. He gave me spectacles.

A. Spectacle was given to me.
B. Spectacles were given to me by him.
C. I was offered spectacles.
D. He had given me spectacles.

19. His sudden arrival surprised everyone.

A. Everyone became surprised by his sudden arrival.
B. Everybody is surprised by his sudden arrival.
C. Everyone was surprised at his sudden arrival.
D. Everyone were surprised at his sudden arrival.

Directions (Qs. No. 20-22): *In the following passage some of the words have been left out. Read the passage carefully and choose the correct answer for the given blank out of the four alternatives.*

In a recent ____20____, the Madras High Court ruled that courts should not be influenced by ____21____ that children are likely to lie in cases of sexual abuse or that they are tutored by parents to make false statements in court. While these observations are welcome, the attitude of the defence lawyer in this case was seriously _____22_______.

20. In a recent ____20____, the Madras High Court ruled.

A. report
B. promotion
C. judgement
D. notice

21. Courts should not be influenced by ____21____.

A. misconceptions B. facts
C. theories D. None of these

22. While these observations are welcome, the attitude of the defence lawyer in this case was seriously _______22_________.

A. supplied B. problematic
C. minute D. edible

Directions (Qs. No. 23-25): *Read the passage carefully and choose the best answer to each question out of the four alternatives.*

Facing a shortfall of 2,277 doctors, Uttar Pradesh's primary health centres (PHCs) have the worst patient-doctor ratio. With 942 of these centres working without electricity, regular water supply or all-weather motorable approach roads, the State's PHCs has the worst infrastructure in the country.

The States that have shown poor PHC ratings include Chhattisgarh, Odisha, Karnataka and Bihar, show the Rural Health Statistics, 2018, quoted by the Ministry.

The data note that while Uttar Pradesh requires 3,621 doctors for its PHCs, the backbone of health delivery, it has only 1,344 doctors, showing a deficit of 2,277. Though the sanctioned strength is 4,509, there are 3,165 vacancies.

The State also has the worst infrastructure with 213 centres without electricity supply, 270 without regular water supply and 459 without all-weather motorable approach roads. The States that have poor infrastructure based on the same parameters include Jammu and Kashmir, Chhattisgarh, Odisha, Assam and Uttarakhand.

In its reply, the Ministry noted that public health and hospitals being a State subject, all administrative and personnel matters, including recruitment of doctors at the PHCs, lie with the State governments. The shortage of doctors in public health facilities varies from State to State, depending on their policies and context.

23. Which state's primary health centres (PHCs) have the worst patient-doctor ratio?

A. Chhattisgarh B. Uttar Pradesh
C. Odisha D. Bihar

24. Which among the following parameters is not used to rate the States that have poor infrastructure?
A. Regular water supply
B. Electricity supply
C. Medicine supply
D. All-weather motorable roads

25. How many doctors do Uttar Pradesh's primary health centres have?
A. 1344 B. 3621
C. 4509 D. 2277

26. Where is headquarter of International Civil Aviation Council is located?
A. Montreal B. Paris
C. New York D. Washington D.C.

27. How many players are there in Kabaddi team?
A. 7 B. 5
C. 12 D. 10

28. With which among the following sports the "C.K Nayudu Trophy" is associated?
A. Basketball B. Cricket
C. Hockey D. Badminton

29. Which among the following city of India hosted first Asian games held in India?
A. Bengaluru B. Hyderabad
C. Kolkata D. New Delhi

30. Under which Delhi sultanate ruler, the territorial expansion was maximum in India?
A. Alauddin Khilji
B. Balban
C. Muhammad bin Tughlaq
D. Ghiyasuddin Tughlaq

31. Which among the following is the 25th state of India?
A. Goa
B. Mizoram
C. Nagaland
D. Arunachal Pradesh

32. Who was the first sultan of Delhi to issue coins in Delhi sultanate?
A. Iltutmish
B. Qutb al-Din Aibak
C. Alauddin Khalji
D. Firoz Shah Tughlaq

33. With which among the following sports the term "half nelson" is associated?
A. Basketball B. Polo
C. Wrestling D. Rugby

34. Which among the following is the capital of Brunei?
A. Manila
B. Hanoi
C. Phnom Penh
D. Bandar Seri Begawan

35. Which among the following gas is used in the soda?
A. Carbon dioxide
B. Nitrogen
C. Hydrogen
D. Sulphur dioxide

36. Who among the following is the author of "One Indian Girl"?
A. Durjoy Dutta B. Chetan Bhagat
C. Ravinder Singh D. Amit Nangia

37. Who among the following has built the Sanchi Stupa?
A. Ashoka B. Rudradaman
C. Amoghavarsha D. Krishnadevaraj

38. Who among the following presided Haripura session of Indian National Congress in 1938?
A. Mahatma Gandhi
B. Subhash Chandra Bose
C. Jawaharlal Nehru
D. Rajendra Prasad

39. Which among the following the launch date of "Apple Satellite"?
A. 19 May 1981 B. 19 June 1983
C. 19 June 1981 D. 19 May 1983

40. Which among the following is the southernmost point of Indian territory?
A. Kanyakumari B. Indira Point
C. Kalapani D. Port Blair

41. Which among the following country is not the part of G-7 countries?
A. Canada B. Japan
C. Germany D. Russia

42. Which among the following is also known as silent killer gas?
A. Carbon Monoxide
B. Sulphur Dioxide
C. Nitrogen Dioxide
D. Nitrous Oxide

43. With which among the following sports the name of "Yasin Merchant" is related?
A. Wrestling B. Snooker
C. Table Tennis D. Polo

44. Which latitude is also known as greater circle?
A. Tropic of Cancer
B. Tropic of Capricorn
C. Equator
D. Arctic Circle

45. Who was the first cricketer to take hat trick in the test cricket?
A. Fred Spofforth B. Bapu Nadkarni
C. Sir Ian Botham D. Wally Hammond

46. With which among the following dance the name "Sanjukta Panigrahi" is related?
A. Kathak B. Kathakali
C. Bharatnatyam D. Odissi

47. Which Gupta ruler was also known for playing veena?
A. Chandragupta-II B. Samudragupta
C. Kumaragupta D. Skandagupta

48. Which among the following rivers fall in the Arabian sea?
A. Narmada B. Luni
C. Mahanadi D. Godavari

49. Bombay High famous for ________.
A. mining B. petroleum
C. uranium reserve D. gold

50. Who was the last ruler of Mughal dynasty?
A. Farrukhsiyar
B. Bahadur Shah Zafar
C. Akbar II
D. Shah Alam II

51. With which among the following games "Durand Cup" is associated?
A. Football B. Cricket
C. Lawn Tennis D. Badminton

52. Where is Indian Military Academy is located?
A. Dehradun B. Shimla
C. Hyderabad D. Gaya

53. Rangaswami Cup is associated with:
A. Wrestling B. Football
C. Hockey D. Golf

54. Fundamental Rights of constitution is taken from which country?
A. UK B. USA
C. Australia D. USSR

55. "Joule" is the unit of ________.
A. Power B. Voltage
C. Energy D. Current

56. A can do a work in 10 days. A work for 4 days and B finished the remaining work in 9 days. Together they will finish the work in how many days?
A. 12 B. 6
C. 8 D. 10

57. P & Q completes the work in 10 days, Q & R in 15 days and R & P in 20 days. Find individual time taken by them.
A. 12, 14, 72 B. 120, 24, 100
C. 120, $17\frac{1}{7}$, 24 D. 15, 13011, 14

58. Two trains start from Pune to Goa towards each other at speed of 50 km/hr and 40 km/hr respectively at same time. Find at what distance they will meet from Pune if the total distance between Pune and Goa is 600 km.
A. $\frac{1000}{3}$ km B. $\frac{800}{3}$ km
C. $\frac{700}{3}$ km D. 340 km

59. The length of Head of a fish is 12 cm. The length of Tail is equal to Head's length and 13rd of body length. Find the length of Body if length of Body = Length of Head + Length of Tail.
A. 24 cm B. 36 cm
C. 25 cm D. 20 cm

60. Two bikes ride in opposite directions around a circular track, starting at the same time from the same point. Biker A rides at a speed of 16 km/hr and the biker B rides at a speed of 14 km/hr. If the track has a diameter of 30 km, after how much time (in hours) will the two bikers meet?

A. 3.14 hr B. 12 hr
C. 4.5 hr D. 2.25 hr

61. A person spend 20% on food, 20% of the remaining on charity and 20% of the remaining on house and left with ₹ 576. Find the original amount he had?

A. ₹ 1100 B. ₹ 1125
C. ₹ 1200 D. ₹ 1340

62. Two man rows boat at speed of 5 km/hr and 10 km/hr toward each other and at a distance of 20 km. Find how far apart in km all they 1 minute before they collide.

A. 250 m B. 120 m
C. 240 m D. 380 m

63. A man buys 4 pizza and 3 burger for ₹ 4500 and 4 pizza and 6 burger for ₹ 6000 find how much should he pay to buy 1 pizza and 2 burger?

A. ₹ 2300 B. ₹ 2200
C. ₹ 1750 D. ₹ 2350

64. A man buys two article of ₹ 560. He sells on at 10% per cent loss and other at 15 percent profit and had no profit no loss. Find cost price of each article

A. 280, 280 B. 330, 230
C. 336, 224 D. None of the above

65. Divide ₹ 6000 into two parts so that simple interest on first part for 2 year at 6% p.a. may be equal the simple interest on the second part for 3 year at 8% p.a.

A. 2500, 3500 B. 4000, 2000
C. 3000, 3000 D. 2200, 3800

66. A cyclist starts at a speed of 8 km/hr and second cyclist start after 2 hours at speed of 12 km/hr. Find how much distance will the second cyclist travel?

A. 48 km B. 44 km
C. 36 km D. 51 km

67. There are total five numbers. The average of first four numbers is 26 and average of last four numbers is 25. Find the average of difference of first and last number.

A. 4 B. 6
C. 2 D. 2.5

68. India borrowed a loan from IMF at the rates of 6 per cent for first five year, 8 per cent for next five year and 10 per cent for beyond 5 years. If at the end of fifteen years the total amount paid was 144 billion U.S. dollars. Find the amount borrowed in billion U.S dollars?

A. 48 B. 58.75
C. 75 D. 65.45

69. The average of father and his twin son is 28. Find the age of father if the ratio of age of father and one son is 8 : 3.

A. 36 years B. 37.5 years
C. 48 years D. 40 years

70. A purchased a toy in ₹ 2400. He paid ₹ 1000 in cash and remaining in two equal installments of ₹ 840 each per month. Find out the rate of interest for each installment.

A. 10% B. 20%
C. 25% D. 12.5%

71. A man completes a certain journey by car. If he covered 30% of the distance at the speed of 20 km/hr. 60% of the distance at 40 km/hr and the remaining distance at 10 km/hr. His average speed is:

A. 35 B. 22
C. 30 D. 25

72. There are X pens in the shop. If person A buys 20% and person B buys 15% from the remaining and C buys 10% of the remaining pens then he is left with 612 pens. Then how much pen was there initially?

A. 1280 B. 870
C. 1000 D. 930

73. If length of a rectangle is increased by 15% and breadth is decreased by 10%. What will be impact on perimeter?

A. $\frac{20}{3}$ % B. 7.5%
C. 12% D. 6%

74. Seismology : Study of Earthquake : : Penology : ?
A. Study of Pen
B. Study of Punishment of Crime
C. Study of Stationery
D. Study of Exo-planets

75. Coal : Thermal Energy : : Water : ?
A. Hygro Energy B. Water Energy
C. Hematology D. Hydro Energy

76. One who collects coins : Numismatic : : One who collects postage stamps : ?
A. Philatelist B. Bibliophile
C. Canophilia D. Astrogeology

77. Energy : Joule : : Current : ?
A. Ohm B. Watt
C. Kelvin D. Ampere

78. Engineer : Machine : : Doctor : ?
A. Diseases B. Hospital
C. Patient D. Nurse

79. Find the odd-one out from:
A. Khora B. Khasi
C. Garo D. Mizo

80. Which of the following does not belong to North America?
A. Mexico B. Cuba
C. Morocco D. Honduras

81. Mallet : Polo : : Break out : ?
A. Football B. Hockey
C. Cricket D. Rugby

82. Vijay Hazare Trophy : Cricket : : Durand Cup : ?
A. Football B. Hockey
C. Kho-Kho D. Kabaddi

83. USA : Dollar : : Chile : ?
A. Pound B. Euro
C. Yuan D. Peso

84. France : Paris : : Ghana : ?
A. Maputo B. Windhoek
C. Accra D. Kampala

85. Find the odd-one out from.
A. Colonel B. Commodore
C. Major D. Brigadier

86. MJS : PLT : : NKW : ?
A. QMX B. QNK
C. WQM D. QNM

87. Which of the following represents: Earth, Sun, Moon?
A.  B. 
C. 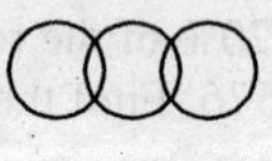 D.

88. Which of the following represents: Men, Indian, Black hair?
A.  B. 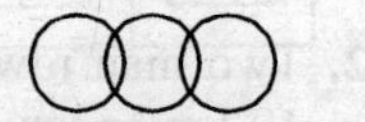
C.  D.

89. OPEN : NEOP : : TAPE : ?
A. EPTA B. PETA
C. EPAT D. PEAT

90. Which of the following represents: warm blooded animals, cold blooded animals, mammals?
A.  B. 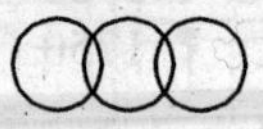
C.  D.

91. 6, 11, 21, 36, ?
A. 51 B. 41
C. 56 D. 46

Directions (Qs. No. 92-94): *In each question, which one of the alternative figures will complete the given figure pattern?*

92. Pattern

Alternative figures

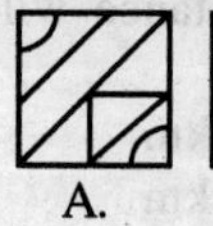

A. B. C. D.

93. Pattern

Alternative figures

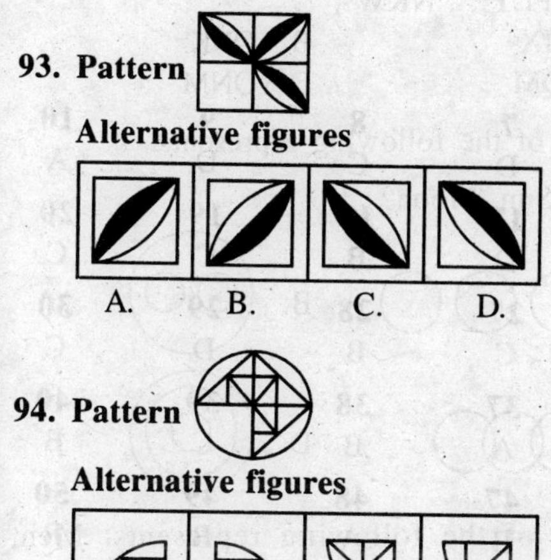

A. B. C. D.

94. Pattern

Alternative figures

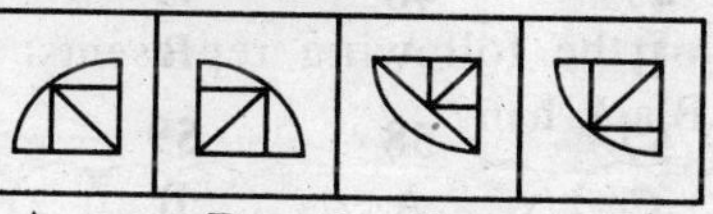

A. B. C. D.

Directions (Qs. No. 95 & 96): *In the questions given below a figure is given. From the given alternatives select the one in which the given figure is embedded.*

95.

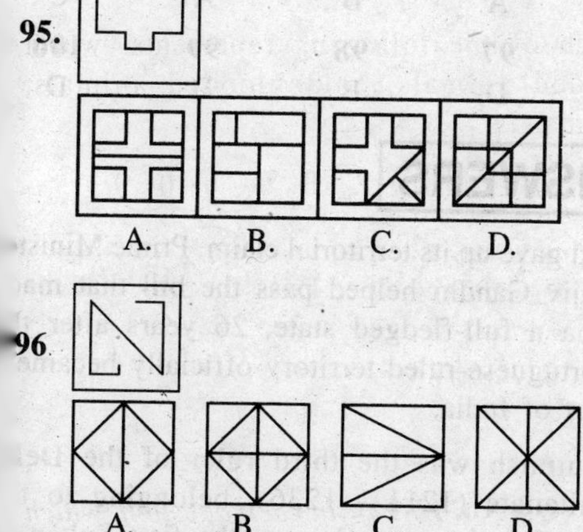

A. B. C. D.

96.

A. B. C. D.

Directions (Qs. No. 97 & 98): *In each question given below which one would be the mirror image of the given figure when the mirror is placed along the line shown in each figure.*

97. Problem Figure

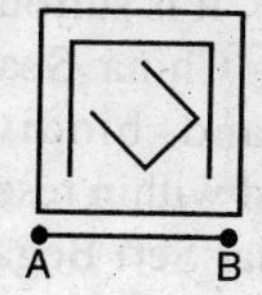

Answer Figures

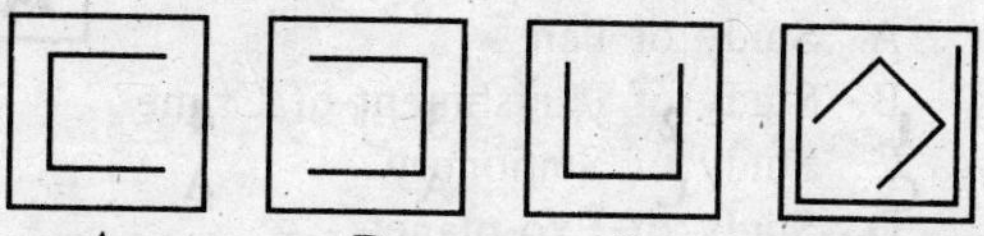

A. B. C. D.

98. Problem Figure

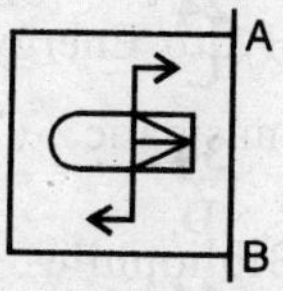

A

B

Answer Figures

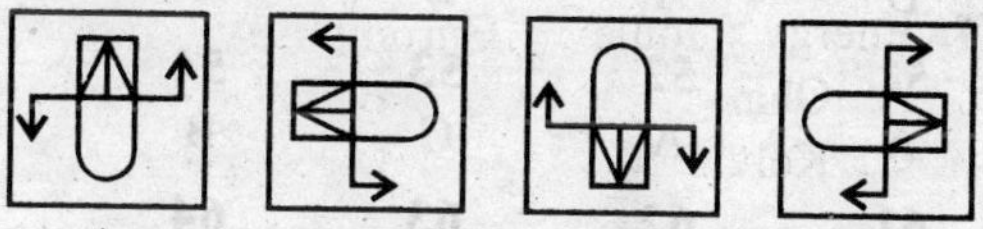

A. B. C. D.

Directions (Qs. No. 99 & 100): *The second figure in the first unit of the Problem Figures bears a certain relationship to the first figure. Similarly, one of the figures in the Answer Figures bears the same relationship to the first figure in the second unit of the Problem Figures. Locate the figure which would fit the question mark.*

99. Problem Figures

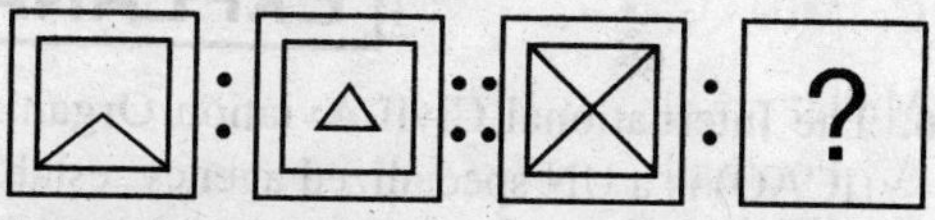

: :: : ?

Answers Figures

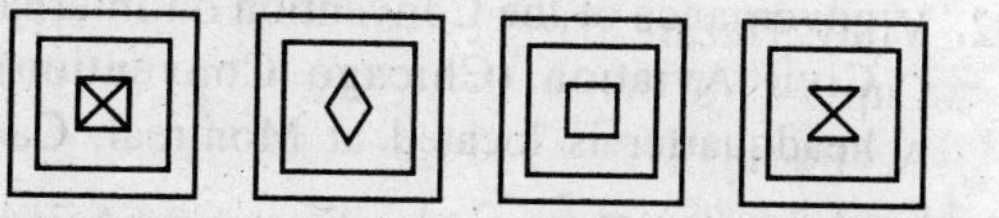

A. B. C. D.

100. Problem Figures

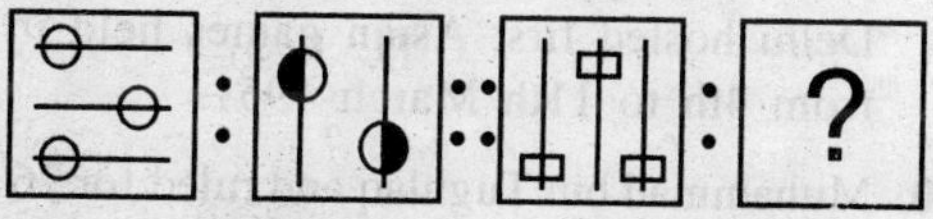

: :: : ?

Answer Figures

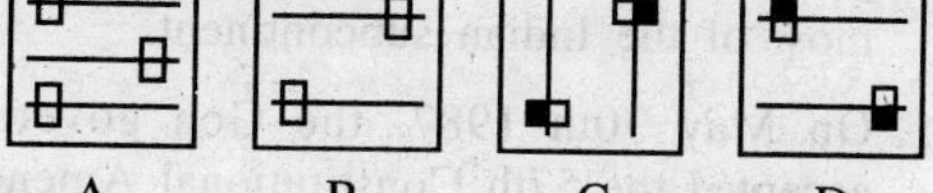

A. B. C. D.

ANSWERS

1	2	3	4	5	6	7	8	9	10
C	C	A	A	A	C	D	C	D	A
11	**12**	**13**	**14**	**15**	**16**	**17**	**18**	**19**	**20**
A	C	B	B	B	C	D	B	C	C
21	**22**	**23**	**24**	**25**	**26**	**27**	**28**	**29**	**30**
A	B	B	C	A	A	C	B	D	C
31	**32**	**33**	**34**	**35**	**36**	**37**	**38**	**39**	**40**
A	A	C	D	A	B	A	B	C	B
41	**42**	**43**	**44**	**45**	**46**	**47**	**48**	**49**	**50**
D	A	B	C	A	D	B	A	B	B
51	**52**	**53**	**54**	**55**	**56**	**57**	**58**	**59**	**60**
A	A	C	B	C	B	C	A	B	A
61	**62**	**63**	**64**	**65**	**66**	**67**	**68**	**69**	**70**
B	A	C	C	B	A	C	D	C	A
71	**72**	**73**	**74**	**75**	**76**	**77**	**78**	**79**	**80**
D	C	A	B	D	A	D	A	A	C
81	**82**	**83**	**84**	**85**	**86**	**87**	**88**	**89**	**90**
B	A	D	C	B	A	A	B	A	C
91	**92**	**93**	**94**	**95**	**96**	**97**	**98**	**99**	**100**
C	C	B	C	A	D	D	B	D	D

EXPLANATORY ANSWERS

26. The International Civil Aviation Organization (ICAO) is a UN specialized agency, established in 1944 to manage the administration and governance of the Convention on International Civil Aviation (Chicago Convention). It's headquarter is located at Montreal, Canada.

29. The Asian Games, also known as Asiad, is a continental multi-sport event held every four years among athletes from all over Asia. New Delhi hosted first Asian games held in India from 4th to 11th March 1951.

30. Muhammad bin Tughlaq and ruled for 26 years. During his rule, Delhi Sultanate reached its peak in terms of geographical reach, covering most of the Indian subcontinent.

31. On May 30th 1987, the Goa government accepted the 57th Constitutional Amendment and gave up its territorial claim. Prime Minist Rajiv Gandhi helped pass the bill that mac Goa a full-fledged state, 26 years after th Portuguese-ruled territory officially became part of India.

32. Iltutmish was the third ruler of the Del Sultanate (1211 - 1236), belonging to t Mamluk dynasty. He was the first Sultan Delhi to issue regular currency and decla Delhi as the capital of his empire in place Lahore. He introduced the silver coin (tank and copper coin (jital).

34. Brunei, a south east Asian country is a ti nation on the island of Borneo. It is surrounc by Malaysia and the South China Sea. known for its beaches and biodive rainforest, much of it protected within reserv The capital of Brunei is Bandar Seri Begaw

35. Carbon dioxide is used in the soda. It comes in the form of the fizz that bubbles up when a can of soda is opened. It is added because dissolved carbon dioxide is carbonic acid, which adds a pleasantly acidic flavour and an interesting mouth-feel. When it's not present, the drink tastes flat.

37. Sanchi Stupa is a memorial built in the city of Sanchi, Madhya Pradesh. It is located 46 km from Bhopal. It is one of the oldest stone structures in India, and an important monument of Indian architecture. It was originally commissioned by the emperor Ashoka in the 3rd century BCE. He commissioned the inception of Stupas to redistribute the mortal remains of Lord Buddha.

39. The Ariane Passenger PayLoad Experiment (APPLE), was an experimental communication satellite with a C-Band transponder launched by the Indian Space Research Organisation on June 19, 1981 by Ariane, a launch vehicle of the European Space Agency (ESA) from Centre Spatial Guyanais near Kourou in French Guiana.

41. The Group of Seven (G7) is an international intergovernmental economic organization consisting of the seven IMF—advanced economies in the world: Canada, France, Germany, Italy, Japan, the United Kingdom and the United States. Hence, Russia is not the part of G-7 countries.

42. Carbon monoxide (CO) is a gas that can kill a person quickly. It is called the "silent killer" because it is colourless, odourless, tasteless and non-irritating. If the early signs of CO poisoning are ignored, a person may lose consciousness and be unable to escape the danger.

44. The equator is the circle that is equidistant from the North Pole and South Pole. It divides the Earth into the Northern Hemisphere and the Southern Hemisphere. Of the parallels or circles of latitude, it is the longest, and the only 'great circle' (a circle on the surface of the Earth, centered on Earth's center).

46. Sanjukta Panigrahi was a dancer from India, who was the foremost exponent of Indian classical dance Odissi. Sanjukta was the first Odia woman to embrace this ancient classical dance at an early age and ensure its grand revival.

47. Samudragupta, the second emperor of the Gupta dynasty, is known to one of India's best rulers. His brilliant leadership and valiant victories earned him the title of 'Napoleon of India'. He was a great musician and played the veena, an Indian stringed instrument resembling the lyre or lute, with great aplomb. He was also a highly intellectual person and an accomplished poet.

48. Narmada rises from Amarkantak Plateau near Anuppur district. It forms the traditional boundary between North India and South India and flows westwards before draining through the Gulf of Khambhat into the Arabian Sea.

50. Bahadur Shah Zafar was the last Mughal emperor. He became the successor to his father, Akbar II on 28th September 1837. Following his involvement in the Indian Rebellion of 1857, the British exiled him to Rangoon in British-controlled Burma (now in Myanmar), after convicting him on several charges.

51. The Durand Football Tournament or Durand Cup is a football competition in India which was first held in 1888 in Annadale, Shimla. It is co-hosted by the Durand Football Tournament Society (DFTS) and Osians. The Tournament is the oldest football tournament in Asia and one of the oldest in the world.

53. Rangaswamy Cup is associated with hockey. Introduced in 1928, the Rangaswami Cup, was originally known as Inter-Provincial Tournament meant to pick up players for the national team for the Olympics.

54. The constitution of India borrowed the concept of Fundamental Rights from USA. Other features borrowed from USA constitution are independence of judiciary, judicial review, impeachment of the president, removal of Supreme Court and high court judges and post of Vice President.

56. A's 1 day's work = $\frac{1}{10}$

$\therefore$ A's 4 day's work = $\frac{4}{10} = \frac{2}{5}$

Remaining work = $1 - \frac{2}{5} = \frac{3}{5}$

B's 9 day's work = $\frac{3}{5}$

$\therefore$ B's 1 day's work = $\frac{3}{5 \times 9} = \frac{1}{15}$

$\therefore$ (A + B)'s 1 day's work = $\frac{1}{10} + \frac{1}{15} = \frac{3+2}{30}$

$= \frac{5}{30} = \frac{1}{6}$

Hence, together they will finish the work in 6 days.

57. (P + Q)'s 1 day's work = $\frac{1}{10}$

(Q + R)'s 1 day's work = $\frac{1}{15}$

and, (R + P)'s 1 day's work = $\frac{1}{20}$

Adding, we get, 2(P + Q + R)'s 1 day's work

$= \frac{1}{10} + \frac{1}{15} + \frac{1}{20} = \frac{6+4+3}{60} = \frac{13}{60}$

(P + Q + R)'s 1 day's work = $\frac{13}{120}$

P's 1 day's work = $\frac{13}{120} - \frac{1}{15} = \frac{13-8}{120}$

$= \frac{5}{120} = \frac{1}{24}$

P's time = 24 days

Q's 1 day's work = $\frac{13}{120} - \frac{1}{20} = \frac{13-6}{120} = \frac{7}{120}$

Q's time = $\frac{120}{7} = 17\frac{1}{7}$ days

R's 1 day's work = $\frac{13}{120} - \frac{1}{10} = \frac{13-12}{120} = \frac{1}{120}$

R's time = 120 days.

58. Here, distance = 600 km

Relative speed = 50 + 40 = 90 km/hr

$\therefore$ Time = $\frac{\text{Distance}}{\text{Speed}} = \frac{600}{90} = \frac{20}{3}$ hour

Hence, they will meet after $\frac{20}{3}$ hour

Distance they will meet from Pune

$= 50 \times \frac{20}{3} = \frac{1000}{3}$ km.

59. Here, length of Head = 12 cm

T = H + $\frac{1}{3}$ of B

Given, B = H + T

$\therefore$ B = H + H + $\frac{1}{3}$B

$\Rightarrow$ $B - \frac{1}{3}B = 2H \Rightarrow \frac{2}{3}B = 2 \times 12$

$\Rightarrow$ $B = 24 \times \frac{3}{2} = 36$ cm

Hence, the length of body = 36 cm.

60. Given, Diameter of the track = 30 km

$\Rightarrow$ $2r = 30$ km

Distance of the track = $2\pi r = 30\pi$ km

Relative speed = 16 + 14 = 30 m

Time = $\frac{\text{Distance}}{\text{Speed}} = \frac{30\pi}{30}$

= π hours = 3.14 hours

Hence, the two bikers meet after 3.14 hours.

61. Let the original amount = ₹ x

Then, $x \times \frac{100-20}{100} \times \frac{100-20}{100} \times \frac{100-20}{100} = 576$

$\Rightarrow x \times \frac{80}{100} \times \frac{80}{100} \times \frac{80}{100} = 576$

$\Rightarrow x \times \frac{4}{5} \times \frac{4}{5} \times \frac{4}{5} = 576$

$\Rightarrow x = \frac{576 \times 125}{64}$

= 9 × 125 = ₹ 1125.

62. Distance = 5 + 10 = 15 km

$= 15 \times \frac{5}{18} \times 60$ meter = 250 m.

63. Let 1 Pizza = x and 1 burger = y

Then, $4x + 3y =$ ₹ 4500 ...(*i*)

and $4x + 6y =$ ₹ 6000

$\Rightarrow$ $2x + 3y =$ ₹ 3000 ...(*ii*)

From (*i*) – (*ii*), we get,

$2x = 1500$

or, $x =$ ₹ 750

From (*ii*), $3y = 3000 - 1500 = 1500$

or, $y =$ ₹ 500

$\therefore$ 1 Pizza + 2 burger = $x + 2y$

= 750 + 1000 = ₹ 1750.

64. Let C.P. of one article = ₹ x

then, C.P. of other article = ₹ $(560 - x)$

According to question,

$$x \times \frac{100-10}{100} + (560-x) \times \frac{100+15}{100} = 560$$

$$\Rightarrow \quad x \times \frac{9}{10} + (560-x) \times \frac{23}{20} = 560$$

$$\Rightarrow \quad \frac{9x}{10} + 28 \times 23 - \frac{23x}{20} = 560$$

$$\Rightarrow \quad \frac{9x}{10} - \frac{23x}{20} = 560 - 644$$

$$\Rightarrow \quad \frac{18x - 23x}{20} = -84$$

$$\Rightarrow \quad -5x = -84 \times 20$$

$$\Rightarrow \quad x = \frac{84 \times 20}{5} = 84 \times 4$$

$\Rightarrow$ $x =$ ₹ 336

and $(560 - x) = 560 - 336 =$ ₹ 224

Hence, cost price of each article are ₹ 336 and ₹ 224.

65. Let first part = ₹ x

Then, second part = ₹ $(6000 - x)$

$$\therefore \quad \frac{x \times 2 \times 6}{100} = \frac{(6000-x) \times 3 \times 8}{100}$$

$$\Rightarrow \quad 12x = 6000 \times 24 - 24x$$

$$\Rightarrow \quad 12x + 24x = 144000$$

$$\Rightarrow \quad 36x = 144000$$

$$\Rightarrow \quad x = \frac{144000}{36} = 4000$$

$\Rightarrow$ $x =$ ₹ 4000

and ₹ $(600 - x) = 6000 - 4000 =$ ₹ 2000.

66. Distance travelled in 2 hours by first cyclist

= 2 × 8 = 16 km

Distance travelled in 6 hours

= 6 × 8 = 48 km

Distance travelled in 4 hours by second cyclist

= 4 × 12 = 48

Hence, Distance travelled by second cyclist

= 48 km.

67. The sum of first four numbers

= 4 × 26 = 104

and the sum of last four numbers

= 4 × 25 = 100

The average of difference of first and last number

$$= \frac{104-100}{2} = \frac{4}{2} = 2.$$

68. $$\frac{P \times 6 \times 5}{100} + \frac{P \times 8 \times 5}{100} + \frac{P \times 10 \times 5}{100} + P = 144$$

$$\Rightarrow \quad \frac{30P}{100} + \frac{40P}{100} + \frac{50P}{100} + P = 144$$

$$\Rightarrow \quad \frac{120P}{100} + P = 144$$

$$\Rightarrow \quad \frac{120P + 100P}{100} = 144$$

$$\Rightarrow \quad 220P = 144 \times 100$$

$$\Rightarrow \quad P = \frac{14400}{220} = 65.45$$

Hence, the amount borrowed in billion U.S. dollars = 65.45.

69. Let the present age of the father and the son be x and y years respectively.

Then, $x + y + y = 28 \times 3$

$\Rightarrow$ $x + 2y = 84$ ...(*i*)

Given, $\frac{x}{y} = \frac{8}{3} \Rightarrow y = \frac{3x}{8}$ ...(*ii*)

From (*i*) and (*ii*), we get

$$x + 2.\frac{3x}{8} = 84 \Rightarrow x + \frac{3x}{4} = 84$$

$$\Rightarrow \quad \frac{4x + 3x}{4} = 84$$

$$\Rightarrow \quad 7x = 84 \times 4$$

$$\Rightarrow \quad x = \frac{84 \times 4}{7} = 12 \times 4 = 48$$

Hence, the age of father = x years = 48 years.

70. The value of two equal installments

$= 840 \times 2 = ₹\ 1680$

and the remaining amount after paid

$= 2400 - 1000 = ₹\ 1400$

$\therefore$ Interest = ₹ 16800 − ₹ 1400 = ₹ 280

According to question,

$$\frac{1400 \times 2 \times r}{100} = 280 \Rightarrow r = \frac{280}{28} = 10\%$$

Hence, the rate of interest = r = 10%.

71. Let the distance = 100 km $\left[\text{Speed} = \frac{\text{Distance}}{\text{Time}}\right]$

Then, the average speed

$$= \frac{100}{\frac{30}{20} + \frac{60}{40} + \frac{10}{10}} \text{ km/hr} = \frac{100}{\frac{3}{2} + \frac{3}{2} + 1}$$

$$= \frac{100}{3+1} = \frac{100}{4} = 25 \text{ km/hr.}$$

72. $$x \times \frac{100 - 20}{100} \times \frac{100 - 15}{100} \times \frac{100 - 10}{100} = 612$$

$$\Rightarrow x \times \frac{4}{5} \times \frac{17}{20} \times \frac{9}{10} = 612$$

$$\Rightarrow \quad x = \frac{612 \times 25 \times 10}{17 \times 9} = \frac{36 \times 25 \times 10}{9}$$

$$= 4 \times 25 \times 10 = 1000$$

Hence, the number of pens in shop = x = 1000.

73. Let the original length = 20 and breadth = 10

Then original perimeter = $2\ (l + b)$

$= 2\ (20 + 10) = 60$

Again, increased length = $20 \times \frac{115}{100} = 23$

and decreased breadth = $10 \times \frac{90}{100} = 9$

$\therefore$ Perimeter = 2 (23 + 9) = 64

$\therefore$ Impact on Perimeter

$$= \frac{4}{60} \times 100\% = \frac{100}{15}\% = \frac{20}{3}\%.$$

74. Seismology is the study of earthquakes. Similarly, Penology is the 'study of the punishment of crime and of prison management'.

75. Coal produces Thermal Energy. Similarly, Water produces Hydro Energy.

76. One who collects coins is called Numismatic. Similarly, One who collects stamps is called Philatelist.

77. Energy is measured in Joule. Similarly, Current is measured in Ampere.

78. Engineer is related to Machine in the same way Doctor is related Diseases.

79. Khasi, Garo, Mizo are ethnic group from India.

80. Morocco belongs to Africa continent. Other three belong to North America.

81. The term "Mallet" is used in Polo. Similarly, "Break out" is used in Hockey.

82. Vijay Hazare Trophy is a Cricket Tournament. Similarly, "Durand Cup" is a Football Tournament.

83. Currency of USA is Dollar. Similarly, Currency of Chile is Peso.

84. Capital of France is Paris. Similarly, Capital of Ghana is Accra.

85. Colonel, Major, Brigadier are Army ranks whereas Commodore is a naval rank.

86. M + 3 = P

J + 2 = L

S + 1 = T

Similarly, N + 3 = Q

K + 2 = M

W + 1 = X.

Previous Paper (Solved)

Air Force Common Admission Test (AFCAT)—2/2019*

1. Who is the UEFA Winner 2019?
A. Liverpool FC
B. Valencia
C. Tottenham Hatspur
D. None of these

2. How many overs are there in the 1st Power Play in T20 Cricket?
A. 5 overs B. 6 overs
C. 7 overs D. 9 overs

3. Tunnel that Connects Jammu to Kashmir path:
A. Pir Panjal Railway Tunnel
B. Karbude Railway Tunnel
C. Rohtang Tunnel
D. Chenani Nashri Tunnel

4. Who was the 1st Governor General of India?
A. Lord William Bentinck
B. C. Rajagopalachari
C. Lord Curzon
D. Warren Hastings

5. Who is writer of Life of Pie?
A. Tom Clancy B. Anne Golon
C. Yann Martel D. Joseph Heller

6. Who is considered the father of Indian revolutionary ideas?
A. Mahatma Gandhi
B. Subhash Chandra Bose
C. Ras Bihari Bose
D. Bal Gangadhar Tilak

7. Who is known as the Bradman of Women's Cricket?
A. Ellyse Perry
B. Elizabeth Rebecca Wilson
C. Poonam Raut
D. Heather Knight

8. Which female athlete won Gold in 2014 CWG in Weightlifting (48 Kg)?
A. Babita Kumari
B. Jitu Rai
C. Sanjita Chanu
D. Kumukcham Sanjita

9. Which Satellite is being launched by NASA to Mars in 2020?
A. Mars 2020 rover mission
B. Artemis Program
C. Artemis-2
D. All of these

10. Satyamev Jayate is part of which Upanishad?
A. Chandogya
B. Prashna
C. Mundaka
D. Mandukya

11. 'CANT' is related to which sport?
A. Football B. Kabaddi
C. Hockey D. Volleyball

12. Who is the writer of Padmavat Poem?
A. Ali Ahmad
B. Ziauddin Barani
C. Malik Muhammad Jayasi
D. Al-Biruni

13. Name of ISROs Space Program with the highest number of Satellites.
A. PSLV-C37 B. PSLV-C41
C. PSLV-C40 D. PSLV-C36

14. Which European league won UEFA 3 times in a row?
A. Real Madrid B. Benfica
C. Milan D. None of these

* Based on memory.

15. What is the Capital of Bosnia?
A. Azerbaijan B. Eritrea
C. Slovakia D. Sarajevo

16. How many medals have been won by Micheal Phelps?
A. 29 B. 28
C. 25 D. 32

17. Which dynasty established the Ajanta & Ellora caves?
A. Kanva Dynasty
B. Shunga Dynasty
C. Hindu Satavahana Dynasty
D. None of these

18. Which text of the Vedas refers to Medicine?
A. Atharvaveda B. Samaveda
C. Yajurveda D. Rigveda

19. Which cricketer reached fastest 10000 runs in ODI?
A. MS Dhoni B. Sachin Tendulkar
C. Virat Kohli D. Ricky Ponting

20. What is the Capital of Colombia?
A. Bogota B. Praia
C. Moroni D. Zagreb

21. Where is the Headquarter of WHO located?
A. Montreal, Canada B. New York, USA
C. Geneva, Switzerland D. Vienna, Austria

22. The Khilafat Movement was merged with which movement?
A. Quit India Movement
B. Non-Cooperation Movement
C. Swaraj Movement
D. None of these

23. Which lines run parallel to the equator?
A. Latitude B. Longitude
C. Both A and B D. None of these

24. Who Invented Electricity?
A. Guglielmo Marconi
B. Wilhelm Rontgen
C. Joseph Henry
D. Benjamin Franklin

25. Sun occupies how much percentage of area?
A. 98.0 B. 99.86
C. 90 D. 56

Direction (Qs. No. 26-30): *Each of the following questions consist of problem figures followed by answer figures. Select a figure from amongst the answer figures which will continue the same series or pattern as established by the problem figures.*

26. Problem Figures

Answer Figures

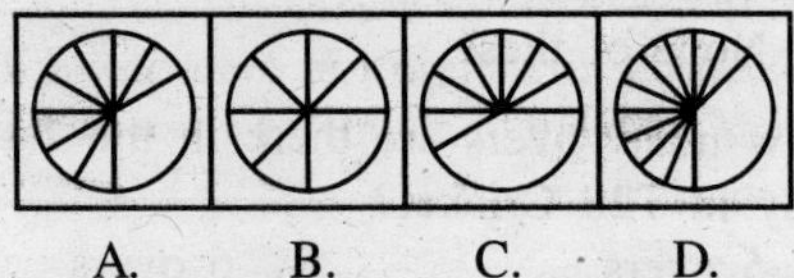

A. B. C. D.

27. Problem Figures

Answer Figures

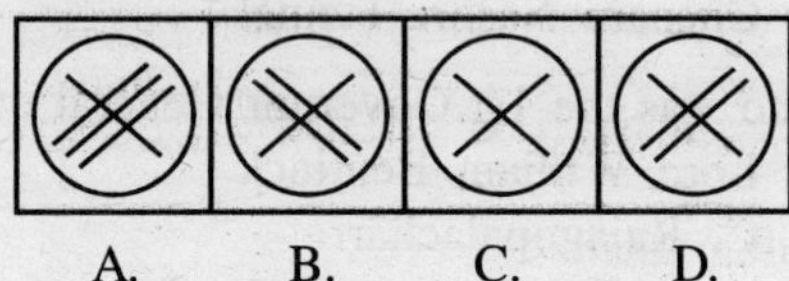

A. B. C. D.

28. Problem Figures

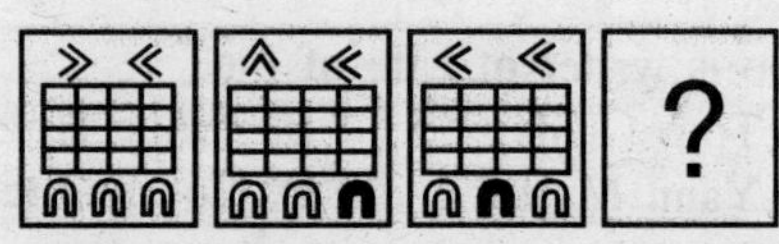

Answer Figures

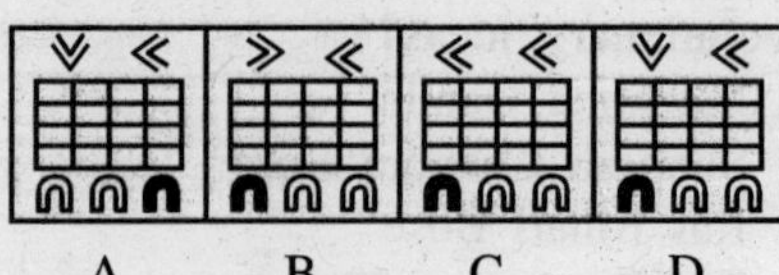

A. B. C. D.

29. Problem Figures

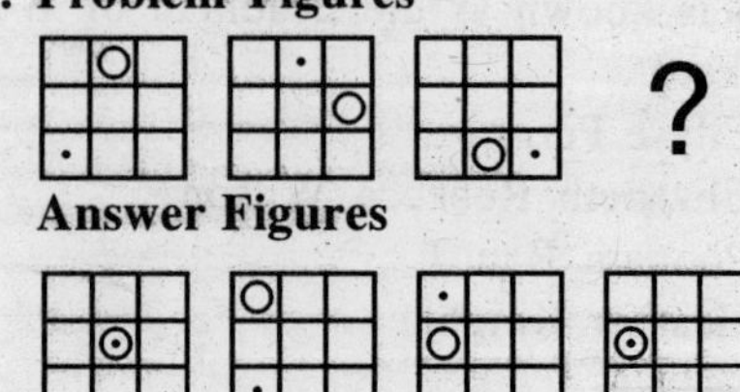

Answer Figures

A. B. C. D.

30. Problem Figures

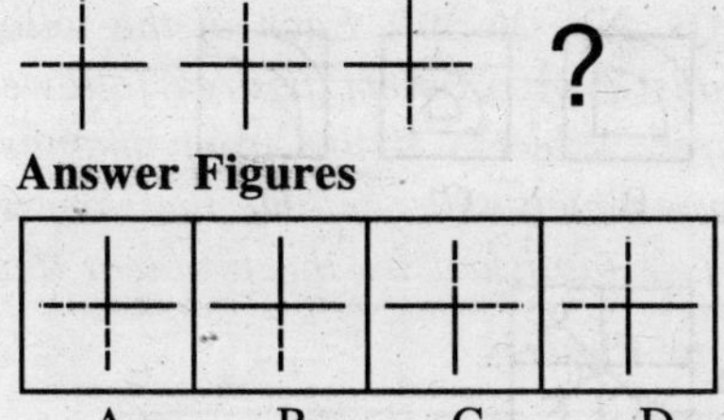

Answer Figures

A. B. C. D.

Directions (Qs. No. 31-35): *The second figure in the first unit of the Problem Figures bears a certain relationship to the first figure. Similarly, one of the figures in the Answer Figures bears the same relationship to the first figure in the second unit of the Problem Figures. Locate the figure which would fit the question mark.*

31. Problem Figures

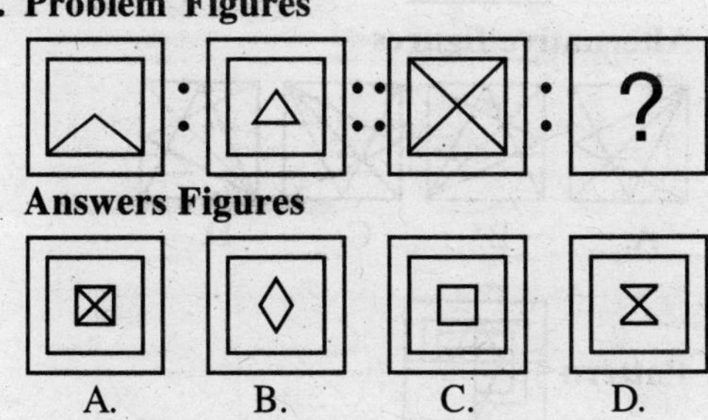

Answers Figures

A. B. C. D.

32. Problem Figures

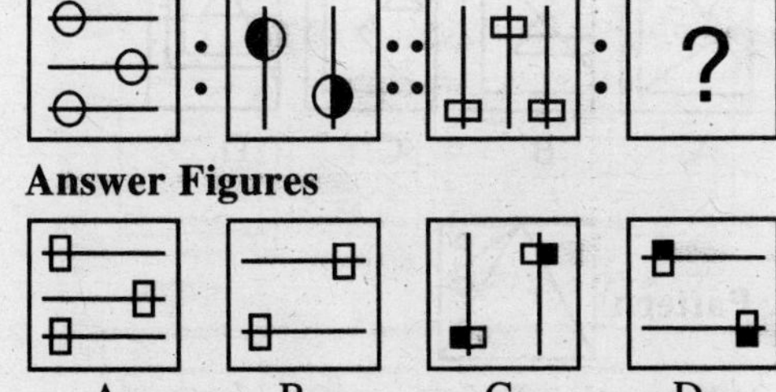

Answer Figures

A. B. C. D.

33. Problem Figures

Answer Figures

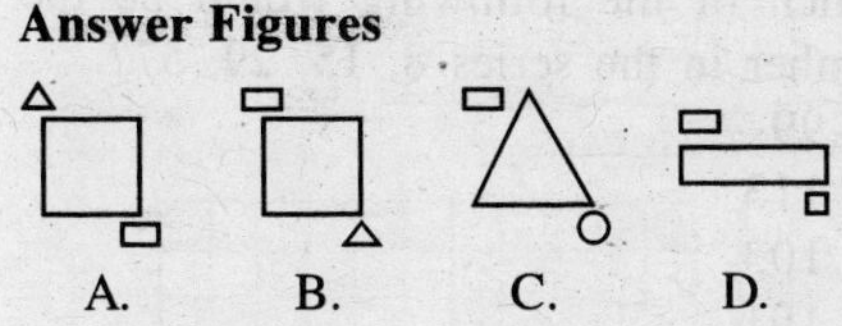

A. B. C. D.

34. Problem Figures

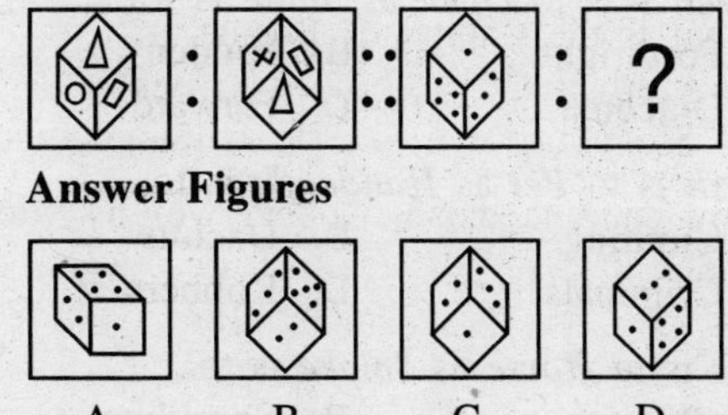

Answer Figures

A. B. C. D.

35. Problem Figures

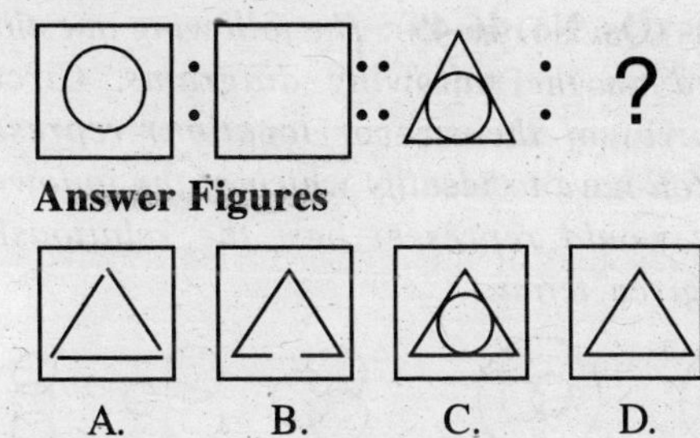

Answer Figures

A. B. C. D.

Directions (Qs. No. 36-40): *In each of the following questions, three words are alike in some manner. Spot the odd one out.*

36. A. Green B. Red
C. Colour D. Orange

37. A. Stable B. Hole
C. Canoe D. Sty

38. A. Nose B. Eyes
C. Skin D. Teeth

39. A. Venus B. Moon
C. Pluto D. Mars

40. A. Happy B. Gloomy
C. Lively D. Cheerful

Directions (Qs. No. 41-45): *In the questions given below establish the relationship between the two words. Then from the given options select one which has the same relationship as of the given two words.*

41. *Mania* is to *Craze* as *Phobia* is to .....
A. Desires B. Hobbies
C. Want D. Fear

42. *Stammering* is to *Speech* as *Deafness* is to.....
A. Ear B. Hearing
C. Noise D. Silence

43. *Secretive* is to *Open* as *Snide* is to.....
A. Forthright B. Hidden
C. Outcome D. Forward

44. *Leash* is to *Pet* as *Handcuffs* is to.....
A. Cunning B. Dacoits
C. Criminals D. Robbers

45. *Ride* is to *Horse* as *Smoke* is to.....
A. Chimney B. Sparkling
C. Pipe D. Ashes

Directions (Qs. No. 46-49): *The following questions are based on the following diagrams. Circles (irrespectives of the size or location) represent objects. You have to identify which of the following diagrams would represent best the relationship between given terms.*

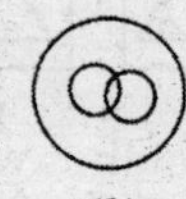

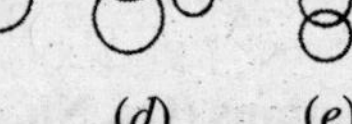

(*a*) (*b*) (*c*) (*d*) (*e*)

46. Which of the above five diagrams would best represent—Musicians, Instrumentalists, Violinists?
A. (*a*) B. (*b*)
C. (*c*) D. (*e*)

47. Which of the above five diagrams would best represent—People, Painters, Boys?
A. (*e*) B. (*d*)
C. (*a*) D. (*b*)

48. Which of the above five diagrams would best represent—Mothers, Fathers and Teachers?
A. (*a*) B. (*b*)
C. (*d*) D. (*e*)

49. Which of the above five diagrams would best represent—Men, Women and Children?
A. (*a*) B. (*c*)
C. (*e*) D. None

Directions (Qs. No. 50-54): *In each question, which one of the alternative figures will complete the given figure pattern?*

50. Pattern

Alternative figures

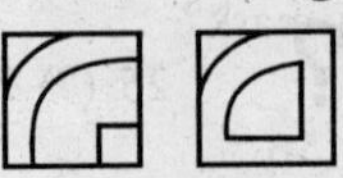

A. B. C. D.

51. Pattern

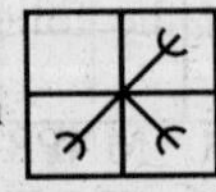

Alternative figures

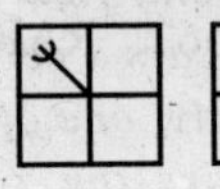
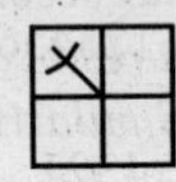
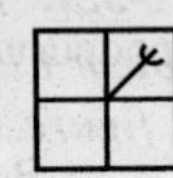
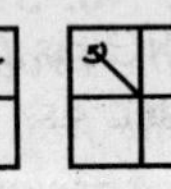

A. B. C. D.

52. Pattern

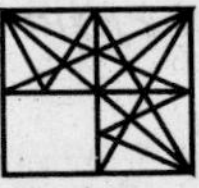

Alternative figures

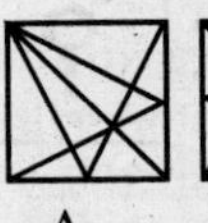
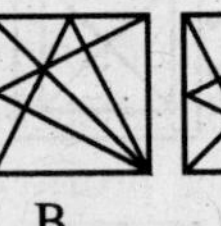
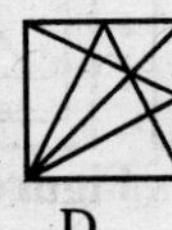

A. B. C. D.

53. Pattern

Alternative figures

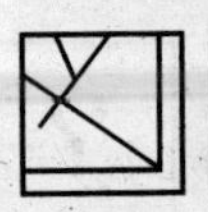
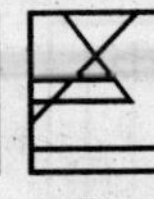
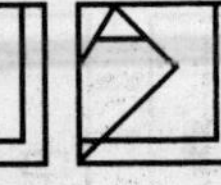

A. B. C. D.

54. Pattern

Alternative figures

A. B. C. D.

55. Which of the following would be the next number in the series 8, 15, 29, 57?
A. 99
B. 113
C. 103
D. 101

56. Which of the following numbers will be inserted in place of the (?) mark?
35 (78) 40   45 (97) 35   25 (?) 30
A. 66   B. 56
C. 67   D. 71

57. Find the missing term in the following:
ACEG : DFHJ : : QSUV : ?
A. TVXY   B. MNPR
C. OQST   D. KMNP

58. If 'BEARING' is coded as 1234567. 'RARE' will be coded as:
A. 4234   B. 4321
C. 4345   D. 4342

59. If RADIO is coded as 'UDGLR', PHOTO will be coded as:
A. OIPWR   B. OTOPT
C. SKRWR   D. SKPWR

60. A manufacturer sells a cooler to a distributor at a profit of 18%. The distributor sells the same to a retailer at a profit of 20%. The retailer, in turns sells it to a customer for ₹ 2124 thereby earning a profit of 25%. What is the cost price for the manufacturer?
A. ₹ 1200
B. ₹ 1300
C. ₹ 1400
D. ₹ 1450

61. A manufacturer's list price of a table is ₹ 4750. He sells it to a retailer with successive discounts of 15% and 10% with terms : cash 4, 2/20. If the retailer pays the bill on 10th day, what is his cost price?
A. ₹ 1356.08
B. ₹ 3361.08
C. ₹ 3561.08
D. ₹ 4616.10

62. A and B are two alloys of gold and copper prepared by mixing metals in proportions 7 : 2 and 7 : 11 respectively. If equal quantities of the alloys are melted to form a third alloy C, the proportion of gold and copper in C will be:
A. 5 : 9   B. 5 : 7
C. 7 : 5   D. 9 : 5

63. The price of cooking oil has increased by 25%. The percentage of reduction that a family should effect in the use of cooking oil so as not to increase the expenditure on this account is:
A. 25%   B. 30%
C. 20%   D. 15%

64. In an examination 80% of the students passed in Mathematics and 70% passed in English, while 10% students failed in both the subjects. If 360 students passed in both the subjects, find the total number of students who appeared in the examination.
A. 400   B. 600
C. 630   D. 640

65. Two vessels A and B contain mixture of milk and water in the ratio 4 : 1 and 9 : 11 respectively. They are mixed in the ratio of 3 : 2. Find the ratio of milk : water in the resulting mixture.
A. 34 : 16
B. 33 : 17
C. 16 : 34
D. 17 : 33

66. A vessel contains mixture of liquids A and B in the ratio 3 : 2. When 20 litres of the mixture is taken out and replaced by 20 litres of liquid B, the ratio changes to 1 : 4. How many litres of liquid A was there initially present in the vessel?
A. 12 litres
B. 18 litres
C. 24 litres
D. 22 litres

67. If $\frac{x^2+y^2+z^2-64}{xy-yz-zx} = -2$ and $x + y = 32$, then find the value of z.
A. 5   B. 4
C. 3   D. 2

68. If $a + b + c = 13$, $a^2 + b^2 + c^2 = 69$, then what is the value of $(ab + bc + ca)$.
A. 75   B. 69
C. 50   D. 60

69. If 3 men and 5 women can do a piece of work in 8 days and 2 men and 7 boys can do the same work in 12 days. Find the number of boys, the work done by whom can equate the work done by 10 women.

A. 19 boys B. 21 boys
C. 23 boys D. 15 boys

70. A and B can together finish a work in 30 days. They worked together for 20 days and then B left. After another 20 days, A finished the remaining work. In how many days A alone can finish the job?

A. 60 days B. 54 days
C. 50 days D. 40 days

71. $\dfrac{4\frac{1}{7}-2\frac{1}{4}}{3\frac{1}{2}+1\frac{1}{7}} \div \dfrac{1}{2+\dfrac{1}{2+\dfrac{1}{5-\frac{1}{5}}}} = ?$

A. 3 B. $\frac{1}{8}$
C. 8 D. 1

72. $\frac{1}{1\cdot 2\cdot 3}+\frac{1}{2\cdot 3\cdot 4}+\frac{1}{3\cdot 4\cdot 5}+\frac{1}{4\cdot 5\cdot 6}$ is simplified to:

A. $\frac{17}{30}$ B. $\frac{13}{30}$
C. $\frac{11}{30}$ D. $\frac{7}{30}$

73. A cricket team won 3 matches more than they lost. If a win gives them 2 points and loss (–1) point. If their score is 23, then how many matches in all have they played?

A. 40 B. 37
C. 20 D. 17

74. Starting from a point at a speed of 4 km/hr a man reaches at a cerain place and returns back to the point from where he had started journey on bicycle at the speed of 16 km/hr. His average speed during the entire journey will be:

A. 6.4 km/h B. 8.4 km/h
C. 5.4 km/h D. 10 km/h

75. Start from his house one day Saurabh walks at a speed of $2\frac{1}{2}$ km/hr and reaches his school 6 minutes late. Next day he increases his speed by 1 km/hr and reaches the school 6 minutes early. What is the distance of the school from his house?

A. 2 km B. $1\frac{3}{4}$ km
C. $1\frac{1}{2}$ km D. 1 km

76. If a, b, c, d, e are five consecutive odd numbers, their average is:

A. $5(a + 4)$
B. $\frac{abcde}{5}$
C. $5(a + b + c + d + e)$
D. None of these

77. A pupil's marks were wrongly entered as 83 instead of 63. Due to that the average marks for the class got increased by half. What is the number of pupils in the class?

A. 73 B. 40
C. 50 D. 10

Directions (Qs. Nos. 78 to 81): *In questions, sentences given with blanks to be filled in with an appropriate word(s). Four alternatives are suggested for each question. Choose the correct alternative out of the four and indicate it by blackening the appropriate oval [●] in the Answer Sheet.*

78. He was ______ by nature and so avoided all company.

A. anti-social B. cordial
C. gregarious D. timid

79. The United Kingdom _____ England, Wales, Scotland and Northern Ireland.

A. comprises B. combines
C. comprises of D. consists

80. Jyoti refused to be _____ by her long illness.

A. dispensed B. dispirited
C. dispersed D. dispatched

81. Jim suffered a ____ of fortune.

A. reversal B. revert
C. regress D. reverse

Directions (Qs. Nos. 82 to 84): *In questions, some parts of the sentences have errors and some are correct. Find out which part of a sentence has an error and blacken the oval [●] corresponding to the appropriate letter (A, B, C). If a sentence is free from error, blacken the oval corresponding to (D) in the Answer Sheet.*

82. (A) We have finished our work/(B) three hours ago and have been waiting/(C) for you since then./(D) No error.

83. (A) A study is going under way/(B) to determine the exact concentration/(C) of lead in the water supply./(D) No error.

84. (A) Several guests noticed Mr. Sharma/(B) falling back in his chair/(C) and gasping for breath. /(D) No error.

Directions (Qs. Nos. 85 to 87): *In questions, four alternatives are given for the Idiom/Phrase underlined in the sentence. Choose the alternative which best expresses the meaning of the Idiom/ Phrase and mark it in the Answer Sheet.*

85. 'I am going to stay at home because I am feeling under the weather today.'

A. depressed B. irritated
C. unhappy D. sick

86. He and his neighbour are always at loggerheads.

A. abusing each other
B. agree on everything
C. aloof from each other
D. disagreeing on everything

87. Even in the middle of the fire he kept a level head.

A. was sensible B. was crazy
C. was self-centred D. was impulsive

Directions (Qs. No. 88 and 89): *Read the passage carefully and answer these questions.*

The capitalist system does not foster healthy relations among human beings. A few people own all the means of production and others have to sell their labour under conditions imposed upon them. The emphasis of capitalism being on the supreme importance of material wealth, the intensity of its appeal is to the acquisitive tendency. It promotes worship of economic power with little regard to the means employed for its acquisition and the end that it serves. By its exploitation of human beings to the limits of endurance its concentration is on the largest profit rather than maximum production. Thus, the division of human society is done on the basis of profit motive. All this is injurious to human dignity. And when the harrowed poor turn to the founders of religion for succour, they rather offer a subtle defence for the established order. They promise future happiness for present suffering. They conjure up visions of paradise to soothe the suffering majority and censure the revolt of the tortured men. The system imposes injustice, the religion justifies it.

88. The passage indicates that the capitalist system is:

A. ambitious B. prosperous
C. dehumanising D. fair

89. In a capitalist system of society each man wishes:

A. to produce maximum wealth
B. to have visions of paradise
C. to soothe the sufferings of other
D. to acquire maximum wealth

Directions (Qs. Nos. 90 to 92): *In questions, out of the four alternatives, choose the one which best expresses the meaning of the given word and mark it in the Answer Sheet.*

90. RESURGENCE

A. renewal B. reluctance
C. repletion D. relocation

91. INGENUOUS

A. crafty B. candid
C. careless D. creative

92. DAMP

A. light B. wet
C. clear D. complicated

Directions (Qs. Nos. 93 to 95): *In questions, choose the word opposite in meaning to the given word and mark it in the Answer Sheet.*

93. ZENITH

A. shallow B. nadir
C. low D. bottom

94. ARROGANT

A. laughty B. proud
C. selfish D. modest

95. ECCENTRIC

A. carefree B. peculiar
C. normal D. unusual

Directions (Q. Nos. 96-100): *In the following passage there are blanks, each of which has been numbered. These numbers are printed below the passage and against each, five words are suggested, one of which fits the blank appropriately. Find out the appropriate word in each case.*

Visual experiences can ...(96)... children, teenagers and even adults learn and absorb more due to its highly stimulating and ...(97)... engaging impact. It is for this reason that we are seeing an increase in schools across the globe ...(98)... content provider programmes into their class curriculum to ...(99)... lessons through video. Visual excursions and school collaborations are ...(100)... by advances in high definition video, high fidelity audio and content sharing, allowing students to experience a richer and more stimulating learning experience.

96. A. help B. aiding
C. prescribe D. feature

97. A. plus B. lonely
C. ably D. deeply

98. A. incorporating B. pressing
C. following D. parting

99. A. make B. demand
C. impart D. vision

100. A. dissolved B. enhanced
C. measured D. failed

ANSWERS

1	2	3	4	5	6	7	8	9	10
A	B	D	A	C	D	B	D	A	C
11	12	13	14	15	16	17	18	19	20
B	C	A	A	D	B	C	A	C	A
21	22	23	24	25	26	27	28	29	30
C	B	A	D	B	C	D	D	D	A
31	32	33	34	35	36	37	38	39	40
D	D	A	C	D	C	C	D	B	B
41	42	43	44	45	46	47	48	49	50
D	B	A	C	A	A	D	D	D	B
51	52	53	54	55	56	57	58	59	60
A	D	D	A	B	B	A	D	C	A
61	62	63	64	65	66	67	68	69	70
C	C	C	B	B	B	B	C	B	A
71	72	73	74	75	76	77	78	79	80
D	D	B	A	B	D	B	D	A	B
81	82	83	84	85	86	87	88	89	90
A	A	A	D	D	D	A	C	D	A
91	92	93	94	95	96	97	98	99	100
B	B	B	D	C	A	D	A	C	B

EXPLANATORY ANSWERS

26. Clockwise, the circle is turned by 30° and also one radial line segment is removed.

27. The diagonal line segments are removed one by one in a set order.

28. The 'V' shape on the top left is rotated 90° anticlockwise. The three figures at the bottom are shaded one at a time beginning from the right figure and moving to the left.

29. The circle and the dot are moved two and three sections clockwise respectively.

30. The cross is turned 90° clockwise at each step.

31. The triangle in the first figure is moved to the centre of the second figure. Similarly, the two triangles joined at the apex are moved to the centre in answer figure.

32. The first figure is turned by 90° one of the bars is removed and opposite sides of the element attached to the bar are shaded to get the second figure.

33. The element at the bottom is moved to the diagonal corner, the element in the top is enlarged and moved to the centre and element in the middle is reduced and moved to the bottom right corner.

34. The view of the cube is changed from top to bottom. The design on the right side remains unchanged while the design on the left side is changed.

35. The inner shape in the first figure is removed to get the second figure.

36. All others are types of colour.

37. Canoe is a boat. Other are resting places of birds/animals.

38. All others are sense organs.

39. All others are planets.

40. All others are expressions of joy.

41. The related words are snynonyms.

42. Defect in speech causes stammering and in hearing causes deafness.

43. The related words are antonyms.

44. Leash is used to tie a pet, handcuffs to tie criminals.

45. Horse is the object of action 'to ride' and Chimney is the object of action 'to smoke'.

46. All violinists are instrumentalist and all instrumentalists are Musician.

47. Some painters may be boys and some boys may be painters. But all painters and boys are people.

48. Some mothers and some fathers may be teachers but a father can not be a mother and vice-versa.

49. No diagram can represent the given words.

50. 

51. 

52. 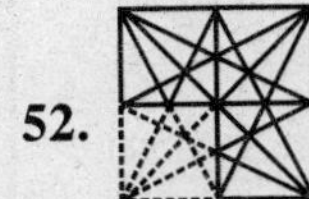

53. 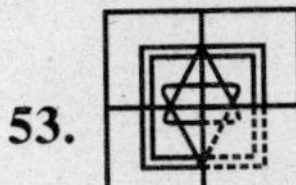

54. 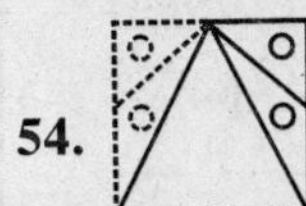

55. 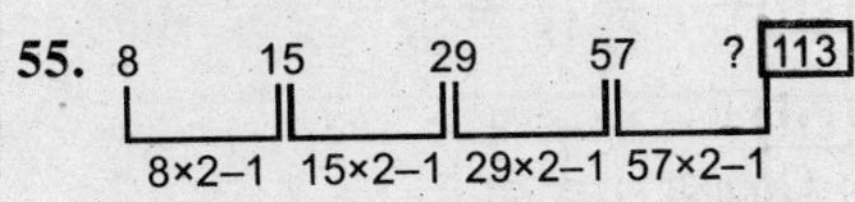

Hence, required number = 113.

57. 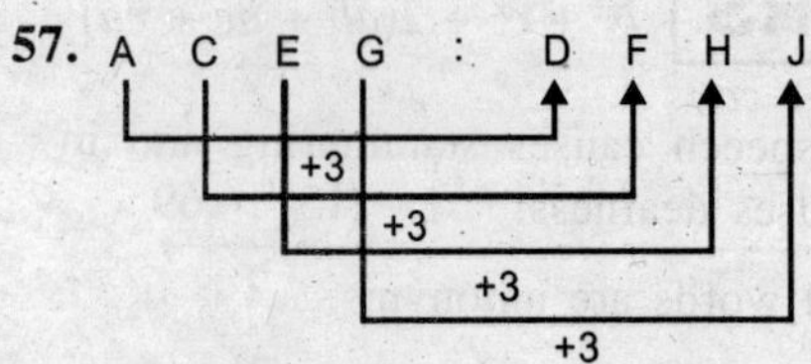

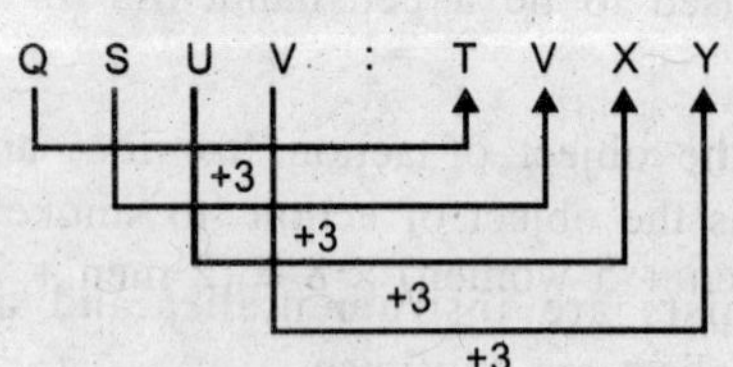

58. B E A R I N G → 1 2 3 4 5 6 7 ; R A R E → 4 3 4 2

60. Required C.P. $= \frac{100}{118} \times \frac{100}{120} \times \frac{100}{125} \times 2124$

$= ₹\ 1200.$

61. Here, retailer pays the bill on 10th day, so discount will be 2%.

Hence, required cost price

$= \frac{85}{100} \times \frac{90}{100} \times \frac{98}{100} \times 4750$

$= \frac{142443}{40}$

$= ₹\ 3561.08.$

62. Gold in C $= \left(\frac{7}{9} + \frac{7}{18}\right)$

$= \frac{21}{18} = \frac{7}{6}$

Copper in C $= \left(\frac{2}{9} + \frac{11}{18}\right)$

$= \frac{15}{18} = \frac{5}{6}$

$\therefore$ Gold : Copper $= \frac{7}{6} : \frac{5}{6}$

$= 7 : 5.$

63. Required reduction

$= \left[\frac{r}{(100+r)} \times 100\right]$

$= \left(\frac{25}{125} \times 100\right)\% = 20\%.$

64. Here, percentage of students failed in Mathematics and English be 30% and 20% respectively.

Percentage of students failed either one or both subjects

$= 30 + 20 - 10$

$= 40\%$

Hence, percentage of pass students

$= 100 - 40$

$= 60\%$

Now, $60\% = 360$

$\therefore \quad 100\% = \frac{360}{60} \times 100$

$= 600.$

65. Fraction is

	Milk	*Water*
A :	$\frac{4}{5}$	$\frac{1}{5}$
B :	$\frac{9}{20}$	$\frac{11}{20}$

(3A + 2B) = A and B : $\left(\frac{12}{5} + \frac{9}{10}\right) \left(\frac{3}{5} + \frac{11}{10}\right)$

$= \frac{33}{10} \qquad \frac{17}{10}$

So, Ratio of milk : water in the resulting mixture = 33 : 17.

66. % of liquid B initially present in the vessel

$= \frac{2}{3+2} \times 100 = 40\%$

% of liquid B finally present in the vessel

$= \frac{4}{1+4} \times 100$

$= 80\%$

The second solution is liquid B which is being mixed and it has 100% liquid B.

80% of liquid B present in the resultant mixture may be taken as average percentage. So, using rule of alligation on liquid B per cent, we can write,

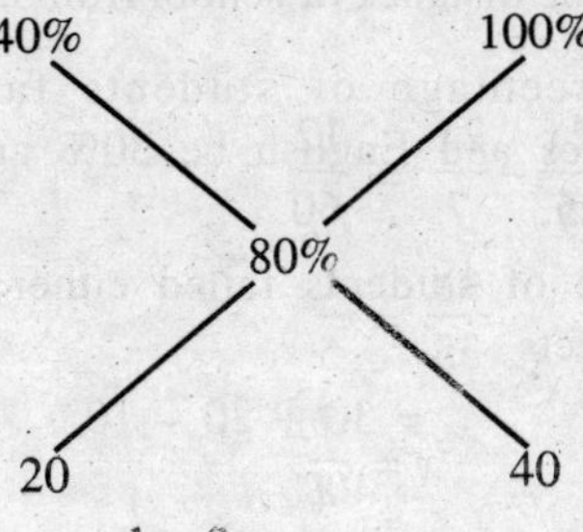

or 1 : 2

The ratio of liquid left in the vessel to liquid B being mixed = 1 : 2

Since the quantity of liquid B being mixed is 20 litres, the quantity of liquid left in the vessel is 10 litres.

Therefore, the total quantity of liquid initially present in the vessel

$= 10 + 20$

$= 30$ litres

Quantity of liquid A

$= \frac{3}{2+3} \times 30 = 18$ litres.

67. $\frac{x^2+y^2+z^2-64}{xy-yz-zx} = -2$

$\therefore x^2 + y^2 + z^2 - 64$

$= -2(xy - yz - zx)$ ...(*i*)

Now, $(x + y - z)^2$

$= x^2 + y^2 + z^2 + 2(xy - yz - zx)$

$\Rightarrow (3z - z)^2 = x^2 + y^2 + z^2 + 2(xy - yz - zx)$

$(\because x + y = 3z)$

$\therefore x^2 + y^2 + z^2 - 4z^2$

$= -2(xy - yz - zx)$ ...(*ii*)

From (*i*) and (*ii*), we get,

$4z^2 = 64$

$\Rightarrow z^2 = 16$

$\therefore z = 4.$

68. $(a + b + c)^2 = a^2 + b^2 + c^2 + 2(ab + bc + ca)$

$\therefore ab + bc + ca$

$= \frac{(a+b+c)^2-(a^2+b^2+c^2)}{2} = \frac{(13)^2-69}{2}$

$= \frac{169-69}{2}$

$= \frac{100}{2} = 50.$

69. Here, (3 men + 5 women) × 8 ≡ (2 men + 7 boys) × 12

$\Rightarrow$ 40 women ≡ 84 boys

$\therefore$ 10 women ≡ $\frac{84}{40} \times 10$

= 21 boys

Hence, work done by 10 women

= work done of 21 boys.

70. (A + B)'s 20 days' work = $\frac{20}{30} = \frac{2}{3}$

Remaining part of work = $1 - \frac{2}{3} = \frac{1}{3}$,

which will be done by A alone in 20 days.

Hence, whole work will be done by A alone in 20 × 3 = 60 days.

71. $\dfrac{4\frac{1}{7}-2\frac{1}{4}}{3\frac{1}{2}+1\frac{1}{7}} \div \dfrac{1}{2+\dfrac{1}{2+\dfrac{1}{5-\frac{1}{5}}}}$

$= \dfrac{\frac{29}{7}-\frac{9}{4}}{\frac{7}{2}+\frac{8}{7}} \div \dfrac{1}{2+\dfrac{1}{2+\dfrac{1}{\frac{24}{5}}}}$

$= \dfrac{\frac{29\times4-9\times7}{28}}{\frac{7\times7-8\times2}{14}} \div \dfrac{1}{2+\dfrac{1}{2+\frac{5}{24}}}$

$$= \frac{\frac{116-63}{28}}{\frac{49-16}{14}} \div \frac{1}{2+\frac{1}{\frac{53}{24}}}$$

$$= \frac{\frac{53}{28}}{\frac{65}{14}} \div \frac{1}{2+\frac{24}{53}}$$

$$= \frac{53 \times 14}{28 \times 65} \div \frac{1}{\frac{130}{53}}$$

$$= \frac{53}{130} \div \frac{53}{130}$$

$$= \frac{53}{130} \times \frac{130}{53} = 1.$$

72. $\frac{1}{1\cdot2\cdot3} + \frac{1}{2\cdot3\cdot4} + \frac{1}{3\cdot4\cdot5} + \frac{1}{4\cdot5\cdot6}$

$$= \frac{120+30+12+6}{1\cdot2\cdot3\cdot4\cdot5\cdot6}$$

$$= \frac{168}{720} = \frac{7}{30}$$

73. Let the number of matches, they lost be x.

Now,

$(x + 3) \times 2 - x \times 1 = 23$

$\Rightarrow \quad x = 17$

Total number of matches

$= (x + 3) + x$

$= (17 + 3) + 17$

$= 37.$

74. Average speed during the entire journey

$$= \frac{2xy}{x+y} = \frac{2 \times 4 \times 16}{4+16}$$

$$= \frac{8 \times 16}{20} = 6.4 \text{ km/hr.}$$

75. Let x km be distance of school from his house; then

$$\frac{2x}{5} - \frac{2x}{7} = \frac{12}{60}$$

$$\Rightarrow \quad \frac{4x}{35} = \frac{1}{5}$$

$$\therefore \quad x = \frac{7}{4}$$

$$= 1\frac{3}{4} \text{ km.}$$

76. Clearly,

$b = a + 2,\ c = a + 4,\ d = a + 6,\ e = a + 8$

$\therefore$ Required Average

$$= \frac{a+(a+2)+(a+4)+(a+6)+(a+8)}{5}$$

$$= \frac{5a+20}{5}$$

$= (a + 4).$

77. Let the total number of pupils in the class be x; then,

$$\frac{83-63}{x} = \frac{1}{2}$$

$$\Rightarrow \quad \frac{20}{x} = \frac{1}{2}$$

$$\therefore \quad x = 40.$$

NUMERICAL ABILITY

1

SIMPLIFICATION

BODMAS - RULE

This rule is very important for the arithmetical simplification. When vinculum, brackets, of, division, multiplication, addition and subtraction all or two or more than two operations are present in any question, then we can find out the result (answer) with the help of **BODMAS** - rule. Details of BODMAS- rule are given below :

Order	*Abbreviated Letter Used in rule*	*Meaning*	*Notation*
1.	V	Vinculum or Bar	——
2.	B	Brackets	[ ], { }, ( )
3.	O	Of	of
4.	D	Division	÷
5.	M	Multiplication	×
6.	A	Addition	+
7.	S	Subtraction	−

Note :

(*i*) Order of the letter which is used in BODMAS - rule is always fixed.

(*ii*) Absence of any operation or more than one operations does not change the order of BODMAS.

(*iii*) 'Of' means multiplication.

BRACKETS

When all brackets are present in a question, in that condition **ViCiCuSq-Rule** is applied. This ViCiCuSq-Rule stands for brackets and represents the order of calculation of brackets. Details are given below :

Order	*Abbreviated Letter Used in rule*	*Meaning*	*Notation*
1.	Vi	Vinculum	——
2.	Ci	Circular Bracket	( )
3.	Cu	Curly Bracket	{ }
4.	Sq	Square Bracket	[ ]

Note : This order of brackets (ViCiCuSq) is also fixed and not variable.

ADDITION

In the problem of addition we have two main factors (speed and accuracy) under consideration. We will discuss a method of addition which is faster than the method used by most people and also has a higher degree of accuracy. In the latter part of this chapter we will also discuss a method of checking and double-checking the results.

Meaning of Addition

Addition is the operation of finding a single number taken together. The result obtained by adding two or more numbers is termed as the sum or total. The numbers to be added are called 'addends'. The sign used for addition is '+' (*i.e.,* plus).

We know that addition is a very simple process. Everybody knows to add but not many of those do know the correct way (time) to get the correct answer. Many of us have time consuming ways of adding numbers.

First of all while adding numbers, we avoid to say 7 plus 7 equal to 14 and 18 plus 12 equal to 30 etc. Instead as soon as we see 7 and 7 to be added , simply say '14'. Similarly for 18 and 12, merely say '30'.

It is also necessary that when we see a number like 151, we avoid saying one hundred and fifty one, simply say one fifty one.

As far as possible we use double columns method. But before going to use double columns method let us see how a single column method is used.

Rule I : Addition of Single Column Method

The time saving device is to place a dot (°) for each ten to be carried and add only units.

Example 1 :

6° + 3 + 7° + 9° + 4 + 8° + 5° + 9 = 51

Step VII Step VI Step V Step IV Step III Step II Step I

(*a*) 51 (*b*) 49
(*c*) 52 (*d*) 50
(*e*) None of these

Ans. (*a*)

Explanation : Starting from the right

Step I : 9 + 5 = 14. Here, we say the unit figure only (only say 4). We place a dot for ten figure and take 4 for next step.

Step II : 4 + 8 = 12. Again we take 2 for the next step and put a dot for ten figure.

Step III : 2 + 4 = 6. We take only 6 because there is not a ten figure.

Step IV : 6 + 9 = 15, We take 5 for the next step and put a dot for ten figure.

Step V : 5 + 7 = 12. We take 2 for next step and place a dot for ten figure.

Step VI : 2 + 3 = 5. Take 5 for next step.

Step VII : 5 + 6 = 11. Here, we put a dot for ten figure and write only unit figure 1 in the answer.

There are five dots in (Step I + Step II + Step IV + Step V + Step VII), so, we place the number 5 at the ten figure digits. Thus, our answer will be 51.

Example 2 : Example 1 in another way

6°
3
7°
9°
4
8°
5°
9
51

(*a*) 50 (*b*) 51
(*c*) 52 (*d*) 53
(*e*) None of these

Ans. (*b*)

Explanation : Here, starting from the bottom instead of 14, 22, 26. etc. we say the unit figure only placing a dot next to the number when we exceed 10. Thus, we say 4, 2, 6, 5, 2, 5, 1. The five dots indicate 50. Thus, 50 plus the last unit figure 1 is equal to 51.

Rule II : Addition of Double Columns Method

This method is very essential for quick work. Here, we add from 'tens' and then add its unit place as :

Example 1 :

98
65
32
87
54
21
357

(*a*) 355 (*b*) 356
(*c*) 358 (*d*) 357
(*e*) None of these

Ans. (*d*)

Explanation : The addition proceeds 21 + 50 (of 54), *i.e.,* 71 and then 4 giving 75. 75 to 80 (of 87), *i.e.,* 155 and then 7 gives 162, 162 + 30 (of 32), *i.e.,* 192 and then 2 giving 194, 194 + 60 (of 65), *i.e.,* 254 and then 5 giving 259, 259 + 90 (of 98) is 349 and then 8 giving 357.

Here, the figure which our eyes see and recognize should be 71, 75, 62, 94, 59, 57. The hundreds that we get during the process of addition can be placed beside the number where the total comes to a hundred.

Note : Starting from the top, we get the same process and same result.

Example 2 : We may apply the Double Columns Method for taking addition with more columns.

4 6 9 7 8
5 4 1 2 2
2 8 5 7 9
5 6 1 4 2
4 5 2 1 3
23 10 34
Step III Step II Step I

(*a*) 231134 (*b*) 231034

(*c*) 231132 (*d*) 231032

(*e*) None of these

Ans. (*b*)

Explanation : Starting from the bottom right

Step I : First double column

(*i.e.*, right 2 columns)

13 + 42 = 55, 55 + 79 = 134

34 + 22 = 56, 56 + 78 = 134

Total = 234

(*i.e.*, 34 written and 2 carried for next step)

Step II : Second double column

2 + 52 + 61 = 115, 15 + 85 = 100

00 + 41 = 41 , 41 + 69 = 110

Total = 310

(10 written and 3 carried for next step)

Step III : Last column

3 + 4 = 7, 7 + 5 = 12, 12 + 2 = 14,

14 + 5 = 19, 19 + 4 = 23

Here, we write 23

or

3 + 4 = 7 , 7 + 5 = 12, 2 + 2 = 4

4 + 5 = 9, 9 + 4 = 13 (3 for unit figure)

Total 23

Thus, Result = 231034.

Rule III : Addition of Double Columns Method Horizontally

By double columns method, it is easy to add numbers horizontally even when the numbers of digits in each numbers are different.

Example :

36925 + 4563 + 321659 + 884 = ?

(*a*) 363140 (*b*) 364030

(*c*) 364031 (*d*) 364040

(*e*) None of these

Ans. (*c*)

Explanation :

Step I : First double column (starting from right hand side).

84 + 59 = 143, 43 + 63 = 106,

6 + 25 = 31, Total = 231

(Here, we write 31 and carried 2 for next step)

Step II : Second double column is

2 + 8 = 10, 10 + 16 = 26, 26 + 45 = 71,

71 + 69 = 140 Total = 140

(We write 40 and carried 1 for next step)

Step III : Last double column is

1 + 32 = 33, 33 + 3 = 36 (36 written)

The result is 364031.

Rule IV : Addition Including Decimal

For addition of numbers containing decimals addition should be used.

Example :

456.073 + 2.45 + 0.04 + 0.0004 + 485 = ?

(*a*) 943.5666 (*b*) 943.555

(*c*) 943.5634 (*d*) 943.56

(*e*) None of these

Ans. (*c*)

Explanation: Starting from right hand side of every term.

Step I : First double column is 04 + 30 = 34

(Written 34, no carried)

Step II : Second double column is

04 + 45 = 49 + 07 = 56

(Written 56 and no carried)

Step III : Third double column is

85 + 2 = 87, 87 + 56 = 143

(Written 43 and carried 1 for next step)

Step IV : Fourth column is

1 + 4 = 5, 5 + 4 = 9

(Written 9 and no carried)

The decimal is placed after counting numbers from right hand side.

Thus, our result will be 943.5634.

Rule V : Sum of Consecutive *n*-natural Numbers

The sum of consecutive *n*-natural numbers

$$= \frac{n\,(n+1)}{2}$$

Example : 1 + 2 + 3 + 4 + 5 + 6 + 7 + 8 + 9 + 10 = ?

Here, $n = 10$

$$\text{Thus, sum} = \frac{10\,(10+1)}{2} = \frac{10 \times 11}{2} = 55$$

Rule VI : Sum of X^{nth} Terms = ?

$$\textit{The sum of the } X^{nth} \textit{ terms} = \frac{X.n\,(n+1)}{2}$$

Example 1 : Give the sum of the $2^{10\text{th}}$

Here, $X = 2$ and $n = 10$, then

$$\text{Sum} = \frac{2 \times 10\,(10+1)}{2} = 110$$

Example 2 : Give the sum of the 4^{20th} terms = ?

Here, $X = 4$ and $n = 20$ then

$$\text{Sum} = \frac{4 \times 20 \times (20+1)}{2} = \frac{4 \times 20 \times 21}{2} = 840$$

Rule VII : Sum of Squares of Consecutive *n*-natural Numbers

Sum of the squares of consecutive *n* - natural numbers $= \frac{n(n+1)(2n+1)}{6}$

Example :

$1^2 + 2^2 + 3^2 + 4^2 + 5^2 + ... + (10)^2 = ?$

Here, $n = 10$, so

$$\text{sum} = \frac{10(10+1)(20+1)}{6} = \frac{10 \times 11 \times 21}{6} = 385$$

Rule VIII : Sum of Cubes of consecutive *n*-natural Numbers

Sum of the cubes of consecutive *n*-natural numbers $= \left[\frac{n(n+1)}{2}\right]^2$

Example : $1^3 + 2^3 + 3^3 + 4^3 + 5^3 + ... + (10)^3 = ?$

$$\text{sum} = \left[\frac{10(10+1)}{2}\right]^2 = 3025$$

Rule IX : Sum of Even Numbers

Sum of the consecutive *n*-even numbers $= X(X+1)$

Note : Here, $X = n/2$

Example : $2 + 4 + 6 + 8 + 10 = ?$

Here, $n = 10$, then $X = 5$

Thus, sum $= 5(5+1) = 30$

Rule X : Sum of Odd Numbers

The sum of consecutive *n*-odd numbers $= \left[\frac{n+1}{2}\right]^2$

Example : $1 + 3 + 5 + 7 + 9 + 11 = ?$

Here, $n = 11$, so sum $= \left[\frac{11+1}{2}\right]^2 = 36$

SUBTRACTION

Subtraction is the operation of finding what number is left when a smaller number is taken out from a greater number. The greater number is called minuend and the smaller number is called as the subtrahend and the number left is called the remainder or the difference. The sign used for this operation is '–'.

Rule 1 : Borrowing and Paying Back Method

This method is the quickest method of subtraction. This method is also called equal additions method.

Example : Suppose we have to subtract 55 from 91. Mentally, we have to increase the number to be subtracted to the nearest multiple of 10, *i.e.*, increase 55 to 60 by adding 5 to it. Mentally increase the other quantity by the same amount, *i.e.*, by 5. Therefore, the problem is 96 minus 60 *i.e.*, our answer is 96 – 60 = 36.

Rule II : Vinculum Method

Note : But it is not necessary that we will get a positive number as we did this in the above example. Now, when we get the negative answer then, this method is :

```
   8 1 2
 – 5 3 4 2
   8 3 1 8
 – 1 1 3 1
  ↓II ↓I
   2 7 4 3
or 2 6 5 7
```

(*a*) 2547 (*b*) 2678
(*c*) 2657 (*d*) 2675
(*e*) None of these

Ans. (*c*)

Explanation : Starting from right top position.

Step I : First double column

$12 - 42 = -30$ (or $\overline{30}$),

$-30 + 18 = -12$(or $\overline{12}$)

$-12 - 31 = -43$ (or $\overline{43}$)

written $\overline{43}$, no carry.

Step II : Second double column

$8 - 53 = -45$ (or $\overline{45}$), $-45 + 83 = 38$

$38 - 11 = 27$, 27 written and no carry.

Here, we write $27\overline{43}$

The first double column total = – 43 or $\overline{43}$ and second double column total 27.

The answer is written as 27 $\overline{43}$. (The line above 43 is called a Vinculum). Then the value of this number is obviously,

2700 – 43 = 2657 which is our answer.

This method is known as VINCULUM METHOD.

Rule III : Double Column Addition and Subtraction Method

This method is useful when there is a series of additions and subtractions to be performed in a line.

```
   8 9 7 8
 – 1 4 3 2
 + 7 8 7 6
 – 4 3 7 8
 + 1 4 3 2
  12 4  7 6
     ↓   ↓
     II  I
```

(*a*) 12380 (*b*) 13380
(*c*) 12476 (*d*) None of these

Ans. (*c*)

Explanation : We should keep looking at the sign before the number and then adding and subtracting as the case may be starting from the top right position.

Step I : First double column

78 – 32 = 46 , 46 + 76 = 122,
22 – 78 = – 56, – 56 + 32 = – 24

Total 1 $\overline{24}$, 1 $\overline{24}$ means 100 – 24 = 76
So, 76 written and 0 carried.

Step II : Second double column

89 – 14 = 75, 75 + 78 = 153, 53 – 43 = 10,
10 + 14 = 24
Total 124 which is written.
Thus, our answer will be 12476.

Example 2 :

```
     2 8 6
   – 4 6 8 3
   + 5 3 8 1
   – 2 8 7 6
   + 8 3 2 3
     6 4 3 1
     ↓   ↓
     II  I
```

(*a*) 1634 (*b*) 3461
(*c*) 6431 (*d*) 5471
(*e*) None of these

Ans. (*c*)

Explanation : We should keep looking at the sign before the number and then adding and subtracting as the case may be.

Starting from the top right position.

Step I : First double column

+ 86 – 83 = 3, 3 + 81 = 84,
84 – 76 = 8
8 + 23 = 31 written 31 and no carry.

Step II : Second double column

2 – 46 = – 44, – 44 + 53 = 9, 9 – 28 = – 19
– 19 + 83 = 64 written 64 and no carry.
Thus, our answer will be 6431.

Rule IV : Subtraction by Complementary Addition

This method is useful for those problems in which it is said that what should be added to a number to make a second number.

Example 1: $\underbrace{5748 + 3059 + ?}_{\text{I}} = \underbrace{9090}_{\text{II}}$

Step I : Using double columns method

Starting from right position
59 + 48 = 107 + 83 = 190
83 written and 1 carried.

Here, we add 83 because 83 is the lowest number which gives 190 when added to 107.

(190 because 90 is the last number of 9090).

Step II : 1 + 57 = 58 + 30 = 88 + 2 = 90

Here, we write 2 and no carry.
The answer will be 283.

Rule V : Austrian Method of Subtraction

Suppose we want to subtract a smaller number from a larger number then this method is useful for us. This is also very useful for those students who are appearing in the Banking Examination or Banking based Examination.

```
Example :  +  6  3  2  4  8
           –     1  7  6  5
           –     2  4  3  2
           –     3  1  8  7
           –     8  8  7  6
              T  S  R  Q  P
              ↓  ↓  ↓  ↓  ↓
              4  6  9  8  8
```

Mental Work : Different steps are involved.

Step I : Starting from bottom right 6 + 7 + 2 + 5 = 20. The number 8 is in front of 20. Here, we choose a number in which unit figure is 8 and this is nearest to 20 (Just greater than 20). Let this number be 28.

Then we subtract 20 from 28 (28 – 20 = 8) and write this number below P and carry 2 for next step.

Step II : 2 + 7 + 8 + 3 + 6 = 26

The number 4 is in front of 26. Here, again we choose a number whose unit figure is 4 and is nearest to 26 (Just greater than 26). Let this number be 34. We subtract 26 from 34 (34 – 26 = 8) and write this number below Q. Then we carry 3 for next step.

Step III : 3 + 8 + 1 + 4 + 7 = 23.

The number 2 is in front of 23. Here, we choose such a number in which unit figure is 2 and is nearest to 23. This number is 32 (Just greater than 23). We subtract 23 from 32 (32 – 23 = 9). Write this number below R and carried 3 for next step.

Step IV : 3 + 8 + 3 + 2 + 1 = 17.

The number 3 is in front of 17. Here, again we choose such a number that unit figure will be 3 and is just nearest to 17. This number is 23. We subtract 17 from 23 (23 – 17 = 6) and write this number below S and carried 2 for next step.

Step V : 2 + 0 = 2. Here, 6 is in front of 2. We write 6 – 2 = 4 below T.

Then the number below T S R Q P = 46988 is our required result.

Some Special Type Questions Based on Banking Examinations and their Tricky Solutions

If two given numbers are opposite, the unit digit (figure) of first is the tens digits (figure) of second and tens digit of first is the unit digit (figure) of second such that 34 and 43, then sum of the numbers is the addition of both figures of any number multiplied by 11 and difference of the numbers is the subtraction of higher figure minus lower figure of any number multiplied by 9.

> Sum = (Addition of both the figures of any number) × 11

and

> Difference = (Subtraction of higher figure – lower figure of any number) × 9

Example : Find the sum and difference of the numbers 43 and 34.

Here, 43 and 34 are opposite. The unit figure of first is 3 and is the tens figure of second. And tens figure of first is 4 and is the unit figure of second.

So, using the formula, sum = (4 + 3) × 11 = 77.

And difference = (4 – 3) × 9 = 9

MULTIPLICATION

We suggest you to remember the tables up to 30 because it saves some valuable time during calculation. Multiplication should be well commanded, because it is needed in almost every question of our concern.

Multiplication is the operation of finding the sum of a given number repeated as many times as there are units in the other given number. The sum thus obtained is called the 'product' of the two numbers. The number to be repeated or multiplied is called 'multiplicand'. The number which indicated how often the multiplicand is to be repeated is called the 'multiplier'.

Different Short-Cut Rules for Multiplication : Multiplication by 11

Step I : We prefix a zero to the multiplicand.

Step II : We write the answer one figure at a time, from right to left as in any multiplication. The figures of the answer are obtained by adding to each successive digit of the multiplicand its right neighbour.

If in the process of addition, we get a 2 digit number, we set down only the right digit thereof and carry the left digit. Some examples are here :

Example 1 : 5892 × 11 = ?

Solution :

Step I : Put down the last figure of 5892 as the right hand figure of the answer :

$$\frac{5892 \times 11}{2}$$

Step II : Each successive figure of 5892 is added to its right-hand neighbour. 9 plus 2 is 11, put 1 below the line and carry over 1. 8 plus 9 plus 1 is 18, put 8 below the line and carry over 1. 5 plus 8 plus 1 is 14, put 4 below the line and carry over 1.

$$\frac{5892 \times 11}{12}$$ (9 + 2 = 11, put 1 below the line and carry over 1)

$$\frac{5892 \times 11}{812}$$ (8 + 9 + 1 = 18, put 8 below the line and carry over 1)

$$\frac{5892 \times 11}{4812}$$ (5 + 8 + 1 = 14, put 4 below the line and carry over 1)

Step III : The first figure of 5892, 5 plus 1, becomes the left-hand figure of the answer :

$$\frac{5892 \times 11}{64812}$$. The answer is 64812.

As you see, each figure of the long number is used twice. It is first used as a 'number', and then, at the next step, it is used as a neighbour. Looking carefully, we can use just one rule instead of three rules, and this one rule can be called as "add the right neighbour" rule.

We must first write a zero in front of the given number, or at least imagine a zero there.

Then we apply the idea of adding the neighbour to every figure of the given number in turn :

$$\frac{05892 \times 11}{2}$$

As there is no neighbour on the right, so we add nothing.

$$\frac{05892 \times 11}{4812}$$ As we did earlier

$$\frac{05892 \times 11}{64812}$$ zero plus 5 plus carried over 1 to 6.

This example shows why we need the zero in front of the multiplicand. It is to remind us not to stop too soon. Without the zero in front, we might have neglected the last 6, we might then have thought that the answer was one 4812. The answer is longer than the given number by one digit, and the zero in front takes care of that.

Multiplication by 12

This method is exactly the same as in the case of 11 except that we double each number before adding the right neighbour.

Example : 5324 × 12

Step I : $$\frac{05324 \times 12}{8}$$

(double the right hand figure and add zero, as there is no neighbour)

Step II : $$\frac{05324 \times 12}{88}$$ (double the 2 and add 4)

Step III : $$\frac{05324 \times 12}{888}$$ (double the 3 and add 2)

Step IV : $$\frac{05324 \times 12}{3888}$$

(double the 5 and add 3, put 3 below the line and carry over 1)

Step V : $$\frac{05324 \times 12}{63888}$$

(zero doubled is zero, plus 5 plus carried over 1)

The answer is 63888. If you go through it yourself you will find that the calculation goes very fast and is very easy.

Rule I : Short - Cut Method for Two-digit Multiplication

General Formula :

$$\begin{array}{cc} A & B \\ C & D \\ \hline \end{array}$$

$$A \times C / A \times D + B \times C / B \times D$$

Here, there are three steps :

Step I : B × D   Step II : A × D + B × C

Step III : A × C

Example 1 : 35 × 72

$$\begin{array}{r} 35 \\ \times 72 \\ \hline 2520 \end{array}$$

Step I : 5 × 2 = 10 Here, write 0 and carry 1 for next step.

Step II : (3 × 2 + 7 × 5) + 1 = 41 + 1 = 42, we write 2 and again carry 4 for next step.

Step III : (7 × 3) + 4 = 21 + 4 = 25, we write 25 and then we get our result

35 × 72 = 2520.

Example 2 : 41 × 75

Last step	Middle step	First step
30	7	5

So, 41 × 75 = 3075

Thus, we see that during the process of multiplication if the result obtained contains more than one digit, then we put down only the right digit and carry the remaining digit to the left.

Multiplication by 13

To multiply any number by 13, we

" Treble each digit in turn and add its right neighbour".

This is the same as multiplying by 12 except that now we "treble" the "number" before we add its "neighbour".

If we want to multiply 9483 by 13, we proceed like this :

Step I : $\dfrac{09483 \times 13}{9}$

(treble the right hand figure and write it down as there is no neighbour on the right)

Step II : $\dfrac{09483 \times 13}{79}$

($8 \times 3 + 3 = 27$, write down 7 and carry over 2)

Step III : $\dfrac{09483 \times 13}{279}$

($4 \times 3 + 8 + 2 = 22$, write down 2 and carry over 2)

Step IV : $\dfrac{09483 \times 13}{3279}$

($9 \times 3 + 4 + 2 = 33$, write down 3 and carry over 3)

Step V : $\dfrac{09483 \times 13}{123279}$

($0 \times 3 + 9 + 3 = 12$, write it down)

The answer is 1,23,279.

Rule II : Multiplication of 2, Three digit Numbers

$$\begin{array}{r} ABC \\ \times\ DEF \\ \hline \end{array}$$

General Formula :

Step I : $C \times F$

Step II : $B \times F + C \times E$

Step III : $A \times F + C \times D + B \times E$

Step IV : $A \times E + B \times D$

Step V : $A \times D$

The required answer: $A \times D / A \times E + B \times D / A \times F + C \times D + B \times E / B \times F + C \times E / C \times F$

Example : 123×456

Solution :

$$\begin{array}{r} 123 \\ \times 456 \\ \hline 56088 \end{array}$$

Step I : $3 \times 6 = 18$, we write 8 and carry 1 for next step.

Step II : $(2 \times 6 + 3 \times 5) + 1 = 27 + 1 = 28$, we write 8 and carry 2 for next step.

Step III : $(1 \times 6 + 3 \times 4 + 2 \times 5) + 2 = 28 + 2 = 30$, we write 0 and carry 3 for next step.

Step IV : $(1 \times 5 + 2 \times 4) + 3 = 13 + 3 = 16$, we write 6 and carry 1 for next step.

Step V : $(1 \times 4) + 1 = 4 + 1 = 5$

Thus required answer is 56088.

Rule III : Multiplication of 2, Four digit Numbers

General Formula :

$$\begin{array}{r} AB\ \ CD \\ \times\ EF\ \ GH \\ \hline \end{array}$$

Step I : $D \times H$

Step II : $C \times H + D \times G$

Step III : $B \times H + F \times D + C \times G$

Step IV : $A \times H + E \times D + B \times G + C \times F$

Step V : $A \times G + C \times E + B \times F$

Step VI : $A \times F + B \times E$

Step VII : $A \times E$

The required answer : $D \times H / C \times H + D \times G / B \times H + F \times D + C \times G / A \times H + E \times D + B \times G + C \times F / A \times G + C \times E + B \times F / A \times F + B \times E / A \times E$

Example :

$$\begin{array}{r} 2\,3\,2\,4 \\ \times\ 5\,2\,6\,7 \\ \hline 122\,4\,0\,5\,0\,8 \end{array}$$

Step I : $4 \times 7 = 28$, We write 8 and carry 2 for Step II.

Step II : $2 \times 7 + 4 \times 6 + 2 = 40$

Again write 0 and then carry 4 for Step III.

Step III : $3 \times 7 + 4 \times 2 + 2 \times 6 + 4 = 45$.

We write 5 and carry 4 for Step IV.

Step IV : $2 \times 7 + 4 \times 5 + 3 \times 6 + 2 \times 2 + 4 = 60$.

We write 0 and carry 6 for Step V.

Step V : $2 \times 6 + 2 \times 5 + 3 \times 2 + 6 = 34$.

Write down 4 and carry 3 for Step VI.

Step VI : $2 \times 2 + 3 \times 5 + 3 = 22$

Write down 2 and carry 2 for Step VII.

Step VII : $2 \times 5 + 2 = 12$.

We write 12 finally and then get our result 12240508.

Rule VI : Special case when the units figures of the multiplicand and the multiplier together total 10 and the other figures are the same

Example : $45 \times 45 = ?$
Tens figure × (Tens figure + 1)
Unit figure × unit figure
$45 \times 45 = 4\,(4 + 1)\,(5 \times 5) = 2025$

Step I : To obtain the right part of the answer, multiply the unit (*i.e.,* the extreme right) digits of the two numbers.

Step II : To obtain the left part of the answer, multiply the other (*i.e.,* the tens digit) by one more than itself/themselves.

Rule VII : If the unit figure is same and the sum of tens figure is 10. Then the rule is

General Rule :

Tens figure × Tens figure + Unit figure
(Unit figure)^2 ← Last two digits of the product.

For Example : $86 \times 26 = 8 \times 2 + 6,\ 6 \times 6 = 2236$
$52 \times 52 = 5 \times 5 + 2,\ 2 \times 2 = 2704$

Rule VIII : The sum of unit figures is 5 and the tens figures are equal. Then the rule is :

General Rule :

(Tens figure)^2 + $\frac{1}{2}$ × Tens figure
(Unit figure)^2 ← Last two digits of the product.

[**Note :** Tens digit must be an even number.]

Example: $83 \times 82 = 8^2 + ½ \times 8,\ 3 \times 2 = 6806.$

Rule IX : If the unit figures are same and the sum of tens figures is 5. Then

Rule = Tens figure × Tens figure + 1/2 × Unit figure
(Unit figure)^2 ← Last two digits of the product.

[**Note :** Ones digit must be an even number.]

For Example : $36 \times 26 = (3 \times 2 + \frac{1}{2} \times 6),\ (6 \times 6)$
$= 936$

Rule X : If the unit figures are 5 and difference between tens figure is 1, then the rule is

Rule = (Larger tens figure + 1) × (smaller tens figure), 75

Example : $35 \times 45 = (4 + 1) \times 3,\ 75 = 1575.$

Rule XI : If sum of the right digits (in sets of 2) of numbers is 50 and the other digits are the same

The method is

1 421
<u>429</u>

180609 $(4 \times 4 + \frac{1}{2} \times 4$ and $21 \times 29)$

2 9918
<u>9932</u>
$9850\frac{1}{2}$ <u>0576</u> = 98505576

$(99 \times 99 + \frac{1}{2} \times 99$ and $18 \times 32)$

Rule XII : The same method is useful for multiplying mixed fractions whose fractional parts together total 1 and whose integral parts are the same

$6\frac{1}{2} \times 6\frac{1}{2} = 42\frac{1}{4}$ (*i.e.,* 6×7 and $\frac{1}{4}$)

$5\frac{1}{4} \times 5\frac{3}{4} = 30\frac{3}{16}$

Rule XIII : Special Method for Squaring Numbers, Ending from 5

$(15)^2$	=	225	1 × 2/25
$(25)^2$	=	625	2 × 3/25
$(35)^2$	=	1225	3 × 4/25
$(45)^2$	=	2025	4 × 5/25
$(95)^2$	=	9025	9 × 10/25
$(875)^2$	=	765625	87 × 88/25
$(995)^2$	=	990025	99 × 100/25
$(1005)^2$	=	1010025	100 × 101/25
$(1245)^2$	=	1550025	124 × 125/25

Rule XIV : In two numbers, if sum of fractional parts is 1/2 and integral parts of both numbers are same

$8\frac{1}{4} \times 8\frac{1}{4} = 68\frac{1}{16}$

$(8 \times 8 + \frac{1}{2} \times 8$ for the integral part and $\frac{1}{4} \times \frac{1}{4}$ for the fractional part)

Rule XV : Multiplication of a given number by a power of 5.

We put as many zeros to the right of multiplicand as is the number of the power of 5 and we divide the number so formed by 2 to the same power as is the number of 5.

Example: $1478 \times 625 = ?$

We know $625 = 5^4$

$$\therefore \quad 1478 \times 625 = \frac{14780000}{2^4}$$

$$= \frac{14780000}{16} = 923750$$

Rule XVI : Multiplication of a given number by 9, 99, 999, 9999, 99999 etc.

We place as many zeros to the right of the multiplicand as is the number of nines and from the number so formed, subtract the multiplicand to get the answer.

Example: $7832 \times 9999 = ?$

So, $7832 \times 9999 = 78320000 - 7832 = 78312168$

Rule XVII : Multiplication by Repeating Number 1

Example : $5423 \times 111 = ?$

Step I : We write down the first right side digit of 5423 *i.e.*, 3.

Step II : We write down the sum of two right side digit of 5423 *i.e.*, $2 + 3 = 5$.

Step III : Again write down the sum of the three right side digit of 5423 *i.e.*, $4 + 2 + 3 = 9$.

[Here, we never exceed from three because 111 is made of three numbers.]

Step IV : We write down the sum of next three right side digits 5423 *i.e.*, $5 + 4 + 2 = 11$.

Step V : We write down the sum of next two digits $5 + 4$ and add $1 = 10$ of the number 5423.

Step VI : At last we write the last digit $5 + 1 = 6$.

Required answer = 601953

$5423 \times 111 = ?$

V	U	T	Z	Y	X
5 + 1	5 + 4 + 1	5 + 4 + 2	4 + 2 + 3	2 + 3	3
6	10	11	9	5	3
↓	↓	↓	↓	↓	↓
6th Step	5th Step	4th Step	3rd Step	2nd Step	1st Step

Required answer = 601953.

Rule XVIII : Multiplication by Repeating Number 2

In this process the multiplication and general rule both are same, like Rule XVII but only difference is that we multiply every digit of XYZT..... by 2.

Example : $234 \times 22 = ?$

T	Z	Y	X
2 × 2 + 1	2 (2 + 3) + 1	2 (3 + 4)	2 × 4
↓	↓	↓	↓
5	1	4	8
4th Step	3rd Step	2nd Step	1st Step

Required answer = 5148.

DIVISION

We now go on to the quicker Math's of at-sight division which is based on long-established Vedic process of mathematical calculations. Different from "for the special cases", it is capable of immediate application to all cases and it can be described as the "crowning gem of all" for the universality of its applications.

Rule I : Test of divisibility by 2

A given number is divisible by 2, if the unit digit in the number is any of 2, 4, 6, 8 and 0.

Example : The numbers 96712, 34504, 26436, 648, 243980 end in 2, 4, 6, 8 and 0 respectively so they all are divisible by 2.

Rule II : Test of Divisibility by 3

A given number is divisible by 3, if the sum of the digits of a number is divisible by 3.

Example : The number 537240 is divisible by 3 because sum of its digits $= 5 + 3 + 7 + 2 + 4 + 0 = 21$ which is divisible by 3.

Rule III : Test of divisibility by 4

A given number is divisible by 4, if the number formed by last two digits is divisible by 4.

Example : The number 539624 is divisible by 4, since the number formed by last two digits is 24, which is divisible by 4.

And the number 674238 is not divisible by 4 since the number formed by last two digits is 38, which is not divisible by 4.

Rule IV : Test of Divisibility by 5

A given number is divisible by 5 if the unit digit is either 0 or 5.

Example : The number 5176580 and 672385 end in 0 and 5 respectively so both of them are divisible by 5.

Rule V : Test of divisibility by 6

A given number is divisible by 6 if this number is divisible by 2 and 3 both.

Example : 24 is divisible by 6 because 24 is divisible by 2 and 3 both.

Rule VI : Test of divisibility by 8

A given number is divisible by 8, if the number formed by last three digits is divisible by 8.

Example : The number 36597512 is divisible by 8, since the number formed by the last three digits is 512 which is divisible by 8. But the number 31527412 is not divisible by 8, since the number formed by the last three digits is 412, which is not divisible by 8.

Rule VII : Test of Divisibility by 9

A given number is divisible by 9, if the sum of the digits of a number is divisible by 9.

Example : The number 586431 is divisible by 9 because sum of its digits = 5 + 8 + 6 + 4 + 3 + 1 = 27 which is divisible by 9.

The number 586432 is not divisible by 9 because sum of digits 5 + 8 + 6 + 4 + 3 + 2 = 28, which is not divisible by 9.

Rule VIII : Test of Divisibility by 10

Any number that ends in zero is divisible by 10.

Example : The number 87670 is divisible by 10 because this number ends in zero.

Rule IX : Test of Divisibility by 11

A given number is divisible by 11, if the difference of the sum of its digits in odd places and the sum of its digits in even places, is either zero or divisible by 11.

Example : The number 4832718 is divisible by 11 because sum of digits in odd places = 8 + 7 + 3 + 4 = 22.

Sum of digits in even places = 1 + 2 + 8 = 11

Difference = 22 – 11 = 11, which is divisible by 11, Hence, 4832718 is divisible by 11.

Rule X : Test of Divisibility by 12

A given number is divisible by 12 if the number is divisible by 3 and 4 both.

Example : The number 96 is divisible by 12, because this number is divisible by 3 and 4 both.

Rule XI : Multiples of a Number

A number which is divisible by a given number '*a*' is called its multiple *i.e.,* 3, 6, 9, 12 etc. are all multiples of 3.

Rule XII : If in any number the digit repeats thrice then this number will be divisible by 3 and 37

Example : 222, 777, 131313, 212121

Rule XIII : If in a number any digit repeats six times then this number must be divisible by 3,7,11,13

Example : 222222, 777777,

Rule XIV : If any number is divided in three groups and the difference between the numbers at even places and odd places is 0 or divisible by 7 then this number must be divisible by 7.

Example : 231622342 divides into three groups as

231	622	342
1st group	2nd group	3rd group
odd	even	odd

$$\underset{even}{622} - \underset{odd}{(231+342)} = 49$$

which is divisible by 7.

Other Points :

(1) Dividend : The number to be divided is called the dividend.

(2) Divisor : The number by which it is divided is called the divisor.

(3) Quotient : The number which tells how many times the divisor is contained in the dividend is called the quotient.

(4) Remainder : If the dividend does not contain the divisor on exact number of times and we take away from the dividend as many times the divisor as we can, what is left is called the remainder. When there is no remainder, the division is called to be exact.

(5) In inexact division

Dividend = (Divisor × Quotient + Remainder)

(6) In exact division

Dividend ÷ Divisor = Quotient

(7) Quotient × Divisor = Dividend

(8) $\text{Divisor} = \dfrac{\text{Dividend} - \text{Remainder}}{\text{Quotient}}$

(9) True Remainder = (First Remainder) + (Second Remainder × First Divisor) + (Third Remainder × First divisor × Second Divisor) and so on.

If a given number is divided by another number using factors, then the true remainder is obtained from successive remainders by using the above formula.

Example : A number when divided by 899 gives a remainder 63. The remainder, when the same number is divided by 29 is

Number $= 899 \times \text{Quotient} + 63$

$= 29 \times 31 \text{ Quotient} + 2 \times 29 + 5$

So, the remainder obtained by dividing the number by 29 is clearly 5.

Rule I : Division by 9, 99, 999, ... etc.

Rule II : Division by 5, 15, 35 and 45

If we want to divide a number by 5, 15, 35 and 45 then first of all we multiply the given number by 2 and then divide it by 10, 30, 70, 90 respectively, after calculation we get the result.

Step I : The given number is multiplied by 2.

Step II : Divide the number (found from step 1) by 10, 30, 70, 90 for 5, 15, 35, 45, respectively.

Example : $285 \div 45$.

Step I : Multiply the dividend by 2, *i.e.,* $285 \times 2 = 570$.

Step II : Divide the result of step 1 by 90 *i.e.,* $570 \div 90 = 6.3$.

Rule III : Division by 100000, 10000, 1000, 100, 10

If we want to divide any number by 10, 100, 1000, 10000, 100000, ... etc., then first of all we count the zeros. Write the number which is to be divided, count the digits of the number from the right hand side which is equal to the number of zeros and put decimal at that point. The right hand side of the decimal is known as remainder and left hand side of the decimal is known as quotient.

Example : $66666 \div 100 = ?$

Step I : 'Count the zero'. There are two zeros here.

Step II : In the dividend a decimal is given as the digits of the number from R.H.S. which is equal to the number of zeros.

666.66

Step III : R.H.S. of the number is 66 which is known as Remainder.

Step IV : L.H.S. of the number is 666 which is required Quotient.

Rule IV : Division by 25 and 75

If we want to divide any number by 25 and 75 then first of all, we multiply the number by 4 and then divide by 100 and 300 respectively for finding real remainder, we divide the remainder by 4. The process same as Rule II.

Step I : Multiply the number by 4.

Step II : Divide the number (from step 1) by 100 or 300.

Step III: Divide remainder by 4 to get the real remainder.

Example : $7878 \div 25 = ?$

Step I : Multiply the number by 4

$7878 \times 4 = 31512$

Step II : Divide the number (from step 1) by 100

$31512/100 = 315.12$

Step III : Real remainder $12/4 = 3$.

Rule V : Division by two digit Number

Example : $1701 \div 21 = ?$

As before, separate the divisor 21 into parts as 2/1

This means that

(1) We have to put a decimal after one place from the right in the dividend, *i.e.,* as 170.1 and

(2) That we are going to divide only by the left digit 2 (of the divisor 21) and not by 21 itself.

Our 1st A.D. is the first digit 1 of 1701 but since 1 will not go in 2, we bring down the 1st 2 digits 17 as the A.D. (as in any conventional division). To indicate that 17 has been brought down, the 17 had been underlined in the working. The subsequent steps are shown below :

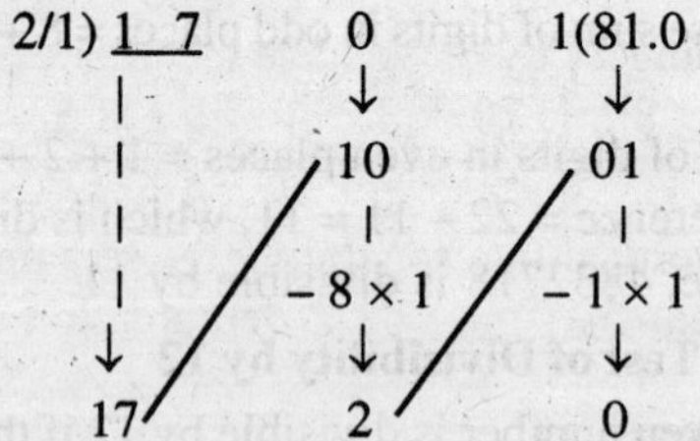

Rule VI : Three Digit divisors

Example : Divide 7031985 by 823.

Step I : Here, the divisor is of 3 digits. All the difference which we make is to put the last two digits (23) of divisor on top. And there are two flag-digits (23), We will separate two digits (85) for remainder.

8^{23} | 70 3 1 9 | 85

Step II : We divide 70 by 8 and put down 8 and 6 in their proper places.

8^{23}	70	$_6 3$	1	9	85
	8				

Step III : Now, our gross dividend is 63. From that we subtract 16, the product of the first of the flag-digits, *i.e.,* 2, and the first quotient-digit, *i.e.,* 8, and get the remainder 63 – 16 = 47 as the actual dividend. And, dividing it by 8, we have 5 and 7 as Q and R respectively and put them at their proper places.

8^{23}	70	$_6 3$	$_7 1$	9	85
	8	5			

Step IV : Now our gross dividend is 71, and we deduct the cross-products of two flag-digits 23 and the two quotient digits (8 and 5), *i.e.,* 2 × 5 + 3 × 8 = 10 + 24 = 34; and our remainder is 71 – 34 = 37. We then continue to divide 37 by 8. We get Q = 4 & R = 5

8^{23}	70	$_6 3$	$_7 1$	$_5 9$	85
	8	5	4		

Step V : Now our gross dividend is 59. And actual dividend is equal to 59 minus cross- product of 23 and 54, *i.e.,* 59 – (2 × 4 + 3 × 5) = 59 – 23 = 36

Dividing 36 by 8, our Q = 4 and R = 4

8^{23}	70	$_6 3$	$_7 1$	$_5 9$	$_4 85$
	8	5	4	4	

Step VI : Actual dividend = 48 – (3 × 4 + 2 × 4)
= 48 – 20 = 28

Dividing it by 8, our Q = 3 and R = 4

8^{23}	70	$_6 3$	$_7 1$	$_5 9$	$_4 8 _4 5$
	8	5	4	4	3

Step VII : Actual dividend = 45 – (3 × 4 + 2 × 3)
= 45 – 18 = 27.

Dividing 27 by 8, we have Q = 3 and R = 3.

8^{23}	70	$_6 3$	$_7 1$	$_5 9$	$_4 8 _4 5_3$
	8	5	4	4	3 3

The vertical line separating the remainder from the quotient part may be a demarcation point for decimal.

Ans. 8544.33

Our answer can be 8544.33, but if we want the quotient and remainder, the procedure is somewhat different. In that case, we do not need the last two steps, *i.e.,* the calculation up to the stage

8^{23}	70	$_6 3$	$_7 1$	$_5 9$	$_4 85$
	8	5	4	4	

is sufficient to answer the question.

Quotient = 8544 ; Remainder = 485 – 10 × (Cross multiplication of 23 and 44) * – last digit of flag × last digit of quotient

= 485 – 10 (4 × 2 + 4 × 3) – 3 × 4
= 485 – 200 – 12 = 273

Application of Algebraic Formula in Simplification

In competitive examinations some questions can be solved very easily maintaining speed and accuracy by using algebraic formulae than the use of the other method.

Example :

$$\frac{0.05 \times 0.05 \times 0.05 + 0.04 \times 0.04 \times 0.04}{0.05 \times 0.05 - 0.05 \times 0.04 + 0.04 \times 0.04} = ?$$

(*a*) 0.09 (*b*) 0.01
(*c*) 0.009 (*d*) 0.01
(*e*) None of these

Solution : General method

$$\frac{0.05 \times 0.05 \times 0.05 + 0.04 \times 0.04 \times 0.04}{0.05 \times 0.05 - 0.05 \times 0.04 + 0.04 \times 0.04} =$$

$$= \frac{0.000125 + 0.000064}{0.0025 - 0.002 + 0.0016} = \frac{0.000189}{0.0021}$$

$$= \frac{0.000189}{0.002100} = \frac{189}{2100} = \frac{189}{21 \times 100} = \frac{9}{100} = 0.09$$

By using Algebraic formula

$$\frac{0.05 \times 0.05 \times 0.05 + 0.04 \times 0.04 \times 0.04}{0.05 \times 0.05 - 0.05 \times 0.04 + 0.04 \times 0.04} = ?$$

$$= \frac{(0.05)^3 + (0.04)^3}{(0.05)^2 - 0.05 \times 0.04 + (0.04)^2}$$

$= 0.09$

$$\left[\frac{a^3 + b^3}{a^2 - ab + b^2} = a + b\right]$$

It is clear that this problem is solved in the minimum time by using algebraic formula.

So, algebraic formulae are very useful in the field of simplification. Therefore candidates are suggested to remember these important algebraic formulae for fast calculation and accuracy :

* Cross multiplication of two flag digits and last two digits of quotient.

1. $a^2 - b^2 = (a + b)(a - b)$

2. $\dfrac{a^2 - b^2}{a + b} = a - b$

3. $\dfrac{a^2 - b^2}{a - b} = a + b$

4. $(a + b)^2 + (a - b)^2 = 2(a^2 + b^2)$

5. $(a + b)^2 - (a - b)^2 = 4ab$

6. $\dfrac{a^3 - b^3}{a^2 + ab + b^2} = a - b$

7. $\dfrac{a^3 + b^3 + c^3 - 3abc}{a^2 + b^2 + c^2 - ab - ac - bc} = a + b + c$

8. $(a + b)^3 = a^3 + 3ab(a + b) + b^3$
$= a^3 + 3a^2b + 3ab^2 + b^3$

9. $(a - b)^3 = a^3 - 3ab(a - b) - b^3$
$= a^3 - 3a^2b + 3ab^2 - b^3$

10. $a^3 - b^3 = (a - b)(a^2 + ab + b^2)$

11. $a^3 + b^3 = (a + b)(a^2 - ab + b^2)$

12. $(a + b)^2 = a^2 + 2ab + b^2$

13. $(a - b)^2 = a^2 - 2ab + b^2$

EXERCISE

1. ? % of 150 + 250 = 280
(*a*) 30 (*b*) 10
(*c*) 20 (*d*) 40
(*e*) None of these

2. 25 % of 40 ÷ 4 % of 25 = ?
(*a*) 10 (*b*) 1
(*c*) 0 (*d*) 2
(*e*) None of these

3. 75 % of 96 = ? × 12
(*a*) 72 (*b*) 6
(*c*) 12 (*d*) 96
(*e*) None of these

4. 73.85 + 215.345 – 167.2134 = ?
(*a*) 456.4084 (*b*) 121.2166
(*c*) 120.8296 (*d*) 121.6711
(*e*) None of these

5. 30 % of 270 + 5/8 of 64 = ?
(*a*) 121 (*b*) 81
(*c*) 40 (*d*) 242
(*e*) None of these

6. $\dfrac{2.4 \times 3.2 + 4.32}{0.5 \times 24} = ?$
(*a*) 4 (*b*) 0.5
(*c*) 1.504 (*d*) 1
(*e*) None of these

7. 9.75 + 25.88 + ? = 41.18
(*a*) 5.55 (*b*) 5.75
(*c*) 6.57 (*d*) 4.23
(*e*) None of these

8. $\dfrac{1344 \div 24 + 104}{202.1 - 198.9} = ?$
(*a*) 50 (*b*) 500
(*c*) 0.50 (*d*) 25
(*e*) None of these

9. $\dfrac{17.82 + 17.18 - 5}{(30)^2 \div 3} = ?$
(*a*) 10/1 (*b*) 1/10
(*c*) 10/100 (*d*) 100/30
(*e*) None of these

10. $22 + 5\dfrac{1}{3} + 1\dfrac{1}{2} - 9\dfrac{3}{5} \div \dfrac{2}{5} = ?$
(*a*) $4\dfrac{1}{2}$ (*b*) $3\dfrac{1}{2}$
(*c*) $2\dfrac{1}{3}$ (*d*) $5\dfrac{1}{6}$
(*e*) None of these

11. 3.6 – 1.2 ÷ 5.76 = ?
(*a*) 3.381 (*b*) 3.401
(*c*) 4.391 (*d*) 2.391
(*e*) None of these

12. $\dfrac{11 - 4 \times 3 + 7}{20 - 5 \times 4 + 12} = ?$
(*a*) 0.1 (*b*) 0.2
(*c*) 0.3 (*d*) 0.4
(*e*) None of these

13. $\dfrac{\sqrt{324}}{36} \times \dfrac{\sqrt{729}}{9} \times \dfrac{\sqrt{25}}{196} = ?$
(*a*) 135/14 (*b*) 18/5
(*c*) 18/7 (*d*) 9/17
(*e*) None of these

14. 13.243 + 5.409 + ? = 24.71

(*a*) 5.78 (*b*) 4.718
(*c*) 4.818 (*d*) 5.818
(*e*) None of these

15. 16 % of 40 = ? % of 1

(*a*) 6.40 (*b*) 0.640
(*c*) 640 (*d*) 450
(*e*) None of these

16. 7.02 + 7.2 − 2.2 = ?

(*a*) 12.2 (*b*) 12.0
(*c*) 12.02 (*d*) 12.002
(*e*) None of these

17. ? % of 346 = 10.38

(*a*) 5 (*b*) 7
(*c*) 9 (*d*) 4
(*e*) None of these

18. $3\frac{1}{3} + ? - 2\frac{3}{4} = 2\frac{29}{36}$

(*a*) $2\frac{7}{9}$ (*b*) $\frac{7}{9}$
(*c*) $1\frac{1}{7}$ (*d*) $1\frac{17}{18}$
(*e*) None of these

19. 288 ÷ 24 ÷ 0.12 = ?

(*a*) 100 (*b*) 12
(*c*) 12.12 (*d*) 1.44
(*e*) None of these

20. $\frac{8+6\times2-9}{3+7\times3-9} = ?$

(*a*) $1\frac{1}{4}$ (*b*) 4/9
(*c*) 11/15 (*d*) 19/21
(*e*) None of these

21. 1/2 + 1/3 + ? = 3/2

(*a*) $2\frac{1}{5}$ (*b*) $1\frac{1}{10}$
(*c*) $\frac{2}{3}$ (*d*) $1\frac{1}{3}$
(*e*) None of these

22. 60 % of 30 = ? % of 200

(*a*) 18 (*b*) 36
(*c*) 40 (*d*) 9
(*e*) None of these

23. 5/4 × 200/67 ÷ 20/67 = ?

(*a*) 0.125 (*b*) 125
(*c*) 12.5 (*d*) 1250
(*e*) None of these

24. $\frac{36+6-2\times2}{72-14\times5} = ?$

(*a*) 1/2 (*b*) 1/240
(*c*) 15/2 (*d*) 3
(*e*) None of these

25. $\frac{\sqrt{625}}{5} \times \frac{\sqrt{144}}{3} \times 0.07 = ?$

(*a*) 140 (*b*) 14.0
(*c*) 0.140 (*d*) 1.40
(*e*) None of these

EXPLANATORY ANSWERS

1. (*c*) : x % of 150 + 250 = 280

$\therefore \frac{x \times 150}{100} = 30$

$\therefore x = \frac{30 \times 100}{150} = 20.$

2. (*a*) : $\frac{25 \times 40}{100} \times \frac{100}{25 \times 4} = 10.$

3. (*b*) : $\frac{75}{100} \times 96 = 12x \;\therefore\; x = \frac{96 \times 75}{12 \times 100} = 6.$

4. (*e*) : 121.9816.

5. (*a*) : $\frac{30}{100} \times 270 + \frac{5}{8} \times 64 = 81 + 40 = 121$

6. (*d*) : $\frac{2.4\times3.2+4.32}{0.5\times24} = \frac{7.68+4.32}{12} = \frac{12}{12} = 1$

7. (*a*) : $X = 41.18 - 9.75 - 25.88 = 5.55.$

8 (*a*) : $\frac{56+104}{3.2} = \frac{160}{32} \times 10 = 50.$

9. (*b*) : $\frac{35-5}{900+3} = \frac{30}{300} = \frac{1}{10}$.

10. (*e*) : $22 + \frac{16}{3} + \frac{3}{2} - \frac{48}{5} \times \frac{5}{2} = \frac{29}{6} = 4\frac{5}{6}$.

11. (*e*) : $3.6 - \frac{120}{576} = 3.6 - 0.208 = 3.392$.

12. (*e*) : $\frac{11-12+7}{20-20+12} = \frac{6}{12} = 0.5$.

13. (*e*) : $\frac{18}{36} \times \frac{27}{9} \times \frac{5}{196} = \frac{15}{392}$.

14. (*e*) : 6.058.

15. (*c*) : $x = \frac{16 \times 40}{100} \times 100 = 640$.

16. (*c*) : $14.22 - 2.2 = 12.02$.

17. (*e*) : $\frac{x}{100} \times 346 = 10.38$

$\therefore\ x = \frac{1038}{346} \times \frac{100}{100} = 3$.

18. (*e*) : $3\frac{1}{3} + x - 2\frac{3}{4} = 2\frac{29}{36}$

$\Rightarrow\ x = 2\frac{29}{36} + 2\frac{3}{4} - 3\frac{1}{3}$

$= 2 + 2 - 3 + (29/36 + 3/4 - 1/3)$

$= 1 + 44/36 = 1 + \frac{11}{9} = 1\frac{11}{9}$

19. (*a*) : $288 \div 24 \div 0.12$

$= 288 \times \frac{1}{24} \times \frac{1}{0.12}$

$= \frac{12}{12} \times 100 = 100$

20. (*c*) : $\frac{8+12-9}{3+21-9} = \frac{20-9}{24-9} = \frac{11}{15}$.

21. (*c*) : $1/2 + 1/3 + ? = 3/2$

$\therefore\ x = 3/2 - 5/6$

$= \frac{9-5}{6} = \frac{4}{6} = \frac{2}{3}$.

22. (*d*) : $\frac{60}{100} \times 30 = \frac{x}{100} \times 200$

$\Rightarrow\ 18 = 2x$

$\Rightarrow\ x = 9$

23. (*c*) : $\frac{5}{4} \times \frac{200}{67} \times \frac{67}{20} = \frac{25}{2} = 12.5$.

24. (*e*) : $\frac{36+6-4}{72-70} = \frac{38}{2} = 19$.

25. (*d*) : $\frac{25}{5} \times \frac{12}{3} \times 0.07 = 1.40$.

2

POWERS AND ROOTS

SQUARE, CUBE, INDICES, SURDS SQUARING

Squaring of a number is largely used in mathematical calculations. There are so many rules for special cases. But we will discuss a general rule for squaring which is capable of universal application.

Squaring is multiplying the number by itself. For example,

$25^2 = 25 \times 25 = 625$

When the number is large, squaring by simple multiplication is obviously not very easy.

You should remember the following squares which will help you in taking square roots :

$1^2 = 1$	$11^2 = 121$	$21^2 = 441$
$2^2 = 4$	$12^2 = 144$	$22^2 = 484$
$3^2 = 9$	$13^2 = 169$	$23^2 = 529$
$4^2 = 16$	$14^2 = 196$	$24^2 = 576$
$5^2 = 25$	$15^2 = 225$	$25^2 = 625$
$6^2 = 36$	$16^2 = 256$	$26^2 = 676$
$7^2 = 49$	$17^2 = 289$	$27^2 = 729$
$8^2 = 64$	$18^2 = 324$	$28^2 = 784$
$9^2 = 81$	$19^2 = 361$	$29^2 = 841$
$10^2 = 100$	$20^2 = 400$	$30^2 = 900$

Short Methods in Squaring

Let *a, b* denote numbers

$a^2 = a^2 - b^2 + b^2 = (a^2 - b^2) + b^2$

or $a^2 = [(a + b)(a - b)] + b^2$ ...(I)

$(a + b)^2 = a^2 + b^2 + 2ab$ ..(II)

$(a - b)^2 = a^2 + b^2 - 2ab$ ...(III)

These are very useful as we can write the given number as sum or difference of two convenient numbers.

Example : Find $(1213)^2$ = ?

$= [(1213 - 13)(1213 + 13)] + (13)^2$

$= (1200 \times 1226) + 169 = 1471200 + 169$

$= 1471369$

Squaring of a number ending in 5

Multiply the number formed after deleting 5 at the units place with the number, one higher than it. Annex 25 on the right side of the product and you will get the square of the given number.

Example : Find $(165)^2$ = ?

Solution : $16 \times 17 = 272$

So, $(165)^2 = 27225$

Properties of Squares

1. It cannot be a negative number.
2. It cannot have odd number of zeros at its end.
3. It cannot end with 2, 3, 7 or 8.
4. Square of an even number is always an even number.
5. Square of an odd number is always an odd number.
6. Every square number is either a multiple of 3 or exceeds multiple of 3 by unity.
7. Every square number is either a multiple of 4 or exceeds multiple of 4 by unity.
8. If a square number ends in 9, the digit preceding 9 must be either zero or even.
9. 1, 5, 6 and 0 at the end of a number reproduce themselves as the last digit in their squares.

Square of Decimal Number

Find the square of the number ignoring the decimal point. Put the decimal point leaving double the number of digits (from the right) as compared to that in the given number. In other words, the position of decimal place in the square is double of that in the original number. The square will lie between the square of integral part and the square of the number, one higher than the integral part.

Example : Find the square of 14.52 = ?

Solution : $(1452)^2 = 2108304$; $(14.52)^2 = 210.8304$

Square of Fraction :

$$\left(\frac{p}{q}\right)^2 = \frac{p^2}{q^2}$$

Square of $1\frac{1}{2}, 2\frac{1}{2}, 3\frac{1}{2}, 4\frac{1}{2}$ etc.

Multiply the integral part by one more than it. Add $\frac{1}{4}$ to the product and you will get the square of the given half fraction.

Example : Find the square of $4\frac{1}{2}$.

Solution : $\left(4\frac{1}{2}\right)^2 = 4\times5+\frac{1}{4} = 20+\frac{1}{4}$

$= \frac{81}{4} = 20\frac{1}{4}$

Square of Number Consisting of 9s only

Let the number consists of n 9s.

Write down $(n-1)$ 9*s*, followed by one 8, then $(n-1)$ zeros and finally annex 1 at the end.

Example : Find $(99999)^2$.

Solution : The given number consists of five 9s.

So, we will write four 9s followed by 8, then four zeros and finally 1.

i.e., $(99999)^2 = 9999800001$.

SQUARE ROOT

Square root is inverse of square. Square root of a given number may be defined as the number whose square is equal to the given number. In other words, square root of a given number is the number, which when multiplied by itself, gives the product equal to the given number.

Example : $\sqrt{4} = 2$ and $2\times2 = 4$,

$\sqrt{9} = 3$ and $3\times3 = 9$

There are two methods of finding square root of a number.

Method I : By Factorization

This method is generally used where the given number is a perfect square or when the number can be written as product of such factors whose square roots are known.

You should know following common square roots:

$\sqrt{0} = 0$	$\sqrt{15} = 3.873$
$\sqrt{1} = 1$	$\sqrt{16} = 4$
$\sqrt{2} = 1.414$	$\sqrt{17} = 4.123$
$\sqrt{3} = 1.732$	$\sqrt{19} = 4.359$
$\sqrt{4} = 2$	$\sqrt{21} = 4.583$
$\sqrt{5} = 2.236$	$\sqrt{22} = 4.690$
$\sqrt{6} = 2.449$	$\sqrt{23} = 4.796$
$\sqrt{7} = 2.646$	$\sqrt{25} = 5$
$\sqrt{9} = 3$	$\sqrt{36} = 6$
$\sqrt{10} = 3.162$	$\sqrt{49} = 7$
$\sqrt{11} = 3.317$	$\sqrt{64} = 8$
$\sqrt{13} = 3.606$	$\sqrt{81} = 9$
$\sqrt{14} = 3.742$	$\sqrt{100} = 10$

In factorization method, we write the given number as product of prime factors and take the product of prime factors, choosing one out of every pair.

Note :

1. Square root of a number greater than or equal to 1 but less than 100 consists of only one digit.
2. Square root of a number greater than or equal to 100 but less than 10000 consists of two digits.
3. In general, if the given number has '*n*' digits, its square root will have $n/2$ digits when n is even and $\frac{n+1}{2}$ digits when n is odd. This holds good for the case of pure decimal fractions too.

Some properties of exact square roots (*i.e.*, square roots are whole numbers)

1. A pure square number ending in 1 must have 1 or 9 as the last digit in its square root.

   For example, $\sqrt{81} = 9$; $\sqrt{121} = 11$.
2. If a square ends in 4, its square root must have 2 or 8 as the last digit.

   For example, $\sqrt{64} = 8$; $\sqrt{144} = 12$.
3. If a square ends in 5 or 00, its square root must have 5 or 0 respectively as the last digit.

   For example, $\sqrt{625} = 25$; $\sqrt{100} = 10$.
4. A square ending in 9 has 3 or 7 as the last digit in its square root.

   For example, $\sqrt{169} = 13$; $\sqrt{729} = 27$.

Method II : By Division

is the most general method of finding square roots and is applicable to all cases.

Step I : Mark-off groups of two digits, starting from right. The extreme group may be either single digit or a pair.

Step II : Start division process from the extreme left group.

Step III : For the second stage, add the quotient the divisor. The divisor of this stage will be equal this sum with the quotient for this stage suffixed it. The next dividend is always obtained by annexing the next pair of digits (of the dividend) to the remainder.

Step IV : For the next stage, again add the divisor and the quotient of the previous stage. The divisor this stage will be formed in the same manner as explained for the second stage in step III.

Step V : Continue step IV till all the groups get exhausted, in case a remainder is left, annex two zeros it and put a decimal point in the quotient.

At every stage after this we will annex two zeros the remainder.

Continue to the number of decimal places required in the result. The quotient is equal to the square root of the given number.

CUBE ROOTS

If $a^3 = x$, then $a = \sqrt[3]{x}$; a is the cube root of x

Cube root of $8 = \sqrt[3]{2 \times 2 \times 2} = 2$

"Cube root of" $27 = \sqrt[3]{27} = \sqrt[3]{3 \times 3 \times 3} = 3$

"Cube root of" $216 = \sqrt[3]{6 \times 6 \times 6} = 6$

"Cube root of" $0.000064 = \sqrt[3]{0.04 \times 0.04 \times 0.04} = 0.04$

Example : Evaluate $\sqrt[3]{1325 + \sqrt{20 + \sqrt{256}}}$

Solution : $\sqrt[3]{1325 + \sqrt{20 + 16}}$ $\quad (\because \sqrt{256} = 16)$

$= \sqrt[3]{1325 + \sqrt{36}}$

$= \sqrt[3]{1325 + 6}$ $\quad (\because \sqrt{36} = 6)$

$= \sqrt[3]{1331} = \sqrt[3]{11 \times 11 \times 11} = 11$

EXERCISE

1. The largest number of five digits which is a perfect square, is :
   (*a*) 99999 (*b*) 99764
   (*c*) 99976 (*d*) 99856
   (*e*) None of these

2. The value of $\sqrt{2}$ up to three places of decimals is :
   (*a*) 1.410 (*b*) 1.412
   (*c*) 1.413 (*d*) 1.414
   (*e*) None of these

3. $\dfrac{(\sqrt{7} + \sqrt{5})}{\sqrt{7} - \sqrt{5}}$ is equal to :
   (*a*) $6 + \sqrt{35}$ (*b*) $6 - \sqrt{35}$
   (*c*) 2 (*d*) 1
   (*e*) None of these

4. The least number by which 294 must be multiplied to make it a perfect square, is :
   (*a*) 2 (*b*) 3
   (*c*) 6 (*d*) 5
   (*e*) None of these

5. The least number to be added to 269 to make it a perfect square , is :
   (*a*) 31 (*b*) 16
   (*c*) 7 (*d*) 20
   (*e*) None of these

6. What is the smallest number by which 3600 be divided to make it a perfect cube?
   (*a*) 9 (*b*) 50
   (*c*) 300 (*d*) 450
   (*e*) None of these

7. The smallest number of 4 digits, which is a perfect square is :
   (*a*) 1000 (*b*) 1016
   (*c*) 1024 (*d*) 1036
   (*e*) None of these

8. $\sqrt{10} \times \sqrt{250} = ?$
   (*a*) 46.95 (*b*) 43.75
   (*c*) 50.25 (*d*) 50
   (*e*) None of these

9. $\sqrt{?}/200 = 0.02$

(*a*) 0.4 (*b*) 4
(*c*) 16 (*d*) 1.6
(*e*) None of these

10. $\sqrt{.04} = ?$

(*a*) .02 (*b*) .2
(*c*) .002 (*d*) 1.2
(*e*) None of these

11. The greatest number of four digits which is a perfect square, is :

(*a*) 9996 (*b*) 9801
(*c*) 9900 (*d*) 9604
(*e*) None of these

12. $\sqrt[3]{?}\ / 200 = 0.02$

(*a*) 0.4 (*b*) 64
(*c*) 16 (*d*) 1/64
(*e*) None of these

13. If $\sqrt{256} \div \sqrt[3]{x} = 2$, then x is equal to :

(*a*) 64 (*b*) 128
(*c*) 512 (*d*) 1024
(*e*) None of these

14. $112/\sqrt{196} \times \sqrt{576}/12 \times \sqrt{256}/8 = ?$

(*a*) 8 (*b*) 12
(*c*) 16 (*d*) 32
(*e*) None of these

15. $(2\sqrt{27} - \sqrt{75} + \sqrt{12})$ is equal to :

(*a*) $\sqrt{3}$ (*b*) $2\sqrt{3}$
(*c*) $3\sqrt{3}$ (*d*) $4\sqrt{3}$
(*e*) None of these

16. $\sqrt{50} \times \sqrt{98}$ is equal to :

(*a*) 65.95 (*b*) 63.75
(*c*) 70.25 (*d*) 70
(*e*) None of these

17. The largest four-digit number which is a perfect cube, is :

(*a*) 9999 (*b*) 9261
(*c*) 8000 (*d*) 8467
(*e*) None of these

18. If $\sqrt{2} = 1.4142$, the square root of $\dfrac{(\sqrt{2}-1)}{\sqrt{2}+1}$ i equal to :

(*a*) 0.732 (*b*) 0:3652
(*c*) 1.3142 (*d*) 0.4142
(*e*) None of these

19. $\dfrac{\sqrt{121} \times 0.9}{1.1 \times 0.11} = ?$

(*a*) 2 (*b*) $\dfrac{900}{11}$
(*c*) 9 (*d*) 11
(*e*) None of these

20. $\sqrt{25}/15625 = \sqrt{?}/30625$

(*a*) 2 (*b*) 3.5
(*c*) 96.04 (*d*) 1225
(*e*) None of these

21. $\sqrt{3.61/10.24} = ?$

(*a*) 29/32 (*b*) 19/72
(*c*) 19/32 (*d*) 29/62
(*e*) None of these

22. $\dfrac{\sqrt{32} + \sqrt{48}}{\sqrt{8} + \sqrt{12}} = ?$

(*a*) $\sqrt{2}$ (*b*) 2
(*c*) 4 (*d*) 8
(*e*) None of these

23. $\dfrac{1}{\sqrt{9} - \sqrt{8}} = ?$

(*a*) $1/2\,(3 - \sqrt{2})$ (*b*) $1/3 + 2\sqrt{2}$
(*c*) $(3 - 2\sqrt{2})$ (*d*) $(3 + 2\sqrt{2})$
(*e*) None of these

EXPLANATORY ANSWERS

1. (*d*) : Largest number of 5 digits is 99999.

```
3 ) 99999 ( 316
   -9
61 ) 99 (
    -61
626 ) 3899 (
      3756
      -143
```

So, required number $= (99999 - 143) = 99856$.

2. (*d*) :

```
1 ) 2.000000 ( 1.414
   -1
24 ) 100 (
    -96
281 ) 400 (
     -281
2824 ) 11900 (
      -11296
```

So, $\sqrt{2} = 1.$

3. (a) : $\dfrac{\sqrt{7}+\sqrt{5}}{\sqrt{7}-\sqrt{5}} = \dfrac{\sqrt{7}+\sqrt{5}}{\sqrt{7}-\sqrt{5}} \times \dfrac{\sqrt{7}+\sqrt{5}}{\sqrt{7}+\sqrt{5}}$

$= \dfrac{\left(\sqrt{7}+\sqrt{5}\right)^2}{7-5} = \dfrac{7+5+2\sqrt{7}\times\sqrt{5}}{2}$

$= \dfrac{12+2\sqrt{35}}{2} = 6+\sqrt{35}$.

4. (c) : $294 = 7\times7\times2\times3$. To make it a perfect square it must be multiplied by 2×3, *i.e.*, 6.

5. (d) :

```
   1 ) 269 ( 16
      -1
  26 ) 169 (
     - 156
        13
```

Required number to be added $= (17)^2 - 269 = 20$.

6. (d) : $3600 = 2\times2\times2\times2\times3\times3\times5\times5$.
To make it a perfect cube, we must divide it by $2\times5\times5\times3\times3 = 450$

7. (c) : Smallest number of 4 digits = 1000

```
   3 ) 1000 ( 31
      -9
  61 ) 100 (
     - 61
       39
```

So, required number $= (32)^2 = 1024$.

8. (d) : $\sqrt{10}\times\sqrt{250} = \sqrt{2500} = 50$.

9. (c) : Let $\sqrt{x}/200 = 0.02$

Then, $\sqrt{x} = 200\times0.02 = 4$
So, $x = 16$.

10. (b) : $\sqrt{.04} = \sqrt{4/100} = 2/10 = 0.2$

11. (b) : Greatest number of four digits = 9999
Now, $9999 = (99)^2 + 198$
So, $(99)^2 = 9999 - 198 = 9801$,
So, required number = 9801.

12. (b) : Let $\sqrt[3]{x}/200 = 0.02$

Then, $\sqrt[3]{x} = 200\times0.02 = 4$,
So, $x = 4\times4\times4 = 64$.

13. (c) : $\sqrt{256}/\sqrt[3]{x} = 2 \Rightarrow 16 = 2\sqrt[3]{x}$

$\Rightarrow \sqrt[3]{x} = 8 \Rightarrow x = 512$

14. (d) : Given expression
$= (112/14\times 24/12\times16/8) = 32$

15. (c) : $2\sqrt{27}-\sqrt{75}+\sqrt{12}$

$= 2\sqrt{9\times3}-\sqrt{25\times3}+\sqrt{4\times3}$

$= 6\sqrt{3}-5\sqrt{3}+2\sqrt{3} = 3\sqrt{3}$

16. (d) : $\sqrt{50}\times\sqrt{98} = \sqrt{4900} = 70$

17. (b) : Clearly, 9261 is a perfect cube.

18. (d) : $\dfrac{\sqrt{2}-1}{\sqrt{2}+1} = \dfrac{\sqrt{2}-1}{\sqrt{2}+1}\times\dfrac{\sqrt{2}-1}{\sqrt{2}-1} = \dfrac{\left(\sqrt{2}-1\right)^2}{1}$

So $\sqrt{\dfrac{\sqrt{2}-1}{\sqrt{2}+1}} = \sqrt{2}-1 = 1.4142-1 = 0.4142$

19. (b) : Given expression $= \dfrac{\sqrt{121}\times0.9}{1.1\times0.11}$

$= \dfrac{11\times9\times1000}{11\times11\times10} = \dfrac{900}{11}$

20. (c) : $\dfrac{\sqrt{25}}{15625} = \dfrac{\sqrt{x}}{30625} \Rightarrow \sqrt{x} = \dfrac{30625\times5}{15625} = 9.8$

$\therefore\ x = 96.04$.

21. (c) : $\sqrt{3.61/10.24} = \sqrt{361/1024}$

$\dfrac{\sqrt{19\times19}}{\sqrt{32\times32}} = 19/32$

22. (b) : $\dfrac{\sqrt{32}+\sqrt{48}}{\sqrt{8}+\sqrt{12}} = \dfrac{\sqrt{16\times2}+\sqrt{16\times3}}{\sqrt{4\times2}+\sqrt{4\times3}}$

$= \dfrac{4\sqrt{2}+4\sqrt{3}}{2\sqrt{2}+2\sqrt{3}} = \dfrac{4\left(\sqrt{2}+\sqrt{3}\right)}{2\left(\sqrt{2}+\sqrt{3}\right)} = \dfrac{4}{2} = 2$

23. (d) : $\dfrac{1}{\sqrt{9}-\sqrt{8}} = \dfrac{1}{\sqrt{9}-\sqrt{8}}\times\dfrac{\sqrt{9}+\sqrt{8}}{\sqrt{9}+\sqrt{8}}$

$= \dfrac{3+2\sqrt{2}}{9-8} = 3+2\sqrt{2}$.

LCM AND HCI

LEAST COMMON MULTIPLE (LCM)

LCM of two or more numbers is the least among the numbers which are common multiples of the given numbers. In other words, LCM of given numbers is the smallest number which is exactly divisible by each of them. In the above examples, the LCM for

2 and 5 is 10

2 and 3 is 6

4 and 6 is 12

We can find LCM by two methods.

Method 1:

Step I : Write the numbers as product of prime factors.

Step II : Find the product of the highest powers of the prime factors, which will be the LCM

Note : Do not repeat any factor while writing the product in Step II.

Example : Find the LCM of 36, 56, 105 and 108.

Step I : $36 = 2^2 \times 3^2$

$56 = 2^3 \times 7$

$105 = 3 \times 5 \times 7$

$108 = 2^2 \times 3^3$

Step II: The LCM must contain every prime factor of each of the numbers. Also it must include the highest power of each prime factor which appears in any of them. So, it must contain 2 or it would not be a multiple of 56, it must contain 3 or it would not be a multiple of 108, it must contain 5 or it would not be a multiple of 105, and it must contain 7 or it would not be a multiple of 56 or of 105.

Therefore, the LCM $= 2^3 \times 3^3 \times 5 \times 7 = 7560$

Method 2 :

This is quicker method to find the prime factors and hence LCM In this method there can be mo than one arrangement for the same numbers.

Step I : Write the numbers in a row and strike o those numbers which are factors of any other numb in the set.

Step II : Write the factor on the left hand si which can divide maximum of the numbers.

Step III : Write in the next row the quotie obtained and also those numbers (as they are) whi are not divisible by that factor. You can strike c from any row 1, if it appears.

Step IV : Repeat steps II and III until we get a where no two numbers have a common factor or di sor, *i.e.,* all the numbers in the row are prime to ea other, though individually they may not be pri numbers.

Step V : Multiply all the factors or divisors a the numbers left in the last row. The product gi the LCM of the given numbers.

Let us now see how it works and how simple i

Example : Find LCM of 48, 108 and 140.

Method 1: Factorization Method

Factors of 48 $= 2 \times 2 \times 2 \times 2 \times 3 = 2^4 \times 3$

Factors of 108 $= 2 \times 2 \times 3 \times 3 \times 3 = 2^2 \times 3^3$

Factors of 140 $= 2 \times 2 \times 5 \times 7 = 2^2 \times 5 \times 7$

LCM = Highest power of 2 × Highest power (× Highest power of 5 × Highest power of 7

$= 2^4 \times 3^3 \times 5 \times 7 = 15120$

Method 2 : By Division Method

2	48, 108, 140
2	24, 54, 70
3	12, 27, 35
	4, 9, 35

So, LCM $= 2 \times 2 \times 3 \times 4 \times 9 \times 35 = 15120$.

L.C.M of Decimals

To find the LCM of decimal numbers first of all we find out the LCM of numbers without decimal. And then we see the number in which the decimal is given in the minimum digits from right to left. We put the decimal in our result which is equal to that number of digits.

Example : Find the LCM of 0.16, 5.4 and .0098.

First of all we find out the LCM of 16, 54, 98.

Here, LCM of 16, 54, 98 is 21168.

In numbers 0.16, 5.4, 0.0098, the minimum digits from right to left is 5.4.

Here, in 5.4 the decimal is given of one digit from right to left is 5.4.

So, we put decimal in our result such that: = 21168 = 2116.8.

Example : Find the LCM of 48, 10.8 and 0.140.

LCM of 48, 108 and 140 = 15120

So, LCM of 48, 10.8, and 0.140 = 1.5120.

L.C.M of Fractions

If *a/b, c/d, e/f* be the proper fractions then their LCM is given by

$$= \frac{\text{L.C.M of numerators } a, c, e}{\text{H.C.F of denominators } b, d, f}$$

Example : Find the LCM of 3^5, 3^8 ,3^{12} , 3^{15} ,3^{20}

If the base of these numbers is same then LCM of these numbers will be equal to maximum power of these numbers.

So, LCM = 3^{20}

> **Imp :** If *A* and *B* be the two numbers then the product of their LCM and HCF is equal to the product of the two numbers. *i.e.*,
>
> $\text{LCM} \times \text{HCF} = A \times B$
>
> $\text{So, L.C.M} = \frac{A \times B}{\text{H.C.F}}$

To Find LCM By Multiples

If we want to find LCM of 3 and 4 then first of all we find the multiples of 3 and 4. Then the lowest common multiples of both of them is their LCM

Multiples of 3: 3, 6, 9, 12, 15, 18, ...

Multiples of 4: 4, 8, 12 , 16, 20, ...

Here, lowest common multiple is 12 which is our LCM.

HIGHEST COMMON FACTOR (HCF)

A number which is a factor of two or more numbers is said to be a common factor or common measure of the numbers. We exclude unity which is common measure of all numbers. The greatest number which will divide each of two or more numbers is called their Highest Common Factor or Greatest Common Measure and is denoted by the letters HCF or GCM(Greatest Common Measure).

Example: Find the HCF of 8 and 12.

Factors of 8 are 1, 2, 4, 8 and

Factors of 12 are 1, 2, 3, 4, 6, 12

The common factors are 1, 2, 4 but highest of these is 4. Hence, 4 is the HCF.

By Factorization Method

Factor method has discussed above or, we express each given number as the product of primes. Now, we take the product of common factors which is our required HCF.

Example : Find the HCF of 144, 336 and 2016.

Factors of 144 = $2^4 \times 3^2$

Factors of 336 = $2^4 \times 3 \times 7$

Factors of 2016 = $2^5 \times 7 \times 3^2$

So, HCF of given numbers = $2^4 \times 3 = 48$.

By Division Method

Step I : We divide the greater number by the smaller and find out the remainder.

Step II : Then divide the first divisor by remainder and find the second remainder.

Step III : Then divide the second divisor by the second remainder.

Step IV : We repeat this process till no remainder is left. The last divisor is our required HCF.

Example : HCF of 513 and 783.

```
513 ) 783 ( 1
      513
      270 ) 513 ( 1
            270
            243) 270 (1
                 243
                 27 ) 243 ( 9
                      243
                       ×
```

So, HCF = 27.

HCF of Decimals

Here, first of all we find HCF of the given numbers without decimals and then put decimal.

Example : Find the HCF of 0.0012, 1.6, and 28.

Here, HCF of 12, 16 and 28 is 4.

The decimal is given at maximum digits from right to left.

So, HCF = 0.0004.

HCF of Fractions

If *a/b*, *c/d*, *e/f* be the proper fractions then their HCF is given by

$$= \frac{\text{H.C.F of numerators } a, c, e \ldots}{\text{L.C.M of denominators } b, d, f \ldots}$$

Example : Find the HCF of 2/5, 8/35, 4/15 and 6/25.

$$\text{HCF} = \frac{\text{H. C. F. of } 2, 8, 4, 6}{\text{L. C. M. of } 5, 35, 15, 25} = \frac{2}{525}.$$

EXERCISE

1. HCF of 11, 0.121, 0.1331 is :
(*a*) 0.0011 (*b*) 0.121
(*c*) 0.1331 (*d*) 12.21
(*e*) None of these

2. The L.C.M of 22, 54, 108, 135 and 198 is :
(*a*) 330 (*b*) 1980
(*c*) 5940 (*d*) 11880
(*e*) None of these

3. HCF of 8^{-2}, 8^{-3}, 8^{-4}, 8^{-5} is :
(*a*) 8^{-2} (*b*) 8^{-3}
(*c*) 8^{-4} (*d*) 8^{-5}
(*e*) None of these

4. The sum of two numbers is 528, and their HCF is 33. How many pairs of such numbers can be formed?
(*a*) 4 (*b*) 5
(*c*) 8 (*d*) 2
(*e*) None of these

5. HCF of 4^5, 4^{11} and 4^{15} is :
(*a*) 4^5 (*b*) 4^{11}
(*c*) 4^{15} (*d*) 4
(*e*) None of these

6. The HCF of 2^3, 3^2, 4 and 15 is :
(*a*) 2^3 (*b*) 3^2
(*c*) 1 (*d*) 360
(*e*) None of these

7. HCF of 15, 45, 90 is :
(*a*) 12 (*b*) 13
(*c*) 13 (*d*) 15
(*e*) None of these

8. The GCM of 9/45, 15/20, 16/20 and 15/25 is :
(*a*) 1/20 (*b*) 1/40
(*c*) 1/60 (*d*) 1/15
(*e*) None of these

9. GCM of 3556 and 3444 is :
(*a*) 25 (*b*) 26
(*c*) 27 (*d*) 28
(*e*) None of these

EXPLANATORY ANSWERS

1. (*a*) **:** HCF of 11, 121, 1331 is 11.
So, HCF of 11, 0.121 and 0.1331 is = 0.0011.

2. (*c*) **: Method 1**

2	22, 54, 108, 135, 198
11	11, 27, 54, 135, 99
9	1, 27, 54, 135, 9
3	1, 3, 6, 15, 1
	1, 1, 2, 5, 1

So, LCM = 2 × 11 × 9 × 3 × 2 × 5 = 5940

Method 2

Factors of 22 = 2 × 11
Factors of 54 = 2 × 3 × 3 × 3 = 2×3^3
Factors of 108 = 2 × 2 × 3 × 3 × 3 = $2^2 \times 3^3$
Factors of 135 = 5 × 3 × 3 × 3 = 5×3^3
Factors of 198 = 2 × 3 × 3 × 11 = $2^1 \times 3^2 \times 11^1$
So, LCM = Max. power of 2 × Max. power of 3 × Max. power of 5 × Max. power of 11 = $2^2 \times 3^3 \times 5 \times 11$ = 5940

3. (*d*) **:** HCF of the given numbers = 8^{-5}

4. (*a*) : Trick :

Let the numbers be 33 a and 33 b

Now, $33a + 33b = 528$

$\Rightarrow \quad 33(a + b) = 528 \qquad a + b = 16$

The possible values of a and b are (1, 15); (3, 13) ; (5, 11) ; and (7, 9).

So, the possible pairs of numbers are (33, 495); (99, 429); (165, 363); (231, 297).

5. (*a*) : HCF of the given numbers = 4^5

Minimum power of 4.

6. (*c*) : Trick :

HCF of 2^3, 3^2, 4 and 15

Here by factorization method we see that 1 is the HCF of given numbers

$$\left.\begin{array}{ll} 2^3 & = 2^3 \\ 3^2 & = 3^2 \\ 4 & = 2^2 \\ 15 & = 3 \times 5 \end{array}\right] = 1$$

7. (*d*) : By Factorization Method

Factors of 15 = 3×5

Factors of 45 = $3^2 \times 5$

Factors of 90 = $3^2 \times 5 \times 2$

So, HCF = $3 \times 5 = 15$.

8. (*a*) : GCM of the given fractions

$$= \frac{\text{G.C.M of } 9, 15, 16, 15}{\text{L.C.M of } 45, 20, 20, 25} = \frac{1}{900}$$

9. (*d*) : Trick :

HCF =

$$\begin{array}{l} 3444\,)\,3556\,(\,1 \\ \quad\;\; -3444 \\ \quad\;\;\; 112\,)\,3444\,(\,30 \\ \qquad\qquad -360 \\ \qquad\qquad\; 84\,)\,112\,(\,1 \\ \qquad\qquad\qquad -84 \\ \qquad\qquad\qquad 28\,)\,84\,(\,3 \\ \qquad\qquad\qquad\quad\;\; 84 \\ \qquad\qquad\qquad\quad\;\; \times \end{array}$$

HCF = 28.

4

RATIO AND PROPORTION

RATIO

When we say that the length of a line *AB* is 5 centimetres, we mean that a unit of length called 1 centimetre is contained in *AB* five times. If we have two lines *AB* and *CD* and their lengths be 2 and 3 centimetres respectively, we say that the length of *AB* is 2/3 of the length of *CD*.

Ratio is a relation between two quantities in the same units which shows that one quantity is how many times of another quantity. Suppose A and B are two persons who have ₹ 50 and ₹ 100 respectively. Here 50 and 100 are two quantities in the same unit, rupees. It is clear that ₹ 50 is half of ₹100. Thus we can say in term of ratio that ratio of ₹ 50 and ₹ 100 is 1: 2.

A ratio may be expressed in the form of simplest fraction (If numerator and denominator have no common factor except 1, then fraction is in the simplest or lowest form).

Sign of ratio = (:) read as "Is To" So, ratio of two quantities ₹ 50 and ₹ 100 = 50/100 = 1/2 = 1 : 2 (Pronounced as 1 is to 2).

Memorable Points

1. Here in 1 : 2, '1' is called *Antecedent* of the ratio.
2. '2' is called *Consequent* of the ratio.

PROPORTION

The equality of two ratios is called *proportion*. Suppose, we have two ratios for example, 3 : 2 and 15 : 10. Here, 3 : 2 = 15 : 10. Thus this equality of these two given ratios is called proportion.

Sign of Proportion

Sign of proportion is : :

Therefore the above mentioned example is written as 3 : 2 : : 15 : 10 (it means 3/2 = 15/10)

The terms 3, 2, 15 and 10 are called proportional and named as the 1st, 2nd, 3rd and 4th proportional respectively.

In a proportion, the 1st and 4th terms are known as *extremes*, while 2nd and 3rd terms are known as *means.*

So, in given example 3 and 10 are extremes, while 2 and 15 are means.

In the concised way, all these terms are shown below :

3 : 2 : : 15 : 10

1st Ratio (3 : 2) — Proportion (: :) — 2nd Ratio (15 : 10)

Note : (1) It is not necessary that all four terms (proportional) are in the same unit. But in this condition, 1st and 2nd and 3rd and 4th terms must have same unit.

(2) 3 : 2 : : 15 : 10 is also written as
3/2 = 15/10

Memorable Points

We can find out the value of a unknown proportional, when values of three proportional are known by applying the following methods :

1. 1st proportional $= \frac{2nd \times 3rd}{4th}$

Example : ? : 190 : : 840 : 40

Solution : ? (1st proportional)

$$= \frac{190 \times 840}{40} = 3990.$$

2. 2nd proportional $= \frac{1st \times 4th}{3rd}$

Example : 50/ ? = 20/60

Solution : 50/ ? = 20/60

50 : ? : : 20 : 60

$$? = \frac{50 \times 60}{20} = 150$$

3. 3rd proportional = $\frac{\text{1st} \times \text{4th}}{\text{2nd}}$

Example : 3/4 = ? / 56

Solution : 3 : 4 :: ? : 56

$$\Rightarrow \quad ? = \frac{3 \times 56}{4} = 42$$

4. 4th proportional = $\frac{\text{2nd} \times \text{3rd}}{\text{1st}}$

Example : 500/1200 = 500/?

Solution : 500 : 1200 : : 500 : ?

$$\Rightarrow \quad ? = \frac{1200 \times 500}{500} = 1200$$

Some other Terms and their Formulae of Ratio and Proportion

***1.* Mean proportional of '*a*' and '*b*' =** $\sqrt{ab}$

Example : Find the mean proportional between 0.32 and 0.02.

Solution : Mean proportional between 0.32 and 0.02

$$= \sqrt{0.32 \times 0.02} = \sqrt{0.0064} = 0.08$$

***2.* Duplicate Ratio of** $a : b = a^2 : b^2$

Example : Find duplicate ratio of $7\sqrt{3} : 4\sqrt{2}$

Solution : Duplicate ratio of $7\sqrt{3} : 4\sqrt{2}$

$$= \left(7\sqrt{3}\right)^2 : \left(4\sqrt{2}\right)^2 = 49 \times 3 : 16 \times 2 = 147 : 32.$$

***3.* Sub-duplicate Ratio of** $a : b = \sqrt{a} : \sqrt{b}$

Example : Find sub-duplicate ratio (S.D.R) of 200 : 392.

Solution : S.D.R of 200 : 392 = $\sqrt{200} : \sqrt{392}$

$$= \frac{\sqrt{200}}{\sqrt{392}} = \sqrt{\frac{200}{392}}$$

$$= \sqrt{\frac{100}{196}} = \frac{10}{14} = \frac{5}{7} = 5 : 7$$

***4.* Triplicate Ratio of** $a : b = a^3 : b^3$

Example : Find triplicate ratio of 4 : 5.

Solution : Triplicate ratio of 4 : 5

$$= 4^3 : 5^3 = 64 : 125$$

***5.* Sub-Triplicate Ratio of** $a : b = \sqrt[3]{a} : \sqrt[3]{b}$

Example : Find sub-triplicate Ratio of 27 : 1.

Solution : S.T.R of 27 : 1 = $\sqrt[3]{27} : \sqrt[3]{1}$

$$= \sqrt[3]{3^3} : \sqrt[3]{1} = 3 : 1.$$

***6.* Inverse or Reciprocal Ratio of** $a : b = 1/a : 1/b$

Example : Find reciprocal ratio of 4 : 5.

Solution : Reciprocal ratio of 4 : 5 = 1/4 : 1/5

***7.* Third Proportional to '*a*' and '*b*' =** b^2/a

Example : Find the third proportional to 0.8 and 0.2.

Solution : Third proportional to 0.8 and 0.2

$$= \frac{(0.2)^2}{0.8} = \frac{0.04}{0.8} = \frac{4}{80} = 0.05.$$

***8.* Compound Ratio of** $a : b, c : d, e : f$

$$= \frac{\text{Product of all first terms of all ratio}}{\text{Product of all second terms of all ratio}}$$

$$= \frac{a \times c \times e}{b \times d \times f}$$

Example : Find compound ratio of 8 : 2, 2 : 1 and 9 : 3.

Solution : Compound ratio = $\frac{8 \times 2 \times 9}{2 \times 1 \times 3}$

$$= \frac{24}{1} = 24 : 1.$$

***9.* If** $A : B = x : y$ **and** $B : C = m : n$ **then**

(*I*) $A : C = \frac{x \times m}{y \times n}$

(*II*) $A : B : C = mx : ym : yn$

Example : If $A : B = 2 : 3$ and $B : C = 4 : 5$ then $C : A$ is equal to

$$A : C = \frac{2 \times 4}{3 \times 5} = \frac{8}{15} = 8 : 15$$

$$\left[\because \text{In Formula } A : C = \frac{x \times m}{y \times n} \right]$$

So, $C : A = 15 : 8$.

10. If $A : B : C = x : y : z$ and $C : D = m : n$ Then $A : B : C : D = m(x : y) : z(m : n)$

Example : If $A : B : C = 2 : 3 : 4$ and $C : D = 5 : 6$, then $A : B : C : D$ is equal to

Solution : $A : B : C : D = m(x : y) : z(m : n)$

So, $A : B : C : D = 5(2 : 3) : 4(5 : 6)$

$= 10 : 15 : 20 : 24$

EXERCISE

1. The students in three classes are in the ratio 2 : 3 : 5. If 20 students are increased in each class, the ratio changes to 4 : 5 : 7. What is the total number in the three classes before the increase?

(*a*) 100 students (*b*) 75 students
(*c*) 150 students (*d*) 50 students
(*e*) None of these

2. The ratio between two numbers is 3 : 4. If each number be increased by 2, the ratio becomes 7 : 9. Find the numbers.

(*a*) 12, 16 (*b*) 16, 12
(*c*) 12, 15 (*d*) 13, 14
(*e*) None of these

3. Divide ₹ 1540 among *A, B, C* so that *A* shall receive 2/9 as much as *B* and *C* together, and *B* 3/11 of what *A* and *C* together do. Find the share of A, B and C.

(*a*) 285, 330, 830 (*b*) 280, 330, 930
(*c*) 280, 330, 980 (*d*) 330, 380, 980
(*e*) None of these

4. In a fort there is provision for 40 days for 275 persons. If after 16 days, 125 persons leave the fort, for how many more days the provision will now last?

(*a*) 45 days (*b*) 35 days
(*c*) 44 days (*d*) 53 days
(*e*) None of these

5. A fort has provision for 35 days. If after 5 days 225 more persons joined and the food lasts 25 days, how many men are there in the fort?

(*a*) 1225 persons (*b*) 1572 persons
(*c*) 1125 persons (*d*) 1229 persons
(*e*) None of these

6. The ratio between the ages of Rahim and Karim is 3 : 5 and the sum of their ages is 56 years. What was the ratio of their ages 7 years ago?

(*a*) 1: 2 (*b*) 3 : 2
(*c*) 3 : 4 (*d*) 4 : 3
(*e*) None of these

7. The prices of a scooter and television set are in the ratio 3 : 2. If a scooter costs ₹ 6,000 more than the television set, what is the price of the television set?

(*a*) ₹ 12,000 (*b*) ₹ 8,000
(*c*) ₹ 10,000 (*d*) ₹ 5,000
(*e*) None of these

8. The prices of scooter and a moped are in the ratio of 9 : 5. If a scooter costs ₹ 4200 more than a moped, find the price of the moped.

(*a*) ₹ 5052 (*b*) ₹ 5250
(*c*) ₹ 5053 (*d*) ₹ 5060
(*e*) None of these

9. A sum of money is divided between two persons in the ratio of 3 : 5. If the share of one person is ₹ 20 less than that of the other, find the sum.

(*a*) ₹ 75 (*b*) ₹ 90
(*c*) ₹ 80 (*d*) ₹ 85
(*e*) None of these

EXPLANATORY ANSWERS

1. (*a*) : $4 - 2 = 5 - 3 = 7 - 5 = 2.$

As we know 20 students are increased in each class.

So, $(2 + 3 + 5) = \dfrac{20}{2} \times 10$

$= 100$ students.

2. (*a*) : Let numbers are $3x$ and $4x$

$$\frac{3x+2}{4x+2} = \frac{7}{9}$$

$\Rightarrow \quad 27x + 18 = 28x + 14$

$\Rightarrow \quad x = 4$

Hence, numbers are $3 \times 4 = 12$ and $4 \times 4 = 16$.

3. (*b*) : A's share : $(B + C)$'s share = 2 : 9 ... (1)
B's share : $(A + C)$'s share = 3 : 11 ... (2)
Now dividing ₹ 1540 in the ratio of 2 : 9 and 3 : 11
A's share 2/11 of ₹ 1540 = ₹ 280
B's share = 3/14 of ₹ 1540 = ₹ 330
C's share = ₹ 1540 – (₹ 280 + ₹ 330) = ₹ 930

4. (*c*) : Reasoning
More men less days, less men more days
So, 275 : x : : (275 – 125) : (40 – 16)

So, $x = \frac{275 \times 24}{150} = 44$ days.

5. (*c*) : Let the number of persons be x.
$(35 - 5)\, x = 25\,(x + 225)$
$\Rightarrow 30x - 25x = 25 \times 225$

$\Rightarrow \quad x = \frac{25 \times 225}{5}$

$\Rightarrow \quad x = 1125$ persons.

6. (*a*) : Present age of Rahim = 56/8 × 3 = 21 years
Present age of Karim = 56/8 × 5 = 35 years
So, ratio of ages 7 years ago
= (21 – 7) : (35 – 7)
= 14 : 28 = 1 : 2

7. (*a*) : Let the price of a scooter = $3x$ and the price of a television set = $2x$.
$\because \quad 3x - 2x = 6000$
$\Rightarrow \quad x = 6000$
So, price of television set = $2x = 2 \times 6000$
= ₹ 12000

8. (*b*) : We have, $9x - 5x = 4200$
$\Rightarrow \quad 4x = 4200$

$\Rightarrow \quad x = \frac{4200}{4} = 1050$

So, price of the moped = $5x = 5 \times 1050$
= ₹ 5250.

9. (*c*) : $\frac{\text{Sum}}{\text{Difference}} = \frac{\text{Sum}}{20} = \frac{3+5}{5-3}$

$\text{Sum} = \frac{8}{2} \times 20 =$ ₹ 80

5

PARTNERSHIP

MEANING OF PARTNERSHIP

Partnership is an association of two or more persons who put their money together in order to carry on a certain business. It is of two kinds :

1. Simple
2. Compound

1. Simple Partnership : If the capitals of the partners are invested for the same period, the partnership is called *simple.*

2. Compound Partnership : If the capitals of the partners are invested for different lengths of time, the partnership is called *compound.*

Sleeping Partner : One who simply invests money, but does not attend to the business is called a *sleeping partner.*

Working Partner : One who invests money as well as attends to the business is called a *working partner.*

A working partner receives a fixed salary from the profits for managing the business.

In order to solve the problems regarding partnership, remember this special trick :

$$\frac{\text{A's capital} \times \text{A's time in partnership}}{\text{B's capital} \times \text{B's time in partnership}} = \frac{\text{A's profit}}{\text{B's profit}}$$

Example : Rahim and Rohan enter into a speculation. Rahim puts in ₹ 50 and Rohan puts in ₹ 45. At the end of 4 months Rahim withdraws half of his capital. Sanju then enters with a capital of ₹ 70. At the end of 12 months in what ratio will the profit be divided?

Solution :

Rahim's share : Rohan's share : Sanju's share

$= 50 \times 4 + 25 \times 8 : 45 \times 12 : 70 \times 8$

$= 400 : 540 : 560$

$= 20 : 27 : 28$

Therefore, the profit will be divided in the ratio of 20 : 27 : 28.

EXERCISE

1. Bhavana began a business with ₹ 2100 and is joined afterwards by *Y* with ₹ 3,600. After how many months did *Y* join, if the profit at the end of the year is divided equally?

(*a*) 3 months (*b*) 4 months
(*c*) 5 months (*d*) 6 months
(*e*) 8 months

2. A and B enter into a partnership. A contributes ₹ 3,500 for 8 months and B contributes ₹ 4,000. If they share the profits equally, then how long B's capital was used?

(*a*) 7 months (*b*) 5 months
(*c*) 8 months (*d*) 4 months
(*e*) None of these

3. A and B start a business with initial investments in the ratio of 12 : 11 and their annual profits were in the ratio of 4 : 1. If A invested the money for 11 months, then B invested the money for :

(*a*) 3 months (*b*) 2 months
(*c*) 4 months (*d*) 1 month
(*e*) None of these

4. A started a business with ₹ 30,000 and 4 months later B joins. If at the end of the year, the profits are divided in the ratio of 9 : 4, then what was B's capital?

(*a*) ₹ 20,000 (*b*) ₹ 35,000
(*c*) ₹ 30,000 (*d*) ₹ 19,000
(*e*) None of these

5. A invests ₹ 3,000 for one year in a business, how much B should invest in order that the profit after 1 year may be divided in the ratio of 2 : 3?

(*a*) ₹ 2,000 (*b*) ₹ 1,800
(*c*) ₹ 3,600 (*d*) ₹ 4,500
(*e*) None of these

6. ₹120 is divided between A, B and C, so that A's share is ₹ 20 more than B's and ₹ 20 less than C's. What is B's share?

(*a*) ₹ 10 (*b*) ₹ 15
(*c*) ₹ 20 (*d*) ₹ 25
(*e*) None of these

7. Ram, Puja and Manisha hired a car for ₹ 520 and they used it 7, 8 and 11 hours respectively. The amount of hire charges paid by Puja was :

(*a*) ₹ 140 (*b*) ₹ 160
(*c*) ₹ 180 (*d*) ₹ 220
(*e*) None of these

8. A began business with ₹ 1,250 and is joined afterwards by B, with ₹ 3,750. When did B Join, if the profit at the end of the year is divided equally?

(*a*) After 6 months (*b*) After 8 months
(*c*) After 4 months (*d*) After 7 months
(*e*) None of these

9. A's capital is twice that of B's capital and B's capital is thrice that of C's capital. What is the ratio of the capitals of A,B and C?

(*a*) 1 : 2 : 3 (*b*) 2 : 1 : 3
(*c*) 1 : 3 : 6 (*d*) 6 : 3 : 1
(*e*) None of these

10. Madan and Sunil are partners in a business. Madan invests ₹ 5,000 for 5 months and Sunil invests ₹ 6,000 for 6 months. If the profit is ₹ 610, then Sunil's share in the profit is :

(*a*) ₹ 250 (*b*) ₹ 360
(*c*) ₹ 520 (*d*) ₹ 630
(*e*) None of these

EXPLANATORY ANSWERS

1. (*c*) : $\frac{2100 \times 12}{3600 \times x} = \frac{1}{1}$

$\Rightarrow \quad x = 7$

Hence, *y* joins after 12 – 7 = 5 months.

2. (*a*) : Now, $\frac{3500 \times 8}{4000 \times x} = \frac{1}{1} \Rightarrow x = 7$ months.

3. (*a*) : $\frac{12 \times 11}{11 \times x} = \frac{4}{1}$

So, *x* = 3 months.

4. (*a*) : $\frac{30000 \times 12}{x \times 8} = \frac{9}{4}$

So, *x* = ₹ 20,000.

[Using Formula

$\frac{\text{A's capital} \times \text{A's time in partnership}}{\text{B's capital} \times \text{B's time in partnership}} = \frac{\text{A's profit}}{\text{B's profit}}$]

5. (*d*) : $\frac{3000 \times 12}{x \times 12} = \frac{2}{3}$

$\Rightarrow \quad x = 4500$

6. (*c*) : A : B : C

$x : (x - 20) : (x + 20)$

According to the question,

$x + (x - 20) + (x + 20) = 120$

$\Rightarrow \quad x = ₹\ 40$

∴ B's share = 40 –20 = ₹ 20

7. (*b*) : Charges paid by Puja = 8/26 × ₹ 520 = ₹ 160.

8. (*b*) : **Trick :** $\frac{1250 \times 12}{3750 \times x} = \frac{1}{1}$

$\Rightarrow \quad x = 4$

9. (*d*) : *A* : *B* : *C* are in the ratio 6 : 3 : 1.

10. (*b*) : Madan : Sunil

5000 × 5 : 6000 × 6 = 25 : 36

So, Sunil's share = 36/61 × 610 = ₹ 360.

6

PERCENTAGE

The term per cent means for every hundred. It can best be defined as :

" A fraction, whose denominator is 100, is called a *percentage*, and the numerator of the fraction is called *the rate per cent.*"

Suppose, a man says that he gains forty per cent (40 %) profit after selling a watch. It means his profit is ₹ 40 for every hundred rupees.

So, by definition of the percentage, the meaning of 40 per cent of the percentage, the meaning of 40 per cent is 40/100.

To Convert Fraction into Percentage

Process : 1. Fraction is multiplied by 100.

2. Result (Fraction × 100) takes sign of per cent (%) after it.

Therefore, Rule :

Value in % = (Fraction × 100) %

Example :

	Value in fraction	Rule (Fraction × 100) %	Value in per cent
1.	4/25	(4/25 × 100) %	16 %
2.	2/3	(2/3 × 100) %	66.66 %
3.	3/40	(3/40 × 100) %	7.5 %

To Convert Percentage into Fraction

Process :

1. Given value or term is divided by 100.
2. Sign of per cent (%) is eliminated or removed.

Rule :

$$\text{Fraction} = \frac{\text{Digit of Per cent}}{100}$$

Example :

Value in percentage	Rule $\left(\frac{\text{Digit of \%}}{100}\right)$	Fraction
1. 9 %	9/100	9/100
2. 0.3 %	0.3/100	3/1000
3. 36 %	36/100	9/25

To Convert Percentage into Decimal

Process :

1. Given value (in percentage) is divided by 100 and we take result in decimal.

2. Sign of per cent (%) is eliminated.

Example :

Value in per cent	Using Process	Value in decimal
0.03 %	0.03/100	= 0.0003

Rule : Short-cut Method to Convert Percentage into Decimal.

Decimal is placed at two digits from right to left side in given value eliminating sign of per cent (%).

Example : 25 %

According to rule, decimal will take place after two digits (5 and 2) from right to left. Thus decimal value of 25 % will be 0.25.

Other Example : 34 % = 0.34
126 % = 1.26
9 % = 0.09
(Here, second digit is '0')

To Convert Decimal into percentage

Process : 1. Given value is multiplied by 100

2. Sign of per cent (%) is added after the product

Rule :

Value in per cent =(Value in decimal) × 100 %

Example :

	Value in decimal	Rule	Value in per cent
1.	0.218	(0.218 × 100) %	21.8 %

Memorable Point :

If Y % of X = Z, then XY/100 = Z

In above mathematical relation, there are three terms, X, Y and Z. If values of any two terms are known then we can obtain the value of rest term.

1. $X = \frac{Z}{Y} \times 100$ 2. $Y = \frac{Z}{X} \times 100$

3. $Z = \frac{X}{Y} \times 100$

Example : 35 % of 160 + 60 % of 80 = ? % of 312

Solution : 35 % of 160 + 60 % of 80 = ? of 312

⇒ 160 × 35/100 + 80 × 60/100 = ?/100 × 312

$$\Rightarrow \quad \frac{(56+48)\times 100}{312} = ?$$

$$\Rightarrow \quad ? = \frac{100}{3} = 33\frac{1}{3}$$

Facts To Remember

Remember the following results. Their direct use help in solving objective type problems on percentage.

Sl. No.	*Value in %*	*Value in Fraction*	Sl. No.	*Value in %*	*Value in Fraction*
1.	100%	1	11.	10 %	1/10
2.	50 %	1/2	12.	90 %	9/10
3.	25 %	1/4	13.	130 %	13/10
4.	20 %	1/5	14.	$6\frac{1}{4}$ %	1/16
5.	30 %	3/10	15.	$12\frac{1}{2}$ %	1/8
6.	40 %	2/5	16.	$37\frac{1}{2}$ %	3/8
7.	80 %	4/5	17.	$62\frac{1}{2}$ %	5/8
8.	120 %	6/5	18.	$66\frac{2}{3}$ %	2/3
9.	70 %	7/10	19.	$87\frac{1}{2}$ %	7/8
10.	1 %	1/100			

EXERCISE

1. (?) × 15 = 37.5 % of 220

(*a*) 11 (*b*) 81.5

(*c*) 5.5 (*d*) 815

(*e*) None of these

2. 67 % of 89 ÷ 89 % of 67 = ?

(*a*) 5163 (*b*) 5963

(*c*) 0 (*d*) 1

(*e*) None of these

3. 80 % of 1200 + 40 % of 20 = ?

(*a*) 960 (*b*) 1760

(*c*) 968 (*d*) 96,800

(*e*) None of these

4. 0.75 + ? = 1350 % of 50

(*a*) 746.25 (*b*) 674.25

(*c*) 576.25 (*d*) 467.25

(*e*) None of these

5. 10 % of ? = 0.101

(*a*) 10.1 (*b*) 0.101

(*c*) 101 (*d*) 1.01

(*e*) None of these

EXPLANATORY ANSWERS

1. (*c*) : In the given expression

$$? = 220 \times \frac{37.5}{100} \times \frac{1}{15} = 5.5$$

2. (*d*) : The given expression can be written as

? = 89 × 67/100 ÷ 67 × 89/100

= 89 × 67/100 × 100/67 × 89 = 1

3. (*c*) : In the given expression

? = 1200 × 80/100 + 20 × 40/100

= 960 + 8 = 968.

4. (*b*) : In the given expression

? = 1350 % of 50 – 0.75

= 1350/100 × 50 – 0.75

= 675 – 0.75

= 674.25.

5. (*d*) : Given expression can be written as

? × 10/100 = 0.101

$$\Rightarrow ? = \frac{0.101\times 100}{10} = 1.01.$$

Some Special Rules For Quantitative Questions

Rule I :

First time X % is increased and second time X % is decreased, then loss % = $[X^2/100]\%$

Example : The price of a book is increased by 30% and after some days decreased by 30%. Decreased or increase per cent is :

(*a*) 0.0009% increase (*b*) 0.09% decrease
(*c*) 90% decrease (*d*) 9% increase
(*e*) None of these

Solution : (*e*) Loss % = $[(30)^2/100]$ = 9%.

Rule II :

In price increase of *x* % reduced per cent to have no extra expenditure = [*x*/ (100 + *x*) × 100] %

Example : If the price of milk is increased by 1%, how much per cent must a man reduce his consumption of milk to have no extra expenditure?

(*a*) 100/101 % (*b*) 101/100 %
(*c*) 1/101 % (*d*) 1 %
(*e*) None of these

Solution. (*a*) : Reduced per cent
= [1/100 + 1× 100]% = 100/101%.

Rule III :

(1) If *P*'s salary is *r* % more than *Q*'s, then *Q*'s salary less than *P*'s

$$= \left[\frac{r}{(100+r)} \times 100\right] \%$$

(2) If *P*'s salary is *r* % less than *Q*'s, then *Q*'s salary more than *P*'s

$$= \left[\frac{r}{(100-r)} \times 100\right] \%$$

Example : P's salary is 50 % below *Q*'s. How much per cent is *Q*'s salary above *P*'s ?

(*a*) 0 % (*b*) $16\frac{2}{3}$ %
(*c*) 50 % (*d*) 100 %
(*e*) None of these

Solution. (*d*) : *Q*'s salary above *P*'s

$$= \left[\frac{50}{(100-50)} \times 100\right] \% = 100\ \%$$

Rule IV :

In price decrease of *x* %, increase per cent in consumption to maintain same expenditure

$$= \left[\frac{x}{(100-x)} \times 100\right] \%$$

Example : The price of sugar is reduced by 40 %. Find by how much per cent must its consumption be increased so that the expenditure remains the same as before?

(*a*) 45 % (*b*) $66\frac{2}{3}$%
(*c*) $16\frac{2}{3}$% (*d*) $33\frac{1}{3}$%
(*e*) None of these

Solution. (*b*) : Increase per cent

$$= \left[\frac{40}{100-40} \times 100\right] \% = \frac{200}{3} \% = 66\frac{2}{3} \%$$

Rule V :

First time *x* % is increased and second time *y* % is increased, then increase in per cent

$$= \left[(x+y)+\frac{xy}{100}\right]\%$$

Example : The price of a TV is increased by 30 % before budget and 20 % after budget. Then total increase in price will be

(*a*) 50 % (*b*) 56 %
(*c*) 55 % (*d*) 59 %
(*e*) None of these

Solution. (*b*) : Increase per cent

$$= \left[(30+20)+\frac{30\times 20}{100}\right]\%$$
$$= 50 + 6 = 56\ \%$$

Rule VI :

First time *x* % decreased and second time *y*% decreased, then decrease per cent

$$= \left[(x+y)-\frac{xy}{100}\right]\%$$

Example : The price of a commodity is reduced two times as 40% and 10% respectively. What is percentage decrease in the price?

(*a*) 48 (*b*) 46
(*c*) 45 (*d*) 51
(*e*) None of these

Solution. (*b*) : Percentage decrease

$$= \left[(40+10)-\frac{40\times 10}{100}\right]\% = 46\%$$

EXERCISE

1. $\frac{20\% \text{ of } 740}{?} = 1036$
   (*a*) 7 (*b*) 2/7
   (*c*) 1/7 (*d*) 3/7
   (*e*) None of these
2. 12 % of 200 = ?
   (*a*) 24 (*b*) 25
   (*c*) 27 (*d*) 28
   (*e*) 23
3. The tax on a commodity is diminished by 10% and its consumption increased by 10%. The effect on the revenue derived from it is :
   (*a*) 0.1% decrease (*b*) 1% decrease
   (*c*) 1% increase (*d*) 0.1% increase
   (*e*) None of these
4. A reduction of 20% in the price of coffee enables a purchaser to obtain 4 kg more for ₹ 80. The reduced price per kg of coffee is
   (*a*) ₹ 5 (*b*) ₹ 6
   (*c*) ₹ 4 (*d*) ₹ 5.50
   (*e*) None of these
5. A student has to secure 40% marks to get through. If he gets 40 marks and fails by 40 marks, find the maximum marks set for the examination.
   (*a*) 200 (*b*) 150
   (*c*) 300 (*d*) 100
   (*e*) None of these
6. Due to increase of 40% in the price of a radio, selling is reduced 60%, then how much percentage increase or decrease will be in income?
   (*a*) 74% increase (*b*) 44% increase
   (*c*) 44% decrease (*d*) 62% increase
   (*e*) None of these
7. If the length of a rectangle is decreased by 40 % and the breadth is increased by 30 %, then what is increase or decrease per cent in the area of rectangle?
   (*a*) 22% increase (*b*) 22% decrease
   (*c*) 28% increase (*d*) 27% decrease
   (*e*) None of these

EXPLANATORY ANSWERS

1. (*c*) : $= \frac{740 \times 20}{? \times 100} = 1036$

$\Rightarrow \quad ? \times 1036 = 74 \times 2$

$? = \frac{74 \times 2}{1036} = \frac{1}{7}.$

2. (*a*) : $\frac{12}{100} \times 200 = 24$

3. (*b*) : Trick : Effect = $(10^2/100)$ % = 1 % decrease.

4. (*c*) : Trick : Reduced price per kg

$= \frac{80 \times 20}{100 \times 4} = ₹ 4$

5. (*a*) : Maximum marks = $\frac{100\,(40+40)}{40} = 200$

6. (*c*) : Trick : $= \left[(40-60) - \frac{40 \times 60}{100}\right]\%$

$= -20 - 24$

$= -44 = 44$ % decrease,

7. (*b*) : Trick : Percentage increase or decrease

$= \left[(30-40) - \frac{30 \times 40}{100}\right]\%$

$= -22 = 22\%$ decrease

Note: Negative sign shows decrease and positive sign shows increase.

7

Average and Age Related Problems

An average or more accurately an arithmetic mean is, in crude terms, the sum of n different data divided by n :

Example : If one earns ₹ 40 on Monday, ₹ 50 on Tuesday and ₹ 60 on Wednesday, then his average income for 3 days is equal to :

(*a*) ₹ 50 (*b*) ₹ 100
(*c*) ₹ 30 (*d*) ₹ 40
(*e*) None of these

Solution. (*a*) : $\frac{40+50+60}{3} = ₹ 50$

The two formulae used in this chapter are :

$$\text{Average} = \frac{\text{Sum of observations}}{\text{Number of observations}}$$

Sum of observations

= Average × Number of observations

Example : If the marks obtained by Mohan in History, Sanskrit and English are 62, 73 and 69 respectively, then his average marks are :

(*a*) 73 (*b*) 66.2
(*c*) 68 (*d*) 63.9
(*e*) None of these

Solution. (*c*) : Average marks $= \frac{62+73+69}{3}$

$= \frac{204}{3} = 68$

Type 1 (Average Speed)

I. Average speed = $\frac{\text{Total distance travelled}}{\text{Total time taken}}$

Example : A man walks 2000 metres in 30 minutes, 1500 metres in 40 minutes and 500 metres in 10 minutes. Then what is the average speed for whole walking distance or journey?

(*a*) 50 metres / minute
(*b*) 55 metres/ minute
(*c*) 60.5 metres/minute
(*d*) 50.5 metres/minute
(*e*) None of these

Solution. (*a*) : Average speed

$= \frac{(2000+1500+500) \text{ metres}}{(30+40+10) \text{ minutes}}$

$= \frac{4000}{80} = 50$ m/minute

II. If equal distances are travelled at the rate x and y, then Average speed $= \frac{2xy}{x+y}$

Example : Madhu goes to his school at 5 km per hour and returns at 8 km per hour crossing same route. Then her average speed is :

(*a*) $7\frac{1}{3}$ km/hr (*b*) $5\frac{3}{4}$ km/hr
(*c*) $6\frac{2}{3}$ km/hr (*d*) $6\frac{2}{13}$ km/hr
(*e*) None of these

Solution. (*d*) :

Average speed $= \frac{2\times5\times8}{5+8}$ km/hr

$= \frac{80}{13}$ km/hr $= 6\frac{2}{13}$ km/hour.

Type 2 (Average Age)

Conditional Trick

A. *When a person leaves a group and another person joins the group in the place of person left, then*

I. In the case of increasing of average age, Age of the new comer = Age of person left + no. of persons in the group x increase in average age.
II. In the case of decreasing of average age, Age of the new comer = Age of person left – no. of persons in the group x decrease in average age.

Example : The average age of 8 men is increased by 4 years when one of them whose age is 30 years is replaced by a new man. What is the age of new man?

(*a*) 55 years (*b*) 62 years
(*c*) 42 years (*d*) 69 years
(*e*) None of these

Solution. (*b*) : The age of new man = $30 + 8 \times 4$
$= 62$ years

Example : The average age of 45 persons is decreased by 1/9 years when one of them whose age is 60 years replaced by new comer. What is the age of new comer?

(*a*) 40 years (*b*) 62 years
(*c*) 55 years (*d*) 59 years
(*e*) None of these

Solution. (*c*) : Age of new comer = $60 - 45 \times 1/9$
$= 60 - 5$
$= 55$ years.

B. When a person joins a group without replacing any previous person from that group, then

I. In the case of increasing of average age
Age of the new comer = Previous average age + no. of all persons (including new comer) × increase in average age.

II. In the case of decreasing of average age,
Age of the new comer = Previous average age – no. of all persons (including new comer) × decrease in average age.

Example : The average age of 6 women is 32 years which is increased by 1 year when a new woman joins the group. Then what is the age of new woman?

(*a*) 42 years (*b*) 35 years
(*c*) 45 years (*d*) 39 years
(*e*) None of these

Solution. (*d*) : Age of new woman = $32 + (6 + 1) \times 1$
$= 32 + 7$
$= 39$ years.

Example: The average age of 20 teachers is 45 years which is decreased by 6/7 years when a student joins this group. Then what is the age of that student?

(*a*) 15 years (*b*) 27 years
(*c*) 18 years (*d*) 25 years
(*e*) None of these

Solution. (*b*) : Age of the student
$= 45 - (20 + 1) \times 6/7$
$= 45 - 18 = 27$ years

C. When a person leaves the group but nobody joins this group, then

I. In the case of increasing of average age,
Age of man left = Previous average age – no. of present persons × increase in the average age.

II. In the case of decreasing of average age,
Age of man left = Previous average age + no. of present persons × decrease in average age.

Example : The average age of 10 girls in a hostel is 19 years. But one girl left the hostel and average age is increased by 1/2 year. Then how many years old is she?

(*a*) $14\frac{1}{2}$ years (*b*) 15 years
(*c*) $15\frac{1}{2}$ years (*d*) 18 years
(*e*) None of these

Solution. (*a*) : Age of the girl left

$$= 19 - (10 - 1) \times \frac{1}{2}$$

$$= 19 - 9 \times \frac{1}{2} = 14\frac{1}{2} \text{ years.}$$

Example : The average age of 26 labours is 30 years. It is decreased by 1/5 years, when a labour went home. Then the age of that labour is

(*a*) 30 years (*b*) 32 years
(*c*) 24 years (*d*) 35 years
(*e*) None of these

Solution : Age of the labour left

$$= 30 + (26 - 1) \times \frac{1}{5}$$

$$= 30 + 25 \times \frac{1}{5} = 35 \text{ years.}$$

Type 3 (Average of Numbers)

A. Average related to Natural Numbers

I. Average of consecutive n natural numbers $= \frac{(n+1)}{2}$

For example, Average of consecutive natural numbers till 7 $= \frac{7+1}{2} = 4$.

II. Average of squares of n natural numbers $= \frac{(n+1)(2n+1)}{6}$

For example, Average of square of numbers till 11

$$= \frac{(11+1)(2\times 11+1)}{6} = \frac{12\times 23}{6} = 46.$$

III. Average of cubes of n consecutive natural numbers $= \frac{n(n+1)^2}{4}$

For example, Average of $1^3, 2^3, 3^3, 4^3 = \frac{4(4+1)^2}{4}$
$= 25$

B. Average related to Even Numbers

I. Average of n consecutive even numbers $= n + 1$

For example, Average of 4 consecutive even numbers $= 4 + 1 = 5$.

II. Average of consecutive even numbers till n $= (n/2 + 1)$

Note : When n is even.

For example, Average of consecutive even numbers till 10 $= (10/2 + 1) = 6$.

III. Average of squares of n consecutive even numbers $= \frac{2(n+1)(2n+1)}{3}$

For example, Average of 2, 4, 6, 8

$$= \frac{2(4+1)(2\times 4+1)}{3} = \frac{2\times 5\times 9}{3} = 30$$

IV. Average of squares of consecutive even numbers till $n = \frac{(n+1)(n+2)}{3}$

For example, Average of squares of consecutive even numbers till 16

$$= \frac{(16+1)(16+2)}{3} = 102.$$

C. Average related to Odd numbers

I. Average of n consecutive odd Numbers $= n$

For example, Average of 7 consecutive odd numbers = 7.

II. Average of consecutive odd numbers till n $= \frac{(n+1)}{2}$

Note : When n is odd.

For example, Average of consecutive odd numbers till 13

$$= \frac{13+1}{2} = 7.$$

III. Average of squares of consecutive odd numbers till n $= \frac{n(n+2)}{3}$

For example, Average of squares of consecutive odd numbers till 9

$= \text{average of } 1^2, 3^2, 5^2, 7^2, 9^2 = \frac{9(9+2)}{3} = 33$

EXERCISE

1. A person reached Delhi from Jaipur by his car at a speed of 60 km per hour and returned to Jaipur along the same route at a speed of 40 km per hour. What is his average speed?

(*a*) 50 km per hour (*b*) 45 km per hour
(*c*) 48 km per hour (*d*) 55.5 km per hour
(*e*) None of these

2. The average weight of 8 persons is increased by 2.5 kg When one of them whose weight is 56 kg is replaced by a new man. The weight of new man is :

(*a*) 66 kg. (*b*) 75 kg.
(*c*) 67.6 kg. (*d*) 76 kg.
(*e*) None of these

3. The average of consecutive natural numbers from 1 to 49 is :
(*a*) 28 (*b*) 50
(*c*) 48 (*d*) 49
(*e*) None of these

4. Raju's average daily expenditure is ₹ 15 during September, ₹ 20 during October and ₹ 13 during November. What is the average daily expenditure for the three months?
(*a*) ₹ 16 approximately
(*b*) ₹ 18 approximately
(*c*) ₹ 19.50 approximately
(*d*) ₹ 17 approximately
(*e*) None of these

5. The average of first five multiples of 3 is :
(*a*) 15 (*b*) 9
(*c*) 12 (*d*) 3
(*e*) None of these

6. If difference between age of Ritu and Ram is 15 years and ratio of their ages is 3 : 2, then the age of Ram is :
(*a*) 25 years (*b*) 20 years
(*c*) 28 years (*d*) 30 years
(*e*) None of these

7. The sum of the ages of husband and wife is 70 years and ratio of their ages is 3 : 2. The age of the wife is :
(*a*) 32 years (*b*) 25 years
(*c*) 28 years (*d*) 27 years
(*e*) None of these

8. The average score of a cricket for 10 matches is 49.9 runs. If the average for the first six matches is 49, then what is average score for the last 4 matches?
(*a*) 48.7 (*b*) 49.8
(*c*) 46.4 (*d*) 50
(*e*) None of these

9. The present age difference between father and son is 14 years. The ratio of their age will be 4 : 3 after 11 years. How old is son now?
(*a*) 25 years (*b*) 31 years
(*c*) 30 years (*d*) 28 years
(*e*) None of these

EXPLANATORY ANSWERS

1. (*c*) : Average speed $= \dfrac{2xy}{x+y} = \dfrac{2 \times 60 \times 40}{60+40}$
$= 48$ kmph

2. (*d*) : Weight of new man $= 56 + 8 \times 2.5$ kg
$= (56 + 20)$ kg $= 76$ kg

3. (*e*) : Average $= \dfrac{(n+1)}{2} = \dfrac{49+1}{2} = 25.$

4. (*a*) : Average daily expenditure

$= \dfrac{\text{Total expenditure}}{\text{Total days}}$

$= \dfrac{15 \times 30 + 20 \times 31 + 13 \times 30}{30 + 31 + 30}$

$= \dfrac{1460}{91} =$ ₹ 16 approximately

5. (*b*) : The average of first five multiples of 3

$= \dfrac{3+6+9+12+15}{5} = \dfrac{45}{5} = 9$

6. (*d*) : Let Ritu's age $= 3x$ years
Ram's age $= 2x$ years
$3x - 2x = 15 \Rightarrow x = 15$
Ram's age $= 2 \times 15 = 30$ years.

7. (*c*) : The age of the wife $= \dfrac{2}{(3+2)} \times 70$
$= 28$ years.

8. (*e*) : Average score $= \dfrac{(10 \times 49.9 - 6 \times 49)}{4}$

$= \dfrac{499 - 294}{4} = \dfrac{205}{4}$
$= 51.25$ runs.

9. (*b*) : Let present age of father be x years.
Present age of son $= (x - 13)$ years
According to the question,

$$\frac{x+11}{(x-13)+11} = \frac{4}{3}$$

$\Rightarrow \quad 3x + 33 = 4x - 8$
$\Rightarrow \quad x = 41$
Thus, present age of son $= 41 - 13$
$= 28$ years.

8

PROFIT & LOSS

In this chapter, the use of *"Rule of Fraction"* is dominant. We should understand this rule very well because it is going to be used in almost all the questions.

The Rule of Fraction

If our required value is greater than the supplied value we should multiply the supplied value with a fraction which is more than one. And if our required value is less than the supplied value, we should multiply the supplied value with a fraction which is less than one.

1. If there is a gain of $X\%$, the calculating figures would be 100 and $(100 + X)$.

2. If there is a loss of $Y\%$, the calculating figures would be 100 and $(100 - Y)$.

3. If the required value is more than the supplied value, our multiplying fractions should be

$$\frac{100+X}{100}, \frac{100}{100-Y} \text{ (both are greater than 1).}$$

4. If the required value is less than the supplied value, our multiplying fractions should be

$$\frac{100}{100+X}, \frac{100-Y}{100} \text{ (both are less than 1).}$$

Some Defined Terms

1. *Cost Price (CP):* It is price at which an article is purchased. Profit and loss both are calculated at cost price.

2. *Selling Price (SP):* It is the price at which the article is sold.

3. (*I*) *Profit or Gain.* If SP is greater than CP, there is profit or gain.
Profit = SP – CP

(*II*) *Loss.* If SP is less than the CP, there is loss.
Loss = CP – SP

(*III*) *If SP = CP* Then there is no loss or gain.

4. Gain on ₹ 100 is gain per cent and loss on ₹ 100 is loss per cent.

General Formula :

1. $\text{Gain \%} = \left(\frac{\text{Gain}}{\text{CP}} \times 100\right)\%$

2. $\text{Loss \%} = \left(\frac{\text{Loss}}{\text{CP}} \times 100\right)\%$

3. $\text{SP} = \left(\frac{100 + \text{Gain \%}}{100}\right) \times \text{CP}$

4. $\text{SP} = \left(\frac{100 - \text{Loss \%}}{100}\right) \times \text{CP}$

5. $\text{CP} = \left(\frac{100}{100 + \text{Gain \%}}\right) \times \text{SP}$

6. $\text{CP} = \left(\frac{100}{100 - \text{Loss \%}}\right) \times \text{SP}$

Formula For Short-cut Solution :

Type 1 :

Conditional Trick

If cost price of X goods = Selling price of Y goods then,

I. $\text{Gain \%} = \frac{X-Y}{Y} \times 100$ (In case of $X > Y$)

II. $\text{Loss \%} = \frac{Y-X}{Y} \times 100$ (in case of $X < Y$)

Type 2 :

I. If X_1 and X_2 both are the rate of gain or both are the rate of loss, then, CP = $\left(\frac{100}{X_1 - X_2}\right)\times$ amount of difference between SPs.

II. If in X_1 and X_2 one is the rate of gain and another is the rate of loss, then CP = $\left(\frac{100}{X_1 + X_2}\right)\times$ amount of difference between SPs

Type 3 :

Miscellaneous Trick

I. When a man buys two things on equal price and in those things one is sold on the profit of *X* % and another is sold on the loss of *X* %, then there is no loss or gain per cent.

Example : If Ravi buys two cows at ₹ 824 each and sells one at a gain of 14 % and another one at a loss of 14%. How much does he gain or loss in the whole transaction?

Ans. No loss, no gain.

II. When a man sells two things at the same price each and in this process his loss on first thing is *X* % and gain on second thing is *X* % then in such type of questions, there is always a loss.

$$\text{Loss \%} = X\text{ \% of }X = \frac{X^2}{100} = \left(\frac{X}{10}\right)^2$$

Example : A man sold two watches at ₹ 450 each. He sold one at a loss of 15 % and the other at a gain of 15 %. His loss or gain is

(*a*) 15 % gain
(*b*) 2.25 % loss
(*c*) 30 % loss
(*d*) Neither loss nor gain
(*e*) None of these

Ans. (*b*) Loss % = $\left(\frac{15}{10}\right)^2$ = 2.25%

III. Dishonest dealer and less weight

$$\text{Gain\%} = \frac{\text{Error}}{\text{True value} - \text{Error}} \times 100$$

Where, error = 1000 gm – used weight of goods

Example : Dealer professes to sell his goods at cost price, but used a weight of 950 gms for a kilogram weight. His real gain per cent is

(*a*) 5 % (*b*) 5.26 %
(*c*) 4 % (*d*) 4.75 %
(*e*) None of these

Solution. (*b*) :

$$\text{Gain \%} = \frac{50}{1000-50}\times 100 = \frac{50}{950}\times 100 = 5.26\%$$

IV. If *A* sells a thing to *B* at a gain of R_1 %, *B* sells it to *C* at a gain of R_2 % and *C* sells it to *D* at a gain of R_3% then, CP for *D* = CP for *A* $(1 + R_1/100)(1 + R_2/100)(1 + R_3/100)$

Example : *A* sells a watch to *B* at a gain of 20%, *B* sells it to *C* at a gain of 25% and *C* sells it to *D* at a gain of 10%. If *D* pays ₹ 330, what did it cost *A* ?

(*a*) ₹ 250 (*b*) ₹ 300
(*c*) ₹ 200 (*d*) ₹ 225
(*e*) None of these

Solution. (*c*) :

$$330 = X(1 + 20/100)\times(1 + 25/100)\times(1 + 10/100)$$

$$\Rightarrow X = \frac{330\times100\times100\times100}{120\times125\times110} = ₹\,200$$

Where *X* is supposed the cost price of *A*.

V. If *A* sells a thing to *B* at a loss of R_1 %, *B* sells it to *C* at a loss of R_2 % and *C* sells it to *D* at a loss of R_3 % then, CP for *D* = CP for *A* $(1 - R_1/100)(1 - R_2/100)(1 - R_3/100)$

Example : *A* sells a radio to *B* at a loss of 20%, *B* sells it to *C* at a loss of 30% and *C* sells it to *D* at a loss of 10%. If A pays ₹ 2,000 then cost price for *D* is

(*a*) ₹ 1280 (*b*) ₹ 1190
(*c*) ₹ 1305 (*d*) ₹ 1008
(*e*) None of these

Solution. (*d*) : CP for *D*

$$= 2000\times(1 - 20/100)(1 - 30/100)(1 - 10/100)$$

$$= \frac{2000\times80\times70\times90}{100\times100\times100} = ₹\,1008$$

EXERCISE

1. By selling 66 metres of cloth, a person gains the cost of 22 metres. Find his gain %.
(a) $33\frac{1}{2}\%$ (b) $33\frac{1}{3}\%$
(c) 33% (d) $34\frac{1}{3}\%$
(e) None of these

2. Madan buys 87 goods at the cost of ₹ 890 and sell 60 goods at the same cost of ₹ 890. What is the value of gain per cent?
(a) 55.5% (b) 50.9%
(c) 40% (d) 45%
(e) None of these

3. If an article is sold at a loss of 34.8% instead of at a loss of 17.8% then the seller gets ₹ 19.50 less. The CP of the article is :
(a) ₹ 330.50 (b) ₹ 337.50
(c) ₹ 300.70 (d) ₹ 331.50
(e) None of these

4. A motorcycle is sold at a gain of 18%. If it had been sold for ₹ 490 more, 23% would have been gained. The cost price of the motor cycle is :
(a) ₹ 10,500 (b) ₹ 9,500
(c) ₹ 9,800 (d) ₹ 12,000
(e) None of these

5. A man buys two horses for ₹ 1350, he sells one as to lose 6% and the other so as to gain 7.5 %. On the whole he neither gains nor loses. What does each horse cost?
(a) ₹ 750, ₹ 600 (b) ₹ 650, ₹ 500
(c) ₹ 700, ₹ 650 (d) ₹ 600, ₹ 750
(e) None of these

6. *K* sells a book to *L* at a gain of 20%, *L* sells it to *M* at a gain of 10% and *M* sells it to *N* at a gain of 12.5 %. If *N* pays ₹ 14.85, then what is the selling price of this book for *K*?
(a) ₹ 8.75 (b) ₹ 12.50
(c) ₹10 (d) ₹ 15
(e) None of these

7. Each of the two cars is sold at the same price. A profit of 10% is made on the first and a loss of 7% is made on the second. What is the combined loss or gain?
(a) 160/206 % gain (b) 160/203 % gain
(c) 160/205 % loss (d) 160/203 % loss
(e) None of these

8. A man purchased two cows for ₹ 500. He sells the first at 12 % loss and the second at 8% gain. In this bargain, he neither gains nor loses. Find the selling price of each cow.
(a) ₹ 176, 324 (b) ₹ 175, 325
(c) ₹ 324, 180 (d) ₹ 176, 325
(e) None of these

9. An article is marked for sale at ₹ 275. The shopkeeper allows a discount of 5% on the marked price. His net profit is 4.5%. What did the shopkeeper pay for the article?
(a) ₹ 250 (b) ₹ 300
(c) ₹ 350 (d) ₹ 225
(e) None of these

10. A shopkeeper bought 15 kg rice at the rate of ₹9.50 per kg and 25 kg rice at the rate of ₹ 7.25 per kg. He sold mixture of both types of rice at the rate of ₹ 10.50 per kg. In this transaction his profit is :
(a) ₹ 96.25 (b) ₹ 105.20
(c) ₹ 95.00 (d) ₹ 108.45
(e) None of these

EXPLANATORY ANSWERS

1. (b): Gain % = $\frac{22}{66} \times 100 = 33\frac{1}{3}\%$.

2. (d): Gain % = $\left(\frac{87-60}{60} \times 100\right)\% = 45\%$.

3. (e): CP = ₹$\left(\frac{100}{34.8-17.8}\right) \times 19.50 =$ ₹ 114.70

4. (c): CP = ₹$\left(\frac{100}{23-18}\right) \times 490 =$ ₹ 9,800.

5. (*a*) : Loss on one horse = gain on the other

So, 6 % of the cost of first horse

= 7.5 % of the cost of the second horse

So, $\frac{\text{Cost of first horse}}{\text{Cost of second horse}} = \frac{7.5\%}{6\%}$

$= \frac{15}{12} = \frac{5}{4}$

Cost of first horse = $\frac{5}{9} \times 1350$ = ₹ 750

Cost of second horse = $\frac{4}{9} \times 1350$ = ₹ 600

6. (*c*) : Trick : CP for *N*

$= \text{CP of } K\left(1+\frac{20}{100}\right)\left(1+\frac{10}{100}\right)\left(1+\frac{12.5}{100}\right)$

$\Rightarrow 14.85 = X\,(120/100) \times (110/100) \times (225/200)$

$\Rightarrow \quad X = ₹\,\frac{14.85 \times 100 \times 100 \times 200}{120 \times 110 \times 225}$

= ₹ 10

7. (*b*) : $\frac{100\,(10-7) - 2 \times 10 \times 7}{200 + 10 - 7}$

$= \frac{300-140}{203} = \frac{160}{203}\ \%$

gain as the sign is + ve.

8. (*a*) : Cost price of first cow = $\frac{500 \times 8}{12+8}$ = ₹ 200

So, SP of first cow = $200\left(\frac{100-12}{100}\right)$ = ₹ 176

And CP of second cow = $\frac{500 \times 12}{12+8}$ = ₹ 300

So, SP of second cow = 300 (108/100)

= ₹ 324

9. (*a*) : We know that if the shopkeeper marked *X* % higher then

$4.5 = X - 5 - \frac{5X}{100} \Rightarrow X = 10\ \%$

Therefore, cost price = $275\left(\frac{100}{100+10}\right)$

= ₹ 250

10. (*a*) : Trick : Profit = SP – CP

= (15 + 25) 10.50 – (15 × 9.50 + 25 × 7.25)

= 420.00 – 323.75 = ₹ 96.25

9

SIMPLE INTEREST

SIMPLE INTEREST

Interest is that extra money which is paid by the borrower to the lender for the use of money lent for a specified period. The sum borrowed is called the *Principal* and the total sum of principal and the interest is called the *Amount*. Interest is usually calculated at a *rate per cent* for a certain period (*time*).

If the interest on a certain sum borrowed for a certain period is reckoned uniformly, then it is called *Simple Interest,* denoted by SI = Simple Interest

Thus, if A = Amount, P = Principal, I = Interest, T = Time (in years), R = rate per cent per annum

Then, we can recognized the following useful relations :

1. $I = \dfrac{P \times R \times T}{100}$
2. $P = \dfrac{100 \times \text{SI}}{T \times R}$
3. $T = \dfrac{100 \times \text{SI}}{P \times R}$
4. $R = \dfrac{100 \times \text{SI}}{P \times T}$
5. $P = \dfrac{100 \times A}{100 + RT}$
6. $A = P + \text{SI}$

Short-Cut

SI = (Rate × Time) per cent of Principal

Rate = Interest as the percentage of the Principal.

EXERCISE

1. At what rate per cent, a sum of money doubles itself in 15 years?

(*a*) 25% (*b*) 6%
(*c*) 6.66% (*d*) 8%
(*e*) None of these

2. A sum becomes 28/25 of itself in 5 years, find the rate of interest.

(*a*) 3% (*b*) 5%
(*c*) 12% (*d*) 2.40%
(*e*) None of these

3. If ₹ 900 amounts to ₹ 1,080 in 4 years at simple interest, what sum will amount to ₹ 1,275 in 5 years at the same rate?

(*a*) ₹ 1,020 (*b*) ₹ 1,050
(*c*) ₹ 1,080 (*d*) ₹ 1,200
(*e*) None of these

4. A sum of money doubles itself in 7 years, in how many years it will become four fold?

(*a*) 10 years (*b*) 35 years
(*c*) 14 years (*d*) 21 years
(*e*) 28 years

5. A certain sum of money amounted to ₹ 575 at 5% in a time in which ₹ 750 amounted to ₹ 840 at 4%. The rate being the simple interest, what was the sum?

(*a*) ₹ 650 (*b*) ₹ 625
(*c*) ₹ 500 (*d*) ₹ 475
(*e*) None of these

6. ₹ 4,000 is divided into two parts such that if one part be put out at 3 % and the other at 5%, the annual interest from both the investments be ₹ 144. Find the first part.

(*a*) ₹ 3,000 (*b*) ₹ 2,800
(*c*) ₹ 2,500 (*d*) ₹ 1,200
(*e*) None of these

7. A sum of money amounts to ₹ 767 in 3 years and ₹ 806 in 4 years at the rate of 6%. What is the sum?
(*a*) ₹ 600 (*b*) ₹ 650
(*c*) ₹ 700 (*d*) ₹ 675
(*e*) None of these

8. In how many years will a sum of money double itself at 12% per annum?
(*a*) 6 years 9 months (*b*) 8 years 4 months
(*c*) 7 years 6 months (*d*) 8 years 6 months
(*e*) None of these

9. What annual payment will discharge a debt of ₹580 due in 5 years, the rate being 8% per annum?
(*a*) ₹ 166.40 (*b*) ₹ 65.60
(*c*) ₹ 100 (*d*) ₹ 120
(*e*) None of these

10. *A* lent ₹ 600 to *B* for 2 years and ₹ 150 to *C* for 4 years and received altogether from both ₹ 90 as simple interest. The rate of interest is :
(*a*) 12% (*b*) 4%
(*c*) 5% (*d*) 10%
(*e*) None of these

EXPLANATORY ANSWERS

1. (*c*) : Suppose principal = P, ∴ Amount = $2P$

$$SI = 2P - P = P,\ P = \frac{P \times 15 \times r}{100}$$

Where r = rate

So, $r = 100/15 = 20/3 = 6.66\%$.

Trick: Rate = 100/ time = 100/15 = 6.66%

2. (*d*) : Suppose, principal = P

Amount = $28/25\ P$

$$SI = \frac{28}{25}P - P = 3\,P/25$$

$$\frac{3P}{25} = \frac{P \times 5 \times r}{100}$$

$$\Rightarrow \quad r = \frac{3 \times 100}{25 \times 5} = \frac{12}{5} = 2.4\%$$

3. (*a*) : SI = ₹ 180

$$r = \frac{180 \times 100}{4 \times 900} = 5\%$$

Let P = ₹ 100

$$SI = \frac{100 \times 5 \times 5}{100} = ₹\,25$$

$A = 100 + 25 = 125$

when amount is 125 then, $P = 100$

$$\text{when amount is 1275 then, } P = \frac{100}{125} \times 1275 = ₹\,1020$$

4. (*d*) : **Trick :** Rate = 100 / 7

$$\text{So, Time} = \frac{3 \times 100 \times 7}{100} = 21 \text{ years}$$

5. (*c*) : SI = 840 − 750 = ₹ 90

$$T = \frac{90 \times 100}{750 \times 4} = 3 \text{ years}$$

$$P = \frac{100 \times 575}{100 + 3 \times 5} = \frac{57500}{115} = ₹\,500.$$

6. (*b*) : **Trick :**

Let first part be x

second part = $4000 - x$

According to the question,

$$\frac{x \times 3 \times 1}{100} + \frac{(4000 - x) \times 5 \times 1}{100} = 144$$

$$\Rightarrow \quad \frac{3x}{100} + \frac{20000}{100} - \frac{5x}{100} = 144$$

$$\Rightarrow \quad \frac{-2x}{100} = 144 - 200$$

$$\Rightarrow \quad x = \frac{5600}{2} = 2800$$

Hence, first part x = ₹ 2800

7. (*b*) : S.I. = 806 − 767 = 39

$$\therefore P = \frac{39 \times 100}{1 \times 6} = ₹\,650.$$

8. (*b*) : Time = 100/ rate = 100/12 = 25/3 years = 8 years 4 months.

9. (*c*) : Suppose, every instalment = ₹ 100

So, $(100 + 8 \times 4) + (100 + 8 \times 3) + (100 + 8 \times 2) + (100 + 8 \times 1) + 100 = ₹\,580$

When it is ₹ 580 then instalment = ₹ 100.

10. (*c*) :

$$\frac{600 \times r \times 2}{100} + \frac{150 \times r \times 4}{100} = ₹\,90$$

$$\Rightarrow \quad 12r + 6r = 90$$

$$\Rightarrow \quad r = \frac{90}{18} = 5\%$$

So, $r = 5\%$.

10

COMPOUND INTEREST

COMPOUND INTEREST

Money is said to be lent on **Compound Interest (CI)** when at the end of a year or other fixed period the interest that has become due is not paid to the lender, but is added to the sum lent, and the amount thus obtained becomes the principal for the next period. The process is repeated until last period. The difference between the original principal and the final amount is called **Compound Interest (CI).**

IMPORTANT FORMULA

Let principal = ₹ P, Time = t yrs and Rate = r % per annum

Case I : When interest is compounded annually :

$$\text{Amount} = P\left[1+\frac{r}{100}\right]^t$$

Case II : When interest is compounded half-yearly.

$$\text{Amount} = P\left[1+\frac{r/2}{100}\right]^{2t} = P\left[1+\frac{r}{200}\right]^{2t}$$

Case III: When interest is compounded quarterly:

$$\text{Amount} = P\left[1+\frac{r/4}{100}\right]^{4t} = P\left[1+\frac{r}{400}\right]^{4t}$$

Case IV : When rate of interest is r_1 %, r_2 % and r_3 % for 1st year, 2nd year and 3rd year respectively.

$$\text{Amount} = P\left[1+\frac{r_1}{100}\right]\times\left[1+\frac{r_2}{100}\right]\times\left[1+\frac{r_3}{100}\right]$$

The above mention formulae are not new for you. We think that all of you know their uses. When dealing with the above formula, some mathematical calculations become lengthy and take more time. To simplify the calculations and save the valuable time we are giving some extra information. Study the following sections carefully and apply them during your calculations.

The problems are generally asked up to the period of 3 years and the rates of interest are 10%, 5% and 4%. We have the basic formula :

$$\textit{Amount} = \textit{Principal}\left(1+\frac{r}{100}\right)^t$$

If the principal is ₹ 1, the amount for first, second and third years will be

$$\left(1+\frac{r}{100}\right), \left(1+\frac{r}{100}\right)^2 \text{ and } \left(1+\frac{r}{100}\right)^3 \text{ respectively.}$$

And if the rate of interest is 10 %, 5 % and 4 %, these values will be

$(11/10)$, $(11/10)^2$, $(11/10)^3$, $(21/20)$, $(21/20)^2$, $(21/20)^3$ and $(26/25)$, $(26/25)^2$, $(26/25)^3$ respectively.

The above information can be put in the tabular form as given below : Principal = ₹ 1, then A :

	1 Year	*2 Years*	*3 Years*
r	$(1 + r/100)$	$(1 + r/100)^2$	$(1 + r/100)^3$
10	11/10	121/100	1331/1000
5	21/20	441/400	9261/8000
4	26/25	676/625	17576/15625

The above table should be remembered. The use of the above table can be seen in the following example.

Example : ₹ 7500 is borrowed at CI at the rate of 4 % per annum. What will be the amount payable after 2 yrs?

(*a*) ₹ 8112 (*b*) ₹ 8111
(*c*) ₹ 8002 (*d*) ₹ 5000
(*e*) None of these

Solution. (*a*) : As the rate of interest is 4 % per annum and the time is 2 yrs, our concerned fraction would be $\frac{676}{625}$. So after 2 yrs ₹ 7500 will produce

$7500 \times \frac{676}{625} =$ ₹ 8112.

EXERCISE

1. The compound interest on a certain sum for 2 years is ₹ 41 and the simple interest is ₹ 40. What is the rate per cent?

(*a*) 4% (*b*) 5%
(*c*) 6% (*d*) 8%
(*e*) Data is insufficient

2. A sum of money at compound interest amounts to thrice itself in 3 years. In how many years will it be 9 times itself?

(*a*) 18 years
(*b*) 12 years
(*c*) 9 years
(*d*) 6 years
(*e*) None of these

3. The difference between simple and compound interest on a sum of ₹ *P* for 2 years at *r* % per annum will be :

(*a*) $\frac{\left(\frac{r}{100}\right)^2}{P}$ (*b*) $\frac{\left(\frac{100}{r}\right)^2}{P}$

(*c*) $\frac{P}{\left(\frac{100}{r}\right)^2}$ (*d*) $P\left(\frac{100}{r}\right)^2$

(*e*) None of these

4. A sum of money placed at compound interest doubles itself in 4 years. In how many years will it amount to eight times itself?

(*a*) 16 years (*b*) 8 years
(*c*) 12 years (*d*) 20 years
(*e*) None of these

5. The difference between the compound interest and the simple interest on a certain sum at 5 % per annum for 2 years is ₹ 1.50, the sum is :

(*a*) ₹ 600 (*b*) ₹ 500
(*c*) ₹ 400 (*d*) ₹ 300
(*e*) None of these

6. The difference between the compound interest and simple interest on a certain sum of money for 2 years at 10 % per annum is ₹ 15. find the sum of money.

(*a*) ₹ 1,500 (*b*) ₹ 1,800
(*c*) ₹ 2,100 (*d*) ₹ 1,950
(*e*) None of these

7. Find the sum lent at CI at 5 % per annum will amount to ₹ 441 in 2 years?

(*a*) ₹ 400 (*b*) ₹ 400
(*c*) ₹ 375 (*d*) ₹ 380
(*e*) None of these

8. The difference between simple and compound interest on a certain sum of money for 2 years at 4 % per annum is ₹ 1. Find the sum.

(*a*) ₹ 675 (*b*) ₹ 1,625
(*c*) ₹ 750 (*d*) ₹ 625
(*e*) None of these

9. A sum is invested at compound interest payable annually. The interest in two successive years was ₹ 225 and ₹ 236.25. Find the rate of interest.

(*a*) 5% (*b*) 6%
(*c*) 7% (*d*) 4%
(*e*) None of these

10. The simple interest on a sum of money for 3 years is ₹ 240 and the compound interest on the same sum at the same rate for 2 years is ₹ 170. The rate of interest is :

(*a*) $12\frac{1}{2}$ % (*b*) $29\frac{1}{6}$ %
(*c*) 5% (*d*) 8%
(*e*) None of these

EXPLANATORY ANSWERS

1. (b) : Trick :

$$\text{Rate }\% = \frac{41-40}{20}\times 100 = 5\%$$

$$\left[CI = SI\left(1+\frac{R}{100}\right) \quad \textbf{Note: } \text{When } t = 2 \text{ years}\right]$$

2. (d) : $\because \quad 3P = P(1 + r/100)^3$

$\Rightarrow \quad 3 = (1 + r/100)^3$

$3^2 = 9 = (1 + r/100)^{3\times 2}$

$= (1 + r/100)^6$

In 6 years the sum will amounts to a times of itself.

3. (c) : Required difference

$$= P\left[\left(1+\frac{r}{100}\right)^2 - 1\right] - \frac{P\times r\times 2}{100}$$

$$= P\left[i+\left(\frac{r}{100}\right)^2 + \frac{2r}{100} - 1\right] - \frac{2\,\text{Pr}}{100}$$

$$= P\left[\left(\frac{r}{100}\right)^2 + \frac{2r}{100} - \frac{2r}{100}\right]$$

$$= P\left[\frac{r}{100}\right]^2 = \frac{P}{\left(\frac{100}{r}\right)^2}$$

4. (c) : Trick :

$2 = (1 + r/100)^4$

$\Rightarrow \quad 2^3 = 8 = (1 + r/100)^{4\times 3}$

i.e., $4 \times 3 = 12$ years.

5. (a) : $P\times\left(\frac{5}{100}\right)^2 = 1.50$

$\Rightarrow \quad P\times\frac{25}{10000} = 1.50$

$\Rightarrow \quad \frac{P}{400} = 1.50$

$\Rightarrow \quad P = 400 \times 1.50$

6. (a) : $P\times\left(\frac{10}{100}\right)^2 = 15$

$P = 15 \times 100 = 1500$

7. (b) : As the rate of interest is 5% per annum and time is 2 years, our concerned fraction would be $\frac{441}{400}$.

$$P = \frac{441}{441}\times 400 = ₹400$$

8. (d) : $P\left(\frac{4}{100}\right)^2 = 1$

$P = 25 \times 25 = ₹625$

9. (a) : Difference in interest = 236.25 – 225

= ₹11.25

This difference is the simple interest over ₹225 for one year. Hence, rate of interest

$$= \frac{11.25\times 100}{225\times 1} = 5\%.$$

10. (a) : S.I. for one year = 240/3 = ₹80

S.I. for 2 years = 2 × 80 = ₹160

Difference of CI and S.I. for 2 years = 170 – 160 = ₹10

So, rate = $\frac{10}{80}\times 100 = 12\frac{1}{2}\%$.

11

ALLIGATION OR MIXTURE

Alligation Rule : When two or more quantities of different values are mixed together to produce a mixture of a mean value, the ratios of their amounts are inversely proportional to the differences of their values from the mean value. Thus,

$$\frac{\text{Amount of Quantity of Smaller value}}{\text{Amount of Quantity of Larger value}} = \frac{\text{Larger value} - \text{Mean value}}{\text{Mean value} - \text{Smaller value}}$$

Similarly, if two ingredients (one cheeper and the other dearer) are mixed in a ratio, then

$$\frac{\text{Quantity of Cheaper Article}}{\text{Quantity of Dearer Article}} = \frac{\text{CP of Dearer Article} - \text{Mean price}}{\text{Mean price} - \text{CP of Cheaper Article}}$$

or

Cost Price of a unit quantity of cheaper article (c)		Cost Price of a unit quantity of dearer article (d)
	Mean Price (m)	
(d – m)		(m – c)

(Cheaper quantity) : (Dearer quantity) = (d – m) : (m – c)

The Alligation Rule has its application in the following situations :

1. When we have to find the proportion in which different ingredients of known values are to be mixed to produce a mixture of a given mean value.
2. When we have to find the mean value of a mixture when the proportion and value of its ingredients are known.
3. When we have to find the mean or average price of a mixture when the proportion and value of its ingredients are known.

EXERCISE

1. If goods be purchased for ₹ 450 and one - third be sold at loss of 10%, what per cent of profit should be taken on the remainder so as to gain 20% on the whole transaction?
   (*a*) 35% (*b*) 30%
   (*c*) 40% (*d*) 45%
   (*e*) None of these
2. Kamal mixes 80 kg sugar worth ₹ 6.75 per kg with 120 kg sugar worth of ₹ 8 per kg. At what rate should he sell the mixture to gain 20%?
   (*a*) ₹ 7.50 (*b*) ₹ 9
   (*c*) ₹ 8.20 (*d*) ₹ 8.85
   (*e*) None of these
3. A merchant has 50 kg of sugar, part of which he sells at 8% profit and the rest at 18% profit. He gains 14% on the whole. The quantity sold at 18% profit is :
   (*a*) 20 kg (*b*) 30 kg
   (*c*) 15 kg (*d*) 35 kg
   (*e*) None of these
4. A man travelled a distance of 60 km in 7 hours partly on foot at the rate of 8 km per hour and

partly on bicycle at 16 km per hour. Distance travelled by foot is :

(a) 52 km (b) 48 km
(c) 36 km (d) 44 km
(e) None of these

5. In what ratio should water and wine be mixed so that after selling the mixture at the cost price a profit of 20% is made?

(a) 1 : 5 (b) 1 : 6
(c) 1 : 7 (d) 1 : 9
(e) None of these

6. Find the quantity of rice @ ₹ 10 per kg which should be mixed with 25 kg of rice @ ₹ 8 per kg, so that on selling the mixture @ ₹ 15 per kg there is 80% profit.

(a) 6 kg (b) 7 kg
(c) 3 kg (d) 5 kg
(e) None of these

7. A trader has 50 kg of rice, a part of which he sells at 14% profit and the rest at 6% loss. On the whole his loss is 4 %. What are the quantities sold at 14% profit and that at 6% loss?

(a) 5 kg and 45 kg (b) 5 kg and 55 kg
(c) 5 kg and 50 kg (d) 5 kg and 40 kg
(e) None of these

8. A sum of rupees 210 made up of coins consisting of rupee, 50 *P* and 25 *P*, of which the numbers are proportional to 5, 6 and 8. How many of rupee coins are there?

(a) 63 (b) 168
(c) 105 (d) 100
(e) None of these

9. A vessel of 80 litre is filled with milk and water 70% of milk and 30 % of water is taken out of the vessel. It is found that the vessel is vacated by 55% . The initial quantity of milk and water was

(a) 50 litres and 35 litres
(b) 50 litres and 30 litres
(c) 50 litres and 40 litres
(d) 50 litres and 45 litres
(e) None of these

10. Two equal glasses are respectively 1/4 and 1/ full of milk. They are then filled up with wate and contents mixed in a tumbler. The ratio c milk and water in the tumbler is :

(a) 3 : 11 (b) 7 : 17
(c) 9 : 23 (d) 11 : 23
(e) None of these

EXPLANATORY ANSWERS

1. (a) : 1st Part 2nd Part

–10% x%

20%

1/3 2/3 Ratio = 1 : 2

We see that 20 – (–10) = 20 + 10 = 30.

As 2 is written in place of 30, there should be 15 in place of 1.

Therefore, $x = 20 + 15 = 35\%$.

2. (b) : Total CP = 80 × 6.75 + 120 × 8 = ₹ 1500

$$\text{SP per kg} = \frac{120 \times 1500}{100 \times 200} = ₹ 9.$$

3. (b) : 8 18

14

4 6 Ratio = 4 : 6 = 2 : 3

$$\text{Quantity sold on 18\% profit} = \frac{50}{5} \times 3$$

= 30 kg.

4. (a) : Let the distance travelled by bicycle be *x* km

∴ The distance travelled on foot will be $(60 - x)$ km.

According to question, $\frac{60-x}{8} + \frac{x}{16} =$

$$\Rightarrow \frac{120 - 2x + x}{16} = 7$$

$$\Rightarrow x = 8$$

Distance travelled on foot = 60 – 8 = 52 k

5. (a) : Water : Wine = 20 : 100 = 1 : 5.

6. (d) : 8 10

$\frac{25}{3}$

$\frac{5}{3}$ $\frac{1}{3}$

$$\text{CP of the mixture} = 15 \times \frac{100}{180} = ₹ \frac{25}{3} \text{ per}$$

$$\frac{\text{Quantity of rice @ ₹ 8 per kg}}{\text{Quantity of rice @ ₹ 10 per kg}} = \frac{5/3}{1/3} = \frac{5}{1}$$

$$\text{Quantity of rice @ ₹ 10 per kg} = 25 \times \frac{1}{5}$$

$$= 5 \text{ kg}$$

7. (*a*) : I Part II Part

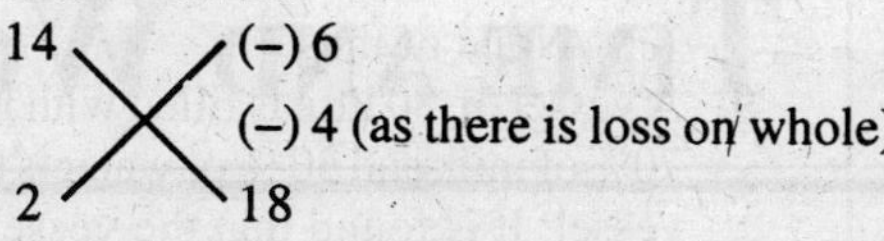

So, ratio of quantities sold at 14% profit and 6% loss = 2 : 18 = 1 : 9

So, quantity sold at 14% profit = $\frac{50}{10} \times 1$

= 5 kg and sold at 6% loss = 50 – 5 = 45 kg

8. (*c*) : Ratio = 5 : 6 : 8, Value = 5 : 3 : 2

Number of rupee coins = $\frac{210}{10} \times 5 = 105.$

9. (*b*) : Here, the % values of milk and water that is taken from the vessel should be taken into consideration.

(Milk) 70% (Water) 30%

55%

25% 15% ⇒ 5 : 3

Ratio of milk to water = 5 : 3

So, quantity of milk = $\frac{80}{8} \times 5 = 50$ litres

and quantity of water = $\frac{80}{8} \times 3 = 30$ litres

10. (*b*) : Quantity of milk in tumbler = 1/4 + 1/3 = 7/12

Quantity of water in tumbler

= (1 – 1/4) + (1 – 1/3) = 3/4 + 2/3 = 17/12

So, ratio of milk and water = 7/12 : 17/12

= 7 : 17.

12

TIME AND WORK

The problem on Time and Work are based on the calculation of time required by a given number of workforce (which may include men, women and children) to complete the given period of time. Thus, it can be said that the problems on time and work fall in two categories:

(*i*) To find the time required to complete a given job.

(*ii*) To find the work done in given period of time.

- It is important to consider the capacity of a man doing work in terms of the part of the work he can do in one day. For instance, if a man can do a piece of work in 6 days, then 1/6th of work is done in one day. The whole work can be finished in 6 days.
- Again, if *A* can do a work in 4 days and *B* in 7 days, the ratio of the work done by *A* and *B* in the same time is 7 : 4.
- If *A* is twice as good a workman as *B*. *A* will take half of the time taken by *B* to do certain piece of work. It means the ratio of the work done by *A* and *B* is 2 : 1.

Wages are paid in proportion to units of job done by each in the same time.

All the above points can be summarized as given below :

If '*M*' number of people take' *D*' days to complete the given job, the total number of 'Man-Days' required to complete the given job are given by the product of '*M*' and '*D*'. This product '*MD*' now remains unchanged. Thus, if '*M*' changes into 'M_1', '*D*' will change into 'D_1' in such a way that $MD = M_1D_1$. Similarly, if '*D*' changes to 'D_2' '*M*' will change to 'M_2' in such a way that $MD = M_2D_2$.

1. This is the basic relationship and all-in one formula. We can also derive :
2. More men-less days and conversely, more days-less men.
3. More men-more work and conversely, more work-more men.
4. More days-more work and conversely, more work-more days.
5. Number of days required to complete the given work = $\dfrac{\text{Total work}}{\text{One day's work}}$

Note : Since the total work is assumed to be One (unit), the number of days required to complete the given work would be the reciprocal of the one day's work.

Sometimes the problems on Time and Work can be solved using proportional rule :

(Man × Day × Hour × 1/work) in one situation
= (Man × Day × Hour × 1/work) in another situation.

EXERCISE

1. *A* can do a piece of work in 25 days and *B* can finish it in 20 days. They work together for 5 days and then *A* goes away. In how many days will *B* finish the work?

(*a*) 10 days (*b*) 11 days (*c*) 20 days (*d*) $33\frac{1}{11}$ days

(*e*) None of these

2. *A* can do a piece of work in 25 days which *B* alone can do in 20 days. *A* started the work and was joined by B after 10 days. The work lasted for :

(a) 15 days (b) $12\frac{1}{2}$ days

(c) $16\frac{1}{2}$ days (d) $14\frac{2}{9}$ days

(e) None of these

3. A can do a piece of work in 40 days. He worked at it for 5 days and B finished the remaining work in 21 days. In how many days can A and B together finish the work?

(a) 13 days (b) 15 days

(c) $6\frac{2}{3}$ days (d) $18\frac{1}{7}$ days

(e) None of these

4. A is thrice as good a workman as B. Together they can do a job in 15 days. In how many days B will finish it alone?

(a) 60 days (b) 45 days

(c) 20 days (d) 40 days

(e) None of these

5. A can do a work in 8 days and B in 6 days. A and B can do the work on alternate days. If A begins the work, then the work can be finished in how many days?

(a) 5 days (b) 7 days

(c) $6\frac{3}{4}$ days (d) $7\frac{1}{2}$ days

(e) None of these

6. A can do a piece of work in 6 days and B alone can do it in 8 days. A and B undertook to do it for ₹ 320 and with the help of C they finished it in 3 days. How much is paid to C?

(a) ₹ 80 (b) ₹ 60

(c) ₹ 37.50 (d) ₹ 40

(e) None of these

7. A, B, C are employed to do a piece of work for ₹ 529. A and B together are supposed to do 19/23 of the work, what should C be paid?

(a) ₹ 82 (b) ₹ 92

(c) ₹ 437 (d) ₹ 300

(e) None of these

8. Eight children and 12 men complete a certain piece of work in 9 days. Each child takes twice the time taken by a man to finish the work. In how many days will 12 men finish the same work?

(a) 8 days (b) 15 days

(c) 9 days (d) 12 days

(e) None of these

9. A cistern can be filled by pipes A and B in 12 minutes and 16 minutes respectively. When full, the tank can be emptied by a third pipe C in 8 minutes only. If all the taps be turned on at the same time, the cistern will be full in :

(a) 20 min (b) 24 min

(c) 36 min (d) 48 min

(e) None of these

10. If 30 men working 7 hours a day can do a piece of work in 18 days, in how many days will 21 men working 8 hours a day do the same piece of work?

(a) 25 days (b) 20 days

(c) $22\frac{1}{2}$ days (d) 30 days

(e) None of these

EXPLANATORY ANSWERS

1. (b) : $(A + B)$'s 5 days' work = $(1/25 + 1/20) \times 5$
$= 9/20$

Remaining work = $1 - 9/20 = 11/20$

B will finish it in = $\frac{11}{20} \times 20 = 11$ days.

2. (e) : A's 10 days' work = $10/25 = 2/5$

Remaining work = $1 - 2/5 = 3/5$

$(A + B)$'s 1 day's work = $1/25 + 1/20 = 9/100$

So, $(A + B)$ complete 3/5 of the work in

$$= \frac{100}{9} \times \frac{3}{5} = 6\frac{2}{3} \text{ days}$$

So, work lasted for = $10 + 6\frac{2}{3} = 16\frac{2}{3}$ days.

3. (b) : A's 5 days' work = $5/40 = 1/8$

Remaining work = $1 - 1/8 = 7/8$

B can do a piece of work in $= \dfrac{8}{7} \times 21$

$= 24$ days

i.e., $A = 1/40$, $B = 1/24$

So, $(A + B)$ can complete the work in

$$= \frac{40 \times 24}{40 + 24} = 15 \text{ days.}$$

4. (*a*) : $A = 3B$

So $(A + B)$'s 1 day's work $= 1/15$

$4B$'s 1 day's work $= 1/15$

B's 1 day work $= 1/15 \times 4 = 1/60$

So, B alone will complete the work in 60 days.

5. (*b*) : Trick : Numbers of days $= \dfrac{8+6}{2} = 7$ days.

6. (*d*) : C's share of work $= 1 - \left(\dfrac{3}{6} + \dfrac{3}{8}\right) = \dfrac{1}{8}$

So, C's share $= \dfrac{1}{8} \times 320 =$ ₹ 40.

7. (*b*) : Trick : C's share $= 529 \times (1 - 19/23)$

$= 529 \times 4/23 =$ ₹ 92

8. (*d*) : Trick : 2 children = 1 man

So, (8 children + 12 men) = 16 men

So, 12 men will complete the same work

in $\dfrac{16 \times 9}{12} = 12$ days.

9. (*d*) : (A + B + C)'s 1 min work

$$= \frac{1}{12} + \frac{1}{16} - \frac{1}{8}$$

$$= \frac{4 + 3 - 6}{48} = \frac{1}{48}$$

Hence, cistern will full in 48 min.

10. (*c*) : Trick : Man × Day × hours

Number of days $= \dfrac{30 \times 18 \times 7}{21 \times 8}$

$= 22\dfrac{1}{2}$ days.

13

TIME AND DISTANCE

The following rules/tricks should be remembered for solving problems on the Time and Distance :

A. *Basic Formulae :*

(*i*) Distance Travelled = Average speed × Time Taken

(*ii*) $\text{Average Speed} = \dfrac{\text{Distance Travelled}}{\text{Time Taken}}$

(*iii*) $\text{Time Taken} = \dfrac{\text{Distance Travelled}}{\text{Average Speed}}$

Trains passing a telegraph post or a stationary man

Example 1 : How many seconds will a train 100 metres long running at the rate of 36 km per hour take to pass a certain telegraph post?

Solution : In passing the post the train must travel its own length.

Now, 36 km/hr = 36 × 5/18 = 10 m/sec

So, required time = 100/10 = 10 seconds

Trains crossing a bridge or passing a railway station

Example 2 : How long does a train 110 metres long running at the rate of 36 km/hr take to cross a bridge 132 metres in length?

Solution : In crossing the bridge the train must travel its own length plus the length of the bridge. Now, 36 km/hr = 36 × 5/18 = 10 m/sec.

So, required time = 242/10 = 24.2 seconds

Trains running in opposite directions

Example 3 : Two trains 121 metres and 99 metres in length respectively are running in opposite directions, one at the rate of 40 km/hr and the other at the rate of 32 km/hr. In what time will they be completely clear of each other from the moment they meet?

Solution : As the two trains are moving in opposite directions their relative speed = 40 + 32 = 72 km/hr, or 20 m/sec.

So, the required time = $\dfrac{\text{Total length}}{\text{Relative speed}}$

$= \dfrac{121+99}{20} = 11$ sec

Trains running in the same direction

Example 4 : In Example 3 if the trains were running in the same direction, in what time will they be clear of each other?

Solution: Relative speed = 40 – 32

$= 8 \text{ km/hr} = \dfrac{20}{9}$ m/sec

Total length = 121 + 99 = 220 m

So, required time = $\dfrac{\text{Total length}}{\text{Relative speed}} = \dfrac{220}{20} \times 9$

= 99 sec

Train passing a man who is walking

Example 5 : A train 110 metres in length travels at 60 km/hr. In what time will it pass a man who is walking at 6 km/hr (*i*) against it (*ii*) in the same direction?

Solution : This question is to be solved like the above examples 3 and 4, the only difference being that the length of the man is zero.

(*i*) Relative speed = 60 + 6 = 66 km/hr = $\dfrac{55}{3}$ m/sec.

So, required time = $\dfrac{110}{55} \times 3 \times 3 = 6$ seconds

(*ii*) Relative speed = 60 – 6 = 54 km/hr = 15 m/sec.

So, required time = 110/15 = $7\dfrac{1}{3}$ seconds.

EXERCISE

1. The speed of a 100 m long running train *A* is 40 % more than the speed of another 180 m long train *B* running in the opposite directions. To find out the speed of train *B*, which of the information given in statements *P* and *Q* is/are sufficient?
   P : The two trains cross each other in 6 seconds
   Q : The difference between the speeds of the two trains was 26 kmph.
   (*a*) Only P is sufficient
   (*b*) Only Q is sufficient
   (*c*) Both P and Q are needed
   (*d*) Both P & Q are not sufficient
   (*e*) None of these

2. Two stations *A* and *B* are 110 km apart on a straight line. One train starts from *A* at 7 a.m. and travels towards *B* at 20 kmph. Another train starts from *B* at 8 a.m. and travels towards *A* at a speed of 25 kmph. At what time will they meet?
   (*a*) 9 am (*b*) 10 am
   (*c*) 11 am (*d*) 10:30 am
   (*e*) None of these

3. The length of the train that takes 8 seconds to pass a pole when it runs at a speed of 36 km/hr is :
   (*a*) 70 m (*b*) 80 m
   (*c*) 85 m (*d*) 90 m
   (*e*) None of these

4. A train running at certain speed crosses a stationary engine in 20 seconds. To find out the speed of the train, which of the following information is necessary :
   (*a*) Only the length of the train
   (*b*) Only the length of the engine
   (*c*) Either the length of the train or the length of the engine
   (*d*) Both the length of the train and the length of the engine
   (*e*) None of these

5. How long will a train 60 m long travelling at 40 km/hr take to pass through a station whose platform is 90 m long?
   (*a*) 12.5 seconds
   (*b*) 13.5 seconds
   (*c*) 14.5 seconds
   (*d*) 15.5 seconds
   (*e*) None of these

6. A train overtakes two persons who are walking in the same direction in which the train is going, at the rate of 2 kmph and 4 kmph and passes them completely in 9 and 10 seconds respectively. The length of the train is :
   (*a*) 72 m (*b*) 54 m
   (*c*) 50 m (*d*) 45 m
   (*e*) None of these

7. Two trains of equal lengths take 10 seconds and 15 seconds respectively to cross a milestone. If the length of each train be 120 metres, in what time (in seconds) will they cross each other travelling in opposite direction?
   (*a*) 20 sec (*b*) 15 sec
   (*c*) 12 sec (*d*) 10 sec
   (*e*) None of these

8. A train is running at the rate of 40 kmph. A man is also going in the same direction parallel to the train at the speed of 25 kmph. If the train crosses the man in 48 seconds, the length of the train is :
   (*a*) 100 m (*b*) 200 m
   (*c*) 300 m (*d*) 400 m
   (*e*) None of these

9. A train 700 m long is running at 72 kmph. If it crosses a tunnel in 1 minute, the length of the tunnel is
   (*a*) 700 m (*b*) 600 m
   (*c*) 550 m (*d*) 500 m
   (*e*) None of these

EXPLANATORY ANSWERS

1. (*a*) : Let speed of B be x kmph.

Then, speed of $A = \frac{140x}{100} = \frac{7x}{5}$ kmph

Relative speed

$$= \left(x + \frac{7x}{5}\right) \text{ kmph}$$

$$= \frac{12x}{5} \times \frac{5}{18} \text{ m/sec}$$

$$= \frac{2x}{3} \text{ m/sec}$$

Time taken to cross each other

$$= [(100 + 180) \times \frac{3}{2x}] \text{ sec.} = \frac{420}{x} \text{ sec}$$

Now, $420/x = 6 \Rightarrow x = 70$ kmph.

Thus, only P is sufficient.

2. (*b*) : Suppose they meet in x hours after 7 a.m.

Distance covered by A in x hours $= 20x$ km

Distance covered by B in $(x - 1)$ hours $= 25(x - 1)$ km

$\because 20x + 25(x - 1) = 110$

$\Rightarrow \quad 45x = 135$

$\Rightarrow \quad x = 3$

So, they meet at 10 a.m.

Quicker Maths (Direct formula) :

They will meet at

$$8 \text{ a.m.} + \frac{110 - (8 \text{ a.m.} - 7 \text{ a.m.})20}{20 + 25}$$

$= 8$ a.m. $+ 2$ hr $= 10$ a.m.

3. (b) : 36 km/hr $= 36 \times 5/18 = 10$ m/s

Distance covered by train in 8 seconds = length of train

$= 8 \times 10 = 80$ m

4. (d) : Since the sum of the lengths of the train and the engine is needed, both the lengths must be known.

5. (*b*) : Speed $= 40$ km/hr $= 40 \times \frac{5}{18}$ m/s

So, Time $= \frac{(60 + 90)}{40 \times 5} \times 18$

$$= \frac{150 \times 18}{40 \times 5} = 13.5 \text{ seconds.}$$

6. (*c*) : 2 kmph $= (2 \times 5/18)$ m/sec $= 5/9$ m/sec

and 4 kmph $= \left(4 \times \frac{5}{18}\right)$ m/sec $= 10/9$ m/sec

Let the length of the train be x metres and its speed be y m/sec

Then $\frac{x}{(y - 5/9)} = 9$ and $\frac{x}{(y - 10/9)} = 10$

So, $9y - 5 = x$ and $10(9y - 10) = 9x$

So, $9y - x = 5$ and $90y - 9x = 100$

On solving we get : $x = 50$

So, length of the train is 50 m.

7. (*c*) : Speed of first train $= \frac{120}{10} = 12$ m/s

Speed of second train $= \frac{120}{15} = 8$ m/s

Their relative speed $= 12 + 8 = 20$ m/s

Hence, required time $= \frac{120 + 120}{20} = \frac{240}{20}$

$= 12$ sec

8. (*b*) : Length of train = Relative speed × time

$$= (40 - 25)\left(\frac{5}{18}\right) \times 48$$

$$= \frac{15 \times 5 \times 48}{18}$$

$= 200$ m

9. (*d*) : Let length of the tunnel be x m;

speed $= (72 \times 5/18)$ m/ sec $= 20$ m/sec

Time $= 60$ sec

$\because \quad 60 = \frac{700 + x}{20} \Rightarrow 700 + x = 1200$

$\Rightarrow \quad x = 500$ m

14

STREAMS

Normally by speed of the boat or swimmer we mean the speed of the boat (or swimmer in still water). If the boat (or the swimmer) moves against the stream then it is called *upstream* and if it moves with the stream, it is called *downstream*.

If the speed of the boat (or the swimmer) is x and if the speed of the stream is y then, while upstream the effective speed of the boat $= x - y$ and while downstream the effective speed of the boat $= x + y$.

Theorem : If x km per hour be the man's rate in still water, and y km per hour the rate of the current. Then,

$x + y$ = man's rate with current

$x - y$ = man's rate against current.

Adding and subtracting and then dividing by 2

$x = 1/2$ (man's rate with current + his rate against current)

$y = 1/2$ (man's rate with current – his rate against current)

Hence, we have the following two facts :

(*i*) A man's rate in still water is half the sum of his rates with and against the current.

(*ii*) The rate of the current is half the difference between the rates of the man with and against the current.

Tricks For Boats and Streams Related Problems

Suppose,

x = Speed of a boat or man in still water.

y = Speed of the stream or the current or the river.

Then,

Type I :

1. Speed of boat or man with the stream (downstream)

   = Down rate = $x + y$

2. Speed of boat or man against the stream (up stream)

   = Up rate = $x - y$

Type II :

1. $x = 1/2$ (Down rate + Up rate)
2. $y = 1/2$ (Down rate – Up rate)

Special Hints :

1. If a body covers a distance at the rate of x kmph and another equal distance at the rate of y kmph. Then,

   $$\textbf{Average Speed} = \frac{2xy}{x+y}$$

2. If a man changes his speed in the ratio of $U : V$, then the ratio of the time taken to cover the same distance is $V : U$.

Precautions :

1. All given quantities (speed or distance) should be in the same manner *i.e.*, either in kilometre (distance) and kilometre per hour (speed) or in metre (distance) and in metre per second (speed).
2. Sometimes we have to change the unit of given quantity according to the need of the question. It must be remembered.

EXERCISE

1. The current of stream runs at 1 kmph. A motorboat goes 35 km upstream and back again to the starting point in 12 hours. The speed of the motorboat in still water is :
   (*a*) 6 km/hr (*b*) 7 km/hr
   (*c*) 8 km/hr (*d*) 8.5 km/hr
   (*e*) None of these
2. A man can row 5 kmph in still water. If the river is running at 1 kmph, it takes him 75 minutes to row to a place and back. How far is the place?
   (*a*) 3 km (*b*) 2.5 km
   (*c*) 4 km (*d*) 8.5 km
   (*e*) None of these
3. A man can row upstream at 7 kmph and downstream at 10 kmph. Find man's rate in still water and the rate of current.
   (*a*) 2.5 , 1.5 km/hr (*b*) 8.5, 1.5 km/hr
   (*c*) 3, 2.5 km/hr (*d*) 3.5, 2.5 km/hr
   (*e*) None of these
4. A man can row 9 1/3 km/hr in still water and he takes thrice as much time to row up than as to row down the same distance in river. The speed of the current is :
   (*a*) 5 km/hr (*b*) $4\frac{2}{3}$ km/hr
   (*c*) $5\frac{1}{4}$ km/hr (*d*) $4\frac{1}{4}$ km/hr
   (*e*) None of these
5. A boat travels upstream from *B* to *A* and downstream from *A* to *B* in 3 hours. If the speed of the boat in still water is 9 km/hr and the speed of the current is 3 km/hr, the distance between *A* and *B* is :
   (*a*) 10 km (*b*) 12 km
   (*c*) 11 km (*d*) 13 km
   (*e*) None of these
6. A man can row upstream at 8 kmph and downstream at 13 kmph. The speed of the stream is :
   (*a*) 5 km/hr (*b*) 2.5 km/hr
   (*c*) 10.5 km/hr (*d*) 4.2 km/hr
   (*e*) None of these
7. A man rows 13 km upstream in 5 hours and also 28 km downstream in 5 hours. The speed of the stream is :
   (*a*) 1.5 km/hr (*b*) 2 km/hr
   (*c*) 2.5 km/hr (*d*) 3 km/hr
   (*e*) None of these
8. A man can row a boat at 10 kmph in still water. If the speed of the stream is 6 kmph the time taken to row a distance of 80 km down the stream is :
   (*a*) 8 hours (*b*) 5 hours
   (*c*) 10 hours (*d*) 20 hours
   (*e*) None of these
9. If a man rows at 6 kmph in still water and 4.5 kmph against the current, then his rate along the current is :
   (*a*) 7.5 km/hr (*b*) 6 km/hr
   (*c*) 8 km/hr (*d*) 9 km/hr
   (*e*) None of these

EXPLANATORY ANSWERS

1. (*a*) : Let the speed of motorboat in still water be *x* kmph.

Then, speed upstream = $(x-1)$ kmph

speed downstream = $(x+1)$ kmph

$$\because \quad \frac{35}{x-1}+\frac{35}{x+1}=12$$

$$\Rightarrow \quad \frac{35x+35+35x-35}{x^2-1}=12$$

$$\Rightarrow \quad 6x^2-35x-6=0$$

$$\Rightarrow (x-6)(6x+1)=0 \Rightarrow x=6$$

Hence, the speed of motor boat in still water = 6 kmph.

2. (*a*) : Speed downstream = $(5+1)$ km/hr = 6 km/hr

Speed upstream = $(5-1)$ km/hr = 4 km/hr

Let the required distance be *x* km.

$$\text{Then,} \quad \frac{x}{6}+\frac{x}{4}=\frac{75}{60}$$

$$\Rightarrow \quad \frac{2x+3x}{12}=\frac{5}{4}$$

$$\Rightarrow \quad 2x+3x=15$$

$$\Rightarrow \quad x=3$$

So, required distance = 3 km.

3. (*b*) : Rate of man in still water = 1/2 (10 + 7) km/hr = 8.5 km/hr

Rate of current = 1/2 (10 – 7) km/hr
= 1.5 km/hr

4. (*b*) : Let the speed of current = x km/hr
Then, 28/3 + x = 3 (28/3 – x)

$$\Rightarrow \quad 4x = 28 - \frac{28}{3}$$

$$\Rightarrow \quad x = \frac{14}{3} = 4\frac{2}{3} \text{ km/hr.}$$

5. (*b*) : Let the distance be x km.
Now, upstream speed = 9 – 3 = 6 km/hr.
and downstream speed = 9 + 3 = 12 km/hr
Total time taken in upstream and downstream journey

$$\frac{x}{6} + \frac{x}{12} = 3 \quad \Rightarrow \frac{3x}{12} = 3$$

$$\Rightarrow \quad x = 12 \text{ km}$$

Quicker Maths (Direct formula) :

Distance = Total time ×

$$\left\{\frac{(\text{speed of boat in still water})^2 - (\text{speed of current})^2}{2 \times \text{speed of boat in still water}}\right\}$$

$$= 3 \times \left\{\frac{(9)^2 - (3)^2}{2 \times 9}\right\} = \frac{3 \times 72}{18} = 12 \text{ km}$$

6. (*b*) : Speed of stream = $\frac{1}{2}$ (13 – 8) kmph
= 2.5 kmph

7. (*a*) : Speed upstream = 13/5 kmph
Speed downstream = 28/5 kmph

$$\text{Speed of stream} = \frac{1}{2}\left(\frac{28}{5} - \frac{13}{5}\right) \text{kmph}$$

= 1.5 kmph

8. (*b*) : Speed downstream = (10 + 6) km/hr
= 16 km/hr
Time taken to cover 80 km downstream
= (80/16) hrs = 5 hrs

9. (*a*) : Let the rate of the stream be x kmph.
Then, rate against the current = $(6 - x)$ kmph.

$$\Rightarrow \quad 6 - x = 4.5$$

$$\Rightarrow \quad x = 1.5$$

So, rate of current = 1.5 kmph
Rate along the current = 6 + 1.5 = 7.5 kmph

MISCELLANEOUS EXERCISE

1. A monkey ascends a greased pole 12 metres high. He ascends 2 metres in first minute and slips down 1 metre in the alternate minute. In which minute, he reaches the top?
(*a*) 10th (*b*) 11th
(*c*) 12th (*d*) 13th
(*e*) None of these

2. Two trains start at the same time from Aligarh and Delhi and proceed towards each other at the rate of 16 km/hr and 21 km/hr respectively. When they meet, it is found that one train has travelled 60 km more than the other. The distance between the two stations is :
(*a*) 445 km (*b*) 444 km
(*c*) 440 km (*d*) 450 km
(*e*) None of these

3. A train 100 metres long, moving at a speed of 50 km per hour, crosses a train 120 metres long coming from opposite direction in 6 seconds. What is the speed of the second train?
(*a*) 132 kmph (*b*) 82 kmph
(*c*) 60 kmph (*d*) 50 kmph
(*e*) None of these

4. If I walk at 4 kmph, I miss the bus by 10 minutes. If I walk at 5 kmph, I reach 5 minutes before the arrival of the bus. How far I walked to reach the bus stand?
(*a*) 5 km (*b*) 10 km
(*c*) 7 km (*d*) 4 km
(*e*) None of these

5. Two buses travel to a place at speeds of 45 kmph and 60 kmph respectively. If the second bus takes $5\frac{1}{2}$ hours less than the first for the journey, the length of the journey is :
(*a*) 900 km (*b*) 945 km
(*c*) 990 km (*d*) 1350 km
(*e*) None of these

6. A man leaves a point P at 6 a.m. and reaches the point Q at 10 a.m. Another man leaves the point Q at 8 a.m. and reaches the point P at 12 noon. At what time do they meet?
(*a*) 9 a.m. (*b*) 10 a.m.
(*c*) 8 a.m. (*d*) 7 a.m.
(*e*) None of these

7. A man travels 360 km in 4 hrs, partly by air and partly by train. If he had travelled all the way by air, he would have saved 4/5 of the time he was in train and would have arrived at his destination 2 hours early. Find the distance he travelled by air and train.
(*a*) 260 km and 80 km (*b*) 270 km and 90 km
(*c*) 260 km and 70 km (*d*) 270 km and 95 km
(*e*) None of these

8. A person covers a distance in 40 mintues if he runs at a speed of 45 km per hour on an average. Find the speed at which he must run to reduce the time of journey to 30 minutes.
(*a*) 70 km/hr (*b*) 75 km/hr
(*c*) 60 km/hr (*d*) 65 km/hr
(*e*) None of these

9. A boat moves downstream at the rate of 1 km in 6 minutes and upstream at the rate of 1 km in 10 minutes. The speed of the current is :
(*a*) 2 km/hr (*b*) 3 km/hr
(*c*) 1 km/hr (*d*) 4 km/hr
(*e*) None of these

10. Two trains travel in the same direction at 90 km/hr and 72 km/hr respectively and the faster train passes a man in the slower train in 23 seconds. Find the length of the train that runs faster.
(*a*) 135 m (*b*) 120 m
(*c*) 115 m (*d*) 150 m
(*e*) None of these

1. A man rows upstream 13 km and downstream 28 km taking 5 hours each time. What is the speed of the current?
(*a*) $2\frac{1}{2}$ km (*b*) 1 km
(*c*) $1\frac{1}{2}$ km (*d*) 2 km
(*e*) None of these

2. By walking at 3/4 of his usual speed, a man reaches office 20 minutes later than usual time. What is his usual time?
(*a*) 65 min (*b*) 60 min
(*c*) 70 min (*d*) 64 min
(*e*) None of these

. Ravi runs 15.6 km per hour. How many metres does he run in two minutes?
(*a*) 400 metres (*b*) 520 metres
(*c*) 200 metres (*b*) 450 metres
(*e*) None of these

14. A monkey tries to ascend a greased pole 14 metres high. He ascends 2 metres in first minute and slips down 1 metre in the alternate minute. If he continues to ascend in this fashion, how long does he take to reach the top?
(*a*) 25 min. (*b*) 28 min.
(*c*) 20 min. (*d*) 30 min.
(*e*) None of these

15. Two runners cover the same distance at the rate of 15 km and 16 km per hour respectively. Find the distance travelled when one takes 16 minutes longer than the other.
(*a*) 60 km (*b*) 70 km
(*c*) 64 km (*d*) 80 km
(*e*) None of these

16. Two cars run to a place at the speeds of 45 km/hr and 60 km/hr respectively. If the second car takes 5 hours less than the first for the journey. Find the length of the journey.
(*a*) 1000 km (*b*) 900 km
(*c*) 850 km (*d*) 1200 km
(*e*) None of these

17. A cyclist travels for 10 hours, the first half at 21 km per hour and the other half at 24 kmph. Find the distance travelled.
(*a*) 235 km (*b*) 224 km
(*c*) 255 km (*d*) 275 km
(*e*) None of these

18. On a tour, a man travels at the rate of 64 km an hour for the first 160 km, then travels the next 160 km at the rate of 80 km an hour. What is the average speed in km per hour for the first 320 km of the tour?
(*a*) 75 kmph (*b*) 85 kmph
(*c*) 71.1 kmph (*d*) 75.12 kmph
(*e*) None of these

19. A man can row 4.5 km/hr in still water and he finds that it takes him twice as long to row upstream as to row down the river. Find the rate of stream.
(*a*) 4 km/hr (*b*) 7 km/hr
(*c*) 1.5 km/hr (*d*) 2 km/hr
(*e*) None of these

20. A man can row 5 km per hour in still water. If the river is flowing at 1 km per hour, it takes him 75 minutes to row to a place and back. How far is the place?
(*a*) 3 km (*b*) 2.5 km
(*c*) 4 km (*d*) 5 km
(*e*) None of these

21. A train passes through the stationary man standing on the platform in 7 seconds and passes through the platform completely in 28 seconds. If the length of the platform is 330 metres, what is the length of the train?

(*a*) 82.5 m (*b*) 220 m
(*c*) 110 m (*d*) 100 m
(*e*) None of these

22. A man covers a certain distance between his house and office on scooter. Having an average speed of 30 km/hr, he is late by 10 minutes. However, with a speed of 40 km/hr, he reaches his office 5 minutes earlier. Find the distance between his house and office.

(*a*) 30 km (*b*) 35 km
(*c*) 40 km (*d*) 45 km
(*e*) None of these

23. The distance between two stations, Delhi and Amritsar, is 450 km. A train starts at 4 p.m. from Delhi and moves towards Amritsar at an average speed of 60 km/hrs. Another train starts from Amritsar at 3:20 p.m. and moves towards Delhi at an average speed of 80 km/hrs. How far from Delhi will the two trains meet and at what time?

(*a*) 70 km and 4 p.m.
(*b*) 140 km and 3 p.m.
(*c*) Data is inadequate
(*d*) 170 km and 6:50 p.m.
(*e*) None of these

EXPLANATORY ANSWERS

1. (*e*) : The monkey climbs 1 metre in every 2 minutes, so it will take 20 minutes to climb 10 metres. It will take 1 minute to climb the rest 2 metres and will reach the top. Therefore, it will reach the top in 21st minute.

2. (*b*) : Suppose, they meet after x hours
So, $21x - 16x = 60$;
So, $x = 12$
So, distance $= 16 \times 12 + 21 \times 12 = 444$ km.

3. (*b*) : Suppose, requisite speed = x km/hrs.
Now, $22 \times 60 \times 60 = 6 \times 100\,(50 + x)$
So, $x = 82$ km/hrs.

4. (*a*) : **Trick :** $10 + 5 = 15$ min = 1/4 hour.

$$\text{Requisite distance} = \frac{1}{4} \times \frac{4 \times 5}{5 - 4} = 5 \text{ km}$$

5. (*c*) : **Trick :**

$$\text{Distance} = \frac{11}{2} \times \frac{60 \times 45}{60 - 45} = 990 \text{ km}$$

6. (*a*) : Let the distance $PQ = A$ km.
And they meet x hrs after the first man starts.
Average speed of first man

$$= \frac{A}{10 - 6} = \frac{A}{4} \text{ km/hr.}$$

Average speed of second man

$$= \frac{A}{12 - 8} = \frac{A}{4} \text{ km/hr}$$

$$\text{Distance travelled by first man} = \frac{Ax}{4} \text{ km}$$

They meet x hrs after the first man starts. The second man, as he starts 2 hrs late, meets after $(x - 2)$ hrs from his start. Therefore, the distance travelled by the second man

$$= \frac{A(x-2)\,km}{4}$$

$$\text{Now, } \frac{Ax}{4} + \frac{A(x-2)\,km}{4} = A$$

$$\Rightarrow \quad 2x - 2 = 4$$

$$\Rightarrow \quad x = 3 \text{ hrs.}$$

So, they meet at 6 a.m. + 3 hrs = 9 a.m.

Quicker Approach : Since both the persons take equal time of 4 hrs to cover the distance, their meeting time will be exactly in the middle of 6 a.m. and 12 noon. *i.e.*, at 9 a.m.

But what happens when they take different times? In that case, the following formula works good. They will meet at

$$= \text{First's starting time} + \frac{(\text{Time taken by first})\,(\text{2nd's arrival time} - \text{1st's starting time})}{\text{Sum of time taken by both}}$$

$$= 6 \text{ a.m.} + \frac{(10-6)\,(12-6)}{(10-6) + (12-8)}$$

$$= 6 \text{ a.m.} + \frac{4 \times 6}{4 + 4} = 9 \text{ a.m.}$$

7. (b) : 4/5 of total time in train = 2 hours.

So, total time in train = $2 \times \frac{5}{4}$ = 5/2 hrs

So, total time spent in air = 4 – 5/2 = 3/2 hrs

By the given hypothesis, if 360 km is covered by air, then time taken is (4 – 2) = 2 hrs

So, when 3/2 hrs is spent in air, distance covered

$$= \frac{360}{2} \times \frac{3}{2} = 270 \text{ km}$$

So, distance covered by train = 360 – 270 = 90 km

8. (c) : Theorem : Speed and time taken are inversely proportional.

Therefore, $S_1 T_1 = S_2 T_2 = S_3 T_3$ ...

Where S_1, S_2, S_3, ... are the speeds and T_1, T_2, T_3, ... are the time taken to travel the same distance. Thus in this case :

$45 \times 40 = S_2 \times 30$

$$\therefore \quad S_2 = \frac{45 \times 40}{30} = 60 \text{ km/hrs.}$$

9. (a) : Speed in downstream= $\left(\frac{1}{6} \times 60\right)$ km/hr

= 10 km/hr

Speed in upstream = $\left(\frac{1}{10} \times 60\right)$ km/hr

= 6 km/hr

So, speed of the current = $\frac{1}{2}(10 - 6)$

= 2 km/hrs

10. (c) : Trick : Length of faster train

$$= 23 \times \left(18 \times \frac{5}{18}\right) = 115 \text{ m}$$

11. (c) : Speed in upstream = 13/5 = 2.6 km/hr

Speed in downstream = 28/5 = 5.6 km/hr

So, speed of current = $\frac{1}{2}(5.6 - 2.6)$

$$= 1\frac{1}{2} \text{ km}$$

12. (b) : Let usual speed and time are x min and t sec respectively

$$xt = \frac{3x}{4}(t + 20 \times 60)$$

$4t = 3t + 3600$

$t = 3600$ sec or $\frac{3600}{60} = 60$ min

13. (b) : Requisite distance = $\frac{15600}{60} \times 2$

= 520 metres.

14. (a) : In every 2 minutes, he is able to ascend 2 – 1 = 1 metre. This way he ascends up to 12 metres because when he reaches at the top, he does not slip down. Thus, up to 12 metres, he takes 12 × 2 = 24 minutes and for the last 2 metres, he takes 1 minute. Therefore, he takes 24 + 1 = 25 minutes to reach the top.

15. (c) : Let the distance be x km.

Time taken by the first runner = $\frac{x}{15}$ hrs

Time taken by the second runner = $\frac{x}{16}$ hrs

Now,

$$\frac{x}{15} - \frac{x}{16} = \frac{16}{60}$$

$$\Rightarrow \quad \frac{x(16-15)}{15 \times 16} = \frac{16}{60}$$

$$\Rightarrow \quad x = \frac{16}{60} \times 15 \times 16 = 64 \text{ km}$$

Direct Formula : Distance

$$= \frac{\text{Products of speeds}}{\text{Difference of speeds}} \times$$

Difference in time to cover the distance

$$= \frac{15 \times 16}{(16-15)} \times \frac{16}{60} = 64 \text{ km}$$

16. (b) : "One takes 5 hrs less than the other" means the second takes 5 hrs more than the first to reach the destination. So, the above direct formula works in this case also.

So, distance = $\frac{45 \times 60}{60 - 45} \times 5 = 900$ km

17. (*b*) : Let the total distance be $2x$ km.
According to question,

$$\frac{x}{21}+\frac{x}{24}=10$$

$$24x+21x=21\times 24\times 10$$

$$45x=5040$$

$$x=112$$

Hence, total distance travelled $= 2\times 112$
$= 224$ km

18. (*c*) : Average speed $=\dfrac{2\times 64\times 80}{64+80}$
$= 71.11$ km/hour.

19. (*c*) : Let man's rate with current $= x$ km/hr.

So, $\frac{1}{2}[x+2x]=4.5$

So, $x = 3$ km/hr

i.e., With current = 3 km/hr. and against current = 6 km/hr.

So, rate of current

$=\frac{1}{2}[6-3]=1.5$ km/hr.

20. (*a*) : Suppose, distance $= x$ km

Then, $\frac{x}{6}+\frac{x}{4}=\frac{5}{4}$

$\Rightarrow x = 3$ km

21. (*c*) : Suppose train's length $= x$ metres

So, speed $=\frac{x}{7}$ metres/sec.

So, distance covered in 28 seconds

$=\frac{x}{7}\times 28 = 4x$ metres

Now, $4x - x = 330$

So, $x = 110$ metres.

22. (*a*) : Let the distance be x km

Time taken to cover x km at 30 km/hr

$=\frac{x}{30}$ hrs.

Time taken to cover x km at 40 km/hr

$=\frac{x}{40}$ hrs.

Difference between the time taken = 15 min = 1/4 hr

So, $\frac{x}{30}-\frac{x}{40}=\frac{1}{4}$ or $4x-3x=30$

or $x=30$

Hence, the required distance is 30 km.

Direct Formula :

Required distance

$$=\frac{\text{Product of two speeds}}{\text{Difference of two speeds}}$$

$\times$ Difference between arrival times

Thus in this case, the required distance

$$=\frac{30\times 40}{40-30}\times\frac{15}{60}=30\text{ km}$$

Note : 10 minutes late and 5 minutes earlier make a difference of $10+5=15$ minutes. As the other units are in km/hr, the difference in time should also be changed into hours.

23. (*d*) Suppose the trains meet at a distance of x km from Delhi. Let the trains from Delhi and Amritsar be A and B respectively. Then, [Time taken by B to cover $(450-x)$ km

$-$ [Time taken by A to cover x km] $=\frac{40}{60}$,

$$\frac{450-X}{80}-\frac{X}{60}=\frac{40}{60}$$

So, $3(450-x)-4x=160$

$\Rightarrow 7x=1190$

$\Rightarrow x=170$

Thus, the trains meet at a distance of 170 km from Delhi.

Time taken by A to cover 170 km
$=(170/60)$ hrs = 2 hrs 50 min.

So, the trains meet at 6:50 p.m.

Note : R.H.S. = 4 : 00 pm − 3:20 p.m. = 40 minutes
= 40/60 hr

L.H.S. comes from the fact that the train from Amritsar took 40 minutes more to travel up to the meeting point because it had started its journey at 3:20 p.m. Whereas the train from Delhi had started its journey at 4 p.m. and the meeting time is the same for both the trains.

15

RACES AND GAMES

Race : A contest of speed is called a *race*.

Race-course : The ground or path on which contests are arranged is called a *race-course*.

Dead - heat Race :

If all the persons contesting a race reach the goal exactly at the same time, then the race is called *dead-heat race*.

Now, suppose A and B are two participants in a race. If, before the start of the race, A is at the starting point and B is ahead of A by 25 metres, then A is said to give B a start of 25 metres. To cover a race of 100 metres in this case, A will cover a distance of 100 metres and B will cover 100 – 25 = 75 metres only.

Note : In the above case, we may say that "*A* has given a lead of 25 metres to *B*".

Games : If we say that it is a game of 100, then the person among the participants who scores 100 points first is the winner. If, when A scores 100 while B scores only 80 points, then we say that "*A* can give 20 points to *B*" or, "*A* can give *B* 20 points" in a game of 100.

Example : A is $1\frac{2}{3}$ times as fast as B. If A gives B a start of 60 metres, how long should the racecourse be so that both of them reach at the same time?

Solution : A's speed : B's speed $= 1\frac{2}{3} : 1$

$= 5/3 : 1$

$= 5 : 3$

We may say that A gains 5 – 3 = 2 m in a race of metres.

Therefore, he will gain 60 m in a race of $\frac{5}{2} \times 60$

$= 150$ m

Quicker Maths (Direct formula) :

$$\text{Distance of race-course} = \text{lead}\left(\frac{1}{1-\frac{\text{B's speed}}{\text{A's speed}}}\right)$$

$$= 60\left(\frac{1}{1-3/5}\right) = 60\left(\frac{5}{5-3}\right) = 150 \text{ m.}$$

Example : In a 100 m race, A runs at 5 km/hr. A gives B a start of 8 metres and still beats him by 8 seconds. Find the speed of B.

Solution : Time taken by A to cover 100 m.

$$= 100 \div (5 \times 5/18) = \frac{100 \times 18}{25} = 72 \text{ seconds}$$

So, B covers (100 – 8) or 92 m in (72 + 8) or 80 seconds.

So, speed of $B = \frac{92}{80} \times \frac{18}{5} = 4.14$ km/hr

Quicker Math (Direct Formula) :

$$\text{B's speed} = \frac{100\text{m} - 8\text{m}}{\text{A's time to cover 100m} + 8 \text{ sec}}$$

$$= \frac{92}{72+8} = \frac{92}{80} \text{ m/s} = 4.14 \text{ km/hr.}$$

Example : In a game of billiards, A can give B 12 points in 60 and A can give C 10 in 90. How many can C give B in a game of 70?

Solution : $A : B = 60 : 48 = 90 : 72$

$A : C = 90 : 80 = 90 : 80$

So, $C : B = 80 : 72 = 80\,(70/80) : 72\,(70/80)$

$= 70 : 63$

So, C gives B 7 points in the game of 70 points.

EXERCISE

1. A can run 100 m in 20 seconds and B in 25 seconds. A will beat B by :
   (a) 10 m (b) 20 m
   (c) 25 m (d) 12 m
   (e) None of these
2. At a game of billiards, A can give B 15 points in 60 and A can give C 20 in 60. How many can B give C in a game of 90?
   (a) 10 points (b) 20 points
   (c) 30 points (d) 40 points
   (e) None of these
3. In a 500 m race, the ratio of speeds of two runners A and B is 3 : 4. A has a start of 140 m. Then A wins by :
   (a) 30 m (b) 34 m
   (c) 20 m (d) 10 m
   (e) None of these
4. In a 100 m race, A runs at 6 km/hr. If A gives B a start of 4 m and still beats him by 12 seconds, what is the speed of B?
   (a) 4 km/hr (b) 4.5 km/hr
   (c) 4.8 km/hr (d) 5 km/hr
   (e) None of these
5. Two men A and B run a 4 km race on a course 250 m round. If their rates be 5 : 4, how often does the winner pass the other :
   (a) 1 time (b) 4 times
   (c) 2 times (d) 5 times
   (e) None of these
6. A runs 1.75 times as fast as B. If A gives B a start of 60 m, how far must the winning post be in order that A and B reach at the same time?
   (a) 105 m (b) 80 m
   (c) 140 m (d) 45 m
   (e) 50 m
7. At a game of billiards, A can give B 10 points in 60 and he can give C 15 in 60. How many can B give C in a game of 90?
   (a) 10 points (b) 9 points
   (c) 8 points (d) 7 points
   (e) None of these
8. In a 1000 m race A can give B 100 m and C 280 m. In the same race, B can give C :
   (a) 180 m (b) 200 m
   (c) 270 m (d) 90 m
   (e) None of these
9. A and B run a km and A wins by 1 minute. A and C run a km and A wins by 375 m. B and C run a km and B wins by 30 seconds. Find the time taken by A and B ro run a km race.
   (a) 150, 210 sec (b) 200, 160 sec
   (c) 300, 150 sec (d) 150, 200 sec
   (e) None of these
10. In a race of 300 m A beats B by 15 m or 5 seconds. A's time over the course is :
   (a) 100 sec (b) 95 sec
   (c) 105 sec (d) 90 sec
   (e) None of these

EXPLANATORY ANSWERS

1. (b): Distance covered by B in 5 seconds

$$= \frac{100}{25} \times 5 = 20 \text{ m}$$

So, A beats B by 20 m.

2. (a) : $A : B : C = 60 : 45 : 40$

$$\text{So, } B : C = \frac{45}{40} = \frac{45 \times 2}{40 \times 2} = \frac{90}{80}$$

So, B gives C 10 points in a game of 90.

3. (c) : To reach the winning points A covers 500 – 140 =360 m.

So, B covers 360 (4/3) = 480 m when A reaches the winning point.

So, A reaches the winning point while B remains 20 m behind.

So, A wins by 20 m.

4. (c) : B's speed

$$= \frac{100 \text{ m} - 4 \text{ m}}{A'\text{s time to cover } 100 \text{ m} + 12 \text{ second}}$$

A's time to cover 100 m

$$= 100 \div (6 \times 5/18)$$

$$= \frac{100 \times 18}{6 \times 5} = 60 \text{ sec}$$

So, B's speed $= \frac{96}{60+12} = \frac{4}{3}$ m/s

$$= \frac{4}{3} \times \frac{18}{5} = 4.8 \text{ km/hr.}$$

5. (*a*) : A's rate : B's rate = 5 : 4

⇒ When A makes 5 rounds, B makes 4 rounds

⇒ When A covers $\frac{5 \times 250}{1000} = \frac{5}{4}$ km.

B covers $\frac{4 \times 250}{1000} = 1$ km

⇒ A passes B each time, when A makes 5 rounds.

⇒ In covering 5/4 km, A passes B 1 time.

6. (*c*) : $60 \times \left(\frac{1}{1-4/7}\right)$

$$= 60 \times \frac{7}{3} = 140 \text{ m}$$

7. (*b*) : $A : B = 60 : 50$ $\quad A : C = 60 : 45$

So, $B : C = 50 : 45$

$= 50\,(90/50) : 45\,(90/50) = 90 : 81$

Hence, B gives C 9 points in a game of 90.

8. (*b*) : $A : B : C = 100 : 900 : 720$

$$\text{So, } B : C = \frac{900}{720} = \frac{900 \times \frac{1000}{900}}{720 \times \frac{1000}{900}}$$

$$= \frac{1000}{800} = 1000 : 800$$

So, B can give C 200 m.

9. (*a*) : A beats B by 60 seconds, B beats C by 30 seconds.

So, A beats C by 90 seconds or 375 m (given)

So, C covers 375 m in $\frac{90}{375} \times 1000$

$= 240$ seconds

Thus, time taken by A to cover 1 km

$= 240 - 90 = 150$ sec.

and time taken by B to cover 1 km

$= 240 - 30 = 210$ sec.

10. (*b*) : 15 m is covered by B in 5 seconds

So, 300 m is covered by B in $\frac{5}{15} \times 300$

$= 100$ seconds

Hence, A's time over the course $= 100 - 5$

$= 95$ sec.

16

MENSURATION-I

The fundamental formulae on plane figures (Triangle, Rectangle, Square, Parallelogram, Trapezium, Rhombus, Circle) are reviewed below :

TRIANGLE

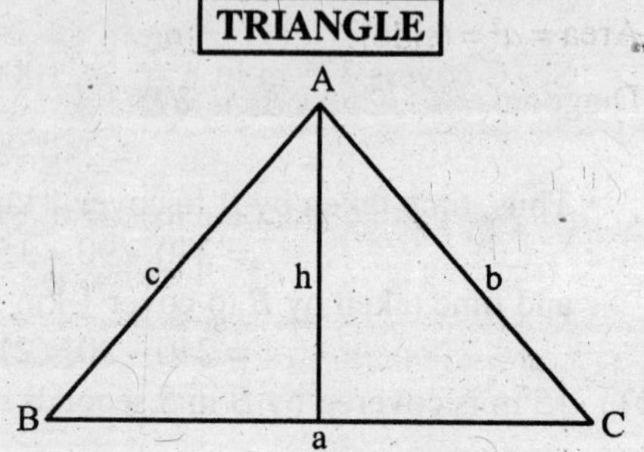

1. Area = $\frac{1}{2}$ × Base × Height

2. Area = $\sqrt{s(s-a)(s-b)(s-c)}$

Where a, b, c are the lengths of the sides of triangle and

$$s = \frac{a+b+c}{2}$$

RIGHT ANGLED TRIANGLE

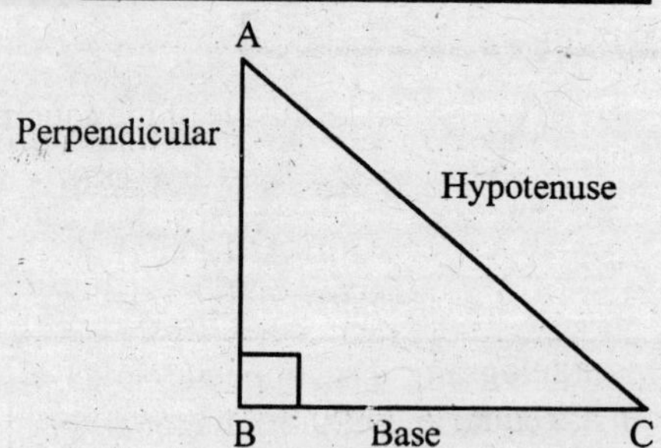

1. Area = $\frac{1}{2}$ × Base × Perpendicular

2. $(\text{Hypotenuse})^2 = (\text{Perpendicular})^2 + (\text{Base})^2$

ISOSCELES TRIANGLE

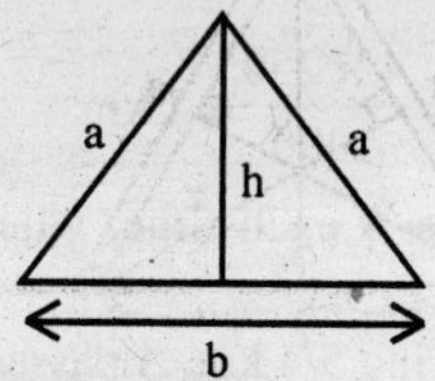

1. Area = $\frac{1}{4} b\sqrt{4a^2 - b^2}$

ISOSCELES RIGHT TRIANGLE

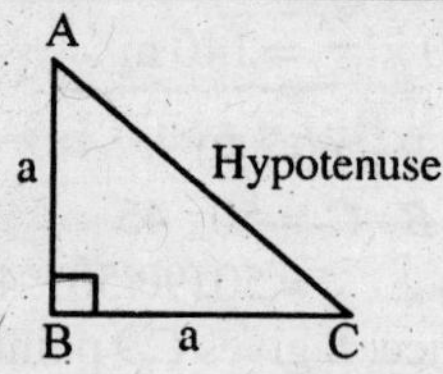

1. Area = $\frac{1}{2} \times (a)^2$

2. Hypotenuse = $a\sqrt{2}$

3. Perimeter = $\sqrt{2}a(\sqrt{2}+1)$

EQUILATERAL TRIANGLE

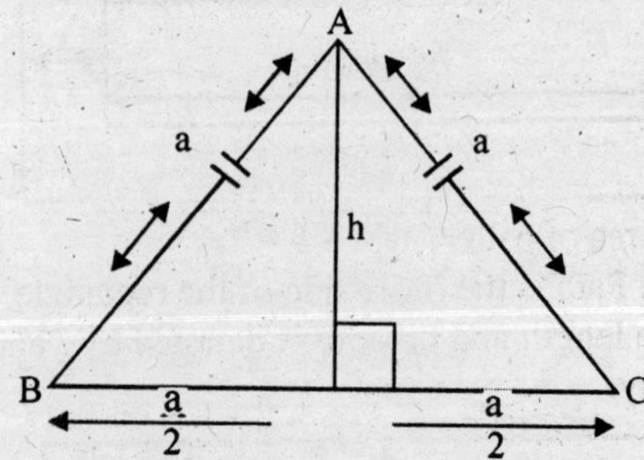

1. Perimeter = $3a$
2. Area = $\frac{\sqrt{3}\, a^2}{4}$
3. Height = $h = \frac{\sqrt{3}\, a}{2}$
4. Area = $\frac{(h)^2}{\sqrt{3}}$

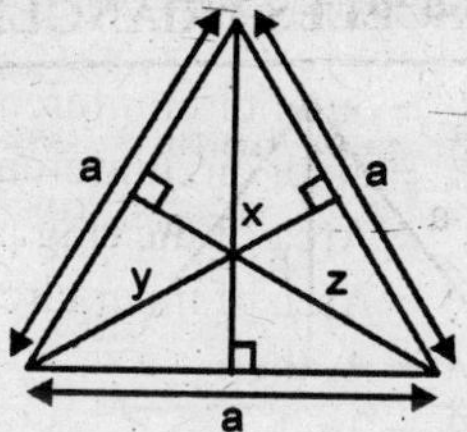

1. $a = \frac{2}{\sqrt{3}}\,(x + y + z)$
2. Area = $\frac{(x+y+z)^2}{\sqrt{3}}$

RECTANGLE

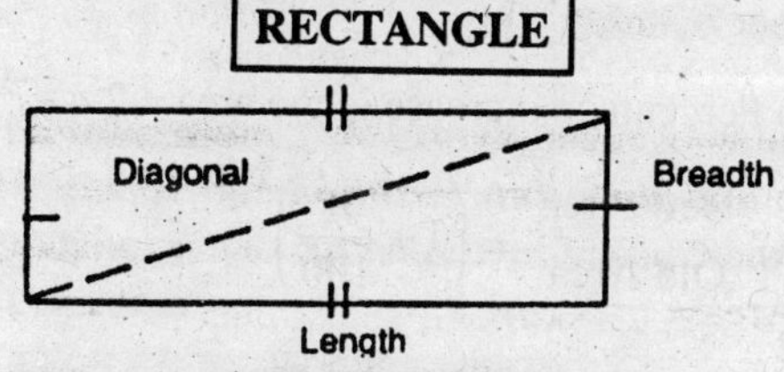

(I) 1. Area = Length × Breadth
2. Perimeter = 2 (Length + Breadth)
3. Diagonal = $\sqrt{(\text{Length})^2 + (\text{Breadth})^2}$

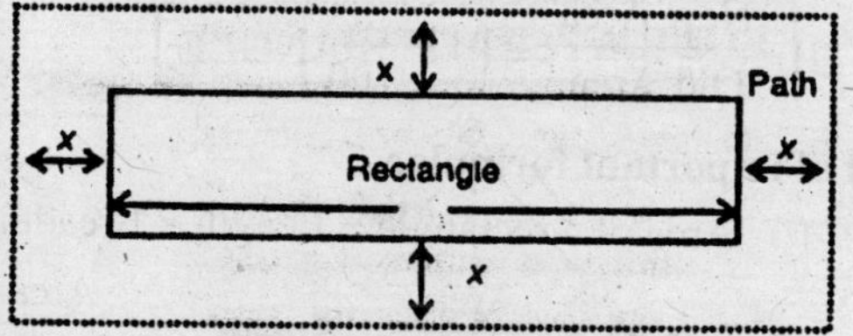

(II) Area of path = $2x\,(l + b + 2x)$

Note : Path is the outer side of the rectangle. Where length and breadth is denoted by l and b pectively.

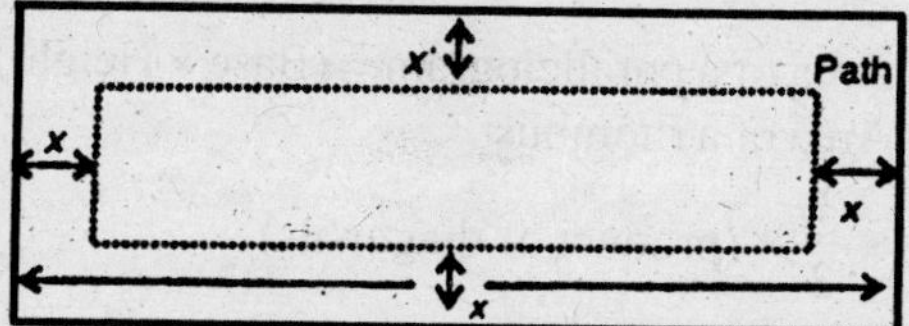

(III) Area of path which is inside of the rectangle
= $2x\,(l + b - 2x)$

SQUARE

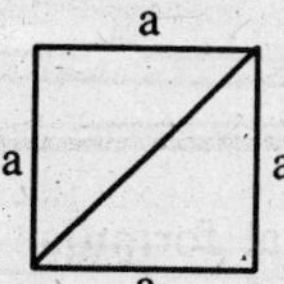

(I)
1. Perimeter = $4a$ = 4 × side
2. Area = a^2 = (side)^2
3. Diagonal = $a\sqrt{2}$ = side × $\sqrt{2}$

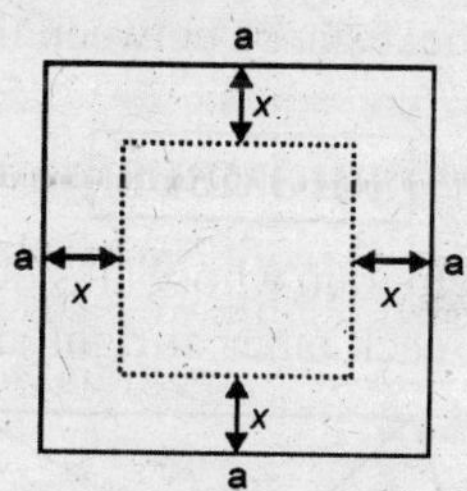

(II) Area of path (which is inside of square)
= $4x\,(a - x)$

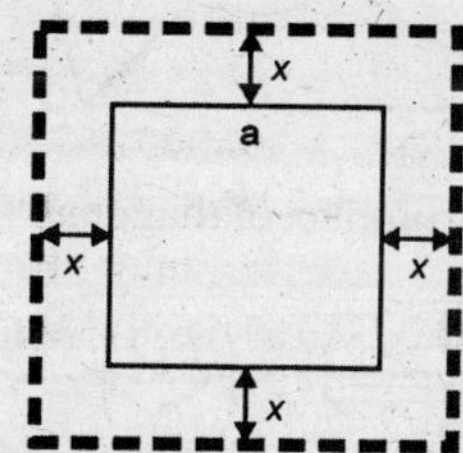

(III) Area of path (which is outside of the square)
= $4x\,(a + x)$

PARALLELOGRAM

A quadrilateral, whose opposite sides are parallel, is called a parallelogram. The opposite sides of a parallelogram are equal and the two diagonals bisect each other.

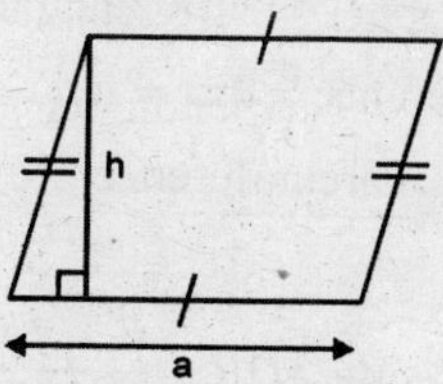

Area = Base × Height = $a \times h$

TRAPEZIUM

It is a quadrilateral whose one pair of opposite sides are parallel and other pair of opposite sides are not parallel.

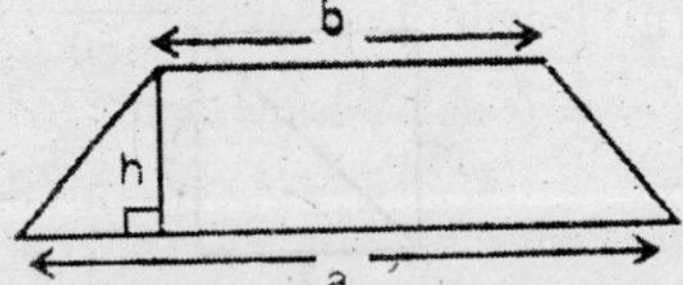

$$\text{Area} = \frac{1}{2} \times \text{height} \times (\text{sum of parallel sides})$$

$$= \frac{1}{2} h (a + b)$$

where h is the distance between the two parallel sides.

RHOMBUS

It is a parallelogram whose all sides are equal. Its diagonals bisect each other at right angles.

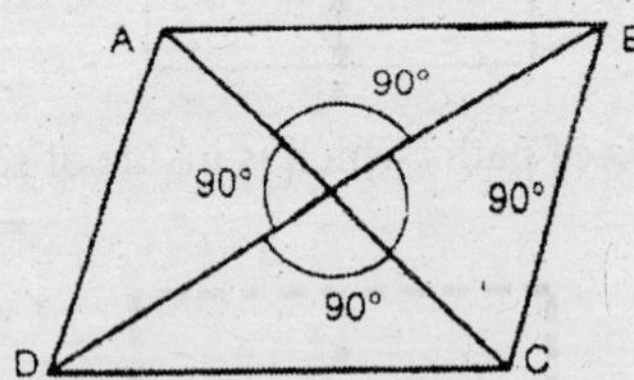

1. $\text{Area} = \frac{1}{2} \times \text{product of diagonals} = \frac{1}{2} \times AC \times BD$
2. $\text{Side} = \sqrt{\left(\frac{AC}{2}\right)^2 + \left(\frac{BD}{2}\right)^2}$
3. Perimeter = 4 × one side

CIRCLE

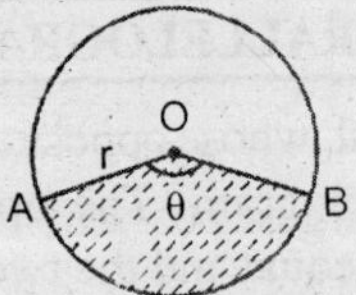

1. Diameter = 2 × radius = 2 r
2. Area = πr^2
3. Circumference = $2\pi r = \pi d$
4. $\text{Radius} = \frac{\text{Circumference}}{2\pi} = \sqrt{\frac{\text{Area}}{\pi}}$
5. $\text{Area of sector } AOB = \frac{\theta \times \pi r^2}{360°}$
6. $\text{Length of the arc } AB = \frac{\theta \times 2 \pi r}{360°}$

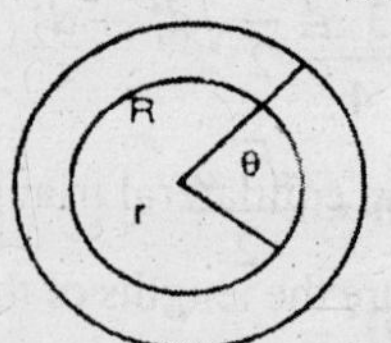

$$\frac{C_1}{C_2} = \frac{R}{r} = \frac{A_1}{A_2} = \frac{R^2 - r^2}{r^2}$$

Where C_1 = outer circumference
C_2 = inner circumference
A_1 = Area of the ring portion
A_2 = Area of inner circle

If $A_1 = A_2$ then
$R = 2r$

Area of the ring = $\pi(R + r)(R - r) = \pi(R^2 - r^2)$

SOME TRICKS FOR PLANE FIGURES

Type 1 :

If each area of related side is increasing by a% then,

(I) Percentage increase in the area = $2a + \frac{a}{100}$

(II) $\frac{\text{New Area}}{\text{Old Area}} = \left(1 + \frac{a}{100}\right)^2$

Type 2 :

If each area of related side is decreasing by a% the

(I) Percentage decrease in area = $2a - \frac{a}{100}$

(II) $\frac{\text{New Area}}{\text{Old Area}} = \left(1 - \frac{a}{100}\right)^2$

List of important formulae

1. (*i*) Area of a rectangle = Length × Breadth

   (*ii*) $\text{Length} = \frac{\text{Area}}{\text{Breadth}}$; $\text{Breadth} = \frac{\text{Area}}{\text{Length}}$

   (*iii*) $(\text{Diagonal})^2 = (\text{Length})^2 + (\text{Breadth})^2$
2. Area of a square = $(\text{side})^2 = 1/2\ (\text{diagonal})^2$
3. Area of 4 walls of a room = 2(Length + Bread × Hei
4. Area of a parallelogram = (Base × Height)
5. Area of a rhombus

   $= \frac{1}{2} \times (\text{product of diagonals})$

When d_1 and d_2 are the two diagonals then side of rhombus

$$= \frac{1}{2}\sqrt{d_1^2 + d_2^2}$$

6. Area of an equilateral triangle $= \frac{\sqrt{3}}{4} \times (\text{side})^2$
7. If a, b, c are the lengths of the sides of a triangle and $s = \frac{1}{2}(a + b + c)$
8. Area of a triangle $= \frac{1}{2} \times$ base $\times$ height.
9. Area of a trapezium $= \frac{1}{2}$(sum of parallel sides) $\times$ distance between them
10. (*i*) Circumference of a circle $= 2\pi r$

    (*ii*) length of arc $AB = \frac{\theta 2\pi r}{360°}$ where $\angle AOB = \theta$ and O is the centre

    (*iii*) Area of sector $AOB = \frac{\pi r^2 \theta}{360°}$

    (*iv*) Area of sector $AOB = \frac{1}{2} \times \text{Arc } AB \times r$

SOLVED QUESTIONS ON AREAS

The formulae given above are sufficient for solving various questions on areas. But in some typical cases we can develop quicker methods for solving questions. We shall explain both these possibilities by way of a few examples.

Problems on Rectangles and Squares :

Type I : Simple questions requiring direct application of formula.

Example 1 : Find the diagonal of a rectangle whose sides are 12 metres and 5 metres.

Solution : The length of the diagonal

$= \sqrt{12^2 + 5^2} = \sqrt{169} = 13$ metres

Type II : Carpeting a floor.

Example 2 : How many metres of a carpet 75 cm wide will be required to cover the floor of a room which is 20 metres long and 12 metres broad?

Solution : Length of carpet

$$= \frac{\text{Length of room} \times \text{breadth of room}}{\text{width of carpet}}$$

$$= \frac{20 \times 12}{0.75} = 320 \text{ m.}$$

What amount needs to be spent in carpeting the floor if the carpet is available at ₹20 per metre?

Quicker method :

Amount required =

$$\text{Rate per metre} \times \frac{\text{length of room} \times \text{breadth of room}}{\text{width of carpet}}$$

$$= 20 \times \frac{20 \times 12}{0.75} = ₹\,6400$$

Type III : **Paving a courtyard with tiles.**

Example 3 : How many paving tiles each measuring 2.5m × 2m are required to pave a rectangular courtyard 30 m long and 16.5 m wide?

Solution : ***Quicker method***

Number of tiles required

$$= \frac{\text{length} \times \text{breadth of courtyard}}{\text{length} \times \text{breadth of each tile}} = \frac{30 \times 16.5}{2.5 \times 2} = 99$$

What amount needs to be spent if the tiles of the aforesaid dimension are available at ₹1 per piece?

Quicker method : Amount required

$$= \text{Price per tile} \times \frac{\text{length} \times \text{breadth of courtyard}}{\text{length} \times \text{breadth of each tile}}$$

$$= 1 \times \frac{30 \times 16.5}{2.5 \times 2} = 99$$

Type IV : **Paving with square tiles : largest tile**

Example 4 : A hall-room 39 m 10 cm long and 35 m 70 cm broad is to be paved with equal square tiles. Find the largest tile so that the tiles exactly fit and also find the number of tiles required.

Solution : ***Quicker Method :***

Side of largest possible tile

= HCF of length and breadth of the room

= HCF of 39.10 and 35.70 = 1.70

Also, number of tiles required

$$= \frac{\text{length} \times \text{breadth of room}}{(\text{HCF of length and breadth of room})^2}$$

$$= \frac{39.10 \times 35.70}{1.70 \times 1.70} = 483$$

Type V : Path around a garden and verandah around a room

Example 5 : A rectangular hall 12 m long and 10 m broad, is surrounded by a verandah 2 metres wide. Find the area of the verandah.

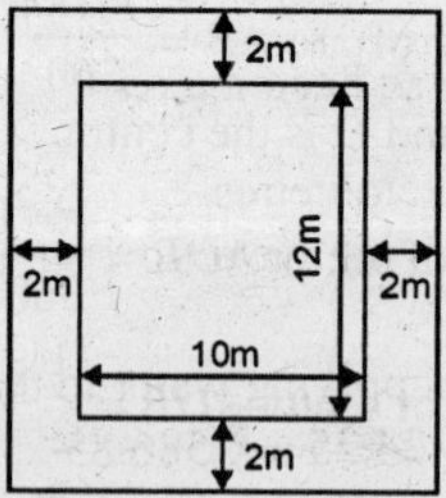

Solution : ***Quicker Method***

In such cases,

(I) When the verandah is outside the room, surrounding it

Area of verandah = 2 (width of verandah) × [Length + breadth of room + 2 (width of verandah)]

(II) When the path is within the garden, surrounded by it

Area of path = 2 (width of path) × [length + breadth of garden – 2(width of path)]

Now in the given question, by formula I, (since the verandah is outside the room, formula I will be applied)

Area of verandah $= 2 \times 2 \times (10 + 12 + 2 \times 2)$

$= 4 \times 26 = 104 \text{ m}^2$

Some more cases on paths :

A. When area of the path is given, to find the area of the garden enclosed (the garden is square in shape).

Example 6 : A path 2 m wide running all round a square garden has an area of 9680 sq m. Find the area of the garden enclosed by the path.

Solution : (***Quicker Method***) **:**

Area of the square garden

$$= \left[\frac{\text{Area of path} - 4 \times (\text{width of path})^2}{4 \times \text{width of path}}\right]^2$$

So, here in the given question,

$$\text{Area of garden} = \left[\frac{9680 - 4 \times (2)^2}{4 \times 2}\right]^2$$

$$= \left[\frac{9664}{8}\right]^2 = (1208)^2 = 1459264 \text{ sqm}$$

B. When area of the path be given, to find the width of the path.

Example 7 : A path all around the inside of a rectangular park 37 m by 30 m occupies 570 sq m. Find the width of the path.

Solution : Area of path

= 2 × width of path × [length + breadth of park – 2 × (width of path)]

$\Rightarrow \quad 570 = 2 \times x \times [37 + 30 - 2x]$

(x is the width of path)

$\Rightarrow \quad 570 = 134x - 4x^2$

$\Rightarrow \quad 4x^2 - 134x + 570 = 0$

On solving this equation we get, $x = 5$ m.

C. Paths crossing each other (important).

Example 8 : An oblong piece of ground measures 19 m 2.5 dm by 12 metres 5 dm. From the centre of each side a path 2m wide goes across to the centre of the opposite side. What is the area of the path? Find the cost of paving these paths at the rate of ₹ 1.32 per sq metre.

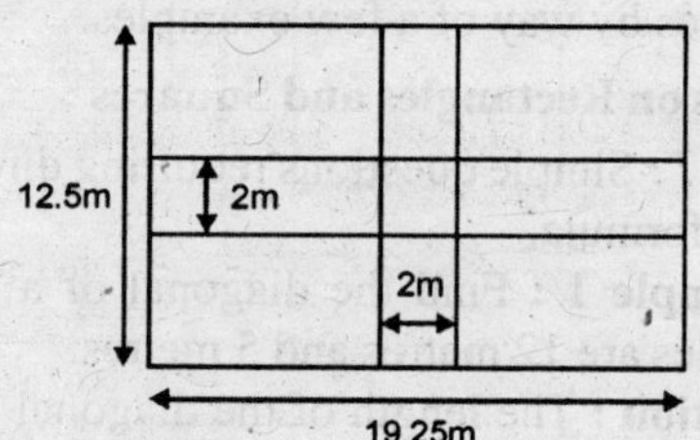

Solution : ***Quicker Method***

In such problems, use the formula given below :

1. **Area of the path**

   = (width of path) (length + breadth of park – width of path)

2. **Area of the park minus the path =**

   (length of park – width of path) × (breadth of park – width of path)

Now, for the given question,

Area of path $= 2 \times (19.25 + 12.5 - 2)$

$= 2 \times 29.75 = 59.5$ sq m

So, cost = rate × area = ₹ (59.5 × 1.32)

= ₹ 78.54.

Type VI : Area and ratio

Example 9 : The sides of a rectangular field of 726 sq m are in the ratio of 3:2, find the sides.

Solution : ***Quicker Method***

Side

$$= \text{One of the given ratios} \times \sqrt{\frac{\text{area}}{\text{product of given ratios}}}$$

So, In the given question,

$$\text{First side } = 3 \times \sqrt{\frac{726}{3 \times 2}} = 3 \times 11 = 33 \text{ m}$$

$$\text{And second side} = 2 \times \sqrt{\frac{726}{3 \times 2}} = 2 \times 11 = 22 \text{ m}$$

Type VII : Some Miscellaneous Cases

Turkey carpet and oilcloth

Example 10 : In the centre of a room 10 square metres, there is a square of turkey carpet, and the rest of the floor is covered with oilcloth. The carpet, and the oilcloth cost ₹ 15 and ₹ 6.50 per square metre respectively, and the total cost of the carpet and the oilcloth is ₹ 1338.50. Find the width of the oilcloth border.

Solution : The area of the square room = 100 sq metres

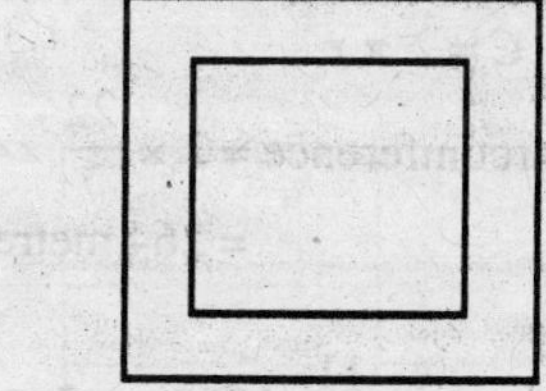

$$\text{The mean cost per sq metre} = ₹\frac{1338.50}{100}$$

$$= ₹\ 13.385$$

Carpet Oilcloth
15 6.50
13.385
6.885 1.615
= 81 : 19

By the Alligation Rule, the area of the square is 81 sq metres.

Therefore, the carpet is 9 metres both in length and breadth.

But the room is 10 metres in length and breadth.

Hence, double the width of the border is (10 – 9) or 1 metre.

So, the width of the border = 1/2 metre = 5 dm.

Problems on Triangles :

Type I : Simple Application of Formula

Example 11 : The base of a triangular field is 880 metres and its height 550 metres. Find the area of the field. Also calculate the charges for supplying water to the field at the rate of ₹ 24.25 per sq hectometre.

Solution : Area of the field = $\frac{\text{Base} \times \text{Height}}{2}$

$= \frac{880 \times 550}{2}$ sq metres

$= \frac{440 \times 550}{100 \times 100}$ sq hectometre

= 24.20 sq hectometres.

Cost of supplying water to 1 sq hectometre = ₹ 24.25

So, cost of supplying water to the whole field = ₹ 24.20 × 24.25 = ₹ 586.85

Problems on Parallelogram, Rhombus and Trapezium:

Type I : Question Requiring Direct Application of Formulae

Example 12 : Find the area of a rhombus one of whose diagonals measures 8 cm and the other 10 cm.

Solution : Area = Product of diagonals

= 8 × 10 = 80 sq cm.

Type II : Some Quicker Methods

A : To find the area of a rhombus with one side and one diagonal given

Example 13 : Find the area of a rhombus one side of which measures 20 cm and one diagonal 24 cm.

Solution : ***Quicker Method***

$$\text{Area of a rhombus} = d_1 \times \sqrt{(\text{side})^2 - \left(\frac{d_2}{2}\right)^2}$$

So, In the given question,

$$\text{Area} = 24 \times \sqrt{(20)^2 - \left(\frac{24}{2}\right)^2}$$

$$= 24 \times \sqrt{400 - 144} = 24 \times 16 = 384 \text{ cm}^2$$

Problems on Regular Polygons :

A regular polygon is a polygon (triangle, quadrilateral, pentagon, hexagon, octagon etc.) which has all sides equal.

The following formula may prove useful :

A. Area of a regular polygon = $\frac{1}{2} \times n \times a \times r$

where, n = number of sides

a = length of side

r = radius of the inscribed circle

and also, $r = \frac{a}{2}\cot\left(\frac{180°}{n}\right)$

B. Area of a hexagon = $\frac{3\sqrt{3}}{2} \times (\text{side})^2$

C. Area of an octagon = $2(\sqrt{2}+1)(\text{side})^2$

Example 14 : Find the area of a regular hexagon whose side measures 9 cm.

Solution : Area of a regular hexagon = $\frac{3\sqrt{3}}{2}a^2$

Here, $a = 9$ cm

So, area = $\frac{3\sqrt{3}}{2} \times 9^2$ sq cm

= 210.4 sq cm approximate.

Problems on Rooms and Walls :

Papering the walls and allowing for doors etc.

Example 15 : A room 8 metres long, 6 metres broad and 3 metres high has two windows each measures $1\frac{1}{2}$ m × 1 m and a door measures 2 m × $1\frac{1}{2}$ m

Find the cost of papering the walls with paper 50 cm wide at 25 p. per metre.

Solution : Area of walls = 2(8 + 6) 3 = 84 sq m

Area of two windows and door

$= 2 \times 1\frac{1}{2} \times 1 + 2 \times 1\frac{1}{2} = 6$ sq m

Area to be covered = 84 – 6 = 78 sq m

So, length of paper = $\frac{78 \times 100}{50} = 156$ m

Total cost of papering the walls with paper

$= \frac{156 \times 25}{100} = ₹\, 39$

Lining a box with metal

Example 16 : A closed box measures externally 9 dm long, 6 dm broad, $4\frac{1}{2}$ dm high, and is made of wood $2\frac{1}{2}$ cm thick. Find the cost of lining it on the inside with metal at 6 P per sq m.

Solution : The internal dimensions are $8\frac{1}{2}$ dm, $5\frac{1}{2}$ dm, 4 dm.

Area of the 4 sides $2(8\frac{1}{2} + 5\frac{1}{2}) \times 4$ sq dm

= 112 sq dm

Area of bottom and top = $2 \times 8\frac{1}{2} \times 5\frac{1}{2}$ sq dm

$= \frac{187}{2}$ sq dm

Total area to be lined = $\left(112 + \frac{187}{2}\right)$ sq dm

= 205.5 sq dm = 2.055 m²

So, cost = 2.055 × 6P = ₹ 12.33.

Problems on Circles :

I. Simple Application of Formula

Example 17 : (*a*) Find the circumference of a circle whose radius is 42 metres.

(*b*) Find the radius of a circular field whose circumference measures 5 1/2 km. (Take $\pi = 22/7$)

Solution : (*a*) $C = 2\pi r$

So, required circumference = $2 \times \frac{22}{7} \times 42$ metres

= 264 metres

(*b*) $r = C/2\pi$

So, required radius = $\frac{\frac{11}{2} \times 1000\, m \times 7}{2 \times 22}$

$= \frac{11 \times 1000 \times 7}{2 \times 2 \times 22} = 875$ m

II. Some Quicker Methods

A. Area of a ring :

Example 18 : The circumference of a circular garden is 1012 m. Find the area. Outside the garden, a road of 3.5 m width runs around it. Calculate the area of this road and find the cost of gravelling at the rate of 32 paise per sq m.

Solution : Circumference = $2\pi r$

$r = \frac{1012 \times 7}{2 \times 22} = 161$ m

Outer radius (R) = 161 + 3.5 = 164.5 m

Area of road = $\pi(R^2 - r^2)$

$= \frac{22}{7}[(164.5)^2 - 161^2]$

$= \frac{22}{7} \times 325.5 \times 3.5$

$= \frac{22}{7} \times 1139.25 = 3580.5$ m²

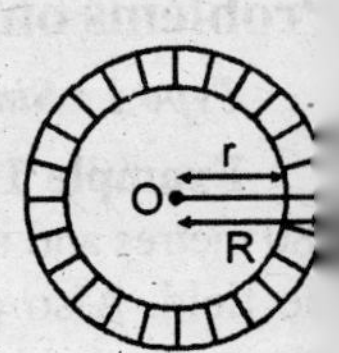

Cost of gravelling the road = ₹ $\dfrac{3580.5 \times 32}{100}$

= ₹ 1145.76

B. Identical circles placed together :

Example 19 : There is an equilateral triangle of which each side is 2 m. With all the three corners as centres of circles each of radius 1 m. (*i*) Calculate the area common to all the circles and the triangle. (*ii*) Find the area of the remaining portion of the triangle.

(Take $\pi = 3.1416$)

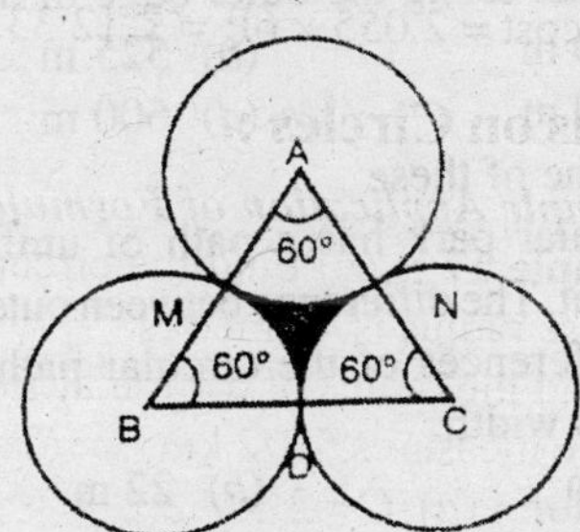

Solution : When the side of the equilateral triangle is double the radius of the circles, all circles touch each other and in such cases the following formula may be used :

$$\text{Area of each sector} = \frac{1}{6}\pi r^2 = \frac{1}{6} \times \pi \times 1^2 = \frac{1}{6}\pi$$

$$\text{Area of 3 sectors} = 3 \times \frac{1}{6}\pi = \frac{\pi}{2}$$

$$= \frac{3.1416}{2} = 1.5708 \text{ m}^2$$

(*i*) So, the area common to all circles and triangle = 1.5708 m^2

(*ii*) Area of remaining portion

= area of equilateral triangle – area of 3 sectors

$$= \frac{\sqrt{3}}{4} \times 2^2 - 1.5708 = 1.732 - 1.5708 = 0.161 \text{ m}^2.$$

Example 20 : The diameter of a coin is 1 cm. If four of these coins be placed on a table so that the rim of each touches that of the other two, find the area of the unoccupied space between them.

(Take $\pi = 3.1416$)

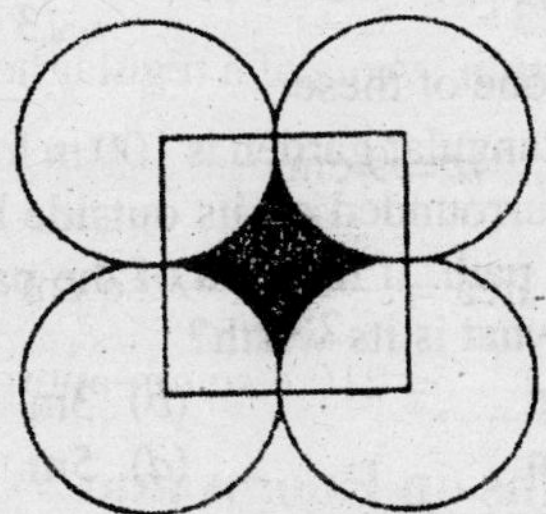

Solution : (***Quicker Method***)

Again, if the circles be placed in such a way that they touch each other and the square's side is double the radius. In such cases the following formula may be used :

$$\text{Area of each sector} = \frac{1}{4}\pi r^2 = \frac{1}{4} \times \pi \times \left(\frac{1}{2}\right)^2$$

$$= \frac{1}{4} \times \pi \frac{1}{4} = \frac{1}{16}\pi$$

Area of unoccupied portion

= area of square – [4 × area of each sector]

$$= 1^2 - \left[4 \times \frac{1}{16}\pi\right] = 1 - \frac{1}{4} \times 3.141$$

$$= 1 - 0.7854 = 0.2146 \text{ cm}^2.$$

EXERCISE

1. The length and breadth of a room are in the ratio 2 : 1. If the cost of cementing the floor at 75 paise per sq metre comes to be ₹ 864 and the cost of polishing the walls at ₹ 3.25 per sq metre comes to be ₹ 884, then the height of the room is :

   (*a*) $2\frac{8}{9}$ m (*b*) $1\frac{8}{9}$ m

   (*c*) $1\frac{2}{9}$ m (*d*) $1\frac{7}{9}$ m

   (*e*) None of these

2. The area of the greatest circle, which can be inscribed in a square, whose perimeter is 120 cm, is:

   (*a*) $\pi \times \left(\frac{7}{2}\right)^2$ cm^2 (*b*) $\pi \times \left(\frac{9}{2}\right)^2$ cm^2

   (*c*) $\pi \times \left(\frac{15}{2}\right)^2$ cm^2 (*d*) $\pi \times (15)^2$ cm^2

   (*e*) None of these

3. The lengths of the perpendiculars drawn from any point in the interior of an equilateral triangle to the respective sides are p_1, p_2 and p_3. The length of each side of the triangle is:

(a) $\frac{1}{3}(p_1+p_2+p_3)$ (b) $\frac{1}{\sqrt{3}}(p_1+p_2+p_3)$

(c) $\frac{2}{\sqrt{3}}(p_1+p_2+p_3)$ (d) $\frac{4}{\sqrt{3}}(p_1+p_2+p_3)$

(e) None of these

4. A rectangular garden is 100 m long, 80 m wide. It is surrounded on its outside by a uniformly broad path. If the area of the path is 1900 m², then what is its width?

(a) 2m (b) 3m
(c) 4m (d) 5m
(e) None of these

5. A piece of wire of 78 cm long is bent in the form of an isosceles triangle. If the ratio of one of the equal sides to the base is 5 : 3, then length of the base is:

(a) 16 cm (b) 17 cm
(c) 18 cm (d) 19 cm
(e) None of these

6. What will be the cost of gardening 1m broad boundary around a rectangular plot having perimeter of 340 m at the rate of ₹ 10 per m²?

(a) ₹ 1720 (b) ₹ 3400
(c) ₹ 3440 (d) ₹ 3540
(e) None of these

7. What is the least number of square tiles required to pave the floor of a room 15m 17 cm long and 9m 2cm broad?

(a) 794 (b) 800
(c) 804 (d) 814
(e) None of these

8. A park square in shape has a 3m wide road inside it running along its sides. The area occupied by the road is 1764 m². Find the perimeter along the outer edge of the road.

(a) 500 m (b) 525 m
(c) 550 m (d) 600 m
(e) None of these

9. A circular park has a path of uniform width around it. The difference between outer and inner circumferences of the circular path is 132 m. Find its width.

(a) 21m (b) 22 m
(c) 23 m (d) 24 m
(e) None of these

10. The circumference of a circle is 100 cm. The side of a square inscribed in the circle is:

(a) $\frac{25\sqrt{2}}{\pi}$ cm (b) $\frac{50\sqrt{2}}{\pi}$ cm

(c) $\frac{75\sqrt{2}}{\pi}$ cm (d) $\frac{100\sqrt{2}}{\pi}$ cm

(e) None of these

EXPLANATORY ANSWERS

1. (b): Suppose the length and the breadth of the room are $2x$ metres and x metres respectively.

$\therefore$ Area of the floor $= 2x \times x = 2x^2$ sq metres

$$\text{Area of the floor} = \frac{864}{75/100} = \frac{864\times100}{75}$$
$$= 1152 \text{ sq. metre}$$

Now, $2x^2 = 1152 \Rightarrow x^2 = \frac{1152}{2} = 576$

Hence, $x = 24$

$\therefore$ Length of the room $= 2 \times 24 = 48$ m

Breadth of the room = 24 m

$$\text{Now, area of the four walls} = \frac{884}{3.25}$$
$$= 272 \text{ sq. metre}$$

Hence, $2 \times h(l+b) = 272$

$\Rightarrow 2 \times h(48+24) = 272$

$$\therefore \quad h = \frac{272}{2\times72} = 1\frac{8}{9} \text{ m}$$

2. (d):

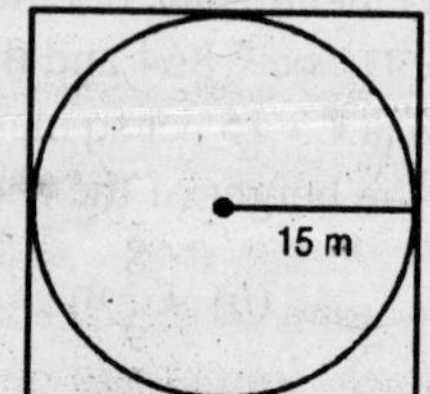

$$\text{Side of square} = \frac{120}{4} = 30 \text{ cm}$$

Hence, radius of the required circle = $\frac{30}{2}$ = 15 cm

Since, area of the circle = $\pi \times (15)^2$ cm²

3. (*c*) : Let side of the equilateral triangle be x. From the figure,

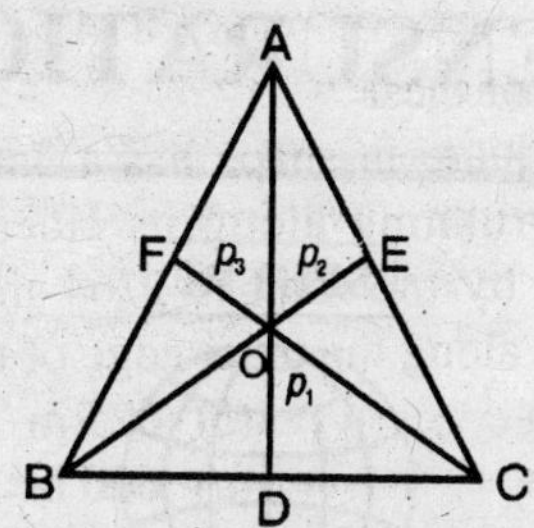

Area of the equilateral triangle ABC
= Area of Δ BOC + Area of Δ AOC + Area of Δ AOB

$$\Rightarrow \frac{\sqrt{3}}{4}x^2 = \frac{1}{2}\times x \times p_1 + \frac{1}{2}\times x \times p_2 + \frac{1}{2}\times x \times p_3$$

$$\Rightarrow \frac{\sqrt{3}}{2}x = p_1 + p_2 + p_3$$

$$\therefore x = \frac{2}{\sqrt{3}}(p_1 + p_2 + p_3)$$

4. (*d*) :

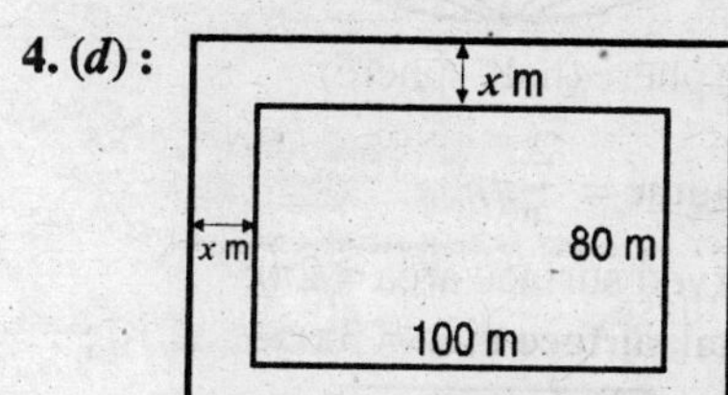

Let width of the road be x m; then,

$(100 + 2x)(80 + 2x) - 100 \times 80 = 1900$

$\Rightarrow 4x^2 + 360x - 1900 = 0$

$\Rightarrow x^2 + 90x - 475 = 0$

$\Rightarrow x^2 + 95x - 5x - 475 = 0$

$\Rightarrow x(x + 95) - 5(x + 95) = 0$

Then, $x = 5$ m

5. (*c*) : Let one of the equal side and base of the isosceles triangle be $5x$ and $3x$ m respectively.

Then, $5x + 5x + 3x = 78 \Rightarrow 13x = 78$

$\therefore x = 6$

Hence, perimeter = 3 × 6 = 18 cm.

6. (*c*) : Here, $2(x + y) = 340$ m

Again, area of boundary

$= [(x+2)(y+2)] - xy = xy + 2(x+y) + 4 - xy$

$= 2(x + y) + 4 = 340 + 4 = 344$ m²

Hence, cost of gardening

= 344 × ₹ 10 = ₹ 3440

7. (*d*) : Length = 15m 17cm = 1517 cm; breadth = 9m 2cm = 902 cm

H.C.F. of 1517 and 902 = 41

Hence, required number of square tiles

$$= \frac{1517 \times 902}{41 \times 41} = 814$$

8. (*d*) : Area of the road $= x^2 - (x - 6)^2 = 1764$

$\Rightarrow 12x - 36 = 1764$

$\Rightarrow 12x = 1800$

$\therefore x = \frac{1800}{12} = 150$ m

Hence, required perimeter = 4 × 150 = 600 m

9. (*a*) : Here, $2\pi R - 2\pi r = 132$ m

$$\therefore R - r = \frac{132 \times 7}{2 \times 22} = 21 \text{ m}$$

Hence, width of the circular path = 21 m

10. (*b*) :

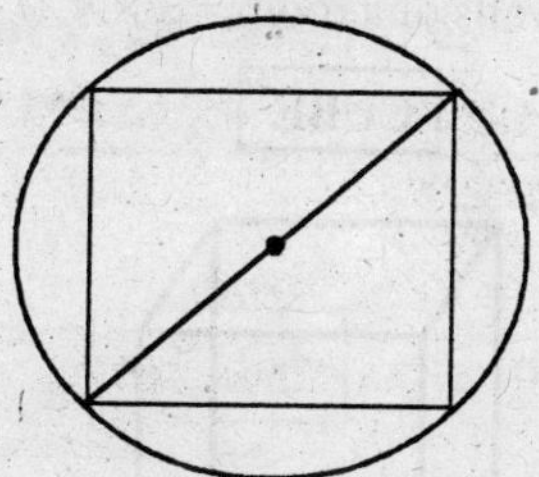

Diameter of the circle = $\frac{100}{\pi}$ cm

So, diagonal of the inscribed square

$= \frac{100}{\pi}$ cm

And, side of the inscribed square

$$= \frac{100}{\sqrt{2}\pi} = \frac{50\sqrt{2}}{\pi} \text{ cm}$$

17

MENSURATION-II

An object which occupies space has usually three dimensions : length, breadth, and depth. Such an object is usually called a *solid*.

Given below are some commonly known solids:

CUBOID

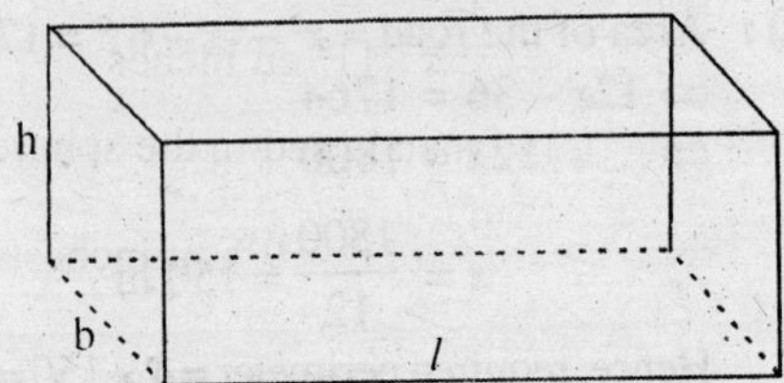

1. Volume = $(l \times b \times h)$
2. Total surface area = $2(lb + bh + lh)$
3. Diagonal = $\sqrt{l^2 + b^2 + h^2}$
4. Area of 4 walls of a room = $2 \times h\ (l + b)$

CUBE

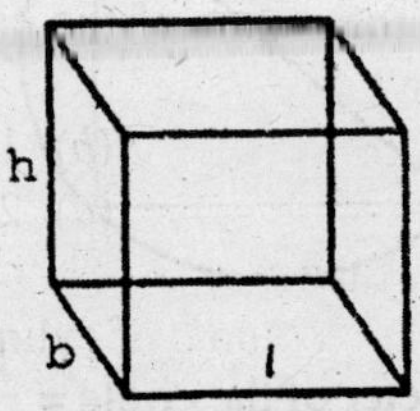

In cube $l = h = b$

1. Volume = $(l)^3$
2. $l = \sqrt[3]{\text{volume}}$
3. Total surface area = $6\,(l)^2$
4. Diagonal = $l\sqrt{3}$

SPHERE

(*i*) Let radius of sphere = r

1. Volume = $\frac{4}{3}\pi r^3$
2. Total surface area = $4\pi r^2$

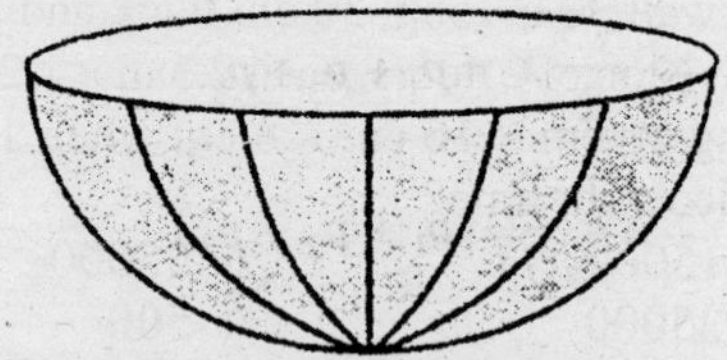

(*ii*) Hemi-sphere (half-sphere)

1. Volume = $\frac{2}{3}\pi r^3$
2. Curved surface area = $2\pi r^2$

Total surface area = $3\pi r^2$

CYLINDER

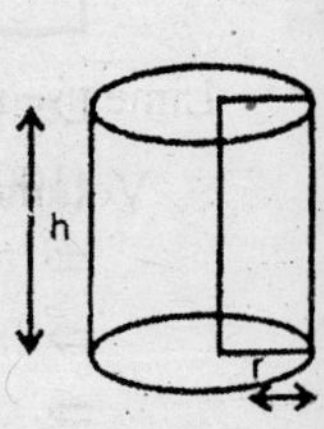

1. Volume = $\pi r^2 h$
2. Curved surface area = $2\pi rh$
3. Total surface area $= 2\pi r(r + h)$

CONE

1. Slant height = $l = \sqrt{r^2 + h^2}$
2. Volume $= \frac{1}{3}\pi r^2 h$
3. Curved surface area = πrl
4. Total surface area = $\pi r(r + l)$

Example 1 : A trench is 10 m long, 5 m broad, and $3\frac{1}{3}$ m deep. The earth dugout from this trench is evenly spread on a road which is 200 m long and 5 m broad. Find the height of the earth spread on the road.

(*a*) $16\frac{2}{3}$ cm (*b*) $6\frac{2}{3}$ cm
(*c*) $16\frac{3}{5}$ cm (*d*) $15\frac{3}{5}$ cm
(*e*) None of these

Solution. (*a*) : Volume of the trench

$$= 10 \times 5 \times \frac{10}{3} = \frac{500}{3} \text{ cu m}$$

The area of the road = 200 × 5 = 1000 sq m.

$$\therefore \text{ Height of the earth spread} = \frac{500}{3} \times \frac{1}{1000}$$

$$= \frac{1}{6} \text{ m} = 16\frac{2}{3} \text{ cm}$$

Example 2 : How many bricks will be required to build a wall 30 m long, 30 cm thick and 5 m high with a provision of 2 doors, each 2.5 m × 1.2 m; each brick being 20 cm × 16 cm × 8 cm when 1/9 of the wall is filled with lime?

(*a*) 15000 (*b*) 25000
(*c*) 35000 (*d*) 500
(*e*) None of these

Solution. (*a*) : Area of wall = 30 × 5 = 150 sq m

Area of 2 doors = 2 × 2.5 × 1.2 = 6 sq m

∴ Remaining area of wall = 150 – 6 = 144 sqm.

$$\text{Volume of wall} = 144 \times \frac{30}{100} = \frac{216}{5} \text{ cu m}$$

$$\text{Lime used in the wall} = \frac{216}{5} \times \frac{1}{9} = \frac{24}{5} \text{ cu m}$$

∴ Volume of the bricks used in the wall

$$= \frac{216}{5} - \frac{24}{5} = \frac{192}{5} \text{ cu m}$$

$$\text{Volume of 1 brick} = \frac{20}{100} \times \frac{16}{100} \times \frac{8}{100} \text{ cu cm}$$

$$= \frac{8}{3125} \text{ cu m.}$$

$$\therefore \text{ Number of bricks} = \frac{\frac{192}{5}}{\frac{8}{3125}} = \frac{192 \times 3125}{40}$$

= 15000.

Example 3 : The inner diameter of a hollow metallic sphere is 18" and its thickness is 2". Find the weight of the sphere, if the weight of 1 cu ft metal is 486 lbs.

(*a*) 701.5 lbs (*b*) 700.0 lbs
(*c*) 709.5 lbs (*d*) 710.5 lbs
(*e*) None of these

Solution. (*c*) : Inner radius of the sphere = $\frac{18}{2}$ = 9 inches

$$\text{Inner volume of the sphere} = \frac{4}{3}\pi r^3$$

$$= \frac{4}{3}\pi \times 9^3 \text{ cu inches}$$

Outer radius of the sphere = 9 + 2 = 11 inches

∴ Outer volume of the sphere

$$= \frac{4}{3}\pi \times 11^3 \text{ cu inches}$$

∴ Volume of the metal used in the sphere

$$= \frac{4}{3}\pi(11^3 - 9^3) \text{ cu inches}$$

$$= \frac{4}{3} \times \frac{22}{7}(1331 - 729)$$

$$= \frac{88 \times 602}{21} = 2522.67 \text{ cu inches}$$

∴ Weight of the sphere

$$= \frac{2522.67}{12 \times 12 \times 12} \times 486 = 709.5 \text{ lbs.}$$

Example 4 : The volume of a cone is equal to that of a cylinder whose height is 9 cm and diameter 60 cm. What is the radius of the base of cone if its height is 108 cm?

(*a*) 10 cm (*b*) 15 cm
(*c*) 20 cm (*d*) 25 cm
(*e*) None of these

Solution. (*b*) : Volume of cylinder = $\pi r^2 h$

$$= \frac{22}{7} \times 30 \times 30 \times 9 \text{ cu cm}$$

$$\text{Volume of a cone} = \frac{1}{3}\pi r^2 \times \text{height}$$

$$= \frac{1}{3} \times \frac{22}{7} \times r^2 \times 108 \text{ cu cm}$$

$$\because \frac{22}{7} \times 30 \times 30 \times 9 = \frac{1}{3} \times \frac{22}{7} \times r^2 \times 108$$

$$\therefore r^2 = \frac{30 \times 30 \times 9 \times 3}{108} = 225 \text{ or } r = 15 \text{ cm}$$

Example 5 : There is a cubical room whose length is 10 m. How many students can it accommodate if each student requires 5 cu m of space?

(*a*) 100 (*b*) 150
(*c*) 200 (*d*) 250
(*e*) None of these

Solution. (*c*) : Volume of room = $(10)^3$ cu m
= 1000 cu m

Space required for a student = 5 cu m

$\therefore$ Required number of students $= \frac{1000}{5} = 200.$

Example 6 : Three cubes whose edges are 3 cm, 4 cm, and 5 cm respectively are melted to form a single cube. The surface of the new cube will be :

(*a*) 100 sq m (*b*) 216 sq m
(*c*) 200 sq m (*d*) 150 sq m
(*e*) None of these

Soltuion. (*b*) : Volume of 1st, 2nd and 3rd cube is 27, 64 and 125 cu cm.

Total volume of all three cubes = 27 + 64 + 125
= 216 cu cm

$\therefore$ Edge of new cube $= \sqrt[3]{216} = 6$ cm

$\therefore$ Surface of the new cube $= 6 \times (6)^2 = 216$ sq cm.

Example 7 : Find the length of the longest rod that can be placed in a room 12 m long 9 m broad and 8 m high.

(*a*) 16 m (*b*) 17 m
(*c*) 15 m (*d*) 12 m
(*e*) None of these

Solution. (*b*) :The longest rod that can be placed in the room is equal to the length of its diagonal.

$\therefore$ Length of the longest rod

$= \sqrt{12^2 + 9^2 + 8^2} = \sqrt{144 + 81 + 64}$

$= \sqrt{289} = 17$ m

Example 8 : Find the volume of a right circular cone whose height is 24 cm and diameter of the base is 20 cm.

(*a*) $2514\frac{2}{7}$ cu cm (*b*) $2004\frac{1}{5}$ cu cm
(*c*) $2510\frac{3}{5}$ cu cm (*d*) $2156\frac{3}{7}$ cu cm
(*e*) None of these

Solution. (*a*) : Volume of cone $= \frac{1}{3}\pi r^2 h$

$= \frac{1}{3} \times \frac{22}{7} \times 10 \times 10 \times 24$

$= \frac{17600}{7}$ cu cm. $= 2514\frac{2}{7}$ cu cm.

Example 9 : Find the height of a right circular cone which is formed by melting a solid cylinder 3.5 m high and 2 m in radius. The radius of the base of the cone being equal to the radius of the cylinder.

(*a*) 11.5 m (*b*) 12.5 m
(*c*) 10.6 m (*d*) 10.5 m
(*e*) None of these

Solution. (*d*) : Volume of the cylinder

$= \frac{22}{7} \times 2 \times 2 \times 3.5 = 44$ cu m

Radius of the base of the cone = 2 m

$\because \quad \frac{1}{3}\pi r^2 h = 44$

$\because \quad h = \frac{3 \times 44 \times 7}{22 \times 2 \times 2} = \frac{21}{2} = 10.5$ m

Example 10 : A spherical iron shell with 21 cm external diameter weighs $22775\frac{5}{21}$ grams. Find the thickness of the shell if the metal weighs 10 gram per cu m.

(*a*) 0.5 cm (*b*) 1.0 cm
(*c*) 2.0 cm (*d*) 2.5 cm
(*e*) None of these

Solution. (*c*) : Let internal radius be r cm.

Internal volume $= \frac{4}{3}\pi r^3$ cu cm.

External radius $= \frac{21}{2}$ cm.

$\therefore$ External volume

$= \frac{4}{3} \times \frac{22}{7} \times \frac{21}{2} \times \frac{21}{2} \times \frac{21}{2} = 4851$ cm

$\therefore$ Volume of the metal of the shell

$= \frac{478280}{21} \times \frac{1}{10} = \frac{47828}{21}$ cu cm.

Internal volume of the metal of the shell

$= \left(4851 - \frac{47828}{21}\right) = \left(\frac{101871 - 47828}{21}\right)$

$= \frac{54043}{21}$ cu cm.

$\frac{4}{3}\pi r^3 = \frac{54043}{21}$

$\frac{4}{3} \times \frac{22}{7} \times r^3 = \frac{54043}{21}$

$\therefore \quad r^3 = \frac{54043 \times 3 \times 7}{21 \times 4 \times 22}$

or $\quad r^3 = 614.125$

or $\quad r = 8.5$ cm

$\therefore$ Thickness = (10.5 – 8.5)

= 2 cm.

EXERCISE

1. A wall 8 m long 6 m high and 22.5 cm thick is made up of bricks each measuring (25 cm × 11.25 cm × 6 cm). The number of bricks required is :

(*a*) 6000 (*b*) 5600
(*c*) 6400 (*d*) 7200
(*e*) None of these

2. The maximum length of rod that can be kept in a rectangular box of dimensions 8 cm × 6 cm × 2 cm, is :

(*a*) $2\sqrt{13}$ cm (*b*) $2\sqrt{14}$ m
(*c*) $2\sqrt{26}$ cm (*d*) $10\sqrt{2}$ m
(*e*) None of these

3. A rectangular block 6 cm × 12 cm × 15 cm is cut up into exact number of equal cubes. The least possible number of cubes will be :

(*a*) 6 (*b*) 11
(*c*) 33 (*d*) 40
(*e*) None of these

4. Three cubes of iron whose edges are 6 cm, 8 cm and 10 cm respectively are melted and formed into a single cube. The edge of the new cube formed is :

(*a*) 12 cm (*b*) 14 cm
(*c*) 16 cm (*d*) 18 cm
(*e*) None of these

5. The surface area of a cube is 600 cm. The length of its diagonal is :

(*a*) $10/\sqrt{3}$ cm (*b*) $10/\sqrt{2}$ cm
(*c*) $10\sqrt{3}$ cm (*d*) $10\sqrt{2}$ cm
(*e*) None of these

6. A beam 9 m long, 40 cm wide and 20 cm high is made up of iron which weighs 50 kg per cubic metre. The weight of the beam is :

(*a*) 56 kg (*b*) 48 kg
(*c*) 36 kg (*d*) 27 kg
(*e*) None of these

7. The sum of the length, breadth and depth of a cuboid is 19 cm and its diagonal is $5\sqrt{5}$ cm. Its surface area is :

(*a*) 361 cm^2 (*b*) 125 cm^2
(*c*) 236 cm^2 (*d*) 486 cm^2
(*e*) None of these

8. Given that 1 cu cm of marble weighs 25 gms, the weight of a marble block 28 cm in width and 5 cm thick is 112 kg. The length of the block is :

(*a*) 36 cm (*b*) 37.5 cm
(*c*) 32 cm (*d*) 26.5 cm
(*e*) None of these

9. The volume of a wall, 5 times as high as it is broad and 8 times as long as it is high, is 12.8 cu metres. The breadth of the wall is :

(*a*) 30 cm (*b*) 40 cm
(*c*) 22.5 cm (*d*) 25 cm
(*e*) None of these

10. In a shower 5 cm of rain falls. The volume of water that falls on 1.5 hectares of ground is :

(*a*) 75 cu m (*b*) 750 cu m
(*c*) 7500 cu m (*d*) 75000 cu m
(*e*) None of these

EXPLANATORY ANSWERS

1. (*c*) : Number of bricks $= \frac{800 \times 600 \times 22.5}{25 \times 11.25 \times 6}$

= 6400.

2. (*c*) : Required length $= \sqrt{(8^2 + 6^2 + 2^2)}$ cm

$= \sqrt{104} = 2\sqrt{26}$ cm

3. (*d*) : Volume of rectangular block = $(6 \times 12 \times 15)$ $= 1080$ cm^3
The side of largest cube = HCF of 6 cm, 12 cm, 15 cm = 3 cm
Volume of cube=$(3 \times 3 \times 3)$ cm^3 = 27 cm^3
Number of cubes = (1080/27) = 40.

4. (*a*) : Volume of the new cube = $[6^3 + 8^3 + (10)^3]$ = 1728 cu cm
Let the edge of new cube be a cm
Then, $a^3 = 1728 = (4 \times 4 \times 4 \times 3 \times 3 \times 3)$
$\Rightarrow \quad a = 12$ cm

5. (*c*) : $6a^2 = 600 \Rightarrow a^2 = 100$ or $a = 10$ cm
So, diagonal = $\sqrt{3}a = 10\sqrt{3}$ cm.

6. (*c*) : Volume$=(9 \times \frac{40}{100} \times \frac{20}{100})$ cu m $= \frac{18}{25}$ cu m
So, weight of the beam = $\left(\frac{18}{25} \times 50\right)$ kg
= 36 kg.

7. (*c*) : $(l + b + h) = 19$ and $\sqrt{l^2 + b^2 + h^2} = 5\sqrt{5}$
and so $(l^2 + b^2 + h^2) = 125$
Given $(l + b + h)^2 = 19^2$
Now $(l^2 + b^2 + h^2) + 2(lb + bh + lh) = 361$
$\Rightarrow 2(lb + bh + lh) = (361 - 125) = 236$
So, surface area = 236 cm^2.

8. (*c*) : Let length = x cm
Then, $x \times 28 \times 5 \times \frac{25}{1000} = 112$
So, $x = \frac{112 \times 1000}{28 \times 5 \times 25} = 32$ cm
So, length of block = 32 cm

9. (*b*) : Let, breadth = x metres . Then,
height = $5x$ metres
and length = $40x$ metres
So, $x \times 5x \times 40x = 12.8$
or $x^3 = \frac{12.8}{200} = \frac{128}{2000} = \frac{64}{1000}$
So, $x = \frac{4}{10}$ m $= \left(\frac{4}{10} \times 100\right)$ cm = 40 cm

10. (*b*) : Area = (1.5×10000) sq . metres
= 15000 sq metres.
Depth = 5/100 m = 1/20 m
So, Volume = (Area × Depth)
= $(15000 \times 1/20) = 750$ cu m.

18
SERIES

A series is a sequence of numbers, where the sequence of numbers is obtained by some particular pre-defined rule and by applying that rule it is possible to find out the next term of the series.

(1) Arithmetic Series : An arithmetic series is one in which successive numbers are obtained by adding (or subtracting) a fixed number to the previous number. For example :

3, 5, 7, 9, 11, ...

(2) Geometric Series : A geometrical series is one in which each successive number is obtained by multiplying (or dividing) the previous number by a fixed number. For example, 4, 8, 16, 32, 64 ....

(3) Series of squares, cubes etc. These series can be formed by squaring or cubing every successive number. For example, 2, 4, 16, 256, ...

Some Important Rules for Number series :

1. The numbers in the series increases or decreases by perfect squares. For example :
   $-(2)^2, -(3)^2, -(5)^2$; $2^2, 3^2, 5^2$
2. The numbers in the series increases or decreases by perfect cubes. For example :
   $-1^3, -2^3, -3^3, -4^3$; $1^3, 2^3, 3^3, 4^3$,
3. The numbers in the series increases or decreases by prime number. For example :
   13, 11, 7, 5, 3, ...
4. The numbers in the series are multiples of a number. For example :
   2, × 3, × 4, × 5, × 6, × 7, × ...
5. The numbers in the series is found by dividing certain numbers. For example :
   2, ÷ 4, ÷ 5, ÷ 8 ....
6. The numbers in the series are in AP. Here, some given numbers are said to be in AP if the difference between two consecutive numbers is same. For example :
   1, 3, 5, 7, 9, 11, ...
7. The numbers in the series are in GP. Here, some given numbers are said to be in GP if the difference between two consecutive numbers follow a certain pattern of multiplication or division or same as the lowest number throughout the series. For example : 32, 16, 8, 4, 2.
8. Some special rules are for special series. This can be found out by observing the series of numbers.
9. In the special series, two series may be mixed.

EXERCISE

Directions (Qs. 1 to 7) : *In the following number series, one of the numbers does not fit into the series. Find the wrong number.*

1. 2, 5, 10, 18, 26, 37, 50

(*a*) 2 (*b*) 5
(*c*) 37 (*d*) 18
(*e*) None of these

2. 3 , 18, 38, 78, 123, 178, 243

(*a*) 123 (*b*) 178
(*c*) 3 (*d*) 38
(*e*) None of these

3. 380, 188, 92, 48, 20, 8, 2

(*a*) 188 (*b*) 92
(*c*) 48 (*d*) 20
(*e*) None of these

4. 5, 11, 23, 47, 96, 191, 383

(*a*) 11 (*b*) 23
(*c*) 47 (*d*) 96
(*e*) None of these

5. 89, 78, 86, 80, 85, 82, 83
(*a*) 78 (*b*) 86
(*c*) 80 (*d*) 85
(*e*) None of these

6. 58, 57, 54, 50, 42, 33, 32
(*a*) 57 (*b*) 54
(*c*) 50 (*d*) 32
(*e*) None of these

7. 2, 20, 27, 44, 64
(*a*) 27
(*b*) 8
(*c*) 20
(*d*) 44
(*e*) None of these

Directions (Qs. 8 to 10) : *Complete the following series.*

8. 1 4 9 16 25 36 49 ....
(*a*) 54 (*b*) 56
(*c*) 64 (*d*) 81
(*e*) None of these

9. 11 13 17 19 23 29 31 37 41 ....
(*a*) 43 (*b*) 47
(*c*) 53 (*d*) 51
(*e*) None of these

10. 3 7 6 5 9 3 12 1 15 ....
(*a*) 18 (*b*) 13
(*c*) −1 (*d*) 3
(*e*) None of these

EXPLANATORY ANSWERS

1. (*d*) : 2 5 10 18 26 37 50
↓ ↓ ↓ ↓ ↓ ↓ ↓
1^2+1 2^2+1 3^2+1 4^2+1 5^2+1 6^2+1 7^2+1
Wrong no. = 18, Correct no. = 17.

2. (*c*) : Only 3 is a prime number.

3. (*c*) : Wrong no. = 48, Correct no. = 44
Each term will be four more than two times the next term.

4. (*d*) : 5 11 23 47 96 191 383

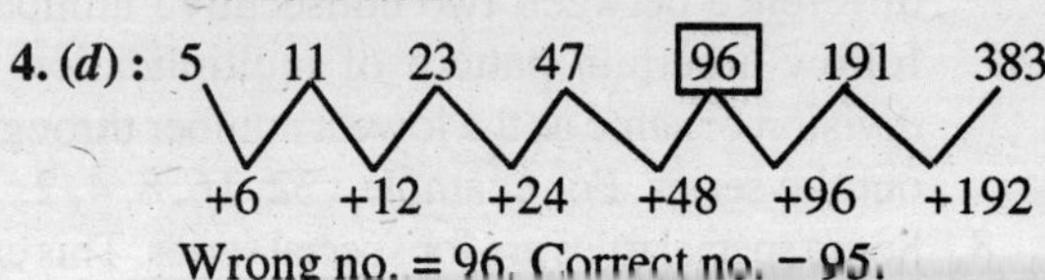

+6 +12 +24 +48 +96 +192
Wrong no. = 96, Correct no. = 95.

5. (*a*) : If 87 is written in place of 78 then tens digit of each term will be 8.

6. (*c*) : 58 57 54 50 42 33 22
−1 −3 −5 −7 −9 −11
Wrong no. = 50, Correct no. = 49.

7. (*c*) : 2 ☐ 20 27 44 64
+11 +14 +17 +20
Wrong no. = 20, Correct no. = 13.

8. (*c*) : Numbers are 1^2, 2^2, 3^2, 4^2, 5^2, 6^2, 7^2.
So, the next number is $8^2 = 64$.

9. (*a*) : Numbers are all primes. The next prime 43.

10. (*c*) : There are two series, beginning respectively with 3 and 7. In one 3 is added and another 2 is subtracted.
The next number is 1 − 2 = −1.

19

APPROXIMATE VALUES

Follow the following Approximation rules :

(1) Replace the large numbers by the numbers which have maximum possible number of zeros in the end.

Example 1:

(*i*) For 110869 use 111000 (if the choices are in thousands)

(*ii*) For 5628 use 5600 (if the choices are in hundreds) and 5630 (if choices are in tens)

(2) If there are two large numbers

568940 + 698219 = ?

Case I : If the choices are in tens, then approximate values to be used should be

568940 + 698219 = ?

We see that the first value is decreased and the second value is increased. This way we reduce the deviation. If we had used 568950 for the first value and also the same increased value for the second, then the deviation would have been 5 + 1 = 6. But in the present case the deviation is 5 – 1 = 4.

Case II : If the choices are in hundreds, then approximate values to be used should be

568900 + 698200

Normally, people will use the approximate numbers as 568900 + 698200

In this case, the deviation (– 45) + (–19) = – 64.

But in our case, the deviation is 55 + (–19) = 36.

Note : The numerical value of deviation is lower in our case,

Case III : If the choices are in thousands, then approximate values to be used should be :

569000 + 698000

The first value is increased and the second is decreased.

(3) If a large number is to be subtracted from another large number then both the numbers should be increased or decreased simultaneously.

Multiplication

Example 2: $904 \times 14 \times 0.04 = ?$

(*a*) 480 (*b*) 490
(*c*) 505 (*d*) 515
(*e*) 520

Solution : First we solve for two smaller values

$14 \times 0.04 = 0.56$

Now, $? = 904 \times 0.56 = 90.4 \times 5.6$

Following the rule :

$90 \times 5 = 450$

$\underline{+0.4 + 0.6 = 56}$ $(= 2 + 54)$

$= 506 = 505$

Division

Example 3: $12675 \div 42 = ?$

(*a*) 300 (*b*) 290
(*c*) 280 (*d*) 305
(*e*) 309

Solution : The divisor is to be decreased by 2, so the dividend should also be decreased and the value of decrease

$= 2 \times 300 = 600$ (approx. value of quotient = 300)

So, $12675 \div 42 = 12000 \div 40 = 300$.

Percentage

Example 4: 105 % of 369 = ?

(*a*) 380 (*b*) 390
(*c*) 400 (*d*) 405
(*e*) 410

Solution : 105% of $369 = 369 + 5 \times 3.69$

$\approx 369 + 5 \times 3.7 \approx 369 + 18 = 387 \approx 390.$

EXERCISE

1. $85432 \div 2106 + 59.5614 = ?$
   (a) 100 (b) 60
   (c) 80 (d) 140
   (e) 200
2. $\sqrt{67621} = ?$
   (a) 320 (b) 260
   (c) 200 (d) 280
   (e) 300
3. 9.7 % of 5011 + 55.03 % of 4991
   (a) 5500 (b) 7200
   (c) 6000 (d) 5000
   (e) 4200
4. $730 \times 199 = ?$
   (a) 350000 (b) 335000
   (c) 300000 (d) 34600
   (e) 400000
5. $.0144 \times 0.36 = ?$
   (a) 0.5 (b) 0.005
   (c) 0.05 (d) 0.005
   (e) 5.0
6. 31% of 1508 + 26% of 2018
   (a) 1500 (b) 2000
   (c) 1000 (d) 1200
   (e) 1600
7. $3015 + 13594 + 3738 = ?$
   (a) 40000 (b) 36000
   (c) 42000 (d) 46000
   (e) 50000
8. $6012 \times 119 = ?$
   (a) 560000 (b) 448000
   (c) 900000 (d) 640000
   (e) 720000
9. $2712.1563 \div 1805.4018 + 3.4982 = ?$
   (a) 9 (b) 8
   (c) 4 (d) 5
   (e) 7
10. $4182.\ 365 \div 20.886 = ?$
    (a) 300 (b) 200
    (c) 150 (d) 250
    (e) 180

EXPLANATORY ANSWERS

1. (a): $85432 \div 2106 + 60 = 40 + 60 = 100$
Therefore (a) is the correct answer.

2. (b): $\sqrt{67621} = \sqrt{67600} = 260$
Therefore (b) is the correct answer.

3. (e): 29.7 % of 5011 + 55.03 % of 4991
= 30 % of 5000 + 55 % of 5000
$= \frac{30}{100} \times 5000 + \frac{55}{100} \times 5000$
$= 1500 + 2750 = 4250 \Rightarrow 4200$
Therefore (e) is the correct answer.

4. (a): $1730 \times 199 = 1730 \times 200$
$= 346000 \Rightarrow 350000$
Therefore (a) is the correct answer.

5. (b): $0.0144 \times 0.36 = 0.0140 \times 0.36 = .005040$
$\Rightarrow .005$
Therefore (b) is the correct answer.

6. (c): 31% of 1508 + 26% of 2018
= 30% of 1500 + 25% × 200
$= \frac{30}{100} \times 1500 + \frac{25}{100} \times 2000$
$= 450 + 500 = 950 \Rightarrow 1000$
Therefore (c) is the correct answer.

7. (a): $23015 + 13594 + 3738$
$= 23000 + 13600 + 3700$
$= 40300 \Rightarrow 40000$
Therefore (a) is the correct answer.

8. (e): $6012 \times 119 = 6000 \times 120 = 720000$
Therefore (e) is the correct answer.

9. (d): $2712.1563 \div 1805.4018 + 3.4982$
$= 2700 \div 1800 + 3.5 = 1.5 + 3.5 =$
Therefore (d) is the correct answer.

10. (b): $4182.\ 365 \div 20.886 = 4200 \div 21 = 200$
Therefore (b) is the correct answer.

20

DATA INTERPRETATION

Data Interpretation is one of the easy sections of Bank PO Examination. It is an extension of Mathematical skills and accuracy. Data Interpretation is nothing but drawing conclusions and inferences from a comprehensive data presented numerically in tabular form by means of an illustration, viz., Graph, Pie chart etc. Sound knowledge of quantitative techniques is a prerequisite for good performance in this section. The thumb rule, as in the case of reading comprehension—read the passage rapidly but carefully and comprehend it at the same time—applies in this section too. However, unlike reading comprehension where one can afford to skip irrelevant portions of the passage, here even the minutest of details cannot be overlooked.

A good grasp of basic geometric as well as arithmetic formulae is must to score high in this section. Since such questions may require a fair amount of calculations, one should be able to multiply and divide quickly using short-cut methods. Familiarity with graphical representation of data like venn diagrams, graphs, pie diagrams, histogram, polygon etc. should be thorough. Once the data are grasped well, questions based on tables and graphs take little time.

In some Bank PO Exams data are presented in more than one table or graph. The aim is to test not only quantitative skills but also relative, comparative and analytical ability. The crux of the matter is to find a relationship between the two tables or graphs before attempting the questions.

EXERCISE

Directions (Qs. 1 to 5): *Study the following tables carefully and answer the questions given below:*

Number of Males and Females staying in various societies

Societies	Males	Females
A	250	350
B	400	150
C	300	275
D	280	300
E	180	250
F	325	300

Percentage of Children (Males and Females) in the societies

Societies	Children	Males	Females
A	25%	40%	60%
B	40%	75%	25%
C	16%	25%	75%
D	25%	80%	20%
E	40%	50%	50%
F	24%	46%	54%

1. What is the respective ratio of the number of the adult females to the total number of female children staying in all the societies together?
(*a*) 82 : 243
(*b*) 243 : 82
(*c*) 71 : 112
(*d*) 112 : 71
(*e*) None of these

2. What is the respective ratio of the total number of adult males in the societies A and B together to the total number of adult males in the societies E and F together?

(a) 14 ; 17 (b) 17 : 14
(c) 75 : 79 (d) 79 : 75
(e) None of these

3. What is the difference between the number of male children in society B and the number of male children in society F?

(a) 14 (b) 26
(c) 84 (d) 96
(e) None of these

4. What is the total number of female children staying in all the societies together?

(a) 314 (b) 343
(c) 410 (d) 433
(e) None of these

5. What is the total number of members staying in all the societies together?

(a) 3000 (b) 3360
(c) 4100 (d) 4289
(e) None of these

Directions (Qs. 6 to 10): *Study the following table carefully and answer the questions given below:*

Quantity of Rice produced by Various states over the years (Quantity in Tonnes)

States ↓	YEARS					
	2003	**2004**	**2005**	**2006**	**2007**	**2008**
A	1500	1480	1620	1700	1540	1650
B	1250	1190	1400	1450	1320	1380
C	1160	1190	1310	1300	1340	1360
D	1520	1500	1480	1590	1630	1580
E	1440	1350	1430	1280	1380	1400
F	1600	1620	1510	1610	1580	1590

6. In which state has the production of rice increased continuously over the years?

(a) B (b) C
(c) D (d) A
(e) None of these

7. Which state produced the lowest quantity of rice over the years?

(a) A (b) C
(c) D (d) E
(e) None of these

8. Rice produced by State C in the year 2006 is approximately what per cent of the rice produced by State A in the same year?

(a) 69% (b) 72%
(c) 76% (d) 82%
(e) None of these

9. In which year was the production of rice the highest in all the states together?

(a) 2005 (b) 2006
(c) 2007 (d) 2008
(e) None of these

10. What is the respective ratio of the average quantity of rice produced by State D to the average quantity of rice produced by State F over the years?

(a) 69 : 79 (b) 138 : 155
(c) 276 : 317 (d) 310 : 317
(e) None of these

EXPLANATORY ANSWERS

1. (b) : In society A:

Number of children

$$= \frac{25}{100} \times (250 + 350) = \frac{1}{4} \times 600 = 150$$

$$\text{Number of male children} = \frac{40}{100} \times 150 = 60$$

$$\text{Number of female children} = 150 - 60 = 90$$

In society B:

Number of children

$$= \frac{40}{100} \times (400 + 150) = \frac{2}{5} \times 550 = 220$$

Number of male children

$$= \frac{75}{100} \times 220 = 165$$

Number of female children
= 220 – 165 = 55

In society C:

Number of children

$$= \frac{16}{100} \times (300 + 275)$$

$$= \frac{4}{25} \times 575 = 92$$

Number of male children = $\frac{25}{100} \times 92 = 23$

Number of female children = 92 – 23 = 69

In society D:

Number of children

$$= \frac{25}{100} \times (280 + 300)$$

$$= \frac{1}{4} \times 580 = 145$$

Number of male children

$$= \frac{80}{100} \times 145 = 116$$

Number of female children
= 145 – 116 = 29

In society E:

Number of children

$$= \frac{40}{100} \times (180 + 250) = \frac{2}{5} \times 430 = 172$$

Number of male children

$$= \frac{50}{100} \times 172 = 86$$

Number of female children
= 172 – 86 = 86

In society F :

Number of children

$$= \frac{24}{100} \times (325 + 300) = \frac{6}{25} \times 625 = 150$$

Number of male children

$$= \frac{46}{100} \times 150 = 69$$

Number of female children
= 150 – 69 = 81

Hence, total number of female children
= 90 + 55 + 69 + 29 + 86 + 81 = 410

Total number of adult females
= (350 + 150 + 275 + 300 + 250 + 300) – 410
= 1625 – 410 = 1215

Hence, required ratio = 1215 : 410 = 243 : 82

2. (*b*) : Total number of adult males in the society A and B = (250 + 400) – (60 + 165)
(As shown in solution : 1)
= 650 – 225 = 425

Total number of adult males in the society E and F = (180 + 325) – (86 + 69)
(As shown in solution : 1)
= 505 – 155 = 350

Hence, required ratio = 425 : 350 = 17 : 14

3. (*d*) : Male children in society B = 165
Male children in society F = 69
(As shown in solution : 1)
Hence, their difference = 165 – 69 = 96

4. (*c*) : Total number of female children = 410
(As shown in solution : 1)

5. (*b*) : Number of members
= (250 + 350) + (400 + 150) + (300 + 275) + (280 + 300) + (180 + 250) + (325 + 300)
= 600 + 550 + 575 + 580 + 430 + 625
= 3360

6. (*e*) : It is clear from the table that none of the state has the production of rice increased continuously over the years.

7. (*b*) : Production of rice by different states over the years:

A → 1500 + 1480 + 1620 + 1700 + 1540 + 1650 = 9490 tonnes

B → 1250 + 1190 + 1400 + 1450 + 1320 + 1380 = 7990 tonnes

C → 1160 + 1190 + 1310 + 1300 + 1340 + 1360 = 7660 tonnes

D → 1520 + 1500 + 1480 + 1590 + 1630 + 1580 = 9300 tonnes

E → 1440 + 1350 + 1430 + 1280 + 1380 + 1400 = 8280 tonnes

F → 1600 + 1620 + 1510 + 1610 + 1580 + 1590 = 9510 tonnes

Hence, the State C produced the lowest quantity of rice.

8. (*c*) : Required percentage

$$= \frac{1300}{1700} \times 100$$

$$= 76.47\% \approx 76\%$$

9. (*d*) : Production of rice in different years by all states together:

2003 → 1500 + 1250 + 1160 + 1520 + 1440 + 1600 = 8470 tonnes

2004 → 1480 + 1190 + 1190 + 1500 + 1350 + 1620 = 8330 tonnes

2005 → 1620 + 1400 + 1310 + 1480 + 1430 + 1510 = 8750 tonnes

2006 → 1700 + 1450 + 1300 + 1590 + 1280 + 1610 = 8930 tonnes

2007 → 1540 + 1320 + 1340 + 1630 + 1380 + 1580 = 8790 tonnes

2008 → 1650 + 1380 + 1360 + 1580 + 1400 + 1590 = 8960 tonnes

Hence, in year 2008 the production of rice was the highest.

10. (*d*) : Average quantity of rice produced by State

$$D = \frac{9300}{6} = 1550 \text{ tonnes}$$

(As shown in soluton : 7)

Average quantity of rice produced by State

$$F = \frac{9510}{6} = 1585 \text{ tonnes}$$

(As shown in soluton : 7)

Hence, required ratio = 1550 : 1585 = 310 : 317

21

BAR GRAPHS AND PIE CHARTS

Bar Graphs

A bar graph may be either horizontal or vertical. The important point to note about bar graphs is their bar length or height; the greater their length or height, the greater their value. Bar graphs usually present categorical and numeric variables grouped in class intervals. They consist of an axis and a series or labelled horizontal or vertical bars. The bars depict frequencies of different values of a variable or simply the different values or simply the different values themselves.

The numbers on the *x*-axis of a bar graph or the *y*-axis of a column graph are called the scale.

Pie Charts

A pie chart is a way of summarising a set of categorical data or displaying the different values of a given variable (*e.g.*, percentage distribution). This type of chart is a circle divided into series of segments. Each segment represents a particular category.

EXERCISE

Directions : *Shown below is the multiple bar diagram depicting the changes in the student's strength of a college in four faculties from* 2000-01 *to* 2002-03. (*Scale* 1 *cm* = 100)

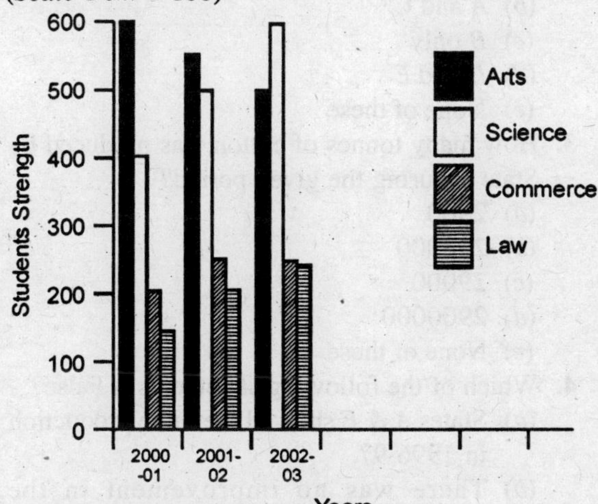

Study the above multiple bar chart and mark a tick against the correct answer in each of the following questions.

1. The percentage of students in science faculty in 2000-01 was :
   (*a*) 26.9 % (*b*) 27.8 %
   (*c*) 29.6 % (*d*) 30.2 %
2. The percentage of students in law faculty in 2002-03 was :
   (*a*) 18.5 % (*b*) 15.6 %
   (*c*) 16.7 % (*d*) 14.8 %
3. How many times the total strength was of the strength of commerce students in 2001-02?
   (*a*) 3 times (*b*) 4 times
   (*c*) 5 times (*d*) 6 times
4. During which year the strength of arts faculty was minimum?
   (*a*) 2000-01 (*b*) 2001-02
   (*c*) 2002-03 (*d*) None of these
5. How much per cent was the increase in science students in 2002-03 over 2000-01?
   (*a*) 50% (*b*) 150%
   (*c*) $66\frac{2}{3}$% (*d*) 75%
6. A regular decrease in students' strength was in the faculty of
   (*a*) Arts (*b*) Science
   (*c*) Commerce (*d*) Law

EXPLANATORY ANSWERS

1. (c) : Total number of students in 2000-01

$= (600 + 400 + 200 + 150) = 1350$

Number of science students in 2000-01 was 400.

Percentage of science students in 2000-01

$= \left[\frac{400}{1350} \times 100\right] \% = 29.6\%$

So, answer (*c*) is correct.

2. (b) : Total number of students in 2002-03

$= (500 + 600 + 250 + 250) = 1600$

Number of law students in 2002-03 is 250.

Percentage of law students in 2002-03

$= \left[\frac{250}{1600} \times 100\right] \% = 15.6\ \%$

So, answer (*b*) is correct.

3. (d) : Total strength in 2001-02

$= (550 + 500 + 250 + 200) = 1500$

So, $\frac{\text{Total strength}}{\text{Strength of commerce students}}$

$= \frac{1500}{250} = 6.$

4. (c) : A slight look indicates that the strength in arts faculty in 2000-01, 2001-02 and 2002-03 was 600, 550 and 500 respectively. So, it was minimum in 2002-03. So, answer (*c*) is correct.

5. (a) : Number of science students in 2000 - 01 was 400.

Number of science students in 2002 - 03 was 600.

$\text{Percentage increase} = \left(\frac{200}{400} \times 100\right) \% = 50\%$

Answer (*a*) is correct.

6. (a) : [Just a look is sufficient.]

EXERCISE

Directions (Qs. 1 to 5) : *Examine the following graph carefully and answer the questions given below it.*

Production of Cotton bales of 100 kg. each in lacs in States *A,B, C,D, and E* during 1995-96, 1996-97, 1997-98

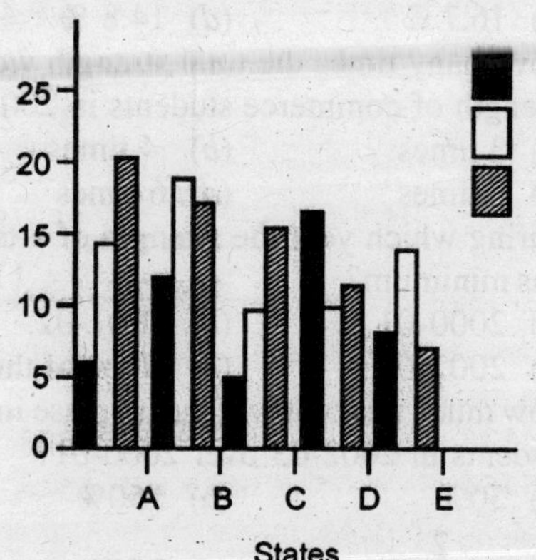

1. The production of State *D* in 1997-98 is how many times its production in 1996-97?

(*a*) 1.33 (*b*) 0.75

(*c*) 0.56 (*d*) 1.77

(*e*) None of these

2. In which states is there a steady increase in the production of cotton during the given period?

(*a*) A and B

(*b*) A and C

(*c*) B only

(*d*) D and E

(*e*) None of these

3. How many tonnes of cotton was produced by State *E* during the given period?

(*a*) 2900

(*b*) 290000

(*c*) 29000

(*d*) 2900000

(*e*) None of these

4. Which of the following statements is False?

(*a*) States *A* & *E* showed the same production in 1996-97.

(*b*) There was no improvement in the production of cotton in State *B* during.

(*c*) State *A* has produced maximum cotton during the given period.

(*d*) Production of states *C* and *D* together is equal to that of State *B* during 1996-97.

(*e*) None of these

Directions (Qs. 5 to 9): *Study the graph carefully to answer the questions that follow:*

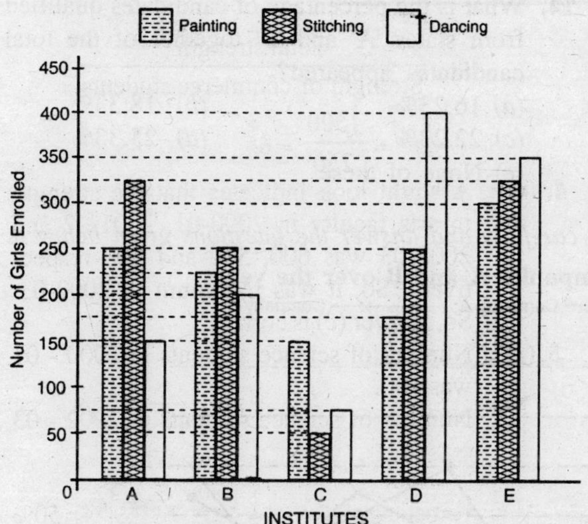

5. What is the respective ratio of total number of girls enrolled in Painting in the institutes A and C together to those enrolled in Stiching in the institutes D and E together?

(a) 5 : 4 (b) 5 : 7
(c) 9 : 8 (d) 16 : 23
(e) None of these

6. What is the respective ratio of total number of girls enrolled in Painting, Stiching and Dancing from all the Institutes together?

(a) 43 : 47 : 48 (b) 44 : 47 : 48
(c) 44 : 48 : 47 (d) 47 : 48 : 44
(e) None of these

7. What is the total number of girls enrolled in Painting from all the Institutes together?

(a) 1100 (b) 1150
(c) 1200 (d) 1275
(e) None of these

8. Number of girls enrolled in Stitching in Institute B forms approximately what per cent of the total number of girls enrolled in Stitching in the Institutes together?

(a) 21% (b) 29%
(c) 33% (d) 37%
(e) None of these

9. Number of girls enrolled in Dancing in Institute A forms what per cent of total number of girls enrolled in all the Hobby classes together in that Institute?

(a) 17.76% (b) 20.69%
(c) 31.23% (d) 33.97%
(e) None of these

Directions (Qs. 10 to 14): *Study the following graph and table carefully and answer the questions given below it:*

Distribution of Candidates appeared in a competitive examination from seven states
Total Candidates appeared = 3 lakh

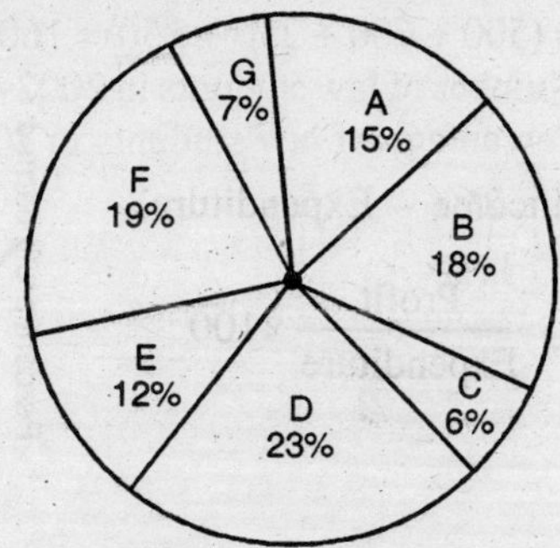

State-wise percentage and ratio of male and female qualified candidates

State	*% Qualified over appeared from a state*	*Ratio of qualified Candidates*
A	49	4 : 5
B	61	6 : 4
C	54	7 : 8
D	45	3 : 2
E	65	7 : 6
F	57	11 : 8
G	48	9 : 11

10. What is the number of male candidates qualified from State 'G'?

(a) 4536 (b) 4568
(c) 5454 (d) 5544
(e) None of these

11. Which of the following pair of states have equal number of qualified male candidates?

(a) A and E (b) B and F
(c) C and E (d) C and G
(e) None of these

12. What is the total number of candidates qualified from states E and D together?
(*a*) 45540 (*b*) 54410
(*c*) 54450 (*d*) 54540
(*e*) None of these

13. What is the total number of female candidates qualified from states A and B together?
(*a*) 24526 (*b*) 25426
(*c*) 26426 (*d*) 26526
(*e*) None of these

14. What is the percentage of candidates qualified from states 'A' and 'B' together of the total candidates appeared?
(*a*) 16.23% (*b*) 18.33%
(*c*) 22.23% (*d*) 25.33%
(*e*) None of these

Directions (Qs. 15 to 19): *Study the following graph carefully and answer the questions given below it.*

Per cent profit earned by two Companies A and B over the years

Profit = Income − Expenditure

$$\text{Profit\%} = \frac{\text{Profit}}{\text{Expenditure}} \times 100$$

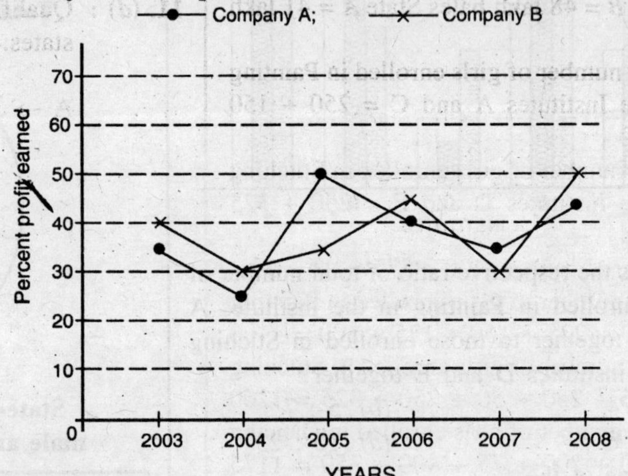

15. If the income of company A in 2005 was ₹ 1,42,500, what was its expenditure in that year?
(*a*) ₹ 95000 (*b*) ₹ 95500
(*c*) ₹ 99,500 (*d*) ₹ 1,05,000
(*e*) None of these

16. If the expenditure of Company 'A' in 2004 was ₹ 75 lakhs and income of Company A in 2004 was equal to its expenditure in 2005. What was the total income (in lakhs ₹) of the Company A in 2004 and 2005 together?
(*a*) 131.25 (*b*) 175
(*c*) 218.75 (*d*) 234.37
(*e*) None of these

17. Total expenditure of companies A & B together in 2008 was ₹ 13.5 lakhs. What was the total income of the two companies (in lakh Rs.) in that year?
(*a*) 19.75
(*b*) 20.25
(*c*) 19.575
(*d*) Cannot be determined
(*e*) None of these

18. Expenditure of company 'B' in 2006 was 90% of its expenditure in 2005. Income of Company 'B' in 2006 was what per cent of its income in 2005?
(*a*) $96\frac{2}{3}$ (*b*) $99\frac{1}{3}$
(*c*) 121.5 (*d*) 130.5
(*e*) None of these

19. Expenditure of company 'B' in years 2003 and 2004 were in the ratio of 5 : 7 respectively. What was the respective ratio of their incomes?
(*a*) 8 : 13 (*b*) 10 : 13
(*c*) 11 : 14 (*d*) 13 ; 14
(*e*) None of these

EXPLANATORY ANSWERS

1. (*b*) : Suppose, it is x times

$$x = \frac{12}{9} = \frac{4}{3}$$

2. (*b*) : It is clear by graph.

3. (*b*) : 8 + 14 + 7 = 29 lakhs

Its weight $= \frac{29 \times 100000}{1000} \times 100$

4. (*c*) : State B = 48 lakh bales State A = 41 lakh bales

5. (*d*) : Total number of girls enrolled in Painting in the Institutes A and C = 250 + 150 = 400

Total number of girls enrolled in Stitching in the Institutes D and E = 250 + 325 = 575

Required ratio = 400 : 575 = 16 : 23

6. (*c*) : Total number of girls enrolled in Painting = 250 + 225 + 150 + 175 + 300 = 1100

Total number of girls enrolled in Stitching = 325 + 250 + 50 + 250 + 325 = 1200

Total number of girls enrolled in Dancing = 150 + 200 + 75 + 400 + 350 = 1175

Hence, required ratio = 1100 : 1200 : 1175 = 44 : 48 : 47

7. (*a*) : Total number of girls enrolled in Painting = 250 + 225 + 150 + 175 + 300 = 1100

8. (*a*) : Number of girls enrolled in Stitching in Institute B = 250

Total number of girls enrolled in Stitching in all the Institutions = 325 + 250 + 50 + 250 + 325 = 1200

Hence, required percentage

$$= \frac{250}{1200} \times 100 = 20.83 \approx 21\%$$

9. (*b*) : Number of girls enrolled in Dancing in Institute A = 150

Total number of girls enrolled in all the Hobby classes together in Institute A = 250 + 325 + 150 = 725

Hence, required percentage $= \frac{150}{725} \times 100$

= 20.69%

10. (*a*) : Number of candidates qualified from State

$$G = \frac{48}{100} \times \frac{7}{100} \times 3{,}00{,}000 = 10080$$

Number of male candidates qualified from

$$\text{State G} = \frac{9}{9+11} \times 10080 = \frac{9}{20} \times 10080$$

$$= 4536$$

11. (*d*) : Qualified Male Candidates from different states:

$$A \rightarrow \frac{4}{9} \times \frac{49}{100} \times \frac{15}{100} \times 300000 = 9800$$

$$B \rightarrow \frac{6}{10} \times \frac{61}{100} \times \frac{18}{100} \times 300000 = 19764$$

$$C \rightarrow \frac{7}{15} \times \frac{54}{100} \times \frac{6}{100} \times 300000 = 4536$$

$$D \rightarrow \frac{3}{5} \times \frac{45}{100} \times \frac{23}{100} \times 300000 = 18630$$

$$E \rightarrow \times \frac{7}{13} \times \frac{65}{100} \times \frac{12}{100} \times 300000 = 12600$$

$$F \rightarrow \frac{11}{19} \times \frac{57}{100} \times \frac{19}{100} \times 300000 = 18810$$

$$G \rightarrow \frac{9}{20} \times \frac{48}{100} \times \frac{7}{100} \times 300000 = 4536$$

Hence, states C and G have equal number of qualified male candidates.

12. (*c*) : Required number of candidates

$$= \frac{65}{100} \times \frac{12}{100} \times 300000 + \frac{45}{100} \times \frac{23}{100} \times 300000$$

= 23400 + 31050 = 54450

13. (*b*) : Required number of female candidates

$$= \frac{5}{9} \times \frac{49}{100} \times \frac{15}{100} \times 300000 + \frac{4}{10} \times \frac{61}{100} \times \frac{18}{100} \times 300000$$

= 12250 + 13176 = 25426

14. (*b*) : Number of candidates qualified from states A and B together

$$= \frac{49}{100} \times \frac{15}{100} \times 300000 + \frac{61}{100} \times \frac{18}{100} \times 300000$$

$= 22050 + 32940 = 54990$

Required percentage $= \frac{54990}{300000} \times 100$

$= 18.33\%$

15. (*a*) : Let expenditure of Company A in 2005 = ₹ x; then

$$x + \frac{50}{100} \times x = 1,42,500 \Rightarrow \frac{3x}{2} = 1,42,500$$

$$\therefore x = \frac{2 \times 1,42,500}{3} = ₹\ 95000$$

16. (*d*) : In 2004, expenditure of Company 'A' = ₹ 75 lakh

Since, income of the Company 'A' in 2004

$$= 75 + \frac{25}{100} \times 75 = ₹\ 93.75 \text{ lakhs}$$

Now, expenditure of the Company 'A' in 2005 = ₹ 93.75 lakhs

Since, income of the Company A in 2005

$$= 93.75 + \frac{50}{100} \times 93.75$$

= ₹ 140.62 lakhs

Hence, total income for both the years = 93.75 + 140.62 = ₹ 234.37 lakhs

17. (*d*) : Here total expenditure of both companies are given while their individual expenditures are needed to determine their incomes. So, the total income of the two companies cannot be determined by the given datas.

18. (*a*) : Let expenditure of Company B in 2005 = ₹ x; then

$$I_1 \text{ (Income)} = x + \frac{35}{100} x = \text{Rs.} \frac{27x}{20}$$

Since, expenditure of Company B in 2006

$$= \frac{90}{100} \times ₹\ x = ₹ \frac{9x}{10}, \text{ then}$$

$$I_2 \text{ (Income)} = \frac{9x}{10} + \frac{45}{100} \times \frac{9x}{10}$$

$$= \frac{9x}{10} + \frac{81x}{200} = ₹ \frac{261x}{200}$$

Hence, required percentage

$$= \frac{261x/200}{27x/20} \times 100 = \frac{290}{3} = 96\frac{2}{3}\%$$

19. (*b*) : Let expenditures of Company B in 2003 and 2004 are ₹ $5x$ and ₹ $7x$ respectively; then

their income in 2003, I_1

$$= 5x + \frac{40}{100} \times 5x = ₹\ 7x$$

Also their income in 2004,

$$I_2 = 7x + \frac{30}{100} \times 7x = ₹ \frac{91x}{10}$$

Hence, the required ratio $= 7x : \frac{91x}{10}$

$= 10 : 13.$

VERBAL ABILITY IN ENGLISH

INTRODUCTION

This section helps to evaluate your practising the English Language and to work with specialized vocabulary. It assesses your ability to understand. A variety of questions are designed to assess the extent of your vocabulary, to measure your ability to use words as tools in reasoning, to test your ability to discern the relationships that exist both within written passages and among individual groups of words. You are tested not only for your use of words but also for reasoning and arguing.

The best method of improving your use of English with this guide is to study the formulae and sample sentences. Then do the practice exercises at the end of each section. Practice carefully.

Common Errors in English

The most common errors in English are of spellings, grammar and usage of words. By regular practice, the errors can be easily spotted and minimised.

I. COMMON ERRORS WITH NOUNS AND NOUN-PHRASES

	Incorrect	**Correct**
1.	I have bought new *furnitures.*	I have bought new *furniture.*
2.	The wages of sin *are* death.	The *wages* of sin is death.
3.	She told these *news* to her mother.	She told her mother this *news.*
4.	He took *troubles* to do his work.	He took *trouble* (or pains) over his work.
5.	The *cattles* were grazing.	The *cattle* were grazing.
6.	He showered *many abuses* on me.	He showered *much abuse* on me.
7.	I spent the holidays with my *family members.*	I spent the holidays with my *family.*
8.	There is no *place* in this compartment.	There is no *room* in this compartment.
9.	Write this new *poetry* in your *copy.*	Write this new *poem* in your *note-book.*
10.	He took *insult* at this	He took *offence* at this.
11.	Put your *sign* here.	Put your *signatures* here.
12.	She is my *cousin sister*	She is my *cousin.*
13.	*Sunil's* my *neighbour's* house was burgled.	*Sunil* my *neighbour's* house was burgled.
14.	I lost a *ten-rupees* note.	I lost *a ten-rupee* note.
15.	Road closed for *repair*	Road closed for *repairs.*
16.	His house is out of *repairs.*	His house is out of *repair*
17.	What is the *reason* of an earthquake ?	What is the *cause* of an earthquake
18.	This building is made of *stones*	This building is made of *stone.*
19.	I disapprove of *these kinds* of games.	I disapprove of *this kind* of games.
20.	Veena's and Sheela's father is ill.	Veena and Sheela's father is ill.

Incorrect	Correct
21. His *son-in-laws* are doctors	His *sons-in-law* are doctors.
22. *Alms* is given to the *poor.*	*Alms* are given to the poor.
23. He always keeps his words.	He always keeps his *word*
24. I carried the *luggages.*	I carried the *luggage.*
25. *Two-third* of the work is left.	*Two-thirds* of the work is left.

II. COMMON ERRORS WITH PRONOUNS

Incorrect	Correct
1. Both did not go	Neither went.
2. We all did not go.	None of us went.
3. Each of these boys play.	Each of these boys plays.
4. Whoever does best he will get a prize.	Whoever does best will get a prize.
5. One should not waste his time.	A man should not waste his time.
6. I and she are sisters	She and I are sisters.
7. He is wiser than me.	He is wiser than I.
8. Between you and I, Anil is not to be trusted.	Between you and me, Anil is not to be trusted.
9. Nobody was there but I.	Nobody was there but me.
10. Who is there ? It is me.	Who is there ? It is I.
11. Only he and me can use this card.	Only he and I can use this card.
12. Let you and I go now.	Let you and me go now.
13. Everyone got one's pay	Everyone got his pay.
14. Everyone is frightened when they see a tiger.	Everyone is frightened when he sees a tiger.
15. These two friends are fond of one another.	These two friends are fond of each other.
16. I did not like him coming at that hour.	I did not like his coming at that hour.
17. Who do you think I met ?	Whom do you think I met ?
18. You should avail this opportunity.	You should avail yourself this opportunity.
19. When you have read these books, please return the same to me.	When you have read the books, please return them to me.
20. They that are humble need fear no fall.	Those that are humble need fear no fall.

III. COMMON ERRORS WITH ADJECTIVES

Incorrect	Correct
1. These all oranges are good.	All these oranges are good.
2. He held the book in the both hands.	He held the book in both hands.
3. Both men have not come.	Neither man has come.
4. That man should do some or other work.	That man should do some work or other
5. He is elder than I.	He is older than I.
6. Shakespeare is greater than any other poets.	Shakespeare is greater than any other poet.

Incorrect	Correct
7. He is a coward man.	He is a cowardly man.
8. Many villagers cannot write his own name.	Many villagers cannot write their own name.
9. Each of us loves our home.	Each of us loves his home.
10. Much efforts bring their reward.	Much effort brings its reward.
11. He found hundred rupees.	He found a hundred rupees.
12. He had leave of four days.	He had four days leave.
13. This is a worth seeing sight.	This is a sight worth seeing.
14. He will spend his future life here.	He will spend the rest of his life here.
15. There is a best teacher in that class.	There is a very good teacher in that class.
16. Of the two plans this is the best.	Of the two plans this is the better.
17. He is becoming strong every day.	He is becoming stronger every day.
18. He is worst than I.	He is worse than I.
19. Jaipur is hot than Delhi.	Jaipur is hotter than Delhi.
20 In our library the number of books is less.	In our library the number of books is small.
21. From the three he is more clever.	He is the cleverest of the three.
22. India is the first peace-loving country in the world.	India is the foremost peace-loving country in the world.
23. Verbal instruction will not do.	Oral instruction will not do.
24. Her command over French is most excellent.	Her command over French is excellent.
25. He has not some money with him.	He has not any money with him.
26. I have visited Bombay many a times.	I have visited Bombay many a time.
27. Death is more preferable to dishonour.	Death is preferable to dishonour.
28. I gave him a few books I had.	I gave him the few books I had.
29. If he wants farther help send him to me.	If he wants further help, send him to me.
30. She is so cunning as a fox.	She is as cunning as a fox.

IV. COMMON ERRORS WITH VERBS

Incorrect	Correct
1. He asked had we taken our luggage.	He asked if we had taken our luggage.
2. She asked what are you doing.	She asked what we were doing.
3. Rama asked to Anil why he is angry.	Rama asked Anil why he was angry.
4. He does not care for his money.	He does not take care of his money.
5. He does not care for his work.	He takes no care over his work.
6. No one cared for him after his mother died.	No one took care of him after his mother died.
7. He got angry before I said a word.	He got angry before I had said a word.
8. I met a man who was my tutor 20 years ago.	I met a man who had been my tutor twenty years ago.
9. I had been for walking yesterday.	I went for a walk yesterday.
10 If I shall do this I shall be wrong.	If I do this I shall be wrong.

Incorrect	Correct
11. I have left trekking.	I have given up trekking.
12. I came to know as to how he did this.	I learnt how he did this.
13. I came to know why he was sad.	I found out why he was sad.
14. He knows to swim.	He knows how to swim.
15. The criminal's head was cut.	The criminal's head was cut off.
16. I said to him to go.	I told him to go.
17. I told the teacher to excuse me.	I asked the teacher to excuse me.
18. He is troubling me.	He is giving me trouble.
19. I have got a hurt on my leg.	I have hurt my leg.
20. She gave a speech.	She made a speech.
21. He has given his examination.	He has sat for his examination.
22. He took out his shoes.	He took off his shoes.
23. I have ordered for a new car.	I have ordered a new car.
24. He would not hear me.	He would not listen to me.
25. I struck a blow on his face.	I struck him in the face.
26. He denied to come.	He refused to come.
27. He lived there for a day.	He stayed there for a day.
28. The book is not found.	The book is lost.
29. Shut the light.	Turn off the light.
30. I must revenge my brother.	I must avenge my brother.

V. COMMON ERRORS IN SUBJECT-VERB AGREEMENT

Incorrect	Correct
1. The owners of this factory is very rich.	The owners of this factory *are* very rich.
2. The pleasures of nature that one can experience at Shimla is beyond description.	The pleasures of nature that one can experience at Shimla *are* beyond description.
3. There is no street lights in our colony.	There *are* no street lights in our colony.
4. He and I am entrusted with the job.	He and I *are* entrusted with the job.
5. Rice and curry are his favourite dish.	Rice and curry *is* his favourite dish.
6. The honour and glory of our country are at stake.	The honour and glory of our country *is* at stake.
7. Time and tide waits for none.	Time and tide *wait* for none.
8. All the passengers with the driver was killed.	All the passengers, with the driver, *were* killed.
9. The teacher, with her students, were going out.	The teacher, with her students, *was* going out.
10. I as well as they am tired.	I as well as they *are* tired.
11. Not only the soldiers but their captain also were captured.	Not only the soldiers but their captain also was captured.

Incorrect	Correct
12. Neither you nor I were selected.	Neither you nor I *was* selected.
13. Either of these two applicants are fit for the job but neither want to accept it.	Either of these two applicants *is* fit for the job but neither wants to accept it.
14. One of these students are sure to stand first.	One of these students *is* sure to stand first.
15. Everyone of these workers want a raise.	Everyone of these workers wants a raise.
16. None of these letters has been answered so far.	None of these letters *have* been answered so far.
17. None of the girls were present at the party.	None of the girls *was* present at the party.
18. Many a battle were fought on Indian soil.	Many a battle *was* fought on Indian soil.
19. A lot of work remain to be done.	A lot of work *remains* to be done.
20. The majority of these girls likes music.	The majority of these girls *like* music.
21. The number of admissions are encouraging.	The number of admissions *is* encouraging.
22. A large number of boys was present.	A large number of boys *were* present.
23. A variety of books was on display.	A variety of books *were* on display.
24. Variety are the spice of life.	Variety *is* the spice of life.
25. lf my estimates are correct. I will need another hundred rupees.	If my estimate is correct, I will need another hun dred rupees.
26. Mathematics are my favourite subject.	Mathematics *is* my favourite subject.
27. 'Gulliver's Travels' are written by Swift.	'Gulliver's Travels' *is* written by Swift.
28. Ten miles are a long distance to cover on foot.	Ten miles *is* a long distance to cover on foot.
29. A new pair of shoes are to be purchased.	A new pair of shoes is to be purchased.
30. The Committee have issued its report.	The Committee *has* issued its report.
31. I, who am your friend, has always been on your side,	I, who am your friend, *have* always been on your side.
32. I am the person who have always stood by you.	I am the person who *has* al- ways stood by you.
33. This is one of the best novels that has been published this year.	This is one of the best novels that *have* been published this year.
34. Less than half the amount have been wasted.	Less than half the amount *has* been wasted.
35. A lot of people has turned up for the show.	A lot of people *have* turned up for the show.
36. Much of their honour are un-deserved.	Much of their honour *is* un-deserved.
37. More than a decade have passed since this house was built.	More than a decade *has* passed since this house was built.
38. Either she or he are mistaken.	Either she or he *is* mistaken.
39. Plenty of information are available on the subject.	Plenty of information *is* available on the subject.
40. Plenty of pamphlets is available on the subject.	Plenty of pamphlets *are* available on the subject.

VI. COMMON ERRORS IN USE OF WILL, SHALL, WOULD, SHOULD, MAY, MIGHT, MUST

	Incorrect	Correct
1.	When I shall see him I shall tell him this.	When I *see* him, I shall tell him this.
2.	If I should do wrong, he would punish me.	If I *did* wrong, he would punish me.
3.	Until he will have confessed his fault, he will be kept in prison,	Until he *has* confessed his fault, he will be kept in prison.
4.	She will obey me.	She *shall* obey me.
5.	You would work hard.	You *should* work hard.
6.	You shall find him in the garden.	You *will* find him in the garden.
7.	He must have died of exposure, but we cannot be certain.	He *might* have died of exposure, but we cannot be certain.
8.	You might not show disrespect to your elders.	You *must* not show disrespect to your elders.
9.	You may take exercise in order to maintain good health,	You *must* take exercise in order to maintain good health.
10.	He must be a crook for all we know.	He *may* be a crook for all we know.

VII. COMMON ERRORS IN THE USE OF ADVERBS

(Very, Much, Too, Enough, Quite, Hardly, Scarcely, Before, Ago, Since, Yet, Still, etc.)

	Incorrect	Correct
1.	He is very much angry.	He is *very* angry.
2.	She was very good enough to help me.	She was *good enough* to help me.
3.	She runs much fast.	She runs *very* fast.
4.	She runs very faster than Seema.	She runs *much* faster than Seema.
5.	It is bitter cold today.	It is *bitterly* cold today.
6.	He is a much learned man.	He is a very learned man.
7	She is thinking very hardly.	She is thinking very hard.
8.	To tell in brief the film was boring.	*In short* the film was boring.
9.	He told the story in details.	He told the story *in detail.*
10.	I did it anyhow.	I *managed to do* it somehow.
11.	Aeroplanes reach Europe soon.	Aeroplanes reach Europe quickly.
12.	Before long there were dinosaurs on the earth.	*Long ago,* there were dinosaurs on the earth.
13.	This book is too interesting.	This book is *very* interesting.
14.	He lives miserly.	He lives in *a miserly* way.
15.	Just I had gone when she came.	I had just gone when she came.

Incorrect	Correct
16. He sings good.	He sings *well.*
17. He sings good than I.	He sings *better* than I.
18. Really speaking it is cold.	*As a matter of fact* it is cold.
19. He is enough tall to reach the ceiling.	He is *tall enough* to reach the ceiling.
20. He went directly to his college.	He went *direct* to his college.
21. He is presently at Delhi	He is at Delhi *at present.*
22. Last night she returned lately.	Last night she *returned late.*
23. He was even blamed by his friends.	He was *blamed even* by his friends.
24. I only employed him for a week.	I employed him for a week only.
25. I met him four months before.	I met him four *months ago.*
26. Anil seldom ever goes to school.	Anil *seldom goes* to school.
27. I will wait here until you do not go.	I will wait here until *you go.*
28. I never remember having met her before.	I *do not remember* having met her before.
29. She has not been here too long to have many friends,	She has not *been here long* enough to have many friends.
30. Hardly I have had any rest since one week.	Hardly have *I had* any rest for a week.
31. Scarcely the water crossed the danger level, the warning signals were sounded.	Scarcely *had the* water *crossed the* danger level, when the warning signals were sounded.
32. She is neat but fairly slow.	She is *neat* but rather slow.
33. It is a rather good film.	It is a *fairly good* film.
34. We yet have time to catch the bus.	We *still have* time to catch the bus.
35. She has not still spent all her money.	She has *not yet* spent all her money.

VIII. COMMON ERRORS IN THE USE OF CONJUNCTIONS

Incorrect	Correct
1. As he is fat so he runs slowly.	As he is fat *he* runs slowly.
2. If he is fat then he will run slowly.	If he is fat, he will run slowly.
3. Though, he is fat still he runs fast.	Though he is fat, *he runs* fast.
4. *As* I pulled the trigger at the sametime he shook my arm.	As I pulled the trigger, he shook my arm.
5. No sooner I had spoken than he left.	No sooner *had* I spoken than he left.
6. Not only he will go, but also he will stay there.	Not only *will he* go, but he *will also* stay there.
7. Neither he comes nor he writes.	Neither *does he* come nor *does he* write.
8. Scarcely he entered the room than the telephone rang.	Scarcely *had* he entered the room *when the* telephone rang.
9. Hardly she had left the house than it began to rain.	Hardly *had she* left the house *when* it began to rain.

Incorrect	Correct
10. He is the fastest runner and he comes last.	He is the fastest runner *but* he comes last.
11. She is as innocent as if she looks.	She is as innocent as she looks.
12. Until he does not try he must be punished.	He must be punished unless he tries
13. I want to know as to why you are late.	I want to know why you are late.
14. I am fond of Chinese food as for example sweet and sour prawns.	I am fond of Chinese food, for example, sweet and sour prawns.
15. He was angry therefore I ran away.	He was angry so I ran away.
16. I was trying to work, at that time he was disturbing me.	While I was trying to work, he was disturbing me.
17. Supposing if he is late, what will happen?	Supposing he is late (or if he is late) what will happen?
18. He asked me that why I was late.	He asked me why I was late.
19. Let us catch a taxi lest we should not get late.	Let us catch a taxi lest we should get late.
20. She dresses herself like the teacher does.	She dresses herself as the teacher does.
21 Wait while I come.	Wait *until* (or *till)* I come.
22. Until, there is corruption in India, there can be little progress.	*As long* as there is corruption in India there can be little progress.
23. I have never told a lie nor cheated anybody.	I have never told a lie *nor have I* cheated anybody.
24. Both Mohan as well as Arun are responsible for this action.	Both Mohan *and* Arun are responsible for this action.
25. Hindus and Muslims both are to blame for the riots.	*Both Hindus* and Muslims are to blame for the riots.
26. I have bought paintings, books, records, and etc.	I have bought paintings, books *and records etc.*
27. He as well as you is a fool.	He as well as you *are* a fool.
28. He is so poor and he cannot save anything.	He is so *poor that* he cannot save anything.
29. Such a' book that you want is not available.	Such a book *as* you want is not available.
30. Such was her condition as everyone was moved to pity.	Such was her condition that everyone was moved to pity.

IX. COMMON ERRORS IN THE USE OF PREPOSITIONS

Incorrect	Correct
1. I will not listen him.	I will not listen *to* him.
2. Copy this word by word.	Copy this word *for* word.
3. He enquired from her where she lived.	He enquired *of* her where she lived.
4. Sign here with ink.	Sign here *in* ink.
5. Has she come in train or by foot?	Has she come *by* train or *on* foot ?
6. She said this at his face.	She said this *to* his face.

	Incorrect	Correct
7.	Open the book on page one	Open the book *at* page one.
8.	I was invited for lunch.	I was *invited to* lunch.
9.	I am ill since three months.	I have been *ill for* three months.
10.	This paper is inferior than that.	This paper is inferior *to* that.
11.	This resembles to that.	This *resembles* that.
12.	My brother is superior than you in strength.	My brother is superior *to* you in strength.
13.	He wrote me	He wrote *to* me.
14.	I shall explain them this.	I shall explain this *to* them.
15.	Send this letter on my address.	Send this letter *to* my address.
16.	He suggested me this.	He suggested this *to* me.
17.	He goes on his work.	He goes *to his* work.
18.	He reached to Nagpur.	He *reached* Nagpur.
19.	He told to me to go.	He told *me* to go.
20	The term begins from July 1st.	The term begins *on* July 1st.
21.	There are many advantages from this.	The advantages *of* this are many.
22.	We waste much time in trifles.	We waste much time *on* (or *over)* trifles.
23.	He sat on a tree.	He sat *in* a tree.
24.	This is a comfortable house to live.	This is a comfortable house to live in
25.	This is the road to go.	This is the road to go *by.*
26.	He married with an Indian lady.	He *married an Indian* lady.
27.	He accompanied with his friend.	He *accompanied his* friend.
28.	He went for doing some business.	He went away *on* business.
29.	He went for riding.	He went *for a ride.*
30.	I pitied on him.	I *pitied* him.
31.	When this was searched it was found.	When this was searched *for* it was found.
32.	I shall inform them this.	I shall inform them *of* this.
33.	Due to illness I cannot go to school.	*Owing* to illness I cannot go to school.
34.	He went to the back side of the house.	He went behind (or to the back of) the house.
35.	I must go; there is no help.	I must go; there is no help *for it.*
36.	I met with your friend there.	I *met your* friend there.
37.	The First World War was fought during 1914-1918.	The First World War was fought *between* 1914-1918.
38.	England grew prosperous between Queen Victoria's reign.	England grew prosperous *during* Queen Victoria's reign.
39.	He asked a holiday.	He asked *for* a holiday.
40.	I am obliged of you for this good turn.	I am obliged *to* you for this good turn.
41.	There is no harm to try.	There is no harm *in trying.*

X. MISCELLANEOUS ERRORS

(Including Ambiguities and Indianisms)

	Incorrect	Correct
1.	Many *homes* are lying vacant.	Many *houses* are lying vacant.
2.	It is cool in the shadow of the tree.	It is cool in the *shade* of the tree.
3.	She *keeps* good health.	She *enjoys* good health.
4.	My leg is paining.	*I am feeling pain* in my leg.
5.	See this word in the dictionary.	*Look up* this word in the dictionary.
6.	The train will arrive *just now*	The train will arrive *shortly*.
7.	They are *pulling* on well.	They are *getting* on well.
8.	The river has *over flown* its bank.	The river has *over flown* its banks.
9.	He was appointed *on* the post.	He was appointed *to* the post.
10.	Last but not *the least,* we have to discuss the problem of over population.	Last but not *least,* we have to discuss the problem of over population.
11.	*Cities* after *cities* fell.	*City* after *city* fell.
12.	What is the use Munir going there?	What is the use of Munir going there?
13.	He *did many mischief.*	He *made much mischief.*
14.	It is exact five *in* my watch.	It is exact five *by* my watch.
15.	I will dine with them on *next Sunday.*	I will dine with them *Sunday next.*
16.	Misfortunes when faced bravely and *manly* become less troublesome.	Misfortunes when faced bravely and *manfully* become less troublesome.
17.	I am *laid down* with fever.	I am *laid up* with fever.
18.	He is habituated to smoking.	He is *addicted* to smoking.
19.	*According to my opinion* he is right.	*In my opinion* (or according *to me)* he is right.
20.	Could you please *open* this knot?	Could you please *untie* this knot?
21.	When five *wars old* his father died.	*When he was five wars old* his father died.
22.	I made him *to* do this work.	I *made him do* this work.
23.	What is the *cost* of this camera ?	What is the *price of* this camera?
24.	He wants *as many as* five kilograms of sugar.	He wants *as much as* five kilograms of sugar.
25.	I have come to a final *conclusion.*	I have come to a *conclusion* (or *to a final decision)*
26.	Do you wish me to teach *you or the principal?*	Do you wish me or the principal to teach you?
27.	The tree was *loaded with* fruit.	The tree was *laden with* fruit.
28.	What sort of a man is he?	What sort of man is he?
29.	My views are different *than* you.	My views are different *from yours.*
30.	I take this opportunity *to thank* you.	I take this opportunity *of thanking* you.

SPOTTING ERRORS

Directions (Qs. 1 to 150): *In this section, each sentence has three parts, indicated by (A), (B) and (C). Read each sentence to find out whether there is an error. If you find an error in any one of the parts (A, B, C), indicate your response by marking the letter related to that part. If a sentence has no error, indicate this by marking '(D)' which stands for "No error". Errors may belong to grammar, usage or idiom. Ignore errors of punctuation, if any.*

1. (A) We are meeting today afternoon/(B) to discuss the matter/(C) and reach a compromise./(D) No error.

2. (A) Either Ram or/(B) you is responsible/(C) for this action./(D) No error.

3. (A) The student flatly denied/(B) that he had copied/(C) in the examination hall./(D) No error.

4. (A) By the time you arrive tomorrow/(B) I have finished/(C) my work./(D) No error.

5. (A) The speaker stressed repeatedly on/(B) the importance of improving/(C) the condition of the slums./(D) No error.

6. (A) The captain with the members of his team/(B) are returning/(C) after a fortnight./(D) No error.

7. (A) After returning from/(B) an all-India tour/(C) I had to describe about it/(D) No error.

8. (A) The teacher asked his students/(B) if they had gone through/(C) either of the three chapters included in the prescribed text./(D) No error.

9. (A) Although they are living in the country/(B) since they were married/(C) they are now moving to the town./(D) No error.

10. (A) Do you know/(B) how old were you/(C) when you came here?/(D) No error.

11. (A) Beware of/(B) a fair-weather friend/(C) who is neither a friend in need nor a friend indeed/(D) No error.

12. (A) Copernicus proved/(B) that Earth/(C) moves round the Sun./(D) No error.

13. (A) Seldom we have been treated/(B) in such a rude manner/(C) by the police personnel./(D) No error.

14. (A) Some men are born great,/(B) some achieve greatness/(C) and some had greatness thrust on them./(D) No error.

15. (A) The property/(B) was divided/(C) among the two brothers./(D) No error.

16. (A) I am quite certain/(B) that the lady is not only greedy/(C) but miserly./(D) No error.

17. (A) The aircraft overloaded/(B) there was something wrong of the battery/(C) and the engine was making a queer noise/(D) No error.

18. (A) A thorough inquiry of the misappropriation of funds/(B) is now imperative/(C) to bring the guilty to book/(D) No error.

19. (A) The brilliant success in the examination/(B) as well as his record in sports/(C) deserves high praise/(D) No error.

20. (A) While travelling by a train/(B) on a cold winter night/(C) an argument rose between two passengers in our compartment/(D) No error.

21. (A) I cannot find/(B) where has he gone/(C) though I have tried may best/(D) No error.

22. (A) If I was/(B) the Prime Minister of India/(C) I would work wonders/(D) No error.

23. Amit's severe bout of flu/(B) debilitated him so much/(C) that he was too tired to do for work for a week./(D) No error.

24. (A) This is the crux of the entire problem;/(B) everything centres on/(C) it being resolved./ (D) No error.

25. (A) One of the major aims of the Air Force/(B) was the complete demolition of all means of transportation/(C) by the bombing of rail lines and terminals./(D) No error.

26. (A) His strong voice cut over/(B) the hum of conversation/(C) like a knife through butter./ (D) No error.

27. (A) Even though they weren't expecting us/ (B) they managed to knock up/(C) a marvellous meal./(D) No error.

28. (A) The celebrated singer was/(B) surrounded by the usual crowd/(C) of lackeys and hanger-ons./(D) No error.

29. (A) If it weren't/(B) for you,/(C) I wouldn't be alive today./(D) No error.

30. (A) He looked like a lion/(B) baulked from/ (C) its prey./(D) No error.

31. (A) Widespread flooding/(B) is effecting/(C) large areas of the villages./(D) No error.

32. (A) She regards/(B) negotiating prices with customers/(C) as her special preserve./(D) No error.

33. (A) Often in political campaigns, a point is reached at which/(B) the candidates take out their gloves./(C) and start slugging with bare fists./(D) No error.

34. (A) If we really set to/(B) we can get the whole house/(C) cleaned in an afternoon./(D) No error.

35. (A) Pieces of rock plummeted/(B) down the mountainside/(C) in the ground below./(D) No error.

36. (A) Since the two parties each won/(B) the same number of seats,/(C) the minority party holds the balance of power./(D) No error.

37. (A) It's arrogant for you/(B) to assume you'll/ (C)win every time./(D) No error.

38. (A) We've paid for our travel and accommodation,/(B) so we need only to take/ (C) some pocket-money with us./(D) No error.

39. (A) There's no evidence to show/(B) that information technology secrets are more/(C) vulnerable in India than Britain or the US./(D) No error.

40. (A) It is shameful that hunting/(B) is still considered sport/(C) by some unscrupulous people in the civilized world./(D) No error.

41. (A) The Prime Minister's good looks won him (B)the election but he has still to prove/(C) that he's not a just pretty face./(D) No error.

42. (A) The two books are the same/(B) except fo the fact that this/(C) has an answer in the back. (D) No error.

43. (A) He estimated his income tax bill/(B) by extrapolation over figures/(C) submitted i previous years./(D) No error.

44. (A) The modern office block/(B) sticks ou like a sore thumb/(C) among the old building in the area./(D) No error.

45. (A) I will try to put over/(B) some feelers t gauge/(C) people's reactions to our proposal (D) No error.

46. (A) A major contribution of Mathura sculptor (B)of that period were the creation an popularization/(C) of the Buddha's image i human form./(D) No error.

47. (A) Amit has been deceiving Mona/(B) f many years but she/(C) has not still tumble to it. (C)/No error. (D)

48. (A) Mahavira was an advocate of nonviolen and vegetarianism,/(B) who revived a reorganized the Jain doctrine/(C) a established rules for their monastic order. (No error.

49. (A) Microwaves are the principle carriers/(of television, telephone and data transmissio (C)between stations on earth and between t earth and satellites./(D) No error.

50. (A) An unit is an abstract idea,/(B) defin either by reference to/(C) a randomly chos material standard or to a natural phenomeno (D) No error.

51. (A) With the crisis deepening,/(B) the critics sense an opportunity/(C) about putting in place a more radical strategy./(D) No error.

52. (A) The salesman gave us/(B) a big spiel about why/(C) we should buy his product./(D) No error.

53. (A) I will need several weeks/(B) to invent the lie of the land before/(C) I can make any decision about the future of the business./(D) No error.

54. (A) You should be cautious/(B) and make a few discrete enquiries about/(C) the firm before you sign anything./(D) No error.

55. (A) Your husband doesn't/(B) believe that you are older/(C) than I./(D) No error.

56. (A) There is a beautiful moon out tonight/(B) and Neeta and I are going for a stroll/(C) — would you like to come along with she and I?/(D) No error.

57. (A) The data on/(B) the divorce case is/(C) on the judge's desk./(D) No error.

58. (A) The stood off/(B) from the crowd/(C) because of her height and flaming red hair./(D) No error.

59. (A) It's stupid to go/(B) to the expense of taking/(C) music lessons if you never practise/(D) No error.

60. (A) You will find it difficult/(B) to explain of your use/(C) of such offensive language/(D) No error.

61. (A) Because of the/(B) extenuating circumstances/(C) the court acquitted him out of the crime/(D) No error.

62. (A) The carpet was badly stained/(B) to such an extent that/(C) you couldn't tell its original colour/(D) No error.

63. (A) It is greatly to Amit's credit/(B) that he gave back the money he found/(C) his honesty does for him credit/(D) No error.

64. (A) A terrific hue and cry/(B) was raised/(C) at the new tax proposals/(D) No error.

65. (A) The former General was/(B) exiled of his country because of/(C) his part in the plot against the government/(D) No error.

66. (A) The company has/(B) set off itself some stiff production/(C) goals for this year/(D) No error.

67. (A) The music was so loud/(B) that we had to bellow over each/(C) other to be heard./(D) No error.

68. (A) When this beautiful girl arrived, (A) all the men in the room/(C) gravitated over her./(D) No error.

69. (A) The children are/(B) really in their element/(C) playing on the beach./(D) No error.

70. (A) The refugees are/(B) badly off for blankets,/(C) and even worse for food./(D) No error.

71. (A) From their vintage-point on the cliff,/(B) the children could watch/(C) the ships coming and going./(D) No error.

72. (A) A cogent remark/(B) compels acceptance because/(C) of their sense and logic./(D) No error.

73. (A) Credit cards have/(B) brought about a revolution/(C) in people's spending habits./(D) No error.

74. (A) In financial matters/(B) it is important to/(C) get disinterested advice./(D) No error.

75. (A) Some women admit that/(B) their principle goal in life/(C) is to marry a wealthy man./(D) No error.

76. (A) Take two spoonsful/(B) of this medicine/(C) every three hours./(D) No error.

77. (A) The film was so disjointed/(B) that I could not tell you/(C) what the story was about./(D) No error.

78. (A) He had been/(B) saved of death as if/(C) by divine intervention./(D) No error.

79. (A) I informed the principal/(B) that I was running temperature/(C) and, therefore, could not attend the meeting./(D) No error.

80. (A) The lady was broken with grief/(B) when she heard the sad news of the train disaster/(C) in which her brother was killed./(D) No error.

81. (A) The farmer is irrigating/(B) his fields/(C) since morning./(D) No error.

82. (A) I could not/(B) answer to/(C) the question./(D) No error.

83. (A) Two years passed/(B) since/(C) my cousin died./(D) No error.

84. (A) He hesitated to accept the post/(B) as he did not think/(C) that the salary would be enough for a man with a family of three (C)/ No error (D)

85. (A) Have you gone through/(B) either of these three chapters/(C) that have been included in this volume?/(D) No error.

86. (A) I am learning English/(B) for ten years/(C) without much effect/(D) No error.

87. (A) Ramesh has agreed/(B) to marry with the girl/(C) of his parent's choice (D) No error.

88. (A) The pity is that/(B) no sooner he had left the place/(C) than the fire broke out/(D) No error.

89. (A) When he was arriving/(B) the party was/(C) in full swing/(D) No error.

90. (A) The Dean wrote he constituted a committee of experts/(B) comprising of five members/(C) before the next meeting took place/(D) No error.

91. (A) Inflation and shortages/(B) have made it very difficult for him/(C) to make his both ends meet./(D) No error.

92. (A) The most studious boy/(B) in the class/(C) was made as the captain./(D) No error.

93. (A) I am participating/(B) in the two-miles race/(C) tomorrow morning./(D) No error.

94. (A) The sum and substance/(B) of his speech/(C) were essentially anti-establishment./(D) No error.

95. (A) It has been such a wonderful evening/(B) I look forward to meet you again/(C) after the vacations./(D) No error.

96. (A) When the boy committed a mistake/(B) the teacher made him to do/(C) the sum again./(D) No error.

97. (A) Unless the government does not revise its policy of liberalization/(B) the growth of the indigenous technology/(C) will be adversely affected./(D) No error.

98. (A) Supposing if you get/(B) a seat in the plane/(C) you will not take more than two hours to reach Mumbai./(D) No error.

99. (A) Whenever a person lost anything/(B) the poor folk around/(C) are suspected./(D) No error.

100. (A) Still impressive is that/(B) we achieve this selective attention/(C) through our latent ability to lip-read./(D) No error.

101. (A) The brakes and steering failed/(B) and the bus ran down the hill/(C) without anyone being able to control it./(D) No error.

102. (A) The polling was marred/(B) at many a place/(C) by attempts at rigging./(D) No error.

103. (A) He wanted to work all right/(B) but we saw that he was completely worn/(C) and so we persuaded him to stop./(D) No error.

104. (A) When a whale is washed ashore by the tide,/(B) the people flock together to see it./(C) wondering how so huge an animal can swim about in the water./(D) No error.

105. (A) Few scientists changed/(B) people's ideas as much as/(C) Darwin with his Theory of Evolution./(D) No error.

106. (A) Were he/(B) to see you,/(C) he would have been surprised./(D) No error.

107. (A) The number of marks carried by each question/(B) are indicated/(C) at the end of the question./(D) No error.

108. (A) An animal/(B) can be just as unhappy in a vast area/(C) or in a small one/(D) No error.

109. (A) It is time/(B) we did something/(C) to stop road accidents./(D) No error.

110. (A) A free press is not a privilege/(B) but the organic necessity/(C) in a free society./(D) No error.

111. (A) The Indian radio./(B) which was previously controlled by the British rulers./(C) is free now from the narrow vested interests./(D) No error.

112. (A) Because of the emergency help/(B) that the patient received./(C) he would have died/(D) No error.

113. (A) At present juncture,/(B) however, the super-computer/(C) would be a costly toy./(D) No error.

114. (A) Students should not take part/(B) in party politics and political demonstrations/(C) as they interfere in serious study./(D) No error.

15. (A) Wherever they go/(B) Indians easily adapt to/(C) local circumstances./(D) No error.

16. (A) According to the Bible/(B) it is meek and humble/(C) who shall inherit the earth./(D) No error.

17. (A) I was there/(B) many a time/(C) in the past./(D) No error.

18. (A) As much as I admire him for his sterling qualities./(B) I cannot excuse him for/(C) being unfair to his friends./(D) No error.

19. (A) Were you/(B) given a choice/(C) or you had to do it?/(D) No error.

20. (A) When he was asked what is wrong with him,/(B) he said that he was not well,/(C) and asked for leave of absence for one day./(D) No error.

21. (A) At the end of the year/(B) every student who had done adequate work/(C) was automatically promoted./(D) No error.

22. (A) Many times the news has been published/(B) in the papers that the end of the world will be certain/(C) if a nuclear war breaks out./(D) No error.

3. (A) Happily, zoos were/(B) unwilling to cooperate/(C) in a scheme that was potentially harmful to animal welfare./(D) No error.

4. (A) We discussed about the problem so thoroughly/(B) on the eve of the examination/(C) that I found it very easy to work it out./(D) No error.

5. (A) She reluctantly said that/(B) if nobody else was doing it/(C) she will do it./(D) No error.

6. (A) He will end up his work/(B) in the city/(C) by the end of the year./(D) No error.

7. (A) Though child marriage/(B) has been banned,/(C) the custom still prevailed among some groups in India./(D) No error.

128. (A) Supposing if/(B) there is no bus,/(C) how will you get there?(D) No error.

129. (A) At the moment the house/(B) was burgled the family/(C) attended a night party in the neighbourhood./(D) No error.

130. (A) On a holiday/(B) Sudha prefers reading/(C) than going out visiting friends/(D) No error.

131. (A) Neither he/(B) nor his father is interested/(C) in joining the party./(D) No error.

132. (A) A group of friends/(B) want to visit/(C) the new plant as early as possible./(D) No error.

133. (A) May I/(B) know who you want/(C) to see please/(D) No error.

134. (A) Myself and Gopal/(B) will take care of/(C) the function on Sunday./(D) No error.

135. (A) I could not put up in a hotel/(B) because the boarding and lodging charges/(C) were exorbitant./(D) No error.

136. (A) He is not coming tomorrow/(B) as he is having a pain in the chest/(C) and has to see a doctor./(D) No error.

137. (A) They have been/(B) very close friends/(C) until they quarrelled./(D) No error.

138. (A) Since India has gained Independence/(B) 49 years ago,/(C) much progress has been made in almost every field./(D) No error.

139. (A) The party chief made it a point to state that/(B) the Prime Minister and the Union Home Minister should also come/(C) and they see what his party men had seen./(D) No error.

140. (A) Due to me being a newcomer/(B) I was unable to get a house/(C) suitable for my wife and me./(D) No error.

141. (A) The reason why/(B) he was rejected/(C) was because he was too young./(D) No error.

142. (A) The scientist must follow/(B) his hunches and his data/(C) wherever it may lead./(D) No error.

143. (A) Firstly you should/(B) think over the meaning of the words/(C) and then use them./(D) No error.

144. (A) Scarcely had/(B) I arrived than/(C) the train left./(D) No error.

145. (A) Unless you stop to make noise at once/(B) I will have no option but to/(C) bring the matter to the attention of the police./(D) No error.

146. (A) He couldn't but help/(B) shedding tears at the plight of the villagers/(C) rendered homeless by a devastating cyclone./(D) No error.

147. (A) Since it was his first election campaign, the candidate was confused;/(B) none could clearly understand/(C) either the principles he stood for or the benefits he promised./(D) No error.

148. (A) It is an established fact that the transcendental American poets and philosophers,/(B) who lived in the latter half of the nineteenth century,/(C) were more influenced by Indian philosophy, in particular by Upanishadic Philosophy./(D) No error.

149. (A) The crew were on board/(B) and they soon busied themselves/(C) in preparing to meet the storm./(D) No error.

150. (A) One of the members/(B) expressed doubt if/(C) the Minister was an athiest./(D) No error.

ANSWERS

1	2	3	4	5	6	7	8	9	10
A	B	D	B	A	B	C	C	B	D
11	**12**	**13**	**14**	**15**	**16**	**17**	**18**	**19**	**20**
D	B	A	C	C	C	B	A	D	C
21	**22**	**23**	**24**	**25**	**26**	**27**	**28**	**29**	**30**
B	A	C	C	B	A	A	C	C	C
31	**32**	**33**	**34**	**35**	**36**	**37**	**38**	**39**	**40**
C	A	A	A	C	A	A	B	D	B
41	**42**	**43**	**44**	**45**	**46**	**47**	**48**	**49**	**50**
C	C	C	D	A	B	C	C	A	A
51	**52**	**53**	**54**	**55**	**56**	**57**	**58**	**59**	**60**
C	D	D	D	C	C	D	A	B	B
61	**62**	**63**	**64**	**65**	**66**	**67**	**68**	**69**	**70**
C	A	C	A	B	B	B	C	B	D
71	**72**	**73**	**74**	**75**	**76**	**77**	**78**	**79**	**80**
A	C	D	D	D	A	B	B	B	A
81	**82**	**83**	**84**	**85**	**86**	**87**	**88**	**89**	**90**
A	B	A	D	B	A	B	B	A	B
91	**92**	**93**	**94**	**95**	**96**	**97**	**98**	**99**	**100**
C	C	B	C	B	B	A	A	A	C
101	**102**	**103**	**104**	**105**	**106**	**107**	**108**	**109**	**110**
C	D	B	D	A	A	B	C	D	B
111	**112**	**113**	**114**	**115**	**116**	**117**	**118**	**119**	**120**
C	A	A	C	B	B	A	A	A	A
121	**122**	**123**	**124**	**125**	**126**	**127**	**128**	**129**	**130**
D	D	C	A	C	A	C	A	A	C
131	**132**	**133**	**134**	**135**	**136**	**137**	**138**	**139**	**140**
D	B	B	A	A	C	A	A	C	A
141	**142**	**143**	**144**	**145**	**146**	**147**	**148**	**149**	**150**
C	C	A	B	A	A	D	C	C	B

SENTENCE COMPLETION

Filling the blanks is such an exercise which starts with the primary schools and continues in the highest level of competitive examinations. One must practise it regularly to score well.

Directions (Qs. 1-150) : *Pick out the most effective word(s) from the given words to fill in the blanks to make the sentence meaningfully complete.*

1. You must ensure the correctness of the information before ....

A. drawing B. enabling
C. learning D. jumping

2. The rocket .... the target and did not cause any casualty.

A. sensed B. reached
C. missed D. exploded

3. It is desirable to take .... in any business if you want to make profit.

A. advice B. risk
C. loan D. recourse

4. They wasted all the money on purchase of some .... items.

A. excellent B. important
C. significant D. trivial

5. When he found the wallet his face glowed but soon it faded as the wallet was ....

A. empty B. vacant
C. recovered D. stolen

6. He has served the country by .... many significant positions.

A. appointing B. creating
C. developing D. holding

7. The frequent errors are a result of the student's ....

A. talent B. smartness
C. carelessness D. perception

8. The robbers eventually .... in breaking into the house.

A. succeeded B. decided
C. caught D. trained

9. I finally .... her to stay another day.

A. advised B. persuaded
C. suggested D. called

10. Most of the people who .... the book exhibition were teachers.

A. witnessed B. presented
C. conducted D. attended

11. One requires great .... to teach and handle little children who are restless.

A. patience B. attitude
C. determination D. knowledge

12. The researchers will .... some of the causes of increasing poverty in the state.

A. fund B. investigate
C. promote D. circulate

13. I usually perform .... when nobody is watching me.

A. alone B. good
C. better D. hard

14. It was .... to everyone that the minister had been drinking.

A. observed B. known
C. discovered D. realised

15. I would rather stay indoors .... the rain stops.

A. so B. waiting
C. until D. usually

16. The process should be completed as far as possible within a week, ... which the matter should be brought to notice of the officer concerned.

A. following B. failing
C. realizing D. referring

17. The officers are ..... to regular transfers.
A. free B. open
C. subject D. available

18. All letters received from Government should ..... be acknowledged.
A. suddenly B. obviously
C. immediately D. occasionally

19. Mumbai office ..... a meeting of senior officials to discuss the high incidence of frauds.
A. attended B. convened
C. reported D. registered

20. The note should be ..... to all the concerned departments for their consideration.
A. regulated B. requested
C. carried D. forwarded

21. Your present statement does not .... what you said last week.
A. accord to B. accord in
C. accord with D. accord for

22. I had a vague .... that the lady originally belonged to Scotland.
A. notion B. expression
C. imagination D. theory

23. The prisoner showed no .... for his crimes.
A. hatred B. obstinacy
C. remorse D. anger

24. It is inconceivable that in many schools children are subjected to physical .... in the name of discipline.
A. violation B. exercise
C. violence D. security

25. We have not yet fully realised the .... consequences of the war.
A. happy B. pleasing
C. grim D. exciting

26. Happiness consists in being .... what we have.
A. contented to B. contented with
C. contented for D. contented in

27. His rude behaviour is a .... his organization.
A. disgrace for B. disgrace on
C. disgrace upon D. disgrace to

28. No child is .... understanding. One has to wait and provide proper guidance.
A. dull to B. dull in
C. dull of D. dull for

29. I am fully .... the problems facing the industry.
A. alive with B. alive to
C. alive for D. alive on

30. The Romans were .... science.
A. bad in B. bad to
C. bad for D. bad at

31. Although I was .... of his plans, I encouraged him, because there was no one else who was willing to help.
A. sceptical B. remorseful
C. fearful D. excited

32. You have no business to .... pain on a weak and poor person.
A. inflict B. put
C. direct D. force

33. Her uncle died in a car accident. He was quite rich. She suddenly .... all her uncle's money.
A. succeeded B. caught
C. gave D. inherited

34. There was a major accident. The plane crashed. The pilot .... did not see the tower.
A. likely B. probably
C. scarcely D. hurriedly

35. The car we were travelling in .... a mile from home.
A. broke off B. broke down
C. broke into D. broke up

36. What are you .... in the kitchen cupboard?
A. looking in B. looking on
C. looking to D. looking for

37. I did not see the point of .... waiting for them, so I went home.
A. hanging around B. hang on
C. hang together D. hanging up

38. He lost confidence and .... of the deal at the last minute.
A. backed out B. backed on
C. backed down D. backed onto

39. To the dismay of all the students, the class monitor was ..... berated by the Principal at a school assembly.
A. critically B. ignominiously
C. prudently D. fortuitously

40. All attempts to revive the fishing industry were ..... failure.
A. foredoomed to B. heading at
C. predicted for D. estimated to

41. There are ..... parked outside than yesterday.
A. fewer cars
B. few cars
C. less cars
D. a small number of cars

42. The minister had to ..... some awkward questions from reporters.
A. fend B. fend at
C. fend out D. fend off

43. The ..... of evidence was on the side of the plaintiff since all but one of the witnesses testified that his story was correct.
A. propensity B. force
C. preponderance D. brunt

44. Attention to detail is ..... of a fine craftsman.
A. hallmark B. stamp
C. seal of authority D. authenticity

45. Behaving in a .... and serious way, even in a .... situation, makes people respect you.
A. Calm, difficult B. steady, angry
C. flamboyant, tricky D. cool astounding

46. Along with a sharp rise in ...., a recession would eventually result in more men, women, and children living in ....
A. crime, apathy
B. fatalities, poor
C. deaths, slums
D. unemployment, poverty

47. The government has .... to provide financial aid to the ones .... by severe floods in the city.
A. desired, troubled B. promised, havoc
C. failed, affected D. wanted, struck

48. An airplane with .... passengers on board made an unscheduled .... as the airport to which it was heading was covered with thick fog.
A. imitable, slip B. faulty, stop
C. variety, halt D. numerous, landing

49. Deemed universities .... huge fees, but have not been successful in providing .... education to our students.
A. collect, maintaining
B. pay, better
C. ask, good
D. charge, quality

50. If the banks desire to .... profit, they should get rid of .... measures.
A. lose, concentrate
B. increase, populist
C. earn, unhealthy
D. maximise, traditional

51. Leadership defines what the future should look like and ...... people with that vision.
A. aligns B. develops
C. trains D. encourages

52. We upset ourselves by responding in an ...... manner to someone else's actions.
A. unabashed B. irrational
C. arduous D. arguable

53. All the people involved in that issue feel a great ...... to his suggestion.
A. contradiction B. adherence
C. indifference D. repugnance

54. These elections will be remembered as much for its anti-incumbency mood as for its ...... mandate
A. invincible B. rational
C. unprecedented D. deliberate

55. How do you expect us to stay in such a ...... building even if it can be hired on a nominal rent?
A. scruffy B. disperate
C. fragmented D. robust

56. ...... efforts from all concerned are required to raise the social and economic conditions of our countrymen.
A. Perpetual B. Dynamic
C. Massive D. Exploring

57. Many companies see technology as a ...... for a whole host of business problems.
A. consideration B. preference
C. linking D. panacea

58. Known as devout and serious person, she also has ...... sense of humour
A. better B. plentiful
C. quick D. good

59. The matter would have become serious if ...... action had not been taken
A. hasty B. fast
C. timely D. unusual

60. The ...... with which he is able to yield the paint brush is really remarkable.
A. ease B. practice
C. majesty D. sweep

61. The speaker did not properly use the time as he went on ...... on one point alone.
A. devoting B. deliberating
C. diluting D. dilating

62. They decided to ...... down their original plans for the bigger house and make it smaller.
A. climb B. turn
C. scale D. play

63. Usha was badly ...... by the news which she got in the letter
A. electrified B. petrified
C. deranged D. shaken

64. In spite of her other ......, she still managed to find time for her hobbies
A. occupations B. preoccupations
C. predilections D. business

65. Success comes to those who are vigilant not to permit ...... from the chosen path
A. distraction B. deviation
C. alienation D. diversion

66. It is advisable to ...... on this issue rather than create unnecessary problem by taking a rigid stand
A. lose B. promise
C. evade D. compromise

67. After a short holiday she came back totally ......
A. rejuvenated B. reborn
C. refurbished D. revamped

68. The victim tried to tell us what had happened but his ...... were not audible.
A. assailants B. sounds
C. letters D. words

69. The ...... between the twins is so slight that it is very difficult to identify one from the other.
A. similarity B. distance
C. resemblance D. difference

70. The members were ...... of the date of the meeting well in advance.
A. communicated B. conveyed
C. ignorant D. informed

71. A ...... of ships was kept ready to scour the sea in case of an emergency.
A. group B. pack
C. unit D. fleet

72. I had not expected to meet him; it was quite an ...... meeting.
A. organised B. intentional
C. undesirable D. accidental

73. The window of our room ...... the rear.
A. overlooks B. opens
C. opposes D. adjoins

74. I could ...... see the sight since it was dark.
A. clearly B. barely
C. obviously D. aptly

75. The top-ranking manager ...... his success in the profession to his Managing Director's guidance.
A. account B. agrees
C. attributes D. claims

76. Does your pride keep you ...... making the decision you know you should?
A. away B. alert
C. from D. quiet

77. Their ...... to scale the mountain peak was an absolute failure.
A. attempt B. desire
C. anxiety D. proposal

78. The writer, like a spider ...... a web; the creatures caught in the web have no substance, no reality.
A. spins B. catches
C. writes D. compiles

79. In a ...... move the Chief Minister today dropped two ministers from the cabinet.
A. secret B. delicate
C. continuous D. surprise

80. In his address to the teachers, the Vice-Chancellor ...... certain measures being taken for improving the quality of college education.
A. declined B. directed
C. advised D. highlighted

81. Change the legal system are inevitable for we are not working for a ...... society.
A. backward B. dynamic
C. stagnant D. modern

82. Modern science began ...... the influence of Copernicus, Kepler, Galileo and Newton.
A. by B. under
C. from D. upon

83. A meeting of senior police officers was held to ...... the law and order situation of the town.
A. review B. curb
C. cover D. support

84. The problems that India's economic development faces are ......
A. myopic B. dubious
C. enormous D. strong

85. In our zeal for progress we should not ...... the executive with more powers.
A. avoid B. arm
C. give D. enhance

86. At present, all over the world, moral standards, ... to have fallen.
A. look B. wish
C. started D. appear

87. He was one of the ...... spirits behind the successful lagitation of the citizens for keeping the city clean.
A. revolving B. moving
C. evolving D. amazing

88. You've never ...... me about your experiences in Scotland.
A. described B. explained
C. told D. said

89. The student ...... that book from the library to study at home.
A. issued B. borrowed
C. hired D. lent

90. I wish I ...... a king.
A. was B. am
C. should be D. were

91. He ...... to listen to my arguments and walked away.
A. denied B. disliked
C. objected D. refused

92. The flow of blood was so ...... that the patient died.
A. intense B. adequate
C. profuse D. extensive

93. When I met her yesterday, it was the first time I ...... her since Christmas.
A. saw B. have seen
C. had seen D. have been seing

94. Can you pay ...... all these articles?
A. for B. of
C. off D. out

95. He ...... the role of the organisation in creating environmental awareness among the people.
A. commanded B. commended
C. commented D. commemorated

96. I ...... you to be at the party this evening.
A. expect B. hope
C. look forward to D. desire

97. The consequence of economic growth has now ...... to the lowest level.
A. flowed B. percolated
C. gone D. crept

98. The employees were unhappy because their salary was not increased ......
A. marginally B. abruptly
C. substantially D. superflously

99. ...... the being a handicapped person, he is very co-operative and self-reliant.
A. Because B. Although
C. Since D. Despite

100. The child broke ...... from his mother and ran towards the painting.
A. away B. after
C. down D. with

101. With his ...... income, he finds it difficult to live a comfortable life.
A. brief B. sufficient
C. meagre D. huge

102. He could ...... a lot of money in such a short time by using his intelligence and working hard.
A. spend B. spoil
C. exchange D. accumulate

103. Though the brothers are twins, they look ......
A. alike B. handsome
C. indifferent D. different

104. Unfavourable weather conditions can ..... illness.
A. cure B. detect
C. treat D. enhance

105. No sooner did the bell ring, ... the actor started singing.
A. when B. than
C. after D. before

106. If I ...... realised it, I would not have acted on his advice.
A. was B. had
C. were D. have

107. Why don't you ...... your work in advance before commencing it.
A. start B. complete
C. finish D. plan

108. Contemporary economic development differs ...... from the Industrial Revolution of the 19th century.
A. usually B. specially
C. literally D. markedly

109. Mounting unemployment is the most serous and ...... problem faced by India today.
A. profound B. intractable
C. unpopular D. dubious

110. Unemployment is not only ...... throughout the emerging world, but is growing worse, especially in urban areas.
A. endemic B. peripheral
C. absorbing D. prolific

111. Manpower is the ...... means of converting other resources to mankind's use and benefit.
A. inimitable B. indivisible
C. indispensable D. inequitable

112. This article tries to ...... us with problems of poor nations so that we help them more effectively.
A. enable B. convince
C. allow D. acquaint

113. Among human beings, language is the principal ...... of communication.
A. methodology B. instrument
C. accomplishment D. theory

114. These essays are intellectually ...... are represent various levels of complexity.
A. persistent B. superior
C. modern D. demanding

115. ...... the doctor's advice he started taking some daily exercise.
A. In B. To
C. On D. Towards

116. Do you ...... giving that book to me for a few days?
A. desires B. mind
C. call D. observe

117. Our volunteers will ...... your donations either in cash or kind and give you a receipt.
A. lend B. gave
C. return D. collect

118. If you need some money, I will ...... the amount from my bank and give you.
A. deposit B. return
C. withdraw D. require

119. ...... he wanted to attend his friend's party, he could not attend it.
A. As B. But
C. Since D. Although

120. The boss considered the situation and ...... only three days leave to him.
A. granted B. submitted
C. sanction D. asked

121. If you want to do well, you must follow strict ...... in your studies.
A. discipline B. belief
C. view D. report

122. It was very difficult to dig as the ground was very ......

A. thin B. soft
C. rigid D. hard

123. He was ...... with a serious crime.

A. condemned B. charged
C. accused D. convicted

124. The oil crisis highlighted the need to develop new ...... of energy and to conserve those which are already in use.

A. means B. preserves
C. methods D. sources

125. The wood always ...... on water.

A. floated B. floats
C. was floating D. float

126. He finds it difficult to ...... between blue and green as he is colour blind.

A. recognise B. see
C. distinguish D. study

127. The bright colour of this shirt has ...... away.

A. faded B. paled
C. disappeared D. gone

128. The ...... animal was on the look out for food.

A. savage B. uncivilised
C. primitive D. wild

129. The bank clerk tried to ...... money from his friend's account.

A. embezzle B. embroil
C. embellish D. empower

130. The movement of the train was so ...... that all the passengers slept very well.

A. noisy B. fast
C. soothing D. distracting

131. That rule is applicable ...... everyone.

A. to B. for
C. about D. with

132. Besides other provisions, that shopkeeper deals ...... cosmetics too.

A. with B. in
C. at D. for

133. The music for event was ...... by A.R. Rahman.

A. made B. composed
C. demonstrated D. displayed

134. The reward is a ...... of her service to mankind.

A. recognition B. witness
C. memorial D. memento

135. The most important task of the Air Force is to ...... the country against an air attack by an enemy.

A. secure B. save
C. defend D. protect

136. The ruling party will have to put its own house ...... order.

A. in B. on
C. to D. into

137. As a general rule, politicians do not ...... centre stage.

A. forward B. forbid
C. forgive D. forsake

138. Shivam ...... classical music. He always prefers Bhimsen Joshi to Asha Bhonsale, and Pandit Jasraj to Kumar Sanu.

A. adores B. apprehends
C. encompasses D. cultivates

139. Indications are that the Government is ...... to the prospect of granting bonus to the striking employees.

A. aligned B. obliged
C. reconciled D. relieved

140. The ...... study on import of natural gas from Iran through a pipeline would be completed shortly.

A. natural B. calculated
C. economic D. feasibility

141. His party is solely to be blamed for the political ...... in the country.

A. devaluation B. revival
C. advocacy D. stalemate

142. We still have not given our ...... to conduct the survey of natural resources in our State.

A. projection B. consent
C. request D. compliance

143. He is the best man for this job. He has mental ...... to carry it out.

A. predilection B. durability
C. adroitness D. persuasion

144. Man is ......; however, he is more in need of mental companionship than of physical companionship.
A. egoistic B. biological
C. emotional D. gregarious

145. We cannot go on strike every year. Now that we have gone on strike we must ...... this issue.
A. clinch B. culminate
C. cross D. canvass

146. I was totally ...... by his line of thinking and could not put forth any argument.
A. demolished B. nonplussed
C. exhausted D. refuted

147. Any problem to be ...... needs to be broken down to small pieces.
A. chosen B. taught
C. tackled D. posed

148. He has ...... people visiting him at his house because he fears it will cause discomfort to neighbours.
A. forbidden B. warned
C. stopped D. request

149. Nowadays, why ...... people so scared of each other?
A. were B. is
C. had D. are

150. If the perceptions of two individuals do not ...... there is bound to be problems.
A. reflect B. differ
C. match D. express

ANSWERS

1	**2**	**3**	**4**	**5**	**6**	**7**	**8**	**9**	**10**
A	C	B	D	A	D	C	A	B	D
11	**12**	**13**	**14**	**15**	**16**	**17**	**18**	**19**	**20**
A	B	C	A	C	B	C	C	B	D
21	**22**	**23**	**24**	**25**	**26**	**27**	**28**	**29**	**30**
C	A	C	C	C	B	D	B	B	D
31	**32**	**33**	**34**	**35**	**36**	**37**	**38**	**39**	**40**
B	C	C	B	C	C	D	A	B	A
41	**42**	**43**	**44**	**45**	**46**	**47**	**48**	**49**	**50**
A	D	D	A	A	D	C	D	C	B
51	**52**	**53**	**54**	**55**	**56**	**57**	**58**	**59**	**60**
A	A	D	C	A	A	D	D	C	A
61	**62**	**63**	**64**	**65**	**66**	**67**	**68**	**69**	**70**
D	C	D	B	A	D	A	D	D	D
71	**72**	**73**	**74**	**75**	**76**	**77**	**78**	**79**	**80**
D	D	A	B	C	C	A	A	D	D
81	**82**	**83**	**84**	**85**	**86**	**87**	**88**	**89**	**90**
C	B	A	C	B	D	B	C	B	D
91	**92**	**93**	**94**	**95**	**96**	**97**	**98**	**99**	**100**
D	C	C	B	B	A	B	C	D	A
101	**102**	**103**	**104**	**105**	**106**	**107**	**108**	**109**	**110**
C	D	D	D	B	B	D	D	B	A
111	**112**	**113**	**114**	**115**	**116**	**117**	**118**	**119**	**120**
C	D	B	D	C	B	D	C	D	A
121	**122**	**123**	**124**	**125**	**126**	**127**	**128**	**129**	**130**
A	D	B	D	B	C	A	D	A	C
131	**132**	**133**	**134**	**135**	**136**	**137**	**138**	**139**	**140**
A	B	B	A	C	A	D	A	C	D
141	**142**	**143**	**144**	**145**	**146**	**147**	**148**	**149**	**150**
D	B	C	D	A	B	C	C	D	C

SYNONYMS AND ANTONYMS

English is the most popular language of the world. It comprises thousands of words. No one can remember all the words and their meanings but everyone must try to read and learn the maximum number of words and their meanings. Readers must keep and use a dictionary religiously.

ABANDON

Syn.: discard, desert, discontinue, renounce, relinquish, abnegate, forsake, surrender, give up, quit.

Ant.: retain, maintain, uphold, stay, remain.

ABATE

Syn.: lessen, decrease, diminish, subside, slacken, subside, allay, reduce, curtail.

Ant.: increase, enlarge, heighten, intensify, raise.

ABBREVIATE

Syn.: shorten, abridge, compress, curtain, condense, contract, prune, truncate, reduce.

Ant.: enlarge, expand, lengthen, extend, elongate, prolong, protract.

ABILITY

Syn.: competence, aptitude, capability, talent, intelligence, cleverness, capacity.

Ant.: inability, incompetence, incapacity, incapability, inaptitude.

ABLE

Syn.: capable, competent, intelligent, talented, efficient, skilful.

Ant.: unable, incapable, inefficient, incompetent.

ABRUPT

Syn.: sudden, curt, steep, hasty, unexpected, disconnected, disjointed, brusque, rough.

Ant.: expected, anticipated, gradual, courteous, smooth.

ABSURD

Syn.: illogical, irrational, inconsistent, silly, inane, unreasonable, funny, ridiculous, laughable, ludicrous, nonsensical, fatuous.

Ant.: logical, reasonable, rational, consistent, sensible, sound, proper, sane.

ACCURATE

Syn.: exact, precise, correct, actual, just, right, correct.

Ant.: incorrect, inexact, improper, fallacious, inaccurate, misleading, erroneous.

ADEQUATE

Syn.: ample, abundant, enough, sufficient, plentiful, copious.

Ant.: inadequate, insufficient, meagre, scant, scantly, skimpy.

AFFABLE

Syn.: urbane, polite, friendly, courteous, amiable, suave, good-tempered.

Ant.: impolite, unfriendly, discourteous, haughty.

AKIN

Syn.: kindred, similar, allied, cognate, alike, related, analogous.

Ant.: dissimilar, unrelated, unallied, unconnected, different, unlike, separate.

ALERT

Syn.: wary, vigilant, watchful, attentive, heedful, cautious, lively, fully awake.

Ant.: unwatchful, sluggish, relaxed, quiet, restful.

ABNORMAL

Syn.: unusual, irregular, anomalous, unnatural, odd, strange, erratic.

Ant.: usual, regular, natural, normal, customary.

ACTIVE

Syn.: brisk, energetic, lively, nimble, agile.

Ant.: inactive, indolent, sluggish, lazy, passive, torpid.

ACTUAL

Syn.: real, genuine, authentic, true, concrete, factual, existing.

Ant.: unreal, implied, assumed, false, imaginary, fictitious.

AMBIGUOUS

Syn.: vague, uncertain, undecided, undefined, obscure, doubtful, indistinct, dubious, perplexing.

Ant.: lucid, plain, clear, obvious, unambiguous, unmistakable, indisputable.

APT

Syn.: appropriate, apposite, suitable, fitting, pertinent, germane, relevant, congruent, harmonious, congruous.

Ant.: inapt, inappropriate, incongruous, improper, unsuitable, inapposite, irrelevant.

ARDENT

Syn.: fervid, fervent, warm, impassioned, plowing, intense, eager, earnest, passionate, hearty, cordial, enthusiastic.

Ant.: cool, indifferent, apathetic, nonchalant, unimpassioned.

ATROCIOUS

Syn.: nefarious, heinous, cruel, outrageous, beastly, horrible, horrendous.

Ant.: noble, humane, honourable, laudable, admirable, moral.

AUDACIOUS

Syn.: bold, daring, fearless, impudent, brash, rash, reckless, impertinent, madcap, insolent, brave, disrespectful, intrepid.

Ant.: cowardly, timid, fearful, meek, humble, afraid, frightened, scared, different, panicky, apprehensive, shy, mousy, timorous, fidgety.

AUTHENTIC

Syn.: genuine, real, trustworthy, true, reliable, accurate, authoritative, sound, tangible, definite, actual, precise, exact, correct, factual, veritable, sterling.

Ant.: apocryphal, unreliable, spurious, false, fictitious, fake, sham, imaginary, counterfeit, baseless, untrue.

BEAUTIFUL

Syn.: catching, prepossessing, fetching, cute, enticing, engaging, attractive, charming, fascinating, captivating, alluring, tempting, lovely, bewitching, reductive, pretty, enchanting, winning, comely.

Ant.: ugly, unattractive, unprepossessing, repulsive, gaunt, haggard, unpleasing, revolting, hideous.

BITTER

Syn.: tart, harsh, pungent, unpalatable, acrid, spiteful, cutting, stinging, sour, unpleasant, sarcastic, resentful, biting, sardonic, caustic, severe, acrimonious, poignant, distasteful.

Ant.: tasty, toothsome, tasteful, palatable, pleasant, delicious, warm.

BRIGHT

Syn.: brilliant, shining, luminous, lustrous, radiant sparkling, quick-witted, cheerful, clever resplendent, flashing, lucid, limpid, sagacious keen, astute, shrewd, brainy, intelligent.

Ant.: dull, ignorant, cheerless, imbecite, murky dark, gloomy, sullen.

BRIEF

Syn.: compendious, concise, short, terse, laconic curt, succinct, condensed, compact, pithy.

Ant.: long, lengthy, prolonged, protracted elongated, lengthened, extended, detailed, prolix verbose, wordy.

BRUTAL

Syn.: atrocious, savage, beastly, brutish, fiendish devilish, barbarous, cruel, ruthless, merciless, crude ferocious, bestial, heinous.

Ant.: humane, gentle, civilised, merciful, polished sympathetic, tender, liberal, considerate, good natured.

CANDID

Syn.: frank, outspoken, sincere, impartial, hones artless, ingenuous, straightforward.

Ant.: sly, wily, insincere, reserved, unfair, evasiv

CAPRICIOUS

Syn.: unpredictable, impulsive, fickle, changeabl inconstant, whimsical.

Ant.: constant, firm, steadfast, unswerving.

CARELESS

Syn.: heedless, inattentive, indifferent, negliger remiss, lax, unmindful.

Ant.: cautious, vigilant, careful, mindful, attentiv

CERTAIN

Syn.: indisputable, reliable, sure, definit undisputed, unmistakable, positive, absolute.

Ant.: uncertain, disputable, doubtful, indefini ambiguous, dubious, questionable.

CHEEK

Syn.: impudence, impertinence, effrontery, gall, temerity, audacity, insolence, sauce, sass.

Ant.: politeness, courtesy, humility, gentleness, respect.

Note: *Cheek* also means either side of the face below the eye.

Examples: She has healthy rosy *cheeks*.
They are dancing *cheek* to *cheek*.

HEERFUL

yn.: genial, happy, jolly, merry, jovial, pleasant, ively, cheery, sunny, jocund, gay.

nt.: cheerless, joyless, dejected, unhappy, doleful, orrowful, mournful, glum, dreary, dismal.

HARM (Verb)

yn.: fascinate, attract, please, delight, influence, ntice, enchant, entrance, enrapture, allure, aptivate, bewitch, ravish, tempt, lure, seduce, eguile, enthral, thrill.

nt.: repel, repulse, rebuff, snub, disgust, deter, isturb, irritate, annoy, alarm, frighten, terrify.

OMFORTABLE

yn.: cosy, snug, pleasant, pleasing, pleasurable, atisfied.

nt.: uncomfortable, disagreeable, dissatisfied, isturbed, displeasing, irritating, miserable, retched, troubled, cheerless.

OMPLETE (Adj)

yn.: whole, thorough, total, entire, full, perfect, haustive, consummate.

nt.: incomplete, imperfect, partial, unfinished, completed, unaccomplished, deficient, skimpy, etchy.

ORDIAL

n.: sincere, friendly, earnest, warm, hearty, ardent, artfelt, amiable, affable.

t.: unfriendly, insincere, cold, distant, formal, served.

URAGE

n.: bravery, boldness, valour, heroism, rlessness, intrepidity, nerve, gallantry, pluck, titude, daring.

t.: cowardice, timidity, pusillanimity, fear, funk.

CURIOUS

Syn.: inquisitive, inquiring, prying, strange, unusual, nosey, meddlesome.

Ant.: incurious, uninquiring, uninquisitive, uninterested, unconcerned, indifferent, common, usual.

CORRECT (Adj)

Syn.: accurate, proper, exact, precise, right, true, regular, perfect.

Ant.: incorrect, improper, inexact, wrong, untrue, irregular, imperfect.

DAFT

Syn.: silly, crazy, irrational, foolish, unreasonable, reckless, insane, imbecile, lumpish.

Ant.: sane, sound, sensible, deft, rational, reasonable.

DAINTY

Syn.: pretty, neat, delicate, refined, tasty, delicious, fastidious, elegant, toothsome, exquisite, cute, tasteful, palatable.

Ant.: inelegant, coarse, vulgar, rough, crude, rude, nasty, dirty.

DEEP

Syn.: abstruse, profound, intense, learned, sagacious, extreme, devious, vivid, submerged, bottomless, unfathomable, abysmal, mysterious, knotty, astute, recondite, intricate.

Ant.: shallow, apparent, familiar, artless, commonplace, ordinary, trite, naive, superficial, cursory, simple, banal.

DELIGHT

Syn.: joy, pleasure, rapture, ecstasy, enjoyment, bliss, gratification, gusto, comfort.

Ant.: displeasure, discomfort, sorrow, distress, misery, anguish, suffering, agony, woe, despair, depression.

DETRIMENTAL

Syn.: harmful, injurious, hurtful, pernicious, damaging, noxious.

Ant.: good, beneficial, valuable, useful, profitable, harmless, inoffensive, unobnoxious.

DIFFICULT

Syn.: hard, troublesome, perplexing, tough, laborious, irksome, toilsome, arduous, knotty, burdensome, uphill, herculean, enigmatic.

Ant.: easy, uncomplicated, intelligible, lucid, plain, simple, facile, manageable, tractable, elementary, rudimentary.

DILIGENT

Syn.: industrious, laborious, hard-working, attentive, assiduous, observant, mindful, vigilant, watchful, wakeful, careful.

Ant.: careless, heedless, inattentive, indifferent, unobservant, unmindful.

DISHONEST

Syn.: untrustworthy, false, fraudulent, deceitful, crooked, tricky, deceptive, treacherous, unjust, unfair, unreliable.

Ant.: trustworthy, reliable, fair, just, candid, frank, sincere, upright, truthful, veracious, honest.

DOCILE

Syn.: pliant, tractable, amenable, teachable, yielding, compliant, tame, submissive, gentle, unresisting, dutiful, passive, acquiescent, unassertive, manageable, governable, obsequious.

Ant.: obstinate, stubborn, intractable, self-willed, dogged, defiant, insolent, resistant, resisting, obdurate, disobedient, wilful, uncompromising, unyielding, refractory, recalcitrant.

DOUBTFUL

Syn.: questionable, uncertain, unsure, unlikely, improbable, disputable, debatable, dubious, controversial, fishy, moot, ambiguous.

Ant.: certain, sure, probable, indisputable. unquestionable, positive, absolute, definite, clear, unmistakable, reliable, trustworthy, undoubted, undeniable, indubitable.

DROLL

Syn.: amusing, laughable, funny, comic, sarcastic, whimsical, comical, odd, queer, farcical, ludicrous, ridiculous, absurd, diverting, rompish.

Ant.: sad, lamentable, lugubrious, tragic, painful, dolorous, hurtful, distressing, grievous, woeful, rueful, mournful, deplorable, touching.

DULL

Syn.: stupid, boring, monotonous, foolish, unintelligent, cheerless, gloomy, uninteresting, spiritless, blunt, doltish, sad, stolid, dismal, dowdy, drab, unfashionable, insensible.

Ant.: sensible, cheerful, bright, intelligent, clever, lively, animated, brilliant, sharp, talented, jolly, merry, joyful, gay, jocund, energetic, keen, active, intense, brisk, lively, trenchant, rousing.

EAGER

Syn.: ardent, earnest, zealous, keen, fervent, fervid, vehement, intent, agog, avid, excited, impatient, curious, anxious, enthusiastic, wistful, hearty, cordial, desirous.

Ant.: indifferent, disinterested, cool, loath, unconcerned, apathetic, reluctant, unwilling, disinclined.

EFFICIENT

Syn.: capable, able, competent, gifted, effective, effectual, efficacious, skilful, proficient, talented, intelligent, adept.

Ant.: inefficient, incompetent, ineffectual, unskilled, inexpert.

ELIGIBLE

Syn.: fit, suitable, desirable, worthy, qualified, acceptable, right.

Ant.: unfit, unsuitable, unworthy, unacceptable, undesirable, unqualified.

EMPHEMERAL

Syn.: short-lived, transitory, transient, fleeting, momentary, fugitive, evanescent, fugacious, temporary.

Ant.: eternal, perpetual, perennial, permanent, intransient, lifelong, everlasting, long-lived, prolonged, protracted.

ENORMOUS

Syn.; immense, gigantic, colossal, huge, vast, gargantuan, monstrous, prodigious, stupendous, plentiful, plenteous, copious.

Ant.: trivial, insignificant, ordinary, average, small little, tiny, diminutive.

ENOUGH

Syn.: plenty, ample, sufficient, abundant, adequate

Ant.: insufficient, inadequate, meagre, scanty deficient, scant, jejune, skimpy.

ENTHUSIASM

Syn.: verve, ardour, zeal, fervour, fanaticism.

Ant.: apathy, indifference, detachment, ennui unconcern, lethargy, weariness, exhaustion lassitude, languor.

EXPERT (Adj)
Syn.: adept, skilled, adroit, proficient, skilful, deft, dexterous, versed, accomplished.
Ant.: inexpert, unskilful, unskilled, maladroit, clumsy, lungling, unqualified, raw, inexperienced, green, incompetent.

FACE (V)
Syn.: confront, oppose, defy, meet, encounter, resist.
Ant.: avoid, shun, elude, avert, eschew.

FAITHFUL
Syn.: loyal, trustworthy, conscientious, true, accurate, devoted, exact, reliable, staunch, steadfast, constant, dependable, compliant.
Ant.: disloyal, untrustworthy, inaccurate, inexact, unreliable, unfaithful, treacherous, undependable, untrue, fickle.

FICKLE
Syn.: inconstant, disloyal, unfaithful, capricious, impulsive, unpredictable, changeable, unstable, variable, vacillating, wavering, fanciful, whimsical, mutable, irresolute, erratic, unreliable, fitful.
Ant.: steady, steadfast, unchangeable, unwavering, constant, loyal, faithful, reliable, dependable, stable, immutable, invariable.

FIT (Adj)
Ant.: suitable, appropriate, proper, advantageous, sound, well, meet, becoming, fitting, qualified, apt, apposite, decent, decorous, congruent, congruous, concordant, harmonious, eligible.
Ant.: unfit, unsuitable, unbecoming, disadvantageous, unwell, indecent, indecorous, improper, inappropriate, inapt, incongruent, ineligible.

FOOLISH
Syn.: silly, stupid, unwise, ridiculous, absurd, asinine, imbecile, indiscreet, irrational, idiotic, brainless, senseless, nonsensical, witless, preposterous, inane, fatuous, imprudent, inconsistent, illogical, laughable, paradoxical, dotty.
Ant.: wise, sane, prudent, discreet, sound, sensible, rational, sagacious, judicious, sage.
Note: Each of the following words means *foolish person.*

FRIENDLY
Syn.: kindly, pleasantly, amicable, cordial, hearty, warm-hearted, affable, genial, well-inclined, good-tempered, amiable, favourable, pleasing, sociable, companionable, nice, neighbourly, benevolent, well-disposed.
Ant.: hostile, unsociable, unfavourable, unfriendly, adverse, inimical, antagonistic, distant, reserved, cool, ill-inclined, ill-disposed, resistant, opposed.

FUNDAMENTAL
Syn.: basic, primary, essential, cardinal, indispensable, original, rudimentary, elementary, radical, most important, prime, chief.
Ant.: secondary, subordinate, minor, inferior, resultant, second-rate, subsidiary.

FUNNY
Syn.: amusing, jocular, jocose, laughable, eccentric, absurd, droll, comical, comic, playful, ludicrous, farcical, humorous, ridiculous, odd, queer, diverting, strange.
Ant.: sad, serious, solemn, sober, sedate, staid, grave, sorrowful, mournful.

GARRULOUS
Syn.: talkative, chatty, verbose, loquacious, communicative, glib, voluble, prolix, wordy, long-winded, diffuse, profuse, discussive, rambling, circumlocutory, maundering, periphrastic.
Ant.: laconic, reticent, silent, taciturn, uncommunicative, terse, reserved, short-spoken.

GENUINE
Syn.: authentic, sound, true, real, pure, veritable, unadulterated, unalloyed, unaffected, natural, factual, actual, legitimate, undistorted, tangible, valid, sterling.
Ant.: sham, spurious, fictitious, artificial, adulterated, alloyed, impure, apocryphal, untrue, fallacious, unsound, invalid.

GIFTED
Syn.: talented, intelligent, sagacious, competent, wise, able, proficient, efficient, capable, shrewd, inventive, skilful, ingenious, experienced.
Ant.: foolish, doltish, silly, stupid, idiotic.

GLORIOUS

Syn.: famous, beautiful, splendid, magnificent, enjoyable, pleasant, grand, exalted, lofty, majestic, sublime, noble, bright, radiant, renowned.

Ant.: base, ignoble, low, ordinary, ridiculous.

GOOD (N)

Syn.: benefit, profit, advantage, virtue, boon, weal, prosperity, blessing, gain, welfare, righteousness, merit.

Ant.: harm, injury, corruption, wickedness, depravity, detriment, disadvantage, ill, calamity, loss, evil, curse.

GRACEFUL

Syn.: elegant, pleasing in style and attitude, polite, considerate, comely, beautiful, attractive, lithe, lissom, svelte, sylphlike, willowy.

Ant.: ungainly, awkward, lumbering, uncouth, ill mannered, not refined.

GRAND

Syn.: august, exalted, stately, splendid, majestic, lofty, superb, imposing, dignified, noble, princely, magnificent, big, pompous, gorgeous, sublime, impressive.

Ant.: mean, common, insignificant, secondary, inferior, unimportant, little, undignified, unimposing, petty, paltry, beggarly, lowly.

GRIM

Syn.: fearful, stern, fierce, ruthless, horrible, determined, strong-willed, horrid, repellent, frightful, ghastly, gristly, gloomy, severe, unrelenting, unpleasant, depressing, determined, repulsive, dingy, drab, savage, appalling, ferocious, ugly, sullen, hideous.

Ant.: handsome, pretty, graceful, elegant, gentle, gracious, friendly, humane, benign, mild, docile, attractive.

GRUFF

Syn.: rough, surly, blunt, harsh, rude.

Ant.: affable, courteous, mild, smooth.

HARMFUL

Syn.: detrimental, pernicious, prejudicial, deleterious, injurious, noxious, hurtful, mischievous, obnoxious, inauspicious, oppressive, baneful, baleful, menacing, malignant, unhealthful, vitiated, damaging.

Ant.: helpful, profitable, beneficial, advantageous, harmless, useful, favourable, good, salutary, healthful, inoffensive, unobnoxious.

HARMONIOUS

Syn.: congruous, concordant, uniform, proportioned, consistent, tuneful, melodious, sweet-sounding, agreeable, friendly, amicable, cordial.

Ant.: unfriendly, hostile, unfavourable, adverse, opposing, opposed, antagonistic, contrary, discordant, conflicting, inconsistent.

HARSH

Syn.: rough, stern, cruel, severe, blunt, coarse, gruff, discordant, raucous, hoarse, rugged, severe, shrill, strident, austere, acrimonious, ungenial, sharp, sour, ungracious, brutal, heartless.

Ant.: gentle, mild, smooth, soft, melodious.

HEALTHY

Syn.: robust, strong, vigorous, lusty, hearty, sound, well, hygienic, salubrious, wholesome, salutary, bracing, invigorating, harmless, healthful, hale and hearty, inoffensive, laudable, moral.

Ant.: diseased, delicate, infirm, injurious, frail, noxious, sick, ailing, ill, sick.

HEARTY

Syn.: warm, earnest, sincere, heartfelt, cordial, sound, ardent, friendly, enthusiastic, cheerful, healthy, fervent, fervid.

Ant.: cool, reserved, taciturn, insincere.

HONEST

Syn.: frank, sincere, direct, fairly earned, truthful, upright, virtuous, right, genuine, trustworthy.

Ant.: dishonest, untrustworthy, tricky, deceitful, fraudulent, insincere.

HONOUR (N)

Syn.: privilege, probity, integrity, glory, distinction, great respect, glory, dignity, reverence, grandeur, high-mindedness, eminence, renown, fame.

Ant.: dishonour, disrespect, contempt, irreverence, disgrace, degradation, slight, infamy, perfidy, treachery, improbity, scorn, disdain.

HUMOROUS

Syn.: droll, amusing, ludicrous, funny, jocular, merry, comic, jocose, waggish, farcical.

Ant.: solemn, serious, sober, grave, composed, sedate, dignified.

IDLE

Syn.: indolent, lazy, inactive, unemployed, useless, unoccupied, slothful, futile.

Ant.: active, busy, occupied, working, industrious, employed.

INDUSTRIOUS

Syn.; diligent, hard-working, laborious, assiduous, sedulous.

Ant.: lethargic, inactive, apathetic, lazy, idle, indolent, slothful, torpid, sluggish, shiftless, slack, lax, supine.

IMPORTANT

Syn.: significant, valuable, weighty, influential, momentous, prominent, material, essential, remarkable, eventful.

Ant.: insignificant, unimportant, petty, trivial, mean, secondary, minor, uninfluential, worthless, valueless, immaterial, inferior.

INGENIOUS

Syn.: adroit, clever, dexterous, quick-witted, skilful, talented, smart, bright, sharp, adept, original, inventive, expert, intelligent.

Ant.: unskilled, dull, foolish, clumsy, awkward, stupid, unskilful, inexpert, maladroit, incompetent, inexperienced, unconversant, ungainly.

INGENUOUS

Syn.: innocent, open, candid, frank, sincere, straightforward, truthful, artless, honest, naive, simple, trusting, unaffected, outspoken.

Ant.: insincere, reserved, sly, wily, contrived, disingenuous, mean, pretentious, sham, affected, priggish.

INFINITE

Syn.: boundless, endless, unlimited, unbounded, limitless, immeasurable, interminable, stupendous, eternal, immense, vast, incalculable, numberless, countless, bottomless, unfathomable, inexhaustible, indefinite, perpetual.

Ant.: finite, limited, restricted, bounded, conditioned, confined, definite, determinate, circumscribed.

INTELLIGENT

Syn.: brainy, clever, bright, brilliant, keen, sagacious, quick-witted, discerning, sharp, shrewd, astute, canny, perspicacious, perceptive, nimble, well-informed, enlightened.

Ant.: foolish, doltish, dull, stupid, unintelligent, stolid, obtuse, silly, inane.

INTEGRITY

Syn.: honesty, probity, uprightness, rectitude, truthfulness, sincerity, trustworthiness, fairness, wholeness, completeness, oneness, totality, entirety, indivisibility.

Ant.: dishonesty, duplicity, unfairness, deceit, fraud, improbity.

IRRITABLE

Syn.: peevish, touchy, irascible, testy, short-tempered, fretful, splenetic, petulant, grumpy, pettish, snappish, choleric, peppery, churlish, cantankerous, fractious, crabbed.

Ant.: calm, composed, agreeable, gracious, cheerful, genial, good-natured, blithe, jaunty, buoyant, lively, animated.

JEALOUS

Syn.: envious, invidious, suspicious, resentful, covetous, jaundiced, distrustful, apprehensive, intolerant.

Ant.: unenvious, unjealous, tolerant, liberal, genial, indifferent, unsuspecting.

JOLLY

Syn.: genial, jovial, jubilant, lively, gay, joyful, merry, mirthful, cheerful, light-hearted, jocular, jocund, blithe.

Ant.: cheerless, joyless, sad, mournful, gloomy, morose, sullen, lugubrious, sorrowful, melancholy, dismal, unhappy.

JUST

Syn.: fair, honest, proper, right, reasonable, well-founded, deserved, impartial, true, upright, exact, precise, proportioned, normal.

Ant.: unfair, unjust, improper, unreasonable, partial, untrue, inexact, abnormal, ill-proportioned, prejudiced, biased.

KEEN

Syn.: acute, sharp, penetrating, astute, clever, cunning, quick, shrewd, wily, eager, enthusiastic, intense, deep, strong, cutting, ardent, nippy, avid, fervent.

Ant.: indifferent, blunt, dull, languid, indifferent, cool, careless, half-hearted, unconcerned, lukewarm, impervious, insouciant.

KIND (Adj)

Syn.: friendly, gentle, mild, obliging, benign, lenient, helpful, sympathetic, favourable, benevolent, amiable, good-natured, cordial, courteous, gracious, warm-hearted, humane, compassionate, generous, philanthropic.

Ant.: unfriendly, unfavourable, discourteous, unkind, harsh, severe, hard, callous, cruel, inhumane.

KNOWLEDGE

Syn.: understanding, learning, information, instruction, acquaintance, cognition, cognizance, awareness, comprehension, apprehension, consciousness, familiarity, ken, enlightenment, experience, attainments, scholarship, education.

Ant.: ignorance, nescience, illiteracy, incomprehension, inexperience, unawareness.

LABORIOUS

Syn.: diligent, hard-working, industrious, toilsome, tedious, tiresome, irksome, arduous, assiduous, wearisome, strenuous, painstaking, uphill.

Ant.: easy, light, feasible, indiligent, lazy, indolent, simple, idle.

LACONIC

Syn.: curt, terse, concise, pithy, short, brief, succinct, crisp, compendious, compact.

Ant.: lengthy, prolix, wordy, circumlocutory, verbose, discursive, long-winded, rambling, roundabout, copious, diffuse.

LAX

Syn.: negligent, careless, remiss, sluggish, inattentive, neglectful, heedless, vague, desultory, unmethodical, loose, slack, relaxed.

Ant.: careful, meticulous, attentive, methodical, severe, strict, heedful, regardful, cautious, prudent, discreet.

LESSEN

Syn.: shorten, abate, curtail, decrease, reduce, diminish, abridge, mitigate, contract, deduct, subtract, shrink, allenuate.

Ant.: increase, enlarge, augment, extend, expand, grow, amplify, enhance, magnify.

LIVELY

Syn.: high-spirited, vigorous, energetic, active, animated, brisk, bright, blithe, frolicsome, merry, playful, spirited, forceful, sprightly, vivacious, joyous, joyful, gay.

Ant.: dull, listless, insipid, vapid, inactive, uninteresting, depressed, languid, torpid, apathetic, indifferent, sluggish, dejected, joyless, cheerless, unlively, spiritless.

LOGICAL

Syn.: cogent, convincing, sound, valid, effective, reasonable, natural, rational, sane, relevant.

Ant.: illogical, invalid, ineffective, unreasonable, unnatural, irrational, insane, irrelevant, fallacious.

MADDEN

Syn.: infuriate, enrage, incense, derange, craze, anger, offend, displease, embitter, exasperate, rankle, affront, irritate, provoke, nettle, inflame, annoy.

Ant.: placate, pacify, soothe, calm, assuage, appease, mollify.

MALICIOUS

Syn.: spiteful, malignant, malevolent, evil-minded, hostile, rancorous, virulent, wicked, malign, pernicious, vicious, harmful, maleficent, ill-disposed, ill-intentioned.

Ant.: benign, kind, good-natured, benevolent, cordial, unselfish, sympathetic, gracious, well-intentioned, humane, warm-hearted, affectionate.

MASTERLY

Syn.: skilful, adept, deft, dexterous, expert, skilled, consummate, perfect, masterful, dominating.

Ant.: unskilled, maladroit, clumsy, inexpert.

METHODICAL

Syn.: orderly, logical, systematic, regular, procedural, planned, arranged, tidy.

Ant.: disorderly, illogical, irregular, unsystematic, unmethodical, untidy, desultory, unarranged, disarranged, sloppy, chaotic, anarchical.

MODEST

Syn.: moderate, inexpensive, not showy or splendid in appearance, not vain or boastful, shy, bashful, humble, meek, reserved, unassuming, unpretentious, diffident, unobtrusive, coy.

Ant.: immodest, showy or splendid in appearance, vain, boastful, ostentatious, pretentious, proud, arrogant, bold, conceited, haughty, disdainful, pert, imperious, domineering, priggish, smug, self-satisfied, egotistic, self-important.

MOMENTOUS

Syn.: important, prominent, significant, weighty, material, pressing, influential, grave, consequential, serious, notable, solemn, memorable, remarkable.

Ant.: unimportant, immaterial, inconsequential, insignificant, mean, petty, trivial, slight, niggling, trifling.

NATURAL

Syn.: innate, inherent, original, normal, spontaneous, unaffected, characteristic, typical, native, unstudied, inborn, naive, ingenuous, inbred, ingrained, usual, intrinsic.

Ant.: unnatural, abnormal, artificial, affected, forced, irregular, unusual, inconsistent, fictitious.

NECESSARY

Syn.: requisite, needful, essential, inevitable, unavoidable, indispensable.

Ant.: unnecessary, optional, unessential, dispensable, voluntary, discretional, casual.

NICE

Syn.: pleasant, agreeable, friendly, kind, fine, subtle, respectable, scrupulous, dainty, attractive, fastidious, tasteful, delicate, choosy, refined, palatable, delectable, pleasing, pleasurable.

Ant.: disagreeable, coarse, unscrupulous, rough, nasty, rueful, mournful, woeful, deplorable, distressing.

NIMBLE

Syn.: agile, sharp, active, brisk, lively, spry, quick.

Ant.: slow, sluggish, clumsy, inert, lazy, indolent, awkward, slothful.

NOVICE

Syn.: beginner, tyro, neophyte, apprentice, greenhorn, learner, acolyte, rookie.

Ant.: expert, adept, master, teacher, trainer, instructor.

OBEDIENT

Syn.: observant, dutiful, complying, compliant, loyal, faithful, devoted, fractable, docile, submissive, pliable, pliant, yielding.

Ant.: disloyal, unfaithful, intractable, uncomplying, incompliant, unruly, unsubmissive, refractory, resisting, contumacious, recalcitrant.

OBSTINATE

Syn.: stubborn, obdurate, dogged, tenacious, persistent, insistent, headstrong, pertinacious, unyielding, determined, self-willed, wilful, resolute.

Ant.: irresolute, subservient, yielding, submissive, amenable, wavering.

OFFENSIVE (Adj)

Syn.: insulting, annoying, disgusting, repulsive, aggressive, distasteful, foul, aggressive, obnoxious, nasty.

Ant.: pleasant, defensive, inoffensive, harmless, blameless, unaggressive, innocuous.

OWN (V)

Syn.: possess, confess, admit, avow, acknowledge, have, hold, concede.

Ant.: deny, disclaim, disavow, renounce, disown, abjure, abandon.

PEEVISH

Syn.: irritable, touchy, testy, tetchy, irascible, fretful, bad-tempered, crabbed, pettish, petulant, snappish, waspish, fractious, hot-headed, crabby, churlish.

Ant.: affable, genial, good-natured, good-tempered, pleasant, cordial, hearty, jolly, soft-spoken, polite, urbane.

PERFECT (Adj)

Syn.: complete, excellent, ideal, exact, precise, total, absolute, thorough, faultless, indefective, indeficient, immaculate, impeccable, sound, spotless, entire, utter, consummate.

Ant.: imperfect, incomplete, inexact, deficient, faulty, unsound, deformed, impaired, blemished, crude.

PLEASANT

Syn.: enjoyable, polite and friendly, pleasurable, agreeable, pleasing, delectable, palatable, delightful, cheerful, delicious, jocular, merry.

Ant.: unpleasant, disagreeable, unlively, lugubrious, dismal, sad, mournful, offensive, unpleasing, disgusting, obnoxious, nasty.

PLENTIFUL

Syn.: ample, abundant, copious, profuse, plenteous, prolific, bounteous, bountiful, lavish.

Ant.: scanty, meagre, limited, skimpy, insufficient, sparing, scarce, deficient, rare.

POMPOUS

Syn.: self-important, ostentatious, high-flown, bombastic, grandiose, arrogant, haughty, grand, imposing, lofty, magnificent, majestic, stately, sublime, dignified, showy, pretentious, assuming, turgid, magniloquent.

Ant.: unassuming, plain-mannered, unpretending, modest, unobtrusive, humble-minded, unpretentious, bashful, coy.

PRECISE

Syn.: exact, accurate, definite, correct, punctitious, fastidious, particular, proper.

Ant.: inexact, inaccurate, indefinite, incorrect, improper, vague, ambiguous, rough, circumlocutory.

PREPOSSESSING

Syn.: attractive, charming, taking, alluring, engaging, winning, appealing, winsome.

Ant.: unattractive, repulsive, ugly, unprepossessing, ill-looking.

PREPOSTEROUS

Syn.: outrageous, absurd, unreasonable, ridiculous, foolish, silly, stupid, inconsistent, irrational, nonsensical, laughable, idiotic, illogical, ludicrous.

Ant.: consistent, reasonable, rational, logical, sensible, sound, just, fair, right, moderate.

PRINCIPAL (Adj)

Syn.: chief, main, foremost, prime, leading, most important, pre-eminent, outstanding, excellent, conspicuous, highest, first-rate, cardinal, fundamental, primary, paramount, supreme, predominant.

Ant.: minor, inferior, subordinate, secondary, auxiliary, subsidiary.

PUSHY

Syn.: aggressive, offensive, forceful, belligerent, bold, impudent, rude, disrespectful, insolent, self-assertive.

Ant.: cowardly, timid, defensive.

QUESTIONABLE

Syn.: doubtful, uncertain, suspicious, dubious, disputable, debatable, arguable, fishy, controversial.

Ant.: certain, indisputable, obvious, evident, unquestionable, sure.

QUICKEN

Syn.: hasten, hurry, speed, accelerate, refresh, animate, rush, expedite.

Ant.: retard, slacken, moderate, curb, shorten, slow, relax, delay, impede, hinder, obstruct.

QUIET (Adj)

Syn.: calm, peaceful, screne, hushed, silent, modest, restrained, subdued, gentle, unostentatious, restful, relaxed, leisurely, unhurried, reposeful, tranquil, quiescent, unobtrusive, passive, undisturbed, motionless, still, mild, modest.

Ant.: loud, agitated, disturbed, perturbed, noisy.

QUIET (N)

Syn.: calm, calmness, hush, peace, repose, rest, silence, stillness, tranquility, serenity, quiescence, quietude.

Ant.: agitation, disturbance, uproar, noise, din, noisiness, loudness, tumult, excitement, turmoil, commotion, unrest.

RAPID

Syn.: speedy, quick, swift, fast, prompt, expeditious, hasty, hurried.

Ant.: slow, sluggish, slack, tardy, leisurely, gradual, languid.

REASONABLE

Syn.: sensible, logical, moderate, tolerable, acceptable, average, sound, fair, rational, inexpensive, sober, temperate.

Ant.: unreasonable, absurd, unfair, illogical, irrational, intolerable, immoderate, expensive, senseless, preposterous, ridiculous, silly, excessive, obstinate.

REGULAR

Syn.: proper, systematic, symetrical, normal, usual, habitual, constant, orderly, steady, methodical, consistent.

Ant.: irregular, improper, abnormal, unusual, disorderly, inconstant, desultory, unmethodical, changeable, erratic, sporadic.

REMARKABLE

Syn.: unusual, exceptional, august, impressive, extra-ordinary, uncommon, splendid, singular, notable, noteworthy, striking, distinguished, wonderful, famous, prominent, conspicuous, imposing.

Ant.: ordinary, average, inconspicuous, normal, usual, common, customary, undistinguished.

RESPONSIBLE

Syn.: answerable, trustworthy, dependable, accountable, liable, chargeable, reliable.

Ant.: irresponsible, untrustworthy, undependable, unreliable, unaccountable, unanswerable.

RICH

Syn.: wealthy, affluent, prosperous, opulent, nourishing, abundant, ample, fruitful, fertile, luxuriant, vivid, bountiful, sumptuous, gorgeous, sonorous, well-to-do, plentiful, fecund, well-heeled, productive, wholesome, nutritious.

Ant.: poor, needy, penniless, beggarly, indigent, destitute, barren, sterile, unfruitful, unproductive, impecunious, hard up, necessitous.

SCHOOL (V)

Syn.: train, teach, direct, lead, guide, educate, instruct, control, discipline, inform, enlighten, tutor.

Ant.: misdirect, mislead, misguide, deceive, delude.

SCRUPULOUS

Syn.: absolutely honest, extremely careful and thorough, paying great attention to details, exact, meticulous, punctitious, upright, moral, conscientious, veracious, truthful, right-minded, high-principled.

Ant.: dishonest, deceitful, tricky, fraudulent, unscrupulous, careless, unprincipled, conscienceless, knavish.

SILLY

Syn.: foolish, doltish, indiscreet, stupid, unwise, childish, inane, fatuous, senseless, absurd, ridiculous, idiotic, nonsensical, irrational, preposterous, outrageous, imprudent.

Ant.: wise, prudent, rational, sane, discreet, sound, intelligent, sensible, sapient, sagacious, discerning, perspicacious, brainy, brilliant, well-advised, judicious, astute, shrewd.

SLY

Syn.: foxy, wily, crafty, cunning, deceitful, secretive, furtive, roguish, mischievous, stealthy, underhand, surreptitious.

Ant.: open, frank, candid, ingenuous, sincere, artless.

SOFTEN

Syn.: mollify, soothe, ease, calm, comfort, quiet, temper, moderate, mitigate, abate, allay, alleviate, assuage, diminish, lessen, extenuate, relieve.

Ant.: harden, stiffen, augment, irritate, increase, aggravate, worsen, enhance, heighten, intensify, infuriate, indurate.

SUITABLE

Syn.: appropriate, proper, fitting, right, becoming, apposite, eligible, seemly, apt, meet, decorous, seasonable.

Ant.: unsuitable, improper, unbecoming, inapt, indecorous, unseemly, ineligible, inappropriate, inapposite.

TEDIOUS

Syn.: boring, tiresome, wearisome, irksome, monotonous, dreary, uninteresting, dull, humdrum, drab.

Ant.: interesting, amusing, entertaining, exciting, delightful, brisk.

TERRIBLE

Syn.: horrible, alarming, fearful, shocking, frightful, awesome, appalling, dreadful, terrifying, frightening, formidable, tèrrific, horrid, terrible, fearsome.

Ant.: pleasing, encouraging, safe, secure, joyous, informidable, unastounding.

TOLERABLE

Syn.: endurable, bearable, passable, sufferable, acceptable.

Ant.: intolerable, unbearable, unacceptable, unendurable.

TOTALLY

Syn.: fully, wholly, completely, entirely, absolutely, thoroughly, perfectly, utterly.

Ant.: partially, partly, incompletely, somewhat.

TRUE

Syn.: accurate, actual, unerring, correct, authentic, exact, real, veracious, constant, faithful, loyal, genuine, precise, veritable, reliable, rightful, sincere, factual, legitimate.

Ant.: untrue, inaccurate, incorrect, inexact, unreal, unfaithful, disloyal, unreliable, insincere, false, spurious, fictitious, erroneous, inconstant, fickle, fallacious, apocryphal.

UNASSUMING

Syn.: modest, reserved, retiring, humble, diffident, bashful, shy, coy, unpretentious, unostentatious.

Ant.: arrogant, boastful, haughty, proud, vain, immodest, pretentious, ostentatious, pert, vainglorious, imperious, smug, priggish, domineering.

URBANE

Syn.: suave, affable, polite, civil, courteous, refined, well-bred, well-mannered, accomplished, sophisticated, courtly, amiable.

Ant.: uncivil, uncouth, rude, ill-mannered, discourteous, impolite, boorish, impertinent.

UTTER (Adj)

Syn.: complete, entire, thorough, full, whole, perfect, absolute, sheer, total, downwright, consummate, arrant.

Ant.: incomplete, imperfect, partial, meagre, lacking, wanting, deficient, sketchy, skimpy.

VALID

Syn.: binding, sound, legal, logical, effective, cogent, operative, weighty, well-grounded, just.

Ant.: invalid, illegal, illogical, unjust, unsound, ineffective, null and void, inoperative.

VANITY

Syn.: pride, egotism, arrogance, conceit, immodesty, self-esteem, smugness, priggishness, vainglory, boasting, boast, bombast, bluster, brag, rodomontade.

Ant.: modesty, humility, meekness, simplicity, unostentatiousness.

VIGOROUS

Syn.: energetic, active, strong, potent, powerful, mighty, forceful, animated, lively, spirited, sprightly, brisk, vivacious, intense.

Ant.: powerless, ineffective, ineffectual, dull, feeble, unsound, impotent, flabby.

VITAL

Syn.: essential, indispensable, necessary, basic, cardinal, paramount, energetic, lively, dynamic.

Ant.: unessential, unimportant, dispensable, immaterial, insignificant.

WELCOME (Adj)

Syn.: pleasing, agreeable, acceptable, gratifying, pleasant, pleasurable.

Ant.: unwelcome, unacceptable, disagreeable, distasteful, unpleasant, offensive, repugnant, repulsive, unpalatable.

WISE

Syn.: prudent, sagacious, sage, learned, profound, well-advised, judicious, scholarly, well-informed, well-read, shrewd.

Ant.: unwise, foolish, shallow, silly, stupid, inane, fatuous, injudicious, imprudent, ill-advised, doltish, uneducated, unschooled.

WRONG (Adj)

Syn.: erroneous, incorrect, unjust, inaccurate, mistaken, faulty, untrue, unprecise, improper, bad, amiss, inappropriate, unsuitable, false, unfair, unfit.

Ant.: right, correct, true, proper, suitable, exact, just, precise, fair, accurate.

YEARLING

Syn.: youngling, colt, filly, cub, whelp, puppy.

Ant.: elder, doyen, old-timer, veteran.

YEARN

Syn.: desire, strongly, pine, long, hanker, grieve, mourn.

Ant.: hate, detest, despise, loathe, dislike, abominate.

YIELDING

Syn.: pliant, tractable, docile, submissive, compliant, flexible, soft, manageable.

Ant.: intractable, unmanageable, awkward, stubborn, obstinate, obdurate, unyielding, inflexible, hard, unruly, recalcitrant.

YOUNG

Syn.: youthful, new, fresh, inexperienced, immature, youngish, teen-age, juvenile, adolescent, green, puerile.

Ant.: old, elderly, experienced, aged, senior mature, full-grown.

ZANY (Adj)

Syn.: ridiculous, eccentric, amusing, ludicrous foolish, doltish, silly, inane, fatuous, stupid, droll funny, whimsical, dull, drab.

Ant.: wise, intelligent, accomplished, well informed, shrewd, brisk, active.

ZANY (N)
Syn.: merry-andrew, buffoon, clown, madcap, fool, comedian, jester, nitwit, dunce, dolt, nincompoop, ninny, simpleton, numskull, oaf, loon, dullard, dunderhead, blockhead, goof, idiot, booby, bonehead, dunce, imbecile.
Ant.: sage, scholar, genius, wise person, intelligent person.

ZEAL
Syn.: enthusiasm, energy, verve, keenness, vim, vigour, heartiness, earnestness, spirit, eagerness, warmth, ardour, fervour, devotion, dash, briskness, alacrity, intensity, vehemence.
Ant.: apathy, indifference, unconcern, ennui, detachment, coldness, torpor, torpidity.

ZEALOUS
Syn.: eager, keen, enthusiastic, deep, strong, intense, earnest, passionate, spirited, ardent, warm, energetic, fervent, fervid, impassioned, vehement.
Ant.: cold, apathetic, indifferent, nonchalant, calm and casual, cool.

ZENITH
Syn.: acme, top, summit, apex, climax, vertex, culmination, peak, prime, highest point.
Ant.: nadir, lowest point or part, base, bottom, foot.

ZEST
Syn.: gusto, relish, enthusiasm, exhilaration, thrill, great enjoyment or excitement.
Ant.: distaste, disrelish, dislike, insipidity.

MULTIPLE CHOICE QUESTIONS

Directions (Qs. 1 to 32): *In the following questions, each word is followed by four options A, B, C and D. Select the option which best expresses the meaning of the given word.*

1. ABSURD
   A. Foolish B. Simple
   C. Courageous D. Silly
2. ABANDON
   A. Lose B. Profit
   C. Vacate D. Foil
3. ADULATION
   A. Embarrassment B. Fawning
   C. Veneration D. Praise
4. ABDICATE
   A. Rude B. Soft
   C. Imperious D. Give up
5. BAFFLE
   A. Abet B. Enlighten
   C. Foil D. Taciturnity
6. BUOYANT
   A. Support B. Unworthy
   C. Desponding D. Cheerful
7. BLEMISH
   A. Eccentric B. Disgrace
   C. Fair D. Youth
8. BOOTY
   A. Buxom B. Loot
   C. Delicate D. Daub
9. CUPIDITY
   A. Shrewd B. Basic
   C. Avarice D. Parody
10. CORRIGIBLE
    A. Amendable B. Oppose
    C. Devise D. Illicit
11. CONNIVE
    A. Overlook B. Grow
    C. Censure D. Defect
12. CAJOLE
    A. Pause B. Lenient
    C. Blast D. Lure
13. HAUGHTY
    A. Imperial B. Imperious
    C. Umpire D. Brave
14. OPPORTUNE
    A. Timely B. Short lived
    C. Occasional D. Temper
15. EXTERMINATE
    A. Extensore B. Rubbing
    C. Soothing D. Extirpate
16. VENERABLE
    A. Watchful B. Lawful
    C. Respectful D. Hateful

17. VORACIOUS
A. Funny B. Venturous
C. Gluttonous D. Hungry

18. INSOLVENT
A. Rich B. Poor
C. Bankrupt D. Penniless

19. REPEAL
A. Pass B. Cancel
C. Sanction D. Dishonour

20. LYNCH
A. Murder B. Shoot
C. Killed D. Hang

21. COMBAT
A. Fight B. Conflict
C. Shoot D. Quarrel

22. LAMENT
A. Condone B. Console
C. Complain D. Contribution

23. DEBACLE
A. Disgrace B. Defeat
C. Collapse D. Decline

24. SHIVER
A. Fear B. Tremble
C. Shake D. Ache

25. TORTURE
A. Terror B. Harassment
C. Torment D. Tranquility

26. LAUDABLE
A. Lovable B. Commendable
C. Profitable D. Oblivious

27. FIXED
A. Sterile B. Static
C. Stubborn D. Parennial

28. FANCIFUL
A. Romantic B. Beautiful
C. Imaginative D. Egoistic

29. QUEER
A. Unfamiliar B. Cute
C. Curious D. Strange

30. OPPRESS
A. Prosecute B. Trouble
C. Persecute D. Perilous

31. ZEST
A. Anticipation B. Optimistic
C. Cruel D. Enthusiasm

32. SUFFICIENT
A. Fit B. Proper
C. Adequate D. Vast

Directions (33–50): *In each of these questions, you find a sentence, a part of which is* ***bold****. For the* ***bold*** *part, four words/phrases are suggested. Choose the word/phrase* ***nearest*** *in meaning to the* ***bold*** *part.*

33. His descriptions are **vivid**.
A. Detailed B. Categorical
C. Clear D. Ambiguous

34. Friends have always **deplored** my unsociable nature.
A. Deprived B. Implored
C. Denied D. Regretted

35. Despite his enormous wealth, the businessman was very **frugal** in his habits.
A. Reckless B. Law-abiding
C. Unpredictable D. Economical

36. He was **engrossed** in writing a story.
A. Absolved B. Absorbed
C. Interested D. Engaged

37. People fear him because of his **vindictive** nature.
A. Violent B. Cruel
C. Revengeful D. Irritable

38. He always has a very **pragmatic** approach to life.
A. Practical B. Proficient
C. Potent D. Patronizing

39. He was not at all **abashed** by her open admiration.
A. Delighted B. Piqued
C. Embarrassed D. Livid

40. Rahul was amazed at how **affable** his new employer was
A. Demanding
B. Polite
C. Repulsive
D. Quality-conscious

41. Since our plans are **amorphous** we shall send you the detailed programme at a later date.
A. Impractical B. Prohibitive
C. Inimical D. Formless

42. Preeti's **arduous** efforts had sapped her energy.
A. Over-ambitious B. Strenuous
C. Sterile D. Apocryphal

43. The manager's **articulate** presentation of the advertising campaign impressed his employers.
A. Well-prepared B. Effective
C. Superficial D. Banal

44. I do not wish to be **beholden** to anyone in this office
A. Dependent B. Opposed
C. Obligated D. Sycophant

45. We must prevent the **proliferation** of nuclear weapons.
A. Use B. Increase
C. Expansion D. Extension

46. The debate has **instigated** a full official enquiry into the incidence.
A. Initiated B. Incited
C. Forced D. Caused

47. The workers were full of **applause** for the new policy of the management.
A. Approval B. Adulation
C. Praise D. Eulogy

48. Her **ostensible** calm masked a deepseated fear.
A. Illusory B. Apparent
C. Dubious D. Visible

49. Sonu is an **inveterate** liar.
A. Effective B. Habitual
C. Frequent D. Familiar

50. The underworld still makes solid profit out of **illicit** liquor.
A. indigenous B. illegitimate
C. illegal D. country

Directions (Qs. 51 to 100): *In each of the sentences given below a word is printed in* **bold**. *Below it four choices are given. Pick up the one which is most nearly the SAME in meaning as the word printed in* **bold** *and can replaces it without altering the meaning of the sentence.*

51. When youngesters do not have good role-models to **emulate** they start searching for them amongst Sportsmen of Filmstars.
A. imitate B. modify
C. molify D. inhabit

52. The **aberration** in the India Economy can be attributed to short-sightedness of its political masters.
A. procrastination B. privilege
C. deviation D. steadfastness

53. The claims of students look hollow when they **attribute** their poor performance to difficulty of examination.
A. infer B. impute
C. inhere D. inundate

54. As soon as he finished his speech, there was **spontaneous** applause from the audience.
A. well-timed B. willing
C. instinctive D. instantaneous

55. The soldier proved his **mettle** in the battlefield.
A. persistence
B. stamina and strength
C. courage and endurance
D. heroism

56. He listened of my request with **indifference**.
A. disinterest B. concern
C. displeasure D. caution

57. The accident occurred due to his **lapse**.
A. trick B. interval
C. error D. ignorance

58. Being a member of this Club, he has certain **rights**.
A. status B. truth
C. virtues D. privileges

59. He is **averse** to the idea of holding elections now.
A. convinced B. angry
C. agreeable D. opposed

60. Silence is **mandatory** for meditation to be effective.
A. compulsory B. necessary
C. required D. needed

61. The underworld still makes solid profit out of **illicit** liquor.
A. indigenous B. illegitimate
C. illegal D. country

62. When I look back over the wartime years I cannot help feeling that time is an inadequate and even **capricious** measure of their duration at one moment they seem so long, at another so short.
A. misleading B. whimsical
C. erratic D. unpredictable

63. The tablet **alleviated** the pain, and the patient was soon feeling much better.
A. mitigated B. moderated
C. removed D. lightened

64. The leader nodded his **approbation**
A. understanding B. approval
C. admiration D. appreciation

65. We should always try to maintain and promote communal **amity**.
A. bondage B. contention
C. friendship D. understanding

66. Many species of animals have become **extinct** during the last hundred years.
A. aggressive B. non-existent
C. scattered D. feeble

67. True religion does not require one to **proselytise** through guile or force.
A. translate B. hypnotise
C. attack D. convert

68. That the plan is both inhuman and **preposterous** needs no further proof.
A. heartless B. impractical
C. absurd D. abnormal

69. She **baffled** all our attempts to find her.
A. defeated B. thwarted
C. foiled D. circumvented

70. Instead of putting up a united front against of common enemy, the medieval states frittered away their energy in **internecine** warfare.
A. mutually destructive
B. baneful
C. pernicious
D. detrimental

71. The bullet wound proved to be **fatal** and the soldier died immediately.
A. grievous B. dangerous
C. serious D. deadly

72. Whatever opinion he gives is **sane.**
A. rational B. obscure
C. wild D. arrogant

73. He **corroborated** the statement of his brother.
A. confirmed B. disproved
C. condemned D. seconded

74. Whatever the **verdict** of history may be, Chaplin will occupy a unique place in its pages.
A. judgement B. voice
C. outcome D. prediction

75. The attitude of the Western countries towards the Third World countries is rather **callous** to say the least.
A. passive B. unkind
C. cursed D. unfeeling

76. The story is too fantastic to be **credible.**
A. believable B. false
C. readable D. praiseworthy

77. Catching snakes can be **hazardous** for people untrained in the art.
A. tricky B. harmful
C. difficult D. dangerous

78. After the **dismal** performance of the team in the series concluded yesterday, the captain offered his resignation to the president of the club.
A. poor B. sorrowful
C. minimum D. short

79. The small boy was able to give a **graphic** description of the thief.
A. picture B. drawing
C. vivid D. broad

80. The prisoner has been **languishing** in the jail for the last many years.
A. convicted B. suffering
C. attempting D. avoiding

81. Some of the Asian countries have been **enmeshed** in an inescapable debt trap.
A. entagled B. hit
C. struck D. ensured

82. In spite of their efforts, the team of scientists could not make much **headway** to solve the problem.
A. progress B. thinking
C. efforts D. start

83. On scrutiny the police officer found out that the documents provided by the landlord were totally **fabricated**.
A. forged B. historical
C. prepared D. genuine

84. The soldier displayed **exceptional** courage and saved the Major from the enemy's hand.
A. avoidable B. unusual
C. strange D. abnormal

85. He found a **lucrative** assignment.
A. good B. profitable
C. excellent D. significant

86. The novel was so interesting that I was **oblivious** of my surroundings.
A. precarious B. unmindful
C. aware D. watchful

87. The great dancer impressed the appreciative crowd by his **nimble** movements.
A. unrhythmic B. lively
C. quickening D. clear

88. The president of the party **deprecated** the move of the Government to introduce electroal reforms in a haste.
A. welcomed B. denied
C. protested D. humiliated

89. It took him a long time to **come round** after the operation.
A. recover B. walk
C. move D. eat

90. Few teachers have been spared the problem of an **obstreperous** pupil in the class.
A. sullen B. unruly
C. lazy D. awkward

91. His visit to foreign countries brought about a **sea-change** in his outlook and his attitude to people.
A. complete change
B. partial change
C. favourable change
D. unfavourable change

92. Swift is known in the world of letters for his **misogynism**.
A. hate for mankind
B. hate for womankind
C. love for the reasonable
D. love for womankind

93. He was warned at the **outset** of his career.
A. end B. beginning
C. middle D. entrance

94. The time I spent in the library was a most **rewarding** one.
A. profitable B. paying
C. serviceable D. precious

95. That young is quite **sanguine** about the result of his competitive examination.
A. depressed B. pessimistic
C. anxious D. optimistic

96. The courage shown by the soldiers at this moment of crisis is **exemplary**.
A. suitable B. clear
C. elementary D. admirable

97. The notice said that the meeting would begin **precisely** at 9.30 a.m.
A. approximately B. exactly
C. accurately D. concisely

98. The inspector was a **vigilant** young man.
A. intelligent B. ambitious
C. watchful D. smart

99. A **rupture** in the relationship of the two brothers is quite apparent.
A. break B. damage
C. breach D. gap

100. "I have learnt a great deal working in factories, and for a time I've been a weaver. Here are my **testimonials,** Mr. Davis."
A. witnesses B. testaments
C. tokens D. credentials

Directions (Qs. 101 to 121): *In the following questions choose the word which is the exact **opposite** of the given word.*

101. DEAR
A. Priceless B. Free
C. Worthless D. Cheap

102. FLAGITIOUS
A. Innocent B. Vapid
C. Ignorant D. Frivolous

103. LIABILITY
A. Property B. Assets
C. Debt D. Teasure

104. VIRTUOUS
A. Wicked B. Corrupt
C. Vicious D. Scandalous

105. ENCOURAGE
A. Dampen B. Disapprove
C. Discourage D. Warn

106. MORTAL
A. Divine B. Immortal
C. Spiritual D. Eternal

107. LEND
A. Borrow B. Cheat
C. Pawn D. Hire

108. COMIC
A. Emotional B. Tragic
C. Fearful D. Painful

109. ADDITION
A. Division B. Enumeration
C. Subtraction D. Multiplication

110. MINOR
A. Big B. Major
C. Tall D. Heavy

111. REPEL
A. Attend B. Concentrate
C. Continue D. Attract

112. ARTIFICIAL
A. Red B. Natural
C. Truthful D. Solid

113. CAPACIOUS
A. Limited B. Caring
C. Foolish D. Changeable

114. PROVOCATION
A. Vocation B. Pacification
C. Peace D. Destruction

115. METICULOUS
A. Mutual B. Shaggy
C. Meretricious D. Slovenly

116. ABLE
A. Disable B. Inable
C. Unable D. Misable

117. COMFORT
A. Uncomfort B. Miscomfort
C. Discomfort D. None of these

118. GAIN
A. Loose B. Fall
C. Lost D. Lose

119. SYNTHETIC
A. Affable B. Natural
C. Plastic D. Cosmetic

120. ACQUITTED
A. Freed B. Burdened
C. Convicted D. Entrusted

121. STRINGENT
A. General B. Vehement
C. Lenient D. Magnanimous

Directions (Qs. 122 to 150) : *Each of the following items consists of a sentence followed by four words. Select the* ***antonym*** *of the word (occuring in the sentence in* ***bold*** *letters) as per the context.*

122. What the critic said about this new book was **absurd**.
A. Interesting B. Impartial
C. Sensible D. Ridiculous

123. The issue raised in the forum can be **ignored**.
A. Removed B. Considered
C. Set aside D. Debated

124. After swallowing it the frog has become **lethargic**.
A. Aggressive B. Dull
C. Active D. Hungry

125. For the first time I saw him speaking **rudely** to her.
A. Softly B. Gently
C. Politely D. Slowly

126. Dust storms and polluted rivers have made it **hazardous** to breathe the air and drink the water.
A. Convenient B. Risky
C. Wrong D. Safe

127. Only hard work can **enrich** our country.
A. Impoverish B. Improve
C. Increase D. Involve

128. He is man of **extravagant** habits.
A. Sensible B. Careful
C. Economical D. Balanced

129. They employ only **diligent** workers.
A. Unskilled B. Lazy
C. Careless D. Idle

130. His success in the preliminary examination made him **complacent**.
A. Discontented
B. Self-satisfied
C. Curious
D. Militant

131. In this competition, he has become the **victor**.
A. Beaten B. Frustrated
C. Disappointed D. Vanquished

132. His behaviour at social gatherings is **laudable**.
A. Condemnable B. Impolite
C. Unpleasant D. Repulsive

133. The characters in this story are not all **fictitious**.
A. Common B. Factual
C. Real D. Genuine

134. The **reluctance** of the officer was obvious.
A. Eagerness B. Hesitation
C. Enjoyment D. Unwillingness

135. He is a **generous** man.
A. Stingy B. Uncharitable
C. Selfish D. Ignoble

136. He showed a marked **antipathy** to foreigners.
A. profundity B. fondness
C. objection D. willingness

137. The authorities took the corrective action with **celerity**.
A. reluctance
B. delay
C. promptness
D. lack of judgement

138. It seems **churlish** to refuse such a generous offer.
A. wise B. sensible
C. polite D. immature

139. A **conscientious** editor, he checked every definition for its accuracy.
A. novice B. careless
C. unscientific D. biased

140. Sharma's **craven** refusal to join the protest was criticised by his comrades.
A. strategic B. bold
C. diplomatic D. well-thought

141. The dictator **quelled** the uprising.
A. fostered B. defended
C. supported D. fomented

142. People are unwilling to **follow** the rules.
A. waive B. neglect
C. dispose D. disregard

143. That was an **impudent** remark.
A. gentle B. mild
C. modest D. unassuming

144. His sudden appearance on the scene was **fortuitous.**
A. circumstantial B. unfortunate
C. sudden D. calculated

145. The batsman gave a **sterling** performance.
A. a risky B. a vital
C. an ordinary D. a match-saving

146. While facing that situation he turned out to be **dauntless**.
A. tactful B. stoical
C. bashful D. cowardly

147. We went to the first floor through the **rickety** wooden stairs.
A. stable B. old
C. narrow D. uncomfortable

148. They made a **profigate** use of scarce resources.
A. proper B. extravagant
C. effective D. thrifty

149. The consultant analysed the proposal carefully before he decided to **jettison** it.
A. abandon B. strengthen
C. accept D. modify

150. The politician was **flummoxed** by the question put to him.
A. comfortable B. annoyed
C. delighted D. disconcerted

ANSWERS

1	2	3	4	5	6	7	8	9	10
D	C	D	D	C	D	B	B	C	A
11	**12**	**13**	**14**	**15**	**16**	**17**	**18**	**19**	**20**
C	D	B	A	D	C	C	C	B	C
21	**22**	**23**	**24**	**25**	**26**	**27**	**28**	**29**	**30**
A	C	C	B	C	B	B	C	D	C
31	**32**	**33**	**34**	**35**	**36**	**37**	**38**	**39**	**40**
D	C	C	D	D	B	C	A	C	B
41	**42**	**43**	**44**	**45**	**46**	**47**	**48**	**49**	**50**
D	B	A	C	B	B	C	B	B	C
51	**52**	**53**	**54**	**55**	**56**	**57**	**58**	**59**	**60**
A	C	B	C	C	A	C	D	D	A
61	**62**	**63**	**64**	**65**	**66**	**67**	**68**	**69**	**70**
C	B	A	B	C	B	D	C	C	A
71	**72**	**73**	**74**	**75**	**76**	**77**	**78**	**79**	**80**
D	A	A	A	D	A	D	A	C	B
81	**82**	**83**	**84**	**85**	**86**	**87**	**88**	**89**	**90**
A	A	A	B	B	B	C	C	A	B
91	**92**	**93**	**94**	**95**	**96**	**97**	**98**	**99**	**100**
A	B	B	A	D	D	B	C	A	D
101	**102**	**103**	**104**	**105**	**106**	**107**	**108**	**109**	**110**
D	A	B	C	C	B	A	B	C	B
111	**112**	**113**	**114**	**115**	**116**	**117**	**118**	**119**	**120**
D	B	A	B	D	C	C	D	B	C
121	**122**	**123**	**124**	**125**	**126**	**127**	**128**	**129**	**130**
C	C	B	C	C	D	A	C	C	A
131	**132**	**133**	**134**	**135**	**136**	**137**	**138**	**139**	**140**
D	A	C	A	A	B	B	C	D	B
141	**142**	**143**	**144**	**145**	**146**	**147**	**148**	**149**	**150**
D	D	A	D	C	D	A	D	C	A

ORDERING OF WORDS

The words form a sentence and convey their meaning only when they are arranged in a proper order. One must study and practise it regularly.

Directions (Qs. 1–100): *In the following questions, some parts of the sentence have been jumbled up. You are required to rearrange these parts which are labelled P, Q, R and S to produce the correct sentence. Choose the option with proper sequence.*

1. We are doing
P : to the people
Q : to give relief
R : all we can
S : but more funds are needed
The correct sequence should be
A. P Q R S B. R Q P S
C. Q P R S D. S P Q R

2. The man
P : when he was
Q : in the office last evening
R : could not finish
S : all his work
The correct sequence should be
A. P Q R S B. Q R S P
C. R Q P S D. R S P Q

3. The people decided
P : they were going
Q : how much
R : to spend
S : on the construction of the school building
The correct sequence should be
A. Q P R S B. P Q R S
C. P R Q S D. S Q P R

4. The man said that
P : those workers
Q : would be given a raise
R : who did not go on
S : strike last month
The correct sequence should be
A. P Q R S B. P R S Q
C. Q P R S D. R S P Q

5. I think
P : the members
Q : are basically in agreement
R : of the group
S : on the following points.
The correct sequence should be
A. R Q P S B. S Q R P
C. P R Q S D. P Q S R

6. While it was true that
P : I had
Q : to invest in industry
R : some lands and houses
S : I did not have ready cash
The correct sequence should be
A. P Q R S B. P R S Q
C. S Q P R D. Q P R S

7. P : But your help
Q : to finish this work
R : it would not have been possible
S : in time
The correct sequence should be
A. P R Q S B. S P Q R
C. R P Q S D. P Q R S

8. The boy
P : in the competition
Q : who was wearing spectacles
R : won many prizes
S : held in our college
The correct sequence should be
A. P Q R S B. R P S Q
C. Q R P S D. Q P S R

9. About 200 years ago,
P : in the south of India
Q : an old king

R : ruled over a kingdom
S : called Rajavarman.
The correct sequence should be
A. Q S R P   B. P Q R S
C. Q P S R   D. Q S P R

10. P : his land
Q : a wooden plough
R : the Indian peasant still uses
S : to cultivate.
The correct sequence should be
A. R Q P S   B. Q P S R
C. S R Q P   D. R Q S P

11. He was a man,
P : even if he had to starve
Q : who would not beg
R : borrow or steal
S : from anyone.
The correct sequence should be
A. P Q R S   B. P R Q S
C. Q R S P   D. Q P R S

12. P : in the progress of
Q : universities play a crucial role
R : our civilization
S : in the present age.
The correct sequence should be
A. S Q P R   B. Q R S P
C. Q R P S   D. S Q R P

13. P : far out into the sea
Q : for the next two weeks there were further explosions
R : which hurled
S : ashes and debris.
The correct sequence should be
A. Q R P S   B. R S P Q
C. Q R S P   D. S R P Q

14. William Shakespeare,
P : in his lifetime
Q : the great English dramatist
R : wrote thirty-five plays
S : and several poems.
The correct sequence should be
A. P Q R S
B. R S P Q
C. Q S R P
D. Q R S P

15. Whenever I am,
P : with an old friend of mine
Q : in New Delhi
R : to have dinner
S : I always try.
The correct sequence should be
A. S Q P R   B. Q S R P
C. R P S Q   D. P R Q S

16. P : I don't know
Q : must have thought
R : what people sitting next to me
S : but I came away.
The correct sequence should be
A. R S Q P   B. R Q S P
C. P Q R S   D. P R Q S

17. P : in estimating the size of the earth
Q : but they were hampered by the lack of instruments of precision
R : ancient astronomers
S : used methods which were theoretically valid
The correct sequence should be
A. R P Q S   B. P R Q S
C. R S Q P   D. R P S Q

18. P : It is a pity that
Q : by offering a handsome dowry
R : a number of parents think that
S : they will be able to ensure the happiness of their daughters
The correct sequence should be
A. S Q R P   B. P R S Q
C. P S R Q   D. P R Q S

19. The common man
P : in nurturing
Q : a more active role
R : communal harmony
S : should play
The correct sequence should be
A. P R S Q   B. S Q P R
C. S Q R P   D. P R Q S

20. The doctor
P : able to find out
Q : what has caused
R : the food poisoning
S : has not been

The correct sequence should be
A. S P R Q B. P R Q S
C. P R S Q D. S P Q R

21. P : was suspended
Q : the officer being corrupt
R : before his dismissal
S : from service

The correct sequence should be
A. Q P S R B. Q P R S
C. R S Q P D. R S PQ

22. With an unsteady hand
P : on my desk
Q : from his pocket
R : he took an envelope
S : and threw it

The correct sequence should be
A. Q R P S B. Q R S P
C. R Q P S D. R Q S P

23. P : she gave her old coat
Q : to a beggar
R : the one with the brown fur on it
S : shivering with cold

The correct sequence should be
A. S Q R P B. S P R Q
C. P R Q S D. P S Q R

24. It is a privilege
P : to pay tax
Q : of every citizen
R : as well as the duty
S : as well as the duty who is well-placed

The correct sequence should be
A. R P S Q B. S P R Q
C. R Q S P D. S Q R P

25. It is not good
P : of the wicked persons
Q : to overthrow
R : to accept the help
S : the righteous persons

The correct sequence should be
A. R S Q P B. Q S R P
C. R P Q S D. Q P R S

26. Life is judged
P : and not by
Q : of work done
R : the longevity of years
S : by the quality

The correct sequence should be
A. Q S P R B. S Q R P.
C. Q S R P D. S Q P R

27. P : When he learns that
Q : you have passed the examination
R : in the first division
S : your father will be delighted

The correct sequence should be
A. Q P S R B. S P Q R
C. Q R S P D. S R Q P

28. P : The journalist
Q : saw
R : countless number of the dead
S : driving across the field of battle

The correct sequence should be
A. P Q S R B. P Q R S
C. P S Q R D. S R Q P

29. P : Jane planned
Q : some stamps
R : to buy
S : this afternoon

The correct sequence should be
A. P R Q S B. P S Q R
C. Q R P S D. Q S P R

30. Her mother
P : when she was
Q : hardly four years old
R : began to teach Neha
S : English

The correct sequence should be
A. R S Q P B. S R P Q
C. R S P Q D. S R Q P

31. P : Bill had
Q : a friend
R : an appointment
S : to meet

The correct sequence should be

A. P S R Q B. P R S Q
C. Q S R P D. Q R S P

32. For fear

P : that may or may not affect them perhaps at first
Q : of upsetting young people
R : only healthy people over 80 should be sequenced
S : about their genetic propensities

The correct sequence should be

A. S Q P R B. Q S R P
C. S Q R P D. Q S P R

33. While traditional

P : under made-up Americans aliases pretending familiarity with a culture and climate
Q : India sleeps a dynamic young cohort of highly skilled articulate professionals
R : they've never actually experienced earning salaries that were undreamt of by their elders
S : work through the night in the call centres functioning on US time

The correct sequence should be

A. P R Q S B. Q S P R
C. P S Q R D. Q R P S

34. IITs are

P : of great self-confidence and competitive advantage for India today
Q : in science and technology which has become a source
R : as they epitomize his creation of an infrastructure for excellence
S : perhaps Jawaharlal Nehru's most consequential legacy

The correct sequence should be

A. Q P S R B. S R Q P
C. Q R S P D. S P Q R

35. As India

P : from nearly 250 years of the British rule in India
Q : first major struggle for independence from the British rule
R : celebrates the Diamond Jubilee of its independence
S : it also observes simultaneously the 150th Anniversary of the Great Indian Mutiny

The correct sequence should be

A. R S P Q B. Q P S R
C. R P S Q D. Q S P R

36. There have been

P : a day after high intensity violence left at least 50 persons
Q : sporadic clashes between
R : dead in the northern city of Tripoli
S : the Lebanese army and militants

The correct sequence should be

A. Q S R P B. S Q R P
C. Q S P R D. S Q P R

37. Although

P : of non-owner managers came to be widely appreciated
Q : political freedom from the British masters
R : came to us in 1947 it was not until
S : well into the following decade that the role

The correct sequence should be

A. S P Q R B. Q R S P
C. S R Q P D. Q P S R

38. Conditions

P : for marketing in the U.S. and Canada
Q : Mexico as a manufacturing base
R : that Indian companies aspiring to tap
S : would have to fulfil include the complex rules of origin

The correct sequence should be

A. R Q P S B. S P Q R
C. R P Q S D. S Q P R

39. Aside

P : of the same three-storey building in the military academy
Q : from eating in the same dining hall
R : half to the north of the entrance half to the south
S : the 206 troops live side by side on the ground floor

The correct sequence should be

A. R P S Q B. Q S P R
C. R S P Q D. Q P S R

40. Russia's test firing
P : to US steps that have sparked an arms race
Q : of an intercontinental ballistic missile on
R : and undermined world security
S : Tuesday was in response

The correct sequence should be

A. S Q P R B. Q S R P
B. S Q R P D. Q S P R

41. Marks, cities, civilization —
P : on the verge of globalization; poised to
Q : the slow ascent to where he is today, poised
R : it is in this order that primitive man made
S : achieve universal prosperity and abundance

The correct sequence should be

A. R Q P S B. P S R Q
B. R S P Q D. P Q R S

42. I bow my head
P : for their sense of the beautiful in
Q : nature and for their foresight in investing beautiful
R : manifestations of nature with a religious significance
S : in reverence to our ancestors

The correct sequence should be

A. Q R S P B. S P Q R
B. Q P S R D. S R Q P

43. With all the crime and sleaze
P : I am not sure how many parents will be able to
Q : how many will have the courage to satisfy the child's uncomfortable queries
R : that dominates the front page of the newspapers today
S : read out the headlines to their children and if they do so

The correct sequence should be

A. R P S Q B. S Q R P
C. R Q S P D. P R S Q

44. The way
P : processes that govern their actions
Q : nutrients become integral parts
R : depends on the physiological and biochemical
S : of the body and contribute to its functions

The correct sequence should be

A. Q R S P B. P S R Q
C. Q S R P D. S P R Q

45. Thus,
P : international surveys would hence forth record
Q : if dirt-poor people in the developing world
R : their wealth of happiness alongside their material poverty
S : display a general sense of well-being

The correct sequence should be

A. S Q R P B. Q S P R
C. S Q P R D. Q S R P

46. It's
P : someone who's grieving but
Q : natural to feel uncomfortable
R : that prevent you from being there
S : or awkward when you have to help

The correct sequence should be

A. Q P S R B. R S P Q
C. Q S P R D. R P S Q

47. Developing countries
P : along the equator, which
Q : could become leaders in energy production
R : are expected to face the brunt of global warming
S : with a solar energy breakthrough

The correct sequence should be

A. Q S P R B. P R Q S
C. Q R P S D. P S Q R

48. A diversified
P : use as a heating or power generation fuel by converting gas into
Q : adding a new dimension to the traditional use of gas
R : of natural gas is emerging

S : amongst other products, high quality diesel transportation fuel virtually free of sulphur.

The correct sequence should be

A. R P Q S B. S Q P R
C. R Q P S D. S P Q R

49. As things stand

P : but a majority still does not have access to English

Q : linguistic edge they are equipped with

R : after globally because of the

S : Indian professionals are much sought

The correct sequence should be

A. R S P Q B. S R Q P
C. R S Q P D. S R P Q

50. While advocates

P : of its provisions with the

Q : there is some misguided concern about a possible clash of some

R : of social reform have generally hailed the new legislation

S : religious and customary practices in vogue in the country

The correct sequence should be

A. R Q P S B. Q R S P
C. R Q S P D. Q R P S

51. He has

P : while has in a reverie

Q : found the book

R : at the bus-stop

S : he lost

The proper sequence should be:

A. Q R S P B. P R Q S
C. Q S R P D. P Q S R

52. Then the women

P : lamenting their evil desire

Q : that had brought

R : wept loudly

S : this sorrow upon them

The proper sequence should be:

A. R P Q S B. R Q P S
C. P Q S R D. P R Q S

53. It is easy to excuse

P : but it is hard

Q : in a boy of fourteen

R : the mischief of early childhood

S : to tolerate even unavoidable faults

The proper sequence should be:

A. R P Q S B. Q R S P
C. Q R P S D. R P S Q

54. I don't remember

P : I saw a man dying in front of a hospital

Q : but when I left Lucknow in 1984

R : hit apparently by a fast moving car

S : the exact date

The proper sequence should be:

A. S Q R P B. S Q P R
C. Q R P S D. S P R Q

55. Since the beginning of history

P : have managed to catch

Q : the Eskimos and Red Indians

R : by a very difficult method

S : a few specimens of this acquatic mammal

The proper sequence should be:

A. Q P R S B. S Q P R
C. S Q R P D. Q P S R

56. I saw that

P : but seeing my host in this mood

Q : I deemed it proper to take leave

R : as I had frequently done before

S : it had been my intention to pass the night there

The proper sequence should be:

A. Q P S R B. Q R P S
C. S P Q R D. S R P Q

57. It was to be

P : before their school examination

Q : which was due to start

R : the last expedition

S : in a month's time

The proper sequence should be:

A. S R Q P B. R Q S P
C. R P Q S D. S P R Q

58. They felt safer

P : to watch the mountain

Q : of more than five miles

R : as they settled down

S : from a distance

The proper sequence should be:
A. R P S Q B. R S Q P
C. P Q S R D. P R S Q

59. If you need help
P : promptly and politely
Q : ask for attendants
R : to help our customers
S : who have instructions
The proper sequence should be:
A. S Q P R B. Q P S R
C. Q S R P D. S Q R P

60. He was so kind and generous that
P : he not only
Q : made others do so
R : but also
S : helped them himself
The proper sequence should be:
A. P S R Q B. S P Q R
C. P R S Q D. Q P R S

61. People
P : at his dispensary
Q : went to him
R : of all professions
S : for medicine and treatment
The proper sequence should be:
A. Q P R S B. R P Q S
C. R Q S P D. Q R P S

62. When it began to rain suddenly on the first of January
P : to celebrate the new year
Q : we ran for shelter
R : to the neighbouring house
S : where many people had gathered
The proper sequence should be:
A. Q R P S B. P S Q R
C. P R S Q D. Q R S P

63. The master
P : who was very loyal to him
Q : punished the servant
R : without giving any valid reason
S : when he left the work unfinished
The proper sequence should be:
A. R Q P S B. R Q S P
C. Q P S R D. Q R P S

64. The appearance
P : this dinosaurs were at their peak
Q : of the first mammals on the earth
R : at the time when
S : went almost unnoticed
The proper sequence should be:
A. S R P Q B. Q S R P
C. Q R P S D. R P Q S

65. It is easier
P : to venture into space
Q : for men
R : beneath their feet
S : than to explore
The proper sequence should be:
A. Q R P S B. Q P S R
C. P S R Q D. P Q S R

66. It is very easy
P : a great deal more than one realises
Q : may mean
R : that a phrase that one does not quite understand
S : to persuade oneself
The proper sequence should be:
A. R S Q P B. S P Q R
C. S R Q P D. R Q P S

67. The national unity of a free people
P : to make it impracticable
Q : for there to be an arbitrary administration
R : depends upon a sufficiently even balance of political power
S : against a revolutionary opposition that is irreconciably opposed to it.
The proper sequence should be:
A. Q R P S B. Q R S P
C. R P Q S D. R S P Q

68. He told us that
P : and enjoyed it immensely
Q : in a prose translation
R : he had read Milton
S : which he had borrowed from his teacher
The proper sequence should be:
A. R S Q P B. Q R P S
C. R Q S P D. R Q P S

69. This time
P : exactly what he had been told
Q : the young man did
R : beyond his dreams
S : and the plan succeeded
The proper sequence should be:
A. Q P R S B. Q P S R
C. P Q S R D. Q S R P

70. As a disease
P : and breaks up marriages
Q : accidents and suicides
R : alcoholism leads to
S : affecting all ages
The proper sequence should be:
A. S R P Q B. R P S Q
C. S R Q P D. R Q P S

71. This majestic mahogany table
P : belongs to an old prince
Q : which has one leg missing
R : who is no impoverished
S : but not without some pride
The proper sequence should be:
A. P Q S R B. Q R S P
C. P R S Q D. Q P R S

72. We have to
P : as we see it
Q : speak the truth
R : there is falsehood and darkness
S : even it all around us
The proper sequence should be:
A. R Q S P B. Q R P S
C. R S Q P D. Q P S R

73. He sat
P : through the Town Hall Park
Q : which flanked a path running
R : under the boughs
S : of a spreading tamarind tree
The proper sequence should be:
A. P Q S R B. R S Q P
C. R S P Q D. P R S Q

74. We went
P : along the railway line
Q : and had a right to
R : where other people were not allowed to go
S : but daddy belonged to the railway
The proper sequence should be:
A. R P Q S B. P R S Q
C. R S Q P D. P R Q S

75. In the darkness
P : the long, narrow beard
Q : was clearly visible with
R : the tall stooping figure of the doctor
S : and the aquiline nose
The proper sequence should be:
A. R Q P S B. P S Q R
C. R S Q P D. Q P R S

76. It is foolish
P : of those who posses them
Q : to believe that
R : will result in victory
S : the use of nuclear weapons.
The correct sequence should be:
A. R S P Q B. Q S R P
C. P R Q S D. S Q P R

77. A distressing fact is that
P : social accountability
Q : are dominated only by greed
R : many people today
S : and there is hardly any
The correct sequence should be:
A. S R P Q B. Q S R P
C. P R Q S D. R Q S P

78. I once had
P : every morning
Q : a client who swore
R : for the past four years
S : she had a headache
The correct sequence should be:
A. P R S Q B. Q S P R
C. R P Q S D. S Q R P

79. People know
P : not only of the smokers themselves,
Q : that smoking tobacco
R : but also of their companions
S : is injurious to the health

The correct sequence should be:
A. P S Q R B. R P S Q
C. Q P R S D. Q S P R

80. He had
P : finished his lunch
Q : hardly
R : at the door
S : when someone knocked

The correct sequence should be:
A. Q P R S B. P Q R S
C. Q P S R D. R P Q S

81. Mr. Sexena was a profound scholar who
P : was held in high esteem by all those
Q : who read his books and visited him regularly
R : till his untimely death
S : though not popular with the general public

The correct sequence should be:
A. P Q R S B. R P Q S
C. S R Q P D. S P Q R

82. The Government wants that
P : by the veterinary surgeons
Q : by the butchers
R : all the goats slaughtered
S : must be medically examined

The correct sequence should be:
A. R P S Q B. Q S R P
C. R Q S P D. P R S Q

83. The general line about television
P : is that it is very exciting,
Q : but also potentially very dangerous
R : immensely powerful
S : that I took myself

The correct sequence should be:
A. P Q R S B. S P R Q
C. P R Q S D. R P Q S

84. The second test of good government is that
P : to every man and woman
Q : and act only with their consent
R : it should give a lot of freedom
S : and should treat their personalities with respect and sympathy

The correct sequence should be:
A. Q S P R B. S R Q P
C. R P S Q D. P Q R S

85. The teacher warned that
P : he would not let
Q : go home
R : those students
S : who do not finish the class work

The correct sequence should be:
A. P Q R S B. P R Q S
C. P R S Q D. R S P Q

86. Towards the end of the eighteenth century, quite a number of economists
P : in the near future
Q : at the possibility of
R : were seriously perturbed
S : the world facing starvation

The correct sequence should be:
A. P R Q S B. R Q S P
C. Q S P R D. R P Q S

87. The best way of understanding our own civilization
P : is to examine
Q : an ordinary man
R : in the life of
S : an ordinary day

The correct sequence should be:
A. P Q R S B. R Q P S
C. P S R Q D. R S P Q

88. What greater thing is there
P : for two human souls to feel
Q : to rest on each other in all sorrow,
R : that they are joined for life,
S : to strengthen each other in all labour

The correct sequence should be:
A. S Q R P B. R P Q S
C. Q R S P D. P R S Q

89. Fame
P : by showing off
Q : to the best advantage
R : one's ability and virtue
S : is earned

The correct sequence should be:
A. P Q R S B. S P R Q
C. P R S Q D. P Q S R

90. When he was a child
P : passed his happiest hours
Q : the boy who was to become Britain's Baron Haden
R : staring out of his apartment window
S : living in New York
The correct sequence should be:
A. Q S P R B. P R Q S
C. S Q P R D. R S Q P

91. P : The teacher had to be specially careful
Q : because he enjoyed the confidence
R : about how he faced up to this problem
S : of all the boys
The correct sequence should be:
A. P R Q S B. Q P S R
C. S P R Q D. P S R Q

92. Movies made in
P : all around the globle
Q : Hollywood in America
R : by people
S : are seen at the same time
The correct sequence should be:
A. Q S R P B. Q R P S
C. P S R Q D. Q P S R

93. P : The foundations of the prosperity of a state
Q : primary health and education but also
R : involves the creation of job oppotunities
S : does not merely rest on
The correct sequence should be:
A. P S Q R B. P Q R S
C. P R Q S D. P S R Q

94. I am pure
P : and will be happy
Q : sooner or later
R : a day will come
S : when all will be equal
The correct sequence should be:
A. Q P R S B. Q S R P
C. R Q S P D. R S Q P

95. P : To do his/her work properly
Q : it should be the pride and honour
R : without anybody forcing him/her
S : of every citizen in India
The correct sequence should be:
A. Q S R P B. P R Q S
C. Q S P R D. P Q R S

96. The person who can state
P : correct than the person who cannot
Q : is more likely to be
R : his antagonist's point of view
S : to the satisfaction of the antagonist
The correct sequence should be:
A. R S Q P B. R Q P S
C. P Q R S D. S Q R P

97. The time has come
P : for future generations to come
Q : that the ideal of peace is a distant ideal
R : or one which can be postponed
S : when man must no longer think
The correct sequence should be:
A. P Q R S B. S Q R P
C. Q R S P D. R S P Q

98. I had been staying with
P : at his cottage among the Yorkshire fells
Q : a friend of mine
R : a delightfully lazy fellow
S : some ten miles away from the railway station
The correct sequence should be:
A. P Q R S B. Q R P S
C. Q R S P D. R Q P S

99. All the evil in this world is brought about by person
P : when they ought to be up
Q : but do not know
R : nor what they ought to be doing
S : who are always up and doing
The correct sequence should be:
A. P Q S R B. Q P R S
C. S Q P R D. P Q R S

100. If all the countries
P : of mankind and agree to obey
Q : work together for the common good
R : with each other and there will be no more war
S : the laws, then they will never fight
The correct sequence should be:
A. P Q R S B. Q S P R
C. Q P S R D. R Q P S

ANSWERS

1	2	3	4	5	6	7	8	9	10
B	D	A	B	C	C	A	C	A	D
11	12	13	14	15	16	17	18	19	20
C	A	C	D	B	D	C	B	B	D
21	22	23	24	25	26	27	28	29	30
B	D	C	C	B	D	B	C	A	B
31	32	33	34	35	36	37	38	39	40
B	D	B	B	C	C	C	A	B	D
41	42	43	44	45	46	47	48	49	50
A	B	A	C	B	C	B	A	B	A
51	52	53	54	55	56	57	58	59	60
C	A	D	B	D	D	C	A	C	A
61	62	63	64	65	66	67	68	69	70
C	D	C	C	B	B	D	C	B	C
71	72	73	74	75	76	77	78	79	80
D	D	B	B	A	B	D	B	D	C
81	82	83	84	85	86	87	88	89	90
D	C	B	C	B	B	C	D	B	C
91	92	93	94	95	96	97	98	99	100
A	A	A	C	C	A	B	B	C	C

ORDERING OF SENTENCES

A Paragraph is formed from sentences, it will convey its true meaning and purpose only when the sentences are arranged in a proper manner. Try and practise it.

Directions (Qs. 1 to 100) : *In these questions, each passage consists of six sentences. The first and the sixth sentences are given in the beginning. The middle four sentences in each passage have been removed and jumbled up. These jumbled sentences are labelled P, Q, R and S. Choose the proper sequence of the four sentences P, Q, R, and S from the alternatives A, B, C and D.*

1. S_1 : I got a colourful bus, filled with all kinds of strange people.

S_6 : It was a gate that neither separated nor connected anything from or to anything.

P : We arrived at a gate like the one in Salvador Dali's paintings.

Q : The bus rode across dirty expanses without roads.

R : At first I wasn't aware that the bus roof was loaded with drugs.

S : Everyone was filled with dust and often the wheels would sink into the soft soil.

The proper sequence should be:

A. S P Q R B. Q R S P
C. R Q S P D. R S P Q

2. S_1 : For the average Indian tourist the mention of Indonesia conjures visions of Bali and little else.

S_6 : it is a pity since otherwise this largest archipelogo in the world has much to offer to the international visitor.

P : With cash flow problems, the airline has had to cut down its overseas operations.

Q : Tourism had not been much of a priority in this predominantly Muslim country of 210 million people.

R : The air connectivity through the national airline is also diminishing.

S : This aspect is evident in the low budget allocated each year to this sector.

The proper sequence should be:

A. Q S R P B. R P S Q
C. Q R S P D. S Q P R

3. S_1 : Man cannot survive except through his mind. He comes on earth unarmed.

S_6 : To plant, he needs a process of thought; to hunt, he needs weapons; and to make weapons the process of thought.

P : Man has no claws, no fangs, no horns and no great strength of muscle.

Q : Animals obtain food by force.

R : He must plant his food or hunt it.

S : His brain is his only weapon.

The proper sequence should be:

A. S Q P R B. P R Q S
C. Q S P R D. P Q S R

4. S_1 : Bill Clinton is the US President.

S_6 : Looking at him, a lot of people are turning vegetarian.

P : But that is not true of Mr. Clinton.

Q : This had led him to be a vegetarian.

R : His philosophy is 'Be simple'.

S : Men as powerful as him usually have lavish tastes.

The proper sequence should be:

A. S P Q R B. S P R Q
C. R Q P S D. P Q S R

5. S_1 : Large parts of Karnataka are located in the drought prone rain shadow of the Western Ghats characterised by low and unreliable rainfall.

S_6 : Once water is made available for irrigation the economic picture of the area would be transformed.

P : The project occupies a triangular area lying between the Krishna and Bheema rivers.

Q : The Upper Krishna Project is being executed in the drought prone north eastern part of Karnataka about 456 kms from Bangalore in the districts of Gulburga, Raichur, Bagalkot and Bijapur.

R : The area though being subjected to vagaries of the monsoons has highly fertile land.

S : The population in this area subsists mainly on agriculture.

The proper sequence should be:

A. R S Q P B. P Q R S
C. Q P R S D. P S Q R

6. S_1: As the icebergs drift away from the poles towards warmer waters, they often invade the paths of ships, and in times of fog cause fearful collisions.

S_6: More than fifteen hundred lives were lost.

P : Striking an iceberg without warning in the fog, she sank quickly.

Q: The Titanic was the largest ship in the world at that time.

R: She was sailing on her maiden voyage from Southampton to New York with more than two thousand passengers and crew.

S : The biggest disaster of this kind ever recorded was that of the Titanic on April 14, 1912.

The proper sequence should be:

A. P Q R S B. S Q R P
C. Q R P S D. Q S P R

7. S_1: The release of atomic energy is the greatest achievement which science has yet attained.

S_6: However, the scientists are gratified by the numerous applications of atomic energy for peaceful and constructive purposes.

P : But the first invention to which their discoveries were applied was a bomb.

Q: The atom was split by physicists whose minds were set on the search for knowledge.

R: It was more deadly than any other weapon invented so far.

S : It is with this dread that scientists regard the first use to which their greatest discovery was put.

The proper sequence should be:

A. P Q R S B. S Q P R
C. Q P R S D. R S Q P

8. S_1: Human beings have the most common trait of airing their individual views and opinions.

S_6: A rigid and blind self-justification, though a common human weakness, will lead nowhere.

P : If everybody starts running after his own point of view without caring for others, civilisation will soon perish.

Q: But we have to live in a society and cooperation is the basis of civilisation.

R: Everybody has a right to live and lead his own life, but one should be tolerant of others' views.

S : What is essential to live happily in this world is a peaceful coexistence—to live and let others live.

The proper sequence should be:

A. P R Q S B. Q P S R
C. R Q P S D. S R P Q

9. S_1: The northeastern region presents a diverse system of habitats ranging from tropical rain forests to alpine meadows.

S_6: The winter temperature in Shillong, for example, varies from 4ºC to 24ºC; in Gangtok, from 9ºC to 23ºC.

P : In eastern Himalayas, the rainfall ranges from 125 to 300 cm; in Assam from 178 to 305 cm.

Q: The temperature in the region varies with location, elevation, topography, rainfall and humidity.

R: This uneven distribution affects the region in two opposite ways, floods and droughts.

S : It is largely a humid tropical region with two periods of rainfall; the winter rains come from the west and the summer rains are brought by the monsoon winds.

The proper sequence should be:

A. Q R S P B. S P R Q
C. P Q R S D. R S Q P

10. S_1: The coconuts are usually picked before they are quite ripe to stop them from falling to the ground or into the water.

S_6: Like this, in a series of jerks, first feet and then hands, he goes right to the top of the tree taking the rope with him.

P : First the fastens a strong piece of rope around his ankles; then, he puts both hands around the smooth tree-trunk and grips it lower down with his bare feet.

Q: It is exciting to watch him climb.

R : To pick them, man climbs up the tree, taking with him only a very sharp knife and a little coil of rope.

S : When he is ready to start, he gives a jerk and moves his feet higher up the trunks, then another jerk and moves his hands.

The proper sequence should be:

A. P R S Q B. S Q P R
C. Q P R S D. R Q P S

11. S_1 : A city tour organised by the airport got our next vote.

S_6 : "We can only grow in height as most of our land is reclaimed from the mud brought from neighbouring countries," said Bernadette.

P : A bumboat ride through the Singapore River gave us a vantage view of the country's prized possession of skyscrapers in the central business district.

Q : The tour is very popular with transit passengers and there are many such buses doing the route.

R : We were greeted into an airconditioned volvo bus with a bottle of chilled water.

S : On the drive through the 'colonial heart' of the city, our guide, Bernadette, pointed out the Parliament House, Supreme Court and City Hall to us.

The proper sequence should be:

A. R S Q P B. P Q S R
C. R Q S P D. P S Q R

12. S_1 : But Bhutan is a curious mix of modern and the medieval.

S_6 : His licence plate reads simply 'BHUTAN'.

P : It was next to a speed limit sign : 8 km an hour.

Q : Even the king zips through in a navy blue Toyota Land Cruiser.

R : I noticed a rusty sign for the Kit Kat chocolate bar and realised it was the only advertisement I had seen.

S : Yet in the cities, most middle class people drive brand new Japanese cars.

The proper sequence should be:

A. S Q R P B. R P S Q
C. S P R Q D. R Q S P

13. S_1 : His usually fretful features composed, Javagal Srinath announced his retirement from international cricket.

S_6 : He finished with 236 wickets in 67 Tests and 315 in 229 One-day Internationals.

P : He had spent the early years of his 13-year career sitting out nine Tests when he was at his quickest, being reminded of everything he was not.

Q : In a classic case of appreciating a good thing when it is gone, the tributes poured in for India's most successful pace bowler after Kapil Dev.

R : Not aggressive enough, not a non-vegetarian, not an all-rounder.

S : Srinath soldiered on, whether wickets were flat or causes lost, as they often were when India toured.

The proper sequence should be:

A. Q P R S B. R S Q P
C. Q S R P D. R P Q S

14. S_1 : However, the flower industry also has its share of thorns.

S_6 : Also, there are no tax concessions from the Government.

P : Most companies have to individually invest in the transport, which is very costly.

Q : Then there are infrastructural bottlenecks—no refrigerated transport or retail chains and ware-houses to store the highly perishable commodity.

R : For one, it is extremely fragmented and dominated by small players who don't have the financial muscle to expand the business.

S : Ferns & Petals claims to be the only flower retailer with a multi-city presence in India.

The proper sequence should be:

A. Q S R P B. R P Q S
C. Q P R S D. R S Q P

15. S_1 : One could well be forgiven for momentarily confusing Spencer Plaza, Chennai, with a Dubai Shopping Mall.

S_6 : Sensing that healthcare plus tourism adds to big opportunities, corporate hospitals, in cooperation with tour operators, are promoting India as a healthcare destination from the Middle East to far East.

P : Having satiated their shopping instincts, many head back, not to a hotel, but to a hospital, and to ailing relatives.

Q : Arabs pour in and out of trendy showrooms, laden with bags full of branded clothes, footwear and cosmetics.

R : It is a scenario being replicated across India.

S : For these are tourists with a difference, attracted to India for its cutting edge medical expertise more than its charms.

The proper sequence should be:

A. Q P S R B. S R Q P
C. Q R S P D. S P Q R

16. S_1 : Now that I am getting old and stiff in the joints, I like to meditate, while grazing in the pasture, on my foal days.

S_6 : When I was old enough, the trainer came and, to my great indignation, fastened a long rope to my head, and then began driving me round and round in circles with his long whip.

P : I had no work to do, and could run about after my mother, who was a fine white Arab mare, without any restraint.

Q : I think that was the happiest part of my life.

R : But that could not last for ever.

S : Most of my time was spent in the fields, where I nibbled the tender grass and capered about, while my mother was steadily grazing.

The proper sequence should be:

A. S-R-Q-P B. Q-P-S-R
C. Q-R-S-P D. S-P-Q-R

17. S_1 : A stamp is, to many people, just a slip of paper that takes a letter from one town or country to another.

S_6 : An album, a packet of hinges, a new supply of stamps, and the time passes swiftly and pleasantly.

P : But they do not realise that there are many who do buy, many who find the effort worth-while and many who, if they do not spend their time collecting stamps, would spend it less profitably.

Q : They are unable to understand why do we stamp collectors find so much pleasure in collecting them.

R : To them it seems a waste of time, a waste of effort and a waste of money.

S : We all seek something to do in our leisure hours and what better occupation is there to keep us out of mischief than that of collecting stamps?

The proper sequence should be:

A. S P R Q B. Q P R S
C. S R P Q D. Q R P S

18. S_1 : The British wanted it to be their answer to the American White House.

S_6 : In the end it earned him a place in the history books.

P : Today, the Head of the Indian Republic occupies just a handful of the 340 rooms.

Q : No wonder Edwin Lutyens didn't mind that the 17-year assignment earned him just £ 5,000.

R : But the 354-acre complex is an apt example of the expertise of a man who wanted the Rashtrapati Bhavan to be an object of admiration forever.

S : Though the answer was good enough, the British didn't anticipate that within

17 years of building the Viceroy House, they would have to leave the country and the architectural wonder would be renamed Rashtrapati Bhavan.

The proper sequence should be:

A. R Q S P B. S P R Q
C. S Q R P D. R P S Q

19. S_1 : And the biggest wonder about the Harappan cities is, simply put, their brick.

S_6 : In other words, the brick was just like the platinum rod kept in Paris to define the world standard of time.

P : Some archaeologists have ventured further.

Q : If at all the size varied in some sites, it still retained the same length – breadth – height proportion everywhere!

R : It had a standard size, be it in Mohenjodaro or Harappa, Kalibangan or Lothal.

S : They say that even the constructions – the houses and the cities – were built in the same proportion as the brick.

The proper sequence should be:

A. R Q P S B. S P Q R
C. R P Q S D. S Q P R

20. S_1 : Freedom and power bring responsibility.

S_6 : That future is not one of ease or resting but of incessant striving so that we may fulfil the pledges we have so often taken and the one we shall take today.

P : Some of these pains continue even now.

Q : Before the birth of freedom we have endured all the pains of labour and our hearts are heavy with the memory of this sorrow.

R : Nevertheless, the past is over and it is the future that beckons to us now.

S : That responsibility rests upon this assembly, a sovereign body representing sovereign people of India.

The proper sequence should be:

A. P R S Q B. S R P Q
C. P Q S R D. S Q P R

21. S_1 : The other day we heard someone smilingly refer to poets as dreamers.

S_6 : Dreams are the sunrise streamers heralding a new day of scientific progress, another forward surge.

P : We must not be so superficial that we fail to discern the practicableness of dreams.

Q : Where they differ from the logician and the scientist is in the temporal sense alone; they are ahead of their time, where logicians and scientists are abreast of their time.

R : The truth is that poets are just as practical as people who build bridges or look into microscopes; and just as close to reality and truth.

S : Now, it is accurate to refer to poets as dreamers, but it is not discerning to infer, as this person did, that the dreams of poets have no practical value beyond the realm of literary diversion.

The proper sequence should be:

A. S P Q R B. Q R S P
C. S R Q P D. Q P S R

22. S_1 : What was his great power over the mind and heart of man due to?

S_6 : That truth made the service of the poor and the dispossessed the passion of his life, for where there is inequality and discrimination and suppression there is injustice and evil and untruth.

P : That truth led him to proclaim without ceasing that good ends can never be attained by evil methods, that the end itself is distorted if the method pursued is bad.

Q : Even we realize that his dominating passion was truth.

R : That truth led him to fight evil and untruth wherever he found them, regardless of the consequences.

S : That truth led him to confess publicly whenever he thought he had made a mistake – Himalayan errors he called some of his own mistakes.

The proper sequence should be:

A. S R Q P B. Q P S R
C. Q R S P D. S P Q R

23. S_1 : Political empowerment apart, the state should recognise the right to life of every citizen.

S_6 : The state should prepare for the seasons ahead, not just winter, and create shelters on a war footing.

P : Places of religious worship play an important role in this respect, providing food and shelter.

Q : Where lives are at stake, resource crunch cannot work as an excuse.

R : It can still intervene to save lives, by ensuring that offices, schools and other institutions that function only during the day are used as night shelters.

S : However, civil society organisations cannot be expected to compensate for state neglect.

The proper sequence should be:

A. S Q R P B. R P S Q

C. S P R Q D. R Q S P

24. S_1 : This is the age of knowledge.

S_6 : Not surprisingly then that we Indians are often labelled as being overly superstitious.

P : Logic and intuition are no longer enemies.

Q : It is also the Age of Aquarius.

R : The two live together comfortably in every Indian household.

S : So why should superstitions be considered out of place in this age of nanotechnology and computers?

The proper sequence should be:

A. Q P S R B. R S P Q

C. Q S P R D. R P S Q

25. S_1 : Sachin has scored centuries against all oppositions, in all countries.

S_6 : But largely, he has been the dictator, giving nightmares to quality bowlers of the world.

P : There have been those rare occasions when he looked entangled at the crease.

Q : In fact, some of his most memorable essays came in adverse conditions.

R : Gavaskar called him "the closest thing to batting perfection this game has ever seen".

S : Sachin has established his stamp over all types of attack.

The proper sequence should be:

A. P Q S R B. R Q S P

C. P S Q R D. R S Q P

26. S_1 : Jagan has been working in our home for over 25 years.

S_6 : Then came the question of raising his children on the paltry sum of money he earned washing cars and sweeping homes.

P : And another

Q : Till finally his wife delivered a son and he declared his innings.

R : I remember the day his first daughter was born.

S : And then came another.

The proper sequence should be:

A. R P S Q B. Q S P R

C. R S P Q D. Q P S R

27. S_1 : Diabetes is a silent killer and because it does not seem as potent as cancer or AIDS is very often overlooked without too much heed by patients.

S_6 : Though diabetes can never be totally cured it can definitely be controlled from causing serious consequences.

P : Worse, as many as a third of them don't even know it.

Q : Untreated diabetes can lead to heart and kidney failure, amputations and even death.

R : Millions of people suffer from diabetes.

S : The early symptoms of diabetes are often confused with other less grave conditions.

The proper sequence should be:

A. S Q R P B. R P S Q

C. S P R Q D. R Q S P

28. S_1 : Ships, built in dry docks are launched amidst chanting of Atharva Veda.

S_6 : The latest INS Mumbai is the tenth reincarnation of its original INS Bombay.

P : Even now newer warships are given names of old decommissioned warships.

Q : One of the enduring superstitions of the Navy is that old ships don't die.

R : In Europe, they break champagne bottles on the bow; in India we break coconuts.

S : It derives from the animistic belief that a ship has a soul that lives on and that it is reborn.

The proper sequence should be:

A. R Q S P B. S P R Q
C. R P S Q D. S Q R P

29. S_1 : Jaswant Singh of 4 Garhwal Rifles was apparently relaxing at 10,000 feet when he spotted a whole battalion of Chinese troops advancing towards an Indian Army post.

S_6 : Versions of the story vary.

P : They surrounded him, captured the three and beheaded them.

Q : Finally the enemy sent a scout party to ascertain the real strength of the Indian defence, and they found just a rifleman and two girls.

R : After the war, the Chinese, impressed by the rifleman's valour, gave his head back to the Indians, who set up a temple for him.

S : With just one 303 and ammunition supplied by two girls from an abandoned dump, he mowed down about 50 enemy troopers.

The proper sequence should be:

A. P Q S R B. S R P Q
C. P R S Q D. S Q P R

30. S_1 : Each creature of the sea has its own significance for seamen.

S_6 : A dead dolphin is a bad omen.

P : One reason could be that dolphins and sharks do not cohabit.

Q : Sighting a dolphin is supposed to bring luck.

R : A dolphin swimming with the ship brings good luck.

S : Upon sighting the first dolphin on a voyage even the admiral will come up on deck to watch it.

The proper sequence should be:

A. S R Q P B. Q P S R
C. S P Q R D. Q R S P

31. S_1 : While crossing a busy road we should obey the policeman on duty.

S_6 : We should never run while crossing a road.

P : We should always cross the road at the zebra crossing.

Q : We must look to the signal lights and cross the road only when the road is clear.

R : If there are no signal lights at the crossing, we should look to the right, then to the left and again to the right before crossing the road.

S : If the road is not clear we should wait.

The proper sequence should be:

A. P S R Q B. P Q R S
C. R Q S P D. Q R P S

32. S_1 : As a dramatist Rabindranath was no[t] what might be called a success.

S_6 : Therefore, drama forms the essential par[t] of the traditional Indian culture.

P : His dramas were moulded more on th[e] lines of the traditional Indian villag[e] dramas than the dramas of the moder[n] world.

Q : His plays were more a catalogue of idea[s] than a vehicle of the expression of actio[n].

R : Actually drama has always been the li[fe] of the Indian people, as it deals wit[h] legends of gods and goddesses.

S : Although in his short stories and nove[ls] he was able to create living and wel[l] defined characters, he did not seem to b[e] able to do so in his dramas.

The proper sequence should be:

A. S R Q P B. Q P S R
C. Q S P R D. R S Q P

33. S_1 : The Hound of Baskervilles was fear[ed] by the people of the area.

S_6 : The Hound of Baskervilles remains unsolved mystery.

P : Some people spoke of seeing a hu[ge] shadowy form of a hound at midnight the moor.

Q : But they spoke of it in tones of horror.
R : Nobody had actually seen the hound.
S : This shadowy form did not reveal any details about the animal.

The proper sequence should be:

A. S P Q R B. S P R Q
C. P S R Q D. P Q R S

34. S_1 : All the land was covered by the ocean.
S_6 : The god moulded the first people out of clay according to his own image and mind.
P : The leading god fought the monster, killed it and chopped its body into two halves.
Q : A terrible monster prevented the gods from separating the land from the water.
R : The god made the sky out of the upper part of the body and ornamented it with stars.
S : The god created the earth from the lower part, grew plants on it and populated it with animals.

The proper sequence should be:

A. P Q R S B. P Q S R
C. Q P S R D. Q P R S

35. S_1 : Over decades, we have made things a lot worse.
S_6 : In the end, it can destroy the entire village.
P : It has proved quite disastrous.
Q : The unregulated spread of borewells was an early form of water privatisation.
R : Many poor farmers have seen their dug wells sucked dry as neighbours collar all the groundwater.
S : The richer you are, the more wells you can sink, the deeper you can go.

The proper sequence should be:

A. Q S P R B. P Q R S
C. Q P R S D. P S Q R

36. S_1 : The fact is that good writing is a craft which can be acquired like any other craft.
S_6 : In short, he has to become a wordsmith.
P : Much the same is the case with the one who aspires to become a good craftsman of English.
Q : Let's take examples.
R : A young man, who wants to become a goldsmith or a silversmith, becomes an apprentice with a seasoned man in that craft.
S : After a few years of apprenticeship, he learns the ins and outs of it and becomes a skillful craftsman.

The proper sequence should be:

A. S P Q R B. Q R S P
C. S R Q P D. Q P S R

37. S_1 : Yet, things are not that bad.
S_6 : Fortune, after all, favours the brave, not the complainers.
P : Some of the successful people started out with more handicaps than us.
Q : It is time we stopped feeling sorry for ourselves and got over our doubts and fears to face the world.
R : If we look around ourselves, we find people who had less than us but went on to make their fortunes.
S : Perhaps we can replicate what they did for themselves.

The proper sequence should be:

A. R Q S P B. S P R Q
C. R P S Q D. S Q R P

38. S_1 : When you have to study for examination, you have many things to do.
S_6 : The final aim, of course, is to pass the examination that is two months away.
P : Suppose you have only two months to do it.
Q : The time-table tells you what you have to do everyday and for how many hours.
R : You have to read a number of books, learn tables and formulas.
S : Then the best way is to make a time-table for yourself.

The proper sequence should be:

A. R P S Q B. S R Q P
C. Q R S P D. P S Q R

39. S_1 : The umpire has to do a lot of hard work before qualifying to supervise a match.
S_6 : So an umpire must keep abreast of time and apply the rules as occasion demands.

P : However, umpires are human and are sometimes prone to make mistakes.

Q : The rules of the game are being constantly changed.

R : The players should gracefully and sportingly accept these mistakes.

S : He is aware of the responsibilities that go with the job.

The proper sequence should be:

A. Q P R S B. S P R Q

C. S R P Q D. Q R P S

40. S_1 : Mohan came to the city to meet a friend.

S_6 : He should not have behaved so rudely.

P : Mohan asked her to join them for tea.

Q : Mohan's friend who had some grudge against Sheila quickly got up and left the restaurant without saying a word.

R : While they were having tea at a restaurant Sheila, a former fellow-student of theirs, came in.

S : Though Sheila knew Mohan's friend was a bad fellow, she accepted the invitation.

The proper sequence should be:

A. P R S Q B. R P S Q

C. P R Q S D. R P Q S

41. S_1 : When the Romans invaded Britain about 2,000 years ago, their calendar was calculated on the phases of the moon.

S_6 : The astronomer's name was Sosigenes and his calendar had a year of 365 days.

P : This calendar had gradually become so out of line with the seasons that it was two or three months behind.

Q : The Emperor Julius Caesar was determined to correct it.

R : Caesar had been to Egypt and seen the advantages of a calendar which used only the sun.

S : So he sought help from a Greek astronomer who lived in the Egyptian city of Alexandria.

The proper sequence should be:

A. R Q P S B. P Q R S

C. P S R Q D. R S P Q

42. S_1 : Education is in great demand today in India.

S_6 : Things have changed considerably now.

P : These people were accustomed to applying their intelligence to the profession of their fathers.

Q : Since independence it has spread to backward classes.

R : They had no idea that they could train themselves to do something else.

S : Besides this training they had little book learning.

The proper sequence should be:

A. P Q R S B. Q P R S

C. P Q S R D. Q P S R

43. S_1 : There was once a king in India.

S_6 : The three sons did not know what to do and where to go.

P : The captain of the king's army wanted the kingdom for himself.

Q : He died leaving three sons.

R : The eldest of the three sons would have become the king.

S : So he drove the three sons away and took everything in the kingdom in his possession.

The proper sequence should be:

A. P R Q S B. P S Q R

C. Q S P R D. Q R P S

44. S_1 : An old man died and left his son a lot of money.

S_6 : He became sad and lonely.

P : Soon the had nothing left.

Q : The son was foolish young man.

R : All his friends left him.

S : He quickly spent all his money.

The proper sequence should be:

A. S Q R P B. Q S P R

C. S Q P R D. Q S R P

45. S_1 : Siberian crane is a migratory bird.

S_6 : They return to Siberia at the onset of summer in India.

P : They remain here for four-five months.

Q : Migrating birds are those which travel to other places for a period of time and then return.

R : They can't sustain in the severe winter of Siberia.

S : So during winters they travel thousands of miles to reach the bird sanctuary in Rajasthan in India.

The proper sequence should be:

A. Q R S P B. Q P S R
C. S R Q P D. S P Q R

46. S_1 : The removal of corruption prevalent in our country is a difficult problem.

S_6 : Corruption can be removed only when we improve our character.

P : None is ready and willing to perform this Herculean task.

Q : It is difficult to prove that Mr. X is corrupt.

R : The legal system of the country provides no solution to it.

S : The investigating officer is himself corrupt and allows the man to remain unpunished.

The proper sequence should be:

A. Q R P S B. P S Q R
C. Q S P R D. P R Q S

47. S_1 : A boy used to play pranks with his mother by hiding himself in a wooden box.

S_6 : Thus the box he used to hide in turned out to be his coffin.

P : The latch accidentally got locked, and the boy, unable to open it, died of asphyxiation.

Q : One day the playful boy, studying in the fifth standard, refused to go to school.

R : In a bid to surprise his mother he got into the empty wooden box and pulled down the lid.

S : His mother was so upset by this that she locked him up in the house and went to work.

The proper sequence should be:

A. Q S R P B. S Q R P
C. Q S P R D. S Q P R

48. S_1 : Abha, along with Gandhi and Patel, hesitated to interrupt.

S_6 : He leaned his forearms on their shoulders and moved forward.

P : Abha, the young wife of Kanu Gandhi, grandson of the Mahatma's cousin, and Manu the grand daughter of another cousin, accompanied him.

Q : Finally, therefore, she picked up the Mahatma's nickel-plated watch and showed it to him.

R : "I must go away", Gandhi remarked, and so saying he rose, went to the adjoining bath room and then started towards the prayer ground.

S : But she knew Gandhi's attachment to punctuality.

The proper sequence should be:

A. S P R Q B. R Q S P
C. S Q R P D. R P S Q

49. S_1 : Soon after he returned to the civilian life, Kennedy wrote a short essay.

S_6 : Such a recurrence would mean increased taxation which, in its turn, would hamper the functioning of free enterprise and affect the chances of full employment.

P : He had his own logic for it.

Q : He advanced an argument that after the war, efforts should be made to prevent the recurrence of an arms-race.

R : In this essay Kannedy tried to draw the Lessons from the ghastly experiences of the war.

S : It was published in February 1945, aptly titled : "Let's try an Experiment in Peace."

The proper sequence should be:

A. P Q R S B. S R Q P
C. P R Q S D. S Q R P

50. S_1 : Radio and television are the two most accessible media.

S_6 : Many of them are led to buy and use cosmetics and edibles they do not need.

P : Their teste and choice have been affected by commercial advertisements that come with sponsored programmes.

Q : The most vulnerable to the influence of this wave are children.

R : This is mainly because of the advertisement wave it has created.

S : Of the two, television has greater impact.

The proper sequence should be:

A. S P Q R B. Q R S P
C. S R Q P D. Q P S R

51. S_1 : She said on the phone that she would report for duty next day.

S_6 : Eventually we reported to the police.

P : We waited for a few days, then we decided to go to her place.

Q : But she did not.

R : We found it locked.

S : Even after that we waited for her for quite a few days.

The proper sequence should be:

A. P R S Q B. Q P S R
C. Q P R S D. S Q P R

52. S_1 : A force of attraction exists between everybody in the universe.

S_6 : The greater the mass, the greater is the earth's force of attraction on it—we call this force of attraction gravity.

P : Normally it is very small but when one of the bodies is a planet, like the earth, the force is considerable.

Q : It has been investigated by many scientists including Galileo and Newton.

R : Everything on or near the surface of the earth is attracted by the mass of the earth.

S : This gravitational force depends on the mass of the bodies involved.

The proper sequence should be:

A. P R Q S B. P R S Q
C. Q S R P D. Q S P R

53. S_1 : Metals are today being replaced by polymers in many applications.

S_6 : Many Indian Institutes of Science and Technology run special programmes on polymer science.

P : Above all, they are cheaper and easier to process, making them a viable alternative to metals.

Q : Polymers are essentially long chains of hydrocarbon molecules.

R : Today polymers as strong as metals have been developed.

S : These have replaced the traditional chromium-plated metallic bumpers in cars.

The proper sequence should be:

A. Q R S P B. R S Q P
C. R Q S P D. Q R P S

54. S_1 : It is regrettable that there is widespread corruption in the country at all levels.

S_6 : This is indeed a tragedy of great magnitude.

P : So there is hardly anything that the government can do about it now.

Q : And there are graft and other malpractices too.

R : The impression that corruption is a universal phenomenon persists and the people do not cooperate in checking this evil.

S : Recently several offenders were brought to book, but they were not given deterrent punishment.

The proper sequence should be:

A. Q S R P B. S Q R P
C. R S Q P D. P Q S R

55. S_1 : It was a dark moonless night.

S_6 : They all seemed to him to be poor and ordinary—mere childish words.

P : He turned over the pages, reading passages here and there.

Q : He heard them on the floor.

R : The poet took down his books of poems from his shelves.

S : Some of them contained his earliest writings which he had almost forgotten.

The proper sequence should be:

A. R P Q S B. R Q S P
C. R S P Q D. R P S Q

56. S_1 : A noise started above their heads.

S_6 : Nearly two hundred lives were lost on the fateful day.

P : But people did not take it seriously.

Q : That was to show everyone that there was something wrong.

R : It was a dangerous thing to do.

S : For, within minutes the ship began to sink.

The proper sequence should be:

A. P Q S R B. P R Q S
C. Q P R S D. Q P S R

57. S_1 : The cooperative system of doing business is a good way of encouraging ordinary workers to work hard.

S_6 : The main object is to maintain the interest of every member of the society and to ensure that the members participate actively in the projects of the society.

P : If the society is to be well run, it is necessary to prevent insincere officials being elected to the committee which is solely responsible for the running of the business.

Q : They get this from experienced and professional workers who are not only familiar with the cooperative system, but also with efficient methods of doing business.

R : To a large extent, many cooperative societies need advice and guidance.

S : The capital necessary to start a business venture is obtained by the workers' contributions.

The proper sequence should be:

A. S Q P R　　B. P Q S R
C. S R Q P　　D. P S R Q

58. S_1 : American private lives may seem shallow.

S_6 : This would not happen in China, he said.

P : Students would walk away with books they had not paid for.

Q : A Chinese journalist commented on a curious institution: the library.

R : Their public morality, however, impressed visitors.

S : But in general they returned them.

The proper sequence should be:

A. P S Q R　　B. Q P S R
C. R Q P S　　D. R P S Q

59. S_1 : The *Bhagavadgita* recognises the nature of man and the needs of man.

S_6 : A man who does not harmonise them, is not truly human.

P : All these three aspects constitute the nature of man.

Q : It shows how the human being is a rational one, an ethical one and a spiritual one.

R : More than all, it must be a spiritual experience.

S : Nothing can give him fulfilment unless it satisfies his reason, his ethical conscience.

The proper sequence should be:

A. P S R Q　　B. R S P Q
C. Q P S R　　D. P S Q R

60. S_1 : I usually sleep quite well in the train, but this time I slept only a little.

S_6 : It was shut all night, as usual.

P : Most people wanted it shut and I wanted it open.

Q : As usual, I got angry about the window.

R : The quarrel left me completely upset.

S : There were too many people and too much luggage all around.

The proper sequence should be:

A. R S Q P　　B. S Q P R
C. S Q R P　　D. R S P Q

61. S_1 : For decades, American society has been called a melting pot.

S_6 : In recent years, such differences—accentuated by the arrival of immigrants from Asia and other parts of the world in the United States—have become something to celebrate and to nurture.

P : Differences remained—in appearance, mannerisms, customs, speech, religion and more.

Q : The term has long been a cliche, and a half-truth.

R : But homogenisation was never achieved.

S : Yes, immigrants from diverse cultures and traditions did cast off vestiges of their native lands and become almost imperceptibly woven into the American fabric.

The proper sequence should be:

A. Q R S P　　B. S Q R P
C. S Q P R　　D. Q S R P

62. S_1 : While talking to a group, one should feel self-confident and courageous.

S_6 : Any man can develop his capacity if he has the desire to do so.

P : Nor is it a gift bestowed by Providence on only a few.

Q : One should also learn how to think calmly and clearly.

R : It is like the ability to play golf.

S : It is not as difficult as most men imagine.

The proper sequence should be:

A. S Q P R B. Q S P R
C. Q R S P D. R S Q P

63. S_1 : In 1934, William Golding published a small volume of poems.

S_6 : But *Lord of the Flies* which came out in 1954 was welcomed as "a most absorbing and instructive tale".

P : During the World War II (1939-45) he joined the Royal Navy and was present at the sinking of the *Bismarck*.

Q : He returned to teaching in 1945 and gave it up in 1962, and is now a full-time writer.

R : In 1939, he married and started teaching at Bishop Wordsworth's School in Salisbury

S : At first his novels were not accepted.

The proper sequence should be:

A. R P Q S B. R P S Q
C. S R P Q D. S Q P R

64. S_1 : Our ancestors thought that anything which moved itself was alive.

S_6 : Therefore some scientists think that life is just a very complicated mechanism.

P : The philosopher Descartes thought that both men and animals were machines.

Q : But a machine such as a motorcar or a steamship moves itself, and as soon as machines which moved themselves had been made, people asked, "Is man a machine?"

R : And before the days of machinery that was a good definition.

S : He also thought that the human machine was partly controlled by the soul action on a certain part of the brain, while animals had no souls

The proper sequence should be:

A. P R S Q B. R P Q S
C. P S Q R D. R Q P S

65. S_1 : But how does a new word get into the dictionary?

S_6 : He sorts them according to their grammatical function, and carefully writes a definition.

P : When a new dictionary is being edited, a lexicographer collects all the alphabetically arranged citation slips for a particular word.

Q : The dictionary makers notice it and make a note of it on a citation slip.

R : The moment a new word is coined, it usually enters the spoken language.

S : The word then passes from the realm of hearing to the realm of writing.

The proper sequence should be:

A. P Q R S B. P R S Q
C. R Q P S D. R S Q P

66. S_1 : The heart is the pump of life.

S_6 : All this was made possible by the invention of the heart-lung machine.

P : They have even succeeded in heart transplants.

Q : Nowadays surgeons are able to stop a patient's heart and carry out complicated operations.

R : A few years ago it was impossible to operate on a patient whose heart was not working properly.

S : If the heart stops we die in about five minutes.

The proper sequence should be:

A. S R Q P B. S P R Q
C. S Q P R D. S R P Q

67. S_1 : Throughout history man has used energy from the sun.

S_6 : This energy comes from inside atoms.

P : Today, when we burn wood or use electric current we are drawing on energy.

Q : However, we now have a new supply of energy.

R : All our ordinary life depends on the sun.

S : This has come from the sun.

The proper sequence should be:

A. S Q P R B. R Q P S
C. Q S R P D. P S R Q

68. S_1 : In India marriages are usually arranged by parents.

S_6 : She felt she was a modern girl and not a subject for bargaining

P : Sometimes girls and boys do not like the idea of arranged marriages.

Q : Most young people accept this state of affairs.

R : Shanta was like that.

S : They assume their parents can make good choices.

The proper sequence should be:

A. S P R Q B. P S R Q
C. Q S P R D. R Q P S

69. S_1 : I had halted on the road.

S_6 : I decided to watch him for a while and then go home.

P : As soon as I saw the elephant I knew I should not shoot him.

Q : It is a serious matter to shoot a working elephant.

R : I knew that his 'mast' was already passing off.

S : The elephant was standing eighty yards from the road.

The proper sequence should be:

A. S P Q R B. P Q S R
C. R Q P S D. S R P Q

70. S_1 : A man can be physically confined within stone walls.

S_6 : No tyranny can intimidate a lover of liberty.

P : But his mind and spirit will still be free.

Q : Thus his freedom of action may be restricted.

R : His hopes and aspirations still remain with him.

S : Hence, he will be free spiritually if not physically.

The proper sequence should be:

A. P Q R S B. S R Q P
C. Q P R S D. Q P S R

71. S_1 : The dictionary is the best friend for your task.

S_6 : Soon you will realize that this is an exciting task

P : That may not be possible always.

Q : It is wise to look it up immediately.

R : Then it must be firmly written on the memory and traced at the first opportunity.

S : Never allow a strange word to pass unchallenged.

The proper sequence should be:

A. P Q R S B. S P Q R
C. Q R P S D. S Q P R

72. S_1 : Far away in a little street there is a poor house.

S_6 : His mother has nothing to give but water, so he is crying

P : Her face is thin and worn and her hands are coarse, pricked by a needle, for she is a seam-stress.

Q : One of the windows is open and through it I can see a poor woman.

R : He has fever and he is asking for oranges.

S : In a bed in a corner of the room her little boy is lying ill.

The proper sequence should be:

A. S R Q P B. P Q S R
C. Q P S R D. R S P Q

73. S_1 : Kolkata unlike other cities, has kept its trams.

S_6 : The foundation stone was laid in 1972.

P : As a result, there is horrendous congestion.

Q : It was going to be the first in South Asia.

R : They run down the centre of the road.

S : To ease in the city decided to build an underground railway line.

The proper sequence should be:

A. P R S Q B. P S Q R

C. S Q R P D. R P S Q

74. S_1 : We now know that oceans are very deep.

S_6 : This reaches from India to the Antarctic.

P : For example, the Indian Ocean has a range called the Indian Ridge.

Q : Much of it is fairly flat.

R : However, there are great mountain ranges as well.

S : On average the bottom is two and a half to three and a half miles down.

The proper sequence should be:

A. S Q P R B. P Q S R

C. R S Q P D. Q P R S

75. S_1 : As he passed beneath her he heard the swish of her wings.

S_6 : The next moment he felt her wings spread outwards.

P : He was not falling head long now.

Q : Then monstrous terror seized him.

R : But it only lasted a minute.

S : He could hear nothing.

The proper sequence should be:

A. P S Q R B. Q S P R

C. Q S R P D. P R Q S

76. S_1 : When a satellite is launched, the rocket begins by going slowly upwards through the air.

S_6 : Consequently, the rocket still does not become too hot.

P : However, the higher it goes, the less air it meets.

Q : As the rocket goes higher, it travels faster.

R : For the atmosphere becomes thinner.

S : As a result there is less friction.

The proper sequence should be:

A. Q P R S B. Q S P R

C. P Q R S D. P Q S R

77. S_1 : Sunbirds are among the smallest of Indian birds.

S_6 : Our common sunbirds are the purple sunbird, the glossy black species and purplerumped sunbird, the yellow and maroon species

P : Though they are functionally similar to the hummingbirds of the New World, they are totally unrelated.

Q : They do eat small insects too.

R : They are also some of the most brilliantly-coloured birds.

S : Sunbirds feed on nectar mostly and help in pollination.

The proper sequence should be:

A. S Q P R B. R P S Q

C. Q P R S D. P S R Q

78. S_1 : Venice is a strange and beautiful city in the north of Italy.

S_6 : This is because Venice has no streets.

P : There are about four hundred old stone bridges joining the island of Venice.

Q : In this city there are no motor cars, no horses and no buses.

R : These small islands are near one another.

S : It is not an island but a hundred and seventeen islands.

The proper sequence should be:

A. P Q R S B. P R Q S

C. S R P Q D. P Q S R

79. S_1 : A ceiling on urban property.

S_6 : Since their value would exceed the ceiling fixed by the Government.

P : No mill-owner could own factories or mills or plants.

Q : And mass circulation papers.

R : Would mean that.

S : No press magnate could own printing presses.

The proper sequence should be:

A. Q S R P B. R P S Q

C. S R P Q D. Q P S R

80. S_1 : The weather-vane often tops a church spire, tower or high building.

S_6 : The weather-vane can, however, give us some indication of the weather.

P : They are only wind-vanes.

Q : Neither alone can tell us what the weather will be.

R : They are designed to point to the direction from which the wind is coming.

S : Just as the barometer only tells us the pressure of the air, the weather-vane tells us the direction of the wind.

The proper sequence should be:

A. P Q R S B. P S R Q
C. P R S Q D. S P Q R

81. S_1 : Most of the universities in the country are now facing financial crisis.

S_6 : The Government should realise this before it is too late.

P : Cost benefit yardstick thus should not be applied in the case of the universities.

Q : The current state of affairs cannot be allowed to continue for long.

R : Universities cannot be equated with commercial enterprises.

S : Proper development of universities and colleges must be ensured

The proper sequence should be:

A. Q R P S B. Q S P R
C. Q R S P D. Q P R S

82. S_1 : I keep on flapping my big ears all day.

S_6 : Am I not a smart, intelligent elephant?

P : They also fear that I will flap them all away.

Q : But children wonder why I flap them so.

R : I flap them so to make sure they are safely there on either side of my head.

S : But I know what I am doing.

The proper sequence should be:

A. S R Q P B. Q P S R
C. Q P R S D. P S R Q

83. S_1 : Urban problems differ from State to State and city to city.

S_6 : There is no underground drainage system in most cities, and the narrow historical roads are already congested.

P : Most of the cities have neither water nor the required pipelines.

Q : The population in these cities has grown beyond the planners' imagination.

R : However, certain basic problems are common to all cities.

S : Only broad macro-planning was done for such cities, without envisaging the future growth, and this has failed to meet the requirements.

The proper sequence should be:

A. P Q S R B. Q P S R
C. R Q P S D. R S Q P

84. S_1 : A gentleman who lived alone always had two plates placed on the table at dinner time.

S_6 : In this way the cat showed her gratitude to her master.

P : One day just as he sat down to dine, the cat rushed into the room.

Q : One plate was for himself and the other was for his cat.

R : She dropped a mouse into her own plate and another into her master's plate.

S : He used to give the cat a piece of meat from his own plate.

The proper sequence should be:

A. Q S P R B. P S R Q
C. Q R S P D. R P Q S

85. S_1 : I took cigarettes from my case.

S_6 : Then he continued to draw on it.

P : But when the fit of coughing was over, he replaced it between his lips.

Q : I lit one of them and placed it between the lips.

R : Then with a feeble hand he removed the cigarette.

S : Slowly he took a pull at it and coughed violently.

The proper sequence should be:

A. P S Q R B. Q P S R
C. Q S R P D. S R P Q

86. S_1 : Forcasting the weather has always been a difficult business.

S_6 : He made his forecasts by watching flights of the birds or the way smoke rose from fire.

P : During a period of drought, streams and rivers dried up, the cattle died from thirst and the crops were ruined.

Q : Many different things affect the weather and we have to study them carefully to make an accurate forecast.

R : Ancient Egyptians had no need of this weather in the Nile valley hardly ever changes.

S : In early times, when there were no instruments, such as thermometer or the barometer, man looked for tell-tale signs in the sky.

The proper sequence should be:

A. P R Q S B. Q P R S
C. Q R P S D. S P Q R

87. S_1 : Once upon a time there lived three young men in a certain town of Hindustan.

S_6 : All of them set out in search of their foe called Death.

P : All the people of the neighbourhood were mortally afraid of them.

Q : They were so powerful that they could catch growling lions and tear them to pieces.

R : Someone told them that they would become immortal if they killed Death.

S : The young men believed themselves to be very good friends.

The proper sequence should be:

A. Q P R S B. S Q P R
C. R S Q P D. S R P Q

88. S_1 : Duryodhana was a wicked prince.

S_6 : This enraged Duryodhana so much that he began to think of removing Bhima from his way.

P : One day Bhima made Duryodhana fall from a tree from which Duryodhana was stealing fruits.

Q : He did not like that Pandavas should be loved and respected by the people of Hastinapur.

R : Duryodhana specially hated Bhima.

S : Among the Pandavas, Bhima was extraordinarily strong and powerful.

The proper sequence should be:

A. P S Q R B. Q P R S
C. Q S R P D. P S R Q

89. S_1 : You know my wife, Madhavi, always urged me to give up smoking.

S_6 : Poor girl!

P : I really gave it up.

Q : And so when I went to jail I said to myself I really must give it up, if for no other reason than of being self-reliant.

R : When I emerged from jail, I wanted to tell her of my great triumph!

S : But when I met her, there she was with a packet of cigarettes.

The proper sequence should be:

A. P S R Q B. S P Q R
C. Q P R S D. R S P Q

90. S_1 : A black-haired, young woman came tripping along.

S_6 : Both disappeared from view.

P : She was leading a young man wearing a hat.

Q : The woman swept it off and tossed it in the air.

R : The child jumped up to catch the hat.

S : The young man tossed his head to shake the hat back.

The proper sequence should be:

A. P S Q R B. R P S Q
C. Q R P S D. S Q R P

91. S_1 : Jawaharlal Nehru was born in Allahabad on 14 Nov., 1889.

S_6 : He died on 27 May, 1964.

P : Nehru met Mahatma Gandhi in February, 1920.

Q : In 1905 he was sent to London to study at a school called Harrow.

R : He became the first Prime Minister of Independent India on 15 August, 1947.

S : He married Kamla Kaul in 1915.

The proper sequence should be:

A. Q R P S B. Q S P R
C. R P Q S D. S Q R P

92. S_1 : An elderly lady suddenly became blind

S_6 : The lady said that she had not been properly cured because she could not see all her furniture.

P : The doctor called daily and every time he took away some of her furniture he liked.

Q : At last, she was cured and the doctor demanded his fee.

R : She agreed to pay a large fee to the doctor who would cure her.

S : On being refused, the doctor wanted to know the reason.

The proper sequence should be:

A. P Q R S B. R P Q S
C. R S P Q D. R Q P S

93. S_1 : The path of Venus lies inside the path of the Earth.

S_6 : When at its brightest, it is easily seen with the naked eye in broad daylight.

P : When at its farthest from the Earth, Venus is 160 million miles away.

Q : With such a wide range between its greatest and least distances it is natural that at sometimes Venus appears much brighter than at others.

R : No other body ever comes so near the Earth, with the exception of the Moon and an occasional comet or asteroid.

S : When Venus is at its nearest to the earth it is only 26 million miles away.

The proper sequence should be:

A. S R P Q B. S Q R P
C. P S Q R D. Q P R S

94. S_1 : Religion is not a matter of mere dogmatic conformity.

S_6 : A man of that character is free from fear, free from hatred.

P : It is not merely going through the ritual prescribed to us.

Q : It is not a question of ceremonial piety.

R : Unless that kind of transformation occurs, you are not an authentically religious man.

S : It is the remaking of your own self, the transformation of your nature.

The proper sequence should be:

A. S P R Q B. Q P S R
C. P S R Q D. S P Q R

95. S_1 : For some time in his youth, Abraham Lincoln was manager of a shop.

S_6 : Never before had Lincoln had so much time for reading as he had then.

P : Then a chance customer would come.

Q : Young Lincoln's way of keeping shop was entirely unlike anyone else's.

R : Lincoln would jump up and attend to his needs and then revert to his reading.

S : He used to lie full length on the counter of the shop eagerly reading a book.

The proper sequence should be:

A. S R Q P B. Q S P R
C. S Q R P D. Q P S R

96. S_1 : Minnie went shopping one morning.

S_6 : She drove home with an empty shopping basket.

P : Disappointed she turned around and returned to the parking lot.

Q : She got out and walked to the nearest shop.

R : She drove her car into the parking lot and stopped.

S : It was there that she realised that she'd forgotten her purse at home.

The proper sequence should be:

A. R S Q P B. R Q S P
C. P Q R S D. Q P R S

97. S_1 : Several sub-cities have been planned around the capital.

S_6 : Hopefully the housing problem will not be as acute as at present after these sub-cities are built.

P : Dwarka is the first among them.

Q : They are expected to alleviate the problem of housing.

R : It is coming up in the south-west of the capital.

S : It will cater to over one million people when completed.

The proper sequence should be:

A. Q P R S B. P R S Q
C. P Q R S D. Q R S P

98. S_1 : Just as some men like to play football or tennis, so some men like to climb mountains.

S_6 : You look down and see the whole country below you.

P : This is often very difficult to do, for mountains are not just big hills.

Q : Paths are usually very steep, and some mountain-sides are straight up and down, so that it may take many hours to climb as little as one hundred feet.

R : There is always the danger that you may fall off and be killed or injured.

S : Men talk about conquering a mountain, and the wonderful feeling it is to reach the top of a mountain after climbing for hours and may be, even for days.

The proper sequence should be:

A. P Q R S B. Q P S R
C. R Q P S D. S R Q P

99. S_1 : Ms. Paras started a petrol pump in Madras.

S_6 : Thus she has shown the way for many others.

P : A total of twelve girls now work at the pump.

Q : She advertised in newspapers for women staff.

R : They operate in two shifts.

S : The response was good.

The proper sequence should be:

A. P Q S R B. S Q P R
C. Q S P R D. P Q R S

100. S_1 : Your letter was a big relief.

S_6 : But don't forget to bring chocolate for Geeta.

P : How did your exams go?

Q : After your result, you must come here for a week.

R : You hadn't written for over a month.

S : I am sure you will come out with flying colours.

The proper sequence should be:

A. P S R Q B. Q R P S
C. R P S Q D. R S P Q

ANSWERS

1	2	3	4	5	6	7	8	9	10
C	C	A	B	C	B	C	B	A	D
11	**12**	**13**	**14**	**15**	**16**	**17**	**18**	**19**	**20**
A	A	A	D	C	D	D	B	A	D
21	**22**	**23**	**24**	**25**	**26**	**27**	**28**	**29**	**30**
C	A	B	C	D	C	B	A	D	B
31	**32**	**33**	**34**	**35**	**36**	**37**	**38**	**39**	**40**
D	C	D	D	A	B	C	A	B	B
41	**42**	**43**	**44**	**45**	**46**	**47**	**48**	**49**	**50**
B	D	D	B	A	D	A	C	B	A
51	**52**	**53**	**54**	**55**	**56**	**57**	**58**	**59**	**60**
C	D	A	A	D	C	A	B	B	B
61	**62**	**63**	**64**	**65**	**66**	**67**	**68**	**69**	**70**
B	B	A	C	A	A	D	C	B	A
71	**72**	**73**	**74**	**75**	**76**	**77**	**78**	**79**	**80**
D	C	D	A	C	A	A	C	B	D
81	**82**	**83**	**84**	**85**	**86**	**87**	**88**	**89**	**90**
A	B	D	A	C	B	B	C	C	A
91	**92**	**93**	**94**	**95**	**96**	**97**	**98**	**99**	**100**
B	B	A	B	B	B	A	A	C	C

COMPREHENSION

Comprehension is a very important part of General English paper. The questions on comprehension lay particular stress on understanding a given passage. You are required to read a passage and answer a few questions based on it. Various comprehension questions are set solely with the objectives named below:

1. To test your ability to detect the central idea or the focal point in the given passage.
2. To test your ability to understand and interpret the given passage.
3. To judge your capability to pick out the various arguments put forward by the writer for or against something.
4. To test your accuracy and richness of vocabulary.
5. To test your academic ability to understand the implied and the clearly and fully expressed ideas of the writer of the passage.
6. To test, occasionally, your power of appreciating critically the views contained in the given passage.

While answering comprehension questions, you must comply with the following important points:

1. First, read the whole passage attentively, carefully and quickly.
2. Read it for the second time, slowly but steadily.
3. Work out the probable meaning of new words, from the context in which they have been used.
4. Underline and look for transitional words and phrases as an aid to comprehension.
5. The process of elimination should be used while selecting the correct answer.
6. Your answers should be brief and to the point.

Directions: *Read the following passages carefully and choose the best answer to each of the questions out of the four alternatives.*

PASSAGE-1

The group of tired dusty riders arrived at a fork in the road. Their leader immediately sprang to the ground after first throwing his rein to one of the others, and began to examine minutely the sandy track. The problem was simple; if the fleeing enemy had taken the left turning, there remained little hope of catching them, since he knew that it led back to a small settlement of native huts where they should be sheltered by the friendly inhabitants. If, on the other hand, they had branched to the right, they would have before them the open desert, not a flat expanse of sand such as they had just crossed, but a country broken by a series of ridges, behind any of which a whole army could hide.

He turned to his companions to see if he could read any solution in their faces. But they were too occupied by their aching limbs and several were taking a quick drink from the flasks which hung at their belts. He realised every minute's delay lessened their chances of overtaking their adversaries. So, with a rapid glance at the sun, he jumped once more into the saddle and with his whip indicated the way they were to go.

Questions

1. Why did the leader look at the sun?
   - A. To estimate what daylight still remained
   - B. He sent a silent prayer to the sun-god to show the way
   - C. To estimate chances of their overtaking their adversaries
   - D. To estimate their position in the desert

2. What, if any, was the difference in the nature of the terrain they had already traversed and the one lying ahead?
   - A. The country-side already traversed was ups and downs

B. There was hardly any difference as it was a vast expanse of unending desert
C. The terrain hitherto was dusty and tiring, the road ahead led back to a habitation
D. What they had crossed was a flat expanse of sand and what they lay ahead to the right was a series of ridges of sand

3. What difficulties did they expect if they took the branch to the right?
A. The open desert ahead promised no oasis to shelter them at night
B. They were absolutely in the dark about what they lay ahead of them
C. Ahead lay a country full of ridges of sand providing cover to the fleeing enemy
D. They would have before them the open desert obstructing pursuit

4. What was the aim of the group of riders?
A. They were fleeing from a pursuing enemy
B. They had a small settlement of native huts as their goal
C. They were exploring a desert
D. They were pursuing a fleeing enemy

5. What difficulties did the pursuers expect if they took to the left hand track?
A. It led through a trackless expanse of unending desert
B. It led to a settlement where the residents would surely shelter the enemy they were after
C. The settlement it led to was hostile to them
D. The leader anticipated a possible revolt among his followers, foot-sore, dust covered and tired as they already were.

6. Where and why did they stop?
A. At a fork in the road to examine the sandy track for foot-prints of the fleeing enemy
B. At the huts of some friendly inhabitants in order to rest their weary limbs
C. At a three-way crossing where the leader wanted to study the position of the sun in the sky
D. At a fork in the road in order to decide whether they should turn left or right

PASSAGE-2

Just as some men like to play football or cricket, so some men like to climb mountains. This is often very difficult to do so, for mountains are not just big hills. Paths are usually very steep. Some mountain sides are straight up and down, so that it may take many hours to climb as little as one hundred feet. There is always the danger that you may fall off and be killed or injured. Men talk about conquering a mountain. It is a wonderful feeling to reach the top of a mountain after climbing for hours and may be, even for days. You look down and see the whole country below you. You feel god-like. Two Italian prisoners of war escaped from a prison camp in Kenya during the war. They did not try to get back to their own country, for they knew that was impossible Instead, they climb to the top of Mount Kenya, and then they came down again and gave themselves up. They had wanted to get that feeling of freedom that one has, after climbing a difficult mountain.

Questions

1. Some men like to climb mountains because
A. They know the trick of climbing
B. They don't like to play football or cricket
C. They want to have wonderful feeling
D. They like to face danger

2. To climb mountains is often difficult because
A. mountains are big hills
B. it consumes more time
C. prisoners often escape from camps and battle there
D. paths are steep and uneven

3. Mountaineering is not a very popular sport like football or cricket because:
A. there are no spectators in this sport
B. it may take many hours or even days
C. not many people are prepared to risk their lives
D. people don't want to enjoy a god-like feeling

4. It is a wonderful feeling .... . It refers to:
A. the steep path
B. the prisoners
C. the mountain
D. mountaineering

PASSAGE-3

Although he was born in a little village near the coast and had gone to school in the nearest sea-side town, Ram Mehar, was not a lover of the sea; even when walking along the sands, he was always afraid of being cut off by the tide. He was not a good swimmer, so perhaps this accounts for it.

After working for some years in Calcutta, he was transferred to a coast resort and, of course, the family outings were often made to the beach. One day his children pleaded to go out into the bay in a boat. The sun shone brightly. There was little wind and the water was calm. So Ram Mehar hired a boat and with his two children rowed out into the bay. Of course, they were tempted to go further than they had intended, past the protecting cliffs and out to the open sea. At first all went well, but when they decided to turn back, they encountered difficulties. A strong breeze had sprung up and the currents here were rather treacherous.

Ram Mehar rowed very hard, but it seemed they were making little progress. The children were waving to attract the attention of the people on the beach. Just then a motor-boat appeared from the direction of the bay. Their plight had been noticed and the boat had come to their rescue.

A line was soon attached and they were towed back round the cliff to the shore. Ram Mehar's dislike of the sea was not diminished by this experience.

Questions

1. What did the children plead to be allowed to do?
- A. Climb the cliff to have a better view of the bay
- B. Go to a coast resort
- C. Go for a outing on the beach
- D. Go out into the bay in a boat

2. Ram Mehar was tempted to go farther away from the land than he had intended because:
- A. he enjoyed rowing in the bright sunshine
- B. the sea was calm, there being little wind
- C. his children wanted to go far out in the sea
- D. he encountered no danger while rowing the boat

3. What accounted for his dislike of the sea?
- A. Being not a good swimmer, he feared that he might get drowned in the sea
- B. The protruding cliffs made navigation dangerous
- C. He was accustomed to comfortable city life
- D. Many a tragedy had occurred in the past near the sea coast

4. Ram Mehar was nervous of walking along the sands because:
- A. he had no love for the sea
- B. there the sea was infested with deadly monsters
- C. he feared that tide may cut him off from the land
- D. the sea was too deep even near the coast

PASSAGE-4

The bulk of our population is poor and illiterate. Their sorry condition poses a problem. On one hand, there is a shortage of teachers for adult education and, on the other, the adults feel shy of starting to learn at a late age and atttend classes like children. Moreover, the adult villagers have little time to spare for attending classes. The job of a farmer is very strenuous and he needs ample rest and relaxation. In addition, he finds that what is taught at adult centres of education has no bearing on his daily needs and therefore he has become cynical about adult education. It is necessary to make adult education in villages agriculture-oriented so as to make it more meaningful for the farmer. In towns and cities also, adult education needs to be made work-based. It should comprise types of system in which earning and learning go together side-by-side. Efforts should be made to discourage the tendency of the village folk to migrate to the towns.

Another aspect of the problem is the confinement of industry to cities and towns. What is called the *industrial area* is entirely the monopoly of the cities. For expansion of education and literacy in the rural areas, it is necessary that industry should be dispersed in the villages also. An important development that has taken place in the countryside is the phenomenal success of the Green Revolution.

Questions

1. What is needed for adult education in villages is that:
   A. it should be made agriculture-oriented
   B. it should be free
   C. it should be made compulsory
   D. it should be available in every village
2. The main problem in educating the adult villagers is:
   A. their financial helplessness to purchase books, etc. required for studies
   B. they hardly find time to attend classes
   C. their inability to read and write
   D. there is no room for schools in villages
3. A farmer has grown cynical about education because:
   A. what is taught in such schools is mostly of no use in his daily life
   B. there is no one in his family to look after his cultivation when he goes to attend the classes.
   C. he has no time to go to school
   D. he has no money to pay the fees for education
4. One of the main problems of adult education in the country is:
   A. poor financial condition of the people
   B. shortage of teachers for such schools
   C. shortage of school buildings
   D. want of funds with the government for such schools

PASSAGE-5

Just as it is vital for parents to live their own lives as fully as possible and to deepen their understanding of themselves to the utmost, so it is important for teachers and educators to do the same. When children go to school their teachers become, during school hours, substitutes for their parents. The children transfer to the teacher some of the feelings they have for their parents and are influenced in their turn by the personalities of the teachers. This mutual relationship is of more importance than any teaching method, and a child's ability to learn is continually hampered if the relationship is unsatisfactory. Again, if teachers really want to be educators, to help children to develop into satisfactory men and women, and not simply to *stuff them with knowledge*, they will only be really successful if they themselves have sound personalities. No amount of preaching, however well done, no principles however sound, no clever technique of mechanical aids can replace the influence of a well-developed personality.

Questions

1. Teachers will be real educators by:
   A. adopting advanced teaching methods
   B. stuffing children with knowledge
   C. developing sound personalities of their own
   D. through good teaching aid
2. The central idea of the passage is that:
   A. teachers should develop sound personalities of their own to be able to influence the children
   B. informal education is better than formal education
   C. there should be more research done in education
   D. parents should have the right relationship with teachers of their children
3. The writer recommends to the teachers to deepen their understanding of themselves on the assumption that it:
   A. will earn them a name of nation-builder
   B. is their duty
   C. will make them earn more
   D. helps to build a well-developed personality
4. The teachers and educators are important to the children because:
   A. without them they would remain ignorant
   B. they help them to get jobs
   C. they serve as substitutes for parents in schools
   D. they preach good principles

PASSAGE-6

Once a man saw that three masons along with some labourers were constructing a temple. He observed the masons for some days and found that though the three of them were doing the same kind of work, there was a marked difference in their approach to their job.

He saw that the first mason reported for his work late, did his work half-heartedly and sluggishly, enjoyed longer respite, frequently checked the time on his wrist-watch and left the work before time.

The second mason was very punctual in arriving and leaving, and did his work methodically and conscientiously.

The third mason, however, would come before time, took little rest in the interval and often worked over-time.

The man naturally got curious and wanted to know the three masons' outlook on their work. He asked them what they were doing. The first mason tapped his protruding belly with his hand and said, *I am earning fuel for this bloody belly.* The second said, *I am constructing a building.* The third looked at the stately edifice and said, *I am building the house of God.*

Questions

1. The first mason was:
   A. lazy B. sick
   C. hard-working D. active
2. The first mason was concerned only with his:
   A. wages B. job
   C. time D. rest
3. The masons and labourers were building a:
   A. club B. monastery
   C. school D. temple
4. The third mason approached his work with:
   A. zest B. skill
   C. duty D. dedication

PASSAGE-7

Scarcity not created by war; it is a permanent characteristic of all human society and is the basis of the problem that faces, and always had faced, the human race whatever its form of organisation. It springs from the fact that the material resources of the world are limited and that our ability to make use of those resources is even more limited by our ignorance.

Everthing that we need to satisfy our wants has to be derived finally from two sources --- the natural resources that are available and the human ability to make use of them. As our knowledge grows and we increase our skill, we can exploit more and more of the opportunities that nature offers us. The increase in communications, for example, has made accessible many minerals from depths below the earth's surface that could not be reached by earlier generations. But whatever the rate of development may be, there is, at any one time, a limit to the total of what can be produced. Here and now, there is only so much of the material resources of the world accessible to us and there are only so many people capable of work and endowed with the capacities and skills that they have developed. No doubt we waste a lot by stupidity even if the very best possible use is made of all the resources we can reach, there is still a limit to what can be produced out of them, and it is out of that total that we must all satisfy our wants.

Questions

1. Some of the material resources are:
   A. wasted by man's stupidity
   B. neglected by man
   C. accessible to man
   D. stored for the future
2. The first sentence of the passage tells us that scarcity is:
   A. created by war
   B. caused by human beings
   C. not permanent
   D. present in all human societies
3. The main idea of the passage is:
   A. the cause of scarcity
   B. the need to work hard
   C. how to overcome scarcity
   D. the need to increase our knowledge

4. The cause of scarcity is:
   A. limited natural resources and still more limited knowledge of how to use them
   B. the limitation of man's knowledge
   C. human ignorance of natural resources
   D. the limitation of various natural resources

PASSAGE-8

The great Acharyas have said that having discovered a great goal, surrender yourself to that goal and act towards it drawing your inspiration from that goal whereby you will get a new column of energy. Do not allow this energy to be dissipated in the futile memories of the past regrets or failures, nor in the imagined sorrows of the future, nor in the excitement of the present. And this bring that entire focus into activity. That is the highest creative action in the world outside. Thereby, the individual who is till now considered most efficient, finds his way to the highest achievement and success.

This is said very easily in a second. But in order to train our mind to this attitude, it needs considerable training because we have already trained the mind wrongly to such an extent that we have become perfect in imperfections. Not knowing the art of action, we have been master artists in doing the wrong thing. The totality of activity will bring the country to a wrong end indeed.

If each one is given a car to achieve an ideal socia-listic pattern and nobody knows how to drive, what would be the condition on the road? Everybody has equal right on the public road. Then each car must necessarily dash against the other, and there is bound to be a jumble. This seems to be very apt pattern of life that we are heading to. Everyone of us is a vehicle. We know how to go forward. The point is that intellect is very powerful and everyone is driving, but nobody seems to know to control the mental energy and direct it properly or guide it to the proper destination.

Questions

1. Which of the following is the source of energy?
   A. A column that supports a building
   B. Stimulation obtained from a set aim
   C. Highest creative action
   D. Proper training of the mind to achieve perfection
2. Which of the following could lead to success?
   A. Cherishing the memories of the past
   B. Preparing oneself to face the probable sorrow of the future
   C. Bringing all the energy into activity
   D. Being alert about the excitement of the present
3. What is the effect of the wrong training of the mind?
   A. We have become perfect in all aspects
   B. Art of action too much emphasized
   C. Each of us could become master artist
   D. We could avoid wastage of our energy
   E. None of these
4. The author's chief aim is:
   A. establishment of socialistic pattern
   B. the car accidents resulting from each of driving skill
   C. discovery of a great goal in life
   D. regulation of energy in proper direction

PASSAGE-9

In our boyhood we beheld the dying rays of that intimate sociability which was characteristic of the last generation. Neighbourly feelings were then so strong that the informal gatherings were a necessity, and those who could contribute its amenities were held in great respect. People now-a-days call on each other on business, or as a matter of social duty, but not to foregather by way of informal gatherings. They have not the time, nor are there the same intimate relations. What goings and comings we used to see, how merry were the rooms and verandahs with the hum of conversation and the snatches of laughter. The faculty our predecessors had of becoming the centre of groups and gatherings, of starting and keeping up animated and amusing gossip, has vanished. Man still come and go, but those same verandahs and rooms seem empty and deserted. In those days everything from furniture to festivity was designed to be enjoyed by the many, so that whatever of pomp or magnificence there might have been did not savour of hauteur. These appendages have since increased in quantity, but they have become unfeeling and know not the art of making high and low alike feel at home. The barebodied, the indigently clad, no longer have the right to use and occupy them, without a permit, on the strength of their smiling faces alone. Those whom we now-a-days seek to imitate in our house-building and furnishing, they have their own society, with its wide hospitality. The mischief with us is that we have lost what we had but have not the means of building up afresh on the European standard, with the result that our home-life has become joyless. We still meet for business or political purposes, but never for the pleasure of simply meeting one another. We have ceased to contrive opportunities to bring men together simply because we love our fellow-men. I can imagine nothing more ugly than this social miserliness, and, when I look back on those whose ringing laughter, coming straight from their hearts, used to lighten for us the burden of household cares, they seem to have been visitors from some other world.

Questions

1. Which of the following is social miserliness according to the author?
   A. Diminishing intimate sociability
   B. Increasing social inequality
   C. Bare-bodied, half-starved masses
   D. We don't wish to incur expenditure merely to get people together
2. Why does the author feel that the rooms and verandahs have lost their charm?
   A. The rooms and verandahs have been deserted by the people
   B. They have been crowded by gatherings of gossiping people
   C. The conversational quality our predecessors had has now vanished
   D. Unlike in the past, no facilities for arranging meetings are available
3. People whom do which of the following now would look like visitors from some other world?
   A. Eradication of poverty and establishing social equality
   B. Strengthening the ties of love and affection through recurring informal meetings
   C. Reducing the burden of household cares by extending monetary assistance
   D. Enhancing business opportunities with European countries
4. How is the meeting of people of present generations different from the meeting of the people of the past?
   A. Intimate sociability has crept in
   B. Neighbourly feelings have now been strengthened
   C. Informal gossiping is not considered ethical these days
   D. People now do not meet merely for the pleasure of meeting one another
5. The approach of the author seems to be:
   A. extremely critical about our indifference towards the past generation
   B. emphatic about the need for informal social interaction
   C. cynical about our blindly imitating the Western style
   D. pessimistic about our business and political avenues
6. Why, according to the author, has our home life become joyless?
   A. We have lost the means of building up houses on the European standards
   B. Complete imitation of the West is not possible owing to different climatic conditions
   C. We have lost interpersonal intimacy and sociability. We do not have the means to build up afresh on the European standards
   D. Most people are bare-bodied and half-starved
7. Which of the following statements is definitely true in the context of the passage?
   A. Poor people in the past generation did not have the right to enjoy anything without permission

B. We have ceased to bring people together solely for the pleasure of meeting them

C. Dying rays of intimate sociability was the characteristic of the last generation

D. The gap between different strata of the present society is on the increase

PASSAGE-10

A recent report in New York Times says that in American colleges, students of Asian origin outperform not only the minority group students but the majority Whites as well. Many of these students must be of Indian origin, and their achievement is something we can be proud of. It is unlikely that these talented youngsters will come back to India, and that is the familiar brain drain problem. How-ever, recent statements by the nation's policy makers indicate that the perception of this issue is changing. *Brain bank* and not *brain drain* is the more appropriate idea, they suggest, since the expertise of Indians abroad is only deposited in other places and not lost.

This may be so, but this brain bank, like most of the banks, is one that primarily serves customers in its neighbourhood. The skills of the Asians now excelling in America's colleges will mainly help the USA. No matter how significant, what Non-Resident Indians do for India and what their counterparts do for other Asian countries is only a by-product. But it is also necessary to ask, or be reminded, why Indians study more fruitfully when abroad. The Asians whose accomplishments New York Times records would have probably had a very different fate if they had studied in India. In America they found elbow room, books and facilities not available and not likely to be available here. The need to prove themselves in their new country and the competition of an international standard they faced there must have cured mental and physical laziness. But other things helping them in America can be obtained here if we achieve a change in social attitudes, especially towards youth.

We need to learn to value individuals and their unique qualities more than conformity and respectability. We need to learn the language of encouragement to add to out skill in flattery. We might also learn to be less liberal with blame and less tight-fisted with appreciation, especially to those showing signs of independence.

Questions

1. Among the many groups of students in American colleges, Asian students:

A. are often written about in newspapers like New York Times

B. are the most successful academically

C. have proved that they are as good as the Whites

D. have only a minority status like the Blacks

2. The students of Asian origin in America include:

A. a fair number from India

B. a small group from India

C. persons from India who are very proud

D. Indians who are the most hardworking of all

3. In general, the talented young Indian studying in America:

A. have a reputation for being hardworking

B. have the opportunity to contribute to India's development

C. can solve the brain drain problem becaus of recent changes in policy

D. will not return to pursue their careers i India

4. There is talk now of the *brain bank*. Thi idea:

A. is a solution to the brain drain problen

B. is a new problem caused partly by th brain drain

C. is a new way of looking at the role c qualified Indians living abroad

D. is based on a plan to utilise foreig exchange remittances to stimula research and development

5. The brain bank has limitations like all ban in the sense that:

A. a bank's services go mainly to those ne it

B. small neighbourhood banks are not viable in this age of multinationals

C. only what is deposited can be withdrawn and utilised

D. no one can be forced to put his assets in a bank

6. The author feels that what Non-Resident Indians do for India:

A. will have many useful side-effects

B. will not be their main interest and concern

C. can benefit other Asian countries, as a lay-product

D. can help American colleges be of service of the world community

PASSAGE-11

Gandhi was not born great. He was a blundering boy, a mediocre student, a poor lawyer, an ordinary individual until he remade himself. He was a self-remade man. He had faith in himself. But above all, he had a deep, touching faith in the peasants, miners, labourers, and young unformed men and women whom he drew into his work. He fed them all an elixir of growth which often transformed nameless, uneducated people into leonine heroes. The elixir was fearlessness.

Questions

1. Consider the following assumptions:

1. Gandhi was a great man throughout his life.
2. Men are not born great, but they are made great by self effort.
3. Gandhi liked the ordinary people and neglected the rich.
4. Gandhi transformed the ordinary masses into great heroes.

Which of the above assumptions can be drawn from the above passage?

A. 2 and 4 B. 1 and 2

C. 3 and 4 D. None of these

2. Gandhi transformed the uneducated people by teaching them

A. work-mindedness B. self-confidence

C. fearlessness D. heroism

3. Gandhi's attitude to the labour class was one of

A. generosity B. pity

C. compassion D. fearlessness

4. The word 'leonine' in the passage means

A. lean B. courageous

C. timid D. learning

PASSAGE-12

The dog fence in Australia has been erected to keep out hostile invaders, in this case hordes of yellow dogs called dingoes. The empire it preserves is that of wool growers. Yet the fence casts a much broader ecological shadow. For the early explorers, a kangaroo or a wallaby sighting marked a noteworthy event. Now try ***not*** to see one. Without a native predator there is no check on the marsupial population. The kangaroos are now cursed more than the dingoes. They have become rivals of sheep, competing for water and grass. The State Governments now cull more than three million kangaroos a year to keep Australia's natural symbol from over running the pastoral lands.

Questions

1. The Fence is meant to keep the:

A. kangaroo in and the dingo out.

B. kangaroo in and the sheep out.

C. sheep in and the kangaroo out.

D. sheep in and the dingo out.

2. Australia's national symbol is:

A. Kangaroo B. Wallaby

C. Sheep D. Dingo

3. What has led to the unchecked growth of the marsupial population?

A. The building of fences

B. The absence of native predator

C. The culling of kangaroos

D. The availability of water and grass

4. The marsupial population is up in Australia because:

A. both wallaby and kangaroo count as marsupials.

B. the kangaroo consumes the water and grass of the sheep.

C. the dingo cannot get at the kangaroo.

D. the kangaroos are fenced out.

PASSAGE-13

Not all nocturnal animals have good eyesight. Many of them concentrate on the other senses for finding their way about and for finding food. The sense of touch is very well developed in many nocturnal animals, whether they have good eyes or not. The large hairs or whiskers on the faces of cats and mice are sense organs and the animals react rapidly if these whiskers are touched. The sense of smell is also very important for nocturnal animals such as hedgehogs and field mice. The moist night air holds scent much better than dry air does.

Questions

1. Which one of the following statements is correct?
   A. All nocturnal animals are blind
   B. Many nocturnal animals do not have good eyesight
   C. Most nocturnal animals can not see any thing in the dark
   D. No nocturnal animal has good eyesight
2. The cat's whiskers are organs associated with the sense of
   A. taste B. touch
   C. hearing D. smell

PASSAGE-14

When we talk of education in our present age, we think largely in terms of schools and colleges. The man who is well-to-do spends money in sending his son to foreign lands, in the belief that some wonderful process will take place there transforming a dull fellow into a genius. Yet the products of expensive schools and universities often fail to make good. One the other hand, the poor man who has struggled against adversity often earns the highest honour. The fact is that the true background of early education is the home. The home, the influence of the mother, the inspiring examples that are held before the child at an age while he is impressionable, are the true groundwork of character.

Questions

1. According to the passage, who helps in ou character-building?
   A. A foreign university
   B. A well-to-do man
   C. Examples that inspire
   D. A man who has earned honour.
2. The proper background of early education is
   A. a school.
   B. a college.
   C. a religious institution.
   D. the home.
3. From the passage, we get an impression tha the highest honour is earned by
   A. a man who has received education in a foreign country.
   B. a man who has struggled against adversity
   C. a man who has seen prosperity alone.
   D. the son of a prosperous man.
4. A well-to-do man sends his son to foreig lands
   A. because it is the fashion of the day.
   B. in the belief that his dull son will b transformed into a genius.
   C. so that the son may learn the customs c those countries.
   D. in order to make his son familiar with th persons and places of those countries.
5. The expression "the products of expensiv schools and universities often fail to mak good" means
   A. they fail to make a mark in life.
   B. they fail to become intelligent.
   C. they fail to earn proper living.
   D. they do not earn good reputation.

PASSAGE-15

The functional declines of advancing age a depressing. The heart's ability to pump blood dro about one per cent: blood flow to arms and le decreases by thirty to forty per cent in old age. T amount of air a person can exhale after a deep brea lessens and the chest wall stiffens with age. However, recent studies have shown that most of these age-associated declines can be delayed by exercise. Exercise lowers the resting heart-rate and increases the amount of blood pumped with each beat in older people. When stress is placed on bones through exercise, calcium content rises, with the result that resistance to fracture is improved.

Questions

1. Old age is generally a depressing period, because

A. old people worry more than others.
B. old people tend to regret their past.
C. various organs of the body function less efficiently.
D. old people do very little work.

2. The strength of bones can be increased by exercise, because it

A. increases the amount of blood pumped by the heart.
B. increases calcium content in bones.
C. increases the amount of air exhaled by a person.
D. lessens the stiffness of the chest wall.

3. The word 'exhale' means

A. breathe in. B. breathe out.
C. breathe slowly. D. breath fast.

4. Which one of the following statements is correct?

A. Exercise delays natural decay of old age
B. Old-age problems increase due to exercise
C. Exercise increases the heartbeat which is dangerous
D. Exercise creates stress which is harmful to bones.

5. The chest wall becomes stiff in old age, because

A. the heart's ability to pump blood to it drops about one per cent
B. the blood flow to various organs decreases
C. the resting heart-rate becomes high
D. the person's ability to exhale sufficient air lessens

PASSAGE-16

No doubt, the 'green revolution' has led to self-sufficiency in food production but it has also brought with it the formidable problem of poisoning of food grains and other eatables. This is caused by excessive use of chemicals on crops and pesticide residues. It has also created havoc by exterminating the species of useful parasites and viruses which keep pests under control. Scientists are now worried about the resurgence of such formidable pests in menacing proportions which seem to undermine all that they have achieved in agricultural production.

Questions

1. From the reading of the passage, which one of these statements do you think is correct?

A. The 'green revolution' has solved all problems in agriculture
B. Application of chemicals has resulted in everlasting preservation of grains
C. The 'green revolution' is a mixed blessing
D. Scientists are satisfied with achievements in agricultural production

2. The statement that "the green revolution has also created havoc by exterminating the species of useful parasites and viruses" means

A. all parasites and viruses keep pests under control
B. pesticides and chemicals kill parasites and viruses, which control pests
C. the pests are controlled by parasites
D. application of chemicals to grains has created havoc

3. Which one of the following statements best reflects the underlying implication of the passage?

A. Man's effort to control nature to his advantage has always created unseen dangers side by side
B. Research in one area leads to a challenge for further research in the same field
C. At present, research in preservation of agricultural production is at the cross-roads
D. The excessive use of chemicals and pesticides is dangerous

4. Which one of these phrases best helps to brings out the precise meaning of 'menacing proportions'?
   A. To an extent which becomes threatening
   B. Assuming dimensions that cause concern
   C. Unimagined, dangerous proportion
   D. Harmful size

PASSAGE-17

Water is the basis of life. Every animal and every plant contains a substantial proportion of free or combined water in its body, and no kind of physiological activity is possible in which this fluid does not play an essential part. Water is, of course, necessary for animal life, while moisture in the soil is equally imperative for the life and growth of plants and trees, though the quantity necessarily varies enormously with the species. The conservation and utilization of water is thus fundamental to human life. Apart from artesian water, the ultimate source in all cases is rain or snowfall.

Questions

1. Water is the basis of life, because
   A. it is seen everywhere on the earth
   B. it is obtained from the sea and rain
   C. it helps living things to exist
   D. it is necessary for the birth and growth of all living things
2. No kind of physiological activity is possible without water, because
   A. water is fluid
   B. water plays very important role in it
   C. water flows easily
   D. water does not play any role at all
3. The passage is on
   A. the use of water in day-to-day life
   B. the use of water in agriculture
   C. the use of wastewater
   D. the importance of water in human life

PASSAGE-18

The importance of early detection of tuberculosis (TB), regular treatment and nutritious food are just not known widely enough. Often TB victims discontinue the treatment when the symptoms disappear, without waiting for a complete cure; the next attack is more virulent from bacteria which have thus become drug-resistant.

Anti-TB drugs are produced in India. The capability to meet the country's requirements of anti-TB drugs in full already exists. Yet millions of Indians suffer from TB and thousands of them die every year. Voluntary organizations and government agencies are doing commendable work. But we have so far tackled only the fringe of the problem. What is now needed is a nation-wide determination to fight TB. India eradicated smallpox with a national campaign. We can eradicate TB too.

Questions

1. Treatment is discontinued by TB victims, when
   A. they think that the disease is completely cured
   B. the apparent signs of TB are no longer visible to them
   C. they run out of resources like money or medicine
   D. they are attacked by drug-resistant bacteria
2. Millions of Indians suffer from TB, because
   A. People discontinue the treatment too soon or do not start the treatment early enough
   B. India does not produce anti-TB drugs of the required quality
   C. anti-TB drugs are not available at a reasonable price
   D. people do not have nutritious food
3. When the treatment of TB is discontinued too early
   A. the old symptoms reappear
   B. the patient gradually gets better, although slowly
   C. the disease appears in a new, more dangerous form
   D. the patient must get good, nutritious food
4. 'The fringe of the problem' means
   A. the basic cause of the problem
   B. the root of the problem
   C. the side effects of the drugs
   D. the edge of the problem, not the main point

5. Who or what become 'drug-resistant', according to the passage?
   A. TB patients who are treated for a long time
   B. People who do not want to take medicine for their illness
   C. TB bacteria that have not been fully eradicated
   D. Patients who have discontinued the treatment

PASSAGE-19

We have built up an energy intensive society such that hundreds of daily acts are dependent on having energy at our ready command. Most of that energy comes from fossil fuels. Yet, within two centuries we will have used up nearly all of the fossil fuel that has been built up over millions of years of earth time. Furthermore, the extraction and consumption of fossil fuels is a major polluter of our environment. Our appetite for energy is seemingly insatiable. We are now searching for it in different places and using methods that inevitably upset and pollute the environment. Since fossil energy will soon be gone we are searching for alternative sources.

Questions

1. Today we are dependent on energy for everything. What is the most likely factor that contributes to this situation?
   A. Sufficient quantity of energy is available at present.
   B. We have developed a society which makes intensive use of energy.
   C. Energy is the most convenient and easy to use.
   D. We have no alternatives.
2. The author seems to disapprove further extraction and consumption of fossil fuels. Which of the following is the most likely reason for that?
   A. Further extraction of fossil fuel is a costly affair.
   B. Further extraction and consumption of fossil fuel may lead to conflict between countries.
   C. We do not have the technical know-how for further extraction of fossil fuels.
   D. Further extraction and consumption of fossil fuels will lead to world-wide environmental pollution.
3. According to the author, we are searching for alternative sources of energy. What is the most likely reason for this?
   A. Alternative sources of energy are cheaper.
   B. It is feared that fossil energy will soon be exhausted.
   C. A number of alternative energy sources are easily available.
   D. Alternative sources of energy will not cause any environmental problems.

PASSAGE-20

Books are, by far, the most lasting product of human effort. Temples crumble into ruins, pictures and statues decay, but books survive. Time does not destroy the great thoughts which are as fresh today as when they first passed through their authors' minds ages ago. The only effect of time has been to throw out of currency the bad products, for nothing in literature can long survive but what is really good and of lasting value. Books introduce us into the best society; they bring us into the presence of the greatest minds that have ever lived, we hear what they said and did; we see them as if they were really alive, we sympathise with them, enjoy with them, and grieve with them.

Questions

1. According to the passage, books live for ever because :
   A. they have productive value.
   B. time does not destroy great thoughts.
   C. they are in printed form.
   D. they have the power to influence people.
2. According to the passage, temples, pictures and statues belong to the same category because :
   A. all of them are beautiful.
   B. all of them are substantial.
   C. all of them are likely to decay.
   D. all of them are fashioned by men.

3. "Lasting value" in the passage means :
A. Something which has survived the passage of time.
B. Something which has been lost with the passage of time.
C. Something which has relevance for the present.
D. Something which had relevance for the past.

ANSWERS

Passage-1

1	2	3	4	5	6
A	D	C	D	C	D

Passage-2

1	2	3	4
C	D	C	D

Passage-3

1	2	3	4
D	B	A	C

Passage-4

1	2	3	4
A	B	A	B

Passage-5

1	2	3	4
C	A	D	C

Passage-6

1	2	3	4
B	D	D	D

Passage-7

1	2	3	4
C	D	C	A

Passage-8

1	2	3	4
B	C	C	D

Passage-9

1	2	3	4	5	6
D	C	E	D	B	C
7					
B					

Passage-10

1	2	3	4	5	6
B	A	D	C	D	C

Passage-11

1	2	3	4
A	C	A	B

Passage-12

1	2	3	4
A	A	B	A

Passage-13

1	2
B	B

Passage-14

1	2	3	4	5
C	D	B	B	A

Passage-15

1	2	3	4	5
C	B	B	A	D

Passage-16

1	2	3	4
C	B	D	A

Passage-17

1	2	3
C	B	D

Passage-18

1	2	3	4	5
B	D	C	D	C

Passage-19

1	2	3
B	D	B

Passage-20

1	2	3
B	C	A

CLOSET TEST

Directions (Qs. 1–210): *In the following passages, there are blanks, each of which has been numbered. These numbers are printed below the passage and against each, four words are suggested, one of which fits the blank appropriately. Find out the appropriate word in each case.*

PASSAGE-1

Seed quality is an ...(1)... aspect of crop production. For ages, farmers have traditionally been selecting and ...(2)... good quality seed, since it was in their interest to do so. They knew and understood the importance of quality seed in production.

However, with the advent of green revolution technology, based ...(3)... on the high-yielding dwarf varieties of wheat and rice, mainstream thinking changed. Agricultural scientists, for reasons that remain ...(4)... began to doubt, the ability of farmers to maintain seed quality ...(5)... . Aided by the World Bank, the Ministry of Agriculture launched a National Seeds Project in 1967. Under the project spread into three phases, seed processing plants werre ...(6)... up in nine states. Six states were covered under phase three. All that the huge processing plants were ...(7)... to do was to provide 'certified' seeds of food crops, mainly self- pollinating crops, to farmers. In mid-1980s, the International Rice Research Institute (IRRI) in the Philippines concluded a study which ...(8)... that there was hardly any difference in the crop yields from transplanted rice and from the crop sown by broad casted seeds. One would wonder why, in the first instance, were the farmers, asked to ...(9)... over to transplanting paddy? The answer is simple–probably, to help the mechanical industries grow. Since rice, is the staple food in Asia, tractor sales could only grow if there was a way to move the machine in the rice fields. No wonder, the sales of tractors, puddlers, reapers and other associated ...(10)... soared in the rice growing areas.

1. A. irrational B. main C. brilliant D. important

2. A. maintaining B. trusting C. selling D. processing

3. A. necessarily B. exceptionally C. primarily D. regularly

4. A. unexplained B. doubt C. some D. true

5. A. himself B. sometimes C. proper D. improve

6. A. established B. created C. set D. wound

7. A. tried B. mattered C. meaning D. supposed

8. A. renounced B. showed C. passed D. negated

9. A. shift B. make C. turn D. switch

10. A. sell B. equipments C. people D. techniques

PASSAGE-2

The world's climate has always changed and species have evolved accordingly to survive it. The surprising fact about the ...(11)... between evolution and global warming ...(12)... that it is not linear. ...(13)... temperatures alone are not ...(14)... of evolution. Evolution is also the ...(15)... of seasonal changes. As the environment ...(16)... those species which don't adapt ...(17)... to exist. But the sheer ...(18)... of manmade climate change today is ...(19).... 'Bad things are happening' and by one ...(20)... global warming could threaten up to one-third of the world's species if left unchecked. In fact; a lot of the species which will be able to survive are the ones we consider pests like insects and weeds.

11. A. difference B. similarity
C. argument D. relationship

12. A. being B. seems
C. mainly D. is

13. A. However B. Mounted
C. Rising D. Elevating

14. A. means B. triggers
C. responses D. threats

15. A. result B. precursor
C. resistance D. cause

16. A. conserves B. stifles
C. predicts D. changes

17. A. continue B. halt
C. cease D. terminate

18. A. luck B. value
C. collapse D. pace

19. A. threatened B. pursued
C. unprecedented D. record

20. A. forecast B. chance
C. pattern D. imagination

PASSAGE-3

The large number of natural disasters within a few days in late September has led to two assumptions. First, we are experiencing more natural calamities today **...(21)...** ever before, and second, the distribution of disasters **...(22)...** unequal. A UN report studied natural disasters **...(23)...** 1975 and 2007 found that not only is the **...(24)...** of catastrophes increasing because of climate change and environmental **...(25)...** but also that the brunt of tragedies is borne **...(26)...** poor countries least equipped to deal with such **...(27)...** It is true that some countries are disaster-prone but some **...(28)...** Japan for example have managed to overcome their geographical disadvantages.

...(29)... to UN estimates, equivalent populations in the Philippines and Japan **...(30)...** the same number of cyclones each year but 17 times more people perish in the Philippines than in Japan. In some ways natural disasters give developed economies an excuse for technological improvement while in poorer ones it feeds a vicious cycle–since they are constantly struggling to recover from natural calamities they cannot afford the disaster prevention measures needed.

21. A. as B. than
C. not D. of

22. A. being B. are
C. often D. is

23. A. after B. prior
C. between D. separating

24. A. response B. dances
C. occurring D. frequency

25. A. degradation B. protection
C. detriment D. audit

26. A. of B. by
C. with D. for

27. A. calm B. misbelieve
C. misfortunes D. faith

28. A. inspite B. even
C. since D. like

29. A. Thanks B. Comparing
C. Similar D. According

30. A. endure B. incite
C. enjoys D. trigger

PASSAGE-4

On October 2, 1983 the Grameen Bank Project **...(31)...** the Grameen Bank. We invited the Finance Minister to be the Chief Guest at our **...(32)...** ceremony. But when the Ministry came to **...(33)...** that the ceremony would take place in a remote district, they said it would not be an **...(34)...** place to launch a Bank and that the ceremony should be **...(35)...** in Dhaka so that all the top Government Officials could **...(36)...** We stood firm and **...(37)...** to them that we did not work in urban areas so it made no **...(38)...** to have the ceremony in a city **...(39)...** we had no borrowers. We had the ceremony in a big open field with the Finance Minister present as Chief Guest. For all of us who had worked so hard to **...(40)...** this it was a dream come true.

31. A. reorganised B. merged
C. named D. became

32. A. opening B. closing
C. dedicated D. inaugurate

33. A. reveal B. know
C. aware D. inform

34. A. excellent B. available
C. inauspicious D. appropriate

35. A. invited B. assembled
C. done D. held

36. A. present B. accompany
C. attend D. involve

37. A. apologised B. told
C. explained D. denied

38. A. difference B. sense
C. difficulty D. meaning

39. A. where B. while
C. that D. however

40. A. obey B. achieve
C. discover D. built

PASSAGE-5

Decades ago, China ...(41)... the concept of 'barefoot doctors'. They were community healthcare workers who successfully ...(42)... the health of China's villages. Following this example, many African, Asian and Latin American countries have started ...(43)... programmes. The largest of such community health efforts is India's National Rural Health Mission. In ...(44)... over three years, the programme has mobilized over fifty thousand new community health workers, each ...(45)... as 'Asha'. This is short for 'Accredited Social Health Activist' and translated into Hindi is the word ...(46)... hope.

Today technology companies and foundations are also joining the ...(47)... to support community health workers. Mobile phone companies are ...(48)... these workers with phones and support systems to obtain up to date medical information, call ambulances etc. In the ...(49)... years, community health workers can thus help ...(50)... the spread of many devastating but curable diseases.

41. A. gives B. researches
C. introduced D. originates

42. A. improved B. entrusted
C. fought D. cured

43. A. thousands B. alike
C. imitated D. similar

44. A. course B. less
C. approximate D. just

45. A. referred B. known
C. perceived D. regarded

46. A. denotes B. describes
C. for D. explains

47. A. business B. membership
C. scope D. effort

48. A. provided B. buying
C. equipped D. empowering

49. A. coming B. next
C. past D. few

50. A. overlook B. curb
C. protect D. enrich

PASSAGE-6

Jamshedji Tata is ...(51)... to be the path-finder of modern industrial builders. He is known as the grandfather of the Indian industry for his acumen and enthusiasm. Nobody else could have ...(52)... of the new industries started by Jamshedji at that time when industrial ...(53)... and revolution was yet to come to India.

Jamshedji's father Nasarvanji Tata used to trade in jute with China and Britain. He started ...(54)... from India. Jamshedji started a cloth mill in Nagpur more than hundred years ago. At that time almost all the ...(55)... used to come from Lancashire in England. What Jameshdji ...(56)... was praiseworthy.

Jamshedji ...(57)... very well that an industrial revolution can only be brought in the country by setting up iron and steel industry ...(58)... he did not live to see the industry he had in mind, he had done all ...(59)... work. In fact, he laid the ground work for it. He had planned the entire steel city now known as Jamshedpur, complete with streets, roads, schools, parks, play grounds, temples, mosques, churches, etc. His ...(60)... was fulfilled by his sons, Sir Dorabji Tata and Sir Rattan Tata, when they started the Tata Iron & Steel Factory in 1907 just after three years of his death.

51. A. rewarded B. agreed
C. empowered D. considered

52. A. absolved B. thought
C. ventured D. set

53. A. imports B. acts
C. machinery D. awakening

54. A. export B. industries
C. import D. trade

55. A. goods B. imports
C. cloth D. machines

56. A. did B. dreamt
C. agreed D. told

57. A. felt B. advocated
C. planned D. knew

58. A. Because B. Although
C. Surprisingly D. Luckily

59. A. insignificant B. complete
C. trivial D. preliminary

60. A. need B. task
C. dream D. industry

PASSAGE-7

Rabbits are among the most ...(61)... of all animals. The rabbit of a colony, once had a ...(62)... to discuss this ...(63)... of theirs. They came to the ...(64)... that as their timidity would never leave them, they were condemned to a miserable existence and it would be better to drown themselves and end their ...(65)... once and for all. Accordingly, they began to move towards a large lake.

When the frogs in the lake saw a large number of rabbits ...(66)... they were filled with ...(67)... and made for the deepest part of the lake. Seeing this, the ...(68)... of the rabbits stopped and said to his fellow-creatures: "It is true we are timid, but here are animals more timid than us. There is still some ...(69)... for us. Let us all go back to our homes," and the ...(70)... of rabbits headed back to their colony.

61. A. skilled B. calm
C. expensive D. timid

62. A. meeting B. lecture
C. assembly D. festival

63. A. tradition B. gene
C. trait D. virtue

64. A. decision B. finate
C. point D. conclusion

65. A. torture B. misery
C. bad luck D. life

66. A. attending B. retreating
C. approaching D. swimming

67. A. sympathy B. tear
C. empathy D. gratitude

68. A. group B. army
C. leader D. captain

69. A. ray B. refuge
C. doubt D. hope

70. A. multiple B. manifold
C. leader D. herd

PASSAGE-8

Once, in a forest there was a little tree covered with pointed leaves. "Ah"! It said to itself one day, "my neighbours are happy. They have leaves that are pleasing to see. Mine are like needles, I wish I could have ...(71)... of gold!" Soon it was night and the little tree dozed, the next morning it was transformed! "What joy," it cried, "I'm covered with gold! No other tree in the forest has a similar grab." But towards evening a man came by, he threw a fearful look around him, and seeing that nobody was ...(72)... him, took off the golden leaves, put them in a sack and ...(73)...

"Oh," said the little tree, "I miss those lovely golden leaves which ...(74)... in the sunlight, but leaves of glass could be just as brilliant. I would like to have leaves of glass." That evening the little tree slept, and the next morning it was ...(75)... again. From its branches hung leaves of glass. "Ah", it said, "this is a pretty attire, my neighbours have nothing like it." But that very day, some black clouds gathered in the sky, the wind blew strongly and a storm came in. All the glass leaves from the little tree fell and broke.

"Alas," sighed the tree. This foliage that I was ambitious for is very elegant, but very ...(76)... It would be better to have a ...(77)... of good green leaves, some nice fragrant ones." The little tree slept that night, and the next morning it was dressed as it vied. But the scent of its fresh leaves attracted the ...(78)... who came to nibble them, and standing up on their hind paws, they nibbled all the way to the top of the little tree and left it entirely ...(79)... When it went to sleep that night, it longed for its original leaves, and the next morning ...(80)... to see them reappear on its branches. They had neither the splendour of gold, nor the luminous transparency of glass, nor the attraction of aromatic plants; but they were solid, nobody came to take them off and the tree had them throughout the season.

71. A. designs B. leaves C. branches D. fruits

72. A. beside B. with C. inspecting D. watching

73. A. exclaimed B. continued C. wished D. fled

74. A. dried B. sheltered C. glistened D. warmed

75. A. new B. created C. transformed D. awake

76. A. costly B. fragile C. attractive D. good

77. A. bunch B. forest C. collection D. substitute

78. A. neighbours B. bees C. hunters D. trees

79. A. lonely B. sad C. bare D. depressed

80. A. excited B. proclaimed C. rejoiced D. eager

PASSAGE-9

As the country embarks on planning ...(81)... the 12th Plan (2012-17) period, a key question mark ...(82)... hangs over the process is on the energy requirements.

Growh is energy hungry, and the aspirations of growing at 9-10% will ...(83)... huge demands on the energy resources of the country. In this energy jigsaw, renewable energy will ...(84)... like never before in the 12th Plan and ...(85)....

By the rule of the thumb, India will ...(86)... about 100 gigawatts (Gw)-100,000 megawatts-of capacity addition in the next five years. Encouraging trends on energy efficiency and sustained ...(87)... by some parts of the government—the Bureau of Energy Efficiency in particular needs to be complimented for this—have led to substantially lesser energy intensity of economic growth. However, even the tempered demand numbers are ...(88)... to be below 80 Gw. As against this need the coal supply from domestic sources is unlikely to support more than 25 Gw equivalent capacity. Imported coal can add some more, but at a much ...(89)... cost. Gas-based electricity generation is unlikely to contribute anything substantial in view of the unprecedented gas supply challenges. Nuclear will be ...(90)... in the foreseeable future. Between imported coal, gas, large hydro and nuclear, no more than 15-20 Gw equivalent can be ...(91)... to be added in the five-year time block.

...(92)... ...(93)... this, capacity addition in the renewable energy based power generation has touched about 3 Gw a year. In the coming five years, the overall capacity addition in the electricity grid ...(94)... renewable energy is likely to range between 20 Gw and 25 Gw. Additionally, over and above the grid-based capacity, off-grid electricity applications are reaching remote places and ...(95)... lives where grid-based electricity supply has miserably failed.

81. A. against B. for C. onwards D. at

82. A. that B. inside C. always D. who

83. A. forward B. subject
C. place D. demand

84. A. pass B. publish
C. feature D. find

85. A. likewise B. publicity
C. next D. after

86. A. waste B. require
C. highlight D. generate

87. A. structures B. efforts
C. projections D. practices

88. A. sure B. unsure
C. unexpected D. unlikely

89. A. nominal B. excelled
C. higher D. lower

90. A. failure B. success
C. dangerous D. marginal

91. A. certain B. linked
C. remarked D. expected

92. A. When B. But
C. However D. As

93. A. for B. with
C. is D. against

94. A. through B. project
C. versus D. against

95. A. lightening B. making
C. touching D. saving

PASSAGE-10

The Right of Children to Free and Compulsory Education (RTE) Act, 2009, which came ...(96)... effect in April this year, is meant to transform the education sector and take India closer to the goal of universal schooling. But with admissions to the new academic session just ...(97)... the corner, it is fast becoming clear that ...(98)... well-intentioned ideas into ...(99)... will take some doing. For a start, the guidelines for admissions under the RTE prohibit schools from conducting any sort of student profiling. The stress on a random yet justifiable admission process means that schools will have to resort to something as quirky as a lottery system. However, leaving admission to a good school to pure ...(100)... will only incentivise manipulations, defeating the very essence of RTE.

The main problem facing the education sector is that of a resource crunch. The provisions for ensuring universal access to education are all very well, ...(101)... we have the infrastructure in place first. Brick and mortar schools need to precede open admission and not the ...(102)... way around. In that sense, legislators' assessment of ground realities is ...(103)... target when they endorse the closure of tens of thousands of low-cost private schools for not meeting the minimum standards of land plot, building specifications and playground area as laid out in the RTE Act. Instead of bearing down ...(104)... on private schools for failing to conform to abstract bureaucratic criteria, efforts to bring about universal education should focus on upgrading and expanding the existing government school infrastructure to accommodate all. Only then can we ensure the much-needed supply-demand ...(105)... in the education sector.

96. A. with B. for
C. on D. into

97. A. around B. near
C. into D. about

98. A. forming B. translating
C. having D. taking

99. A. affect B. ideas
C. practice D. concept

100. A. benefit B. merit
C. chance D. basis

101. A. unless B. until
C. executed D. provided

102. A. other B. any
C. two D. differ

103. A. on B. of
C. often D. off

104. A. soft B. more
C. less D. hard

105. A. need B. equilibrium
C. expectation D. attempt

PASSAGE-11

The U.S. is in the ...(106)... of a cleanup of toxic financial waste that will ...(107)... taxpayers hundreds of billions of dollars, at the very least. The primary manufacturers of these hazardous products ...(108)... multimillion-dollar paychecks for their efforts. So why shouldn't they ...(109)... to pay for their mop-up? This is, after all, what the U.S. Congress ...(110)... in 1980 for ...(111)... of actual toxic waste. Under the Superfund law ...(112)... that year, polluters ...(113)... for the messes they make. Environmental lawyer E. Michael Thomas sees no ...(114)... lawmakers couldn't demand the same of financial polluters and ...(115)... them to ante up some of the bank bailout money.

106. A. range B. depth
C. midst D. essence

107. A. benefit B. cost
C. earn D. facilitate

108. A. donated B. demanded
C. dwindled D. pocketed

109. A. hesitate B. come
C. defy D. have

110. A. decreed B. refrained
C. commented D. admonished

111. A. consumers B. advocates
C. exponents D. producers

112. A. revoked B. forced
C. squashed D. enacted

113. A. regain B. claim
C. pay D. demand

114. A. practice B. reason
C. compensation D. issue

115. A. force B. plead
C. appeal D. dupe

PASSAGE-12

A day light can be seen ...(116)... very small holes, so little things will ...(117)... a person's character. Indeed consists in little acts well and ...(118) performed; daily life being the ...(119)... from which build it up and rough ...(120)... the habits which form it. One of the more marked test of character is the manner in which we ...(121)... ourselves towards others, a graceful behaviour, towards superiors, inferiors, and ...(122)... is constant source of pleasure. It pleases others because it indicates ...(123)... for their personality, but it gives tenfold more ...(124)... to our selves. Every man may, to large extent be a self educator in good ...(125)... as in every else, he can be civil and kind if he thinks he has not a penny in his purse.

116. A. through B. out of
C. in D. by

117. A. darken B. characterise
C. adorn D. illustrate

118. A. equally B. honourably
C. roughly D. officially

119. A. house B. livelihood
C. quarry D. relation

120. A. spouse B. give up
C. new D. watch

121. A. conduct B. manage
C. nature D. present

122. A. equals B. juniors
C. seniors D. superiors

123. A. happiness B. honour
C. regard D. respect

124. A. force B. requirement
C. pleasure D. dedication

125. A. status B. behaviour
C. character D. career

PASSAGE-13

With the U.S. military tied down on two fronts and the rest of the world growing ...(126)... to American power, the challenges for Rice are as ...(127)... as they have been for any Secretary of State in the past three decades. After six years of tussling with others on Bush's national-security team, Rice has seen off her rivals and ...(128)... as the principal spokes-person for Bush's foreign ...(129).... Her reward has been to ...(130)... responsibility for selling a failed policy in Iraq and ...(131)... a legacy for Bush at a time when ...(132)... in the world are in the mood to help her. "Bush is severely ...(133)... and has very little ...(134)... or support at home or abroad," says Leslie Gelb, former president of the Council on Foreign Relations. "That is ...(135)... true for his Secretary of State. So they are ...(136)... flailing around."

That's a grim assessment, since the ...(137)... to international order are ...(138)... today than at any 'other' time since the end of the cold war. The most immediate source of ...(139)... emanates from Iraq, where the country's civil war risks ...(140)... a region-wide conflict.

126. A. resistant B. subservient
C. immune D. cordial

127. A. obvious B. trivial
C. superfluous D. daunting

128. A. renamed B. emerged
C. appointed D. visited

129. A. aid B. recognition
C. policy D. acceptability

130. A. shirk B. avoid
C. transfer D. inherit

131. A. focusing B. framing
C. escaping D. salvage

132. A. people B. few
C. diplomats D. autocrats

133. A. intensified B. master-minded
C. weakened D. projected

134. A. credibility B. difficulty
C. majority D. enthusiasm

135. A. not B. uniformly
C. remotely D. also

136. A. effectively B. inadvertently
C. basically D. aimlessly

137. A. admirations B. threats
C. pleasantries D. demands

138. A. louder B. fewer
C. magnificent D. bigger

139. A. instability B. fuel
C. energy D. atrocity

140. A. defusing B. demolishing
C. terminating D. igniting

PASSAGE-14

The ...(141)... of Bengal tigers left in the world has ...(142)... from 100,000 to 4,000 over the last century. The main threats are ...(143)... of habitat, poaching and the trade in tiger parts for Eastern medicines. Most Bengal tigers live in protected areas of India. Anti-poaching task-force have been ...(144)... up and there is also a trade ...(145)... on tiger products in many countries, as a measure to save this rare species.

141. A. from B. kind
C. glory D. number

142. A. limited B. shrunk
C. abolished D. eliminated

143. A. prevention B. encroaching
C. condition D. loss

144. A. set B. brought
C. swept D. deployed

145. A. agreement B. contract
C. ban D. link

PASSAGE-15

Human Resources Development Department has ...(146)... heads of all Central Office Departments to ...(147)... to the notice of the employees ...(148)... to their departments ...(149)... the availability of professional counsellor engaged by our organization on contract basis to ...(150)... counselling services to employees of Mumbai. HRDD has also sought the ...(151)... of all the employees to ...(152)... the fears and unfounded notions, if any, about counselling so that employees were ...(153)... to come forward and avail of it. Counselling facility for employees was ...(154)... in Mumbai in Septembe 21 with the help of a professional counsellor. The counsellor is ...(155)... on Mondays in the Main Building Mumbai.

146. A. reported B. indicated
C. referred D. advised

147. A. tell B. ask
C. show D. bring

148. A. affected B. absolved
C. attached D. affixed

149. A. regarding B. about
C. upon D. aforesaid

150. A. decide B. determine
C. provide D. takeover

151. A. availability B. presence
C. support D. permission

152. A. dissolve B. disperse
C. dispel D. displace

153. A. asked B. directed
C. diverted D. encouraged

154. A. obstructed B. observed
C. started D. laid

155. A. ready B. available
C. accessible D. attainable

PASSAGE-16

From the time I started writing this book I have come to see it as personal ...(156)... to an outstanding fellow Indian, whose ...(157)... and compassion have often moved me. Insight, not objectivity, is the key to understanding of a life as multi-layered as that of Swami Vivekananda and in the ...(158)... of writing this book, I have often felt ...(159)... by the realization that a historian may not always be a good biographer. I have also been ...(160)... by the several inconsistencies and ...(161)... of Vivekananda's life, and only by bringing these out more sharply, I felt, could one consciously ...(162)... from the hagiography that ...(163)... biographical work on him. It is impossible to reach an understanding of a personality as complex as Vivekananda's without studying his ambiguities and shifting ...(164)... on various issues. In trying to integrate these in a ...(165)... assessment of Vivekananda, I have largely gone by what the Swami has himself suggested – judge a man ultimately by his strengths, not his weaknesses.

156. A. justice B. devotion
C. contribution D. tribute

157. A. deliberation B. projection
C. vivacity D. acknowledgement

158. A. course B. manifestation
C. objective D. implementation

159. A. represented B. relieved
C. compensated D. burdened

160. A. absorbed B. perplexed
C. carried D. ventured

161. A. duplications B. paradoxes
C. assumptions D. levels

162. A. desist B. estranged
C. distinguish D. depart

163. A. evolves B. focuses
C. permeates D. empowers

164. A. positions B. engagements
C. possibilities D. provocations

165. A. modern B. conducive
C. commensurate D. holistic

PASSAGE-17

Actually, everyday we all engage in this business of 'reading' people. We do it ....(166).... We want to figure others out. So we ...(167)... make guesses about what others think, value, want and feel and we do so based on our ....(168).... beliefs and understanding about human nature. We do so because if we can figure out ....(169).... and intentions of others the possibility of them ....(170).... or hurting us, ...(171).... and this well help us to ....(172).... a lot of unnecessary pain and trouble. We also make second-guesses about what they will do in future, how they will ....(173).... if we make this or that response. We do all this second guessing based upon our ....(174).... of what we believe about the person's inner nature ....(175).... his or her roles and manners. We mind-read their ....(176).... motives.

Also everyday we misguess and misread. Why? Because of the complexity, ...(177).... and multi-dimensional functioning of people. After all how well do you 'read' your own thoughts, aims, values, motives, beliefs, etc.? How well do you know your own structuring process— your own thinking and ....(178).... styles.

166. A. vehemently B. practically
C. actually D. incessantly

167. A. ably B. constantly C. partly D. largely

168. A. futuristic B. proactive C. reactive D. assumptive

169. A. manifestations B. expressions C. motives D. hopes

170. A. tricking B. blaming C. furthering D. alarming

171. A. lessens B. happens C. questions D. deepens

172. A. approach B. direct C. avoid D. implement

173. A. solve B. apply C. plan D. respond

174. A. projection B. exhibition C. situation D. prediction

175. A. organising B. underneath C. appreciating D. outside

176. A. cunning B. visible C. deeper D. obvious

177. A. abnormality B. angularity C. focus D. layeredness

178. A. proposing B. developing C. upbringing D. emoting

PASSAGE-18

Man has always cosidered himself to be the ruler of his planet. This ...**(179)**... and the attendant superiority feeling has made him look down ...**(180)**... other creatures who co-exist with human on this earth. The so-called 'civilized' human race has ...**(181)**... and ill-treated small and large animal species and birds in an attempt to prove his ...**(182)**... . It is common knowledge that ...**(183)**... number of animals have been ...**(184)**... for centuries under the ...**(185)**... of conducting scientific experiments or for sports. Till recently, in the ...**(186)**... of scientific experiments monkeys and frogs have been ...**(187)**... to dissection and ...**(188)**... in the laboratory.

179. A. pleasure B. fact C. achievement D. arrogance

180. A. in B. upon C. with D. for

181. A. criticised B. devalued C. protected D. abused

182. A. supremacy B. wisdom C. cleverness D. instinct

183. A. tall B. plenty C. countless D. diverse

184. A. tourtured B. exposed C. treated D. vanished

185. A. projection B. criticism C. pretext D. game

186. A. matter B. set C. scheme D. name

187. A. confined B. subjected C. condemned D. allied

188. A. cruelty B. deformation C. study D. vivisection

PASSAGE-19

Organisation ...**(189)**... is a very broad subject that appears frequently in recent management studies. Organisations have many ...**(190)**... to improve whatever it is that they do. They can reflect on their operations, study their products, ...**(191)**... to cutsomers, and encourage ...**(192)**... parts of the organisation to share knowledge as well as the results of their ...**(193)**... efforts. All firms have these opportunities, although few companies take full ...**(194)**... of them Good firms everywhere ...**(195)**... their processes and ...**(196)**... in order to learn from past successes as well as ...**(197)**... . They measures and benchmark what they do. They try to get different parts of the organisation to ...**(198)**... with one another.

189. A. learning B. system C. building D. structure

190. A. systems B. incentives C. opportunities D. methods

191. A. call B. refer C. please D. listen

192. A. significant B. different C. all D. some

193. A. approved B. separate C. all D. individualistic

194. A. benefit B. credit
C. recourse D. advantage

195. A. critique B. protect
C. design D. innovate

196. A. projects B. finances
C. people D. products

197. A. breaks B. limitations
C. gaps D. failures

198. A. expand B. develop
C. cooperate D. grow

PASSAGE-20

With the U.S. military tied down on two fronts and the rest of the world growing ...(199)... to American power, the challenges for Rice are as ...(200)... as they have been for any Secretary of State in the past three decades. After six years of tussling with others on Bush's national-security team, Rice has seen off her rivals and ...(201)... as the principal spokes- person for Bush's foreign ...(202).... Her reward has been to ...(203)... responsibility for selling a failed policy in Iraq and ...(204)... a legacy for Bush at a time when ...(205)... in the world are in the mood to help her. "Bush is severely ...(206)... and has very little ...(207)... or support at home or abroad," says Leslie Gelb, former president of the Council on Foreign Relations. "That is ...(208)... true for his Secretary of State. So they are ...(209)... flailing around."

That's a grim assessment, since the ...(210)... to international order are bigger today than at any 'other' time since the end of the cold war. The most immediate source of atrocity emanates from Iraq, where the country's civil war risks igniting a region-wide conflict.

199. A. resistant B. subservient
C. immune D. cordial

200. A. obvious B. trivial
C. superfluous D. daunting

201. A. renamed B. emerged
C. appointed D. entrusted

202. A. aid B. recognition
C. policy D. acceptability

203. A. shirk B. avoid
C. transfer D. inherit

204. A. focusing B. framing
C. escaping D. salvage

205. A. people B. few
C. diplomats D. autocrats

206. A. intensified B. master-minded
C. weakened D. projected

207. A. credibility B. difficulty
C. majority D. enthusiasm

208. A. not B. uniformly
C. remotely D. also

209. A. effectively B. inadvertently
C. basically D. aimlessly

210. A. admirations B. threats
C. pleasantries D. demands

ANSWERS

1	2	3	4	5	6	7	8	9	10
D	B	C	A	B	C	D	B	D	B
11	**12**	**13**	**14**	**15**	**16**	**17**	**18**	**19**	**20**
D	D	C	B	A	D	C	D	C	D
21	**22**	**23**	**24**	**25**	**26**	**27**	**28**	**29**	**30**
B	D	C	D	A	B	C	D	D	A
31	**32**	**33**	**34**	**35**	**36**	**37**	**38**	**39**	**40**
D	A	B	D	D	C	C	B	A	B
41	**42**	**43**	**44**	**45**	**46**	**47**	**48**	**49**	**50**
C	A	D	D	C	C	D	D	A	B

51	52	53	54	55	56	57	58	59	60
D	B	B	A	C	A	D	B	D	C
61	**62**	**63**	**64**	**65**	**66**	**67**	**68**	**69**	**70**
D	A	D	D	B	C	B	C	D	D
71	**72**	**73**	**74**	**75**	**76**	**77**	**78**	**79**	**80**
B	D	D	D	C	B	C	B	C	C
81	**82**	**83**	**84**	**85**	**86**	**87**	**88**	**89**	**90**
B	C	C	C	D	B	B	D	C	D
91	**92**	**93**	**94**	**95**	**96**	**97**	**98**	**99**	**100**
D	D	D	A	C	D	A	B	C	C
101	**102**	**103**	**104**	**105**	**106**	**107**	**108**	**109**	**110**
D	A	D	D	B	C	B	D	D	A
111	**112**	**113**	**114**	**115**	**116**	**117**	**118**	**119**	**120**
D	D	C	B	A	A	D	B	C	C
121	**122**	**123**	**124**	**125**	**126**	**127**	**128**	**129**	**130**
A	A	D	C	B	A	D	D	C	D
131	**132**	**133**	**134**	**135**	**136**	**137**	**138**	**139**	**140**
D	A	C	D	D	D	D	D	D	D
141	**142**	**143**	**144**	**145**	**146**	**147**	**148**	**149**	**150**
D	B	D	A	C	D	D	C	A	C
151	**152**	**153**	**154**	**155**	**156**	**157**	**158**	**159**	**160**
B	C	D	C	B	D	C	A	B	A
161	**162**	**163**	**164**	**165**	**166**	**167**	**168**	**169**	**170**
B	D	C	A	D	D	B	D	C	A
171	**172**	**173**	**174**	**175**	**176**	**177**	**178**	**179**	**180**
A	C	D	A	D	C	B	D	D	B
181	**182**	**183**	**184**	**185**	**186**	**187**	**188**	**189**	**190**
B	A	C	A	C	D	B	D	B	C
191	**192**	**193**	**194**	**195**	**196**	**197**	**198**	**199**	**200**
D	B	D	D	D	A	D	D	A	D
201	**202**	**203**	**204**	**205**	**206**	**207**	**208**	**209**	**210**
B	C	D	D	A	C	D	D	D	D

WORD ANALOGY

Directions (Qs. 1–25): *Tick the most appropriate pair in each set in the spirit of the one given at the top :*

1. Lunatic : Asylum

A. The poor : palace
B. Soldiers : barracks
C. Flowers : fields
D. Crops : garden

2. Soldier : Rifle

A. Blacksmith : anvil
B. Thief : ladder
C. Watchman : uniform
D. Barber : hair

3. Frog : Tadpoles

A. Man : sons
B. Woman : daughters
C. Cat : kids
D. Elephant : calves

4. Lizards : Reptiles

A. Frogs : amphibians
B. Tree : fruit
C. Earth : moon
D. Man : woman

5. Earthworm : Segments

A. Tree : wood
B. Crocodiles : scales
C. Apple : juice
D. Earth : moisture

6. Mosquito : Malaria

A. Rabid dog : rabies
B. House fly : AIDS
C. Cockroach : influenza
D. Virus : diabetes

7. Fish : Water

A. Man : air
B. Cat : mouse
C. Lion : flesh
D. Tree : roots

8. Impulsive : Cautious

A. Liberty : bondage
B. Tyrant : bully
C. Tremble : quake
D. Vulgar : indecent

9. Weighty : Voluminous

A. Jolly : dismal
B. Loyalty : perfidy
C. Wealth : opulence
D. Odd : normal

10. Innocent : Guilty

A. Kill : produce
B. Suspect : doubt
C. Depress : discourage
D. Contract : condense

11. Useless : Cheap

A. Late : unpunctual
B. Real : illusive
C. Just : unfair
D. Humble : proud

12. Loyal : Faithful

A. Treacherous : devoted
B. Just : fair
C. Yield : suppress
D. Uncertain : sure

13. Cancel : Confirm

A. Certain : ambiguous
B. Vulgar : crude
C. Reliable : trustworthy
D. Obscure : anonymous

14. Gloomy : Bright

A. Pleasant : delightful
B. Funny : comic

C. Condemn : blame
D. Hard : flexible

15. Modern : Ancient
A. Happy : joyful
B. Service : slavery
C. Mild : harsh
D. assumed : unreal

16. Dexterous : Clumsy
A. Cheap : worthless
B. Usual : common
C. Zenith : acme
D. True : false

17. Luscious : Sweet
A. Above : below
B. Absolve : penalise
C. Lucrative : profitable
D. Adopt : abandon

18. Fraud : Duplicity
A. Inferior : cheap
B. Delicious : abhorrent
C. Desire : detest
D. Diligent : lackadiasical

19. Weired : Ordinary
A. Vacant : void
B. Vivid : clear
C. Vivid : dim
D. Wicked : unvirtuous

20. Build : Demolish
A. Abide : persist
B. Compel : coax
C. Odious : hateful
D. Claim : demand

21. Passionate : Impassive
A. Deter : discourage
B. Folly : stupidity
C. Polite : rude
D. Fanciful : whimsical

22. Gauche : Attractive
A. True : exact
B. Tough : hard
C. Tasteful : palatable
D. Insipid : delicious

23. Existence : Life
A. Silence : noise
B. Risk : shield
C. Enormous : immense
D. Rural : urban

24. Belief : Suspicion
A. Unravel : unweave
B. Profuse : insufficient
C. Urge : spur
D. Use : occupy

25. Violent : Calm
A. Tranquil : peaceful
B. Reticent : quiet
C. Even : smooth
D. Disdain : reverence

ANSWERS

1	2	3	4	5	6	7	8	9	10
B	A	D	A	B	A	A	A	C	A
11	**12**	**13**	**14**	**15**	**16**	**17**	**18**	**19**	**20**
A	B	A	D	C	D	C	A	C	B
21	**22**	**23**	**24**	**25**					
C	D	C	B	D					

REASONING & MILITARY APTITUDE TEST

LETTER ANALOGY

Directions : *In the questions given below one term is missing. Based on the relationship of the two given words find the missing term from the given options.*

1. GFC : CFG : : RPJ : ?
   A. JRP B. JPR
   C. PJR D. RJP
2. BCF : DEG : : MNQ : ?
   A. OPR B. PQS
   C. OPP D. QRT
3. NATION : ANITNO : : HUNGRY : ?
   A. HNUGRY B. UNHGYR
   C. YRNGUH D. UHGNYR
4. SSTU : MMNO : : AABC : ?
   A. GGHH B. IJKK
   C. XXYZ D. NOOP
5. ACE : FGH : : LNP : ?
   A. QRS B. PQR
   C. QST D. MOQ
6. UVW : SXU : : LMN : ?
   A. JOL B. KNM
   C. JKL D. MLO
7. EIGHTY : GIEYTH : : OUTPUT : ?
   A. UTOPTU B. UOTUPT
   C. TUOUTP D. TUOTUP
8. TSR : FED : : WVU : ?
   A. CAB B. MLK
   C. PQS D. GFH
9. CJDL : FMGR : : IKJR : ?
   A. OQPT B. RSTU
   C. OQRT D. KRMO
10. BOQD : ERTG : : ANPC : ?
    A. DQSF B. FSHU
    C. SHFU D. DSQF
11. BaBy : TaTa : : LiLy : ?
    A. PooL B. ROse
    C. HaNd D. DoWN
12. ABCD : RSTU : : JKLM : ?
    A. UVWX B. EFHG
    C. SRTU D. QSRP
13. AEI : LPT : : CGK : ?
    A. OSV B. RUY
    C. TXC D. FJN
14. RUX : TRP : : BEH : ?
    A. SQN B. QON
    C. QOM D. QNL
15. CART : ART : : FOUR : ?
    A. RUN B. TWO
    C. QUE D. OUR
16. FIK : JGO : : DFR : ?
    A. BIO B. HDV
    C. GCU D. FLP
17. LJH : KKI : : CIA : ?
    A. BJB B. DHB
    C. BJC D. BBJ
18. ACE : HIL : : MOQ : ?
    A. SVW B. TUX
    C. RTW D. WUS
19. BCDE : WVUT : : QRST : ?
    A. EFHG B. JIHG
    C. POML D. GEDC
20. PNLJ : IGEC : : USQO : ?
    A. HJLN B. LNJH
    C. NLJH D. JHNL
21. DIMO : DMIO : : JUVR : ?
    A. JVRU B. JRVU
    C. JVUR D. JUVR
22. RRS : XMW : : ITB : ?
    A. PNE B. NOG
    C. RSW D. OOF
23. ODRS : OSRD : : PAGJ : ?
    A. PJGA B. PJAG
    C. PGJA D. PGAJ

24. MEQI : JUOD : : ANIW : ?
A. RUKE B. URIA
C. EUIO D. PTRE

25. AKU : AJS : : CRD : ?
A. BQE B. CQB
C. DSB D. APC

26. LOM : NMK : : PKI : ?
A. RNK B. RSM
C. RMP D. RIG

27. ARQ : DTR : : JNG : ?
A. MPH B. PHJ
C. LPI D. GLE

28. ODL : LOD : : PWN : ?
A. WNP B. NWP
C. NPW D. NMP

29. MAR : RAMP : : INS : ?
A. NEST B. SNIP
C. TINS D. SNAP

30. SUW : RST : : DFH : ?
A. DEF B. FGH
C. CDE D. GHI

31. PYG : OZF : : SBJ : ?
A. QDJ B. PEG
C. OFH D. RCI

32. ABC : ZYX : : IJK : ?
A. RST B. RQP
C. RTS D. RPQ

33. DMT : FNS ; : HRJ : ?
A. ISK B. JSI
C. JTK D. JTI

34. ABDH : ZYWS : : EFHL : ?
A. USOV B. VOSU
C. VUSO D. TSUV

35. BYDW : FVHT : : GQIO : ?
A. JLNP B. QSTR
C. KMOL D. KNML

36. CIRCLE : RICELC : : SQUARE : ?
A. UQSERA B. QUSERA
C. QSUERA D. UQSAER

37. PSQR : CFED : : JMKL : ?
A. UXVW B. WZYX
C. YVXZ D. YZWX

38. JKLM : XYZA : : NOPQ : ?
A. BCDE B. RSTU
C. YZAB D. IJKL

39. EGI : NPR : : HJL : ?
A. RTW B. FGI
C. NQT D. TVX

40. TPNX : XNP : : BUCW : ?
A. WUC B. CUW
C. WCU D. COW

41. CNO : FLP : : WHF : ?
A. GFZ B. ADH
C. ZFG D. YGF

42. DUST : BUSY : : JOIN : ?
A. ROIT B. SOON
C. RIOT D. COST

43. FHJL : VTRP : : MOQS : ?
A. JHFD B. HGFD
C. IGED D. JHED

44. SWZ : XTA : : DGM : ?
A. JEO B. IDN
C. HCM D. NDI

45. NBRC : CRAB : : TYDA : ?
A. DRAY B. ADAY
C. DATB D. YDAB

46. BdNf : JnLo : : OrGh : ?
A. GhnM B. WbDq
C. NMoh D. FwbF

47. GNTB : GTNB : : WROX : ?
A. WORX B. RONX
C. WYOX D. RWOX

48. JMP : GOQ : : DBL : ?
A. BCN B. AEN
C. BDN D. ADM

49. UCFH : VEIL : : RXDJ : ?
A. RYFM B. TAHO
C. SZNG D. SZGN

50. ICHQ : HCIT : : PMBK : ?
A. BMYR B. BMPN
C. MBPY D. MPBS

ANSWERS

1	2	3	4	5	6	7	8	9	10
B	A	D	C	A	A	D	B	A	A
11	**12**	**13**	**14**	**15**	**16**	**17**	**18**	**19**	**20**
C	A	D	C	D	B	A	B	B	C
21	**22**	**23**	**24**	**25**	**26**	**27**	**28**	**29**	**30**
C	D	A	A	B	D	A	C	B	C
31	**32**	**33**	**34**	**35**	**36**	**37**	**38**	**39**	**40**
D	B	B	C	D	A	B	A	D	C
41	**42**	**43**	**44**	**45**	**46**	**47**	**48**	**49**	**50**
C	A	A	B	B	B	A	D	D	B

EXPLANATORY ANSWERS

1. The letters of the first group are reversed.

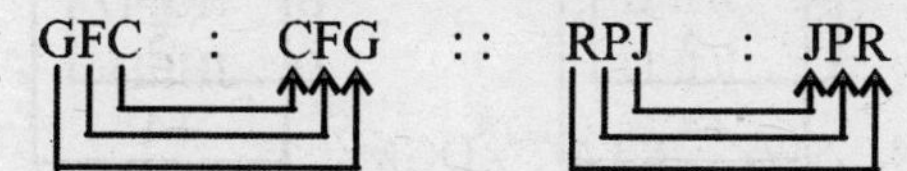

2. The three letters are moved 2, 2 and 1 steps forward respectively.

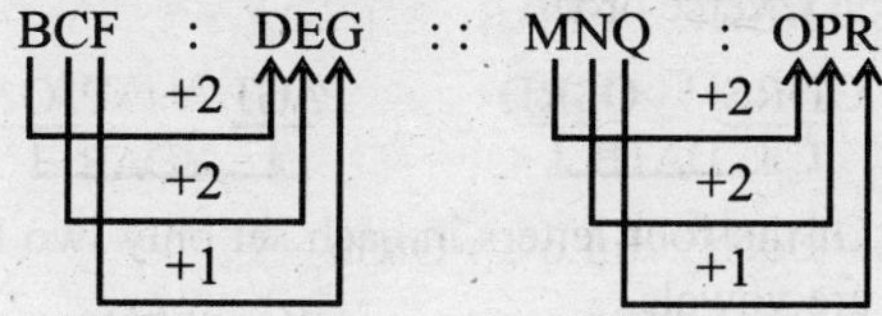

3. The word is divided in sections of two letters and the letters are reversed.

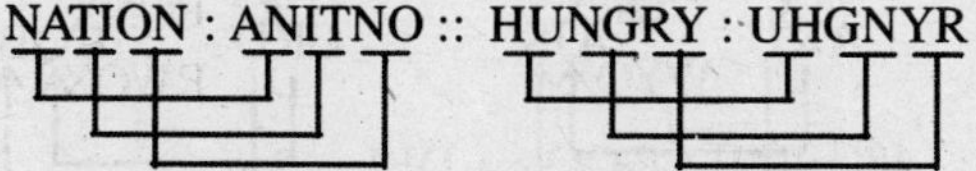

4. The first letter in each group is repeated and followed by two consecutive letters.

5. The three letters are moved 5, 4, and 3 steps forward respectively.

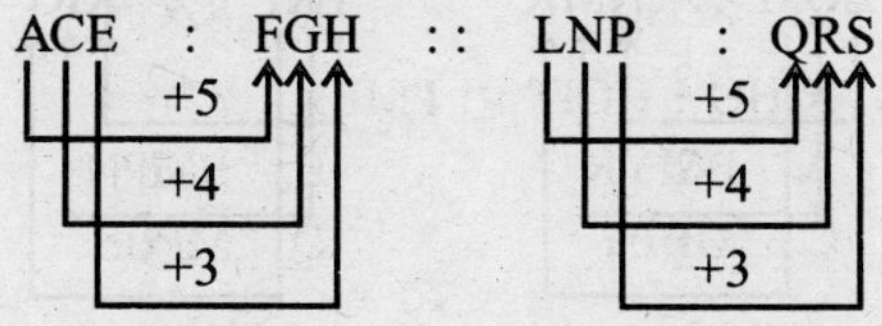

6. The three letters are moved –2, +2 and –2 steps respectively.

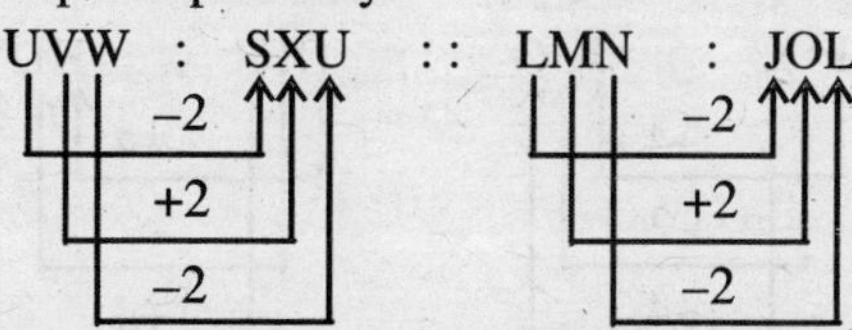

7. The word is divided in the sections of three letters and the letters are written backwards.

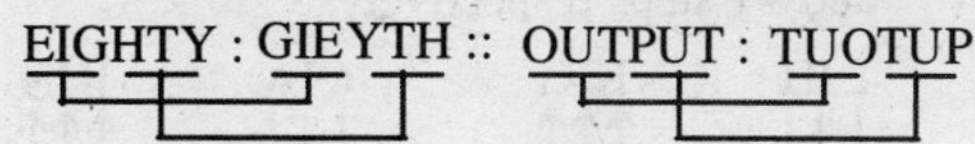

8. The letters are consecutive and written in reverse order.

9. In each set of letters, the 1st and 3rd letters are consecutive.

10.

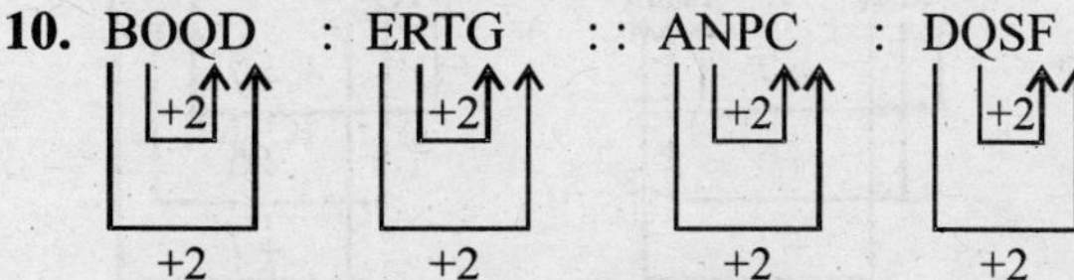

11. In each group the alternate letters are capitals.

12. In each group the first three letters are consecutive and they follow the fourth letter.

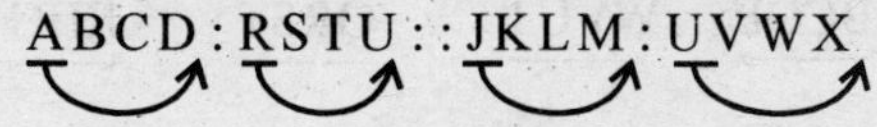

13. In each group the letters jump three letters between them, *i.e.,* they are moving to the fourth letter.

A E I : L P T :: C G K : F J N

+4 +4   +4 +4   +4 +4   +4 +4

14. The letters in first set are jumping two letters, *i.e.,* moving three steps forward and in the second they are jumping one letter, *i.e.* moving two steps backward.

R U X : T R P :: B E H : Q O M

+3 +3   –2 –2   +3+3   –2 –2

15. The first set of letters drop the first letter to get the second set.

C A R T : A R T :: F O U R : O U R

16. The three letters in first set are moved +4, –2, and +4 steps respectively.

FIK : JGO :: DFR : HDV

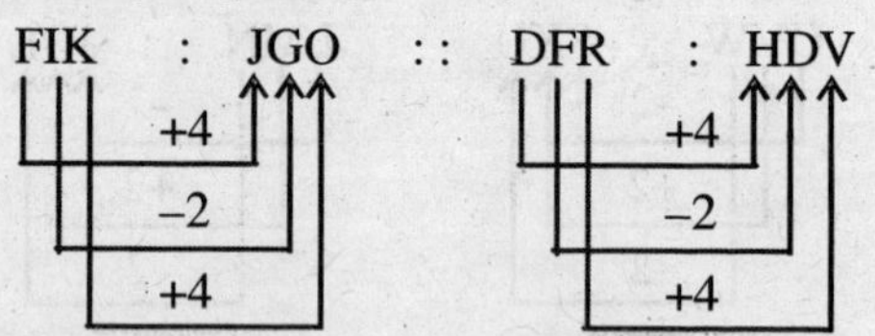

17. The letters in the first set are moved –1, +1 and +1 steps respectively.

LJH : KKI :: CIA : BJB

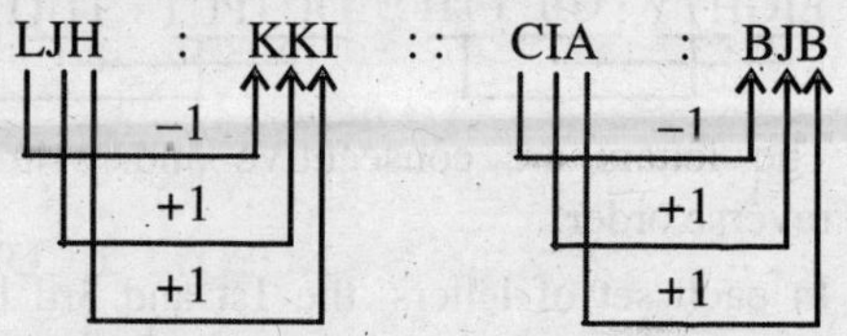

18. The three letters are moved +7, +6 and +7 steps forward respectively.

ACE : HIL :: MOQ : TUX

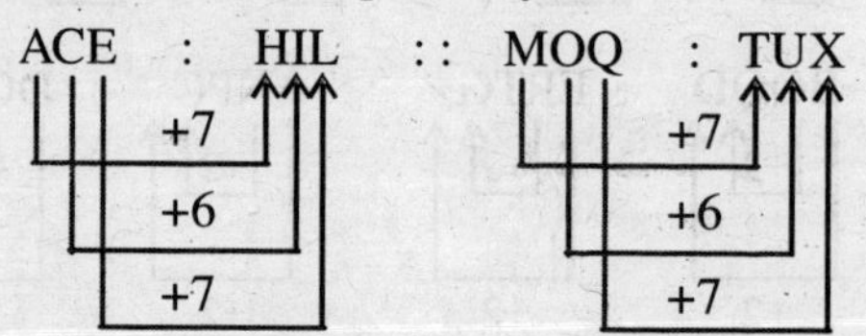

19. The consecutive letters in the first set are in natural order and in the second set, they are in reverse order.

BCDE : WVUT :: QRST : JIHG

20. The letters are moved seven steps backwards.

PNLJ : IGEC :: USQO : NLJH

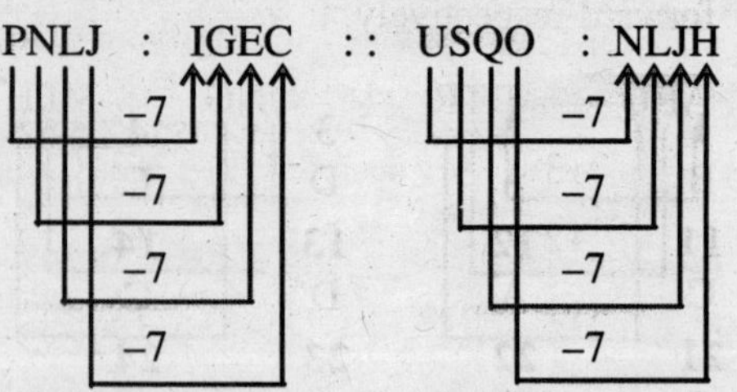

21. Only the middle letters are reversed to obtain the second set of letters.

DIMO : DMIO :: JUVR : JVUR

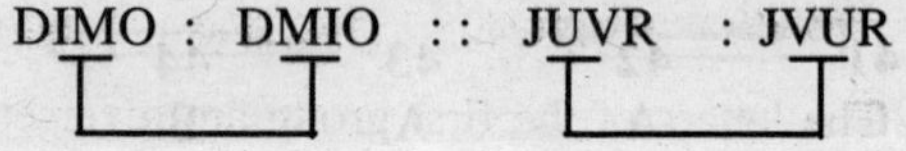

22. The three letters are moved +6, –5 and +4 steps respectively.

RRS : XMW :: ITB : OOF

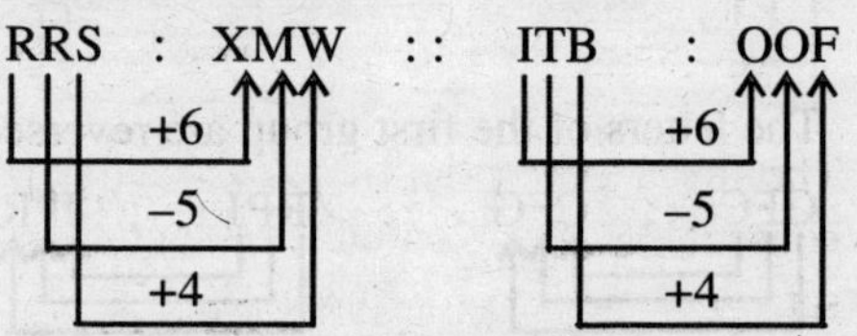

23. Of the four letters the first letter is left at its place while the other three letters are written in reverse order.

ODRS : OSRD :: PAGJ : PJGA

24. Of the four letters in each set only two letters are vowels.

25. Of the three letters the first letter is left as it is and the other letters are moved one and two steps backward respectively.

AKU : AJS :: CRD : CQB

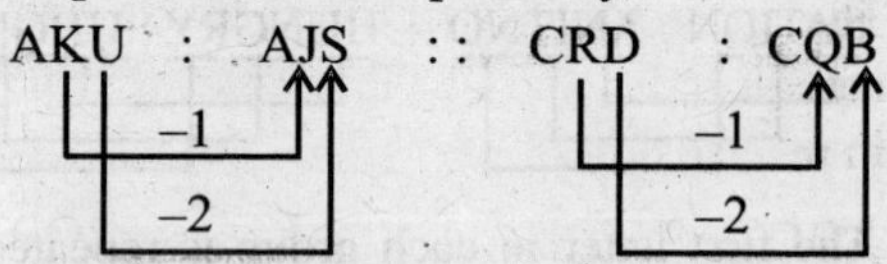

26. The first letter is moved two steps forward and the second and third letters two steps backward.

LOM : NMK :: PKI : RIG

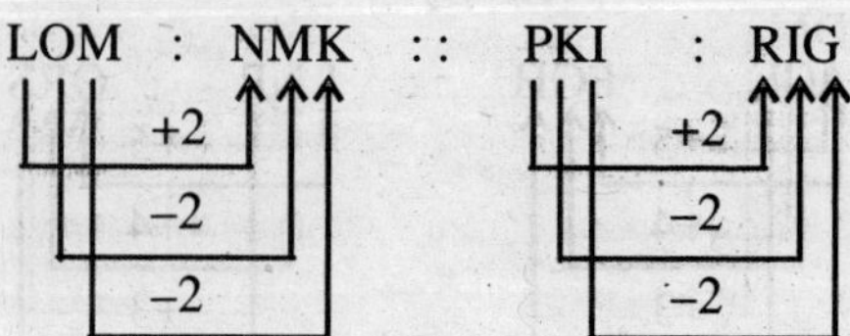

27. The three letters are moved 3, 2 and 1 step forward respectively.

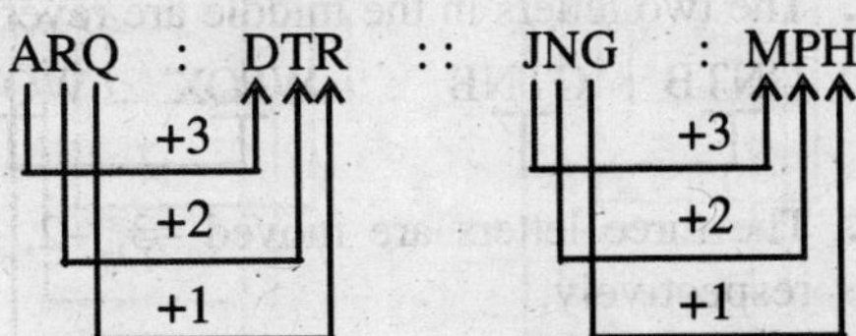

28. The third letter is placed ahead of the first and second letters.

29. The letters of the first group are reversed and letter P added in the end.

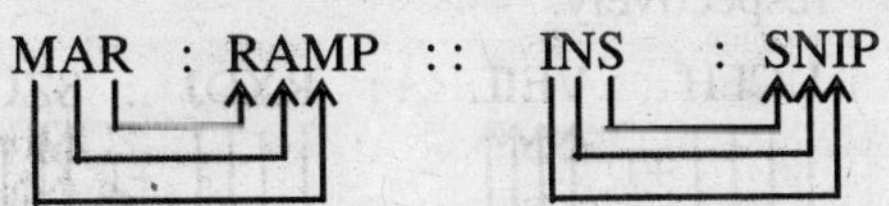

30. The first letter in the first set of letters has its consecutive letters on either side in the second set.

31. The three letters are moved –1, +1, –1 steps respectively.

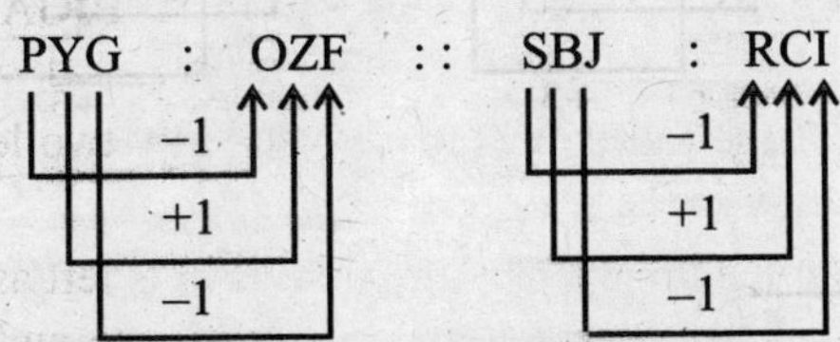

32. The consecutive letters in the first set are in natural order and in the second set, they are in reverse order.

ABC : ZYX :: IJK : RQP

33. The three letters are moved +2, +1, –1 steps respectively.

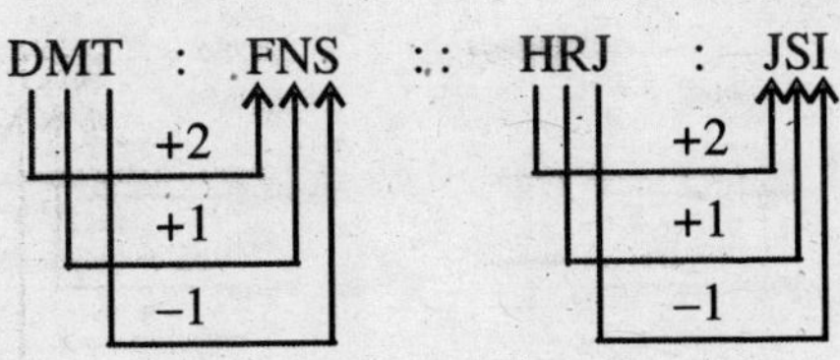

34. A B D H : Z Y W S :: E F H L : V U S O

+1 +2 +4   –1 –2 –4   +1 +2 +4   –1 –2 –4

35. The letters are moved +4, –3, +4, –3 steps respectively.

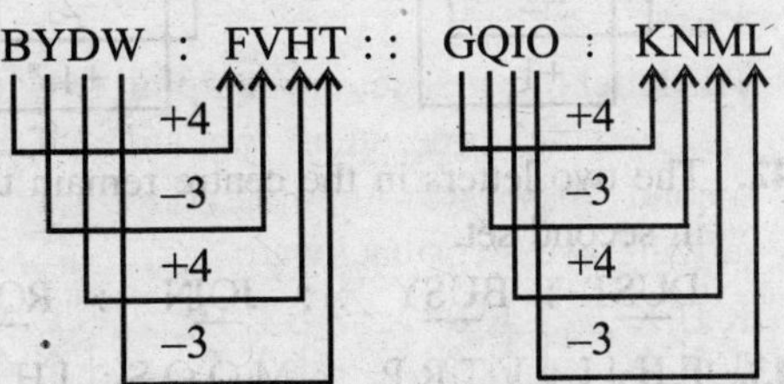

36. The word is divided into two equal parts and then the letters are reversed.

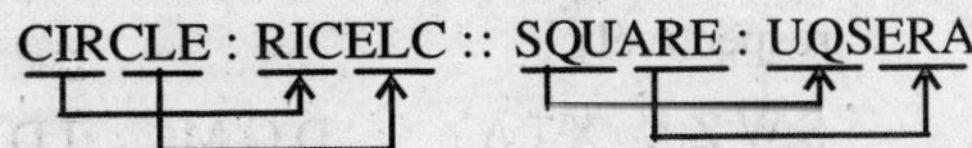

37. In the first set the first, third, fourth and second positioned letters are in consecutive order. In the second set the first, fourth, third and second positioned letters are in consecutive order.

PSQR : CFED :: JMKL : WZYX

38. The letters are consecutive and the first letter of the first set is moved 14 steps 'or' the last letter of the first set is moved 11 steps forward to get the first letter of the second set.

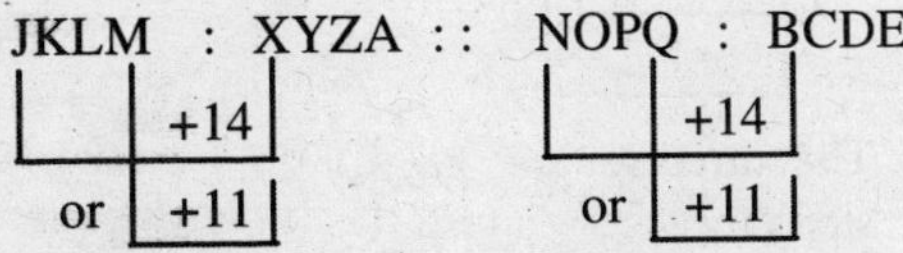

39. The letters are in natural order and skip one letter in between.

E G I : N P R :: H J L : T V X

+1 +1   +1 +1   +1 +1   +1 +1

40. The first letter is dropped and the remaining three letters are reversed.

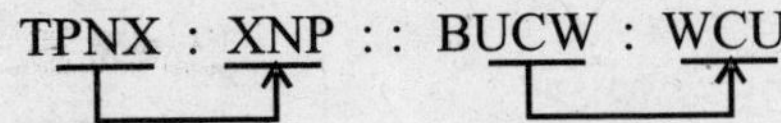

41. The letters are moved +3, –2, +1, steps respectively.

42. The two letters in the centre remain the same in second set.

DUST : BUSY :: JOIN : ROIT

43. F H J L : V T R P :: M O Q S : J H F D

+2 +2 +2   –2 –2 –2   +2 +2 +2   –2 –2 –2

44. The three letters are moved +5, –3, +1 steps respectively.

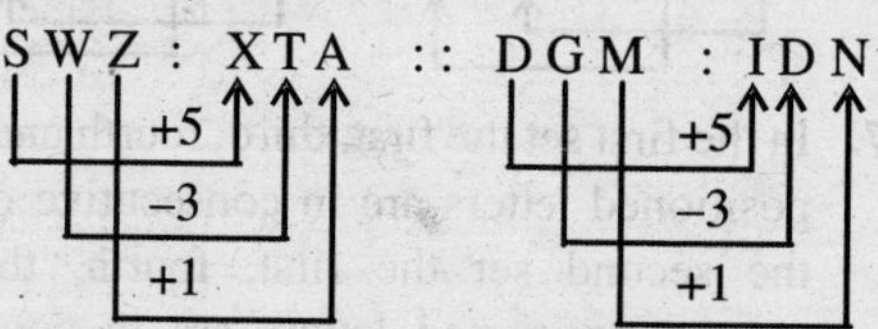

45. The first letter is dropped, the remaining three letters are reversed and letter 'A' placed in between the second and third letters.

N BRC : CRAB :: TYDA : ADAY

46. The first and the third letters are capita letters.

47. The two letters in the middle are reversed.

GNTB : GTNB :: WROX : WORX

48. The three letters are moved –3, +2, +1 ste respectively.

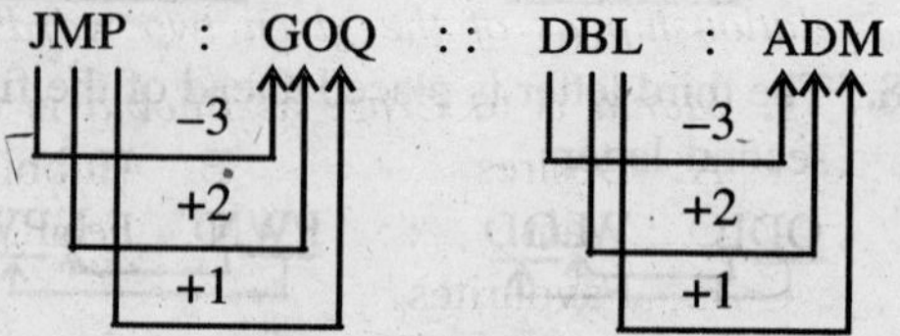

49. The letters are moved 1, 2, 3, 4 steps forwa respectively.

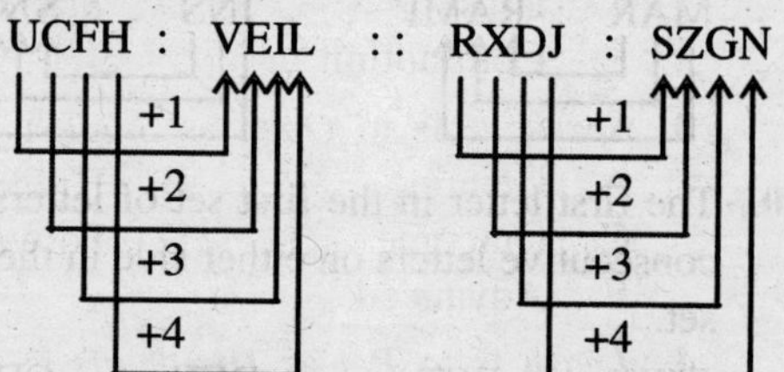

50. The first three letters are reversed and the la letter moved three steps forward.

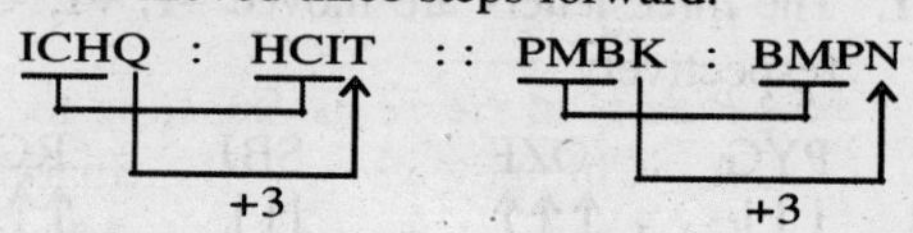

WORD ANALOGY

Directions : *In the questions given below establish the relationship between the two words. Then from the given options select one which has the same relationship as of the given two words.*

1. *Mania* is to *Craze* as *Phobia* is to .....
A. Desires B. Hobbies
C. Want D. Fear
E. Favourites

2. *Stammering* is to *Speech* as *Deafness* is to.....
A. Ear B. Hearing
C. Noise D. Silence
E. Commotion

3. *Secretive* is to *Open* as *Snide* is to.....
A. Genuine B. Hidden
C. Outcome D. Forward
E. Advanced

4. *Leash* is to *Pet* as *Handcuffs* is to.....
A. Cunning B. Dacoits
C. Criminals D. Robbers
E. Accused

5. *Ride* is to *Horse* as *Smoke* is to.....
A. Chimney B. Sparkling
C. Cigar D. Ashes
E. Fire

6. *Squander* is to *Money* as *Dissipate* is to....
A. Light B. Finance
C. Savings D. Energy
E. Banking

7. *Tipsy* is to *Drunken* as *Walk* is to.......
A. Stroll B. Exercise
C. Stride D. Tired
E. Run

8. *Sphere* is to *Circle* as *Cube* is to........
A. Prism B. Cylinder
C. Square D. Trapezium
E. None of these

9. *Leader* is to *Follower* as ..... is to *Soldier*.
A. Captain B. Unit
C. Army D. Barrack
E. Cavalry

10. *Guilt* is to *Past* as *Hope* is to.....
A. Present B. Future
C. Today D. Despair
E. Hopeless

11. .... is to *Liquid* as *Mile* is to *Distance*.
A. Unit B. Kilo
C. Scale D. Litre
E. Mercury

12. *Gum* is to.... as *Socket* is to *Eye*.
A. Tree B. Paper
C. Tooth D. Stick
E. None of these

13. *Court* is to *Judges* as *Cockpit* is to.......
A. Attorney B. Pilot
C. Lawyer D. Ruler
E. Administrator

14. *Stars* are to *Night* as *Sun* is to....
A. Noon B. Dawn
C. Day D. Light
E. Dusk

15. ..... is to *Nose* as *Touch* is to *Skin*.
A. Smell B. Face
C. Breath D. Perfume
E. Nostril

16. *Spasm* is to *Pain* as *Flash* is to.....
A. Wind B. Light
C. Signal D. Fire
E. Rain

17. *War* is to..... as *Smoke* is to *Pollution*.
A. Alliance B. Peace
C. Victory D. Treaty
E. Destruction

18. *Treatment* is to...... as *Education* is to *Teacher*.
A. Doctor B. Matron
C. Hospital D. Clinic
E. Chemist

19. *Mammals* is to *Man* as *Aves* is to.....
A. Aeroplanes B. Birds
C. Pigeons D. Fruit
E. Winds

20. *Mango* is to *Fruit* as ... is to *Monument.*
A. Remains B. Tombs
C. Red Fort D. History
E. Pillars

21. *Statue* is to *Shape* as *Song* is to.....
A. Singer B. Lyrics
C. Composer D. Poetry
E. Tune

22. *Train* is to *Track* as *Bullet* is to....
A. Barrel B. Kill
C. Firing D. Ammunition
E. Weapon

23. *Psychology* is to *Emotions* as *Philosophy* is to.....
A. Dreams B. Scholar
C. Research D. Wisdom
E. Learning

24. *Mermaid* is to *Fish* as *Centaur* is to.....
A. Pegasus B. Unicorn
C. Deer D. Cat
E. Horse

25. *Punishment* is to *Imprisonment* as *Reward* is to......
A. Freedom B. Remand
C. Money D. Rebuke
E. Award

26. *Surgeon* is to *Scalpel* as *Sculptor* is to....
A. Pastle B. Chisel
C. Pallet D. Engraving
E. Hammer

27. *Backbone* is to *Back* as ... is to *Belly.*
A. Kidney B. Navel
C. Ribs D. Femur
E. Lungs

28. *Star* is to......as *Drop* is to *Ocean.*
A. Galaxy B. Shine
C. Earth D. Twinkle
E. None of these

29. .... is to *Strike* as *Whisper* is to *Shout.*
A. Slap B. Touch
C. Anger D. Noisy
E. Kill

30. .... is to *Dumb* as *Light* is to *Blind.*
A. Voice B. Language
C. Speech D. Tongue
E. None of these

31. *Physicist is to Physics as .... is to Anatomy.*
A. Botany B. Botanist
C. Body D. Biologist
E. Medicine

32. *Love* is to *Hate* as *Friend* is to.......
A. Trust B. Companion
C. Enemy D. Despise
E. Adore

33. *Flower* is to *Petal* as ... is to *Arm.*
A. Hand B. Weapon
C. Clock D. Law
E. Body

34. *Sweep* is to ...... as *Wash* is to *Soap.*
A. Broom B. Dust
C. Floor D. Water
E. Clean

35. *Dull* is to..... as *Intelligent* is to *Clever.*
A. Bright B. Foolish
C. Insane D. Mad
E. Slow

36. *Scales* is to *Fish* as *Feathers* is to.....
A. Hat B. Birds
C. Prune D. Fly
E. Light

37. *Burn* is to *Ointment* as *Grief* is to.....
A. Sorrow B. Adversity
C. Consolation D. Pity
E. Sentiment

38. *Frequently* is to *Always* as *Seldom* is to......
A. Often B. Rarely
C. Occasionally D. Never
E. None of these

39. *Mine* is to *I* as *His* is to......
A. Him B. Their
C. Them D. Me
E. He

40. *Delhi* is to *Haryana* as *Orissa* is to ....
A. Jammu & Kashmir

B. Andhra Pradesh
C. Tamil Nadu
D. Nagaland
E. Punjab

41. *Pen* is related to *Stationery* in the same way as *Chair* is related to.....

A. Wood
B. Rest
C. Room
D. Position
E. Furniture

42. *Tailor* is related to *Cloth* in the same way as *Cobbler* is related to ....

A. Machine
B. Leather
C. Stiching
D. Mending
E. Making

43. As *Dam* is to *Mad* so also *Drab* is to....

A. Barb
B. Brab
C. Bard
D. Badr
E. Brda

44. As *Cassock* is to *Priest* so also .... is to *Graduate*.

A. Gown
B. Cap
C. Tie
D. Coat
E. Degree

45. As *Dilatory* is to *Expeditious* so also *Direct* is to....

A. Straight
B. Tortuous
C. Curved
D. Circumlocutory
E. Perfect

46. *Intelligent* is related to *Clever* in the same way as *Dull* is related to.......

A. Light
B. Cunning
C. Slow
D. Foolish
E. Bright

47. As *Boat* is to *Sails* so also *Balloon* is to...

A. Rubber
B. Nylon
C. Rope
D. Hot air
E. Wind

48. As *Horse* is to *Grass* so also *Automobile* is to.......

A. Smoke
B. Petrol
C. Brake oil
D. Mobil oil
E. Water

49. *Crime* is related to *Court* in the same way as *Disease* is related to.....

A. Lawyer
B. Punishment
C. Hospital
D. Doctor
E. Medicine

50. *Millionaire* is related to *Wealth* in the same way as *Genius* is related to........

A. Capability
B. Smartness
C. Intelligence
D. Awareness
E. Alertness

51. *Needle* is related to *Thread* in the same way as *Pen* is related to.......

A. Write
B. Ink
C. Cap
D. Paper
E. Word

52. As *Paw* is to *Cat* so also *Hoof* is to.......

A. Horse
B. Lamb
C. Elephant
D. Lion
E. Hen

53. *House* is related to *Mason* in the same way as *Furniture* is related to.......

A. Wood
B. Chair
C. Table
D. Seat
E. Carpenter

54. *Bullet* is to *Rifle* as *Arrow* is to.......

A. Archer
B. Bow
C. Target
D. Cord
E. Bull's eye

55. *Page* is related to *Book* in the same way as *Brick* is related to.......

A. Heap
B. Building
C. Clay
D. Mason
E. Mud

56. *Walk* is related to *Run* in the same way as *Breeze* is related to.......

A. Cold
B. Dust
C. Air
D. Wind
E. Smoke

57. *Driving* is related to *Bus* in the same way as *Flying* is related to.......

A. Air
B. Kite
C. Bird
D. Aeroplane
E. Paper

58. What is related to *Elbow* in the same way as *Knee* is related to *Leg*?

A. Palm
B. Fingers

C. Shoulder D. Hand
E. Head

59. What is related to *Fruit* in the same way as *Cabbage* is related to *Vegetable*?
A. Ginger B. Orange
C. Carrot D. Capsicum
E. Potato

60. *Centimetre* is related to *Metre* in the same way as *Paisa* is related to.......
A. Capital B. Rupee
C. Coin D. Wealth
E. Money

61. *Top* is related to *Bottom* in the same way as *Sky* is related to.......
A. Cloud B. Air
C. Earth D. Water
E. Land

62. *Yes* is related to *No* in the same way as *Alive* is related to.......
A. Dead B. Life
C. Live D. Funeral
E. Gone

63. *Kathak* is related to *Uttar Pradesh* in the same way as *Odissy* is related to.......
A. Assam B. Gujarat
C. Orissa D. Maharashtra
E. Punjab

64. *Table* is related to *Carpenter* in the same way as *Building* is related to.......
A. Craftsman B. Contractor
C. Mason D. Architect
E. Cobbler

65. *House* is related to *Shelter* in the same way as *Soap* is related to.......
A. Washerman B. Bathroom
C. Water D. Fragrance
E. Cleanliness

66. *Hot* is related to *Oven* in the same way as *Cold* is related to.......
A. Air-conditioner B. Refrigerator
C. Ice-cream D. Snow
E. Ice-cube

67. *Swim* is related to *Fish* in the same way as *Walk* is related to.......
A. Man B. Bird
C. Legs D. Foot
E. Athlete

68. *Jungle* is related to *Zoo* in the same way as *Sea* is related to.......
A. Harbour B. Water
C. Aquarium D. Fishery
E. Oceanarium

69. *Metal* is related to *Conduction* in the same way as *Plastic* is related to.......
A. Petro Chemicals
B. Industries
C. Inflammation
D. Insulation
E. Induction

70. *Patient* is related to *Doctor* in the same way as *Student* is related to ....
A. School B. Teacher
C. Book D. Classmates
E. Studies

ANSWERS

1	2	3	4	5	6	7	8	9	10
D	B	A	C	C	D	E	C	A	B
11	**12**	**13**	**14**	**15**	**16**	**17**	**18**	**19**	**20**
D	C	B	C	A	B	E	A	B	C
21	**22**	**23**	**24**	**25**	**26**	**27**	**28**	**29**	**30**
E	A	D	E	C	B	C	A	B	C
31	**32**	**33**	**34**	**35**	**36**	**37**	**38**	**39**	**40**
D	C	E	A	B	B	C	D	E	B

41	42	43	44	45	46	47	48	49	50
E	B	C	A	D	D	D	B	C	C
51	**52**	**53**	**54**	**55**	**56**	**57**	**58**	**59**	**60**
B	A	E	B	B	D	D	D	B	B
61	**62**	**63**	**64**	**65**	**66**	**67**	**68**	**69**	**70**
C	A	C	C	E	B	A	A	D	B

EXPLANATORY ANSWERS

1. The related words are synonyms.

2. Defect in speech causes stammering and in hearing causes deafness.

3. The related words are antonyms.

4. Leash is used to tie a pet, handcuffs to tie criminals.

5. Horse is the object of action 'to ride' and cigar is the object of action 'to smoke'.

6. Squander is misuse of money and dissipate is misuse of energy.

7. As tipsy is lesser degree of drunken so is walk to run.

8. Two-dimensional view of a sphere is circle and that of cube a square.

9. As followers are guided by their leader so are soldiers by their captain.

0. Feeling of guilt comes with mistakes in past and that of hope for a good future.

1. Liquid is measured in litres and distance in miles.

2. As gum holds the tooth in place so socket holds the eye.

3. The judges work from court and pilots from cockpit.

. Stars are seen during the night and sun during day.

. Sense organ skin senses the touch and nose senses smell.

. A second's spur of pain is spasm and that of light is flash.

. Smoke causes pollution and war causes destruction.

18. Education is sought by the teacher and treatment by doctor.

19. Species of man is mammals and that of birds aves.

20. Mango is a specified fruit; Red Fort a specified monument.

21. Shape of an object forms the statue and tune of lyrics forms the song.

22. Track is the path of train, barrel is of bullet.

23. Psychology is the study of emotions as philosophy is of wisdom.

24. Mermaid is a mythological fish and centaur a mythological horse.

25. Imprisonment is the form of punishment, money a kind of reward.

26. As scalpel is an instrument used by a surgeon so is chisel of a sculptor.

27. Backbone supports the back and ribs support the belly.

28. A single drop is a very tiny part in an ocean so is a star in the galaxy.

29. The lesser degree of shout is whisper and that of strike is touch.

30. Blind cannot see the light and dumb cannot give speech.

31. Physicist deals with the subject Physics and biologist with subject anatomy.

32. The related words are antonyms.

33. Petal is a part of flower, arm is a part of body.

34. Soap is the object of action 'to wash' and broom is 'to sweep'.

35. One who is clever is intelligent and one who is foolish is dull.

36. As fish is covered with scales so are birds with feathers.

37. As ointment soothes the burn, so does consolation to grief.

38. The related words are near opposites.

39. The related words are noun–pronoun.

40. The related words are neighbouring States.

41. Pen is a type of stationery, chair is a type of furniture.

42. Tailor makes clothes from cloth, cobbler makes shoes from leather.

43. Letter of the related words are written backwards.

44. The dress worn on attaining Priesthood is a cassock, the dress worn on becoming a graduate is a gown.

45. The related words are opposites.

46. The related words are synonyms.

47. Sails are needed to sail a boat, hot air is needed to float a balloon in air.

48. Horse depends on grass for food and energy, automobile on petrol for energy.

49. Crime is taken care of in a court by punishment, disease is taken care of in a hospital by treatment.

50. A millionaire has lots of wealth, a genius has lots of intelligence.

51. Needle uses thread for sewing, pen uses ink for writing.

52. Cat's leg is a paw, horse's leg is a hoof.

53. House is made by a mason, furniture is made by a carpenter.

54. Bullet is shot with a rifle, arrow is shot with a bow.

55. Page is a part of the book, brick is a part of a building.

56. A 'fast walk' is - 'run', a 'fast breeze' is 'wind'.

57. Mode of conveyance, bus, is driven and mode of conveyance, aeroplane, is flown.

58. Knee is a joint in the leg, elbow is a joint in the hand.

59. Cabbage is a vegetable, orange is a fruit.

60. Centimetre is one hundred part of a metre, paisa is one hundredth part of a rupee.

61. The related words are opposites.

62. The related words are opposites.

63. Kathak is a dance form of Uttar Pradesh and Oddisi of Orissa.

64. Table is made by a carpenter, a building is made by a mason.

65. House provides shelter, soap provides cleanliness.

66. Food remains hot in an oven, and cold in a refrigerator.

67. Fishes swim, man walks.

68. Zoo is the part of jungle where wild animals are kept for the public to see and where they are studied, bred and protected. Similarly, oceanarium is the part of sea where sea creature are kept to be seen by the public or to be studied by scientists.

69. Metal is a good conductor and plastic a good insulator of heat.

70. Problem of patient is attended by a doctor, problem of student is attended by the teacher.

CODING & DECODING

Directions : *In the following questions select the right option which indicates the correct code for the word or letter given in the question.*

1. If CORRESPONDENCE is coded as NUTTRAXUPQRPNR in a certain code, how will SCOPE be coded?
A. AUXNR B. ANUXR
C.. RNUXA D. XUPAR

2. In a certain code language SECRET is written as UIIZOF. How will MYSTERY be written in the same code?
A. OCYANCN B. OCYBOCM
C. OCYAODM D. OCYBODM

3. In a certain code LOCATE is written as 981265 and SPARK as 47230, CASKET will be coded in the same manner as :
A. 124056 B. 210465
C. 164025 D. 124506

4. If HALT is coded as SZOG in a certain code, how will STOP be coded in the same manner?
A. GFLK B. HGLK
C. HGKJ D. IHML

5. In a certain code language ABIXV is coded as DELAY. In the same code what will BXOIV stand for?
A. EARTH B. EARNS
C. EARLY D. ELDER

6. In a certain code FLOWER is coded as EIJPVG. How will ROSE be coded?
A. QMOW B. QLOX
C. QKNX D. QLNX

7. If SPORTS is coded in a certain manner as TOPQUR, then TENNIS will be coded as :
A. SFMOJT B. UFONHT
C. SDOMJR D. UDOMJR

8. If BROTHER is coded as IYVAOLY, then SISTER will be coded as :
A. ZQZALY B. ZOZBLY
C. ZPZALY D. ZPZLAY

9. In a certain language SFTVMU is coded as RESULT. In that language what does GJSTU mean?
A. FLIRT B. HURTS
C. FIRST D. FIRED

10. In a certain code APPROACH is coded as CHOAPRAP. How will RESTRICT be coded?
A. CTRISTER B. ERTSIRTC
C. CTRISTRE D. TCIRSTRE

11. If EDUCATION is written as DECUTAOIN, then COLLEGE will be written as :
A. OCLLGEE B. OCLGEEL
C. COELLEG D. EOLCGLE

12. In a certain code VILLA is coded as YKOND, then HOUSE will be coded in the same manner as :
A. KQYTG B. KQXUH
C. JPWTG D. LRYVI

13. SCIENTIST is coded in a certain language as ICSTNETSI. AMBULANCE will be coded in the same language as :
A. MBUALNCEA B. BMAALUECN
C. MAUBALCNE D. UBMLAECNA

14. In a certain code ELECTION is written as GLGCVIQN, then VOTER will be coded as :
A. XOVET B. VOXET
C. WPUFU D. VQTGR

15. EXCURTION is coded as CXEURTNOI, OUTBURSTS will be coded in the same manner as :
A. UTBTRUTSS B. OUTRUBSTS
C. TUOBURSTS D. TUOBRSUTS

16. If ADD is coded as WOO, SUM as QJM and TOTAL as KPKWX, then TOADS will be coded as :
A. KPOWQ B. KPWQO
C. KPWOQ D. KPWOJ

17. If BOMBAY is coded as GLRYFV, then MADRAS will be coded as :

A. RIXOIP B. RXIOXP
C. RXIOGQ D. RXIOFP

18. If QVOJTI is written in a certain code as PUNISH, what will SFXBSE mean?

A. RETARD B. REWARD
C. ROTARY D. REBUKE

19. If ADMIRE is coded as AIDRME, then ADORES will be coded as :

A. AODRSE B. ARDESO
C. ARDEOS D. AREDOS

20. FAILURE is coded as OHRSDYN, then SUCCESS will be coded in the same manner as:

A. BBNNZBB B. BBLJNZB
C. BLNNZZB D. BLNNZBB

21. If PURCHASE is coded as UPCRAHES, then HIRE will be coded in the same manner as :

A. RHIE B. HIER
C. HERI D. IHER

22. If is UZWV coded as FADE, then what does IFHG stand for in the same code?

A. RUST B. PORT
C. QUIT D. ROSE

23. ACTOR is coded in a certain language as EGXSV. How will STAGE be coded in the same language?

A. VWFLJ B. XYFLJ
C. WXEKI D. WYDJH

24. If DRINK is coded as IMNIP, then COKE will be coded as :

A. GIOA B. HJPZ
C. HIOA D. GJPZ

25. HORSE is written in a certain code as BUNGY and CAT as HOW, how will CHEST be written in the same code?

A. OBYGW B. WYGBN
C. UNHBY D. HBYGW

26. If MOTHERLAND is coded as 9206314758, then NORTH will be coded as :

A. 72406 B. 52406
C. 52360 D. 52106

27. If BAD is coded in a certain language as 514, GIVE as 3068 and FOR as 729, then how will VIDEO be written?

A. 60482 B. 03482
C. 30214 D. 60487

28. In a certain code language CHILD is written as IMOQJ. How will BABE be written in the same language?

A. HFHJ B. FGFK
C. FFGJ D. HFGJ

29. QUOTE is coded as OWMVC, how will WRITE be coded?

A. TSFUB B. UTGVC
C. VUHWD D. TUFWC

30. VACATE is coded as YEFEWI, OCCUPY will be coded as :

A. QEEXRB B. SHGZTD
C. SFGXTC D. RGFYSC

31. If CHART stands for GLEVX, then BOARD will stand for :

A. FSEVH B. HVESF
C. VESFH D. SEVHF

32. If BOOK is coded as CNPJ, then MOON will be coded as :

A. MPNN B. NNPM
C. PNMN D. NMPN

33. If PAPER stands for QBQFS, then what will GLASS stand for?

A. MTBHT B. MHTBT
C. HMBTT D. HMTBT

34. If DOWN is coded as FQYP, then the word WITH will be coded as :

A. KYJV B. IJYK
C. YKVJ D. JKVY

35. If CHAIR stands for EJCKT, then TABLE would stand for :

A. NGDC B. VCDNG
C. DCGNV D. GNVCD

36. If the word CLERK is coded as EOIWQ, then how would you code the word TABLE?

A. VCDNG B. VCDGN
C. VDFQK D. VDFOK

37. If the word TRADE is coded as XVEHI, then how should the word PUBLIC be coded?

A. TYFMPG B. SXEOLF
C. TYFPMG D. SXLLOP

38. If the word PENCIL is coded as LICNEP, then how would the word INKPOT be coded?
A. TOPINK B. JOLQPU
C. HMKOPS D. TOPKNI

39. If the word TRAIN is coded as WUDLQ, then how will the word BUS be coded?
A. EXU B. DWU
C. EXV D. VXE

40. If the word UNITED is coded as SLGRCB, then how should the word DISOWN be coded?
A. BGQMUL B. CGRLTK
C. CGRTLK D. BGQLUM

41. In a certain code TRANSMISSION is written as RTANMSISISON. How will COMMUNICATIONS be written in the same code?
A. OCMMUNCIATIONS
B. OCMMNUICTAIONS
C. OCMMNUICTAISNO
D. OCMMNUICTAIOSN

42. In a certain code REGISTRY is written as VAKEWPVU. How will ENTRY be written in the same code?
A. IJXNC B. ARPVW
C. ARPVU D. IJXMC

43. AUSTRALIA is written in a certain code language as 973609429 and CANADA as 591989. How should CRUST be written in the same code?
A. 50763 B. 53076
C. 50376 D. 50736

44. DAZE is written as 41265 in a certain code. How will BOY be written in the same code?
A. 41425 B. 5120
C. 21525 D. 359

45. If MEDAL is coded as XPOLW, then how will CADGE be coded in the same manner?
A. NLORP B. PNQTR
C. LJMPN D. MLOQP

46. The code for certain letters are indicated in the following words: BRAIN–12345, GRADE–72308, DRAIN–02345, STATE–78388. What is the code for 'D'?
A. 3 B. 2
C. 0 D. 4

47. If in a certain code FIRST is represented as 36509, TOP as 154, MORE as 4837 and MERIT as 83579, then what is the code for 'R'?
A. 8 B. 3
C. 9 D. 7

48. Certain letters are coded as : TODAY–45738, WROTE–10542, DATE–7342 and DIRTH–79046, what does the code number '5' stand for?
A. D B. R
C. O D. T

49. In a certain code language certain words are coded as given below : JOKER–29750, TRUMP–45813, PROJECT–1572064. What is the code for 'C'?
A. 6 B. 7
C. 5 D. 0

50. If FACE is coded as 6135, BIG as 297, HAD as 814 and BADGE as 21475, then what is the code for 'A'?
A. 3 B. 1
C. 2 D. 4

51. In a certain code certain words are coded as follows : ACTION–014853, FORCE–25916, REGAIN–967083. Which of the following letters is coded as '7'?
A. A B. N
C. R D. G

52. In a certain code WORK is written as 0918, ROUND as 19354, KIND as 8654, BRING as 71652 and BROOD as 71994. Which of the following is represented by '2'?
A. R B. G
C. N D. B

53. Certain words are coded as follows : BEAR–9218, DRUM–0863, PRY–485 and DOOR–7998. What is the code for 'R'?
A. 9 B. 3
C. 8 D. 4

54. FRANK is coded as 93210, AFTER as 29463, MUFFET as 879964, FERRY as 96335 and REEF as 3669. What is the code for 'F'?

A. 9 B. 3
C. 6 D. 1

55. If SAY is coded as 069, ASK as 608, YES as 930, DYE as 493 and EYE as 393, then what is the code for 'Y'?
A. 0 B. 9
C. 3 D. 6

56. If STABILITY is coded as 321956527 and RESTICATE as 403258120, what is 'I' coded as?
A. 6 B. 2
C. 5 D. 9

57. If EXAMINATION is coded as 83690567045, the codes for 'N' and 'A' are :
A. 7, 5 B. 5, 6
C. 6, 5 D. 5, 7

58. In a certain code BEAUTY is coded as 835247, DEVIL as 03916 and ABIDE as 58103. What does '3' stand for?
A. E B. D
C. B D. A

59. Certain words are coded in the following manner : BARK–0375, DIRT–4972, WAGE–4086, RISK–7518. What is the code for 'R'?
A. 2 B. 7
C. 5 D. 0

60. The code for certain letters are indicated in the following words : TRADE–54321, BADGE–93271, GRADE–74321, QUEUE–80101. What is the code for 'G'?
A. 7 B. 4
C. 2 D. 8

ANSWERS

1	2	3	4	5	6	7	8	9	10
B	D	A	B	C	D	D	C	C	C
11	**12**	**13**	**14**	**15**	**16**	**17**	**18**	**19**	**20**
A	B	B	A	C	C	D	B	C	B
21	**22**	**23**	**24**	**25**	**26**	**27**	**28**	**29**	**30**
D	A	C	B	D	D	A	A	B	D
31	**32**	**33**	**34**	**35**	**36**	**37**	**38**	**39**	**40**
A	B	C	C	B	C	C	D	C	A
41	**42**	**43**	**44**	**45**	**46**	**47**	**48**	**49**	**50**
D	A	D	C	A	C	B	C	A	B
51	**52**	**53**	**54**	**55**	**56**	**57**	**58**	**59**	**60**
D	B	C	A	B	C	B	A	B	A

EXPLANATORY ANSWERS

1. Since,

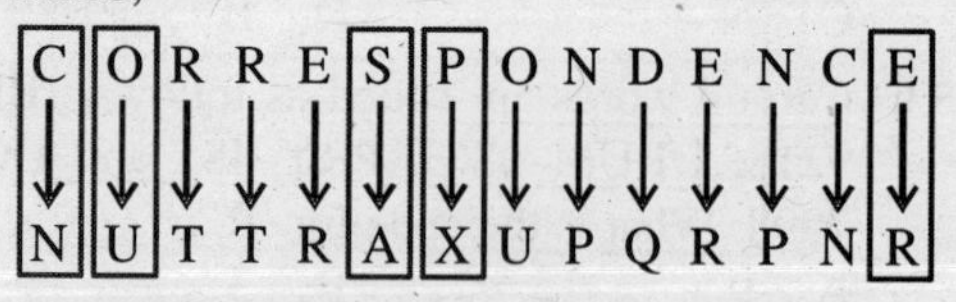

Therefore,

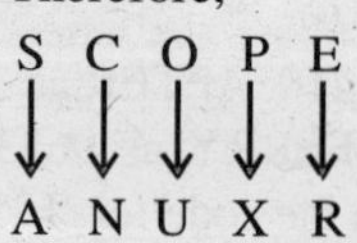

2. The word is coded by moving the letters forward by consecutive even numbered steps.

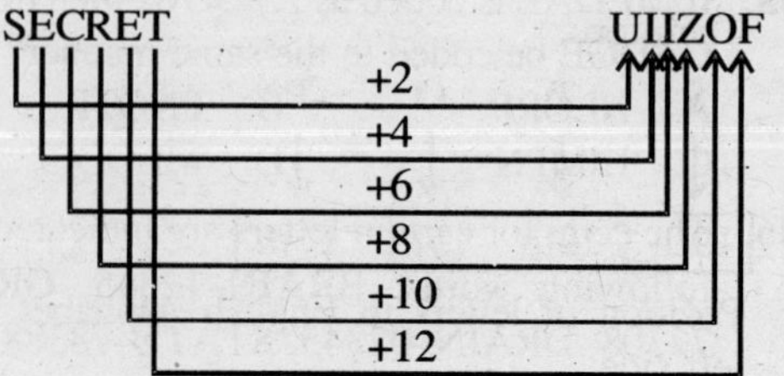

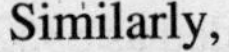

Similarly,

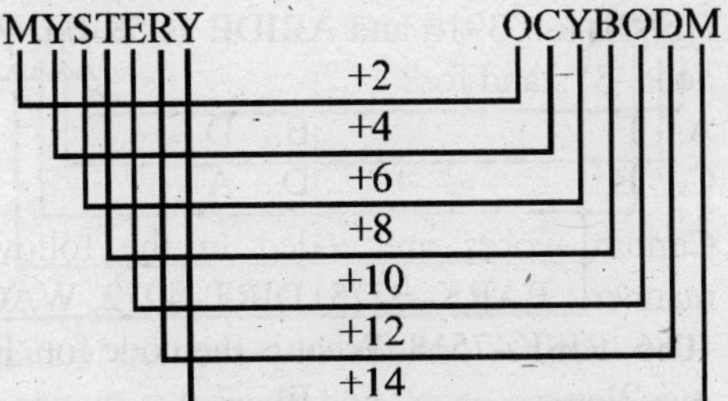

3. Since,

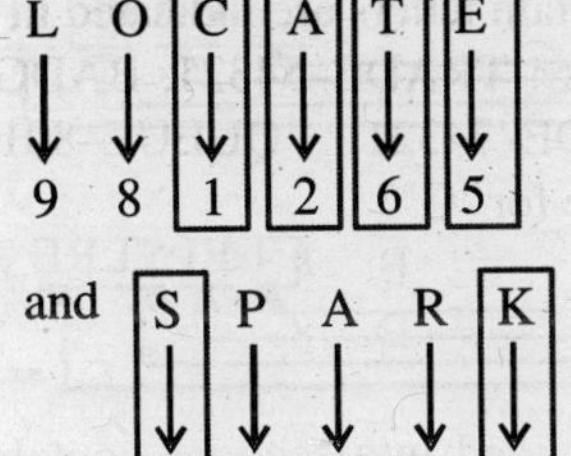

Therefore,

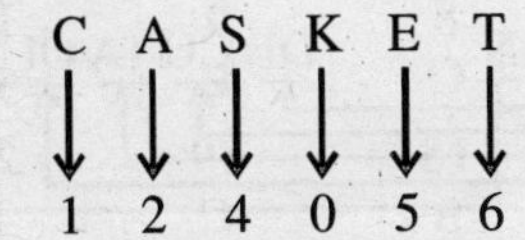

4. Since,

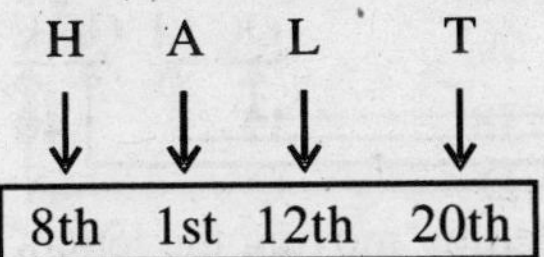

Position of letters in English Alphabet from left side

and

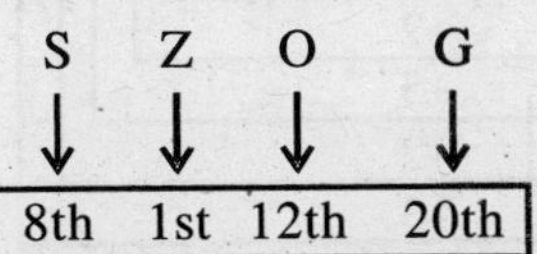

Position of letters in English Alphabet from right side

Therefore,

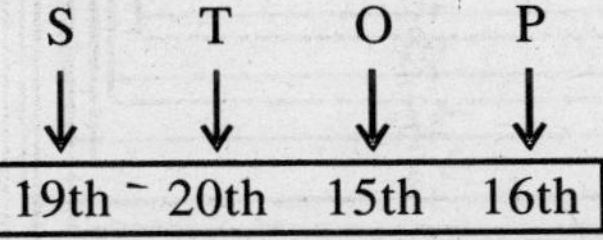

Position of letters in English Alphabet from left side

and

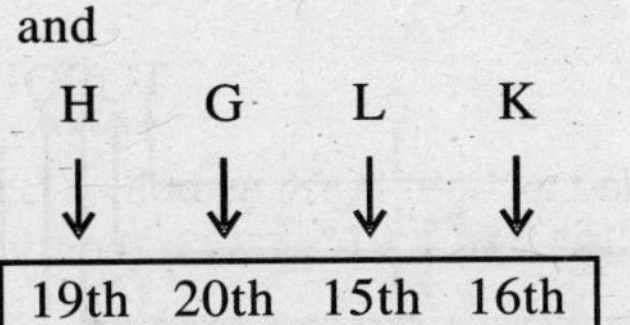

Position of letters in English Alphabet from right side

5. Since,

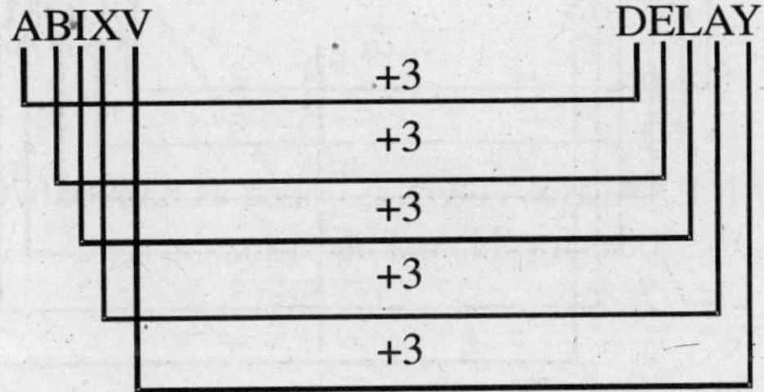

Therefore,

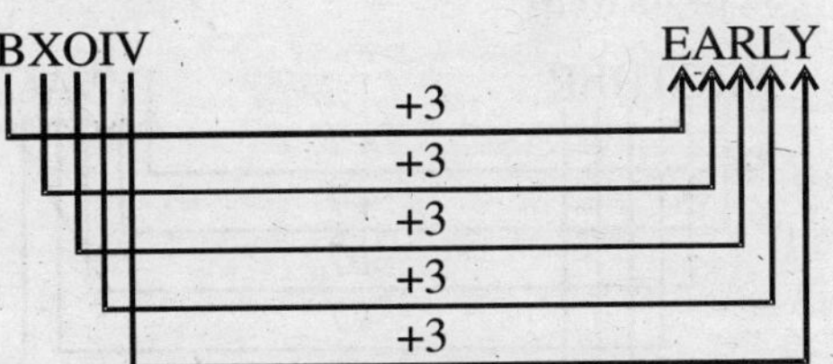

6. The word is coded by moving the letters, consecutive odd numbered steps backwards.

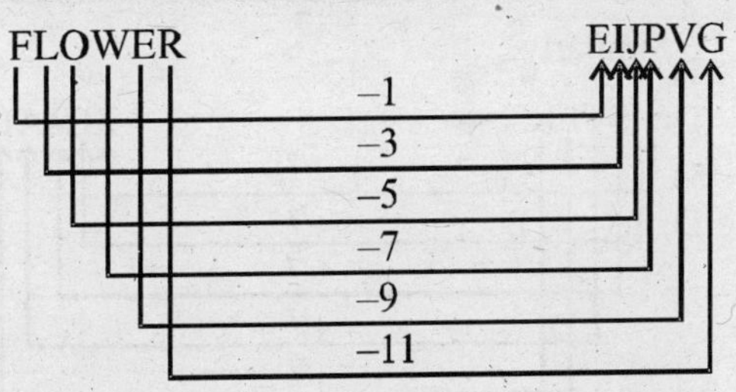

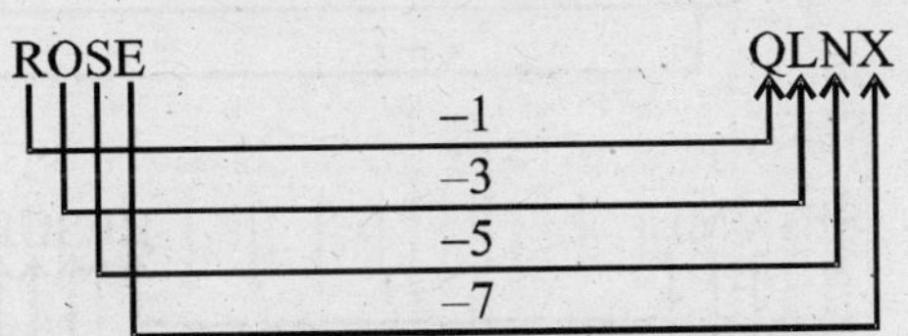

(The series restarts from Z on reaching A)

7. The word is coded by moving the letters one step forward and one step backward alternately.

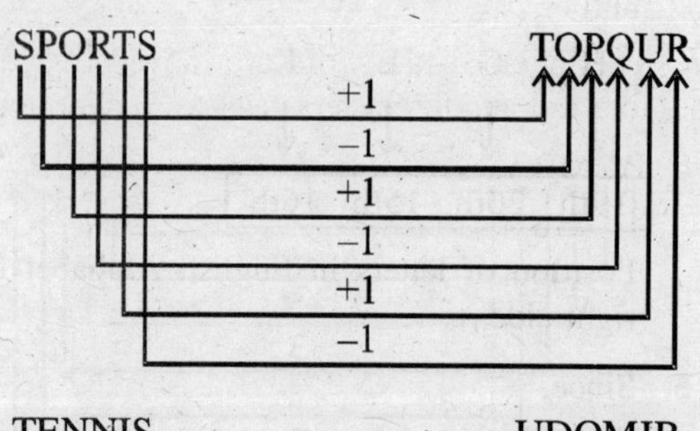

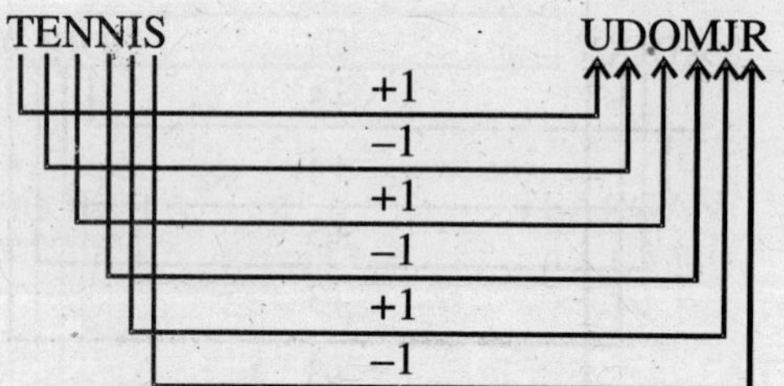

8. The word is coded by moving the letters seven steps forward.

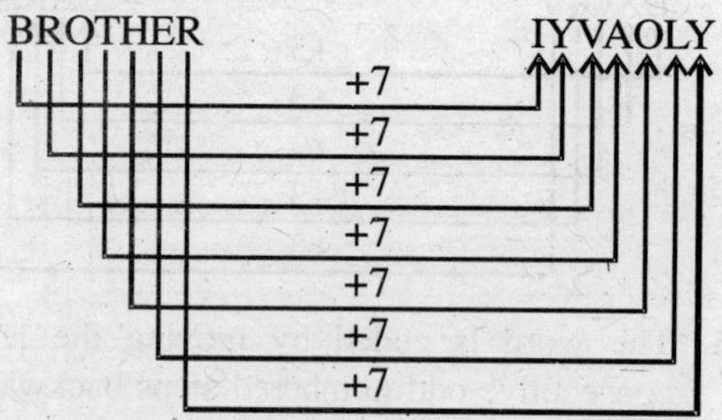

Similarly,

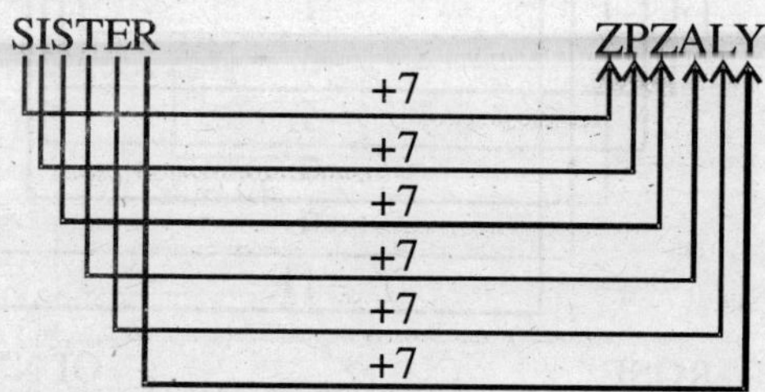

9. Since,

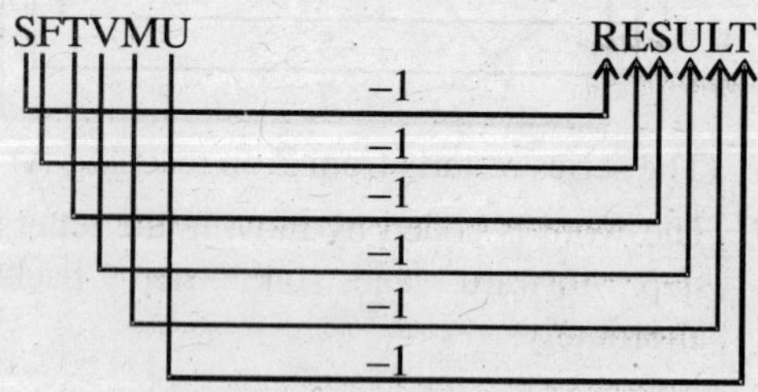

Therefore,

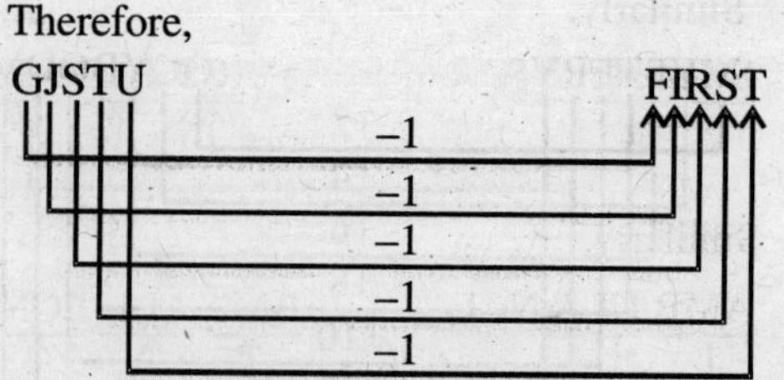

10. The word is divided into sections containing two letters each, and then the sections are written backwards.

11. The word is divided into sections containing two letters each and the positions of the letters are interchanged.

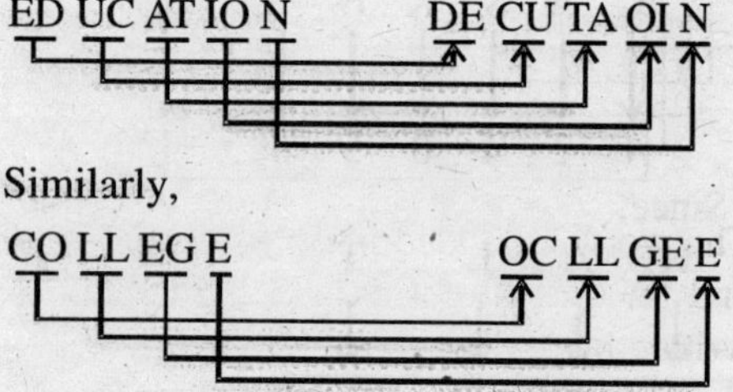

12. The word is coded by moving the letters three and two steps forward alternately.

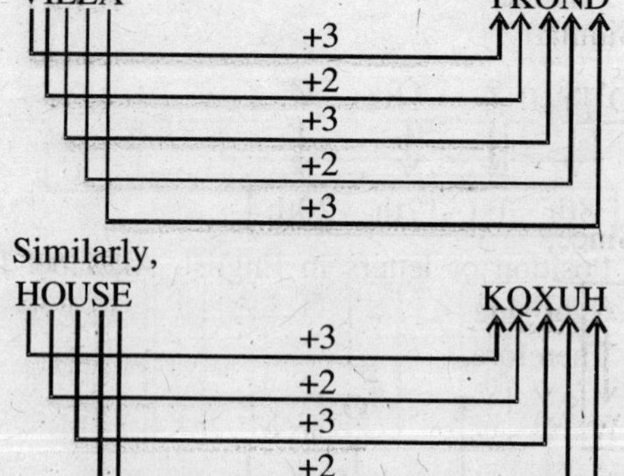

13. The word is divided into three equal sections and the letters in each section are written backwards.

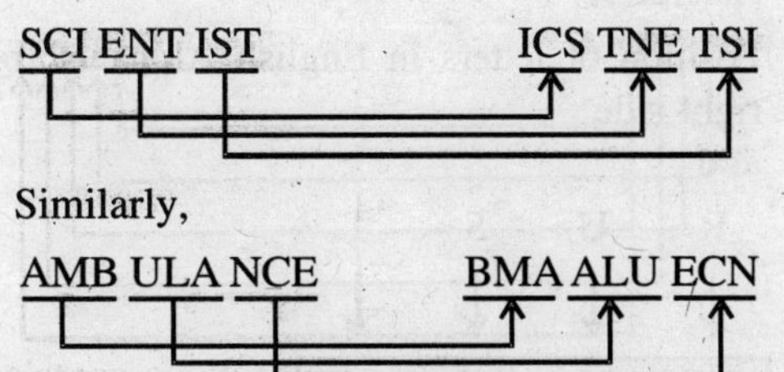

Similarly,

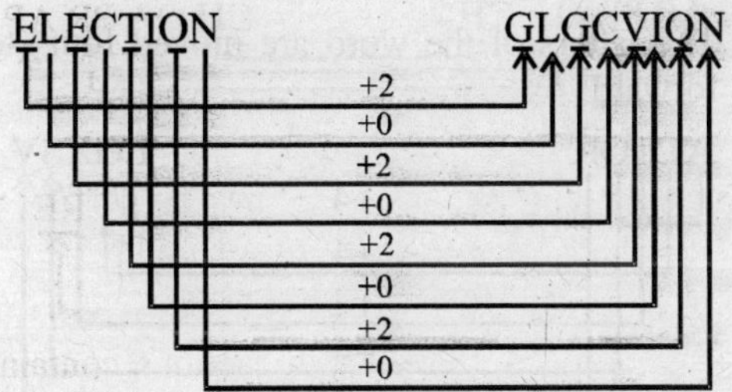

14. Only the letters at the odd positions are moved two steps forward.

Similarly,

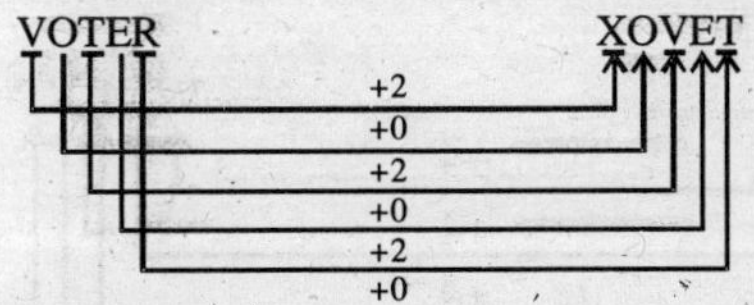

15. The word is divided into three equal sections, and the letters of first and third sections are written backwards.

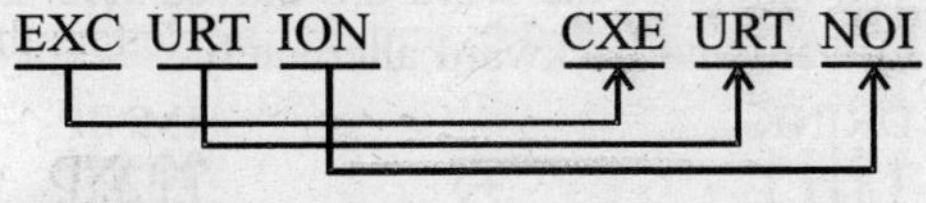

Similarly,

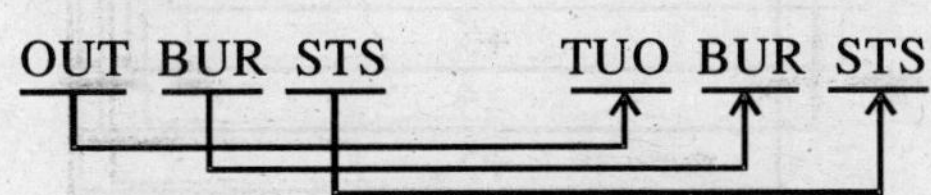

16. Since,

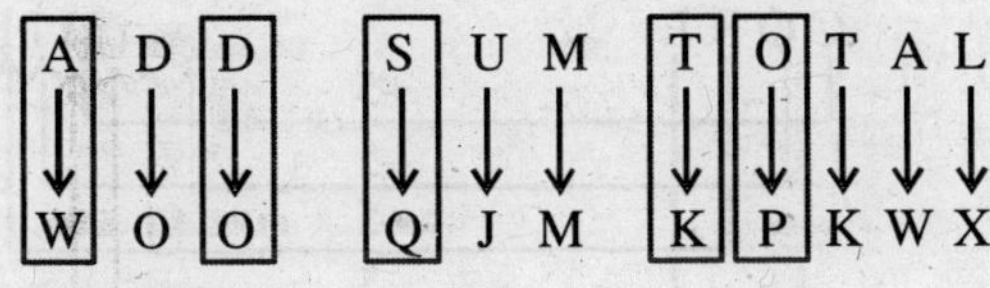

Therefore,

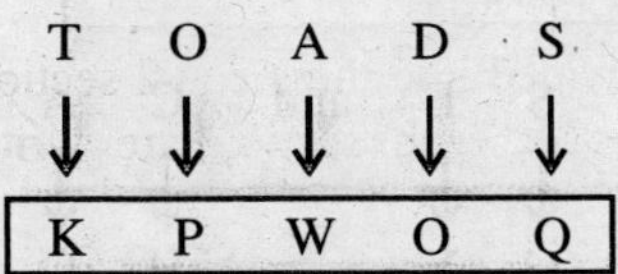

17. The letters of the word are moved five steps forward and three steps backward alternately.

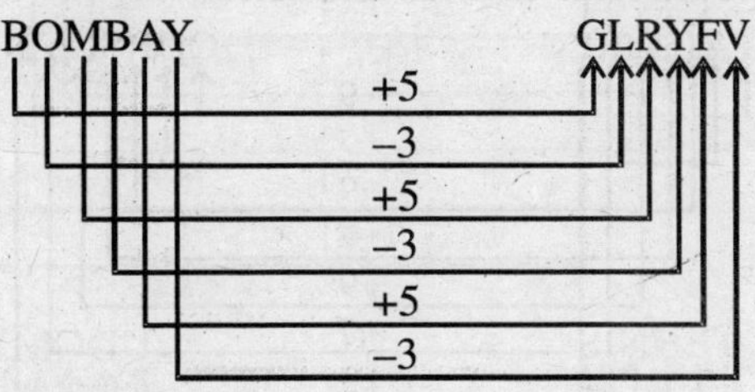

Similarly,

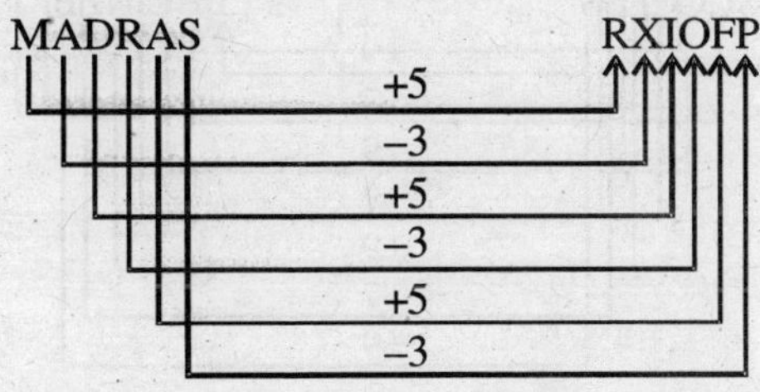

18. Since,

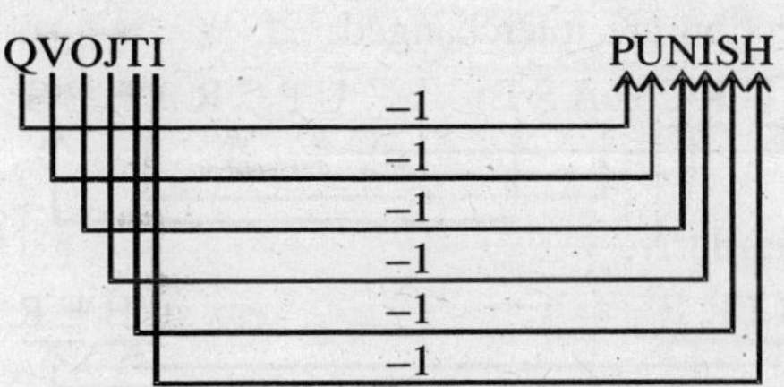

Therefore,

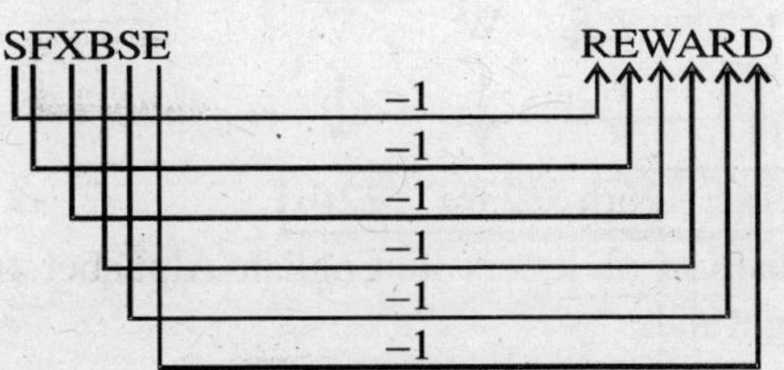

19. Since,

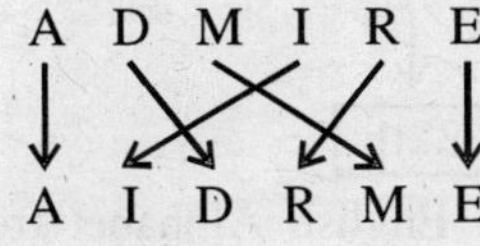

Therefore,

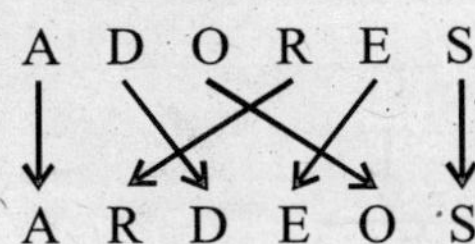

20. The letters of the word are moved nine and seven steps forward alternately.

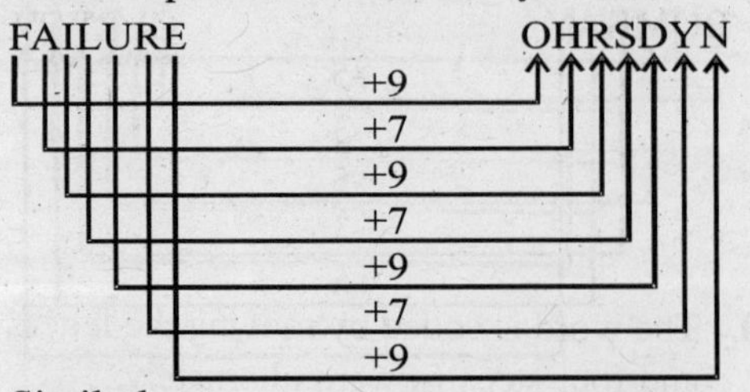

Similarly,

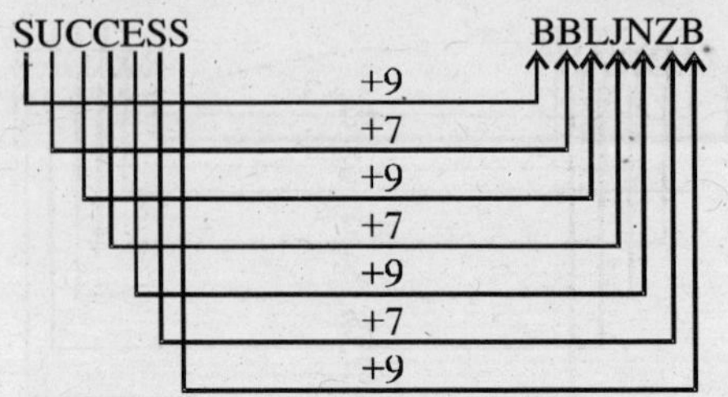

21. The word is divided into sections of two letters, and then the places of letters in each section are interchanged.

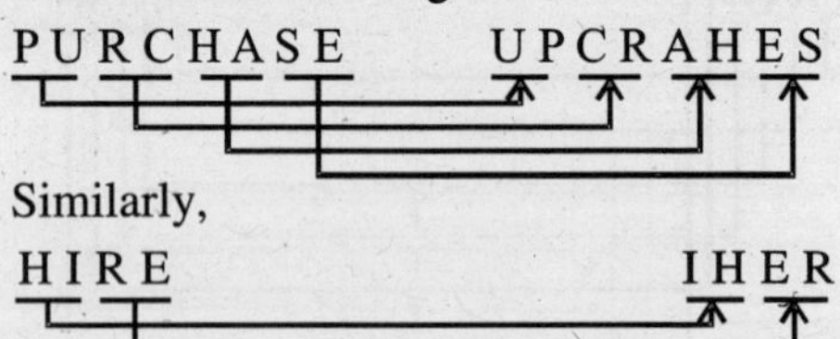

22. Since,

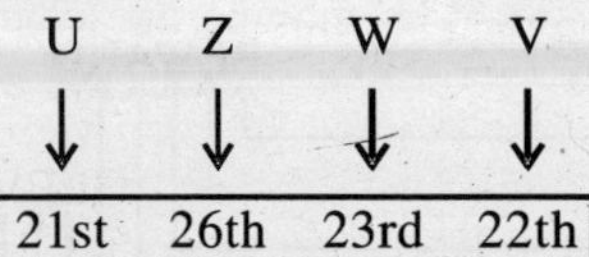

Position of letters in English Alphabet from right side

and

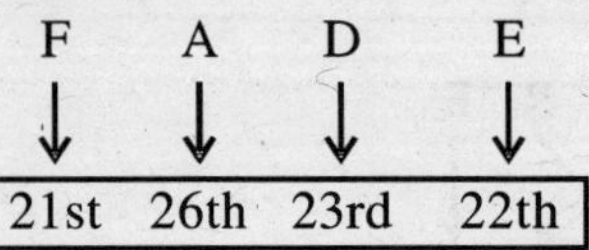

Position of letters in English Alphabet from left side

Therefore,

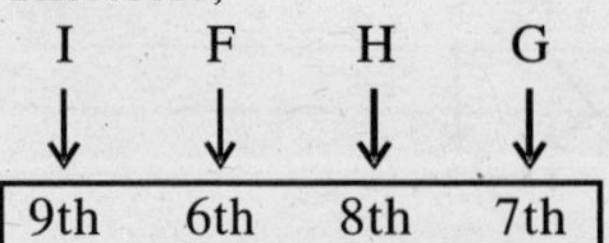

Position of letters in English Alphabet from right side

and

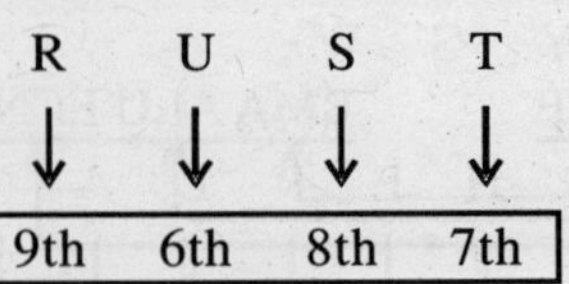

Position of letters in English Alphabet from left side

23. The letters of the word are moved four steps forward.

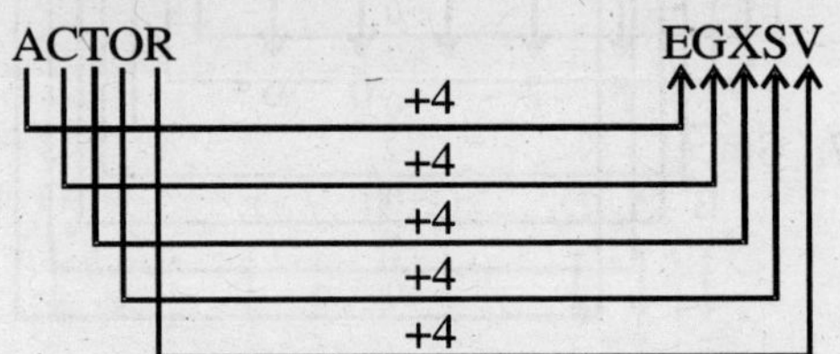

Similarly,

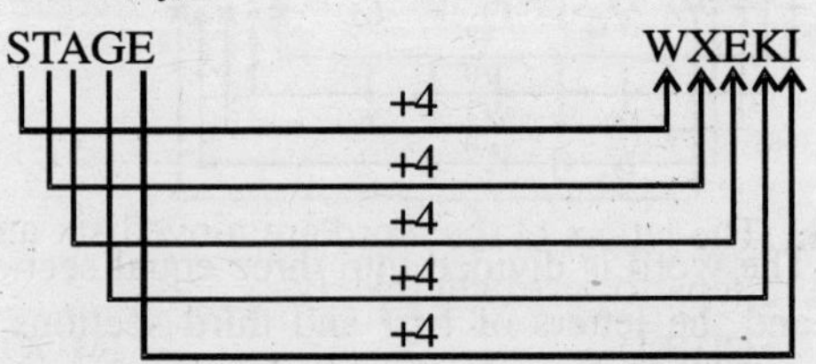

24. The letters of the word are moved five steps forward and backward alternately.

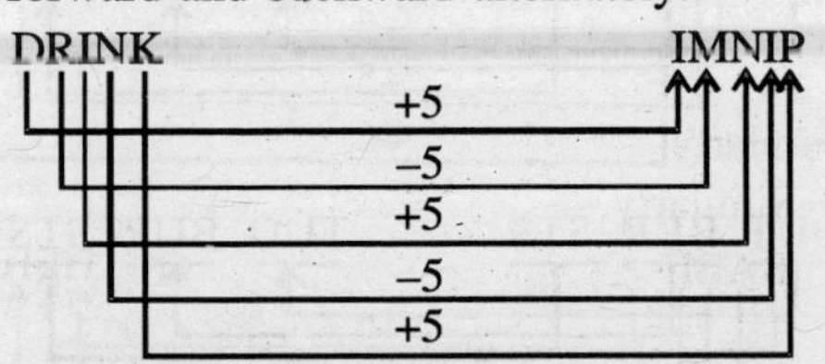

Similarly,

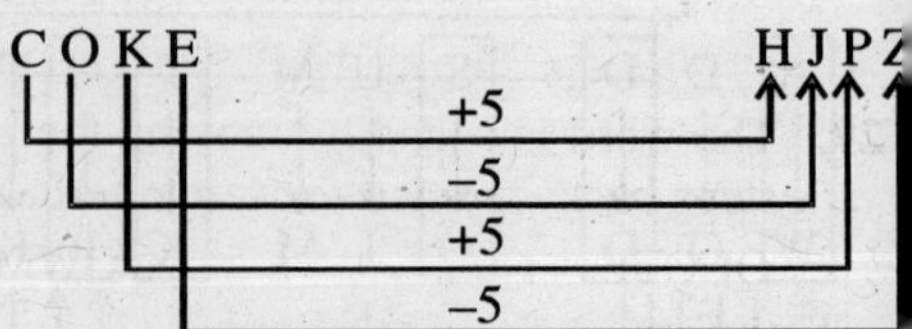

25. Since,

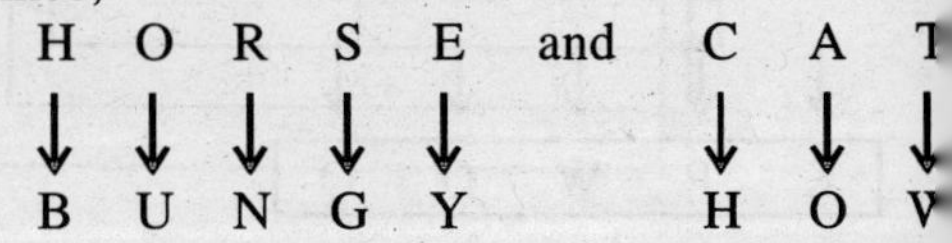

Therefore,

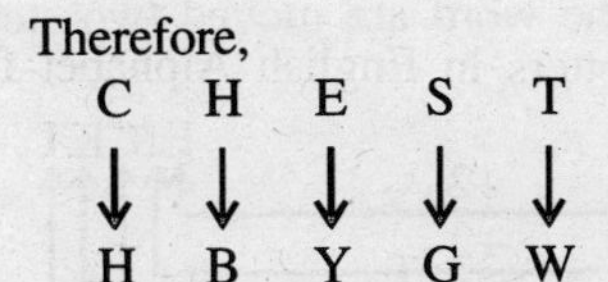

26. Since,

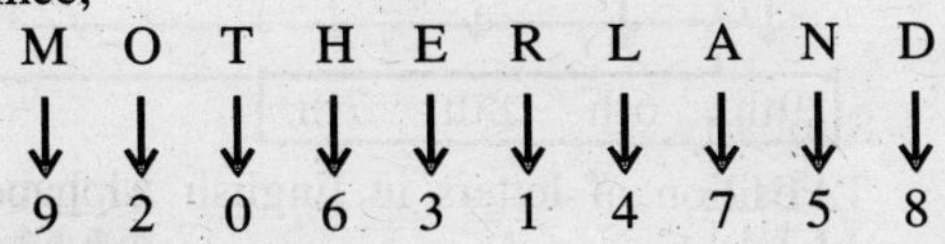

Therefore,

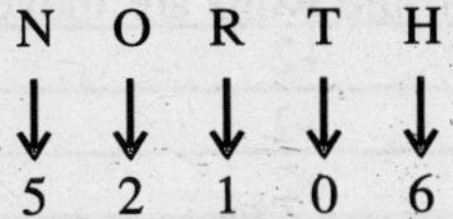

27. Since,

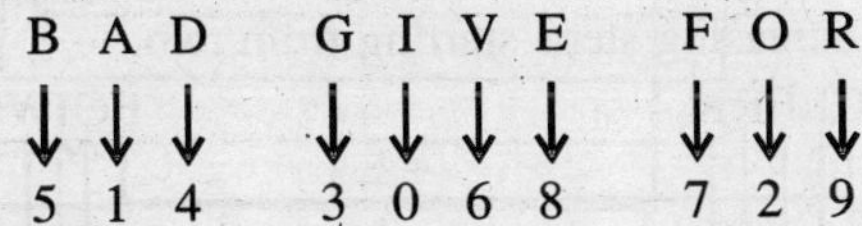

Therefore,

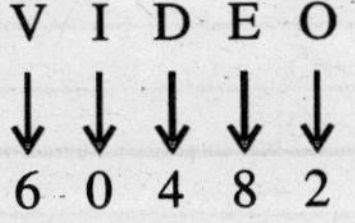

28. The letters of the word are moved six and five steps forward alternately.

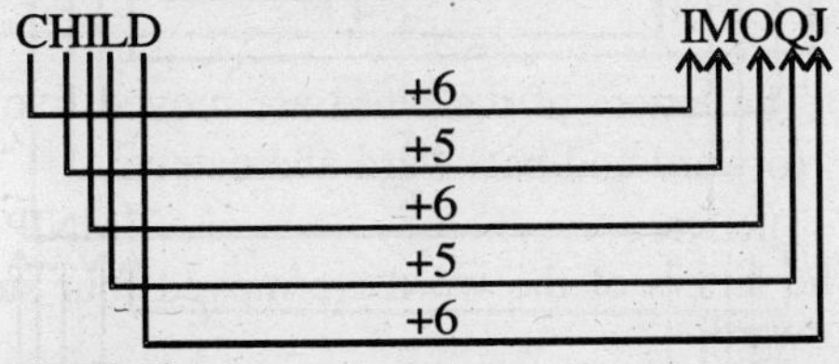

Similarly,

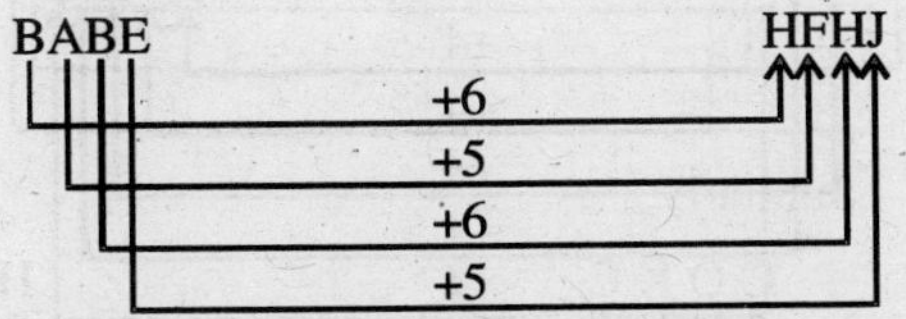

29. The word is coded by moving the letters two steps backward and forward alternately.

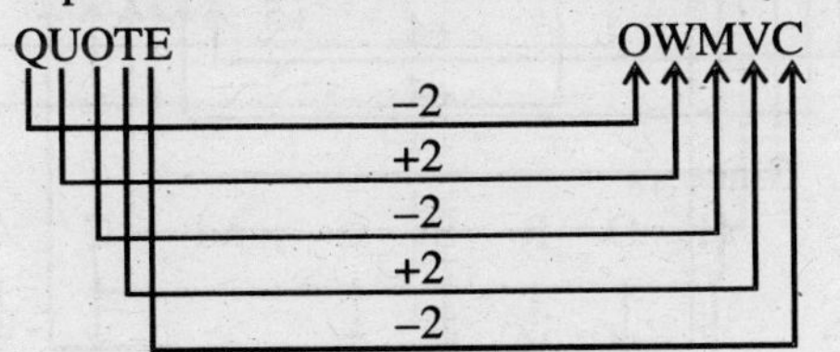

Similarly,

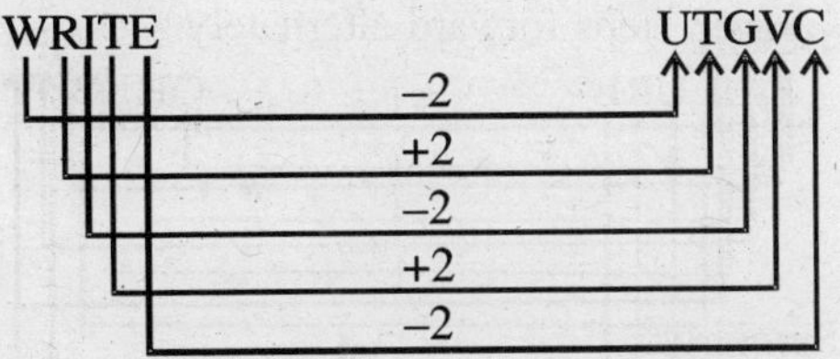

30. The word is coded by moving the letters three and four steps forward alternately.

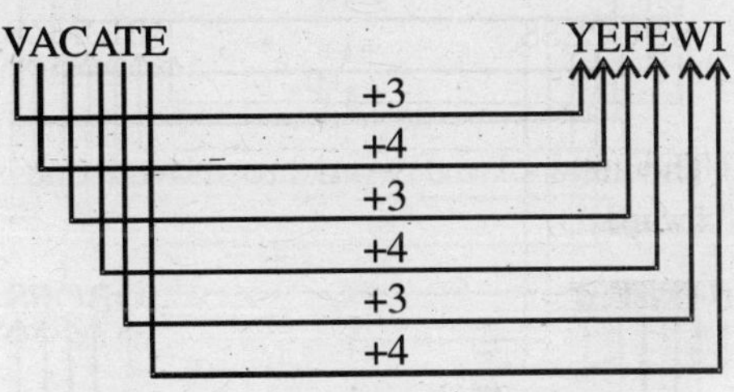

Similarly,

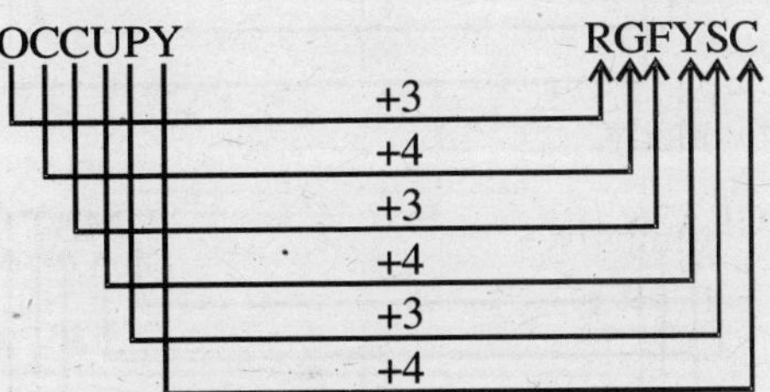

31. The word is coded by moving the letters four steps forward.

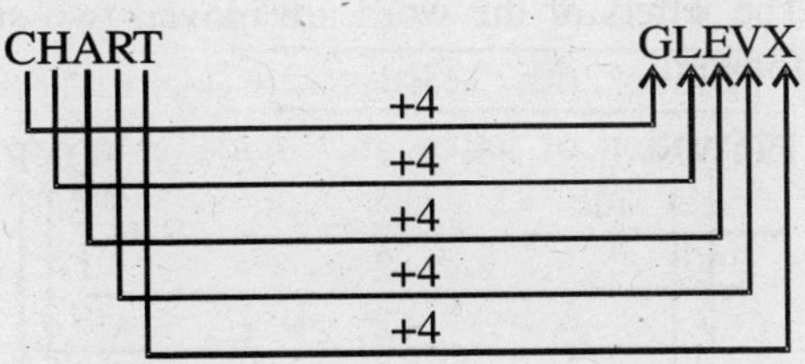

Similarly,

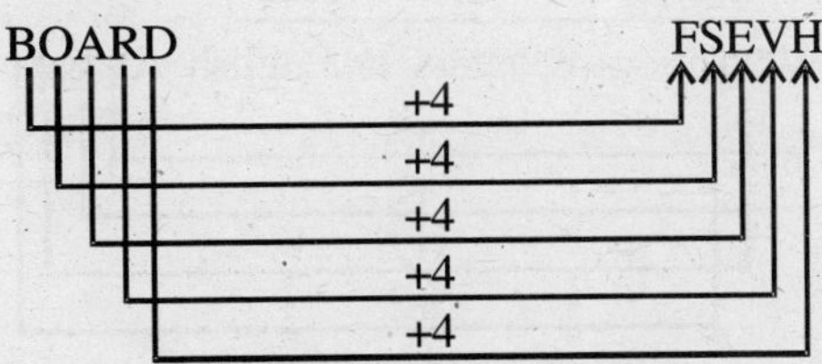

32. The word is coded by moving the letters one step forward and backward alternately.

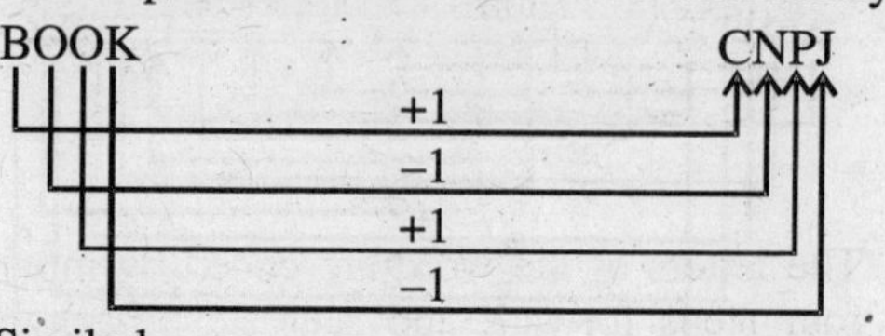

Similarly,

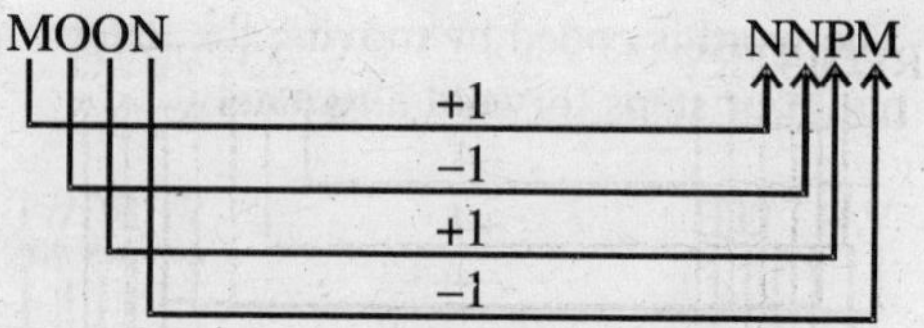

33. The letters of the word are moved one step forward.

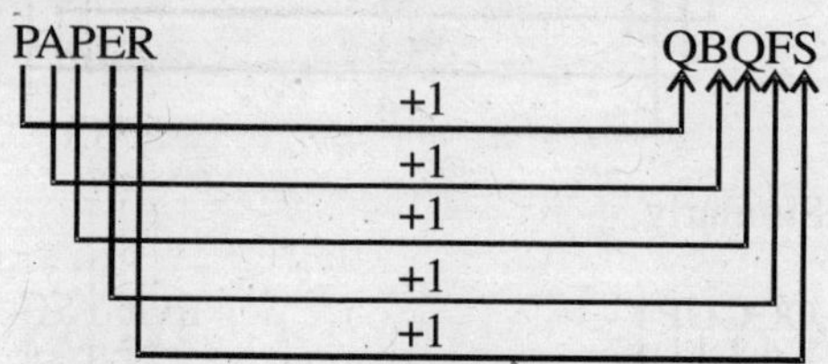

Similarly,

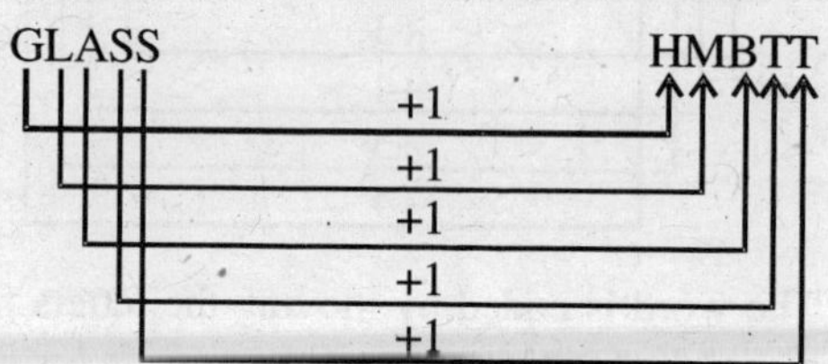

34. The letters of the word are moved two steps forward.

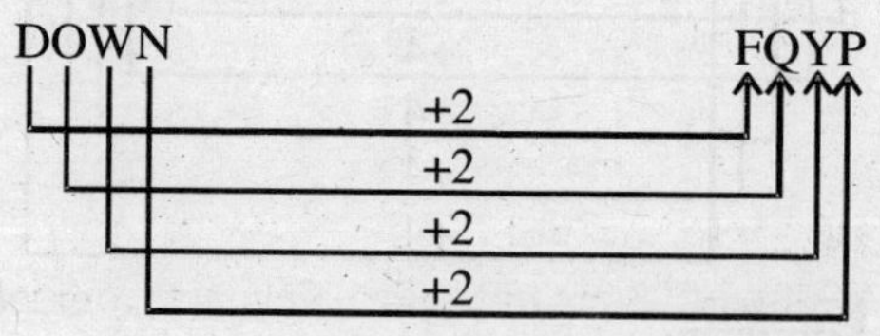

Similarly,

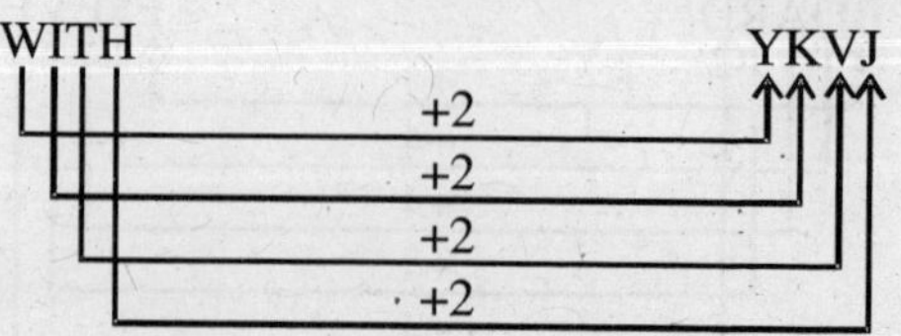

35. The letters of the word are moved two steps forward.

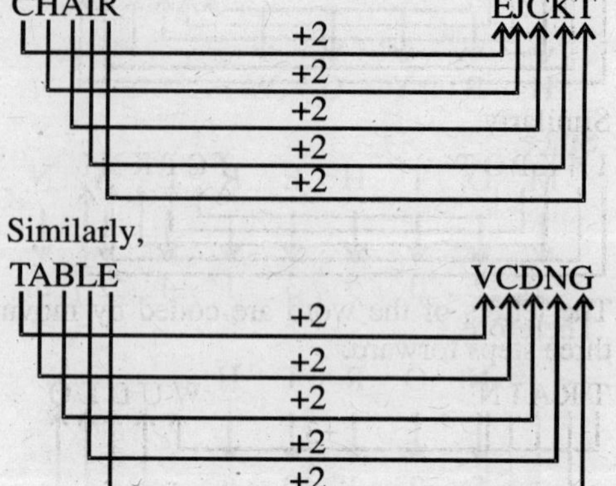

36. The letters of the word are moved forward by increasing steps starting from two.

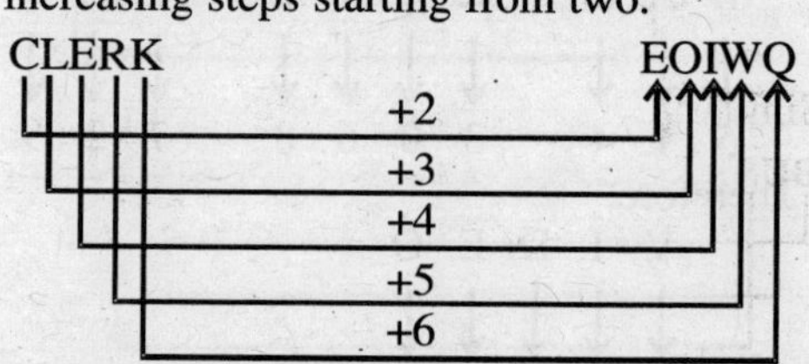

Similarly,

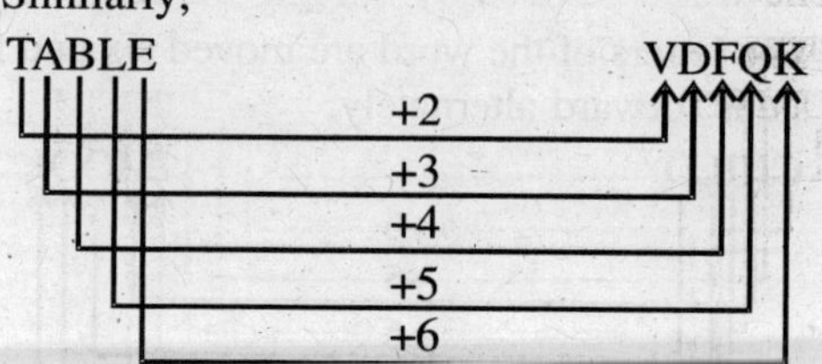

37. The letters of the word are moved four steps forward.

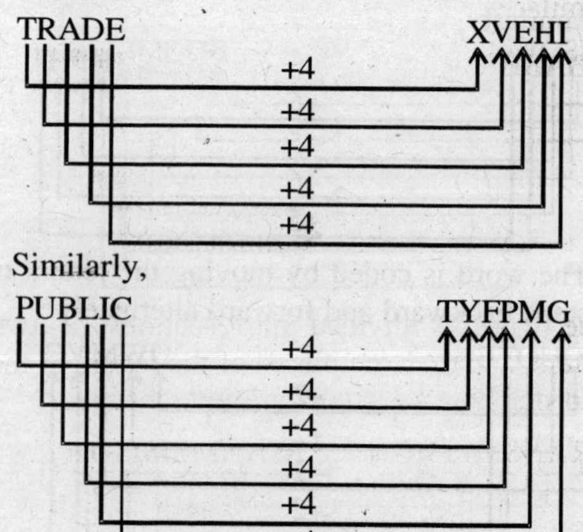

38. The letters of the word are written backward.

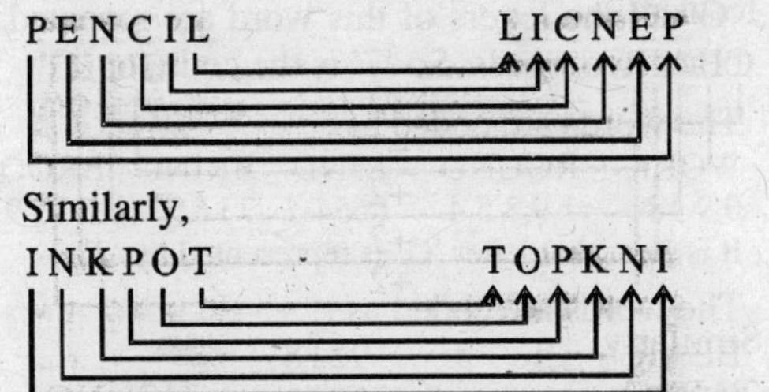

Similarly,

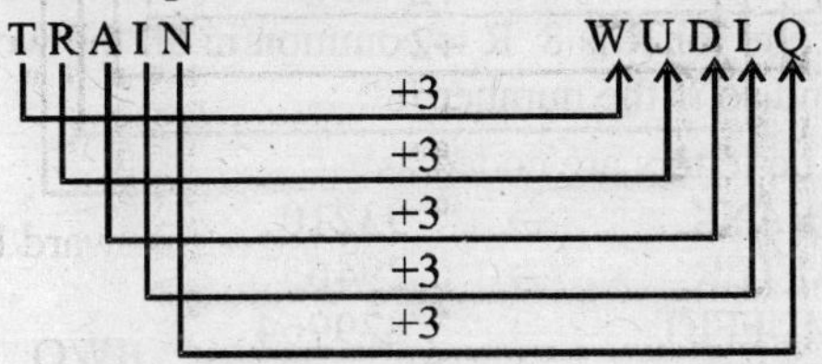

39. The letters of the word are coded by moving three steps forward.

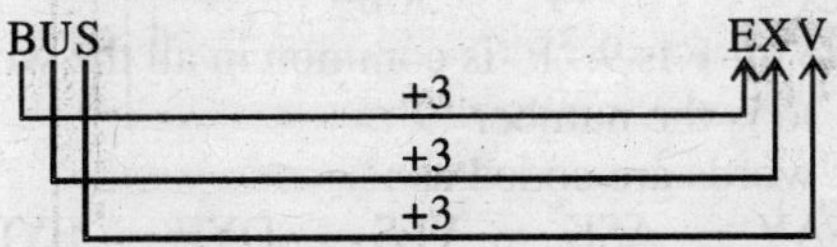

Similarly,

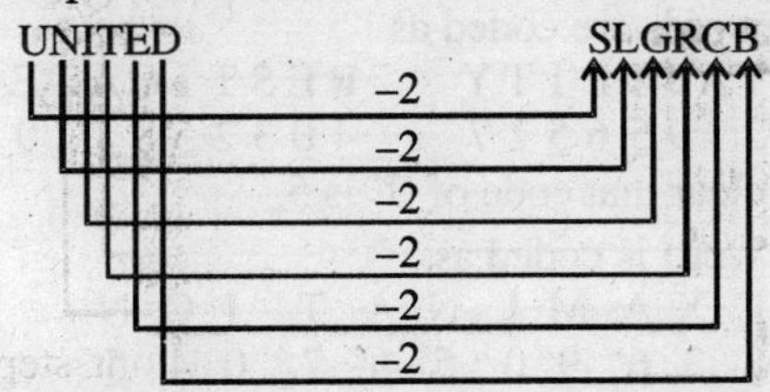

40. The word is coded by moving the letters two steps backward.

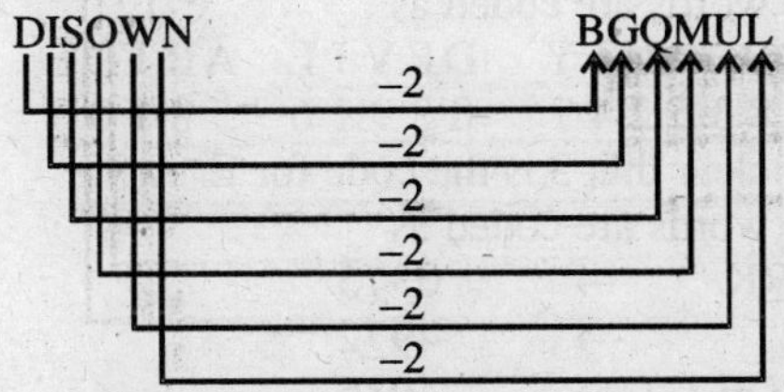

Similarly,

41. The word is divided into sections of two letters, and then the places of the letters of the odd numbered sections are interchanged.

Similarly,

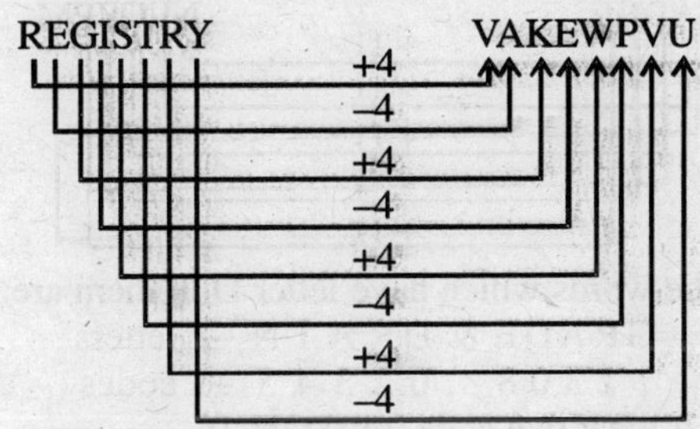

42. The letters of the word are coded by moving four steps forward and four steps backward alternately.

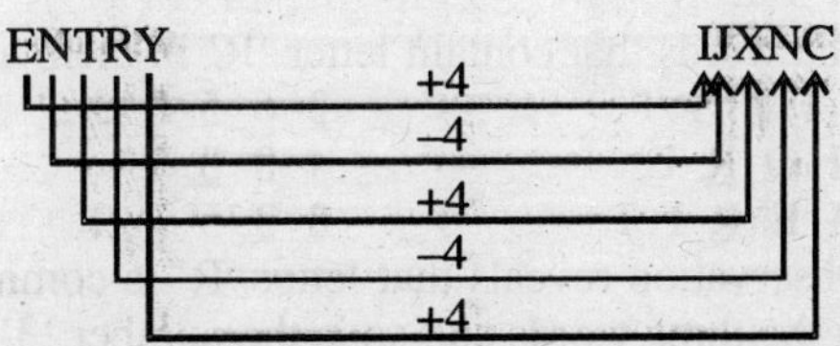

43. Since,

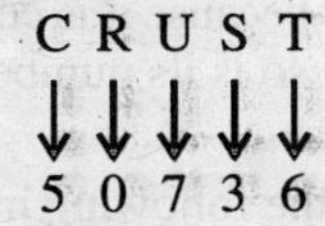

Therefore,

44. Since,

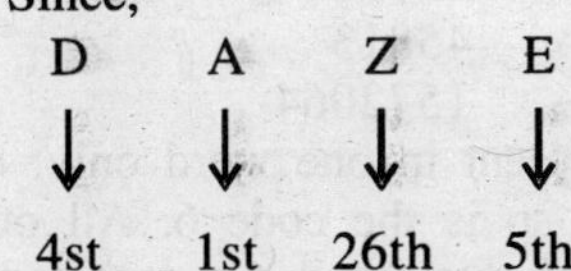

Position of letters in english alphabet from left side

Therefore,

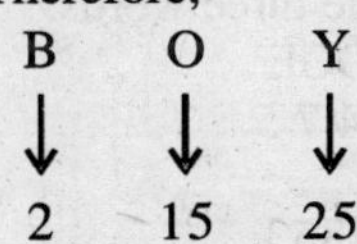

Position of letters in english alphabet from left side

45. The word is coded by moving the letters eleven steps forward.

MEDAL XPOLW

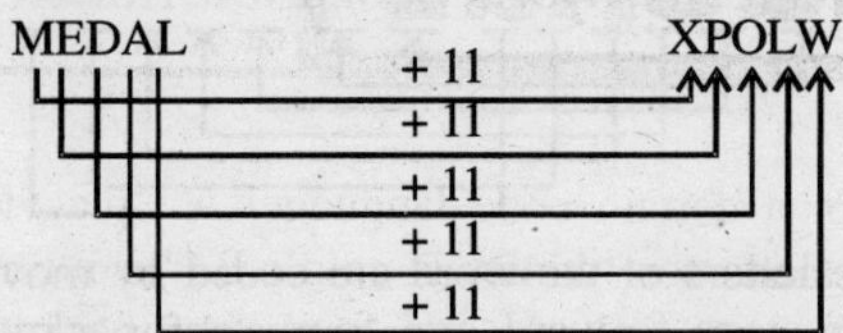

Similarly,

CADGE NLORP

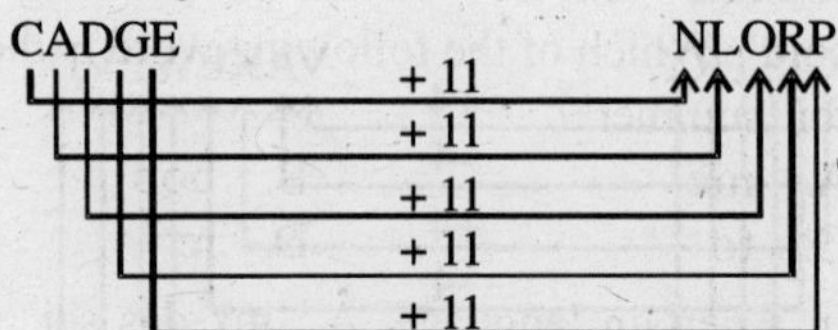

46. The words which have letter D in them are:

GRADE & DRAIN → letters
7 2 3 0 8 0 2 3 4 5 → codes

It is clear that code for 'D' is '0'.

47. The words that contain letter 'R' in them are :

F I R S T → 3 6 5 0 9
M O R E → 4 8 3 7
M E R I T → 8 3 5 7 9

Observation reveals that letter 'R' is common in the three words and so is the number '3'.

48. The manner of coding is :

TODAY WROTE DATE DIRTH
4 5 7 3 8 1 0 5 4 2 7 3 4 2 7 9 0 4 6

The number '5' is common in words TODAY and WROTE, and so is the letter 'O'. Letter 'T' cannot be the answer because it is common in all the four words and so is its number code '4'.

49. The words are coded in the following manner:

JOKER → 29750
TRUMP → 45813
PROJECT → 1572064

Letter 'C' is present in one word only, *i.e.*, PROJECT, and so is the code 6. All other number codes of this word are repeated in codes for JOKER and TRUMP.

50. The letter 'A' is present in three words and so is the number '1' in all the three words.

FACE HAD BADGE
6 135 8 1 4 2 1 4 7 5

51. The words are coded as :

ACTION → 014853
FORCE → 25916
REGAIN → 967083

Number 7 is present only in REGAIN. Except 'G' all the letters of this word are repeated in other two words. So '7' is the code for 'G'.

52. The words are coded as :

WORK ROUND KIND BRING BROOD
0 9 1 8 1 9 3 5 4 8654 71652 71994

It is clear that letter 'G' is represented by '2'.

53. The words are coded as :

BEAR → 9218
DRUM → 0863
PRY → 485
DOOR → 7998

Code for R is 8. R is common in all the words and so is the number '8'.

54. The letters are coded as :

FRANK → 93210
AFTER → 29463
MUFFET → 879964
FERRY → 96335
REEF → 3669

Code for F is 9. 'F' is common in all the words and so is the number '9'.

55. The words are coded as :

SAY ASK YES DYE EYE
069 608 930 493 393

It is clear that code for 'Y' is 9.

56. The words are coded as :

STABILITY RESTICATE
3 2 1 9 5 6 5 2 7 4 0 3 2 5 8 1 2 0

It is clear that code of 'I' is 5.

57. The word is coded as :

E X A M I N A T I O N
8 3 6 9 0 5 6 7 0 4 5

Code for N is 5 and for A is 6.

58. The words are coded as :

BEAUTY DEVIL ABIDE
8 3 5 2 4 7 0 3 9 1 6 5 8 1 0 3

It is clear that 3 is the code for E.

59. The words are coded as :

BARK → 0375
DIRT → 4972
WAGE → 4086
RISK → 7518

'R' is common in three words and so is the number '7'.

60. The words with the letter G are :

BADGE & GRADE
9 3 2 7 1 7 4 3 2 1

It is clear that code for G is 7.

CODING LANGUAGE

Directions : *In the following questions study the coded patterns and then select the right option from the given alternatives.*

1. In a certain language, A. 'go ju mi' stands for 'plenty of money'; B. pao ju go nei vu' for 'money creates lots of problems'; C. 'kol vu nei' for 'problems create tension'; and D. 'sol tun ju haw' for 'still money is needed'. Which of the following words stand for 'money'?

   A. nei B. ju
   C. haw D. go

2. In a certain language, A. 'FOR' stands for 'old is gold'; B. 'ROT' stands for 'gold is pure'; C. 'ROM' stands for 'gold is costly'. How will 'pure old gold is costly' be written?

   A. TFROM B. FOTRM
   C. FTORM D. TOMRF

3. In a certain code '415' means 'milk is hot'; '18' means 'hot soup'; and '895' means 'soup is tasty'. What number will indicate the word 'tasty'?

   A. 9 B. 8
   C. 5 D. 4

4. In a certain code '643' means 'she is beautiful', '593' means 'he is handsome', and '567' means 'handsome meets beautiful'. What number will indicate the word 'meets'?

   A. 5 B. 3
   C. 7 D. 6

5. In a certain code language, A. 'dugo hui mul zo' stands for 'work is very hard'; B. 'hui dugo ba ki' for 'Bingo is very smart'; C. 'nano mul dugo' for 'cake is hard', and D. 'mul ki qu' for 'smart and hard'. Which of the following words stand for 'Bingo'?

   A. jalu B. dugo
   C. ki D. ba

6. In a certain code language, A. 'pic vic nic' stands for 'winter is cold'; B. 'to nic re' for 'summer is hot'; C. 're pic boo' for 'winter and summer' and D. 'vic tho pa' for 'nights are cold'. Which of the following word is the code for 'summer'?

   A. nic B. boo
   C. to D. re

7. In a certain language, A. 'mx das sci' means 'good little frock'; B. 'jm coz sci' means 'girl behaves good'; C. 'ngv drs coz' means 'girl makes mischief'; and D. 'das gp coz' means 'little girl fell'. What is the code for 'frock' in this language?

   A. mx B. das
   C. sci D. gp

8. In a certain language 'mu mit es' means 'who is she' and 'elb mu es' means 'where is she'. What is the code for 'where' in this language?

   A. es B. elb
   C. mu D. mit

9. In a certain code language '069' means 'grapes are sweet', '476' means 'very sweet fruit' and '509' means 'grapes are ripe'. Which of the following digits means 'ripe' in that language?

   A. 0 B. 5
   C. 9 D. 7

10. In a certain code language 'roi ja kyo twa' means 'Moody is writing letters', 'pok ju ja twa' means 'Woody is writing cards', 'trn kyo pos un' means 'they are writing letters', and 'koi rus pok' means 'gifts and cards'. What is the code word for 'Moody'?

    A. ja B. twa
    C. roi D. kyo

11. In a certain code language 'wre asi amoh kedo' means 'Polo is drinking tea', 'wre epu uki' means 'Polo buys books', and 'buen eld kedo'

means 'Libbo drinks tea'. Which of the following code words mean 'Polo' and 'tea' in the above language?

A. kedo and wre B. asi and buen
C. wre and kedo D. amoh and wre

12. In a certain code, (i) 'juka lal mit sut' stands for 'Hello, how are you?'; (ii) 'mudi sut em nif' for 'Where are they going?'; (iii) 'hu zul met sut' for 'What are their names?'; and (iv) 'lal sut zul pe' for 'Are you going too?'. Which of the following words in the above code language stand for 'are you'?

A. sut mit B. mudi sut
C. juka nif D. sut lal

13. In a certain code 'gri chri' means 'brand new', 'gyp twoh' means 'very old', 'gri bur twoh' means 'old and new' and 'chri deh twoh' means 'old brand car'. Which of the following codes means 'new car'?

A. chri gri B. gri deh
C. deh gyp D. twoh deh

14. If 'luma papa jano' stands for 'he speaks softly', 'papa lo hedi lami' for 'wind blows softly downhill'; and 'lo puki luma jano lami sod' for 'he speaks like wind blows whisper; then what word will be written for 'downhill'?

A. papa B. lami
C. hedi D. lo

15. In a certain language, A. 'sun shines brightly' is written as 'ba lo sul'; B. 'houses are brightly lit' as 'kado udo ari ba'; and C. 'light comes from sun' as 'dapi kup lo nro'. What words will be written for 'sun' and 'brightly'?

A. lo, ba B. ba, lo
C. snl, lo D. ba, sul

16. In a certain code language, (1) 'lo ni hie pun' stands for 'he is drinking coke'; (2) 'hol ful gui pun' stands for 'she is eating food'; and (3) 'ne ful ni lo' stands for 'drinking coke and food'. Which of the following words is the code for 'he'?

A. hie B. lo
C. pun D. ni

17. In a certain code language,

1. Gor Paku Means 'Best Gift'
2. Mull Gor Sot Means 'Gift of Love'
3. Sol Hed Paku Means 'Best of Luck' and
4. Hed Sot Paku Means 'Love is Best'

Which of the following codes stand for the word 'Love'?

A. Paku B. Hed
C. Sot D. Mull

18. In a certain code language, 'pe sa de mi' means 'yes well no mean' and 'pa mi sa de' means 'sell mean well no'. What would 'yes' mean in that language?

A. de B. pe
C. mi D. sa

19. In a certain code 'hua pih uf pu' means 'he is very intelligent'; 'pih hua kup kit' means 'she is very fair'; 'luck uf hua' means 'Jai is intelligent'; and 'uf kit pod' means 'fair and intelligent'.

Which of the following codes stand for 'Jai'?

A. kit B. hua
C. luck D. pih

20. In a certain code language 'jo mi rei ma' stands for 'rest work no play'; 'rei kol puihi mesi' for 'less ground play tour'; and 'puihi ma jo mati' for 'rest group ground work'.

Which of the following codes stand for word 'no'?

A. mi B. mesi
C. rei D. jo

21. In a certain code '7 8 6' means 'bring me apple', '9 5 8' means 'peel green apple' and '6 4 5' means 'bring green fruit'. Which of the following is the code for 'me'?

A. 8
B. 6
C. 7
D. Cannot be determined

22. If 'ish lto inm' stands for 'neat and tidy'; 'qpr inm sen' stands for 'small but neat'; 'hsm sen rso' stands for 'good but erratic'; what would 'but' stand for?

A. inm B. sen
C. qpr D. hsm

23. If 'nso ptr kli chn' stands for 'Sharma gets marriage gift': 'ptr lnm wop chn' stands for 'wife gives marriage gift': 'tti wop nhi' stands for 'he gives nothing'; what would 'gives' stand for?

A. wop B. ptr
C. nhi D. chn

24. In a certain code language, 'col tip mot' means 'singing is appreciable', 'mot baj min' means 'dancing is good' and 'tip nop baj' means 'singing and dancing'. Which of the following means 'Good' in that code language?

A. mot
B. min
C. baj
D. Cannot be determined

25. In a certain code '7 8 6' means 'study very hard', '9 5 8' means 'hard work pays' and '6 4 5' means 'study and work', which of the following is the code for 'very'?

A. 8
B. 6
C. 7
D. Cannot be determined

26. In a certain code language '1 2 3' means 'hot filter coffee', '3 5 6' means 'very hot day' and '5 8 9' means 'day and night'. Which digit in that language means 'very'?

A. 8 B. 6
C. 9 D. 5

27. In a certain code, '3 5 7' means 'get me toy', '8 4 3' means 'bring good toy' and '7 4 6' means 'bring me water'. Which of the following digits represents 'good' in that code?

A. 7 B. 6
C. Data inadequate D. None of these

28. In a certain code 721 means 'good college life'. 526 means 'you are good' and 257 means 'life are good', which digit stands for 'you' as the code?

A. 6 B. 5
C. 7 D. None of these

29. In a certain code language 'dom pul ta' means 'bring hot food', 'pul tir sop' means 'food is good' and 'tak da sop' means 'good bright boy'. Which of the following does mean 'hot' in that language?

A. dom
B. pul
C. ta
D. Cannot be determined

30. In a certain code '3 7' means 'which class' and '5 8 3' means 'caste and class'. What is the code for 'caste'?

A. 3 B. 7
C. Either 5 or 3 D. Either 5 or 8

31. In a code language 'mu kay cit' means 'very lucky person' and 'dis hu mu' means 'fortunate and lucky'. Which is the word in that language for 'lucky?'

A. mu B. kay
C. cit D. dis

Directions : (Qs. 32-33) : *In a code language, A. 'pit dar na' means 'you are good'; B. 'dar tok pa' means 'good and bad'; C. 'tim na tok' means 'they are bad'.*

32. In that language, which word stands for 'they'?

A. na B. tok
C. tim D. None of these

33. To find the answer to the above question, which of the following statements can be dispensed with?

A. Only A B. Only B
C. A or B D. None of these

Directions : (Qs. 34-35) : *In a certain code language :*

A. 'tom na rod' means 'give me sweet'.
B. 'jo ta rod' means 'you and me'.
C. 'pot ta noc' means 'you are good'.
D. 'jo mit noc' means 'good and bad'.

34. Which of the following represents 'bad' in that language?

A. mit B. noc
C. jo D. None of these

35. To arrive at the answer to the above question which of the following can be dispensed with?

A. All are necessary B. A or B only
C. A or C only D. None of these

Directions: (Qs. 36-37) : *In a certain code language :*

A. 'pit na som' means 'bring me water'.
B. 'na jo tod' means 'water is life'.
C. 'tub od pit' means 'give me toy'.
D. 'jo lin kot' means 'life and death'.

36. Which of the following represents 'is' in that language?

A. jo B. na
C. tod D. lin

37. To find out the answer to the above question, which of the following statements can be dispensed with?

A. A only B. C only
C. D only D. B or C only

Directions : (Qs. 38 to 40) : *In a certain code language :*

A. '1 3 4' means 'you are well'
B. '7 5 8' means 'they go home'
C. '8 3 9' means 'we are home'.

38. Which of the following represents 'they' in that code language?

A. 5 B. 7
C. 3 D. Data inadequate

39. Which of the statements can be dispensed with while answering the above question?

A. A only B. B only
C. A or C only D. B and C only

40. Which of the following represents 'are' in that code language?

A. 1 B. 3
C. 4 D. 7

41. In a certain code **nee tim see** means 'how are you'; **ble nee see** means 'where are you'. What is the code for 'where'?

A. nee
B. tim
C. see
D. None of these

42. In a certain code language, **pit nae tom** means 'apple is green'; **nae ho tap** means 'green and white' and **ho tom ka** means 'shirt is white'. Which of the following represents 'apple' in that language?

A. nae B. tom
C. pit D. ho

43. If in a certain language, **mxy das zci** means 'good little frock'; **jmx cos zci** means 'girl behaves good'; **nvg drs cos** means 'girl makes mischief' and **das ajp cos** means 'little girl fell'; which word in that language stands for 'frock'?

A. zci B. das
C. nvg D. None of these

44. In a certain code language, **Mink Yang Pe** means 'fruits are ripe'; **Pe Lao May Mink** means 'oranges are not ripe' and **May Pe Nue Mink** means 'mangoes are not ripe'. Which word in that languages means 'Mangoes'?

A. May B. Pe
C. Nue D. Mink

45. In a certain code language, **pul ta nop** means 'fruit is good'; **nop ki tir** means 'tree is tall' and **pul ho sop** means 'eat good food'. Which of the following means 'fruit' in that language?

A. pul B. ta
C. nop D. Data inadequate

46. In a certain code language, **Tom Kun Sud** means 'dogs are barking'; **Kun Jo Mop** means 'dogs and horses'; and **Mut Tom Ko** means 'donkeys are mad'. Which word in that language means 'barking'?

A. Sud B. Kun
C. Jo D. Tom

47. If **cinto baoli tsi nzro** means 'her village is Sarurpur'; **mhi cinto keepi tsi oind** means 'her first love is literature'; and **oind geit tsi cinto pki** means 'literature collection is her hobby' which word would mean 'literature'?

A. cinto B. baoli
C. oind D. geit

48. In a certain code language, **Pat Zoo Sim** means 'eat good mangoes'; **Pus Sim Tim** means 'mangoes and sweets' and **Tim Zoo Kit** means 'purchase good sweets'. Which word in that language means 'good'?

A. Zoo B. Pus
C. Sim D. Tim

49. In a certain code language, **pic vic nic** means 'winter is cold'; **to nic re** means 'summer is hot'; **re pic boo** means 'winter and summer'; and **vic tho pa** means 'nights are cold'. Which word in that language represents 'summer'?

A. nic B. re
C. to D. pic

50. In a certain code language, **kew xas huma deko** means 'she eating apples'; **kew tepo qua** means 'she sells toys' and **sul lim deko** means 'i like apples'. Which word in that language means 'she' and 'apples'?

A. xas and deko
B. xas and kew
C. kew and deko
D. kew and xas

51. In a certain code language '389' means 'run very fast', '964' means 'come back fast' and '487' means 'run and come'. Which digit in the language means 'come?

A. 7 B. 9
C. 4 D. 8

52. If 'Men are very busy' means '1234', 'Busy persons need ecouragement' means '4567', 'encouragement is very important' means '3589' and 'Important persons are rare' means '2680' what is the code for 'encouragement'?

A. 5 B. 6
C. 8 D. 9

53. In a certain code language, 743 means **Mangoes are good**; 657 means **Eat good food**; and 934 means **Mangoes are ripe**. Which digit means ripe in that language?

A. 5 B. 4
C. 9 D. 7

54. In a certain code, 253 means **books are old** 546 means **man is old**; and 378 means **buy good books**. What stands for 'are' in that code?

A. 2 B. 4
C. 5 D. 6

55. In a certain code language, 123 means **bright little boy**; 145 means **tall big boy** and 637 means **beautiful little flower**. Which digit in that language means 'bright'?

A. 1 B. 3
C. 4 D. None of these

56. In a certain code language, 'Monday is a holiday' is written as 'sa da pa na' and 'they enjoy a holiday' is written as 'da na ta ka'. How is 'Monday' written in that code language?

A. sa
B. pa
C. sa or pa
D. Data inadequate

57. In a certain code 'Hit Bit Mit' means 'Git Rit Nit' 'Sit Pit Mit' means 'Lit Git Tit' and 'Fit Zit Pit' means 'Dit Vit Tit'. What does 'Sit' stand for in that code language?

A. Vit B. Dit
C. Rit D. Lit

Directions (58) : *In a certain code language*

A. *'pit na sa' means 'you are welcome'*
B. *'na ho pa la' means 'they are very good'*
C. *'ka da la' means 'who is good'*
D. *'od ho pit la' means 'they welcome good people'*

58. Which of the following means 'people' in that code language?

A. ho B. pit
C. la D. od

59. In a code language "1 3 5 7" means "We are very happy", "2 6 3 9" means "They are extremely lucky" and "794" means "Happy and Lucky". Which digit in that code language stands for "very"?

A. 1 B. 5
C. 7 D. Data inadequate

60. In a certain code '5 6 9' means 'nice little car', '8 3 5' means 'he is nice' and '9 3 7' means 'he has car', which of the following means 'has' in that code?

A. 3 B. 9
C. 7 D. 3 or 7

ANSWERS

1	2	3	4	5	6	7	8	9	10
B	A	A	C	D	D	A	B	B	C
11	**12**	**13**	**14**	**15**	**16**	**17**	**18**	**19**	**20**
C	D	B	C	A	A	C	B	C	A
21	**22**	**23**	**24**	**25**	**26**	**27**	**28**	**29**	**30**
C	B	A	B	C	B	D	A	D	D
31	**32**	**33**	**34**	**35**	**36**	**37**	**38**	**39**	**40**
A	C	D	A	D	C	B	D	A	B
41	**42**	**43**	**44**	**45**	**46**	**47**	**48**	**49**	**50**
D	C	D	C	B	A	C	A	B	C
51	**52**	**53**	**54**	**55**	**56**	**57**	**58**	**59**	**60**
C	A	C	A	D	C	D	D	D	C

EXPLANATORY ANSWERS

1.

Code	*Sentence*
1. go *ju* mi	plenty of *money*
2. pao *ju* go nei vu	*money* creates lots of problems
3. kol vu nei	problems create tension
4. sol tun *ju* haw	still *money* is needed

In 1st, 2nd and 4th codes and their sentences the word 'ju' is repeated and so is 'money'.

2.

Code	*Sentence*
1. FOR	old is gold
2. ROT	gold is pure
3. ROM	gold is costly

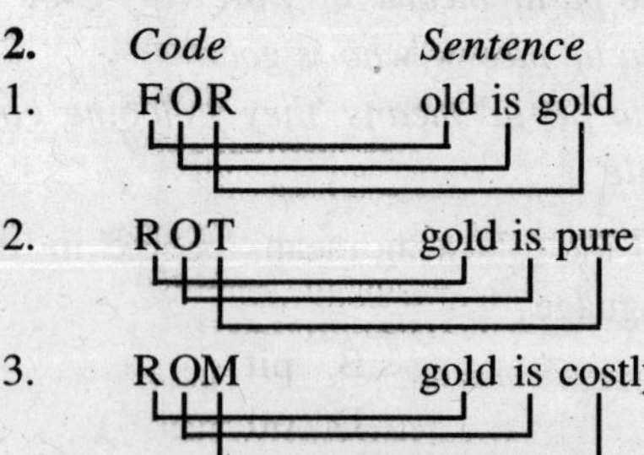

Therefore,

F stands for old
O stands for is
R stands for gold
T stands for pure
M stands for costly

So, 'pure old gold is costly' will be written a 'TFROM'.

3.

Code	*Sentence*
1. 415	milk is hot
2. 18	hot soup
3. 895	soup is *tasty*

From 3rd code and its sentence neither numbe '9' is repeated nor the word 'tasty'.

4.

Code	*Sentence*
1. 643	she is beautiful
2. 593	he is handsome

3. 567 handsome *meets* beautiful

From 3rd code and its sentence, neither number '7' nor the word 'meets' is repeated.

5.

Code	*Sentence*
1. *dugo hui* mul zo	work *is very* hard
2. *hui dugo* **ba** *ki*	**Bingo** *is very smart*
3. nano mul *dugo*	cake is *hard*
4. mul *ki* qu	*smart* and hard

From 2nd code and its sentence, neither 'ba' nor 'Bingo' is repeated.

(Words repeated are in italics)

6.

Code	*Sentence*
1. pic vic nic	winter is cold
2. to nic *re summer* is hot	
3. *re* pic boo	winter and *summer*
4. vic tho pa	nights are cold

The word 'summer' is common in 2nd and 3rd sentences and so is the code 're'.

7.

Code	*Sentence*
1. **mx** *das sci*	*good little* **frock**
2. jm coz *sci*	girl behaves *good*
3. ngv drs coz	girl makes mischief
4. *das* gp coz	*little* girl fell

Word 'frock' is only in the 1st sentence. The code word 'das' is repeated in 4th sentence and 'sci' in 2nd sentence. So, 'mx' is the code for 'frock'.

8.

Code	*Sentence*
1. *mu* mit *es*	who *is she*
2. **elb** *mu* es	**where** *is she*

The code words 'mu' and 'es' are repeated in Ist sentence. The only code left is 'elb' which means 'where'.

9.

Code	*Sentence*
1. *069*	*grapes are* sweet
2. 476	very sweet fruit
3. **509**	*grapes are* **ripe**

The code numbers '0' and '9' are repeated in 1st and 3rd sentences. The only code remaining is '5' which stands for 'ripe'.

10.

Code	*Sentence*
1. **roi** *ja kyo twa*	**Moody** *is writing letters*
2. pok ju *ja twa*	Woody *is writing* cards
3. trn *kyo* pos un	they are writing *letters*
4. koi rus pok	gifts and cards

'Moody' is in 1st sentence only. The code words 'ja' and 'twa' are repeated in 2nd sentence and 'kyo' in 3rd sentence. Only code word 'roi' remains which stands for 'Moody'.

11.

Code	*Sentence*
1. *wre* asi amoh **kedo**	*Polo* is drinking **tea**.
2. *wre* epu uki	*Polo* buys books
3. buen eld **kedo**	Libbo drinks **tea**

The word 'Polo' is common in 1st and 2nd sentence and so is the code 'wre'. The word 'tea' is common in 1st and 3rd sentences and so is the code 'kedo'.

12.

Code	*Sentence*
1. juka *lal* mit **sut**	hello, how **are** *you*?
2. mudi **sut** em nif	where **are** they going?
3. hu zul met **sut**	what **are** their names?
4. *lal* **sut** zul pe	**are** *you* going too?

The word 'are' is present in all the four sentences and so is the code 'sut. The word 'you' is common in 1st and 4th sentences and so is the code 'lal'.

13.

Code	*Sentence*
1. **gri** chri	brand **new**
2. gyp twoh	very old
3. **gri** bur twoh	old and **new**
4. chri *deh* gyp	old brand *car*

The word 'new' is present in 1st and 3rd sentences and so is the code 'gri. The word 'car' is only in the 4th sentence and code 'deh' is not repeated in any other sentence.

14.

Code		*Sentence*
1. luma *papa* jano	→	he speaks *softly*
2. *papa lo* **hedi** *lami*	→	*wind blows softly* **downhill**
3. *lo* puki luma jano *lami* sod	→	he speaks like *wind blows* whisper

Code 'papa' is repeated in 1st and 2nd sentence but the word 'downhill' is not. Of the other coded words in 2nd sentence 'lo' and 'lami' are repeated in 3rd sentence, but again the word 'downhill' is not. The only code remaining is 'hedi' which should mean 'downhill'.

15. *Sentence* → Code

1. *sun* shines **brightly** → **ba** *lo* sul
2. houses are **brightly** lit → kado udo ari **ba**
3. light comes from *sun* → dapi kup *lo* nro.

In 1st and 3rd sentences, the word 'sun' is repeated and so is the code 'lo'. Similarly, in 1st and 2nd sentences the word 'brightly' is repeated and so is the code 'ba'.

16. *Code* → *Sentence*

1. *lo ni* **hie** *pun* → **he** *is drinking coke*
2. hol ful gui *pun* → she *is* eating food
3. ne ful *ni lo* → *drinking coke* and food

In the 1st and 2nd sentences, the code 'pun' for 'is' is repeated but the word 'he' is not. In the 1st and 3rd sentences, the codes 'ni' and 'lo' are repeated. So, the code 'hie' stands for 'he'.

17. *Code* → *Sentence*

1. Gor Paku → Best Gift
2. Mull Gor *Sot* → Gift of *Love*
3. Sol Hed Paku → Best of Luck
4. Hed *Sot* Paku → *Love* is Best

Only in sentences 2nd and 4th, the word 'Love' is repeated and the only code repeated is 'Sot'.

18. *Code* → *Sentence*

1. **pe** *sa de mi* → **yes** *well no mean*
2. pa *mi sa de* → sell *mean well no*

In both the sentences, "well no mean" is repeated and so the coded words 'sa de mi' So, only 'pe' stands for 'yes'.

19. *Code* → *Sentence*

1. *hua* pih uf pu → he *is* very intelligent
2. pih *hua* kup kit → she *is* very fair
3. **luck** *uf hua* → **Jai** *is intelligent*
4. *uf* kit pod → fair and *intelligent*

The word 'Jai' is in 3rd sentence. Of the three codes, 'hua' is repeated in 1st and 2nd sentences and 'uf' is repeated in 3rd and 4th sentences. So, code 'luck' stands for 'Jai'.

20. *Code* → *Sentence*

1. *jo* **mi** *rei ma* → *rest work* **no** *play*
2. *rei* kol puihi mesi → less ground *play* tour
3. puihi *ma jo* mati → *rest* group ground *work*

The word 'no' is only in 1st sentence. Of the other codes 'rei' is repeated in 2nd sentence and 'jo' and 'ma' are repeated in 3rd sentence. So, 'mi' code stands for word 'no'.

21. *Code* — *Sentence*

1. *7*8*6* — *bring* **me** *apple*
2. 95*8* — peel green *apple*
3. *6*45 — *bring* green fruit

The word 'me' is in 1st sentence only. The word 'bring' is common in 1st and 3rd sentences and so is the code 6. The word 'apple' is common in 1st and 2nd sentences and so is the code 8. Only word remaining is 'me' and its code is 7.

22. *Code* — *Sentence*

1. ish lto inm — neat and tidy
2. qpr inm *sen* — small *but* neat
3. hsm *sen* rso — good *but* erratic

In 2nd and 3rd sentences word 'but' is repeated and so is the code 'sen'.

23. *Code* — *Sentence*

1. nso ptr kli chn — Sharma gets marriage gift
2. ptr lnm *wop* chn — wife *gives* marriage gift
3. tti *wop* nhi — he *gives* nothing

In 2nd and 3rd sentences word 'gives' is repeated and so is the code 'wop'.

24. *Code* — *Sentence*

1. col tip *mot* — singing *is* appreciable
2. *mot baj* **min** — *dancing is* **good**
3. tip nop *baj* — singing and *dancing*

The word 'good' is in 2nd sentence only. The word 'dancing' is common in 2nd and 3rd sentences and so is the code 'baj'. The word 'is' is common in 1st and 2nd sentences and so is the code 'mot'. The only code remaining is 'min' which stands for 'good'.

Code	*Sentence*
1. **7***86*	*study* **very** *hard*
2. 95*8*	*hard* work pays
3. *6*45	*study* and work

The word 'very' is in 1st sentence only. The word 'study' is common in 1st and 3rd sentences and so is the code '6'. The word 'hard' is common in 1st and 2nd sentences and so is the code '8'. The only code remaining is '7' which stands for 'very'.

Code	*Sentence*
1. 12*3*	*hot* filter coffee
2. *3***5***6*	**very** *hot day*
3. *5*89	*day* and night

The word 'very' is in 2nd sentence only. The word 'hot' is common in 1st and 2nd sentences and so is the code '3'. The word 'day' is common in 2nd and 3rd sentences and so is the code '5'. The only code remaining is '6' which stands for 'very'.

Code	*Sentence*
1. *3*57	get me *toy*
2. **8***43*	*bring* **good** *toy*
3. 7*4*6	*bring* me water

The word 'good' is in 2nd sentence only. The word 'bring' is common in 2nd and 3rd sentences and so is the code '4'. The word 'toy' is common in 1st and 2nd sentences and so is the code '3'. The only code remaining is '8' which stands for 'good'.

Code	*Sentence*
1. 721	good college life
2. *52***6**	**you** *are good*
3. *25*7	life *are good*

The word 'you' is in 2nd sentence only. The words 'are good' are common in 2nd and 3rd sentences and so are the codes '2' and '5'. The only code remaining is '6' which stands for 'you'.

Code	*Sentence*
1. dom *pul* ta	bring **hot** *food*
2. *pul* tir sop	*food* is good
3. tak da sop	good bright boy

From 1st and 2nd codes and sentences it is clear that code for 'food' is 'pul'. Neither the words 'bring' and 'hot' are repeated nor the codes 'dom' and 'ta'. So, the codes for the words cannot be detected.

30.

Code	*Sentence*
1. *3*7	which *class*
2. 58*3*	caste and *class*

In both the codes and sentences code '3' stands for 'class'. So the code for 'caste' can be either '5' or '8'. The same applies for word 'and'. More information is needed.

31.

Code	*Sentence*
1. *mu* kay cit	very *lucky* person
2. dis hu *mu*	fortunate and *lucky*

In both the codes and sentences word 'lucky' is common and so is the code 'mu'.

32.

Code	*Sentence*
A. pit dar *na*	you *are* good
B. dar *tok* pa	good and *bad*
C. **tim** *na tok*	**they** *are bad*

The word 'they' is in sentence C only. The word 'are' is repeated in sentence A and so is the code 'na'. The word 'bad' is repeated in sentence B and so is the code 'tok'. The only code remaining is 'tim' which stands for 'they'.

33. The answer to the above question was arrived at only after comparing all the three codes and sentences.

34.

Code	*Sentence*
A. tom na rod	give me sweet
B. *jo* ta rod	you *and* me
C. pot ta *noc*	you are *good*
D. *jo* **mit** *noc*	*good* and **bad**

The word 'bad' is in sentence 'D' only. The word 'good' is repeated in sentence 'C' and so is the code 'noc'. The word 'and' is repeated in sentence 'B' and so is the code 'jo'. The only code remaining is 'mit' which stands for 'bad'.

35. The answer to the above question was arrived at by comparing codes and sentences B, C and D. Only sentence 'A' could be dispensed with.

36.

Code	*Sentence*
A. pit *na* som	bring me *water*
B. *na jo* **tod**	*water* **is** *life*
C. tub od pit	give me toy
D. *jo* lin kot	*life* and death

The word 'is' is in Sentence 'B' only. The word 'water' is repeated in Sentence 'A' and so is the code 'na'. The word 'life' is repeated in sentence 'D' and so is the code 'jo'. The only code remaining is 'tod' which stands for 'is'.

37. The answer to the above question was arrived at by comparing codes and sentences A, B and D. Only sentence 'C' could be dispensed with.

38.

Code	*Sentence*
A. 134	you *are* well
B. 758	they go *home*
C. 839	we *are home*

In codes and sentences B and C the word 'home' is repeated and so is the code '8'. The code for word 'they' can be either '7' or '5'. The same applies for 'go'. More information is needed.

39. Sentence 'A' has nothing in common with sentence 'B'.

40. In codes and sentences A and C the word 'are' is repeated and so is the code '3'.

41. In the first and second statements, the common code words **nee** and **see** mean 'are' and 'you'. So, in the second statement, the remaining code **ble** means 'where'.

42. In the first and second statements the common code word is **nae** and the common word is **green**. So, **nae** means **green**.

In the first and third statements, the common code word is **tom** and the common word is **is**. So, **tom** means **is**. Therefore in the first statement **pit** means **apple**.

43. In the first and second statements, the common code word is **zci** and the common word is **good**. So, **zci** means **good**.

In the first and fourth statements, the common code word is **das** and the common word is **little**. So, **das** means **little**. Thus, in the first statement **mxy** means **frock**.

44. In the second and third statements, the common code words are **Pe**, **Mink** and **May** and the common words are **are**, **not** and **ripe**. So, in the third statement, **Nue** stands for mangoes.

45. In the first and second statements, th common code word is **nop** and the comm word is **is**. So, **nop** means **is**.

In the first and third statements, the comm code word is **pul** and the common word good. So, **pul** means **good**. Thus, in the fi statement, **ta** means **fruit**.

46. In the first and second statements, t common code word is **Kun** and the comm word is **Dogs**. So, **Kun** means **Dogs**.

In the first and third statements, the comm code word is **Tom** and the common word **are**. Therefore in the first statement, S means **barking**.

47. In the first and second statements, t common code words are **cinto** and **tsi** and common words are **her** and **is**.

In the second and third statements, **cinto** a **tsi** mean **her** and **is**. Another common co word is **oind** and the common word **literature**. So, **oind** would mean **literatu**

48. In the first and third statements, the comm code word is **Zoo** and the common word **Good**. So, **Zoo** means **Good**.

49. In the second and third statements, common code word is **re** and the comm word is **summer**. So, **re** represents **summ**

50. In the first and second statements, common code word is **kew** and the comr word is **she**. So, **kew** means **she**.

In the first and third statements, the comr code word is **deko** and the common wor **apples**. So, **deko** means **apples**.

51. In the second and third sentences, com number is '4' and common code is 'cor Hence, number '4' stands for 'come'.

52. In the second and third sentences, com word is 'encouragement' and the com number is '5'. Hence, number '5' stands 'encouragement'.

3. In the first and third statements, the common code digits are 4 and 3, and the common words are 'Mangoes' and 'are'. So, 4 and 3 are the codes for 'Mangoes' and 'are'. Thus in the third statement, 9 means 'ripe'.

4. In the first and second statements, the common code digit is 5 and the common word is 'old'. So, 5 stands for 'old'.

In the first and third statements, the common code digit is 3 and the common word is 'books'. So, 3 stands for 'books'. Thus, in the first statement, 2 stands for 'are'.

5. In the first and second statements, the common code digit is 1 and the common word is 'boy'. So, 1 means 'boy'.

In the first and third statements, the common code digit is 3 and the common word is 'little'. So, 3 means 'little'. Thus in the first statement, 2 means 'bright'.

[illegible]. Monday is [a holiday] → sa [da] pa [na]

they enjoy [a holiday] → [da na] ta ka

Thus, Monday → sa or pa.

57. Hit Bit (Mit) → (Git) Rit Nit

Sit [Pit] (Mit) → Lit (Git) [Tit]

Fit Zit [Pit] → Dit Vit [Tit]

Therefore, 'Sit' stands for 'Lit'.

58.

(i) (pit) △are sa → you △are (welcome)

(ii) △na ⬠ho pa [la] → ⬠they △are very [good]

(iii) ka da [la] → who is [good]

(iv) od ⬠ho (pit) [la] → ⬠they (welcome) [good] people

It is clear that 'od' stands for 'people'.

59. We are very [happy] → 1 3 5 [7]

They are extremely (lucky) → 2 6 3 (9)

[Happy] and (lucky) → [9] (9) 4

∴ We vary → 1, 5

Hence, data inadequate

60. 5 (9) 6 → nice little (car)

8 [3] 5 → [he] is nice

(9) [3] 7 → [he] has (car)

It is clear that '7' stands for 'has'.

ODD ONE OUT

Directions : *In each of the following questions, four words/letter groups/numbers/number groups are alike in some manner. Spot the odd one out.*

1. A. Green B. Red C. Colour D. Orange
2. A. Stable B. Hole C. Canoe D. Sty
3. A. Nose B. Eyes C. Skin D. Teeth
4. A. Venus B. Moon C. Pluto D. Mars
5. A. Happy B. Gloomy C. Lively D. Cheerful
6. A. Cone B. Circle C. Triangle D. Rectangle
7. A. Lead B. Mercury C. Copper D. Iron
8. A. Kite B. Bird C. Radar D. Jet
9. A. Knee B. Shoulder C. Ankle D. Palm
10. A. Deluge B. Calamity C. Catastrophe D. War
11. A. Cub B. Chicken C. Pig D. Pup
12. A. Rabbit B. Crocodile C. Earthworm D. Snail
13. A. Tree B. Leaf C. Bush D. Herb
14. A. Doctor B. Teacher C. Engineer D. Diver
15. A. Trot B. Equestrian C. Derby D. Grunt
16. A. Ornate B. Pleasant C. Decorate D. Beautify
17. A. Polo B. Chess C. Ludo D. Squash
18. A. Tutor B. Principal C. Pupil D. Professor
19. A. Pond B. River C. Stream D. Brook
20. A. Quotation B. Duty C. Tax D. Octroi
21. A. Root B. Tree C. Branch D. Flower
22. A. Mumbai B. Chandigarh C. Lucknow D. Hyderabad
23. A. Immortal B. Eminence C. Perpetual D. Everlasting
24. A. Spinach B. Potato C. Carrot D. Ginger
25. A. Van B. Aeroplane C. Helicopter D. Transport
26. A. Fathom B. Marine C. Deep D. Lacuna
27. A. Attorney B. Lawyer C. Judge D. Liquidator
28. A. Sparrow B. Kingfisher C. Kiwi D. Parrot
29. A. Arrow B. Daggar C. Knife D. Sword
30. A. Mathematics B. Algebra C. Trigonometry D. Geometry
31. A. Irish B. Iranian C. Eastern D. Chinese
32. A. December B. June C. January D. March

33. A. Boxer B. Wrestler
C. Jockey D. Player

34. A. Mature B. Outdo
C. Ripen D. Bloom

35. A. Kanpur B. Haridwar
C. Varanasi D. Lucknow

36. A. Adore B. Like
C. Love D. Covet

37. A. Greedy B. Rapacious
C. Endear D. Avaricious

38. A. Club B. Heart
C. Spade D. Ace

39. A. Permit B. Allow
C. Agree D. Confess

40. A. Stool B. Wood
C. Table D. Chair

41. A. ACE B. LOR
C. GIK D. VXZ

42. A. TSR B. LKJ
C. PQO D. HGF

43. A. EF LM B. KJ SR
C. XW HG D. ED YX

44. A. JOPK B. BOPC
C. QOPR D. TOPS

45. A. DfH B. MoQ
C. UwY D. InO

46. A. JKkL B. OPpQ
C. DEEf D. VWwX

47. A. BdfH B. FHJL
C. RTvX D. uVwX

48. A. DFHEG B. TWXUV
C. OQSPR D. JLNKM

49. A. FEUV B. DCXW
C. BAZY D. HGTS

50. A. UTSR B. XYZW
C. ONML D. IHGF

51. A. MKGA B. PNID
C. RPLF D. VTPJ

52. A. ABJNM B. QRTUZ
C. IXYOQ D. WGFPO

53. A. BFJQ B. RUZG
C. GJOV D. ILQX

54. A. CS B. OU
C. EV D. QO

55. A. EFGH B. IRST
C. ULMN D. JKLO

56. A. LNP B. ECA
C. JLN D. RTV

57. A. SU B. BD
C. PN D. WY

58. A. KI B. SQ
C. CA D. VX

59. A. SC B. FT
C. MK D. HV

60. A. END B. PUT
C. ARM D. OWL

61. A. CFIL B. ABCD
C. ACDF D. EFGH

62. A. SPQR B. MKLN
C. WUVX D. FDEG

63. A. HK B. DG
C. NK D. UX

64. A. MLKA B. HGFA
C. RQPA D. STUA

65. A. KNOS B. QTUY
C. DFGJ D. BEFJ

66. A. 1948 B. 2401
C. 966 D. 1449

67. A. 182 B. 169
C. 130 D. 158

68. A. 129 B. 130
C. 131 D. 132

69. A. 3215 B. 9309
C. 4721 D. 2850

70. A. 1776 B. 2364
C. 1976 D. 3776

71. A. 64 B. 84
C. 16 D. 36

72. A. 24 B. 90
C. 54 D. 36

73. A. 7658 B. 1234
C. 9876 D. 6543

74. A. 3 B. 9
C. 5 D. 7

75. A. 6450 B. 1776
C. 2392 D. 3815

76. A. 24 B. 48
C. 42 D. 12

77. A. 616 B. 252
C. 311 D. 707

78. A. 18 B. 12
C. 30 D. 20

79. A. 3730 B. 6820
C. 5568 D. 4604

80. A. 2587 B. 7628
C. 8726 D. 2867

81. A. 63 B. 29
C. 27 D. 25

82. A. 23 B. 37
C. 21 D. 31

83. A. 18 B. 9
C. 21 D. 7

84. A. 9875432 B. 98765
C. 98756 D. 9876543

85. A. 602 B. 431
C. 530 D. 813

86. A. 4 B. 6
C. 7 D. 10

87. A. 3456 B. 2345
C. 5467 D. 5678

88. A. 10 B. 11
C. 15 D. 16

89. A. 336 B. 213
C. 436 D. 819

90. A. 258 B. 326
C. 224 D. 339

91. A. Chair - Furniture
B. Shirt - Garment
C. Necklace - Jewellery
D. Bogie - Engine

92. A. Crayon - Paper B. Pencil - Lead
C. Pen - Ink D. Brush - Paint

93. A. War - Peace B. Real - Natural
C. Premiere - First D. Wrath - Anger

94. A. Finger - Thimble B. Head - Cap
C. Waist - Tiara D. Foot - Shoe

95. A. Day - Night B. Clever - Foolish
C. Clear - Blurred D. Arrive - Come

96. A. Quintal - Gallon
B. Bouquet - Flowers
C. Book - Pages
D. Parliament - Members

97. A. Birds - Chirp B. Horses - Hum
C. Lions - Roar D. Snakes - Hiss

98. A. Niece - Nephew B. Husband - Wife
C. Brother - Sister D. Father - Mother

99. A. Petrol - Car B. Oil - Lamp
C. Diesel - Wood D. Wax - Candle

100. A. Ganga - Narmada
B. Thar - Gobi
C. Stomach - Hands
D. Everest - Mountain

101. A. Medicine - Doctor
B. Flower - Artist
C. Shoes - Cobbler
D. Skin - Dermatologist

102. A. Authority - Sanction
B. Repel - Attract
C. Finicky - Choosy
D. Breath - Entity

103. A. Polo - Rink B. Golf - Lawn
C. Tennis - Court D. Chess - Board

04. A. Ecstacy - Fantasy
B. Price - Thrice
C. Crime - Prune
D. Both - Oath

05. A. Army - General
B. College - Principal
C. Ship - Captain
D. Navy - Lieutenant

06. A. Train - Tracks B. Birds - Fly
C. Aeroplane - Sky D. Submarine - Sea

07. A. Jelly - Gentle B. Stone - Hard
C. Fur - Soft D. Glass - Smooth

08. A. Branch - Tree
B. Minute - Hour
C. Sentence - Paragraph
D. Student - Teacher

09. A. Sum - Total B. Now - Present
C. Big - Notion D. Yes - Agree

0. A. Four - Foursome
B. Three - Triplet
C. Two - Double
D. One - Single

1. A. Brahmaputra - River
B. Sahara - Desert
C. Aravalli - Ocean
D. Europe - Continent

2. A. Much - Most B. Bad - Worse
C. Simple - Simpler D. Little - Less

3. A. Ripe - Crude B. Close - Near
C. Warm - Tender D. Believe - Trust

4. A. Giraffe - Tall
B. Snail - Heavy
C. Jet - Fast
D. Ant - Industrious

. A. Nine - Twine B. Fire - Liar
C. Honey - Money D. Rust - Crest

. A. FGH - HIJ B. PQR - RST
C. MNO - OPQ D. CDE - DEF

117. A. JuM - jUm B. iLo - Ilo
C. PSa - psA D. ZeX - zEx

118. A. NQT - JMP B. CFI - RUX
C. ADG - FGH D. SVY - ORU

119. A. DXD - XDX B. KUK - UKU
C. FHF - EHE D. RSR - SRS

120. A. AYT - BZU B. FNG - EMF
C. RWO - QVN D. HJD - GIC

121. A. POT - TOP B. TAN - ANT
C. BIN - NIB D. DUB - BUD

122. A. LT - HF B. IN - VA
C. ZE - XM D. RB - SC

123. A. MQU - CGK B. BGL - TYD
C. RWB - FKP D. JOT - DIN

124. A. JLN - KMO B. GIK - HJL
C. DFJ - EGI D. OQS - PRT

125. A. URS - UrS B. JPL - JpL
C. PQM - PqM D. MoN - MON

126. A. PQR - HGF B. RST - ONM
C. IJK - CBE D. WXY - FED

127. A. JM - KL B. QP - RS
C. EH - FG D. MP - NO

128. A. AE - OL B. UI - OE
C. IO - UE D. EA - OU

129. A. VWX - OCU B. IFH - SGQ
C. LAN - BDR D. EJP - ZTY

130. A. MEAL - LAME B. BARK - KERB
C. SPOT - TOPS D. RUBY - BURY

131. A. 91, 10 B. 57, 12
C. 69, 15 D. 72, 13

132. A. 20, 10 B. 45, 27
C. 15, 12 D. 30, 18

133. A. 7, 3 B. 13, 9
C. 11, 7 D. 17, 8

134. A. 10, 20 B. 40, 50
C. 30, 40 D. 50, 60

135. A. 16, 26 B. 3, 4
C. 26, 24 D. 27, 25

136. A. 39, 13 B. 57, 19
C. 64, 16 D. 72, 26

137. A. 16, 43 B. 29, 56
C. 53, 82 D. 71, 98

138. A. 7, 47 B. 5, 25
C. 3, 9 D. 4, 16

139. A. 92, 46 B. 77, 38.5
C. 30, 16 D. 42, 21

140. A. 13, 65 B. 18, 90
C. 17, 95 D. 24, 120

141. A. 63, 52 B. 75, 64
C. 80, 69 D. 32, 12

142. A. 17, 37 B. 8, 13
C. 5, 13 D. 23, 7

143. A. 55, 10 B. 76, 13
C. 92, 14 D. 83, 11

144. A. 7, 343 B. 8, 514
C. 5, 125 D. 6, 216

145. A. 42, 14 B. 56, 19
C. 69, 23 D. 108, 36

ANSWERS

1	**2**	**3**	**4**	**5**	**6**	**7**	**8**	**9**	**10**
C	C	D	B	B	A	B	C	D	D
11	**12**	**13**	**14**	**15**	**16**	**17**	**18**	**19**	**20**
C	A	B	D	D	B	A	C	A	A
21	**22**	**23**	**24**	**25**	**26**	**27**	**28**	**29**	**30**
A	B	B	A	D	D	D	C	A	A
31	**32**	**33**	**34**	**35**	**36**	**37**	**38**	**39**	**40**
C	B	D	B	D	D	C	D	D	[illegible]
41	**42**	**43**	**44**	**45**	**46**	**47**	**48**	**49**	**50**
B	C	A	D	D	C	D	B	A	[illegible]
51	**52**	**53**	**54**	**55**	**56**	**57**	**58**	**59**	**60**
B	C	A	C	D	B	C	D	A	[illegible]
61	**62**	**63**	**64**	**65**	**66**	**67**	**68**	**69**	**70**
C	A	C	D	C	A	D	C	B	[illegible]
71	**72**	**73**	**74**	**75**	**76**	**77**	**78**	**79**	**80**
B	A	A	B	D	C	C	A	B	[illegible]
81	**82**	**83**	**84**	**85**	**86**	**87**	**88**	**89**	**90**
B	C	D	C	D	C	C	B	C	[illegible]
91	**92**	**93**	**94**	**95**	**96**	**97**	**98**	**99**	**100**
D	A	A	C	D	A	B	A	C	[illegible]
101	**102**	**103**	**104**	**105**	**106**	**107**	**108**	**109**	**110**
B	B	A	C	D	B	A	D	C	[illegible]
111	**112**	**113**	**114**	**115**	**116**	**117**	**118**	**119**	**120**
C	A	A	B	D	D	B	C	C	[illegible]
121	**122**	**123**	**124**	**125**	**126**	**127**	**128**	**129**	**130**
B	D	A	C	D	C	B	A	D	[illegible]
131	**132**	**133**	**134**	**135**	**136**	**137**	**138**	**139**	**140**
D	A	D	A	A	D	C	A	C	[illegible]
141	**142**	**143**	**144**	**145**					
D	B	C	B	B					

EXPLANATORY ANSWERS

1. All others are types of colour.
2. Canoe is a boat. Others are resting places of birds/animals.
3. All others are sense organs.
4. All others are planets.
5. All others are expressions of joy
6. All others are geometrical figures.
7. All others are solid metals.
8. All others are flying objects. Radar traces the objects in sky.
9. All others are joints in human body.
10. All others are nature-bound. Only war is man-made.
11. All others are young ones of animals.
12. All others are crawling animals.
13. All others are types of vegetation.
14. All others are professions, but only Diver's profession comprises of diving under water.
15. All other terms are related with activities of a horse.
16. All other words have the same meaning.
17. All others are indoor games.
18. All others are instructors. Pupil learns from the instructor.
19. All others are running forms of water.
20. All others are forms of taxes.
21. All others are parts of tree which are above the ground.
22. All are capitals but Chandigarh is the capital of two states.
23. All others have the same meaning.
24. All others are underground vegetables.
25. All others are means of transport.
26. All others words are related to sea.
27. All others are legal professionals.
28. Only Kiwi is a flightless bird.
29. Only arrow needs a bow. Others can be used by hand.
30. All others are branches of mathematics.
31. All others refer to people from particular country.
32. All other months have 31 days.
33. All others are players.
34. All other words have the same meaning.
35. Only Lucknow is a capital city.
36. All other words refer to modes of attachment or liking.
37. All others are synonyms of greedy.
38. All others are four kinds of cards in the pack.
39. All other words convey permission to do something.
40. All other objects are made of wood.
41. The sequence in each group is +2. Only option B has sequence in +3, *i.e.,*

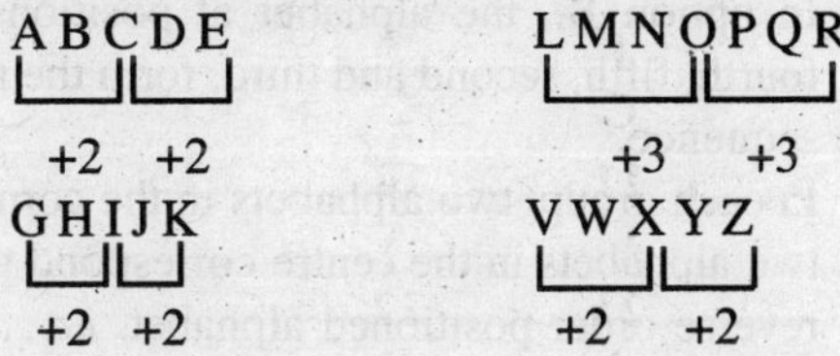

42. The sequence of alphabet in each group is in reverse order. Only option C has sequence in disturbed order.
43. Two consecutive alphabet in each group are in reverse sequence (–1), *i.e.,*

    KJ SR ; XW HG ; ED YX

    –1 –1 –1 –1 –1 –1

    Only in option A. the sequence is in natural order (+1), *i.e.,*

44. In each group, letters 'OP' are common. The two corner alphabet are in natural order (+1); *i.e.,*

    JOPK ; BOPC ; QOPR

    +1 +1 +1

    Only in option D. they are in reverse order (–1); *i.e.,*

    TOPS

    –1
45. In other groups, only the alphabet in the centre is of lower case. In this option letter 'L' on the left is also in lower case.

46. In other groups, the third letter which is a repeat of the second alphabet is in lower case.

47. In each group, the sequence of the alphabet, irrespective of the case, is +2; *i.e.*,

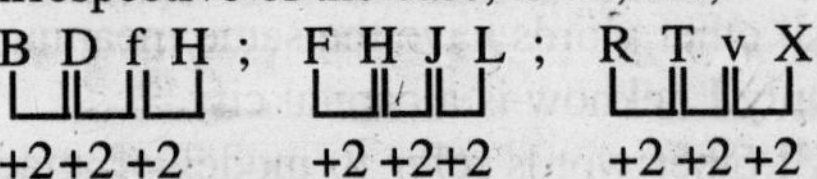

Only in option D. the sequence is in natural order (+1), *i.e.*,

u V w X

+1 +1 +1

48. In each group; the alphabet at positions-first, fourth, second, fifth and third, form a natural sequence.

In option B., the alphabet at positions first, fourth, fifth, second and third, form the natural sequence.

49. In each group, two alphabets in the corner and two alphabets in the centre correspond to their reverse order positioned alphabet. *i.e.*,

natural order → A B C D E F G H I J K L M
reverse order → Z Y X W V U T S R Q P O N
natural order → N O P Q R S T U V W X Y Z
reverse order → M L K J I H G F E D C B A

As such—

D corresponds with W and
C corresponds with X.
B corresponds with Y and
A corresponds with Z.
H corresponds with S and
G corresponds with T.

Similarly,

F should correspond with U and
E should correspond with V;
i.e. letters 'UV' should be written as 'VU'

50. In each group, the alphabet are in reverse order.

In option B., the order is disturbed.

51. The sequence of alphabet in each group follows the reverse pattern of –2, –4, –6, *i.e.*,

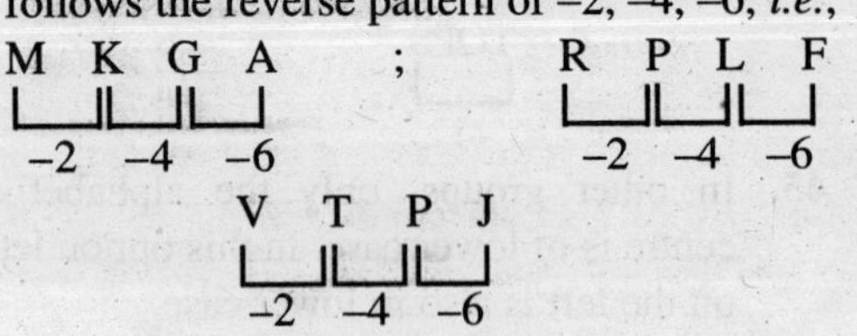

In option B., the pattern is

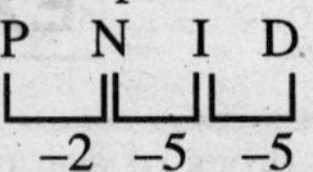

The correct pattern should be→P N J D

−2 −4 −6

52. In each group at least two pairs of alphabet are in sequence, *i.e.*,

In option C. only one pair is in sequence

IXYOQ

53. The sequence of alphabet in each group follows the natural pattern of +3, +5, +7, *i.e.*,

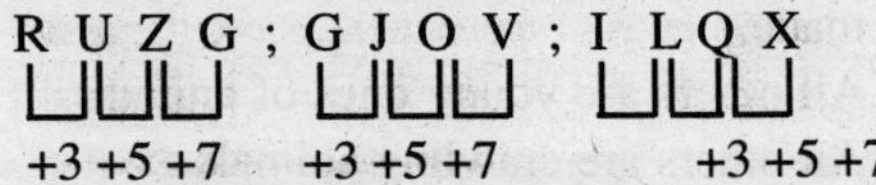

Note : The alphabetical series restarts from letter 'A' on reaching letter 'Z'.

In option A., the pattern is

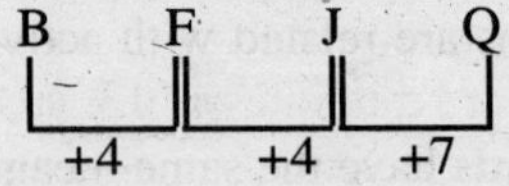

54. Only this group has letters made by straight lines.

55. In all other groups the first letter is a vowel followed by three consecutive letters.

56. In all other groups the alternate letters are in natural alphabet order.

57. In all other groups the alternate letters are in natural alphabet order.

58. In all other groups the alternate letters are in reverse alphabet order.

59. Only this group has letters made by curved lines.

60. In all other groups the first letter is a vowel.

61. In all other groups the difference between the consecutive letters is even. *i.e.*,

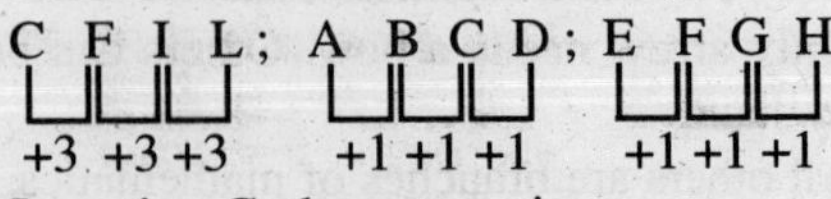

In option C. the pattern is :

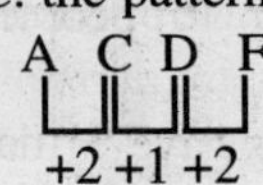

62. In all other groups the alphabet at positions second, third, first and last form a natural sequence. In option A., the alphabet at positions second, third, fourth and first form the natural sequence.

63. In all other groups the letters skip two letters in between and are in natural order. In option C. they are in reverse order.

64. In all other groups the first three letters are in reverse order followed by A at the last position. In option D. the three letters are in natural order.

65. The sequence in all other groups is +3, +1, +4, *i.e.*,

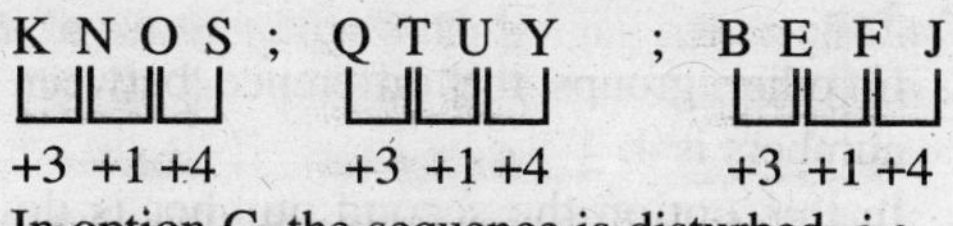

In option C. the sequence is disturbed, *i.e.*,

D F G J

+2 +1 +3

66. Other numbers are divisible by 7.

67. Other numbers are multiples of 13.

68. 131 is a prime number.

69. In other numbers, no digit is repeated.

70. In other numbers the last two digits are same.

71. All other numbers are perfect squares.

72. In other numbers, the sum of both the digits is 9.

73. In others, the digits are consecutive in natural or reverse series.

74. All others are prime numbers.

75. All other numbers are divisible by 2.

76. All other numbers are multiples of 12.

77. In other numbers, the first and last digits are same.

78. The other numbers are $3^2 + 3 = 12$, $5^2 + 5 = 30$, $4^2 + 4 = 20$

79. In all other numbers, two digits are same.

80. Other numbers are made with digits 2, 6, 7 and 8.

81. 29 is a prime number.

82. All other numbers are prime numbers.

83. All other numbers are divisible by 3.

84. In all other numbers the sequence of digits after 987 is in decreasing order.

85. In all other numbers the total of digits is 8.

86. All other numbers are even numbers.

87. In all other numbers the digits are in increasing order.

88. 11 is a prime number.

89. In all other numbers the digit on the right is the sum of two digits on the left.

90. In all other numbers the digit on the right is the product of two digits on the left.

91. Bogie is a part of train which is a type of conveyance. Chair, Shirt and Necklace are types of furniture, garment and jewellery respectively.

92. The medium used for writing with pencil is lead, with pen it is ink and with brush, it is paint. With crayon it should be wax.

93. The pair of words are opposite. Other pairs are synonyms.

94. Tiara is worn on the head.

95. Other words are opposite to each other.

96. In all other groups the first word is the collection of the second.

97. In all other groups the second word is the sound of the first. Horses neigh.

98. The related pairs are first masculine and then feminine. In A., it is opposite.

99. Petrol is used to run a car, oil to burn a lamp and wax for candle. Diesel and wood have no relation.

100. The related pairs have same identity. A. has rivers, B. deserts and C. parts of body. In D., mountain identifies the first word - Everest.

101. Doctor deals with medicine, cobbler with shoes and dermatologist with skin. Person dealing with flowers should be gardener or a horticulturist.

102. The other pairs of words have same meaning. Repel and attract are opposites.

103. The related words are the games and the places where they are played. Polo is played on ground.

104. The other pairs of words are rhyming words.

105. The head of the Navy is Commander.

106. Birds fly in sky as train runs on its tracks, aeroplane flies in sky and submarine runs under sea. Birds are living objects.

107. The second words shows the quality of the first word. Jelly is tender or wobbly.

108. In other groups the first word is a part of the second.

109. The other pairs share the same meaning.

110. Three is thrice or threesome.

111. Aravallis are Mountains.

112. All other words are combinations of positive and comparative degrees of comparisons. Option A. has a pair of positive and superlative degree of comparison.

113. All other pair of words have the same meaning.

114. In all other pairs the second word is the characteristic feature of the first. Snail should be slow.

115. The other pair of words are rhyming words.

116. In all other groups the letters are in natural series and the last letter of first part is the first letter of the second part.

117. In all other groups only the vowel is in lower case in the first part and in second part the case is reversed.

118. In all other groups the letters jump two letters in between them.

119. In all other groups the single letter in first part is repeated in the second and vice versa.

120. In all other groups the letters in the first part are one step forward than the corresponding letters in the second part.

121. In all other groups the letters in the first part are written backwards in the second part.

122. All other groups have letters made by straight lines only.

123. In all other groups the letters jump four letters in between them.

124. In all others groups the letters jump one letter between them.

125. In all other groups the second part is same as first except that the middle letter is changed to small letter.

126. In all other groups the letters in first part are in natural series and in second part in reverse series.

127. In all other groups the two letters on the right fit between the two letters on the left.

128. All other pairs have only vowels.

129. In other groups, the letters on the left are made with straight lines and the letters on the right have curved lines.

130. In other groups, the letters on the left are used to form a new word on the right.

131. In all other pairs the second number is the sum of the digits of the first number.

132. In all other pairs the numbers are divisible by 3.

133. In other groups the difference between the numbers is 4.

134. In this option the second number is double the first number. In other groups the difference between the two numbers is 10.

135. In other groups the first digits of the two numbers are same (consider 3 and 4 as 03 and 04).

136. In other pairs the first number is divisible by the second number.

137. In other pairs the difference between the two numbers is 27.

138. The second number in other pairs is the square of the first number.

139. The second number in other pairs is half of the first number.

140. The second number in other pairs is five times the first number.

141. The difference in each pair is of 11. In this option, it is 10.

142. 8 is not a prime number.

143. The second number in other groups is the sum of digits of the first number.

144. The second number in other groups is the cube of the first number.

145. In all other pairs, the first number is divided by 3 to get the second number.

RELATIONSHIPS

rections : *In each of the following questions nly study the relationship mentioned between persons, and then from the given options select right relationship as the answer.*

1. 'A' is the father of 'B' and 'C'. 'B' is the son of 'A' but 'C' is not the son of 'A'. What is 'C's' relation with 'A'?

A. Daughter B. Son
C. Niece D. Nephew

2. A lady said, "The person standing there is my grandfather's only son's daughter". How is the lady related to the standing person?

A. Sister B. Mother
C. Aunt D. Cousin

3. Ravi is the brother of Amit's son's son. What is Amit's relation to Ravi?

A. Cousin B. Father
C. Grandfather D. Son

4. Mayank said, "My mother is the sister of Rajat's brother." What is Rajat's relation with Mayank?

A. Cousin
B. Maternal uncle
C. Uncle
D. Brother-in-law

Introducing Lily, Raghav said, "Her father is my mother's only son". How is Lily related to Raghav?

A. Aunt B. Daughter
C. Mother D. Sister

Ajay is the brother of Vijay. Mili is the Sister of Ajay. Sanjay is the brother of Rahul and Mehul is the daughter of Vijay. Who is Sanjay's Uncle?

A. Rahul B. Ajay
C. Mehul D. Data inadequate

7. Aditya is Bhavi's brother, Bharat is Jayant's father. Ella is Bhavi's mother. Aditya and Jayant are brothers. What is Ella's relationship with Bharat?

A. Sister B. Mother
C. Daughter D. Wife

8. A man introduced the boy coming with him as "He is son of the father of my wife's daughter". What relation did the boy bear to the man?

A. Son-in-law B. Son
C. Brother D. Father

9. A and B are two brothers. C is sister of B. D is sister of E. E is son of A. Who is D's uncle?

A. D B. E
C. B D. C

10. Varun said pointing towards Arun, "He is my sister's only brother's son". How is Arun related to Varun?

A. Son B. Brother
C. Nephew D. Data insufficient

11. Pointing to a man, a lady said, "His brother's father is my grandfather's only son." How is the lady related to the man?

A. Mother B. Sister
C. Daughter D. Aunt

12. Vidya is the wife of Gopi and Gopi is the brother of Akhil. Akhil is the uncle of Vijay. What is Vijay's relation with Vidya?

A. Son B. Nephew
C. Brother-in-law D. Brother

13. If Amit's father is Billoo's father's only son and Billoo has neither a brother nor a daughter, what is the relationship between Amit and Billoo?

A. Uncle - Nephew
B. Father- Daughter
C. Father - Son
D. Cousins

14. A is the sister of B. B is the son of C, and E is the daughter of D, and sister of A. What is D to C?
A. Brother
B. Husband
C. Wife
D. Data is inadequate

15. A man said to a lady, "Fagu's mother is the only daughter of your father". How is the lady related to Fagu?
A. Daughter B. Sister
C. Wife D. Mother

16. Pointing to a man, a woman said, "He is the only son of my mother's mother". How is the woman related to the man?
A. Aunt B. Daughter
C. Niece D. Sister

17. If B's mother was A's mother's daughter, how was A related to B?
A. Uncle
B. Aunt
C. Sister
D. Data is insufficient

18. Pointing to a woman in the photograph a man said, "She is the daughter of my grandmother's only son. How is the woman related to the man?
A. Mother B. Daughter
C. Sister-in-law D. Sister

19. A man and a woman are sitting in a room. Man's mother-in-law and woman's mother-in-law are mother and daughter respectively. Man is the .... of the woman.
A. Father
B. Father-in-law
C. Uncle
D. Grandfather-in-law

20. Pointing to Suman, Amit said, "He is my sister's only brother's son". How is Suman related to Amit?
A. Grandson
B. Son
C. Nephew
D. Cannot be determined

21. Pointing to someone, I said, "She is my father's sister and she is the only daughter" How many children did my paternal grand parents have in all?
A. Two sons
B. One daughter
C. One son and one daughter
D. Cannot be determined

22. Pointing to a photograph, a woman said, "Sh is the only daughter of my mother's father. How is the woman related to the person in th photograph?
A. Mother
B. Grandmother
C. Daughter
D. Cannot be determined

23. Sandip's mother is the only daughter Rekha's father. How is Rekha's husba related to Sandip?
A. Uncle B. Brother
C. Grandfather D. Father

24. If P is the husband of Q and R is the moth of S and Q, what is R to P?
A. Mother
B. Sister
C. Aunt
D. Mother-in-law

25. Ram is the brother of Shyam and Mahesh the father of Ram. Jagat is the brother of Pri and Priya is daughter of Shyam. Who is uncle of Jagat ?
A. Shyam
B. Mahesh
C. Ram
D. Data insufficient

26. Pointing to a photograph, a woman says, "This man's son's sister is my mother-in-law". How is the woman's husband related to the man in the photograph ?

A. Son-in-law B. Son
C. Grandson D. Nephew

27. Pointing towards a person in a photograph, Aruna said, "He is the only son of the father of my sister's brother". How is that person related to Aruna?

A. Mother
B. Maternal Uncle
C. Father
D. None of these

28. If Vijay says "Viju's mother is the only daughter of my mother", how is Vijay related to Viju ?

A. Brother
B. Grandfather
C. Father
D. None of these

29. Pointing to a photograph a lady tells Mohan, "I am the only daughter of this lady and her son is your maternal uncle." How is the speaker related to Mohan's father ?

A. Wife
B. Sister-in-law
C. Either of the two
D. Neither of the two

30. Q's mother is sister of P and daughter of M. S is daughter of P and sister of T. How is M related to T ?

A. Father
B. Grandfather
C. Grandmother
D. Grandfather or Grandmother

31. A is the mother of B'. B's father C has three children. Based on this information, state which of the following statements is definitely true ?

A. C has three daughters
B. C has three sons
C. B is a male child
D. None of these

32. Daya has a brother Anil. Daya is a son of Chandra. Bimal is Chandra's father. In terms of relationship, what is Anil of Bimal ?

A. Grandfather B. Brother
C. Grandson D. Son

33. 'A' is the brother of 'B', 'C' is the sister of 'B'. How is 'B' related to 'A'?

A. Cousin
B. Sister
C. Brother
D. Cannot be determined

34. Pointing to Snehal, Mahesh said, "Her mother's only daughter is my daughter". How is Mahesh related to Snehal?

A. Brother B. Uncle
C. Son D. Father

35. Is 'C' mother of 'D'? To find out the answer which of the following informations given in the statements 'A' and 'B' is/are sufficient?

(A) B has two children of which D is one.
(B) D's sister is daughter of C.

A. Both A and B together are needed
B. Both A and B together are not sufficient
C. Only A is sufficient
D. Only B is sufficient

36. A is B's brother. A is C's brother. To find out how B is related to C, which of the following is the minimum further information necessary, is any?

I. C's sex II. B's sex

A. Only I is necessary
B. Only II is necessary
C. Either I or II is necessary
D. Both I and II are needed

37. Is D brother of F? To find out the answer which of the following informations given in the statements A and B is/are sufficient?

(A) B has two sons of which F is one.

(B) D's mother is married to B.

A. Both A and B together are needed
B. Both A and B together are not sufficient
C. Only A is sufficient
D. Only B is sufficient

38. Neera is daughter of Mahender. Mala, Achla's sister has a son Mohan and daughter Sushila. Kamla is maternal aunt of Sushila and mother of Krishna. Mohan is cousin of Krishna. Krishna is brother of Neera. How is Achla related to Mahender?

A. Cousin
B. Sister-in-law
C. Niece
D. Daughter

39. B is maternal uncle of A. C is maternal grandfather of B. D is grandson of C. How is D related to A?

A. Maternal uncle
B. Cousin brother
C. Nephew
D. Maternal grandfather

40. Introducing a man, a woman said, "His wife is the only daughter of my father". How is the man related to the woman?

A. Husband
B. Father
C. Father-in-law
D. Brother

41. B's mother is the only daughter of A's mother. How is A related to B?

A. Niece B. Brother
C. Father D. Uncle

42. Introducing a man to her husband, a woman said, "His brother's father is the only son of my grandfather." How is the woman related to the man?

A. Aunt B. Mother
C. Daughter D. Sister

43. A said to B that B's mother was the mother-in-law of A's mother. How is A's mother related to B's mother?

A. Mother
B. Daughter-in-law
C. Daughter
D. Cousin

44. If A is the mother of B and C, and D is the husband of C, then what is A to D?

A. Aunt
B. Mother-in-law
C. Sister-in-law
D. Sister

45. Introducing a man, a woman said, "His mother is the only daughter of my father." How is the man related to the woman?

A. Father B. Uncle
C. Husband D. Son

46. If Maya is the only daughter of Richa's grandmother's brother, how is Maya's daughter related to Richa?

A. Niece
B. Cousin
C. Aunt
D. Mother

47. Pointing to a woman, a man said, "Her husband's mother is the wife of my father's only son". How is the man related to the woman?

A. Son
B. Brother-in-law
C. Uncle
D. Father-in-law

48. Bela is the mother of Chinu and Miki. If Kavind is the husband of Miki, what is Bela to Kavind?

A. Daughter
B. Sister
C. Mother
D. Mother-in-law

49. Pointing to a woman, a man says, "Her mother is the only daughter of my mother-in-law". How is the woman related to the man?

A. Sister
B. Daughter
C. Aunt
D. Data is insufficient

50. Introducing a lady, a man said that her mother's husband's sister is his mother. What is the man's relationship with the lady?
A. Cousin
B. Nephew
C. Father
D. Data insufficient

ANSWERS

1	2	3	4	5	6	7	8	9	10
A	A	C	B	B	D	D	B	C	A
11	**12**	**13**	**14**	**15**	**16**	**17**	**18**	**19**	**20**
B	B	C	D	D	C	D	D	B	B
21	**22**	**23**	**24**	**25**	**26**	**27**	**28**	**29**	**30**
D	C	D	D	C	C	D	D	A	D
31	**32**	**33**	**34**	**35**	**36**	**37**	**38**	**39**	**40**
D	C	D	D	B	D	A	B	A	A
41	**42**	**43**	**44**	**45**	**46**	**47**	**48**	**49**	**50**
D	D	B	B	D	B	D	D	B	A

EXPLANATORY ANSWERS

1.

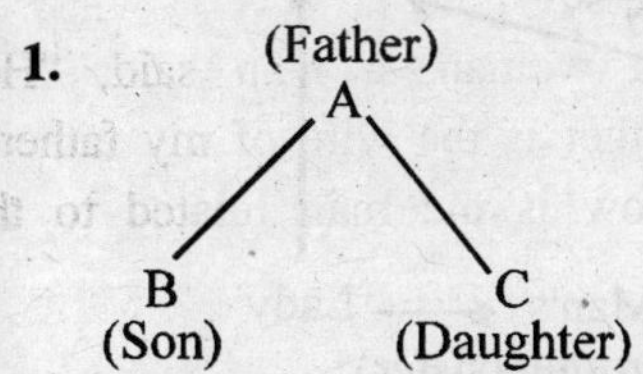

'C' is not the son of 'A', but 'A' is the father of 'C'. So, 'C' is the daughter of 'A'.

2.

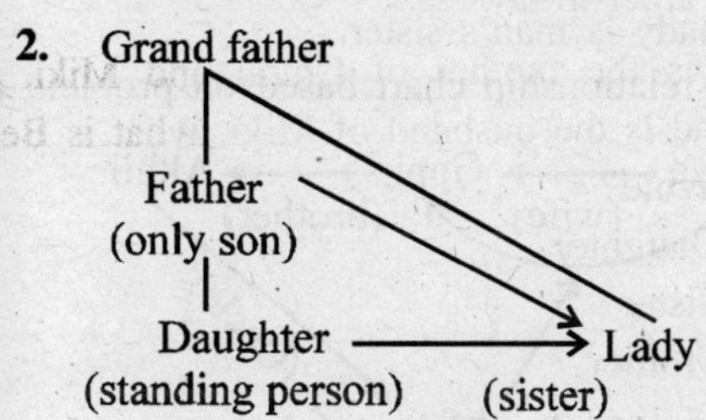

Lady's grandfather's son is lady's father and father's daughter will only be lady's sister.

3.

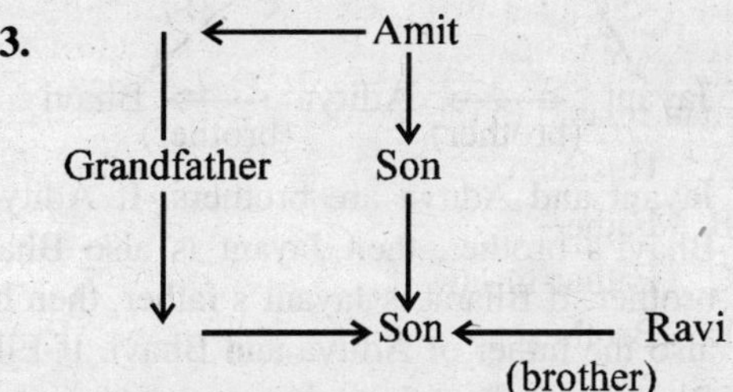

Amit's son's son is Amit's grandson. Ravi is the brother of Amit's son's son. So, Amit is also the grandfather of Ravi.

4.

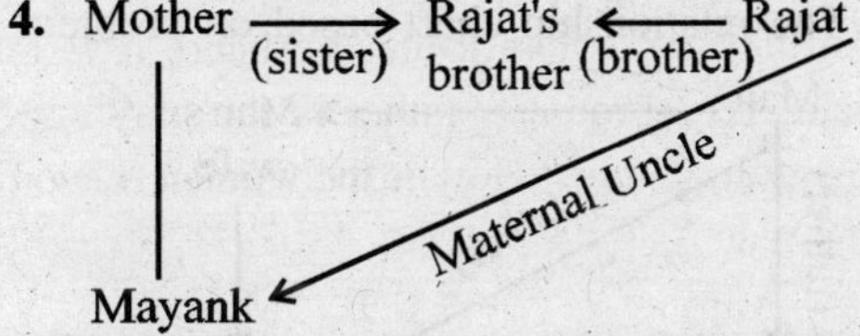

Mayank's mother is the sister of Rajat's brother. So Rajat is also the brother of

Mayank's mother. Relation of the brother with his sister's child is maternal. So Rajat is Mayank's maternal uncle.

5. The relation is : Mother
↑ (Son)
Raghav
↓ (Father)
Lily (Daughter)

'My mother's only son' means Raghav himself. 'Her father' means Lily's father; *i.e.* Raghav and so, Lily is Raghav's daughter.

6. 1. Mili ——→ Ajay ——→ Vijay ↓ Mehul (daughter)
(sister) (brother)

2. Sanjay ——→ Rahul
(brother)

There are two sets of relationship. Information given is incomplete and no relation can be established between the two sets.

7. The relationship chart based on problem is

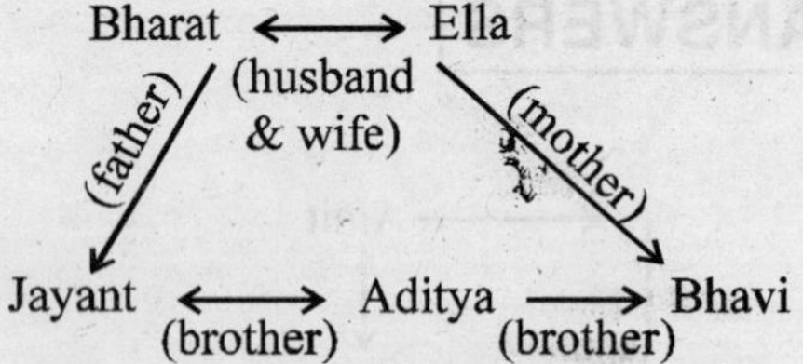

Jayant and Aditya are brothers. If Aditya is Bhavi's brother, then Jayant is also Bhavi's brother. If Bharat is Jayant's father, then he is also the father of Aditya and Bhavi. If Ella is Bhavi's mother, then she is also the mother of Aditya and Jayant. This means Bharat and Ella are husband and wife and the parents of three.

8. The relationship chart based on problem is :

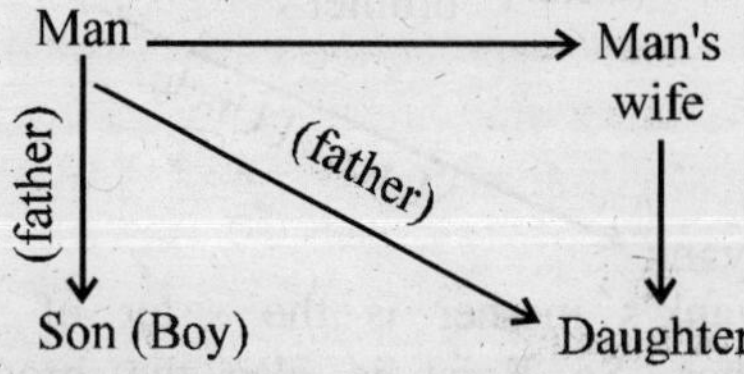

'Father of the man's wife's daughter' is the man himself and the boy in question is the man's son.

9. The relationship chart based on the problem is :

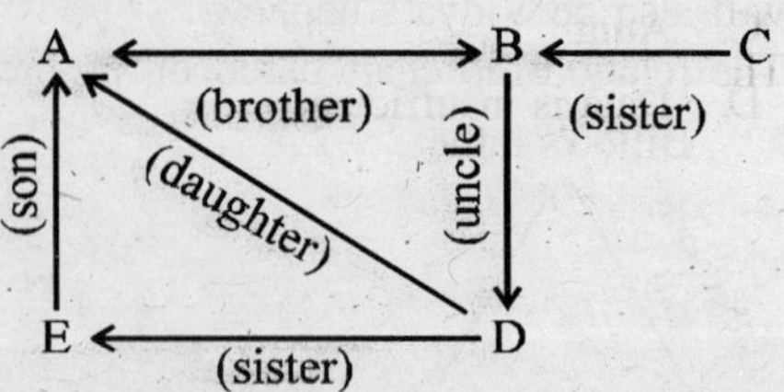

When D is sister of E, who is son of A the D is daughter of A. Brother of A is B and so B is D's uncle.

10.

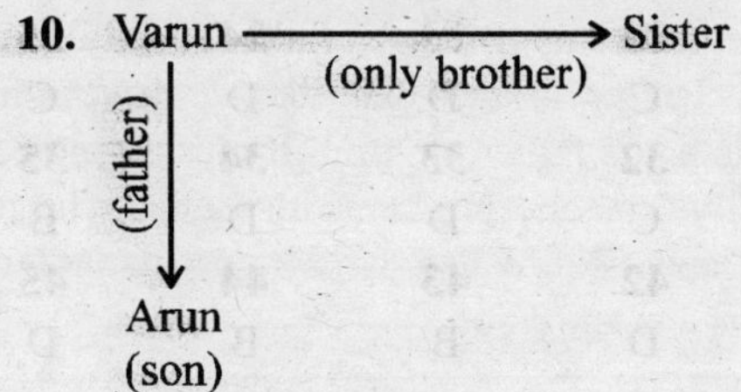

Varun's sister's only brother is Varun himse and Arun is his son.

11.

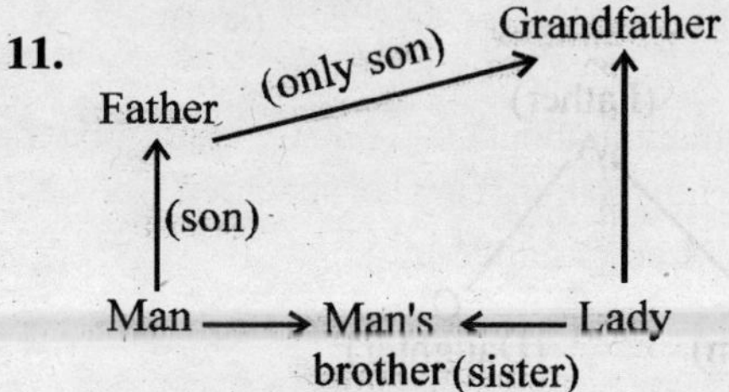

Man's brother's father is also the lady's fath as he is the only son of lady's grandfather. S the lady is man's sister.

12. The relationship chart based on problem i

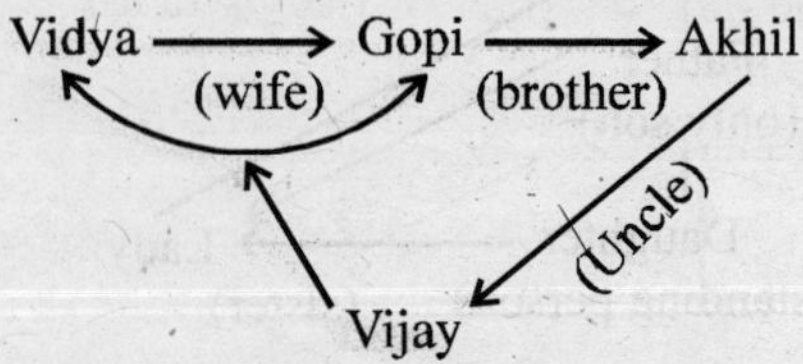

Vidya is wife of Gopi who is brother of Ak So, Vidya is sister-in-law of Akhil. If Akhi uncle of Vijay then Gopi will naturally be uncle of Vijay as it is not specified that a of the mentioned persons are Vijay's parents. Now, when Vijay is Gopi's nephew then he will also be Vidya's nephew.

13. The relationship chart based on problem is :

Billoo's father

(father's only son)

Amit's father/Billoo

↑

Amit

Amit's father is Billoo's father's only son means Billoo is the only son in question also, he is the father of Amit. It must be noted that Billoo has no brother which means he is single and also, when he has no daughter, Amit is his only son.

14.

D → E (daughter) —(sister)→ A —(sister)→ B (son) ← C

Information about 'D' and 'C' is not given as such no relation can be specified.

15. Lady's father

↑

Fagu's Mother (the only daughter) /Lady

↑

Fagu

The only daughter of Lady's father is Fagu's mother.

16. Grandmother ← (only son) Man

↑

Mother —(sister)→ Man

↑

Woman ← (niece) Man

The man is the brother of the woman's mother. So, the woman is man's niece.

17. A's mother

(daughter) B's mother → A's mother → A

B's mother → B

Sex of 'A' is not known. Either option A or B is correct.

18. Man's Grandmother

↓

Grandmother's only son

A

↓

Man (sister) Daughter

'My grandmother's only son' is the father of the man, and 'daughter of my grand-mother's only son' is the sister of the man.

19.

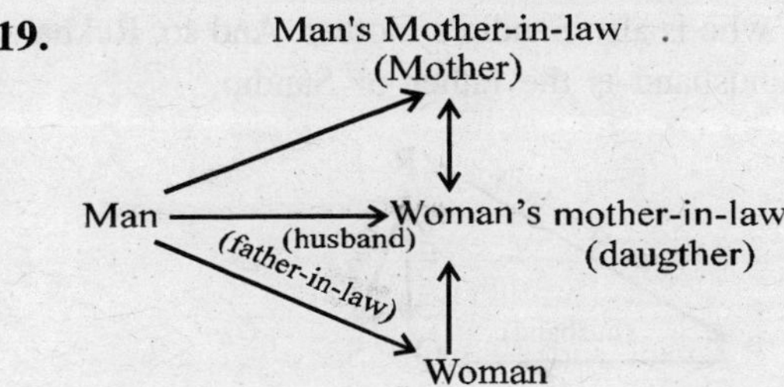

Woman's mother-in-law is the daughter of Man's mother-in-law. So, the man is the husband of woman's mother-in-law and the father-in-law of the woman.

20. Amit (only brother) ⟷ Amit's Sister

↓

Son (Suman)

'My sister's only brother's is Amit himself and 'Sister's only brother's son' is the son of Amit *i.e.,* Suman is the son of Amit.

21. My father ← Father's sister (only daughter)

Myself ↗ My father

Nothing can be determined from this information.

22.

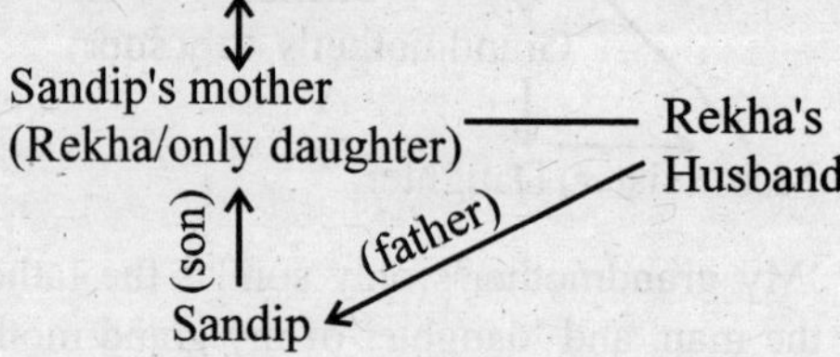

'Only daughter of my mother's father' is the person in the photograph and she is also the mother of the woman. So, the woman is the daughter of the person in the photograph.

23.

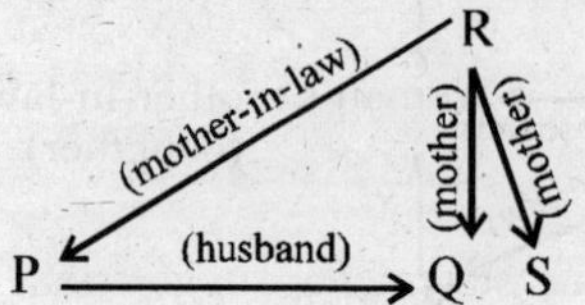

'Only daughter of Rekha's father's is Rekha who is also Sandip's mother. And so, Rekha's husband is the father of Sandip.

24.

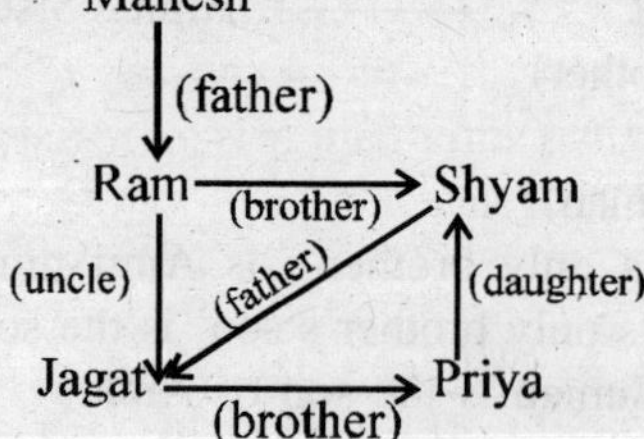

P is the husband of Q and R is the mother of Q. So, Q is the daughter of R and R is the mother-in-law of daughter's husband P.

25.

Jagat is brother of Priya and Priya is daughter of Shyam. So Shyam is also the father of Jagat. Ram is the brother of Shyam. So, Jagat's father's brother Ram is the uncle of Jagat.

26.

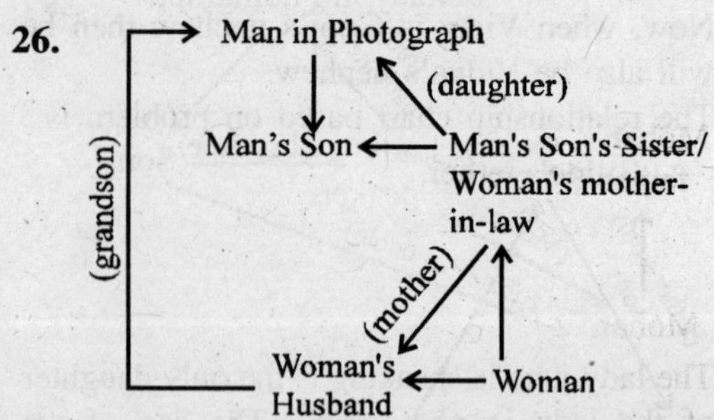

'Man's son's sister' is the daughter of the man and is also the mother-in-law of the woman. Woman's husband will be the son of the woman's mother-in-law. As the woman's mother-in-law is the daughter of the man in photograph, woman's husband will be the grandson of the man in photograph.

27.

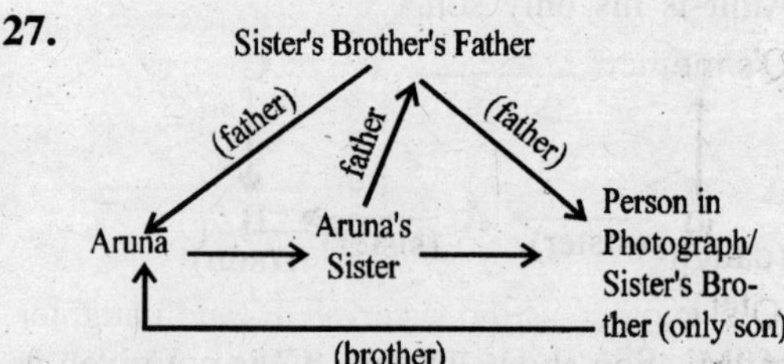

'The only son of the father of my sister's brother' is the brother himself. Aruna's sister's brother is also the brother of Aruna.

28.

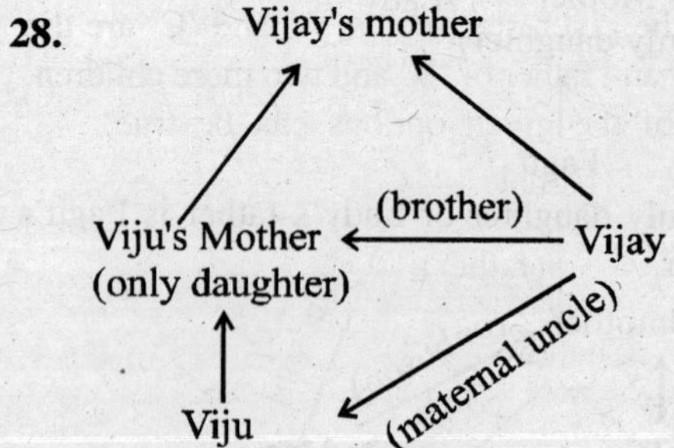

Only daughter of my mother *i.e.* Viju's mother is the sister of Vijay. And so, Vijay who is the brother of Viju's mother is Viju's maternal uncle.

29. Lady in Photograph

(only daughter) — Son

Mohan's father ← (wife) Lady Speaker ← (brother) Son

(Mother) (maternal uncle)

Mohan

The lady who is speaking is the only daughter of the lady in photograph. The son of the lady in photograph is the brother of lady who is speaking. If the brother of the lady speaker is the maternal uncle of Mohan, then the lady speaker is the mother of Mohan, and so she is also the wife of Mohan's father.

30. M

(daughter) (child of)

Q's mother → (sister) P ← (child of)

Q (daughter) S → T (sister)

'Q's' mother is the sister of 'P' and daughter of 'M'. So, 'P' is also the child of 'M'. 'S' is the daughter of 'P' and sister of 'T'. So 'T' is also the child of 'P'; who is the child of 'M'. As the sex of the members is not given 'M' can be either the grandfather or the grandmother of 'T'.

31. From the given statements 'A' and 'C' are the mother and father of 'B' and two more children. None of the given options can be true.

32.

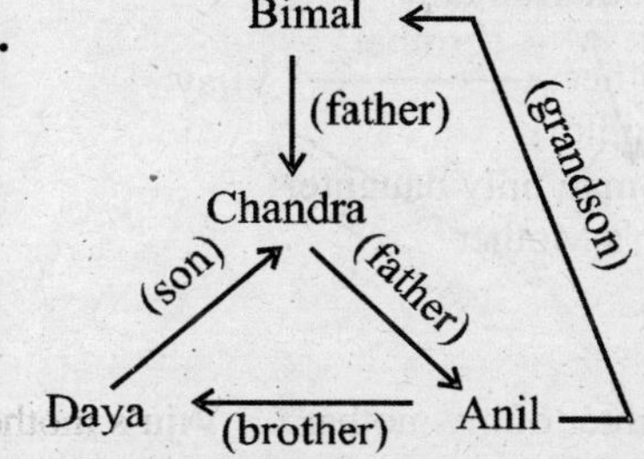

Daya is the son of Chandra. So, Daya's father Chandra is also the father of Daya's brother Anil. Bimal is the father of Chandra. So, Anil who is the son of Chandra is the grandson of Biman.

33. A → B ← C

(brother) (sister)

As the sex of 'B' is not known, 'B's' relationship with 'A' cannot be determined.

34

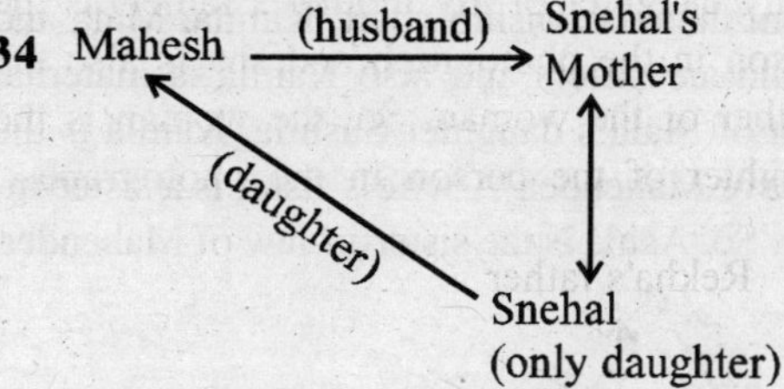

'Her (Snehal's) mother's only daughter' is Snehal herself. So Snehal is the daughter of Mahesh who in turn is her father.

35.

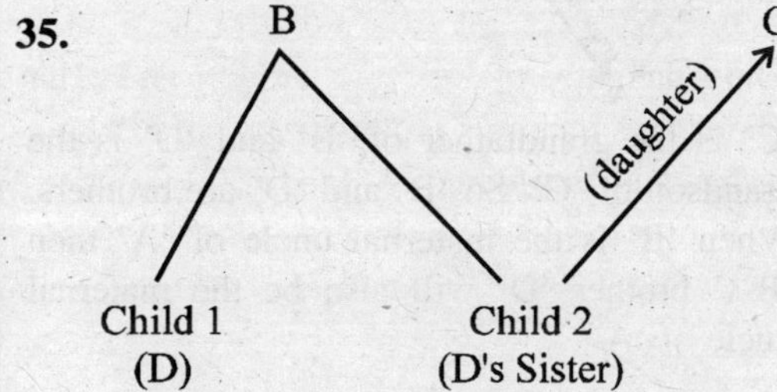

Though both the statements suggest that 'B' and 'C' are the parents of the two children; it cannot be said for certain that 'C' is the mother of 'D' as the sex of 'B' and 'C' is not given.

36.

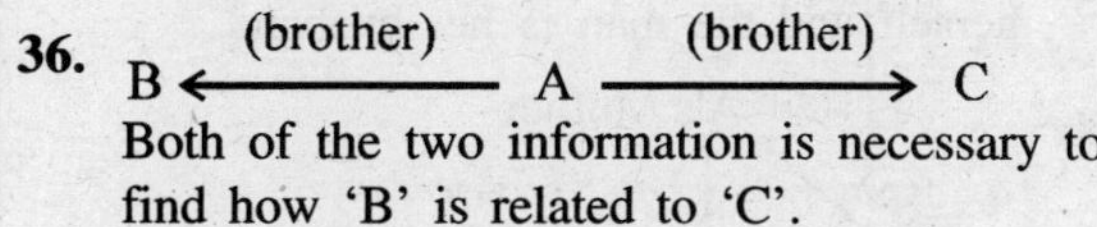

Both of the two information is necessary to find how 'B' is related to 'C'.

37.

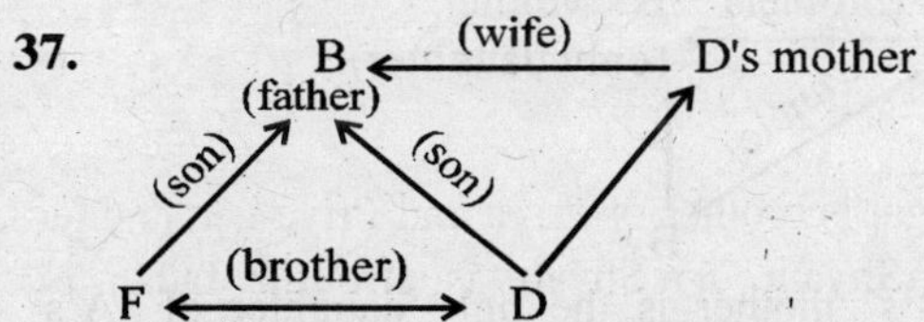

Both the statements are needed to know that 'D' is the brother of 'F'.

38.

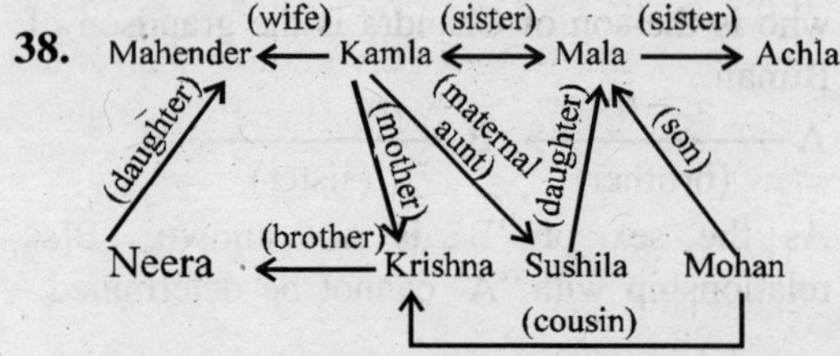

From the relationship chart, Kamla, Mala and Achla are sisters and also Kamla is maternal aunt of Mala's daughter Sushila. Kamla is the wife of Mahender. A wife's sister is a sister-in-law. So, Achla is the sister-in-law of Mahender.

39.

C
(maternal grandfather)
(grandson)
B (brothers) D
(maternal uncle)
(maternal uncle)
A

'C' is the grandfather of 'B' and 'D' is the grandson of 'C'. So 'B' and 'D' are brothers. When 'B' is the maternal uncle of 'A' then 'B's' brother 'D' will also be the maternal uncle of 'A'.

40.

Woman's Father
(husband)
Man → Man's wife (only daughter)

'Only daughter of my father' is the woman herself and the man is her husband.

41.

A's Mother
(son)
(brother)
A → B's Mother (only daughter)
(uncle)
B

'B's' mother is the only daughter of 'A's' mother. So 'A' is the son. As 'A' is also the brother of 'B's' mother, he is the uncle of 'B'.

42.

Woman's Grandfather
Man's Brother's Father (only son)
(father)
(father)
Woman (sister) → Man → Man's Brother

'Only son of my grandfather' is the father of the woman. 'His brother's father' is also the father of the man. So, the woman is the sister of the man.

43.

B's Mother/Mother-in-Law of A's mother
(daughter-in-law)
B
A's Mother
A

'B's' mother is the mother-in-law of 'A's' mother. So, 'A's' mother is the daughter-in-law of 'B's' mother.

44.

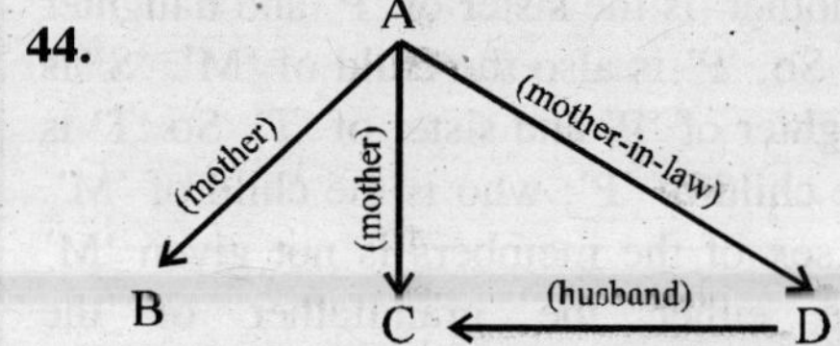

'A' is the mother of 'C' and 'D' is the husband of 'C'. So, 'A' is the mother-in-law of 'C's' husband 'D'.

45. E. :

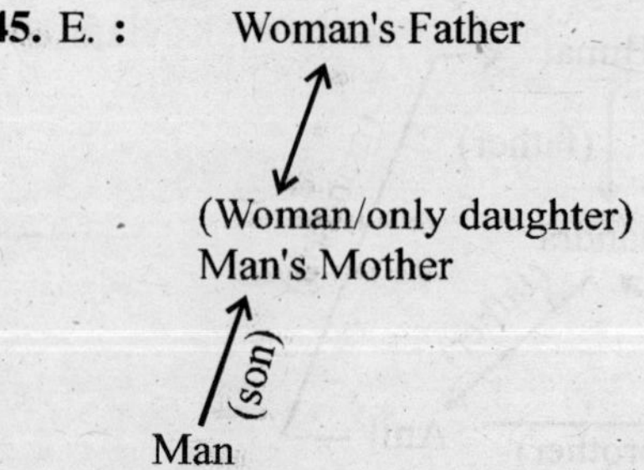

'Only daughter of my father' is the woman herself and 'His mother' means the man's mother. So, the man is the son of the woman.

46.

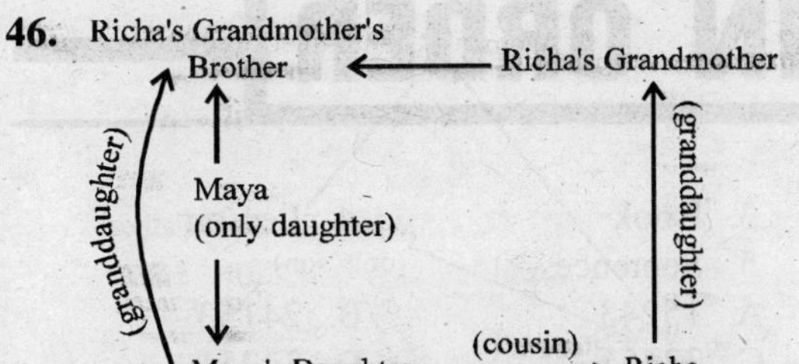

Both Maya's Daughter and Richa are granddaughters of a brother and a sister respectively. So Maya's daughter is the cousin of Richa.

47. Man's Father

Woman's Husband's Mother (wife) Man (only son)

(father) (father-in-law)

Woman's Husband (wife) Woman

'My father's only son' is the man himself. 'Her husband's mother' is the wife of the man and so the man is the father of the woman's husband. As the woman is the wife of man's son, the man is the father-in-law of the woman.

48. The relationship chart based on the problem is :

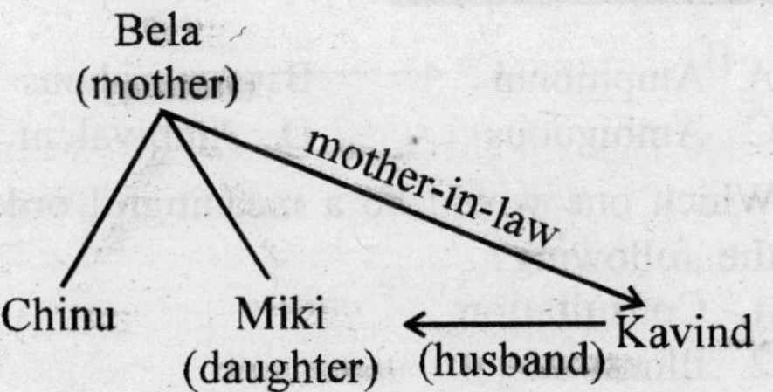

Bela is mother of Miki. Kavind is Miki's husband. So, Bela is Kavind's mother-in-law as wife's mother is the husband's mother-in-law.

49. The relationship chart based on the given statements is :

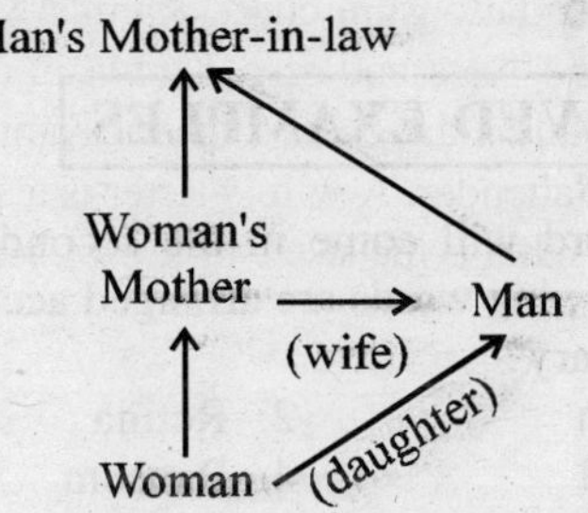

The woman, who is pointed out is the man's daughter and the man's mother-in-law's only daughter is man's wife.

50. The relationship chart based on problem is :

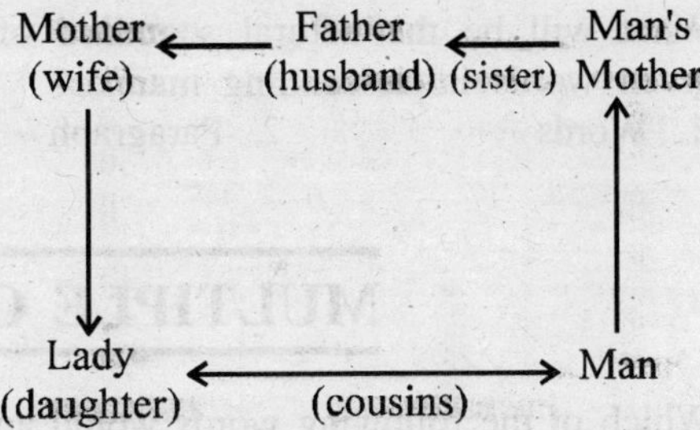

As the children of brother and sister are cousins, so are the man and the lady. Lady is the daughter of brother of man's mother and man is the son of brother's sister.

ARRANGING IN ORDER

In these type of questions arrangement of given options is done on the basis of dictionary, size, rank, weight, natural sequence etc in ascending or descending order.

SOLVED EXAMPLES

1. Which word will come in the second place if the following words are arranged according to dictionary?

1. Reason 2. Retina
3. Regard 4. Ransom
5. Ration

A. Retina B. Ration
C. Regard D. Ransom

Ans. B : The order of words according to dictionary is Ransom, Ration, Reason, Regard, Retina.

2. What will be the natural sequence of the given words in descending manner?

1. Words 2. Paragraph
3. Book 4. Lesson
5. Sentence

A. 15243 B. 24153
C. 32451 D. 34251

Ans. D : A book contains many lessons, a lesson contains many paragraphs, a paragraph contains many sentences and a sentence contains many words.

(**Note** : Option *A.* is in ascending manner.)

3. What word will come in the middle if the following words one arranged in ascending order of weight?

1. Paperweight 2. Pencil
3. Chair 4. Knife
5. Pin

A. Pin B. Knife
C. Pencil D. Paperweight

Ans. B : According to ascending order of weight the arrangement will be - Pin, Pencil, Knife, Paperweight, Chair.

MULTIPLE CHOICE QUESTIONS

1. Which of the following words would appear in the third if they are arranged as in the dictionary order?

A. Delude B. Delirium
C. Defer D. Delete

2. Which one would be a meaningful order of the following?

1. Key 2. Door
3. Lock 4. Room
5. Switch on

A. 5 1 2 4 3 B. 4 2 1 5 3
C. 1 3 2 4 5 D. 1 2 3 5 4

3. If the following words are rearranged in the alphabetical order as in a dictionary, which will be the third word?

A. Amphibian B. Amorphous
C. Ambiguous D. Ambivalent

4. Which one would be a meaningful order of the following?

1. Consultation
2. Illness
3. Doctor
4. Treatment
5. Recovery

A. 4 3 1 2 5 B. 2 3 4 1 5
C. 5 1 4 3 2 D. 2 3 1 4 5

5. In a telephone directory, which of the following names will appear in the third?

A. Randhir B. Randesh
C. Rama D. Ramesh

6. What would be a meaningful order of the following?

1. Andhra Pradesh 2. Universe
3. Tirupathi 4. World
5. India

A. 1 5 3 2 4 B. 4 1 5 3 2
C. 5 4 2 1 3 D. 3 1 5 4 2

7. Which one would be a meaningful order of the following?

1. Mother 2. Child
3. Milk 4. Cry
5. Smile

A. 3 2 1 5 4 B. 2 4 1 3 5
C. 1 5 2 4 3 D. 2 4 3 1 5

8. Which would be the proper order of the following?

1. Rainbow 2. Rain
3. Sun 4. Happy
5. Child

A. 4 2 3 5 1 B. 4 5 1 2 3
C. 2 1 4 3 5 D. 2 3 1 5 4

9. Which one will be a meaningful order of the following :

1. Birth 2. Death
3. Funeral 4. Marriage
5. Education

A. 1 3 4 5 1 B. 4 5 3 1 2
C. 1 5 4 2 3 D. 2 3 4 5 1

10. In a telephone directory which of the following names will appear in the second?

A. Sajewet B. Sajewat
C. Segvan D. Salwar

11. Which would be the proper order of the following? (in ascending order)

1. Trillion 2. Thousand
3. Billion 4. Hundred
5. Million

A. 4 2 5 3 1 B. 1 5 3 2 4
C. 4 2 3 5 1 D. 1 2 3 4 5

12. What would be the meaningful order of the following?

1. Table 2. Tree
3. Wood 4. Seed
5. Plant

A. 1 3 2 4 5 B. 4 5 3 2 1
C. 4 5 2 3 1 D. 1 2 3 4 5

13. Which one would be a meaningful order of the following?

1. Snake 2. Grass
3. Eagle 4. Frog
5. Insect

A. 3 2 1 4 5 B. 5 2 1 4 3
C. 2 5 4 1 3 D. 2 4 5 3 1

14. Which one would be a meaningful order of the following?

1. Windows 2. Walls
3. Floor 4. Foundation
5. Roof 6. Room

A. 4 2 1 5 3 6 B. 4 3 5 6 2 1
C. 4 5 3 2 1 6 D. 4 1 5 6 2 3

15. Which would be a meaningful order of the following?

1. Index 2. Contents
3. Title 4. Chapters
5. Introduction

A. 2 3 4 5 1 B. 3 2 5 4 1
C. 5 1 4 2 3 D. 3 2 5 1 4

16. If the following words are arranged in their natural sequence in descending order, which word will occur in the second place?

1. Book 2. Paragraph
3. Library 4. Alphabet
5. Page

A. Page B. Paragraph
C. Book D. Library

17. What would be the proper order of the following :

1. Decameter 2. Meter
3. Kilometer 4. Centimeter
5. Milimeter

A. 1 4 3 2 5 B. 5 4 1 2 3
C. 5 4 3 2 1 D. 5 4 2 1 3

18. If the following words are arranged in natural order then what will come in the second place?

1. Producer 2. Raw material
3. Seller 4. Consumer
5. Distributor

A. Producer B. Seller
C. Consumer D. Distributor

19. If the words are arranged in ascending order which word will occur in the fourth place?
1. Youth 2. Infant
3. Adult 4. Childhood
5. Teenager
A. Teenager B. Childhood
C. Adult D. Youth

20. If the following words are arranged according to dictionary, what will be the correct order?
1. Martial 2. Marital
3. Matrimony 4. Material
5. Matriarch
A. 2 1 4 5 3 B. 2 4 5 1 3
C. 3 4 1 5 2 D. 2 1 5 3 4

21. What would be the proper order of the following words in descending order?
1. Gram 2. Decigram
3. Hectagram 4. Kilogram
5. Centigram
A. 4 3 1 2 5 B. 4 2 3 1 5
C. 5 2 1 4 3 D. 4 3 2 1 5

22. What will be the middle word in natural order of the words given?
1. Medication 2. Patient
3. Diagnosis 4. Recuperation
5. Doctor
A. Doctor B. Patient
C. Medication D. Diagnosis

23. Which would be the proper order of the following?
1. Country 2. Furniture
3. Forest 4. Wood
5. Trees
A. 4 3 2 1 5 B. 2 4 1 5 3
C. 1 3 5 4 2 D. 1 2 3 4 5

24. If the following words are arranged in natural order, what will come in the last place in ascending order?
1. Captain
2. Brigadier
3. Major
4. Lieutenant-General
5. Lieutenant
A. Lientenant-General B. Brigadier
C. Captain D. Major

25. What will be the natural order of the following words according to speed?
1. Jet 2. Bus
3. Cycle 4. Aeroplane
5. Train
A. 3 5 2 4 1 B. 3 2 5 1 4
C. 3 2 5 4 1 D. 3 2 1 4 5

26. If these words are arranged according to dictionary then what word will come in the third place?
1. Originality 2. Originally
3. Originator 4. Original
5. Originate
A. Originality B. Originator
C. Originate D. Originally

27. Which word will come in the third place in the natural sequence of the following words in descending order?
1. Town 2. Country
3. Family 4. Neighbourhood
5. State
A. Town B. Country
C. State D. Neighbourhood

28. What will be the natural order of the following words?
1. Digest 2. Cut
3. Chew 4. Purchase
5. Cook
A. 4 5 2 3 1 B. 4 2 5 1 3
C. 4 5 3 1 2 D. 4 2 5 3 1

29. If the following words are arranged according to dictionary what will come in the last?
1. Institutist 2. Institutional
3. Institute 4. Institutor
5. Institutionalism
A. Institutist B. Institutor
C. Institutionalism D. Institutional

30. What will be the natural order of the following?
1. Independence Day
2. Christmas
3. Diwali
4. Holi
5. Republic Day
A. 5 4 1 3 2 B. 5 1 4 3 2
C. 4 1 5 3 2 D. 2 3 4 1 5

31. What will be the natural order of the following words according to weight?

1. Drum 2. Pin
3. Paper weight 4. Pebble
5. Coffee cup

A. 4 2 3 5 1 B. 2 4 5 3 1
C. 4 2 5 1 3 D. 2 4 3 5 1

32. What word will come in the third place if these words are arranged in descending order?

1. Judge 2. Listen
3. Act 4. Analyse
5. Observe

A. Listen B. Observe
C. Act D. Analyse

33. If the following words are arranged in ascending order what word will be in the fourth place?

1. Air commodore
2. Wing Commander
3. Pilot Officer
4. Squadron Leader
5. Air Marshal

A. Air Marshal B. Air Commodore
C. Wing Commander D. Pilot Officer

34. If the following words are arranged in natural sequence in descending order, what will come in the second place from the last?

1. Teacher 2. Lecturer
3. Dean 4. Tutor
5. Reader

A. Dean B. Lecturer
C. Tutor D. Teacher

35. If the words are arranged according to dictionary, what will come in the second place from the last?

1. Spastically 2. Spasmatic
3. Spasticity 4. Spastic
5. Spasmodical

A. Spastic B. Spasmodical
C. Spastically D. Spasmatic

36. What will be the natural order of the following words according to size?

1. Dog 2. Horse
3. Ant 4. Giraffe
5. Mouse

A. 3 5 1 2 4 B. 3 1 5 2 4
C. 3 5 1 4 2 D. 3 5 2 1 4

37. What will be the natural order of the following in descending order?

1. Hut 2. Skyscraper
3. Palace 4. Room
5. House

A. 2 3 1 5 4 B. 4 1 5 3 2
C. 2 3 5 1 4 D. 3 2 5 4 1

38. Which would be the proper order of the following?

1. Euphoria 2. Happiness
3. Ambivalence 4. Ecstasy
5. Pleasure

A. 3 4 1 2 5 B. 3 2 5 4 1
C. 5 4 1 3 2 D. 3 5 2 1 4

39. What will be the proper order of the words according to dictionary?

1. Rural 2. Rugby
3. Rugged 4. Rummage
5. Ruffle

A. 5 3 2 4 1 B. 5 2 3 1 4
C. 5 2 4 3 1 D. 5 2 3 4 1

40. Which name will come in the middle if these names are arranged in a telephone directory?

1. Priyanka 2. Priyana
3. Priti 4. Pratima
5. Protima

A. Priti B. Pratima
C. Protima D. Priyana

41. Arrange the following in a meaningful sequence :

1. Senescence 2. Infancy
3. Puberty 4. Going adulthood
5. Babyhood

A. 5 3 2 4 1 B. 1 3 4 2 5
C. 2 3 4 5 1 D. 2 5 3 4 1

42. Arrange the following words in the sequence in which they occur in dictionary :

Liver	Long	Late	Load	Luminous	Letter
1	2	3	4	5	6

A. 3 6 1 4 2 5 B. 3 6 1 2 4 5
C. 3 1 6 2 4 5 D. 3 1 6 2 5 4

43. Which number-sequence of the following represents a correct sequence from small to big?

1. Bungalow 2. Flat

3. Cottage 4. House
5. Palace 6. Mansion
A. 3 2 1 4 6 5 B. 3 2 4 1 6 5
C. 3 2 4 1 5 6 D. 5 6 4 1 2 3

44. Arrange the following words in a meaningful order :
1. Gold 2. Iron
3. Sand 4. Platinum
5. Diamond
A. 3 2 1 5 4 B. 2 4 3 5 1
C. 5 4 3 2 1 D. 4 5 1 3 2

45. Arrange the following words in a meaningful order :
1. Site 2. Plan
3. Rent 4. Money
5. Building
A. 2 3 5 1 4 B. 4 1 2 5 3
C. 1 2 3 5 4 D. 3 4 2 5 1

46. Which one would be a meaningful order of the following?
1. Probation 2. Interview
3. Selection 4. Appointment
5. Advertisement 6. Application
A. 5 6 4 2 3 1 B. 5 6 3 2 4 1
C. 5 6 2 3 4 1 D. 6 5 4 2 3 1

47. What would be a meaningful order of the following?
1. Caste
2. Family
3. Newly-married couple
4. Clan
5. Species
A. 3 4 5 1 2 B. 5 2 1 4 3
C. 2 3 1 4 5 D. 4 5 3 2 1

48. Which one would be a meaningful order of the following?
1. College 2. Child
3. Salary 4. School
5. Employment
A. 1 2 4 3 5 B. 4 1 3 5 2
C. 2 4 1 5 3 D. 5 3 2 1 4

49. What will be the dictionary order of these words?
Bungling, 1 Burgling, 2 Bubble, 3
Bundle, 4 Bushy, 5 Bully 6
A. 2 4 5 6 1 3 B. 5 6 1 4 3 2
C. 1 4 6 5 2 3 D. 3 6 4 1 2 5

50. Which word would be in the second place if the following are arranged in a natural sequence?
1. Noon 2. Night
3. Evening 4. Dusk
5. Dawn
A. Night B. Noon
C. Dusk D. Evening

ANSWERS

1	2	3	4	5	6	7	8	9	10
B	C	B	D	B	D	B	D	C	A
11	**12**	**13**	**14**	**15**	**16**	**17**	**18**	**19**	**20**
A	C	C	A	B	C	D	A	D	A
21	**22**	**23**	**24**	**25**	**26**	**27**	**28**	**29**	**30**
A	D	C	A	C	D	A	D	B	A
31	**32**	**33**	**34**	**35**	**36**	**37**	**38**	**39**	**40**
B	D	B	D	C	A	C	D	D	D
41	**42**	**43**	**44**	**45**	**46**	**47**	**48**	**49**	**50**
D	A	B	A	B	C	B	C	D	D

EXPLANATORY ANSWERS

1. The dictionary order of word is — Defer, Delete, **Delirium,** Delude.
2. With the Key you open a Lock, then open the Door to enter the Room and Switch on the light.
3. The dictionary order of the words is — Ambiguous, Ambivalent, **Amorphous,** Amphibian.
4. An Ill person goes to a Doctor for Consultation who prescribes Treatment for Recovery.
5. In telephone directory the order of names is — Raamesh, Rana, **Randesh,** Randhir.
6. Tirupathi is in Andhra Pradesh which is a state in India and India is a part of the World which is in Universe.
7. When a Child Cries the Mother gives him Milk and then he Smiles.
8. When it rains in the Sun a Rainbow is formed and the Child is Happy to see it.
9. After the Birth of a child, his Education is important. When he is grown up he is Married. When he is old he Dies and is taken for the Funeral.
10. In telephone directory the order of names is—Sajewat, **Sajewet**, Salwar, Segvan.
11. The words are arranged in order of increasing amount.
12. From a Seed a Plant is grown into a Tree whose Wood is used to make a Table.
13. In the Grass there are many Insects. Frog who eats them is a prey of Snake who in turn is the prey of an Eagle.
14. The order of words depict the right order of constructing a building/room.
15. A Title comprises Contents of Introduction for Chapter Index.
16. The words in descending order of natural sequence are—Library, **Book,** Page, Paragraph, Alphabet. Library is a collection of Books, a Book is a collection of many Pages, in a Page there are many Paragraphs which contain a lot of Alphabet.
17. The proper order of measurement in increasing order is—Milimeter, Centimeter, Meter, Decameter, Kilometer.
18. The natural order of words is—Raw material, **Producer,** Distributor, Seller, Consumer. Raw material is used by the Producer to make a product which its Distributor gives to the Seller from whom the Consumer can purchase it.
19. The words in ascending order depict the natural growth of a human being — Infant, Childhood, Teenager, **Youth,** Adult.
20. The dictionary order of words is — Marital, Martial, Material, Matriarch, Matrimony.
21. The arrangement of weights in descending order is — Kilogram, Hectagram, Gram, Decigram, Centagram.
22. The words in natural order are — Patient, Doctor, **Diagnosis,** Medication, Recupera-tion. A Patient goes to the Doctor who gives the Diagnosis and Prescribes the Medication for Recuperation.
23. The proper order of the words is—Country, Forest, Trees, Wood, Furniture. In a Country there are Forests comprising Trees the Wood of which are used to make Furniture.
24. The arrangement of ranks in ascending order is—Lieutenant, Captain, Major, Brigadier, **Lieutenant-General.**
25. The natural order of modes of transport according to increasing speed is — Cycle, Bus, Train, Aeroplane, Jet.
26. The dictionary order of words is — Original, Originality, **Originally,** Originate, Originator.
27. The words in natural sequence of descending order are — Country, State, **Town,** Neighbour-hood, Family.

In a country there are many States which comprises of many Towns wherein in the Neighbourhood live Families.

28. The natural order of the words is — Purchase, Cut, Cook, Chew, Digest. After Purchasing vegetables we Cut them, then Cook them and while eating Chew them and Digest them in our stomach.

29. The dictionary order of words is — Institute, Institutional, Institutionalism, Institutist, **Institutor**.

30. The natural order of National Holidays in Calendar is — Republic Day (January), Holi (March), Independence Day (August), Diwali (October/November), Christmas (December).

31. The arrangement of words according to weight in ascending order is — Pin, Pebble, Coffee Cup, Paper Weight, Drum.

32. The arrangement of words in descending order is — Act, Judge, **Analyse,** Observe, Listen *Or* Act, Judge, **Analyse,** Listen, Observe.

33. The arrangement of ranks in ascending order is — Pilot Officer, Squadron Leader, Wing Commander, **Air Commodore,** Air Marshal.

34. The arrangement of educational posts in descending order is — Dean, Reader, Lecturer, **Teacher,** Tutor.

35. The dictionary order of words is — Spasmatic, Spasmodical, Spastic, **Spastically,** Spasticity.

36. The natural order of living beings according to increasing size is — Ant, Mouse, Dog, Horse, Giraffe.

37. The words in descending order are — Sky-scraper, Palace, House, Hut, Room.

38. The order of expressions of feeling of joy is — Ambivalence, Happiness, Pleasure, Euphoria, Ecstacy.

39. The dictionary order of words is — Ruffle, Rugby, Rugged, Rummage, Rural.

40. Order of names in telephone directory is — Pratima, Priti, **Priyana**, Priyanka, Protima.

41. The meaningful sequence of the words is— Infancy, Babyhood, Puberty, Going Adulthood, Senescence.

42. The dictionary order of words is — Late, Letter, Liver, Load, Long, Luminous.

43. The sequence of letters from small to big is — Cottage, Flat, House, Bungalow, Mansion, Palace.

44. The meaningful order of words is — Sand Iron, Gold, Diamond, Platinum. (The order is based on the dearness.)

45. The meaningful order of words is — Money Site, Plan, Building, Rent — based on prope planning.

46. The meaningful order of the words is — Advertisement, Application, Interview Selection, Appointment, Probation.

47. The meaningful order of words is — Species Family, Caste, Clan, Newly-married Couple

48. The meaningful order of words is — Chil School, College, Employment, Salary.

49. The dictionary order of words is—Bubble Bully, Bundle, Bungling, Burgling, Bush

50. The natural order of words is— Dawn, Noo Evening, Dusk, Night.

CALENDAR, CLOCK, TIME, DISTANCE

These are mathematical problem based on calculations of time by a clock or calendar and computations of speed or distances.

SOLVED EXAMPLES

1. If day-after-tomorrow is Sunday, what was day-before-yesterday?

A. Wednesday

B. Thursday

C. Friday

D. Saturday

Ans. A :

Day-after-tomorrow	—	Sunday
Tomorrow	—	Saturday
Today	—	Friday
Yesterday	—	Thursday
Day-before-yesterday	—	Wednesday

2. If the next day after 3rd Monday in a month is 16th, what will be the date on day before 5th Monday?

A. 27 B. 28

C. 29 D. 30

Ans. B. : Next day after 3rd Monday is 16th

So Monday is 15th

4th Monday is 22nd.... (15 + 7)

5th Monday is 29th .... (15 + 14) or (22 + 7)

So, date on day before 5th Monday is 28th

3. How many times in 12 hours the hands of a clock will be at right angles?

A. 12 B. 16

C. 18 D. 24

Ans. D : In every hour the hands are at right angles twice.

4. If a train runs at a speed of 92.7 km/hr, then the distance covered in metres in 20 minutes will be :

A. 3009 B. 308.9

C. 309 D. 30900

Ans. D : Speed of the train is 92.7 km/hr *i.e.* 92700 metres in 60 minutes

In 20 minutes the distance covered will be :

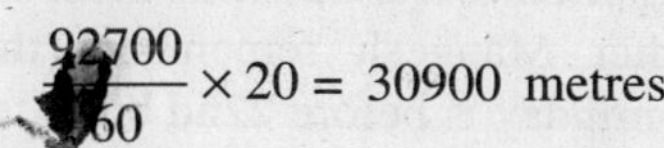

$$\frac{92700}{60} \times 20 = 30900 \text{ metres}$$

5. Prabhat remembers that his mother's birthday is after seventeenth April but before twenty-first April, whereas his sister Urmila remembers that their mother's birthday is after nineteenth but before twenty-fourth April. Which of the following days in April is definitely their mother's birthday?

A. Nineteenth

B. Twenty-first

C. Twenty-second

D. Twentieth

Ans. D : Mother's birthday in the month of April :

According to Prabhat: is from

17th 21st

19th 24th

According to Urmila: is from

It is clear that the mother's birthday is between 19th and 21st April and so the definite date is 20th April.

MULTIPLE CHOICE QUESTIONS

1. If the day before yesterday was Thursday, when will Sunday be?
   A. Tomorrow
   B. Day after tomorrow
   C. Today
   D. Two days after today
2. If the seventh day of a month is three (3) days earlier than Friday, what day will it be on the nineteenth day of the month?
   A. Sunday B. Monday
   C. Wednesday D. Friday
3. Radha remembers that her father's birthday is after 16th but before 21st of March, while her brother Mangesh remembers that his father's birthday is before 22nd but after 19th of March. On which date is the birthday of their father?
   A. 19th
   B. 20th
   C. 21st
   D. Cannot be determined
4. A man is three (3) years older than his wife and four (4) times as old as his son. If the son attains an age of fifteen (15) years after three (3) years, what is the present age of the mother?
   A. 60 years B. 51 years
   C. 48 years D. 45 years
5. A clock is so placed that at 12 noon its minute hand points towards north-east. In which direction does its hour hand point at 1.30 P.M.?
   A. East B. West
   C. North D. South
6. If in the above question clock is turned through an angle of 135° in an anticlockwise direction, in which direction will its minute hand point at 8.45 P.M.?
   A. East B. West
   C. North D. South
7. A couple married in 1980 had two children, one in 1982 and the other in 1984. Their combined ages will equal the years of the marriage in?
   A. 1986 B. 1985
   C. 1987 D. 1988
8. **Manoj left home for the bus stop 15 minute earlier than the usual time. It takes 10 minute to reach the stop. He reached the stop at 8.4 a.m. What time does he usually leave hom for the bus stop?**
   A. 8.30 a.m. B. 8.55 a.m.
   C. 8.45 p.m. D. None of these
9. Mamuni went to the movies nine days ag She goes to the movies only on Thursda What day of the week is today?
   A. Sunday B. Tuesday
   C. Thursday D. Saturday
10. If Thursday was the day after the day befo yesterday five days ago, what is the lea number of days ago when Sunday was thr days before the day after tomorrow?
    A. Two days ago B. Three days ago
    C. Four days ago D. Five days ago
11. 1.12.91 is the first Sunday. Which is t fourth Tuesday of December 91?
    A. 31.12.91 B. 24.12.91
    C. 17.12.91 D. 26.12.91
12. If the third day of a month is Monday, whi of the following will be the fifth day fr 21st of that month?
    A. Tuesday B. Monday
    C. Wednesday D. Thursday
13. If 15 horses eat 15 bags of gram in 15 da in how many days will one horse eat one b of grain?
    A. 15 days B. 1/15 days
    C. 1 day D. 30 days
14. A century leap year is divisible by :
    A. 4 B. 16
    C. 40 D. 400
15. If the fifth day of a month is Friday, wh of the following will be the Seventh from 10th of that month?
    A. Tuesday B. Monday
    C. Wednesday D. Thursday

16. Day after tomorrow is my birthday. On the same day next week falls 'Holi'. Today is Monday. What will be the day after 'Holi'?

A. Wednesday B. Thursday
C. Friday D. Saturday

17. A clock shows the time as 3 : 30 p.m. If the minute hand gains 2 minutes every hour, how many minutes will the clock gain by 4 a.m.?

A. 23 Minutes B. 24 Minutes
C. 25 Minutes D. 26 Minutes

18. Two brothers were expected to return home on the same day. Rajat returned 3 days earlier but Rohit returned 4 days later. If Rajat returned on Thursday, what was the expected day when both the brothers were to return home and when did Rohit Return?

A. Wednesday, Sunday
B. Thursday, Monday
C. Sunday, Thursday
D. Monday, Friday

19. A train started from station 'A' and proceeded towards station 'B' at a speed of 48 km/hr. Forty-five minutes later another train started from station 'B' and proceeded towards station 'A' at 50 km/hr. If the distance between the two stations is 232 km, at what distance from station 'A' will the trains meet?

A. 132 km B. 144 km
C. 108 km D. 160 km

20. A, B and C are pipes attached to a cistern. A and B can fill it in 10 and 15 minutes respectively, while C can empty it in 20 minutes. If A, B and C be kept open successively for 1 minute each, find the last integral number of minutes required for the cistern to get filled.

A. 20 B. 23
C. 25 D. 26

21. How many minutes does the minute hand gain in every one hour?

A. 55 B. 60
C. 65 D. No gain

22. A 260 metres long train runs at a speed of 55 kmph. How much time will it take to cross a platform 290 metres long?

A. 20 seconds B. 36 seconds
C. 18 seconds D. 60 seconds

23. Bunny's brother Sunny is 562 days older to him while his sister Jenny is 75 weeks older to Sunny. If Jenny was born on Tuesday, on which day was Bunny born?

A. Monday B. Tuesday
C. Friday D. Thursday

24. My uncle shall visit me after 64 days of my father's birthday. If my father's birthday falls on Tuesday, what shall be the day on my Uncle's visit?

A. Wednesday B. Sunday
C. Tuesday D. Monday

25. If 21st November falls five days before Wednesday then what will be the day on 25th December?

A. Wednesday B. Sunday
C. Friday D. Thursday

26. How much time will 160 m long train travelling at a speed of 40 km/hr take to cross a man going in the same direction with a speed of 4 km/hr?

A. 15 seconds B. 40 seconds
C. 24 seconds D. 16 seconds

27. If in a clock the numbers 1 to 12 are replaced with alphabet starting from F, then which of the following options shall indicate the time as 9'o clock?

A. M - P B. Q-N
C. P - M D. N - Q

28. If 3rd December 1999 is Sunday, what day is 3rd January 2000?

A. Tuesday B. Wednesday
C. Thursday D. Friday

29. Prabir starts for office every morning at 9.15 a.m. and reaches there at 9.55 a.m. On Wednesday he started five minutes later than the time he started on Friday. Three days out of five days in the week he started late, out of which Friday was one of the days. On how many days he started in time?

A. Two B. Three
C. Four D. One

30. In the question above, at what time did he start on Wednesday?

A. 9.25 a.m. B. 9.15 a.m.
C. Data inadequate D. 9.20 a.m.

Directions (Qs. 31-33) : *Read the following information and answer the questions given below :*

(I) Kundanmal is available at home between 12 noon to 4 p.m. on Tuesday, Thursday and Sunday.

(II) His younger brother Nainamal is available at home on Monday, Thursday, Friday and Sunday between 10 a.m. to 2 p.m.

(III) The eldest brother Jethamal is available between 9 a.m. to 12 noon on Monday, Wednesday and Thursday and 2 p.m. to 4 p.m. on Friday, Saturday and Sunday.

31. On which day(s) of a week, the youngest and the eldest brothers are available at home at the same time?

A. Only Monday
B. Only Thursday
C. Only Friday
D. Both Monday and Thursday

32. At a time, on which day of a week all the three brothers are available at home?

A. Sunday
B. Thursday
C. None
D. Can't be determined

33. For how many days only one brother is available at a particular time in a week?

A. Four B. Three
C. Two D. None of these

Directions (Qs. 34-37) : *Read the following information and answer the questions given below :*

(i) A city bus company operates 7 buses M, N, O, P, Q, R and S each once for daily 4 hours sight-seeing tours.

(ii) From Monday to Friday first bus leaves at 8 a.m. sharp, subsequent bus leaves alternatively after a gap of 45 minutes, followed by 30 minutes, again 45 minutes and 35 minutes and so on.

(iii) On Saturday and Sunday, first bus leaves at 7.30 a.m. and others follows regularly after a gap of 1 hour.

(iv) Bus 'Q' leaves immediately after 'M' and is immediately followed by 'S'.

(v) Bus 'O' is not followed by any other bus.

(vi) Bus 'R' leaves immediately before 'M' but not immediately after 'P'.

34. At what time, bus 'M' leaves on Saturday

A. 10 a.m. B. 9.45 a.m.
C. 10.30 a.m. D. Data inadequate

35. On Sunday, when bus 'P' completes its tour which of the following buses begins its tour

A. Q B. S
C. O D. Data inadequate

36. If the time gap after bus 'M' leaves on Saturday Sunday is increased by 30 minutes for the subsequent trips, at what time, tour of bus 'O' will be completed?

A. 3 p.m. B. 2 p.m.
C. 6 p.m. D. 7 p.m.

37. If the time gap between two buses is uniform kept as 45 minutes from Monday to Frida then the beginning of tour of bus 'O' w mark completion of tour of which of th following buses?

A. N B. R
C. M D. None of these

Directions (Qs. 38-40) : *Read the followi information and answer the questions given belov*

(i) Eight doctors P, Q, R, S, T, U, V and W vi a charitable dispensary run by Shram-Man Trust every day except on a holiday, i Monday.

(ii) Each doctor visits for 1 hour from Tuesd to Sunday except Saturday. The timings a 9 a.m. to 1 p.m. and 2 p.m. to 6 p.m., 1 p. to 2 p.m. is lunch break.

(iii) On Saturday, it is open only in the morni *i.e.,* 9 a.m. to 1 p.m. and each doctor vis for only half an hour.

(iv) No other doctor visits the dispensary bef doctor 'Q' and after doctor 'U'.

(v) Doctor 'W' comes immediately after lu break and is followed by 'R'.

(vi) 'S' comes in the same order as 'P' in afternoon session.

38. At what time the visit of Doctor 'T' would be over on Saturday?

A. 10 a.m.
B. 11 a.m.
C. Either 10 a.m. or 11 a.m.
D. Data inadequate

39. Doctor 'P' visits in-between which of the following pairs of doctors?

A. R and W
B. S and T
C. U and W
D. None of these

40. If the lunch break and subsequent visiting hours are reduced by 15 minutes, at what time Doctor 'U' is expected to attend the dispensary?

A. 3.15 p.m.
B. 4.15 p.m.
C. 4.45 p.m.
D. 4 p.m.

ANSWERS

1	2	3	4	5	6	7	8	9	10
A	A	B	D	A	D	A	C	D	A
11	**12**	**13**	**14**	**15**	**16**	**17**	**18**	**19**	**20**
B	C	A	D	C	B	C	C	A	D
21	**22**	**23**	**24**	**25**	**26**	**27**	**28**	**29**	**30**
A	B	D	A	D	D	D	B	A	C
31	**32**	**33**	**34**	**35**	**36**	**37**	**38**	**39**	**40**
D	C	D	C	A	D	D	C	D	D

EXPLANATORY ANSWERS

1. Thursday —Day-before-yesterday
Friday —Yesterday
Saturday —Today
Sunday — Tomorrow

2. 7th day is 3 days earlier than Friday so, 10th day is Friday, so also is 17th.
∴ 19th day will be 2nd day ahead of Friday, *i.e.,* Sunday.

3. Father's birthday

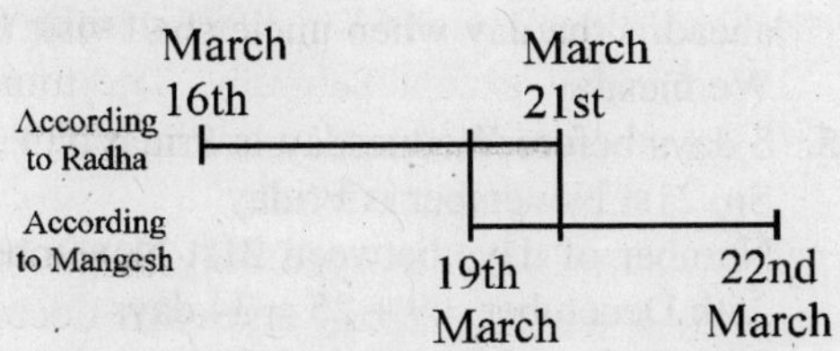

∴ Their father's birthday is on 20th March.

4. Present age of son is 15-3 = 12 years. Age of the man is 4 times the age of son, *i.e.,* 12 × 4 = 48 years
Man is 3 years elder to his wife/son's mother. So Age of the mother is 48 – 3 = 45 years

5.

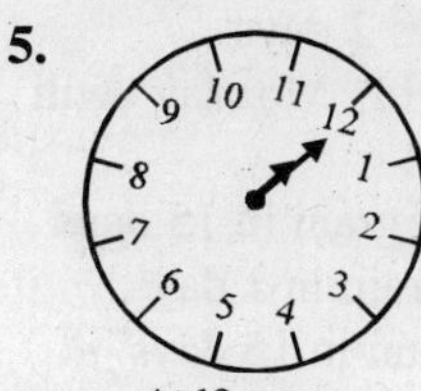

At 12 noon

At 1.30 p.m. the hour hand will point towards East.

6.

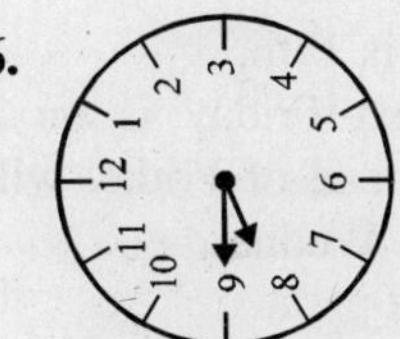

After rotating the clock in earlier question, its minute hand will point towards South at 8:45 p.m.

7. 1982 — 2 years later — 1st child
1984 — 4 years later — 2nd child
Total age of children — 2 years.
1985 — 5 years later — Total age of children : 4 years.

1986 — 6 years later — Total age of children : 6 years.

8. Manoj reached the bus stop at 8.40 a.m. He left his home at 8:40 – 10 minutes = 8:30 a.m. He left 15 minutes earlier than usual, so his actual time of leaving home is 8:30 am + 15 minutes = 8:45 a.m.

9. Mamuni goes to the movies on Thursday, so nine days ago was Thursday.
∴ Two days ago was also Thursday. So, today is Saturday.

10. Day after the day-before-yesterday five days ago is the 6th day which is Thursday. And so, the 3rd day will be Sunday. Three days before the day-after-tomorrow is Yesterday which is the 1st day of the five days. So, two days ago was Sunday.

11. First Sunday is on 1st December
First Tuesday is on 3rd December
3 weeks later, Fourth Tuesday will be on 3 + (7 × 3) = 24th December.

12. 3rd day of the month is Monday
5th day from 21st is 26th
26 – 3 = 23 days
23 days later, 23/7 leaves 2 days.
So, two days ahead of Monday will be Wednesday.

13. 15 horses eat 15 bags of grain in 15 days
15 horses eat 1 bag of grain in 1 day
1 horse eats 1 bag of grain in 15 days

14. A leap year is divisible by 4 and a century leap year is divisible by 400.

15. Seventh day from 10th is 17th.
5th day is Friday. Next Friday is on 12th
17 – 12 = 5, 5 days ahead of Friday will be Wednesday. So, 17th is Wednesday.

16. Today is Monday
Day-after-tomorrow is Wednesday
Next week 'Holi' is also on Wednesday
So, Day after Holi is Thursday.

17. Hours between 3:30 p.m. and 4 a.m. are — 12½ hours. Number of minutes gained will be 12½ × 2 = 25 minutes.

18. Rajat returned on Thursday. 3 days later was the day of expected return, *i.e.,* Sunday. Rohit returned 4 days after Sunday *i.e.* Thursday.

19. $\xleftarrow{\quad d \quad}\!\!\!\!\!\xrightarrow{}|\xleftarrow{\quad 232-d \quad}\!\!\!\!\!\xrightarrow{}$

i.e., $\frac{d}{48} = \frac{232-d}{50} + \frac{3}{4}$

$\frac{d}{48} = \frac{464-2d+75}{100}$

$100\,d = (539 - 2d)\,48$

$100\,d = 25872 - 96\,d$

$196\,d = 25872$

$d = 25872 \div 196 = 132$ km.

20. In 3 minutes the cistern filled by A, B and C

$= \frac{1}{10} + \frac{1}{15} - \frac{1}{20} = \frac{7}{60}$ th.

Time taken to fill the cistern completely

$= \frac{60}{7} \times 3 = 25\frac{5}{7}$ minutes

21. In every hour the minute hand moves 60 minutes whereas the hour hand moves 5 minutes.

22. Total length to be covered = 260 + 290 = 550 metres.
Time taken to cross the platform

$= \frac{550}{55} \times \frac{3600}{1000} = 36$ seconds

23. Jenny is older to Sunny by 75 × 7 = 525 days.
Jenny is older to Bunny by 525 + 562 = 1087 days
1087 ÷ 7 gives 2 as remainder.
So, if Jenny was born on Tuesday, then Bunny was born 2 days later, *i.e.,* on Thursday.

24. My father's birthday is on Tuesday.
64 ÷ 7 gives 1 as remainder
So, 63rd day will be Tuesday and one day ahead is the day when uncle shall visit *i.e.,* on Wednesday.

25. 5 days before Wednesday is Friday.
So, 21st November is Friday
Number of days between 21st November and 25th December = 9 + 25 = 34 days
34 ÷ 7 gives 6 as remainder
∴ 28th day will be Friday and 6 days ahead will be Thursday.
So, 25th December will be Thursday.

26. Relative speed of the train will be 40 – 4 = 36 km/hr or 10 m/sec as both, the train and the man, are moving in same direction.

Time taken by the train to cross the man 160 ÷ 10 = 16 seconds.

27. 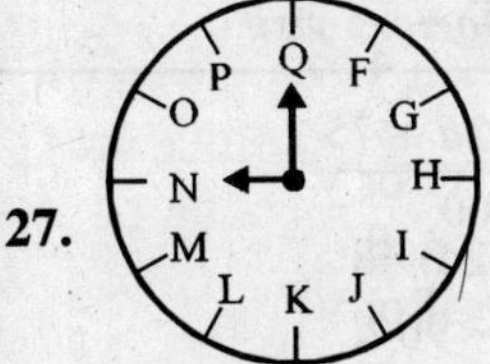

Note : Q – N will indicate the time as Quarter to twelve *i.e.* 11:45

28. 3rd December 1999 is Sunday. Number of days in-between 3rd December 1999 and 3rd January 2000 = 28 + 3 = 31 days 31 ÷ 7 gives 3 is remainder

So, 31st December 1999 will be Sunday and 3rd January 2000 will be 3 days ahead *i.e.* Wednesday.

31. The availability of brothers in a week is :

	Jethamal	*Kundanmal*	*Nainamal*
Monday	9 a.m. - 12 noon	x	10 a.m. - 2 p.m.
Tuesday	x	12 noon - 4 p.m.	x
Wednesday	9 a.m. - 12 noon	x	x
Thursday	9 a.m. - 12 noon	12 noon - 4 p.m.	10 a.m. - 2 p.m.
Friday	2 p.m. - 4 p.m.	x	10 a.m. - 2 p.m.
Saturday	2 p.m. - 4 p.m.	x	x
Sunday	2 p.m. - 4 p.m.	12 noon - 4 p.m.	10 a.m. - 2 p.m.

34.

Order in which the buses leave Monday to Friday	*Leaving Time from and Sunday*	*Leaving Time on Saturday*
P	8: a.m.	7:30 a.m.
N	8:45 a.m.	8:30 a.m.
R	9:15 a.m.	9:30 a.m.
M	10 a.m.	10:30 a.m.
Q	10:35 a.m.	11:30 a.m.
S	11:20 a.m.	12:30 p.m.
O	12 noon	1:30 p.m.

35. Bus P leaves at 7:30 a.m. and completes its four hours sight-seeing tour at 11:30 a.m. Bus Q begins its tour at 11:30 a.m.

36. Bus M leaves at 10:30 am. If time gap of 1 hr is increased by 30 minutes, bus Q will leave at 12 noon; bus S at 1:30 p.m. and bus O at 3 p.m. Bus O will complete its four hours tour at 7 p.m.

37. Bus N will leave at 8:45 a.m., R at 9:30 a.m., M at 10:15 a.m., Q at 11 a.m., S at 11:45 a.m, and O at 12:30 p.m. 4 hours before 12:30 p.m. is 8:30 a.m. No bus starts at 8:30 a.m.

38.	Timings on Monday to Friday and Sunday		Timings on Saturday	The Order in which the Doctors visit
	9 am	– 10 am	9 am - 9:30 am	Q
	10 am	– 11 am	9:30 am - 10 am	T or V
	11 am	– 12 noon	10 am - 10:30 am	S
	12 noon	– 1 pm	10:30 am - 11 am	T or V
	(Lunch 1 pm	– 2 pm)		
	2 pm	– 3 pm	11 am - 11:30 am	W
	3 pm	– 4 pm	11:30 am - 12 noon	R
	4 pm	– 5 pm	12 noon - 12:30 pm	P
	5 pm	– 6 pm	12:30 pm - 1 pm	U

40. The new lunch timings for the doctors will be :

Lunch	—	1 pm	-	1:45 pm
W	—	1:45 pm	-	2:30 pm
R	—	2:30 pm	-	3:15 pm
P	—	3:15 pm	-	4 pm
U	—	4 pm	-	4:45 pm

Doctor U will attend the dispensary at 4 pm.

ROWS AND RANKS

These type of problems need easy calculations to find out the number of objects in a row, lane or queue or to find a person's rank in a class of certain number of students; or to find the total number of students.

SOLVED EXAMPLES

1. In a row of trees, one tree is 8th from one end and 3rd from the other. How many trees are there in the row?

A. 11 B. 9
C. 10 D. 12

Ans. C : The number of trees in the row is :

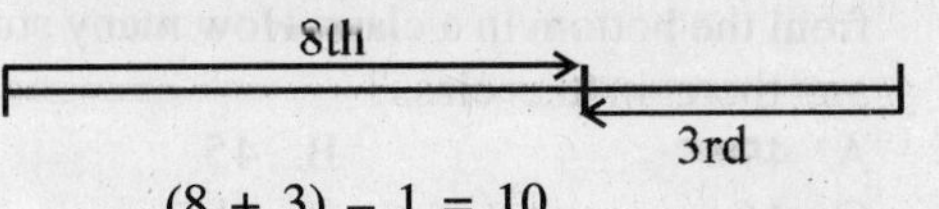

(8 + 3) – 1 = 10

2. If Janki is 12 ahead in rank of Pallavi who ranks 15th from last, then how many students are there in the class if Janki ranks 4th in order of merit?

A. 23
B. 27
C. 31
D. 33

Ans. C : After calculations the answer will be :

The total number of students are : 4 + 12 + 15 = 31

MULTIPLE CHOICE QUESTIONS

1. In a row of trees, one tree is fifth from either end of the row. How many trees are in the row?

A. 11 B. 8
C. 10 D. 9

2. Jaya ranks 5th in a class of 53. What is her rank from the bottom in the class?

A. 49th B. 48th
C. 47th D. 50th

3. Mohan ranks twenty-first in a class of sixty-five students. What will be his (Mohan's) rank if the lowest candidate is assigned rank 1?

A. 44th B. 45th
C. 46th D. Data inadequate

4. If Rahul finds that he is 12th from the right in a line of boys and 4th from the left, how many boys should be added to the line such that there are 28 boys in the line?

A. 12 B. 14
C. 20 D. 13

5. In a row of boys, Rajan is tenth from the right and Suraj is tenth from the left. When Rajan and Suraj interchange their positions, Suraj will be twenty-seventh from the left. Which of the following will be Rajan's position from the right?

A. Tenth B. Twenty-sixth
C. Twenty-ninth D. None of these

6. Mahesh and Suresh are ranked 11th and 12th respectively from the top in a class of 41 students. What will be their respective ranks from the bottom?

A. 32nd and 33rd B. 29th and 30th
C. 30th and 31st D. 31st and 30th

7. Uma ranked 8th from the top and 37th from bottom in a class. How many students are there in the class?

A. 47 B. 46
C. 45 D. None of these

8. In a queue, Sadiq is 14th from the front and Joseph is 17th from the end, while Jane is in between Sadiq and Joseph. If Sadiq be ahead of Joseph and there be 48 persons in the queue, how many persons are there between Sadiq and Jane?

A. 5 B. 6
C. 7 D. 8

9. Rohan ranked eleventh from the top and twenty-seventh from the bottom among the students who passed the annual examination in a class. If the number of students who failed in the examination was 12, how many students appeared for the examination?

A. 48
B. 49
C. 50
D. Cannot be determined

10. Some boys are sitting in a row. P is sitting fourteenth from the left and Q is seventh from the right. If there are four boys between P and Q, how many boys are there in the row?

A. 19 B. 21
C. 25 D. 23

11. There are five different houses, A to E, in a row. A is to the right of B and E is to the left of C and right of A, and B is to the right of D. Which of the houses is in the middle?

A. B B. A
C. D D. E

12. Madhav ranks seventeenth in a class of thirtyone. What is his rank from the last?

A. 13 B. 14
C. 15 D. 16

13. Veena ranks 73rd from the top in a class of 182. What is her rank from the bottom if 22 students have failed the examination?

A. 88 B. 108
C. 110 D. 90

14. Rakesh ranked 9th from the top and 38th from the bottom in a class. How many students are there in the class?

A. 47 B. 45
C. 46 D. 48

15. John ranks 19th in class and is 36th from the last. How many students are there in the class?

A. 53 B. 54
C. 51 D. 50

ANSWERS

1	2	3	4	5	6	7	8	9	10
D	A	B	D	D	D	D	D	B	C
11	**12**	**13**	**14**	**15**					
B	C	A	C	B					

EXPLANATORY ANSWERS

1.

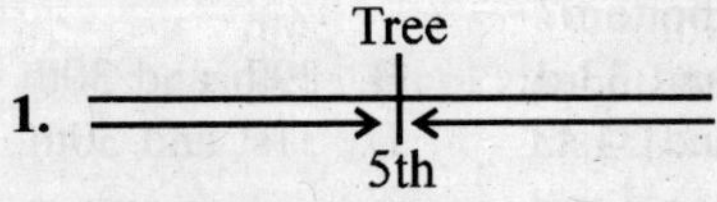

Total number of trees in the row are :
(5 + 5) –1 =9

2. Jaya 53rd 5th

Jaya's rank from the bottom is :
(53 – 5) +1 = 49th.

3.

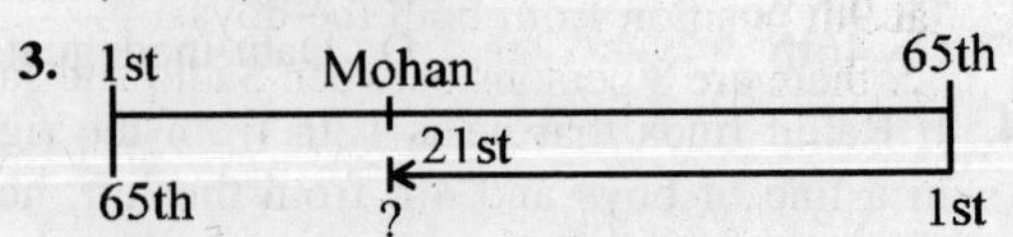

Note : Mohan's rank from the last or the question asked means the same.

Mohan's rank is (65 – 21) +1 = 45th

4.

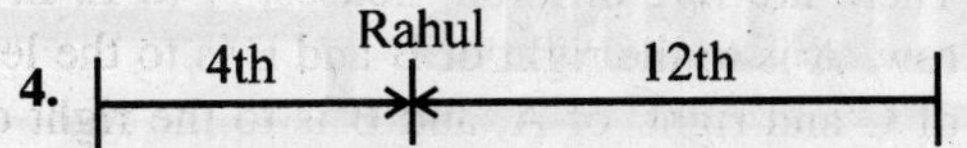

The number of boys in the line are :
(4 + 12) – 1 = 15
To make a line of 28 boys, (28 –15) *i.e.* 13 more boys are needed.

5.

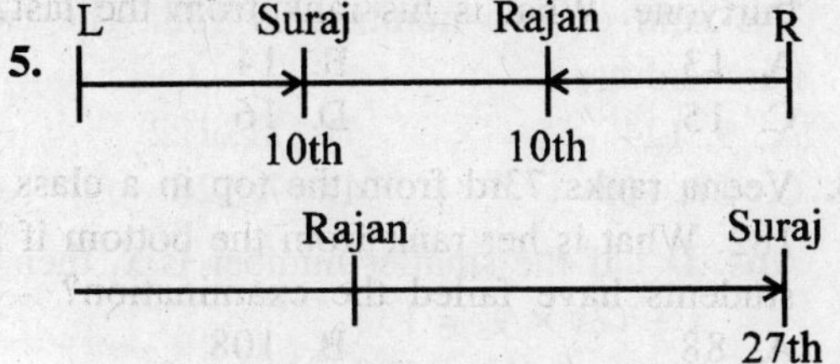

As the position of boys is equal from both ends, Rajan will also be 27th from the right after changing positions.

6.

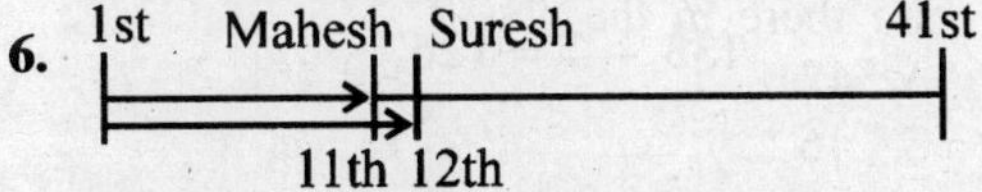

Mahesh's position from bottom is :
(41 – 11) + 1 = 31st
Suresh's position from bottom is :
(41 – 12) +1 = 30th

7.

Uma
8th 37th

Total number of students in the class are :
(8 + 37) – 1 = 44

8.

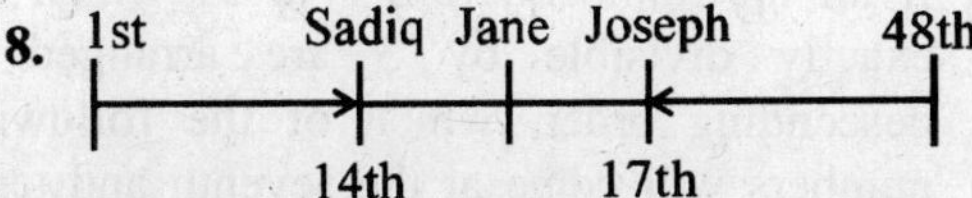

Sadiq's position from last is :
(48 – 14) + 1 = 35th
Number of persons between Sadiq and Joseph are (35 – 17) – 1 = 17th.
Jane is in-between Sadiq and Joseph *i.e.,* she's at 9th position from both the boys.
∴ there are 8 persons between Sadiq and Jane.

9.

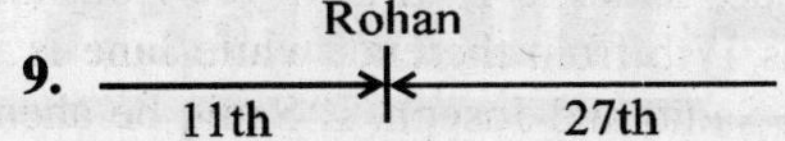

Number of students who passed the examination (11+ 27) – 1 = 37
Those who failed = 12
Total number of students who appeared in the examination = 37 + 12 = 49.

10.

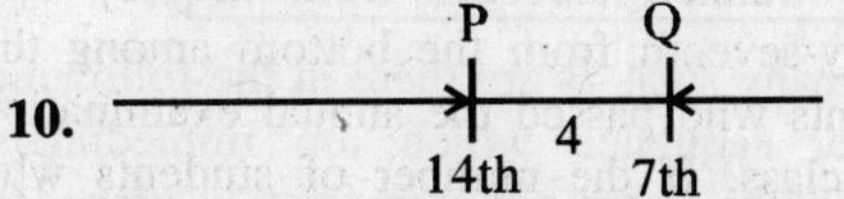

The number of boys in the row are :
(14 + 4 + 7) = 25

11. The houses in the row are :
D B A E C

12.

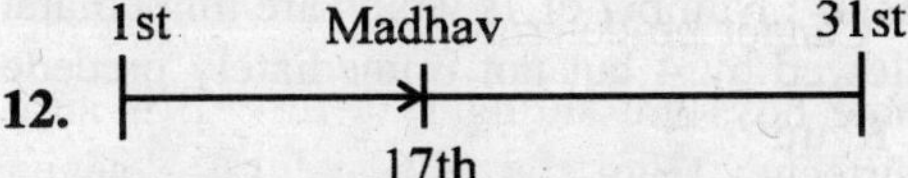

Madhav's rank from the last is :
(31 – 17) + 1 = 15th

13.

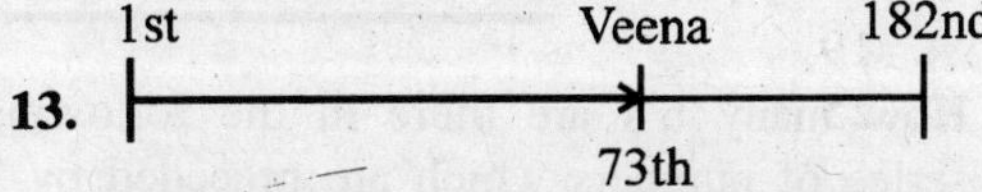

Number of students who failed is 22. Number of students who passed
= 182–22 = 160. So Veena's rank from the bottom will be : (160 – 73) + 1 = 88th

14.

Rakesh
9th 38th

Number of students in the class is :
(9 + 38) – 1 = 46

15.

John
19th 36th

Number of students in the class is :
(19 + 36) – 1 = 54

NUMBER PROBLEMS

Number problems consists of number sequences, problems with algebraic expressions, mathematical calculations and other compatiable problems.

SOLVED EXAMPLES

1. How many such 7s are there in the following number sequence which are immediately followed by 4 but not immediately preceded by 8?

5 4 7 8 9 7 4 3 8 7 5 7 4 8 7 4 1 2 7 4 5 7 9 4

A. Two B. Three

C. Four D. Five

Ans. B : Number of 7s which are immediately followed by 4 but not immediately preceded by 8 are :

5 4 7 8 9 7 4 3 8 7 5 7 4 8 7 4 1 2 7 4 5 7 9 4

(1: 9 7 4; 2: 5 7 4; 3: 2 7 4)

2. A number is 9 times twice the other number. The sum of two numbers is 133. The two numbers are :

A. 9, 124 B. 11, 122

C. 17, 166 D. 7, 126

Ans. D : If the smaller number is x, then

$$x + (2x \times 9) = 133$$
$$x + 18x = 133$$
$$19x = 133$$
$$x = 133 \div 19 = 7$$

If one number is 7, the other number is :

$$133 - 7 = 126$$

MULTIPLE CHOICE QUESTIONS

1. How many 6's are there in the following series of numbers which are preceded by 7 but not immediately followed by 9?

6 7 9 5 6 9 7 6 8 7 6 7 8 6 9 4 6 7 7 6 9 5 7 6 3

A. One B. Two

C. Three D. Four

2. In a chess tournament each of six players will play every other player exactly once. How many matches will be played during the tournament?

A. 12 B. 15

C. 30 D. 36

3. How many 4's are there in the following series which are preceded by 7, but are not preceded by 8?

3 4 5 7 4 3 7 4 8 5 4 3 7 4 9 8 4 7 2 7 4 1 3 6

A. 1 B. 2

C. 3 D. 4

4. How many even numbers are there in the following series of numbers, each of which is immediately preceded by an odd number, but not immediately followed by an even number?

5 3 4 8 9 7 1 6 5 3 2 9 8 4 3 5

A. Nil B. 1

C. 2 D. 3

5. If all the numbers from 1 to 51 which are exactly divisible by 3 are arranged in descending order, which of the following numbers will come at the seventh and tenth places from the top?

A. 33 & 27 B. 33 & 21

C. 21 & 30 D. 33 & 24

6. Nitin was counting down from 32. Shasank was counting upwards, the numbers starting from 1 and he was calling out only the odd numbers. Which common number will they call out at the same time if they were calling out at the same speed?

A. 21

B. 22

C. 19
D. They will not call out the same number

7. In the following list of numerals, how many 3s are followed by 3, but NOT preceded by 3?
2 4 6 3 3 1 5 7 8 3 3 3 4 6 2 3 3 3 3 9 7 2 3
A. 1 B. 2
C. 3 D. 4

8. If in a given number 5 8 9 4 3 2 7 6 1 4, we interchange the first and the second digits, the third and the fourth, the fifth and the sixth and so on, then counting from the right end, which digit will be sixth?
A. 3 B. 2
C. 4 D. 5

9. Aparna cuts a cake into two halves and cuts one-half into smaller pieces of equal size. Each of the small pieces is twenty grams in weight. If she has seven pieces of the cake in all with her, how heavy was the original cake?
A. 140 grams B. 280 grams
C. 240 grams D. 120 grams

10. In the following number sequence how many such even numbers are there which are exactly divisible by its immediate preceding number but not exactly divisible by its immediate following number?
3 8 4 1 5 7 2 8 3 4 8 9 3 9 4 2 1 5 8 2
A. Two B. Three
C. Four D. More than four

11. How many 7s are there in the following series which are not immediately followed by 3 but immediately preceded by 8?
8 9 8 7 6 2 2 6 3 2 6 9 7 3 2 8 7 2 7 7 8 7 3 7 7 9 4
A. Nil B. One
C. Two D. Three

12. How many 9's are there in the following sequence which are neither preceded by 6 nor immediately followed by 3?
9 3 8 6 9 9 5 9 3 7 8 9 9 9 3 9 6 3 9
A. One B. Two
C. Three D. Four

13. If a number is five times as great as another number which is four less than forty, then the number is :
A. 220 B. 180
C. 144 D. 200

14. If 2/3rd of a number is 96, what will be the 3/4th of that number?
A. 108 B. 198
C. 128 D. 48

15. If such numbers which are divisible by 5, and also those which have 5 as one of the digits are eliminated from the numbers 1 to 60, how many numbers would remain?
A. 53 B. 47
C. 40 D. 45

16. How many 8's are there in the following number series which are exactly divisible by its immediately preceding and also exactly divisible by immediately succeeding numbers?
8 2 4 5 1 7 2 8 4 8 4 2 2 8 2 6 9 8 4 5 4 8 3 2 8 4 3 1 8 3
A. 1 B. 2
C. 3 D. 4

17. How many such 3's are there in the following number sequence which are immediately preceded by an odd number and immediately followed by an even number?
5 3 8 9 4 3 7 2 3 8 1 3 8 4 2 3 5 7 3 4 2 3 6
A. One B. Two
C. Three D. Four

18. Count each 7 which is not immediately preceded by 5 but is immediately followed by either 2 or 3. How many such 7's are there?
5 7 2 6 5 7 3 8 3 7 3 2 5 7 2 7 3 4 8 2 6 7 8
A. 2 B. 3
C. 4 D. 5

19. A number is four less than two times the other number. If their difference is 21, what is the greater number?
A. 50 B. 46
C. 31 D. 21

20. Of the two digits number the total of the digits of the number is 6. If these digits are reversed there is an increasing difference of 18. What is the number?

A. 12 B. 24
C. 42 D. 36

21. Sony and Johnny caught 60 fishes. Sony caught four times as many as Johnny. How many fishes did Johnny catch?

A. 12 B. 16
C. 34 D. 38

22. 10 years ago Neha's mother was 4 times older than Neha. After 10 years Neha's mother will be twice Neha's age. How old is Neha now?

A. 10 years B. 15 years
C. 17 years D. 20 years

23. The sum of two consecutive numbers is 87. Which is the larger number?

A. 42 B. 43
C. 44 D. 45

24. How many numbers from 11 to 50 are there which are exactly divisible by 7 but not by 3?

A. 2 B. 4
C. 5 D. 6

25. How many 3's are there in the following sequence which are neither preceded by 6 nor immediately followed by 9?

9 3 6 6 3 9 5 9 3 7 8 9 7 6 3 9 6 3 9

A. One B. Two
C. Three D. Four

26. If the odd numbers between 20 to 40 are arranged in a row, what will be the 6th number from the right?

A. 27 B. 31
C. 33 D. 29

27. How many numbers from 1 to 50 will be left out if the numbers which are exactly divisible by 7 and having 7 as one of the digits are removed?

A. 43 B. 30
C. 42 D. 39

28. How many numbers are there between 20 and 60 which are divisible by 3 and the total of two digits is 9?

A. 4 B. 3
C. 2 D. 1

29. The sum of odd numbers between 20 and 30 is :

A. 105 B. 120
C. 125 D. 140

30. If such numbers which are divisible by 7 and also those which have 7 as one of the digits are eliminated from the numbers 5 to 50, how many numbers would remain?

A. 34 B. 35
C. 36 D. 37

31. My age is two years more than twice that of Ram. If I am 34 years old, how old is Ram?

A. 20 B. 18
C. 16 D. 14

Directions (Qs. 32 and 33) : *Study the following number sequence and answer the questions given below it :*

5 1 4 7 3 9 8 5 7 2 6 3 1
5 8 6 3 8 5 2 2 4 3 4 9 6

32. How many odd numbers are there in the sequence which are immediately preceded and also immediately followed by an even number?

A. 1 B. 2
C. 3 D. 4

33. How many even numbers are there in the sequence which are immediately preceded by an odd number but immediately followed by an even number?

A. 1 B. 2
C. 3 D. 4

34. How many numbers amongst the numbers 7 to 41 are there which are exactly divisible by 9 but not by 3?

A. Nil B. 1
C. 2 D. 3

35. In the series given below, how many even numbers are immediately preceded by 6 as well as immediately followed by 3?

6 6 5 6 8 3 9 4 3 6 7 3 6 4 3 2 8 6 4 6 2 6 6 3

A. 1 B. 2
C. 3 D. 4

36. The sum of odd numbers between 0 and 10 is :

A. 15 B. 20
C. 25 D. 30

37. In a certain match all the teams were to play with each other. If there are 10 teams, how many matches will have to be played?

A. 30 B. 45
C. 60 D. 90

38. How many repeat sequence of three consecutive numbers are there in the given sequence?

6 9 6 2 4 2 9 6 2 9 2 6 9 4 9 6 2 6 9 2 4

A. 3 B. 2
C. 1 D. 4

39. How many numbers are immediately preceded and immediately followed by different numbers?

7 7 7 5 7 5 7 5 7 7 7 7 5 7 5 7 5 7 7 7 7 7 5 7 5

A. 2 B. 3
C. 4 D. 5

40. How many 8's are there in the given sequence which are not immediately preceded by 09 and not immediately followed by 90?

9 0 8 0 9 0 9 8 9 0 8 9 0 8 0 9 8 9 0 9 8 0 9 8 9 0 8 9 0

A. 1 B. 2
C. 3 D. More than 3

41. Which pair of numbers has least and maximum frequency in the given sequence?

8 7 5 6 4 5 8 3 8 6 7 2 3 5 8 3 5 7 6 4 7 6 5

A. 4 and 5
B. 2 and 6
C. 3 and 8
D. 2 and 5

42. Number of Prime numbers between 30 and 50 is :

A. 4 B. 5
C. 6 D. 7

43. Which is the middle even number between 9 and 23?

A. 14 B. 16
C. 18 D. 20

44. A number which is divided by 9 gives 15 as quotient and 3 as remainder. Find that number.

A. 205 B. 108
C. 138 D. 132

45. A number is four less than six times the other number. If the sum of both the numbers is 38, what are the numbers?

A. 6, 32 B. 7, 31
C. 5, 33 D. 4, 34

46. The sum of two numbers is 99. If the two digits of a number are interchanged, the difference between the two numbers is 9. What is the larger number?

A. 54 B. 63
C. 72 D. 78

47. The average age of 5 persons is 40 years while the average age of some other 10 persons is 25 years. The average age of all the 15 persons is :

A. 27 years B. 32 years
C. 37 years D. 30 years

48. A, B, C, D and E play a game of cards. A says to B, "If you give me three cards, you will have as many as E has and if I give you three cards, you will have as many as D has." A and B together have 10 cards more than what D and E together have. If B has two cards more than what C has and the total number of cards be 133, how many cards does B have?

A. 35 B. 25
C. 23 D. 22

49. When I was born, my mother was 23 years of age. After 6 years, when my sister was born, my father was 34 years of age. What is the difference between the ages of my parents?

A. 5 years B. 6 years
C. 11 years D. 17 years

50. A father tells his son, "I was of your present age when you were born." If the father is 36 now, how old was the boy 5 years back?

A. 15 years B. 13 years
C. 17 years D. 20 years

ANSWERS

1	2	3	4	5	6	7	8	9	10
C	B	D	C	D	D	C	B	C	A
11	**12**	**13**	**14**	**15**	**16**	**17**	**18**	**19**	**20**
C	D	B	A	C	D	C	A	B	B
21	**22**	**23**	**24**	**25**	**26**	**27**	**28**	**29**	**30**
A	D	C	B	C	D	D	A	C	B
31	**32**	**33**	**34**	**35**	**36**	**37**	**38**	**39**	**40**
C	D	C	A	C	C	B	A	D	B
41	**42**	**43**	**44**	**45**	**46**	**47**	**48**	**49**	**50**
D	B	B	C	A	A	D	B	A	B

EXPLANATORY ANSWERS

1. 6 7 9 5 6 9 7 6 8 7 6 7 8 6 9 4 6 7 7 6 9 5 7 6 3
1 2 3

2. When all the players have to play with each other then the method of calculating the number of matches to be played is $\frac{n(n-1)}{2}$ where *'n'* is the number of players playing the match. So, the number of matches played will be :
$(6 \times 5) \div 2 = 30 \div 2 = 15$

3. 3 4 5 7 4 3 7 4 8 5 4 3 7 4 9 8 4 7 2 7 4 1 3 6
1 2 3 4

4. 5 3 4 8 9 7 1 6 5 3 2 9 8 4 3 5
1 2

5. The numbers divisible by 3 in descending order are :
51, 48, 45, 42, 39, 36, 33, 30, 27, 24, 21,
7th 10th
18, 15, 12, 9, 6, 3.

6. When Nitin is on count 22, Shasank is on 21 and when Nitin is on count 21, Shasank is on 23.

7. 2 4 6 3 3 1 5 7 8 3 3 3 4 6 2 3 3 3 3 9 7 2 3
1 2 3

8. The new number after interchanging the digits is :
8 5 4 9 2 3 6 7 4 1
6th

9. There is one bigger piece and six smalle pieces. One small piece weighs 20 gm. Tota weight of six smaller speices is 120 gm.
∴ Weight of the bigger piece = 120 gm
∴ Weight of the original cake = 240 gm

10. 3 8 4 1 5 7 2 8 3 4 8 9 3 9 4 2 1 5 8 2
1 2

11. 8 9 8 7 6 2 2 6 3 2 6 9 7 3 2 8 7 2 7 7 8 7 3 7 7 9 4
1 2

12. 9 3 8 6 9 9 5 9 3 7 8 9 9 9 3 9 6 3 9
1 2 3 4

13. Number four less than forty is 40 – 4 = 36
Five times the number is = 36 × 5 = 180

14. If the number is x, then

$$\frac{2}{3}x = 96$$

$$x = \frac{96 \times 3}{2} = 144$$

$\frac{3}{4}$th of the number is $144 \times \frac{3}{4} = 108$

15. The eliminated twenty numbers are : 5, 10, 1: 20, 25, 30, 35, 40, 45 and 50 to 60. Th remaining numbers are 60 – 20 = 40.

16. 8 2 4 5 1 7 2 8 4 8 4 2 2 8 2 6 9 8 4 5 4 8
1 2 3
3 2 8 4 3 1 8 3
4

17. $\underline{538}9437238\underline{138}42357\underline{34}236$

1 2 3

18. $57265738\underline{373}257\underline{273}482678$

1 2

19. If smaller number is x, then

$$(2x - 4) - x = 21$$
$$2x - x = 21 + 4$$
$$x = 25$$

The greater number is

$$(25 \times 2) - 4 = 46$$

20. If the digit at the unit is x and at the tens is y, then

$$(10x + y) - (10y - x) = 18$$
$$9(x - y) = 18$$

i.e. $x - y = 2$

What is given is $x + y = 6$

What is obtained is $x - y = 2$

$$2x = 8$$

Now $x = 8/2$ *i.e.*, $x = 4$

Then $y = 6 - 4 = 2$

So, the number is 24.

21. Out of 5 fishes Sony caught 4 and Johnny 1.

Out of 60 Sony caught $\frac{60}{5} \times 4 = 48$ fishes and

Johnny caught $\frac{60}{5} \times 1 = 12$ fishes

22. If Neha's age be x, ten years ago her age was $x - 10$ and her mother's age $4(x - 10)$. After ten years Neha's age will be $x + 10$ and her mother's age $4(x - 10) + 20$ or $2(x + 10)$

$$\therefore \quad 4(x - 10) + 20 = 2(x + 10)$$
$$4x - 40 + 20 = 2x + 20$$
$$4x - 2x = 20 + 20$$
$$2x = 40$$
$$x = \frac{40}{2} = 20 \text{ years}$$

23. If the smaller number is x, then

$$x + (x + 1) = 87$$
$$2x + 1 = 87$$
$$2x = 86$$
$$x = 86/2 = 43$$

The larger number is $x + 1$ or $43 + 1$ *i.e.*, 44.

24. The numbers divisible by 7 but not by 3 are : 14, 28, 35, 49

25. $\underline{936}6395\underline{937}8976396 39$

1 2

27. The eleven numbers removed are—7, 14, 17, 21, 27, 28, 35, 37, 42, 47, 49. The remaining numbers are 50 – 11 = 39

28. The numbers divisible by 3 and having 9 as the total of their digits are : 27, 36, 45, 54

29. 21 + 23 + 25 +27 + 29 + = 125

30. The eleven numbers eliminated are — 7, 14, 17, 21, 27, 28, 35, 37, 42, 47, 49

The remaining numbers are 46 – 11 = 35

31. If the age of Ram is x, then

$$2x + 2 = 34$$
$$2x = 32$$
$$x = 32/2 = 16 \text{ years.}$$

32. $514739857263158\underline{638}522\underline{434}96$

1 2 3 4

33. $514739857\underline{726}31\underline{586}38\underline{522}43496$

1 2 3

34. Number divisible by 9 is also divisible by 3.

35. $665\underline{683}943673\underline{643}2864682\underline{663}$

1 2 3

36. $1 + 3 + 5 + 7 + 9 = 25$

37. The number of matches played will be —

$(10 \times 9) \div 2 = 90 \div 2 = 45$

38. $6\underline{962}42\underline{962}92694\underline{962}6924$

1 2 3

39. $7\underline{775}757\underline{577}\underline{775}757\underline{577}7\underline{775}75$

1 2 3 4 5

40. $\underline{90809}09890\underline{890809}8909809890890$

1 2

41. 2 appears only once and 5 appears five times

$87\underline{5}64\underline{5}83867\underline{2}3\underline{5}83\underline{5}76476\underline{5}$

1 2 1 3 4 5

42. The prime numbers are—31, 37, 41, 43, 47

43. The even numbers between 9 and 23 are : 10, 12, 14, 16, 18, 20, 22 and the middle even number is 16.

44. The method for calculating the number will be :

(Divisor × Quotient) + Remainder = Number

$\therefore (9 \times 15) + 3 = 135 + 3 = 138$

45. If one number is x, then

$x + (6x - 4) = 38$

$7x = 38 + 4$

$\therefore \quad x = 42/7 = 6$

The other number is $(6 \times 6) - 4 = 36 - 4 = 32$.

46. If one number is x and the other number is y, then

$x + y = 99$

$x - y = 9$

$2x = 108$

$x = 108/2 = 54$

$y = 99 - 54 = 45$

The two numbers are 45 and 54 of which the later is the larger number.

47. Total of the ages of 5 persons is

$5 \times 40 = 200$

Total of the ages of 10 persons is

$10 \times 25 = 250$

Total of the ages of above 15 persons is 450 and their average age is 450/15 = 30 years

48. As per given information :

(1) $B - 3 = E$

(2) $B + 3 = D$

(3) $A + B = D + E + 10$

(4) $B + 2 = C$

(5) Total number of cards

i.e. A+B+C+D+E = 133

(6) According to (1) and (2) : $B - 3 = E$

$B + 3 = D$

$2B = D + E$

(7) According to (3) and (6) $A + B$

$= D + E + 1$

or $\quad A + B = 2B + 10$

i.e. $\quad A = B + 10$

Now, Substituting (4), (6) and (7) in (5) we ge the expression :

$(B+10) + B + (B - 2) + 2B = 133$

So, $\quad 5B + 8 = 133$

$5B = 133 - 8$

$B = 125/5 = 25$

$\therefore$ B has 25 cards

Mother's age when I was born = 23 years

49. Father's age when sister was born = 34 years

Father's age when I was born = 34 – 6 = 28 yea

Difference between the ages of my paren = 28 – 23 = 5 years

50. If boy's present age is 'x' then father's ag when the boy was born is also 'x'.

So, $\quad x + x = 36$

$2x = 36$

$x = 36/2 = 18$

5 year's back the boy was 18 – 5 = 13 yea old.

PERMUTATIONS AND COMBINATIONS

In these type of questions the only factor essential is alertness. In every question a word is given. By using the letters of this given word the options are formed. The candidates are required to find from the given options the word *(i)* which cannot be formed by using the letters of the given word or *(ii)* which can be formed by using the letters of the given word.

SOLVED EXAMPLES

1. Find out the one word among the options which cannot be formed by using the letters of the word given.

MATURITY

A. MART B. TRAY
C. TRUE D. TRAM

Ans. Option '*c*' has the word formed also by using the letter 'E' which is not used in the word MATURITY.

2. Find out the one word among the options which can be formed by using the letters of the word REASONABLE.

A. STONE B. LONER
C. BRACE D. OPERA

Ans. Option '*b*' alone is formed by using the letters in the word given. From other options letters 'T', 'C' and 'P' are new.

MULTIPLE CHOICE QUESTIONS

Directions : *Find out the one word among the options which cannot be formed by using the letters of the word as given in each question.*

1. ROTATION
   A. TORN B. NOTE
   C. TART D. RAIN
2. PHILOSOPHY
   A. SOIL B. SHIP
   C. SOLO D. SPIN
3. SLAVATION
   A. SNORT B. LATVIA
   C. SALIVA D. AVAIL
4. ACADEMY
   A. DEMY B. MACE
   C. DIRE D. MADE
5. INCOGNITO
   A. GOING B. INACTION
   C. IGNITION D. TONGO
6. JUDICIARY
   A. INJURY B. CADDY
   C. DICY D. ACRID
7. DOCTRINE
   A. CRUST B. DOCTOR
   C. TIRED D. CREED
8. EDUCATED
   A. DATE B. CUTE
   C. EAST D. DUCT
9. INSUFFICIENT
   A. ENTICE B. SCENT
   C. SUFFICE D. THENCE
10. DECEMBER
    A. REDEEM B. DECREE
    C. BRACED D. MEMBER
11. FUGITIVE
    A. EXIT B. FIVE
    C. GIVE D. GIFT

12. CATASTROPHE
A. TASTE B. CHEAP
C. POUCH D. STARE

13. TORRENTIAL
A. TRAIL B. MENTAL
C. LEARN D. RETAIL

14. INFRASTRUCTURE
A. RAPTURE B. INSECURE
C. CRAFTS D. STRUCTURE

15. RECOMMEND
A. MEND B. ROME
C. CANE D. OMEN

16. MISCREANTS
A. SCREAM B. CRIME
C. ASCENT D. MIRAGE

17. CREDENTIAL
A. CREATE B. DENTAL
C. TENDRIL D. LOITER

18. MASTERPIECE
A. MINCE B. TRAMP
C. PESTER D. SPRITE

19. PERFECTIONIST
A. OFTEN B. CARTON
C. STINT D. ENTER

20. VAGABOND
A. BOND B. DONG
C. VAIN D. AVON

21. SUPERANNUATE
A. NATURE B. PRANT
C. TRENDS D. SENNATE

22. DIFFERENTIAL
A. LITER B. FARCE
C. DRAIN D. TIRED

23. BENEVOLENT
A. BELT B. OVAL
C. EVEN D. LOBE

24. WITHSTAND
A. THIRD B. THAWS
C. STAND D. STAIN

25. YEOMAN
A. MANY B. OMEN
C. NAME D. YAWN

26. DICTATORSHIP
A. SHORT B. CRASH
C. TERSE D. PORCH

27. RELUCTANT
A. REGLANT B. CULTURE
C. TREAT D. CREATE

28. TUBERCULOSIS
A. TUMBLES B. SUCROSE
C. CLUSTER D. ORBITS

29. JUXTAPOSE
A. TAXES B. PASTE
C. TEASE D. JOIST

30. MANIPULATION
A. MANUAL B. NATION
C. IMPLANT D. PANEL

31. BILLIONAIRE
A. BLARE B. BANGO
C. BORNE D. BRAIN

32. TENACIOUS
A. ENACT B. SCENT
C. TRAIN D. COAST

33. ANTIQUATED
A. QUIET B. ANTIQUE
C. ACQUIT D. EQUATE

34. INTERROGATE
A. ORANGE B. GREATER
C. RINGER D. TEASING

35. HABITATION
A. HABIT B. ACTION
C. THAN D. BOTH

36. AUTOMATICALLY
A. CALAMITY B. LACUNA
C. TOMATO D. MALTA

37. CARPENTER
A. CARPET B. PAINTER
C. REPENT D. NECTAR

38. MIRACULOUS
A. LOCUS B. SCAR
C. SOLACE D. MOLAR

39. PROGNOSTICATION
A. RONTGEN B. SPITOON
C. ROGATION D. START

40. TRANSLOCATION
A. START B. COAL
C. TRACTOR D. TALCUM

41. DISSEMINATION
A. INDIA B. NATIONS
C. MENTION D. ACTION

42. COMMENTATOR
A. COMMON B. MOMENT
C. COSMOS D. TART

43. PHARMACEUTICAL
A. RHEUMATIC B. CRITICAL
C. PRACTICE D. METRIC

44. CHOREOGRAPHY
A. GEOGRAPHY B. GRAPH
C. PHOTOGRAPHY D. OGRE

45. PARAPHERNALIA
A. RENAL B. PRAISE
C. PENAL D. PEAR

46. ADAPTABILITY
A. ABILITY B. DATA
C. PALATE D. PITY

47. COMPETITION
A. TOTEM B. POETIC
C. COMPOSE D. OPINE

48. OBSTETRICIAN
A. SIREN B. RETAIN
C. TERMITE D. SOBER

49. DEVELOPMENT
A. PEDANT B. ENVELOPE
C. VOLTE D. ELOPE

50. CARDIOGRAM
A. AEROGRAM B. RADIO
C. DIAGRAM D. CARGO

51. EQUIVOCATION
A. VOCATION B. LOCATION
C. EQUATION D. VATICAN

52. PORTFOLIO
A. FORT B. TROOP
C. POLIO D. FRAIL

53. APPORTIONMENT
A. METEOR B. APPOINT
C. PROBATION D. PEPPERMINT

54. HINDERLAND
A. DANCER B. HERALD
C. HINDER D. INLAND

55. PENTSTEMON
A. STONE B. TENET
C. PISTON D. MENSE

56. BOISTEROUS
A. STEREO B. SHOUT
C. BOOSTER D. TRESS

57. DISSOPPOINTMENT
A. TENAMENT B. OPPOSE
C. OINTMENT D. POSITION

58. TABERANACLE
A. BRACE B. CARNIVAL
C. CATER D. TRANCE

59. KALEIDOSCOPE
A. CLASP B. PRICK
C. SCOOP D. CLOCK

60. ELECTRIFYING
A. FRYING B. ENGINE
C. ENIGMA D. RECTIFY

61. BATHYGRAPHICAL
A. PARAGRAPH B. PHYLLARY
C. TYPICAL D. THEORETICAL

62. SUBORDINATE
A. BOARD B. SUBMIT
C. URBANE D. NATURE

63. GORGEOUS
A. SOUR B. ROAR
C. URGE D. EROS

64. ECONOMICALLY
A. COMICAL B. ECONOMY
C. AMORAL D. ALIMONY

65. HEMOGLOBIN
A. NIMBLE B. GLOBIN
C. BELONG D. MOVING

66. DOCUMENTATION
A. ACUMEN B. DONATE
C. MENTAL D. COUNT

67. WHOLESOME
A. SHOVE B. WHEEL
C. LOOSE D. HOLES

68. IMPORTANT
A. TRUMP B. IMPART
C. PRINT D. TRAIN

69. YIELDING
A. GLIDE B. INLAY
C. YELL D. DENY

70. PROPAGATE
A. PRATE B. PAGER
C. GRAFT D. AGATE

71. RATIONALLY
A. LATER B. RATION
C. TRAIL D. ORALLY

72. COMPROMISING
A. GRAIN B. COMING
C. PRISM D. SPOON

73. GRIEVANCE
A. AVENGE B. ENDURE
C. GRIEVE D. CAVERN

74. DEMONSTRATE
A. STREAM B. MODERN
C. EASTER D. RATTLE

75. INEXPENSIVE
A. EXPENSE B. NEXUS
C. PENSIVE D. VIXEN

Directions : *Find out the one word among the options which can be formed by using the letters of the word as given in each question.*

76. INVESTIGATE
A. INVERT B. GLIDE
C. STING D. ACTED

77. MAJORITY
A. MORE B. JURY
C. READ D. TRAY

78. WATFRMELON
A. MAKER B. WRITE
C. TOWER D. NOVEL

79. PREDICTION
A. DESIRE B. CREDIT
C. ACTION D. PICKED

80. BARGAIN
A. GRAIN B. BARGE
C. ANGRY D. TRING

81. THERMOSTAT
A. MOTHER B. STAMEN
C. THRUST D. HOIST

82. LEARNED
A. DREAM B. CLEAR
C. ELDER D. DRAPE

83. ADVENTURE
A. AWARE B. EVENT
C. TRUCE D. DRIED

84. THANKSGIVING
A. AVENGE B. HAUNTS
C. GRAINS D. SAVING

85. NOCTURNAL
A. CRUST B. TRAIL
C. CORAL D. OCEAN

86. CHARMED
A. HEAD B. CHUM
C. DECK D. MORE

87. ULTIMATUM
A. AUTUMN B. LIMPID
C. UTMOST D. TUMULT

88. HARBINGER
A. BIRTH B. RANCH
C. ABODE D. GRAIN

89. OTHERWISE
A. SHORT B. WASTE
C. HOVER D. ITEMS

90. DERELICT
A. TRACE B. CREED
C. LINER D. ERODE

91. SINISTER
A. TIMER B. SISTER
C. TEASE D. STRAIN

92. WORKSHOP
A. SHOCK B. ROWER
C. PORCH D. WHOOP

93. DEVELOPING
A. PLAIN B. GREED
C. DEVIL D. VOICE

94. RESIDENTIAL
A. GRIND B. TRADE
C. LOVER D. STRAP

95. BLANDISHMENT
A. BOARD B. METAL
C. SHAPE D. CRASH

96. PAINSTAKER
A. POKER B. STALK
C. TAKEN D. PRIDE

97. BELLIGERENT
A. GREEN B. LEGAL
C. BLOAT D. INFER

98. UNDISCHARGED
A. CHANGED B. DISARMED
C. GROUNDED D. SHARPEN

99. LEVIGATE
A. VEIN B. GLAD
C. EAST D. GIVE

100. MELANCHOLY
A. CHIME B. MELON
C. MADLY D. CRANE

ANSWERS

1	2	3	4	5	6	7	8	9	10
B	D	A	C	B	A	A	C	D	C
11	**12**	**13**	**14**	**15**	**16**	**17**	**18**	**19**	**20**
A	C	B	A	C	D	D	A	B	C
21	**22**	**23**	**24**	**25**	**26**	**27**	**28**	**29**	**30**
C	B	B	A	D	C	A	A	D	D
31	**32**	**33**	**34**	**35**	**36**	**37**	**38**	**39**	**40**
B	C	C	D	B	B	B	C	A	D
41	**42**	**43**	**44**	**45**	**46**	**47**	**48**	**49**	**50**
D	C	B*	C	B	C	C	C	A	A
51	**52**	**53**	**54**	**55**	**56**	**57**	**58**	**59**	**60**
B	D	C	A	C	B	A	B	B	C
61	**62**	**63**	**64**	**65**	**66**	**67**	**68**	**69**	**70**
D	B	B	C	D	C	A	A	B	C
71	**72**	**73**	**74**	**75**	**76**	**77**	**78**	**79**	**80**
A	A	B	D	B	C	D	C	B	A
81	**82**	**83**	**84**	**85**	**86**	**87**	**88**	**89**	**90**
A	C	B	D	C	A	D	D	A	B
91	**92**	**93**	**94**	**95**	**96**	**97**	**98**	**99**	**100**
B	D	C	B	B	C	A	A	D	B

ote : *Ans 43: The word CRITICAL is ruled out on the grounds that the given word has only one I

ARTIFICIAL VALUES AND MISSING NUMBERS

Playing with numbers and mathematical skills are needed to attempt these type of tests. The candidates have to work out the right combination of arithmetical symbols to arrive at the answer options which will take the place of the interrogation sign in the given questions.

SOLVED EXAMPLES

1. Select the right option which can be placed at the sign of interrogation?

16 17 32 5 25 11

13 22 49 81 50 34

68 167 ?

A. 65 B. 120

C. 116 D. 192

Ans. B : The number inside the circle is the sum of the other four numbers, *i.e.,*

16 + 17 + 13 + 22 = 68

32 + 5 + 49 + 81 = 167, similarly

25 + 11 + 50 + 34 = 120

2. Which one number can be placed at the sig of interrogation?

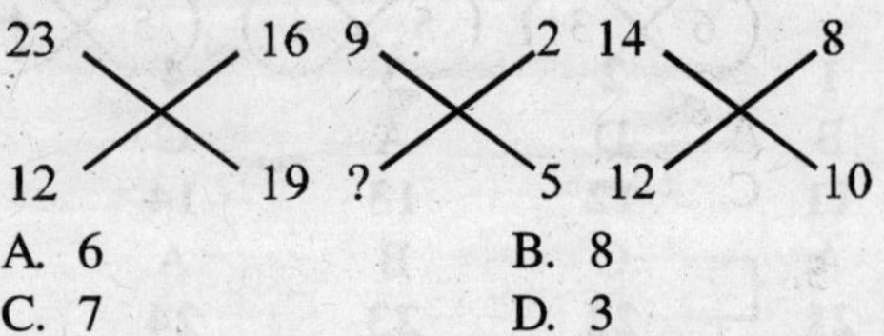

A. 6 B. 8

C. 7 D. 3

Ans. A : The difference between two opposi numbers is 4, *i.e.,*

23 − 19 = 4 and 16 − 12 = 4

14 − 10 = 4 and 12 − 8 = 4, similarly

9 − 5 = 4 and 6 − 2 = 4.

There are no definite rules to reach the rig answer. Try solving the questions in the exercis given below to learn more about the differe ways of getting the correct answer.

MULTIPLE CHOICE QUESTIONS

Directions : *In each question given below which one number can be placed at the sign of interrogation?*

1.

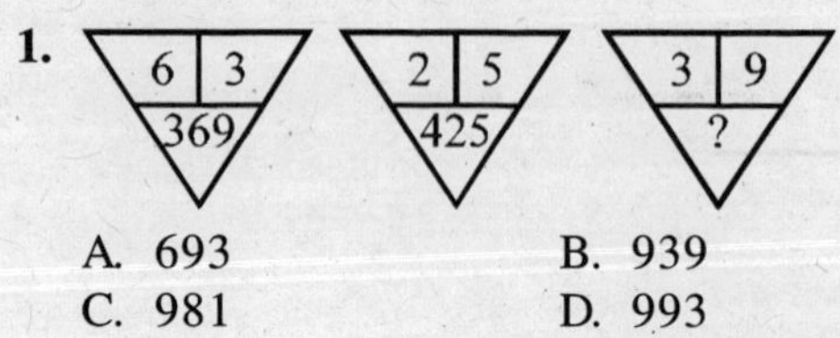

A. 693 B. 939

C. 981 D. 993

2.

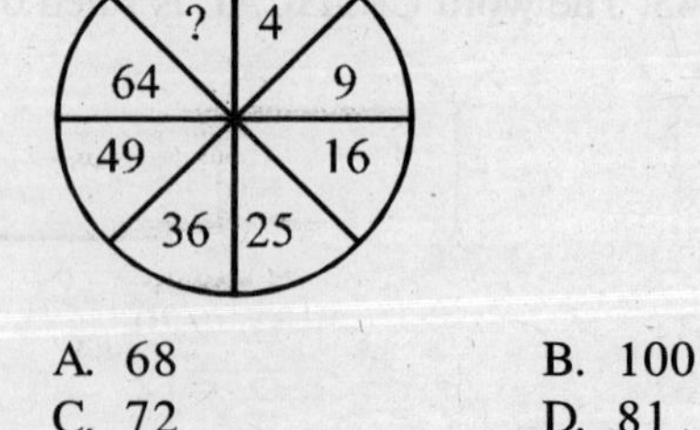

A. 68 B. 100

C. 72 D. 81

3.

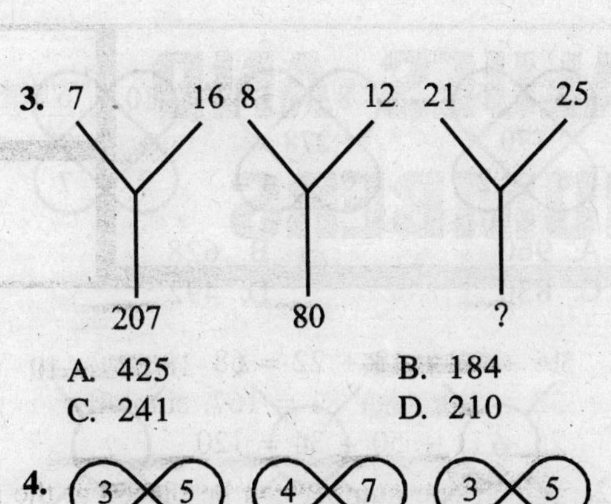

A. 425 B. 184
C. 241 D. 210

4.

A. 35 B. 37
C. 45 D. 48

5.

7 5
6

5 21
13

24 4
?

A. 4 B. 8
C. 20 D. 14

6.

14	9	4
12	7	2
10	5	0
16	11	?

A. 9 B. 6
C. 3 D. 7

7.

29, 27, 39, 80, 33, 45, 43

29, 30, 42, 70, 31, 43, 44

59, 40, ?, 80, 10, 39, 20

A. 69 B. 49
C. 50 D. 60

8.

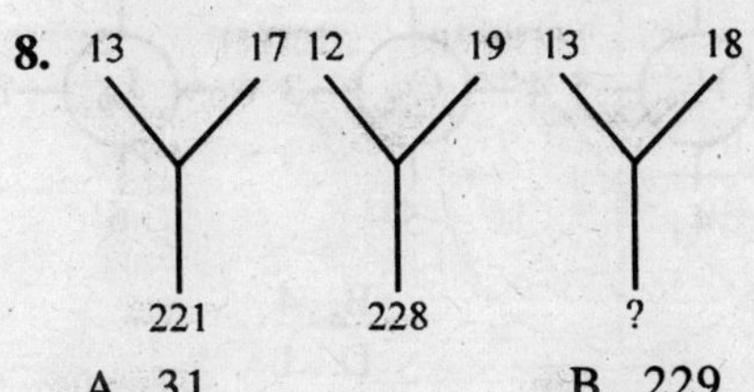

A. 31 B. 229
C. 234 D. 312

9.

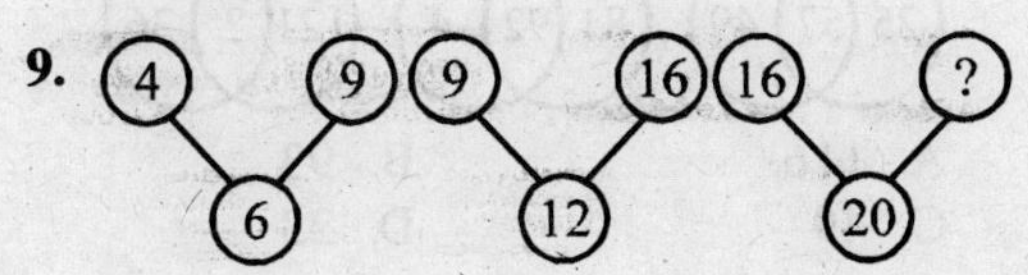

A. 21 B. 25
C. 50 D. 60

10.

51	(11)	61
64	(30)	32
35	(?)	43

A. 25 B. 27
C. 32 D. 37

11.

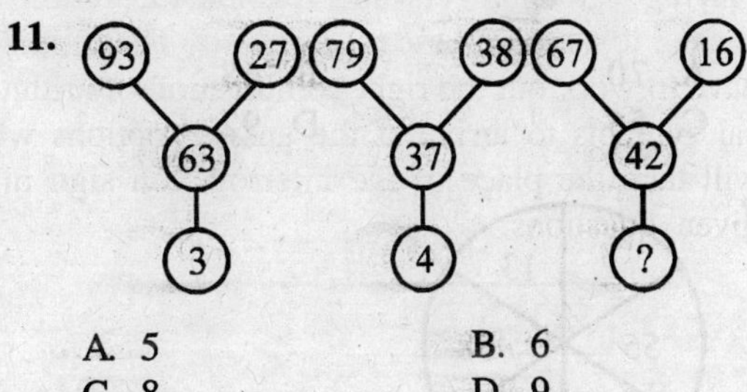

A. 5 B. 6
C. 8 D. 9

12.

4, 6, 14, 8, 10, 18

8, 6, 14, 8, 14, 22

5, 6, ?, 4, 11, 15

A. 8 B. 14
C. 10 D. 6

13.

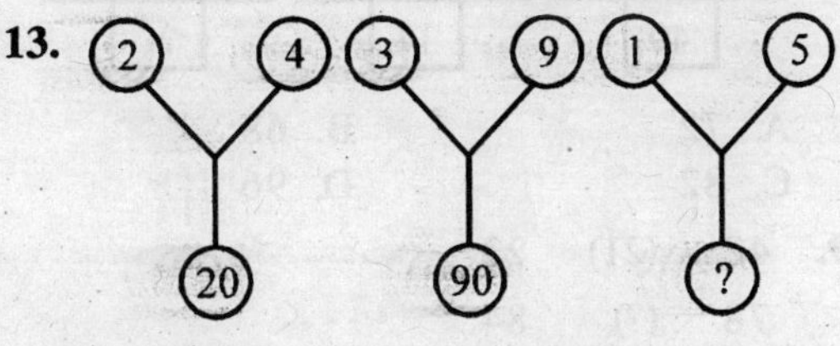

A. 20 B. 25
C. 26 D. 75

14.

27	22	50
13	12	26
9	2	?

A. 12 B. 39
C. 18 D. 24

15.

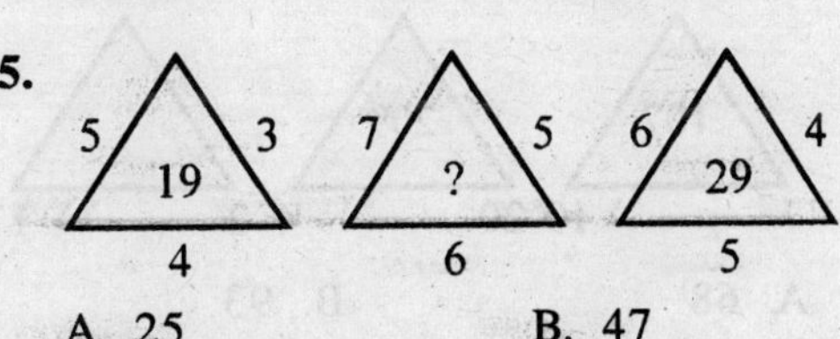

A. 25 B. 47
C. 37 D. 41

16.

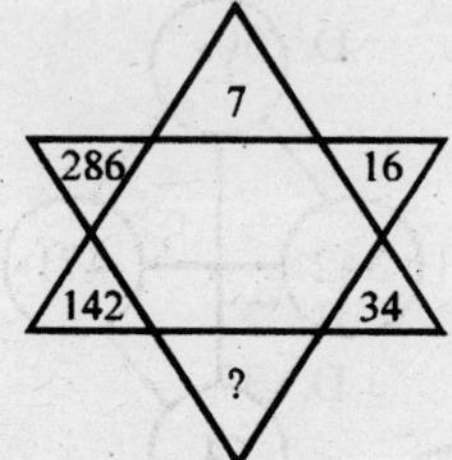

A. 70
B. 68
C. 56
D. 92

17.

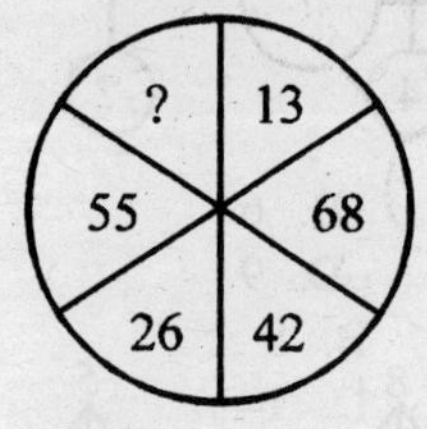

A. 41
B. 37
C. 29
D. 25

18.

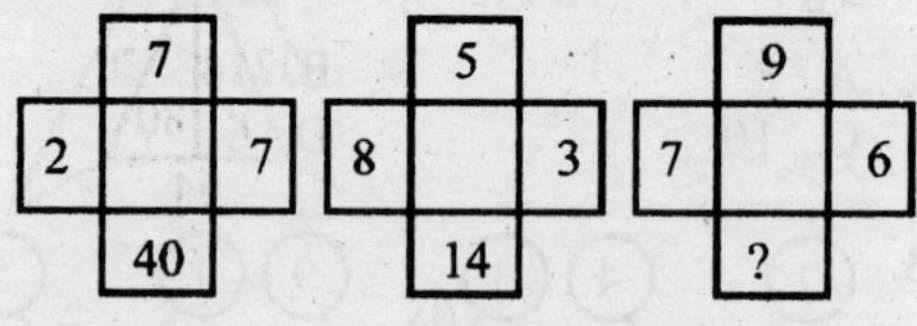

A. 72
B. 68
C. 82
D. 96

19.

42	(21)	22
78	(?)	84
162	(18)	99

A. 12
B. 13
C. 60
D. 72

20.

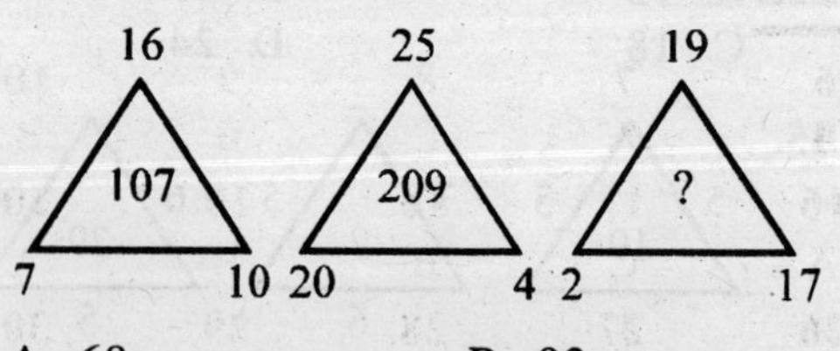

A. 68
B. 93
C. 175
D. 217

21.

10 6 ? 2 7

A. 960
B. 628
C. 830
D. 492

22.

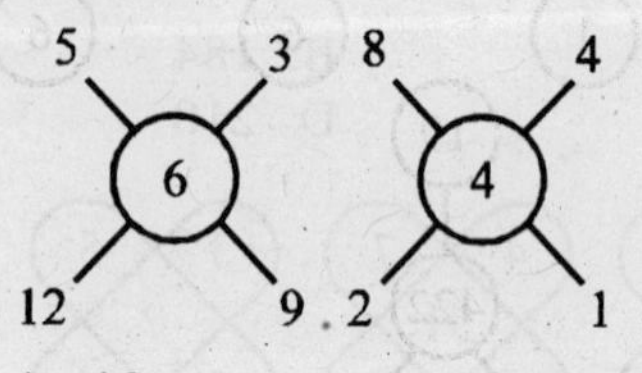

A. 18
B. 10
C. 36
D. 24

23.

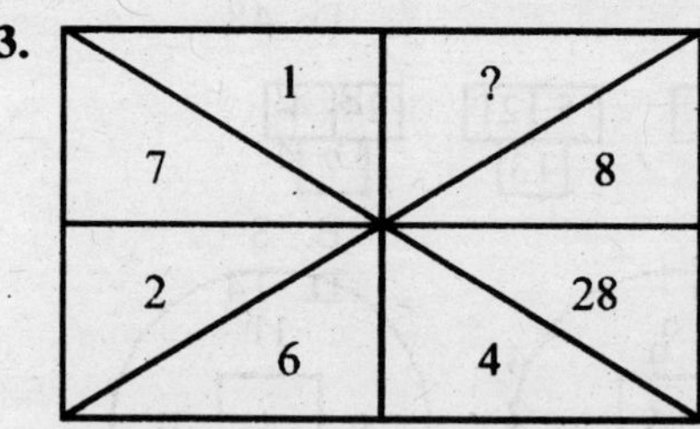

A. 24
B. 10
C. 32
D. 12

24.

6	(40)	4
3	(12)	3
7	(?)	2

A. 51
B. 36
C. 22
D. 4

25.

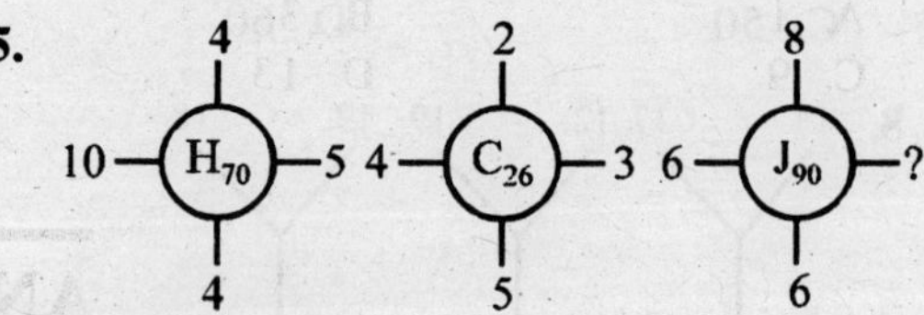

A. 5
B. 4
C. 2
D. 1

26.

25 (57) 49 81 (92) 4 121 (?) 36

A. 116
B. 93
C. 49
D. 23

27.

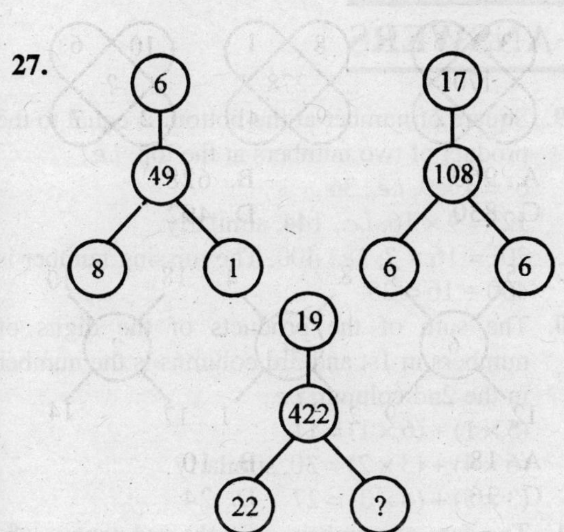

A. 0 B. 2
C. 3 D. 4

28.

9
2 19 M
5

11
9 4 B
2

3
? 6 E
7

A. 1 B. 3
C. 9 D. 13

29.

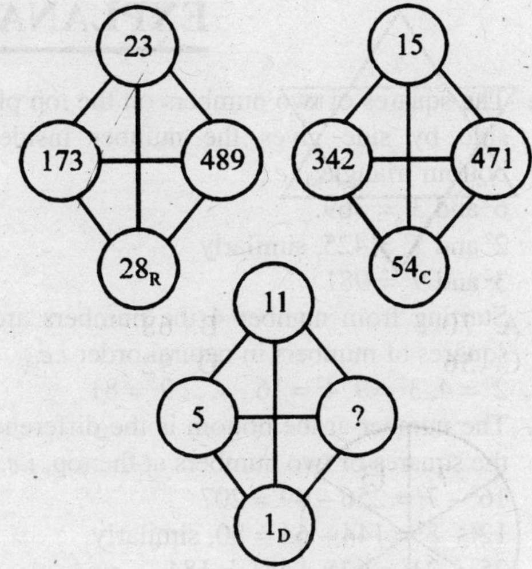

A. 3 B. 8
C. 10 D. 14

30.

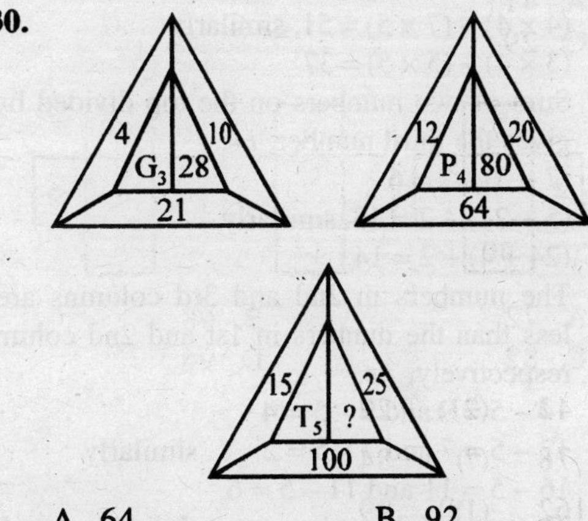

A. 64 B. 92
C. 120 D. 146

ANSWERS

1	2	3	4	5	6	7	8	9	10
C	D	B	B	D	B	A	C	B	B
11	**12**	**13**	**14**	**15**	**16**	**17**	**18**	**19**	**20**
D	C	C	A	D	A	C	B	B	A
21	**22**	**23**	**24**	**25**	**26**	**27**	**28**	**29**	**30**
C	D	A	A	B	A	D	B	C	C

EXPLANATORY ANSWERS

1. The squares of two numbers on the top placed side by side gives the number inside the bottom triangle, *i.e.*,
6^2 and $3^2 = 369$
2^2 and $5^2 = 425$, similarly
3^2 and $9^2 = 981$.
2. Starting from number 4 the numbers are the squares of numbers in natural order *i.e.*,
$2^2 = 4, 3^2 = 9, 4^2 = 16 \ldots\ldots 9^2 = 81$
3. The number at the bottom is the difference of the squares of two numbers at the top, *i.e.*,
$16^2 - 7^2 = 256 - 49 = 207$
$12^2 - 8^2 = 144 - 64 = 80$, similarly
$25^2 - 21^2 = 625 - 441 = 184$
4. The number in the centre is the sum of the products of diagonal numbers, *i.e.*,
$(3 \times 3) + (5 \times 6) = 39$
$(4 \times 4) + (7 \times 5) = 51$, similarly
$(3 \times 4) + (5 \times 5) = 37$
5. Sum of two numbers on the top divided by 2 gives the third number, *i.e.*,
$(7 + 5) \div 2 = 6$
$(5 + 21) \div 2 = 13$, similarly
$(24 + 4) \div 2 = 14$
6. The numbers in 2nd and 3rd columns are 5 less than the nunbers in 1st and 2nd columns respectively, *i.e.*,
$14 - 5 = 9$ and $9 - 5 = 4$
$12 - 5 = 7$ and $7 - 5 = 2, \ldots$ similarly
$16 - 5 = 11$ and $11 - 5 = 6$.
7. The sum of 3 numbers in each line in one figure is same, *i.e.*,
$29 + 80 + 43$ or $39 + 80 + 33$
or $45 + 80 + 27 = 152$
$29 + 70 + 44$ or $42 + 70 + 31$
or $43 + 70 + 30 = 143$, similarly
$59 + 80 + 20$ or $39 + 80 + 40 = 159$.
The missing number is :
$159 - (80 + 10) = 69$
8. The number at the bottom is the product of two numbers at the top, *i.e.*,
$13 \times 17 = 221$
$12 \times 19 = 228$, similarly
$13 \times 18 = 234$
9. Square of number at the bottom is equal to the product of two numbers at the top, *i.e.*,
$6^2 = 4 \times 9$, *i.e.*, 36
$12^2 = 9 \times 16$, *i.e.*, 144, similarly
$20^2 = 16 \times ?$, *i.e.*, 400. The missing number is $400 \div 16 = 25$
10. The sum of the products of the digits of numbers in 1st and 3rd columns is the number in the 2nd column, *i.e.*,
$(5 \times 1) + (6 \times 1) = 11$
$(6 \times 4) + (3 \times 2) = 30$, similarly
$(3 \times 5) + (4 \times 3) = 27$
11. The sum of numbers on right and centre subtracted from the number on the left gives the number at the bottom, *i.e.*,
$93 - (27 + 63) = 3$
$79 - (38 + 37) = 4$, similarly
$67 - (16 + 42) = 9$
12. The number inside each triangle is the difference of the numbers at its base *i.e.*
$10 - 4 = 6$, $18 - 4 = 14$ and $18 - 10 = 8$
$14 - 8 = 6$, $22 - 8 = 14$ and $22 - 14 = 8$, similarly
$11 - 5 = 6$, $15 - 5 = 10$ and $15 - 11 = 4$.
13. The sum of squares of two numbers at the top gives the third number below, *i.e.*,
$2^2 + 4^2 = 20$
$3^2 + 9^2 = 90$, similarly
$1^2 + 5^2 = 26$
14. The sum of numbers in 1st and 2nd column plus 1 is the number in the 3rd column, *i.e.*,
$27 + 22 + 1 = 50$
$13 + 12 + 1 = 26$, similarly
$9 + 2 + 1 = 12$
15. The product of numbers on either side of the triangle plus the number at the base is the number inside the triangle, *i.e.*,
$(5 \times 3) + 4 = 19$
$(6 \times 4) + 5 = 29$, similarly
$(7 \times 5) + 6 = 41$
16. Clockwise starting from number 7, the nex number is obtained by doubling the numbe and adding 2, *i.e.*,

$(7 \times 2) + 2 = 16$
$(16 \times 2) + 2 = 34$ . . ., similarly
$(34 \times 2) + 2 = 70$
$(70 \times 2) + 2 = 142$
$(142 \times 2) + 2 = 286$

17. The difference between the numbers in opposite sectors is 13, *i.e.*,
$26 - 13 = 13$
$68 - 55 = 13$, similarly
The missing number is $42 - 13 = 29$
($42 + 13 = 55$ is not given as option)

18. The number at the bottom is obtained by subtracting the sum of two numbers in the centre grid line from the square of the number at the top, *i.e.*,
$7^2 - (2 + 7) = 40$
$5^2 - (8 + 3) = 14$, similarly
$9^2 - (7 + 6) = 68$

19. The number inside the brackets is obtained by multiplying the number on the left by 2 and then dividing the product by the sum of digits of number on the right, *i.e.*,
$(42 \times 2) \div (2 + 2) = 21$
$(162 \times 2) \div (9 + 9) = 18$, similarly
$(78 \times 2) \div (8 + 4) = 13$

20. Subtracting the sum of squares of two numbers at the base from the square of number at the apex gives the number inside the triangle, *i.e.*,
$16^2 - (7^2 + 10^2) = 107$
$25^2 - (20^2 + 4^2) = 209$, similarly
$19^2 - (2^2 + 17^2) = 68$

21. The number in the centre is the product of all the 4 numbers minus 10, *i.e.*,
$(3 \times 5 \times 2 \times 6) - 10 = 170$
$(8 \times 1 \times 4 \times 9) - 10 = 278$, similarly
$(10 \times 6 \times 7 \times 2) - 10 = 830$

22. The number inside the circle is the product of difference of two numbers above and difference of two numbers below, *i.e.*,
$(5 - 3)(12 - 9) = 6$
$(8 - 4)(2 - 1) = 4$, similarly
$(18 - 10)(17 - 14) = 24$

23. Starting from number 1 anticlockwise the number in the diagonally opposite section is its multiplication by 4, *i.e.*,
$1 \times 4 = 4, 7 \times 4 = 28, 2 \times 4 = 8$, similarly $6 \times 4 = 24$.

24. Square of the number on the left plus the number on the right is the number within brackets, *i.e.*,
$6^2 + 4 = 40$
$3^2 + 3 = 12$, similarly
$7^2 + 2 = 51$

25. Letter H is 8th in order of alphabetical series. Taking the sum of numbers placed vertically outside the circle + 8; multiplying it by the number on the right; then subtracting from the product the number on the left, gives the number inside the circle, *i.e.*,

Step I → $4 + 8 + 4 = 16$
Step II → $16 \times 5 = 80$
Step III → $80 - 10 = 70$

Letter C is 3rd in order, so

Step I → $2 + 3 + 5 = 10$
Step II → $10 \times 3 = 30$
Step III → $30 - 4 = 26$

Similarly, J is 10th in order, so

Step I → $8 + 10 + 6 = 24$
Step II → $24 \times ?$
Step III → $(24 \times ?) - 6 = 90$

Simplifying the above equation :
$24 \times ? = 90 + 6$, *i.e.*, 96
$? = 96 \div 24 = 4$

26. The digits in the centre are obtained from the root of numbers on both sides *i.e.*
$\sqrt{25} = 5$ and $\sqrt{49} = 7$
gives 57
$\sqrt{81} = 9$ and $\sqrt{4} = 2$ gives 92
Similarly
$\sqrt{121} = 11$ and $\sqrt{36} = 6$ gives 116

27. The number in the centre divided by the number on the top gives the quotient in the lower left circle and remainder on the lower right, *i.e.*,

6) 49 (8 Quotient
48
1 Remainder

17) 108 (6 Quotient
102
6 Remainder

Similarly,

$$\begin{array}{r} 19\ )\ 422\ (\ 22 \text{ Quotient} \\ \underline{38} \\ 42 \\ \underline{38} \\ 4 \text{ Remainder} \end{array}$$

28. Letter M is 13th in order of aphabetical series. So 13 (= M) × 2 (number on the opposite side) = 9 × 5 (product of numbers above and below the square) – 19 (number inside the square) *i.e.*

$13 \times 2 = (9 \times 5) - 19$

$26 = (45 - 19)$

$26 = 26$

Letter B is 2nd in order, so

$2 \times 9 = (11 \times 2) - 4$

$18 = 22 - 4$

$18 = 18$

Similarly, letter E is 5th in order

$5 \times ? = (3 \times 7) - 6$

$5 \times ? = 21 - 6$

$5 \times ? = 15$

$? = 15 \div 5 = 3$

29. Letter R is 18th in order of aphabetical series. So the product of vertically opposite numbers + 18 (= R) = the sum of two horizontally opposite numbers, *i.e.*,

$(28 \times 23) + 18 = 173 + 489$

$644 + 18 = 662$

$662 = 662$

Letter C is 3rd in order, so

$(54 \times 15) + 3 = 342 + 471$

$810 + 3 = 813$

$813 = 813$

Similarly, letter D is 4th in order

$(1 \times 11) + 4 = 5 + ?$

$11 + 4 = 5 + ?$

$15 = 5 + ? \text{ or } 5 + ? = 15$

So, $? = 15 - 5 = 10$

30. Letter G is 7th in order of alphabetical series. Starting from left section of the big triangle the order is G – 3, *i.e.*, 7 – 3 = 4; G + 3, *i.e.*, 7 + 3 = 10 and G × 3, *i.e.*, 7 × 3 = 21. The number in the right section of inner triangle is the sum of outer numbers minus G, *i.e.*, (4 + 10 + 21) – 7 = 35 – 7 = 28

Letter P is 16th in order so

16 – 4 = 12; 16 + 4 = 20; 16 × 4 = 64; further

(12 + 20 + 64) – 16 = 96 – 16 = 80;

Similarly,

letter T is 20th in order so

20 – 5 = 15; 20 + 5 = 25; 20 × 5 = 100 further

(15 + 25 + 100) – 20 = 140 – 20 = 120

LOGICAL DIAGRAMS

In these type of questions, a set of five different figures is given as options. Each figure represents a logical pattern of certain groups of related words wherein each word represents a class. One has to identify the most appropriate logical figure for the set of words given. Some of the relationships represented by these diagrams are given below. Understand the relationship patterns and then attempt the exercise following the explanation.

SOLVED EXAMPLES

1. The given classes have nothing in common.
Example : Milk, Eggs.

Milk Eggs

2. The given classes have something in common, but neither of them is completely contained in the other.
Example : Colour, Red

Colour Red

3. Of the two given classes, one is wholly contained in the other, but not vice–versa.
Example : Fruits, Apples

Fruits Apples

4. Same logic as figure 2.
Example : Tall, Men, Educated

Tall Men Edu-cated

5. Of the three given classes, one is completely contained in the other and not vice–versa while the third class has nothing in common with either of the two classes.
Example : Water, Solids, Liquids

Liquids Water Solids

6. Two classes are wholly contained in the third class, but not vice–versa, also the two contained classes have nothing in common.
Example : Punjab, Agra, India

India Punjab Agra

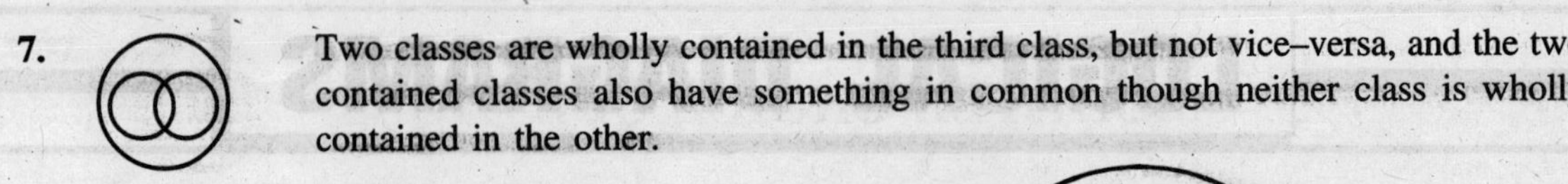

7. **Two classes are wholly contained in the third class, but not vice–versa, and the two contained classes also have something in common though neither class is wholly contained in the other.**

Example : Mothers, Sisters, Females

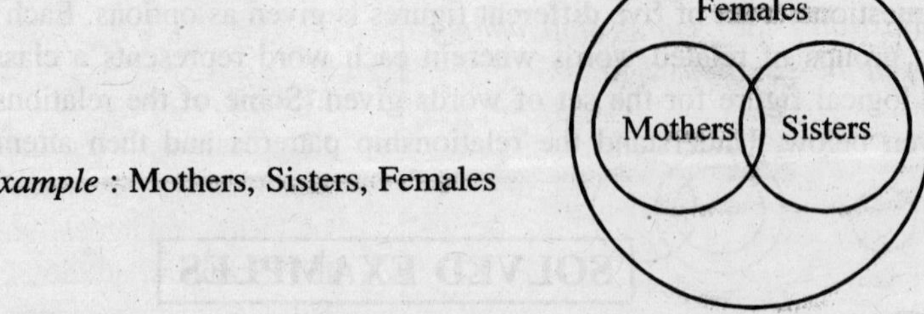

8. **The first class is contained wholly in the other two classes, but not vice–versa. The second is wholly contained in the third and partially in the first. A part of third class is contained in the second of which some is contained in the first.**

Example : Preposition, From, Grammer.

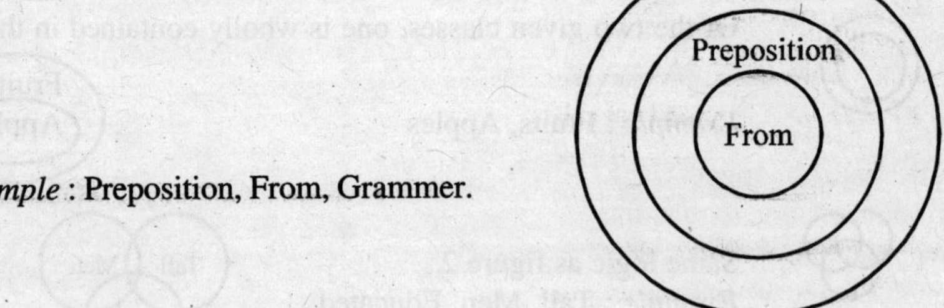

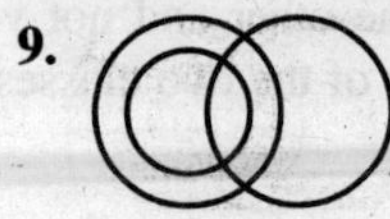

9. **First class is wholly contained in the second and not vice–versa. The third class is partially contained in the other two classes.**

Example : Sugar, Sweet, Tea

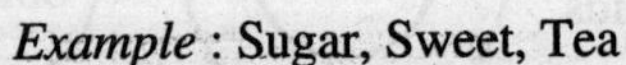

Note : Some people drink tea without Sugar.

10. **The first and second class have some part in common, and so have the second and third class, but the first and the third class have nothing in common.**

Example : Rich, Men, Famous.

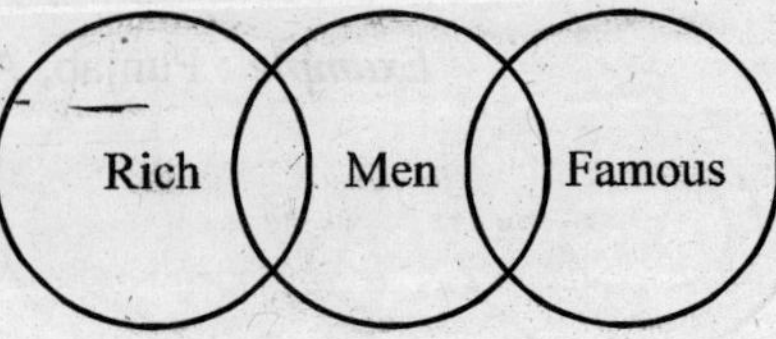

MULTIPLE CHOICE QUESTIONS

Directions : *From the five logical Diagrams, select one which best illustrates the relationship among three given classes in the questions 1 to 10.*

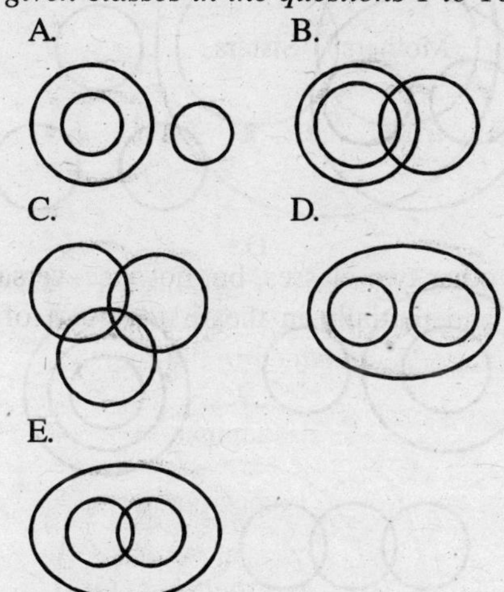

1. Birds, fruits, mangoes
2. Criminals, lawyers, bandits
3. Swimmers, bachelors, men
4. Smart, engineers, women
5. Vegetables, potatoes, brinjals
6. Grapes, sweet, fruit
7. Doctors, architects, humans
8. Scholars, people, Indians
9. Children, naughty, studious
10. Pens, pencils, stationery

Directions : *From the five logical diagrams select one which best illustrates the relationship among three given classes in questions 11 to 20.*

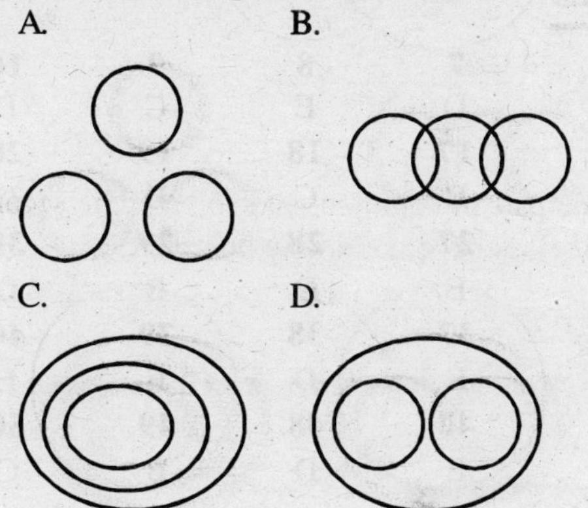

E.

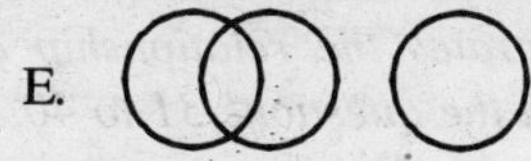

11. Ink, crayons, red
12. Canines, dogs, pups
13. Table, chair, stool
14. Ripe, mangoes, basket
15. Scholars, studious, illiterates
16. Cars, ships, means of conveyance
17. Age, number, thirteen
18. Country, state, continent
19. Father, parent, mother
20. Iron, metal, mercury

Directions : *From the five logical diagrams select one which best illustrates the relationship among three given classes in the questions 21 to 30.*

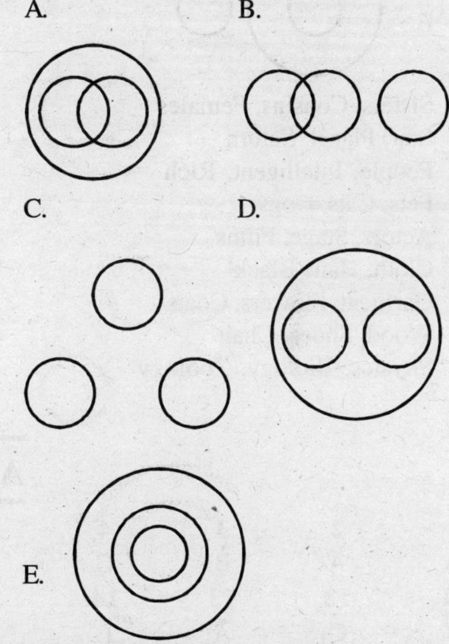

21. Lizards, Reptiles, Crocodiles
22. Whales, Tortoise, Fishes
23. Birds, Crows, Parrots
24. Sisters, Women, Mothers
25. Plants, Scientists, Men
26. Novels, Album, English
27. Sentences, Words, Paragraph

28. Beef, Mutton, Flesh
29. Principal, Student, Parent
30. Lily, Rose, Flower.

Directions : *From the five logical diagrams select one which best illustrates the relationship among three given classes in the questions 31 to 40.*

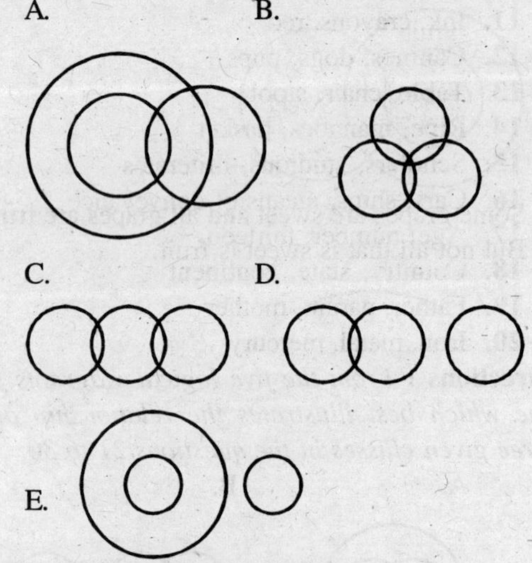

31. Sisters, Cousins, Females
32. Star, Planet, Saturn
33. People, Intelligent, Rich
34. Pets, Cats, Dogs
35. Actors, Stage, Films
36. Cloth, Hair, Black
37. Garment, Flowers, Coats
38. Wood, Shoes, Chair
39. Physics, Biology, Zoology
40. Police, Criminal, Thief

Directions : *From the five logical diagrams select one which best illustrates the relationship among three given classes in the questions 41 to 50.*

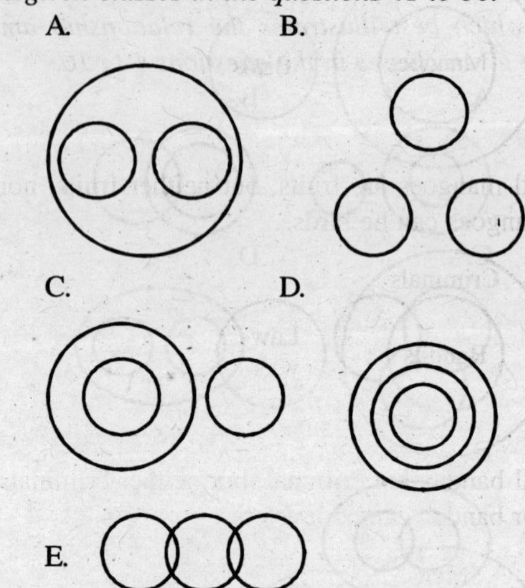

41. Country, Nepal, India
42. Body, Blood, Veins
43. Chess, Games, Hockey
44. Tractor, Aircraft, Cart
45. Oriental, Continental, Mughlai
46. Delhi, Lucknow, Uttar Pradesh
47. Russian, People, German
48. Days, Months, Years
49. Stamp, Pen, Chalk
50. Marble, Animal, Goat

ANSWERS

1	2	3	4	5	6	7	8	9	10
A	A	B	C	D	B	D	E	C	D
11	**12**	**13**	**14**	**15**	**16**	**17**	**18**	**19**	**20**
B	C	A	E	E	D	B	C	D	D
21	**22**	**23**	**24**	**25**	**26**	**27**	**28**	**29**	**30**
D	C	D	A	B	B	E	D	B	D
31	**32**	**33**	**34**	**35**	**36**	**37**	**38**	**39**	**40**
A	D	B	C	B	C	E	D	E	E
41	**42**	**43**	**44**	**45**	**46**	**47**	**48**	**49**	**50**
A	D	A	B	B	C	E	D	B	C

EXPLANATORY ANSWERS

1. 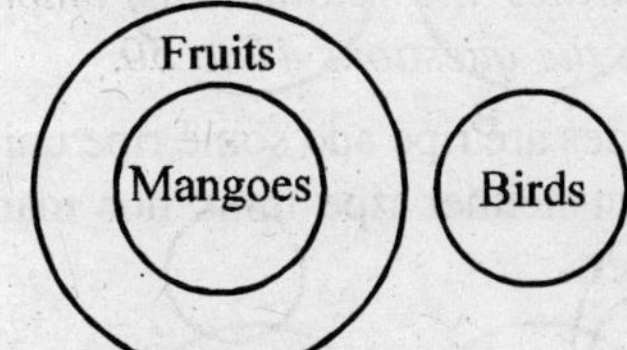

All mangoes are fruits, but neither fruits, nor mangoes can be birds.

2. 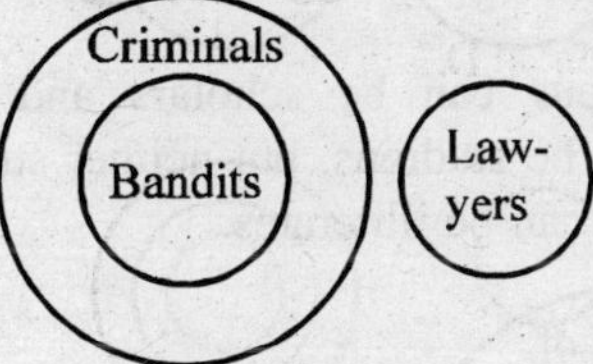

All bandits are criminal, but neither criminals nor bandits can be lawyers.

3. 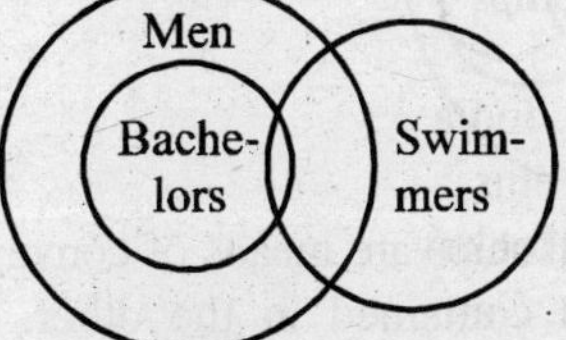

All bachelors are men and some men and bachelors can be swimmers.

4. 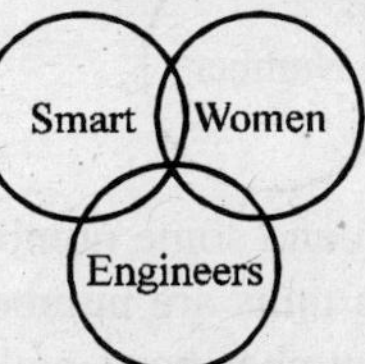

Some women can be smart and some women can be engineers and vice–versa. Some engineers can be women and some engineers can be smart and vice–versa.

5. 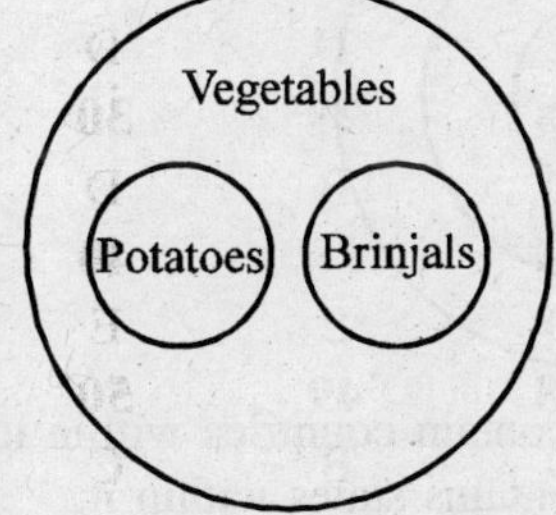

Potatoes and brinjals are vegetables but they have nothing in common. Some vegetables are potatoes and some are brinjals.

6. 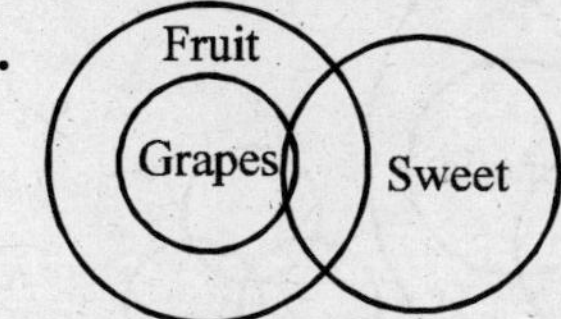

Some grapes are sweet and all grapes are fruit. But not all that is sweet is fruit.

7. 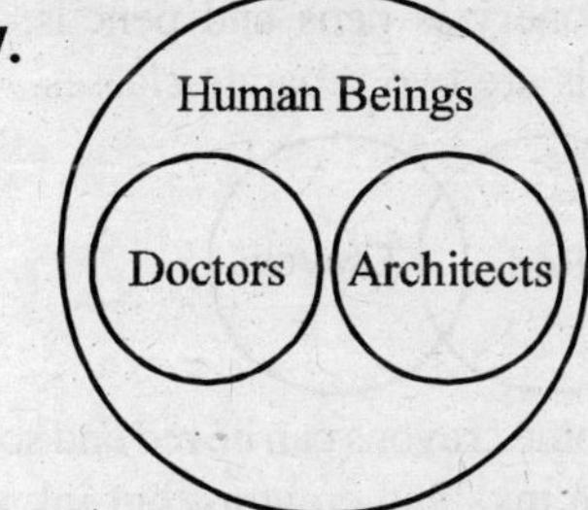

Doctors and architects are two separate classes, but all doctors and architects are humans and some humans are either doctors or architects.

8. 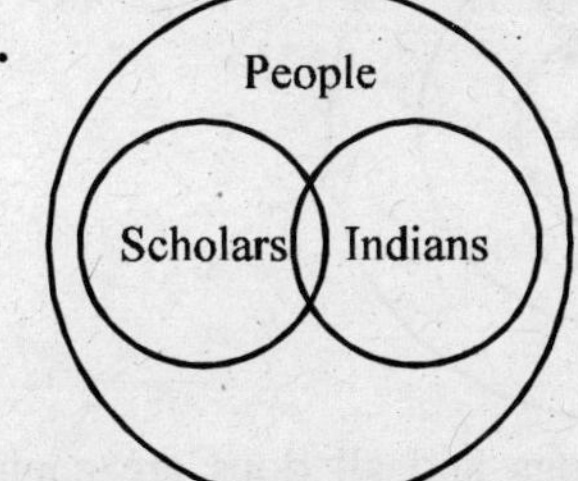

Some Indians can be scholars and some scholars can be Indians. All scholars and Indians are people.

9. 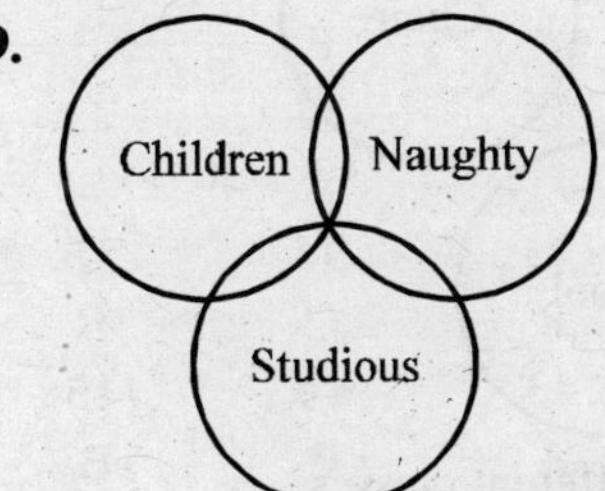

Some children can be naughty and some can be studious, some studious can be children and some naughty. Some naughty can be studious and some children.

10.

Stationery
Pens
Pencils

Pens and pencils both are items of stationery and some stationery is pens and pencils, but pens and pencils are two separate classes.

11.

Inks
Red
Crayons

Some ink and some crayons can be red and some red units can be inks and crayons, but ink and crayon have nothing in common.

12.

Canines
Dogs
Pups

All pups are dogs and all dogs are canines. Some canines are dogs, of which some are pups.

13.

Table
Chair
Stool

All three are different classes.

14.

Ripe
Mangoes
Baskets

Some mangoes are ripe and some ripe units a mangoes, but neither ripe units nor mango can be baskets.

15.

Studious
Scholars
Illiterates

Some studious can be scholars and sor scholars can be studious, but neither studio nor scholars can be illiterates.

16.

Means of Conveyance
Cars
Ships

All cars and all ships are means of conveyan but neither is contained in the other. So means of conveyance are cars and some shi

17.

Age
Thirteen
Number

Some are aged thirteen and some numbers thirteen. Some thirteen units are numbers a some ages. Age and number have nothing common.

18.

Continents
Countries
States

All continents contain countries within it each country contains states within it.

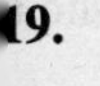

19.

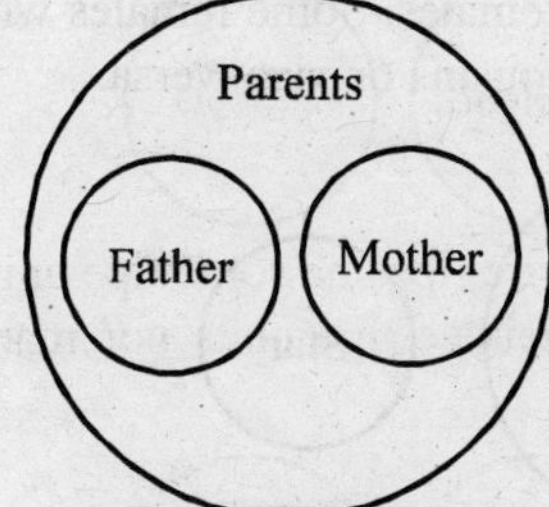

All fathers and mothers are parents, but they are two separate classes. Some of the parents are fathers and some are mothers.

0.

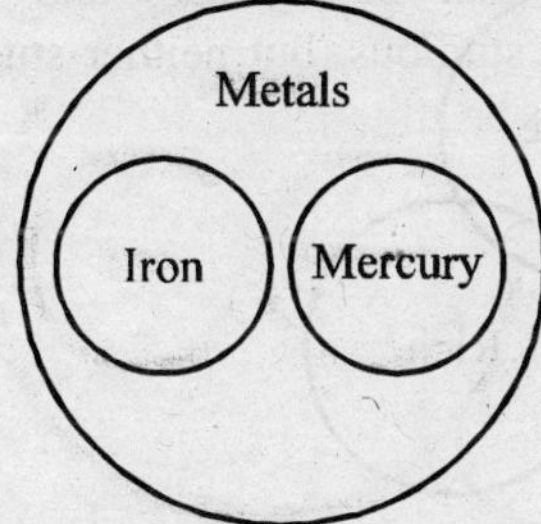

Iron and mercury are metals, but they have nothing in common. Some metals are iron and some mercury.

1.

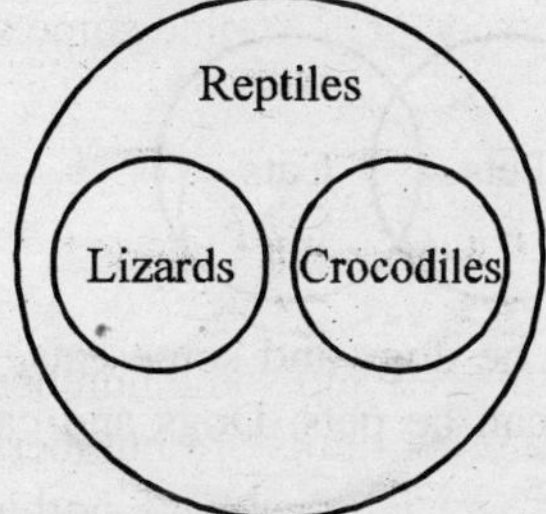

All lizards and crocodiles are reptiles, but neither is contained in the other. Some reptiles are lizards and some crocodiles.

.

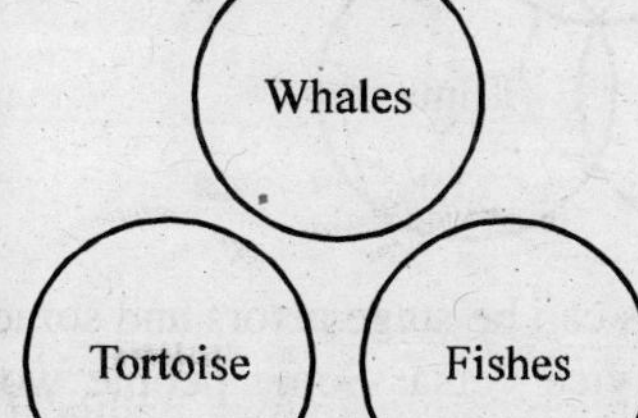

All three are different classes.

23.

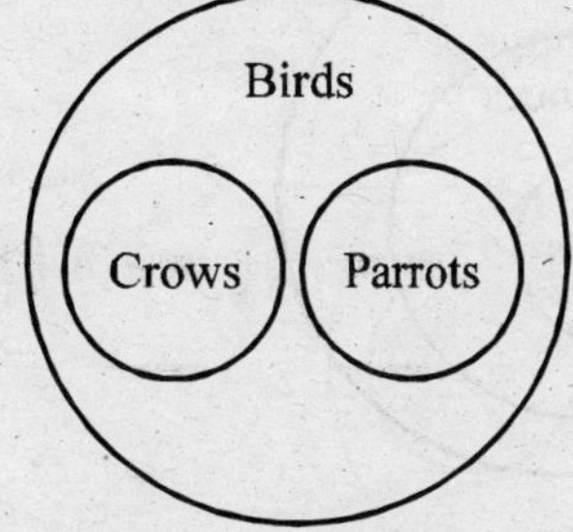

All crows and parrots are birds but neither is contained in the other. Some birds are crows and some parrots.

24.

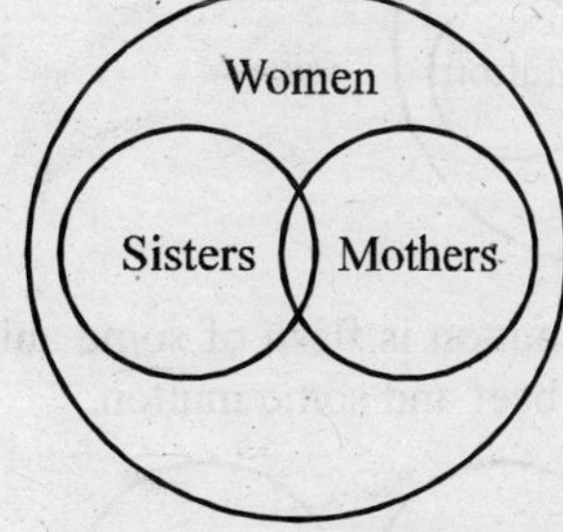

Some sisters can be mothers and some mothers can be sisters. All sisters and mothers are women.

25.

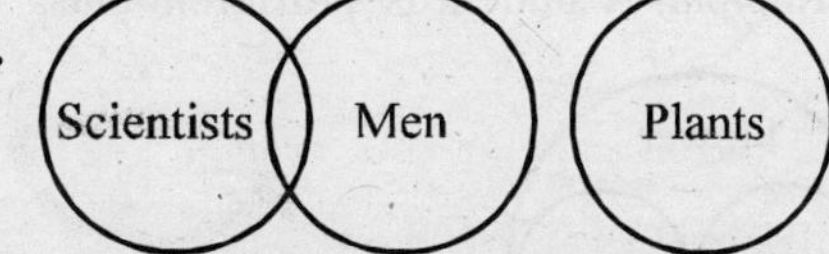

Some scientists can be men and some men can be scientists, but neither scientists nor men can be plants.

26.

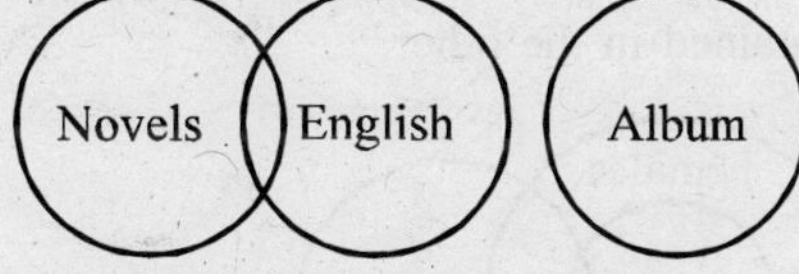

Some novels can be in English and some written material in English can be novels, but neither novels nor English can be album.

27.

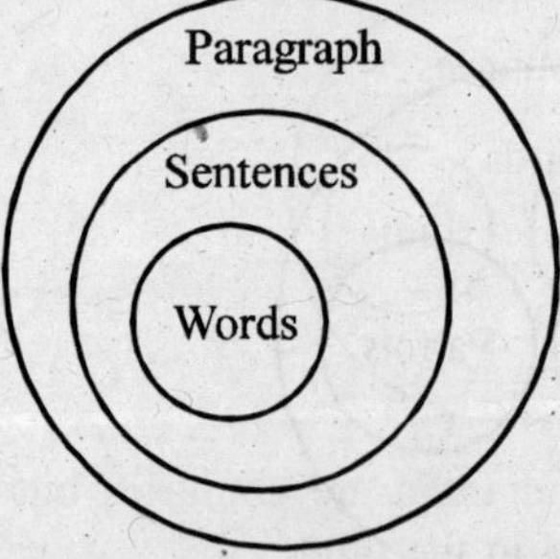

All paragraphs contain sentences within it and all sentences contain words within it.

28.

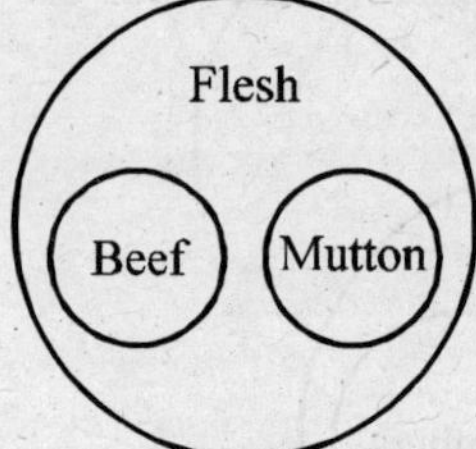

All beef and mutton is flesh of some animals. Some flesh is beef and some mutton.

29.

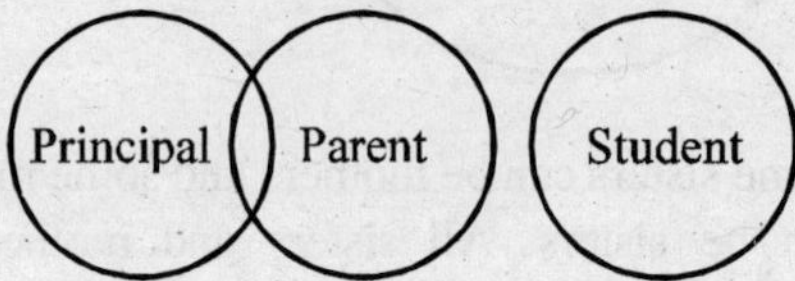

A Principal can be a parent and parent can be a principal. A student is a different class.

30.

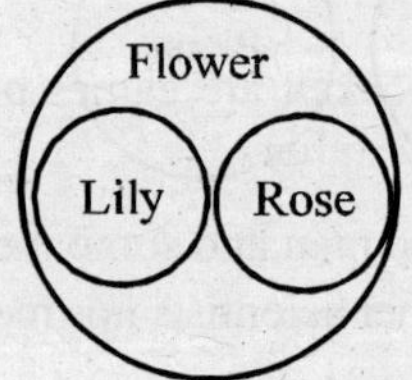

Both lily and rose are flowers. But neither is contained in the other.

31.

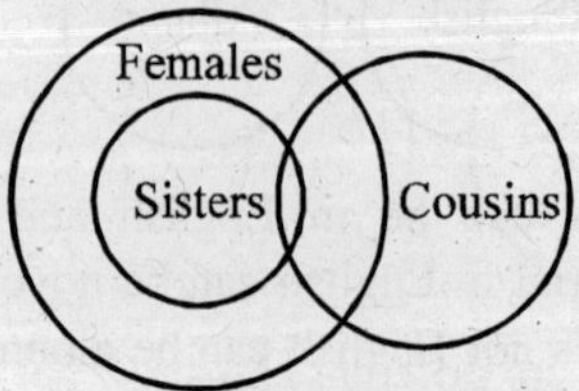

All sisters are females. Some females who a sisters can be cousins or vice–versa.

32.

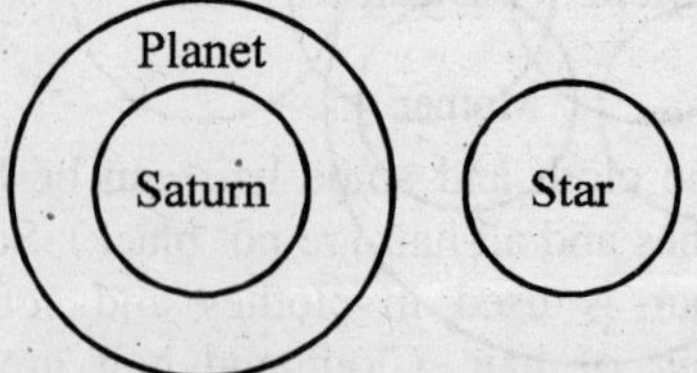

Saturn is a planet. One of the planets is Satu Star is a different class.

33.

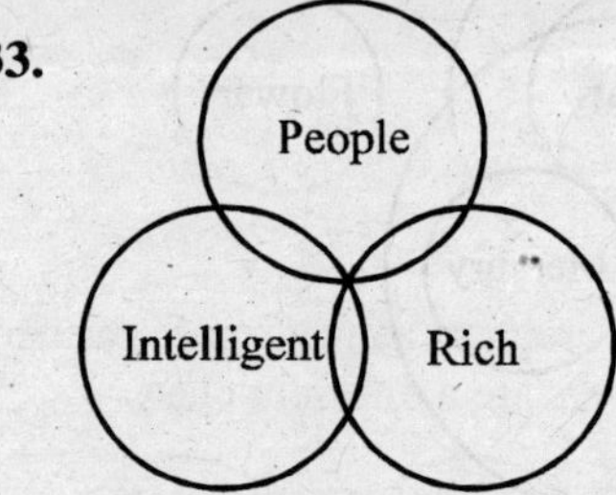

Some people can be intelligent and some be rich and vice–versa. Some intelligent be rich and some intelligent beings can people and vice versa.

34.

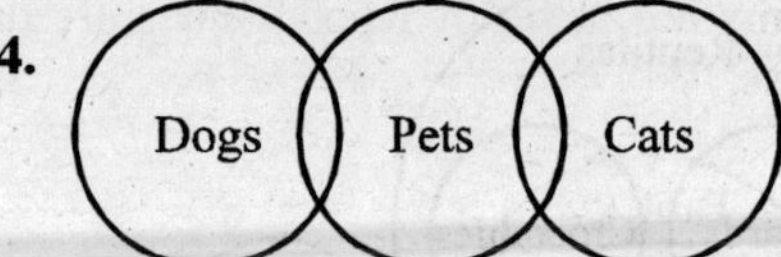

Some pets can be dogs and some cats. Sc dogs and cats can be pets. Dogs and cats different classes.

35.

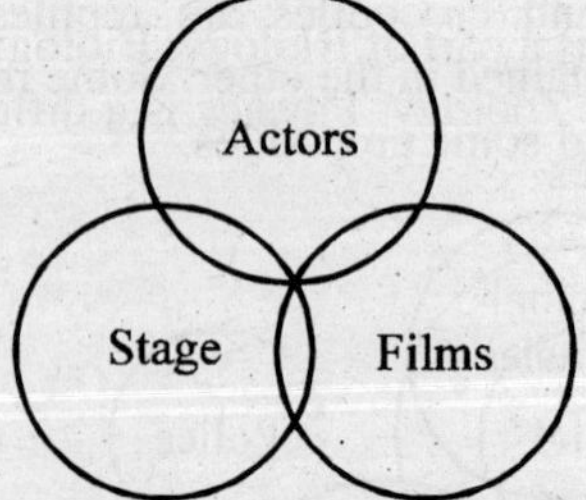

Some actors can be stage actors and some actors and vice versa. Some people wor in films can be actors and some can als stage actors and vice versa.

36.

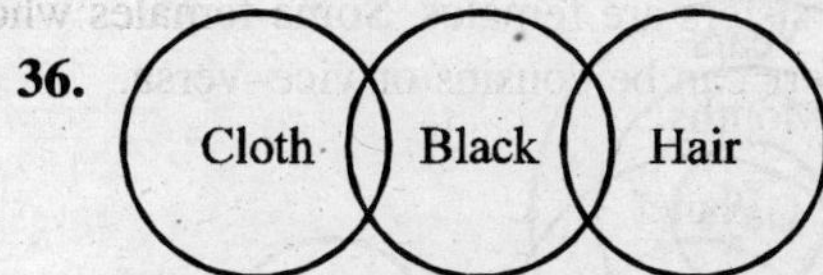

Some cloth and some hair can be black. (all clothes and all hair are not black). Some black colour is used in clothes and some is the colour of hair. Cloth and hair are different classes.

37.

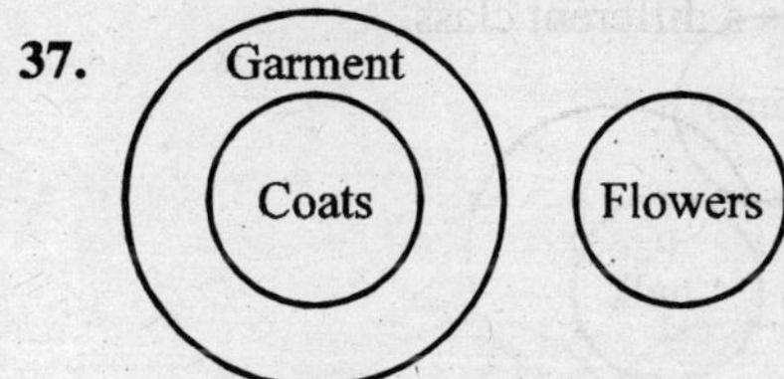

All coats are garments. Some garments are coat. Flowers are a different class.

38.

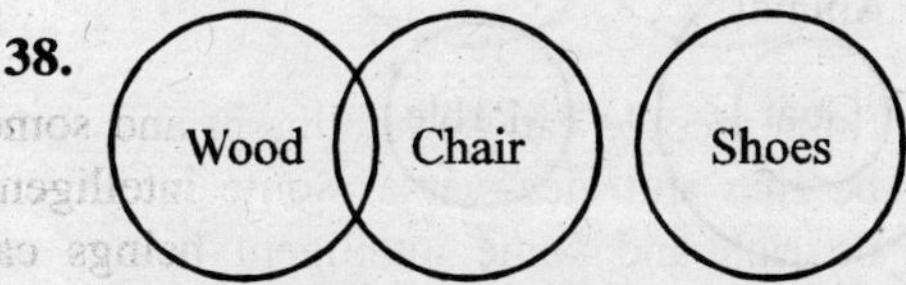

Some wood is used for making chair. Some chairs are made of wood. Shoes are different class.

39.

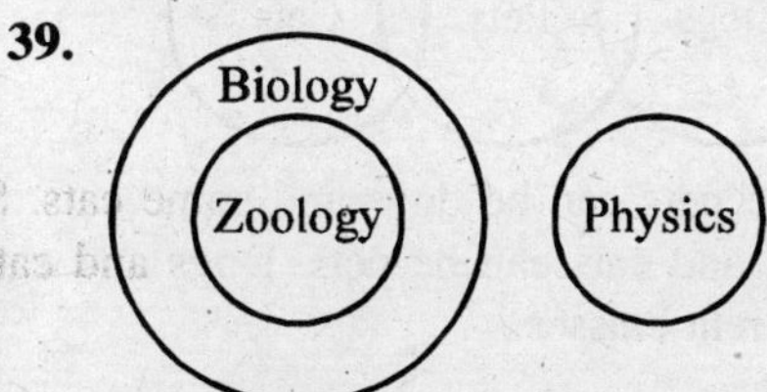

Zoology is a part of Biology. Biology contains the study Zoology. Physics is a different field of sciences.

40.

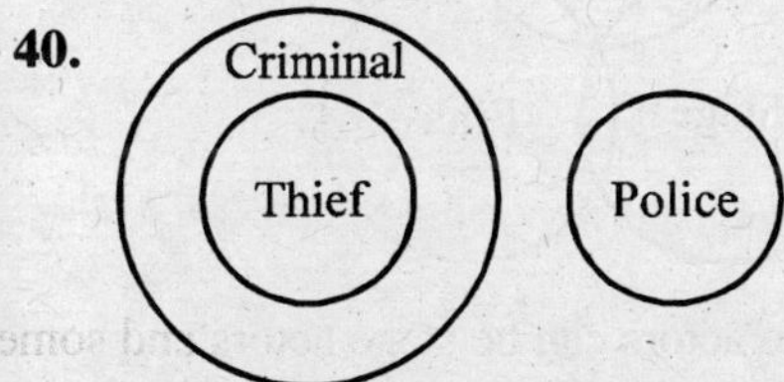

Thief is a criminal. Some criminals can be thieves. Police is a different class.

41.

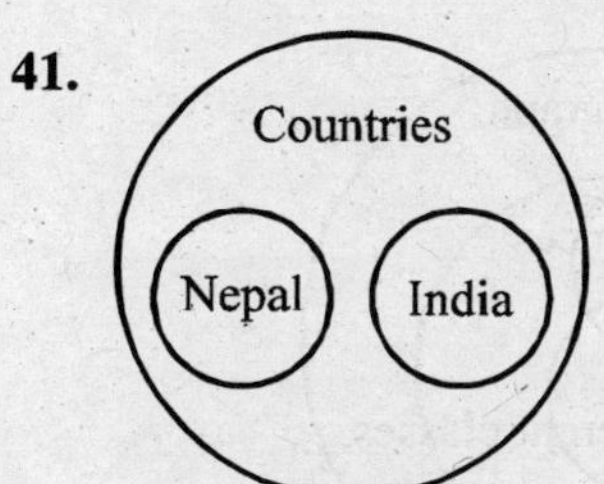

Nepal and India are countries but neither is contained in the other.

42.

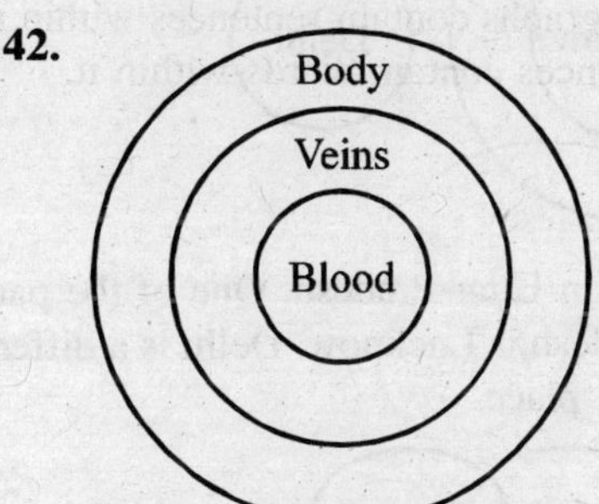

Body contains veins within it and all veins contain blood within it.

43.

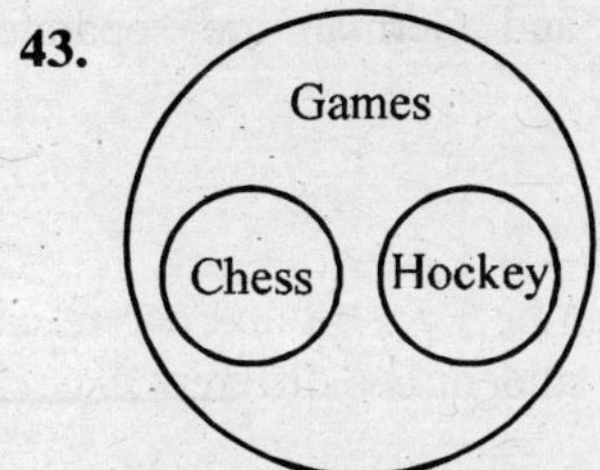

Both chess and hockey are games but neither is contained in the other.

44.

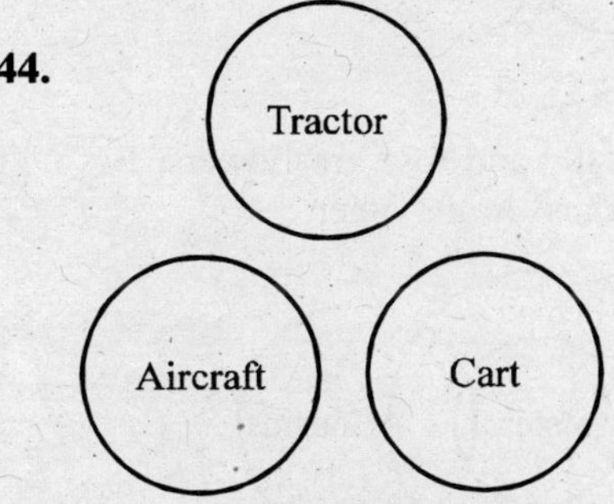

All three are different classes.

45.

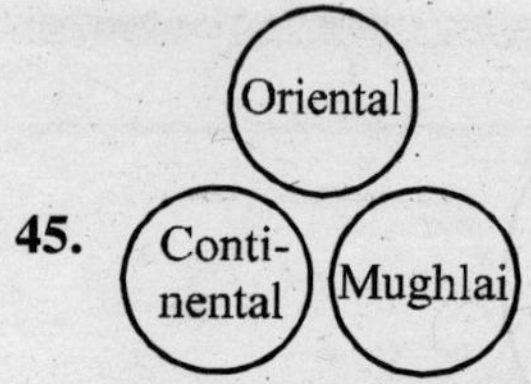

All three are different classes.

46.

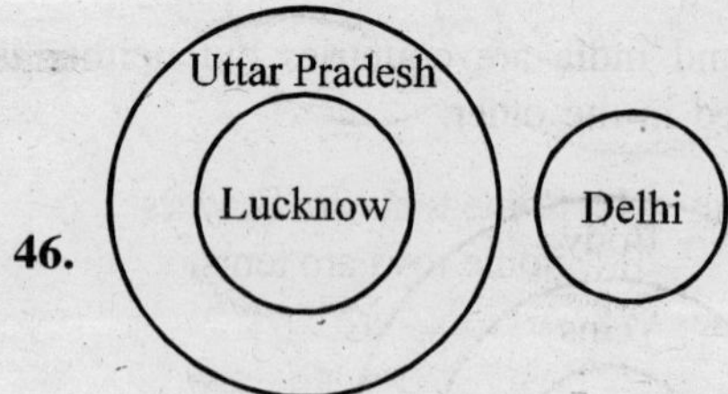

Lucknow is in Uttar Pradesh. One of the part of Uttar Pradesh is Lucknow. Delhi is a different /separate place.

47.

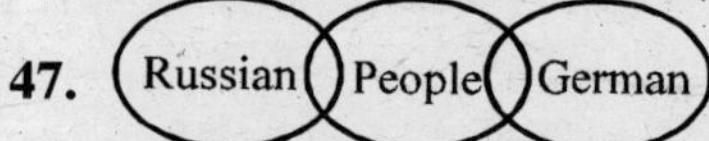

Some Russian and some German can be people. Some people can be Russian and some German. Russian and German are separate classes.

48.

Years have months contained within it and months have days contained within it.

49.

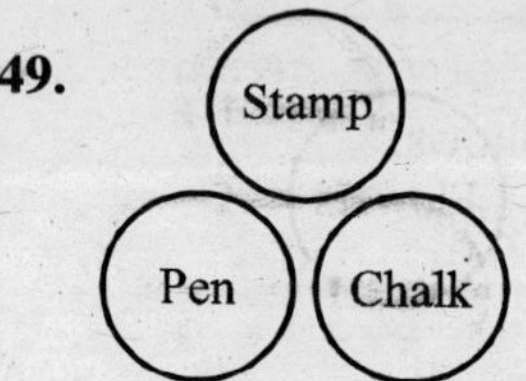

All three are different classes.

50.

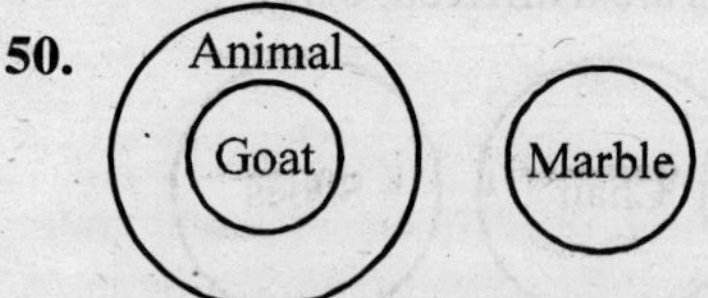

Goat is an animal. Some animals are goats. Marble is a different class.

SYLLOGISM

In this reasoning pattern the two premises are followed by two conclusions drawn from them. Four options A, B, C and D are given as answers. Based on the two statements the candidate has to select the right option as answer.

SOLVED EXAMPLES

In the questions below the answer is given as :

A. if only conclusion I follows.

B. if only conclusion II follows.

C. if either I or II follows, and

D. if neither I nor II follows.

1. Statements I : All officers are lazy.

II : Some men are officers.

Conclusions I : All lazy are men.

II : Some men are lazy.

Ans. B : When all officers are lazy and some men are officers then some men must be lazy. Therefore, conclusion II is correct.

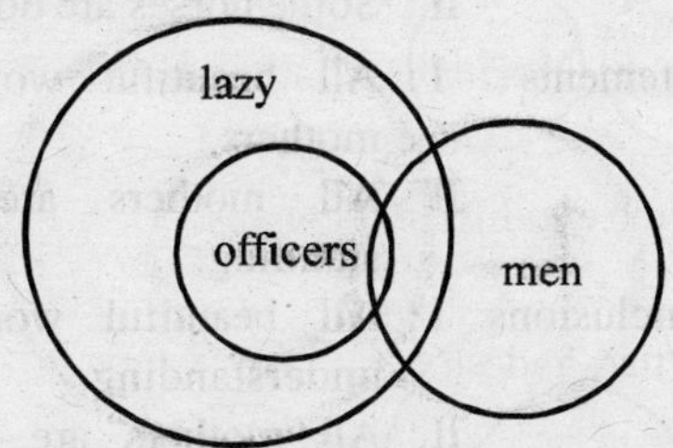

2. Statements I : Some tents are flowers.

II : Some toys are tents.

Conclusions I : All tents are toys.

II : All flowers are tents.

Ans. D : Some tents are flowers so some flowers can be tents. Some toys are tents so some tents can be toys. All tents and all flowers cannot be toys and tents respectively. Therefore, neither of the conclusion is correct.

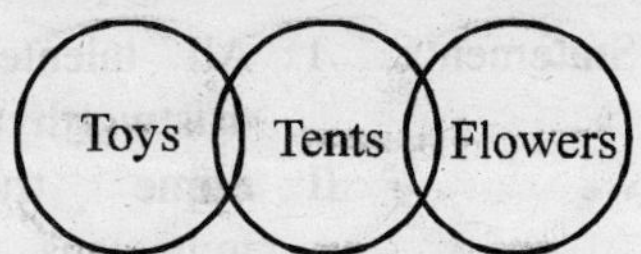

MULTIPLE CHOICE QUESTIONS

Directions : *In each question below are given two statements followed by two conclusions numbered I and II. You have to take the two given statements to be true even if they seem to be at variance from commonly known facts and then decide which of the given conclusions logically follows from the two given statements, disregarding commonly known facts. Read both the statements and—*

Give answer A if only conclusion I follows; give answer B if only conclusion II follows; give answer C if either I or II follows and give answer D if neither I nor II follows.

1. Statements I : All painters are smilling.

II : Some authors are painters.

Conclusions I : All smiling authors are painters.

II : Some authors are smiling.

2. Statements I : All peons in this office are efficient.

II : Ramu is not efficient.

Conclusions I : Ramu is not peon in this office.

II : Ramu should be more efficient.

3. Statements I : All weavers are hard working.

II : No hard working men are foolish.

Conclusions I : No weavers are foolish.

II : Some foolish are weavers.

4. Statements I : Some dogs are pups.
II : All horses are pups.
Conclusions I : Some dogs are horses.
II : Some horses are dogs.

5. Statements I : All beautiful women are mothers.
II : All mothers are understanding.
Conclusions I : All beautiful women are understanding.
II : All mothers are beautiful women.

6. Statements I : Some toys are tables.
II : No table is black.
Conclusions I : Some toys are black.
II : Some toys are not black.

7. Statements I : All men are horses.
II : All horses are elephants.
Conclusions I : All men are elephants.
II : All elephants are men.

8. Statements I : All talented persons are trustworthy.
II : Some trustworthy are musicians.
Conclusions I : All talented persons are musicians.
II : Some musicians are not talented person.

9. Statements I : Alcoholic drinks are injurious to health.
II : All old women drink whisky.
Conclusions I : All old women have poor health.
II : All young women are in good health.

10. Statements I : Some engineers are teachers.
II : Some engineers are efficient.
Conclusions I : Some teachers are efficient.
II : All efficient are engineers.

11. Statements I : Some foods are sweet.
II : Some foods are sour.
Conclusions I : All foods are either sweet or sour.
II : Some sweet are sour.

12. Statements I : All hair are black.
II : Some black are long.
Conclusions I : Some hair are long.
II : No hair is long.

13. Statements I : Some phones are watches.
II : All watches are guns.
Conclusions I : All guns are watches.
II : Some guns are phones.

14. Statements I : All umbrellas are aeroplanes
II : Some aeroplanes are birds.
Conclusions I : Some umbrellas are birds.
II : Some birds are umbrellas.

15. Statements I : All puppets are dolls.
II : All dolls are toys.
Conclusions I : Some toys are puppets.
II : All toys are puppets.

16. Statements I : Some fat are thin.
II : No thin is tall.
Conclusions I : Some fat are tall.
II : Some fat are not tall.

17. Statements I : Some doors are windows.
II : Some windows are pencils.
Conclusions I : All doors are pencils.
II : Some pencils are doors.

18. Statements I : Some boys are tables.
II : Some tables are chairs.
Conclusions I : Some boys are chairs.
II : Some chairs are boys.

19. Statements I : All dogs are jackals.
II : Some jackals are crows.
Conclusions I : Some dogs are crows.
II : All dogs are crows.

20. Statements I : All trees are parrots.
II : No parrots is cat.
Conclusions I : No tree is cat.
II : Some cats are trees.

21. Statements I : All cars are cats.
II : All fans are cats.
Conclusions I : All cars are fans.
II : Some fans are cars.

22. Statements I : Many scooters are trucks.
II : All trucks are trains.
Conclusions I : Some scooters are trains..
II : No truck is a scooter.

23. Statements I : All sharks are ferocious.
II : No ferocious is harmful.
Conclusions I : Some sharks are harmful.
II : Some ferocious are not sharks.

24. Statements I : Some doctors are institutes.
II : Some croocks are institutes.
Conclusions I : All institutes are doctors.
II : Some institutes are crooks.

25. Statements I : All pilots are experts.
II : All authors are pilots.
Conclusions I : All authors are experts.
II : No expert is a author.

ANSWERS

1	2	3	4	5	6	7	8	9	10
B	A	A	D	A	C	A	B	D	D
11	**12**	**13**	**14**	**15**	**16**	**17**	**18**	**19**	**20**
D	D	B	D	A	B	D	D	D	A
21	**22**	**23**	**24**	**25**					
D	A	B	B	A					

EXPLANATORY ANSWERS

1. When all painters are smiling and some authors are painters, then some authors are smiling. Therefore, only conclusion II is correct.

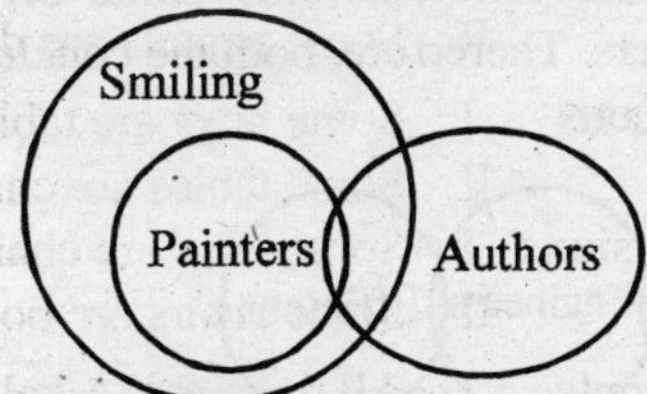

2. When all the peons of the office are efficient, then Ramu cannot be a peon in this office. Therefore, only conclusion I is correct.

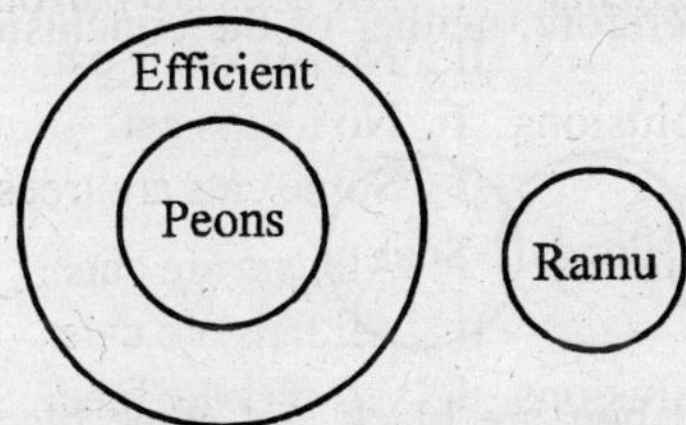

3. When all weavers are hardworking and no hardworking men are foolish, then no weavers are foolish. Therefore, only conclusion I is correct.

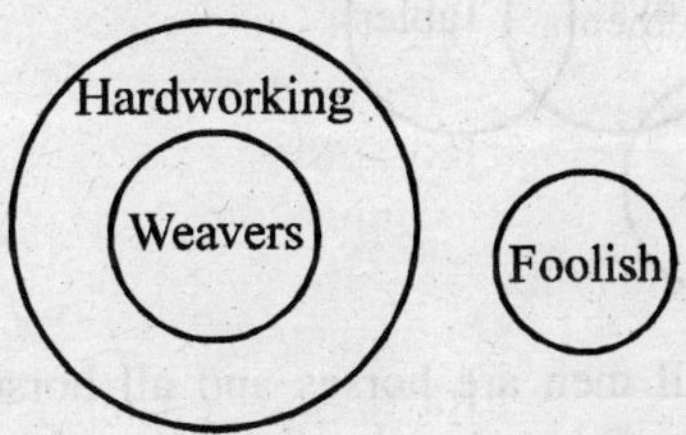

4. No relationship can be established between the two statements. Therefore, neither conclusion I nor conclusion II is correct.

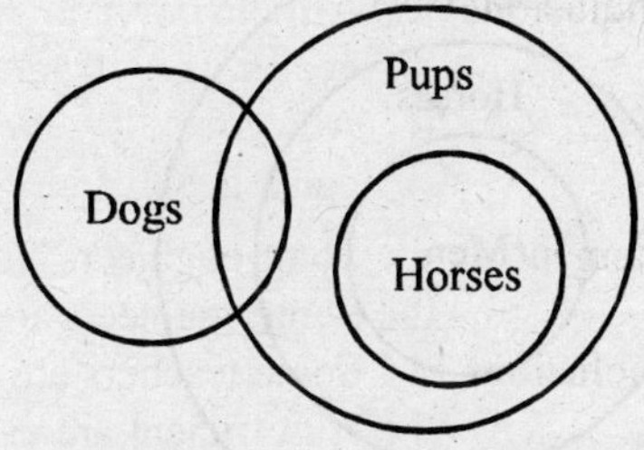

5. When all beautiful women are mothers and all mothers are understanding, then naturally all beautiful women are understanding. All mothers need not be beautiful women. Therefore, only conclusion I is correct.

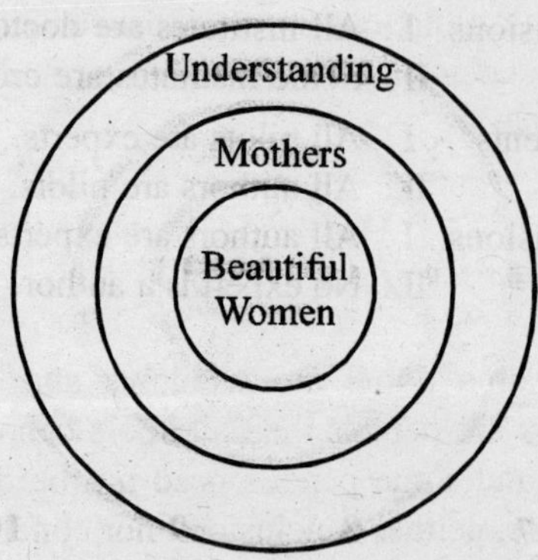

6. When some toys are tables and no table is black, then it is indicated that some toys can be black, as all toys are not tables. On the other hand, some toys may not be black. Therefore, there is a possibility that some toys may or may not be black. As such, either conclusion I or conclusion II can be correct.

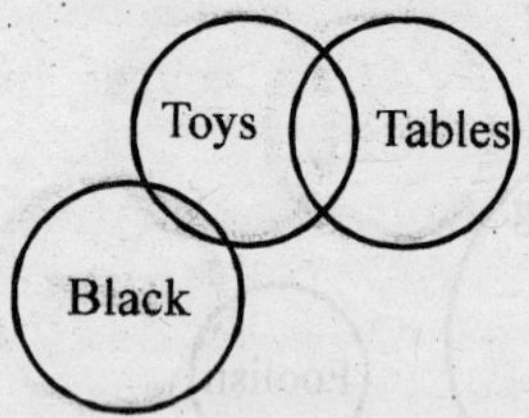

7. When all men are horses and all horses are elephants then, naturally all men are elephants, but all elephants need not be men. Therefore, only conclusion I is correct.

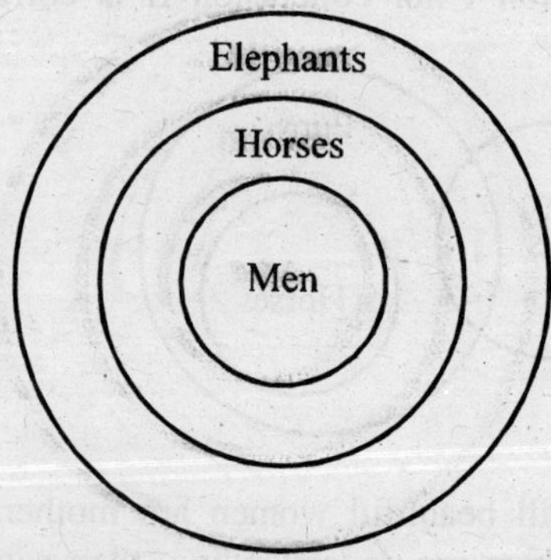

8. When only some trustworthy are musicians, then all talented persons cannot be musicians. In the same logical way, when some trustworthy are musicians, then some musicians are not talented. Therefore, only conclusin II is correct.

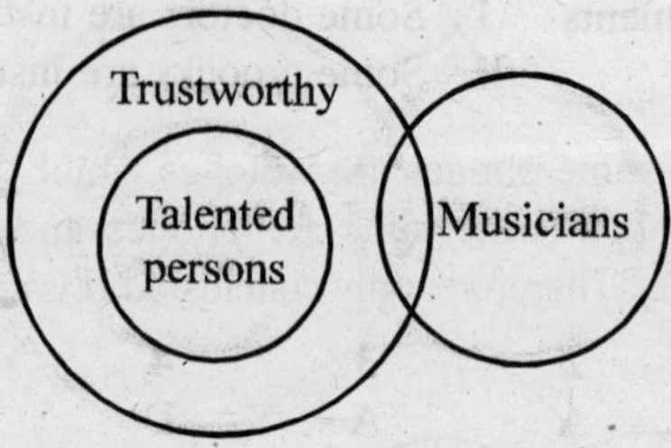

9. Even though alcoholic drinks are injurious to health and all old women drink whisky, which is an alcoholic drink, it does not necessarily mean that all old women must have poor health and that all young women are in good health, because they do not take alcoholic drinks. Therefore, neither conclusion I nor conclusion II is correct.

10. When some engineers are teachers, then some teachers are engineers. Also, when some engineers are efficient, only some efficient are engineers. Thererfore, both the conclusions are incorrect.

11. When some foods are sweet and some foods are sour, then all foods are not necessarily sweet or sour and what is sweet need not be sour. Therefore, neither of the conclusions is correct.

12. When all hair are black and some black are long, then it is not for certain that some hair are long or no hair is long. Some hair that are black may or may not be long. Therefore, neither of the conclusions is correct.

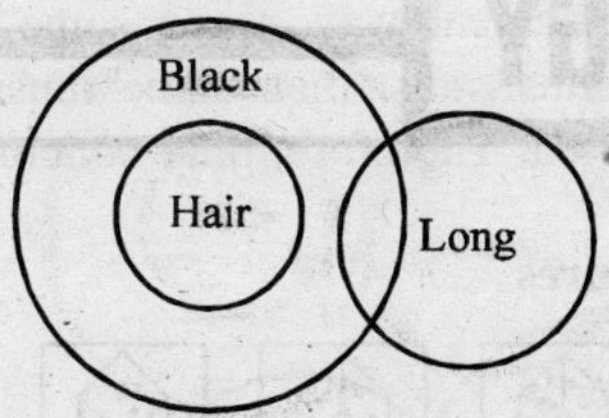

13. When some phones are watches which are all guns, then some guns are phones and some watches. Therefore, only conclusion II is correct.

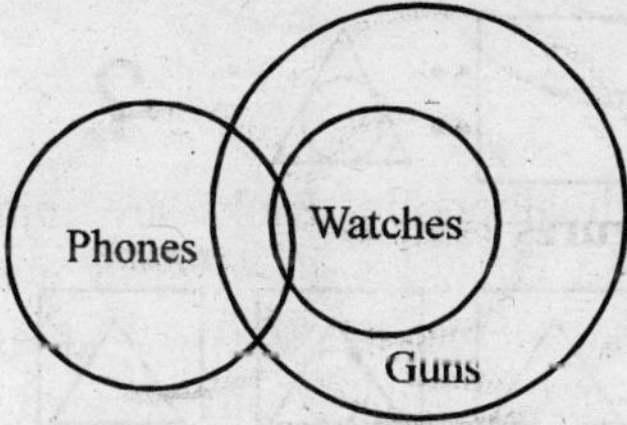

14. All umbrellas are aeroplanes and some aeroplanes are birds, then the umbrellas are not necessarily birds or vice versa. Therefore, neither conclusion I nor conclusion II is correct.

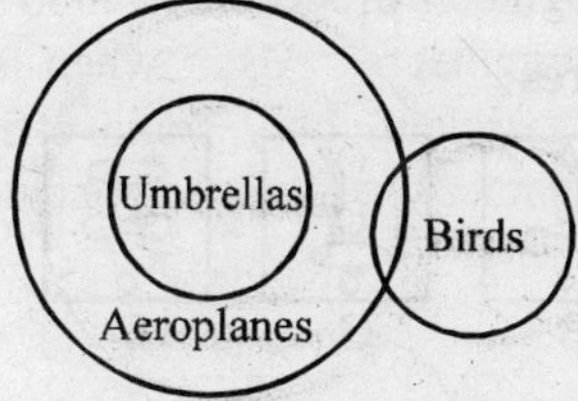

15. When all puppets are dolls which are all toys, then only some (not all) toys are necessarily puppets. Therefore, only conclusion I is correct.

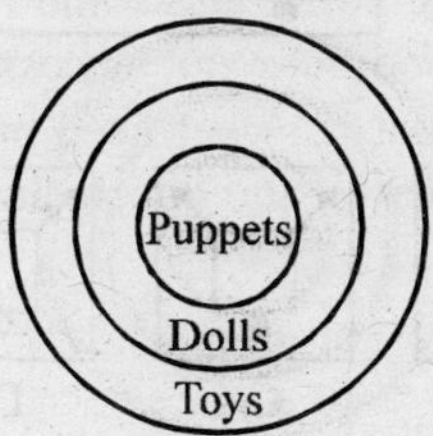

16. No relationship can be established between the two statements. Therefore, only conclusion II is correct.

17. When some doors are windows and some windows are pencils then all doors cannot be pencils and some pencils need not be doors. Therefore, neither conclusion I nor conclusion II is correct.

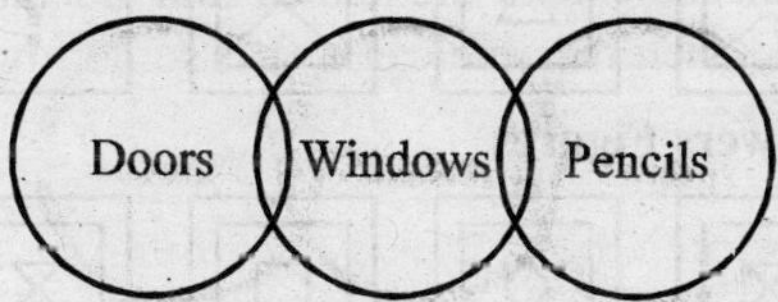

18. When some boys are tables and some tables are chairs then some boys need not be chairs or vice versa. Therefore, neither of the conclusions is correct.

19. When all dogs are jackals and some jackals are crows then some dogs need not be crows and all dogs cannot be crows. Therefore, neither of the conclusions is correct.

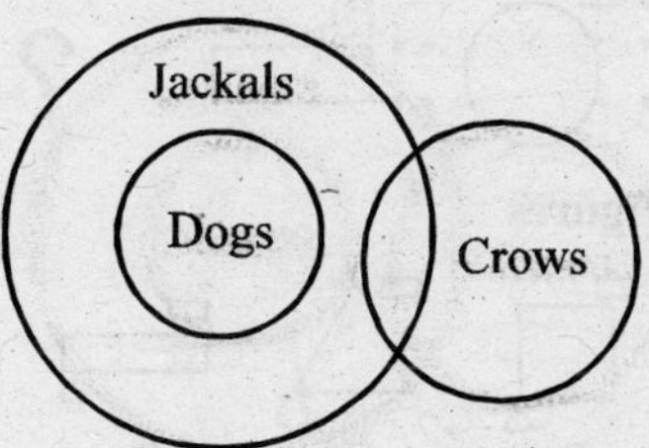

NON-VERBAL ANALOGY

Directions : *The second figure in the first unit of the Problem Figures bears a certain relationship to the first figure. Similarly, one of the figures in the Answer Figures bears the same relationship to the first figure in the second unit of the Problem Figures. Locate the figure which would fit the question mark.*

1. Problem Figures

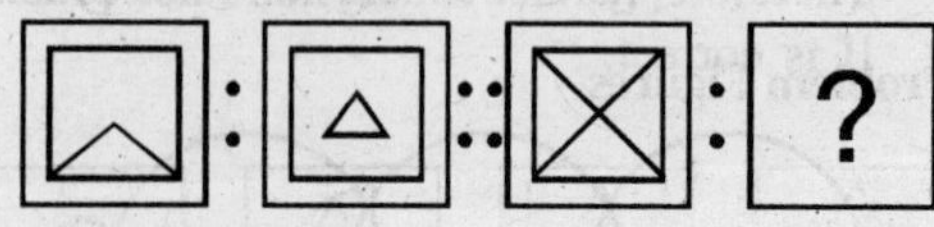

Answers Figures

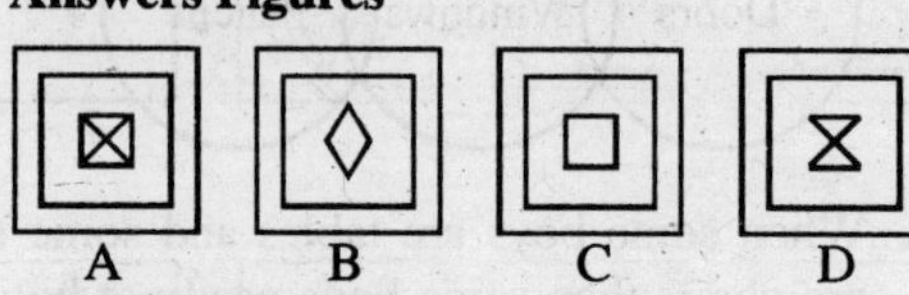

2. Problem Figures

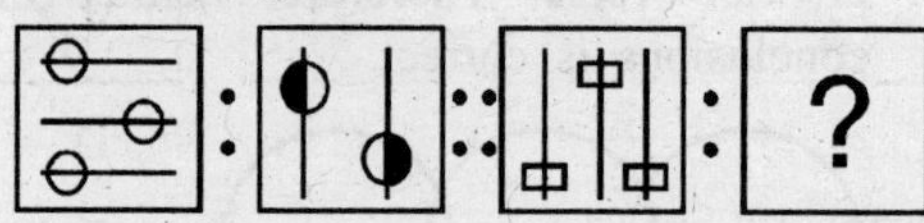

Answer Figures

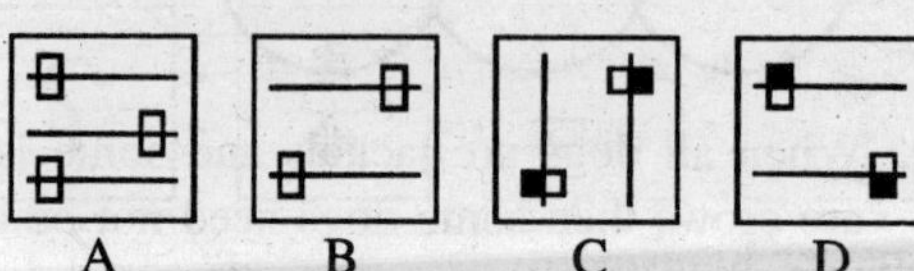

3. Problem Figures

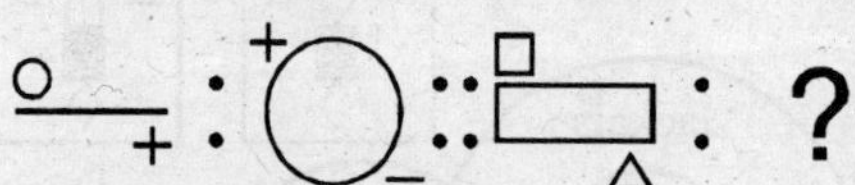

Answer Figures

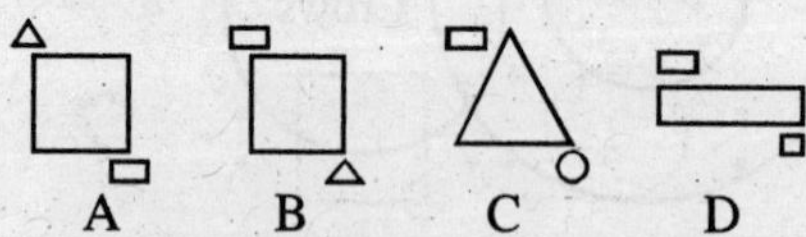

4. Problem Figures

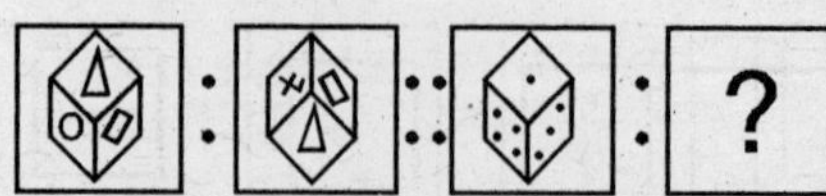

Answer Figures

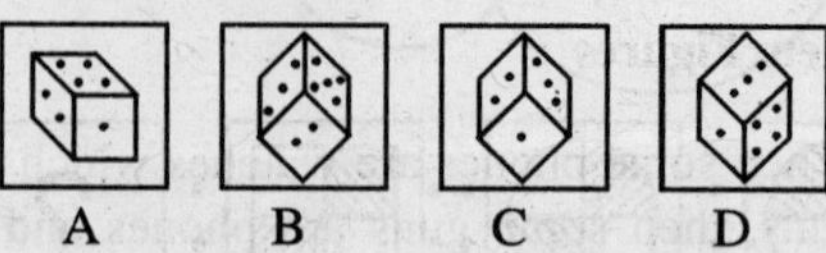

5. Problem Figures

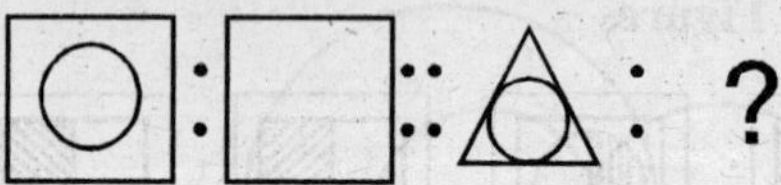

Answer Figures

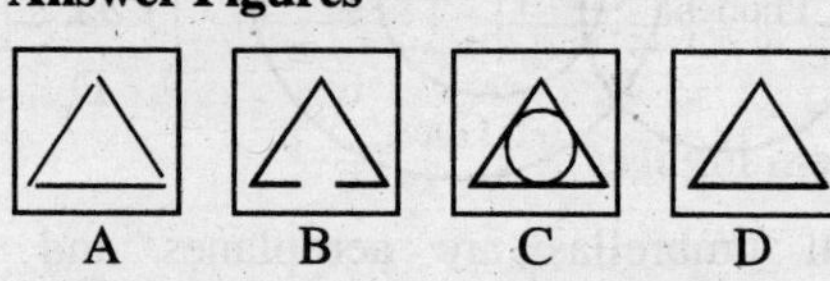

6. Problem Figures

Answer Figures

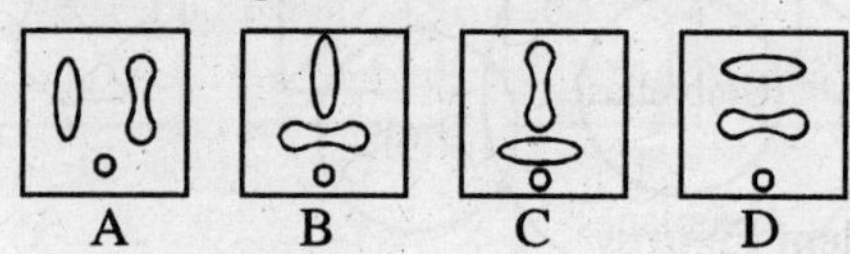

7. Problem Figures

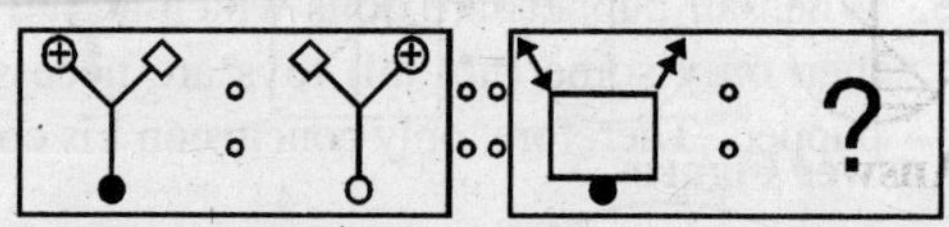

Answer Figures

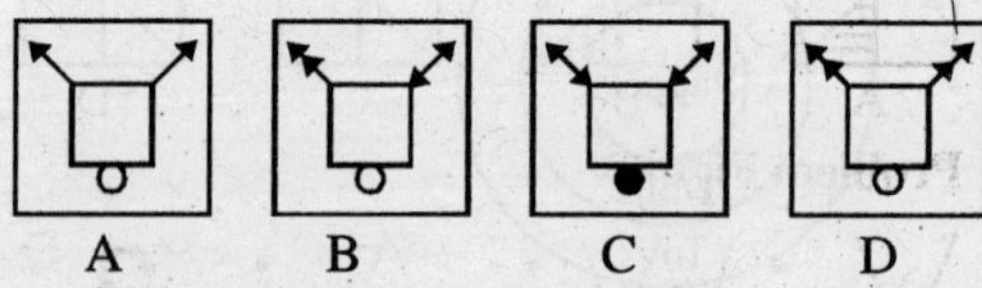

8. Problem Figures

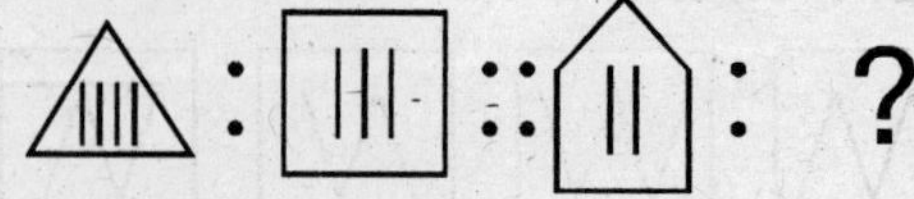

Answer Figures

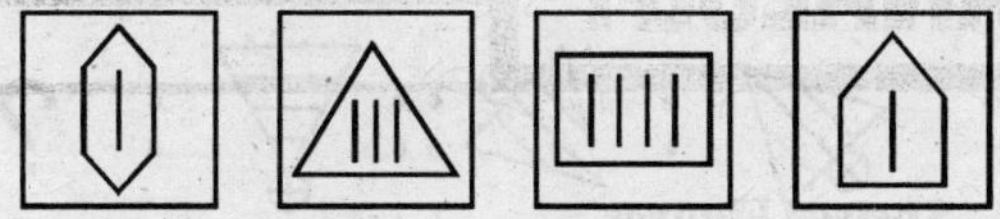

A B C D

9. Problem Figures

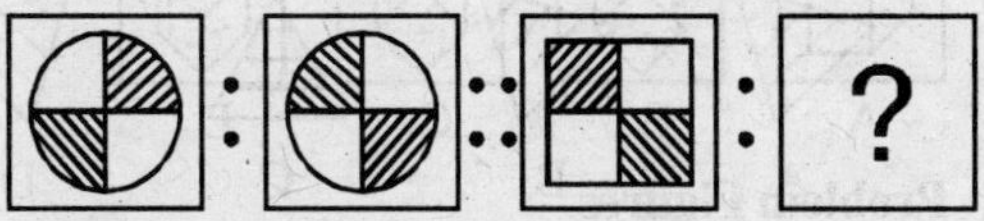

Answer Figures

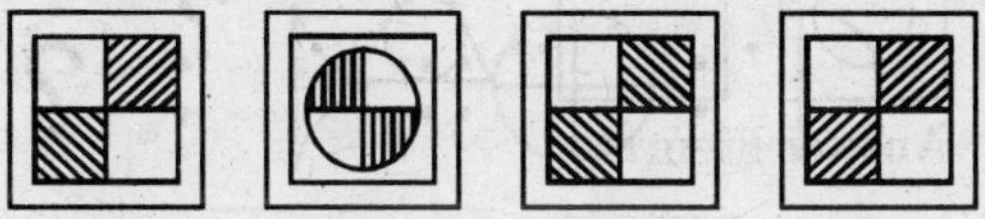

A B C D

10. Problem Figures

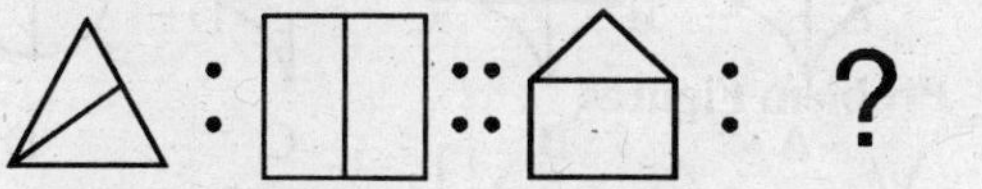

Answer Figures

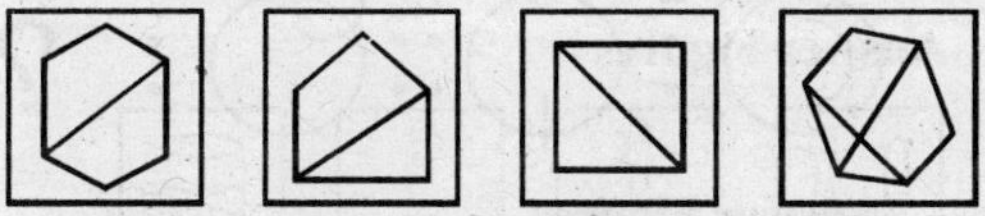

A B C D

1. Problem Figures

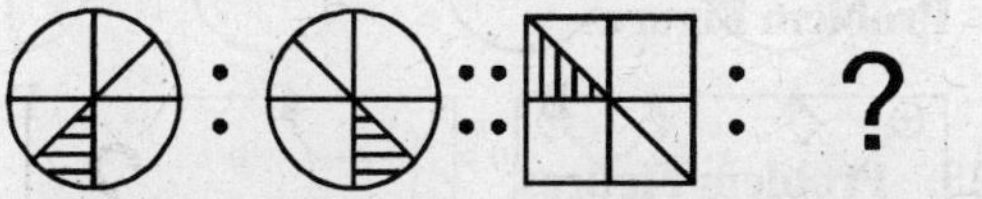

Answer Figures

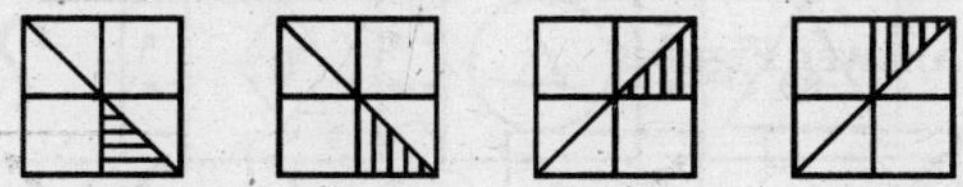

A B C D

2. Problem Figures

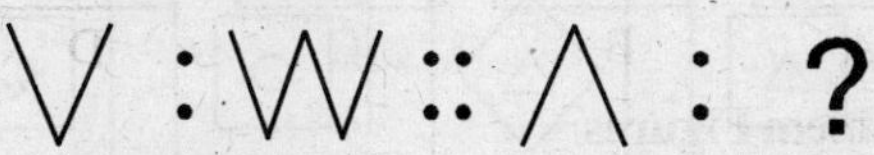

Answer Figures

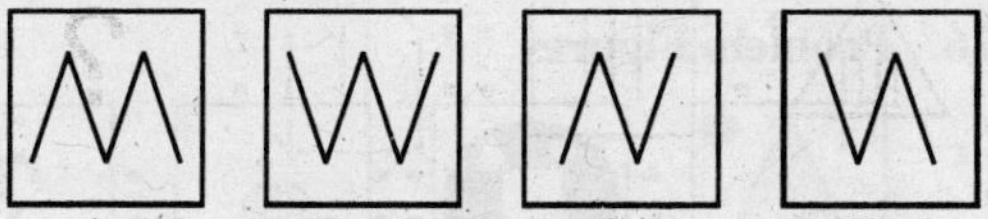

A B C D

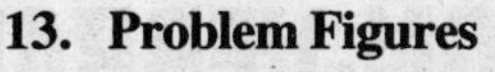

13. Problem Figures

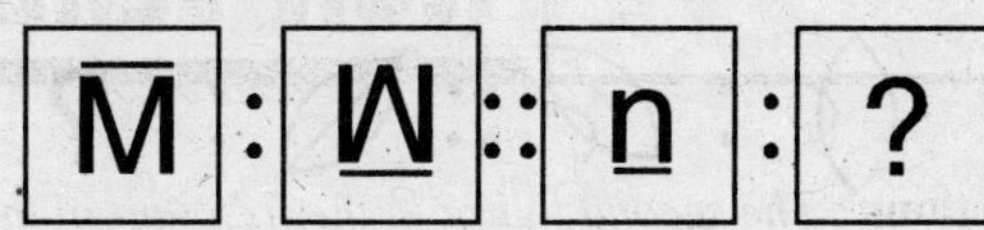

Answer Figures

A B C D

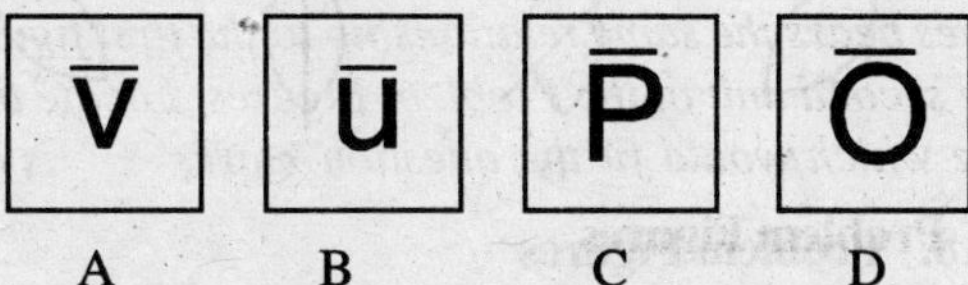

14. Problem Figures

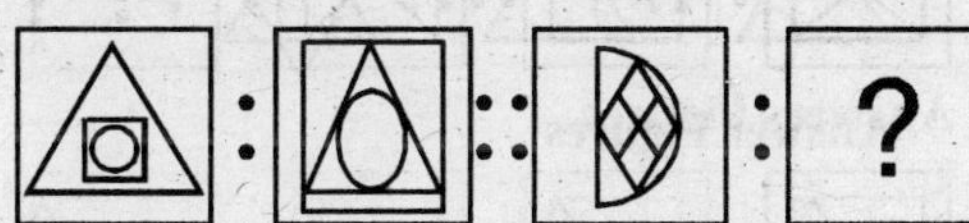

Answer Figures

A B C D

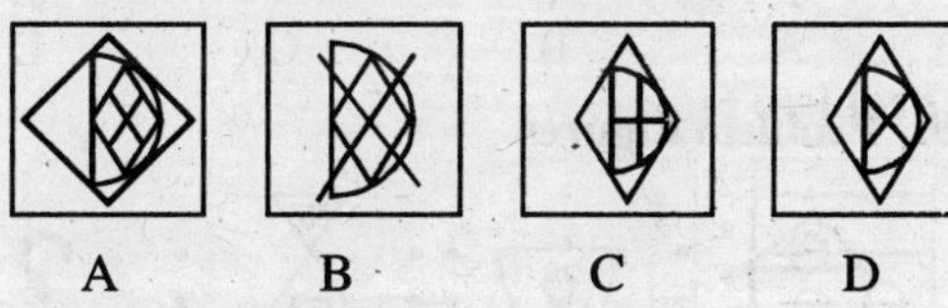

15. Problem Figures

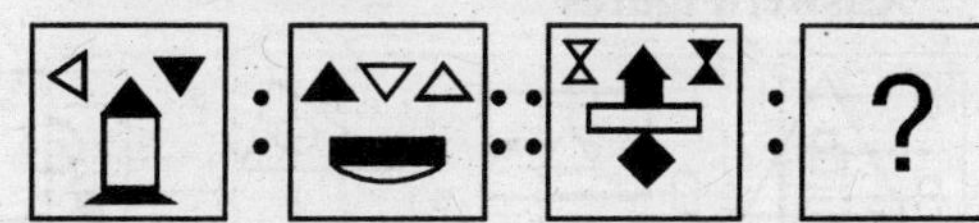

Answer Figures

A B C D

16. Problem Figures

Answer Figures

A B C D

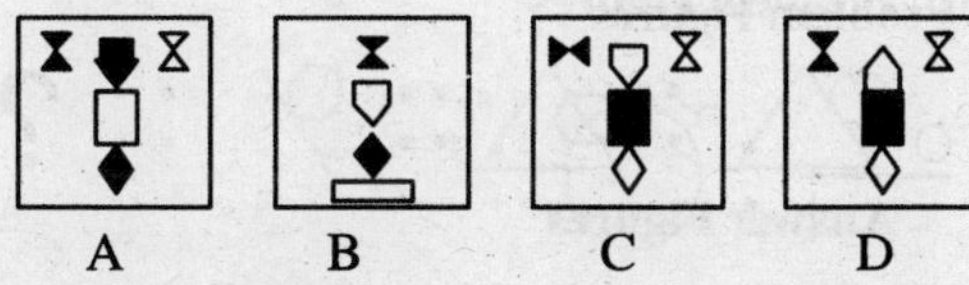

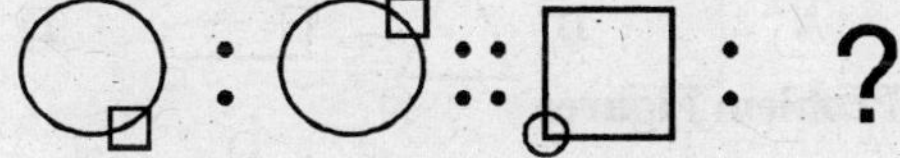

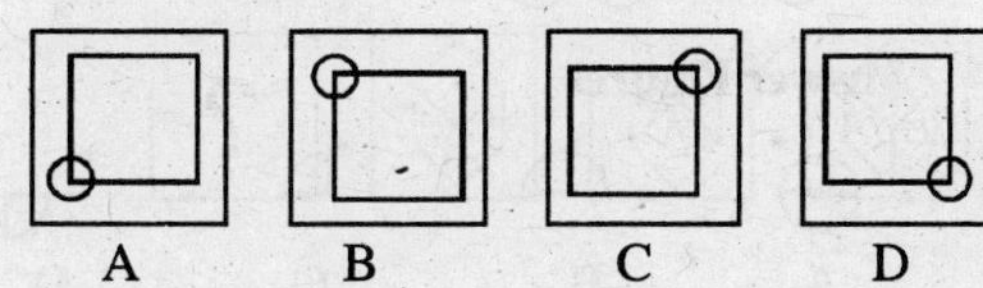

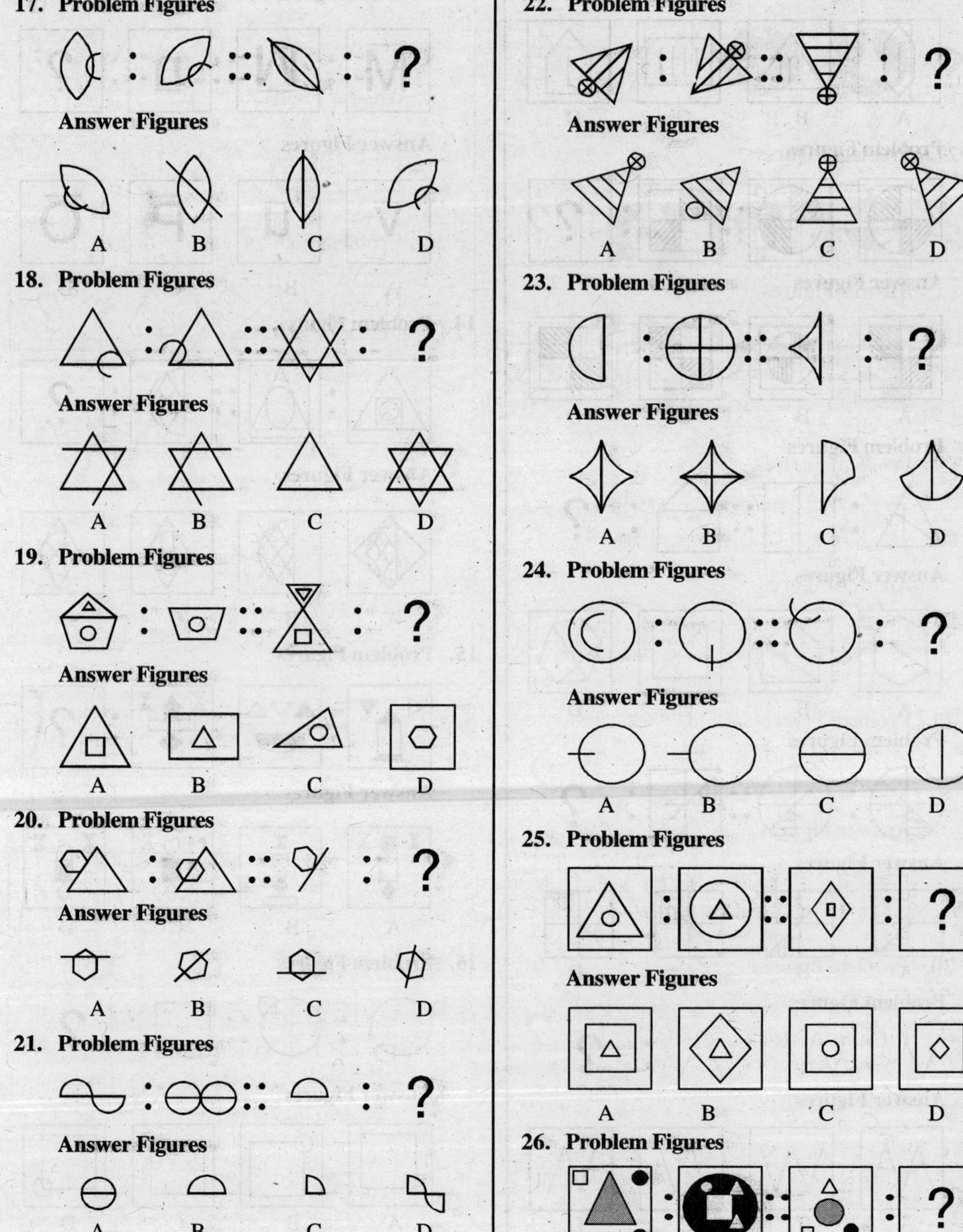
17. Problem Figures
Answer Figures
A B C D
18. Problem Figures
Answer Figures
A B C D
19. Problem Figures
Answer Figures
A B C D
20. Problem Figures
Answer Figures
A B C D
21. Problem Figures
Answer Figures
A B C D
22. Problem Figures
Answer Figures
A B C D
23. Problem Figures
Answer Figures
A B C D
24. Problem Figures
Answer Figures
A B C D
25. Problem Figures
Answer Figures
A B C D
26. Problem Figures

Answer Figures

  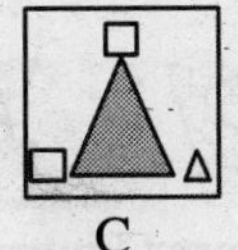 

A B C D

27. Problem Figures

   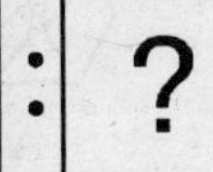

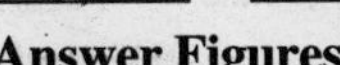

Answer Figures

A B C D

28. Problem Figures

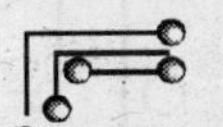   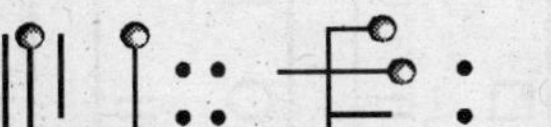

Answer Figures

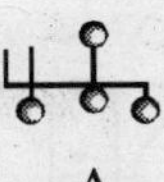   

A B C D

29. Problem Figures

  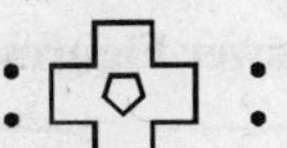 

Answer Figures

A B C D

30. Problem Figures

Answer Figures

A B C D

31. Problem Figures

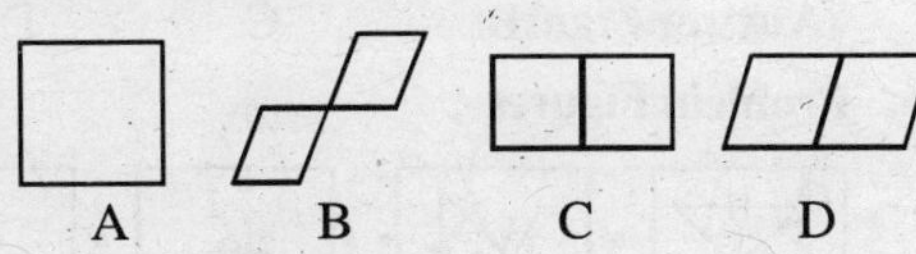

Answer Figures

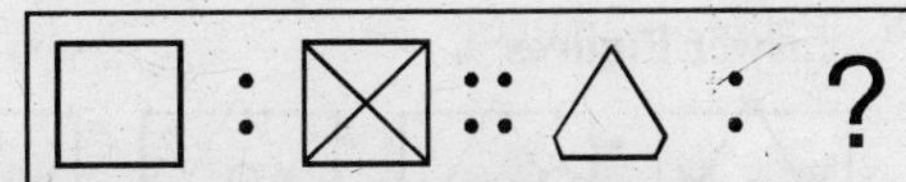

A B C D

32. Problem Figures

Answer Figures

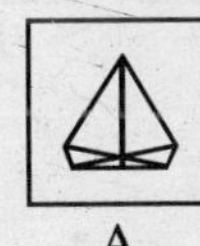 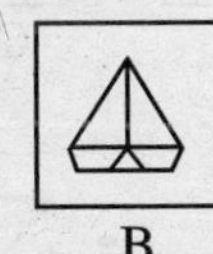  

A B C D

33. Problem Figures

Answer Figures

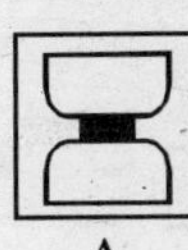 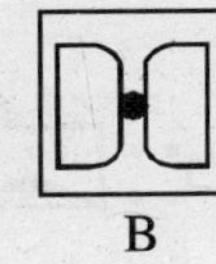 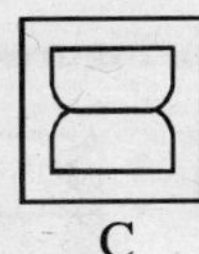 

A B C D

34. Problem Figures

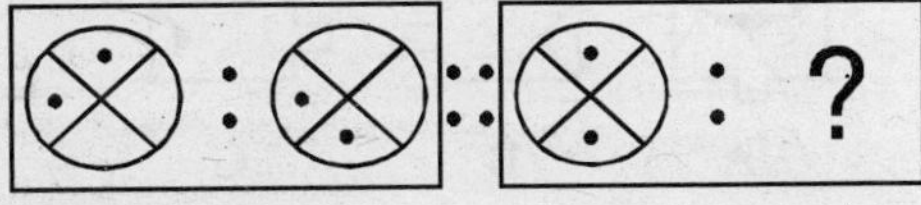

Answer Figures

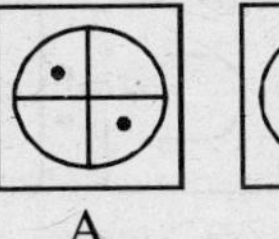 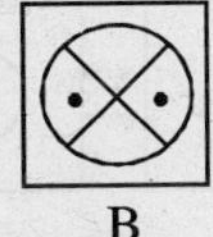  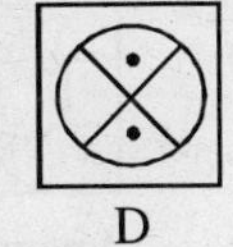

A B C D

35. Problem Figures

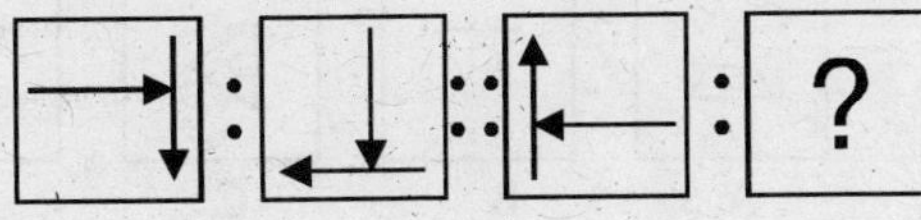

Answer Figures

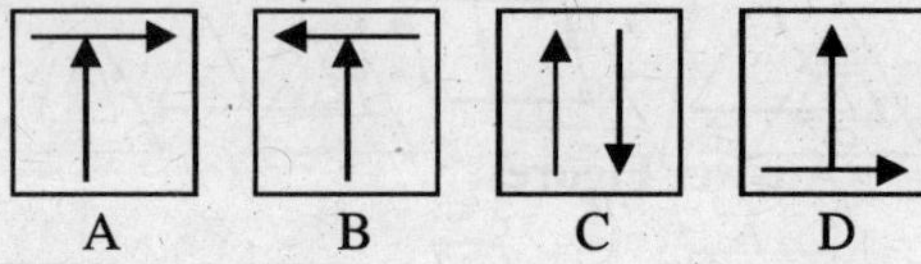

36. Problem Figures

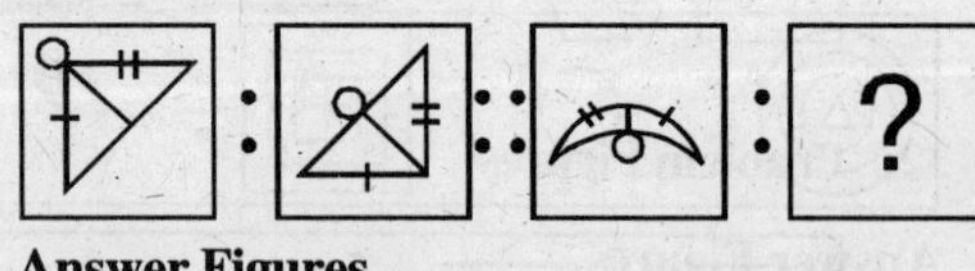

Answer Figures

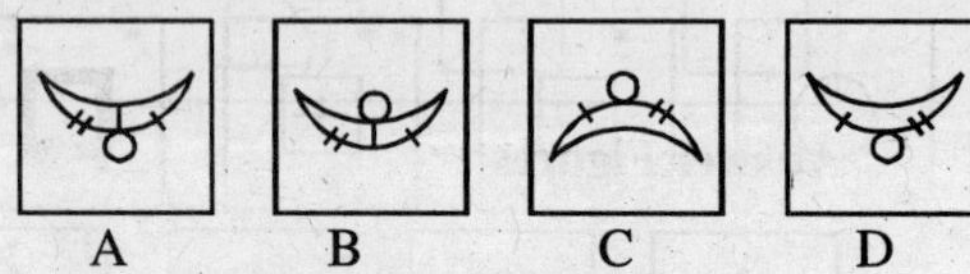

37. Problem Figures

Answer Figures

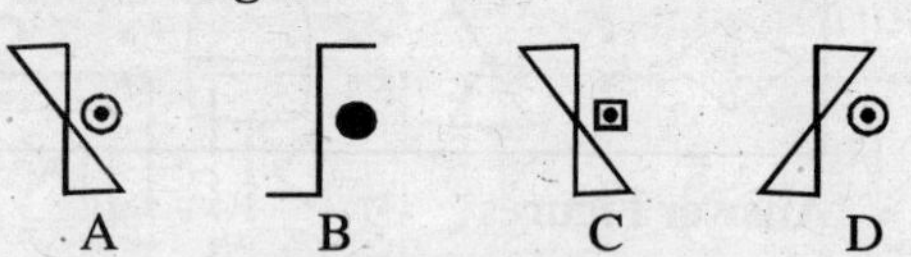

38. Problem Figures

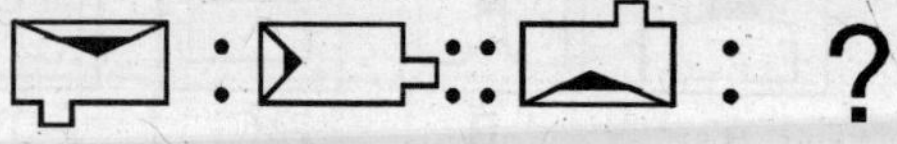

Answer Figures

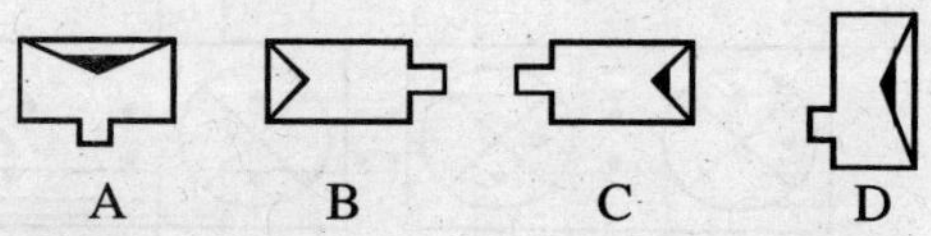

39. Problem Figures

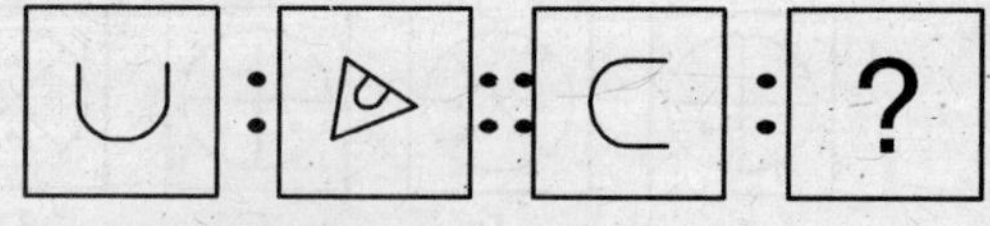

Answer Figures

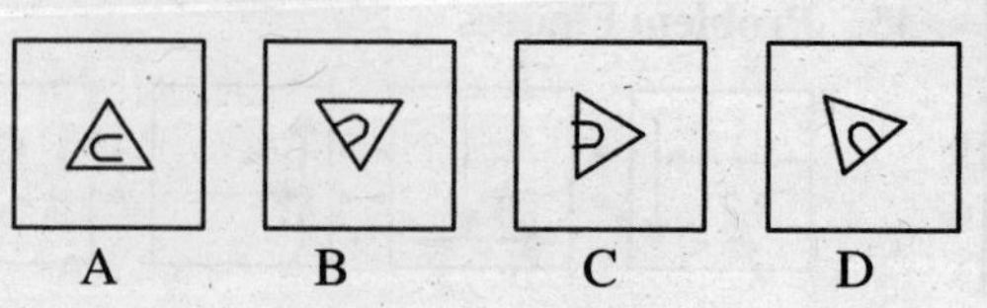

40. Problem Figures

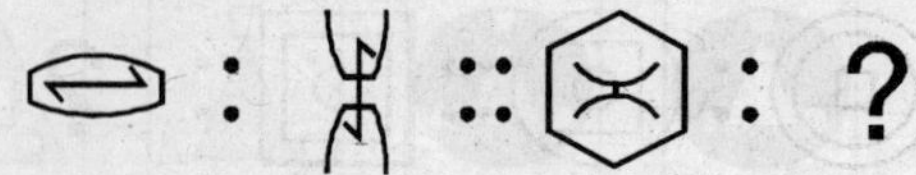

Answer Figures

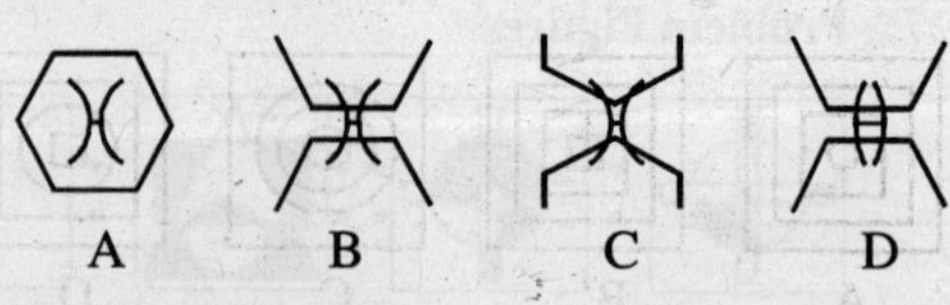

41. Problem Figures

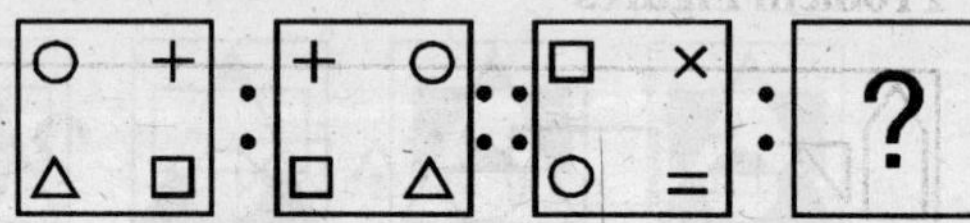

Answer Figures

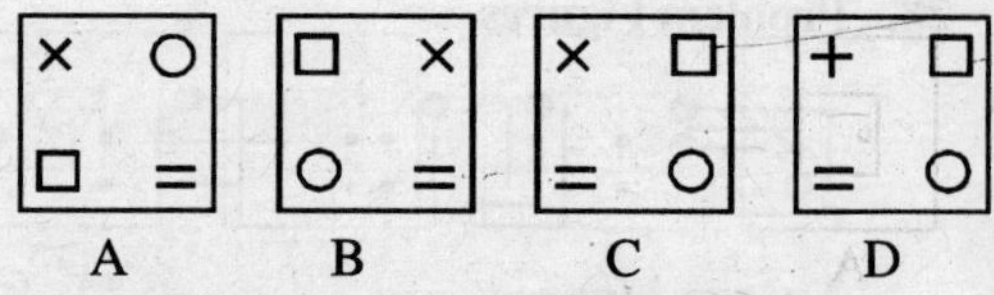

42. Problem Figures

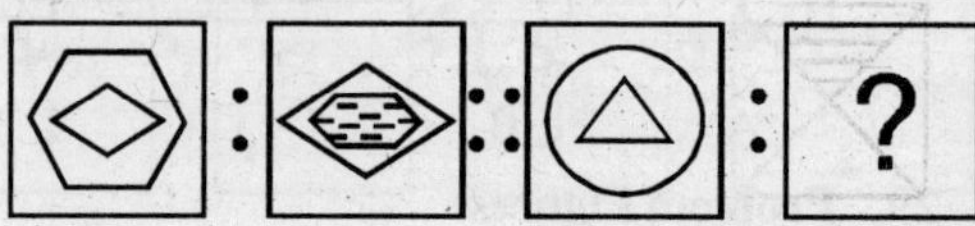

Answer Figures

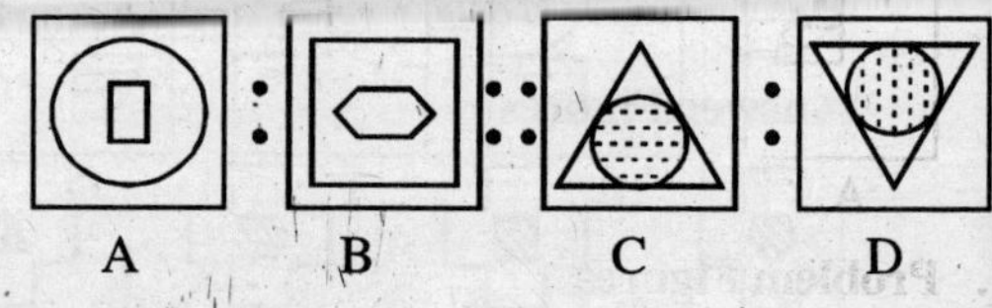

43. Problem Figures

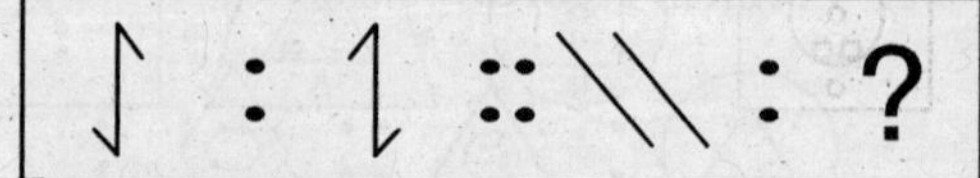

Answer Figures

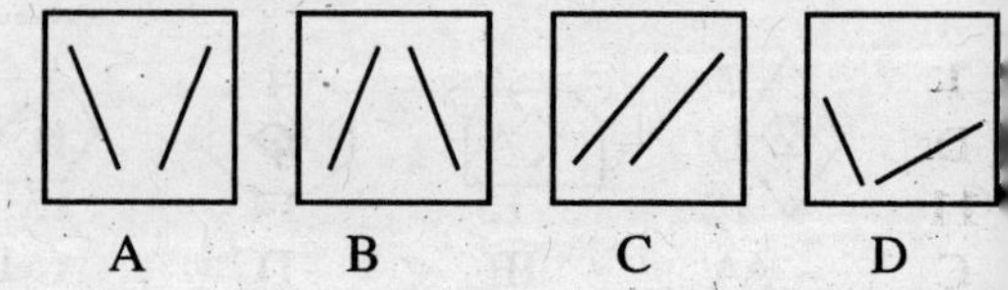

4. Problem Figures

Answer Figures

5. Problem Figures

Answer Figures

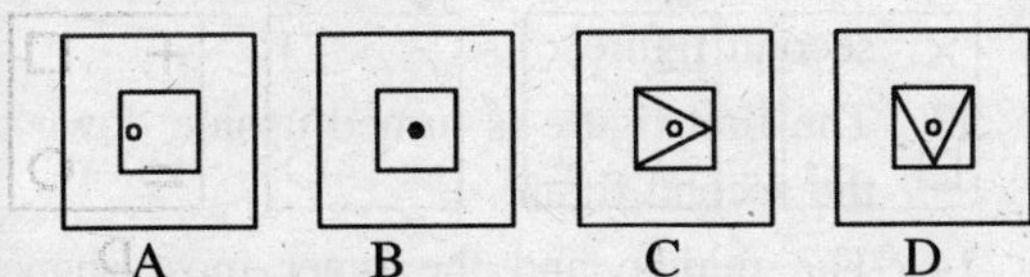

6. Problem Figures

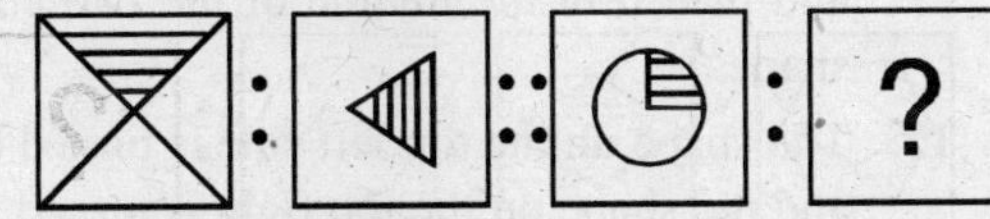

Answer Figures

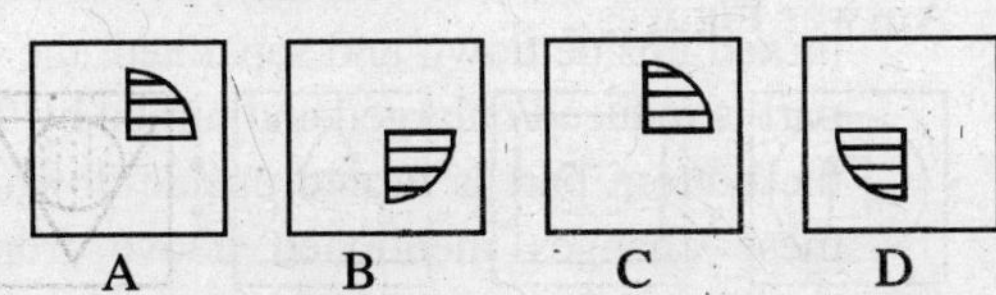

7. Problem Figures

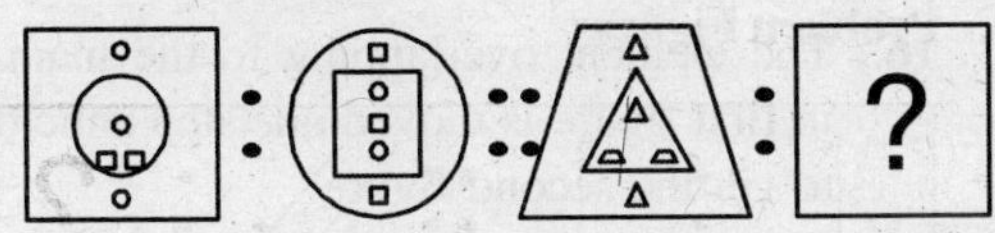

Answer Figures

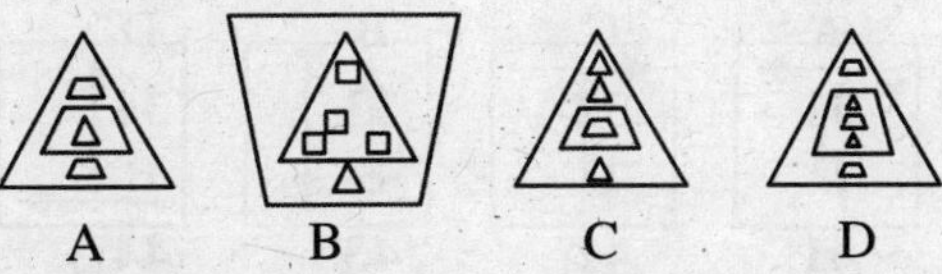

48. Problem Figures

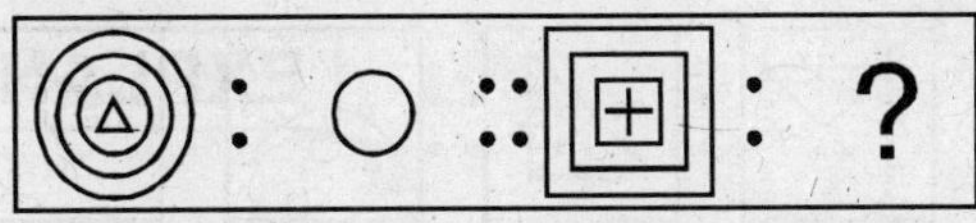

Answer Figures

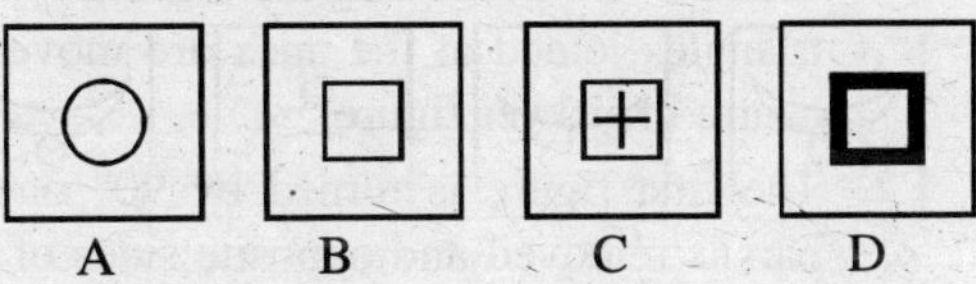

49. Problem Figures

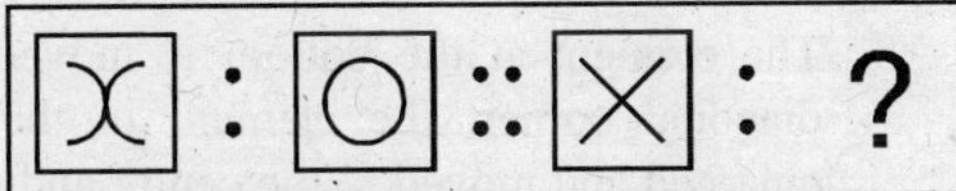

Answer Figures

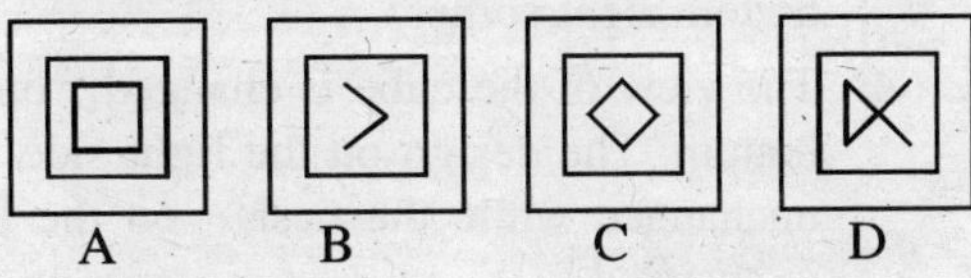

50. Problem Figures

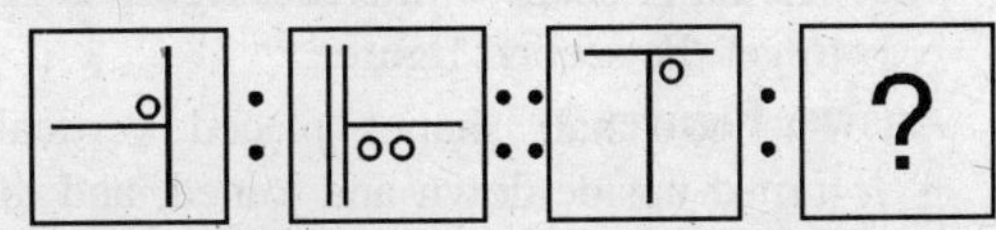

Answer Figures

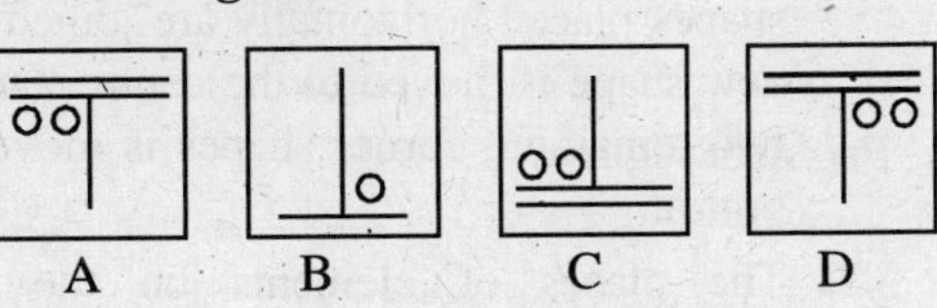

ANSWERS

1	2	3	4	5	6	7	8	9	10
D	D	A	C	D	B	B	A	A	A
11	**12**	**13**	**14**	**15**	**16**	**17**	**18**	**19**	**20**
C	A	B	D	C	D	C	B	A	A

21	22	23	24	25	26	27	28	29	30
A	C	B	D	D	A	D	A	C	C
31	**32**	**33**	**34**	**35**	**36**	**37**	**38**	**39**	**40**
D	D	B	B	A	A	D	C	D	C
41	**42**	**43**	**44**	**45**	**46**	**47**	**48**	**49**	**50**
C	C	C	D	B	B	D	B	C	C

EXPLANATORY ANSWERS

1. The triangle in the first figure is moved to the centre of the second figure. Similarly, the two triangles joined at the apex are moved to the centre in answer figure.

2. The first figure is turned by 90° one of the bars is removed and opposite sides of the element attached to the bar are shaded to get the second figure.

3. The element at the bottom is moved to the diagonal corner, the element in the top is enlarged and moved to the centre and element in the middle is reduced and moved to the bottom right corner.

4. The view of the cube is changed from top to bottom. The design on the right side remains unchanged while the design on the left side is changed.

5. The inner shape in the first figure is removed to get the second figure.

6. The two half shapes placed vertically are turned upside down and joined, and this new shape is moved to the top. The two curved shapes placed horizontally are joined and this new shape is moved to the centre. One of the two remaining corner shapes is moved to the bottom.

7. The places of elements on the top are interchanged and the shade inside the circle is removed.

8. One of the vertical lines is removed and the number of lines making the second figure is increased by one.

9. First figure is rotated 90° anticlockwise to get the second figure.

10. The number of lines making the second fi is one more than the number of lines ma the first figure.

11. The diagonal line is turned by 90° and the segments are moved to the horizon opposite section.

12. The design in first figure is doubled to ge second figure.

13. The first figure is turned upside down to the second figure.

14. The middle and the inner most shapes enlarged and the outermost shape is red and placed in the middle of the two enla shapes.

15. The shape on the top left side is turned by and the shape on the top right is turned up down. The top part of the vertical desig turned upside down and separated, the mi part is reduced/enlarged and turned by 90 the bottom part is turned upside down. I these changes mentioned above from figure to the second, the black areas are white and vice versa.

16. The element overlapping to the main d in first figure is moved one step anticlock to get the second figure.

17. The first figure is rotated 45° clockwise t the second figure.

18. The incomplete element in first figu moved two steps anti clockwise and t 135° anti-clockwise to get the second fi

19. The top half of the design in first fig removed to get the second figure.

The element on the left in first figure crosses the line it is attached to so that it is divided into two equal parts in second figure.

The incomplete design in first figure is completed in the second figure.

The design in first figure is turned by 180° to get the second figure.

The design in first figure is completed and divided into four equal parts in the second figure.

The arc inside the circle in first figure is replaced by a line segment cutting the circle in second figure. By the same logic, the arc cutting the circle in first figure should be replaced by a line segment inside the circle in the answer figure.

The outer design is reduced and enclosed within the inner design which is enlarged to get the second figure.

The square is replaced by circle, circle by triangle and triangle by square, without changing the positions in a dark circle.

The shaded positions are made blank and vice versa to get the second fgure.

The figure is rotated 90° anticlockwise and the circles are reversed at other end of lines.

The number of lines making the inner design in first figure is increased by one and this new design is shaded by slant lines in the second figure.

The size and place of both the designs in first figure are swapped and the inner design is shaded in second figure.

Each triangle in first figure is replaced by a parallelogram in second figure.

Second figure contains all the diagonal lines that can be drawn inside the first figure.

The design is turned by 90°, the two half parts are turned against each other and joined by a dot.

The dots are moved anticlockwise. One section each.

Both the arrows are turned by 90° and moved one step clockwise. The arrow touching the side is made free and the free arrow touches the side.

36. The circle is moved to the opposite middle end and the design is inverted at the line with the circle.

37. The design in first figure is laterally inverted to get the second figure.

38. The triangle with the shaded apex and the protruding square moved anticlockwise one step each.

39. The U shapped element in first figure is turned 45° clockwise and enclosed inside a triangle in second figure.

40. The first figure is turned by 90°, the inner shape is laterally inverted and the two halves of the outer shape are turned away from each other to get the second figure.

41. The places of elements are interchanged vertically.

42. The size and place of both the designs in the first figure are swapped and the inner design is shaded. Note, that the triangle will not change its position.

43. The shape in first figure is laterally inverted to get the second figure.

44. The size and place of the inner most and middle designs in the first figure are swapped to get the second figure.

45. The two pieces in first figure are joined together to get the second figure as a whole.

46. The second figure contains only the shaded portion of the first figure turned 90° clockwise.

47. The shapes of both elements in the figure are interchanged while one of the two identical elements in the innermost part is moved to the top and all three innermost elements are arranged vertically. As circle becomes square and vice versa, so does triangle becomes a quadrant and vice versa.

48. Second figure contains only one of the three identical forms in first figure.

49. The two vertically half positions of the figure are laterally inverted and joined.

50. The first figure is turned by 180° and one line segment and a circle are added in second figure.

SPOTTING EMBEDDED FIGURES

Directions (Qs. 1 to 47) : *In the questions given below a figure is given. From the given alternatives select the one in which the given figure is embedded.*

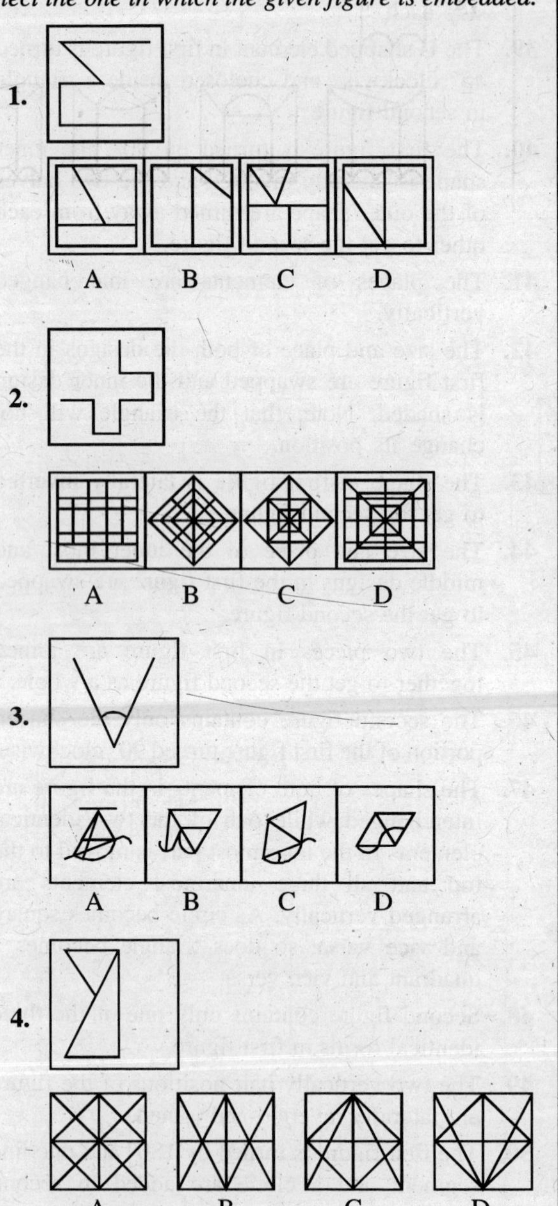

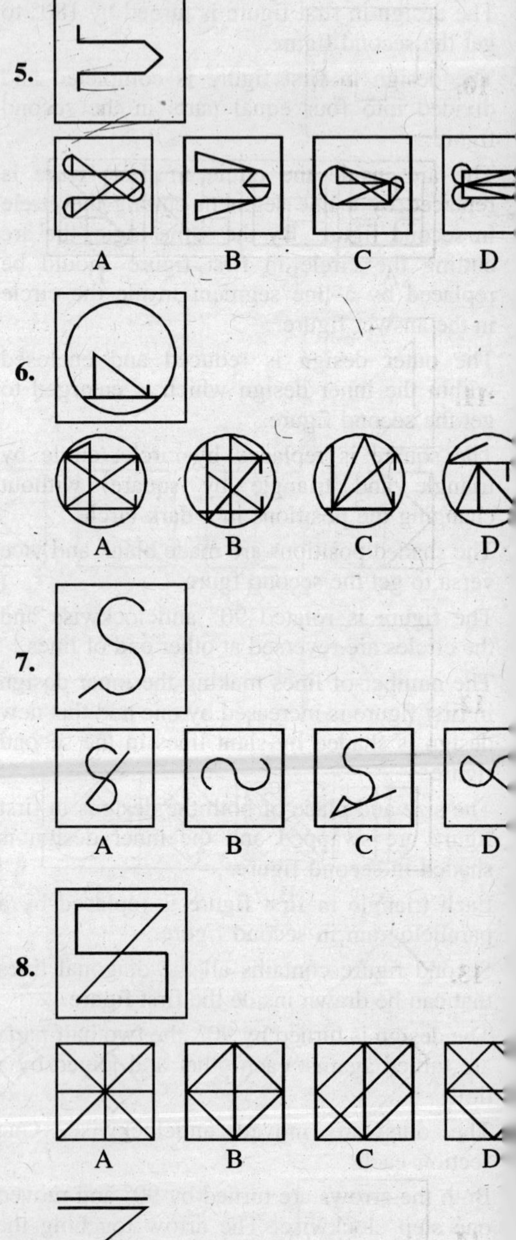

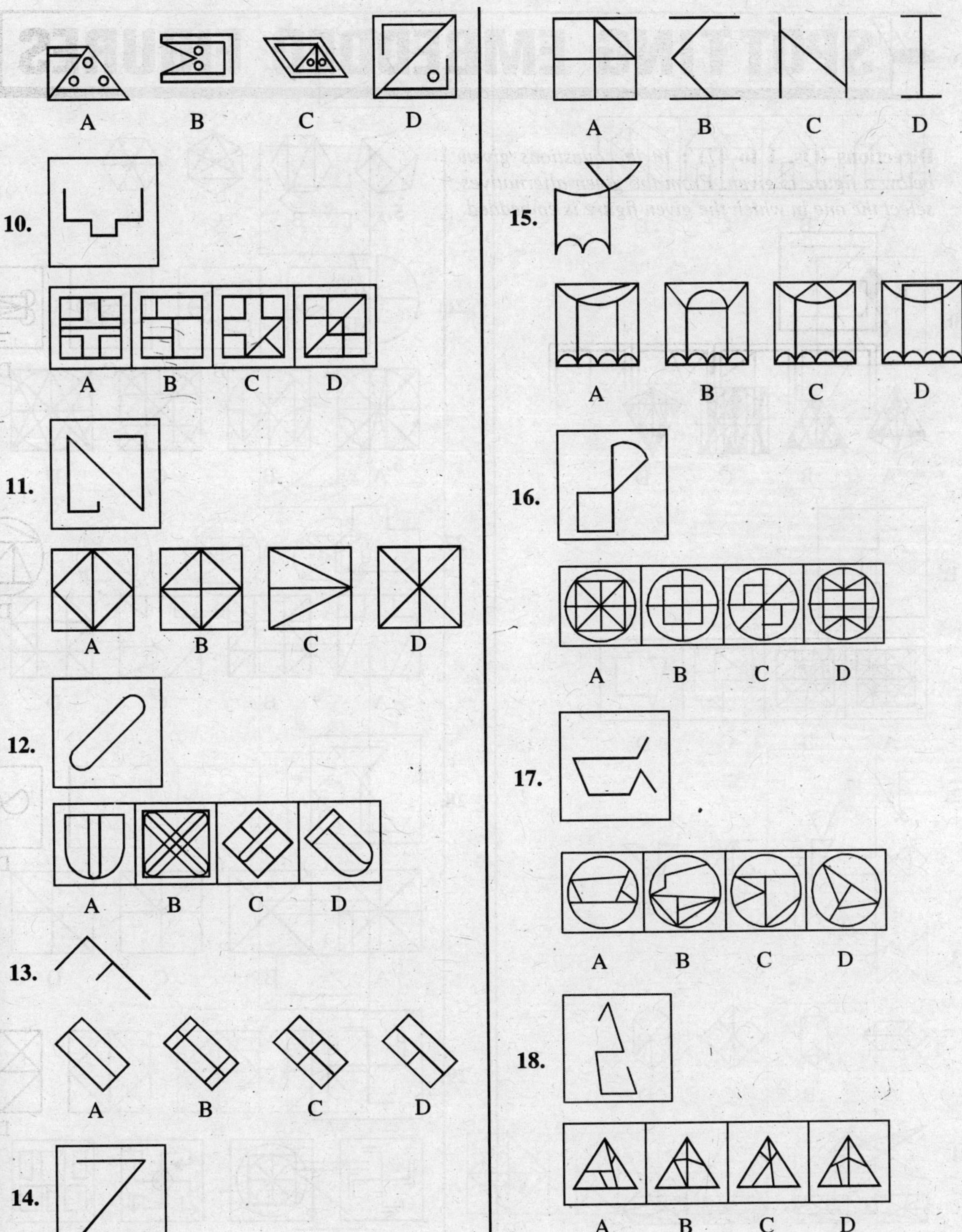
A
B
C
D
10.
A
B
C
D
11.
A
B
C
D
12.
A
B
C
D
13.
A
B
C
D
14.
A
B
C
D
15.
A
B
C
D
16.
A
B
C
D
17.
A
B
C
D
18.
A
B
C
D

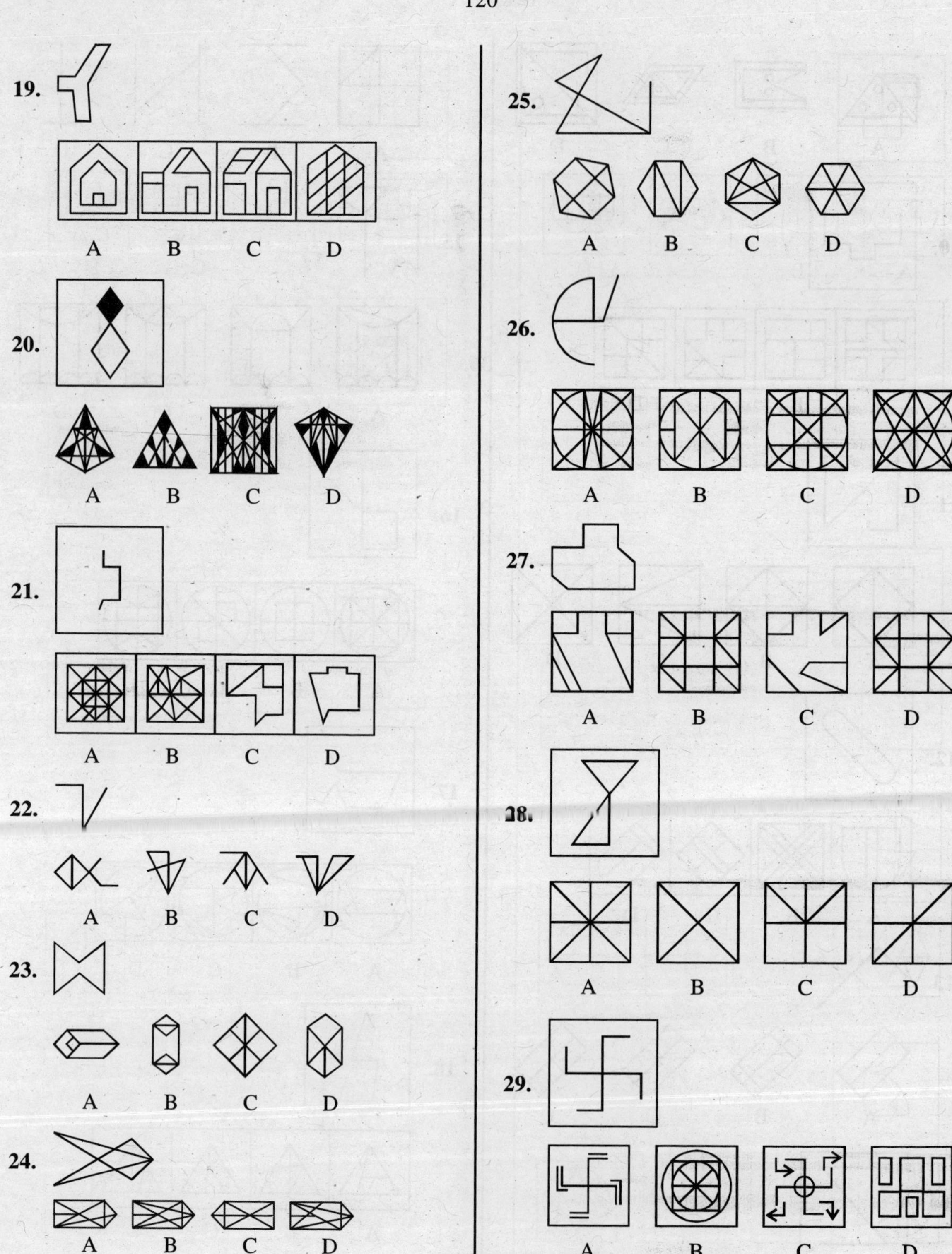
19.
A
B
C
D
20.
A
B
C
D
21.
A
B
C
D
22.
A
B
C
D
23.
A
B
C
D
24.
A
B
C
D
25.
A
B
C
D
26.
A
B
C
D
27.
A
B
C
D
28.
A
B
C
D
29.
A
B
C
D

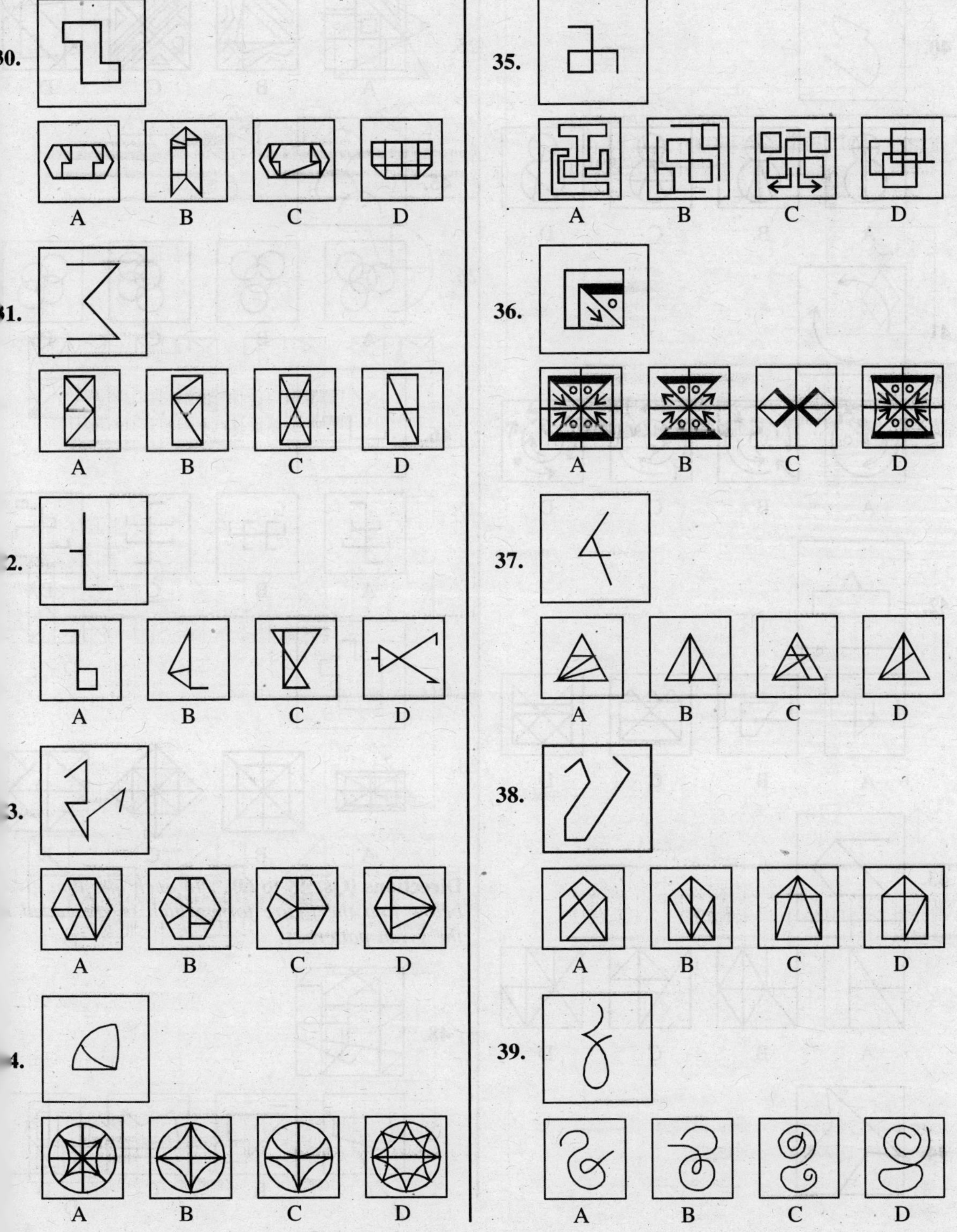
30.
A
B
C
D
31.
A
B
C
D
2.
A
B
C
D
3.
A
B
C
D
4.
A
B
C
D
35.
A
B
C
D
36.
A
B
C
D
37.
A
B
C
D
38.
A
B
C
D
39.
A
B
C
D

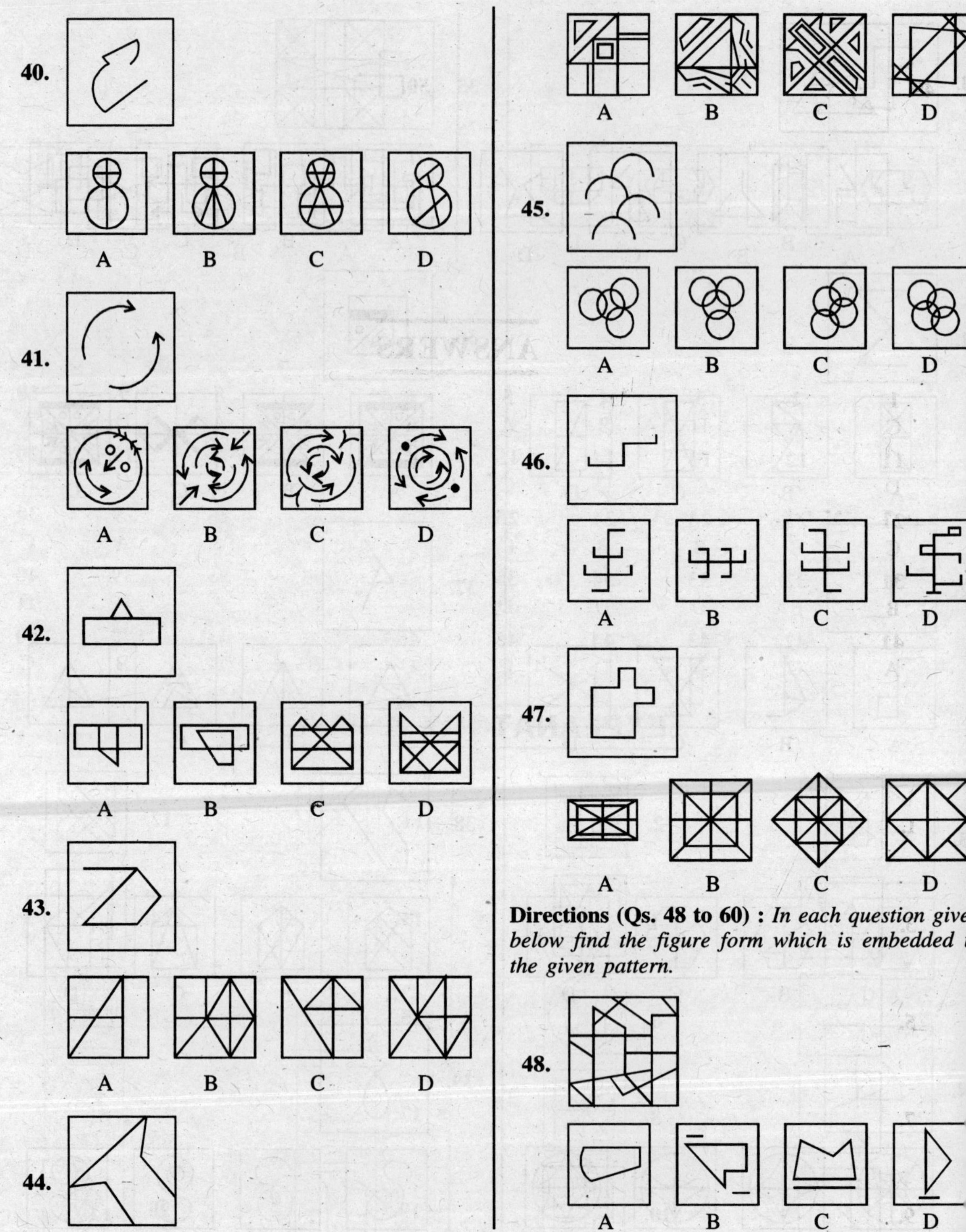

Directions (Qs. 48 to 60) : *In each question given below find the figure form which is embedded in the given pattern.*

49.

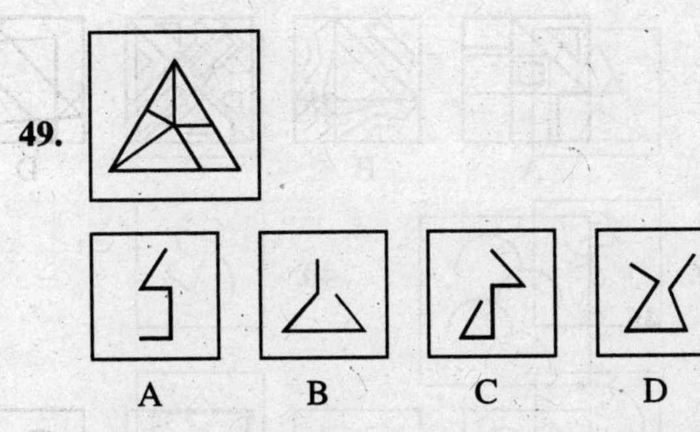

50.

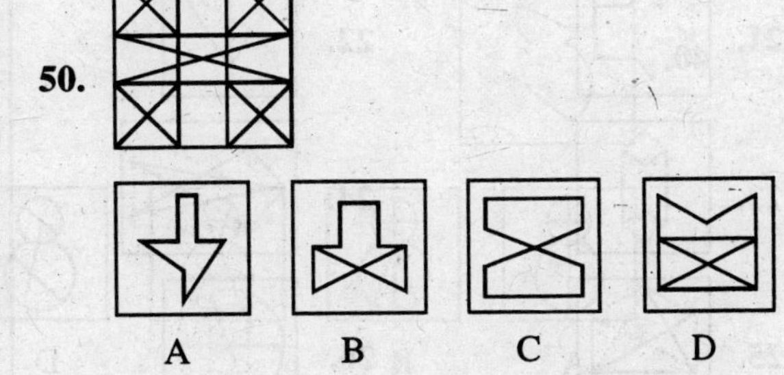

ANSWERS

1	2	3	4	5	6	7	8	9	10
C	A	D	B	A	B	C	A	D	A
11	**12**	**13**	**14**	**15**	**16**	**17**	**18**	**19**	**20**
D	B	C	C	C	D	A	A	C	B
21	**22**	**23**	**24**	**25**	**26**	**27**	**28**	**29**	**30**
C	B	B	B	C	A	B	A	A	C
31	**32**	**33**	**34**	**35**	**36**	**37**	**38**	**39**	**40**
B	B	D	D	D	A	C	A	B	D
41	**42**	**43**	**44**	**45**	**46**	**47**	**48**	**49**	**50**
A	C	B	D	C	C	B	D	B	C

EXPLANATORY ANSWERS

1.

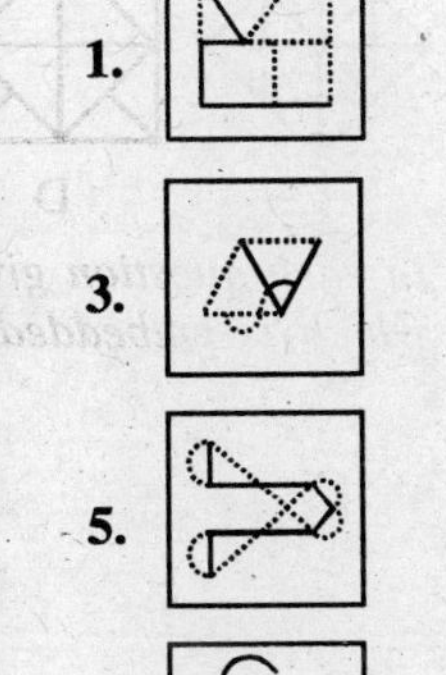

2.

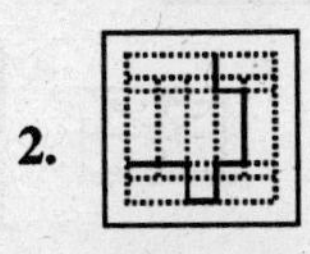

3.

4.

5.

6.

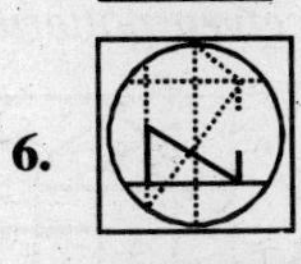

7.

8.

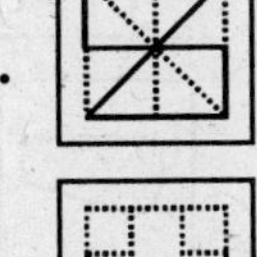

9.

10.

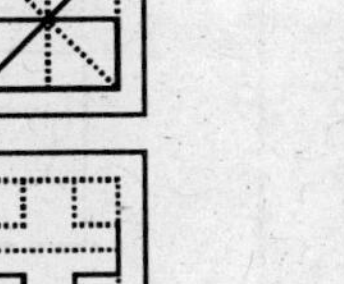

11.

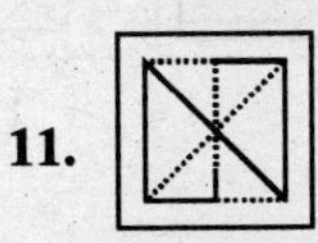

12.

13.

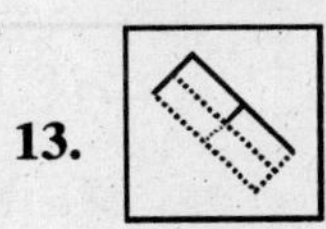

14.

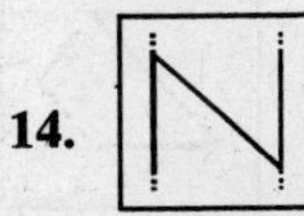

15.

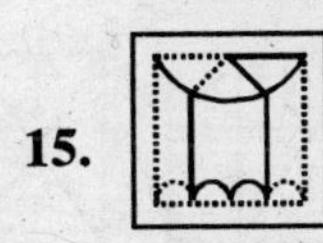

16.

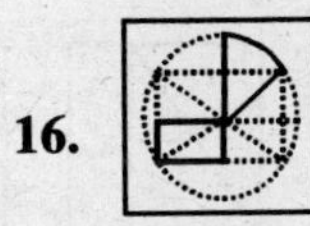

17.

18.

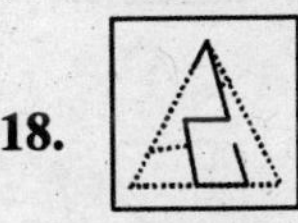

19.

20.

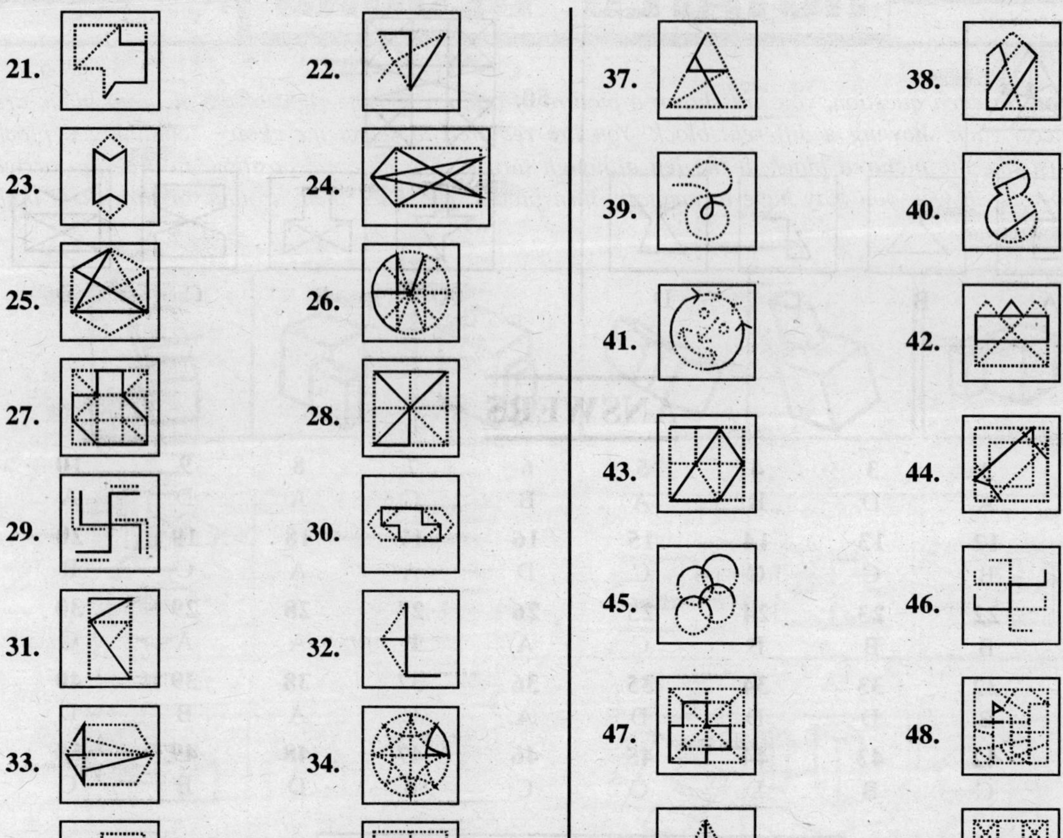

21.
22.
23.
24.
25.
26.
27.
28.
29.
30.
31.
32.
33.
34.
35.
36.
37.
38.
39.
40.
41.
42.
43.
44.
45.
46.
47.
48.
49.
50.

ROTATED BLOCKS

Directions: *In each question, you are shown a picture of a block. To the right of the pictured block are five choices, each showing a different block. You are required to select the choice containing a block that is just like the pictured block at the left although turned in a different position. In order to arrive at the correct answer, you may have to mentally turn blocks over, turn them around, or turn them both over and around.*

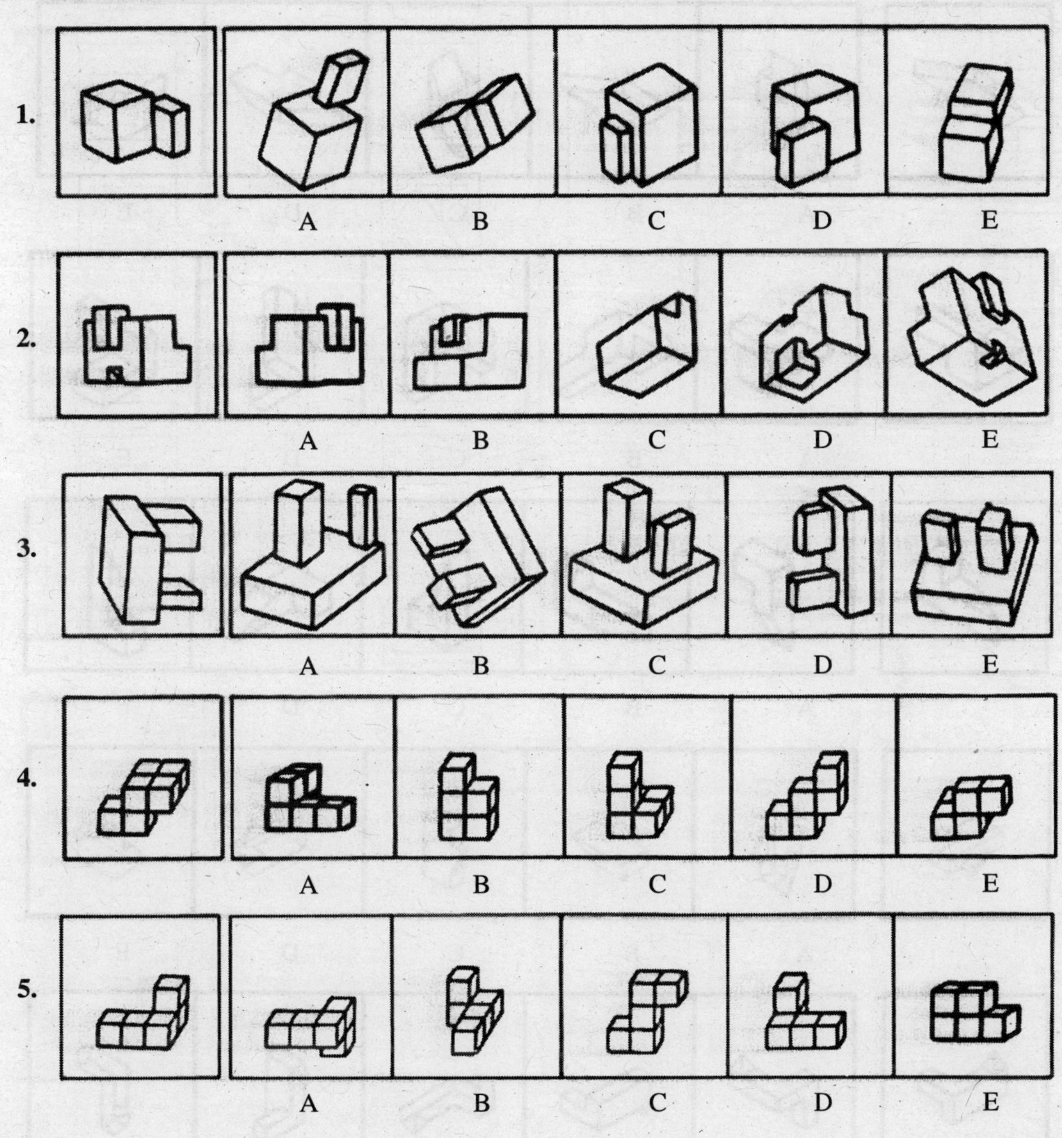

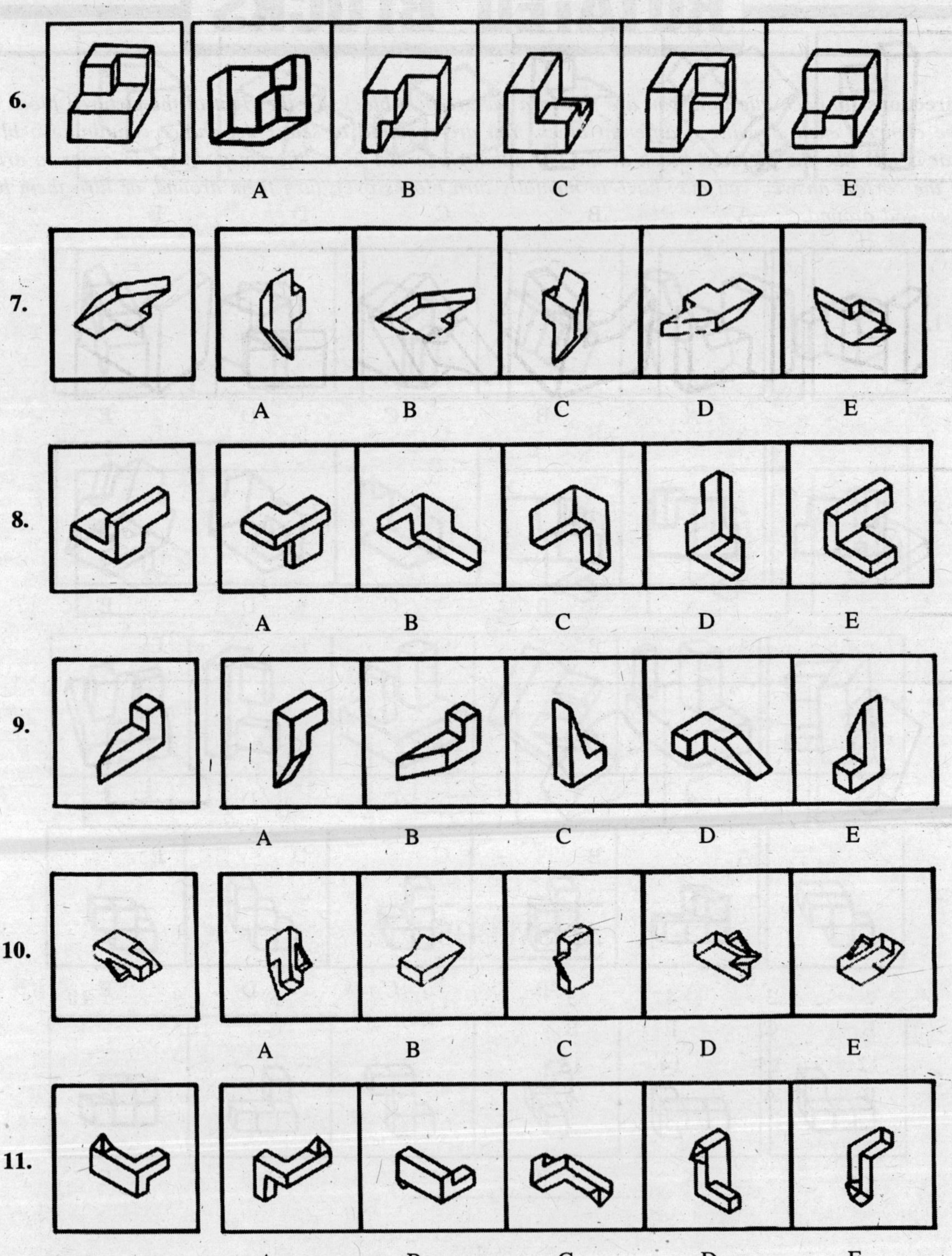
6.
A
B
C
D
E
7.
A
B
C
D
E
8.
A
B
C
D
E
9.
A
B
C
D
E
10.
A
B
C
D
E
11.
A
B
C
D
E

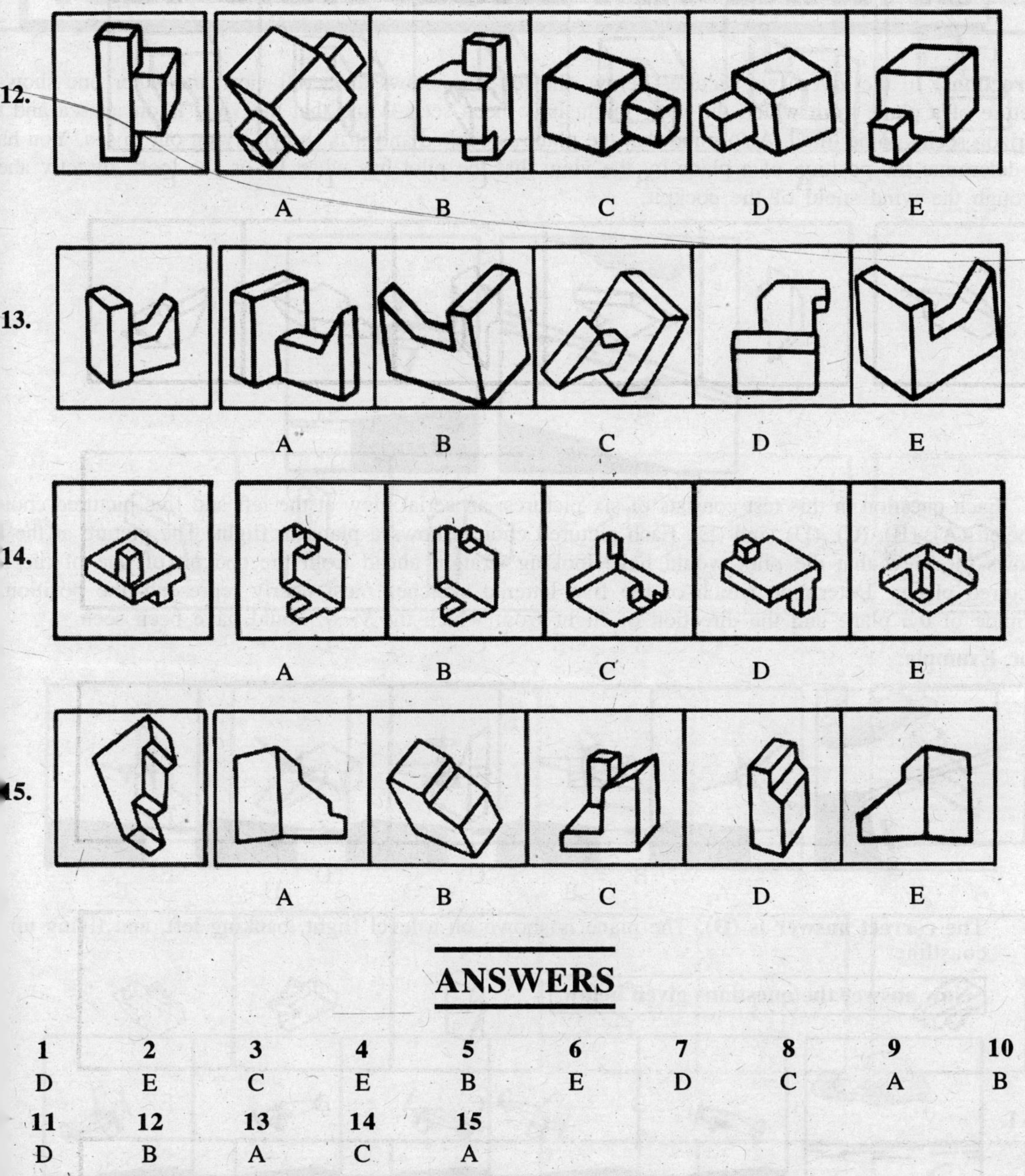

ANSWERS

1	2	3	4	5	6	7	8	9	10
D	E	C	E	B	E	D	C	A	B
11	**12**	**13**	**14**	**15**					
D	B	A	C	A					

SPATIAL APPERCEPTION TEST

Directions: In the given two pictures below, the left one shows an aerial view and other one shows picture of a plane from which the view might have been seen. Mind that the view is out at sea and t horizon seems to be tilted. Also mind that the plane is banked and it is shown flying out to sea. You ha to determine the position of a plane by the view that the pilot has when he or she looks directly ahe through the wind stield of the cockpit.

Each question in this test consists of six pictures: an aerial view at the left and five pictured choi labeled (A), (B), (C), (D), and (E). Each pictured choice shows a plane in flight. The picture at the shows the view that the pilot would have looking straight ahead from the cockpit of one of the f pictured planes. Determine which of the five lettered sketches most nearly represents the position attitude of the plane and the direction of flight from which the view would have been seen.

For Example:

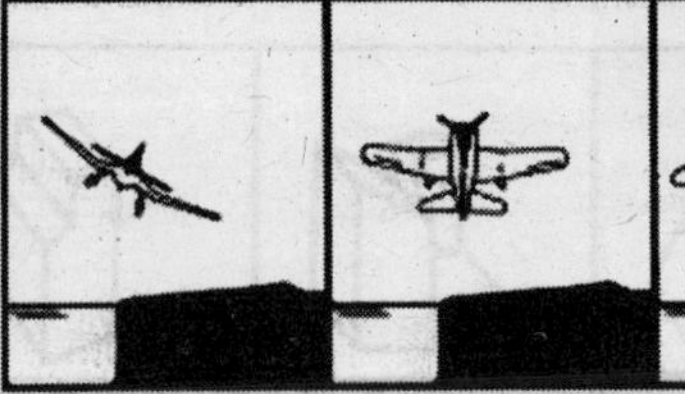

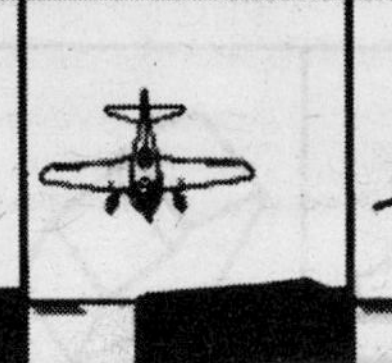

A B C D E

The correct answer is (D). The plane is shown on a level flight, banking left, and flying up coastline.

Now answer the questions given below

1.

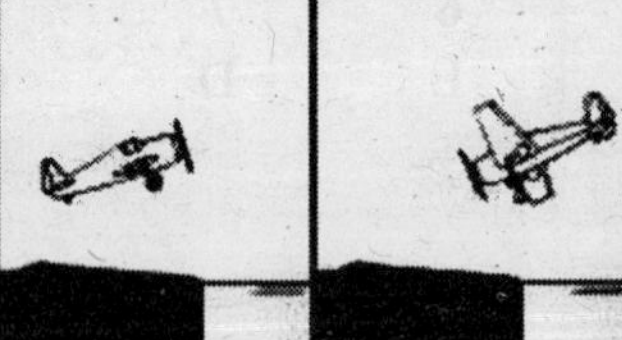

A B C D E

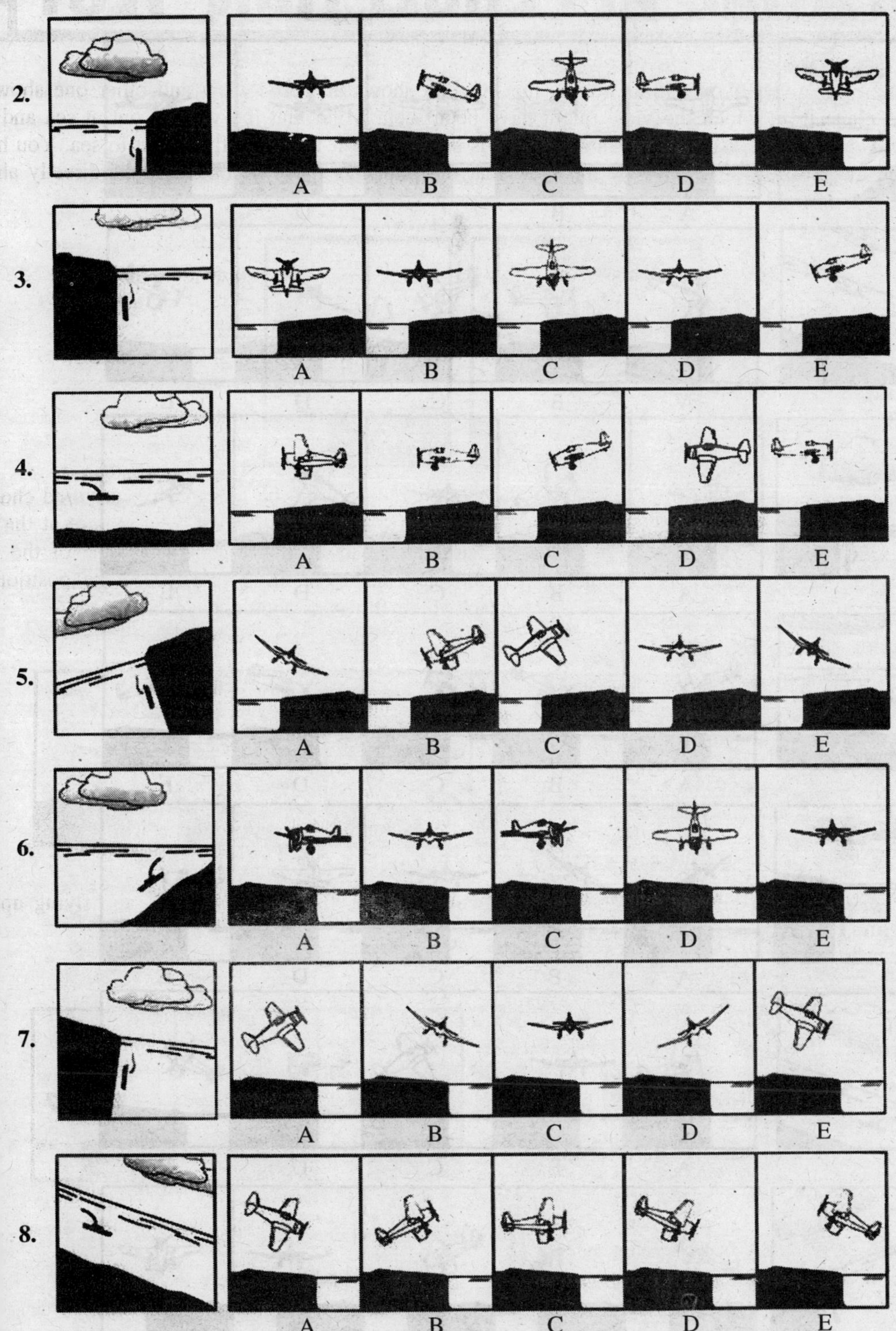
2.
A B C D E
3.
A B C D E
4.
A B C D E
5.
A B C D E
6.
A B C D E
7.
A B C D E
8.
A B C D E

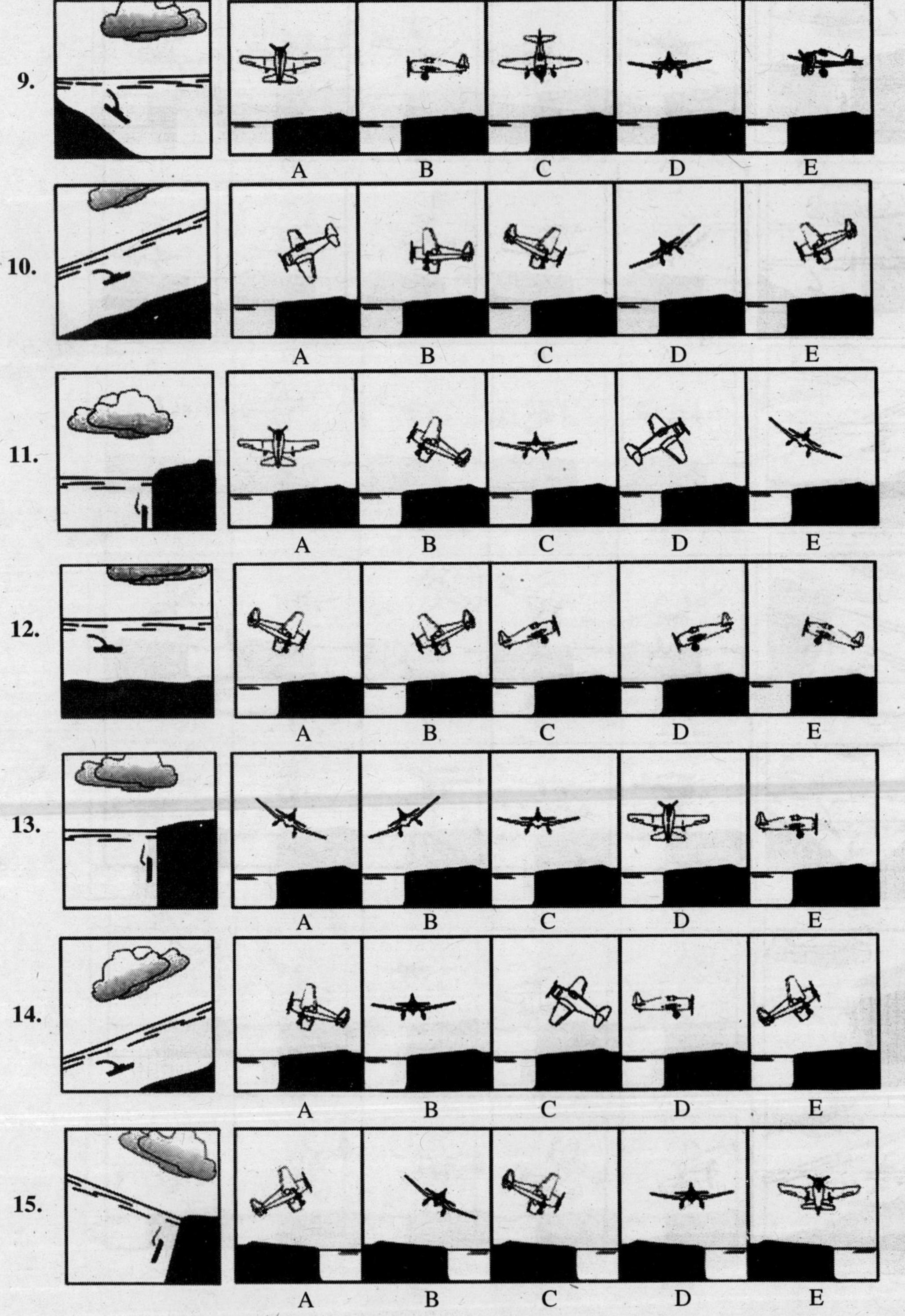
9.
A
B
C
D
E
10.
A
B
C
D
E
11.
A
B
C
D
E
12.
A
B
C
D
E
13.
A
B
C
D
E
14.
A
B
C
D
E
15.
A
B
C
D
E

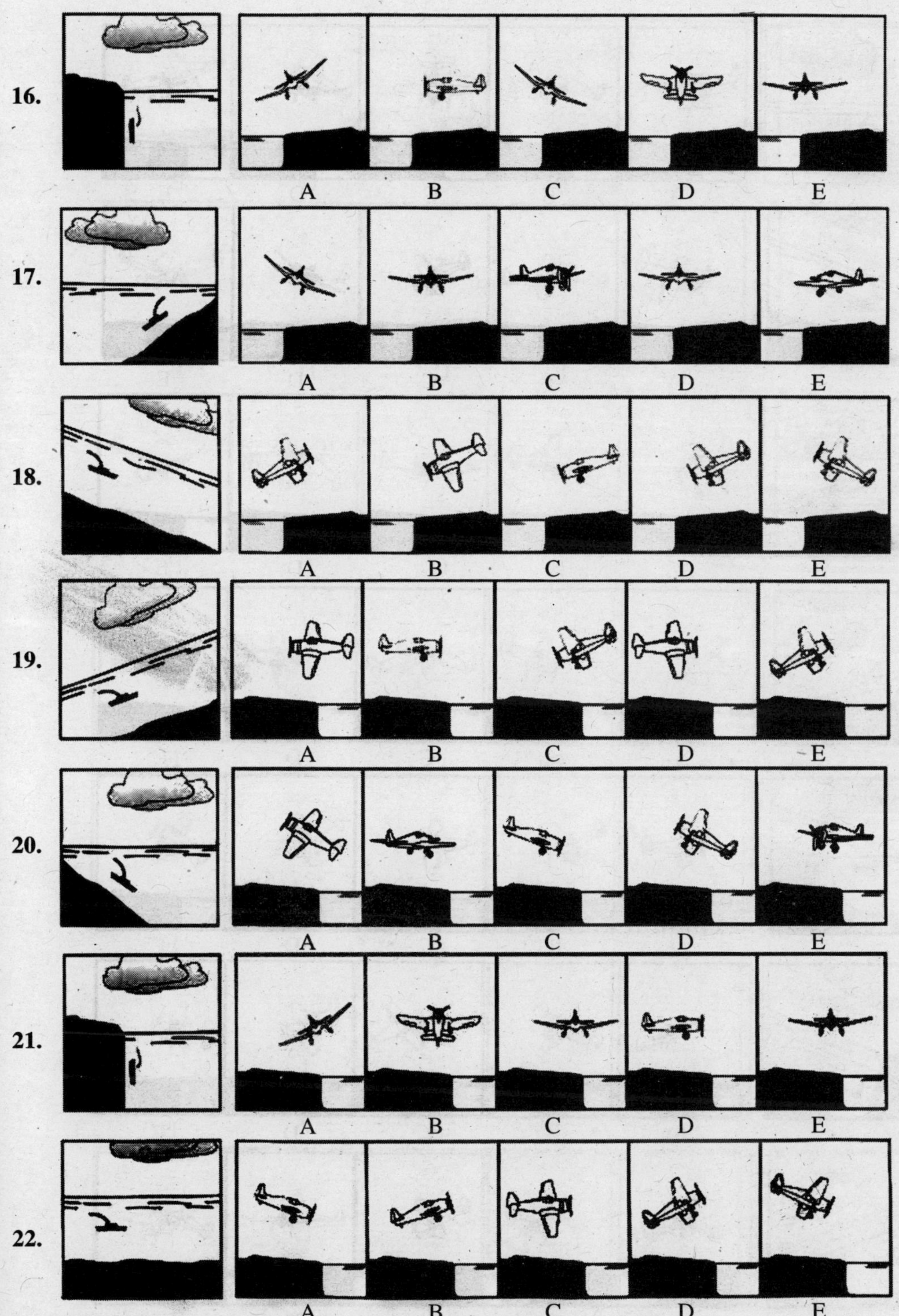
16.
A
B
C
D
E
17.
A
B
C
D
E
18.
A
B
C
D
E
19.
A
B
C
D
E
20.
A
B
C
D
E
21.
A
B
C
D
E
22.
A
B
C
D
E

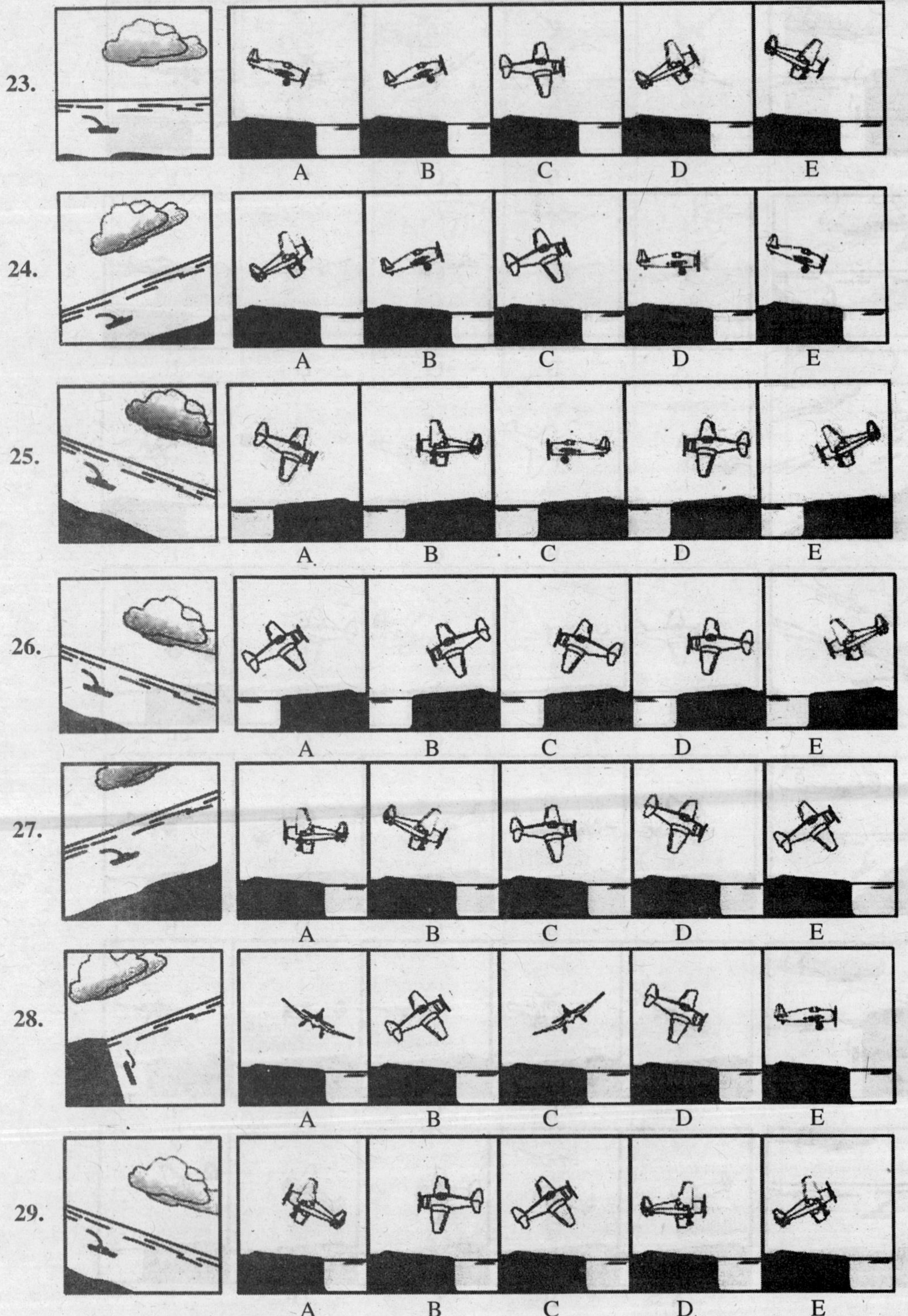
23.
A
B
C
D
E
24.
A
B
C
D
E
25.
A
B
C
D
E
26.
A
B
C
D
E
27.
A
B
C
D
E
28.
A
B
C
D
E
29.
A
B
C
D
E

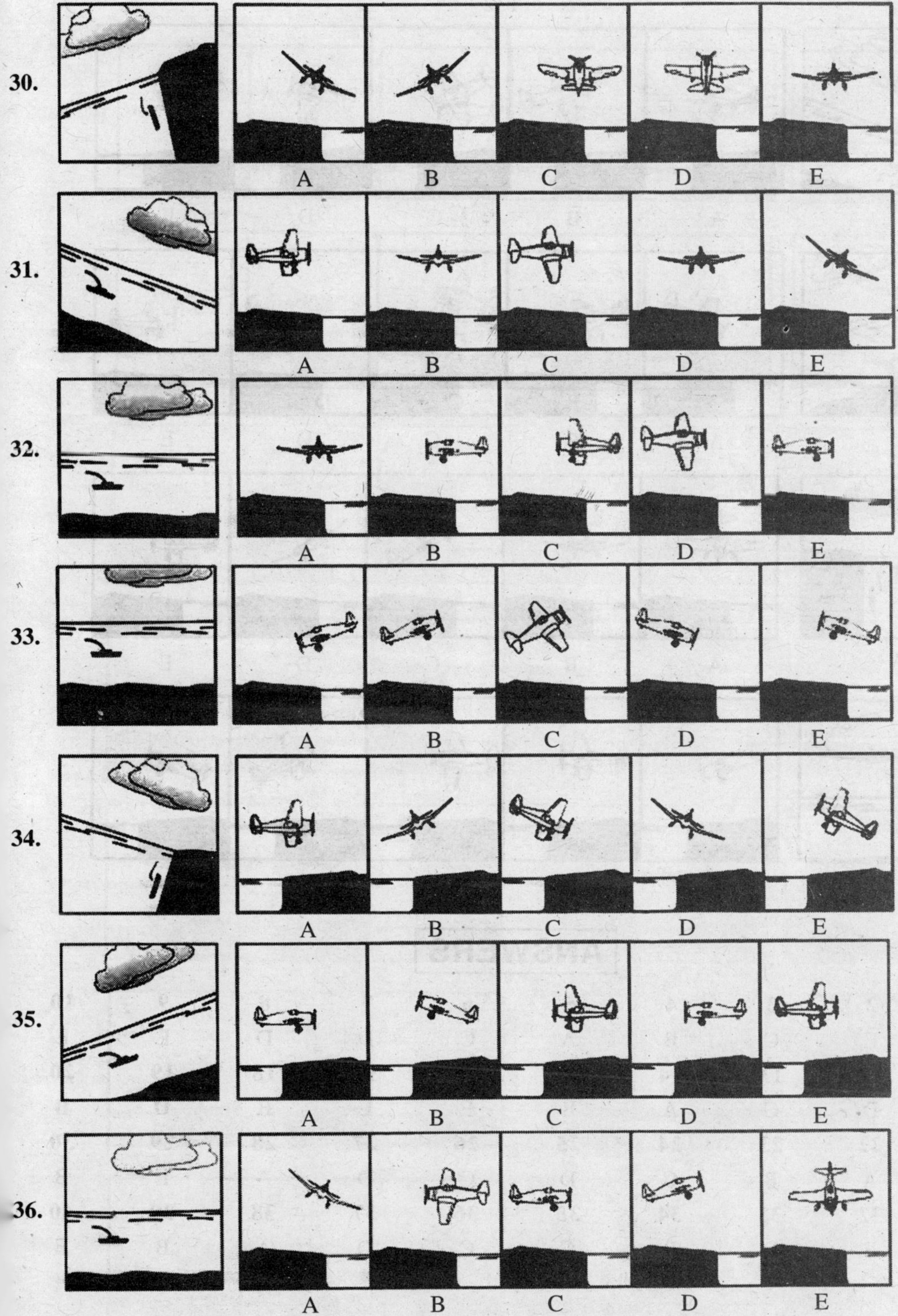
30.
A
B
C
D
E
31.
A
B
C
D
E
32.
A
B
C
D
E
33.
A
B
C
D
E
34.
A
B
C
D
E
35.
A
B
C
D
E
36.
A
B
C
D
E

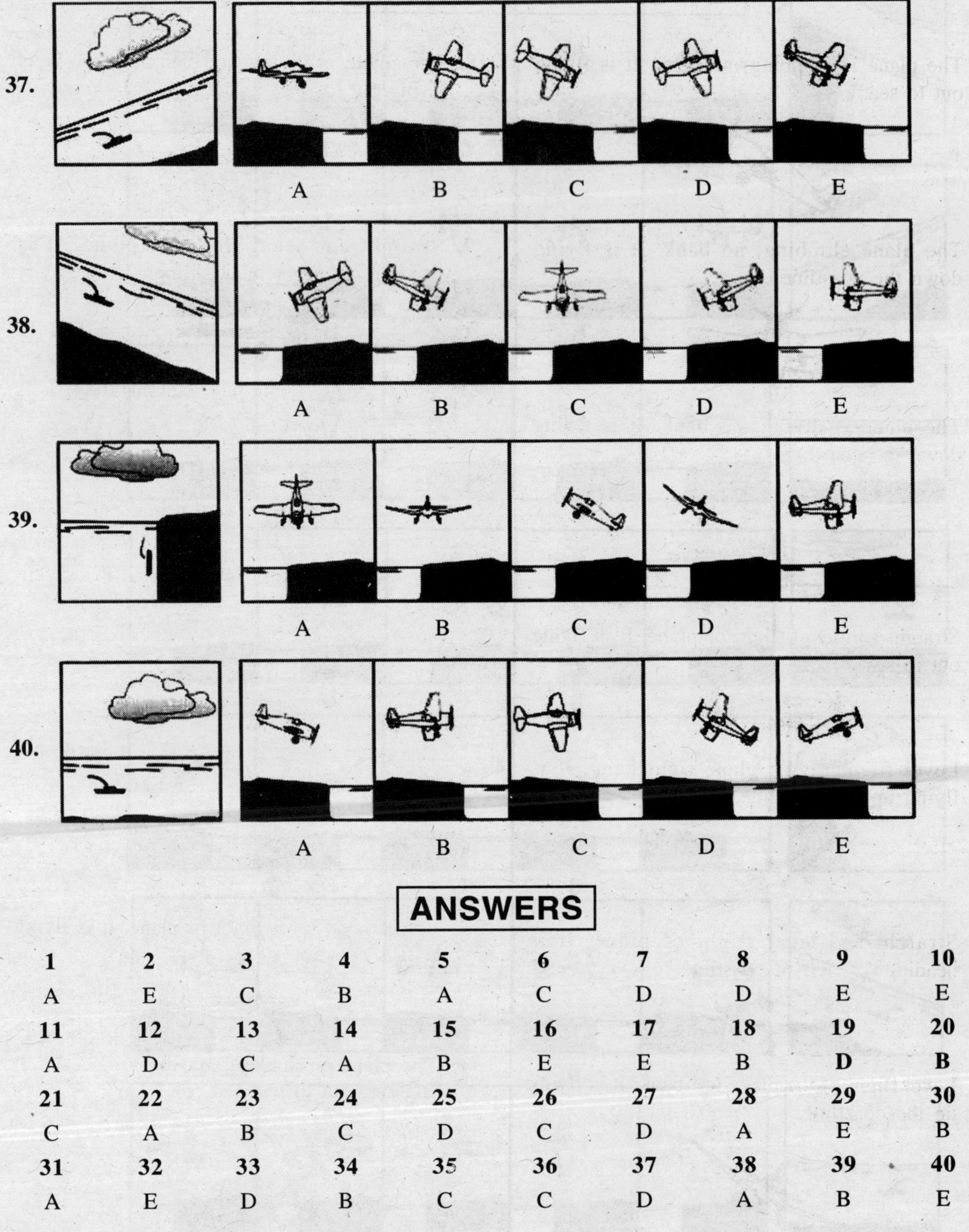

ANSWERS

1	2	3	4	5	6	7	8	9	10
A	E	C	B	A	C	D	D	E	E
11	**12**	**13**	**14**	**15**	**16**	**17**	**18**	**19**	**20**
A	D	C	A	B	E	E	B	**D**	**B**
21	**22**	**23**	**24**	**25**	**26**	**27**	**28**	**29**	**30**
C	A	B	C	D	C	D	A	E	B
31	**32**	**33**	**34**	**35**	**36**	**37**	**38**	**39**	**40**
A	E	D	B	C	C	D	A	B	E

EXPLANATORY ANSWERS

1. The plane is climbing; no bank. It is flying out to sea.

2. The plane climbing; no bank. It is flying down the coastline.

3. The plane is diving; no bank. It is flying down the coastline.

4. Straight-and-level flight of plane. It is flying out to sea.

5. Level flight of the plane right bank. It is flying up the coastline.

6. Straight-and-level flight of plane. It is heading 45° left of coastline.

7. Level flight of the plane left bank. It is flying up the coastline.

8. The plane is diving and banking left. It is flying out to sea.

9. Straight-and-level flight of plane. It is heading 45° right of coastline.

10. The plane is diving and banking right. It is flying out to sea.

11. The plane is climbing; no bank. It is flying up the coastline.

12. The plane is diving; no bank. It is flying out to sea.

13. Straight-and-level flight of plane. It is flying up the coastline.

14. The plane is climbing and banking right. It is flying out to sea.

15. Level flight of the plane, left bank. It is flying down the coastline.

16. Straight-and-level flight of plane. It is flying down the coastline.

17. Straight-and-level flight of plane. It is heading 45° left of coastline.

18. The plane is diving; banking left. It is flying out to sea.

19. Level flight of the plane right bank. It is flying out to sea.

20. Straight-and-level flight of plane. It is heading 45° right of coastline

21. Straight-and-level flight of plane. It is flying up the coastline.

22. The plane is diving; no bank. It is flying out to sea.

23. The plane is climbing; no bank. It is flying out to sea.

24. The plane is Climbing and banking right. It is flying out to sea.

25. Level flight of the plane; left bank. It is flying out to sea.

26. The plane is climbing and banking left. It i flying out to sea.

27. The plane is diving and banking right. It i flying out to sea.

28. Level flight of the plane; right bank. It flying up the coastline.

29. The plane is climbing and banking left. It is flying out to sea.

30. Level flight of the plane, right bank. It is flying down the coastline.

31. Level flight of the plane, left bank. It is flying out to sea.

32. Straight-and-level flight of plane. It is flying out to sea.

33. The plane is diving; no bank. It is flying out to sea.

34. Level flight of the plane left bank. It is flying up the coastline.

35. Level flight of the plane right bank. It is flying out to sea.

36. Straight-and-level flight of the plane. It is heading out of sea.

37. The plane is climbing and banking right. It is heading out of sea.

38. The plane is diving and banking to the lelt. It is heading out of sea.

39. Straight and level flight of the plane along the coastline.

40. The plane is climbing, no bank. It is flying out of sea.

TEMPERAMENT TEST

Directions 1–21: *In each question given below there is a statement. You have to consider the statement and decide how much do you agree with the statement. Give answer :*

A. If you strongly agree with the statement.
B. If you agree with the statement.
C. If you are neutral with the statement.
D. If you disagree with the statement.
E. If you strongly disagree with the statement.

1. Decision should not be affected by emotion.

2. Since parents have given us the life therefore their every decision should be obeyed.

3. We should give the priority to relation than profession.

4. We should ignore the difficult problem if it comes. Because it obstructs our development.

5. We should put off problems as long as we can.

6. We should work in group because it becomes easy if we work collectively.

7. We should work alone because others can take away the contribution.

8. The stressful situations often confuse us.

9. We know that negative thinking is not good but sometimes we think negatively.

10. We should work different even if it is improper because different things attract people and we can easily get the popularity.

11. Corruption is acceptable now. Because most of the people thrive through it.

12. Regular exercise is wastage of time.

13. Quick decision is not good.

14. We should live in limited social circle because broad relationship is unnecessary involvement.

15. Beggars should be turned out from society.

16. Honesty is not the best policy now-a-days.

17. Politeness is a kind of timidness.

18. We should leave the seat in train, for a women even if we are at long journey.

19. Real friends are rare.

20. Now-a-days deep knowlegde is not necessary.

21. Enthusiasm defeats poverty.

Directions 22-92: *Each question given below consists of two options and a statement. Consider the statement and choose the best option.*

22. At work, is it more natural for you to
A. point out mistakes
B. try to please others

23. Are you more comfortable
A. before a decision
B. after a decision

24 Are you more
A. routinized than whimsical
B. whimsical than routinized

25. Do you tend to notice
A. opportunities for change
B. disorderliness

26. Is it preferable mostly to
A. make sure things are arranged
B. just let things happen naturally

27. Do you feel better about
A. keeping your options open
B. coming to closure

28. Would you say you are more
A. easy going
B. serious and determined

29 Do you usually want things
A. settled and decided
B. just penciled in

30. Are you inclined to be more
A. leisurely than hurried
B. hurried than leisurely

31. Do you tend to choose
A. rather carefully
B. somewhat impulsively

32. Do you prefer to work
A. to deadlines
B. just whenever

33. When finishing a job, do you like to
A. tie up all loose ends
B. move on to something else

34. In most situations are you more
A. spontaneous than deliberate
B. deliberate than spontaneous

35. Are you prone to
A. nailing things down
B. exploring the possibilities

36. Do you more often prefer
A. final unalterable statements
B. tentative preliminary statements

37. On the job, do you want your activities
A. unscheduled
B. scheduled

38. Are you more satisfied having
A. work in progress
B. a finished product

39. Do you prefer contracts to be
A. settled on a handshake
B. signed, sealed, and delivered

40. Is it your way to
A. pick and choose at some length
B. make up your mind quickly

41. Is clutter in the work place something you
A. take time to straighten up
B. tolerate pretty well

42. Do you see yourself as basically
A. thin-skinned
B. thick-skinned

43. Which do you wish more for yourself
A. strength of will
B. strength of emotion

44. Are you swayed more by
A. a touching appeal
B. convincing evidence

45. Which seems the greater fault
A. to be too compassionate
B. to be too dispassionate

46. Do you value in yourself more that you are
A. reasonable
B. devoted

47. Do you think of yourself as a
A. tough-minded person
B. tender-hearted person

48. In hard circumstances, are you sometimes
A. too sympathetic
B. too unsympathetic

49. It is worse to be
A. hard-nosed
B. a softy

50. Which rules you more
A. your thoughts
B. your feelings

51. Which is more of a compliment
A. "There's a logical person"
B. "There's a sentimental person"

52. Are you more often
A. a warm-hearted person
B. a cool-headed person

53. When in charge of others do you tend to be
A. firm and unbending
B. forgiving and lenient

54. Is it better to be
A. just
B. merciful

55. In a heated discussion do you
A. look for common ground
B. stick to your guns

56. If you must disappoint someone are you usually
A. warm and considerate
B. frank and straightforward

57. Which appeals to you more
A. consistency of thought
B. harmonious relationships

58. In sizing up others, do you tend to be
A. friendly and personal
B. objective and impersonal

59. In making up your mind are you more likely to go by
A. desires
B. data

60. Are you more comfortable in making
A. critical judgments
B. value judgments

61. With people are you usually more
A. gentle than firm
B. firm than gentle

62. Is it easier for you to
A. identify with others
B. put others to good use

63. In stories, do you prefer
A. action and adventure
B. fantasy and heroism

64. Are you drawn more to
A. overtones
B. fundamentals

65. Do you prize in yourself
A. a vivid imagination
B. a strong hold on reality

66. Are you more inclined to feel
A. somewhat removed
B. down to earth

67. Are you more likely to trust
A. your conceptions
B. your experiences

68. Do you more often see
A. what's right in front of you
B. what can only be imagined

69. Are you inclined to take what is said
A. more figuratively
B. more literally

70. Do you speak more in
A. particulars than generalities
B. generalities than particulars

71. Are you more frequently
A. a fanciful sort of person
B. a practical sort of person

72. Children often do not
A. make themselves useful enough
B. exercise their fantasy enough

73. Common sense is
A. frequently questionable
B. usually reliable

74. Do you find visionaries and theorists
A. somewhat annoying
B. rather-fascinating

75. Facts
A. illustrate principles
B. speak for themselves

76. Do you like writers who
A. say what they mean
B. use metaphors and symbolism

77. Do you tend to be more
A. factual than speculative
B. speculative than factual

78. Are you more interested in
A. what is possible
B. what is actual

79. Are you more
A. ideational than sensible
B. sensible than ideational

80. Is it worse to
A. be in a rut
B. have your head in the clouds

81. Are you more
A. observant than introspective
B. introspective than observant

82. Are you inclined to be
A. somewhat reserved
B. easy to approach

83. Do you consider yourself
A. a good conversationalist
B. a good listener

84. At work do you tend to
A. keep more to yourself
B. be sociable with your colleagues

85. Are you the kind of person who
A. doesn't miss much
B. is rather talkative

86. Do you think of yourself as
A. a private person
B. an outgoing person

87. Do you tend to
A. say right out what's on your mind
B. keep your ears open

88. Does interacting with strangers
A. tax your reserves
B. energize you

89. At a party, do you
A. interact with a few friends
B. interact with many, even strangers

90. Waiting in line, do you often
A. stick to business B. chat with others

91. When the phone rings, do you
A. hope someone else will answer it
B. hurry to get to it first.

92. Your gender is:
A. Female
B. Male

Directions 93-164: *The following questions consist of a statement. You have to consider the statement and decide whether you agree or not with the statement.*

93. You are almost never late for your appointments
A. YES B. NO

94. You like to be engaged in an active and fast-paced job
A. YES B. NO

95. You enjoy having a wide circle of acquaintances
A. YES B. NO

96. You feel involved when watching TV soaps
A. YES B. NO

97. You are usually the first to react to a sudden event: the telephone ringing or unexpected question
A. YES B. NO

98. You are more interested in a general idea than in the details of its realization
A. YES B. NO

99. You tend to be unbiased even if this might endanger your good relations with people
A. YES B. NO

100. Strict observance of the established rules is likely to prevent a good outcome
A. YES B. NO

101. It's difficult to get you excited
A. YES B. NO

102. It is in your nature to assume responsibility
A. YES B. NO

103. You often think about humankind and its destiny
A. YES B. NO

104. You believe the best decision is one that can be easily changed
A. YES B. NO

105. Objective criticism is always useful in any activity
A. YES B. NO

106. You prefer to act immediately rather than speculate about various options
A. YES B. NO

107. You trust reason rather than feelings
A. YES B. NO

108. You are inclined to rely more on improvisation than on careful planning
A. YES B. NO

109. You spend your leisure time actively socializing with a group of people, attending parties, shopping, etc.
A. YES B. NO

110. You usually plan your actions in advance
A. YES B. NO

111. Your actions are frequently influenced by emotions
A. YES B. NO

112. You are a person somewhat reserved and distant in communication
A. YES B. NO

113. You know how to put every minute of your time to good purpose
A. YES B. NO

114. You readily help people while asking nothing in return
A. YES B. NO

115. You often contemplate about the complexity of life
A. YES B. NO

116. After prolonged socializing you feel you need to get away and be alone
A. YES B. NO

117. You often do jobs in a hurry
A. YES B. NO

118. You easily see the general principle behind specific occurrences
A. YES B. NO

119. You frequently and easily express your feelings and emotions
A. YES B. NO

120. You find it difficult to speak loudly
A. YES B. NO

121. You get bored if you have to read theoretical books
A. YES B. NO

122. You tend to sympathize with other people
A. YES B. NO

123. You value justice higher than mercy
A. YES B. NO

124. You rapidly get involved in social life at a new workplace
A. YES B. NO

125. The more people with whom you speak, the better you feel
A. YES B. NO

126. You tend to rely on your experience rather than on theoretical alternatives
A. YES B. NO

127. You like to keep a check on how things are progressing
A. YES B. NO

128. You easily empathize with the concerns of other people
A. YES B. NO

129. Often you prefer to read a book than go to a party
A. YES B. NO

130. You enjoy being at the center of events in which other people are directly involved
A. YES B. NO

131. You are more inclined to experiment than t follow familiar approaches
A. YES B. NO

132. You avoid being bound by obligations
A. YES B. NO

133. You are strongly touched by the stories abou people's troubles
A. YES B. NO

134. Deadlines seem to you to be of relative, rathe than absolute, importance
A. YES B. NO

135. You prefer to isolate yourself from outsic noises
A. YES B. NO

136. It's essential for you to try things with yo own hands
A. YES B. NO

137. You think that almost everything can analyzed
A. YES B. NO

138. You do your best to complete a task on tir
A. YES B. NO

139. You take pleasure in putting things in ord
A. YES B. NO

140. You feel at ease in a crowd
A. YES B. NO

141. You have good control over your desires a temptations
A. YES B. NO

142. You easily understand new theoretic principles
A. YES B. NO

143. The process of searching for a solution is m important to you than the solution itself
A. YES B. NO

144. You usually place yourself nearer to the s than in the center of the room
A. YES B. NO

145. When solving a problem you would rat follow a familiar approach than seek a r one
A. YES B. NO

146. You try to stand firmly by your principles
A. YES B. NO

147. A thirst for adventure is close to your heart
A. YES B. NO

148. You prefer meeting in small groups to interaction with lots of people
A. YES B. NO

149. When considering a situation you pay more attention to the current situation and less to a possible sequence of events
A. YES B. NO

150. You consider the scientific approach to be the best
A. YES B. NO

151. You find it difficult to talk about your feelings
A. YES B. NO

152. You often spend time thinking of how things could be improved
A. YES B. NO

153. Your decisions are based more on the feelings of a moment than on the careful planning
A. YES B. NO

154. You prefer to spend your leisure time alone or relaxing in a tranquil family atmosphere
A. YES B. NO

155. You feel more comfortable sticking to conventional ways
A. YES B. NO

156. You are easily affected by strong emotions
A. YES B. NO

157. You are always looking for opportunities
A. YES B. NO

158. Your desk, workbench etc. is usually neat and orderly
A. YES B. NO

159. As a rule, current preoccupations worry you more than your future plans
A. YES B. NO

160. You get pleasure from solitary walks
A. YES B. NO

161. It is easy for you to communicate in social situations
A. YES B. NO

162. You are consistent in your habits
A. YES B. NO

163. You willingly involve yourself in matters which engage your sympathies
A. YES B. NO

164. You easily perceive various ways in which events could develop
A. YES B. NO

Directions 165-170: *Each question in this section consists of a statement that may be considered to be somewhat controversial. Select one of the following choices that best describes the extent to which you agree or disagree with each statement:*
A. Strongly agree B. Tend to agree
C. Tend to disagree D. Strongly disagree

165. Generally speaking, people get the recognition they deserve.
A. Strongly agree B. Tend to agree
C. Tend to disagree D. Strongly disagree

166. There is too much power concentrated in the hands of labour union officials.
A. Strongly agree B. Tend to agree
C. Tend to disagree D. Strongly disagree

167. Acid rain is one of the most serious environmental problems facing us today.
A. Strongly agree B. Tend to agree
C. Tend to disagree D. Strongly disagree

168. Success at work depends on hard work; luck has very little to do with it.
A. Strongly agree B. Tend to agree
C. Tend to disagree D. Strongly disagree

169. Most people use politeness to cover up what is actually ruthless competition.
A. Strongly agree B. Tend to agree
C. Tend to disagree D. Strongly disagree

170. Breaking the law is hardly ever justified.
A. Strongly agree B. Tend to agree
C. Tend to disagree D. Strongly disagree

PERSONALITY TEST

Directions 1-21: *In each question given below there is a statement. You have to consider the statement and decide how much do you agree with the statement. Give answer :*

A. If you strongly agree with the statement.
B. If you agree with the statement.
C. If you are neutral with the statement.
D. If you disagree with the statement.
E. If you strongly disagree with the statement.

1. I tell a lie if it is needed.

2. I give some time to social services.

3. I get imotional when a beloved person goes away.

4. I don't like to take someone's obligation.

5. I don't loose patience during hardship.

6. I try to solve my problems alone.

7. I feel good if someone comes to meet me.

8. I feel awkward among strangers.

9. I like solitary life.

10. I get irritated if someone shows a non-sense behaviour.

11. I take seriously even a minor thing.

12. I start my work at eleventh hour.

13. I want to lead my group.

14. I remain always ready to extempore.

15. I like to accept responsibility.

16. I like to remain the centre of attraction in the crowd.

17. I get perplexed if a complex situation comes.

18. I don't like too busy life.

19. I am conservative.

20. I believe in God up to superstition.

21. In my opinion humanity is more important than nationality.

Directions 22–41: *The questions in this section consist of sets of five descriptive words from which you are to select the choice that most accurately describes you or the choice that least describes you.*

22. Which of the following *most* accurately describes you?
A. Adventurous B. Energetic
C. Impetuous D. Impulsive
E. Restless

23. Which one of the following *least* describes you?
A. Adventurous B. Energetic
C. Impetuous D. Impulsive
E. Restless

24. Which one of the following *most* accurately describes you?
A. Ambitious B. Emotional
C. Logical D. Resourceful
E. Sentimental

25. Which one of the following *least* describe you?
A. Ambitious B. Emotional
C. Logical D. Resourceful
E. Sentimental

26. Which one of the following *most* accurately describes you?
A. Cautious B. Deliberate
C. Impatient D. Impulsive
E. Patient

27. Which one of the following *least* describe you?
A. Cautious B. Deliberate
C. Impatient D. Impulsive
E. Patient

28. Which one of the following *most* accurate describes you?
A. Competent B. Gifted
C. Intelligent D. Quick-witted
E. Skillful

29. Which one of the following *least* describes you?
A. Competent B. Gifted
C. Intelligent D. Quick-witted
E. Skillful

30. Which one of the following *most* accurately describes you?
A. Compromising B. Dependable
C. Independent D. Sincere
E. Studious

31. Which one of the following *least* describes you?
A. Compromising B. Dependable
C. Independent D. Sincere
E. Studious

32. Which one of the following *most* accurately describes you?
A. Condescending B. Friendly
C. Pleasant D. Polite
E. Reserved

33. Which one of the following *least* describes you?
A. Condescending B. Friendly
C. Pleasant D. Polite
E. Reserved

34. Which one of the following *most* accurately describes you?
A. Courteous B. Curious
C. Patronizing D. Studious
E. Thoughtful

35. Which one of the following *least* describes you?
A. Courteous B. Curious
C. Patronizing D. Studious
E. Thoughtful

36. Which one of the following *most* accurately describes you?
A. Discreet B. Jealous
C. Loyal D. Open-minded
E. Suspicious

37. Which one of the following *least* describes you?
A. Discreet B. Jealous
C. Loyal D. Open-minded
E. Suspicious

38. Which one of the following *most* accurately describes you?
A. Economical B. Extravagant
C. Lavish D. Sensible
E. Thrifty

39. Which one of the following *least* describes you?
A. Economical B. Extravagant
C. Lavish D. Sensible
E. Thrifty

40. Which one of the following *most* accurately describes you?
A. Generous B. Intolerant
C. Judgmental D. Opportunistic
E. Sensitive

41. Which one of the following *least* describes you?
A. Generous B. Intolerant
C. Judgmental D. Opportunistic
E. Sensitive

Directions 42–61: *The items in this section consist of questions that are to be answered by either "Yes" or "No."*

42. Did you generally start each new school year with a great deal of enthusiasm?
A. Yes B. No

43. Do you readily trust people?
A. Yes B. No

44. Do you generally have a strong opinion on most matters?
A. Yes B. No

45. Do you tend to speak rapidly?
A. Yes B. No

46. Do you like sports?
A. Yes B. No

47. Are you often in low spirits?
A. Yes B. No

48. Do you find off-colour language offensive?
A. Yes B. No

49. Do you often find yourself finishing sentences for other people?
A. Yes B. No

50. Do you like to visit museums?
A. Yes B. No

51. Are you frequently in a hurry?
A. Yes B. No

52. Do you get much time to keep up with the things you like to do?
A. Yes B. No

53. When under pressure, do you tend to lose your temper?
A. Yes B. No

54. Did you enjoy going to school dances?
A. Yes B. No

55. Do you become upset when you think something is taking too long?
A. Yes B. No

56. Do you have trouble going to sleep at night?
A. Yes B. No

57. Do you wish you could do over some of the things you have done?
A. Yes B. No

58. Did you ever build a model airplane?
A. Yes B. No

59. Did you ever build a model airplane that could fly?
A. Yes B. No

60. Did you ever fly in a helicopter?
A. Yes B. No

61. Did you ever fly in a glider or pilot a hang glider?
A. Yes B. No

Directions 62-91: *The items in this section consist of a listing of many occupations. Some may appeal to you; others may not. For each of the listed occupations you would like for a life career, answer by selecting "Like." For each of the listed occupations you would not like for a life career, answer by selecting "Don't like."*

62. Artist
A. Like B. Don't like

63. Author
A. Like B. Don't like

64. Bank Teller
A. Like B. Don't like

65. Clothing Designer
A. Like B. Don't like

66. Electrician
A. Like B. Don't like

67. Explorer
A. Like B. Don't like

68. Inventor
A. Like B. Don't like

69. Investigator
A. Like B. Don't like

70. Lawyer
A. Like B. Don't like

71. Musician
A. Like B. Don't like

72. Nurse
A. Like B. Don't like

73. Politician
A. Like B. Don't like

74. Professional Ballplayer
A. Like B. Don't like

75. Prison Warden
A. Like B. Don't like

76. Research Scientist
A. Like B. Don't like

77. Sales Manager
A. Like B. Don't like

78. School Principal
A. Like B. Don't like

79. Singer
A. Like B. Don't like

80. Social Worker
A. Like B. Don't like

81. Teacher
A. Like B. Don't like

82. Professor
A. Like B. Don't like

83. Farmer
A. Like B. Don't like

84. Jeweller
A. Like B. Don't like

85. Doctor
A. Like B. Don't like

86. Broker
A. Like B. Don't like

87. Beggar
A. Like B. Don't like

88. Sweeper
A. Like B. Don't like

89. Editor
A. Like B. Don't like

90. Engineer
A. Like B. Don't like

91. Coolie
A. Like B. Don't like

Directions 92-100: *The questions in this section consist of pairs of statements describing personal characteristics and preferences. For each question, select the statement that describes you better.*

92. A. I feel happy most of the time.
B. I rarely see the bright side of life.

93. A. I have a great deal of self-confidence.
B. I try to avoid getting together with people.

94 A. I prefer working with people.
B. I prefer working with equipment or my hands.

95 A. New and different experiences excite me.
B. New and different experiences frighten me.

96. A. I prefer to work with competent coworkers.
B. I prefer to work with congenial coworkers.

97. A. I enjoy engaging actively in athletic sports.
B. I enjoy watching athletic events.

98. A. One of my most important career goals is security.
B. One of my most important career goals is high income.

99. A. I rarely worry about what other people think of me.
B. It bothers me that people have wrong ideas about me.

100. A. I prefer having a few close friends.
B. I prefer having many friends.

Directions (Qs. 101-192) : *In the questions given below three/four alternatives have been given below each one of them. You have to select the right alternative according to your aptitude and mark it in your answer sheet.*

101. I found a purse full of money in college premise. I
A. donated the amount among poors
B. gave it to the principal
C. none of these

102. I am punctual regarding
A. going to bed B. time
C. meals

103. I was travelling on a boat which capsized. Firstly, I
A. rescued others B. saved myself
C. closed my eyes

104. When someone asks you for help in odd situations then:
A. you give him/her all possible help
B. you promise him/her help
C. you do not help him/her

105. In case my wrist watch is out of order, I
A. would try to repair it myself
B. would give it to watch maker
C. would buy a new watch

106. Often I change my opinion in the last moment.
A. Yes B. No
C. Some times

107. Generally I am extrovert and well behaved
A. Yes B. No
C. Some times

108. I like to use new technique of work
A. Yes B. No
C. Some times

109. When someone considers you wrong then:
A. you do not react
B. you consider him/her wrong
C. you try to ward off the misunderstanding on proper occasion.

110. If you are a female and you are talking with a male:
A. You hide your age
B. You are afraid
C. You talk without hesitation

111. I do like rules and regulations
A. Yes B. No
C. Some times

112. Excellent ideas come to my mind:
A. while working alone
B. while working in group
C. I do not know

113. Whenever my little baby cries loudly, then I
A. beat him/her
B. feed milk to him/her
C. make him/her sleep

114. When I see a mad person, I
A. approach towards him/her
B. maintain distance from him/her
C. throw stone at him/her

115. While driving my car I offer lift who ask for the lift
A. always B. some times
C. never

116. When someone tries to convince you then:
A. You get convinced
B. You do not get convinced
C. You hear him/her passionately

117. Whenever someone knocks on my closed door then firstly I
A. open the door
B. peep through the lens fitted in the door
C. do not open the door

118. I speak to others about my expectation and dreams:
A. rarely B. often
C. some times

119. When I do any foolish work then :
A. I feel ashamed
B. I feel proud of my self
C. Nothing happens

120. If I were correspondent of any newspaper then I would write on the following subject
A. Cinema and theatre
B. Political events
C. Neither, A nor B

121. If I were not human being then :
A. I wish to be a bird
B. I wish to be a horse
C. Can not say

122. Suppose, you have worn a new shirt and your friend passed a comment that it is not looking good on you. You
A. will change the shirt immediately
B. will take it lightly as it is your style
C. will not change the shirt but feel offended

123. I wish to live alone always.
A. Yes B. No
C. Some times

124. I want to spend my spare (extra) time :
A. in reading interesting books
B. in reading comics
C. None of these

125. Before doing any work I ask myself 'Is i appropriate'?
A. Yes B. No
C. Some times

126. If I see the GOD, I will ask for
A. huge wealth B. honesty
C. love

127. People call you selfish:
A. Always B. Sometimes
C. Never

128. While talking to friends I do not like t express my very personal matters.
A. Yes B. No
C. Sometimes

129. Consultation with others helps me to take ar decision.
A. Yes B. No
C. I get confused

130. After failure:
A. One repents
B. One tries again to succeed
C. Nothing special is happened

131. I want to be convinced by arguments
A. Yes B. No
C. Some times

132. If an argument starts with someone, then I invariably
A. listen to the viewpoint of that person carefully and then, speak what is in my mind
B. state my view at the very outset
C. start saying whatever comes to my mind
D. become confused and perplexed

133. If you were a woman and if it were within your control, then what would you like to become?
A. Miss World
B. A player of international level
C. Politician
D. Actress

134. I like to fight the intricate problems
A. Only sometimes B. No
C. Yes D. Never

135. I read such books in leisure which deal with:
A. moral values B. sex
C. violence D. any theme

136. Whenever I join a new group, then
A. I am not able to understand them
B. I take some time to understand people
C. I feel pretty soon that I have known all of them
D. I take some time to identify and understand them

137. After having a meal to my heart's content, if someone requests me to eat a sweet, then I
A. refuse politely
B. eat some of the sweets
C. do not care about the proposition
D. Scold the person who makes a request

138. When I accomplish a task in a foolish manner, then
A. I feel proud
B. I like the action very much
C. I feel ashamed of it
D. nothing happens

139. Best ideas come to my mind
A. when I work in a group
B. when I work alone
C. never
D. do not know when they come

140. You inform your close friend
A. all the important issues
B. all the bad issues
C. all the thoughts going on in your mind
D. nothing at all

141. Normally, I am an extrovert and gregarious
A. Sometimes B. No
C. Yes D. Never

142. Sometimes I feel disappointed:
A. Yes B. Cannot say
C. No D. Off and On

143. I inspire from the biographies of great personalities:
A. Often B. Sometimes
C. Never D. Regularly

144. When my bicycle goes out of order, then I
A. show it to the bicycle mechanic
B. try to repair it myself
C. tell my friends to repair it
D. buy a new bicycle

145. I search for the possibilities of the solution of every problem.
A. Sometimes B. Never
C. Yes D. No

146. If a person takes away my things without getting my permission, then I feel pain.
A. Yes B. Sometimes
C. No D. Never

147. Whenever I talk to somebody, then I
A. look at his face
B. look into his eyes
C. look at the things around him
D. look at his feet

148. Whenever someone interrupts my speech, then I
A. do not pay attention to him
B. start speaking at a faster pace than before
C. stop my speech and let him speak
D. nothing is certain

149. You have adorned a new shirt. Your companion passes a remark that your shirt is misfit for your persona. So, you will
A. start scolding him in the presence of all others
B. change the shirt immediately

C. not change the shirt but singe from the heart of your hearts
D. laugh away the remark, starting that it is your style

150. I always take care of ..... in my life.
A. sleeping
B. time
C. taking meal
D. making enjoyments

151. When you go to buy cloth for yourself, then what is the most important issue/factor looked after by you?
A. The cloth must be suitable for you
B. The cloth that is stated to be good by the shopkeeper
C. The costliest cloth
D. The design of the cloth should be different from those of all others

152. If I were to acquire a lot of money, then I will
A. distribute it among neighbours
B. spend it and have whale of a time
C. save most of it for the future
D. cannot say anything about it

153. If I were a bat, then I would
A. fly during the day
B. fly during the night
C. fly during the day as well as the night
D. increase the number of ultrasonic waves

154. During the period of difficulty, I invariably take the help of another person.
A. Never B. Yes
C. No D. Sometimes

155. I like to meet new people:
A. Always B. Sometimes
C. Never D. Can't say

156. If you are a woman, then, while talking to others ;
A. you fly into a rage when the talk related to age is commenced
B. you tell your age by reducing a few years from the actual age
C. refrain from giving any set of information related to age
D. you inform about your correct age, if asked about the same

157. I love to live alone.
A. Sometimes B. Yes
C. No D. Never

158. Excessive consumption of ghee and oil is
A. tasty for the health
B. beneficial to the health
C. injurious to the health
D. cannot state anything in this context

159. The secret of my success is
A. studying newspaper
B. awakening at night
C. hard labour
D. gossiping

160. When my little child cries loudly, then I
A. give him food
B. thrash him with vigour
C. make him sleep
D. give him feed of milk

161. I like to use new procedures of work.
A. Never B. Yes
C. Sometimes D. No

162. During winter days, I
A. get up at a fixed time
B. get up only in the morning
C. get up late
D. get up at an uncertain time

163. I like to be convinced by facts.
A. Sometimes B. No
C. Yes D. Never

164. When someone tells me to make a promise then I
A. never make a promise
B. think before finally making a promise
C. make a promise immediately
D. cannot say anything in this context

165. I do remember God
A. in distress B. in happier time
C. always D. off and on

166. If I were the correspondent of a magazine then I would write on the following subjec
A. Health
B. Cinema and theatre
C. Political events
D. None of these

167. The house of my hate-worthy neighbour is on fire. I
- A. am very happy to learn about this
- B. am going to put out the fire
- C. am not going to put out the fire
- D. am still thinking

168. I get help when I discuss things/issues with others
- A. Sometimes
- B. No
- C. Yes
- D. I get into a fix

169. Upon seeing a lunatic, I
- A. start making hue and cry
- B. throw stones on him
- C. go near him
- D. keep myself away from him

170. I like pre-defined rules and regulations.
- A. Sometimes
- B. No
- C. Yes
- D. According to the occasion

171. I myself open the door of the car to enable my wife to sit inside the car.
- A. If I am happy
- B. Sometimes
- C. Never
- D. Always

72. Before starting my scooter, first of all, I
- A. check its brakes
- B. check the quantity of petrol in the fuel tank
- C. check air in the tyres
- D. check the headlight

73. When I decide something, then I
- A. get into a fix
- B. think about the decision
- C. feel myself to be contented and satisfied
- D. change my decision afterwards

74. When I am alone at my home, then, quite often, I
- A. sing a song
- B. sleep
- C. watch television
- D. read literature

75. I like to explore various possibilities/ opportunities, even though it may lead to delay in the piece of work.
- A. Sometimes
- B. Yes
- C. No
- D. Never

176. Before doing any piece of work, I ask myself, "Is it correct?"
- A. Sometimes
- B. Yes
- C. No
- D. Never

177. In the interview the quality which is sought mostly is:
- A. handsomeness
- B. clothing
- C. personality
- D. hair style

178. While talking to my friends, I do not like to express my personal feelings
- A. Sometimes
- B. Yes
- C. No
- D. It depends of the gravity of feelings

179. When I go by the car, I always give lift to hitch-hikers.
- A. Only to ladies
- B. Always
- C. Never
- D. Sometimes

180. If put under pressure, I give emphasis on giving myself more time so that I may be able to think more clearly.
- A. I get into a fix
- B. Yes
- C. No
- D. Sometimes

181. The boat I was travelling in, sank midway. First of all, I
- A. started coaxing the boatman
- B. saved others
- C. saved myself
- D. closed my eyes

182. While doing work, invariably, I
- A. remain in a dilly-dally situation—"to do or not to do"
- B. feel difficulty during the beginning
- C. find the end to be tedious
- D. start doing it immediately

183. I like to carry out the agricultural work according to the scientific method
- A. For some time
- B. Always
- C. Sometimes
- D. Never

184. If I find two persons fighting each other, on my way, I
- A. try to help them arrive at a truce/ settlement of the dispute
- B. start fighting on behalf of the weaker person

C. let them fight and move on
D. watch the show

185. If I were not a man, then I
A. would like to be a cow
B. would become a horse in a big stable
C. would like to be a bird
D. cannot say any thing in this context

186. Whenever some one demands any thing from me, I
A. return him empty-handed
B. abuse him
C. give something
D. do not talk to him

187. It is necessary for progress:
A. to deceive others
B. to resort to unlawful means
C. to be sincere towards one's own duty
D. No need of special attention.

188. Whenever I take a decision, then I
A. do not change it B. change it
C. never change it D. do not know

189. Any dispute can be solved by
A. quarrelling B. dialogue
C. court D. can't say

190. While driving during night there must be
A. helmet B. light source
C. smooth road D. controlled spee

191. I like to
A. wander
B. study
C. watch television
D. indulge in gossips

192. When I go to appear in an interview, the
wear a clean
A. shirt B. pantaloon
C. dress D. underwear

GENERAL KNOWLEDGE

INDIAN HISTORY

ANCIENT INDIA

INDUS VALLEY CIVILISATION (2500-1750 BC)

The earliest excavations in the Indus valley were done at Harappa in the West Punjab and Mohenjodaro in Sindh. Both places are now in Pakistan.

Important Sites

The most important sites are Kot Diji in Sindh, Kalibangan in Rajasthan, Ropar in the Punjab, Banawali in Haryana, Lothal, Surkotada and Dhaulavira, all the three in Gujarat.

Mohenjodaro is the largest of all the Indus cities and it is estimated to have spread over an area of 200 hectares.

Indus Valley Civilisation : An Objective Study

Major Sites	*Excavators*	*Year*	*River*	*Location*	*Important Findings*
1. Harappa	D.R. Sahni	1921	Ravi	West Punjab (Pakistan)	Granaries, Virgin Goddess, Cemetery, Stone symbol of Lingam and Yoni
2. Mohenjodaro	R.D. Banerjee	1922	Indus	Sindh (Pakistan)	Great Bath, Great Granary, Assem bly Hall, Proto-Shiva, Brick Kilns, Mesopotamian seals
3. Chanhudaro	N.G. Mazumdar	1931	Indus	Sindh (Pakistan)	Bronze toy cart, Ink-pot, Lipstick, City without a citadel
4. Kalibangan	B.B. Lal & B.K. Thapar	1953	Ghaggar	Ganganagar (Rajasthan)	Decorated bricks, ploughed field surface, Firealtars
5. Lothal	S.R. Rao	1957	Bhogwa	Ahmedabad (Gujarat)	Dockyard, Rice husk, Fire altars, Double burial
6. Banawali	R.S. Bist	1973	Ghaggar	Hissar (Haryana)	Toy plough, Gridiron pattern of Town planning.
7. Dholavira	R.S. Bist	1990	Luni	Kutchh (Gujarat)	A Large well & a bath, A stadium
8. Surkotada	J. Joshi	1964	—	Gujarat	Bones of Horse, Pot burials

Salient Features of the Harappan Culture

The Harappan Civilization was primarily Urban.

Mohenjodaro and Harappa were the planned cities.

The large-scale use of burnt bricks in almost all kinds of constructions are the important characteristics of the Harappan culture.

Another remarkable feature was the underground drainage system connecting all houses to the street drains which were covered by stone slabs or bricks.

The most important public place of Mohenjodaro is the Great Bath measuring 39 feet length, 23 feet breadth and 8 feet depth.

Agriculture was the most important occupation. In the fertile soils, farmers cultivated two crops a year. They were the first who had grown paddy.

Wheat and barley were the main crops grown besides sesame, mustard and cotton.

Animals like sheep, goats and buffalo were domesticated. The use of horse is not yet firmly established.

Bronze and copper vessels are the outstanding examples of the Harappan metal craft.

A large number of seals numbering more than 2000 have been discovered.

Social Life

Jewelleries such as bangles, bracelets, fillets, girdles, anklets, ear-rings and finger rings were worn by women. These ornaments were made of gold, silver, copper, bronze and semi precious stones.

Fishing was a regular occupation while hunting and bull fighting were other pastimes.

Manufacture of terracotta (burnt clay) was a major industry of the people.

Figures of animals such as sacred bull and dove were discovered. The figures of Mother Goddesses were used for religious purposes.

Most of the inscriptions were engraved on seals. It is interesting to note that the Indus script has not yet been deciphered.

The Pipal tree was used as a religious symbol.

The origin of the '*Swastika*' symbol can be traced to the Harrapan Civilization.

The chief male deity was Pasupati, (proto-Siva) represented in seals as sitting in a yogic posture with three faces and two horns.

THE VEDIC PERIOD

RIG VEDIC AGE (1500 - 1000 B.C.)

The Early Vedic period is known from the *Rig Veda.*

The *Rig Veda* refers to Saptasindhu or the land of seven rivers. This includes the five rivers of the Punjab, namely, Jhelum, Chenab, Ravi, Beas and Sutlej along with the Indus and Saraswati. Historians view that the Aryans came from Central Asia. They entered India through the Khyber pass between 2000 B.C. and 1500 B.C. They first settled in seven places in the Punjab region which they called Sapta Sindhu. Slowly, they moved towards the Gangetic Valley.

The Aryan Civilisation was a rural civilisation.

Vedic Literature

The word 'Veda' is derived from the root 'vid', which means to know and signifies 'superior knowledge'.

The Vedic literature consists of the four Vedas – Rig, Yajur, Sama and Atharva.

The *Rig Veda* is the earliest of the four Vedas divided into 10 mandalas and it consists of 1028 hymns. The hymns were sung by *Hotri* in praise of various gods.

The *Yajur Veda* consists of various details of rules to be observed at the time of sacrifice. Its hymns were recited by *Adharvayus*.

The *Sama Veda* is set to tune for the purpose of chanting during sacrifice. It is called the book of chants and the origins of Indian music are traced in it. Its hymns were recited by *Udgatri*.

The *Atharva Veda* contains details of rituals.

Besides the Vedas, there are other sacred works like the Brahmanas, the Aranyakas, the Upanishads, and the epics Ramayana and Mahabharata.

Political Organisation

During this period, the kingdom was tribal in character. Each tribe formed a separate kingdom.

The basic unit of political organisation was *kula* or family.

The highest political unit was called *jana* or tribe.

There were several tribal kingdoms during the Rig Vedic period such as Bharatas, Matsyas, Yadus and Purus. The head of the kingdom was called as *rajan* or king.

There were two popular bodies called the *Sabha* and *Samiti*. The former seems to have been a council of elders and the latter, a general assembly of the entire people.

Social Life

Family was the basis of the society.

The head of the family was known as *grihapathi*.

Economic Condition

The Rig Vedic Aryans were pastoral people and their main occupation was cattle rearing. Their wealth was estimated in terms of their cattle.

Carpentry was another important profession.

RELIGION

The important Rig Vedic gods were Prithvi (Earth), Agni (Fire), Vayu (Wind), Varuna (Rain) and Indra (Thunder).

Indra was the most popular among them during the early Vedic period.

There were also female gods like Aditi and Ushas.

There were no temples and no idol worship during the early Vedic period.

Rigvedic Rivers

River	Name in Rigveda
Indus	Sindhu
Jhelum	Vitasta
Chenab	Asikni
Ravi	Parushini
Beas	Vipasa
Sutlej	Sutudri
Gomati	Gomal
Saraswati	Sarasvati
Ghaggar	Prishadavati

LATER VEDIC PERIOD (1000–600 B.C.)

This age is also called as the Epic Age because the two great epics the Ramayana and Mahabharata were written during this period.

The Sama, Yajur, Atharva Vedas, Brahmanas, Aranyakas, Upanishads and the two epics are the sources of information for this period.

Political Organisation

Larger kingdoms were formed during the later Vedic period.

The king performed various rituals and sacrifices to strengthen his position. They include Rajasuya (consecration ceremony), Asvamedha (horse sacrifice) and Vajpeya (chariot race).

Kingship became hereditary.

Kings assumed titles like Ekrat, Samrat and Sarvabhauma.

Economic Condition

Iron was used extensively in this period and this enabled the people to clear forests and to bring more land under cultivation. Agriculture became the chief occupation.

Taxes like Bali, Sulk and Bhaga were collected from the people.

Wealth was calculated in terms of cows.

Social Life

The four divisions of society (Brahmins, Kshatriyas, Vaisyas and Sudras) or the Varna system was thoroughly established during the Later Vedic period.

The Ashrama system was formed to attain 4 purusharthas. They were *Dharma*, *Artha*, *Kama* and *Moksha*.

Religion

Gods of the Early Vedic period like Indra and Agni lost their importance. Prajapathi (the creator), Vishnu (the protector) and Rudra (the destroyer) became prominent during the Later Vedic period.

JAINISM AND BUDDHISM

JAINISM

Jainism originated in the 6th century B.C. It rejected Vedic religion and avoided its rituals.

Founded by Rishabha Deva. Rishabha Deva was succeeded by 23 Thirthankaras (prophets). Mahavira was the 24th Thirthankara.

Vardhamana Mahavira (540-468 B.C.)

Vardhamana was born in a village called Kundagrama near Vaishali in Bihar.

His father was *Siddhartha*. He was the head of a famous Kshatriya clan.

His mother was *Trisala*. She was a princess of the Lichchhavi clan. She was the sister of the ruler of Vaishali.

Vardhamana was married to *Yasoda,* a princess. They had a daughter.

At the age of 30, he left his home and family. He became an ascetic (monk). He wandered from place-to-place in search of truth for 12 years.

In the 13th year of his penance, he attained the highest spiritual knowledge called Kevalya or Jnana. Thereafter, he was called Mahavira and Jina. His followers were called Jains and his religion Jainism.

He died at the age of 72 in 468 B.C. at a place called Pavapuri near modern Rajgir in Bihar.

Teachings of Jainism

The three principles of Jainism, also known as Triratnas (three gems), are:

1. right faith.
2. right knowledge.
3. right conduct.

Mahavira preached his disciples to follow the five principles. They are:

1. Ahimsa—not to injure any living beings
2. Satya—to speak the truth
3. Asteya—not to steal
4. Tyag—not to own property
5. Brahmacharia—to lead a virtuous life.

Spread of Jainism

Mahavira preached his religion in Prakrit language which was the language of the masses.

Chandragupta Maurya, Kharavela of Kalinga and the royal dynasties of south India such as the Gangas, the Kadambas, the Chalukyas and the Rashtrakutas patronised Jainism.

Jainism was divided into two sects after Vallabhi Council, namely *Svetambaras* (wearing white dresses) under Sthulbhadra and *Digambaras* (naked) under Bhadrabahu.

The first Jain Council was convened at Pataliputra by Sthulabahu, the leader of the *Digambaras*, in the beginning of the 3rd century B.C.

The second Jain Council was held at Vallabhi in 5th century A.D. The final compilation of Jain literature called *Twelve Angas* was completed in this council.

BUDDHISM

Gautama Buddha (563-483 B.C.)

Buddha's original name was *Siddhartha*.

Siddhartha was born in the Lumbini Garden near Kapilavastu in Nepal. His father was Suddhodana. He was a Sakya chief of Kapilavastu. His mother, Mayadevi, died when Siddhartha was only seven days old. He was brought up by his step mother Mahaprajapati Gauthami.

At the age of sixteen Siddhartha, married Yasodhara and gave birth to a son, Rahul.

The sight of an old man, a diseased man, a corpse and an ascetic turned him away from worldly life. He left home at the age of twenty-nine in search of Truth.

He wandered for seven years and at last, he sat under a bodhi tree at Bodh Gaya in Bihar and did intense penance, after which he got Enlightenment (Nirvana) at the age of thirty-five. Since then, he became known as the Buddha or 'the Enlightened One'.

Buddha delivered his first sermon at Sarnath near Banaras (now Varanasi).

He died at the age of 80 in 483 B.C. at Kushinagar in Uttar Pradesh.

Teachings of Buddha

The Four Noble Truths of Buddha are:

1. The world is full of suffering.
2. The cause of suffering is desire.
3. If desires are get rid off, suffering can be removed.
4. This can be done by following the Eightfold Path.

The Eightfold Path consists of:

1. Right Thought.
2. Right Belief.
3. Right Speech.

4. Right Action.
5. Right Living.
6. Right Efforts.
7. Right Knowledge.
8. Right Meditation.

Buddhist Literature

In Pali language.

Buddhist scriptures in Pali are commonly referred to as *Tripitakas, i.e.*, 'Three Baskets'.

Vinaya Pitaka: Rules of discipline in Buddhist monasteries.

Sutta Pitaka: Largest, contains collection of Buddha's sermons.

Abidhamma Pitaka: Explanation of the philosophical principles of the Buddhist religion.

Main Buddhist Councils

Buddhist Council	Time	Place	Chairman	Patron
First	483 BC	Rajagriha	Mahakashyapa	Ajatasatru
Second	383 BC	Vaishali	Sabakamuni	Kalashoka
Third	250 BC	Patliputra	Moggaliputta Tissa	Ashoka
Fourth	AD 72	Kundalvana	Vasumitra, Ashwaghosa	Kanishka

The Mahajanapadas

Mahajanapadas	Capital
1. Kashi	Varanasi
2. Kosala	Shravasti
3. Anga	Champanagri
4. Magadh	Girivraj or Rajgriha
5. Vajji	Vaishali
6. Malla	Kushinagar and Pavapuri
7. Chedi	Shuktimati
8. Vatsa	Kaushambi
9. Kuru	Hastinapur, Indraprastha and Isukara
10. Panchal	Ahichchhatra and Kampilya
11. Matsya	Viratnagar
12. Surasen	Mathura
13. Asmaka	Paudanya
14. Avanti	Ujjaini
15. Gandhara	Taxila
16. Kamboj	Rajpur (Hatak)

DYNASTIES OF ANCIENT INDIA

HARYANKA DYNASTY

Bimbisara was the founder of Haryanka Dynasty. He was a contemporary of both Vardhamana Mahavira and Gautama Buddha.

During his rule, Darius I, the Achaemenian emperor, conquered the Indus Valley area.

Ajatasatru imprisoned his father Bimbisara.

The first Buddhist Council was convened by Ajatasatru at Rajgir.

The immediate successor of Ajatasatru was Udayin.

Udayin laid the foundation of the new capital at Pataliputra situated at the confluence of the two rivers, the Ganges and the Sone.

Shishunaga was the founder of Shishunaga dynasty.

After Shishunaga, the mighty empire began to collapse. His successor was Kakavarman or Kalasoka. During his reign, the second Buddhist Council was held at Vaishali.

Kalasoka was killed by the founder of the Nanda dynasty.

NANDAS

The fame of Magadha scaled new heights under the Nanda dynasty.

Mahapadmananda was the founder of Nanda rule in Magadha.

The last Nanda ruler was Dhana Nanda. Alexander invaded India during his rule.

MAURYAN EMPIRE

CHANDRAGUPTA MAURYA (322–298 B.C.)

Chandragupta Maurya was the founder of the Mauryan Empire. He overthrew Nanda dynasty with the help of Chanakya.

Chandragupta defeated Seleukos Nikator, the Greek general of Alexander, in a battle in 305 B.C.

Seleukos sent Megasthenes as Greek Ambassador to the Court of Chandragupta. Megasthenes wrote *Indica*.

Chandragupta was a follower of Jainism.

He came to Sravana Belgola, near Mysore with a Jain monk called Bhadrabahu. The hill in which he lived until his death is called Chandragiri.

Chanakya served as prime minister during the reigns of Chandragupta and Bindusara.

BINDUSARA (298–273 B.C.)

Chandragupta Maurya was succeeded by his son Bindusara.

Bindusara was called by the Greeks as "*Amitraghatha*" meaning, slayer of enemies.

ASHOKA (273–232 B.C.)

Ashoka was the most famous ruler of the Mauryan dynasty.

The most important event of Ashoka's reign was his victorious war with Kalinga in 261 B.C.

Ashoka convened the Third Buddhist Council at Pataliputra around 250 B.C. in order to strengthen the *Sangha*. It was presided over by Moggaliputta Tissa.

Ashoka's edicts and inscriptions were deciphered by James Prinsep in 1837.

The last Mauryan king, Brahadratha was killed by his minister Pushyamitra Sunga. It put an end to the Mauryan Empire.

SUNGAS

The founder of the Sunga dynasty was *Pushyamitra Sunga*, who was the commander-in-chief under the Mauryas.

He ascended the throne of Magadha in 185 B.C.

Pushyamitra was a staunch follower Brahmanism. He performed two asvamed sacrifices.

After the death of Pushyamitra, his son Agnimi became the ruler.

Agnimitra was a great conqueror. He was also hero of the play *Malavikagnimitram* written Kalidasa.

KANVA

The last Sunga ruler was Devabhuti, who v murdered by his minister Vasudeva Kanva, founder of the *Kanva dynasty*.

The Kanva dynasty ruled for 45 years. After fall of the Kanvas, the history of Magadha v a blank until the establishment of the Gu dynasty.

SATAVAHANAS

The founder of the Satavahana dynasty v Simuka.

The greatest ruler of the Satavahana dynasty *Gautamiputra Satakarni*.

The greatest port of the Satavahanas was Kaly on the west Deccan. Gandakasela and Ganjam the east coast were the other important seapo

The fine painting at Amaravathi a Nagarjunakonda caves belong to this perioc

SANGAM AGE
(300 B.C. TO A.D. 300)

The Sangam Age constitutes an important cha in the history of South India.

According to Tamil legends, there existed th Sangams (Academy of Tamil poets) in anc Tamil Nadu popularly called Muchchang These Sangams flourished under the rc patronage of the Pandyas.

The first Sangam, held at then Madurai, cha by Agastya.

The second Sangam was held at Kapadapur chaired by Tolkappiyar.

The third Sangam at Madurai was founded Mudathirumaran.

Political History

The Tamil country was ruled by three dynasties namely the Chera, Chola and Pandyas during the Sangam Age.

CHERAS

The Cheras ruled over parts of modern Kerala. Their capital was Vanji and their important seaports were Tondi and Musiris.

The greatest Chera King was *Senguttuvan*.

CHOLAS

The Chola kingdom of the Sangam period extended from modern Tiruchi district to southern Andhra Pradesh.

Their capital was first located at Uraiyur and then shifted to Puhar. Kaveripattinam served as their port.

GUPTA PERIOD

The Gupta period is considered as the *Golden Age* in the history of India because this period witnessed all round developments in Religion, Literature, Science, Art and Architecture.

CHANDRAGUPTA I (320-334 A.D.)

In the beginning of the 4th Century A.D., Sri Gupta established a small Kingdom at Pataliputra. He is considered as the founder of the Gupta dynasty.

The first notable ruler of the Gupta dynasty was Chandragupta I. He assumed the title *Maharajadhiraja*. The Meherauli Iron Pillar inscription mentions his extensive conquests.

Chandragupta I is considered to be the founder of the Gupta era which starts with his accession in A.D. 320.

SAMUDRAGUPTA (335-380 A.D.)

Samudragupta was the greatest of the rulers of the Gupta dynasty. The Allahabad Pillar inscription provides a detailed account of his reign.

Because of his military achievements, Samudragupta was hailed as '*Indian Napoleon*'.

CHANDRAGUPTA II (380-414 A.D.)

Samudragupta was succeeded by his son Chandragupta II Vikramaditya.

The greatest of the military achievements of Chandragupta II was his war against the Saka *satraps* of western India.

The famous Chinese pilgrim, Fahien visited India (A.D. 399 - A.D. 414) during the reign of Chandragupta II.

SUCCESSORS OF CHANDRAGUPTA II

Kumaragupta (415-455) was the son and successor of Chandragupta II. His reign was marked by general peace and prosperity.

Kumaragupta was the founder of the Nalanda University.

Kumaragupta was followed by *Skandagupta* who ruled from A.D. 456 to A.D. 468.

After Skandagupta's death, many of his successors like Purugupta, Narasimhagupta, Buddhagupta and Baladitya could not save the Gupta empire from the Huns. Ultimately, the Gupta power totally disappeared due to the Hun invasions and later by the rise of Yasodharman in Malwa.

PUSHYABHUTI DYNASTY (600 - 647 A.D.)

The greatest king was *Harshavardhana*, son of Prabhakar Vardhana of Thaneshwar. He shifted the capital to *Kannauj*.

Hieun Tsang visited during his reign.

He established a large monastery at Nalanda. Banabhata adorned his court, wrote Harshacharita and Kadambari. Harsha himself wrote three plays–Priyadarshika, Ratnawali and Nagananda.

PALLAVAS

The Pallavas established their kingdom in Tondaimandalam by Simhavishnu with its capital at Kanchipuram.

Other great Pallava rulers were Mahendravarman I, Narasimhavarman I, and Narasimhavarman II.

The *Kailasanatha temple* at Kanchipuram is the greatest architectural masterpiece of the Pallava art.

CHALUKYAS (543-755 A.D.)

Pulakesin I was the founder of the Chalukya dynasty. He established a small kingdom with Vatapi or Badami as its capital.

The structural temples of the Chalukyas exist at Aihole, Badami and Pattadakal (Virupaksha temple). Cave temple architecture was also famous under the Chalukyas. Their cave temples are found in Ajanta, Ellora and Nasik.

RASHTRAKUTAS (755-975 A.D.)

The art and architecture of the Rashtrakutas were found at Ellora and Elephanta.

CHOLAS

Cholas became prominent in the ninth century and established an empire comprising the major portion of South India. Their capital was Tanjore. The founder of the Chola kingdom was Vijayalaya.

Rajaraja Chola built the famous Brihadeeswara temple at Tanjore.

Dancing Figure of Shiva (Nataraja) belong to Chola period.

MEDIEVAL INDIA

ARAB CONQUEST OF SIND

In 712 A.D., Muhammad bin Quasim invaded Sind. Quasim defeated Dahir, the ruler of Sind and killed him in a well-contested battle.

Mahmud of Ghazni

In 1024, Mahmud marched from Multan across Rajaputana, defeated the Solanki King Bhimadeva I, plundered Anhilwada and sacked the famous temple of Somanatha. This was his last campaign in India. Mahmud died in 1030 A.D.

Mahmud patronized art and literature. *Firdausi* was the poet-laureate in the court of Mahmud.

Muhammad Ghori

Prithviraj Chauhan defeated Ghori in the first battle of Tarain near Delhi in 1191 A.D.

In the Second Battle of Tarain in 1192, Muhammad Ghori thoroughly routed the army of Prithiviraj, who was captured and killed.

After his brilliant victory over Prithviraj at Tarain, Muhammad Ghori returned to Ghazni leaving behind his favourite general Qutb-ud-din Aibak to make further conquests in India.

SULTANATE PERIOD

SLAVE DYNASTY (1206-1290)

The Slave dynasty was also called Mamluk dynasty. Mamluk was the Quranic term for slave.

Qutb-ud-din Aibak

Qutb-ud-din Aibak was a slave of Muhammad Ghori, who made him the Governor of his Indian possessions.

After the death of Ghori in 1206, Aibak declared his independence. He assumed the title Sultan and made Lahore his capital.

Muslim writers call Aibak Lakh Baksh or giver of lakhs because he gave liberal donations to them.

He built the famous Quwat-Ul-Islam mosque at Delhi. He began the construction of the famous Qutb Minar at Delhi but did not live long to complete it. It was later completed by Iltutmish.

Iltutmish (1210-1236 A.D.)

Iltutmish belonged to the Ilbari tribe and hence his dynasty was named as Ilbari dynasty.

He shifted his capital from Lahore to Delhi.

He organised the *Iqta system* and introduced reforms in civil administration and army.

Raziya (1236-1240 A.D.)

She appointed an Abyssinian slave Yakuth as Master of the Royal Horses.

In 1240, Altunia, the governor of Bhatinda revolted against her. She went in personally to suppress the revolt but Altunia killed Yakuth and took Raziya prisoner.

Bahram Shah, son of Iltutmish killed her.

Balban (1266-1286 A.D.)

Balban introduced rigorous court discipline and new customs such as prostration and kissing the Sultan's feet to prove his superiority over the nobles.

He also introduced the Persian festival of *Nauroz* to impress the nobles and people with his wealth and power.

He established a separate military department - *diwan-i-arz* – and reorganized the army.

KHILJI DYNASTY (1290-1320 A.D.)

The founder of the Khilji dynasty was Jalaluddin Khilji.

Ala-ud-din Khilji was the greatest ruler of the Khilji Dynasty.

He was the first Muslim ruler to extend his empire right upto Rameshwaram in the South.

The Sultan had built a new city called Siri near Delhi.

Amir Khusrau the great Persian poet, patronised by Balban, continued to live in Ala-ud-din Khilji's court also.

He introduced the system of *dagh* (branding of horses) and prepared *huliya* (descriptive list of soldiers).

Ala-ud-din Khilji maintained a large permanent standing army and paid them in cash from the royal treasury.

UGHLAQ DYNASTY

Ghiyas-ud-din Tughlaq was the founder of the Tughlaq dynasty.

To have the capital at the centre of the empire and safe from the Mongol raids, Tughlaq chose Devagiri as his new capital in A.D. 1327. The Sultan renamed the new capital Daulatabad.

In 1329-30, Muhammad-bin-Tughlaq introduced a token currency.

Firoz Shah Tughlaq became Sultan after the death of Muhammad-bin-Tughlaq in A.D. 1351.

He was the first Sultan to impose irrigation tax.

He had built new towns of Firozabad, Jaunpur, Hissar and Firozpur.

Timur—Mongol leader of Central Asia, ordered general massacre in Delhi (AD 1398) at the time of Nasiruddin Mahmud (later Tughlaq king).

SAYYID DYNASTY

Before his departure from India, Timur appointed Khizr Khan as governor of Multan. He captured Delhi and founded the Sayyid dynasty in 1414.

Mubarak Shah, Mohammed Shah and Alam Shah were some of the other important noteworthy rulers of Sayyid Dynasty.

LODHI DYNASTY

The Lodhis were Afghans.

Bahlol Lodhi was the first Afghan ruler while his predecessors were all Turks. He died in 1489 and was succeeded by his son, Sikandar Lodhi.

In 1504, Sikandar Lodhi founded the city of Agra and transferred his capital from Delhi to Agra.

Babar marched against Delhi and defeated and killed Ibrahim Lodhi in the first battle of Panipat (1526).

BAHMANI AND VIJAYANAGAR KINGDOMS

The break up of the Delhi Sultanate provided an opportunity for the rise of a number of kingdoms in the Deccan.

After the decline of the Tughlaqs, there arose two important kingdoms in the Deccan. They were the Bahmani and Vijayanagar kingdoms.

VIJAYANAGAR EMPIRE

The Vijayanagar Kingdom was set up in A.D. 1336. Its aim was to check the spread of Muslim power and protect Hindu Dharma in South India.

Four dynasties – Sangama, Saluva, Tuluva and Aravidu – ruled Vijayanagar from A.D. 1336 to 1672.

Vijayanagar was founded in 1336 by Harihara and Bukka of the Sangama dynasty.

The Moroccan traveller, Ibn Batuta, Venetian traveller Nicolo de Conti, Persian traveller Abdur Razzak and the Portuguese traveller Domingo Paes were among them who left valuable accounts on the socio-economic conditions of the Vijayanagar Empire.

The Hampi ruins and other monuments of Vijayanagar provide information on the cultural contributions of the Vijayanagar rulers.

KRISHNA DEVA RAYA (1509-1530)

The Tuluva dynasty was founded by Vira Narasimha.

The greatest of the Vijayanagar rulers, Krishna Deva Raya belonged to the Tuluva dynasty.

Krishna Deva Raya himself authored a Telugu work, *Amukthamalyadha* and Sanskrit works, *Jambavati Kalyanam* and *Ushaparinayam*.

He built the famous *Vittalaswamy* and *Hazara Ramaswamy* temples at Vijayanagar.

Krishna Deva Raya renovated Virupaksha temple in A.D. 1510.

After his death the enemies of Vijayanagar joined together and defeated the Vijayanagar ruler in the battle of Talaikota.

BAHMANI KINGDOM

The founder of the Bahmani kingdom was Alauddin Bahman Shah also known as Hasan Gangu in 1347. Its capital was Gulbarga.

Ahmad Wali Shah shifted the capital from Gulbarga to Bidar.

Gol Gumbaj was built by *Muhammad Adil Shah*; it is famous for the so called '*Whispering Gallery*'.

Quli Qutub Shah built the famous *Golcunda Fort*.

MUGHAL EMPIRE (1526-1707 AD)

BABAR (1526-1530 AD)

Babar was the founder of the Mughal Empire in India.

On 21st April, 1526 the first Battle of Panip took place between Babar and Ibrahim Lodi who was killed in the battle.

Babar was the first one to use guns or artillery a battle on the Indian soil.

Babar defeated Rana Sanga of Mewar in t battle of Kanwah in A.D. 1527.

Babar was a soldier-scholar and wrote his ov autobiography called Babar Nama in Turki language.

HUMAYUN (1530-1556 AD)

Sher Shah defeated Humayun at Chausa in A. 1539 and again at Kannauj in A.D. 1540.

After losing his kingdom, Humayun became exile for the next fifteen years.

In 1555, Humayun defeated the Afghans a recovered the Mughal throne. After six mont he died in 1556 due to his fall from the stairc of his library.

Gulbadan Begum, Humayun's half-sister wr *Humayun-nama*.

SHER SHAH SURI

The founder of the Sur dynasty was Sher Sh whose original name was Farid.

Sher Shah became the ruler of Delhi in 154

Sher Shah organized a brilliant administra system. The central government consisted several departments.

He built a new city on the banks of the ri Yamuna near Delhi. Now the old fort ca Purana Quila and its mosque is alone surviv

He built a Mausoleum at Sasaram, whic considered as one of the master pieces of Inc architecture.

AKBAR (1556-1605 AD)

When Akbar ascended the throne in A.D. 1 he was only 14 years old. His guardian Bai Khan served him as a faithful minister and tu Bairam Khan, along with Akbar met Hemu ir second Battle of Panipat in 1556. Hemu initially successful, but lost his conscious after an arrow hit him. Akbar killed him.

Battle of Haldighati, was fought between Rana Pratap of Mewar and Mughal army led by Man Singh. Some hisorian say that this battle was indecisive but some say that Rana Pratap was defeated.

Akbar abolished the pilgrim tax and in 1562, he abolished Jaziya.

Akbar evolved a new faith called Din-i-Illahi or Divine Faith.

AHANGIR (1605-1627 AD)

When Akbar died, Prince Salim succeeded with the title Jahangir (Conqueror of World) in 1605.

Jahangir's eldest son, Khusrau, rebelled against him. He was arrested and put into prison. *Guru Arjun Dev, the fifth Sikh Guru* was executed by Jahangir.

In 1611, Jahangir married Mehrunnisa who was known as Nurjahan (Light of World).

Jahangir died in A.D. 1627.

HAHJAHAN (1628-1658 AD)

The reign of Shahjahan is generally considered as the *Golden Age* of the Mughal period.

Shahjahan is called as the *Prince of Builders*. He had built the Jama Masjid and Red Fort in Delhi and Taj Mahal in Agra.

Fine arts like painting, music and literature reached high level of development during Shahjahan's time.

RANGAZEB (1658-1707 AD)

Aurangazeb was the last great Mughal ruler. He ascended the throne after killing his three brothers Dara, Shuja and Murad in a fratricidal war.

Aurangazeb defeated Sikandar Shah of Bijapur and annexed his kingdom.

Aurangazeb was against the Sikhs and he executed the ninth Sikh Guru Tegh Bahadur.

He was called *Darvesh* or a *Zinda Pir*. He forbade *Sati*. Conquered Bijapur (AD 1686) and Golconda (AD 1687) and reimposed Jaziya and Pilgrim tax in AD 1679.

He built *Biwi ka Makbara* on the tomb of his queen *Rabaud-Durani* at Aurangabad; *Moti Masjid* within Red Fort, Delhi; and the Jami or Badshahi Mosque at Lahore.

Aurangazeb died in A.D. 1707.

LATER MUGHALS / FALL OF THE MUGHALS

Bahadur Shah (1707-1712)

- Assumed the title of *Shah Alam I*.

Jahandar Shah (1712-1713)

- First puppet Mughal emperor. He abolished *jaziya*.

Farrukhsiyar (1713-1719)

Mohammad Shah (1719-1748)

- Nadir Shah (*of Iran*) defeated him in the Battle of Karnal (1739) and took away *Peacock throne* and *Kohinoor diamond*.

Ahmad Shah (1748-1754)

Alamgir II (1754-1759),

Shah Alam II (1759-1806)

Akbar II (1806-1837)

- He gave Ram Mohan Roy the title '*Raja*'. He sent Raja Ram Mohan Roy to London to seek a raise in his allowance.

Bahadur Shah II (1837-1857)

- He was confined by the British to the Red Fort. During the revolt of 1857, he was proclaimed the Emperor by the rebels. He was deported to Rangoon after that.

Literature of Mughal Period

Author	Work
Babar	Tuzuk-i-Babari
Abul Fazal	Ain-i-Akbari, Akbarnamah
Jahangir	Tuzuk-i-Jahangiri
Hamid	Padshahnama
Darashikoh	Majm-ul-Bahrain
Mirza Md Qasim	Alamgirnama

THE MARATHAS

SHIVAJI (1627-1680 AD)

- Shivaji was born at Shivner in 1627. His father was Shahji Bhonsle and mother Jija Bai.

His religious teacher was Samarth Ramdas and guardian was Dadaji Kondadev.

In 1674, Shivaji crowned himself at Raigarh and assumed the title Chatrapathi.

Ashtapradhan (eight ministers) helped in administration. These were Peshwas, Sar-i-Naubat (Military), Mazumdar or Amatya (Accounts); Waqenavis (Intelligence); Surnavis (Correspondence); *Dabir* or *Sumanta* (Ceremonies); *Nyayadhish* (Justice); and *Panditrao* (Charity).

Successors of Shivaji were Shambhaji, Rajaram and *Shahu* (fought at Battle of Khed in AD 1708).

THE PESHWAS

Balaji Vishwanath was the first Peshwa. He began his career as a small revenue official and became Peshwa in 1713.

Baji Rao I was the eldest son of Balaji Vishwanath. He was considered as the "greatest exponent of guerilla tactics after Shivaji".

It was during reign of Balaji Baji Rao (Nanasaheb) when the Marathas lost the Third Battle of Panipat.

Baji Rao II (last Peshwa) was the first Maratha to have fled from the British attacks instead of fighting with them. Baji Rao II surrendered to Sir John Malcom.

THE SIKH

Guru Nanak Dev was the founder of Sikhism, the religion that draws its elements from both Hinduism and Islam.

Name of the ten Sikh Gurus and their works are given below:

1. **Guru Nanak Dev (1469-1539AD):** The founder of Sikhism.
2. **Guru Angad Dev (1504-1552AD):** Developed Gurmukhi.
3. **Guru Amar Das (1479-1574AD):** Struggled against Sati system and Purdah system.
4. **Guru Ram Das (1534-1581AD):** Founded Amritsar, the holy city of Sikhism.
5. **Guru Arjun Dev (1563-1606AD):** He built the *Swarn Mandir* (Golden Temple).
6. **Guru Hargobind (1595-1644 AD):** Established Akal Takht.
7. **Guru Har Rai (1630-1661 AD)**
8. **Guru Har Krishan (1656-1664 AD)**
9. **Guru Tegh Bahadur (1621-1675 AD)**
10. **Guru Gobind Singh (1666-1708 AD):** Founded the Khalsa and Sikh baptism composed many poems, and nominated the Sikh sacred text as the final and enduring Guru.

MODERN INDIA

THE ADVENT OF THE EUROPEANS

THE PORTUGUESE

Vasco-da-Gama, a Portuguese explorer, sailed through the route of Cape of Good Hope and reached near Calicut on 20th May 1498 A.D. during the reign of King Zamorin (Hindu King of Calicut).

Vasco-da-Gama founded a factory at Cannanore on his second visit to India in 1501. In due course, Calicut, Cochin and Cannanore became the Portuguese trading centres.

Francisco Almeida came to India in 1505. He was the first Governor of Portuguese possessions in India.

The real founder of Portuguese power in India was *Alfonso de Albuquerque*. He captured Goa from the rulers of Bijapur in 1510. It was made their headquarters.

THE DUTCH

The United East India Company of the Netherlands founded a factory at Masulipatnam in 1605. They built their first fort on the main land of India at Pulicut in 1609, near Madras (Chennai). They captured Nagapattinam from the Portuguese.

They made Agra, Surat, Masulipatnam and Chinsura in Bengal as their trading centres.

THE DANES

The Danish East India Company was established in 1616 in Denmark.

They came to South India and founded a factory at Tranquebar (Tharangambadi) in 1620. They also made settlements at Serampore near Calcutta (Kolkata).

THE ENGLISH

The English East India Company was formed in 1599 under a charter granted by Queen Elizabeth in 1600.

The East India Company sent Sir William Hawkins to the court of the Mughal Emperor Jahangir in 1609 to obtain permission to erect a factory at Surat.

In 1615, Sir Thomas Roe, another British merchant, came to Jahangir's court. He stayed for three years and succeeded in getting permission to set up their trading centres at Agra, Surat, Ahmedabad and Broach.

In 1690, the British got permission from Aurangazeb to build a factory on the site of Calcutta. In 1696 a fort was built at that place. It was called Fort William.

THE FRENCH

The French East India Company was established in 1664 under the inspiring and energetic leadership of Colbert, the economic adviser of the French King Louis XIV.

In 1667, the first French factory was established at Surat by Francis Caron who was nominated as Director-General.

French were defeated by English in the *Battle of Wandiwash* (1760).

EAST INDIA COMPANY

After the Battle of Plassey in 1757 and the Battle of Buxar in 1764, the East India Company became a political power.

India was under the East India Company's rule till 1858 when it came under the direct administration of the British Crown.

Robert Clive was the first Governor of Fort William under the Company's rule.

GOVERNOR-GENERALS OF BENGAL

Warren Hastings (1772-85 AD)

In 1772, the Company appointed Warren Hastings as the Governor of Fort William.

The Dual System introduced by Robert Clive was abolished by Warren Hastings.

Warren Hastings was known for his expansionist policy. His administration witnessed the Rohilla War, the First Anglo-Maratha War and the Second Anglo-Mysore War.

Pitt's India Act (1784) was passed.

Lord Cornwallis (1786-93 AD)

Cornwallis inaugurated the policy of making appointments mainly on the basis of merit thereby laying the foundation of the Indian Civil Service.

Lord Cornwallis introduced Permanent Revenue Settlement.

Tipu Sultan signed the Treaty of Srirangapatnam in 1792 with the British.

Sir John Shore (1793-98 AD)

Played an important role in the introduction of Permanent Settlement.

Battle of Kharda between the Nizams and the Marathas (1795).

Wellesley (1798-1805)

Wellesley came to India with a determination to launch a forward policy that he adopted to achieve his object is known as the 'Subsidiary Alliance'.

The Fourth Anglo-Mysore War started in 1799. The war was short and decisive. Tipu fought till his capital Srirangapatnam was captured and he himself was shot dead.

Peshwa Baji Rao II signed the *Treaty* of *Bassein* with the British in 1802. It was a subsidiary treaty and the Peshwa was recognized as the head of the Maratha kingdom.

The Treaty of Deogaon(1803) was signed between Bhonsle and Wellesley.

Lord Minto (1807-1813)

Lord Minto concluded the Treaty of Amritsar with Ranjit Singh of Punjab in 1809.

The Charter Act of 1813 was passed during this period.

Lord Hastings (1813-1823)

Anglo Nepal War (1814-1816) and Treaty of Sugauli (1816).

Third Maratha War (1817-18), dissolution of Maratha confederacy and creation of Bombay Presidency.

He encouraged the freedom of the Press and abolished the censorship introduced in 1799.

GOVERNOR-GENERALS OF INDIA

Lord William Bentinck (1828-1835)

Charter Act of 1833 was passed and he was made the first Governor-General of India. Before him, the designation was Governor-General of Bengal.

The social reforms of William Bentinck made his name immortal in the history of British India. These include the abolition of *Sati*, the suppression of Thugs and the prevention of female infanticide.

The Government Resolution in 1835 made English the official and literary language of India.

Lord Metcalfe (1835-36 AD)

Known as liberator of press in India.

Lord Auckland (1836-42 AD)

First Afghan War (1838-42), a disaster for the English.

Lord Ellenborough (1842-44 AD)

Brought an end to Afghan war. War with Gwalior (1843), *Annexation of Sind* by Charles Napier (1843).

Lord Hardinge (1844-48 AD)

First Anglo-Sikh War (1845-46) and Treaty of Lahore (1846). Gave preference to English educated persons in employment.

Lord Dalhousie (1848-1856)

The Doctrine of Lapse was applied by Dalhousie.

The first railway line connecting Bombay with Thane was opened in 1853.

VICEROYS OF INDIA

Lord Canning (1856-62 AD)

Lord Canning became the first Viceroy of India in 1858.

Revolt of 1857, Mutiny took place. Indian Penal Code 1860 was passed.

Lord Elgin (1862 AD)

Wahabi Movement.

Lord John Lawrence (1864-69 AD)

Established the *High Courts* at Calcutta, Bombay and Madras in 1865.

Telegraphic communication was opened with Europe. Created the Indian Forest Department.

Lord Northbrooke (1872-76 AD)

Kuka Rebellion in Punjab, Famine in Bihar.

Lord Lytton (1876-80)

In 1878, the Vernacular Press Act was passed. This Act empowered a Magistrate to secure an undertaking from the editor, publisher and printer of a vernacular newspaper that nothing would be published against the English Government. This Act crushed the freedom of the Indian press.

In 1878, the Arms Act was passed. This Act prevented the Indians to keep arms without appropriate license.

Lord Lytton also held a Darbar at Delhi in 1877 in which Queen Victoria was declared as the Empress of India. This extravagant Darbar cost millions of ruppes.

In 1878, the Statutory Civil Service was established exclusively for Indians.

Lord Ripon (1880-84 AD)

Lord Ripon repealed the Vernacular Press Act and earned much popularity among Indians.

Ripon appointed a Commission in 1882 under the chairmanship of Sir William Hunter.

The Commission came to be known as the Hunter Commission. The Commission recommended for the expansion and improvement of the elementary education of the masses.

Ripon was founder of local self-government in modern India.

Lord Dufferin (1884-88 AD)

Third Burmese War (1885-86 AD). Establishment of the Indian National Congress in 1885.

Lord Lansdowne (1888-94 AD)

Factory Act of 1891 granted weekly holiday and stipulated working hours for women and children.

Lord Elgin II (1894-99 AD)

Southern uprisings of 1899. Great famine of 1896-1897 and Lyall Commission on famine was established.

Lord Curzon (1899-1905 AD)

Curzon instituted in 1902, a Universities Commission to go into the entire question of university education in the country.

On the basis of the findings and recommendations of the Commission, Curzon brought in the Indian Universities Act of 1904, which brought all the universities in India under the control of the government.

Lord Minto (1905-10 AD)

Swadeshi Movement (1905-08); foundation of Muslim League (1906); Surat Session and split in the Congress (1907). Morley-Minto Reforms (1909).

Lord Hardinge (1910-16 AD)

Capital shifted from Calcutta to Delhi (1911); Delhi Durbar; Partition of Bengal was cancelled. The Hindu Mahasabha was founded in 1915 by Pandit Madan Mohan Malaviya.

Lord Chelmsford (1916-21 AD)

Gandhi returned to India (1915) and founded the Sabarmati Ashram (1916), Champaran Satyagraha, Satyagraha at Ahmedabad (1981), Kheda Satyagraha (1918).

Rowlatt Act (March, 1919) and the Jallianwala Bagh Massacre (13th April, 1919).

Khilafat Committee was formed and Khilafat Movement started (1919-20).

Non-Cooperation Movement started (1920-22).

Lord Reading (1921-26)

Moplah Rebellion (1921) took place. *Kakori Train* Robbery on 1st August, 1925. *Communal Riots* of 1923-25 in Multan, Amritsar, Delhi etc.

Lord Irwin (1926-31 AD)

Lahore Session of Congress and *Poorna Swaraj* Declaration (1929).

Simon Commission visited India in 1927.

Dandi March (12th March, 1930). Civil Disobedience Movement (1930).

First Round Table Conference was held in England in 1930. Gandhi-Irwin Pact.

Lord Willingdon (1931-36 AD)

Second Round Table Conference in London in 1931 and *third* in 1932.

Lord Linlithgow (1936-43 AD)

Congress Ministries resignation celebrated as '*Deliverance Day*' by the Muslim League (1939), the Lahore Resolution (23rd March, 1940) of the Muslim League demanding separate state for the Muslims. (It was at this session that Jinnah propounded his Two-Nation Theory). Outbreak of World War II in 1939. Cripps Mission in 1942. Quit India Movement (8th August, 1942).

Lord Wavell (1943-47 AD)

Cabinet Mission Plan (16th May, 1946).

First meeting of the Constituent Assembly was held on 9th December, 1946.

Arranged the Shimla Conference on 25th June, 1945 with Indian National Congress and Muslim League but failed.

Lord Mountbatten (March to Aug, 1947)

Last viceroy of British India and the first Governor-General of free India.

Partition of India decided by the 3rd June Plan or Mountbatten Plan.

NATIONAL MOVEMENT (1885-1947)

INDIAN NATIONAL CONGRESS (1885)

Allan Octavian Hume, a retired civil servant in the British Government took the initiative to form an all-India organization. Thus, the Indian National Congress was founded and its first session was held at Bombay in 1885. W.C. Banerjee was its first president. It was attended by 72 delegates from all over India.

The second session was held in Calcutta in 1886 and the third in Madras in 1887.

Between 1885 and 1905, the Congress leaders were moderates. The Moderates had faith in the British justice and goodwill. They were called moderates because they adopted peaceful and constitutional means to achieve their demands.

In 1905, Gopal Krishna Gokhale founded the Servants of India Society to train Indians to dedicate their lives to the cause of the country.

Partition of Bengal (1905)

By Lord Curzon on 16th October, 1905 through a royal proclamation, reducing the old province of Bengal in size by creating East Bengal and Assam out of the rest of Bengal.

The partition of Bengal in 1905 provided a spark for the rise of extremism in the Indian National Movement.

Curzon's real motives behind this partition were:

- To break the growing strength of Bengali nationalism since Bengal was the base of Indian nationalism.
- To divide the Hindus and Muslims in Bengal.
- To show the enormous power of the British Government in doing whatever it liked.

Swadeshi Movement (1905)

The Swadeshi Movement involved programmes like the boycott of government service, courts, schools and colleges and of foreign goods. It was both a political and economic movement.

Lal, Bal, Pal and Aurobindo Ghosh played an important role.

Muslim League (1906)

In December 1906, Muslim delegates from all over India met at Dacca for the Muslim Educational Conference.

Taking advantage of this occasion, Nawab Salimullah of Dacca proposed the setting up of an organisation to look after the Muslim interests. The proposal was accepted.

The All-India Muslim League was finally set up on December 30, 1906.

Minto Morley Reforms (1909)

Minto, the Viceroy and Morley, the Secretary of State for India jointly proposed reforms to the Indian Councils. An Act, called the Indian Councils Act or the Minto-Morley Reforms Act was passed in 1909.

A separate communal electorate was introduced for the Muslims.

The Lucknow Pact (1916)

During the 1916 Congress session at Lucknow two major events occurred. The divided Congress became united. An understanding for joint action against the British was reached between the Congress and the Muslim League and it was called the Lucknow Pact.

The signing of the Lucknow Pact by the Congress and the Muslim League in 1916 marked an important step in the Hindu-Muslim unity.

The Home Rule Movement (1916)

Two Home Rule Leagues were established, one by B.G. Tilak at Poona in April 1916 and the other by Mrs. Annie Besant at Madras in September 1916.

While Tilak's Movement concentrated on

Maharashtra, Annie Besant's Movement covered the rest of the country.

August Declaration

On 20 August, 1917, Montague, the Secretary of State in England, promised the gradual development of self-governing institutions in India.

This August Declaration led to the end of the Home Rule Movement.

Rowlatt Act (1919)

In 1917, a committee was set up under the presidentship of Sir Sydney Rowlatt to look into the militant Nationalist activities. On the basis of its report the Rowlatt Act was passed in March 1919 by the Central Legislative Council. As per this Act, any person could be arrested on the basis of suspicion. No appeal or petition could be filed against such arrests.

This Act was called the Black Act and it was widely opposed. An all-India hartal was organized on 6 April, 1919.

Jallianwala Bagh Massacre (13 April, 1919)

On 13th April, the Baisakhi day (harvest festival), a public meeting was organized at the Jallianwala Bagh (garden). Gen. Dyer marched in and without any warning opened fire on the crowd. The firing continued for about 10 to 15 minutes and it stopped only after the ammunition exhausted.

According to official report 379 people were killed and 1137 wounded in the incident. There was a nationwide protest against this massacre and Rabindranath Tagore renounced his knighthood as a protest.

Khilafat Movement (1920)

The chief cause of the Khilafat Movement was the defeat of Turkey in the First World War.

The Muslims in India were upset over the British attitude against Turkey and launched the Khilafat Movement.

Ali brothers, *Mohd Ali* and *Shaukat Ali* started this movement. It was jointly led by the Khilafat leaders and the Congress.

Non-Co-operation Movement (1920-22)

Mahatma Gandhi announced his plan to begin Non-Cooperation with the government as a sequel to the Rowlatt Act, Jallianwala Bagh massacre and the Khilafat Movement. It was approved by the Indian National Congress at the Nagpur session in December, 1920.

The Congress observed the Non-Co-operation movement in 1920. The main aim of this movement was to attain Swaraj through non-violent and peaceful means.

The whole movement was abruptly called off on 11th February, 1922 by Gandhi following the Chauri-Chaura incident in the Gorakhpur district of U.P. Many top leaders of the country were stunned at this sudden suspension of the Non-Co-operation Movement.

On 5th February an angry mob set fire to the police station at *Chauri-Chaura* and twenty two police men were burnt to death.

Swaraj Party

Leaders like Motilal Nehru and Chittranjan Das formed a separate group within the Congress, known as the Swaraj Party on 1 January, 1923.

The Swarajists wanted to contest the council elections and wreck the government from within.

Simon Commission (1927)

The Act of 1919 included a provision for its review after a lapse of ten years. However, the review commission under the chairmanship of Sir John Simon was appointed by the British Government two years earlier of its schedule in 1927.

Indian leaders opposed the commission, as there were no Indians in it, they cried *Simon Go Back*.

The government used brutal repression and at Lahore, *Lala Lajpat Rai* was severely beaten in lathi-charge.

Nehru Report (1928)

The Secretary of State, Lord Birkenhead, challenged the Indians to produce a Constitution that would be acceptable to all. The challenge was accepted by the Congress, which convened an all party meeting on 28 February, 1928.

A committee consisting of eight was constituted to draw up a blueprint for the future Constitution of India. It was headed by Motilal Nehru. The Report published by this Committee came to be known as the Nehru Report.

Lahore Session (1929)

On Dec. 19, 1929, under the Presidentship of J.L. Nehru, the INC, as its Lahore session, declared Poorna Swaraj (Complete Independence) as its ultimate goal.

On Dec. 31, 1929, the newly adopted tricolour flag was unfurled and Jan. 26, 1930 was fixed as the First Independence Day, which was to be celebrated every year.

Dandi March (1930)

On 12th March, 1930, Gandhi began his famous March to Dandi with his chosen 79 followers to break the salt laws. He reached the coast of Dandi on 5 April, 1930 after marching a distance of 200 miles and on 6 April formally launched the Civil Disobedience Movement by breaking the salt laws.

Civil Disobedience Movement

Countrywide mass participation by women.

The Garhwal soldiers refused to fire on the people at Peshawar.

Round Table Conference

The first Round Table Conference was held in November 1930 at London and it was boycotted by the Congress.

On 8th March, 1931 the Gandhi-Irwin Pact was signed. As per this pact, Mahatma Gandhi agreed to suspend the Civil-Disobedience Movement and participate in the Second-Round Table Conference.

In September 1931, the Second Round Table Conference was held at London. Mahatma Gandhi participated in the Conference but returned to India disappointed.

In January 1932, the Civil-Disobedienc Movement was resumed.

Poona Pact (1932)

The idea of separate electorate for the depresse classes was abandoned, but seats reserved fo them in the provincial legislature were increased

Thus, Poona Pact agreed upon a joint electorat for upper and lower castes.

Demand for Pakistan

Chaudhary Rehmat Ali gave the term *Pakista* in 1933.

In March 1940, the Muslim League demande the creation of Pakistan.

Cripps Mission (1942)

The British Government in its effort to secu Indian co-operation in the Second World W sent Sir Stafford Cripps to India on 23 Marc 1942. This is known as Cripps Mission.

The main recommendations of Cripps was t promise of Dominion Status to India.

Congress rejected it. Gandhi called Cripp proposals as a "Post-dated Cheque".

Quit India Movement (1942-1944)

The All India Congress Committee met Bombay on 8th August, 1942 and passed t famous Quit India Resolution. On the same da Gandhi gave his call of 'do or die'.

On 8th and 9th August, 1942, the governme arrested all the prominent leaders of the Congre Mahatma Gandhi was kept in prison at Poon Pandit Jawaharlal Nehru, Abul Kalam Azad, a other leaders were imprisoned in t Ahamednagar Fort.

Quit India Movement was the final attempt f country's freedom.

Indian National Army (INA)

On July 2, 1943, Subhash Chandra Bose reach Singapore and gave the rousing war cry of *'D Chalo'*. He was made the President of Indi Independence League and soon became t supreme commander of the Indian National Army. He gave the country the slogan of *Jai Hind.*

INA had three fighting brigades named after Gandhi, Azad and Nehru. Rani of Jhansi Brigade was an exclusive women force. INA headquarters were at Rangoon and Singapore.

Cabinet Mission (1946)

The Cabinet Mission put forward a plan for solution of the constitutional problem. A proposal was envisaged for setting up an Interim Government, which would remain in office till a new government was elected on the basis of the new Constitution framed by the Constituent Assembly.

Elections were held in July 1946 for the formation of a Constituent Assembly.

Muslim league observed the *Direct Action Day* on 16 August, 1946.

An Interim Government was formed under the leadership of Jawaharlal Nehru on 2 September, 1946.

Mountbatten Plan (1947)

On 20 February 1947, Prime Minister Atlee announced in the House of Commons the definite intention of the British Government to transfer power to responsible Indian hands by a date not later than June 1948.

Lord Mountbatten armed with vast powers became India's Viceroy on 24 March, 1947. The partition of India and the creation of Pakistan appeared inevitable to him.

After extensive consultation Lord Mountbatten put forth the plan of partition of India on 3 June, 1947. The Congress and the Muslim League ultimately approved the Mountbatten Plan.

Indian Independence Act, 1947

The salient features of this Act was the partition of the country into India and Pakistan would come into effect from 15 August, 1947.

On 15th August, 1947 India, and on the 14th August Pakistan came into existence as two independent states.

Lord Mountbatten was made the first Governor General of Independent India, whereas Mohammad Ali Jinnah became the first Governor General of Pakistan.

C. Rajagopalachari became the first and last Indian Governor-General of India. When India became a Republic on 26 January, 1950 Dr. Rajendra Prasad became the first President of our country.

Socio-Religious Movements and Organisation

Name of the Organisation	*Founder*	*Year*	*Place*
Atmiya Sabha	Ram Mohan Roy	1815	Calcutta
Brahmo Samaj	Ram Mohan Roy	1828	Calcutta
Dharma Sabha	Radhakanta Dev	1829	Calcutta
Tattvabodhini Sabha	Debendranath Tagore	1839	Calcutta
Nirankaris	Dayal Das, Darbara Singh, Rattan Chand etc.	1840	Punjab
Manav Dharma Sabha	Durgaram Manchharam	1844	Surat
Paramhansa Mandli	Dadoba Pandurung	1849	Bombay
Namdharis	Ram Singh	1857	Punjab
Radha Swami Satsang	Tulsi Ram	1861	Agra
Brahmo Samaj of India	Keshab Chandra Sen	1866	Calcuttá
Dar-ul-Ulum	Maulana Hussain Ahmed	1866	Deoband
Prarthna Samaj	Atmaram Pandurung	1867	Bombay
Arya Samaj	Swami Dayanand Saraswati	1875	Bombay
Theosophical Society	Madam H.P. Blavatsky and Col. H.S. Olcott	1875	New York (USA)
Sadharan Brahmo Samaj	Anand Mohan Bose	1878	Calcutta

Deccan Education Society	G.G. Agarkar	1884	Pune (Poona)
Muhammadan Educational Conference	Syed Ahmad Khan	1886	Aligarh
Indian National Conference	M.G. Ranade	1887	Bombay
Deva Samaj	Shivnarayan Agnihotri	1887	Lahore
Nadwah-ul-Ulama	Maulana Shibli Numani	1894	Lucknow
Ramakrishna Mission	Swami Vivekananda	1897	Belur
Servents of Indian Society	Gopal Krishna Gokhale	1905	Bombay
Poona Seva Sadan	Mrs. Ramabai Ranade and G.K. Devadhar	1909	Pune (Poona)
Social Service League	N.M. Joshi	1911	Bombay
Seva Samiti	H.N. Kunzru	1914	Allahabad

Newspapers and Journals

Bengal Gazette (1780) (India's first newspaper)—James Augustus Hikky

Kesari—B.G. Tilak

Maratha—B.G. Tilak

Sudharak—G.K. Gokhale

Amrit Bazar Patrika—Shishir Kumar Ghosh and Motilal Ghosh

Yugantar—Bhupendranath Datta and Birender Kumar Ghosh

Bombay Chronicle—Firoze Shah Mehta

New India (Daily)—Annie Besant

Books and Authors

Causes of the Indian Mutiny—Sir Syed Ahmed Khan

Ghulam Giri—Jyotiba Phule

Anandmath—Bankim Chand Chatterjee

Satyarth Prakash—Swami Dayanand

Unhappy India—Lala Lajpat Rai

India Divided—Dr. Rajendra Prasad

The Discovery of India—J.L. Nehru

Neel Darpan—Dinbandhu Mitra

Hind Swaraj—M.K. Gandhi

What Congress and Gandhi have done to the untouchables—Dr. B.R. Ambedkar

Important Sayings

'Back to Vedas'—Dayanand Saraswati

'Dilli Chalo!'—Subhash Chandra Bose's battle cry of *Azad Hind Fauj*

'Do or Die'—Mahatma Gandhi (while launching Quit India movement in 1942)

'Give me blood and I will give you freedom'—Subhash Chandra Bose (in his address to soldiers of *Azad Hind Fauj)*

'My ultimate aim is to wipe every tear from every eye'—Jawaharlal Nehru

'Swaraj is my birthright and I will have it'—Ba Gangadhar Tilak

'Inqualab Zindabad'—Bhagat Singh

'Jai Jawan, Jai Kisan'—Lal Bahadur Shastri

'Sarfaroshi ki tamanna Ab Hamare Dil mei Hai'—Ram Prasad Bismill

'Saare Jahan Se Achcha, Hindusta Hamara'—Dr. Mohammed Iqbal

'Hindi, Hindu, Hindustan'—Bhartend Harishchandra

'Vande Mataram'—Bankim Chandra Chatterje

GEOGRAPHY

WORLD GEOGRAPHY

THE UNIVERSE

Existing matter and energy are together known as **Universe.**

GALAXY

A galaxy is a huge system of billions of stars and clouds of dust and gases.

Our solar system is a part of *Milky Way* galaxy. There are millions of galaxies that make the Universe.

STARS

Stars account for 98 per cent of the matter in a galaxy. The stars nearest to the earth are *Proxima Centauri, Alpha Centauri, Barnard's Star, Sirius* and so on. Of these, *Sirius* is the brightest.

LIGHT YEAR

Light year is the distance travelled by light in one year at a speed of 2,99,792.5 km. per second.

SOLAR SYSTEM

The Sun, eight planets, satellites and some other celestial bodies known as asteroids and meteoroids form the solar system.

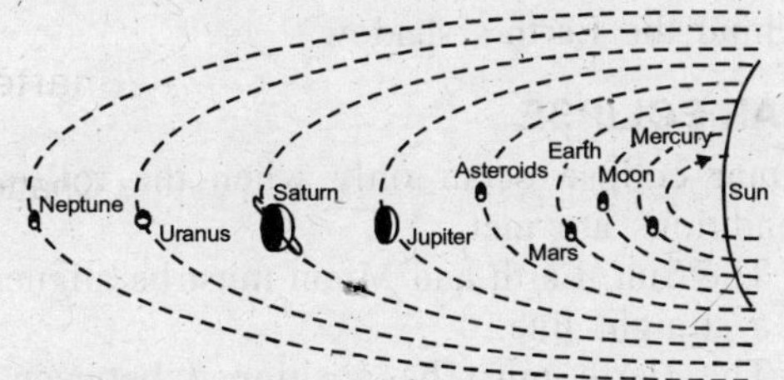

SUN

The Sun is in the centre of the solar system. The Sun is a mixture of gases. It consists of 92% hydrogen, 7.8% helium and 0.2% other gases. The Sun is about 150 million km away from the earth.

The sun is an ultimate source of energy for life on Earth.

Sunlight takes 8 min 16.6 sec to reach earth.

Facts about Sun

Diameter	— 1.392 × 10^6 km
Volume	— 1.304 × 106 times the volume of earth
Temperature	— 6000°C at surface and 15 million degree C at the centre
Relative density	— 1.4
Gravitational Pull	— 28 times the gravitational pull of the earth

Facts about Planets

Closest to Sun	*Mercury*
Farthest from Sun	*Neptune*
Heaviest	*Jupiter*
Hottest	*Venus*
Inner	*Mercury, Venus, Earth, Mars*
Largest	*Jupiter*
Smallest	*Mercury*
Moons, None	*Mercury, Venus*
Moon; Largest	*Ganymede (Jupiter), larger than Mercury*
Nearest to Earth	*Venus*
Orbits; Order	*Mercury (closest to Sun), Venus, Earth, Mars, Jupiter, Saturn, Uranus, Neptune.*
Rings/largest number	*Saturn*
Spin; Backwards	*Venus (East to West)*

COMETS

It has a head and a tail. Its tail originates only when it gets closer to the sun. The tail can be 20-30 million km long. It always point away from the sun because of the force exerted by solar wind and radiation on the cometory material.

THE EARTH

- The earth is the third nearest planet to the Sun.
- From the outer space, the earth appears blue because its two-thirds surface is covered by water. It is, therefore, called a blue planet.
- It is the densest of all planets.
- Rotation is the movement of the earth on its axis. Due to this rotation, day and night occur.
- The earth takes about 23 hours 56 minutes and 4 seconds to complete one rotation around its axis.
- Earth takes 365¼ days (one year) to revolve around the sun.

THE EARTH: FACTS AND FIGURES

- *Mass of Earth*—5.972 × 10^{21} tonnes
- *Density of Earth*—5.517 times that of water
- *Volume of Earth*—1.083 × 10^{11} cubic km
- *Equatorial circumference*—4.007 × 104 km
- *Polar Diameter*—12,714 km
- *Equatorial Diameter*—12756 km
- *Polar or Meridional circumference*—4.0 × 10^4 km
- *Estimated Age*—At least 4600 million years
- *Land Surface*—148,951,000 sq km
- *Water Surface*—361,150,000 sq km (71 per cent of total area)
- *Highest Point of the land surface*—Mt. Everest (8,848 metres)
- *Lowest point of the land surface*—Shores of the Dead Sea (396 metres below the sea level)
- *Greatest Ocean depth*—Mariana Trench, East of Philippines (11,033 metres below the sea level)

THE MOON

- Earth has only one satellite, that is, the moon.
- Its diameter is only one-quarter that of the earth. It is about 3,84,400 km away from us.
- The moon moves around the earth in about 27 days. It takes exactly the same time to complete one spin. As a result, only one side of the moon (only 59% of its surface) is visible to us on the earth.
- Moonlight takes 1.3 sec. to reach earth.

LATITUDE

- Imaginary lines drawn parallel to the equator. Measured as an angle whose apex is at the centre of the earth.
- The equator represents 0° latitude, while the North Pole is 90°N and the South Pole 90°S.
- 23½°N represents Tropic of Cancer while 23½°S represents Tropic of Capricorn.

LONGITUDE

- It is the angular distance measured from the centre of the earth. On the globe the lines of longitude are drawn as a series of semicircles that extend from the North Pole to the South Pole through the equator. They are also called meridians.
- The distance between any two meridians is not equal. At the equator, 1 degree = 111 km. At 30°N or S, it is 96.5 km. It goes on decreasing this way until it is zero at the poles.

INTERNATIONAL DATE LINE

- It is the 180° meridian running over the Pacific Ocean, deviating at Aleutian Islands, Fiji, Samoa and Gilbert Islands.
- Travellers crossing the Date Line from west to east repeat a day and travellers crossing it from east to west lose a day.

INDIAN STANDARD TIME (IST)

- Indian Standard Time is calculated on the basis of 82.5°E longitude which passes through Uttar Pradesh, Madhya Pradesh, Odisha, Chattisgarh and Andhra Pradesh.

ECLIPSES

- Sun is the only source of light for both the Earth and Moon. Eclipses occur when the light thus received is either blocked by the earth or by the Moon.
- Eclipses occur when either the Earth moves behind the Moon's shadow or the Moon moves behind the Earth's shadow.

LUNAR ECLIPSE

- Lunar eclipse occur only when the following conditions are met.
  1. The Sun, Earth and Moon must be aligned in a straight line.
  2. The Earth must be positioned between the Sun and the Moon.
  3. The Moon must be in its full phase (Full Moon).

SOLAR ECLIPSE

- Solar eclipses occur only when the following conditions are met.
  1. The Sun, Earth and Moon must be aligned in a straight line.

2. The Moon must be positioned between the Sun and the Earth.
3. Must be a New Moon day.

ROCKS

Rocks are composed of many minerals such as silica, aluminium, iron and magnesium. The nature of the rock is determined by the presence of its minerals.

Rocks can be classified into three types:

1. ***Igneous rocks*** are formed by magma that reaches the earth's surface along deep cracks and at volcanic vents. e.g., Mica, Granite etc.
2. ***Sedimentary rocks*** are formed by the accumulation and cementation of mud, silt, or sand derived from weathered igneous rock fragments. e.g., Gravel, Peat, Gypsum etc.
3. ***Metamorphic rocks*** are igneous or sedimentary rocks that have been altered by heat and/or pressure, either because they have been buried and folded deep in the crust, or because they have come into contact with molten igneous rock, e.g., Gneiss, Marble, Quartzite etc.

VOLCANOES

Sudden eruption of hot magma (molten rock), gases, ash and other material from inside the Earth to its surface.

Active which erupts frequently, e.g., Mauna Loa (Hawaii), Etna (Sicily), Vesuvius (Italy), Stromboli (Mediterranean Sea).

Dormant Not erupted for quite sometime, e.g., Fujiyama (Japan), Krakatoa (Indonesia), Barren Island (Andamans).

Extinct Not erupted for several centuries, e.g., Arthur's Seat, Edinburgh, Scotland.

EARTHQUAKES

Earthquakes are a form of wave energy that is transferred through bedrock. It is transmitted from the point of the earthquake focus, as spherical seismic waves. They travel in all directions outward.

The intensity of earthquake waves is recorded by *Seismograph*.

LANDFORMS

There are three major landforms: mountains, plateaus and plains.

MOUNTAINS

A mountain can be defined as an area of land that rises abruptly from the surrounding region.

There are three types of mountains- *Fold Mountains, Block Mountains* and the ***Volcanic Mountains***.

Himalayas, Alps, Andes, Rockies, Atlas, etc are examples of Fold Mountains.

The Aravali range in India is one of the oldest **fold mountain** systems in the world.

The Rhine valley and the Vosges mountain in Europe are examples of such mountain systems.

Volcanic mountains are formed due to volcanic activity.

Mt. Kilimanjaro in Africa and Mt. Fujiyama in Japan are examples of such mountains.

Major Mountain Ranges of the World

Range	Location	Highest Peak (m)	Length (km)
Andes	South America	6,960	7,200
Himalayas-Karakoram-Hindukush	South Central Asia	8,848	4,800
Rockies	North America	4,401	4,800
Great Dividing Range	East Australia	2,228	3,600
Western Ghat	Western India	2,637	1,610
Caucasus	Europe	5,642	1,200
Alaska	USA	6,194	1,130
Alps	Europe	4,808	1,050
Apennines	Europe	2,912	—
Ural	Asia	1,895	—
Atlas	North West Africa	—	1,930

PLATEAUS

A plateau is an elevated flat land. It is a flat-topped table land standing above the surrounding area.

Principal Mountain Peaks of the World

Mountains	Height in Metres
1. Mount Everest	8,848
2. K-2 (Godwin Austen)	8,611
3. Kanchenjunga	8,597
4. Lhotse	8,511
5. Makalu I	8,481
6. Dhaulagiri I	8,167
7. Mansalu I	8,156
8. Chollyo	8,153
9. Nanga Parbat	8,124
10. Annapurna I	8,091
11. Gasherbrum I	8,068
12. Broad Peak I	8,047
13. Gasherbrum II	8,034
14. Shisha Pangma (Gosainthan)	8,014
15. Gasherbrum III	7,952

PLAINS

A relatively low-lying and flat land surface with least difference between its highest and lowest points is called a Plain.

OCEANS

Oceans of the world is classified into four groups: the Pacific, the Atlantic, the Arctic and the Indian. The Pacific is the largest ocean, being twice the size of the Atlantic. It covers about a third of the Earth's surface, and contains more than half the water on the planet.

Oceans of the World

Names	Area (Sq. Km.)	Greatest Depth
Pacific	166,240000	Mariana Trench
Atlantic	86,560000	Puerto Rico Trench
Indian	73430000	Java Trench
Arctic	13230000	—

Major Rivers of the World

River	Origin	Falls in	Length (Km.)
Nile	Victoria lake	Mediterranean Sea	6,650
Amazon	Andes (Peru)	Atlantic Ocean	6,428
Yangtze	Tibetan Kiang Plateau	China Sea	6,300
Mississippi Missouri	Itaska lake (USA)	Gulf of Mexico (USA)	6,275
Yenisei	Tannu-Ola Mts.	Arctic Ocean	5,539
Hoang Ho	Kunlun Mts.	Gulf of Chibli	5,464
Ob	Altai Mts., Russia	Gulf of Ob	5,410
Congo	Lualaba & Luapula rivers	Atlantic Ocean	4,700
Amur	Northeast China	Sea of Okhotsk	4,444
Lena	Baikal Mts	Laptev Sea	4,400
Mekong	Tibetan Highlands	South China Sea	4,350
Mackenzie	Great Slave Lake	Beaufort Sea	4,241
Niger	Guinea	Gulf of Guinea	4,200

Major Gulfs of the World

Names	Area (Sq. Km.)	Names	Areas (Sq. Km.)
Gulf of Mexico	15,44,000	Gulf of St. Lawrence	2,37,000
Gulf of Hudson	12,33,000	Gulf of California	1,62,000
Arabian Gulf	2,38,000	English Channel	89,900

Important Straits of the World

Straits	Water Bodies joined	Area
Bab-al-Mandeb	Red Sea & Arabian Sea	Arabia & Africa
Bering	Arctic Ocean & Bering Sea	Alaska & Asia
Bosphorus	Black Sea & Marmara Sea	Turkey
Dover	North Sea & Atlantic Ocean	England & Europe
Florida	Gulf of Mexico & Atlantic Ocean	Florida & Bahamas Islands
Gibralter	Mediterranean Sea & Atlantic Ocean	Spain & Africa
Malacca	Java Sea & Bay of Bengal	India & Indonesia
Palk	Bay of Bengal & Indian Ocean	India & Sri Lanka
Magellan	South Pacific & South Atlantic Ocean	Chile
Sunda	Java Sea & Indian Ocean	Indonesia

Important Lakes of the World

Lake	Location	Area (Sq. Km.)
Caspian	Russia and CIS	371000
Superior	Canada and USA	82414
Victoria	Tanzania (Africa)	69485
Huron	Canada and USA	59596
Michigan	USA	58016
Tanganyika	Africa	32892
Baikal	Russia (CIS)	31502
Great Bear	Canada	31080
Malawi	Malawi (Tanzania)	30044
Great Slave	Canada	28438

Highest Waterfalls of the World

Name(s) (Foreign)	Location
Angel (Salto Angel)	Canaima Nat'l Park, Venezuela
Tugela	Natal Nat'l Park, South Africa
Utigord (Utigordsfoss)	Norway
Monge (Mongefoss)	Marstein, Norway
Gocta Cataracts	Chachapoyas, Peru
Mutarazi (Mtarazi)	Nyanga Nat'l Park, Zimbabwe
Yosemite	Yosemite Nat'l Park, California, U.S.
Espelands (Espelandsfoss)	Hardanger Fjord, Norway
Lower Mar Valley (Ostra Mardolafoss)	Eikesdal, Norway
Tyssestrengene	Odda, Norway

Important Cities on River Banks (World)

City	Country	River
Adelaide	Australia	Torrens
Amsterdam	Netherlands	Amsel
Alexandria	Egypt	Nile
Ankara	Turkey	Kazil
Bangkok	Thailand	Chao Praya
Basra	Iraq	Eupharates and Tigris
Baghdad	Iraq	Tigris
Berlin	Germany	Spree
Bonn	Germany	Rhine
Budapest	Hungary	Danube
Bristol	UK	Avon
Buenos Aires	Argentina	Laplata
Chittagong	Bangladesh	Majyani
Canton	China	Si-Kiang
Cairo	Egypt	Nile
Chung King	China	Yang-tse-kiang
Cologne	Germany	Rhine
Dandzing	Germany	Vistula
Dresden	Germany	Elbe
Dublin	Ireland	Liffy
Hamburg	Germany	Elbe
Kabul	Afghanistan	Kabul
Karachi	Pakistan	Indus
Khortoum	Sudan	Confluence of Blue & White Nile
Lahore	Pakistan	Ravi
Leningrad	Russia	Neva

City	Country	River
Lisbon	Portugal	Tagus
Liverpool	England	Messey
London	England	Thames
Moscow	Russia	Moskva
Montreal	Canada	St. Lawrence
Nanking	China	Yang-tse-kiang
New Orleans	U.S.A.	Mississipi
New York	U.S.A.	Hudson
Ottawa	Canada	Ottawa
Paris	France	Seine
Philadelphia	U.S.A	Delaware
Perth	Australia	Swan
Prague	Czech Republic	Vitava
Quebec	Canada	St. Lawrence
Rome	Italy	Tiber
Rotterdam	The Netherlands	New Moss
Stalingrad	Russia	Volga
Shanghai	China	Yang-tse-kiang
Sidney	Australia	Darling
Saint Louis	U.S.A	Mississippi
Tokyo	Japan	Arakava
Vienna	Austria	Danube
Warsaw	Poland	Vistula
Washington D.C.	U.S.A.	Potomac
Yangoon	Myanmar	Irawaddy

World's Geographical Surnames

City of Sky-scrapers—New York

City of Seven Hills—Rome

City of Dreaming Spires—Oxford

City of Golden Gate—San Francisco

City of Magnificent Buildings—Washington D.C.

City of Eternal Springs—Quito (S. America)

China's Sorrow—Hwang Ho

Cockpit of Europe—Belgium

Dark Continent—Africa

Emerald Isle—Ireland

Eternal City—Rome

Empire City—New York

Forbidden City—Lhasa (Tibet)

Garden City—Chicago

Gate of Tears—Strait of Bab-el-Mandeb

Gift of the Nile—Egypt

Granite City—Aberdeen (Scotland)

Hermit Kingdom—Korea

Herring Pond—Atlantic Ocean

Holy Land—Jerusalem

Island Continent—Australia

Islands of Cloves—Zanzibar

Isle of Pearls—Bahrein (Persian Gulf)

Key to the Mediterranean—Gibralter

Land of Cakes—Scotland

Land of Golden Fleece—Australia

Land of Maple Leaf—Canada

Land of Morning Calm—Korea

Land of Midnight Sun—Norway

Land of the Thousand Lakes—Finland

Land of the Thunderbolt—Bhutan

Land of White Elephant—Thailand

Land of Thousand Elephants—Laos

Land of Rising Sun—Japan

Loneliest Island—Tristan De Gunha (Mid-Atlantic)

Manchester of Japan—Osaka

Pillars of Hercules—Strait of Gibraltar

Pearl of the Antilles—Cuba

Playground of Europe—Switzerland

Quaker City—Philadelphia

Queen of the Adriatic—Venice

Roof of the World—The Pamirs, Central Asia

Sugar bowl of the world—Cuba

Venice of the North—Stockholm

Windy City—Chicago

Whiteman's grave—Guinea Coast of Africa

Yellow River—Huang Ho (China)

Sickman of Europe—Turkey

Important Boundaries

Durand Line	Pakistan & Afghanistan
MacMohan Line	India & China
Radcliff Line	India & Pakistan
Maginot Line	France & Germany
Oder Niesse Line	Germany & Poland
Hindenberg Line	Poland & Germany (at the time of First World War)
38th Parallel	North & South Korea
49th Parallel	USA & Canada

Continents: Some Facts

Continent	Biggest Counrty	Highest Peak	Longest River
Asia	China	Mt. Everest (8848 m)	Yangtze Kiang
Africa	Algeria	Mt. Kilimanjaro (5895 m)	Nile
North America	Canada	Mt. Mckinley (6194 m)	Mississippi Missouri
South America	Brazil	Mt. Acancagua (6960 m)	Amazon
Europe	Russia	Mt. Elbrus (5642 m)	Ob
Australia	Australia	Mt. Coscuisco (2228 m)	Darling
Antarctica	—	Vinson Massif (5140 m)	—

INDIAN GEOGRAPHY

AREA AND LOCATION

- India is in the southern parts of the Asian continent. In the west of India lies the Arabian Peninsula while in the east lies the Indo-China Peninsula.
- India extends between 8°4' N and 37°6' N latitudes and between 68°7' E and 97°2' E longitudes.
- India, has a total geographic area of 32,87,263 sq. km. This is only 2.42 % of the total geographic area of the world but holds 17 per cent of the world's population.
- The 23½°N, which is the Tropic of Cancer, runs across the country.
- India has a length of 3214 km from north to south and 2933 km from east to west. It has a land frontier of 15200 km.
- The total length of the coastline of the mainland, Lakshadweep Islands and Andaman and Nicobar Islands is 7,516.6 km.
- India ranks seventh among the countries of the world, in terms of the geographical extent.
- India is bordered on three sides by water and on one by land, it is also a peninsula.
- India shares its common border with Afghanistan and Pakistan in the north-west, China and Bhutan in the north, and Bangladesh in the east. In the south, Sri Lanka is separated from India by a strait, known as the Palk Strait.
- There are 28 States (After reorganisation of J&K in 2019) and 8 Union Territories (After merger of Dadra & Nagar Haveli and Daman & Diu in 2020).
- 82°30' E longitude is considered as the Indian Standard Meridian. The local time of this longitude is taken as the Indian Standard Time (IST). This is 5½ hours ahead of the Greenwich Mean Time.

THE INDIAN STATES ON INTERNATIONAL BOUNDARIES ARE:

- ***Bordering Pakistan:*** Jammu and Kashmir, Punjab, Rajasthan, Gujarat.
- ***Bordering China:*** Ladakh, Himachal Pradesh, Uttarakhand, Sikkim, Arunachal Pradesh.
- ***Bordering Nepal:*** Bihar, Uttarakhand, UP, Sikkim, West Bengal.
- ***Bordering Bangladesh:*** West Bengal, Mizoram, Meghalaya, Tripura, Assam.
- ***Bordering Bhutan:*** West Bengal, Sikkim, Arunachal Pradesh, Assam.
- ***Bordering Myanmar:*** Arunachal Pradesh, Nagaland, Manipur, Mizoram.
- ***Bordering Afghanistan:*** Jammu and Kashmir (Pakistan-occupied area).

Important Passes

Jammu and Kashmir	Burzi-La
Himachal Pradesh	Bara La, Cha-La, Shipki-La
Uttarakhand	Niti-La, Lipu-Lekh-La
Sikkim	Jelep-La, Nathu-La
Arunachal Pradesh	Bomdi-La
Ladakh	Joji-La

Heighest Mountain Peaks of India

Peaks	Elevation• (in mts.)
Godwin Austin (K2)	8611
Kanchenjunga	8598*
Nanga Parvat	8126*
Gasherbrum	8068*
Broad Peak	8047*
Dastegil	7885*
Masherbrum (East)	7821*
Nanda Devi	7817
Masherbrum (West)	7806*
Rakoposhi	7788*
Kamet	7756
Saser Kangdi	7672

• *Above mean sea level in metres.*

* *Situated in Pak occupied Kashmir (PoK).*

Towns at River Banks

Town	River
Agra	Yamuna
Prayagraj	Confluence of the Ganges and the Yamuna
Ayodhya	Saryu
Badrinath	The Ganges
Kolkata	Hooghly
Cuttuck	Mahanadi
Delhi	Yamuna
Dibrugarh	Brahmaputra
Ferozepur	Satluj
Guwahati	Brahmaputra
Hardwar	The Ganges
Hyderabad	Musi
Jabalpur	Narmada
Kanpur	The Ganges
Kota	Chambal
Kurnool	Tungbhadra
Lucknow	Gomti
Ludhiana	Sutlej
Nasik	Godavari
Pandharpur	Bhima
Patna	The Ganges
Sambalpur	Mahanadi
Srinagar	Jhelum
Srirangapattam	Cauveri
Surat	Tapti
Varanasi	The Ganges
Vijaywada	Krishna

Waterfalls of India

Waterfall	Hgt (Mt.)	River	State
Jog/Gersoppa	260	Sharavati	Karnataka
Rakim Kund	168	Gaighat	Bihar
Chachai	127	Bihad	Madhya Pradesh
Kevti	98	Mahanadi	Madhya Pradesh
Sivasamudram	90	Cauveri	Karnataka
Kunchikal	455	Varahi	Karnataka

Important Lakes of India

Name of lake	State/UT
Pulicat Lake	Tamil Nadu & Andhra Pradesh Border
Sambhar Lake	Rajasthan
Tso Moriri Lake	Jammu & Kashmir
Vembanad Lake	Kerala
Wular & Dal Lakes	Jammu and Kashmir
Chilka Lake	Odisha
Kolleru Lake	Andhra Pradesh
Loktak Lake	Manipur
Lonar Lake	Maharashtra
Pangong Lake	Jammu and Kashmir

Rivers of India

Name	Originates From	Falls Into
Yamuna	Yamunotri	Ganga
Chambal	Singar Chouri Peak, Vindhyan escarpment	Yamuna
Ghaghara	Matsatung Glacier	Ganga

Name	Originates From	Falls Into
Kosi	Near Gosain Dham Peak	Ganga
Sabarmati	Aravalis	Gulf of Khambat
Krishna	Western Ghats	Bay of Bengal
Godavari	Nasik district in Maharashtra	Bay of Bengal
Caurey	Brahmagir Range of Western Ghats	Bay of Bengal
Tungabharda	Western Ghats	Krishna
Ganges	Combines Sources	Bay of Bengal
Sutlej	Mansarovar Rakas lakes	Chenab
Indus	Near Mansarovar Lake	Arabian Sea
Ravi	Kullu Hills near Rohtang Pass	Chenab
Beas	Near Rohtang Pass	Sutlej
Jhelum	Verinag in Kashmir	Chenab
Son	Amarkantak	Ganga
Brahmaputra	Near Mansarovar Lake	Bay of Bengal
Narmada	Amarkantak	Gulf of Khambat
Tapti	Betul District in Madhya Pradesh	Gulf of Khambat
Mahanadi	Raipur District in Chhattisgarh	Bay of Bengal
Luni	Aravallis	Rann of Kuchchh
Ghaggar	Himalayas	Near Fatehabad
Betwa	Vindhyanchal	Yamuna

Geographical Surnames

Bengal's Sorrow	Damodar River
City of Palaces	Kolkata
Gateway of India	Mumbai
Pink City	Jaipur
Paris of India	Jaipur
Manchester of India	Ahmedabad
Kashmir of South	Kerala
Son of Sea	Lakshadweep
Queen of Mountains	Mussourie
Iron City	Jamshedpur
Hollywood of India	Mumbai
Scotland of East	Meghalaya
City of Nababs	Lucknow
City of Temples & Ghats	Varanasi
Land of Five Rivers	Punjab
City of Golden Temple	Amritsar
Garden of India	Bangaluru
Spice Garden of India	Kerala
City of Lakes	Srinagar
Twin City	Hyderabad-Secunderabad
City of Seven Islands	Mumbai
Diamond Harbour	Kolkata
Switzerland of India	Kashmir
Rice Bowl	Chhattisgarh
Fruit Bowl	Himachal Pradesh
Ganga of South	Cauvery
Pitsburg of India	Jamshedpur
City of Bridges	Srinagar
Residence of God	Allahabad
A Cross-road (Quadrivial) of National Highways	Kanpur
Heart of India	Delhi
Black River	Sharda
City of Festivals	Madurai
Queen of Deccan	Pune
Sorrow of Bihar	Kosi River

Some Major Irrigational and Multipurpose Projects

S.No.	Name of Project	Related State	River
1.	Bargi Project	Madhya Pradesh	Bargi
2.	Beas	Joint Venture of Haryana, Punjab and Rajasthan	Beas
3.	Bhadra	Karnakata	Bhadra
4.	Bhakra Nangal	Haryana, Punjab and Rajasthan	Sutluj
5.	Bhima I	Maharashtra	Pawana
6.	Bhima II	Maharashtra	Krishna
7.	Chambal	Joint Project of M.P. and Rajasthan	Chambal
8.	Damodar Valley Project	West Bengal and Bihar	Damodar
9.	Dulhasti Power Project	Jammu and Kashmir	Chenab
10.	Farakka	West Bengal	Hooghly
11.	Gandak	Bihar and U.P.	Gandak
12.	Ghataprabha	Karnataka	Ghataprabha
13.	Hasdeo Bango Project	Madhya Pradesh, Chhattisgarh	Hasdeo
14.	Hirakud	Odisha	Mahanadi
15.	Jayakwadi	Maharashtra	Godavari
16.	Kakrapara	Gujarat	Tapti
17.	Kangsbati	West Bengal	Kangsbati and Kumari
18.	Karjan	Gujarat	Karjan
19.	Kosi	Bihar	Kosi
20.	Koyana	Maharashtra	Koyana
21.	Krishna Project	Maharashtra	Krishna
22.	Kukadi	Maharashtra	Kukadi
23.	Left Bank Ghagra Canal	Uttar Pradesh	Ghagra
24.	Madhya Ganga Canal	Uttar Pradesh	Ganga
25.	Mahanadi Delta Scheme	Odisha	(The irrigation scheme will utilise releases from Hirakund Reservoir)
26.	Mahi	Gujarat	Mahi
27.	Malaprabha	Karnataka	Malaprabha
28.	Mayurakshi	West Bengal	Mayurakshi
29.	Nagarjunasagar	Andhra Pradesh	Krishna
30.	Panam	Gujarat	Panam
31.	Parambikulam Aliyar	Tamil Nadu and Kerala	Perimbikulam
32.	Pochampad	Andhra Pradesh	Godavari
33.	Pong Dam	Punjab	Beas
34.	Ramganga	Uttarakhand	Ramganga
35.	Ranjit Sagar Dam (Thein Dam)	Punjab	Ravi
36.	Rihand	Uttar Pradesh	Rihand
37.	Sabarmati	Gujarat	Sabarmati

S.No.	Name of Project	Related State	River
38.	Sharda Sahayak	U.P.	Ghagra
39.	Sone High Level Canal	Bihar	Sone
40.	Tawa	Madhya Pradesh	Tawa
41.	Tehri Dam	Uttarakhand	Bhagirathi
42.	Tungabhadra	Andhra Pradesh and Karnataka	Tungabhadra
43.	Ukai	Gujarat	Tapti
44.	Upper Krishna	Karnataka	Krishna
45.	Upper Penganga	Maharashtra	Penganga
46.	Uri Power Project	Jammu and Kashmir	Jhelum

Major Indian Crops

Crops	Temp(°c)	Water(cm)	States where Produced
Wheat	15°-25°	60-90	Uttar Pradesh, Punjab, Haryana.
Rice	24°-26°	80-200	West Bengal, Uttar Pradesh, Andhra Pradesh, Bihar, Punjab
Maize	18°-21°	50-60	Karnataka, Uttar Pradesh, Maharashtra
Jowar	20°-35°	40-60	Maharashtra, Madhya Pradesh, Karnataka
Soyabean	25°-27°	50-120	Madhya Pradesh
Cotton	20°-30°	80-150	Maharashtra, Gujarat, Karnataka, Madhya Pradesh
Tobacco	20°-25°	75-80	Andhra Pradesh, Madhya Pradesh, Gujarat, Karnataka, Maharashtra, Uttar Pradesh
Tea	24°-30°	100-200	Assam, West Bengal, Kerala, Tamil Nadu, Uttar Pradesh
Ground Nut	15°-25°	60-130	Gujarat, Maharashtra

Mineral Wealth at a Glance (Metallic Minerals)

Mineral	Chief Producers
Bauxite	Odisha, Gujarat, Jharkhand
Chromite	Odisha, Karnataka
Coal	Jharkhand, Odisha
Copper	Rajasthan, Madhya Pradesh
Diaspore	Uttar Pradesh, Madhya Pradesh
Gold	Karnataka
Iron	Odisha, Karnataka, Goa
Lead	Rajasthan, Andhra Pradesh
Lignite	Tamil Nadu, Jammu & Kashmir
Manganese	Odisha, Karnataka
Natural Gas	Gujarat, Assam
Petroleum	Gujarat, Assam, Andhra Pradesh
Silver	Rajasthan, Jharkhand, Gujarat
Tungsten	Rajasthan
Zinc	Rajasthan, Maharashtra

Zones and Headquarters of Indian Railways

S.No.	Zone	Headquarters
1.	Central	Mumbai (Victoria Terminus)
2.	Eastern	Kolkata
3.	Northern	New Delhi
4.	North-Eastern	Gorakhpur
5.	North-East Frontier	Maligaon, Guwahati
6.	Southern	Chennai
7.	South-Central	Secunderabad
8.	South-Eastern	Kolkata
9.	Western	Mumbai, Churchgate
10.	East Coast	Bhubaneswar
11.	East Central	Hajipur
12.	North Central	Allahabad
13.	North Western	Jaipur
14.	South Western	Bengaluru (Hubli)
15.	West Central	Jabalpur
16.	South East Central	Bilaspur
17.	Metro Railway	Kolkata
18.	South Coast Railway	Vishakhapatnam (Proposed)

Major National Highways

N H	Connects
NH 1	New Delhi-Ambala-Jalandhar-Amritsar
NH 2	Delhi-Mathura-Agra-Kanpur-Allahabad-Varanasi-Kolkata
NH 3	Agra-Gwalior-Nasik-Mumbai
NH 4	Thane and Chennai *via* Pune and Belgaum
NH 5	Kolkata-Chennai
NH 6	Kolkata-Dhule
NH 7	Varanasi-Kanyakumari (2369 km)
NH 8	Delhi-Mumbai (*via* Jaipur, Baroda and Ahmedabad)
NH 9	Mumbai-Vijaywada
NH 10	Delhi-Fazilka
NH 24	Delhi-Lucknow
NH 26	Lucknow-Varanasi

Major Ports of Country

1. Syama Prasad Mookerjee (Kolkata)
2. Mumbai
3. J.L. Nehru Port (Nhava Sheva)
4. V.O. Chidambarnar (Tuticorin)
5. Chennai
6. Mormugao
7. New Mangalore
8. Paradeep
9. Deendayal (Kandla)
10. Vishakhapatnam
11. Cochin
12. Haldia
13. Kamarajar (Ennore).

Major International Airports in India

International Airports	City
Indira Gandhi International Airport	Delhi
Anna International Airport	Chennai
Sri Guru Ram Das Jee International Airport	Amritsar
Rajiv Gandhi International Airport	Hyderabad
Calicut International Airport	Kozhikode
Chhatrapati Shivaji International Airport	Mumbai
Kempegowda International Airport	Bengaluru
Dabolim International Airport in Vasco di Gama City	Goa
Netaji Subash Chandra Bose International Airport	Kolkata
Trivendrum International Airport	Thiruvananthapuram
Lokpriya Gopinath Bordoloi International Airport	Guwahati
Sardar Vallabhbhai Patel International Airport	Ahmedaba

❒ ❒ ❒

INDIAN POLITY

INDIAN CONSTITUTION

Demand for a Constituent Assembly composed of the people of India officially asserted by the Congress for the first time in 1935.

The election for Indian Constitution Assembly held in 1946 according to the *Cabinet Mission Plan*.

The first session of the Assembly was held in New Delhi on December 9, 1946. *Sachidanand Sinha* was elected provisional chairman of the session.

On December 11, 1946, Dr. Rajendra Prasad was elected as the Permanent Chairman of the Constituent Assembly.

The Constitution was framed by the Constituent Assembly of India, set-up in December 1946, in accordance with the Cabinet Mission Plan, under the Chairmanship of Sachidanand Sinha, initially.

The total membership of Constituent Assembly after partition was 299, among them 70 were representatives from the Indian states and others from British India.

The Chairman of the Drafting Committee was **Dr. BR Ambedkar**, also called the Father of the Constitution.

The Constituent Assembly took 2 years, 11 months and 18 days to complete the Constitution.

The Constitution, adopted on 8th November, 1949, contained 395 Articles and Schedules.

The Constitution was delayed till 26th January because, in 1929, on this day Indian National Congress demanded Poorna Swaraj in Lahore Session under JL Nehru.

Indian Constitution is a comprehensive document and it is the lengthiest written Constitution in the World.

THE PREAMBLE

The Preamble of the Constitution: "We the people of India, having solemnly resolved to Constitute India into a Sovereign, Socialist, Secular Democratic Republic and to secure to all its citizen:

Justice, Social, economic and political;

Liberty of thought, expression, belief, faith and worship;

Equality of status and of opportunity; and to promote among them all;

Fraternity assuring the dignity of the individual and the unity and integrity of the nation;

In our Constituent Assembly, this twenty-sixth day of November, 1949, do hereby adopt, enact and give to ourselves this constitution."

Foreign Sources of Indian Constitution

Foreign Sources	Subject
Britain	Parliamentary system, collective responsibilities of Cabinet
America	Fundamental right, Independent Judiciary, Judicial review
Canada	Division of powers
Ireland	Directive principles
Germany	Emergency provisions
Russia	Fundamental duties
Australia	Concurrent list

IMPORTANT ARTICLES

PART - I

UNION AND ITS TERRITORIES (ARTICLE 1 - 4)

The Constitution says, "India, that is Bharat, shall be a Union of States".

Parliament has the power to create any State, reduce it, change the name of boundaries of any State.

PART - II

CITIZENSHIP (ARTICLE 5 - 11)

The Constitution provides for a single Citizenship.

Indian Citizenship can be acquire:

1. by birth
2. by descent
3. by registration
4. by naturalisation
5. by incorporation of territory

Indian Citizenship can be lost by:

1. renunciation;
2. termination — it takes place if a citizen of India voluntary acquires the citizenship of another country; and
3. deprivation — if the Government terminates the citizenship.

PART - III

FUNDAMENTAL RIGHTS (ARTICLE 12 - 35)

Following fundamental rights are enjoyed by every Indian citizen, irrespective of caste, colour, creed and sex:

1. ***Right to Equality:*** No special privileges, no distinction on grounds of religion, caste, creed and sex.
2. ***Right to Freedom:*** The right to freedom of expression and speech, the right to choose one's own profession, the right to reside in any part of the Indian Union.
3. ***Right to Freedom to Religion:*** Except when it is in the interest of public order, morality, health or other conditions, everybody has the right to profess, practice and propagate his religion freely.
4. ***Cultural and Educational Rights:*** The Constitution provides that every community can run its own institutions to preserve its own culture and language.
5. ***Right against Exploitation:*** Traffic in human beings and forced labour and the employmen of children under 14 years in factories o mines, are punishable offences.
6. ***Rights to Constitutional Remedies:*** When citizen finds that any of his fundamental right has been encroached upon, he can move th Supreme Court, which has been empowere to safeguard the fundamental rights of a citize (Article 32).

PART - IV

DIRECTIVE PRINCIPLES OF STATE POLIC (ARTICLE 36 - 51)

Directive principles are not enforceable throug courts. Main aim of Directive principles is provide social and economic base of a genuir democracy.

Some Important Directive Principles:

Provisions for adequate means of livelihood f all citizens (Art. 39).

Right to work (Art. 41).

Right to human condition of work and materni relief (Art. 42).

Right to a living wage and condition of wo ensuring decent standard of life of worker (A 43).

Common Civil Code (Art. 44).

Prohibit consumption of liquor (Art. 47).

Prevent slaughter of useful cattle (Art. 48).

Organise Panchayati Raj (Art. 40).

Separate the judiciary from the executive (Art. 5

Protect and maintain places of histor monuments (Art. 49).

International peace (Art. 51).

PART - IV A

FUNDAMENTAL DUTIES (ARTICLE 51A)

The fundamental duties for the Indian citize have been incorporated in the Constituti through the Constitution (42nd) Amendment A 1976. These duties are:

1. to abide by the Constitution and respect ideals and institutions, the National Flag a the National Anthem;

2. to cherish and follow the noble deeds which inspired our national struggle for freedom;
3. to uphold and protect the sovereignty, unity and integrity of India;
4. to defend the country and render national service when called upon to do so;
5. to promote harmony and the spirit of common brotherhood amongst all the people transcending religious, regional or sectional diversities and to renounce practices derogatory to the dignity of women;
6. to value and preserve the rich heritage of our composite culture;
7. to protect and improve natural environment including forests, lakes, rivers and wildlife, and to have compassion for living creatures;
8. to develop the scientific temper, humanism and the spirit of inquiry and reform;
9. to safeguard public property and to abjure violence;
10. to strive towards excellence in all spheres of individual and collective activity so that the nation constantly rises to higher levels of endeavour and achievement.
11. who is parent or guardian to provide opportunities for education to his child or, as the case may be, ward between age of six and fourteen years.

PART - V

UNION (ARTICLE 52 - 151)

The President

The President is the Constitutional head of the Republic of India. He is more or less the titular head of the executive.

- He is the constitutional head but not the real executive. The real power is vested in the hands of the Council of Ministers.
- President is the first citizen of India.
- ***Qualifications:*** (i) Indian citizen, (ii) age not less than 35 years, (iii) should have qualification for election to Lok Sabha, (iv) should not hold any office of profit, (v) should not be a Member of Parliament or State Legislature.
- ***Election:*** Indirectly elected through Electoral College consisting of elected members of both the Houses of the Parliament and elected members of the Legislative Assemblies of the States.
- According to the 70th Amendment Act, 1992, the expression 'States' include the National Capital Territory of Delhi and the Union Territory of Puducherry. Members of the Legislative Councils have no right to vote in the Presidential election.
- ***Powers:*** He makes appointments to all the constitutional posts.
- He can address either House of Parliament and dissolve Lok Sabha.
- All Bills passed by Parliament must receive his assent to become an Act.
- He issues ordinances when Parliament is not in session. No Money Bill can be introduced in Lok Sabha without his recommendation.
- He appoints 12 members of special repute in the Rajya Sabha.
- He has the power of *Pardon* to a criminal in special cases.
- The President holds the office for a period of five years. He is eligible for re-election.
- He is also entitled to rent free official residence called Rashtrapati Bhawan.

Vice-President

- ***Article 63*** of the Constitution stipulates a Vice-President for India.
- The Vice-President acts as the ex-officio Chairman of the Council of States (Rajya Sabha).
- He is elected by an electoral college consisting of the members of both Houses of Parliament in accordance with the system of proportional represen-tation by means of the single trans-ferable vote. He must be a citizen of India, not less than 35 years of age, and should be eligible for election as a member of the Council of States.

isputes in connection with election of a resident or a vice-president are to be a dealt ith in accordance with Article-71. Such disputes iall be decided by the Supreme Court.

Council of Ministers

he Constitution of India provides for a arliament system of government under which e President is only Constitutional ruler and the eal power is exercised by the Council of Ministers, headed by the Prime Minister.

Council of Ministers is composed of all Union Ministers—the Prime Minister, Cabinet Ministers and Ministers of State.

The Council of Ministers is Collectively responsible to the Lok Sabha.

The Prime Minister is a link between the President and the Council of Ministers.

Prime Minister

The Prime Minister is the leader of the majority party in the Parliament.

He is appointed by the President. Other Ministers are appointed by the president on his advice.

The Prime Minister is the head of the Government and the head of the Council of Ministers.

Jawaharlal Nehru was the first Prime Minister and the longest serving so far.

Union Legislature

- The Legislature of the Union, which is called 'Parliament' consists of the President and the two Houses of Parliament known as the Council of states (Rajya Sabha) and the House of the People (Lok Sabha).

RAJYA SABHA

- The Rajya Sabha is the Upper House of the Parliament and it is constituted of representatives from the States or the Constituent units of the Indian Union.
- It is a permanent body, one third of its members retiring after every two years.
- Its maximum strength is 250. Out of these, twelve members are nominated by the President from well-known personalities in the realm of Science, Art, Literature and Social Service. Rest of 238 representatives of the States and Union Territories are elected.
- Currently, the strength of the Rajya Sabha is 245.

LOK SABHA

- The Lok Sabha whose life is five years, is the Lower House of Parliament and comprises of members directly elected by the people.
- The House of the people (Lok Sabha) at present consists of 543 members directly elected from the states and Union Territories. (By the 104th amendment of the constitution the reservation for two members of Anglo Indian Community nominated by President have been abolished).
- The House of the People shall continue for five years (unless sooner dissolved) from the date of its meeting and no longer and the expiry of the said period of 5 years shall operate as dissolution of the House.

Parliamentary Committees

- There are several Parliamentary Committees to assist the Parliament in its deliberations.
- These are appointed or elected by the respective Houses of Lok Sabha and Rajya Sabha on a motion made or are nominated by their presiding officers.
- Among the Standing Committees, three are financial Committees:
  (*i*) Public Account Committee;
  (*ii*) Estimate Committee;
  (*iii*) Public undertaking Committee.

Speaker of Lok Sabha

- Speaker is elected by the Lok Sabha from among its members.
- The Speaker will have the final power to maintain order within the House of the People and to interpret its rules of procedure.
- A Deputy-Speaker is also elected to officiate in absence of the Speaker.
- *G.V. Mavlankar* was the first Speaker of the Lok Sabha (1952-1956).

Supreme Court

The Constitution provides for the Supreme Court, which consists of Chief Justice and 33 judges. They are appointed by the President of India.

Qualification and Tenure

Eligibility conditions for a judge of the Supreme Court are that he must be : (i) a citizen of India; (ii) a judge of a high court for a minimum period of 5 years; or (iii) an advocate of a high court for at least ten years or a distinguished jurist.

- Judges hold office till the age of 65.

They can resign earlier or can be removed by the President on the recommendation of the two Houses of the Parliament by 2/3rd majority of the members present and voting.

Powers

Original jurisdiction: Cases involving Government of India and the states or cases involving the enforcement of Fundamental Rights fall under original jurisdiction.

- *Appellate Jurisdiction:* In cases which are brought to it in the form of appeals against the judgement of the lower courts—It hears appeals in civil and criminal cases.

Advisory functions: the Supreme Court advises the President on the constitutionality of a particular legal matter. However, its advice is not binding on the President.

Other Powers:

1. it is a court of record and can punish for contempt of itself;
2. it can make rules for regulating the practice and procedure of courts with the approval of the President; and
3. it can recommend to the President the removal of chairman and members of the UPSC. Supreme Court enjoys the power of judicial review (right of the court which declares as unconstitutional, the laws passed by the legislature and orders issued by executive) though it is not specifically mentioned in the Constitution.

The first Chief Justice of India was H.J. Kania (1950-51).

Comptroller and Auditor General (CAG) (Article 148-151)

- The Comptroller and Auditor General of India is guardian of the public purse.
- It is his duty to see that not a *paisa* is spent out of consolidated fund of India or of a state without the authority of the appropriate legislature.
- He is appointed by President of India.
- A person with long administrative experience and knowledge of accounts is appointed.
- Holds office for 6 yrs or till 65 yrs of age.
- The President can remove him only on the recommendation of the 2 houses of Parliament (as in case of judge of Supreme Court).
- The CAG submits its reports to the President (in case of accounts relating to the Union Government) or to the State Governors (for State Government Accounts).
- The first CAG of India was *V Narahari Rao* (1948-1954).
- The CAG is not eligible for further office under the Union or State Governments. The expenses of the office of the CAG is charged to the Consolidated Fund of India.

Attorney General of India

- The Attorney General of India is the first law officer of the Government of India.
- Though he is not a member of cabinet he has the right to speak in the House of Parliament, but he has no right to vote.
- The Attorney General of India shall be appointed by the President and shall hold office during his pleasure.
- His duty shall be to give advice on such legal matter from time-to-time as may be referred to him by the President.
- To be appointed as Attorney General, a candidate must be qualified to be appointed as a Judge of the Supreme Court.
- The Attorney General can participate in proceedings of the Parliament without the Right to Vote (Article 88).
- The first Attorney General of Independent India was MC Setalvad (1950-1963).

PART - VI

THE STATES (ARTICLE 152 - 237)

THE GOVERNOR

- The Governor is appointed by the President and holds office during the pleasure of the President.
- Apart from the power to appoint the council of ministers, if the governor finds that the government of state cannot be carried on in accordance with the provisions of the constitution (Art. 356), he may send his report to the President who may assume to himself the functions of the government of the state. (This is popularly known as 'President's Rule').
- Article 161 gives the Governor the power to grant pardons, reprieves, remission of punishment to persons convicted under the state law.
- Article 171 states that the States where Legislative Councils exists, the Governor can nominate some members from amongst those distinguished in literature, science, arts, cooperative movement and social service.

STATES LEGISLATURE (ARTICLE 168 - 212)

- The state legislature consists of Governor and legislative assembly.
- In some state like *Bihar, Maharashtra, Andhra Pradesh, Karnataka, Uttar Pradesh and Telangana* have a legislative council.
- The membership of the council should not be more than *one-third* of the legislative assembly but not less than 40.
- The legislative assembly of each state shall be composed of members chosen by direct election on the basis of adult suffrage and the number of members shall not be more than 500 or less than 60.
- The assembly of Sikkim, Goa, Puducherry and Mizoram have less than 60 members.

HIGH COURTS (ARTICLE 214-232)

- The High Court stands at the apex of the State Judiciary.
- As per the Constitution, there shall be a High Court in each State. But there may be a common High Court for two or more States and Union Territory, if it is provided by a law of the Parliament. For example, the Chennai High Court has its Jurisdiction over the State of Tamil Nadu and the Union Territory of Puducherry.
- The State Government has no control over it.
- There are 25 High Courts in India.
- The Calcutta High Court, established in 1862, is the oldest High Court in India.

THE PANCHAYATS (ARTICLE 243-243 O)

- Panchayati Raj was introduced in India with a view to associate the people with administration at grass-root level.
- It is a three-tier system as recommended by Balwant Rai Mehta Committee.
- Introduced by the 73rd Amendment Act, 1992 which envisaged a three tier system of local governance.

  These are:

  1. Gram Panchayat at the village level
  2. Panchayat Samiti at the block level
  3. Zila Parishad at the district level.

Jurisdiction and Seat of High Courts

Name	Year	Territorial Jurisdiction	Seat
Allahabad	1866	Uttar Pradesh	Prayagraj (Bench at Lucknow)
Bombay	1862	Maharashtra, Goa, Dadar and Nagar Haveli and Daman and Diu	Mumbai (Benches at Nagpur, Panaji and Aurangabad)
Calcutta	1862	West Bengal and Andaman & Nicobar	Kolkata (Circuit Benches at Port Blair and Jalpaiguri)
Chhattisgarh	2000	Chhattisgarh	Bilaspur

Name	Year	Territorial Jurisdiction	Seat
Delhi	1966	Delhi	Delhi
Guwahati	1948	Assam, Nagaland, Mizoram and Arunachal Pradesh	Guwahati (Benches at Kohima, Aizawl and Itanagar)
Gujarat	1960	Gujarat	Ahmedabad
Himachal Pradesh	1971	Himachal Pradesh	Shimla
Jammu & Kashmir and Ladakh	1928	Jammu & Kashmir, Ladakh	Srinagar and Jammu
Jharkhand	2000	Jharkhand	Ranchi
Karnataka	1884	Karnataka	Bengaluru (Circuit Benches at Dharwar and Gulbarga)
Kerala	1958	Kerala & Lakshadweep	Kochi (Ernakulam)
Madhya Pradesh	1956	Madhya Pradesh	Jabalpur (Benches at Gwalior and Indore)
Madras	1862	Tamil Nadu & Puducherry	Chennai (Bench at Madurai)
Orissa	1948	Odisha	Cuttack
Patna	1916	Bihar	Patna
Punjab and Haryana	1966	Punjab, Haryana and Chandigarh	Chandigarh
Rajasthan	1949	Rajasthan	Jodhpur (Bench at Jaipur)
Sikkim	1975	Sikkim	Gangtok
Uttarakhand	2000	Uttarakhand	Nainital
Tripura	2013	Tripura	Agartala
Meghalaya	2013	Meghalaya	Shillong
Manipur	2013	Manipur	Imphal
Telangana	2019	Telangana	Hyderabad
Andhra Pradesh	2019	Andhra Pradesh	Amravati

HE MUNICIPALITIES (ARTICLE 243 P-243 ZG)

Big cities have municipal corporations headed by the elected Mayor.

For small towns there are elected boards or councils, in turn, elect their Presidents.

Introduced by the 74th Amendment Act, 1993 which envisages three types of urban local bodies, namely, municipality (nagar palika), city council (nagar panchayat).

Municipal governance in India was first introduced in Madras in 1688.

PART - XIII

RTICLE 301 - 307)

In this part from Article 301-307 trade, commerce and intercourse within the territory of India are given.

PART - XIV

RTICLE 308 - 323)

In this part services under the union and the states are given.

- ***Article 312:** All India Services* and ***Article 315:*** Public Service Commissions for the Union and for the States.
- The first Public Service Commission was set up in 1926, on the recommendations of the Lee Commission.

UNION PUBLIC SERVICE COMMISSION (UPSC)

- This Commission is responsible for:
  1. recruitment to all civil services and posts, under the Union Government by written examinations, interviews and promotions, and
  2. advising the Government on all matters relating to methods of recruitment, principles to be followed in making promotions and transfers. Its Chairman is appointed by the President.

STAFF SELECTION COMMISSION (SSC)

- The Union Government has constituted a Staff Selection Commission for recruitment to non-technical Class III posts in the central government and in subordinate offices.

- The Administrative Reforms Commission had recommended the setting up of such a Commission.
- The Commission has also been entrusted with the responsibility of making recruitment to Group 'B' services like Assistants' and Stenographers Grade 'C'.
- The Commission has a chairman and two members.

ELECTIONS (ARTICLE 324-329)

- The Constitution provides for an independent election commission to ensure free and fair election to the Parliament, the State legislature and the offices of President and Vice-President.
- Consists of Chief Election Commissioner +2 Election Commissioners. They all enjoy equal powers.
- The Chief Election Commissioner and other Election Commissioners are appointed by the President.
- Election Commissioners are appointed for a term of 5 yrs.
- They are not eligible for re-appointment. Also, they cannot hold any office of profit after their retirement.
- The Election Commission was established on 25th January, 1950 under Article 324 of the Constitution.
- The first Chief Election Commissioner was *Sukumar Sen.*

Functions

- Preparation of electoral rolls and keeping voters list updated.
- Recognition of various political parties and allotment of election symbols.

NITI AAYOG

- The Indian government has replaced Planing Commission with a new institution named **NITI Aayog (National Institution for Transforming India).**
- The Niti Aayog will comprise the following:
  1. Prime Minister of India as the Chairperson.
  2. Governing Council comprising the Chief Ministers of all the States and Lt. Governors of Territories.
  3. Regional Councils will be formed to address specific issues and contingencies impacting more than one state or a region. These will be formed for a specified tenure. The Regional Councils will be convened by the Prime Minister and will comprise of the Chief Ministers of States and Lt. Governors of Territories in the region. These will be chaired by the Chairperson of the NITI Aayog or his nominee.
  4. Experts, specialists and practitioners with relevant domain knowledge as special invitees nominated by the Prime Minister.
- The full-time organizational framework will comprise of, in addition to the Prime Minister as the Chairperson:
  1. Vice-Chairperson : To be appointed by the Prime Minister.
  2. Members : Full-time. : 3
  3. Part-time members : Maximum of 2 from leading universities research organizations and other relevant institutions in an ex-officio capacity. Part time members will be on a rotational basis.
  4. Ex Officio members : Maximum of 4 members of the Council of Ministers to be nominated by the Prime Minister.
  5. Chief Executive Officer : To be appointed by the Prime Minister for a fixed tenure, in the rank of Secretary to the Government of India.
  6. Secretariat as deemed necessary.

FINANCE COMMISSION

- The constitution of the Finance Commission is laid down in Art. 280.
- The chairman must be a person having experience in public affairs; and the other four members also having wide experience in financial matters.

It consists of Chairman and 4 other members.

- It shall be the duty of the Finance Commission to advice the President on matters such as the distribution between the Union and States of the net proceeds of taxes that is required to be shared. The Finance Commission is not a permanent body. It is dissolved after it has submitted its recommendations.

Important Amendments to the Constitution

First Amendment, 1951	:	Added Ninth Schedule.
Twenty-second Amendment, 1969	:	Formation of Meghalaya within the state of Assam was facilitated.
Twenty-sixth Amendment, 1971	:	The privy and privileges of the former rulers of Indian States were abolished.
Thirty-first Amendment, 1973	:	The upper limit of representation of states was raised from 500 to 525. The upper limit for representation of the UTs was reduced from 25 to 20.
Thirty-sixth Amendment, 1975	:	Sikkim was made a full-fledged state of Indian Union and it was included in the First Schedule.
Thirty-eight Amendment, 1975	:	This act led to the amendment of Article 123, Article 213 and Article 352 which stated that the satisfaction of President or of Governor contained in these Articles would be called in question in any court of law.
orty-second Amendment, 1976	:	This amendment was done in accordance with the recommendations of Swaran Singh Committee and included a number of amendments.
orty-third Amendment, 1977	:	It provided for the restoration of the Jurisdiction of the Supreme Court and High Courts, curtailed by the enactment of the Constitution (Forty-Second Amendment) Act, 1976.
orty-fourth Amendment, 1978	:	The right to property was deleted as Fundamental Right and was made a legal right.
ifty-third Amendment, 1986	:	The Act grants statehood to the Union Territory of Mizoram, thus making it the 23rd State of the Indian Unions.
ifty-sixth Amendment, 1987	:	The UT of Goa converted into Goa state through this amendment whereas Daman and Diu were organised under a new UT.
eventy-third Amendment, 1992	:	It is concerning Panchayati Raj.
eventy-fourth Amendment, 1992	:	It is regarding Municipal Boards and Corporations.
ighty-ninth Amendment, 2003	:	It provides for constitution of a separate National Commission for Scheduled Tribes. (Earlier, there was a combined National Commission for both SC/STs).
inety-first Amendment, 2003	:	It is regarding restricting the total number of Ministers including Prime Minister/Chief Minister in Lok Sabha and State Legislatures to 15% of the total number of the Union or State Legislatures.
nety-sixth Amendment, 2011	:	Amendment of 8th Schedule, it replaces 'Orissa' with 'Odisha'.
nety-eight Amendment, 2013	:	(Insert Article 371 J) To empower the Governor of Karnataka to take steps to develop Hydrabad Karnataka Region.

Ninety-ninth Amendment, 2015	:	The amendment is in toto quashed by Supreme Court on 16 October, 2015.
One hundredth and first Amendment, 2016	:	The act amends the Constitution to introduce "The Goods and Services Tax (GST)."
One hundredth and Third Amendment, 2019	:	The Act providing 10 per cent reservation in government jobs and educational institutions to Economically Weaker Sections (EWS) of General Category, came into effect on January 14, 2019.
One hundredth and Fourth Amendment, 2019	:	This Act ceased the reservation of seats for Anglo-Indians in the Lok Sabha and Legislative assemblies and extended reservation for SCs and STs for up to ten years.

NATIONAL SYMBOLS

STATE EMBLEM

- State Emblem of India is an adaptation from the Sarnath Lion Capital of Ashoka. It was adopted by the Government of India on January 26, 1950. In the adapted form, only three lions are visible, the fourth being hidden from the view.
- The wheel (Dharma Chakra) appears in relief in the centre of the abacus with a bull on the right and a horse on the left.
- The bell-shaped lotus has been omitted. The words "Satyameva Jayate" meaning "Truth alone triumphs" are inscribed below the Emblem in Devanagari script.

NATIONAL FLAG

- The National Flag of India is a horizontal tricolour of deep saffron (Kesari), white and dark green in equal proportion.
- In the centre of the white band there is a wheel in navy blue colour. It has 24 spokes.
- The ratio of the length and the breadth of the flag is 3 : 2. Its design was adopted by the Constituent Assembly of India on July 22, 1947.

NATIONAL ANTHEM

- Rabindranath Tagore's song 'Jana-gana-mana' was adopted by the Constituent Assembly as the National Anthem of India on January 24, 1950.

Jana-gana-mana-adhinayaka jaya he,
Bharata-bhagya-vidhata
Punjab-Sindh-Gujarat-Maratha-
Dravida-Utkala-Banga
Vindhya-Himachala-Yamuna-Ganga
Uchhala-jaladhi-taranga.
Tava subha name jage,
Tava subha asisa mange,
Gahe tava jaya gatha,
Jana-gana-mangala-dayak,
jaya he Bharata bhagya vidhata,
Jaya he, jaya he, jaya he,
Jaya jaya jaya, jaya he.

NATIONAL SONG

- Bankim Chandra Chatterji's 'Vande Matara which was a source of inspiration to the peo in their struggle for freedom, has been adop as National Song. It has an equal status with National Anthem.

Vande Mataram
Sujalam, suphalam, malayaja-shitalam,
Shasya shyamalam, Mataram
Shubhrajyotsna, pulkita yaminim,
Phulla kusumita drumadalashobhinim,
Subhasinim sumadhura—bhashinim,
Sukhadam, Varadam, Mataram.

- **National Bird and Animal of India:** Peac and Tiger.
- **National Aquatic Animal:** Dolphin
- **National Flower:** Lotus
- **National Calendar:** It was adopted on M: 22, 1957. It has 365 days in the year and the month of the year is Chaitra.

❐ ❐ ❐

GENERAL SCIENCE

PHYSICS

PHYSICAL QUANTITIES

Physical quantities may be divided in two classes:
1. Scalar Quantities 2. Vector Quantities

A scalar quantity is one which has only magnitude.

A vector quantity has both magnitude and direction.

Force, Velocity, Momentum, Acceleration are examples of vector quantities.

Mass, length, time, volume, speed, energy, work are examples of scalar quantities.

UNITS

All measurements in physics require standard units.

In 1960, the General Conference of Weights and Measures recommended that a metric system of measurements called the International System of Units, abbreviated as SI units, be used.

Some Important Units

S.No.	Units	Quantity
1.	Metre	Length
2.	Kilogram	Mass
3.	Second	Time
4.	Ampere	Electric Current
5.	Candela	Luminous Intensity
6.	Newton	Force
7.	Joule	Workdone
8.	Watt	Power
9.	Coulomb	Electric Charge
10.	Volt	Potential Difference
11.	Ohm	Electrical Resistance
12.	Farad	Capacitance
13.	Henry	Inductance
14.	Lumen	Luminous Flux

Very small distances are measured in micro-meters or (microns) (μm), angstroms (Å), nanometers (nm) and femtometres (fm).

MOTION

When a body changes its position with respect to something else as time goes on, we say the body is in motion.

There are two types of motion—translational (linear) and rotational (spin).

The motion of a car on a road is translational whereas the motion of a top, spinning on its axis is rotational.

SPEED

It is a scalar form of velocity and is defined as the distance travelled in one second.

$$\text{Speed} = \frac{\text{distance travelled}}{\text{time required}}$$

SI unit of speed is m/s.

VELOCITY

The distance covered by an object in a specified direction in unit time interval is called velocity.

The SI unit of velocity is m/s.

Velocity is a vector quantity.

ACCELERATION

The velocity of a body changes due to change in its speed or direction or both. The rate of change of the velocity of a body is called its acceleration.

$$\text{Acceleration} = \frac{\text{change in velocity}}{\text{time taken}}$$

FORCE AND MOTION

GRAVITATIONAL FORCE

It is the force of attraction between two masses.

It is gravitational force that holds the moon in its orbit round the earth and the earth in its orbit round the sun.

Newton's Law of Universal Gravitation states that every particle in the universe attracts every other particle with a force that is directly proportional to the product of their masses and inversely proportional to the square of the distance between them.

The value of G is 6.67×10^{-11} SI units.

CENTRIPETAL FORCE

The force acting towards the centre on a particle executing uniform circular motion is called centripetal force and is given by

$$F = \frac{mv^2}{r}$$

where, m = Mass of the object

v = Speed

r = Radius of the Circular Path

In case of the moon, gravitational force between the earth and the moon acts as the centripetal force.

Centripetal force always acts on the particle performing circular motion.

CENTRIFUGAL FORCE

The pseudo force that balances the centripetal force in uniform circular motion is called centrifugal force.

Centrifugal force is directed away from the centre along the radius.

The centrifugal force is zero exactly at the poles and maximum at the equator.

WEIGHT

The weight of a body is the force with which the earth attracts the body towards its centre.

The mass of a body is a constant quantity whereas its weight varies slightly from place-to-place on the earth.

The weight of a body is maximum at the poles and minimum at the equator. This variation in weight is due to:

1. the shape of the earth.
2. the rotation of the earth about its axis.

The weight of an object is less at high elevations than at sea level.

At the centre of the earth, the weight of a body would be zero.

On the surface of the moon the value of the acceleration due to gravity is nearly one-sixth of that on earth and, therefore, an object on the moon would weigh only one-sixth its weight on the earth. The mass of an object on the moon would be the same as on earth.

The weight of a body would be more if the earth stopped rotating. Conversely, if the speed of rotation were higher, the weight would be less.

A person weighs more in a lift, which is accelerating upward.

An astronaut feels weightless in a spaceship because he is not pushing against anything.

FRICTION

Friction is the force which opposes the relative motion of two surfaces in contact.

It is friction between the ground and the soles of our shoes that makes walking possible and it is lack of friction that makes our feet slip on highly polished surfaces.

Friction in machines wastes energy and also causes wear and tear. This friction is reduced by using (1) lubricants, and (2) ball bearings.

NEWTON'S LAWS OF MOTION

First Law

Every object continues in its state of rest or uniform motion in a straight line if no net force acts upon it. It is also known as *law of inertia*.

Examples: 1. An unwary passenger in a fast moving bus falls forward when it stops suddenly. This happens because the feet of the passenger come to rest suddenly whereas his upper part of body continues to be in motion. 2. A person getting down from a moving bus has to run some distance, in the direction of the bus, before stopping. If he does not run he is bound to fall because his feet come to rest whereas his body continues to be in motion.

Momentum

The momentum of a body is defined as the product of its mass and velocity.

Second Law

This law states that "the rate of change of momentum of a body is proportional to the applied force and takes place in the direction of the force."

If we express force (F) in Newtons, mass (*m*) in kilograms and acceleration (*a*) in metres per second squared, we can write the second law as; $F = ma$.

In travelling the same distance, a car consumes more fuel on a crowded road than on a free road. This happens because the car has to stop and start quite often on a crowded road. The repeated acceleration requires a force (second law), which ultimately comes from the fuel. On a free road the car runs at almost uniform speed requiring fewer accelerations and hence less fuel consumption.

Third Law

This law states that "to every action there is an equal and opposite reaction."

When a bullet is fired from a gun, equal and opposite forces are exerted on the bullet and the gun.

The engine in a jet aeroplane works on the same principle as a rocket but there is a difference in the method of obtaining the high velocity as jet.

IMPULSE

If a force acts on a body for a very short time, then the product of force and time is called the impulse.

Impulse= Change in momentum

= Force × Time

Application of Impulse

1. A cricket player draws his hand back while catching.
2. A person jumping on hard cement floor receives more injuries than a person jumping on muddy or sandy floor.

WORK, POWER AND ENERGY

WORK

Whenever a force acting on a body displaces it, work is said to be done.

Work = Force × Distance moved in the direction of force.

Work is a scalar quantity and its SI unit is Joule (J).

POWER

Power is defined as the rate of doing work.

$$\text{Power} = \frac{\text{Work done}}{\text{Time taken}}$$

The SI unit of power is Watt (W) and is also measured in horse power.

1 HP = 746 W

ENERGY

Energy is defined as the capacity to do work.

Kinetic Energy

The energy possessed by an object due to its motion is called kinetic energy and is described by the expression

$KE = \frac{1}{2}mv^2$; where, m = mass of the object

v = speed

Potential Energy

Potential energy is the energy possessed by the body by virtue of its position, configuration or any condition of stress or strain.

There are many examples of potential energy. A stone held at some height above the ground has potential energy. Water in an elevated reservoir possesses potential energy.

Transformation of Energy

S.No.	Equipment	Transformation
1.	Dynamo	Mechanical energy into electrical energy
2.	Microphone	Sound energy into electrical energy
3.	Loud Speaker	Electrical energy into sound energy
4.	Electric Bulb	Electrical energy into light and heat energy
5.	Battery	Chemical energy into electrical energy
6.	Electrical Motor	Electrical energy into mechanical energy

CENTRE OF GRAVITY

The centre of gravity of a body is the point where the whole weight of the body can be considered to act:

Racing cars are build low and with wide wheel bases to reduce the risk of overturning at sharp bends.

While crossing a river in a boat, passengers are not allowed to stand. This keeps the CG of the system (boat and passengers) low and ensures stability.

ARTIFICIAL SATELLITES

In the case of a satellite, the centripetal force is provided by the gravitational pull of the earth.

If the speed of a satellite is more than 11.2 km/s or 25,000 miles/hour, the satellite would escape the earth entirely and would never come back. This is called escape velocity.

The existence of gaseous atmosphere on the earth is due to the high value of its escape velocity.

Geostationary Satellites

Geostationary satellites are stationary with respect to an observer on the earth. Their time period is 24-hour. There height above the surface of earth is 36,000 km. They are always in equatorial plane and their orbits are circular. They are also called parking orbits.

DENSITY AND RELATIVE DENSITY

DENSITY

The mass per unit volume of a substance is calle its density.

$$\text{Density} = \frac{\text{Mass}}{\text{Volume}}$$

The SI unit of density is kilogram per metr cubed (kg/m^3).

The relative density of a substance is the ratio o the density of the substance to the density o water.

Relative density has no unit.

PRESSURE

Pressure is defined as force acting per unit are

$$\text{Pressure} = \frac{\text{Force}}{\text{Area}}$$

The SI unit of pressure is newton per metr squared or pascal.

Broad wooden sleepers are placed below the rai to reduce the pressure exerted by the weight o a train.

The pressure of water increases with dept therefore bottom of a dam is made much thicke than the top.

The pressure exerted on an enclosed liquid one place is transmitted equally throughout t liquid. This is called Pascal's Principle.

Hydraulic presses, hydraulic brakes, hydraul door closers, etc. are applications of the Pascal Principle.

At high attitudes where atmosphere pressure less nose bleeding may occur due to the great pressure of blood.

In an aircraft flying at high altitude, norm atmospheric pressure is maintained by the use air pumps. If this were not done, the crew a passengers would experience difficulty breathing and consequently face dangers.

Atmospheric pressure is measured with instrument called the *Barometer*.

ARCHIMEDE'S PRINCIPLE

- This principle states that when a body is wholly or partially immersed in a fluid, it experiences an upthrust (upward force) equal to the weight of the fluid displaced.
- An iron nail sinks in water whereas a ship made of iron and steel floats. This is due to the fact that a ship is hollow and contains air and, therefore, its density is less than that of water.
- The density of sea water is more than that of river water, due to this a ship sinks less in sea water. It is for this reason that a ship rises a little when it enters a sea from a river.
- It is because of the higher density of sea water that it is easier to swim in the sea.
- A balloon filled with a light gas, such as hydrogen, rises because the average density of the balloon and the gas is less than that of air. The balloon cannot rise indefinitely because the density of the air decreases with increasing altitude. At a certain height, where the density of air is equal to the average density of the balloon, it ceases to rise and drifts sideways with the wind.
- When an ice block floats in water the water level will remain the same when all the ice melts into water.
- A *hydrometer* is an instrument used for measuring the relative density of liquids.
- A special type of a hydrometer called *Lactometer* is used for testing milk by measuring its density.

SURFACE TENSION

- Surface tension is that property of liquids owing to which they tend to acquire minimum surface area.
- Surface tension is caused by molecular attractions.
- When a paint brush is dipped in water all its hair spread out but when it is taken out it is covered with a thin film of water which contracts due to surface tension and pulls the hair together.
- Liquid drops, such as raindrops, oildrops, drops of molten metals, dewdrops etc. are all spherical because their surface tend to contract in order to have minimum surface area. For a given volume, a sphere has the minimum surface area.
- Soaps and detergents lower the surface tension of water. This increases the wetting power of water or its ability to detach dirt particles from clothes and untensils.
- The force of attraction between unlike molecules is called **adhesion** and that between like molecules **cohesion.**
- The melted wax of a candle is drawn up into the wick by capillary action. Oil rises up a lamp wick for the same reason.
- If one end of a sugar cube is dipped into tea, the entire cube is quickly wet on account of capillary action.

VISCOSITY

- The force which opposes the relative motion between different layers of liquid or gases is called viscous force.
- Viscosity is the property of liquids and gases both.

BERNOULLI'S THEOREM

- According to Bernoulli's theorem, in case of streamline flow of incompressible and non-viscous fluid (ideal fluid) through a tube, total energy (sum of pressure energy, potential energy and kinetic energy) per unit volume of fluid is same at all points.

  1. When a bowler spins a ball, it changes its direction (swings) in the air due to unequal pressure acting on it.

HEAT

- Heat is that form of energy which flows from one body to other body due to difference in temperature between the bodies. The amount of heat contained in a body depends upon the mass of the body.

TEMPERATURE

- The temperature of a body is the quantity that tells how hot or cold it is with respect to some standard body.

MEASUREMENT OF TEMPERATURE

- Temperature is measured by a thermometer.
- A thermometer may be graduated in following scales—
  1. The upper and lower points of centigrade scale are 100°C and 0°C.
  2. The upper and lower points of Fahrenheit scale are 212°F and 32°F.
  3. The upper and lower points of Reaumur scale are 80°R and 0°R.
  4. The upper and lower points of Kelvin scale are 373K and 273K.
  5. The upper and lower points of Rankine scale are 672° Ra and 460° Ra.
- At –40 degrees both celsius and Fahrenheit scales will show identical readings.
- Water cannot be used in a thermometer becaues it freezes at 0°C and also because of its irregular expansion.

THERMAL EXPANSION

- Solids, liquids and gases generally expand when heated and contract when cooled.
- Gaps have to be left in railway tracks to make allowance for expansion, otherwise the rails will buckle. Allowance is made for the expansion of long steel bridges. One end of such bridge is fixed while the other rests on rollers.
- Telephone wires sag more in summer than in winter due to thermal expansion.

EXPANSION OF WATER

- Water has its minimum volume and maximum density at 4°C.

TRANSMISSION OF HEAT

- There are three ways of heat transmission: 1. Conduction; 2. Convection; 3. Radiation.

Conduction

- In this process, heat is transferred from one place to other place by the successive vibration of the particles of the medium without bodily movement of the particles of the medium.
- Conduction takes place mainly in solids.
- Air is a very bad conductor of heat. The goo insulating properties of wool, cotton, etc. ar mainly due to the air spaces they contain.

Convection

- In this process, heat is transferred by the actua movement of particles of the medium from on place to other place.
- In liquids and gases heat is transmitted b convection.

Radiation

- In this mode of heat transmission heat i transferred from one place to another withou effecting the intervening medium.

HEAT CAPACITY

- The heat capacity of a body is defined as th heat required to raise the temperature of the bod by 1K. Its SI unit is J/K.

SPECIFIC HEAT CAPACITY

- The specific heat capacity of a substance is th heat required to raise the temperature of a uni mass of the substance by 1K.
- Its SI unit is J/kg K.
- It is because of its high specific heat capacit that water is used as a cooling liquid in ca engine.

LATENT HEAT

- It is defined as the amount of heat absorbed o given out by a body during the change of state
- Each gram of ice that melts absorbs 336 J o heat.

EVAPORATION

- Water can change into the vapour state either b boiling or by evaporation at lower temperatures
- When sweat evaporates from the skin it draw much heat from the body and produces a coolin sensation.
- In summer, water is stored in pitchers for cooling Water oozes out of the pores of the pitchers an cools on evaporation.

The rate of evaporation increases with increase in temperature.

REFRIGERATOR

In a refrigerator, cooling is produced by the evaporation of a volatile liquid, freon, inside a copper coil (evaporator), which surrounds the freezer.

The cooling unit (freezer) in a refrigerator is fitted near the top to cool the whole of the interior.

RELATIVE HUMIDITY

Relative humidity is defined as the ratio of the mass of water vapour in a given volume of air to the mass required for saturating the same volume of air at the same temperature.

Relative humidity is measured with an instrument called the hygrometer.

PRESSURE COOKER

The boiling point of a liquid depends on external pressure.

When the atmospheric pressure is 76 cm of mercury, water boils at 100°C. But when the pressure is increased, the boiling point of water is raised.

In a pressure cooker, water boils at temperatures higher than 100°C due to increased pressure. The increased boiling temperature allows water to hold more heat which cooks food faster.

At higher altitudes, atmospheric pressure is reduced. This lowers the boiling point of water and food takes much longer to cook.

WAVE MOTION

Wave motion may be defined as the transfer of energy without the net transfer of matter.

If the particles of the medium vibrate perpendicular to the direction of propagation of wave, the wave is called transverse wave.

Light waves are transverse waves.

If the particles of the medium vibrate in the direction of propagation of wave, the wave is called longitudinal wave.

Sound waves are longitudinal waves.

ELECTROMAGNETIC WAVE

- Electromagnetic waves include an enormous range of frequencies—from radio waves with frequencies less than 10^5 Hz to gamma rays having frequencies greater than 10^{20} Hz.
- All electromagnetic wave have the same speed (3×10^8 m/s) in vacuum. The relation $v = n\lambda$ holds good for all electromagnetic waves.

RADIO AND TELEVISION TRANSMISSION

- Radio waves sent out by radio stations are reflected by the ionosphere and can be received anywhere on the earth.
- At night the radio reception improves because the layers of the ionosphere are not exposed to sunlight and are more settled.
- Radar (Radio detection and ranging) employs high frequency radio waves for detecting objects like ships and aeroplanes.
- In microwave oven, when the waves fall on the food, these are absorbed by water, fats, sugars and certain other molecules whose consequent vibrations produce heat. Since heating occurs inside the food, without warming the surrounding air, the cooking time is greatly reduced.
- In microwave oven, food cannot be cooked in metal vessels because the metal blocks out the microwaves.

LIGHT

- Light is a form of energy which is propagated as electromagnetic waves.
- Light is a transverse wave.
- Speed of light in vacuum is 3×10^8 m/s.
- Light takes 8 minute 16.6 second to reach from sun to earth.

REFLECTION

- When light is incident upon a surface, part of it is reflected. But certain surfaces like mirrors and polished metals reflect almost all the light incident upon them.
- The law of reflection states that the angle of incidence is equal to the angle of reflection.

- To see full image in a plane mirror, a person requires a mirror of at least half of his height.

INCLINED MIRROR (NO. OF IMAGES)

- When an object is placed between two inclined mirrors, several images of the object are formed.

CURVED MIRRORS

- There are two types of curved spherical mirrors— 1. Concave Mirror, 2. Convex Mirror.
- Concave mirror can concentrate the sun's radiation falling on it at one point, it can be used as a burning glass.
- Concave mirrors are also used in solar cookers.
- Large concave mirrors are used in reflecting telescopes for observing and photographing distant stars and other heavenly bodies.
- Concave mirror is also used as a shaving or make-up mirror.
- Small concave mirrors are used by dentists for examining teeth.
- Concave parabolic mirrors are used in searchlight and headlamps of cars.
- Convex mirrors are also used as rear view mirrors in vehicles.

REFRACTION

- When a ray of light passes from one medium to other it suffers a change in direction at the boundary of separation of two media. This phenomenon is called refraction.
- When a ray passes from one medium to another optically denser medium, e.g., from air to water or glass, it bends towards the normal. Conversely, a ray passing from water or glass into air is bent away from the normal.
- Rivers appear shallow, coin in a beaker filled with water appears raised, due to refraction.
- Another effect of refraction is the apparent upward bending of the immersed portion of a stick when dipped in water.
- It is due to refraction, produced by the earth's atmosphere, that the sun is visible for several minutes after it has set below the horizon. Thus, atmospheric refraction tends to lengthen the day.
- When the sun (or moon) is near the horizon, appears elliptical, i.e., with the vertical diamet less than the horizontal diameter. This happe because rays from the lower edge of the sun a bent more than those from the upper ed (Atmospheric Refraction).
- One of the most interesting effects of atmosphe refraction and Mirage is a combined effect atmospheric refraction and total intern reflection.

DISPERSION

- White light consists of seven colours—viol indigo, blue, green, yellow, orange and red. The colours are called the spectrum of the white lig
- Violet has the minimum wavelength (or maximu frequency) and red the maximum wavelength (minimum frequency).
- Due to different speeds, the colours are refract through different angles and therefore, when narrow beam of white light passes through glass prism, it is split up into its constitu colours. This separation of light into colours called dispersion.

COLOUR OF OBJECTS

- We see objects because of the light they refle
- When a rose is viewed in white light, its pet appear red and the leaves appear green, beca the petals reflect the red part of the white li and leaves reflect the green part. The remain colours are absorbed. When the same rose viewed in green light, the petals will app black and the leaves green. In blue or yell light both the petals and leaves will appear bla
- Red, blue and green are primary colours.

LENSES

- There are mainly two types of lenses:
  1. Convex or Converging Lens
  2. Concave or Diverging Lens
- Converging or convex lens is used a magnifying glass.
- Power of a lens is its capacity to deviate a

Power of a lens is measured as the reciprocal of the focal length.

$$P = \frac{1}{f}$$

SI unit of power of lens is dioptre (D).

The power of a converging lens is positive and that of a diverging lens is negative.

For all positions of the object, the images formed by diverging (concave) lens are virtual, erect and diminished.

YE

The light entering the eye is focused by the eye-lens to form an image on the retina.

In front of the eye, lens is the coloured part of eye, called the iris, which automatically adjusts the size of the pupil to the intensity of light falling on it.

In bright light the iris automatically shuts tighter, reducing the amount of light entering the pupil. This protects the retina from getting damaged.

When a person enters a dark room after being in bright light, he is not able to see clearly for a while because the iris is unable to dilate the pupil immediately.

Least distance of distinct vision is 25 cm.

EFECTS OF VISION

A person suffering from long sight (hypermetropia) can clearly see objects at infinity but cannot see near objects clearly. This defect is caused by the eyeball being too short and can be corrected by wearing converging lenses.

In the case of a person suffering from short sight (myopia), the eye ball is too long and distant objects are focused in front of the retina. This defect can be corrected by wearing diverging lenses.

Astigmatism: Curvature of cornea becomes irregular and image is not clear. Cylindrical lens is used.

CATTERING OF LIGHT

When light falls on atoms and molecules, it is scattered in all directions.

- Scattering of light is maximum for violet colour and minimum for red colour.
- Blue colour of sky is due to scattering of light.
- In the evening, the sun is lower in the sky and its light has to traverse a longer path through the atmosphere to reach an observer. Thus, at sunset, blue, green and other colours having been scattered only red and some orange light reach us and the sun appears a deep orange-red.
- In outerspace, *i.e.,* beyond the atmosphere, there is nothing to scatter the sunlight and therefore the sky appears dark and stars are visible even in the presence of the sun.

INTERFERENCE OF LIGHT

- The superposition of two (or more) waves of the same kind that pass the same point in space at the same time is called interference.
- Beautiful colours seen in soap bubbles and oil films on water are produced due to the interference of white light reflected by these surfaces.
- LASER (Light Amplification by Stimulated Emission of Radiation) is an optical device which produces an intense beam of coherent monochromatic light.
- Examples of Interference of Light: Holography, Laser.

DIFFRACTION OF LIGHT

- When a beam of light passes through a narrow slit or an aperture, it spreads out to a certain extent into the region of geometrical shadow. This is an example of diffraction, *i.e.,* of the failure of light to travel in a straight line.

SOUND

- Sound waves are longitudinal and cannot travel in vacuum. The transmission of sound requires a medium : air, liquid or solid.
- The longitudinal mechanical waves which lie in the frequency range 20 Hz to 20,000 Hz are called audible or sound waves. These waves are sensitive to human ear.

- The longitudinal mechanical waves having frequencies less than 20 Hz are called Infrasonic. These waves are produced by sources of bigger size such as earthquakes, volcanic eruptions, ocean waves etc.
- The longitudinal waves having frequencies greater than 20,000 Hz are called ultrasonic waves. Human ear cannot detect these waves. But some animals such as cats, dogs, bats can detect these waves.

PITCH

- The pitch (shrillness of a sound) depends on its frequency.
- A sound of higher frequency has a higher pitch.
- The pitch of a woman's voice is higher than that of a man.

LOUDNESS

- The relative loudness of a sound is measured in decibels (db).
- All stringed instruments, such as the violin, sitar, guitar, etc. have sound boxes attached to increase the loudness.

SPEED OF SOUND

- The presence of water vapour in the air increases the speed of sound.
- Sound travels faster through warm air than through cold air. The speed of sound is higher on a hot day than on a cold day.
- Thunder is heard much after the flash of lightning is seen because of the wide difference in the speeds of light and sound.

REFLECTION OF SOUND

- When a sound wave is reflected by a distant obstacle, such as a wall or a cliff, an echo is heard.
- To hear echo, the minimum distance between the observer and reflector should be 17 m.
- Exploration of underwater gas and oil is done by detecting the echoes of shock waves produced by explosions on the water surface.
- Bats emit ultrasonic waves of frequencies up to 80,000 Hz and use the reflection of these waves (echoes) to determine the presence and distance of objects on their way and from them respectively.

DOPPLER EFFECT

- The Doppler effect is the change in frequency of a wave (sound or light) due to the motion of the source or observer.
- It is due to the Doppler effect that the whistle of a train appears shriller when it approaches a listener than when it moves away from him.

ELECTRICITY

- Electricity produced by friction between two dissimilar objects is known as static electricity. Depending on the nature of the objects, one acquires a positive charge and the other an equal negative charge. For example, if a glass rod is rubbed with silk, the rod acquires positive charge and the silk an equal negative charge.
- *Lightning* is a gigantic electric discharge occurring between two charged clouds or between a charged cloud and the earth.

CONDUCTOR

- Conductors are those materials which allow electricity (charge) to pass through themselves.
- Metals conduct electricity because they have a large number of conduction or free electrons.

INSULATORS

- Insulators are those materials which do not allow electricity to flow through themselves. Insulators have no free electrons.

SUPER CONDUCTORS

- The resistance of metals to flow of electricity reduces with decreasing temperature. At temperatures near absolute zero, metals have almost zero resistance and became super conductors.

SEMI-CONDUCTORS

- Certain materials, such as silicon and germanium have electrical resistivity intermediate between those of conductors and insulators. These materials are termed as semi-conductors.

Semi-conductors are good insulators in their pure crystalline form but their conductivity increases when small amounts of impurities are added to them.

ELECTRIC CURRENT

Electric current is simply the flow of electric charge. In solid conductors the flow of electrons and in fluids the flow of ions as well as electrons constitute the current.

SI units of electric current is Ampere (A).

ELECTRICAL RESISTANCE

When electric current flows through a conductor, e.g., a metallic wire, it offers some obstruction to the current. This obstruction offered by the wire is called its electrical resistance.

SI unit of Resistance is ohm.

OHM'S LAW

If physical conditions like temperature, intensity of light etc. remains unchanged then electric current flowing through a conductor is directly proportional to the potential difference across its ends.

ELECTRIC MOTOR

In an electric motor, electrical energy is converted into mechanical energy.

Electric fans, mixers, washing machines, etc. work on electric motors.

INVERTER

An inverter is a device which converts DC to AC. The inverters used in homes and offices are specially designed to:

1. Convert DC from a battery to AC, and
2. Charge the battery.

FUSE

Electric fuse is a protective device used in series with an electric appliance to save it from being damaged due to high current.

A fuse is a short piece of wire made of a tin-lead alloy, which has a low melting point.

Fuses are always connected in the live wire in series.

COST OF ELECTRICITY

- The consumption of electrical energy in a house is measured in the unit kWh.
- Kilowatt hour is equal to the energy consumed in the circuit at the rate of 1 kilowatt for 1 hour.

MAGNETISM

- A magnet attracts and holds pieces of iron but does not attract pieces of copper.
- Iron, cobalt, nickel and certain alloys are strongly magnetic whereas copper, wood, glass, etc. are non-magnetic.
- Our earth behaves as a powerful magnet whose south pole is near the geographical north pole and whose north pole is near the geographical south pole.

ATOMIC & NUCLEAR PHYSICS

- Atom consists of three fundamental particles electron, proton and neutron. All the protons and neutrons are present in the central core of atom called nucleus. Electrons revolve around the nucleus.
- The total number of protons in the nucleus is called atomic number (Z).
- The total number of proton and neutrons in the nucleus is called mass number (A).
- Ernest Rutherford, discovered nucleus by the scattering of α-particles from gold foil.

RADIOACTIVITY

- Henry Bacquerel (1896) observed that a photographic plate blackened, when placed near double sulphate of potassium and uranium. He further observed that uranium emitted special kind of rays. They were called Becqueral rays.
- Pierre and Marie Curie observed that the radiation from pitchblende was four times stronger than uranium. In 1898, they finally discovered two new substances—Polonium and Radium. These newly discovered substances were called radioactive substances and this property of these substances was named radioactivity.
- No radioactive substance emits both α and β particles simultaneously.

X-RAYS

- X-rays are electromagnetic radiations having wavelength from a fraction of an Angestrom to about 100Å. They were discovered by Rontgen during his studies on the electrical discharge phenomena in gases—he found that an unknown radiation was produced when electrons collided with the walls of the tubes.

ATOMIC ENERGY

- India today ranks sixth in the atomic energy programmes. It has developed the required know-how and expertise to manufacture nuclear weapons, but it believes in the peaceful uses of atomic power. The Atomic Energy Commission was set-up in the country in 1948 under the Chairmanship of Dr. H. J. Bhabha.
- ***Bhabha Atomic Research Centre (BARC):*** The Bhabha Atomic Research Centre at Trombay near Mumbai (Maharashtra) has four research reactors: (*i*) APSARA—It is the first atomic reactor in Asia; (*ii*) CIRUS—It is a joint Indo-Canadian project; (*iii*) PURNIMA II—a zero energy fast reactor, and (*iv*) DHRUVA—a high power completely indigenous nuclear research reactor with most advanced laboratories in the world. Another fast breeder reactor KAMINI at Kalpakkam has been constructed. Today India is the seventh country in the world and the first developing nation to have mastered the fast breeder reactor technology.
- **Nuclear Power:** Under Nuclear Power Corporation of India Limited (NPCIL) there are seven nuclear power stations in operation in six States: (*i*) Tarapur—Maharashtra, (*ii*) Rawatbhata —Rajasthan, (*iii*) Kalpakkam—Tamil Nadu, (*iv*) Narora—U.P., (*v*) Kakrapara—Gujarat, (*vi*) Kaiga—Karnataka and (*vii*) Kudankulam—Tamil Nadu.
- **Heavy Water:** Heavy water is one of the essential input for Pressurised Heavy Water Reactors (PHWRs) used both as a coolant and moderator. The first heavy water plant was set-up in 1962 in Nangal. Subsequently 7 more plants have been set-up at (*i*) Baroda, (*ii*) Tuticorin, (*iii*) Kota, (*iv*) Talcher, (*v*) Thal, (*vi*) Hazira and (*vii*) Manuguru.
- **Research and Development Centres:** Four research centres namely (*i*) Bhabha Atomic Research Centre, Trombay (Maharashtra), (*ii*) Indira Gandhi Centre for Atomic Research, Kalpakkam (Tamil Nadu), (*iii*) Centre for Advanced Technology, Indore (Madhya Pradesh). (*iv*) Variable Energy Cyclotron Centre at Kolkata (West Bengal) are focal points of research and development work in nuclear energy and related discipline.
- **India's Nuclear Explosions:** On May 18, 1974 India conducted her first underground nuclear explosion at Pokhran (Rajasthan) in the Thar desert, 20 km. away from Jaisalmer, at a depth of more than 100 metres. The successful explosion made India the sixth nuclear nation in the world.
- India conducted 5 nuclear explosion tests at Pokhran in two phases on May 11 and May 13 1998 and became a nuclear power state.

IMPORTANT INVENTIONS

Name of Invention	*Inventor*	*Nationality*	*Year*
Aeroplane	Orville & Wilbur Wright	U.S.A.	1903
Ball-Point Pen	John J. Loud	U.S.A.	1888
Barometer	Evangelista Torricelli	Italy	1644
Bicycle	Kirkpatrick Macmillan	Britain	1839-40
Bifocal Lens	Benjamin Franklin	U.S.A.	1780
Car (Petrol)	Karl Benz	Germany	1888
Celluloid	Alexander Parkes	Britain	1861
Cinema	Nicolas & Jean Lumiere	France	1895

Name of Invention	Inventor	Nationality	Year
Clock (mechanical)	I-Hsing & Liang Ling-Tsan	China	1725
Diesel Engine	Rudolf Diesel	Germany	1895
Dynamo	Hypolite Pixii	France	1832
Electric Lamp	Thomas Alva Edison	U.S.A.	1879
Electric Motor (DC)	Zenobe Gramme	Belgium	1873
Electric Motor (AC)	Nikola Tesla	U.S.A.	1888
Electro-magnet	William Sturgeon	Britain	1824
Electronic Computer	Dr. Alan M. Turing	Britain	1943
Film (moving outlines)	Louis Prince	France	1885
Film (musical sound)	Dr. Le de Forest	U.S.A.	1923
Fountain Pen	Lewis E. Waterman	U.S.A.	1884
Gramophone	Thomas Alva Edison	U.S.A.	1878
Helicopter	Etienne Oehmichen	France	1924
Jet Engine	Sir Frank Whittle	Britain	1937
Laser	Charles H. Townes	U.S.A.	1960
Lift (Mechanical)	Elisha G. Otis	U.S.A.	1852
Locomotive	Richard Trevithick	Britain	1804
Machine Gun	James Puckle	Britain	1718
Microphone	Alexander Graham Bell	U.S.A.	1876
Microscope	Z. Janssen	Netherlands	1590
Motor Cycle	G. Daimler	Germany	1885
Photography (on film)	John Carbutt	U.S.A.	1888
Printing Press	Johann Gutenberg	Germany	c.1455
Razor (safety)	King C. Gillette	U.S.A.	1895
Refrigerator	James Harrison & Alexander Catlin	U.S.A.	1850
Safety Pin	Walter Hunt	U.S.A.	1849
Sewing machine	Barthelemy Thimmonnier	France	1829
Ship (steam)	J.C. Perier	France	1775
Ship (turbine)	Hon. Sir C. Parsons	Britain	1894
Skyscraper	W. Le Baron Jenny	U.S.A.	1882
Slide Rule	William Oughtred	Britain	1621
Steam Engine (condenser)	James Watt	Britain	1765
Steel Production	Henry Bessemer	Britain	1855
Steel (stainless)	Harry Brearley	Britain	1913
Submarine	David Bushnell	U.S.A.	1776
Tank	Sir Ernest Swinton	Britain	1914
Telegraph	M. Lammond	France	1787
Telegraph Code	Samuel F.B. Morse	U.S.A.	1837
Telephone (perfected)	Alexander Graham Bell	U.S.A.	1876
Television (mechanical)	John Logie Baird	Britain	1926
Television (electronic)	P.T. Farnsworth	U.S.A.	1927
Thermometer	Galileo Galilei	Italy	1593.
Transformer	Michael Faraday	Britain	1831
Transistor	Bardeen, Shockley & Brattain	U.S.A.	1948
Washing Machine (elec.)	Hurley Machine Co.	U.S.A.	1907
Zip-Fastener	W.L. Judson	U.S.A.	1891

Important Discoveries

Discovery	*Discoverer*	*Nationality*	*Year*
Aluminium	Hans Christian Oerstedt	Denmark	1827
Atomic number	Henry Moseley	England	1913
Atomic structure of matter	John Dalton	England	1803
Chlorine	C.W. Scheele	Sweden	1774
Electromagnetic induction	Michael Faraday	England	1831
Electromagnetic waves	Heinrich Hertz	Germany	1886
Electromagnetism	Hans Christian Oersted	Denmark	1920
Electron	Sir Joseph Thomson	England	1897
General theory of relativity	Albert Einstein	Switzerland	1915
Hydrogen	Henry Cavendish	England	1766
Law of electric conduction	Georg Ohm	Germany	1827
Law of electromagnetism	Andre Ampere	France	1826
Law of falling bodies	Galileo	Italy	1590
Laws of gravitation & motion	Isaac Newton	England	1687
Laws of planetary motion	Johannes Kepler	Germany	1609-10
Magnesium	Sir Humphry Davy	England	1808
Neptune (Planet)	Johann Galle	Germany	1846
Neutron	James Chadwick	England	1932
Nickel	Axel Cronstedt	Sweden	1751
Nitrogen	Daniel Rutherford	England	1772
Oxygen	Joseph Priestly, C.W. Scheele	England, Sweden	1772
Ozone	Christian Schonbein	Germany	1839
Pluto	Clyde Tombaugh	U.S.A	1930
Plutonium	G.T. Seaborg	U.S.A	1940
Proton	Ernest Rutherford	England	1919
Quantum Theory	Max Planck	Germany	1900
Radioactivity	Antoine Bacquerel	France	1896
Radium	Pierre & Marie Curie	France	1898
Silicon	Jons Berzelius	Sweden	1824
Special theory of relativity	Albert Einstein	Switzerland	1905
Sun as centre of solar system	Copernicus	Poland	1543
Uranium	Martin Klaproth	Germany	1789
Uranus (Planet)	William Herschel	England	1781
X-rays	Wilhelm Roentgen	Germany	1895

Scientific Instruments

Name of Instrument	*Used for*
Altimeter	measuring altitude
Ammeter	measuring strength of an electric current
Anemometer	measuring the velocity of wind
Audiometer	measuring level of hearing
Barometer	measuring atmospheric pressure
Callipers	measuring the internal and external diameters of tubes
Calorimeter	measuring quantity of heat
Compass	finding out direction
Dynamo	converting mechanical energy into electrical energy
Galvanometer	detecting and determining the strength of small electric currents
Hydrometer	measuring specific gravity of a liquid
Hygrometer	measuring the humidity in the atmosphere
Lactometer	measuring the purity of milk
Manometer	measuring the gaseous pressure
Micrometer	measuring minute distances, angles, etc.
Microscope	seeing magnified view of very small objects
Photometer	measuring intensity of light from distant stars
Pyrometer	measuring high temperatures
Radar	detecting and finding the presence and location of moving objects like aircraft, missile, etc.
Radiometer	measuring the emission of radiant energy
Rain Gauge	measuring the amount of rainfall
Seismograph	measuring and recording the intensity and origin of earthquake shocks
Sextant	measuring altitude and angular distances between two objects or heavenly bodies
Spectrometer	measuring the refractive indices
Spherometer	measuring the curvature of spherical objects/surface
Sphygmomanometer	measuring blood pressure
Stethoscope	ascertaining the condition of heart and lungs by listening to their function
Stroboscope	viewing objects that are moving rapidly with a periodic motion as if they were at rest
Tachometer	measuring the rate of revolution or angular speed of a revolving shaft
Telescope	viewing magnified images of distant objects
Thermocouple	measuring the temperature inside furnaces and jet engines
Thermometer	measuring human body temperature
Thermostat	regulating constant temperature
Ultrasonoscope	measuring utrasonic sounds
Viscometer	measuring the viscosity of a fluid
Voltmeter	measuring potential difference between two points.

CHEMISTRY

ELEMENTS

- An element may be defined as a substance which is made by same type of atoms and it can neither be broken into, nor built from two or more simpler substances by any known physical or chemical methods, e.g., copper, silver, hydrogen, carbon, oxygen, nitrogen, gold, iron etc.

COMPOUNDS

- A compound may be defined as a substance which contains two or more elements combined in some fixed proportion by weight and which can be decomposed into two or more elements by any suitable method.
- The properties of a compound are entirely different from those of the elements from which it is made.
- Some common examples of compounds are water, sugar, salt, aspirin, chloroform, alcohol and ether.

MIXTURES

- A material containing two or more elements or compounds in any proportion is a mixture.
- The components of a mixture can be separated by physical means like filtration, sublimation and distillation.

ATOMIC STRUCTURE

ATOM

- Atom is the smallest part of the element that takes part in a chemical reaction. Atom of an element can not be changed into that of another element by a chemical or physical means. It does not exist in free state.

MOLECULE

- A molecule is the smallest part of an element or compound that is capable of existing independently.

ATOMIC WEIGHT (OR ATOMIC MASS)

- The atomic mass of an element is the number of times its atom is heavier than 1/12th of the mass of carbon (C^{12}) atom.
- The unit used to measure atomic mass is called atomic mass unit, *i.e.*, amu.

ELECTRON

- The electron is a fundamental particle of an atom which carries a unit negative charge. It was discovered by J.J. Thomson in 1897.

PROTON

- It is a fundamental particle of an atom carrying a unit positive charge. It was discovered by Rutherford and Goldstein in 1886.

NEUTRON

- It is a fundamental particle of an atom carrying no charge. It was discovered by Chadwick in 1932.

ISOTOPES

- The atoms of the same element having different mass numbers are called isotopes.

ISOBARS

- Elements having the same atomic mass but differ in atomic number are called isobars.

ISOTONES

- Elements having the same number of neutrons are called isotones.

OXIDATION AND REDUCTION

- Oxidation is a process in which a substance adds on oxygen or loses hydrogen. In modern terms oxidation is the process in which a substance loses electrons.
- Reduction is a process in which a substance adds on hydrogen or loses oxygen. In modern terms reduction is the process in which a substance gains electrons.
- Oxidation and reduction always occur simultaneously. If one substance is oxidised another is reduced. The reaction in which this oxidation-reduction process occurs is called a redox reaction.

- Oxidising agents are substances which bring about the oxidation of other substances, e.g., Potassium Permanganate, Potassium Dichromate, Nitric Acid, Hydrogen Peroxide, etc.
- Reducing agents are substances which bring about the reduction of other substances, e.g., hydrogen sulphide, hydrogen, carbon, sulphur dioxide, etc.

ACIDS, BASES AND SALTS

ACID

- An acid is any compound that can react with a base to form a salt, the hydrogen of the acid being replaced by positive metallic ion. According to modern theory, an acid is a compound which yields hydrogen ions (protons) to a base in a chemical reaction. In a water solution, an acid tastes sour, turns blue litmus red and produces free hydrogen ions.

Acid	Sources
Citric Acid	Lemons or Oranges (Citrus Fruits)
Lactic acid	Sour milk
Tartaric acid	Grapes
Acetic acid	Vinegar
Maleic acid	Apples
Oxalic acid	Tomato
Formic acid	Red ants

BASES

- Such compounds which gives salt and water with acid known as bases. Bitter in taste, turns red litmus paper into blue, contains replaceable hydroxyl group.
- Some important bases are sodium hydroxide, potassium hydroxide, sodium carbonate and ammonium hydroxide.
- All alkalies are bases but all bases are not alkalies because all bases are not soluble in water.

SALTS

- Salts are ionic compounds containing a positive ion (cation) and a negative ion (anion).
- When an acid reacts with a base, a salt and water are formed. This reaction is called neutralization since the acid and base neutralize each other's effect.

ELECTROLYSIS

- The process of decomposition of an electrolyte by the passage of an electric current through its molten state or its aqueous solution is called electrolysis.
- Device through which electric current is passed known as electrodes.

METALLURGY

- Metals occur in nature, in the native (in free state) as well as in the combined state.
- Naturally occurring materials containing metals are called minerals.
- A mineral from which a given metal is obtained economically is called an ore.
- The process of extraction of a metal in a pure state on a large scale from its ore by Physical and Chemical means is called metallurgy.
- The rocky and siliceous matter that associated with the ore is known as gangue.
- Substance that is added to ore to remove the gangue is known as flux.
- The process of removal of gangue from the ore is known as concentration.
- Calcination is the heating of the ore in the absence of air. This method is employed for obtaining the metal oxides from carbonates and hydroxides.
- Roasting is the heating of the ore in the presence of air. On roasting, part of the ore is oxidised to form an oxide. This oxide is then reduced to the metal.
- The industrial reduction process for obtaining metal from the treated ore is called smelting.

AMALGUM

- An alloy in which one of the component metals is mercury is known as amalgum.

IRON AND STEEL

- Iron is extracted from its ores by the blast furnace process.

- Iron obtained from blast furnace is called pig iron or cast iron containing about 5% carbon.
- Pure iron is called wrought iron which does not contain carbon more than 0.2%, or any other impurities or constituents.
- Steel contains 0.25% – 2% carbon and varying amounts of other elements.

CARBON AND ITS COMPOUNDS

ALLOTROPY

- Such substances which having the same chemical properties, but differ in physical properties, known as allotropes and this property is called allotropy.

DIAMOND

- Diamond is the purest form of carbon.
- It is non-conductor of heat and electricity.
- It is the hardest natural substance.
- It burns in air at 900°C and gives out CO_2.

GRAPHITE (BLACK LEAD)

- It is good conductor of heat and electricity.
- Graphite is used in making lead pencils.
- Graphite is also used as electrodes, lubricant, moderators, electrotyping and carbon arc.

AMORPHOUS FORMS OF CARBON

1. Wood Charcoal – Obtained from wood
2. Sugar Charcoal – Obtained from cane sugar
3. Bone or Animal Charcoal – Obtained from animal bones
4. Coke Charcoal – Obtained from coal

CARBON MONOXIDE (CO)

- Carbon monoxide is an active poison and is very dangerous as it is a colourless and odourless gas and can not, therefore, be easily detected.
- The extremely poisonous nature of carbon monoxide is a result of its combining with the haemoglobin of the blood to form carboxyhaemoglobin, which is not decompassed by any of the processes in the body.

HYDROCARBONS

- Compounds of carbon and hydrogen are called hydrocarbon.
- A natural source of hydrocarbon is petroleum obtained from sedimentary rocks.
- Compounds having the same molecular formula but differ in properties due to different structural formula known as isomers and this property is called isomerism.

SATURATED HYDROCARBONS (ALKANES)

- Containing single covalent bonds only.
- Such compounds are, in general, called alkanes for instance, Methane, Ethane, Propane, Butane.

UNSATURATED HYDROCARBONS

- Containing multiple bonds.
- Compounds with double bonds are called alkenes, e.g. ethylene, propyene etc. and triple bond containing compounds are called alkynes e.g. acetylene, propyne etc.
- Benzene is an unsaturated cyclic hydrocarbon with the structure.
- Compounds derived from benzene are called aromatic compounds.

FUELS

Solid Fuels

- These contain carbon and, during combustion form mainly carbon dioxide and carbon monoxide with a large amount of heat.
- Examples of solid fuels are wood, coal, coke and paraffin wax.

Liquid Fuels

- These are basically mixtures of several hydrocarbons. During combustion, they form carbon dioxide and water.
- Liquid fuels are obtained as different fraction during the distillation of petroleum.
- Examples of liquid fuels are kerosene oil, petrol diesel oil and alcohol.

Gaseous Fuels

- Gaseous fuels do not leave ash on burning and have high content of heat.
- The main gaseous fuels are liquefied petroleum gas (LPG, mainly a mixture of propane and

butane and used in homes for cooking, water gas ($CO + H_2$), producer gas ($CO + N_2$), coal gas (mixture of hydrogen, methane, ethylene, carbon monoxide, nitrogen, oxygen and carbon dioxide) and natural gas (mixture of methane, ethane, propane and butane with traces of higher hydrocarbons obtained from oil well, above petroleum).

PETROLEUM AND NATURAL GAS

- Natural gas contains about 80% methane and 10% ethane, the remaining 10% being a mixture of higher gaseous hydrocarbons.
- Compressed Natural Gas (CNG) is natural gas filled in cylinders under high pressure.
- The quality of petrol for use in car engines is denoted by their anti-knock properties.
- To increase octane number, tetra ethyl lead (TEL) is added to petrol.

HEAVY WATER

- Chemically heavy water is deuterium oxide.
- Heavy water is used in nuclear reactors as a moderator because it slows the fast moving neutrons.

Hard and Soft Water

- Water which produces lather with soap solution readily is called soft water.
- Water which does not produce lather with soap solution readily is called hard water.
- The hardness of water is due to presence of the bicarbonates, chlorides and sulphates of calcium and magnesium.
- Temporary hardness of water is due to the presence of bicarbonates of calcium and magnesium.
- Permanent hardness of water is due to presence of sulphates, chlorides, nitrates of calcium and magnesium.

GLASS

- Ordinary glass is solid mixture of silica, sodium silicate and calcium silicate.
- Soft glass is a soda-lime silicate glass. It melts at low temperature. It is used in manufacturing of bottles, test tubes etc.
- Hard glass is potash lime silicate and melts at high temperature in comparison to soft glass and is used in manufacturing of flask etc.
- Flint glass is a lead potash silicate and is used in manufacturing of prism, lens and optical instruments.
- Pyrex glass is a mixture of sodium aluminium borosilicates. It is used in manufacturing of high quality equipments in laboratory because it does not melt at very high temperature.
- Safety glass is prepared by placing a layer of transparent plastic glass between two layers of glass by means of a suitable adhesive. It is used in making wind screen of automobiles, aeroplanes, trains etc.

CEMENT

- The approximate composition of Portland cement is:
  1. Calcium Oxide → 62%
  2. Silica → 22%
  3. Alumina → 7.5%
  4. Magnesia → 2.5%
  5. Ferric Oxide → 2.5%
- A small amount of gypsum is added to slow down the setting of cement.
- Cement containing excess amount of lime cracks during setting while cement containing less amount of lime is weak in strength.
- Cement containing no iron is white but hard to burn.

POLYMERS AND PLASTICS

- A polymer is a large molecule, built up from many hundreds of thousands of small unit called monomeric units or monomers.
- The process of formation of polymers from monomers is called polymerization.
- Plastics are cross-linked polymers and very tough.
- Some examples of plastics are — Celluloid, Bakelite and Vinyl Plastics.

RUBBER

- Natural and Synthetic rubbers are examples of polymers.
- Natural rubber is isomer of isoprene.

- When the natural rubber is heated along with sulphur called vulcanisation. The resulting rubber is elastic, hard and strong.
- Synthetic rubbers are made by polymerisation of chloroprene, styrene and butadiene mixtures and isobutylene.

SOAPS

- The soaps are sodium salts of higher fatty acids. They are useful only in soft water as they form an insoluble precipitate in hard water. This precipitate consists of salts of calcium and magnesium of higher fatty acids. No lather or emulsion is formed and washing is not possible.

Some Importants Alloys

Alloys	Composition
Brass	Cu, Zn
Bronze	Cu, Sn
Gun metal	Cu, Sn, Zn
Bel metal	Cu, Sn
German silver	Cu, Zn, Ni
Dutch metal	Cu, Zn
Aluminium	Al, Cu
Nichrome	Ni, Fe, Cr, Mn
Chromium steel	Cr, C, Fe

Chemical Formulae, Commercial Name of Chemical Compounds

Commercial Name	Chemical Compounds	Chemical formulae
Common salt	Sodium chloride	$NaCl$
Baking soda	Sodium bicarbonate	$NaHCO_3$
Washing soda	Sodium carbonate	$Na_2CO_3 . 10H_2O$
Caustic soda	Sodium hydroxide	$NaOH$
Chilli salt peter	Sodium nitrate	$NaNO_3$
Soda ash	Sodium carbonate	Na_2CO_3
Hypo	Sodium thiosulphate	$Na_2S_2O_3 . 5H_2O$

BIOLOGY

BRANCHES OF BIOLOGY

(*a*) **Anthropology:** Deals with the scientific study of man and the mankind.

(*b*) **Agronomy:** Deals with the management of farms and science of crop production.

(*c*) **Apiculture:** Deals with the process of bee keeping for commercial purposes.

(*d*) **Entomology:** Deals with the structure, habits and classification of insects.

(*e*) **Eugenics:** Deals with improving the human race.

(*f*) **Pathology:** Deals with the nature of disease, their causes, symptoms, effects, their cure and control.

(*g*) **Physiotherapy:** Deals with the treatment of diseases, body weakness or defects with help of massage and exercise etc.

(*h*) **Sericulture:** Deals with the production of r silk from silkworm.

(*i*) **Pharmacology:** Deals with the knowledge manufacture of drugs.

(*j*) **Occupational therapy:** Deals with treat the physically handicapped or injured pers through exercise etc.

(*k*) **Psychology:** Deals with the study of hun mind, its behaviour and mental qualities.

(*l*) **DNA finger printing:** Technique to h identify a person on the basis of genes.

ANIMALS/PLANTS

- The organisms that closely resemble one ano

re placed in one group, the groups which have milarities are combined together into larger roups, and these into still larger ones. The most iclusive category is kingdom. Other major ategories, in descending order are: phylum, class, rder, family, genus, and species. Man belongs Animal kingdom, chordata division or phylum, lammalia class, Primates order, Hominidae mily, Homo genus and Sapiens species.

CELL THEORY

ell is the basic unit of structure of all living ganisms. According to the cell theory, all ganism are composed of cells and cell products d growth and development results from the vision and differentiation of cells.

ells membrane surrounds all living cells.

icleus is the most important cell organelle iich controls and coordinates all cell activities d also concerned with the transmission of redity characters.

itochondria, ribosomes, lysosomes and tyosomes are present in plant and animal cells.

ly plant cells have cell wall, chloroplast and cuole.

ruses constitute a difficulty since in many ways y are intermediate between living and dead tter.

e cell is said to be made up of a substance led Protoplasm which has two main nstituents cytoplasm and nucleus, and is inded by a cell membrane on outside.

ls take up the raw materials for metabolism ough the cell membrane from extracellular d surrounding them.

oplasm inside is responsible for maintaining internal distribution of organelles and also free cell movements.

ochondria inside provides energy for reactions de the cell. Ribosomes are responsible for the thesis of proteins.

Endoplasmic Reticulum helps in addition of er sugar units to proteins and their sportation to other parts of the cell.

FOOD

- It is a nutritive substance taken by an organism for growth, work, repair and maintaining life processes. It provides energy to do work and maintain body heat, provides materials for the growth of the body, makes necessary materials for reproduction and provides materials for the repair of damaged cells and tissues of our body.
- **Carbohydrates:** For a normal person, 400 to 500 gms of carbohydrates are required daily but for sportspersons, growing children and nursing mothers, it is on higher side.
- **Proteins:** They are complex organic compounds made up of carbon, hydrogen, oxygen and nitrogen. The building blocks of Protein are Amino acids and there are large number of amino acids.
- Proteins are essential for the growth of children and teenagers, and for maintenance and making good the wear and tear of the body tissues in adults.
- An adult needs about 1 gm of protein per kg of body weight.
- **Fats:** They are esters of long chain fatty acids and an alcohol called glycerol. Fats also contain atoms of carbon, hydrogen and oxygen.
- The main function of fats in the body is to provide a steady source of energy and for this purpose, they are deposited within the body.
- One gm of fat gives 37 kilojoules of energy which is more than double of that given by carbohydrates.
- Fats, the richest source of energy to our body, can be stored in the body for subsequent use. Fats, soluble in organic solvents and insoluble in water, also supply fat-soluble vitamins to our body.
- **Minerals:** Some of the important minerals needed by our body are — iron, iodine, calcium, phosphorus, sodium, potassium, zinc, copper, magnesium, chloride, fluoride and sulphur.
- We get most of the minerals in combined form from plant sources. Deficiency of these minerals causes many diseases.
- **Energy Requirements:** The energy requirement of a body varies according to age, sex, lifestyle, occupation, climate and special situations like pregnancy and lactation.

Age	Energy requirements
5 years	6000 kJ per day
11 years	9000 kJ per day
18 years	11000 kJ per day
Adult (normal work)	9600 kJ per day
Adult (heavy work)	12000 kJ per day
Adult (very heavy work)	16000 kJ per day

- **Vitamins:** They act as catalysts in cert chemical reactions of metabolism in our bo
- They don't provide energy to our body nor f body tissues.
- More than 15 types of vitamins are known only 2 vitamins — D and K can be formed in body.

Vitamin	Necessity	Source
Vitamin A	For maintaining healthy eyesight, normal skin and hair	Cod liver oil, fish, eggs, milk, carrot, leafy vegetables.
Vitamin B_1	For growth, carbohydrate metabolism, functioning of heart, nerves and muscles.	Milk, soya-food, meat, whole cereals, green vegetables.
Vitamin C	For keeping teeth, gums and joints healthy, for increasing resistance of body to infection	Citrus fruits, guava, tomatoes.
Vitamin D	For normal growth of bones and teeth	Milk, eggs, butter, cod liver oil, sun
Vitamin E	For normal reproduction, functioning of muscles and protection of liver	Green leafy vegetables, milk, butter, tomato.
Vitamin K	For normal clotting of blood and normal functioning of liver	Green leafy vegetables, soyabean, to

- **Roughage:** Though it does not provide any energy to the body, yet keeps the digestive system in order, by helping in retaining water in the body and preserving constitution.
- The main source of roughage are salads, cabbage, corn cob, porridge, vegetables and fruits with stems.

DISEASES

COMMUNICABLE DISEASES

- They are the diseases which can be transmitted from reservoirs of infection or infected person to the healthy but susceptible persons.
- The disease causing agent or the pathogen can be transmitted directly or indirectly.

DEFICIENCY DISEASES

- These occur due to deficiency of some nutrients in the diet or some hormone due to hypo activity or damage to endocrine glands.

Diet Deficiency	Disease
Protein	Kwashiorkor
Protein-energy malnutrition	Marasmus
Vitamin A	Night-blindness, Xerophthalmia
Vitamin B_1	Beri-Beri
Vitamin B_2	Cheilosis
Vitamin B_5	Pellagra
Vitamin C	Scurvy
Vitamin D	Rickets (in childrer (in adult) Osteoma
Vitamin K	Hypothrombinemia
Iron	Anaemia
Iodine	Goitre
Fluoride	Dental caries
Calcium and phosphorus	Affects formation of bones and teet

Hormone Deficiency	Disease
Insulin	Diabetes
Thyroxine	Cretinism (child),
STH	Dwarfism, Gigantis

ALLERGIC DISEASE

- In these diseases, body becomes hypersen to some foreign agents, allergens, which inflammation when come in contact wi body or enter inside the body.

oreign agents can be dust, pollens, certain-foods, erum, certain drugs or fabrics.

he unfavourable response of the body to llergens is called allergic reaction. Asthma and ay fever are allergic diseases.

TERIAL DISEASES

acteria are minute organisms which are known cause a number of diseases:

ease	Incubation period	Spread through
erculosis	2-10 weeks	Air-borne,droplet infection
heria	2-6 days	Air-borne droplet infection
era	6 hours to 2-3 days	Contaminated food and water. House flies are the vectors
osy	Upto 5 years	Prolonged and intimate contact
oping h	7-14 days	Droplet infection
nus	3-21 days	Entry of cysts through any wound made by sharp object, dog bite or fall on the road
oid	1-3 weeks	Directed and Contact
ue	2-6 days	Rats and bed-bugs transmit the germs
monia	1-3 days	Air-borne

L DISEASES

ase	Incubation period	Spread through
ken-pox	12-20 days	Direct contact with infected persons or infected objects
pox	12 days	Droplet infection
nyalitis	7-14 days	Direct and oral
les	10 days	Droplet infection
os	12-26 days	Droplet infection
es	1-3 months	Bite of rabied animal like dogs, monkeys, cats
nza	24-28 hours	Air-borne

ASES CAUSED BY PROTOZOA

noebiasis (Amoebic dysentery), Malaria, Kala-r, Trypanosomiasis and Giardiasis are main eases caused by Protozoans.

laria is a parasitic infection.

SYSTEM OF HUMAN BODY

DIGESTIVE SYSTEM

- The digestive system consists of alimentary canal and digestive glands. Alimentary canal is about 8-10 meters long tube of varying diameter. Food is taken in through mouth.
- The tongue helps in ingestion, chewing, tasting and swallowing of food and mixing of food and saliva.
- Salivary glands secret saliva which helps in digestion of starch. Gastric glands present in the mucosa of the stomach, provide acidic medium for the food digestion.
- Liver, the largest sized, reddish brown gland of body, secrets bile. Liver is present in the right upper part of the abdomen. The bile secreted by the liver is stored in gall bladder. It helps in the emulsification and digestion of fats.
- Pancreas is the second largest gland in human body and secretes pancreatic juices. Intestine also secret juices.

RESPIRATORY SYSTEM

- Oxygen is needed for the oxidation and expelling of carbon dioxide is necessary to avoid its-accumulation. This process of exchange of gases between the environment and the body, is called respiration.
- In some unicellular organisms like aerobic bacteria, amoeba, hydra, etc. there is direct exchange of gases between the carbon dioxide of the body and oxygen of water.
- There is no blood for transport of gases. However, in larger and complex form of animals, specialised respiratory organs are developed.
- Amphibians respire through skin, fishes through gills and mammals, birds and reptiles through lungs.
- A normal adult inspires or expires about 500 ml of gas with each breath and about 72 breathes per minutes.

CIRCULATORY SYSTEM

- Main components of the circulatory system are heart, blood vessels and blood.

- Heart is a thick, muscular, contractile and automatic pumping organ. In birds and mammals, heart is divided into four chambers.
- Arteries are thick walled blood vessels which always carry the blood away from the heart to various body parts.
- Veins are thin walled blood vessels which always carry the blood from various parts generally to the heart.
- In an adult healthy person, the normal rate of heart beat at rest is about 70-72 times per minute.

BLOOD

- It is red, opaque, somewhat sticky and viscous fluid in the body of animals.
- It is slightly alkaline (pH = 7.4), heavier than water (sp gr = 1.05) and five times more viscous than distilled water.
- Blood forms 6 to 10% of the body weight.
- An adult, on average, has about 6.8 litres of blood.
- Blood contains plasma and blood corpuscles with the former occupying 55-60% of the volume.
- Plasma transports food components, metabolic wastes and hormones; keeps constant level of pH of blood, maintains body temperature and helps in blood clotting.
- Erythrocytes or red blood corpuscles (RBCs), leukocytes or white blood corpuscles (WBCs) and blood platelets are other parts of the blood.
- Due to the presence of iron containing pigment haemoglobin, RBCs are red in colour. The RBCs are crucial for ex-change of oxygen and carbon dioxide. WBCs are nucleated and non-pigmented cells. They are larger in size than RBCs but far less in number (1 : 600).
- WBCs play an important role in immune system of the body. Blood platelets cause the coagulation of blood and clot formation to prevent excessive bleeding.
- Human blood is divided into four main Groups—A, B, AB and O.
- The plasma of Group A blood contains an anti-B factor and vice-versa, so that people of Groups A and B cannot accept each other's blood.
- Group AB contains neither anti-A nor an factor and people with this group can rec transfusions from both but can give to neit
- Group O contains both anti-A and anti-B can receive blood only from Group O but donate blood to all Groups. Group O is ca universal donor because they can donate t the Groups.
- Group AB is called universal acceptor bec they can accept blood from all Groups.

SKELETON SYSTEM

- The frame or the hard structure of the hu body is composed from the bones and the or of making such frame are called skeleton sys

Bones

- Bone is the hardest tissue of the body and the largest section of the body weight.
- Bones contain organic as well as inorg matters. With advancing age, the inorg matter's share increases, causing the bon become more brittle.
- Long bones such as humerus and femur are h while small bones are solid.

EXCRETORY SYSTEM

- In men, excretory system is formed of one p kidneys, one pair of ureters, a urinary bl and a urethra. Kidney is about 10 cm long, shaped, dark-red and slightly flattened stru
- Sweet glands, oil glands, lungs and liver al as additional excretory organ.
- In case of kidney failure, a man can treat hemodialysis or transplantation of a kidney a donor's body.

NERVOUS SYSTEM

- The system which controls and coordinat body functions, retains memory and receive sends signals, is called the nervous systen
- The nervous system comprises brain, spinal nerves and nerve fibres.
- Human brain weighs about 1200 to 140 Main parts of the brain are cerebrum, cereb and medulla oblongata.

'erebrum controls voluntary function and is site f intelligence, will power, emotions, etc.

'erebellum controls involuntary functions like eart beat, respiration, etc.

pinal cord is about 45 cm long and about 35 n in weight. It conducts impulses to and from e brain and controls reflex actions of the body.

arious cranial (arising from ending into brain) nd spinal nerves (arising from spinal cord) ntrol smell, vision, movements of body parts, ste and hearing.

RODUCTION SYSTEM

this type of reproduction, there is formation d fusion of sex cells, called gametes.

rganism develops from the zygote through nbryo formation.

generally involves two parents — male and nale.

e offsprings are different from the parent as riations appear due to new combinations of nes. So, it plays an important role in evolution.

higher plants and animals reproduce sexually.

OMOSOMES

nts and animals have fixed number of omosomes per cell.

nes are located on chromosomes and are ponsible for transfer of characteristics from cell to the next either in the same organism from parents to offspring.

n has 23 pairs of chromosomes, of which one r is sex chromosomes.

les child inherits X chromosomes from the nale parent and Y from the male parent.

nale child receives a X chromosome each from er of its parents.

ndel was the first scientist to explain smission of units from reproductive cells of parents to the off-springs.

NG

the process of producing genetically identical es of a biological material, starting from a le cell. The original genes are transplanted and thus one can produce organisms of known and desirable characteristics.

GENETIC ENGINEERING

- It is the method of artificial synthesis of new genes and their subsequent transplantation or methods of correcting the defective genes.
- It has helped in producing plants and animals with specific characters.
- So, crippling hereditary diseases can also be cured like hemophilia etc.

DNA FINGERPRINTING

- It consists of examining repetitive DNA in the genome for variations in the length of restriction fragments.
- Every individual has his own pattern, so that fingerprinting can match blood to a particular person, and patterns are inherited from parent to child, allowing the method to identify relationships between individuals.

IN-VITRO FERTILIZATION

- When a sperm and an egg are made to fertilize outside a living body (usually a test tube), it is called in-vitro fertilization.
- This process has been used to impregnate several females who could not do so through natural means.

Diseases and the Parts of Body they Affect

AIDS—Immune system of body	*Gout*—Joints of bone
Arthritis—Inflammation of joints	*Jaundice*—Liver
Asthma—Lungs	*Meningitis*—Brain or spinal cord
Cataract—Eyes	*Pleurisy*—Pleura (inflammation of)
Conjunctivitis—Eyes	*Polio*—motor neurons
Diabetes—Pancreas	*Pneumonia*—Lungs
Diphtheria—Throat	*Pyorrhoea*—Sockets of teeth
Glaucoma—Eyes	*Tuberculosis*—Lungs
Eczema—Skin	*Typhoid*—Intestine
Goitre—Front of the neck (due to enlargement of thyroid gland)	*Malaria*—Spleen
	Leukaemia—Blood
	Rickets—Bones

SPACE RESEARCH

First in Space

✶ First creator of rules regarding space research	Isaac Newton
✶ First artificial satellite launched in space	Sputnik-1 (1957)
✶ First living being sent in space	Louika (a dog)
✶ Firstever manned spacecraft	Vostok-I
✶ First man in space	Yuri Gagarin U.S.S.R. (1961)
✶ First woman in space	Valentina Tereshkova U.S.S.R. (June 1
✶ First man who moved in space out of the spacecraft	Alexi Livonov U.S.S.R. (June 1965)
✶ First person to land on moon	Neil Armstrong, America (21st July, 19
✶ First fourwheeled carriage without human being on moon	Leunokhev-I U.S.S.R. (1970)
✶ First space lab in orbit	Skylab (America, 1973)
✶ First space shuttle	Columbia (America, 1981)
✶ First Indian (man) in space	Squadron leader—Rakesh Sharma (13th April, 1984)
✶ First Indian (Woman) in space	Kalpana Chawla (19th Nov., 1997)
✶ First American woman in space	Sailyride (1983)
✶ First spacecraft on Mars	Pathfinder (6 July, 1997)
✶ First woman who lead spacecraft	Allin Collis (America)
✶ First spacecraft without man	Shenzoo, China (20th Nov. 1999)

Indian Space Programme : At a Glance

Satellite	*Date*	*Type*	*Launch Vehicle*	*Resu*
Aryabhatta	19-04-75	Scientific	Cosmos	success
Bhaskara I	07-06-79	Geosurvey	Cosmos	success
Rohini	10-08-79	Geosurvey	S.L.V.3	unsucce
Rohini D-1	18-07-80	Geosurvey	S.L.V.3	success
Rohini	31-05-81	Scientific	S.L.V.3	success
Apple	19-06-81	Communication	Ariane	success
Bhaskara II	20-11-81	Geosurvey	Cosonos	success
INSAT-1A	10-04-82	Multipurpose	Delta	unsucc
Rohini	17-04-83	Scientific	S.L.V.3	success
INSAT-1B	30-08-83	Multipurpose	Space Shuttle	success
SROSS I	24-03-87	Technical	ASLV-D1	unsucc
IRS-1A	17-03-88	Remote sensing	Vostok	success
SROSS II	17-07-88	Technical	ASLV-D2	unsucc
INSAT-1C	21-07-88	Multipurpose	Ariane-4	unsucc
INSAT-1D	12-06-90	Multipurpose	Delta	succes
IRS-1B	29-08-91	Remote sensing	Vostok	succes
INSAT-2A	10-07-92	Multipurpose	Ariane	succes
INSAT-1D	12-06-90	Multipurpose	Delta	succes
IRS-1B	29-08-91	Remote sensing	Vostok	succes
INSAT-2A	10-07-92	Multipurpose	Ariane	succes
IRS-ID	29-09-97	Remote sensing	PSLV	succes
INSAT-3B	22-03-2000	Multipurpose	Ariane	succes

tellite	Date	Type	Launch Vehicle	Result
SAT-1	18-04-2001	Multipurpose	GSLV-D	successful
SAT-3E	28-09-2003	Communication	Ariane-5	successful
rtosat-1 & hamsat	05-05-2005	Maping and Communication	PSLV-C6	successful
andrayaan-I	22-10-2008	Maping and Scientific	PSLV-C11	successful
RTOSAT-2B	12-07-2010	Communication	PSLV-C15	successful
SAT-12	15-07-2011	Communication	PSLV-C17	successful
SAT-1	26-04-2012	Remote Sensing	PSLV-C19	successful
SAT-7	30-08-2013	Defence	Ariane-5	successful
OM	5-11-2013	Mapping	PSLV-C25	successful
NSS-1B	04-04-2014	Mapping and Scientific	PSLV-C24	successful
SAT-16	07-12-2014	Communication	Ariane-5	successful
NSS-1D	28-03-2015	Mapping and Scientific	PSLV-C27	successful
NSS-1E	20-01-2016	Mapping and Scientific	PSLV-C31	successful
rtosat-2 & others	22-06-2016	Mapping and Scientific	PSLV-C34	successful
atsat-1 & others	26-09-2016	Multipurpose	PSLV-C35	successful
ESOURCESAT-2A	07-12-2016	Remote Sensing	PSLV-C36	successful
RTOSAT-2 & 103 others	15-02-2017	Multipurpose	PSLV-C37	successful
SAT-17	29-06-2017	Earth observation Satellite	Ariane-5 ECA	successful
rtosat-2F & others	12-01-2018	Multipurpose	PSLV-C40	successful
SAT-6A	29-03-2018	Communication	GSLV-F08	successful
SAT-7A	19-12-2018	Military Satellite	GSLV-MK-II-F11	successful
rtosat-3	27-11-2019	Earth Imagine Satellite	PSLV-C47	successful
SAT-30	17-01-2020	Communication	Ariane-5	successful
OS-01	07-11-2020	Earth Observation	PSLV-C49	successful
MS-01/GSAT-12R	17-12-2020	Communication	PSLV-XLC50	successful
nejonia and 19 others	28-02-2021	Communication	PSLV-C51	successful
OS-04	14-02-2022	Earth Observation	PSLV-C52	successful
SAT-24"	23-06-2022	Communication	Ariane-5	successful
S-E0 and others	30-06-2022	Mapping	PSLV-C53	successful
eansat-3 and 8 others	26-11-2022	Earth observation Satellite	PSLV-C54	successful
OS-07	10-02-2023	Earth observation Satellite	SSLV-02	successful
LEOS-2 and LUMILITE-4	22-04-2023	Communication	PSLV-C55	successful
andrayaan-3	14-07-2023	Lunar observation	LVM-3	successful
S-SAR and 6 others	30-07-2023	Earth observation	PSLV-C56	successful
itya-L1	02-09-2023	Solar Mission	PSLV-C57	successful
oSat	01-01-2024	Earth observation	PSLV-C58	successful
SAT-3DS	17-02-2024	Meteorological	GSLV-F14	successful
OS-08	16-08-2024	Earth observation	SSLV-D3	successful
oba-3	05-12-2024	Earth Observation	PSLV-C59	successful
'S-02	29-01-2025	Navigation	GSLV-F15	successful
SAR	30-07-2025	Earth Observation	GSLV-F16	successful
1S-03	02-11-2025	Communication	LVM3-M5	successful

COMPUTER

- The computer is the system of that electronic device through which various informations are processed on the basis of a definite set of instructions called program and mathematical (numerical) and non-mathematical both types of informations are processed.
- The first mechanical computer was composed or fabricated by Blaise Pascal in 1642 and it is called Pascalene.
- But in 1833, Charles Babbage first time conceived an automatic calculator or computer.
- Charles Babbage is called the father of modern computer.
- Herman made an electronic tabulating machine based on punch cards which operates automatically.
- In 1937, first mechanical computer Mark-I was fabricated by Howard Akeen.
- The most outstanding contribution in the development of modern computer goes to John Wan Newmaan who brought the 2nd revolution in the area of computer in 1951.
- He discovered EDVAC (Electronic Discrete Variable Automatic Computer) and utilised the stored program and the binary number system in the computer.

FUNCTIONS OF COMPUTER

- 1. Collection and composition (input) of datas;
  2. Storage of datas.
  3. Processing of datas.
  4. Retrieval or output of the proccessed informations and datas.

UNITS OF COMPUTER

1. Input unit.
2. Central processing unit–CPU.
3. External Memory unit.
4. Output unit.

- The CPU of the computer is called brain of the computer and sometimes CPU is also called Micro Processor of the computer.
- The data is entered through the input unit in computer and through the central processing with the help of External Memory Unit datas arranged and processed.
- Ultimately by the output unit these data informations are issued or released.

PARTS OF COMPUTER

- **Monitor :** The monitor of the computer is li television in which the picture appears in form of doted points on the screen and these called pixels.
- **Hard Disc and Floppy Disc :** The Hard Di the permanent disc in the computers while Floppy Disc is the disc utilised when data informations are to be transferred from computer to another.
- **Mouse :** The mouse of the computer is like remote control of TV through which compu directly regulated or controlled without util the key-board.
- **Printer :** The printer is a device which prints documents or processed informations of computer.

SOME HIGH LEVEL LANGUAGES

1. **FORTRAN :** This language was devel for solving the mathematical formulae quickly and conveniently.
2. **COBOL :** This language was develope the commerical purposes. For the proce of this language a group of sentenc selected called paragraph and all parag composed are called a section, whil sections composed are called a divisio
3. **BASIC :** In basic a definite part o prescribed instruction is only inserted i computer.
4. **ALGOL :** This was basically fabricate designed for the complex alge calculations.
5. **PASCAL :** It is an amplified and mod form of ALGOL.

6. **COMAL :** This computer language is used for the students of secondary level.
7. **LOGO :** This language is used for children and kids for drawing Graphic line diagrams.
8. **PROLOG :** This language is developed in 1973 in France and is used for Artificial Intelligence which is capable and equivalent to the logical program.
9. **FORTH :** This language was invented by Charles Mure which is frequently used in all types of the works in the computer.

MPUTER VIRUS

The computer virus is an electronic code which is used to abolish or erradicate the inclusive informations or programs of the computer.

Some important computer viruses are Micheleanjalo, Dork Avangor, kilo, filip, Macmug, Scores, Casecade, Jeruslem, Date crime, Coloumbs crime, Internet virus, Pachcom, Pach EXE, COM-EXE, Marizuana, C-brain, bloody, Chenge Mungu and Desi etc.

MPUTER NETWORKING

There are two types of networkings which are usually occur—Local Area Networking (LAN) and Wide Area Networking (WAN)..

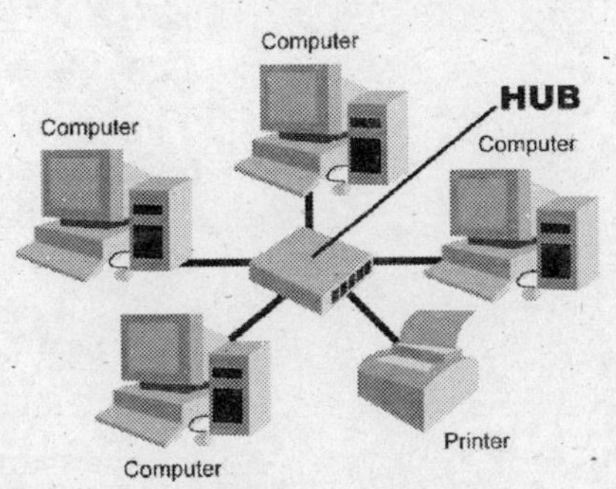

By LAN all the computers of the same buildings are connected like the computers of university premises, computers of offices etc.

By WAN all the comptuers of a large area are connected like the computers of all the offices of a city or town etc.

- In India a very large computer network namely INDONET has been installing through which all the main towns and cities has to be interlinked.

COMPUTER TERMINOLOGY

- **Bit :** The bit is a unit of measurement of the electronic data. One bit is either 0 or 1 but not both. On composing 8 bits, 1 byte is formed.
- **Bug :** The Bug is the error in the computer program or system and its eradication is called Debug.
- **Byte :** Total eight bits compose a byte. Thus 8 bits = 1 byte.
- **CD-ROM :** A CD like of music CD in which data can be stored substantially called CD-ROM. In a CD with comparison to floppy extremely more datas can be stored but one problem in it is that one time recorded data can not be deleted or modified.
- **Chip :** It is a thin slice on which by a special mechanism a circuit is designed which is normally made from Silicon.
- **Memory System :** The place where computer data and program are temporarily kept is called Memory system. Usually memory is implied from RAM.
- **Modem :** The device which converts digital signals into analogue signals and vice-versa is called Modem.
- **RAM :** It is Random Access Memory (a place) where datas to be processed are kept temporarily and it is unstable memory.
- **ROM :** It is Read Only Memory and it is stable or Non-valatile memory which doesn't ended after power off.
- **Scanner :** It is a device through which graphic image is transformed to digital image and the scanners are of usually two types one desktop and another hand operating.

PROGRAMING

- Computers perform phenomenal feats of calculation, but they do not do so in a complicated way.

- They actually carry out very simple operations, such as addition and subtraction.
- They achieve their fantastic computing power by carrying out these operations at incredible speed.
- The programme, or set of instructions for operating the computer, is therefore written as a sequence of very simple steps.

Several computer languages have b developed for different applications, inclu BASIC, COBOL, FORTRAN and PASC Writing programmes is very skilled and ti consuming work.

- But for most typical computer applicati ready-written programmes are available, ca "packages".

GENERAL KNOWLEDGE

FIRST IN THE WORLD

First Chinese visitor to India	*Fahien*
First foreign invader of India	*Alexander, the Great (Greek)*
First person to climb Mt. Everest	*Tenzing Norgay (India) and Edmund Hillary (New Zealand) (1953)*
First atom bomb dropped at	*Hiroshima (Japan)*
First man in the space	*Yuri Gagarin (former USSR)*
First woman in the space	*Valentina Tereshkova (former USSR)*
First person to walk in the space	*Alexei Leonov (former USSR)*
First person to land on the moon	*Neil Armstrong (USA)*
First and the only woman to have climbed Mt. Everest twice	*Santosh Yadav (Indian; May, 1992; May, 1993)*
First person on Mt. Everest without oxygen	*Phu Dorjee (Indian; May 9, 1984)*
First person to climb Mt. Everest twice	*Nawang Gombu*
First President of the USA	*George Washington*
First woman Prime Minister	*Sirimavo Bandaranaike (Sri Lanka)*
First person to swim across English Channel	*Mathew Webb*
First woman to swim across English Channel	*Gertrude Caroline Ederle*
First woman to climb Mt. Everest	*Junko Tabei (Japan)*
First woman to climb Mt. Everest alone and without oxygen supplies	*Alison Hargreaves (Britain: May 13, 1995)*
First Aeroplane to fly around the world without refuelling	*Voyager (Dec. 1986)*
First test-tube Baby	*Louise Brown (UK; 1978)*
First all-talking Film	*Jaz Singer (1927)*
First Secretary-General of the UN	*Trygve Lie (Norway: 1946-53)*
First woman President of the UN General Assembly	*Vijayalakshmi Pandit (India: 1953)*
First woman to reach North Pole	*Ann Bancroft (1986)*
First person to reach North Pole	*Robert Peary*
First person to reach South Pole	*Amundsen (1911)*
First woman to command Spacecraft in Space	*Ellin Collins*

SUPERLATIVES (WORLD)
(The Largest, Biggest, Smallest, Longest, Highest)

Airport	*Largest*	King Fahd International Airport, Dammam (Saudi Arab
Animal,	*Tallest*	Giraffe (Average height 6.09 m)
	Largest and Heaviest	Blue Whale (190 tonnes)
	Longest recorded	Boot lace Worm (55 m)
	Fastest	Cheetah (Approximately 100 km/hr)
Bay,	*With max. shore line*	Hudson Bay (Canada: 12268 km)
	With maximum area	Bay of Bengal (India: 217 million hc)
Building,	*Tallest*	Burj Khalifa (Dubai, 818 meter)
Canal,	*Big ship (longest)*	Suez Canal (160 km)
	Busiest	Kiel Canal (North Sea)
Canyon/Gorge,	*Deepest*	Hells Canyon, Snake River (Idaho : 7900 ft)
	Largest	Grand Canyon (Colarado River; USA; 446 km)
Church,	*Largest*	Basilica of St. Peter (Vatican City Rome– Area 23000 sq.m
City,	*Largest in Area*	Jiuquan Gansu, China (Area 1,67,996 Sq km)
Continent,	*biggest*	Asia (30,928,605 km^2)
	Smallest	Australia Mainland (Area 8,426,635 km^2)
Country,	*Largest in Population*	China (over 138.5 crore)
	Largest in Area	Russia (17,075,000 sq. km)
	With largest electorate	India (over 90 crores)
	Smallest independent	State of Vatican City (109 acre)
Delta,	*Largest*	Sundarban's Ganga-Brahmaputra delta (1,05,000 sq. k
Desert,	*Largest*	Sahara (N. Africa; maximum length 5,150 km EW; maximu width 3,200 km NS)
Dome,	*Largest*	Singapore National Stadium (310 m)
Epic,	*Longest*	Mahabharata
Fish,	*Largest fresh water*	Plabeuk (China, Laos and Thailand)
	Most abundant	Bristle mouth
	Most venomous	Stone Fish (Indo-Pacific Waters)
Film,	*Most Oscars*	Ben Hur (11 Oscars–1959); Titanic (11 Oscars–1998); Th Lord of Rings : The Return of the King (11 Oscars—2003
Fountain,	*Tallest*	King Fahd's Fountain (Jeddah, Saudi Arabia)

it,	*Most nutritive*	Avocado (Vitamins A, C, E and Proteins; Central and South America)
	Least nutritive	Cucumber
f,	*Largest*	Gulf of Mexico (1,544,000 sq. km)
nd,	*Biggest*	Greenland (Kalaatdlit Nunaat–2,175,000 sq km)
ke,	*Largest*	Caspian Sea (Azerbaijan, Russia, Iran border: 37.18 lakh km^2)
	Deepest	Baikal (Siberia)
	Largest (fresh water)	Superior Lake (USA–Canada border: 82,350 km^2)
rary,	*Biggest*	United States Library of Congress (Washington D.C. founded in 1800, contains 101 million items)
	Biggest non-statutory	New York Public Library
untain,	*Highest peak*	Mt. Everest (8848 m; Nepal)
	Highest range	Himalayas, Asia (upto 4200 m)
	Greatest mountain range	Himalaya-Karakoram (96 out of 109 peaks over 7315 m are here)
seum,	*Largest*	American Museum of Natural History, New York
ean,	*Largest and Deepest*	The Pacific (Area: 166,240,000 km^2; Depth: 10,924 m)
insula,	*Largest*	Arabia (3.25 million sq. km)
ces,	*Coldest (annual mean)*	Polus Nedostupnosti (Antarctica –58°C)
	Driest (annual mean)	Desierto de Atacame (near Calama; Chile; rainfall nil)
	Hottest (annual mean)	Dallol (Ethiopia; 34.4°C mean temperature)
	Rainiest (annual mean)	Mowsyrnam near Cherapunji (Meghalaya; India; 11873 mm)
	Windiest	The Commonwealth Bay (Gales reach 320 km/ph)
net,	*Biggest*	Jupiter (equatorial diameter 142984 km)
	Brightest, hottest and nearest to Earth	Venus
	Nearest to Sun	Mercury
eau,	*Highest*	Tibetan Plateau (Central Asia: 4900 m)
form,	*Longest (rail)*	Shree Siddharoodha Swamiji Railway Station Hubballi, Karnataka, India (1507 m. long)
way Line,	*Longest*	Trans-Siberian Railway (Moscow-Nakhodka: 9438 km)
way Station,	*Largest*	Grand Central Terminal (New York City; 19 hc)

Religion,	*Oldest*	Hinduism
Religion,	*Largest*	Christianity
Rivers,	*Longest*	(i) Nile (6650 km) (ii) Amazon (6437 km)
Road,	*Longest*	Pan American Highway (from Alaska-Brasila: 24140 k
Sea,	*Largest*	Philippine Sea (5,695,000 sq. km)
Star,	*Brightest*	Sirius A (also called Dog Star)
Swimming	*Longest*	English Channel
Telescope,	*Largest (radio)*	Five Hundred meter Apertune Spherical Telescope (FAS China.
Temple,	*Largest*	Angkor Wat (Cambodia: 402 acres)
Tunnel,	*Longest (railway)*	Gotthard Base Rail Tunnel (Switzerland; 57.1 km)
	Largest (road)	Laerdal, Norway (24.51 km)
Volcano	*Greatest concentration in*	Indonesia
	Highest (extinct)	Cerro Aconcagua (6960 m; Andes)
	Highest (dormant)	Volcan Llullaillaco (6723 m; Argentina-Chile)
	Highest (active)	Ojos del Salado (Chile-Argentina)
Waterfall,	*Highest*	Salto-Angel (in Venezuela on a branch of river Carr depth 807 m.)
	Largest	Khone Falls (Laos; width 10.8 km)

CAPITAL & CURRENCIES

Country	Capital	Currency
∗ Afghanistan	Kabul	Afghani
∗ Albania	Tirana	Lek
∗ Algeria	Algiers	Dinar
∗ Angola	Luanda	New Kwanza
∗ Argentina	Buenos Aires	Peso
∗ Armenia	Yeravan	Dram
∗ Australia	Canberra	Dollar
∗ Austria	Vienna	Euro
∗ Azerbaijan	Baku	Manat
∗ Bahrain	Manama	Dinar
∗ Bangladesh	Dhaka	Taka

Country	Capital	Currency
∗ Barbados	Bridgetown	Dollar
∗ Belarus	Minsk	Ruble
∗ Belgium	Brussels	Euro
∗ Benin	Porto Novo	Franc
∗ Bhutan	Thimphu	Ngultrum[1]
∗ Bolivia	La paz	Dollar
∗ Botswana	Gaborone	Pula
∗ Brazil	Brasilia	Real
∗ Bosnia Herzegovina	Sarajevo	Dinar
∗ Bulgaria	Sofia	Lev

Country	Capital	Currency
Cambodia	Phnom-Penh	Riel
Canada	Ottawa	Dollar
Chile	Santiago	Peso
China	Beijing	Yuan
Colombia	Bogota	Peso
Congo	Brazzaville	Franc CFA
Republic		
Croatia	Zagreb	Kuna
Cuba	Havana	Peso
Cyprus	Nicosia	Euro
Czech	Prague	Koruna
Republic		
Denmark	Copenhagen	Krone
Ecuador	Quito	Sucre
Egypt	Cairo	Pound
Estonia	Tallinn	Euro
Ethiopia	Addis Ababa	Birr
iji	Suva	Dollar
inland	Helsinki	Euro
rance	Paris	Euro
Georgia	Tbilisi	Lari
Germany	Berlin	Euro
Ghana	Accra	Cedi
Greece	Athens	Euro
Guatemala	Guatemala	Quetzal
	City	
Guyana	George Town	Dollar
Hungary	Budapest	Forint
eland	Reykjavik	Krona
dia	New Delhi	Rupee
donesia	Jakarta	Rupiah
an	Teheran	Rial
aq	Baghdad	Dinar
eland	Dublin	Euro
rael	Jerusalem	Shekel
aly	Rome	Euro
amaica	Kingston	Dollar
apan	Tokyo	Yen
ordan	Amman	Dinar
azakhstan	Akmola	Tenge

Country	Capital	Currency
* Kenya	Nairobi	Shilling
* Korea (S)	Seoul	Won
* Korea (N)	Pyongyang	Won
* Kyrgyzstan	Bishkek	Som
* Kuwait	Kuwait City	Dinar
* Laos	Vientiane	Kip
* Latvia	Riga	Euro
* Lebanon	Beirut	Pound
* Liberia	Monrovia	Dollar
* Libya	Tripoli	Dinar
* Lithuania	Vilnius	Litas
* Luxembourg	Luxembourg	Euro
* Macedonia	Skopje	Dinar
* Malawi	Lilongwe	Kwacha
* Malaysia	Kuala Lumpur	Ringgit
* Maldives	Male	Rufiyaa
* Mali	Bamako	Franc
* Mauritius	Port Louis	Rupee
* Mexico	Mexico City	Peso
* Moldavia	Chisinau	Leu
* Mongolia	Ulan Bator	Tugrik
* Morocco	Rabat	Dirham
* Mozambique	Maputo	Metical
* Myanmar	Nay Pyi Taw	Kyat
* Namibia	Winohoek	Dollar
* Nepal	Kathmandu	Rupee
* Netherlands	Amsterdam	Euro
* New Zealand	Wellington	Dollar
* Nigeria	Abuja	Naira
* Norway	Oslo	Krone
* Oman	Muscat	Rial
* Pakistan	Islamabad	Rupee
* Panama	Panama City	Balboa
* Peru	Lima	New Sole
* Philippines	Manila	Peso
* Poland	Warsaw	Zloty
* Portugal	Lisbon	Euro
* Qatar	Doha	Riyal
* Romania	Bucharest	Leu
* Russia	Moscow	Ruble

Country	Capital	Currency
✶ Saudi Arabia	Riyadh	Rial
✶ Senegal	Dakar	Franc
✶ Slovakia	Bratislava	Euro
✶ Spain	Madrid	Euro
✶ Sri Lanka	Colombo	Rupee
✶ Sudan	Khartoum	Dinar
✶ Suriname	Paramaribo	Guilder
✶ Sweden	Stockholm	Krona
✶ Switzerland	Berne	Swiss Francs
✶ Syria	Damascus	Pound
✶ South Africa	Capetown (Legislative) Pretoria *(Administrative)*	Rand
✶ Tadzhikistan	Dushanbe	Ruble
✶ Taiwan	Taipei	Dollar
✶ Tanzania	Dodoma	Shilling
✶ Thailand	Bangkok	Baht
✶ Tunisia	Tunis	Dinar
✶ Turkiye	Ankara	Lira
✶ Turkmania	Ashikabad	Manat
✶ Uganda	Kampala	Shilling
✶ Ukraine	Kiev	Hyrvnia
✶ United Arab Emirates	Abu Dhabi	Dirham
✶ U.K.	London	Pound Ster
✶ U.S.A.	Washington	Dollar
✶ Uruguay	Montevideo	Peso
✶ Uzbekistan	Tashkent	Som
✶ Venezuela	Caracas	Bolivar
✶ Vietnam	Hanoi	Dong
✶ Yemen	Sana'a	Rial
✶ Zimbabwe	Harare	Dollar
✶ Congo (Democratic Republic)	Kinshasa	Franc
✶ Zambia	Lusaka	Kwacha

GEOGRAPHICAL EXPLORATIONS/DISCOVERIES

Place	Explorer/Discoverer	Nationality	Year
America	Christopher Columbus	Italy	1492
Hawaii Islands (Sandwich Islands)	Captain James Cook	England	1778
Newfoundland	John Cabot	England	1497
New Zealand	Abel Janszoon Tasman	Holland	1642
North Pole	Robert Peary	USA	1909
Sea Route to India (via Cape of Good Hope)	Vasco da Gama	Portugal	1498
South Pole	Roald Amundsen	Norway	1911

NATIONAL MONUMENTS OF SOME FAMOUS COUNTRIES

Monument	Country	Monument	Country
Great Wall of China	China	Pyramid (Giza)	Egypt
Taj Mahal (Agra)	India	Kinder Disk	Denmark
Emperial Palace (Tokyo)	Japan	Leaning Tower of Pisa	Italy
Opera House (Sydney)	Australia	Statue of Liberty (New York)	USA
Eiffel Tower (Paris)	France	Kremlin (Moscow)	Russia

INTELLIGENCE AGENCIES OF SOME PROMINENT COUNTRIES

Country	Intelligence Agency
India	*Research & Analysis Wing (RAW), Intelligence Bureau (I.B.), Central Bureau of Investigation (C.B.I.)*
Pakistan	*Inter Service Intelligence (I.S.I.)*
U.S.A.	*Central Intelligence Agency (CIA), Federal Bureau of Investigation (FBI)*
Britain	*Military Intelligence (M.I.)-5 and 6, Special Branch, Ultra, Joint Intelligence Organisation*
srael	*Mosad*
Egypt	*Mukhabarat*
Japan	*Nicho*
Russia	*K.G.B. (Komitel Gosudarstvennoy Bezopasnosty) (Committee for State Security)*
Canada	*Security Intelligence Service (SIS)*
S. Africa	*Bureau of State Security (BSS)*
ran	*Sabak*
raq	*Al-Mukhabarat*
ustralia	*Australian Security and Intelligence Organisation (ASIO)*
rance	*S.D.E.C.E.*
pain	*C.E.S.I.D.*

JOR LANGUAGES OF THE WORLD AND THEIR SPEAKERS

ing the languages spoken by approximately of humankind (those spoken by more than 000,000 people), this table enumerates akers of each tongue as a primary language.

anguage	Speakers (millions)
hinese	1,322
panish	471
nglish	369
rabic	349
indi	342
ortuguese	232
engali	228
ussian	153
panese	126
hnda	99
njabi (Western)	93
vanese	84
arathi	83
lugu	82
rkish	82
alay	81
ench	79
rean	77
∗ Tamil	77
∗ German	76
∗ Vietnamese	76
∗ Urdu	69
∗ Italian	64
∗ Persian	65

Source : The World Almanac 2022

IMPORTANT NEWS AGENCIES OF THE WORLD

Agency	Country
PTI, UNI, UNIVARTA	India
Antara	Indonesia
Tanjug	Serbia
Associated Press (AP)	America
Reuters, NAFEN	United Kingdom
Angence France Press (AFP)	France
TASS	Russia

NAME OF PARLIAMENTS OF SOME COUNTRIES

Country	Name of Parliament	Country	Name of Parliament
Afghanistan	Shora	Norway	Storting
Argentina	National Congress	Poland	Sejm
Australia	Federal Parliament	Russia	Federal Assembly (Council of the Federatic State Duma
Austria	National Assembly		
Bangladesh	Jatiya Sansad		
India	Lok Sabha and Rajya Sabha	South Africa	National Assembly and S
Bhutan	Tshogdu (National Assembly)	Spain	Cortes Generales
Britain	House of Commons and House of Lords	Sweden	Riksdag
		Switzerland	Federal Assembly (Nati and Standerat)
Canada	House of Commons and Senate		
		North Korea	Supreme People's Assembly
China	National People Congress		
Denmark	Folketing	South Korea	National Assembly
Iran	Majlis (Islamic Consultative Assembly)	U.S.A.	Congress (Senate and of Representatives)
Israel	Knesset	Ethiopia	Federal Council and Ho Representatives
Japan	Diet		
Myanmar	Pyithu Hluttaw (People's Assembly)	Iceland	Alpingi
		Bulgaria	National Assembly
Nepal	Rashtriya Panchayat	Cuba	National Assembly of P Power
The Netherlands	States-General		

LARGEST AND SMALLEST COUNTRIES (Top 5)

Largest Country (Area-wise)	Largest Country (Population-wise)	Smallest Country (Area-wise)	Smallest Cou (Population-w
Russia	China	Vatican City	Vatican City
Canada	India	Monaco	Tuvalu
China	USA	Nauru	Nauru
United States	Indonesia	Tuvalu	Palau
Brazil	Brazil	San Marino	San Marino

MAJOR RELIGIONS OF THE WORLD

Religion	Member	Percentage	Religion	Member	Percen
Christianity	2.5 billion	32.2%	Buddhism	545 million	6.9'
Islam	1.9 billion	24.7%	Sikhism	27 million	0.27'
Hinduism	1.0 billion	13.5%	Jews	14 million	0.14'

NATIONAL EMBLEMS OF IMPORTANT COUNTRIES

untry	National Emblem	Country	National Emblem
nerica	Golden Rod	Australia	Kangaroo
land	Shamrock	Italy	White Lily
ael	Candelabrum	Iran	Rose
nada	White Lily	Great Britain	Rose
ile	Candor and Huemul	Germany	Corn Flower
pan	Chrysanthemum	Zimbabwe	Zimbabwe Bird
nmark	Beach	Turkey	Crescent and Star
e Netherlands	Lion	New Zealand	Kiwi, Fern Southern Cross
rway	Lion	Nepal	Kukri
kistan	Crescent	Poland	Eagle
nce	Lily	Belgium	Lion
ngladesh	Water Lily	Mongolia	The Soyombo
ssia	Double headed eagle	Lebanon	Cedar Tree
dan	Secretary Bird	Syria	Eagle
a	Lioned Capital		

FIRST IN INDIA

he first Indian to get the Nobel Prize for Literature	*Rabindra Nath Tagore*
he first Indian to get the Nobel Prize for Physics	*C.V. Raman*
he first Indian to get the Nobel Prize for Peace	*Mother Teresa*
he first Indian to get the Nobel Prize for Economics	*Amartya Sen*
he first Indian to get Special Oscar award (1992)	*Satyajit Ray*
he first and the last Indian Governor-General of ee India	*C. Rajagopalachari*
he first woman to become the Governor of a State	*Smt. Sarojini Naidu*
he first Indian Commenders-in-Chief	*General K.M. Cariappa*
he first ever woman to become the Chief Minister a State	*Smt. Sucheta Kripalani*
he first Indian woman President of UN General Assembly	*Smt. Vijaylakshmi Pandit*
e first Indian to become the President of ernational Court of Justice	*Dr. Nagendra Singh*
e first Indian woman to swim across the glish Channel	*Ms. Aarti Saha*
e first Indian girl to become Miss Universe	*Miss Sushmita Sen*
e first Indian girl to become Miss World	*Rita Faria*
e first Indian to swim across the English Channel	*Mihir Sen*
e first Field Marshal	*S.H.F.J. Manekshaw*
e first Indian recipient of Victoria Cross	*Khudadad Khan*
e first Indian to conquer Mt. Everest	*Sherpa Tenzing (May 29, 1953)*
e first Indian Cosmonaut (man)	*Rakesh Sharma (April 3, 1984)*

∗ The first Indian Cosmonaut (woman)	*Kalpana Chawla (Nov. 19, 1997)*
∗ The first woman to climb Mt. Everest	*Miss Bachendri Pal (May 23, 198*
∗ The first ICS	*Satyendranath Tagore*
∗ The first to address the UN General Assembly in Hindi	*Atal Bihari Vajpayee*
∗ The first Newspaper	*Bengal Gazette (Jan 27, 1780)*
∗ The first Postage Stamp issued	*In 1852*
∗ The first Telegraph line laid	*In 1851 (Calcutta-Diamond Harb*
∗ The first Railways run	*April 16, 1853 (Bombay-Thane)*
∗ The first Electric Train run	*1925 (Bombay-Kurla)*
∗ The first Atomic Power Station	*Tarapore (Maharashtra)*
∗ The first passenger-cum-cargo ship made in India	*Harshavardhan*
∗ The first Satellite	*Aryabhatta (1975)*
∗ The first President of the Indian National Congress	*W.C. Banerjee*
∗ The first President of Indian Republic	*Dr. Rajendra Prasad*
∗ The first woman judge of the Supreme Court	*Ms Fatima Bibi*
∗ The first to climb Everest without oxygen	*Phu Dorjee (1987)*
∗ The first film (movie)	*Raja Harishchandra*
∗ The first film (talkie)	*Alam Ara*
∗ The first Metro Railway	*Calcutta Metro Railway*
∗ The first Test-tube baby, scientifically documented	*Born on August 6, 1986 at K.E.M. Hospital, Bombay*
∗ The first TV Centre	*At Delhi*
∗ The first Indian to get an Oscar	*Bhanu Athaiya*
∗ The first woman pilot in IAF	*Ms Harita Kaur Deol*
∗ The first woman to get Olympic Medal	*Karnam Malleswari*
∗ The first woman Foreign Secretary	*Chokila Iyer*

SUPERLATIVES (INDIA)

Highest, Biggest, Largest and Longest in India

∗ Award for Gallantry, highest	*Param Vir Chakra*
∗ Award, highest civilian	*Bharat Ratna*
∗ Bank, with largest number of branches	*State Bank of India*
∗ Road Bridge, Longest	*Bhupen Hazarika Bridge, Assam (9.15 km)*
∗ Road and Rail Bridge, Longest	*Bogibeel Bridge, Brahmaputra River, Assam*
∗ Cattle Fair, Largest	*Sonepur (Bihar)*
∗ City, Most Populous	*Mumbai metropolis*
∗ Corridor, Longest	*Rameshwaram Temple corridor (4,000 ft.)*
∗ Desert, Largest	*Thar (Rajasthan)*
∗ Dam, Longest	*Hirakud Dam (Odisha)*
∗ Delta, Largest	*Sunderban's Delta*

ome, Largest	*Gol Gumbaj (Bijapur)*
am, Highest	*Tehri Dam (260 m)*
ateway, Highest	*Buland Darwaja at Fatehpur Sikri (176 ft.)*
resh Water Lake, Largest	*Wular Lake (Kashmir)*
teracy, Highest	*Kerala (94%)*
useum, Largest	*Indian Museum (Kolkata)*
osque, Biggest	*Jama Masjid (Delhi)*
eak, Highest**	*K-2 (Pak-Occupied Kashmir)*
ailway Platform, Longest	*Shree Siddharoodha Swamiji Railway Station Hubballi, Karnataka (1507 m. long)*
ailway Bridge, longest	*Vembanad Bridge, Kerala (4.6 km)*
ver, Longest***	*The Ganges (2525 Km)*
ainfall, Highest (annual mean)	*Mowsynram near Cherrapunji (1178 cm)*
oad Longest	*NH-44 (3,745 km)*
ate, with maximum forest cover	*Madhya Pradesh*
ate, with maximum density of population	*Bihar*
lescope, Largest in Asia	*Vainu Bappu Telescope (at Kavalur: Chennai) 2.34m*
nnel, Longest (Road)	*Dr. Shyama Prasad Mukherjee Tunnel (9.28 kms, J & K)*
nnel, Longest (Railway)	*T-50 Tunnel, Khari-Sumber section (12.77 kms) Jammu & Kashmir.*
llest Minaret	*Qutub Minar (Delhi 72.5 m.)*
aterfall, Highest	*Kunchikal Waterfall (Karnataka: 455 m.)*
o, Largest	*Arignar Anna Zoological Park, Chennai, Tamil Nadu*

est peak in the world is Mount Everest, which is in Nepal. K-2 is the second highest peak in the world. It is 8,611 metres high.
s and Brahmaputra (each 2900 km). Both of them, however, cover a long distance outside India.

TABLE OF PRECEDENCE

President
Vice-President
Prime Minister
Governors of States within their respective states
Former Presidents
Deputy Prime Minister
Chief Justice of India, Speaker of Lok Sabha
Cabinet Ministers of the Union, Chief Ministers of States within their respective States
Deputy Chairman NITI Aayog, former Prime Ministers
Leaders of opposition in Rajya Sabha and Lok Sabha
Holders of the Bharat Ratna Decoration
Ambassadors Extraordinary and Plenipotentiary and High Commissioners of Commonwealth Countries accredited to India, Chief Ministers of States outside their respective States
Judges of the Supreme Court
Deputy Chairman Rajya Sabha, Deputy Chief Minister of States, Deputy Speaker Lok Sabha, Members of the NITI Aayog, Minister of State of the Union and Other Minister in the Ministry of Defence.

BOOKS AND AUTHORS

FOREIGN

Book	Author
✶ As You Like It	William Shakespeare
✶ A Tale of Two Cities	Charles Dickens
✶ Ben Hur	Lewis Wallace
✶ Das Kapital	Karl Marx
✶ David Copperfield	Charles Dickens
✶ Hamlet	William Shakespeare
✶ Iliad	Homer
✶ Inferno	A. Dante
✶ In Memoriam	Lord Tennyson
✶ Ivanhoe	Walter Scott
✶ Julius Caesar	William Shakespeare
✶ Lady Chatterley's Lover	D.H. Lawrence
✶ Lajja	Taslima Nasreen
✶ Les Miserable	Victor Hugo
✶ Leviathan	Thomas Hobbes
✶ Lolita	V. Nobokov
✶ Lycidas	John Milton
✶ Mein Kampf	Adolf Hitler
✶ Moor's Last Sigh	Salman Rushdie
✶ Mother	Maxim Gorky
✶ Mother India	Katherine Mayo
✶ Nana	Emile Zola
✶ Odyssey	Homer
✶ Origin of Species	Charles Darwin
✶ Othello	William Shakespeare
✶ Paradise Lost	John Milton
✶ Paradise Regained	John Milton
✶ Path to Power	Margaret Thatcher
✶ Pickwick Papers	Charles Dickens
✶ Razor's Edge	Somerset Maugham
✶ Republic	Plato
✶ The Tempest	William Shakespeare
✶ Time Machine	H.G. Wells
✶ Tom Sawyer	Mark Twain
✶ Treasure Island	R.L. Stevenson
✶ Twelfth Night	William Shakespeare
✶ Unto This Last	John Ruskin
✶ Utopia	Thomas More
✶ Wealth of Nations	Adam Smith
✶ Wonder that was India	A.L. Basham

INDIAN

Book	Author
✶ Ain-i-Akbari	Abul Fazal
✶ Anand Math	Bankim Chandra Chatterjee
✶ Arthashastra	Kautilya
✶ A Suitable Boy	Vikram Seth
✶ Bhagwat Gita	Ved Vyas
✶ Chidambara	Sumitranandan Pan
✶ Devdas	Sarat Chandra Chatte
✶ Discovery of India	Jawaharlal Nehru
✶ Ganadevata	Tarashankar Bandopadhyaya
✶ Geet Govind	Jaya Dev
✶ Geetanjali	R. N. Tagore
✶ Glimpses of World History	Jawaharlal Nehru
✶ Godaan	Prem Chand
✶ Gul-e-Nagma	Firaq Gorakhpuri
✶ Harsh Charita	Bana Bhatta
✶ India Divided	Dr. Rajendra Prasa
✶ Justice of Peace ke Aansu	Janardan Prasad Si
✶ The Judgement	Kuldip Nayyar
✶ Kadambari	Bana Bhatta
✶ Kagaz Te Kanwas	Amrita Pritam
✶ Kamayani	Jai Shankar Prasa
✶ Kitni Nawon Mein Kitni Bar	S. H. Vatsyayan
✶ Kumar Sambhav	Kalidas
✶ Mahabharata	Ved Vyas
✶ Malgudi Days	R.K. Narayan
✶ Meghdoot	Kalidas
✶ Mritunjaya	B.K. Bhattacharya
✶ Mudrarakshasa	Vishakhadatta
✶ Prison Diary	Jaya Prakash Narayan
✶ Raghuvansha	Kalidas
✶ Rajtarangini	Kalhana
✶ Ramayana	Balmiki
✶ Ramcharit Manas	Tulsidas
✶ Rukh Te Rishi	Harbhajan Singh
✶ Satyarth Prakash	Swami Dayanand
✶ Sur Sagar	Surdas
✶ The Guide	R.K. Narayan

IMPORTANT DATES AND DAYS OF THE YEAR

ANUARY

11 Road Safety Week
12 National Youth Day
15 Army Day
21 Pin Code Week
23 National Day of Patriotism
26 Republic Day
30 Martyr's Day

EBRUARY

14 Oil Conservation Fortnight
14 Valentine's Day

ARCH

4 National Safety Day
8 International Women's Day
15 Consumers' Day
16 Immunisation Day
21 World Forest Day
22 World Day for Water
24 World Meteorological Day
-7 Preservation of Blindness Week

PRIL

7 World Health Day
3 Handloom Week
20 Fire Service Week
8 World Heritage Day
2 World Earth Day

AY

1 May Day
5 National Labour Day
8 World Red Cross Day
1 National Technology Day
5 International Day of the Family
7 World Telecommunication Day
4 Commonwealth Day
1 World No-Tobacco Day

NE

5 World Environment Day
1 World Yoga Day
6 International Day against Drug Abuse and Illicit Trafficking

LY

1 World Population Day

∗ AUGUST

1-7 World Breast feeding Week
10 Sanskrit Divas
15 Independence Day
20 Sadbhavana Divas

∗ SEPTEMBER

1-7 National Nutrition Week
5 Teachers' Day
8 International Literary Day
14 Hindi Diwas
23 World Deaf Day
27 World Tourism Day

∗ OCTOBER

2 Gandhi Jayanti
International Day of Non Violence
Anti-Leprosy Day
4 World Animal Day
6 World Habitat Day *(Ist Monday)*
8 Indian Air Force Day
14 World Standard Day
15 International Day of Rural Women
16 World Food Day
24 United Nations Day
27 Infantry Day
28 World Thrift Day
31 Anti-Terrorism Day

∗ NOVEMBER

2 All Saints Day
14 Children's Day
15-21 National Cooperative Week
19-25 Quami Ekta Week
20 Child Rights Day
26 Constitution Day

∗ DECEMBER

1 World AIDS Day
3 World Day for the Disabled
4 Naval Day
7 Flag Day
8 SMRC Day
10 Human Rights Day
14 National Energy Conservation Day

INDIAN DEFENCE

- The Supreme Command of the Armed Forces is vested in the hands of the President of the Country.
- The responsibility for national defence, however, rests with the Cabinet. All important questions having a bearing on defence are decided by the Cabinet Committee on Political Affairs, which is presided over by the Prime Minister.
- The Defence Minister is responsible to Parliament for all matters concerning the Defence Services.
- All the administrative and operational control of Armed Forces are exercised by the Ministry of Defence. The three services—Army, Navy and Air Force function through their respective service head-quarters headed by the chief of Staff. The post of Chief of Defence Staff (CDS) was created in 2019.

Indian Army Commands

Command	*HQ Location*
Eastern Command	Kolkata
Western Command	Chandigarh
Northern Command	Udhampur
Southern Command	Pune
Central Command	Lucknow
Training Command	Shimla
South-Western Command	Jaipur

Indian Air Force Commands

Command	*HQ Location*
Western Air Command	New Delhi
Sout-Western Air Command	Gandhinagar
Central Air Command	Allahabad
Eastern Air Command	Shillong
Southern Air Command	Thiruvananthapu
Training Command	Bengaluru

Indian Navy Commands

Command	*HQ Location*
Eastern Naval Command	Vishakhapatnam
Western Naval Command	Mumbai
Southern Naval Command	Cochin

Commissioned Ranks in Defence Services

Army	*Navy*	*Air Force*
General	Admiral	Air Chief Marshal
Lieutenant-General	Vice-Admiral	Air Marshal
Major-General	Rear-Admiral	Air Vice-Marshal
Brigadier	Commodor	Air Commodor
Colonel	Captain	Group Captain
Lieutenant-Colonel	Commander	Wing Commander
Major	Lt.Commander	Squadron Leader
Captain	Lieutenant	Flight Lieutenant
Lieutenant	Sub-Lieutenant	Flying Officer

Internal Security Organisations of India

S. No.	*Name of Organisation*	*Year of Creation*	*Headquarters*
1.	Assam Rifles (A.R.)	1835	Shillong
2.	Central Reserve Police Force (CRPF)	1939	New Delhi
3.	Territorial Army	1948	In different States
4.	Indo-Tibetan Border Police	1962	New Delhi
5.	Home Guard	1962	In different States

No.	Name of Organisation	Year of Creation	Headquarters
6.	Coast Guard	1978	New Delhi
7.	Border Security Force (B.S.F.)	1965	New Delhi
8.	Central Industrial Security Force (CISF)	1969	New Delhi
9.	National Security Guard	1984	New Deihi
0.	Police	—	In different States

Army Institutes

1.	Sainik Schools upto +2 Level	33 places in India
2.	Rashtriya Indian Military College (prepare for entrance to N.D.A.)	Dehradun
3.	National Defence Academy (three services)	Khadakwasla, Pune
4.	Indian Military Academy (Army)	Dehradun
5.	Officers Training Academy (3 services) Short Courses	Chennai
6.	National Defence College	New Delhi
7.	The College of Combat	Mnow
8.	The College of Military Englneering	Kirkee
9.	Military College of Telecommunication Engineering	Mhow
10.	The Armoured Corps Centre and School	Ahmed Nagar
11.	The School Artillery	Deolali
12.	The Infantry School	Mhow and Belgaum
13.	College of Material Management	Jabalpur

Air Force Institutions

ir Force Academy	Hyderabad	✶ Helicopter Training School	Hakimpet
ying Instructors School	Tambaram, Chennai	✶ The College of Air Warfare	Secunderabad
ir Force Administrative College	Coimbatore	✶ Air Force Technical College	Jalahalli

UNITED NATIONS (UN)

The United Nations (UN) is an association of states which have pledged themselves to maintain international peace and security and cooperate in solving international political, economic, social cultural and humanitarian problems towards achieving this end.

Trygve Lie of Norway (1946-52) was the first Secretary-General of the UN.

Origin: UN Charter was signed by 50 members on June 26, 1945. Poland signed the charter later to become one of the original 51 member-states. It officially came into existence on October 24, 1945.

- ***UN Charter:*** The Charter is the Constitution of the UN and contains its aims and objectives and rules and regulations for its functioning.
- ***Aims and Objectives:*** They are security, welfare and human rights.
- ***Headquarters:*** New York.
- ***Flag:*** The flag is light blue in colour, and emblazoned in white, in its centre is the UN symbol—a polar map of world embraced by twin olive branches open at the top.
- ***Official Languages:*** The official languages of the UN are: English, French, Chinese, Russian, Arabic and Spanish. However, working languages are English and French only.

- ***Present Membership:*** At present 193 countries are members of the UN. South Sudan is the latest entrant to this world organisation.
- ***Main Organs of the UN:*** There are six main organs:
  1. General Assembly
  2. Security Council
  3. Economic and Social Council
  4. Trusteeship Council
  5. International Court of Justice, and
  6. Secretariat.

1. *General Assembly:* It consists of representative of all members of the UN. Each member country has only one vote. It meets once a year and passes UN Budget. It is the main place for discussions and policy making in the UN.
2. *Security Council:* It is the Executive body of the UN and is mainly responsible for maintaining international peace and securi[ty]. It has 15 members, 5 of which (USA, U[K], France, Russia and China) are permane[nt] members. The 10 non-permanent members a[re] elected by General Assembly for two-year te[rm] and are not eligible for immediate re-electio[n].
3. *Economic and Social Council:* It has [...] members elected by General Assembly.
4. *Trusteeship Council:* It looks after interest [of] the people in areas not yet independent a[nd] leads them towards self-government.
5. *International Court of Justice:* It has [...] judges, no two of whom may be nationals [of] the same state. They are elected by Gener[al] Assembly and Security Council for a term [of] 9 years. The Court elects its President a[nd] Vice-President for a 3-year term.
6. *Secretariat:* It is the Secretariat of the UN a[nd] is headed by the Secretary General.

Some Important UN Agencies

UN Agencies	Headquarters	Year of Establishment
✶ United Nations (U.N.)	New York	1945
✶ International Monetary Fund (I.M.F.)	Washington D.C.	1945
✶ World Health Organisation (W.H.O.)	Geneva	1948
✶ Food & Agricultural Organisation (FAO)	Rome	1945
✶ International Labour Organisation (ILO)	Geneva	1919
✶ UNESCO	Paris	1946
✶ Universal Postal Union (UPU)	Berne	1874
✶ UNIDO	Vienna	1966
✶ International Atomic Energy Agency (IAEA)	Vienna	1957
✶ United Nations Development Programme (UNDP)	New York	1965
✶ UNICEF	New York	1946
✶ International Maritime Organisation (IMO)	London	1958
✶ World Meteorological Organisation (WMO)	Geneva	1950
✶ International Telecommunication Union (ITU)	Geneva	1865
✶ World Trade Organisation (WTO)	Geneva	1995
✶ International Development Association (IDA)	Washington D.C.	1960
✶ World Intellectual Property Organisation (WIPO)	Geneva	1967

Famous International Organisations

International Organisations	Headquarters	Year of Establishment
International Court of Justice	The Hague	1946
International Civil Aviation Organisation (ICAO)	Montreal	1947
International Finance Corporation (IFC)	Washington D.C	1956
Arab League	Cairo	1945
Commonwealth of Nations	London	1949
International Bank for Reconstruction and Development (IBRD)	Washington D.C.	1945
Organisation of Islamic Cooperation (OIC)	Jeddah (Saudi Arabia)	1969
Red Cross	Geneva	1863
Interpol	Lyons	1923
Asian Development Bank (ADB)	Manila	1966
North Atlantic Treaty Organisation (NATO)	Brussels	1949
Association of South East Asian Nations (ASEAN)	Jakarta	1967
South Asian Association for Regional Cooperation (SAARC)	Kathmandu	1985
Asia-Pacific Economic Cooperation (APEC)	Singapore	1989
Organisation for Economic Cooperation and Development (OECD)	Paris	1961
Organisation of Petroleum Exporting Countries (OPEC)	Vienna	1960
Commonwealth of Independent States (CIS)	Minsk	1991
International Olympic Committee (IOC)	Lausanne (Switzerland)	1894
European Union (EU)	Brussels	Changed form of EEC Established in 1958
Amnesty International (AI)	London	1961
Shanghai Cooperation Organisation (SCO)	Beijing	2001
BRICS Development Bank	Shanghai	2014

AWARDS AND HONOURS

NATIONAL AWARDS

BHARAT RATNA

- Bharat Ratna is India's highest Civilian Award.
- It was first awarded in 1954.
- The actual award is designed in the shape of a *peepal* leaf with Bharat Ratna inscribed in Devanagri script in the Sun Figure.
- This is India's highest civilian award. It is given for exceptional work on art, literature, science and recognition of public service of the highest order.
- The emblem, the Sun and the rim are of platinum.
- The inscriptions are in burnished bronze.
- Government servants are not eligible for it.

.EPUBLIC DAY AWARDS

Padma Awards

They fall in line after the Bharat Ratna. They are also discontinued in 1977 along with the Bharat Ratna and award was started again in 1980.

There are three Padma Awards:

- ***Padma Vibhushan:*** This award is given for exceptional and distinguished service in any field, including service rendered by Govt. servants.
- ***Padma Bhushan:*** This award is given for distinguished service of a high order in any field, including service rendered by Govt. servants.
- ***Padma Shri:*** This award is given for distinguished service in any field, including service rendered by Government servants.

Gallantry Awards

- ***Param Vir Chakra:*** The highest award for bravery or some daring and pre-eminent act of valour or self-sacrifice in the presence of the enemy, whether on land, at sea or in the air.
- ***Mahavir Chakra:*** It is the second highest decoration and is awarded for acts of conspicuous gallantry in the presence of the enemy, whether on land, at sea or in the air.
- ***Vir Chakra:*** It is the third in order of awards given for acts of gallantry in the presence of enemy, whether on land, at sea or in the air.
- ***Ashok Chakra:*** This medal is awarded for the most conspicuous bravery or some daring or pre-eminent act of valour or self-sacrifice on land, at sea or in the air but not in the presence of enemy.
- ***Vishishta Sewa Medal:*** It is awarded to personnel of all the three Services in class I, II and III in recognition of distinguished service of the "most exceptional" and "exceptional" and a "high" order respectively. Prefixes Parma and Ati are added before first two categories of medals respectively.
- ***Jeewan Raksha Padak:*** Awarded for meritorious acts or a series of acts of a human nature displayed in saving life from drowning, fire and rescue operations in mines etc.

OTHER NATIONAL AWARDS

SAHITYA AKADEMI AWARDS

- These prizes are awarded annually to the auth of the most outstanding books of literary me published in each of the 22 languages which a specified in the Eighth Schedule of t Constitution.
- There are also two awards for Rajasthani a English. The award, in form of a casket containi an inscribed copper plate and a cheque of ₹ lakh is given to the author or his/her heir.

DADA SAHEB PHALKE AWARD

- The award carries a cash prize of ₹ 15 lakh, Shawl and Swarna Kamal.
- Mrs Devika Rani Roerich was the first person receive Dadasaheb Phalke Award in 1969.

BHARATIYA JNANPITH AWARD

- Instituted in 22nd May, 1961, carries a ca prize of ₹ 21 lakh, a citation and a bronze repli of Vagdevi (Saraswati).
- Instituted by a literary organisation in India.

SARASWATI SAMMAN

- Given for outstanding literary works, valu ₹ 15 lakh.

VYAS SAMMAN

- This is awarded by KK Birla Foundation f outstanding Hindi Literary work by an India citizen that was published in the past decad This carries a cash prize of ₹ 4.0 lakh.

BHARTENDU HARISHCHANDRA AWARDS

- The Bhartendu Harishchandra Awards we instituted in 1983, by the Ministry of Informatio and Broadcasting for original Hindi writing o any subject in mass communications lik journalism, publication, advertising, broadcastin films, etc.

KALIDAS SAMMAN

- Instituted by the Madhya Pradesh Governmen the award is of the value of ₹ 2 lakh.

ABIR SAMMAN

The award is conferred annually on a person of literature of very high order on the basis of his or her superb creativity and consistent commitment to the most recent and latest trends of literary creation in any of the Indian languages. The award carries ₹ 3 lakh and a letter of citation.

INTERNATIONAL AWARDS

OBEL PRIZES

These Prizes were instituted in 1901 by a Swedish scientist, Dr. Alfred Nobel; the discoverer of Dynamite.

Six prizes are awarded annually for (i) Chemistry, (ii) Physics, (iii) Medicine, (iv) Literature, (v) Peace and (vi) Economics —started since 1969.

Indians Honoured with Nobel Prize: So far, following Indians have been honoured with these prizes. Their names are (i) Rabindra Nath Tagore for Literature, for his book 'Gitanjali', in 1913, (ii) Dr. C.V. Raman for Physics in 1930, for his discovery of 'Raman Effect', (iii) Mother Teresa for Peace in 1979, (iv) Prof. Amartya Sen in 1998 for Economics and (v) Kailash Satyarthi for Peace in 2014.

In addition, four non-resident Indians have also been awarded the Nobel Prize. They are: (i) Hargobind Khurana for Medicine in 1968, (ii) Subramanian Chandrasekhar for Physics in 1983, (iii) Venkatraman Ramkrishnan for Chemistry in 2009, (iv) Abhijit Vinayak Banerjee for Economics in 2019.

ANDHI PEACE PRIZE

The government instituted this ₹ 1 crore prize on the lines of the Nobel Peace Prize in 1995.

It is the highest Civilian International award by the Govt. of India.

AMON MAGSAYSAY AWARD

The Ramon Magsaysay Award, named after a Philippines President, who died in an air crash in 1957, is given annually to Asian nationals or institutions who have made worthy contributions to public service, community leadership, journalism, literature and the creative arts and international understanding. It carries a gold medal, a certificate and US$ 50,000. It is awarded on August 31, every year. The Ramon Magsaysay Award is Asia's highest honor and is widely regarded as the region's equivalent of the Nobel Prize. It celebrates the memory and leadership example of the third Philippline president after whom the award is named, and is given every year to individuals or organizations in Asia who manifest the same selfless service and transformative influence that ruled the life of the late and beloved Filipino leader.

INDIRA GANDHI PRIZE FOR PEACE, DISARMAMENT AND DEVELOPMENT

- The award was instituted in the memory of Mrs. Indira Gandhi to foster creative cooperation among nations of the world.

MISS WORLD

- This competition was established in 1951 by the 'Miss World Incorporation'. The Winner of this competition gets cash as prize and she is selected on her physical and intellectual genius.

MISS UNIVERSE

- This competition was established in year 1952 by 'Miss Universe Incorporation'. The winner of this competition gets cash as prize. The most beautiful girl is selected in this competition on the basis of her beauty and multifarious genius.

Highest Honours of Some Countries

Country	Highest Honour
India	Bharat Ratna
Pakistan	Nishan-e-Pakistan
Kuwait	Mubarak-Al-kabir Medal
Saudi Arabia	Shah Abdul Aziz Medal
Argentina	The Order of Sona Martin
Nicaragua	Augusto-Caesar Sandino Order
Vietnam	The Order of the Golden Star
Hungary	The Order of Banner
Britain	Member of British Empire, Victoria Cross
Japan	Order of Moulovenice Sun
Denmark	Order of Diana Brog
France	Legend of Honour
America	Presidential Medal of Freedom
Germany	Pore Lee Merit Iron Cross
The Netherlands	Netherlands Lion

SPORTS

OLYMPICS

- First of all these games were held by the Greeks in 776 B.C. on Mount Olympus in honour of the Greek God Zeus. In this way, the history of Olympic Games is about twenty eight hundred years old. These games continued to be held every four years until 394 A.D. when these games were stopped by a royal order of the emperor of Rome.
- The modern Olympic Games which started in Athens in 1896, are the result of the devotion and dedication of a French educator Baron Pierre de Coubertin and the first Olympic meet in the modern series was held in 1896 in Athens, the Capital of Greece. Since then, they are being held every four years except for breaks during world wars.
- The Olympic flag is white in colour with five coloured rings, each ring symbolic of a continent. Summer as well as Winter Olympics are held in the same year.
- The official Olympic Motto is *Citius, Altius, Swifter, Higher, Stronger*. The Head Office of International Olympic Committee (IOC) is at Lausanne (Switzerland).

COMMONWEALTH GAMES

- The Commonwealth Games are held every four years, in the year in which Asian Games are held. All the Commonwealth Countries (former colonies of Britain) can take part in it.
- The first Commonwealth Games were held in 1930 at Hamilton (Canada). There are currently 54 members of the Commonwealth of Nations, and 71 teams participated in the games.

ASIAN GAMES

- After the Second World War, most of the Asian Countries gained independence. On the lines of Olympic Games, Asian Games were planned every four years. India hosted the first Asian Games in 1951.

WORLD CUP CRICKET

- The first Cricket World Cup was organised in England in 1975. A separate women's Cricket World Cup has been held every 4 years since 1973.

HOCKEY WORLD CUP

- The first Hockey World Cup was organise[d] Barcelona (Spain) in 1971. Women's Hoc[key] World Cup has been held since 1974.

FOOTBALL WORLD CUP

- The Football World Cup is organised by F[IFA] (Federation of International Football Associati[on]) The World Cup is called 'Jules Rimet C[up]' named after the name of FIFA President J[ules] Rimet. The first Football World Cup [was] organised in Uruguay in 1930.
- In 1942 and 1946, the Football World Cup [was] not played due to World War II.

SPORTS TERMS

- ✶ ***Badminton:*** Mixed doubles; Deuce; Dr[...] Smash; Let; Foot work; Setting.
- ✶ ***Base Ball:*** Pitcher; Put out, Strike; Home; B[...]
- ✶ ***Billiards:*** Cue; Jigger; Pot; Break; In Baulk[...] Off; Cannons.
- ✶ ***Boxing:*** Upper cut; Round; Punch; Bout; Kn[ock] down; Hitting below the belt; Ring.
- ✶ ***Bridge:*** Finesse; Dummy; Revoke; Grand Sl[am;] Little Slam; No Trump; Rubber.
- ✶ ***Chess:*** Bishop, Gambit; Checkmate; Stalem[ate]
- ✶ ***Cricket:*** L.B.W. (leg before wicket); Crea[se;] Popping-creases; Stumped; Bye; Leg-B[ye;] Googly; Hattrick; Maiden over; Drive; Bowl[ing;] Duck; Follow-on; No ball; Leg Break; S[...] point; Cover point; Hit-wicket; Late-cut; S[...] Off-spinner; In-swing.
- ✶ ***Football:*** Off Side; Block; Drop-kick; Pena[lty] kick (or goal kick); Corner-kick; Free-ki[ck;] Dribble; Thrown-in; Foul.
- ✶ ***Golf:*** Boggy; Foursome; Stymic; Tee; Put; H[...] Niblic; Caddie; Links; The green; Bunker.
- ✶ ***Hockey:*** Carried; Short Corner; Bully; Sti[ck;] Off side; Roll in; Striking Circle; Under-cutti[ng;] Dribble.
- ✶ ***Horse racing:*** Jockey; Punter.
- ✶ ***Polo:*** Bunker; Chukker; Mallet.
- ✶ ***Tennis:*** Back hand drive; Volley; Smash; H[alf] volley; Deuce; Service; Let; Grand Slam.

ALL THE HEROES

Sportsman	Game
Anand Amritraj	Tennis
Arati Saha	Swimming
Ashok Malik	Golf
Althea Gibson	Tennis
Ashe Arthur	Tennis
Mohd. Azharuddin	Cricket
A.K. Ghosh	Chess
Anju Dua	Gymnastics
Balbir Singh	Hockey
Bannerji, P.K.	Football
Bedi, B.S.	Cricket
Bapu Nadkarni	Cricket
Benaud, Richie	Cricket
Ben Johnson	Athletics
Bobby Fischer	Chess
Boris Becker	Tennis
Bharat Ram	Golf
Chetan Baboor	Table Tennis
Borde, Chandu	Cricket
Budding, Ingo	Tennis
Bungert, Williams	Tennis
Chandrashekhar	Cricket
Chandgi Ram	Wrestling
Charanjit Singh	Hockey
Carl Lewis	Athletics
Chuni Goswami	Football
Clandius	Hockey
Clive Loyd	Cricket
Connoly	Tennis
Chris Evert	Tennis
Dhyan Chand	Hockey
Dara Singh	Wrestling
Dinesh Khanna	Badminton
Diwan, G.	Table Tennis
Dolly Zazir	Swimming
Durrani, Salim	Cricket
Das, Susan	Tennis
Don Bradman	Cricket
Emerson, Roy	Tennis
Erlend Kops	Badminton
Elena Shushunova	Gymnastics
Flash Gordon	Wrestling
Florence Griffith Joyner	Athletics
Gurang Mehta	Chess

Sportsman	Game
Goolagong, Even	Tennis
Ghose, A.L.	Golf
Hamida Bano	Wrestling
Haneef	Cricket
Harbans Singh	Wrestling
Harnek Singh	Hockey
Hasan Sardar	Hockey
Hazare, V.	Cricket
Henry Cotton	Golf
Hutton, Len	Cricket
Imran Khan	Cricket
Ivan Lendle	Tennis
Jaideep Mukherjee	Tennis
Jasjit Singh	Tennis
Jarnail Singh	Football
Jayant Vohra	Table Tennis
kapil Dev	Cricket
Maradona	Football
Martina Navratilova	Tennis
Mike Tyson	Boxing
Mohammed Ali Clay	Boxing
Mohammed Shahid	Hockey
Narendra Hirwani	Cricket
Nawab Pataudi	Cricket
Rod Lever	Tennis
RS Gentle	Hockey
Sachin Tendulkar	Cricket
Seth, T. N.	Badminton
Shirley Fry	Tennis
Shonny Liston	Boxing
Shiny Abraham	Athletics
Steffi Graf	Tennis
Sunil Gavaskar	Cricket
Udham Singh	Hockey
Umrigar, Poly	Cricket
Urmila Thapar	Tennis
Usha P.T.	Athletics
Vijay Amrithraj	Tennis
Vivian Richard	Cricket
Wasim Akram	Cricket
Wilson Jones	Billiards
Woong Pong	Badminton
Worrel, Frank	Cricket
Zafar Iqbal	Hockey

IMPORTANT CUPS & TROPHIES

International

- *American Cup* : Yacht Racing
- *Ashes* : Cricket
- *Davis Cup* : Lawn Tennis
- *Derby* : Horse Race
- *Grand National* : Horse Streple Chase Race
- *Jules Rimet Trophy* : World Soccer Cup
- *King's Cup* : Air Races
- *Merdeka Cup* : Football
- *Swaythling Cup* : Table Tennis (Men)
- *Ryder Cup* : Golf
- *Thomas Cup* : Badminton
- *U. Thant Cup* : Tennis
- *Walker Cup* : Golf
- *Wightman Cup* : Lawn Tennis
- *Rothman's Trophy* : Cricket
- *European Champions Cup* : Football
- *Edgbaston Cup* : Lawn Tennis
- *Grand Prix* : Lawn Tennis

National

- *Agha Khan Cup* : Hockey
- *Beighton Cup* : Hockey
- *Bombay Gold Cup* : Hockey
- *C.K. Naydu Trophy* : Cricket
- *Deodhar Trophy* : Cricket
- *Duleep Trophy* : Cricket
- *Durand Cup* : Football
- *Dhyan Chand Trophy* : Hockey
- *Dr. B.C. Roy Trophy* : Football (Junior)
- *Ezra Cup* : Polo
- *Guru Nanak Cup* : Hockey
- *Holkar Trophy* : Bridge
- *Irani Trophy* : Cricket
- *Murugappa Gold Cup* : Hockey
- *Nehru Trophy* : Hockey
- *Nixan Gold Cup* : Football
- *Rani Jhansi Trophy* : Cricket
- *Ranji Trophy* : Cricket
- *Rangaswami Cup* : Hockey
- *Ramanujan Trophy* : Table Tennis
- *Rene Frank Trophy* : Hockey
- *Rohinton Baria Trophy* : Cricket
- *Rovers Cup* : Football
- *Santosh Trophy* : Football
- *Subroto Cup* : Football

Stadiums & Places Associated with Spo

Name of Stadium	Sports	Place
Arun Jaitley Stadium	Cricket	Delhi
Jawaharlal Nehru Stadium	Athletics	Delhi
Shivajee Stadium	Hockey	Delhi
Ambedkar Stadium	Football	Delhi
Brabourne Stadium	Cricket	Mumbai
Wankhede Stadium	Cricket	Mumbai
National Stadium	Hockey etc.	Mumbai
Eden Garden	Cricket	Kolkata
Green Park Stadium	Cricket	Kanpur
Keenan Stadium	Cricket	Jamshed
Barabati Stadium	Cricket	Cuttack
Lords, Oval, Leeds	Cricket	Britain
Hedingle Manchester	Cricket	Britain
Black Heath	Rugby Football	London
Henley	Boat race	England
Wembley Stadium	Football	London
Narendra Modi Stadium	Cricket	Ahmedal
White City	Dog-race	England
Aintree	Horse-race	England
Tentbridge	Cricket	England
Patnee Martlake	Boat-race	England
Tibankham	Rugby Football	England
Sandy Lodge	Golf	Scotlan
Brooklyn	Baseball	New Yo
Melbourne	Cricket	Australia

Name of Playing Compound of Different Games

Name of Compound	Related Sports
Court	Lawn Tennis, Badminton, Net Hand ball, Volleyball, Squash, Kho, Kabaddi
Diamond	Baseball
Ring	Boxing, Skating, Wrestling, Cir Riding display
Course	Golf
Board	Table Tennis
Pool	Swimming
Mat	Judo, Karate II
Arena	Horse Riding
Vellodrum	Cycling
Field	Polo, Football, Hockey
Track	Athletics
Pitch	Cricket, Rugby
Rink	Ice Hockey

❐❐❐

Multiple Choice Questions

Match List-I with List-II and select the correct answer from the codes given below the lists:

List-I

(*a*) Napoleon Bonaparte
(*b*) Jean Jacques Rousseau
(*c*) Croce
(*d*) Madame Roland

List-II

1. 'A history is contemporary history'
2. 'Liberty what crimes are committed in thy name'
3. 'Man is born free but everywhere he is in chains.'
4. 'I am the Child of Revolution'

Codes :

	(*a*)	(*b*)	(*c*)	(*d*)
A.	1	2	3	4
B.	4	3	1	2
C.	3	4	2	1
D.	3	4	1	2

Abraham Lincon was elected the President of United States in:
A. 1862 B. 1860
C. 1875 D. 1855

Who was known as the 'Prince of Humanists'?
A. Francisco Petrarch B. Dante
C. Boccacio D. Erasmus

D-Day is the day when:
A. Germany declared war on Britain
B. US dropped the atom bomb on Hiroshima.
C. Allied Troops landed in Normandy
D. Germany surrendered to the allies

Whose teachings inspired the French Revolution?
A. Locke
B. Rousseau
C. Hegel
D. Plato

6. At a time when empires in Europe were crumbling before the might of Napoleon which one of the following Governor-Generals kept the British flag flying high in India?
A. Warren Hastings B. Lord Cornwallis
C. Lord Wellesley D. Lord Hastings

7. Which one of the following statements regarding Fascism in Italy is *not* true?
A. The Fascists came to power as a result of popular uprising
B. In 1926, all political parties except Mussolini's party were banned
C. The Fascists suppressed the Socialist movement
D. The Fascists were hostile to the Communists

8. The fall of Czar Nicholas-II is known as:
A. Bloody Sunday
B. Bolshevik Revolution
C. February Revolution
D. October Revolution

9. Industrial Revolution took place first in:
A. France B. Germany
C. United Kingdom D. Japan

10. The British Prime Minister at the outbreak of World War II was :
A. Churchill B. Baldwin
C. Attlee D. Chemberlain

11. The 'Great Depression' (1929) economic crisis was met by adopting the policy of
A. Stimulus B. Marshall Plan
C. New Deal D. Open Door

12. The slogan "No taxation wit[illegible] representation" was raised during th[illegible]
A. American War of Independe[illegible]
B. Russian Revolution
C. French Revolution
D. Indian Freedo[illegible]

13. In the nineteenth century the people of Europe started moving from the villages to the cities due to the impact of :
A. Epidemics
B. War
C. Industrialisation
D. Population explosion in villages

14. The important cause of the Civil War in America was:
A. Abolition of slavery
B. Quest for freedom
C. Industrialisation
D. Rebellion by the native Americans

15. Industrial Revolution could not have come about without:
A. Merchant capitalism
B. The Enclosure Movement
C. The services of the proletariat class
D. An agricultural revolution

16. Consider the following statements :
The French Revolution came about mainly due to the :
1. Extreme poverty of the people
2. Impact of the works of great writers
3. Cruelty of the rulers
4. Impact of impulsive reaction
Which of the above statements are correct?
A. 1, 2 and 4 B. 2 and 3
C. 1, 3 and 4 D. 1, 2, 3 and 4

17. Asia's oldest and largest Buddhist monastery is situated in :
A. Tawang (Arunachal Pardesh)
B. Lhasa (Tibet)
C. Trincomallee (Sri Lanka)
D. Ulan Bator (Mongolia)

18. Who was the main architect of the Russian Revolution?
A. Karl Marx B. Lenin
C. Stalin D. Tolstoy

nin is associated with :
Revolution of 1917
olution of 1949
on
1789

20. Which one of the following statement correct?
A. Voltaire believed in Natural Relig
B. Rousseau wrote *Social Contract*
C. Montesquieu authored *The Spirit*
D. Necker believed in 'General Will'

21. 6th April, 1930 is well known in the of India because this date is ass with..........
A. Dandi March by Mahatma Gandh
B. Quit India Movement
C. Partition of Bengal
D. Partition of India

22. Which ruler enforced the system of Control' in India?
A. Mohammad Tughlak
B. Razia Begum
C. Alauddin Khilji
D. Sher Shah Suri

23. The concept of 'Din-e-Elahi' was fou which king?
A. Dara Shikoh B. Akbar
C. Sher Shah Suri D. Shahjahan

24. Who are supposed to be the earliest tants of India? Where did they come
A. Aryans from Central Asia
B. Dravidians from Mediterranean
C. Negroids from Africa
D. Bhils and the Santhals from Wes

25. The one chief characteristic of architecture of the Gupta Age was :
A. Absence of dome
B. Huge size
C. Beautiful carvings
D. absence of a covered courtyard gathering of worshippers

26. The Rigveda consists of :
A. 1000 hymns B. 2028 hym
C. 1028 hymns D. 1038 hym

27. The central point in Ashoka's dharm
A. royalty to kings
B. peace and non-violence
C. respect to elders
D. religious tolerance

e social evil which was conspicuously
sent during ancient India was :

Sati-System B. *Devadasi*-System
Polygamy D. *Purdah*-System

hich, among the following, can be accepted a novelty introduced by Mughal emperors their buildings?

Domes B. Minarets
Arches D. Attached gardens

e first ruler of India who defeated uhammud of Ghur was :

Mularaja II of Gujarat
Prithviraja Chauhan of Delhi
Jayachand of Kannauj
Parmaldeva of Bundelkhand

hat important event happened in India in 11?

Bengal was partitioned
Non-Cooperation movement was launched
India's capital was shifted from Calcutta to Delhi
Mahatma Gandhi presided over the Congress session

e first phase of the Congress Party (1885-05) was characterized by its efforts to cure:

limited independence
complete freedom
Indianization of services
constitutional reforms

e Muslim League demanded a separate meland for the Indian Muslims openly for first time at its annual session held in hore in the year :

1931 A.D. B. 1936 A.D.
1940 A.D. D. 1941 A.D.

der whose governorship did the East India mpany secure the Diwani Rights in Bengal, har and Odisha from Emperor Shah am?

Lord Cornwallis
Lord William Bentinck
Lord Clive
Lord Wellesley

35. The Simon Commission was generally boycotted by the Indian political parties. What was the reason for this general non-cooperation?

A. the Commission aimed at dividing the people
B. it was an 'all white' Commission
C. it came after the Jallianwala Bagh carnage
D. it was an eye wash

36. Aligarh Muslim University was founded by :

A. Dr. Saifuddin Kitchlu
B. Mohammad Ali Jinnah
C. Sir Syed Ahmed Khan
D. Maulana Mohammad Ali

37. Ibn Batutah was an African traveller visiting India during the time of :

A. Alivardi Khan
B. Ala-ud-din Khalji
C. Iltutmish
D. Mohammad-bin-Tughlaq

38. The battle of Wandiawash was fought in :

A. 1726 B. 1760
C. 1818 D. 1857

39. The abolition of *Sati* by government regulation was at the time of :

A. Warren Hastings B. Lord Wellesley
C. Lord Bentinck D. Lord Ahmerst

40. Pick out the wrong combination :

A. Dilwara Temple : Mt. Abu
B. Pashupati Temple : Kathmandu
C. Padmanabh Temple : Bangalore
D. Minakshi Temple : Madurai

41. Match the following:

(*a*) Chanhudaro (*b*) Kalibangan
(*c*) Lothal (*d*) Surkotada

1. Alleged discovery of the skeleton of horse.
2. Bead making.
3. Traces of a dock and ship on seal.
4. Evidence of ploughing the fields.

The Correct code is :

	(*a*)	(*b*)	(*c*)	(*d*)
A.	2	4	3	1
B.	2	1	3	4
C.	1	2	3	4
D.	2	1	4	3

42. Match the Harappan settlements with the banks of rivers on which they were located :

(*a*) Harappa	1. Ravi
(*b*) Mohenjodaro	2. Indus
(*c*) Ropar	3. Sutlej
(*d*) Kalibangan	4. Ghaggar
(*e*) Lothal	5. Bhogava

Codes :

	(*a*)	(*b*)	(*c*)	(*d*)	(*e*)
A.	1	2	3	4	5
B.	1	2	3	5	4
C.	2	1	3	5	4
D.	2	1	4	3	5

43. The Goddess 'Kannagi' whose many temples were erected during the 'Sangam Age' was the goddess of :

A. Chastity B. Love
C. Prowess D. Wisdom

44. The Jain goal of life is to attain deliverance from the fetters of mudane existence, the way to which lies through three jewels. Which one of the following was not included among the 'three jewels' of Jainism?

A. Right faith B. Right action
C. Right knowledge D. Right conduct

45. The most striking feature of the Ashokan pillar is polish. Name the Ashokan pillar which is considered to be the most graceful of all Ashokan pillars.

A. Sarnath
B. Rampurva
C. Laurya-Nandangarh
D. Rummindei

46. Which are the correct statements?

1. The land grants, started in Satavahana period, paved the way for feudal developments in India.
2. Silk and spices were the Chief Indian export articles of Indo-Roman trade.
3. The Guptas issued the largest number of gold coins in ancient India.
4. The first memorial of a 'SATI' dated 510 A.D. is found at Eran in Madhya Pradesh.

A. 1 and 2 B. 1, 3, and 4
C. 1 and 4 D. 1, 2, 3 and 4

47. Who among the following patro 'Gandhara' (Indo-Greek style) Scho

A. Ashoka, the Great
B. Harsha Vardhana
C. Kanishka
D. Chandragupta Vikramaditya

48. The Sultanate of Delhi had fiv dynasties. The dynasty having lor shortest period were :

A. Ilbari and Khalji
B. Tughlaq and Khalji
C. Tughlaq and Sayyid
D. Ilbari and Lodis

49. Which one of the following events t at the last during reign of Muham Tughlaq?

A. Introduction of token currency
B. Increase of land-revenue in Doa
C. Transfer of Capital from Delhi to
D. Conquest of Khurasan and Iraq

50. The most learned medieval Muslim was well versed in various branches o including astronomy, mathema medicine was :

A. Jalaluddin Khilji
B. Sikander Lodi
C. Ghiyasuddin Tughlaq
D. Muhammad-bin-Tughlaq

51. The 'Sufis' had 12 silsilas. They pr the idea of Union with God throu

A. Love B. Rituals
C. Fasts D. Prayers

52. Match the following:

(*a*) Peshwa	1. Foreign affairs
(*b*) Panditrao	2. Audit and accoun
(*c*) Amatya	3. Providing grants t
(*d*) Sumant	4. General supervisi
	5. Military affairs

Select the correct code :

	(*a*)	(*b*)	(*c*)	(*d*)
A.	2	3	4	5
B.	4	1	2	3
C.	4	3	2	1
D.	3	1	4	2

: Regulating Act of 1773 can be regarded he first measure to :
assert the right of British Parliament to legislate for India
separate the legislature from the executive
separate the judiciary from the executive
centralise law-making

at was the exact constitutional status of Indian Republic on 26th January, 1950?
A Democratic Republic
A Sovereign, Democratic Republic
A Sovereign, Secular, Democratic Republic
A Sovereign, Socialist, Secular, Democratic Republic

en the British obtained the grant of Diwani Bengal, Bihar and Odisha they acquired right to :
maintain law and order in these territories
administer civil justice and collect revenue in these territories
collect revenue and establish revenue administration in these territories
militarily defend these territories

ich of the following were responsible for growth of nationalism in India during the ish rule?
Economic exploitation of India.
Impact of western education.
Role of the Press.
ct the correct answer using the codes given ow :
les:
1, 2 and 3 B. 1 and 2
2 and 3 D. 1 and 3

ch one of the following nationalist leaders been described as being radical in politics conservative on social issues?
G.K. Gokhale
B.G. Tilak
Lala Lajpat Rai
Madan Mohan Malviya

vincial Autonomy in British India was saged by the :
Act of 1909 B. Act of 1919
Act of 1935 D. Act of 1947

59. Dyarchy means :
A. double government
B. a government in which the centre is very powerful
C. a government based on division of power between centre and provinces
D. None of the above

60. The Indian National Congress observed 'Independence Day' for the first time on 26th January in :
A. 1920 B. 1925
C. 1930 D. 1947

61. ....is situated near the banks of Sabarmati River
A. Bhavnagar B. Aurangabad
C. Ahmedabad D. Rajkot

62. Sericulture is:
A. science of the various kinds of serum
B. artificial rearing of fish
C. art of silkworm breeding
D. study of various cultures of a community

63. The most abundant constituents of earth's crust are:
A. Igneous rocks
B. Sedimentary rocks
C. Metamorphic rocks
D. Granite

64. Indian Standard Time is based on:
A. 80°E longitude B. 82½°E longitude
C. 110°E longitude D. 25°E longitude

65. Tides in the oceans are caused by :
A. Gravitational pull of the moon on the earth's surface including sea water
B. Gravitational pull of the sun on the earth's surface only and not on the sea water
C. Gravitational pull of the moon and the sun on the earth's surface including the sea water
D. None of these

66. Nagarjunasagar Project is situated on the river:
A. Tungabhadra
B. Cauvery
C. Krishna
D. Godavari

67. The difference between the Indian Standard Time and the Greenwich Mean Time is:
A. – 3½ hours B. + 3½ hours
C. – 5½ hours D. + 5½ hours

68. Which of the following dams is not on Narmada river?
A. Indira-Sagar Project
B. Maheshwar Hydel Power Project
C. Jobat Project
D. Koyna Power Project

69. Which of the following statements is **not true** about the availability of water on the earth, the crisis for which is going to increase in the years to come?
A. About 97.5 per cent of the total volume of water available on the earth is salty
B. 80 per cent of the water available to us for use comes in bursts as monsoons
C. About 2.5 per cent of the total water available on the earth is polluted water and cannot be used for human activities
D. Possibility is that some big glaciers will melt in the coming ten-fifteen years and sea level will rise by 3-4 metres all over the earth

70. Which of the following is **not** a cash crop?
A. Jute B. Paddy
C. Cashewnut D. Sugarcane

71. Through which States does Cauvery River flow?
A. Gujarat, M.P., Tamil Nadu
B. Karnataka, Kerala, Tamil Nadu
C. Karnataka, Kerala, Andhra Pradesh
D. M.P., Maharashtra, Tamil Nadu

72. Indian Standard Time is the local time of 82½°E which passes through :
A. Guntur B. Delhi
C. Allahabad D. Kolkata

73. The 17th parallel defines the boundary between:
A. North and South Korea
B. USA and Canada
C. North and South Vietnam
D. China and Russia

74. During the period of south-west m
Tamil Nadu remains dry because:
A. the winds do not reach this area
B. there are no mountains in this ar
C. it lies in the rain shadow area
D. the temperature is too high to let th
cool down

75. Which country does top in producin
A. Cote d'Ivoire B. Brazil
C. Ghana D. Nigeria

76. The biggest reserves of thorium are
A. India B. China
C. The Soviet Union D. U.S.A.

77. The Girnar Hills are situated in whic
following states?
A. Gujarat B. Karnataka
C. Madhya Pradesh D. Maharasht

78. During December 22nd the sun is
over:
A. Tropic of Cancer
B. Tropic of Capricorn
C. The Equator
D. None of the above

79. Photosphere is described as the :
A. Lower layer of atmosphere
B. Visible surface of the sun fro
radiation emanates
C. Wavelength of solar spectrum
D. None of the above

80. Broadly, there are three layers of the
the crust, the mantle and the core.
forms what percentage of the volu
earth?
A. 0.5% B. 2.5%
C. 7.5% D. 12.5%

81. The grassland of Argentina is know
A. Pampas B. Campos
C. Savanna D. None of t

82. Different seasons are formed becau
A. Sun is moving around the earth
B. of revolution of the earth aroun
on its orbit
C. of rotation of the earth around
D. All of the above

Eskers and Drumlins are features formed by:
A. underground water
B. running water
C. the action of wind
D. glacial action

Match List-I and List-II and select the correct answer using the codes given below the Lists :

List-I (Rivers)	List-II (Towns)
(a) Ghaghara	1. Lucknow
(b) Brahmaputra	2. Hoshangabad
(c) Narmada	3. Ahmedabad
(d) Sabarmati	4. Guwahati
	5. Ayodhya

	(a)	(b)	(c)	(d)
A.	4	5	1	2
B.	5	4	2	3
C.	5	4	3	1
D.	3	5	2	1

Which of the statements as regards the consequences of the movement of the earth is not correct?
A. Revolution of the earth is the cause of the change of seasons.
B. Rotation of the earth is the cause of days and nights.
C. Rotation of the earth causes variation in the duration of days and nights.
D. Rotation of the earth effects the movement of winds and ocean currents.

The world is divided into :
A. 12 time zones
B. 20 time zones
C. 24 time zones
D. 36 time zones

The 'Kiel' canal links the :
A. Pacific and Atlantic Oceans
B. Mediterranean Sea and Red Sea
C. Mediterranean Sea and Black Sea
D. North Sea and Baltic Sea

Match the following :

List-I	List-II
(a) Himadri	1. Outer Himalayas
(b) Shivalik	2. Inner Himalayas
(c) Himanchal	3. Middle Himalayas
(d) Sahyadri	4. Western Ghats

Codes:

	(a)	(b)	(c)	(d)
A.	1	2	3	4
B.	4	2	3	1
C.	2	1	3	4
D.	1	2	3	4

89. The term 'Regur' refers to:
A. Laterite soils
B. Black Cotton soils
C. Red Soils
D. Deltaic Alluvial Soils

90. Location of sugar industry in India is shifting from north to south because of:
A. cheap labour
B. expanding regional market
C. cheap and abundant supply of power
D. high yield and high sugar content in sugarcane

91. Consider the following statements :
1. Ozone is found mostly in the Stratosphere.
2. Ozone layer lies 55-75 km above the surface of the earth.
3. Ozone absorbs ultraviolet radiation from the Sun.
4. Ozone layer has no significance for life on the earth.

Which of the above statements are correct?
A. 1 and 3 B. 2 and 4
C. 2 and 3 D. 1 and 4

92. Match List-I with List-II and select the correct answer using the codes given below the Lists :

List-I (Crops)	List-II (Producer)
(a) Banana	1. Brazil
(b) Cocoa	2. Cote d'Ivoire
(c) Coffee	3. India
(d) Tea	4. China

Codes :

	(a)	(b)	(c)	(d)
A.	2	3	1	4
B.	3	2	1	4
C.	3	2	4	1
D.	2	3	4	1

93. Darjeeling and Dharamsala would be the right places to visit if one wanted to get a clear view respectively of :
A. Kanchanjunga and Dhauladhar ranges
B. Nandadevi and Dhauladhar ranges
C. Kanchanjunga and Nandadevi ranges
D. Nandadevi and Nanga Parvat

94. Atmosphere exists because:
A. The Gravitational force of the Earth
B. Revolution of the Earth
C. Rotation of the Earth
D. Weight of the gases of atmosphere

95. Victoria lake is located in the continent:
A. Africa
B. Asia
C. North America
D. South America

96. The famous Lagoon Lake of India is :
A. Dal Lake B. Chilka Lake
C. Pulicat Lake D. Mansarover

97. Where are most of the earth's active volcanoes concentrated?
A. Indian Ocean B. Pacific Ocean
C. Aral Sea D. Atlantic Ocean

98. Through which of the following states does the river Chambal flow?
A. U.P., M.P., Rajasthan
B. M.P., Gujarat, U.P.
C. Rajasthan, M.P., Bihar
D. Gujarat, M.P., U.P.

99. Which country is called the sugar bowl of the world?
A. Cuba B. India
C. Argentina D. USA

100. The area covered by forest in India as per ISFR-2023 is:
A. 46% B. 33%
C. 21.76% D. 25.50%

101. A closed economy is the one which :
A. does not permit emigration or immigration
B. permits emigration but no immigration
C. engages in no foreign trade
D. engages in no foreign and domestic trade or transit

102. In a developed economy the major sh employment originates in the :
A. primary sector B. tertiary secto
C. secondary sector D. any of the a

103. The Economic and Social Commissi Asia and Pacific (ESCAP) is located a
A. Bangkok B. Kuala Lump
C. Manila D. Singapore

104. Commercial vehicles are not produc which of the following companies in
A. TELCO B. Ashok Leyla
C. DCM Daewoo D. Birla Yamah

105. In India, the Public Sector is most do in:
A. transport
B. steel production
C. commercial banking
D. organised term-lending fin institutions

106. The main argument advanced in fav small scale and cottage industries in I that:
A. cost of production is low
B. they require small capital investme
C. they advance the goal of equ distribution of wealth
D. they generate a large volun employment

107. The most serious economic problems o are:
A. Poverty and unemployment
B. Stagnation, not poverty
C. Unemployment, not poverty
D. Underdevelopment, not poverty

108. Which of the following is not one of th central problems of an economy?
A. What to produce
B. How to produce
C. When to produce
D. For whom to produce

109. Gender Responsive Budgeting has adopted in India in the year:
A. 2017 B. 2004
C. 2014 D. 2005

. In which of the following industries in India are the maximum number of workers employed?
A. Sugar B. Jute
C. Textiles D. Iron and Steel

. Terrace Cultivation is practiced mostly:
A. in urban areas
B. on slopes of mountains
C. on tops of hills
D. in undulating tracts

. Which of the following is a Selective Credit Control method?
A. Bank Rate
B. RBI directives
C. Cash Reserve Ratio
D. Open market operations

. Which of the following taxes is not shared by the Central Government with the States?
A. Union excise duties
B. Customs duty
C. Income tax
D. Estate duty

. ICICI is the name of a:
A. Financial Institution
B. Chemical Industry
C. Cotton Industry
D. Chamber of Commerce and Industry

. Structural Unemployment arises due to
A. Deflationary conditions
B. Heavy industry bias
C. Shortage of raw material
D. Inadequate productive capacity

. Which of the following is the largest single source of the government's earning from tax revenue?
A. Excise duties
B. Customs duties
C. Corporation tax
D. Income tax

. The largest public sector bank in India is:
A. Central Bank of India
B. Punjab National Bank
C. State Bank of India
D. Indian Overseas Bank

118. Which of the following statements best explains the term contraband goods?
A. Goods produced only for exports
B. Goods produced in joint sector only
C. Goods for the trading of which licence is not required
D. Goods that are forbidden, from export, import or even possession, by law

119. Price in the market is fixed by:
A. Stock exchange rates
B. The demand and supply ruling in the market at a particular time
C. The Finance Minister
D. None of the above

120. Devaluation of currency helps to promote:
A. National Income
B. Savings
C. Imports at lower cost
D. Exports

121. Balanced economic growth can be achieved only if:
A. All the sectors of economy grow at the same rate
B. Population growth is arrested
C. All the inter dependent sectors grow in harmony
D. Basic and heavy industries are assigned highest priority

122. Which one of the following contributes most to the National Income in India?
A. Service Sector
B. Industrial Sector
C. Foreign Trade Sector
D. Agricultural Sector

123. IMF is the result of:
A. Brettonwood conference
B. Rome conference
C. Geneva conference
D. Hawana conference

124. Index 'Residex' is associated with:
A. Share Prices
B. Land Prices
C. Mutual Funds Prices
D. None of the above

125. The term 'devaluation' means:
A. Reducing the value of a currency in terms of another currency
B. Increasing the value of a currency
C. Revising the value of a currency
D. None of the above

126. Per capita net availability of pulses has shown a tendency of:
A. Increase over time
B. Decrease over time
C. Constant over time
D. First increase then decrease

127. National Income is the same as:
A. Net national product at market price
B. Net domestic product at market price
C. Net national product at factor cost
D. Net domestic product at factor cost

128. Which one of the following is not an example of indirect tax?
A. Sales tax B. Excise duty
C. Customs duty D. Expenditure tax

129. The major aim of devaluation is to:
A. encourage imports
B. encourage exports
C. encourage both exports and imports
D. discourage both exports and imports

130. Structural unemployment arises due to:
A. deflationary conditions
B. heavy industry bias
C. shortage of raw materials
D. inadequate productive capacity

131. When was the Family Planning Programme officially started in India?
A. 1950 B. 1952
C. 1956 D. 1962

132. When was the Reserve Bank of India nationalised?
A. 1947 B. 1949
C. 1950 D. 1951

133. Which of the following is *not* a feature of the Indian economy?
A. High rate of population growth
B. Disguised unemployment
C. Lowest rate of adult literacy
D. High rate of exports

134. The 'Relative Deprivation' approach measuring poverty has been adopted by:
A. developing countries
B. developed countries
C. under-developed countries
D. None of the above

135. One of the main factors that led to ra expansion of Indian exports is:
A. Imposition of import duties
B. Liberalisation of the economy
C. Recession in other countries
D. Diversification of exports

136. Sustainable economic development means increase in the rate of growth of real:
A. total and per capita product
B. total and per capita product and level literacy rate
C. total and per capita product and l expectancy at birth
D. total and per capita product, taking i account the cost of degradation of quality of environment in this process

137. Functional unemployment occurs when:
A. unemployed have no qualification for
B. people frequently change their job
C. people were thrown out from job due recession
D. None of these

138. Which among the following does **not** hav 'free trade zone'?
A. Kandla B. Mumbai
C. Visakhapatnam D. Thiruvanantpura

139. Sun Belt of USA is important for which of the following industries?
A. Cotton textile
B. Petrochemicals
C. Hi-tech electronics
D. Food Processing

140. Commercial banking system in India is
A. unit banking B. branch banking
C. mixed banking D. None of the ab

141. Who gives recognition to political partie India?
A. Parliament

B. President
C. Supreme Court
D. Election Commission

42. The Quorum of the Legislative Council is :
A. one-fourth of its total membership
B. one-third of its membership
C. one-tenth of its membership
D. 25

43. The Indian Constitution is:
A. federal
B. unitary
C. a happy mixture of the federal and unitary
D. federal in normal times and unitary in times of emergency

44. Universal adult franchise implies a right to vote to all:
A. adult residents of the State
B. adult male citizens of the State
C. residents of the State
D. adult citizens of the State

45. When a resolution prefering a charge against the President has been passed by a specified majority in the House, it is sent to the other House for investigation. If, as a result of such an investigation, a resolution is passed through a specified majority by the other House, declaring that the charge has been sustained, the President shall leave his office. The specified special majority must not be less than :
A. two-third of the members present and voting
B. one-third of the members present and voting
C. three-fourth of the members present and voting and two-third of the total membership
D. two-third of the total membership

46. Which one of the following judicial powers of the President of India has been *wrongly* listed?
A. he appoints the Chief Justice and other judges of the Supreme Court
B. he can remove the judges of the Supreme Court on grounds of misconduct
C. he can consult the Supreme Court on any question of law or fact which is of public importance
D. he can grant pardon, reprieves and respites to persons punished under Union Law

147. The Vice-president of India can be removed from his office before the expiry of his term if :
A. the Rajya Sabha passes a resolution by a majority of its members and the Lok Sabha agrees with the resolution
B. if the Supreme Court of India recommends his removal
C. the President so desires
D. None of the above

148. 'Sengol', installed in the new Parliament building of India, was seen as a symbol of the path of service, duty and nation in which Empire of the past?
A. Gupta Empire B. Shunga Empire
C. Pandyan Empire D. Chola Empire

149. Which of the following statements is constitutionally not true about the passing of the Union Budgets and Finance Bill in India?
1. Under the law, Finance Bill should be adopted by both the Houses of the Parliament within 45 days of its introduction.
2. If the Finance Bill is not adopted within specified period, the government loses its authority to levy the taxes proposed in the budgets.
3. In the absence of full budget, a vote-on-account gives the power to the government to spend.
4. Government cannot raise revenues without a proper approval of the Finance Bill

A. Only 2 B. Only 3
C. Only 4 D. Only 1, 2 and 3

150. Normally, on whose advice the President's Rule is imposed in a State?
A. Chief Minister
B. Legislative Assembly
C. Governor
D. Chief Justice of High Court

151. Which Article of the Indian Constitution deals with Amendment procedure?

A. Article 368   B. Article 358
C. Article 367   D. All of these

152. Government is the agency through which the will of :

A. the state is expressed
B. the people is expressed
C. the head of the state is expressed
D. the majority is expressed

153. In a unitary system of government :

A. The centre is all powerful
B. The centre is weaker than the states
C. The centre and states stand at par
D. The states and centre are supreme in their respective spheres

154. In Cabinet System of Government the real executive authority rests with :

A. The Council of Ministers
B. The Prime Minister
C. The Constitution
D. The Parliament

155. The Head of the State under a parliamentary government:

A. is an elected representative
B. is a hereditary person
C. is a nominated person
D. may be any one of the above

156. In the event of a ministerial proposal being defeated on the floor of the legislature, under the parliamentary system :

A. the government waits for a general no-confidence motion
B. the minister concerned is taken to task by the Prime Minister
C. the minister is forced to resign
D. the whole Council of Ministers resign

157. The "due process of law" is an essential characteristic of the judicial system of:

A. UK   B. France
C. USA   D. India

158. Under the Constitution it is :

A. obligatory for the President to accept the advice of the Council of Ministers but is not obliged to follow it
B. obligatory for the President to accept the advice of the Council of Ministers
C. not obligatory for the President to seek or accept the advice of the Council of Ministers
D. obligatory for the President to seek the advice of the Council of Ministers if his own party is in power

159. Which one of the following statements is correct?

A. the Presiding Officer of Rajya Sabha is elected every year
B. the Presiding Officer of Rajya Sabha is elected for a term of two years at a time
C. the Presiding Officer of Rajya Sabha is elected for a term of six years
D. the Vice-President of India is the ex-officio Presiding Officer of Rajya Sabha

160. The introduction of "no confidence" motion in the Lok Sabha requires the support of at least:

A. 50 members   B. 70 members
C. 60 members   D. 80 members

161. The High Court comes under :

A. State List   B. Union List
C. Concurrent List   D. None of the above

162. Which one of the following has been wrongly listed as a Fundamental Duty of the Indian citizens?

A. to develop scientific temper, humanism and spirit of inquiry and reform
B. to work for raising the prestige of the country in the international sphere
C. to protect and improve the natural environment
D. to strive towards excellence in all spheres of individual and collective activity

163. Which one of the following is not a Fundamental Duty as outlined in Article 51A of the Constitution?

A. to abide by the Constitution and respect its ideals
B. to defend the country and render national service when called upon to do so

C. to work for the moral upliftment of the weaker sections of society
D. to preserve the rich heritage

164. The main characteristics of the Directive Principles of State Policy given in the Indian Constitution are :
A. not enforceable by any court
B. fundamental in the governance of the country
C. 'Like instruments, instructions, political manifesto and a code of moral precepts which have to guide governors of the country'
D. no law can be passed, which is opposed to these principles

165. Of the following which are true?
A. In a State, the Legislative Council is dominant with regard to non-financial bills and the Legislative Assembly with regard to financial (money) bills
B. Vidhan Parishad can virtually block legisla-tion even if the same is passed by the Vidhan Sabha
C. In case of a tie between the two Houses, the Governor is duty-bound to call a joint session of the two Houses to have the issue settled on a majority verdict
D. If a Bill is twice approved by the Vidhan Sabha, it becomes law even if rejected by the Vidhan Parishad

166. Which one of the following types of emergency can be declared by the President?
A. Emergency due to threat of war and external aggresion
B. Emergency due to break-down of constitu-tional machinery in a State
C. Financial emergency on account of threat to the financial credit of India
D. all the three emergencies

167. The chairman of which of the following parliamentary committees is invariably from the members of ruling party?
A. Committee on public undertakings
B. Public accounts committee
C. Estimates committee
D. Committee on delegated legislation

168. Which of the following is not a formally prescribed device available to the members of parliament?
A. Question hour
B. Zero hour
C. Half-an-hour discussion
D. Short duration discussion

169. Which of the following is not a tool of executive control over public administration?
A. Power of appointment and removal
B. Line agencies
C. Appeal to public opinion
D. Civil services code

170. If the Speaker of the State Legislative Assembly decides to resign, he should submit his resignation to the:
A. Judges of the High Court
B. Deputy Speaker
C. Chief Minister
D. Finance Minister

171. The Constitution of India provides for the nomination of two members of Lok Sabha by the President to represent:
A. the Parsis
B. men of eminence
C. the business community
D. the Anglo-Indian community

172. India is a Federal State because of:
A. dual judiciary
B. dual citizenship prevalent here
C. share of power between the Centre and the States
D. rigid Constitution

173. Residuary Subjects are those subjects which are:
A. contained in the State list
B. contained in the Union list
C. contained in the Concurrent list
D. not covered by any of the three lists

174. Which of the following writs can be issued, by the Supreme Court, to enforce Fundamental Rights?
A. Writ of Habeas Corpus
B. Writ of Mandamus
C. Writ of Quo Warranto
D. All of these

175. When the offices of both the President and the Vice-President of India are vacant, who will discharge their functions?
A. Prime Minister
B. Home Minister
C. Chief Justice of India
D. The Speaker

176. The Supreme Court tenders advice to the President of India on a matter of law or fact:
A. on its own
B. only when such advice is sought
C. only if the matter relates to some basic issue
D. only if the issue poses a threat to the unity and integrity of the country

177. Six months shall **not** intervene between two sessions of the Indian Parliament because :
A. it is the customary practice
B. it is the British convention followed in India
C. it is an obligation under the Constitution of India
D. None of the above

178. The States of the Indian Union can be recognised or their boundaries altered by:
A. the Union Parliament by a simple majority in the ordinary process of legislation
B. two-thirds majority of both the Houses of Parliament
C. two-thirds majority of both the Houses of Parliament and the consent of the legislatures of concerned States
D. an executive order of the Union government with the consent of the concerned State governments

179. The Basic Feature theory of the Constitution of India was propounded by the Supreme Court in the case of :
A. Minerva Mills Vs. Union of India
B. Golaknath Vs. State of Punjab
C. Maneka Gandhi Vs. Union of India
D. Keshavananda Vs. State of Kerala

180. Which one of the following writs is issued by a court in case of illegal detention of a person?
A. Habeas corpus B. Mandamus
C. Certiorari D. Quo-warranto

181. Name the instrument with the help of whic a sailor in a submarine can see the objects c the surface of the sea.
A. Telescope B. Periscope
C. Gycroscope D. Stereoscope

182. 'HEMOPHILLIA' is the disease of ....
A. liver B. blood
C. brain D. bones

183. Vitamin A is abundantly found in ....
A. Brinjal B. Tomato
C. Carrot D. Cabbage

184. .... is not soluble in water.
A. Vitamin A B. Vitamin B
C. Vitamin C D. None of these

185. The blood vessels with the smallest diamet are called ....
A. capillaries B. arterioles
C. venules D. lymphatics

186. Out of the following .... has the greate elasticity.
A. steel B. rubber
C. aluminium D. annealed copper

187. Cooking gas is a mixture of which of t following two gases?
A. Carbon Dioxide and Oxygen
B. Butane and Propane
C. Carbon Monoxide and Carbon Dioxid
D. Methane and Ethylene

188. The substance most commonly used as a fo preservative is:
A. sodium carbonate B. tartaric acid
C. acetic acid D. benzoic acid

189. Normally, the substances that fight agai diseases in human systems are known as:
A. dioxyribonucleic acids
B. carbohydrates
C. enzymes
D. antibodies

190. The SI unit of temperature is ....
A. Kelvin B. Celsius
C. Fahrenheit D. None of the abo

191. One of the common fungal diseases of m is :
A. plague B. ringworm
C. cholera D. typhoid

2. A clear sky is blue because:
A. red light is scattered more than blue
B. ultraviolet light has been absorbed
C. blue light is scattered more than red
D. blue light has been absorbed

3. Jenner introduced the method of making people immune to :
A. small pox B. rabies
C. cholera D. polio

4. The largest cell in the human body is :
A. Nerve cell B. Live cell
C. Muscle cell D. Kidney cell

5. What is the device that steps up or steps down the voltage?
A. Dynamo B. Conductor
C. Inductor D. Transformer

6. The protein deficiency disease is known as :
A. Kwashiorker B. Cirrhosis
C. Eczema D. Clycoses

7. Iron deficiency causes :
A. rickets B. anaemia
C. cirrhosis D. goitre

8. Blood group of an individual is controlled by :
A. Haemoglobin B. Shape of RBC
C. Shape of WBC D. Genes

9. In a normal man the amount of blood pumped out by the heart per minute is about :
A. 1 litre B. 3 litres
C. 4 litres D. 5 litres

0. Red/green colour blindness in man is known as :
A. Protanopia
B. Deutetanopia
C. Both A and B above
D. Marfan's syndrome

. The blue colour of the water in the sea is due to :
A. Reflection of the blue light by the impurities in sea water
B. Reflection of the blue sky by sea water and scattering of blue light by water molecules
C. Absorption of other colours by water molecules
D. None of the above

202. The image formed on the retina of the eye is:
A. upright and real
B. larger than the object
C. small and inverted
D. enlarged and real

203. Unit of loudness of sound is:
A. bel B. decibel
C. phon D. none of these

204. Oil rises up the wick in a lamp :
A. because oil is volatile
B. due to the capillary action phenomenon
C. due to the surface tension phenomenon
D. because oil is very light

205. The 'stones' formed in human kidney consist mostly of :
A. calcium oxalate
B. sodium acetate
C. magnesium sulphate
D. calcium

206. We hear the sound later, while the light is seen earlier:
A. because light's speed is more than that of sound
B. because lights travel in a straight direction while sound in a zigzag direction
C. because sound's frequency is lower than light
D. All of the above

207. Which part of an eye is transplanted?
A. Cornea
B. Retina
C. Iris
D. Sciera

208. The Universal donor group of blood is:
A. O B. A
C. B D. AB

209. The green colour of the leaf is due to :
A. Presence of Chloroplast
B. Presence of Chromium
C. Presence of Nicoplast
D. Presence of excess of oxygen

210. Voice of a child is more shrill than that of an elderly person because:
A. the pitch of the child's voice is higher than that of the person
B. the pitch is lower
C. the child is more energetic
D. None of the above

211. Camel uses its hump for :
A. storing water
B. storing fat
C. for balancing the body
D. temperature regulation

212. A man standing in a free falling lift releases a ball from his hand. The ball would be :
A. moving down
B. moving up
C. stationary
D. moving up and down

213. To change the quality of sound produced by an instrument we need to vary the:
A. pitch
B. loudness
C. amplitude
D. number of overtonnes

214. The disease caused by Asbestos is:
A. Emphysema B. Paralysis
C. Diarrhoea D. Dysentery

215. Sweetness of a sound depends upon its
A. wavelength
B. frequency
C. amplitude
D. periodicity and regularity

216. Bats can fly in the dark because :
A. they have a better vision in the dark
B. the pupils of their eyes are very big
C. they are guided by ultrasonic waves produced by them
D. any bird can do so

217. Blood is formed in the human adult by the :
A. heart B. spleen
C. kidney D. bone marrow

218. Pencil 'lead' is made up of:
A. graphite B. charcoal
C. lead oxide D. lampblack

219. The deficiency of which one of the follow vitamins leads to bleeding of gums loosening of teeth?
A. Vitamin D B. Vitamin C
C. Vitamin B D. Vitamin A

220. How much blood does a normal person h in his body?
A. 8 litres B. 4 to 5 litres
C. 10 litres D. 2 litres

221. Match List-I with List-II and select the cor answer using the codes given below the Li

List-I	List-II
(*a*) Visakhadatta	1. Mrichhakatika
(*b*) Shudraka	2. Ritusamhara
(*c*) Kalidasa	3. Kamasutra
(*d*) Vatsyayana	4. Devichandragupta

Codes :

	(*a*)	(*b*)	(*c*)	(*d*)
A.	1	4	2	3
B.	4	1	3	2
C.	1	4	3	2
D.	4	1	2	3

222. In which one of the following langauge the *Dalit* writing more conspicuous?
A. Punjabi B. Assamese
C. Marathi D. Odiya

223. The first writer to use Urdu as the mediu poetic expression was:
A. Amir Khusrau
B. Mirza Ghalib
C. Bahadur Shah Zafar
D. Faiz

224. The religious text of the Zoroastrians is na as:
A. Torah B. The Analects
C. Tripatika D. Zend Avesta

225. Name the music duo which composed n for Raj Kapoor's film 'Bobby'?
A. Laxmikant Pyarelal B. Shankar Jaikis
C. Kalyanji Anandji D. Nadeem Shrav

226. Raja Harishchandra, an early Indian film, produced by :
A. D.G. Phalke B. Ashok Kumar
C. Ardeshir Irani D. None of the a

All films are certificed by .... before they are publicly exhibited.
A. Films Division
B. National Film Development Corporation (NFDC)
C. Directorate of Advertising and Visual Publicity (DAVP)
D. Central Board of Film Certificate (CBFC)

Who among the following was the director of the film 'Taal'?
A. Gulzar B. Shekhar Kapoor
C. Satish Shah D. Subhash Ghai

Who amongst the following actresses has played the leading role in the film Elizabeth?
A. Gwyneth Paltrow B. Cate Blanchett
C. Simi Garewal D. Kim Basinger

The film 'Train to Pakistan' is based on the novel of the same name, written by:
A. Bhishma Sahani
B. Khushwant Singh
C. Amrita Pritam
D. Khwaja Ahmed Abbas

Which of the following is a folk dance form of Jharkhand?
A. Pali B. Jhumar
C. Nati D. Chhau

The first feature film (talkie) to be produced in India was:
A. Hatimtai B. Alam Ara
C. Pundalik D. Raja Harishchandra

Who directed the film "Bombay"?
A. Shyam Benegal B. Meera Nair
C. Shekhar Kapoor D. Mani Ratnam

Late Iftekhar Ahmad was famous in which of the following fields?
A. Acting B. Singing
C. Music D. Literature

Who among the following is the director of the film 'Kaho Na Pyar Hai'?
A. Subhash Ghai
B. Shekhar Kapoor
C. Ramesh Sippy
D. Rakesh Roshan

236. The character played by Jim Carrey in the movie *Man on Moon* is based on:
A. Andy Kaufman B. Edwin Aldrin
C. John Glenn D. Neil Armstrong

237. A popular Hindi film-based on the famous Sanskrit play *Mrichhakatika*, was titled:
A. Meghadoot B. Amrapali
C. Utsav D. Shakuntala

238. Who composed the song 'Zara Yad Karo Kurbani'?
A. Javed Akhtar
B. Pradeep
C. Nusrat Fateh Ali Khan
D. Raghupati Sahay 'Firaq'

239. Who was the producer of the serial 'Mahabharat'?
A. Shyam Benegal B. B.R. Chopra
C. Ramanand Sagar D. Mani Ratnam

240. Which of the following is a folk dance of Rajasthan?
A. Garba B. Dandya
C. Jhumar D. Kathak

241. 'The Colonel' is the nickname of which Indian Test Cricketer?
A. Colonel C.K. Naidu
B. Rahul Dravid
C. Mohinder Amarnath
D. Dilip Vengsarkar

242. The term 'Grandmaster' is used in which of these games?
A. Judo B. Chess
C. Bridge D. Karate

243. The term "Derby" is related with which of the following?
A. Polo B. Swimming
C. Racing D. Horse Racing

244. With which game is Geet Sethi associated?
A. Basketball B. Chess
C. Snooker D. Tennis

245. Beighton Cup is related with which of the following?
A. Hockey B. Polo
C. Cricket D. Soccer

246. Match List-I with List-II and select the correct answer using the codes given below the Lists :

List-I	**List-II**
(*a*) Basketball	1. Lob
(*b*) Bridge	2. Revoke
(*c*) Golf	3. Pivot
(*d*) Tennis	4. Bunker

Codes :

	(*a*)	(*b*)	(*c*)	(*d*)
A.	2	3	1	4
B.	2	3	4	1
C.	3	2	1	4
D.	3	2	4	1

247. The head office of the International Cricket Council (ICC) is situated in :

A. Zimbabwe B. Australia
C. South Africa D. UAE

248. Match the following :

List-I	**List-II**
(*a*) Deodhar Trophy	1. Volleyball
(*b*) Durand Cup	2. Football
(*c*) Davis Cup	3. Cricket
	4. Tennis

Codes:

	(*a*)	(*b*)	(*c*)
A.	3	2	4
B.	3	1	4
C.	2	3	1
D.	1	2	4

249. Which of the following is called 'Grand Slam'?

A. Winning the highest number of medals in the Olympic games
B. Winning the men's singles title in Wimbledon Championship
C. Winning the Wimbledon Singles title successively for two years
D. Winning all the four championships Australian, French, Wimblendon and US

250. With which game is the term 'butterfly stroke' associated?

A. Swimming B. Cricket
C. Gliding D. Skiing

251. Who is the first Indian to win the 'International Grand Master' title in Chess?

A. Anupama Abhayankar
B. Bhagyashree Sathe Thipsay
C. Vishwanathan Anand
D. D.V. Prasad

252. The XXII Commonwealth Games were h 2022 in:

A. Kuala Lumpur B. Bangkok
C. Victoria D. Birmingham

253. The term 'Tee' is associated with which following sports?

A. Golf B. Table Tennis
C. Polo D. Judo

254. The famous woman Tennis player wh stabbed during a match, is

A. Steffi Graf B. Monica Seles
C. Mary Pierce D. Martina Navra

255. The term 'Baseline' is related to which following?

A. Golf B. Hockey
C. Badminton D. Polo

256. In which Indian State did the game of originate?

A. Manipur B. Rajasthan
C. Gujarat D. West Bengal

257. Narendra Modi Stadium is located at:

A. Hyderabad B. Chennai
C. Ahmedabad D. Prayagraj

258. Rafael Nadal is the well-known p associated with:

A. Hockey B. Cricket
C. Tennis D. Chess

259. Neeraj Chopra is the well-known p associated with :

A. Javelin Throw B. Golf
C. Table Tennis D. Chess

260. Eden Garden, a famous Cricket stadiu located in :

A. Kanpur B. Kolkata
C. Jamshedpur D. Pune

261. Maharaja Ranjit Singh Trophy is asso with :

A. Golf B. Hockey
C. Soccer D. Tennis

Harmanpreet Kaur is a distinguished player in which of the following games?
A. Swimming B. Weightlifting
C. Cricket D. Archery

Cricket was an Olympic event at which of the following Olympics?
A. London, 1908 B. Amsterdam, 1928
C. Paris, 1900 D. Melbourne, 1956

WISPA competitions are associated with :
A. Squash B. Yatching
C. Boxing D. Billiards

Ryder Cup is the famous trophy of :
A. Golf B. Chess
C. Boxing D. Polo

Davis Cup is associated with the sport of :
A. Cricket B. Football
C. Tennis D. Hockey

'Volley', 'Chop' and 'Drive Spine' are the term associated with :
A. Lawn Tennis B. Badminton
C. Table Tennis D. Golf

Lal Bahadur Shastri Stadium is located at :
A. Hyderabad B. Chennai
C. Ahmedabad D. Varanasi

The first winner of Major Dhyan Chand Khel Ratna Award was :
A. Geet Sethi
B. Sachin Tendulkar
C. Viswanathan Anand
D. Karnam Malleswari

The winner of 2023 ICC Men's Cricket World Cup is:
A. Australia B. Sri Lanka
C. Bangladesh D. England

The first team event introduced in 1900 at Paris Olympics was :
A. Hockey B. Football
C. Cricket D. Baseball

Which of the following international tennis tournaments is held on grass court?
A. US Open B. French Open
C. Wimbledon D. Australian Open

273. Which cricketer is nicknamed as the pied piper of Punjab?
A. Yuvraj Singh
B. Harbhajan Singh
C. Mohinder Amarnath
D. Navjot Singh Sidhu

274. 'Merdeka Cup' is associated with ....
A. Golf B. Football
C. Squash D. Hockey

275. The first time athletes marched into the stadium behind their nation's flag in Olympics:
A. at St. Louis 1904 B. at London 1908
C. at Antwerp 1920 D. at Paris 1924

276. The "Dronacharya Award" is associated with:
A. Eminent Surgeons B. Famous Sports Person
C. Sport Coaches D. Expert Engineers

277. Which cricketer is nicknamed as 'Jumbo'?
A. Venkatesh Prasad B. Anil Kumble
C. Glenn McGrath D. Shane Warne

278. The first time the Olympic Games were organised by a private company at:
A. Montreal, 1976 B. Los Angeles, 1984
C. Atlanta, 1996 D. Rome, 1960

279. In which Asian Games Cricket was played first?
A. Guangzhou, 2010 B. Doha, 2006
C. Busan, 2002 D. Seoul, 1986

280. The term 'Penalty cick' is used in :
A. Hockey B. Football
C. Baseball D. Golf

281. Which of the following countries is not a member of North Atlantic Treaty Organisation (NATO)?
A. Norway B. United Germany
C. Portugal D. Australia

282. Khmer Rouge is a dictatorial party of :
A. Cambodia B. Indonesia
C. Malaysia D. Thailand

283. Which country is not a member of SAARC?
A. Russia B. Bangladesh
C. Nepal D. Pakistan

284. The headquarters of WTO is located at :
A. Geneva B. Paris
C. The Hague D. Washington

285. The main function of the World Trade Organisation (WTO) is:
A. enforcing of Uruguay Round Agreements
B. facilitating multi-lateral trade relations of member countries and reviewing trade policies
C. administering trade dispute settlement procedures
D. None of the above

286. The Secretary-General of the UNO is appointed by the:
A. General Assembly
B. Security Council
C. Trusteeship Council
D. World Bank

287. The United Nations officially came into existence in 1945 on :
A. November 24 B. October 14
C. October 24 D. November 14

288. Which one of the following is true of the International Court of Justice?
A. The Judges of the Court are appointed according to the discretion of the Secretary General
B. No two Judges may belong to the same country
C. The Court consists of 20 Judges
D. The statute of the International Court of Justice is not an integral part of the UN Charter

289. Which of the following was not among the six founding countries of the European Community?
A. Belgium B. France
C. Germany D. UK

290. The smallest country in South America is:
A. Ecuador B. Guyana
C. Surinam D. Uruguay

291. In which year "Human Rights Resolution" was adopted by the U.N.?
A. 1945 B. 1946
C. 1947 D. 1948

292. Where is the headquarters of INTER located?
A. Berlin B. California
C. Lyons D. Montreal

293. Parliament of which of the following cou is known as Great People's Khural?
A. Malaysia B. Mongolia
C. Thailand D. Indonesia

294. Numbers of major organs of United N are:
A. 3 B. 4
C. 5 D. 6

295. When is the UN Day celebrated?
A. October 24 B. January 24
C. June 24 D. September 24

296. Which one of the following organ of U Nations is known as the 'Policeman c World'?
A. Security Council
B. International Court of Justice
C. The Secretariat
D. General Assembly

297. The members of the NAFTA include:
A. USA, Canada and Mexico
B. USA, Canada, Mexico and UK
C. USA, UK, Russia and Mexico
D. USA, Canada and Brazil

298. The sits of International Court of Just located at :
A. Vienna B. Paris
C. Hague D. New York

299. Which of the following is known a Constitution of the UN?
A. UN Charter
B. UN Assembly
C. UN Security Council
D. UN Secretariat

300. The Headquarters of the Am International is located at :
A. New York
B. London
C. Geneva
D. Addis-Ababa

Who is the author of the book 'PRISON DIARY'?
A. Bal Gangadhar Tilak
B. Rajendra Prasad
C. Jai Prakash Narayan
D. Jawahar Lal Nehru

Who is the author of 'Satanic Verses'?
A. Lewis Carrol B. Salman Rushdie
C. Parry Mason D. Mulk Raj Anand

Who wrote 'Gitanjali'?
A. Kalidas
B. Gopal Das 'Neeraj'
C. Rabindra Nath Tagore
D. Jawahar Lal Nehru

Who, among the following, scholars flourishing during the Gupta Age, was the author of *Dasakumara-Charita?*
A. Asanga B. Dignaga
C. Dandina D. Bhattin

The author of *Gitagovinda* was:
A. Halayudha B. Jayadeva
C. Kalhana D. Jona-raja

"Ingenious Pain" is a book/novel written by:
A. Andrew Miller B. Santa Monica
C. Ben Johnson D. Bill Gates

Who amongst the following is the author of the famous book "An Equal Music"?
A. Salman Rushdie B. Shasthivrata
C. Vikram Seth D. Kamla Markandeya

The famous Moorti Devi Award is given for excellence in which of the following fields?
A. Medicine
B. Science & Technology
C. Social Service
D. Literature

Who has written "Devdas"?
A. Tarasankar Bandyopadhyay
B. Bankim Chandra Chattopadhyay
C. Rabindranath Tagore
D. Sarat Chandra Chattopadhyay

"Ain-i-Akbari" is written by:
A. Todar Mal B. Abul Fazal
C. Sheikh Saadi D. Mirza Ghalib

311. "Alice in Wonderland" is written by :
A. Lewis Carrol B. Chester Bowles
C. Charles Dickens D. Jonathan Swift

312. "Mrichchhakatikam" is written by :
A. Vishakhadatta B. Vatsyayana
C. Sudraka D. Bana Bhatt

313. "My Experiments with Truth" is written by :
A. Jawaharlal Nehru
B. M.K. Gandhi
C. Abul Kalam Azad
D. Rajendra Prasad

314. Who wrote the book "India Wins Freedom"?
A. Maulana Abul Kalam Azad
B. Mahatma Gandhi
C. Sir Mohammad Iqbal
D. Abdul Gaffar Khan

315. Match List-I with List-II and select the correct answer using the codes given below the Lists :

List-I	**List-II**
(*a*) *Emma*	1. Graham Greene
(*b*) *Mother India*	2. E.M. Forster
(*c*) *Human Factor*	3. Jane Austen
(*d*) *Passage to India*	4. Katherine Mayo

Codes :

	(*a*)	(*b*)	(*c*)	(*d*)
A.	2	1	4	3
B.	3	4	1	2
C.	3	1	2	4
D.	4	2	1	3

316. 'Poverty and Un British Rule in India' is written by:
A. R.C. Dutt B. J.L. Nehru
C. D.B. Naoroji D. S.N. Sen

317. Name the author of the book *A Passage to England.*
A. E.M. Forster
B. Nirad C. Choudhuri
C. Vikram Seth
D. Eric Segal

318. The author of the book 'The Struggle in My Life' is:
A. Mandela B. J.L. Nehru
C. Tilak D. Gokhale

319. Which one among the following State capitals is closest to the Equator?
A. Panaji
B. Bhubaneswar
C. Hyderabad
D. Mumbai

320. Which of the following books is not written by Salman Rushdie?
A. The Satanic Verses
B. Shame
C. Naked Face
D. Midnight's Children

321. The different schools of modern socialism derive their strength primarily from the writings of ....?
A. Joseph Stalin B. Leo Tolstoy
C. Mao Tse-tung D. Karl Marx

322. Baba Amte was famous as a ....
A. Painter B. Singer
C. Politician D. Social Worker

323. Central Government says that .... was received well by citizens as 'imandari ka utsav'.
A. Demonetization
B. Goods and Services Tax
C. E-NAM
D. All of the above

324. Mr. Yehudi Menuhin, was a famous:
A. Sitarist B. Cartoonist
C. Journalist D. Violinist

325. Sundarlal Bahuguna, a famous environmentalist, was associated with :
A. Chipko Movement
B. Narmada Bachao Andolan
C. Satyagraha Movement
D. Anti-corruption Movement

326. Mother Teressa's native place was :
A. Albania B. France
C. Greece D. Italy

327. The live polio vaccine which can be taken by mouth was developed by :
A. Albert Sabin B. Edward Jenner
C. Jonas Salk D. Selman Waksman

328. Which of the following language is usec webpage development?
A. FORTRAN
B. C or C++
C. BASIC
D. HTML

329. The "Last Supper" is a famous renaiss painting. It was a masterpiece of :
A. Michael Angelo B. Leonardo da
C. Titian D. Raphael

330. Dhyanchand is associated with which sp
A. Badminton B. Hockey
C. Tennis D. Football

331. 'Man is born free, yet every where he chains'. This was said by:
A. Voltaire B. John Stuart M
C. Rousseau D. Karl Marx

332. Who among the following was a prom social reformer?
A. Baba Gurmukh Singh
B. Raja Mahendra Pratap
C. Bipin Chandra Pal
D. Jotiba Govind Phule

333. Whose real name was Gadadhar Chhat dhyaya?
A. Swami Vivekanand
B. Ram Krishna Paramhansa
C. Dayanand Saraswai
D. Raja Ram Mohan Rai

334. Who was known as "Man of Destiny"?
A. Napoleon B. Nehru
C. Hitler D. Mussolini

335. Who discovered that mosquito served carrier of malaria?
A. Jonas Salk B. Ronald Ross
C. Louis Pasteur D. Robert Koch

336. Who was the first woman Governor Indian State?
A. Sushila Nayar B. Sucheta Krip
C. Sarojini Naidu D. Sulochana M

337. Who among the following founde Bhartiya Jana Sangh?
A. Deen Dayal Upadhyaya